MW01077203

Education Law

Education Law

A Problem-Based Approach

FOURTH EDITION

Scott F. Johnson
Professor of Law
Concord Law School at Purdue University Global

Sarah E. Redfield
Professor Emerita
University of New Hampshire

Carolina Academic Press
Durham, North Carolina

ISBN 978-1-5310-1679-1
eISBN 978-1-5310-1680-7
LCCN 2019941698

Carolina Academic Press
700 Kent Street
Durham, North Carolina 27701
Telephone (919) 489-7486
Fax (919) 493-5668
www.cap-press.com

Printed in the United States of America

To my mother, Sandra M. Johnson, and the memory of my father,
Thomas F. Johnson — SFJ

To Maggie and Lily and those who love them — SER

Contents

Acknowledgements

Professor Johnson would like to thank Sarah E. Redfield for her work on the first and second editions of this book. I would also like to thank Martin Pritikin, Dean of Concord Law School at Purdue University Global, and Shaun Jamison, Associate Dean of Faculty of Concord Law School at Purdue University Global for their support of my work. Last, but not least, thanks to my family for their love, support, and understanding of the time commitment involved in writing this book.

Professor Redfield, of course, thanks Professor Johnson, whose idea this was and without whom it would never have reached reality. She also thanks the University of New Hampshire School of Law for its support of this work and her students for all they have taught her about education, teaching, and writing.

We both would like to thank everyone at Carolina Academic Press for their assistance, particularly Keith Moore for his editorial assistance and guidance through the process.

Please send questions, comments or feedback about the book to scott.johnson@purdueglobal.edu.

Table of Cases

B

C

D

E

N

S

X

Y

Z

Education Law

Chapter 1

Foundational Principles

Synopsis

§ 1.01 Introduction

This book focuses primarily on public elementary and secondary schools in the United States, which are governed by a fairly complex hierarchy of laws at the federal, state, and local level. Each level has different sources of law that public schools, and school officials, must comply with, or face the consequences of judgments by courts and administrative agencies.

The application of the hierarchy of laws to various issues is essential to understanding education law. A basic starting point at the federal level is the fact that the United States Constitution does not speak directly to education. As the United States Supreme Court said in *San Antonio Independent School District v. Rodriguez*, 411 U.S. 1, 35 (1973): "Education, of course, is not among the rights afforded explicit protection under our Federal Constitution. Nor do we find any basis for saying it is implicitly so protected." Although the United States Constitution does not speak directly to education, some of its provisions, particularly the First, Fourth, Fifth, and Fourteenth Amendments, play a major role in education law. Additionally, the United States Supreme Court's jurisprudence interpreting statutory and constitutional requirements is very significant in the education arena. Problem 1 explores some of the bedrock United States Supreme Court cases related to education to help set the foundation for later discussions. Later sections of this Chapter explore each level of the hierarchy, the different sources of law at each level, and the interaction between the different levels that occurs to govern certain issues in public schools.

Problem 1: Education at Risk and Bedrock Cases from the Supreme Court

The following problem materials include some of the foundational Supreme Court cases regarding education. If you were part of a non-profit group interested in general education reform, what strategy would you pursue today to reach your goals based upon these Supreme Court decisions? Would you try to relitigate the underlying question of *Rodriquez* and seek to have the Court recognize education as a fundamental right under the federal Constitution? Would you try to extend the concepts noted in *Brown* or *Plyler* to other situations?

Problem Materials

- ✓ *Brown v. Board of Education*, 347 U.S. 483 (1954) (*Brown I*)
- ✓ *Brown v. Board of Education*, 349 U.S. 294 (1955) (*Brown II*)
- ✓ *San Antonio Independent School District v. Rodriguez*, 411 U.S. 1 (1973) (*Rodriguez*)
- ✓ *Plyler v. Doe*, 457 U.S. 202 (1982)

Brown v. Board of Education (Brown I)

347 U.S. 483 (1954)

The Court rules that segregated public elementary and secondary schools are unconstitutional.

Mr. Chief Justice Warren delivered the opinion of the Court.

These cases come to us from the States of Kansas, South Carolina, Virginia, and Delaware. They are premised on different facts and different local conditions, but a common legal question justifies their consideration together in this consolidated opinion.

In each of the cases, minors of the Negro race, through their legal representatives, seek the aid of the courts in obtaining admission to the public schools of their community on a nonsegregated basis. In each instance, they had been denied admission to schools attended by white children under laws requiring or permitting segregation according to race. This segregation was alleged to deprive the plaintiffs of the equal protection of the laws under the Fourteenth Amendment. In each of the cases other than the Delaware case, a three-judge federal district court denied relief to the plaintiffs on the so-called "separate but equal" doctrine announced by this Court in *Plessy v. Ferguson*, 163 U.S. 537. Under that doctrine, equality of treatment is accorded when the races are provided substantially equal facilities, even though these facilities be separate. In the Delaware case, the Supreme Court of Delaware adhered to that doctrine, but ordered that the plaintiffs be admitted to the white schools because of their superiority to the Negro schools.

The plaintiffs contend that segregated public schools are not "equal" and cannot be made "equal," and that hence they are deprived of the equal protection of the laws. Because of the obvious importance of the question presented, the Court took jurisdiction. Argument was heard in the 1952 Term, and reargument was heard this Term on certain questions propounded by the Court. . . .

In the first cases in this Court construing the Fourteenth Amendment, decided shortly after its adoption, the Court interpreted it as proscribing all state-imposed discriminations against the Negro race. The doctrine of "separate but equal" did not make its appearance in this Court until 1896 in the case of *Plessy v. Ferguson, supra*, involving not education but transportation.[1] American courts have since labored with the doctrine for over half a century. In this Court, there have been six cases involving the "separate but equal" doctrine in the field of public education. . . .

In the instant cases, that question is directly presented. . . . We must look instead to the effect of segregation itself on public education.

In approaching this problem, we cannot turn the clock back to 1868 when the Amendment was adopted, or even to 1896 when *Plessy v. Ferguson* was written. We must consider public education in the light of its full development and its present place in American life throughout the Nation. Only in this way can it be determined if segregation in public schools deprives these plaintiffs of the equal protection of the laws.

Today, education is perhaps the most important function of state and local governments. Compulsory school attendance laws and the great expenditures for education both demonstrate our recognition of the importance of education to our democratic society. It is required in the performance of our most basic public responsibilities, even service in the armed forces. It is the very foundation of good citizenship. Today it is a principal instrument in awakening the child to cultural values, in preparing him for later professional training, and in helping him to adjust normally to his environment. In these days, it is doubtful that any child may reasonably be expected to succeed in life if he is denied the opportunity of an education. Such an opportunity, where the state has undertaken to provide it, is a right which must be made available to all on equal terms.

We come then to the question presented: Does segregation of children in public schools solely on the basis of race, even though the physical facilities and other

---

1. [FN 6] The doctrine apparently originated in *Roberts v. City of Boston*, 59 Mass. 198, 206 (1849), upholding school segregation against attack as being violative of a state constitutional guarantee of equality. Segregation in Boston public schools was eliminated in 1855. Mass. Acts 1855, c. 256. But elsewhere in the North segregation in public education has persisted in some communities until recent years. It is apparent that such segregation has long been a nationwide problem, not merely one of sectional concern.

"tangible" factors may be equal, deprive the children of the minority group of equal educational opportunities? We believe that it does.

In *Sweatt v. Painter*, 339 U.S. 629, *supra*, in finding that a segregated law school for Negroes could not provide them equal educational opportunities, this Court relied in large part on "those qualities which are incapable of objective measurement but which make for greatness in a law school." In *McLaurin v. Oklahoma State Regents*, 339 U.S. 637, *supra*, the Court, in requiring that a Negro admitted to a white graduate school be treated like all other students, again resorted to intangible considerations: ". . . his ability to study, to engage in discussions and exchange views with other students, and, in general, to learn his profession." Such considerations apply with added force to children in grade and high schools. To separate them from others of similar age and qualifications solely because of their race generates a feeling of inferiority as to their status in the community that may affect their hearts and minds in a way unlikely ever to be undone. The effect of this separation on their educational opportunities was well stated by a finding in the Kansas case by a court which nevertheless felt compelled to rule against the Negro plaintiffs:

> Segregation of white and colored children in public schools has a detrimental effect upon the colored children. The impact is greater when it has the sanction of the law; for the policy of separating the races is usually interpreted as denoting the inferiority of the negro group. A sense of inferiority affects the motivation of a child to learn. Segregation with the sanction of law, therefore, has a tendency to [retard] the educational and mental development of negro children and to deprive them of some of the benefits they would receive in a racial[ly] integrated school system.

Whatever may have been the extent of psychological knowledge at the time of *Plessy v. Ferguson*, this finding is amply supported by modern authority.[2] Any language in *Plessy v. Ferguson* contrary to this finding is rejected.

We conclude that in the field of public education the doctrine of "separate but equal" has no place. Separate educational facilities are inherently unequal. Therefore, we hold that the plaintiffs and others similarly situated for whom the actions have been brought are, by reason of the segregation complained of, deprived of the equal protection of the laws guaranteed by the Fourteenth Amendment. This disposition makes unnecessary any discussion whether such segregation also violates the Due Process Clause of the Fourteenth Amendment.

---

2. [FN 11] K. B. Clark, Effect of Prejudice and Discrimination on Personality Development (Midcentury White House Conference on Children and Youth, 1950); Witmer and Kotinsky, Personality in the Making (1952), c. VI; Deutscher and Chein, *The Psychological Effects of Enforced Segregation: A Survey of Social Science Opinion*, 26 J. Psychol. 259 (1948); Chein, *What are the Psychological Effects of Segregation Under Conditions of Equal Facilities?*, 3 Int. J. Opinion and Attitude Res. 229 (1949); Brameld, *Educational Costs, in* Discrimination and National Welfare (MacIver, ed., (1949), 44–48; Frazier, The Negro in the United States (1949), 674–681. And *see generally* Myrdal, An American Dilemma (1944).

Because these are class actions, because of the wide applicability of this decision, and because of the great variety of local conditions, the formulation of decrees in these cases presents problems of considerable complexity. On reargument, the consideration of appropriate relief was necessarily subordinated to the primary question—the constitutionality of segregation in public education. We have now announced that such segregation is a denial of the equal protection of the laws. In order that we may have the full assistance of the parties in formulating decrees, the cases will be restored to the docket, and the parties are requested to present further argument on Questions 4 and 5 previously propounded by the Court for the reargument this Term. The Attorney General of the United States is again invited to participate. The Attorneys General of the states requiring or permitting segregation in public education will also be permitted to appear as amici curiae upon request to do so. . . .

Brown v. Board of Education (Brown II)

349 U.S. 294 (1955)

The Court rules that states must implement its ruling in Brown I and desegregate public elementary and secondary schools with "all deliberate speed."

MR. CHIEF JUSTICE WARREN delivered the opinion of the Court.

These cases were decided on May 17, 1954. The opinions of that date, declaring the fundamental principle that racial discrimination in public education is unconstitutional, are incorporated herein by reference. All provisions of federal, state, or local law requiring or permitting such discrimination must yield to this principle. There remains for consideration the manner in which relief is to be accorded.

. . . .

Full implementation of these constitutional principles may require solution of varied local school problems. School authorities have the primary responsibility for elucidating, assessing, and solving these problems; courts will have to consider whether the action of school authorities constitutes good faith implementation of the governing constitutional principles. Because of their proximity to local conditions and the possible need for further hearings, the courts which originally heard these cases can best perform this judicial appraisal. Accordingly, we believe it appropriate to remand the cases to those courts.

In fashioning and effectuating the decrees, the courts will be guided by equitable principles. Traditionally, equity has been characterized by a practical flexibility in shaping its remedies and by a facility for adjusting and reconciling public and private needs. These cases call for the exercise of these traditional attributes of equity power. At stake is the personal interest of the plaintiffs in admission to public schools as soon as practicable on a nondiscriminatory basis. To effectuate this interest may call for elimination of a variety of obstacles in making the transition to school systems operated in accordance with the constitutional principles set forth in our May 17, 1954, decision. Courts of equity may properly take into account the public interest in the elimination of such obstacles in a systematic and effective manner. But it should go without saying that the vitality of these constitutional principles cannot be allowed to yield simply because of disagreement with them.

While giving weight to these public and private considerations, the courts will require that the defendants make a prompt and reasonable start toward full compliance with our May 17, 1954, ruling. Once such a start has been made, the courts may find that additional time is necessary to carry out the ruling in an effective manner. The burden rests upon the defendants to establish that such time is necessary in the public interest and is consistent with good faith compliance at the earliest practicable date. To that end, the courts may consider problems related to administration, arising from the physical condition of the school plant, the school transportation system, personnel, revision of school districts and attendance areas into compact units to achieve a system of determining admission to the public schools on a nonracial basis, and revision of local laws and regulations which may be necessary in solving the foregoing problems. They will also consider the adequacy of any plans the defendants may propose to meet these problems and to effectuate a transition to a racially nondiscriminatory school system. During this period of transition, the courts will retain jurisdiction of these cases.

The judgments below, except that in the Delaware case, are accordingly reversed and the cases are remanded to the District Courts to take such proceedings and enter such orders and decrees consistent with this opinion as are necessary and proper to admit to public schools on a racially nondiscriminatory basis with all deliberate speed the parties to these cases. The judgment in the Delaware case—ordering the immediate admission of the plaintiffs to schools previously attended only by white children—is affirmed on the basis of the principles stated in our May 17, 1954, opinion, but the case is remanded to the Supreme Court of Delaware for such further proceedings as that Court may deem necessary in light of this opinion.

It is so ordered.

San Antonio Independent School District v. Rodriguez

411 U.S. 1 (1973)

In a case brought by Mexican-American parents challenging the method by which Texas financed public education, the Supreme Court finds no suspect class or fundamental right and upholds, on a rational-basis analysis, the school finance method at issue.

Mr. Justice Powell delivered the opinion of the Court.

This suit attacking the Texas system of financing public education was initiated by Mexican-American parents whose children attend the elementary and secondary schools in the Edgewood Independent School District, an urban school district in San Antonio, Texas. They brought a class action on behalf of schoolchildren throughout the State who are members of minority groups or who are poor and reside in school districts having a low property tax base.... The complaint was filed in the summer of 1968 and a three-judge court was impaneled in January 1969. In December 1971 the panel rendered its judgment in a *per curiam* opinion holding the Texas school finance system unconstitutional under the Equal Protection Clause of the Fourteenth Amendment. For the reasons stated in this opinion, we reverse the decision of the District Court.

. . . .

Texas virtually concedes that its historically rooted dual system of financing education could not withstanding the strict judicial scrutiny that this Court has found appropriate in reviewing legislative judgments that interfere with fundamental constitutional rights or that involve suspect classifications. If, as previous decisions have indicated, strict scrutiny means that the State's system is not entitled to the usual presumption of validity, that the State rather than the complainants must carry a "heavy burden of justification," that the State must demonstrate that its educational system has been structured with "precision," and is "tailored" narrowly to serve legitimate objectives and that it has selected the "less drastic means" for effectuating its objectives, the Texas financing system and its counterpart in virtually every other State will not pass muster. The State candidly admits that "[n]o one familiar with the Texas system would contend that it has yet achieved perfection." Apart from its concession that educational financing in Texas has "defects" and "imperfections," the State defends the system's rationality with vigor and disputes the District Court's finding that it lacks a "reasonable basis."

This, then, establishes the framework for our analysis. We must decide, first, whether the Texas system of financing public education operates to the disadvantage of some suspect class or impinges upon a fundamental right explicitly or implicitly protected by the Constitution, thereby requiring strict judicial scrutiny. If so, the judgment of the District Court should be affirmed. If not, the Texas scheme must still be examined to determine whether it rationally furthers some legitimate, articulated state purpose and therefore does not constitute an invidious discrimination in violation of the Equal Protection Clause of the Fourteenth Amendment.

The District Court's opinion does not reflect the novelty and complexity of the constitutional questions posed by appellees' challenge to Texas' system of school financing. In concluding that strict judicial scrutiny was required, that court relied on decisions dealing with the rights of indigents to equal treatment in the criminal trial and appellate processes, and on cases disapproving wealth restrictions on the right to vote. Those cases, the District Court concluded, established wealth as a suspect classification. Finding that the local property tax system discriminated on the basis of wealth, it regarded those precedents as controlling. It then reasoned, based on decisions of this Court affirming the undeniable importance of education, that there is a fundamental right to education and that, absent some compelling state justification, the Texas system could not stand.

We are unable to agree that this case, which in significant aspects is *sui generis*, may be so neatly fitted into the conventional mosaic of constitutional analysis under the Equal Protection Clause. Indeed, for the several reasons that follow, we find neither the suspect-classification not the fundamental-interest analysis persuasive.

The wealth discrimination discovered by the District Court in this case, and by several other courts that have recently struck down school-financing laws in other States, quite unlike any of the forms of wealth discrimination heretofore reviewed by this Court. Rather than focusing on the unique features of the alleged discrimination, the courts in these cases have virtually assumed their findings of a suspect classification through a simplistic process of analysis: since, under the traditional systems of financing public schools, some poorer people receive less expensive educations than other more affluent people, these systems discriminate on the basis of wealth. This approach largely ignores the hard threshold questions, including whether it makes a difference for purposes of consideration under the Constitution that the class of disadvantaged "poor" cannot be identified or defined in customary equal protection terms, and whether the relative—rather than absolute—nature of the asserted deprivation is of significant consequence. Before a State's laws and the justifications for the classifications they create are subjected to strict judicial scrutiny, we think these threshold considerations must be analyzed more closely than they were in the court below.

The case comes to us with no definitive description of the classifying facts or delineation of the disfavored class. . . .

However described, it is clear that appellees' suit asks this Court to extend its most exacting scrutiny to review a system that allegedly discriminates against a large, diverse, and amorphous class, unified only by the common factor of residence in districts that happen to have less taxable wealth than other districts. The system of alleged discrimination and the class it defines have none of the traditional indicia of suspectness: the class is not saddled with such disabilities, or subjected to such a history of purposeful unequal treatment, or relegated to such a position of political powerlessness as to command extraordinary protection from the majoritarian political process.

We thus conclude that the Texas system does not operate to the peculiar disadvantage of any suspect class. But in recognition of the fact that this Court has never heretofore held that wealth discrimination alone provides an adequate basis for invoking strict scrutiny, appellees have not relied solely on this contention. They also assert that the State's system impermissibly interferes with the exercise of a "fundamental" right and that accordingly the prior decisions of this Court require the application of the strict standard of judicial review.

It is this question—whether education is a fundamental right, in the sense that it is among the rights and liberties protected by the Constitution—which has so consumed the attention of courts and commentators in recent years.

In *Brown v. Board of Education*, 347 U.S. 483 (1954), a unanimous Court recognized that "education is perhaps the most important function of state and local governments." . . .

This theme, expressing an abiding respect for the vital role of education in a free society, may be found in numerous opinions of Justices of this Court writing both before and after *Brown* was decided. . . .

Nothing this Court holds today in any way detracts from our historic dedication to public education. We are in complete agreement with the conclusion of the three-judge panel below that "the grave significance of education both to the individual and to our society" cannot be doubted. But the importance of a service performed by the State does not determine whether it must be regarded as fundamental for purposes of examination under the Equal Protection Clause. . . . Mr. Justice Stewart's response in *Shapiro* to Mr. Justice Harlan's concern correctly articulates the limits of the fundamental-rights rationale employed in the Court's equal protection decisions:

> The Court today does not "pick out particular human activities, characterize them as 'fundamental,' and give them added protection. . . ." To the contrary, the Court simply recognizes, as it must, an established constitutional right, and gives to that right no less protection than the Constitution itself demands.

. . . .

It is not the province of this Court to create substantive constitutional rights in the name of guaranteeing equal protection of the laws. Thus, the key to discovering whether education is "fundamental" is not to be found in comparisons of the relative societal significance of education as opposed to subsistence or housing. Nor is it to be found by weighing whether education is as important as the right to travel. Rather, the answer lies in assessing whether there is a right to education explicitly or implicitly guaranteed by the Constitution.

Education, of course, is not among the rights afforded explicit protection under our Federal Constitution. Nor do we find any basis for saying it is implicitly so protected. As we have said, the undisputed importance of education will not alone cause this Court to depart from the usual standard for reviewing a State's social and economic legislation. It is appellees' contention, however, that education is distinguishable from other services and benefits provided by the State because it bears a peculiarly close relationship to other rights and liberties accorded protection under the Constitution. Specifically, they insist that education is itself a fundamental personal right because it is essential to the effective exercise of First Amendment freedoms and to intelligent utilization of the right to vote. In asserting a nexus between speech and education, appellees urge that the right to speak is meaningless unless the speaker is capable of articulating his thoughts intelligently and persuasively. The "marketplace of ideas" is an empty forum for those lacking basic communicative tools. Likewise, they argue that the corollary right to receive information becomes little more than a hollow privilege when the recipient has not been taught to read, assimilate, and utilize available knowledge.

A similar line of reasoning is pursued with respect to the right to vote. Exercise of the franchise, it is contended, cannot be divorced from the educational foundation of the voter. The electoral process, if reality is to conform to the democratic ideal, depends on an informed electorate: a voter cannot cast his ballot intelligently unless his reading skills and thought processes have been adequately developed.

We need not dispute any of these propositions. The Court has long afforded zealous protection against unjustifiable governmental interference with the individual's rights to speak and to vote. Yet we have never presumed to possess either the ability or the authority to guarantee to the citizenry the most effective speech or the most informed electoral choice. That these may be desirable goals of a system of freedom of expression and of a representative form of government is not to be doubted. These are indeed goals to be pursued by a people whose thoughts and beliefs are freed from governmental interference. But they are not values to be implemented by judicial instruction into otherwise legitimate state activities.

Even if it were conceded that some identifiable quantum of education is a constitutionally protected prerequisite to the meaningful exercise of either right, we have no indication that the present levels of educational expenditures in Texas provide an education that falls short. Whatever merit appellees' argument might have if a State's financing system occasioned an absolute denial of educational opportunities to any of its children, that argument provides no basis for finding an interference with fundamental rights where only relative differences in spending levels are involved and where—as is true in the present case—no charge fairly could be made that the system fails to provide each child with an opportunity to acquire the basic minimal skills necessary for the enjoyment of the rights of speech and of full participation in the political process.

Furthermore, the logical limitations on appellees' nexus theory are difficult to perceive. How, for instance, is education to be distinguished from the significant personal interests in the basics of decent food and shelter? Empirical examination might well buttress an assumption that the ill-fed, ill-clothed, and ill-housed are among the most ineffective participants in the political process, and that they derive the least enjoyment from the benefits of the First Amendment.

We have carefully considered each of the arguments supportive of the District Court's finding that education is a fundamental right or liberty and have found those arguments unpersuasive....

It should be clear, for the reasons stated above and in accord with the prior decisions of this Court, that this is not a case in which the challenged state action must be subjected to the searching judicial scrutiny reserved for laws that create suspect classifications or impinge upon constitutionally protected rights.

We need not rest our decision, however, solely on the inappropriateness of the strict-scrutiny test. A century of Supreme Court adjudication under the Equal Protection Clause affirmatively supports the application of the traditional standard of review, which requires only that the State's system be shown to bear some rational relationship to legitimate state purposes. This case represents far more than a challenge to the manner in which Texas provides for the education of its children. We have here nothing less than a direct attack on the way in which Texas has chosen to raise and disburse state and local tax revenues. We are asked to condemn the State's judgment in conferring on political subdivisions the power to tax local property to supply revenues for local interests. In so doing, appellees would have the Court intrude in an area in which it has traditionally deferred to state legislatures. This Court has often admonished against such interferences with the State's fiscal policies under the Equal Protection Clause.

Thus, we stand on familiar grounds when we continue to acknowledge that the Justices of this Court lack both the expertise and the familiarity with local problems so necessary to the making of wise decisions with respect to the raising and disposition of public revenues. Yet, we are urged to direct the States either to alter drastically the present system or to throw out the property tax altogether in favor of some other form of taxation. No scheme of taxation, whether the tax is imposed on property, income, or purchases of goods and services, has yet been devised which is free of all discriminatory impact. In such a complex arena in which no perfect alternatives exist, the Court does well not to impose too rigorous a standard of scrutiny lest all local fiscal schemes become subjects of criticism under the Equal Protection Clause.

In addition to matters of fiscal policy, this case also involves the most persistent and difficult questions of educational policy, another area in which this Court's lack of specialized knowledge and experience counsels against premature interference with the informed judgments made at the state and local levels. Education, perhaps even more than welfare assistance, presents a myriad of "intractable economic, social, and even philosophical problems." The very complexity of the problems of financing and managing a statewide public school system suggests that "there will be more than one constitutionally permissible method of solving them," and that, within the limits of rationality, 'the legislature's efforts to tackle the problems' should be entitled to respect. On even the most basic questions in this area the scholars and educational experts are divided. Indeed, one of the major sources of controversy concerns the extent to which there is a demonstrable correlation between educational expenditures and the quality of education—an assumed correlation underlying virtually every legal conclusion drawn by the District Court in this case. Related to the questioned relationship between cost and quality is the equally unsettled controversy as to the proper goals of a system of public education. And the question regarding the most effective relationship between state boards of education and local school boards, in terms of their respective responsibilities and degrees of control, is now undergoing searching re-examination. The ultimate wisdom as to these and related problems of education is not likely to be divined for all time even by the scholars who now so earnestly debate the issues. In such circumstances, the judiciary is well advised to refrain from imposing on the States inflexible constitutional restraints that could circumscribe or handicap the continued research and experimentation so vital to finding even partial solutions to educational problems and to keeping abreast of ever-changing conditions.

It must be remembered, also, that every claim arising under the Equal Protection Clause has implications for the relationship between national and state power under our federal system. Questions of federalism are always inherent in the process of determining whether a State's laws are to be accorded the traditional presumption of constitutionality, or are to be subjected instead to rigorous judicial scrutiny. While "[t]he maintenance of the principles of federalism is a foremost consideration in interpreting any of the pertinent constitutional provisions under which this Court examines state action," it would be difficult to imagine a case having a greater potential impact on our federal system than the one now before us, in which we are urged to abrogate systems of financing public education presently in existence in virtually every State.

The foregoing considerations buttress our conclusion that Texas' system of public school finance is an inappropriate candidate for strict judicial scrutiny. . . .

. . . .

We hardly need add that this Court's action today is not to be viewed as placing its judicial imprimatur on the status quo. The need is apparent for reform in tax systems which may well have relied too long and too heavily on the local property tax. And certainly innovative thinking as to public education, its methods, and its funding is necessary to assure both a higher level of quality and greater uniformity of opportunity. These matters merit the continued attention of the scholars who already have contributed much by their challenges. But the ultimate solutions must come from the lawmakers and from the democratic pressures of those who elect them.

Reversed.

MR. JUSTICE STEWART, concurring.

The method of financing public schools in Texas, as in almost every other State, has resulted in a system of public education that can fairly be described as chaotic and unjust. It does not follow, however, and I cannot find, that this system violates the Constitution of the United States. I join the opinion and judgment of the Court because I am convinced that any other course would mark an extraordinary departure from principled adjudication under the Equal Protection Clause of the Fourteenth Amendment. The unchartered directions of such a departure are suggested, I think, by the imaginative dissenting opinion my BROTHER MARSHALL has filed today.

MR. JUSTICE BRENNAN, dissenting.

Although I agree with my BROTHER WHITE that the Texas statutory scheme is devoid of any rational basis, and for that reason is violative of the Equal Protection Clause, I also record my disagreement with the Court's rather distressing assertion that a right may be deemed "fundamental" for the purposes of equal protection analysis only if it is "explicitly or implicitly guaranteed by the Constitution." As my BROTHER MARSHALL convincingly demonstrates, our prior cases stand for the proposition that "fundamentality" is, in large measure, a function of the right's importance in terms of the effectuation of those rights which are in fact constitutionally guaranteed. Thus, "[a]s the nexus between the specific constitutional guarantee and the nonconstitutional interest draws closer, the nonconstitutional interest becomes more fundamental and the degree of judicial scrutiny applied when the interest is infringed on a discriminatory basis must be adjusted accordingly."

Here, there can be no doubt that education is inextricably linked to the right to participate in the electoral process and to the rights of free speech and association guaranteed by the First Amendment. This being so, any classification affecting education must be subjected to strict judicial scrutiny, and since even the State concedes that the statutory scheme now before us cannot pass constitutional muster under this stricter standard of review, I can only conclude that the Texas school-financing scheme is constitutionally invalid.

Mr. Justice White, with whom Mr. Justice Douglas and Mr. Justice Brennan join, dissenting.

The Texas public schools are financed through a combination of state funding, local property tax revenue, and some federal funds. Concededly, the system yields wide disparity in per-pupil revenue among the various districts. In a typical year, for example, the Alamo Heights district had total revenues of $594 per pupil, while the Edgewood district had only $356 per pupil. The majority and the State concede, as they must, the existence of major disparities in spendable funds. But the State contends that the disparities do not invidiously discriminate against children and families in districts such as Edgewood, because the Texas scheme is designed "to provide an adequate education for all, with local autonomy to go beyond that as individual school districts desire and are able. . . ." It leaves to the people of each district the choice whether to go beyond the minimum and, if so, by how much. The majority advances this rationalization: "While assuring a basic education for every child in the State, it permits and encourages a large measure of participation in and control of each district's schools at the local level."

I cannot disagree with the proposition that local control and local decisionmaking play an important part in our democratic system of government. *Cf. James v. Valtierra*, 402 U.S. 137 (1971). Much may be left to local option, and this case would be quite different if it were true that the Texas system, while insuring minimum educational expenditures in every district through state funding, extended a meaningful option to all local districts to increase their per-pupil expenditures and so to improve their children's education to the extent that increased funding would achieve that goal. The system would then arguably provide a rational and sensible method of achieving the stated aim of preserving an area for local initiative and decision.

The difficulty with the Texas system, however, is that it provides a meaningful option to Alamo Heights and like school districts but almost none to Edgewood and those other districts with a low per-pupil real estate tax base. In these latter districts, no matter how desirous parents are of supporting their schools with greater revenues, it is impossible to do so through the use of the real estate property tax. In these districts, the Texas system utterly fails to extend a realistic choice to parents because the property tax, which is the only revenue-raising mechanism extended to school districts, is practically and legally unavailable.

. . . .

The Equal Protection Clause permits discriminations between classes but requires that the classification bear some rational relationship to a permissible object sought to be attained by the statute. It is not enough that the Texas system before us seeks to achieve the valid, rational purpose of maximizing local initiative; the means chosen by the State must also be rationally related to the end sought to be achieved. As the Court stated just last Term in *Weber v. Aetna Casualty & Surety Co.*, 406 U.S. 164, 172, (1972):

> "The tests to determine the validity of state statutes under the Equal Protection Clause have been variously expressed, but this Court requires, at a minimum, that a statutory classification bear some rational relationship to a legitimate state purpose."

Neither Texas nor the majority heeds this rule. If the State aims at maximizing local initiative and local choice, by permitting school districts to resort to the real property tax if they choose to do so, it utterly fails in achieving its purpose in districts with property tax bases so low that there is little if any opportunity for interested parents, rich or poor, to augment school district revenues. Requiring the State to establish only that unequal treatment is in furtherance of a permissible goal, without also requiring the State to show that the means chosen to effectuate that goal are rationally related to its achievement, makes equal protection analysis no more than an empty gesture. In my view, the parents and children in Edgewood, and in like districts, suffer from an invidious discrimination violative of the Equal Protection Clause.

This does not, of course, mean that local control may not be a legitimate goal of a school-financing system. Nor does it mean that the State must guarantee each district an equal per-pupil revenue from the state school-financing system. Nor does it mean, as the majority appears to believe, that, by affirming the decision below, this Court would be "imposing on the States inflexible constitutional restraints that could circumscribe or handicap the continued research and experimentation so vital to finding even partial solutions to educational problems and to keeping abreast of ever-changing conditions." On the contrary, it would merely mean that the State must fashion a financing scheme which provides a rational basis for the maximization of local control, if local control is to remain a goal of the system, and not a scheme with "different treatment be[ing] accorded to persons placed by a statute into different classes on the basis of criteria wholly unrelated to the objective of that statute."

Perhaps the majority believes that the major disparity in revenues provided and permitted by the Texas system is inconsequential. I cannot agree, however, that the difference of the magnitude appearing in this case can sensibly be ignored, particularly since the State itself considers it so important to provide opportunities to exceed the minimum state educational expenditures.

There is no difficulty in identifying the class that is subject to the alleged discrimination and that is entitled to the benefits of the Equal Protection Clause. I need go no further than the parents and children in the Edgewood district, who are plaintiffs here and who assert that they are entitled to the same choice as Alamo Heights to augment local expenditures for schools but are denied that choice by state law. This group constitutes a class sufficiently definite to invoke the protection of the Constitution. They are as entitled to the protection of the Equal Protection Clause as were the voters in allegedly underrepresented counties in the reapportionment cases. . . . Similarly, in the present case we would blink reality to ignore the fact that school districts, and students in the end, are differentially affected by the Texas school-financing scheme with respect to their capability to supplement the Minimum Foundation School Program. At the very least, the law discriminates against those children and their parents who live in districts where the per-pupil tax base is sufficiently low to make impossible the provision of comparable school revenues by resort to the real property tax which is the only device the State extends for this purpose.

MR. JUSTICE MARSHALL, with whom MR. JUSTICE DOUGLAS concurs, dissenting.

The Court today decides, in effect, that a State may constitutionally vary the quality of education which it offers its children in accordance with the amount of taxable wealth located in the school districts within which they reside. The majority's decision represents an abrupt departure from the mainstream of recent state and federal court decisions concerning the unconstitutionality of state educational financing schemes dependent upon taxable local wealth. More unfortunately, though, the majority's holding can only be seen as a retreat from our historic commitment to equality of educational opportunity and as unsupportable acquiescence in a system which deprives children in their earliest years of the chance to reach their full potential as citizens. The Court does this despite the absence of any substantial justification for a scheme which arbitrarily channels educational resources in accordance with the fortuity of the amount of taxable wealth within each district.

In my judgment, the right of every American to an equal start in life, so far as the provision of a state service as important as education is concerned, is far too vital to permit state discrimination on grounds as tenuous as those presented by this record. Nor can I accept the notion that it is sufficient to remit these appellees to the vagaries of the political process which, contrary to the majority's suggestion, has proved singularly unsuited to the task of providing a remedy for this discrimination. I, for one, am unsatisfied with the hope of an ultimate "political" solution sometime in the indefinite future while, in the meantime, countless children unjustifiably receive inferior educations that "may affect their hearts and minds in a way unlikely ever to be undone." *Brown v. Board of Education*, 347 U.S. 483, 494 (1954). I must therefore respectfully dissent.

[The remainder of Justice Marshall's dissent is omitted. You may want to review it online for a different analysis of whether education is a fundamental right.]

Plyler v. Doe

457 U.S. 202 (1982)

The Supreme Court finds a Texas statute that withheld state funds from local school districts for children not "legally admitted" into the country, and that authorized local districts to refuse to enroll those children in school, unconstitutional on equal protection grounds.

JUSTICE BRENNAN delivered the opinion of the Court.

The question presented by these cases is whether, consistent with the Equal Protection Clause of the Fourteenth Amendment, Texas may deny to undocumented school-age children the free public education that it provides to children who are citizens of the United States or legally admitted aliens.

....

In May 1975, the Texas Legislature revised its education laws to withhold from local school districts any state funds for the education of children who were not "legally admitted" into the United States. The 1975 revision also authorized local school districts to deny enrollment in their public schools to children not "legally admitted" to the country.

This is a class action, filed in the United States District Court for the Eastern District of Texas ... on behalf of certain school-age children of Mexican origin residing in Smith County, Tex., who could not establish that they had been legally admitted into the United States....

The Equal Protection Clause directs that "all persons similarly circumstanced shall be treated alike." But so too, "[the] Constitution does not require things which are different in fact or opinion to be treated in law as though they were the same." The initial discretion to determine what is "different" and what is "the same" resides in the legislatures of the States. A legislature must have substantial latitude to establish classifications that roughly approximate the nature of the problem perceived, that accommodate competing concerns both public and private, and that account for limitations on the practical ability of the State to remedy every ill. In applying the Equal Protection Clause to most forms of state action, we thus seek only the assurance that the classification at issue bears some fair relationship to a legitimate public purpose.

But we would not be faithful to our obligations under the Fourteenth Amendment if we applied so deferential a standard to every classification. The Equal Protection Clause was intended as a restriction on state legislative action inconsistent with elemental constitutional premises. Thus we have treated as presumptively invidious those classifications that disadvantage a "suspect class," or that impinge upon the exercise of a "fundamental right." With respect to such classifications, it is appropriate to enforce the mandate of equal protection by requiring the State to demonstrate that its classification has been precisely tailored to serve a compelling governmental interest. In addition, we have recognized that certain forms of legislative classification, while not facially invidious, nonetheless give rise to recurring constitutional difficulties; in these limited circumstances we have sought the assurance that the classification reflects a reasoned judgment consistent with the ideal of equal protection by inquiring whether it may fairly be viewed as furthering substantial interest of the State. We turn to a consideration of the standard appropriate for the evaluation of [the Texas law]. . . .

We reject the claim that "illegal aliens" are a "suspect class." . . . With respect to the actions of the Federal Government, alienage classifications may be intimately related to the conduct of foreign policy, to the federal prerogative to control access to the United States, and to the plenary federal power to determine who has sufficiently manifested his allegiance to become a citizen of the Nation. No State may independently exercise a like power. But if the Federal Government has by uniform rule prescribed what it believes to be appropriate standards for the treatment of an alien subclass, the States may, of course, follow the federal direction. . . .

The children who are plaintiffs in these cases are special members of this underclass. Persuasive arguments support the view that a State may withhold its beneficence from those whose very presence within the United States is the product of their own unlawful conduct. These arguments do not apply with the same force to classifications imposing disabilities on the minor *children* of such illegal entrants. . . . These arguments do not apply with the same force to classifications imposing disabilities on the minor children of such illegal entrants. At the least, those who elect to enter our territory by stealth and in violation of our law should be prepared to bear the consequences, including, but not limited to, deportation. But the children of those illegal entrants are not comparably situated. Their "parents have the ability to conform their conduct to societal norms," and presumably the ability to remove themselves from the State's jurisdiction; but the children who are plaintiffs in these cases "can affect neither their parents' conduct nor their own status." *Trimble v. Gordon*, 430 U.S. 762, 770 (1977).

Even if the State found it expedient to control the conduct of adults by acting against their children, legislation directing the onus of a parent's misconduct against his children does not comport with fundamental conceptions of justice. "[Visiting] . . . condemnation on the head of an infant is illogical and unjust. Moreover, imposing disabilities on the . . . child is contrary to the basic concept of our system that legal burdens should bear some relationship to individual responsibility or wrongdoing. Obviously, no child is responsible for his birth and penalizing the . . . child is an ineffectual—as well as unjust—way of deterring the parent." *Weber v. Aetna Casualty & Surety Co.*, 406 U.S. 164, 175 (1972).

. . . .

Of course, undocumented status is not irrelevant to any proper legislative goal. Nor is undocumented status an absolutely immutable characteristic since it is the product of conscious, indeed unlawful, action. But § 21.031 is directed against children, and imposes its discriminatory burden on the basis of a legal characteristic over which children can have little control. It is thus difficult to conceive of a rational justification for penalizing these children for their presence within the United States. Yet that appears to be precisely the effect of § 21.031.

Public education is not a "right" granted to individuals by the Constitution. *San Antonio Independent School Dist. v. Rodriguez*, 411 U.S. 1, 35 (1973). But neither is it merely some governmental "benefit" indistinguishable from other forms of social welfare legislation. Both the importance of education in maintaining our basic institutions, and the lasting impact of its deprivation on the life of the child, mark the distinction. . . .

In addition to the pivotal role of education in sustaining our political and cultural heritage, denial of education to some isolated group of children poses an affront to one of the goals of the Equal Protection Clause: the abolition of governmental barriers presenting unreasonable obstacles to advancement on the basis of individual merit. Paradoxically, by depriving the children of any disfavored group of an education, we foreclose the means by which that group might raise the level of esteem in which it is held by the majority. But more directly, "education prepares individuals to be self-reliant and self-sufficient participants in society." Illiteracy is an enduring disability. The inability to read and write will handicap the individual deprived of a basic education each and every day of his life. The inestimable toll of that deprivation on the social, economic, intellectual, and psychological well-being of the individual, and the obstacle it poses to individual achievement, make it most difficult to reconcile the cost or the principle of a status-based denial of basic education with the framework of equality embodied in the Equal Protection Clause. What we said 28 years ago in *Brown v. Board of Education*, 347 U.S. 483 (1954), still holds true. . . .

These well-settled principles allow us to determine the proper level of deference to be afforded [the Texas law]. Undocumented aliens cannot be treated as a suspect class because their presence in this country in violation of federal law is not a "constitutional irrelevancy." Nor is education a fundamental right; a State need not justify by compelling necessity every variation in the manner in which education is provided to its population. *See San Antonio Independent School Dist. v. Rodriguez.* But more is involved in these cases than the abstract question whether [the Texas law] discriminates against a suspect class, or whether education is a fundamental right. [The Texas law] imposes a lifetime hardship on a discrete class of children not accountable for their disabling status. The stigma of illiteracy will mark them for the rest of their lives. By denying these children a basic education, we deny them the ability to live within the structure of our civic institutions, and foreclose any realistic possibility that they will contribute in even the smallest way to the progress of our Nation. In determining the rationality of [the Texas law], we may appropriately take into account its costs to the Nation and to the innocent children who are its victims. In light of these countervailing costs, the discrimination contained in [the Texas law] can hardly be considered rational unless it furthers some substantial goal of the State.

It is the State's principal argument, and apparently the view of the dissenting Justices, that the undocumented status of these children *vel non* establishes a sufficient rational basis for denying them benefits that a State might choose to afford other residents. The State notes that while other aliens are admitted "on an equality of legal privileges with all citizens under non-discriminatory laws," the asserted right of these children to an education can claim no implicit congressional imprimatur. Indeed, in the State's view, Congress' apparent disapproval of the presence of these children within the United States, and the evasion of the federal regulatory program that is the mark of undocumented status, provides authority for its decision to impose upon them special disabilities. Faced with an equal protection challenge respecting the treatment of aliens, we agree that the courts must be attentive to congressional policy; the exercise of congressional power might well affect the State's prerogatives to afford differential treatment to a particular class of aliens. But we are unable to find in the congressional immigration scheme any statement of policy that might weigh significantly in arriving at an equal protection balance concerning the State's authority to deprive these children of an education.

. . . .

To be sure, like all persons who have entered the United States unlawfully, these children are subject to deportation. But there is no assurance that a child subject to deportation will ever be deported. An illegal entrant might be granted federal permission to continue to reside in this country, or even to become a citizen. In light of the discretionary federal power to grant relief from deportation, a State cannot realistically determine that any particular undocumented child will in fact be deported until after deportation proceedings have been completed. It would of course be most difficult for the State to justify a denial of education to a child enjoying an inchoate federal permission to remain. We are reluctant to impute to Congress the intention to withhold from these children, for so long as they are present in this country through no fault of their own, access to a basic education. In other contexts, undocumented status, coupled with some articulable federal policy, might enhance state authority with respect to the treatment of undocumented aliens. But in the area of special constitutional sensitivity presented by these cases, and in the absence of any contrary indication fairly discernible in the present legislative record, we perceive no national policy that supports the State in denying these children an elementary education. The State may borrow the federal classification. But to justify its use as a criterion for its own discriminatory policy, the State must demonstrate that the classification is reasonably adapted to *"the purposes for which the state desires to use it."*

. . . .

If the State is to deny a discrete group of innocent children the free public education that it offers to other children residing within its borders, that denial must be justified by a showing that it furthers some substantial state interest. No such showing was made here. Accordingly, the judgment of the Court of Appeals in each of these cases is *Affirmed*.

Post Problem Discussion

1. Do you agree with the Court's decision in *Rodriquez*? Why or why not? What impact does the Court finding education to be important, but not a fundamental right, under the Constitution have on students, public schools, and the laws and policies that govern them? How would things change if the Court overturned *Rodriquez* today and found that education was a fundamental right?

2. What do these cases tell us about the relationship between local, state, and federal governments in regard to education?

3. The *Brown* cases are perhaps the most influential cases in education law. They are discussed in more detail in Chapter 5. State efforts to desegregate schools raised many issues and tested the boundaries of state and federal power and judicial review. Several states, or state officials, at one point or another openly refused to comply with *Brown* and challenged the Court's authority to force desegregation. How does the federal government enforce court decisions that establish constitutional requirements for states and public schools? Are there other enforcement methods that might be more effective than those that are currently employed?

4. In *Rodriquez*, the Court determines that education is not a fundamental right under the United States Constitution. The Court's decision led to school finance cases being pursued in state courts under state constitutional provisions. Some state courts found education to be a fundamental right under state constitutions, and ruled that state education funding systems were unconstitutional. See Chapter 2. In some cases, these state court orders ultimately led to some of the same challenges with enforcing court decisions that occurred in the desegregation cases—this time under state constitutional law principles. See Chapter 2. Why do you think education would be a fundamental right at the state level in some states, but not at the federal level?

5. *Plyler v. Doe* is often referred to as a case where the court applied "rational basis with teeth." Compare the result in *Plyler* to *Kadrmas v. Dickinson Public Schools*, 487 U.S. 450 (1988), where a poor student and her mother challenged the constitutionality of a North Dakota statute which allowed some local school boards to charge a fee for school bus transportation. Using a rational basis standard of review, the Supreme Court upheld the North Dakota law under the Equal Protection Clause, there being no fundamental right or suspect class. How is this situation any different from *Plyler*? Why do we have a different result? Did the rational basis standard or review simply lose its teeth, or are there differences in the cases that justify the different outcomes?

6. What impact do you think the *Plyler* case has had on the ability of states and schools to restrict educational opportunities for illegal alien children? Can they ever do so under *Plyler*? Under *Plyler*, can a public school report the illegal status of a student, to the U.S. Department of Homeland Security Immigration and Customs Enforcement Agency?

§ 1.02 State & Federal Interaction: The Supremacy and Spending Clauses

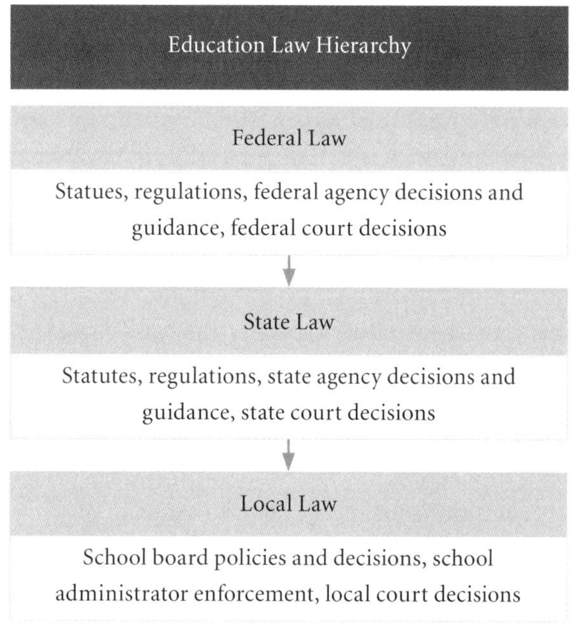

As noted, federal, state, and local laws govern education. These different levels of law operate in a hierarchy with federal law being at the top of the hierarchy under the Supremacy Clause of the United States Constitution. Where the federal government is involved in education—and involved it certainly is—it acts primarily under its power to tax and spend for the "general welfare" under the Spending Clause in Article I, Section 8 of the United States Constitution, and under its authority to assure due process and equal protection under the Fourteenth Amendment of the United States Constitution. Examples of federal statutes that apply to public schools and are based primarily in the Fourteenth Amendment's focus on equality and anti-discrimination include certain provisions of the Americans with Disabilities Act, 42 U.S.C. § 12101, which prohibits discrimination based on disability; Title IV of the Civil Rights of 1964, 42 U.S.C. § 2000c, which prohibits discrimination on the basis of race, color, sex, religion or national origin; and Section 1983, 42 U.S.C. § 1983, a civil rights statute that allows plaintiffs to bring claims for constitutional violations, and for violations of other federal laws.

Examples of Spending Clause statutes include the Individuals with Disabilities Act ("IDEA"), which contains requirements regarding special education services for students with disabilities, 20 U.S.C. § 1400 et seq.; Title I of the Elementary and

Secondary Education Act ("ESEA"), as amended by the Every Student Succeeds Act ("ESSA") in 2015, which has requirements in a number of areas including state-wide student assessment testing and school accountability requirements, 20 U.S.C. § 6301 et seq.; and the Children's Internet Protection Act, which requires schools that accept certain federal funds to implement computer filtering devices to protect students from images that are obscene, pornographic, or harmful to minors, 20 U.S.C. § 6777.

As this itemization suggests, Spending Clause statutes that affect education law have a wide purview. Typically, these statutes set up a process where the federal government offers federal funds to states, and states that accept the funds must agree to comply with certain conditions. The conditions must have a relationship to the purpose of the spending program, and they must be expressly and unambiguously stated so that states can 1) determine whether or not they want to accept the funds, and 2) be aware of the conditions that they will have to follow if they do accept the funds. *South Dakota v. Dole*, 483 U. S. 203 (1987); *Pennhurst State Sch. & Hosp. v. Halderman*, 451 U.S. 1, 17–18 (1981). Within these parameters, the federal authority is primary. If a state accepts the funds, then the state must meet the federal conditions. Theoretically, states can refuse to accept the funds and they would not have to follow the requirements of laws like the IDEA. In reality, this refusal is often discussed, but almost never practiced because the funding amounts are simply too high for states to pass up. What is more common is states, or schools, arguing that certain requirements under the law need not be followed because they were not clearly expressed as conditions for receiving funding.

In most cases, the conditions outlined in a federal Spending Clause approach require a state to adopt an implementation plan, under which the state explains how they will meet the conditions. These plans often include states agreeing to enact state laws and regulations that local school districts and schools must then follow to implement required programs or services that are part of the conditions. In this paradigm, power is often delegated from one level to the next in the hierarchy. As a rule, the state implementing laws must be consistent with federal requirements. However, state laws may sometimes exceed federal requirements, or have requirements that are different from federal law, if the requirements are more protective of student rights. *See, e.g.*, *Burlington v. Department of Educ.*, 736 F.2d 773, 789 (1st Cir. 1984), *aff'd*, 471 U.S. 359 (1985) (holding that IDEA establishes a basic floor of education and states may provide a greater or higher standard of educational services and procedural protection than IDEA requires).

The McKinney-Vento Act, which forms the basis of the next problem, is illustrative. McKinney-Vento requires states that accept funds to meet a number of requirements to ensure that homeless students have certain rights and receive educational services. States may develop their own state laws and regulations to implement these federal requirements, and impose certain obligations on public schools, but the state laws must be consistent with federal requirements.

The following problem provides some of the federal requirements and some illustrative state requirements and asks you to determine if the state laws meet the relevant federal requirements.

Problem 2: Homeless Students

Carla Blake lived in a rural town, Alpine, with her mother last school year and she attended the Alpine Elementary School as a fourth grader. Over the summer, Carla and her mother moved to a slightly larger town, Baron, five miles north of Alpine. The move did not work out as expected and, for various reasons, the Blakes were without a place to live in August. They remained in Baron in September when the school year started, staying at friends' houses, in various campgrounds, and in a small church shelter.

Ms. Blake wants Carla to attend the elementary school in Baron, but the Baron school officials say that she cannot because her "school of origin" is in Alpine. The Alpine School District says Carla can attend Alpine Elementary, but they will not transport Carla from Baron, because it does not do so for students who are not homeless. There is no public transportation, and Carla's mother does not have a car or a way to get Carla to school.

The Baron School District provides the Blakes with an explanation of their right to appeal the decision, and the Blakes follow the indicated process and appeal to the state commissioner of education. Answer the following:

1. Under federal law, what school or schools does Carla have the right to attend? Is the answer any different under state law? If so, is the difference permissible?

2. Where does Carla attend school during the appeal under federal law? Is the answer different under state law? If so, is the difference permissible?

3. What are the obligations under federal law of the Baron and Alpine City school districts to transport Carla if she attends school in Alpine City? Is the answer any different under state law? If so, is the difference permissible?

Problem Materials

✓ McKinney-Vento Act, 42 U.S.C. § 11432

✓ Hypothetical State Law—§ 493:12

✓ *Lampkin v. District of Columbia*, 879 F. Supp. 116 (D.D.C. 1995)

Federal Law 42 U.S.C. § 11432

Grants for state and local activities for the education of homeless children & youths

(a) General authority. The Secretary is authorized to make grants to States in accordance with the provisions of this section to enable such States to carry out the activities described in subsections (d) through (g).

. . . .

(E) Local educational agency requirements. For the State to be eligible to receive the funds described in subparagraph (B), the local educational agency . . . shall—

(i) implement a coordinated system for ensuring that homeless children and youths—

(I) are advised of the choice of schools provided in subsection (g)(3)(A);

(II) are immediately enrolled, in accordance with subsection (g)(3)(C), in the school selected under subsection (g)(3)(A); and

(III) are promptly provided necessary services described in subsection (g)(4), including transportation, to allow homeless children and youths to exercise their choices of schools under subsection (g)(3)(A);

. . . .

(g) State plan.

(1) In general. For any State desiring to receive a grant under this part, the State educational agency shall submit to the Secretary a plan to provide for the education of homeless children and youths within the State. Such plan shall include the following:

(A) A description of how such children and youths are (or will be) given the opportunity to meet the same challenging State academic standards as all students are expected to meet.

(B) A description of the procedures the State educational agency will use to identify such children and youths in the State and to assess their needs.

(C) A description of procedures for the prompt resolution of disputes regarding the educational placement of homeless children and youths.

. . . .

(J) Assurances that the following will be carried out:

(i) The State educational agency and local educational agencies in the State will adopt policies and practices to ensure that homeless children and youths are not stigmatized or segregated on the basis of their status as homeless.

(ii) The local educational agencies will designate an appropriate staff person, able to carry out the duties described in paragraph (6)(A), who may also be a coordinator for other Federal programs, as a local educational agency liaison for homeless children and youths.

(iii) The State and the local educational agencies in the State will adopt policies and practices to ensure that transportation is provided, at the request of the parent or guardian (or in the case of an unaccompanied youth, the liaison), to and from the school of origin, (as determined under paragraph (3), in accordance with the following, as applicable:

(I) If the child or youth continues to live in the area served by the local educational agency in which the school of origin is located, the child's or youth's transportation to and from the school of origin shall be provided or arranged by the local educational agency in which the school of origin is located.

(II) If the child's or youth's living arrangements in the area served by the local educational agency of origin terminate and the child or youth, though continuing the child's or youth's education in the school of origin, begins living in an area served by another local educational agency, the local educational agency of origin and the local educational agency in which the child or youth is living shall agree upon a method to apportion the responsibility and costs for providing the child or youth with transportation to and from the school of origin. If the local educational agencies are unable to agree upon such method, the responsibility and costs for transportation shall be shared equally.

....

(3) Local educational agency requirements

(A) In general. The local educational agency serving each child or youth to be assisted under this part shall, according to the child's or youth's best interest—

(i) continue the child's or youth's education in the school of origin for the duration of homelessness—

(I) in any case in which a family becomes homeless between academic years or during an academic year; and

(II) for the remainder of the academic year, if the child or youth becomes permanently housed during an academic year; or

(ii) enroll the child or youth in any public school that nonhomeless students who live in the attendance area in which the child or youth is actually living are eligible to attend.

(B) School Stability. In determining the best interest of the child or youth under subparagraph (A), the local educational agency shall—

(i) presume that keeping the child or youth in the school of origin is in the child's or youth's best interest, except when doing so is contrary to the request of the child's or youth's parent or guardian, or (in the case of an unaccompanied youth) the youth;

(ii) consider student-centered factors related to the child's or youth's best interest, including factors related to the impact of mobility on achievement, education, health, and safety of homeless children and youth, giving priority to the request of the child's or youth's parent or guardian or (in the case of an unaccompanied youth) the youth;

(iii) if, after conducting the best interest determination based on consideration of the presumption in clause (i) and the student-centered factors in clause (ii), the local educational agency determines that it is not in the child's or youth's best interest to attend the school of origin or the school requested by the parent or guardian, or (in the case of an unaccompanied youth) the youth, provide the child's or youth's parent or guardian or the unaccompanied youth with a written explanation of the reasons for its determination, in a manner and form understandable to such parent, guardian, or unaccompanied youth, including information regarding the right to appeal under subparagraph (E); and

(iv) in the case of an unaccompanied youth, ensure that the local educational agency liaison designated under paragraph (1)(J)(ii) assists in placement or enrollment decisions under this subparagraph, gives priority to the views of such unaccompanied youth, and provides notice to such youth of the right to appeal under subparagraph (E).

(C) Immediate enrollment

(i) In general. The school selected in accordance with this paragraph shall immediately enroll the homeless child or youth, even if the child or youth—

(I) is unable to produce records normally required for enrollment, such as previous academic records, records of immunization and other required health records, proof of residency, or other documentation.; or

(II) has missed application or enrollment deadlines during any period of homelessness.

(ii) Relevant academic records. The enrolling school shall immediately contact the school last attended by the child or youth to obtain relevant academic and other records.

(iii) Relevant health records. If the child or youth needs to obtain immunizations, or other required health records, the enrolling school shall immediately refer the parent or guardian of the child or youth, or (in the case of an unaccompanied youth) the youth, to the local educational agency liaison designated under paragraph (1)(J)(ii), who shall assist in obtaining necessary immunizations or screenings, or immunization or other required health records, in accordance with subparagraph (D).

(E) Enrollment disputes. If a dispute arises over eligibility, or school selection or enrollment in a school—

(i) the child or youth shall be immediately enrolled in the school in which enrollment is sought, pending final resolution of the dispute, including all available appeals;

(ii) the parent or guardian of the child or youth or (in the case of an unaccompanied youth) the youth shall be provided with a written explanation of any decisions related to school selection or enrollment made by the school, the local educational agency, or the State educational agency involved, including the rights of the parent, guardian, or unaccompanied youth to appeal such decisions;

(iii) the parent, guardian, or unaccompanied youth shall be referred to the local educational agency liaison designated under paragraph (1)(J)(ii), who shall carry out the dispute resolution process as described in paragraph (1)(C) as expeditiously as possible after receiving notice of the dispute; and

(iv) in the case of an unaccompanied youth, the liaison shall ensure that the youth is immediately enrolled in the school in which the youth seeks enrollment pending resolution of such dispute.

(F) Placement choice. The choice regarding placement shall be made regardless of whether the child or youth lives with the homeless parents or has been temporarily placed elsewhere.

. . . .

(I) School of origin defined. In this paragraph:

(i) In general. The term "school of origin" means the school that a child or youth attended when permanently housed or the school in which the child or youth was last enrolled, including a preschool.

(ii) Receiving school. When the child or youth completes the final grade level served by the school of origin, as described in clause (i), the term "school of origin shall include the designated receiving school at the next grade level for all feeder schools.

(4) Comparable services. Each homeless child or youth to be assisted under this part shall be provided services comparable to services offered to other students in the school selected under paragraph (3), including the following:

(A) Transportation services.

(B) Educational services for which the child or youth meets the eligibility criteria, such as services provided under title I of the Elementary and Secondary Education Act of 1965 or similar State or local programs, educational programs for children with disabilities, and educational programs for English earners.

(C) Programs in career and technical education.

(D) Programs for gifted and talented students.

(E) School nutrition programs.

(5) Coordination

(A) In general. Each local educational agency serving homeless children and youths that receives assistance under this part shall coordinate—

(i) the provision of services under this part with local social services agencies and other agencies or entities providing services to homeless children and youths and their families, including services and programs funded under the Runaway and Homeless Youth Act (42 U.S.C. 5701 et seq.); and

(ii) transportation, transfer of school records, and other interdistrict activities, with other local educational agencies.

Hypothetical State Law § 493:12[3]

Legal Residence Required.

I. Notwithstanding any other provision of law, no person shall attend school, or send a pupil to the school, in any district of which the pupil is not a legal resident, without the consent of the district or of the school board except as otherwise provided in this section.

. . . .

IV. The term "homeless children and youths" means individuals who lack a fixed, regular, and adequate nighttime residence, and shall include the following:

(a) Children and youths who are sharing the housing of other persons due to loss of housing, economic hardship, or a similar reason; are living in motels, hotels, trailer parks, or camping grounds due to the lack of alternative adequate accommodations; are living in emergency or transitional shelters; are abandoned in hospitals; or are awaiting foster care placement.

(b) Children and youths who have a primary nighttime residence that is a public or private place not designed for or ordinarily used as a regular sleeping accommodation for human beings.

(c) Children and youths who are living in cars, parks, public spaces, abandoned buildings, substandard housing, bus or train stations, or similar settings.

3. The hypothetical statutes in this book are modifications of actual statutes.

. . . .

VI. (a) The commissioner of the department of education, or designee, shall decide residency issues for all pupils, including homeless children and youths, in accordance with this section. If more than one school district is involved in a residency dispute, or the parents who live apart cannot agree on the residence of a minor child, the respective superintendents shall jointly make such decision. In those instances when an agreement cannot be reached, the commissioner of the department of education, or designee, shall make a determination within 14 days of notice of the residency dispute and such determination shall be final. In any case, a written explanation shall be provided to the parties of record and a copy of such explanation shall be kept on file by the department of education. No school district shall deny a pupil attendance or implementation of an existing individual education plan.

(b) A pupil shall remain in attendance in the pupil's school of origin during the pendency of a determination of residency. If a child does not have a school of origin within this state, the child shall be immediately admitted to the school in which enrollment is sought pending determination of the residency dispute, provided such school is in the school district in which the child temporarily resides. For the purpose of this paragraph, "school of origin" means the school the child attended when permanently housed or the school in which the child was last enrolled.

(c) Nothing in this section shall require a district to provide transportation for a student beyond the geographical limits of that district.

Lampkin v. District of Columbia

879 F. Supp. 116 (D.D.C. 1995)

The court finds that the District of Columbia's methods of identifying students as homeless and providing transportation did not comply with federal requirements and orders changes to bring the district into compliance with federal law.

Lamberth, District Judge.

Plaintiffs are homeless mothers in their capacity as legal guardians for their school-age children. They seek timely provision of educational services, including transportation to and from school, for homeless children in the District of Columbia. . . .

Today's opinion marks one modest step in recognition of sentiments expressed by the Supreme Court more than forty years ago. Education is the "very foundation of good citizenship. . . . It is a principal instrument in awakening the child to cultural values . . . and in helping him to adjust normally to his environment. . . . It is doubtful that any child may reasonably be expected to succeed in life if he is denied

[this] opportunity." *Brown v. Board of Education*. Plaintiffs are entitled to declaratory and injunctive relief. The court hereby finds that defendants have violated 42 U.S.C. §§ 11432(e)(3), (8) & (9) by failing to address educational needs of homeless children in a timely fashion. The court further finds that defendants have violated 42 U.S.C. §§ 11432(e)(1)(G) & (9) by failing to provide homeless children with access to adequate transportation to and from school. . . .

Injunctive relief shall be structured as follows: First, the District must identify homeless children at the time they first arrive at an intake center, and refer these children within 72 hours for requisite educational services, including transportation. Second, the District must offer bus tokens to all homeless children who travel more than 1.5 miles to attend primary or secondary school; offer tokens to a homeless parent or other designated adult escort who accompanies a homeless child to or from school; and eliminate any delays occasioned by once-a-week distribution of tokens at homeless shelters. Alternatively, the District may, if it prefers, provide equivalent transportation services through the medium of a dedicated bus system in lieu of public transit. . . .

. . . .

Plaintiffs claim two specific transgressions of the McKinney Act in support of their motion for summary judgment. First, the District purportedly fails to address the educational needs of homeless children until some significant time after they become homeless, in violation of 42 U.S.C. §§ 11432(e)(3), (8) & (9). Second, the District does not provide adequate transportation to and from school for homeless children, in violation of 42 U.S.C. §§ 11432(e)(1)(G) & (9).

Defendants counter that they are in compliance with the Act; they have policies and procedures that assure homeless students in the District access to free public education at schools determined to be in their "best interest" and the District provides greater transportation assistance to homeless students than to non-homeless students.

The District's relevant policies and procedures that address the educational needs of homeless children are enumerated below. Where defendants expand upon or contradict plaintiffs' version of a particular procedure, the differences are noted; but none of these assorted factual disputes are material to the court's resolution of the legal issues.

1. A homeless family first applies for shelter at the District's Office of Emergency Shelter and Support Services ("OESSS"). At that time, an intake worker interviews the applicant and determines the number and ages of any children in the family. The applicant completes a screening questionnaire and is informed of any additional documents that must be obtained before shelter availability is finally determined.

2. The family is not immediately placed in a shelter, but is given a number on a waiting list. Once the number comes to the top of the list, the family returns to OESSS. Then, if the family is determined to be eligible for emergency shelter, it enters the first phase of the District's shelter system, the Center City Hotel. Defendants

observe that the information on a family's application must be verified before the family can qualify for shelter services. Once the verification process is complete, the family enters Center City Hotel the very same day.

3. The Transitory Students Technical Assistance Branch ("TSTAB") is the designated homelessness liaison for the District of Columbia Public Schools. TSTAB does not assume responsibility for addressing the educational needs of homeless children until they have entered the Center City Hotel, or until TSTAB becomes aware that the children are living in "doubled-up" situations (i.e., a family living with another family because of financial problems such as loss of housing). Illustrative of the lead time before TSTAB assumes control: Six of the plaintiffs waited an average of six weeks prior to entry into the shelter system. At the time of oral argument on February 28, 1995, plaintiff Stevenson had been on the waiting list since October 31, 1994—a period of four months.

4. TSTAB does not have staff at OESSS and does not provide services there. Defendants note, however, that OESSS works with TSTAB and provides educational services for families within 24 hours of the time their eligibility is confirmed. For example, if a child is having a problem getting to school, TSTAB may be asked to provide bus tokens (see numbered paragraph 6 below). And if a child is having a problem with school admission, TSTAB will help the child obtain the necessary documents.

5. OESSS assists families in locating a temporary place to stay—e.g., with relatives—while waiting for their number to come up. But the District does not determine that a family is actually homeless and thus eligible for shelter and other services until the family's number reaches the top of the list and the family returns to OESSS for placement. Once in Center City Hotel, the family is interviewed to resolve educational issues in the "best interest" of their children.

6. The District does not provide school bus service, except for special education children. However, the District does offer transportation tokens for homeless children who have to travel more than 1.5 miles to school....

7. On a discretionary basis, OESSS occasionally provides tokens direct to families who bring their children to the intake center and report difficulty in obtaining transportation to school....

The McKinney Act was passed in 1987 in response to "the critically urgent needs of the homeless," 42 U.S.C. § 11301(b)(2) (1988), including the proper education of their children. 42 U.S.C. §§ 11431–35 (Supp. IV 1992). The Act reflected broad congressional policy that "each State educational agency ... assure that each child of a homeless individual and each homeless youth have access to a free, appropriate public education ... [and that] homelessness alone ... not be sufficient reason to separate students from the mainstream school environment." *Id.* § 11431. For purposes of the Act, the District of Columbia is considered to be a state, 42 U.S.C. § 11421(d) (1988), and by accepting federal funds, the District assumed the obligation to comply with the Act's requirements. 42 U.S.C. § 11432(c) (Supp. IV 1992).

Section 11432(e), captioned "State plan," contains the pertinent provisions for purposes of plaintiffs' summary judgment motion. Paragraph (1) describes in general terms the concerns that are to be addressed by the plan. In particular, subparagraph (G) requires the District to adopt procedures designed to "address problems with respect to the education of homeless children and homeless youths, including problems caused by ... transportation issues." *Id.* § 11432(e)(1)(G).

Paragraphs (3) through (9) are devoted to specific means by which educational, health and other needs of the homeless will be confronted. To cite the three provisions that are germane here, paragraphs (3), (8) and (9) read in relevant part as follows:

> (3)(A) The local educational agency of each homeless child and each homeless youth shall either—
>
> (i) continue the child's or youth's education in the school of origin—
>
> (I) for the remainder of the academic year; or
>
> (II) in any case in which a family becomes homeless between academic years, for the following academic year; or
>
> (ii) enroll the child or youth in any school that nonhomeless students who live in the attendance area in which the child or youth is actually living are eligible to attend; whichever is in the child's best interest or the youth's best interest.
>
> ....
>
> (8) Each local educational agency that receives assistance under this subchapter shall designate a homeless liaison to ensure that—
>
> (A) homeless children and youth enroll and succeed in the schools of that agency, and
>
> (B) homeless families, children and youth receive educational services for which they are eligible.
>
> ....
>
> (9) Each State and local educational agency shall review and revise any policies that may act as barriers to the enrollment of homeless children and youth in schools selected in accordance with paragraph (3). In reviewing and revising such policies, consideration shall be given to issues concerning transportation.... Special attention shall be given to ensuring the enrollment and attendance of homeless children and youths who are not currently attending school.

All parties to this litigation agree that as a matter of policy, "best interest" determinations are not made and the remaining panoply of educational services are not provided until some time after a homeless family first reports to the intake center. All parties agree that as a matter of policy, neither dedicated transportation services nor assured access to public transportation is furnished to homeless children for travel to and from school. The question that the court must resolve is whether these acknowledged policies offend the McKinney Act, and if so, what can be done to fashion a remedy.

Plaintiffs declare that delay by the District in commencing educational services to homeless children violates the McKinney Act. The policy neglects a portion of the homeless population—those who have applied for emergency shelter and are on the waiting list for placement in a shelter. During the waiting period, the family remains homeless; yet the District has no mechanism for securing the children's attendance at school.

The pivotal inquiry is: at what point is a child considered to be homeless under the terms of the Act? Section 11302(a) defines "homeless." The pertinent provisions follow.

> For purposes of this chapter, the term "homeless" or "homeless individual" or homeless person includes—
>
> (1) an individual who lacks a fixed, regular, and adequate nighttime residence; and
>
> (2) an individual who has a primary nighttime residence that is—
>
> (A) a supervised publicly or privately operated shelter....

Quite clearly, families who have entered the shelter system are homeless in accordance with § 11302(a)(2)(A). Equally clear is that families who have applied to OESSS and are on the waiting list are also homeless under § 11302(a)(1). They lack a fixed, regular and adequate nighttime residence. It is this latter group that the District, by its policy, ignores when providing educational services. Such a policy manifestly violates the McKinney Act.

Under the Act, the District is required to assess which school is in each child's best interest to attend, giving due consideration to the parent's request. 42 U.S.C. § 11432(e)(3). This requirement is not limited to homeless children in shelters. The District's policy thus violates § 11432(e)(9). By not making a best interest determination or providing tokens to homeless families before they enter Center City Hotel, the District has erected "barriers to the enrollment of homeless children."

....

The court finds that plaintiffs are entitled to injunctive relief....

As plaintiffs have observed, accelerating the timetable for identification of homeless children should not be an overly burdensome task, nor is it outside the scope of procedures that the District presently has in place.... Defendants respond that the McKinney Act requires only that "[e]ach homeless child shall be provided services *comparable* to services offered to other students in the school ... including transportation services." 42 U.S.C. § 11432(e)(5). Since the District does not offer transportation to non-homeless students, it need not, say defendants, offer transportation to the homeless. Plaintiffs reply that non-homeless children, assigned to schools within walking distance of their homes, do not require transportation; while the homeless, relocated to a shelter outside their school's area, cannot walk to school. In order to be "comparable," homeless and non-homeless must be put in nearly the same situation.

Other sections of the statute dispense with the comparability criterion. For example, the District must "address problems with respect to the education of homeless children and homeless youths, including problems caused by . . . transportation issues." *Id.* § 11432(e)(1)(G). Also, the District must "review and revise any policies that may act as barriers to . . . enrollment. . . . In reviewing and revising such policies, consideration shall be given to issues concerning transportation." *Id.* § 11432(e)(9).

The United States Department of Education has provided further evidence that "comparability" is an incomplete standard. In its May 1991 Memorandum to State Coordinators for Education of Homeless Children and Youth, the Department stated:

> [E]ven if "comparable" services are provided, lack of adequate transportation may still act as a barrier to school attendance by homeless children. Many neighborhood schools, for instance, may offer no transportation services at all. Homeless children who attend that school and are temporarily housed some distance from it would find lack of transportation a barrier to attendance.

The Department's memorandum does not constitute a binding regulation nor a formal policy statement, but it is entitled to some weight in light of the Department's oversight authority under section 11432(a) of the Act.

Still, defendants present two possible reasons why they should be deemed to have complied with the relevant statutory provisions. First, the Department of Education memorandum notes explicitly that barriers to transportation are most troublesome for children housed *some distance* from their school. In fact, the District has addressed this specific problem and has instituted a program whereby tokens are made available to children who must travel at least 1.5 miles to school. To be sure, tokens may be less convenient than transportation on a dedicated bus, or walking to school; but it is certainly not incumbent upon the District to eradicate every annoyance faced by a homeless child.

Second, defendants point to 42 U.S.C. §§ 11431(3) & 11432(e)(1)(I) where, respectively, they are commanded not to "separate students from the mainstream school environment" and to "ensure that homeless children and homeless youths are not isolated or stigmatized." Offering dedicated bus service to homeless children, but not to most other students, could conceivably isolate and stigmatize. This argument cannot be casually dismissed, although similar services for special education students would mitigate any isolation or stigma.

The court is sympathetic to plaintiffs' appeal for better access to school transportation for the homeless. Still, a dedicated bus system may be ill-advised on several grounds. It would be a complex remedy, well beyond the expertise of this court (without significant outside assistance) to execute and monitor. Most importantly, the statutory infractions can be redressed without imposing a remedy quite so draconian.

Accordingly, the court orders the District to make transportation tokens available to all homeless children who have to travel more than 1.5 miles to attend primary or secondary school; to make tokens available to a homeless parent or other designated adult escort who accompanies a homeless child to or from school; and to eliminate any delays occasioned by once-a-week distribution of tokens at the shelter.

. . . .

Homelessness has a profound influence on a child's ability to succeed at school. In a large number of cases, failure in school leads ineluctably to adult homelessness and poverty. To help break this cycle, Congress enacted the McKinney Act, directing that homeless children be provided a "free appropriate public education." Lamentably, Congressional goodwill was dissipated by murky statutory draftsmanship. As a result, the Act may not have the encompassing effect than its proponents had hoped. Courts respectful of separation of powers will only apply those provisions of the Act where legislative intent is reliably discernible.

The court's opinion today necessarily proceeds incrementally. By requiring the District to identify homeless children at the time they first arrive at an intake center, and by expanding the coverage of the District's program for providing transportation to and from school, the court takes an exiguous step toward a "free and appropriate public education."

The court is, of course, aware of the District's current budget difficulties. The court's role, however, is to *enforce existing law*, not to recast the statute to ameliorate the District's financial crisis.

Post Problem Discussion

1. Would Carla be considered homeless under the definition of homeless as discussed in *Lampkin*? Why or why not? Is there any difference under the state law? If so, is the difference permissible? For another good case on the definition of homeless, and state compliance issues under the McKinney-Vento Act, see *New Jersey v. New York*, 872 F. Supp. 2d 204 (E.D.N.Y. 2011).

2. Consider the differences, if any, between the problems that may arise for homeless students, and for schools implementing the requirements of the laws in the problem materials, in rural areas and urban areas like the *Lampkin* case, which was decided in Washington, DC. The federal law will be the same. What differences are reasonable in state implementation?

3. What, if any, changes need to be made to the hypothetical state law so that it is in compliance with the applicable provisions of the federal law? Who makes these changes? Can the United States Department of Education force the state to change its laws on educating homeless students? If so, how does it go about doing so?

4. In *Lampkin,* the court issued some very specific remedies for the plaintiffs in that case that will likely have some wide ranging effects on schools and students not involved in the case. If you found that there were some violations of the law in Problem 2, what should the remedy be for Carla?

5. In *Lampkin,* the court noted the potential financial effects of its order, but stated that such effects were subverted by its obligation to enforce the law as it existed. Should the financial impact of a judicial order be something the court considers when fashioning a remedy for a statutory violation? Why or why not?

6. After the court issued its decision in *Lampkin,* the District of Columbia withdrew from McKinney-Vento programs so that it would no longer have to follow the requirements of the law. The District then came back to court and asked the judge to dissolve the injunction issued in *Lampkin*. How do you think the judge ruled on that request? *See Lampkin v. District of Columbia*, 886 F. Supp. 56 (D.D.C. 1995), to find the answer. What impact do you think the decision will have on educating homeless children in the District of Columbia? In other areas of the country?

§ 1.03 Federal Law: Sources & Governance

As the prior sections suggest, the Constitution provides the federal government with a source of power to enact wide-ranging statutes that can filter down the education law hierarchy and impose requirements on schools. When Congress enacts a statute, it typically provides authority for a federal agency to implement that statute. For education matters, that agency is most often the United States Department of Education ("U.S. DOE"), which has its own Office for Civil Rights ("OCR"). 20 U.S.C. § 3413.

The methods of implementation by the U.S. DOE include promulgating federal regulations, issuing agency guidance documents, policy statements, and interpretive letters, and taking enforcement actions. Federal regulations implement and further define the broad goals and requirements of laws like the IDEA and ESSA. When properly adopted, agency rules or regulations themselves have the force and effect of law and must be followed by states and schools in order to maintain federal funding. Agency guidance documents generally provide the Department's interpretation and explanation of what the law means, or how the department will enforce the law's requirements. For example, the Department issued a non-regulatory policy guidance document on the requirements of the McKinney-Vento Homeless Assistance Act discussed in Problem 2. See www.ed.gov/programs/homeless/guidance.pdf.

In addition to rules and guidance documents, the U.S. DOE enforces the laws under its jurisdiction through agency orders resulting from investigations, hearings, and state compliance monitoring. For example, OCR enforces provisions of

Section 504 of the Rehabilitation Act (a law that prohibits schools from discriminating against students with disabilities). Parents who believe that a school did not follow the requirements of Section 504 in dealing with their child may file a complaint with OCR. The agency will investigate and issue a remedial order if it finds a violation.

The Department monitors state compliance by requiring states to submit plans and reports outlining how they will comply (or have complied) with the conditions of laws like the IDEA and ESSA. The Department reviews these documents and may reject a state's plan or require states to make changes in order to receive, or to continue to receive, the federal funds at stake. *See, e.g., Connecticut v. Spellings*, 549 F. Supp. 2d 161 (D. Conn. 2008) (Department rejected the State of Connecticut's plan).

The following table illustrates the federal hierarchy. The Activity following the table illustrates the topics further.

Table 1. The Federal Hierarchy—with examples from education law

United States Constitution	The United States Constitution does *not* have an education clause, but various other provisions of the Constitution, such as the Spending Clause, and the First, Fourth, and Fourteenth Amendments play an important role in education law.
Federal Statutes	The body of education law enacted by the United States Congress is extensive and varied. For example, the Reauthorization of the Elementary and Secondary Education Act ("ESEA"), commonly known as Every Student Succeeds Act ("ESSA"), states that its purpose is "to provide all children significant opportunity to receive a fair, equitable, and high-quality education, and to close educational achievement gaps." 20 U.S.C. § 6301.
Federal rules or regulations	Federal rules or regulations have the force and effect of law. The body of regulations enacted by federal agencies to implement the federal education statutes is also enormous and appears largely within Title 34 of the Code of Federal Regulations ("C.F.R.") starting with the definition sections in34 C.F.R. § 3.1. For example, 34 C.F.R. § 200.5 requires states to administer statewide student assessments under the ESSA in certain grade levels, and in certain subjects. The Administrative Procedure Act, 5 U.S.C. § 553, together with the agency enabling legislation, spell out the process for adoption of agency rules. Typically, the process requires publication of the proposed rule in the Federal Register, an opportunity for comment, and publication of the final rule in the Federal Register followed eventually by codification in the Code of Federal Regulations.
United States Supreme Court	As noted in Problem 1, Supreme Court decisions play a significant role in defining the education landscape in the United States. If the Court finds that a federal statute or regulation is unconstitutional, then the opinion of the Court is elevated above the statute or regulation on the hierarchy, meaning the Court's decision must be followed, and not the unconstitutional statute or regulation. (The same holds true for state and local laws that the Court finds unconstitutional.)

Table 1. The Federal Hierarchy—with examples from education law (*continued*)

Federal court opinion, Circuit Court (for its jurisdictions)	Not all education cases reach the United States Supreme Court. Often, the United States Circuit Court of Appeals opinion for the relevant judicial circuit will be the highest judicial authority on a given question and must be followed in that judicial circuit. For example, for over twenty five years, issues of whether or not diversity was a compelling state interest were governed by the plurality opinion in *Regents of Univ. of Cal. v. Bakke*, 438 U.S. 265 (1978). During this time, the circuit courts were divided on the issue. The Fifth Circuit held that diversity was not a compelling state interest and rejected as unconstitutional a race-conscious admissions policy at the University of Texas School of Law, *Hopwood v. Texas*, 78 F.3d 932 (5th Cir. 1996); the Ninth Circuit held the opposite, finding diversity sufficiently compelling to support the race-conscious approach of the University of Washington Law School, *Smith* v. *University of Wash. Law School*, 233 F.3d 1188 (9th Cir. 2000). As noted in Chapter 5, the Supreme Court took up the difference in the circuits in *Grutter v. Bollinger*, 539 U.S. 306 (2002); but for the time between *Bakke* and *Grutter*, the circuit court opinions controlled in their various circuits.
Federal court opinion, District Court (for its jurisdictions)	In the federal court system, trial-court level decisions are the first level of judicial opinion and control within their own jurisdictions, unless there is a different decision on appeal. District courts are often key decision makers, and their decisions may be long-lived, particularly so where the remedy is an injunction. For example, the history of litigation in Texas about Limited English Proficiency students has gone on for over thirty five years, with the federal district court playing a lead role in ordering and implementing relief, *see, e.g., United States v. Texas*, 321 F. Supp. (E.D. Tex. 1970), continuing through *United States v. Texas*, 572 F. Supp. 2d 726 (E.D. Tex. 2008).
Federal agency orders	Some education cases are decided at the agency level through investigation or adjudication that results in an agency order. As noted in this chapter, the Office for Civil Rights conducts reviews and issues decisions in a variety of civil rights matters, including Section 504.
Federal agency policies, and guidance documents	Federal agencies may also adopt policies and create guidance documents for those governed by federal statutes or within federal programs to help them understand statutory and regulatory requirements. While not having the force and effect of law, such policies are sometimes viewed as a "safe harbor" for those who comply with their provisions.

Activity 1: Federal Scavenger Hunt

Use the sources noted in this section to do the following:

Step One—Find a federal statute that applies to public elementary and/or secondary schools. Examples of federal statutes include the Every Student Succeeds Act ("ESSA"), the Individuals with Disabilities Education Act ("IDEA"), and Titles IV and VI of the Civil Rights Act of 1964, which prohibit discrimination. You do not have to use these examples. You are free to pick any federal statute that you want as long as it applies to public elementary and/or secondary schools.

Review the purposes of the statute you chose, and any other provisions of the statute that you would like to review. Then, write a couple of sentences to explain the statute's requirements for public elementary and/or secondary schools. Write your explanation in a way that someone who is not a lawyer, or a law student, would understand. Be sure to name the statute, and provide a citation for the statute.

Step Two—Find and review a regulation that was promulgated under the authority of the statute that you chose for Step One. Write a couple of sentences to explain how the regulation implements some requirement of the statute that applies to public elementary and/or secondary schools. Write your explanation in a way that someone who is not a lawyer, or law student, would understand. Be sure to provide a citation to the regulation.

Step Three—Find a guidance document issued by the United States Department of Education online. It can be on any topic. It does not have to be related to the statute and regulation you chose in prior steps. Review it and answer the following:

1. What is the document providing guidance about?
2. Does the document help you understand this topic better than you did before you read it?
3. Do you think it would help a school administrator or educator to understand the topic better? Why or why not?
4. Do you agree with the department's interpretations of law governing the topic in the guidance? Why or why not?

Step Four—Find a case from a federal court in your judicial circuit on some education law issue. Provide a one paragraph description of the case and how it impacts schools, school administrators or teachers, and/or students.

§ 1.04 State Law: Sources & Governance

Despite the increasing federal influences on education law, education is still primarily a state and local function under the Tenth Amendment of the United States Constitution, which provides that "The powers not delegated to the United States by the Constitution, nor prohibited by it to the States, are reserved to the States respectively, or to the people." Unlike the United States Constitution, state constitutions often speak directly to the authority and obligation of the state to provide public schools and educate its youth. For example, the New Jersey Constitution provides: "The Legislature shall provide for the maintenance and support of a thorough and efficient system of free public schools for the instruction of all the children in the State between the ages of five and eighteen years." N.J. Const., Art. VIII, Sec. IV, Para. 1.

Much like the federal paradigm, states govern education through statutes, state agency regulations, other agency actions, and state court decisions. Most states have implementing statutes that create a state department of education, and give the department powers over a state education system that includes local school districts, and local schools. States also give local school districts certain powers of their own, as well as delegated responsibility to implement the requirements of state and federal laws. For example, Ohio legislation provides as to the State Board of Education:

> Powers and duties generally; minimum standards
>
> The state board of education shall exercise under the acts of the general assembly general supervision of the system of public education in the state.

ORC Ann. § 3301.07. And as to local districts:

> The board of education of each school district shall be a body politic and corporate, and, as such, capable of suing and being sued, contracting and being contracted with, acquiring, holding, possessing, and disposing of real and personal property, and taking and holding in trust for the use and benefit of such district, any grant or devise of land and any donation or bequest of money or other personal property.

ORC Ann. § 3313.17.

The following table illustrates the state hierarchy. The Activity following the table provides the opportunity to further explore these topics.

Table 2. The State Hierarchy—with examples from education law

State Constitution	State constitutions typically have specific provisions that address education. For example, the Kentucky Constitution provides "The General Assembly shall, by appropriate legislation, provide for an efficient system of common schools throughout the State." Ky. Const. § 183. Some state courts have ruled that such provisions guarantee a fundamental right to an adequate education under state law. *See, e.g., Rose v. Council for Better Educ.*, 790 S.W.2d 186 (Ky. 1989).
State Statutes	Given state constitutional provisions about education, state legislative enactments typically make school attendance compulsory. They also have a variety of other specific requirements regarding public schools and the educational services that must be provided to students. For example, regarding compulsory attendance, Kentucky requires that "(1) Except as provided in KRS 159.030, each parent, guardian, or other person residing in the state and having in custody or charge any child who has entered the primary school program or any child between the ages of six (6) and sixteen (16) shall send the child to a regular public day school for the full term that the public school of the district in which the child resides is in session or to the public school that the board of education of the district makes provision for the child to attend. A child's age is between six (6) and sixteen (16) when the child has reached his sixth birthday and has not passed his sixteenth birthday." KRS § 159.010.

Table 2. The State Hierarchy—with examples from education law (*continued*)

State Administrative Regulations, policies, and guidance documents	Much like federal administrative agencies do at the federal level, state agencies define and implement state statutes by adopting rules and regulations that fill in the details. For example, some of the specifics about school attendance in Kentucky appear in the state regulations at 702 KAR 7:125. "*Pupil attendance*." State departments of education also often produce guidance documents or policies to assist school districts in complying with state and federal requirements. State agencies also adopt guidance documents to help those governed by the laws understand them.
State Supreme Court	State supreme courts interpret state constitutional provisions, state statutes, and state regulations. Much like the federal model, state supreme courts are the final arbiter of state constitutional requirements that do not involve federal issues. *See, e.g., York v. Wahkiakum School Dist. No. 200*, 178 P.3d 995 (Wa. 2008) (ruling from the Washington Supreme Court that a school's drug-testing policy is unconstitutional under the state constitution).
State lower court(s)	Like the federal courts, state lower courts exist at the trial and appellate level, with various levels and names. In some states, these lower court opinions are reported, and in some, they are not. As is the case in federal courts, these lower courts will often be the locus of first orders on an issue. For example, determinations of where a child will attend school in divorce situations.
State agency order	Like federal agencies, state administrative agencies can issue orders after an investigation or hearing. Residency issues are a common area of dispute resolved by state agency orders, see, e.g., the appeals of the Board of Education of the Newburgh City School District in 2008 NY Educ. Dept. LEXIS 83 (N.Y. Educ. Dept. 2008).

Activity 2: State Scavenger Hunt

Step One—Find and review your state statutes on the following topics, and write a couple of sentences to explain these laws in a way that someone who is not a lawyer or law student would understand:

1. Compulsory attendance
2. The duty to provide an education
3. School districts or school administrative units
4. School district annual meeting procedures
5. The authority of your state Board and Department of Education

Step Two—Find a state regulation regarding special education. Does the regulation involve a subject that is required under federal law (IDEA)? Or is it a state requirement that goes beyond the federal requirements? Write a sentence or two explaining how the regulation affects schools, school administrators, educators, parents, and students.

Step Three—How does your state department of education enforce laws within its jurisdiction? Does it have a complaint system and an investigation process? Does it have hearings to resolve disputes between parents and schools? Does it issue public decisions or orders at the conclusion of an investigation or hearing? If so, find an order and review it. What issues does it address? Does the order require a school or the state to take any action? If so what? Do you think that the order correctly interpreted the law and resolved the issue? Why or why not?

Step Four—Find a case from your state supreme court on some education law issue. Provide a one paragraph description of the case and how it affects schools, school administrators or teachers, and students.

§ 1.05 Local Law: Sources & Governance

At the local level, most states have created local public school districts with local public school boards that are comprised of members elected by a public vote. State law defines and limits school board and school district powers.

Public school boards are typically provided with all three types of governmental power: legislative, judicial and executive. Public school boards exercise legislative powers when they create policies. They exercise judicial or adjudicatory powers when they serve as decision-makers in hearings to determine whether students or staff violated particular policies. Common examples are student discipline hearings (discussed in Chapter 8), and teacher non-renewal hearings (discussed in Chapter 3). School boards exercise executive powers in a number of ways, including entering contracts with staff and third party vendors to provide services or equipment and making budgetary decisions.

Some public school boards also have the power to tax in order to fund the school budget, while others just make recommendations for tax amounts and rates to the town or municipality. Often, the local tax to fund the budget is a property tax that must be ratified or affirmed by a public vote. See Chapter 2 for more information about school funding.

Public school districts often have a superintendent who is appointed and supervised at some level by the school board. The superintendent is responsible for the day-to-day operations of the school district. Many states use corporate models, with the superintendent having functions and duties similar to a CEO, and the school board being similar to a corporate board of directors. *See, e.g.*, the Ohio statute mentioned earlier, ORC Ann. § 3319.01 (2008).

In addition to following state and federal statutes and regulations, local school boards, local school districts, local schools, and school personnel must abide by constitutional requirements (both state and United States constitutions). The following table illustrates the local hierarchy. The Activity following the table considers these topics further.

Table 3. The Local Hierarchy—with examples from education law

School Board for the School District	School districts or school administrative units under state law often include a number of schools in a geographical area, typically with one school board for the district. Each school may also have its own school board. School board members are generally elected by a public vote. School boards typically have authority for all three types of governmental power: legislative, judicial and executive. Of particular relevance are the Board's legislative powers, to develop "policies" that the district, schools in the district, and school personnel must follow. These policies can govern every aspect of the district and school operations from employment to vendor contracts to student discipline. Sometimes the policies are challenged as violating state law. For example, the policies of the Wahkiakam School District that all "student athletes must agree to be randomly drug tested as a condition of playing extracurricular sports" were found unconstitutional in the Washington state case mentioned above. *York v. Wahkiakum School Dist. No. 200*, 178 P.3d 995 (2008).
School Administrators for the School District	School districts or school administrative units often have a superintendent appointed by the school board who is responsible for the day-to-day operations of the district.
Local School Board	Schools within a school district or school administrative unit may also have their own school board. These local school boards generally have the same powers over their local school that the school district's school board has over the school district. Policies developed by the local school board must be consistent with school district policies.
Local School Administrators	At the local school level, the administrators are generally the principals, responsible for carrying out and enforcing policies at the school level and overseeing the day-to-day operations of the school.
Local jurisdiction ordinances	Local jurisdictions may have their own equivalent of state legislative acts through municipal ordinances. For example, Camden, New Jersey has a municipal ordinance regarding weapons in schools, Ordinance MC-4209, Ordinance Amending the Camden Code—Weapons Free School Zones, available through the New Jersey State League of Municipalities Electronic Ordinance Library, www.njslom.org/ml012808.html. Local jurisdictions, through their school boards, can also adopt policies with the force and effect of law.
Local Courts	Cities and municipalities often have courts that enforce some state and local laws such as school truancy, juvenile delinquency, and minor criminal violations.

Activity 3: Local Scavenger Hunt

Step One—Refer to the statutes you found in Activity 2 regarding school districts or school administrative units. How are schools organized in your state? Are there school districts? School administrative units? School administrators or superintendents? What are their duties under state law?

Step Two—Find a local school or school district with policies online. What subjects do they address? Do the school policies address school attendance?

School dress codes? Discipline? Bullying or Cyberbullying. Employment? Do you notice any provisions in the policies that may raise constitutional concerns?

Step Three—Find local ordinances or local court decisions on truancy or juvenile delinquency online. Write a couple of sentences to explain what you found in a way that someone who is not a lawyer or law student would understand them.

§ 1.06 Bringing the Pieces Together

As noted, when issues arise in education, federal, state, and local provisions may all apply. The following problem explores some of these issues.

Problem 3: The Boy Scouts Trail Through Sources of Law

The Collins School District allows non-profit and community groups to use its facilities after school hours for meetings and other functions. The school district has, in the past, allowed community groups to use their facilities after school. Some of those groups do not allow gay or transgender students to be members. Two recently elected Collins School Board members are proposing that the school adopt a policy that states:

> The Collins School District does not tolerate, promote, nor support discrimination in any form. Organizations or groups that discriminate based on race, gender/sex, national origin, religion, disability, or sexual orientation may not use school facilities.

The new board members contend that their policy is consistent with the state anti-discrimination law (which is the same as the New Jersey statute in the Problem Materials) and that any other group that discriminates, should change their policies if they want to continue to use school facilities. The remaining three school board members are concerned about the legality of the policy. The board comes to you as their attorney to seek your advice. The board members want to know if the proposed policy complies with state and federal statutory, regulatory, and constitutional requirements. In answering this question, you may find it helpful to trace the various sources of law in the problem and list them in a hierarchical annotation like the charts in this Chapter.

Problem Materials

- ✓ New Jersey Anti-Discrimination Statute, N.J. Stat. Ann. § 10:5-4
- ✓ *Boy Scouts of America v. Dale*, 530 U.S. 640 (2000)
- ✓ *Boy Scouts of America v. Till*, 136 F. Supp. 2d 1295 (S.D. Fla. 2001)
- ✓ Boy Scouts of America Equal Access Act, 20 U.S.C. § 7905
- ✓ Boy Scouts Equal Access Act regulations 34 C.F.R. § 108.1 et seq.

New Jersey Anti-Discrimination Statute

N. J. Stat. Ann. § 10:5-4

Obtaining . . . [public] accommodations . . . without discrimination

This is an excerpt from the N.J. Statute that was the basis for the challenge in Boy Scouts of America v. Dale.

All persons shall have the opportunity to obtain . . . privileges of any place of *public accommodation*, . . . without discrimination because of race, creed, color, national origin, ancestry, age, marital status, affectional or sexual orientation, familial status, or sex, subject only to conditions and limitations applicable alike to all persons. This opportunity is recognized as and declared to be a civil right.

N.J. Stat. Ann. § 10:5-5 Definitions

As used in this act, unless a different meaning clearly appears from the context:. . . .

l. A "place of public accommodation" shall include, but not be limited to: any tavern, roadhouse, hotel, motel, trailer camp, summer camp, day camp, or resort camp, whether for entertainment of transient guests or accommodation of those seeking health, recreation or rest; any producer, manufacturer, wholesaler, distributor, retail shop, store, establishment, or concession dealing with goods or services of any kind; any restaurant, eating house, or place where food is sold for consumption on the premises; any place maintained for the sale of ice cream, ice and fruit preparations or their derivatives, soda water or confections, or where any beverages of any kind are retailed for consumption on the premises; any garage, any public conveyance operated on land or water, or in the air, any stations and terminals thereof; any bathhouse, boardwalk, or seashore accommodation; any auditorium, meeting place, or hall; any theatre, motion-picture house, music hall, roof garden, skating rink, swimming pool, amusement and recreation park, fair, bowling alley, gymnasium, shooting gallery, billiard and pool parlor, or other place of amusement; any comfort station; any dispensary, clinic or hospital; any public library; any kindergarten, primary and secondary school, trade or business school, high school, academy, college and university, or any educational institution under the supervision of the State Board of Education, or the Commissioner of Education of the State of New Jersey. Nothing herein contained shall be construed to include or to apply to any institution, bona fide club, or place of accommodation, which is in its nature distinctly private; nor shall anything herein contained apply to any educational facility operated or maintained by a bona fide religious or sectarian institution, and the right of a natural parent or one in loco parentis to direct the education and upbringing of a child under his control is hereby affirmed; nor shall anything herein contained be construed to bar any private secondary or post-secondary school from using in good faith criteria other than race, creed, color, national origin, ancestry or affectional or sexual orientation in the admission of students.

Boy Scouts of America v. Dale

530 U.S. 640 (2000)

In a 5-4 decision, the Supreme Court of the United States reverses the decision of the Supreme Court of New Jersey and holds that the First Amendment associational rights of the Boy Scouts will not allow the New Jersey public accommodation law to prevent the Boy Scouts from revoking the assistant scoutmaster position of an openly gay young man.

Chief Justice Rehnquist delivered the opinion of the Court.

Petitioners are the Boy Scouts of America and the Monmouth Council, a division of the Boy Scouts of America (collectively, Boy Scouts). The Boy Scouts is a private, not-for-profit organization engaged in instilling its system of values in young people. The Boy Scouts asserts that homosexual conduct is inconsistent with the values it seeks to instill. Respondent is James Dale, a former Eagle Scout whose adult membership in the Boy Scouts was revoked when the Boy Scouts learned that he is an avowed homosexual and gay rights activist. The New Jersey Supreme Court held that New Jersey's public accommodations law requires that the Boy Scouts admit Dale. This case presents the question whether applying New Jersey's public accommodations law in this way violates the Boy Scouts' First Amendment right of expressive association. We hold that it does.

James Dale entered scouting in 1978 at the age of eight by joining Monmouth Council's Cub Scout Pack 142. Dale became a Boy Scout in 1981 and remained a Scout until he turned 18. By all accounts, Dale was an exemplary Scout. In 1988, he achieved the rank of Eagle Scout, one of Scouting's highest honors.

Dale applied for adult membership in the Boy Scouts in 1989. The Boy Scouts approved his application for the position of assistant scoutmaster of Troop 73. Around the same time, Dale left home to attend Rutgers University. After arriving at Rutgers, Dale first acknowledged to himself and others that he is gay. He quickly became involved with, and eventually became the co-president of, the Rutgers University Lesbian/Gay Alliance. In 1990, Dale attended a seminar addressing the psychological and health needs of lesbian and gay teenagers. A newspaper covering the event interviewed Dale about his advocacy of homosexual teenagers' need for gay role models. In early July 1990, the newspaper published the interview and Dale's photograph over a caption identifying him as the co-president of the Lesbian/Gay Alliance.

Later that month, Dale received a letter from Monmouth Council Executive James Kay revoking his adult membership. Dale wrote to Kay requesting the reason for Monmouth Council's decision. Kay responded by letter that the Boy Scouts "specifically forbid membership to homosexuals."

In 1992, Dale filed a complaint against the Boy Scouts in the New Jersey Superior Court. The complaint alleged that the Boy Scouts had violated New Jersey's public accommodations statute and its common law by revoking Dale's membership based solely on his sexual orientation. New Jersey's public accommodations statute prohibits, among other things, discrimination on the basis of sexual orientation in places of public accommodation. N. J. Stat. Ann. §§ 10:5-4 and 10:5-5. . . .

. . . .

The New Jersey Supreme Court affirmed the judgment of the Appellate Division. It held that the Boy Scouts was a place of public accommodation subject to the public accommodations law, that the organization was not exempt from the law under any of its express exceptions, and that the Boy Scouts violated the law by revoking Dale's membership based on his avowed homosexuality. . . .

We granted the Boy Scouts' petition for certiorari to determine whether the application of New Jersey's public accommodations law violated the First Amendment. 528 U.S. 1109 (2000).

In *Roberts v. United States Jaycees*, 468 U.S. 609 (1984), we observed that "implicit in the right to engage in activities protected by the First Amendment" is "a corresponding right to associate with others in pursuit of a wide variety of political, social, economic, educational, religious, and cultural ends." This right is crucial in preventing the majority from imposing its views on groups that would rather express other, perhaps unpopular, ideas. Government actions that may unconstitutionally burden this freedom may take many forms, one of which is "intrusion into the internal structure or affairs of an association" like a "regulation that forces the group to accept members it does not desire." Forcing a group to accept certain members may impair the ability of the group to express those views, and only those views, that it intends to express. Thus, "freedom of association . . . plainly presupposes a freedom not to associate."

The forced inclusion of an unwanted person in a group infringes the group's freedom of expressive association if the presence of that person affects in a significant way the group's ability to advocate public or private viewpoints. But the freedom of expressive association, like many freedoms, is not absolute. We have held that the freedom could be overridden "by regulations adopted to serve compelling state interests, unrelated to the suppression of ideas, that cannot be achieved through means significantly less restrictive of associational freedoms."

To determine whether a group is protected by the First Amendment's expressive associational right, we must determine whether the group engages in "expressive association." The First Amendment's protection of expressive association is not reserved for advocacy groups. But to come within its ambit, a group must engage in some form of expression, whether it be public or private.

Because this is a First Amendment case where the ultimate conclusions of law are virtually inseparable from findings of fact, we are obligated to independently review the factual record to ensure that the state court's judgment does not unlawfully intrude on free expression. The record reveals the following. The Boy Scouts is a private, nonprofit organization. According to its mission statement:

> "It is the mission of the Boy Scouts of America to serve others by helping to instill values in young people and, in other ways, to prepare them to make ethical choices over their lifetime in achieving their full potential.
>
> "The values we strive to instill are based on those found in the Scout Oath and Law:
> "Scout Oath
> "On my honor I will do my best
> To do my duty to God and my country
> and to obey the Scout Law;
> To help other people at all times;
> To keep myself physically strong,
> mentally awake, and morally straight.
> "Scout Law
> "A Scout is:
> "Trustworthy Obedient
> Loyal Cheerful
> Helpful Thrifty
> Friendly Brave
> Courteous Clean
> Kind Reverent."

Thus, the general mission of the Boy Scouts is clear: "To instill values in young people." The Boy Scouts seeks to instill these values by having its adult leaders spend time with the youth members, instructing and engaging them in activities like camping, archery, and fishing. During the time spent with the youth members, the scoutmasters and assistant scoutmasters inculcate them with the Boy Scouts' values—both expressly and by example. It seems indisputable that an association that seeks to transmit such a system of values engages in expressive activity. . . .

Given that the Boy Scouts engages in expressive activity, we must determine whether the forced inclusion of Dale as an assistant scoutmaster would significantly affect the Boy Scouts' ability to advocate public or private viewpoints. This inquiry necessarily requires us first to explore, to a limited extent, the nature of the Boy Scouts' view of homosexuality.

The values the Boy Scouts seeks to instill are "based on" those listed in the Scout Oath and Law. The Boy Scouts explains that the Scout Oath and Law provide "a positive moral code for living; they are a list of 'do's' rather than 'don'ts.'" The Boy Scouts asserts that homosexual conduct is inconsistent with the values embodied in the Scout Oath and Law, particularly with the values represented by the terms "morally straight" and "clean."

Obviously, the Scout Oath and Law do not expressly mention sexuality or sexual orientation. And the terms "morally straight" and "clean" are by no means self-defining. Different people would attribute to those terms very different meanings.

For example, some people may believe that engaging in homosexual conduct is not at odds with being "morally straight" and "clean." And others may believe that engaging in homosexual conduct is contrary to being "morally straight" and "clean." The Boy Scouts says it falls within the latter category.

The New Jersey Supreme Court analyzed the Boy Scouts' beliefs and found that the "exclusion of members solely on the basis of their sexual orientation is inconsistent with Boy Scouts' commitment to a diverse and 'representative' membership ... [and] contradicts Boy Scouts' overarching objective to reach 'all eligible youth.'" The court concluded that the exclusion of members like Dale "appears antithetical to the organization's goals and philosophy." But our cases reject this sort of inquiry; it is not the role of the courts to reject a group's expressed values because they disagree with those values or find them internally inconsistent. . . .

The Boy Scouts asserts that it "teaches that homosexual conduct is not morally straight," and that it does "not want to promote homosexual conduct as a legitimate form of behavior." We accept the Boy Scouts' assertion. We need not inquire further to determine the nature of the Boy Scouts' expression with respect to homosexuality. . . .

We must then determine whether Dale's presence as an assistant scoutmaster would significantly burden the Boy Scouts' desire to not "promote homosexual conduct as a legitimate form of behavior." As we give deference to an association's assertions regarding the nature of its expression, we must also give deference to an association's view of what would impair its expression. . . . That is not to say that an expressive association can erect a shield against antidiscrimination laws simply by asserting that mere acceptance of a member from a particular group would impair its message. But here Dale, by his own admission, is one of a group of gay Scouts who have "become leaders in their community and are open and honest about their sexual orientation." Dale was the copresident of a gay and lesbian organization at college and remains a gay rights activist. Dale's presence in the Boy Scouts would, at the very least, force the organization to send a message, both to the youth members and the world, that the Boy Scouts accepts homosexual conduct as a legitimate form of behavior.

. . . .

Here, we have found that the Boy Scouts believes that homosexual conduct is inconsistent with the values it seeks to instill in its youth members; it will not "promote homosexual conduct as a legitimate form of behavior." . . .

We disagree with the New Jersey Supreme Court's conclusion drawn from these findings.

First, associations do not have to associate for the "purpose" of disseminating a certain message in order to be entitled to the protections of the First Amendment. An association must merely engage in expressive activity that could be impaired in order to be entitled to protection. For example, the purpose of the St. Patrick's

Day parade in *Hurley* was not to espouse any views about sexual orientation, but we held that the parade organizers had a right to exclude certain participants nonetheless.

Second, even if the Boy Scouts discourages Scout leaders from disseminating views on sexual issues—a fact that the Boy Scouts disputes with contrary evidence—the First Amendment protects the Boy Scouts' method of expression. If the Boy Scouts wishes Scout leaders to avoid questions of sexuality and teach only by example, this fact does not negate the sincerity of its belief discussed above.

Third, the First Amendment simply does not require that every member of a group agree on every issue in order for the group's policy to be "expressive association." The Boy Scouts takes an official position with respect to homosexual conduct, and that is sufficient for First Amendment purposes. In this same vein, Dale makes much of the claim that the Boy Scouts does not revoke the membership of heterosexual Scout leaders that openly disagree with the Boy Scouts' policy on sexual orientation. But if this is true, it is irrelevant. The presence of an avowed homosexual and gay rights activist in an assistant scoutmaster's uniform sends a distinctly different message from the presence of a heterosexual assistant scoutmaster who is on record as disagreeing with Boy Scouts policy. The Boy Scouts has a First Amendment right to choose to send one message but not the other. The fact that the organization does not trumpet its views from the housetops, or that it tolerates dissent within its ranks, does not mean that its views receive no First Amendment protection.

Having determined that the Boy Scouts is an expressive association and that the forced inclusion of Dale would significantly affect its expression, we inquire whether the application of New Jersey's public accommodations law to require that the Boy Scouts accept Dale as an assistant scoutmaster runs afoul of the Scouts' freedom of expressive association. We conclude that it does.

State public accommodations laws were originally enacted to prevent discrimination in traditional places of public accommodation—like inns and trains. Over time, the public accommodations laws have expanded to cover more places. New Jersey's statutory definition of "[a] place of public accommodation" is extremely broad. The term is said to "include, but not be limited to," a list of over 50 types of places. N. J. Stat. Ann. § 10:5-5(*l*) (Supp. 2000). Many on the list are what one would expect to be places where the public is invited. For example, the statute includes as places of public accommodation taverns, restaurants, retail shops, and public libraries. But the statute also includes places that often may not carry with them open invitations to the public, like summer camps and roof gardens. In this case, the New Jersey Supreme Court went a step further and applied its public accommodations law to a private entity without even attempting to tie the term "place" to a physical location. As the definition of "public accommodation" has expanded from clearly commercial entities, such as restaurants, bars, and hotels, to membership organizations such as the Boy Scouts, the potential for conflict between state public accommodations laws and the First Amendment rights of organizations has increased.

We recognized in cases such as *Roberts* and *Board of Directors of Rotary Int'l v. Rotary Club of Duarte*, 481 U.S. 537 (1987), that States have a compelling interest in eliminating discrimination against women in public accommodations. But in each of these cases we went on to conclude that the enforcement of these statutes would not materially interfere with the ideas that the organization sought to express. . . .

We thereupon concluded in each of these cases that the organizations' First Amendment rights were not violated by the application of the States' public accommodations laws.

In *Hurley*, we applied traditional First Amendment analysis to hold that the application of the Massachusetts public accommodations law to a parade violated the First Amendment rights of the parade organizers. Although we did not explicitly deem the parade in *Hurley* an expressive association, the analysis we applied there is similar to the analysis we apply here. We have already concluded that a state requirement that the Boy Scouts retain Dale as an assistant scoutmaster would significantly burden the organization's right to oppose or disfavor homosexual conduct. The state interests embodied in New Jersey's public accommodations law do not justify such a severe intrusion on the Boy Scouts' rights to freedom of expressive association. That being the case, we hold that the First Amendment prohibits the State from imposing such a requirement through the application of its public accommodations law.

Justice Stevens' dissent makes much of its observation that the public perception of homosexuality in this country has changed. Indeed, it appears that homosexuality has gained greater societal acceptance. But this is scarcely an argument for denying First Amendment protection to those who refuse to accept these views. The First Amendment protects expression, be it of the popular variety or not. And the fact that an idea may be embraced and advocated by increasing numbers of people is all the more reason to protect the First Amendment rights of those who wish to voice a different view.

. . . .

We are not, as we must not be, guided by our views of whether the Boy Scouts' teachings with respect to homosexual conduct are right or wrong; public or judicial disapproval of a tenet of an organization's expression does not justify the State's effort to compel the organization to accept members where such acceptance would derogate from the organization's expressive message. "While the law is free to promote all sorts of conduct in place of harmful behavior, it is not free to interfere with speech for no better reason than promoting an approved message or discouraging a disfavored one, however enlightened either purpose may strike the government." *Hurley*, 515 U.S. at 579.

The judgment of the New Jersey Supreme Court is reversed, and the cause remanded for further proceedings not inconsistent with this opinion.

Boy Scouts of America v. Till

136 F. Supp. 2d 1295 (S.D. Fla. 2001)

The court enjoins the Broward County School District from applying a policy excluding Boy Scouts from renting facilities after hours due to the Scouts' membership policy, which disallowed homosexuals.

MIDDLEBROOKS, DISTRICT JUDGE.

THIS CAUSE comes before the Court upon Plaintiffs' Complaint and Motion for Preliminary Injunction filed on December 4, 2000.

This case is another chapter in the struggle between private speech and public tolerance. The Broward County School Board permits numerous organizations, including churches, private membership organizations, athletic clubs and other outside groups, to utilize its school facilities for after-hour use. The School Board concedes that this longstanding practice amounts to the creation of a "limited public forum" for purposes of First Amendment analysis. However, the School Board also employs an "anti-discrimination" policy, known as Policy 1341, that prohibits the "rental use or enjoyment of school facilities by any group or organization which discriminates on the basis of age, race, color, disability, gender, marital status, national origin, religion, or *sexual orientation*." For many years, the local arm of the Boy Scouts of America, the South Florida Council, Inc., Boy Scouts of America, has enjoyed the after-hours use of many Broward school facilities....

However, prompted by the Boys Scouts' policy of excluding homosexual children and adults from group membership and the recent United States Supreme Court decision in *Boy Scouts of America v. Dale*, 530 U.S. 640 (2000), the School Board has decided to terminate the partnership agreement with the Scouts. Further, the School Board has concluded that the Scouts are ineligible to rent and lease school facilities like any other private group because the Scouts' membership policies discriminate on the basis of sexual orientation, and therefore violate the School Board's anti-discrimination policy. The Scouts assert that this decision is impermissible viewpoint discrimination under the First Amendment as well as violative of the Equal Protection Clause of the Fourteenth Amendment. The Scouts now bring this lawsuit seeking a preliminary injunction that would prevent the School Board from denying them the after-hours use of school facilities based on their membership policies regarding homosexuals.

Defendants concede that the School Board of Broward County has created a limited public forum by permitting a broad range of organizations and groups to utilize the School District's facilities for after-hours school use. Defendants also do not contest the claim that Boys Scouts have a First Amendment right to freedom of expressive association, including the right to exclude homosexuals as members or leaders in the organization. Defendants recognize that the Boy Scouts have asserted a right to exclude homosexuals for over twenty (20) years. However, in response to Plaintiffs' Motion, Defendants argue that the School Board of Broward County has a compelling governmental interest in enforcing its anti-discrimination policy.

....

In reviewing Plaintiffs' request for injunctive relief, we apply the traditional four-factor test which requires Plaintiffs to demonstrate: "(1) substantial likelihood of success on the merits; (2) irreparable injury will be suffered unless the injunction issues; (3) the threatened injury to the movant outweighs whatever damage the proposed injunction may cause the opposing party; and (4) if issued, the injunction would not be adverse to the public interest." ...

Under the law, there is no question that when government is the speaker, it may make content-based choices. *See Rosenberg v. Rector & Visitors of Univ. of Va.*, 515 U.S. 819, 833 (1995).... Under our constitutional structure, a school board that speaks to promote its own policies or to advance a particular idea is, in the end, accountable to the electorate and the political process for its advocacy. *See Board of Regents of Univ. of Wisconsin System v. Southworth*, 529 U.S. 217, 234 (2000).

Consequently, in this case, the Board, in its disapproval of intolerance towards homosexuality, is free to fashion its own message. It need not assist the Boy Scouts in the solicitation of members through "scouting days" or in any other affirmative acts to "enhance the involvement of this group in the schools" as set forth in the Partnership Agreement. The Board also need not embrace or endorse the Boy Scouts' expression and indeed may fashion its own contrary message.

However, in expressing its own message and setting its example for students to follow, the School Board cannot punish another group for its own message. The government must abstain from regulating speech when the specific motivating ideology or the opinion or perspective of the speaker is the rationale for the restrictions ...

... The School Board concedes that the Boy Scouts have a First Amendment right to freedom of expressive association, which includes the right to exclude homosexuals as members or leaders in the organization.

Yet it is because of the exercise of this right and publicity about the Supreme Court decision that the School Board seeks to bar the Boy Scouts from use of school facilities. There is no question that the School Board, like the private owner of property, may legally preserve the property under its control for the use to which it is dedicated. However, once the state has opened a limited public forum, it may not exclude speech where its distinction is not "reasonable in light of the purpose served by the forum," nor may it discriminate against speech on the basis of its viewpoint. Here, the School Board concedes that in allowing a multitude of groups to use its facilities on a regular basis, it has created a limited public forum.

The facts of this case therefore bring it very close to the decision of the former Fifth Circuit in *Knights of the Ku Klux Klan v. East Baton Rouge Parish School Board*, 578 F.2d 1122 (5th Cir. 1978). There, our predecessor Court of Appeals ordered a preliminary injunction against a school board's policy denying the Ku Klux Klan the use of a high school gymnasium for what the Klan termed a patriotic meeting on a Saturday morning....

....

Moreover, the action taken by the School Board barring the Boy Scouts from use of school facilities does nothing to stop the possible exclusion of students or teachers from scouting. If its purpose is to stop discrimination, the method chosen by the Board is ineffective. Under the law, when government seeks to regulate speech based upon its content, the regulation must achieve the stated governmental purpose, it must be narrowly tailored, and it must be the least restrictive alternative available. For the reasons outlined earlier, I do not believe excluding the Boy Scouts from Broward school facilities based on their anti-gay viewpoint can pass constitutional muster under this standard.

The disposition of this case is controlled by the answer to the first prong of the preliminary injunction test, whether Plaintiffs have shown a substantial likelihood of success on the merits. The School Board's action barring the Boy Scouts from its facilities is a response to membership policies declared by the Supreme Court to be protected by the First Amendment. Under the facts presently before this court, the Boy Scouts have shown a substantial likelihood of success on the merits.... For the foregoing reasons, and because the Boy Scouts have met all four prongs of the test for granting a preliminary injunction, it is hereby

ORDERED and ADJUDGED that an injunction shall issue, pending the hearing on the merits. The Defendants, their agents, employees, and successors in office are enjoined from preventing the Boy Scouts from using Broward County public school facilities and buses during the off school hours by reason of the Boy Scouts' membership policy....

20 U.S.C. § 7905 Equal Access to Public School Facilities

Known as the Boy Scouts of America Equal Access Act, this federal statute was passed into law after the Dale decision. It prohibits public schools from denying the Boy Scouts of America, and other youth groups that meet the definition of being a "patriotic society" under federal law, access to their facilities because of the leadership criteria of such groups.

§ 7905 Equal access to public school facilities

(a) Short title. This section may be cited as the "Boy Scouts of America Equal Access Act".

(b) In general.

(1) Equal access. Notwithstanding any other provision of law, no public elementary school, public secondary school, local educational agency, or State educational agency that has a designated open forum or a limited public forum and that receives funds made available through the Department

shall deny equal access or a fair opportunity to meet to, or discriminate against, any group officially affiliated with the Boy Scouts of America, or any other youth group listed in title 36 of the United States Code (as a patriotic society), that wishes to conduct a meeting within that designated open forum or limited public forum, including denying such access or opportunity or discriminating for reasons based on the membership or leadership criteria or oath of allegiance to God and country of the Boy Scouts of America or of the youth group listed in title 36 of the United States Code (as a patriotic society).

(2) Voluntary sponsorship. Nothing in this section shall be construed to require any school, agency, or a school served by an agency to sponsor any group officially affiliated with the Boy Scouts of America, or any other youth group listed in title 36 of the United States Code (as a patriotic society).

(c) Termination of assistance and other action.

(1) Departmental action. The Secretary is authorized and directed to effectuate subsection (b) by issuing and securing compliance with rules or orders with respect to a public elementary school, public secondary school, local educational agency, or State educational agency that receives funds made available through the Department and that denies equal access, or a fair opportunity to meet, or discriminates, as described in subsection (b).

(2) Procedure. The Secretary shall issue and secure compliance with the rules or orders, under paragraph (1), through the Office for Civil Rights and in a manner consistent with the procedure used by a Federal department or agency under section 602 of the Civil Rights Act of 1964 [42 UCS § 2000d-1]. If the public school or agency does not comply with the rules or orders, then notwithstanding any other provision of law, no funds made available through the Department shall be provided to a school that fails to comply with such rules or orders or to any agency or school served by an agency that fails to comply with such rules or orders.

(3) Judicial review. Any action taken by the Secretary under paragraph (1) shall be subject to the judicial review described in section 603 of the Civil Rights Act of 1964 [42 USC § 2000d-2]. Any person aggrieved by the action may obtain that judicial review in the manner, and to the extent, provided in section 603 of such Act [42 USC § 2000d-2].

(d) Definition and rule.

(1) Definition. In this section, the term "youth group" means any group or organization intended to serve young people under the age of 21.

(2) Rule. For the purpose of this section, an elementary school or secondary school has a limited public forum whenever the school involved grants an offering to, or opportunity for, one or more outside youth or

community groups to meet on school premises or in school facilities before or after the hours during which attendance at the school is compulsory.

34 C.F.R. § 108.3 et seq.

These are the implementing regulations for 20 U.S.C. 7905.

34 C.F.R. § 108.3 Definitions

The following definitions apply to this part:

(a) Act means the Boy Scouts of America Equal Access Act, section 9525 of the Elementary and Secondary Education Act of 1965, as amended by section 901 of the No Child Left Behind Act of 2001, Pub. L. 107-110, 115 Stat. 1425, 1981–82 (20 U.S.C. 7905).

(b) Boy Scouts means the organization named "Boy Scouts of America," which has a Federal charter and which is listed as an organization in title 36 of the United States Code (Patriotic and National Observances, Ceremonies, and Organizations) in Subtitle II (Patriotic and National Organizations), Part B (Organizations), Chapter 309 (Boy Scouts of America).

(c) Covered entity means any public elementary school, public secondary school, local educational agency, or State educational agency that has a designated open forum or limited public forum and that receives funds made available through the Department.

(d) Department means the Department of Education.

(e) Designated open forum means that an elementary school or secondary school designates a time and place for one or more outside youth or community groups to meet on school premises or in school facilities, including during the hours in which attendance at the school is compulsory, for reasons other than to provide the school's educational program.

(f) Elementary school means an elementary school as defined by section 9101(18) of the Elementary and Secondary Education Act of 1965, as amended by section 901 of the No Child Left Behind Act of 2001, Pub. L. 107-110, 115 Stat. 1425, 1958 (20 U.S.C. 7801).

(g) Group officially affiliated with any other Title 36 youth group means a youth group resulting from the chartering process or other process used by that Title 36 youth group to establish official affiliation with youth groups.

(h) Group officially affiliated with the Boy Scouts means a youth group formed as a result of a community organization charter issued by the Boy Scouts.

(i) Limited public forum means that an elementary school or secondary school grants an offering to, or opportunity for, one or more outside youth or community groups to meet on school premises or in school facilities before or after the hours during which attendance at the school is compulsory.

(j) Local educational agency means a local educational agency as defined by section 9101(26) of the Elementary and Secondary Education Act of 1965, as amended by section 901 of the No Child Left Behind Act of 2001, Pub. L. 107-110, 115 Stat. 1425, 1961 (20 U.S.C. 7801).

(k) Outside youth or community group means a youth or community group that is not affiliated with the school.

(l) Premises or facilities means all or any portion of buildings, structures, equipment, roads, walks, parking lots, or other real or personal property or interest in that property.

(m) Secondary school means a secondary school as defined by section 9101(38) of the Elementary and Secondary Education Act of 1965, as amended by section 901 of the No Child Left Behind Act of 2001, Pub. L. 107-110, 115 Stat. 1425, 1965 (20 U.S.C. 7801).

(n) State educational agency means a State educational agency as defined by section 9101(41) of the Elementary and Secondary Education Act of 1965, as amended by section 901 of the No Child Left Behind Act of 2001, Pub. L. 107-110, 115 Stat. 1425, 1965 (20 U.S.C. 7801).

(o) Title 36 of the United States Code (as a patriotic society) means title 36 (Patriotic and National Observances, Ceremonies, and Organizations), Subtitle II (Patriotic and National Organizations) of the United States Code.

(p) Title 36 youth group means a group or organization listed in title 36 of the United States Code (as a patriotic society) that is intended to serve young people under the age of 21.

(q) To sponsor any group officially affiliated with the Boy Scouts or with any other Title 36 youth group means to obtain a community organization charter issued by the Boy Scouts or to take actions required by any other Title 36 youth group to become a sponsor of that group.

(r) Youth group means any group or organization intended to serve young people under the age of 21.

§ 108.4 Effect of State or local law.

The obligation of a covered entity to comply with the Act and this part is not obviated or alleviated by any State or local law or other requirement.

§ 108.5 Compliance obligations.

(a) The obligation of covered entities to comply with the Act and this part is not limited by the nature or extent of their authority to make decisions about the use of school premises or facilities.

(b) Consistent with the requirements of § 108.6, a covered entity must provide equal access to any group that is officially affiliated with the Boy Scouts or is officially affiliated with any other Title 36 youth group. A covered entity may require that any group seeking equal access inform the covered entity whether the group is officially affiliated with the Boy Scouts or is officially affiliated with any other

Title 36 youth group. A covered entity's failure to request this information is not a defense to a covered entity's noncompliance with the Act or this part.

§ 108.6 Equal access.

(a) General. Consistent with the requirements of paragraph (b) of this section, no covered entity shall deny equal access or a fair opportunity to meet to, or discriminate against, any group officially affiliated with the Boy Scouts or officially affiliated with any other Title 36 youth group that requests to conduct a meeting within that covered entity's designated open forum or limited public forum. No covered entity shall deny that access or opportunity or discriminate for reasons including the membership or leadership criteria or oath of allegiance to God and country of the Boy Scouts or of the Title 36 youth group.

(b) Specific requirements.

(1) Meetings. Any group officially affiliated with the Boy Scouts or officially affiliated with any other Title 36 youth group that requests to conduct a meeting in the covered entity's designated open forum or limited public forum must be given equal access to school premises or facilities to conduct meetings.

(2) Benefits and services. Any group officially affiliated with the Boy Scouts or officially affiliated with any other Title 36 youth group that requests to conduct a meeting as described in paragraph (b)(1) of this section must be given equal access to any other benefits and services provided to one or more outside youth or community groups that are allowed to meet in that same forum. These benefits and services may include, but are not necessarily limited to, school-related means of communication, such as bulletin board notices and literature distribution, and recruitment.

(3) Fees. Fees may be charged in connection with the access provided under the Act and this part.

(4) Terms. Any access provided under the Act and this part to any group officially affiliated with the Boy Scouts or officially affiliated with any other Title 36 youth group, as well as any fees charged for this access, must be on terms that are no less favorable than the most favorable terms provided to one or more outside youth or community groups.

(5) Nondiscrimination. Any decisions relevant to the provision of equal access must be made on a nondiscriminatory basis. Any determinations of which youth or community groups are outside groups must be made using objective, nondiscriminatory criteria, and these criteria must be used in a consistent, equal, and nondiscriminatory manner.

§ 108.7 Voluntary sponsorship.

Nothing in the Act or this part shall be construed to require any school, agency, or school served by an agency to sponsor any group officially affiliated with the Boy Scouts or with any other Title 36 youth group.

§ 108.8 Assurances.

An applicant for funds made available through the Department to which this part applies must submit an assurance that the applicant will comply with the Act and this part. The assurance shall be in effect for the period during which funds made available through the Department are extended. The Department specifies the form of the assurance, including the extent to which assurances will be required concerning the compliance obligations of subgrantees, contractors and subcontractors, and other participants, and provisions that give the United States a right to seek its judicial enforcement. An applicant may incorporate this assurance by reference in subsequent applications to the Department.

§ 108.9 Procedures.

The procedural provisions applicable to title VI of the Civil Rights Act of 1964, which are found in 34 CFR 100.6 through 100.11 and 34 CFR part 101, apply to this part, except that, notwithstanding these provisions and any other provision of law, no funds made available through the Department shall be provided to any school, agency, or school served by an agency that fails to comply with the Act or this part.

Post Problem Discussion

1. The Boy Scouts have changed their stance on admitting gay and transgender members. More details can be found in the following article: Kurtis Lee, *Here is how the Boy Scouts has evolved on social issues over the years,* Los Angeles Times, Feb. 5, 2017, http://www.latimes.com/nation/la-na-boy-scouts-evolution-2017-story.html (last accessed on 10/24/18). How do these changes impact the expressive association rights noted in *Dale*?

2. One point to pick up on in the *Dale* case is the Court's explanation of why admitting gay members would violate the Boy Scouts' right to expressive association. Compare the *Dale* case to *Roberts v. Jaycees*, 468 U.S. 609 (1984), where the Court found that admitting women did not violate the Jaycees' right to expressive association. What is the difference in the cases that explains the different outcomes?

3. If you find that the proposed Collins School District Policy does not comply with either state or federal statutory, regulatory, or constitutional requirements, what changes could be made to the policy so that it complied? If the policy complies with state requirements, but not federal requirements, must it be changed? Why or why not?

Chapter 2

School Funding

Synopsis

§ 2.01 Introduction

This Chapter covers various aspects of school funding with a focus on school funding litigation. Most states have state constitutional provisions addressing public education through either an *education clause* that mentions state obligations toward education specifically, or an *equal protection clause*.[1] At least forty-four states have been through some type of litigation concerning their state constitutional requirements.[2] Referred to as school funding or school finance litigation, these cases generally revolve around arguments that state funding for public schools is insufficient, or unequal amongst school districts, which affects the education provided to students in certain school districts.

Some state courts have found that their state constitutional provisions create an obligation to provide and fund an "adequate education." Others have found no such

1. See William E. Thro, *School Finance Reform: A New Approach to State Constitutional Analysis in School Finance Litigation*. 14 J.L. & Politics 525, 538 (1998) (stating that almost all states except Mississippi have constitutional provisions mandating some sort of state educational system).

2. *Id.* at 529–534; *see also* James E. Ryan & Thomas Saunders, *Foreword to Symposium on School Finance Litigation: Emerging Trends or New Dead Ends?*, 22 Yale L. & Pol'y Rev. 463, 472–475 (2004).

requirement. In some states, school funding litigation has continued for extended periods of time, evolving to cover many different issues. This Chapter uses the school funding litigation in New Hampshire as an example to illustrate the issues that can arise in school funding cases.

§ 2.02 Sources of Funding

Public elementary and secondary school funding comes from a variety of federal, state, and local sources. Federal sources include funding from laws passed under the Spending Clause such as the Individuals with Disabilities Education Act ("IDEA"), Every Student Succeeds Act ("ESSA"), and the Perkins Vocational and Technical Education Act. As noted in Chapter 1, federal funding under the Spending Clause includes an obligation to comply with federal conditions.

Diagram 2.1 School Funding Sources

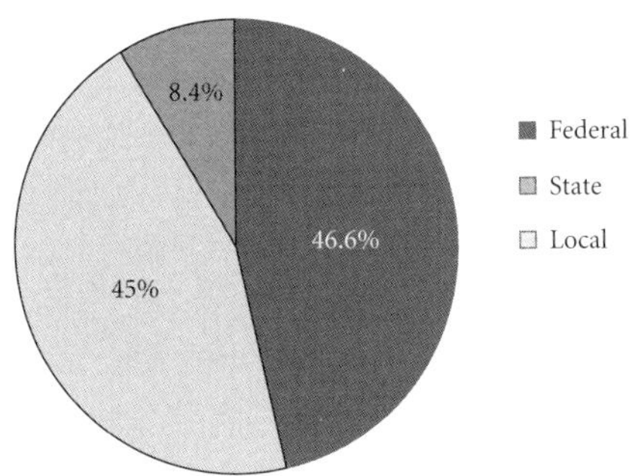

As illustrated in Diagram 2.1, federal funding makes up a small percentage of overall elementary and secondary school funding with the primary sources being state and local funds.[3] State funding often comes from a blend of sources such as sales, income, property, and business taxes. Some states also provide funds from state lottery sales or gambling revenues. Local funding is generally from local property taxes.

§ 2.03 School Funding Litigation — Background

School finance/school funding litigation is often described as existing in three "waves," with some contending that there is a fourth wave.[4] The first two waves dealt primarily with *equal protection or equity arguments* regarding state funding to local school districts. The cases involved claims that some school districts did not receive

3. For fiscal year 20014-15. *See* Thomas D. Snyder, et al., 2010 Digest of Education Statistics 10: NCES 2017-094 (February 2018).

4. *See* Christopher E. Adams, *Is Economic Integration the Fourth Wave in School Finance Litigation?* 56 Emory L.J. 1613, 1636–1659 (2007); William F. Dietz, *Manageable Adequacy Standards in Education Reform Litigation*, 74 Wash. U. L.Q. 1193, 1195–1204 (1996).

sufficient state funding under state and local funding systems and, as a result, had per pupil expenditures that were much lower than other comparable school districts. The cases often involved "property poor" school districts that were not able to keep pace with neighboring "property rich" school districts, because the rich districts could raise more funds with lower property tax rates. These same disparities continue in many places today.

First Wave

The first wave grew out of the first California Supreme Court decision in *Serrano v. Priest* decided in 1971. *Serrano* held California's education funding system, which relied on local property taxes, unconstitutional under the Fourteenth Amendment of the United States Constitution. *Serrano v. Priest*, 487 P.2d 1241, 1263 (Cal. 1971) (*Serrano I*). The California Supreme Court ruled that education was a fundamental right under the Fourteenth Amendment and that the funding system failed strict scrutiny review. *Serrano I*, 487 P.2d at 1258, 1260. The first wave culminated at the federal level with the United States Supreme Court decision in *San Antonio Ind. Sch. Dist. v. Rodriguez*, 411 U.S. 1 (1973), discussed in Chapter 1. In *Rodriguez*, the Court ruled that education was not a fundamental right under the Fourteenth Amendment of the United States Constitution, so it reviewed a challenge to the Texas school funding system using a rational basis level of review. Under the rational basis standard, the Court determined that the disparities in funding between local school districts did not violate the United States Constitution.

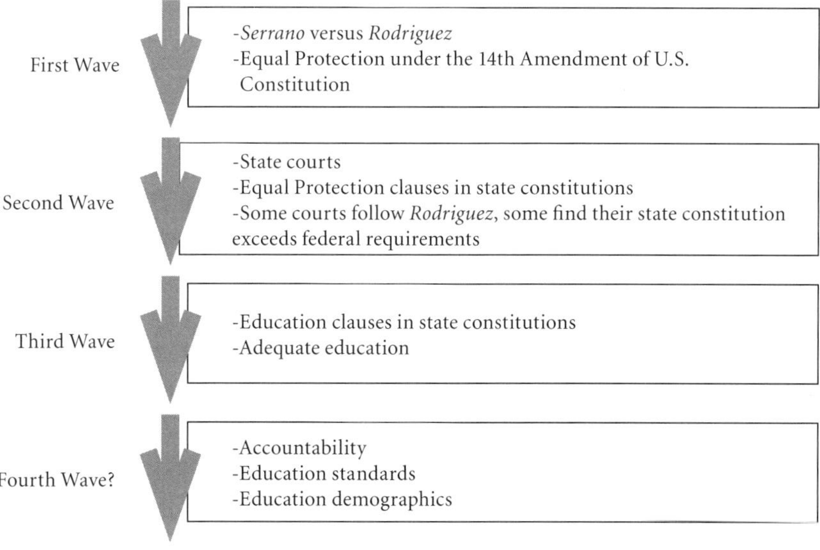

Second Wave

After *Rodriquez*, school funding claims became mostly a state issue and created what is referred to as the second wave of litigation. In this wave, some state courts followed the lead of *Rodriguez* in interpreting their state constitutions, while others found that the *equal protection requirements* in their *state constitutions* were different from the federal requirements. For example, in *Horton v. Meskill*, 376 A.2d 359 (Conn. 1977), the Connecticut Supreme Court found that education was a fundamental right under the Connecticut Constitution's Equal Protection Clause. As a result, the court applied a strict scrutiny analysis and found Connecticut's school funding system unconstitutional because of wide disparities between school districts in per-pupil expenditures, tax rates, and a variety of other factors including teacher salaries.

Some courts in other states came to similar conclusions, while others reached the opposite conclusion. *See, e.g., Danson v. Casey*, 399 A.2d 360 (Pa. 1979) (holding that under rationality review, the state school financing scheme did not violate the state equal protection clause); *Pauley v. Kelly*, 255 S.E.2d 859, 883–884 (W. Va. 1979) (holding that trial court properly concluded that a state is not constrained by the federal constitutional standard, but must examine its own constitution to determine its educational responsibilities); *Serrano v. Priest*, 557 P.2d 929, 952 (Cal. 1976) (*Serrano II*) (holding that strict scrutiny applied in determining whether the statute complied with the state equal protection clause).

Third Wave

Over time, the claims in school funding cases began to focus more on the *education clauses* in state constitutions as opposed to the *equal protection clauses*. This created the third wave of school finance litigation, which focused both on funding and on whether states have a constitutional obligation to provide a certain level or quality of education to students. This qualitative level of education is often referred to as an "adequate education."[5]

Numerous state supreme courts have held that their state constitution requires the state to provide an adequate education to all students. In *Rose v. Council for Better Educ.*, 790 S.W.2d 186 (Ky. 1989), a case some refer to as the "grandmother" of school funding cases, the Kentucky Supreme Court provided some parameters for a constitutionally adequate education and determined that Kentucky's entire educational system was unconstitutional. A number of other state courts followed suit and applied these same criteria. *Campaign for Fiscal Equity v. State of New York*, 801 N.E.2d 326 (N.Y. 2003); *McDuffy v. Secretary of Exec. Off. of Educ.*, 615 N.E.2d 516 (Mass. 1993). In some states, there have been multiple rounds of litigation over the contours of an adequate education with the legislative responses to state court decisions being continually challenged and struck down by state courts as unconstitutional.[6]

---

5. *See* Regina R. Umpstead, *Determining Adequacy: How Courts Are Redefining State Responsibility for Educational Finance, Goals, and Accountability*, 2007 BYU Educ. & L.J. 281, 286–294 (2007); William H. Clune, *Educational Adequacy: A Theory and its Remedies*, 28 U. Mich. J.L. Ref. 481, 485–488 (1995); William E. Thro, *Symposium: Issues in Education Law and Policy: Judicial Analysis During the Third Wave of School Finance Litigation: The Massachusetts Decision as a Model*, 35 B.C. L. Rev 597, 604–609 (1994).

6. New Jersey is often used as the example for this proposition. *See, e.g.*, Paul L. Tractenberg, *Beyond Educational Adequacy: Looking Backward and Forward Through the Lens of New Jersey*, 4 Stan. J. Civ. Rts. & Civ. Liberties 411 (2008).

Because school funding cases involve taxes and large portions of state and local budgets, they are often very political topics. As a result, these cases often involve other constitutional issues like separation of powers and judicial review. In some states, various efforts have been undertaken to undo state supreme court decisions by either replacing or impeaching judges, or by attempting to amend the state constitution.[7] These dynamics are further explored in the context of the school funding litigation in New Hampshire.

§ 2.04 New Hampshire's School Funding Litigation

A. Introduction

New Hampshire's school funding litigation began in the 1980s with a lawsuit that settled before any court decisions were issued. At that time, public schools were funded primarily by local property taxes, with the state providing some supplemental funds to some school districts. The result of the settled lawsuit was a new funding program called the "Augenblick formula" that was supposed to provide more state funds to "property poor" schools.

However, the Augenblick formula was never fully funded, and only provided about eight percent of the funding for New Hampshire's schools, leaving local communities to continue to fund the bulk of educational expenses with local property taxes. The result of the state's funding system was that "property poor" school districts with low property values had much higher tax rates than their "property rich" counterparts, and were still unable to raise similar amounts of funds. The tax and funding differences led to disparities in educational opportunities in property poor and property rich school districts.

In 1989, a group of five school districts, five taxpayers, and five students filed claims in state court challenging the constitutionality of the state's funding system. This group of plaintiffs argued that the disparities in funding, and in educational opportunities, violated the New Hampshire Constitution. New Hampshire's constitution has an *education clause*. It also has a *tax clause* that requires state taxes to be uniform and equal in rate. Named the "*Claremont Lawsuit*" after one of the plaintiff school districts, the litigation spawned ten court decisions and lasted well over a decade. *Claremont* was followed by another lawsuit in New Hampshire with new parties addressing similar education funding issues.

New Hampshire's education funding litigation is a good model to use to gain an understanding of the school funding issues that almost all states have addressed. While there are aspects of some of the issues in the *Claremont* cases that are unique

---

7. Ian Millhiser, *What Happens to a Dream Deferred?: Cleansing the Taint of* San Antonio Independent School District v. Rodriguez, 55 Duke L.J. 405 (2005).

to New Hampshire, most of the issues are the same as the ones that other states have dealt with in school funding cases. These issues include:

✓ Does the state constitution require the state to fund and provide an adequate education?

✓ Is education a fundamental right under the state constitution?

✓ What are the requirements of an adequate education, and how much do they cost?

✓ Does the state have to pay the entire cost of an adequate education, or can it just provide some of the cost, or provide funding only to "property poor" school districts that need financial assistance?

✓ Does the state's education funding system meet constitutional requirements? If not, what must be done to fix it?

✓ Does the state have to ensure that local school districts actually provide students with an adequate education?

The activities, problems, and materials in this Chapter highlight these issues. The following timeline provides a roadmap for New Hampshire's school funding cases:

New Hampshire School Funding Litigation Timeline

Year	Event
1985	School funding case settles before any court decision is issued. The settlement includes the "Augenblick" funding formula.
1989	A group of school districts (including the Claremont school district), students, and taxpayers file a lawsuit in state court challenging the state education funding system under the education and tax clauses in the New Hampshire Constitution. The case becomes known as the "Claremont Lawsuit."
1993	The New Hampshire Supreme Court rules that New Hampshire's Constitution requires the State of New Hampshire to provide and pay for an adequate education. *Claremont Sch. Dist. v. Governor*, 635 A.2d 1375 (N.H. 1993) (*Claremont I*).
1997	The New Hampshire Supreme Court rules that the then-current system of funding education is unconstitutional. It also finds that an adequate education is a fundamental right under the New Hampshire Constitution, and that the state's proposed definition of an adequate education is insufficient. *Claremont Sch. Dist. v. Governor*, 703 A.2d 1353 (N.H. 1997) (*Claremont II*).
1998	One of the defendants asks the court to vacate its *Claremont II* decision because one of the justices who decided the case was over the age of seventy in violation of state constitutional provisions. The court denies the motion, noting that state statutes authorize justices over the age of seventy to sit on the court temporarily to decide individual cases. *Claremont Sch. Dist. v. Governor*, 712 A.2d 612 (N.H. 1998) (*Claremont III*).
1998	The court issues an advisory opinion stating that the tax abatement provisions of a proposed school funding plan called the "ABC plan" would violate the state constitution's tax clause, which requires fair and uniform taxation. *Opinion of the Justices*, 712 A.2d 1080 (N.H. 1998).

New Hampshire School Funding Litigation Timeline (*continued*)

Year	Event
1998	The court denies the state's request for a two year extension to comply with *Claremont II's* deadline for developing a constitutional method of funding education. *Claremont Sch. Dist. v. Governor*, 725 A.2d 648 (N.H. 1998) (*Claremont IV*).
1999	The court issues an advisory opinion stating that a proposed tax plan referendum on a state election ballot would violate New Hampshire's Constitutional provisions requiring a representative form of government. *Opinion of the Justices*, 725 A.2d 1082 (N.H. 1999).
1999	The court rules that an education funding plan with a statewide property tax that is phased in over five years is unconstitutional as it would perpetuate the deficiencies in the school funding system for that five year period. *Claremont Sch. Dist. v. Governor*, 744 A.2d 1107 (N.H. 1999) (*Claremont V*).
1999	The court orders the state to pay the plaintiffs' attorney's fees for their efforts in conferring a substantial benefit to New Hampshire citizens. *Claremont Sch. Dist. v. Governor*, 761 A.2d 389 (N.H. 1999) (*Claremont VI*).
2000	The court rules that a proposal to "target" state education funds only to communities that "need" the funds is unconstitutional as it would require some New Hampshire communities to fund an adequate education with local funds. *Opinion of the Justices*, 765 A.2d 673 (N.H. 2000).
2002	The court rules that the state's constitutional obligation includes developing standards of accountability to ensure that local schools deliver an adequate education, and state efforts to do so were unconstitutional. *Claremont Sch. Dist. v. Governor*, 794 A.2d 744 (N.H. 2002) (*Claremont VII*).
2006	In a case brought by new plaintiffs, the court rules that the state still has not developed a constitutional definition of an adequate education, and orders the state to do so, noting that it may impose various judicial remedies if the state does not develop a definition in the time frame noted by the court. *Londonderry Sch. Dist. SAU No. 12 v. State*, 907 A.2d 988 (N.H. 2006).

B. Constitutional Obligations

The first issue that the New Hampshire Supreme Court addressed in the *Claremont* litigation was whether the New Hampshire Constitution imposed a duty on the state to fund education. At the time of the decision, education was funded primarily by local property taxes, and the state argued that it did not have any constitutional obligation to provide any funds to local schools. The New Hampshire Constitution has an *education clause* that states:

> N.H. Const. pt. II, art. 83. Knowledge and learning, generally diffused through a community, being essential to the preservation of a free government; and spreading the opportunities and advantages of education through the various parts of the country, being highly conducive to promote this end; it shall be the duty of the legislators and magistrates, in all future periods of this government, to cherish the interest of literature and the sciences, and all seminaries and public schools, to encourage private and public institutions,

> rewards, and immunities for the promotion of agriculture, arts, sciences, commerce, trades, manufactures, and natural history of the country; to countenance and inculcate the principles of humanity and general benevolence, public and private charity, industry and economy, honesty and punctuality, sincerity, sobriety, and all social affections, and generous sentiments, among the people: Provided, nevertheless, that no money raised by taxation shall ever be granted or applied for the use of the schools or institutions of any religious sect or denomination.

Based on this language, the trial court in the *Claremont* case stated:

> New Hampshire's Encouragement of Literature Clause contains no language regarding equity, uniformity, or even adequacy of education. Thus, the New Hampshire Constitution imposes no qualitative standard of education, which must be met. Likewise, the New Hampshire Constitution imposes no quantifiable financial duty regarding education; there is no mention of funding or even of "providing" or "maintaining" education. The only "duty" set forth is the amorphous duty "to cherish . . . public schools" and "to encourage private and public institutions." N.H. Const., pt. 2, art. 83. The language of pt. 2, art. 83 is hortatory, not mandatory.

Claremont, 635 A.2d 1375, 1377 (N.H. 1993). However, in *Claremont Sch. Dist. v. Governor* (*Claremont I*), the New Hampshire Supreme Court reversed stating:

> In interpreting an article in our constitution, we will give the words the same meaning that they must have had to the electorate on the date the vote was cast. In doing so, we must "place [ourselves] as nearly as possible in the situation of the parties at the time the instrument was made, that [we] may gather their intention from the language used, viewed in the light of the surrounding circumstances."

Claremont I, 635 A.2d at 1377–78. Using this approach, the court found that part II, article 83 of the New Hampshire Constitution imposed "a duty on the State to provide a constitutionally adequate education to every educable child in the public schools in New Hampshire and to guarantee adequate funding." *Claremont I*, 635 A.2d at 1376.

Activity 1: Find Your State Constitutional Provisions and Court Decisions

Step 1—Read the entire *Claremont Sch. Dist. v. Governor*, 635 A.2d 1375 (N.H. 1993) (*Claremont I*), decision online for an example of a court decision regarding state constitution education clauses. Do you agree that the New Hampshire Constitution requires the state to provide and fund an adequate education? Why or why not?

Step 2—Find your state constitution. Does it have a provision or clause regarding education? If so, how does it compare to New Hampshire's?

Step 3—Research any court decisions interpreting your state constitution's education clause and/or its equal protection clause. Have your state courts interpreted either provision to impose a state constitutional obligation to fund, or to provide, an adequate education? If so, how do the decisions compare to the New Hampshire Supreme Court's decision in *Claremont I*?

C. Constitutionality of the Education Funding System

In a second *Claremont* case in 1997 (*Claremont II*), the New Hampshire Supreme Court ruled that the state education funding system violated two New Hampshire constitutional provisions. One was Part II, Article 83, the state's *education clause*, which the court noted in *Claremont I* required the state to provide and fund an adequate education. The other was the state's *tax clause* in Part II, Article 5 of the state constitution. This clause requires state taxes to be "proportionate and reasonable," and "equal in valuation and uniform in rate." This meant that any tax used to fund the state's obligation to provide an adequate education had to be reasonable and uniform in rate.

Problem 1: Education Funding Systems and Defining Adequacy

You are a state legislator. Review the *Claremont II* decision in the problem materials and consider the following:

1. What kind of education funding system would you propose to meet the court's requirements?
2. How would you go about developing such a system? How would you identify and organize the various factions involved to come to a consensus on a funding system?
3. What do you think would be the largest obstacles in developing an education funding system that complied with the court's decision?

One aspect of the *Claremont II* decision is the state's obligation to define and provide an adequate education under Part II, Article 83. The court ruled that the definition offered by the state was unconstitutional. The court provided some parameters on the constitutional requirements for developing a definition, and for the content of a definition. After reviewing the court's *Claremont II* decision, consider the following in your role as a state legislator:

1. How would you define an adequate education given the requirements noted in the *Claremont II* decision?
2. Given the court's discussion about appealing to a broad constituency when developing the definition, what kind of process do you think the legislature should use to define an adequate education?
3. What groups or organizations do you think should be involved in defining an adequate education?

Problem Materials

✓ *Claremont School District v. Governor*, 703 A.2d 1353 (N.H. 1997) (*Claremont II*)

Claremont School District v. Governor (*Claremont II*)

703 A.2d 1353 (N.H. 1997)

The New Hampshire Supreme Court rules that the current method of funding education, and the proposed definition of an adequate education, violate the New Hampshire Constitution.

Brock, C.J. In this appeal we hold that the present system of financing elementary and secondary public education in New Hampshire is unconstitutional. To hold otherwise would be to effectively conclude that it is reasonable, in discharging a State obligation, to tax property owners in one town or city as much as four times the amount taxed to others similarly situated in other towns or cities. This is precisely the kind of taxation and fiscal mischief from which the framers of our State Constitution took strong steps to protect our citizens. The procedural history of the case and the reasons for our decision follow.

....

Funding for public education in New Hampshire comes from three sources. First, school districts are authorized to raise funds through real estate taxation. Locally raised real property taxes are the principal source of revenue for public schools, providing on average from seventy-four to eighty-nine percent of total school revenue. Second, funds are provided through direct legislative appropriations, primarily in the form of Foundation Aid, Building Aid, and Catastrophic Aid. Direct legislative appropriations account for an average of eight percent of the total dollars spent on public elementary and secondary education, ranking New Hampshire last in the United States in percentage of direct support to public education. Third, approximately three percent of support for the public schools is in the form of federal aid.

At the present time, the State places the responsibility for providing elementary and secondary public education on local school districts. State statutes, rules, and regulations delineate the requirements to be followed by school districts.... For example, school districts are required to provide standard schools for 180 days per year; provide transportation; provide meals to students; purchase and provide textbooks; meet minimum standards for school approval; provide special education services; and participate in the school improvement and assessment program.

To comply with the State's requirements, school districts must raise money for their schools with revenue collected from real estate taxes. Every year, the selectmen of each town are required to assess an annual tax of $3.50 on each $1,000 of assessed value for the support of that district's schools. Each school district then details the sums of money needed to support its public schools and produces a budget that specifies the additional funds required to meet the State's minimum standards. A sum sufficient to meet the approved school budget must be assessed on the taxable real property in the district. The commissioner of revenue administration computes a property tax rate for school purposes in each district. Using the determined rate, city and town officials levy property taxes to provide the further sum necessary to meet the obligations of the school budget. As the trial court noted in its order, the total value of the property subject to taxation for local school revenue varies among the cities and towns of New Hampshire.

To some extent, the amount of revenue that a school district raises is dependent upon the value of the property in that district. This point can be illustrated by a comparison of petitioner district Franklin and its comparison district Gilford. In 1994, Franklin's "equalized property value" (property assessed at 100% of fair market value) per student was $183,626, while Gilford's equalized property value per student was $536,761. As a result, "property rich" Gilford had a significantly greater assessed value upon which taxes could be imposed for the support of its schools than did Franklin. Gilford raised more money per student than Franklin, even while taxing its residents at lower rates.

The plaintiffs argue that the school tax is a unique form of the property tax mandated by the State to pay for its duty to provide an adequate education and that the State controls the process and mechanism of taxation. Because of the purpose of the tax and the control exerted by the State, the plaintiffs contend that the school tax is a State tax that should be imposed at a uniform rate throughout the State. The State argues that "because the school tax is a local tax determined by budgeting decisions made by the district's legislative body and spent only in the district, it meets the constitutional requirement of proportionality." According to the State, "property taxation is a stable and expan[dable] source of revenue which allows the citizens of New Hampshire to decide how to organize and operate their schools in a manner which best meets the needs of their children." The question of whether property taxes for schools are local or State taxes is an issue of first impression.

Part II, article 5 of the State Constitution provides that the legislature may "impose and levy proportional and reasonable assessments, rates, and taxes, upon all the inhabitants of, and residents within, the said state." This article requires that "all taxes be proportionate and reasonable—that is, equal in valuation and uniform in rate." ... "[T]he test to determine whether a tax is equal and proportional is to inquire whether the taxpayers' property was valued at the same per cent of its true value as all the taxable property in the taxing district." ... "[T]he property shall be valued within a reasonable time before the tax is assessed." ...

Determining the character of a tax as local or State requires an initial inquiry into its purpose.

> In order ... that the tax should be proportional ... it is required that the rate shall be the same throughout the taxing district;—that is, *if the tax is for the general purposes of the state, the rate should be the same throughout the state*; if for the county, it should be uniform throughout the county;—and

> the requisite of proportion, or equality and justice, can be answered in no other way.

We find the purpose of the school tax to be overwhelmingly a State purpose and dispositive of the issue of the character of the tax. "[T]he local school district, an entity created by the legislature almost two centuries ago, exists for the public's benefit, to carry out the mandates of the State's education laws." . . . "Indeed, school district monies, a public trust, can only be spent in furtherance of these educational mandates, and to promote the values set forth in the 'Encouragement of Literature' clause, N.H. Const., pt. 2, Art. 83." . . .

Providing an adequate education is thus a duty of State government expressly created by the State's highest governing document, the State Constitution. In addition, public education differs from all other services of the State. No other governmental service plays such a seminal role in developing and maintaining a citizenry capable of furthering the economic, political, and social viability of the State. Only in part II, article 83 is it declared a duty of the legislature to "cherish" a service mandated by the State Constitution. Furthermore, education is a State governmental service that is compulsory. That the State, through a complex statutory framework, has shifted most of the responsibility for supporting public schools to local school districts does not diminish the State purpose of the school tax. Although the taxes levied by local school districts are local in the sense that they are levied upon property within the district, the taxes are in fact State taxes that have been authorized by the legislature to fulfill the requirements of the New Hampshire Constitution. . . . For purposes of analysis under part II, article 5, therefore, the taxing district is the State.

The question then is whether the school tax as presently structured is proportional and reasonable throughout the State in accordance with the requirements of part II, article 5. Evidence introduced at trial established that the equalized tax rate for the 1994–1995 school year in Pittsfield was $25.26 per thousand while the rate in Moultonborough was $5.56 per thousand. The tax rate in Pittsfield, therefore, was more than four times, or over 400 percent, higher than in Moultonborough. Likewise, the equalized tax rate for the 1994–1995 school year in Allenstown was $26.47 per thousand while the rate in Rye was $6.86 per thousand—a difference in tax rates of almost 400 percent. We need look no further to hold that the school tax is disproportionate in violation of our State Constitution. Indeed, the trial court acknowledged that the plaintiffs "presented evidence that the school tax may be disproportionate if it is a state tax."

In addition, we conclude that the school tax as presently assessed is unreasonable. The word "reasonable" as used in part II, article 5 means "just." . . . "[T]he sense of the clause [is], that taxes shall be laid, not merely proportionally, but in due proportion, so that each individual's just share, and no more, shall fall upon him." *Id.*

Because the diffusion of knowledge and learning is regarded by the State Constitution as "essential to the preservation of a free government," N.H. Const. pt. II, art. 83, it is only just that those who enjoy such government should equally assist in contributing to its preservation. The residents of one municipality should not be compelled to bear greater burdens than are borne by others. In mandating that knowledge and learning be "generally diffused" and that the "opportunities and advantages of education" be spread through the various parts of the State, N.H. Const. pt. II, art. 83, the framers of the New Hampshire Constitution could not have intended the current funding system with its wide disparities. This is likely the very reason that the people assigned the duty to support the schools to the State and not to the towns.

There is nothing fair or just about taxing a home or other real estate in one town at four times the rate that similar property is taxed in another town to fulfill the same purpose of meeting the State's educational duty. . . . We hold, therefore, that the varying property tax rates across the State violate part II, article 5 of the State Constitution in that such taxes, which support the public purpose of education, are unreasonable and disproportionate. To the extent that the property tax is used in the future to fund the provision of an adequate education, the tax must be administered in a manner that is equal in valuation and uniform in rate throughout the State.

Following *Claremont I*, the trial court, in the absence of legislative action, accepted a definition of educational adequacy developed by the State Board of Education. This definition provides in part: "An adequate public elementary and secondary education in New Hampshire is one which provides each educable child with an opportunity to acquire the knowledge and learning necessary to participate intelligently in the American political, economic, and social systems of a free government." The definition then establishes at length a system of shared responsibility between State and local government. This definition, however, does not sufficiently reflect the letter or the spirit of the State Constitution's mandate. The constitution places the duty to support the public schools on "the legislators and magistrates." As we said in *Claremont I*, it is for the legislature and the Governor to "fulfill their responsibility with respect to defining the specifics of, and the appropriate means to provide through public education, the knowledge and learning essential to the preservation of a free government." Thus, in the first instance, it is the legislature's obligation, not that of individual members of the board of education, to establish educational standards that comply with constitutional requirements.

Our society places tremendous value on education. Education provides the key to individual opportunities for social and economic advancement and forms the foundation for our democratic institutions and our place in the global economy. The very existence of government was declared by the framers to depend upon the intelligence of its citizens. As the New Hampshire Constitution exists today, education is deemed so essential to the viability of the State that part II, article 83 is one of only two places in the constitution where a duty is affirmatively placed on the legislature. "In these days, it is doubtful that any child may reasonably be expected to succeed in life if he is denied the opportunity of an education." *Brown v. Board of Education*, 347 U.S. 483, 493 (1954).

In this appeal, the plaintiffs ask us to declare a State funded constitutionally adequate public education a fundamental right. . . . When governmental action impinges fundamental rights, such matters are entitled to review under the standard of strict judicial scrutiny. . . .

In determining whether, in New Hampshire, a State funded constitutionally adequate elementary and secondary education is a fundamental right, we are guided by two salient factors: one of constitutional interpretation and the other of practicality and common sense. First and foremost is the fact that our State Constitution specifically charges the legislature with the duty to provide public education. *See* N.H. Const. pt. II, art. 83. This fact alone is sufficient in our view to accord fundamental right status to the beneficiaries of the duty.

It is not the province of this Court to create substantive constitutional rights in the name of guaranteeing equal protection of the laws. Thus, the key to discovering whether education is "fundamental" is not to be found in comparisons of the relative societal significance of education as opposed to subsistence or housing. . . . Rather, the answer lies in assessing whether there is a right to education explicitly or implicitly guaranteed by the Constitution. *San Antonio Independent School District v. Rodriguez*, 411 U.S. 1, 33–34 (1973).

Second, and of persuasive force, is the simple fact that even a minimalist view of educational adequacy recognizes the role of education in preparing citizens to participate in the exercise of voting and first amendment rights. The latter being recognized as fundamental, it is illogical to place the means to exercise those rights on less substantial constitutional footing than the rights themselves. We hold that in this State a constitutionally adequate public education is a fundamental right. . . .

We emphasize that the fundamental right at issue is the right to a State funded constitutionally adequate public education. It is not the right to horizontal resource replication from school to school and district to district. The substance of the right may be achieved in different schools possessing, for example, differing library resources, teacher-student ratios, computer software, as well as the myriad tools and techniques that may be employed by those in on-site control of the State's public elementary and secondary school systems. But when an individual school or school district offers something less than educational adequacy, the governmental action or lack of action that is the root cause of the disparity will be examined by a standard of strict judicial scrutiny. . . .

Mere competence in the basics—reading, writing, and arithmetic—is insufficient in the waning days of the twentieth century to insure that this State's public school students are fully integrated into the world around them. A broad exposure to the social, economic, scientific, technological, and political realities of today's society is essential for our students to compete, contribute, and flourish in the twenty-first century.

We look to the seven criteria articulated by the Supreme Court of Kentucky as establishing general, aspirational guidelines for defining educational adequacy.

A constitutionally adequate public education should reflect consideration of the following:

> (i) sufficient oral and written communication skills to enable students to function in a complex and rapidly changing civilization; (ii) sufficient knowledge of economic, social, and political systems to enable the student to make informed choices; (iii) sufficient understanding of governmental processes to enable the student to understand the issues that affect his or her community, state, and nation; (iv) sufficient self-knowledge and knowledge of his or her mental and physical wellness; (v) sufficient grounding in the arts to enable each student to appreciate his or her cultural and historical heritage; (vi) sufficient training or preparation for advanced training in either academic or vocational fields so as to enable each child to choose and pursue life work intelligently; and (vii) sufficient levels of academic or vocational skills to enable public school students to compete favorably with their counterparts in surrounding states, in academics or in the job market.

Rose v. Council for Better Educ., Inc., 790 S.W.2d at 212; *see McDuffy v. Secretary of Exec. Off. of Educ.*, 615 N.E. 2d 516, 554 (Mass. 1993). We view these guidelines as benchmarks of a constitutionally adequate public education. . . .

We agree with Justice Horton [who issued a dissenting opinion] that we were not appointed to establish educational policy, nor to determine the proper way to finance its implementation. That is why we leave such matters, consistent with the Constitution, to the two co-equal branches of government and why we did so in the unanimous opinion of this court in *Claremont I*. We disagree with him that the taxation of property to support education must reach the level of confiscation before a constitutional threshold is crossed. It is our duty to uphold and implement the New Hampshire Constitution, and we have done so today.

Our decision does not prevent the legislature from authorizing local school districts to dedicate additional resources to their schools or to develop educational programs beyond those required for a constitutionally adequate public education. We recognize that local control plays a valuable role in public education; however, the State cannot use local control as a justification for allowing the existence of educational services below the level of constitutional adequacy. The responsibility for ensuring the provision of an adequate public education and an adequate level of resources for all students in New Hampshire lies with the State. "[W]hile local governments may be required, in part, to support public schools, it is the responsibility of the [State] to take such steps as may be required in each instance effectively to devise a plan and sources of funds sufficient to meet the constitutional mandate." *McDuffy*, 615 N.E.2d at 556.

We agree with those who say that merely spending additional money on education will not necessarily insure its quality. It is basic, however, that in order to deliver a constitutionally adequate public education to all children, comparable funding must be assured in order that every school district will have the funds necessary to provide such education. Imposing dissimilar and unreasonable tax burdens on the school districts creates serious impediments to the State's constitutional charge to provide an adequate education for its public school students.

The State's duty to provide for an adequate education is constitutionally compelled. The present system selected and crafted by the State to fund public education is, however, unconstitutional. While the State may delegate its obligation to provide a constitutionally adequate public education to local school districts, it may not do so in a form underscored by unreasonable and inequitable tax burdens. As the State acknowledged at oral argument, several financing models could be fashioned to fund public education. It is for the legislature to select one that passes constitutional muster.

Decisions concerning the raising and disposition of public revenues are particularly a legislative function and the legislature has wide latitude in choosing the means by which public education is to be supported. The legislature has numerous sources of expertise upon which it can draw in addressing educational financing and adequacy, including the experience of other States that have faced and resolved similar issues. Accordingly, we do not remand for consideration of remedies at this time, but instead stay all further proceedings until the end of the upcoming legislative session and further order of this court to permit the legislature to address the issues involved in this case. We are mindful of the fact that our decision holding the present system of financing public education unconstitutional raises issues concerning the interim viability of the existing tax system. Because the legislature must be given a reasonable time to effect an orderly transition to a new system, the present funding mechanism may remain in effect through the 1998 tax year.

We are confident that the legislature and the Governor will act expeditiously to fulfill the State's duty to provide for a constitutionally adequate public education and to guarantee adequate funding in a manner that does not violate the State Constitution.

Post Problem Discussion

1. In *Claremont II*, the court notes the seven criteria of an adequate education from the *Rose* decision. Do you agree with these criteria? Are there other criteria that you think should be included in the list?

2. In the problem, you were asked to consider things from the perspective of a state legislator. How would your perspective differ if you were a school board member, or a parent, rather than a state legislator in the problem?

3. The *Claremont II* decision had one dissenting judge that the majority noted in its decision. The dissent started by stating:

> I agree that the current financing matrix for education is far from desirable, for many of the reasons expressed in the majority opinion. My problem is that I was not appointed to establish educational policy, nor to determine

> the proper way to finance the implementation of this policy. Those duties, in my opinion, reside with the representatives of the people, the Governor, the legislature, and the respective magistrates and legislative authorities in the respective school and taxing districts.

The full dissent is available online. Review the dissenting opinion and consider which you find more persuasive, the majority or the dissent. If you found any state court decisions on education funding in your state in your answers to Activity 1, did those decisions follow an approach similar to the majority or dissent in *Claremont II*?

4. In *Claremont II*, the New Hampshire Supreme Court ruled that education is a fundamental right under the state constitution. The court distinguishes the *Rodriquez* case, which found that education was not a fundamental right under the United States Constitution. What is the basis for the distinction?

D. Complying with Constitutional Obligations

After the *Claremont II* decision, the state developed a legislative response called the ABC Plan. The plan created a state education property tax rate, but then provided for a "special abatement" that allowed certain towns to have lower tax rates than others depending on their property values. Before the ABC Plan was enacted into law, the Legislature asked the New Hampshire Supreme Court to assess the ABC Plan's constitutionality. In an advisory opinion, the court noted that the proposed legislation would be unconstitutional if enacted into law.

After the court's decision, the state requested a two-year extension from the deadline set in *Claremont II* to develop a constitutional method of funding education. The state argued that it had made a good faith effort to develop the ABC Plan, and now that the court had advised that it would be unconstitutional, the State needed more time to develop a new plan. The court denied the request.

Problem 2: State Education Funding—The ABC Plan

You are an attorney in the New Hampshire Attorney General's office who advises the Legislature and Governor on education funding matters. Legislative leaders and the Governor seek your advice on their options. Specifically, they want to know:

1. What happens if the state does not meet the *Claremont II* deadline?
2. In light of the court's decision about the ABC plan, what type of funding mechanisms could the state use to constitutionally fund an adequate education?
3. There have been some legislative efforts to pass a constitutional amendment to undo the *Claremont II* decision. Legislative leaders and the Governor are now considering supporting this approach. What kind of changes would need to be made to the language of New Hampshire's Constitution in order to allow the state to avoid the requirements of the *Claremont II* decision?

Problem Materials

✓ *Opinion of the Justices* (School Financing), 712 A.2d 1080 (N.H. 1998)

✓ *Claremont School District v. Governor*, 725 A.2d 648 (N.H. 1998) (*Claremont IV*)

Opinion of the Justices (School Financing)

712 A.2d 1080 (N.H. 1998)

The New Hampshire Supreme Court advises that the ABC Plan would be unconstitutional if enacted into law because of its "special abatement" provision.

To the Honorable Senate:

The undersigned justices of the supreme court submit the following reply to your questions of May 21, 1998. Following our receipt of your resolution, we invited interested parties to file memoranda with the court on or before June 2, 1998. Oral argument on the questions presented by the request took place at a special session of the court on June 5, 1998. . . .

Your first question asks, "Would enactment of HB 1280-LOCAL as amended, and its funding allocation formula and property tax abatement scheme violate Part II, Article 5 of the state constitution requiring that all taxes be proportional and reasonable?" Your second question asks whether enactment of HB 1280-LOCAL as amended (the bill) would "violate the express language of this court in *Claremont II*, that to the extent that the property tax is used to fund the provision of an adequate education, to be constitutional, the tax must be administered in a manner that is equal in valuation and uniform in rate throughout the state?" Because *Claremont II* simply explained the meaning and import of Part II, Article 5, we answer these two questions together. Both are answered in the affirmative. In reaching this conclusion, we do not revisit the merits of the issues raised in *Claremont II*. Rather, we advise on the constitutionality of the proposed legislation under the law of this State as expressed therein.

Part II, Article 5 of the State Constitution provides that the legislature may "impose and levy proportional and reasonable assessments, rates, and taxes, upon all the inhabitants of, and residents within, the said state." In *Claremont II*, the court concluded that taxes levied to fund education "are in fact State taxes that have been authorized by the legislature to fulfill the requirements of the New Hampshire Constitution," and are not, in fact, local taxes. Accordingly, the court held that "the varying property tax rates across the State violate part II, article 5 of the State Constitution in that such taxes, which support the public purpose of education, are unreasonable and disproportionate." The court offered further that "[t]o the extent that the property tax is used in the future to fund the provision of an adequate education, the tax must be administered in a manner that is equal in valuation and uniform in rate throughout the State."

The bill, in addition to defining an adequate education, purports to establish a uniform State education tax rate based upon the equalized value of all taxable real property in the State. The tax rate is determined by calculating the total statewide cost for educating all New Hampshire students and dividing this sum by the total statewide equalized property value. The bill also authorizes, however, a "special abatement" for "[t]he amount of state education tax apportioned to each town ... in excess of the product of the statewide per pupil cost of an adequate education ... times the average daily membership in residence for the town." ...

As a result of the special abatement, the effective tax rate is reduced below the uniform State education tax rate in any town that can raise more revenue than it needs to provide the legislatively defined "adequate education" for its children. For example, in those towns where there are no children, the special abatement reduces the effective tax rate to zero. Meanwhile, in any town where the property value is insufficient to support the revenue required to educate local children adequately at the uniform State education tax rate, the effective tax rate remains equal to the uniform State education tax rate. Those towns receive a grant from the State to meet the otherwise unfunded costs of an adequate education. Although such towns would be fully funded, the owners of property therein would pay taxes at a higher rate than those in towns with a surplus of revenue, which would receive the special abatement.

Tax abatements and exemptions are not explicitly recognized in the New Hampshire Constitution. The court has, nevertheless, held that "[i]n the selective process of classifying certain property for taxation and exempting other property the Legislature has a wide discretion." Abatements and exemptions necessarily result in a disproportionate tax burden on the remaining property in the taxing district. Therefore, to satisfy Part II, Article 5, abatements must be supported by good cause and exemptions by just reasons, and thereby "reasonably promote some proper object of public welfare or interest."

When determining whether good cause for an abatement or just reasons for an exemption exist, we leave matters of public policy to the legislature and do not "concern ourselves with the wisdom and practicality of proposed legislation." The court's duty is to safeguard constitutional mandates, *see Opinion of the Justices*, 131 N.H. 640, 642, 557 A.2d 273, 275 (1989), by interpreting the plain and common meaning of the constitution in light of the framers' purpose and intent.

We are not persuaded that the special abatement provision is supported by good cause or just reasons consistent with the constitution. Proponents of the bill would have us construe Part II, Article 5 as permitting the special abatement in order to prevent social discord and because other tax resolutions could be divisive. That all three branches of government must struggle with difficult decisions which may cause social unrest cannot be a factor in the court's constitutional review of the bill. The duty of those of us who are constitutional officers, no matter in what branch of government, is to resolve important issues of the day within the confines of the constitution for the benefit of the people of New Hampshire.

Proponents of the bill also assert that the special abatement is designed to protect towns from financially contributing to the adequate education of children in other towns or school districts. Essentially, the proponents seek to measure proportionality and fairness on a municipality-by-municipality or district-by-district basis, rather than statewide. But, to the extent that a property tax is used to raise revenue to satisfy the State's obligation to provide an adequate education, it must be proportional across the State. *See Claremont II.* While good cause or just reasons can be created by public policy determined by the legislature, public policy cannot undermine the constitutional requirement of proportionality. That is, the purpose of an abatement or an exemption can never be to achieve disproportionality for disproportionality's sake.

Because the diffusion of knowledge and learning is regarded by the State Constitution as "essential to the preservation of a free government," N.H. Const. pt. II, art. 83, it is only just that those who enjoy such government should equally assist in contributing to its preservation. The residents of one municipality should not be compelled to bear greater burdens than are borne by others. This obligation cannot be avoided or lessened by the mere circumstance of a town having few children or a town having a wealth of property value, including wealth generated by the presence of heavy industry.

It should not be forgotten that New Hampshire is not a random collection of isolated cities and towns. Indeed, all of us live in a single State. The benefits of adequately educated children are shared statewide and are not limited to a particular town or district. We live in a highly mobile society such that a child may be educated in Pittsfield and, as an adult, reside in Moultonborough. That adult may serve or influence the town or State as an elected or appointed official, a business or civic leader, or in various other endeavors. The benefits of that citizen's public education and contributions to community may be felt far beyond the boundaries of the educating town or district. Therefore, it is basic to our collective well-being that all citizens of the State share in the common burden of educating our children.

In conclusion, while the bill proposes a tax based on an equalized valuation and initially assigns a uniform rate, clearly some taxpayers would pay a far higher tax rate in furtherance of the State's obligation to fund education than others, due to the special abatement. Application of the special abatement guarantees that property owners paying the full rate bear an increased tax burden compared with property owners who are not assessed the full rate. Because such disproportionality is not supported by good cause or a just reason, it violates both the plain wording of Part II, Article 5 and the express language of *Claremont II.*

. . . .

In interpreting the constitution as we do today, we are mindful that those who crafted the words of Part II, Article 5 had lived under the taxation policies of the British Crown. The framers were thus cognizant of schemes of taxation which were oppressive, unpredictable, and grossly unfair. It undoubtedly was the specter of unfair taxation that prompted the requirement that taxes be both proportional and reasonable. Our interpretation of this language has been consistent and to advise otherwise now would be the first step down a dangerous path leading to frustration of the document upon which our government rests. The language of our constitution commands that taxes be no less than fair, proportional, and reasonable.

....

Our task in the first instance is to interpret the constitution. We have done so in *Claremont I* and *Claremont II*. We repeat what we said in *Claremont II*, that "we were not appointed to establish educational policy, nor to determine the proper way to finance its implementation. That is why we leave such matters, consistent with the Constitution, to the two co-equal branches of government." It is neither our task nor intent to manage the public school systems of the State, or to suggest that the State education system cannot incorporate local elements. In this context, we note the commendable steps taken by the Governor and legislature in reaching their definition of a constitutionally adequate education. The legislature's involvement of a broad cross-section of the community in the process can only lead to a definition that will serve this State's school-age citizens well as they journey toward achievement in the world around them. We applaud the Governor and legislature for the work accomplished to date and in advance for that yet to be undertaken.

Claremont School District v. Governor (*Claremont IV*)

725 A.2d 648 (N.H. 1998)

The court denies the state's request for a two-year extension to develop a constitutional funding plan.

....

In the motion now before us, the State contends that "despite diligent efforts by the executive and legislative branches of government to comply with the extremely tight time frame set in *Claremont II*, [it] has not yet been able to develop and implement an education funding system in response to the *Claremont II* decision." The State suggests that it is in part because of this court's decision in *Opinion of the Justices (School Financing)*, that it has become "practically impossible to meet" the deadlines established in *Claremont II*. Thus, the State seeks a two-year period in which to "create an education funding system to meet the *Claremont II* mandates" and to prevent disruption to the operations of school districts.

The New Hampshire Constitution is the supreme law of this State. Every person chosen governor, councilor, senator, or representative in this State is solemnly committed by oath taken pursuant to Part II, Article 84 to "support the constitutions" of the United States and New Hampshire. Responsibility to act to remedy the constitutional defects articulated by this court in *Claremont II* lies with the Governor and the legislature. That we fulfilled our duty to interpret the constitution and say what the law is, declaring unconstitutional the abatement provision contained in the ABC plan, does not present a convincing reason why the other co-equal branches of government have been unable to remedy the continuing constitutional defect. The executive and legislative branches are "duty bound to devote every effort" to resolution of this matter. *Cooper v. Aaron*, 358 U.S. 1, 7 (1958).

Absent extraordinary circumstances, delay in achieving a constitutional system is inexcusable. The legality of the education funding system in this State has been questioned for at least the past twenty-seven years, and the parties involved in the present action have been engaged in litigation for over seven years. The controlling legal principles are plain. The command of Part II, Article 83 is that the State bears the duty to provide a constitutionally adequate education to every educable child in the State and to guarantee adequate funding. The command of Part II, Article 5 is that taxes be proportional and reasonable, thereby forbidding varying property tax rates across the State to support the public duty to provide education. "[I]t should go without saying that the vitality of these constitutional principles cannot be allowed to yield simply because of disagreement with them." *Brown v. Board of Education*, 349 U.S. 294, 300 (1955). The constitutional rights of the children in this State to an adequate State-funded education and of all taxpaying citizens in New Hampshire to reasonable and proportional taxation are not to be denied any longer. Based on the record and pleadings before us, the motion for extension of deadlines is denied.

Post Problem Discussion

1. As the problem notes, there have been numerous efforts to amend New Hampshire's Constitution to undo or alter the requirements of the *Claremont II* decision. To date, those efforts have been unsuccessful. If you were a state legislator, would you favor that approach? Would your perspective change if you were a school board member, or a school administrator? What are the public policy implications of enacting such a constitutional amendment?

2. Would a constitutional amendment to overturn the *Claremont II* decision also necessarily remove judicial review of future school funding issues? If it did, might that violate other constitutional principles?

3. In denying the request for an extension in *Claremont IV*, the court cited to *Brown v. Board of Educ.* and *Cooper v. Aaron*, two United States Supreme Court school desegregation cases. Having held in *Brown I* that separate but equal education was an unconstitutional denial of equal protection under the Fourteenth Amendment, *Brown v. Board of Educ.*, 347 U.S. 483, 495 (1954), the Supreme Court found in *Brown II* that desegregation efforts should proceed with "all deliberate speed." *Brown v. Board of Educ.*, 349 U.S. 294, 301 (U.S. 1955). In *Cooper v. Aaron*, 358 U.S. 1 (1958), the Supreme Court rejected the argument that the State of Arkansas was not bound by *Brown*, and denied the request by the School Board of Little Rock, Arkansas to postpone implementing their desegregation plan. The petition indicated that because of

> extreme public hostility, which (petitioners) stated had been engendered largely by the official attitudes and actions of the Governor and the Legislature, the maintenance of a sound educational program at Central High

> School, with the Negro students in attendance, would be impossible. The Board therefore proposed that the Negro students already admitted to the school be withdrawn and sent to segregated schools, and that all further steps to carry out the Board's desegregation program be postponed for a period later suggested by the Board to be two and one-half years.

What are the similarities between school funding cases and school desegregation cases? What issues of political power, and separation of powers between the branches of government, are in play in each?

E. State Funding for All?

After the New Hampshire Supreme Court denied the state's request for an extension in *Claremont IV*, the state developed a funding system that included a statewide property tax that itself became a new source of litigation. The statewide property tax also became unpopular politically, and legislative efforts to undo or change the tax began in the very next legislative session. These efforts ultimately focused on providing reduced state dollars overall to allow the state to decrease the statewide property tax rate, in order to appease certain communities whose tax rates increased under the statewide tax.

The approach that the state pursued was called "targeted aid," which means providing state funds only to certain communities that the state determines to be in need of the funds based on available local resources, or a lack thereof. By providing funds to only some communities, the state could reduce the overall amount of state funding, and the overall statewide property tax rate.

Problem 3: Targeted Aid

As an attorney in the Attorney General's office, you are contacted by legislators from communities that are not considered "property rich" or "property poor." Their school board members are contacting them to ask if they will receive funding under targeted aid programs, and if such programs are permitted under the New Hampshire Constitution. Based on the problem materials, what would you advise?

Problem Materials

✓ *Opinion of the Justices, (Reformed Public School Financing System)*, 765 A.2d 673 (N.H. 2000)

Opinion of the Justices (Reformed Public School Financing System)

765 A.2d 673 (N.H. 2000)

The court finds that a funding plan that "targets" funds only to some school districts, and does not fund the costs of an adequate education for all school districts, violates the New Hampshire Constitution.

To the Honorable Senate:

The following response is respectfully returned:

. . . .

Viewed in its entirety, the bill proposes to raise and distribute approximately $750,000,000 of State financial aid to school districts to meet the State's obligation under the decision in *Claremont School District v. Governor*, 142 N.H. 462, 703 A.2d 1353 (1997) (*Claremont II*). Of this sum, $409,000,000 would be raised through a uniform statewide property tax, while $341,000,000 would be raised through other State taxes and general fund sources. The bill would distribute $550,000,000 of "baseline assistance for educational adequacy" among school districts on a weighted per pupil basis. The remaining $200,000,000 would be distributed as "aid to guarantee educational adequacy." This money would be allocated among school districts under a needs-based formula, which would assess the relative financial needs of each community using several factors, including per capita income, local property valuations, and local "tax effort."

We have been requested to give our opinion on two questions. First, whether enactment of the bill would "satisfy the requirements of part II, articles 5, 6, and 83 of the New Hampshire constitution" and, second, whether enactment of the bill would "violate any other provisions of the New Hampshire constitution." . . . We turn, therefore, to the first question, which we answer in the negative.

Part II, Article 5 provides that the legislature may "impose and levy proportional and reasonable assessments, rates, and taxes, upon all the inhabitants of, and residents within, the said state." Part II, Article 6 provides that "[t]he public charges of government, or any part thereof, may be raised by taxation. . . ." Part II, Article 83 provides that "[k]nowledge and learning, generally diffused through a community, being essential to the preservation of a free government; and spreading the opportunities and advantages of education through the various parts of the country, being highly conducive to promote this end; it shall be the duty of the legislators and magistrates, in all future periods of this government, to cherish the interest of literature . . . and all . . . public schools. . . ."

In *Claremont I*, we interpreted Part II, Article 83 to "impose[] a duty on the State to provide a constitutionally adequate education for every educable child in the public schools in New Hampshire and to guarantee adequate funding." In *Claremont II*, we concluded that "the property tax levied to fund education is, by virtue of the State's duty to provide a constitutionally adequate public education, a State tax. . . ." We held that to the extent the property tax is used to comply with the mandate of Part II, Article 5, it must be administered in a manner "that is equal in valuation and uniform in rate throughout the State."

The bill contains legislative findings which acknowledge that its proposed funding mechanism would rely, in part, upon local property taxes to pay for some of the cost of an adequate education. These findings directly contradict the mandate of Part II, Article 83, which imposes upon the State the exclusive obligation to fund a constitutionally adequate education. The State may not shift any of this constitutional responsibility to local communities as the proposed bill would do.

According to the bill, the legislative budget and accounting office (LBA) has projected the statewide cost of an adequate education during fiscal year 2001 at $909,839,861. Under the bill, the State's contribution would be $748,712,651, comprised of: (1) $408,630,541 raised by a $6.10 statewide property tax; (2) $140,063,402 in "baseline grants"; and (3) $200,018,608 in "foundation aid." The balance of $161,127,210 would be funded by local school districts through local property taxes.

The LBA calculations demonstrate that many school districts are left with unfunded gaps between the purported cost of an adequate education and the amount of State aid provided under the bill. These deficiencies would be made up through the imposition of local property taxes. For example, in fiscal year 2001, Franklin would be required to raise $419,618 locally, while Lisbon would need to raise $93,500. Each of the nine largest school districts in the State would have to raise additional money to pay for the cost of an adequate education, ranging from $262,897 in Berlin to $18,877,009 in Nashua.

In towns where no additional money needs to be raised by local taxes to underwrite the cost of an adequate education, the taxpayers would pay the uniform property tax rate of $6.10 per $1,000. In other towns that need to fill the gap, the effective tax rate would be higher. Further, the amounts needed to be raised locally to fund a constitutionally adequate education could increase in any given year as a result of the "adjustment constant" provision in section VII of the bill. This provision allows the legislature to allocate less funding for foundation aid than currently provided by the bill and would, therefore, increase the tax burden on local communities to fund the State's obligation.

As was the case under the system in place when *Claremont II* was decided, if this bill is enacted, taxpayers across the State will be paying real estate taxes at disproportionate and unequal rates to fulfill the State's constitutional duty.

Because the diffusion of knowledge and learning is regarded by the State Constitution as "essential to the preservation of a free government" . . . it is only just that those who enjoy such government should equally assist in contributing to its preservation. The residents of one municipality should not be compelled to bear greater burdens than are borne by others.

"[T]o the extent that a property tax is used to raise revenue to satisfy the State's obligation to provide an adequate education, it must be proportional across the State." Because it may be of some assistance to the legislature, and to the extent there may be any lingering confusion, we take this opportunity to reiterate core holdings from earlier *Claremont* decisions.

First, the New Hampshire Constitution imposes solely upon the State the obligation to provide sufficient funds for each school district to furnish a *constitutionally* adequate education to every educable child. Beyond constitutional adequacy, yet to be defined, the legislature may authorize "local school districts to dedicate additional resources to their schools or to develop educational programs beyond those required."

Second, we have never ruled that constitutional adequacy requires a uniform expenditure per pupil throughout the State. In fact, the cost of a constitutionally adequate education may not be the same in each school district. The constitution mandates statewide adequacy—not statewide equality. It is, however, the State's obligation to underwrite the cost of an adequate education for each educable child.

Third, while local school districts may choose to spend money in varying ways to provide an education for their students, all funds they receive from the State for constitutional adequacy *must* be used for education.

Finally, as articulated in *Claremont I* in 1993, the content of a constitutionally adequate education must be defined, in the first instance, by the legislature. It is not possible to determine the level of funding required to provide the children of this State with a constitutionally adequate education until its essential elements have been identified and defined. The legislature and the Governor have broad latitude to fashion the specifics. Once this critical task has been completed, it is for the legislature to adopt a funding mechanism to ensure that a constitutionally adequate education is provided.

This court has never directed or required the selection of a particular funding mechanism. If the legislature chooses to use a property tax, however, the tax must be equal and proportional across the State.

Post Problem Discussion

1. After the court's decision, political factions still disagreed on whether the state could constitutionally target aid by sending funds only to some communities based on "need," while leaving other communities to pay for some or all of an adequate education with local funds. The New Hampshire Supreme Court addressed the issue again in a subsequent decision involving the state's efforts to define an adequate education, stating:

> Any definition of constitutional adequacy crafted by the political branches must be sufficiently clear to permit common understanding and *allow for an objective determination of cost* whatever the State identifies as comprising constitutional adequacy it must pay for. *None of that financial obligation can be shifted to local school districts*, regardless of their relative wealth or need.

Londonderry Sch. Dist. SAU No. 12 v. State, 907 A.2d 988 (N.H. 2006). After the court's decision, efforts to amend the New Hampshire Constitution increased and came to the forefront in several legislative sessions with the claim now being that the state should amend the Constitution to allow it to target funds to certain communities, and not provide funds to other communities that were considered wealthy enough to fund education on their own. If you were a state legislator, would you support this approach? Why or why not? Would your opinion differ if you were a school board member or a school administrator?

2. As noted, the New Hampshire Supreme Court's decisions require the state to pay for all of the costs of an adequate education, even if the local community has a "wealthy" property base, and could afford to do so with local funds. What are the advantages and disadvantages to this approach? What effect do you think this requirement has on legislative efforts to implement a constitutional financing system?

3. It is important to note that the court's decisions do not require the state to send the same exact amount of funding to each community, as the costs of an adequate education can vary from one community to the next. What are some of the reasons why costs could vary from district to district? What are some ways that the legislature could take these differences into account when providing funds?

§ 2.05 Standards of Adequacy and Accountability

New Hampshire's constitutional obligations regarding education include more than just funding. As the *Claremont* decisions note, the state also has an obligation to provide an adequate education. The State of New Hampshire delegates the responsibility to deliver educational services to local school districts (as opposed to providing them directly at the state level). The New Hampshire Supreme Court eventually addressed the state's constitutional obligation to ensure that local school districts actually provide an adequate education.

Problem 4: State Accountability Obligations

You are legal counsel for the Governor. In response to *Claremont VII*, the state legislature has proposed revising state statutes on accountability. The Governor is deciding whether or not to sign the bill into law. She wants to know if the changes meet the accountability requirements of the *Claremont VII* decision in the problem materials. If your opinion is that the current bill will not, what changes need to be made to it so that it will meet constitutional requirements?

Problem Materials

✓ *Claremont School District v. Governor*, 794 A.2d 744 (N.H. 2002) (*Claremont VII*)

✓ *Proposed RSA 193-E*

Claremont School District v. Governor (*Claremont VII*)

794 A.2d 744 (N.H. 2002)

The court rules that the state has a constitutional obligation to develop an accountability system to ensure that local school districts provide students with an adequate education.

Duggan, J. The issues before this court are: (1) whether the State's obligation to provide a constitutionally adequate public education requires it to include standards of accountability in the educational system; and, if so, (2) whether existing statutes, regulations and/or rules satisfy this obligation. We hold that accountability is an essential component of the State's duty and that the existing statutory scheme has deficiencies that are inconsistent with the State's duty to provide a constitutionally adequate education....

....

The State contends that whether they are obligated to include "standards of accountability" "depends on the meaning of the phrase." The State explains that if "standards of accountability" means the existence of a system to deliver an adequate education, then it agrees that it is obligated to include such standards and further contends that the existing statutes, regulations and rules comply with this requirement. The State is essentially arguing that it is only accountable for devising a system to deliver a constitutionally adequate education. This reformulation of the issue, however, serves only to circumvent the question whether the State is obligated to adopt standards of accountability to *ensure* delivery of a constitutionally adequate education.

Accountability is more than merely creating a system to deliver an adequate education. *Claremont I* did not simply hold that the State should deliver a constitutionally adequate education, but in fact held that it is the State's duty under the New Hampshire Constitution to do so. Accountability means that the State must provide a definition of a constitutionally adequate education, the definition must have standards, and the standards must be subject to meaningful application so that it is possible to determine whether, in delegating its obligation to provide a constitutionally adequate education, the State has fulfilled its duty. If the State cannot be held accountable for fulfilling its duty, the duty creates no obligation and is no longer a duty. We therefore conclude that the State's duty to provide a constitutionally adequate education includes accountability.

This conclusion is consistent with the responses of the executive and legislative branches to the *Claremont* decisions. As recounted above, representations made by the attorney general and efforts made by the Governor and legislature illustrate that the *Claremont* decisions have been generally interpreted to require some form of accountability. Indeed, in 1993 the legislature created an assessment system that would "generate data ... to provide a basis for accountability." RSA 193-C:3, IV(h) (1999). Thus, the legislature's response to *Claremont* demonstrates that it also views accountability as a logical corollary to the State's duty to provide a constitutionally adequate education.

This view is shared by other jurisdictions. In Massachusetts, for example, in response to *McDuffy v. Secretary of Executive Office of Education*, 615 N.E.2d 516 (Mass. 1993), the legislature promulgated a system of accountability whereby the state board of education was given authority to establish specific performance standards and a program for remediation when students' test scores fall below a certain level. *See* Mass. Gen. Laws Ann., ch. 69, § 1B, § 1I (1996). In Ohio, the state supreme court stated that "accountability is an important component of [the educational system]." *DeRolph v. Ohio*, 728 N.E.2d 993, 1018 (2000). In New Jersey, the state supreme court noted that the existence of standards alone is insufficient if "[t]he standards themselves do not ensure any substantive level of achievement." *Abbott by Abbott v. Burke*, 693 A.2d 417, 428 (1997). In Tennessee, the state supreme court said that "[t]he essentials of the governance provisions of the [Basic Educational Program] are mandatory performance standards; local management within established principles; performance audits that objectively measure results; . . . and final responsibility upon the State officials for an effective educational system throughout the State." It is thus widely accepted that establishing standards of accountability is part of the State's duty to provide a constitutionally adequate education.

Having determined that standards of accountability are an essential component of the State's duty to provide a constitutionally adequate education, we must now determine whether the existing statutes, regulations and rules satisfy this obligation. The State argues that these existing laws, which include the definition of an adequate education in RSA 193-E:2; the State's minimum standards for education set forth in the department of education rules, N.H. Admin. Rules, Ed ch. 300; and the New Hampshire Education Improvement and Assessment Program (NHEIAP), RSA ch. 193-C (1999), together provide sufficient standards of accountability. According to the State, "it has given detailed curriculum instruction to schools and school boards, created a test to measure student performance, empowered State agencies to review and improve school performance, and enacted literally thousands of pages of other statutes, regulations, and rules to deliver an adequate education."

The starting point for analyzing the system is RSA 21-N:1, II(c) (2000), which states that "[t]he paramount goal of the state shall be to provide an adequate education for all school-age children in the state, consistent with RSA 193-E." RSA 193-E:1, I, provides:

> It is the policy of the state of New Hampshire that public elementary and secondary education shall provide all students with the opportunity to acquire the knowledge and skills necessary to prepare them for successful participation in the social, economic, scientific, technological, and political systems of a free government, now and in the years to come; an education that is consistent with the curriculum and student proficiency standards specified in state school approval rules and New Hampshire curriculum frameworks.

RSA 193-E:2 sets forth the criteria for an adequate education as follows:

> I. Skill in reading, writing, and speaking English to enable them to communicate effectively and think creatively and critically.
>
> II. Skill in mathematics and familiarity with methods of science to enable them to analyze information, solve problems, and make rational decisions.

III. Knowledge of the biological, physical, and earth sciences to enable them to understand and appreciate the world around them.

IV. Knowledge of civics and government, economics, geography, and history to enable them to participate in the democratic process and to make informed choices as responsible citizens.

V. Grounding in the arts, languages, and literature to enable them to appreciate our cultural heritage and develop lifelong interests and involvement in these areas.

VI. Sound wellness and environmental practices to enable them to enhance their own well-being, as well as that of others.

VII. Skills for lifelong learning, including interpersonal and technological skills, to enable them to learn, work, and participate effectively in a changing society. . . .

A. Minimum Standards

The State argues that as a central part of the system to deliver a constitutionally adequate education, it "dictates certain school approval standards that schools and school districts must meet. These input based standards are enforceable by the State and extend to virtually every aspect of education, from class size to teacher training to detailed curriculum requirements."

The board of education is required by statute to adopt rules relative to "[m]inimum curriculum and educational standards for all grades of the public schools." RSA 186:8, I (1999); *see also* RSA 21-N:9 (2000). These rules are commonly referred to as the State's "minimum standards" or "school approval standards." The minimum standards contain a number of requirements imposed by the State on local school districts so that schools may be approved by the State. For example, the minimum standards set forth the number of days in a standard school year, staff qualifications, maximum class sizes, heating and ventilation requirements, the minimum number of credits required to be offered in certain courses, and the areas of specific substantive materials which must be taught. *See* N.H. Admin. Rules, Ed 302.01–306.41.

The education that the individual schools provide is measured against these standards for approval. *Id.* 306.40. If a school does not meet these standards, it can lose its approval. *Id.* There are four categories of approval: approved with distinction, approved, conditionally approved from one to three years, and unapproved. *Id.* 306.40(b)(1)-(4). If a school is unapproved, the department of education is required to work with the local school board to "correct all deficiencies until such time as an unapproved school meets all applicable standards and is designated as an approved school." *Id.* 306.40(b)(5). The purpose of these rules is to hold school districts accountable for providing an adequate education.

RSA 194:23-c (1999), however, provides that "[t]he state board of education shall have the power to approve for a reasonable period of time a high school that does not fully meet the requirements of RSA 194:23 if in its judgment the financial condition of the school district or other circumstances warrant delay in full compliance." . . .

The financial or emergency conditions which justify a school's or school district's excusal from compliance with the minimum standards include: "(1) Reduction in local tax base; (2) Closing of a major industry; (3) Sudden influx of school-age population; (4) Emergency beyond the control of the school district, such as fire or natural disaster; or (5) Other financial or emergency condition not listed above." *Id.* 306.41(c). The plaintiffs contend that the minimum standards are insufficient to comply with the State's duty to ensure a constitutionally adequate education because by "the express language of Ed 306.41, districts that are too poor to comply with the standards are excused from compliance with the modest standards of the program."

On their face, RSA 194:23-c and N.H. Admin. Rules, Ed 306.41(a) permit a school district to provide less than an adequate education as measured by these minimum standards when the local tax base cannot supply sufficient funds to meet the standards. The statute and the rule also permit noncompliance with the standards under emergency conditions, such as a fire or natural disaster. While it may be permissible to excuse noncompliance under emergency conditions, the statute permits the board of education to also approve a school that does not meet the minimum standards based solely on the "financial condition of the school district." RSA 194:23-c.

Excused noncompliance with the minimum standards for financial reasons alone directly conflicts with the constitutional command that the State must guarantee sufficient funding to ensure that school districts can provide a constitutionally adequate education. As we have repeatedly held, it is the State's duty to guarantee the funding necessary to provide a constitutionally adequate education to every educable child in the public schools in the State. *Claremont I*, 138 N.H. at 184.

The responsibility for ensuring the provision of an adequate public education and an adequate level of resources for all students in New Hampshire lies with the State. While local governments may be required, in part, to support public schools, it is the responsibility of the State to take such steps as may be required in each instance effectively to devise a plan and sources of funds sufficient to meet the constitutional mandate.

There is no accountability when the rules on their face tolerate noncompliance with the duty to provide a constitutionally adequate education. While the State may delegate this duty, *see Claremont II*, 142 N.H. at 476, it must do so in a manner that does not abdicate the constitutional duty it owes to the people, *see State v. Hayes*, 61 N.H. 264, 327 (1881). The State's duty cannot be relieved by the constraints of a school district's tax base or other financial condition. *See Claremont II*, 142 N.H. at 470–71. Apparently the dissenting opinion agrees with this conclusion.

The plaintiffs also allege that, as applied, the minimum standards are insufficient because for the 2001–2002 school year, sixteen schools, including seven high schools, have been granted delays in coming into full compliance with the minimum standards. Although this status is supposed to last for only one year, N.H. Admin. Rules, Ed 306.41(a), at least two elementary schools have been in the "delay in full compliance" category for three years. In all, a total of 12,898 school children in New Hampshire are attending schools that have been granted delayed compliance with the minimum standards. The issue before us, however, does not turn on the particular facts alleged. Rather, the only issue is whether the existing statutes on their face comply with the constitution....

We hold, therefore, that to the extent the minimum standards for school approval excuse compliance solely based on financial conditions, it is facially insufficient because it is in clear conflict with the State's duty to provide a constitutionally adequate education.

B. New Hampshire Education Improvement and Assessment Program

NHEIAP, RSA chapter 193-C, is characterized by the State as "[a]nother important element of the State's system for delivering the opportunity for an adequate education." The goals of the program are to define what students should know and be able to do, develop and implement methods for assessing that learning and its application, report assessment results to all citizens of New Hampshire, help to provide accountability at all levels, and use the results, at both the State and local levels, to improve instruction and advance student learning. RSA 193-C:3, I(a)-(e). The department of education pamphlet describes NHEIAP as the "cornerstone of the state's initiatives to continuously improve education for all students."

The responsibility for administering NHEIAP lies with the department of education. RSA 193-C:3. The commissioner of education is charged with "develop[ing] and implement[ing] this program in conjunction with the state board of education and the legislative oversight committee." *Id.* In fulfilling its duty pursuant to the statutory framework that makes up NHEIAP, the department of education is directed to develop a program that consists of three interlocking components. *See* RSA 193-C:3, I. The first component is a set of educational standards, RSA 193-C:3, III(a), which the department of education has developed and implemented through curriculum frameworks. The second component is a statewide assessment program, which "shall be [a] valid and appropriate representation[] of the standards the students are expected to achieve." RSA 193-C:3, III(b). The final component is the "local education improvement and assessment plan which builds upon and complements the goals established for [NHEIAP]." RSA 193-C:9, I.

The first component, curriculum frameworks that represent the educational standards, is described by the State as "detailed blueprints, which apply to students in kindergarten through 12th grade, defin[ing] what New Hampshire students should know and be able to do at the completion of different levels of their education." The curriculum frameworks, covering more than 700 printed pages, establish lengthy, comprehensive and "challenging benchmarks" in the subject areas tested. RSA 193-C:1, VI. The department of education has developed curriculum frameworks for each of the subject areas described in RSA 193-C:5—reading, language arts, mathematics, science, history and geography.

The second component is the statewide assessment that the department of education is required to administer each year in all school districts in an elementary school grade, a middle school or junior high school grade, and a high school grade. *See* RSA 193-C:6. The assessment tests are directly tied to "curriculum frameworks and are designed to measure whether students are meeting the ambitious standards set forth in those frameworks." The department of education has established four levels of achievement in each subject area—novice, basic, proficient and advanced. According to the department of education, "Students who score at the basic level have successfully demonstrated that they have learned fundamental information and skills. Students at the proficient and advanced levels have demonstrated the attainment of a wide range of knowledge as well as the ability to apply that knowledge."

The final component, a local education improvement and assessment plan for an individual school district, is developed and implemented based on assessment results. RSA 193-C:9, II(a). Through the local improvement assistance program, the department of education "use[s] funds appropriated for th[e] program to provide technical assistance and training to school districts in developing and implementing local education improvement and assessment plans based on assessment results." . . .

In enacting NHEIAP, the legislature recognized that "[i]mprovement and accountability in education are of primary concern to all the citizens of New Hampshire." RSA 193-C:1, I. The statute specifically states that one of "[t]he aims of this program shall be to . . . [h]elp to provide accountability at all levels." RSA 193-C:3, I. The program set forth in RSA chapter 193-C, accordingly, is intended to "serve[] as an effective measure of accountability." RSA 193-C:1, II.

As a measure of accountability, the statute delegates the task of establishing a set of educational standards to the department of education. *See* RSA 193-C:3. The department of education, in turn, created the curriculum frameworks, which "define what New Hampshire students should know and be able to do at the completion of different levels of their education." The assessment "tests, administered at the end of grades three, six, and ten, are developed around the curriculum frameworks and provide vital data that help[] identify strengths in an educational program as well as areas that need improvement." . . .

While the avowed purpose of RSA chapter 193-C is to provide accountability, the statute, together with the reporting requirements of RSA chapter 193-E, is limited to providing: (1) the development of educational standards; (2) statewide assessment through testing; and (3) an opportunity to use the reported assessment results in developing a local education improvement plan. Although the tests measure student performance against the educational standards, the principal use of the assessment results is to generate and compile data. According to the department of education, the "NHEIAP results provide each school and each school district with information on its academic strengths and weaknesses. This allows the community and school district to discuss local results, and then develop a local educational improvement plan for their school or district."

Under RSA 193-C:9, I, however, no school district is required to respond to the assessment results; rather "[e]ach school district in New Hampshire is *encouraged* to develop a local education improvement and assessment plan." (Emphasis added.) This means that even if the assessment results show that all the students in a school are at novice level, neither the school district nor the department of education is required to do anything. Whether an individual school district is providing a constitutionally adequate education or not, it is merely encouraged to develop a local educational improvement plan, and if it opts to do so, the department of education is available to assist. Nothing more is required.

An output-based accountability system that merely encourages local school districts to meet educational standards does not fulfill the State's constitutional duty under Part II, Article 83. While the State may delegate its duty to provide a constitutionally adequate education, the State may not abdicate its duty in the process. The purpose of meaningful accountability is to ensure that those entrusted with the duty of delivering a constitutionally adequate education are fulfilling that duty. When the State chooses to use an output-based tool to measure whether school districts are providing a constitutionally adequate education, that tool must be meaningfully applied. The department of education cannot meaningfully apply the educational standards and assessment tests set out in RSA chapter 193-C when it cannot hold school districts accountable, but instead is limited to using the results to encourage school districts to develop a local education improvement and assessment plan. To the extent the State relies on RSA chapter 193-C to provide for accountability, it must do more than merely encourage school districts to meet the educational standards that are designed to indicate whether students are receiving a constitutionally adequate education.

The State suggests that "[a] student who receives an education of the quality described in [RSA] 193-E:2 and who acquires all of the various skills and types of knowledge expressed there would be well prepared as a citizen to participate in society." While we have no basis to disagree with this statement, the State has not provided a sufficient mechanism to require that school districts actually achieve this goal. We hold that because of deficiencies in the system as set out in this opinion, the State has not met its constitutional obligation to develop a system to ensure the delivery of a constitutionally adequate education.

As the State recognizes, "there are many different ways that the Legislature could fashion an educational system while still meeting the mandates of the Constitution." The development of meaningful standards of accountability is a task for which the legislative branch is uniquely suited. The policy choices to be made are complex, as there are several ways to address this issue. It is for the Governor and the legislature to choose how to measure or evaluate whether a constitutionally adequate education is being provided and what action to take if a school is determined to be deficient. . . .

We conclude that the State "needs to do more work" to fulfill its duty to provide a constitutionally adequate education and incorporate meaningful accountability in the education system. In light of the procedural history of this litigation, including efforts by the executive and legislative branches and their previous statements on this issue, and the application of settled law, this conclusion should be neither surprising nor unanticipated.

We underscore that this court has consistently declined to determine whether the State's definition of an adequate education is constitutional. This issue is not before us now.

We remain mindful that "[w]hile the judiciary has the duty to construe and interpret the word 'education' by providing broad constitutional guidelines, the Legislature is obligated to give specific substantive content to the word and to the program it deems necessary to provide that 'education' within the broad guidelines." We recognize that we are not appointed to establish educational policy and have not done so today.

In 1993, after holding that Part II, Article 83 imposes a duty on the State to provide a constitutionally adequate education to every educable child in the public schools and to guarantee adequate funding, we remanded the case for further proceedings. In 1997, we held that the system for financing elementary and secondary public education in the State was unconstitutional and that the legislature must define and implement a system to provide a constitutionally adequate education. Rather than remanding the case, we retained jurisdiction.

Since that time, both parties have availed themselves of our continuing jurisdiction and sought opinions directly from this court. . . . Therefore, in the nearly nine years since this court issued the decision in *Claremont I*, we have rendered eight subsequent opinions directly related to that initial decision. In each of these decisions, this court considered whether the actions of the State conformed to the governing constitutional principles expressed in *Claremont I* and *Claremont II* that the State must provide and fund a constitutionally adequate public education. At no time has this court deviated from the holdings in *Claremont I* and *Claremont II* or their constitutional underpinnings.

We remain hopeful that the legislative and executive branches will continue to work to satisfy their constitutional duty to ensure the delivery of a constitutionally adequate education to the public school students of this State. As in the past, we are confident that the legislature and the Governor will fulfill their responsibility "to provide through public education, the knowledge and learning essential to the preservation of a free government." *Claremont I*, 138 N.H. at 193.

So ordered.

Proposed RSA 193-E:3 Delivery of an Adequate Education.

I. Annually, beginning with the 2002–2003 school year, each school district shall report data to the department of education at the school and district levels on the indicators set forth in this paragraph. The department of education shall develop a reasonable schedule to phase-in the reporting of new data required by federal law. The requirements for data keeping and the form of the report shall be established in accordance with rules adopted by the state board of education. Indicators shall include the following areas:

(a) Attendance rates.

(b) Annual and cumulative drop-out rates of high school pupils and annual drop-out rates for pupils in grades 7 and 8.

(c) School environment indicators, such as safe-schools data.

(d) Number and percentage of graduating pupils going on to post-secondary education, military service, and advanced placement participation.

(e) Performance on state tests administered pursuant to RSA 193-C and other standardized tests administered at local option.

(f) Expulsion and suspension rates, including in-school and out-of-school suspensions, which shall be reported for each school year.

(g) Number and percentage of classes taught by highly qualified teachers.

(h) Teacher and administrative turnover rates at the school and district levels.

II. The department of education, with the approval of the legislative oversight committee established in RSA 193-C:7, may implement and report data on any additional indicators deemed relevant to the purposes of this section.

III. Not later than December 1, 2003, and annually thereafter, the department of education shall issue a public report on the condition of education statewide and on a district-by-district and school-by-school basis. This report shall be entitled "New Hampshire School District Profiles" and shall be made available at every school administrative unit for public review. It shall include demographic and pupil performance data reported in paragraph I and other relevant statistics as determined by the department of education. Comparisons with state averages shall be provided for all data reported. Comparisons of each district and school to itself based on its own statewide improvement and assessment performance for the prior school year and its most recent 3-year rolling averages shall be provided. Statewide rankings of each district and school shall be provided, including a statewide ranking of each school and school district based on the percentage increase of improvement as compared with the same school district's performance in the previous year. The report shall be organized and presented in a manner that is easily understood by the public and that assists each school district with the identification of trends, strengths, and weaknesses and the development of its local school education improvement plan.

IV. Data reported in paragraph I shall be disaggregated as required by federal law and shall include numbers and percentages of pupils with disabilities, limited English proficient pupils, pupils in advanced placement programs, economically disadvantaged pupils, and pupils of major racial and multi-racial groups.

V. In order to reduce school districts' administrative time and costs, the department of education shall develop and utilize user-friendly, computer forms and programs to collect the data set forth in paragraph I and all enrollment and cost data related to determining the cost of an adequate education.

Post Problem Discussion

1. The New Hampshire Supreme Court's decision regarding accountability was one of the first decisions in the country to expressly recognize a state's constitutional obligation to develop a meaningful accountability system. Why do you think the court determined that the state had such a constitutional obligation?

2. The court goes through the statutes and regulations that the state argued satisfied its accountability obligations and finds that they are not sufficient. What is the court's rationale for these findings?

3. The court notes that the state can use a variety of approaches in its accountability system. What do you think should be included in an accountability system in light of the court's opinion?

4. The court notes that it has continued to provide the Legislature and the Governor with deference in developing a definition of an adequate education, and in developing an accountability system. Why do you think the court provides deference in these areas?

Activity 2: Accountability in Your State

The issue of accountability is one that all states have addressed in one way or another. Often, state accountability requirements are linked with the ESSA's requirements. Complete the following steps to explore this issue in your state:

Step One—Research your state statutes and regulations for those addressing accountability issues like the ones discussed in Problem 4 and *Claremont VII*. Consider the following issues to help focus your research:

1. What factors does your state's accountability system use to assess school or student performance?
2. How does your state determine if schools meet accountability requirements?

3. What steps does your state take when a school or school district is not meeting state accountability requirements?
4. Does your state take any steps to reward schools or school districts that are meeting state accountability requirements?

Step Two—Does your state have a court decision on accountability like *Claremont VII*? If so, does your state's accountability system meet constitutional requirements? If not, do you think your state court would adopt an approach like the court did in *Claremont VII*? Why or why not? If it did, would your state's current accountability system meet the requirements noted in the *Claremont VII* decision?

Step Three—Has your state's accountability system been successful? What factors would you consider in answering this question? How would you gauge success?

Step Four—What changes if any, do you think should be made to your state's accountability requirements?

§ 2.06 Back to the Beginning: Basic Definitions and New Parties

After *Claremont VII*, the state enacted additional statutory provisions and changed the state education funding formula. A new group of plaintiffs sued challenging these laws on a variety of grounds. In this new lawsuit, the New Hampshire Supreme Court initially addressed an old issue, whether the state had developed a constitutional definition of an adequate education. The following problem explores the topic.

Problem 5: Defining Adequacy

In response to the *Londonderry* decision in the problem materials, the state amended its statutes regarding an adequate education. Do the changes meet the constitutional requirements noted in the *Claremont* and *Londonderry* decisions?

Problem Materials

✓ *Londonderry School District SAU No. 12 v. State*, 907 A.2d 988 (N.H. 2006)

✓ *RSA 193-E*

Londonderry School District SAU #12 v. State of New Hampshire

907 A.2d 988 (NH 2006)

The court rules that the state has yet to define an adequate education and orders the state to do so.

Hicks, J. Once again, we are called upon to address the basic educational needs of the children of New Hampshire and the State's obligation to ensure and to fund each educable child's opportunity to obtain a constitutionally adequate education as required by Part II, Article 83 of the New Hampshire Constitution.

The State appeals a decision of the Superior Court finding that the State has failed to fulfill its duty to define a constitutionally adequate education, failed to determine the cost of an adequate education, and failed to satisfy the requirement of accountability, and that House Bill 616 (the current education funding law) creates a non-uniform tax rate in violation of Part II, Article 5 of the New Hampshire Constitution. We affirm the trial court's finding that the State has failed to define a constitutionally adequate education and stay consideration of its remaining findings.

....

Today, the State argues that it has defined a constitutionally adequate education in RSA 193-E:2 (Supp. 2005). That statute, titled "Criteria for an Equitable Education," provides:

> An equitable education shall provide all students with the opportunity to acquire:
>
> I. Skill in reading, writing, and speaking English to enable them to communicate effectively and think creatively and critically.
>
> II. Skill in mathematics and familiarity with methods of science to enable them to analyze information, solve problems, and make rational decisions.
>
> III. Knowledge of the biological, physical, and earth sciences to enable them to understand and appreciate the world around them.
>
> IV. Knowledge of civics and government, economics, geography, and history to enable them to participate in the democratic process and to make informed choices as responsible citizens.
>
> V. Grounding in the arts, languages, and literature to enable them to appreciate our cultural heritage and develop lifelong interest and involvement in these areas.
>
> VI. Sound wellness and environmental practices to enable them to enhance their own well-being, as well as that of others.
>
> VII. Skills for lifelong learning, including interpersonal and technological skills, to enable them to learn, work, and participate effectively in a changing society.

The State argues that this definition of adequacy "accords with the definitions upheld by the judiciaries of other states around the nation," citing West Virginia, Kentucky, Montana and Washington. An examination of the cases and statutes in those states, however, reveals otherwise. In West Virginia, for example, an action was brought by parents of school children contending that the system for financing public schools violated that state's constitutional guarantee of a "thorough and efficient" education. Although the state supreme court of appeals remanded the case "for further evidentiary development," because the case involved "significant and far-reaching public issues," the court proposed certain guidelines to the trial court, including identifying the parameters of a "[t]horough and [e]fficient" educational system, ultimately holding that the legislature has the constitutional duty "to develop a high quality Statewide education system."

On remand the trial court found that the State had failed "to perform its constitutional and statutory duties with respect to formulating high quality standards for education" because the standards promulgated by the board of education were "far too general and minimal to define the elements of a thorough and efficient system of education." The trial court appointed a special master to oversee the development of an educational master plan that contained "an extensive compilation of detailed concepts and standards that defines the educational role of the various state and local agencies, sets forth specific elements of educational programs, enunciates consideration for educational facilities and proposes changes in the educational financing system."

Similarly, in Kentucky, a group of school districts and public school students brought an action challenging whether the Kentucky General Assembly had complied with its constitutional mandate to "provide an efficient system of common schools throughout the state." *Rose v. Council for Better Educ., Inc.*, 790 S.W.2d 186, 189–90 (Ky. 1989) (quotation omitted). The state supreme court declared the system of common schools to be constitutionally deficient and directed the legislature to "re-create . . . and re-establish a system of common schools within this state which will be in compliance with the Constitution." *Id.* at 214. In doing so, the court set out standards for a new system, including identifying seven "capacities" with which each and every child was to be provided through an efficient system of education. *Id.* at 212. The court indicated that the seven characteristics "should be considered as *minimum* goals in providing an adequate education." *Id.* at 214 n.22. The Kentucky legislature subsequently enacted the Kentucky Education Reform Act of 1990, "which radically changed the system of public education" in that state. *Chapman v. Gorman*, 839 S.W.2d 232, 234 (Ky. 1992).

In Montana and Washington, although the applicable statutes contain general definitions of an adequate education, in each state the legislation defines the substantive content of the educational program implementing the general definitions. In Montana, the legislature established five "goals" for public elementary and secondary schools. Mont. Code. Ann. § 20-1-102 (2005). The statutory scheme also identifies "the minimum standards upon which a basic system of free quality public elementary and secondary schools is built," and the "educationally relevant" factors the legislature must consider. Mont. Code Ann. §§ 20-9-309(2)(a), (3); *see* Mont. Code Ann. § 20-9-309(4)(b)(i) (2005).

In Washington, the state supreme court interpreted the constitutional provision that "[i]t is the paramount duty of the state to make ample provision for the education of all children residing within its borders," as creating a judicially enforceable, affirmative duty. *Seattle Sch. Dist. No. 1 of King City v. State*, 585 P.2d 71, 83, 85 (Wa. 1978) (quotation and emphasis omitted). The court held that pursuant to that duty, the legislature has the responsibility to define and give content to a basic education and a basic program of education. *Id.* at 95. The "Basic Education Act," codified in the Washington statutes, requires each school district "to provide opportunities for all students to develop" essential knowledge and skills in four broad categories. Wash. Rev. Code § 28A.150.210 (2004). The state board of education is required to establish a program that includes "the essential academic learning requirements ... and such other subjects and such activities as the school district shall determine to be appropriate for the education of the school district's children," Wash. Rev. Code § 28A.150.220(1)(a), (b), and to "adopt rules to implement and ensure compliance with the program requirements," Wash. Rev. Code § 28A.150.220(4). *See also* Mass. Gen. Laws Ann. ch. 69, § 1 (1996) (intent of statute is to provide "public education system of sufficient quality to extend to all children the opportunity to reach their full potential and to lead lives as participants in the political and social life of the commonwealth and as contributors to its economy"), § 1B (duties of the board of education), § 1D (statewide educational goals and academic standards), § 1E (curriculum frameworks), § 1I (performance reports, evaluation system and assessments); *Hancock v. Commissioner of Educ.*, 822 N.E.2d 1134, 1137–38 (Mass. 2005) (Massachusetts Education Reform Act of 1993 established uniform, objective performance and accountability measures for every public school student, teacher, administrator, school and district in the state). Therefore, although each state noted above provides, as part of a comprehensive statutory scheme, a general definition of an adequate education, each state also establishes a mechanism through which educational content is identified in fulfillment of constitutional duties.

In the case before us, the State asserts that the system of education in New Hampshire goes well beyond constitutional adequacy. In its brief, the State argues that "statutes and regulations ... implement [the definition of adequacy] with a specificity that far exceeds constitutional requirements"; that by complying with the federal No Child Left Behind Act of 2001 and "establishing a comprehensive system for holding its schools accountable, the State has exceeded the constitutional requirements of accountability"; that "the annual testing and statewide performance targets ... far exceed the constitutional standard of adequacy as defined by the legislature in RSA 193-E:2"; and that the "school approval standards go well beyond the constitutional floor of adequacy" and "far surpass the constitutional minimum of adequacy." For purposes of this appeal, we will accept these assertions. These assertions themselves, however, expose the core issue before us. If the statutory scheme that is in place provides for *more* than constitutional adequacy, then the State has yet to isolate what parts of the scheme comprise constitutional adequacy. More specifically, under the statutory scheme there is no way a citizen or a school district in this State can determine the distinct substantive content of a constitutionally adequate education. Consequently, its cost cannot be isolated. Such a system is also impervious to meaningful judicial review.

The task of developing specific criteria of an adequate education is for the legislature. *Claremont II*, 142 N.H. at 475. By failing to do so, the legislature creates the potential for a situation in which a superior court judge, or a special master appointed by this court, will be required to decide what is to be taught in the public schools in order to provide the opportunity to acquire "[s]kill in reading, writing and speaking English," "[s]kill in mathematics and familiarity with methods of science," "[k]nowledge of the biological, physical, and earth sciences," "[k]nowledge of civics and government, economics, geography, and history," "[g]rounding in the arts, languages, and literature," "[s]ound wellness and environmental practices," and "[s]kills for lifelong learning." RSA 193-E:2. Similarly, to assess whether a constitutionally adequate education is being provided, a trial judge would likely have to determine the levels of "skill," "knowledge," "grounding" and "sound wellness" to which an educable child is entitled. Moreover, RSA 193-E:2 mandates that students be provided the "opportunity to acquire" such skills and knowledge. Without more, a trial judge or a special master would have to determine the adequacy of the "opportunity" to be afforded. Determining the substantive educational program that delivers a constitutionally adequate education is a task replete with policy decisions, best suited for the legislative or executive branches, not the judicial branch.

RSA 193-E:2 largely mirrors the seven criteria that we cited with approval in *Claremont II*, 142 N.H. at 474–75. We characterized those criteria as establishing "general" and "aspirational" guidelines for defining educational adequacy and made clear that the legislature was expected to develop and adopt *specific criteria* for implementing the guidelines. In the years since RSA 193-E:2 was adopted, this court and the State have acknowledged that constitutional adequacy has yet to be defined. Standing alone, RSA 193-E:2 does not fulfill the State's duty to define the substantive content of a constitutionally adequate education in such a manner that the citizens of this state can know what the parameters of that educational program are. The right to a constitutionally adequate education is meaningless without standards that are enforceable and reviewable. *See Claremont School Dist. v. Governor (Accountability)*, 147 N.H. at 508 (definition of constitutionally adequate education must have standards subject to meaningful application). Furthermore, without a substantive definition of constitutional adequacy, it will remain impossible for school districts, parents, and courts, not to mention the legislative and executive branches themselves, to know where the State's obligations to fund the cost of a constitutionally adequate education begin and end.

The State further argues that, aside from the constitutionally sufficient definition of adequacy in RSA 193-E:2,

> [t]he Legislature has delegated to the State Board the authority and the duty to prescribe uniform standards for all public schools in New Hampshire. RSA 194:23; RSA 186:8; RSA 21-N:9. The State Board has responded by enacting comprehensive and detailed *minimum* standards for public school approval. Local school boards are required by statute to "comply with the rules and regulations of the state board." RSA 186:5; RSA 186:8. The school

> approval standards are very detailed and demanding; they govern nearly every facet of a school's operation. The standards prescribe how schools must be organized and staffed as well as the particular educational content of each subject taught. These standards are monitored by DOE, which grades individual schools on their compliance with the standards.

If it is the State's position that RSA 193-E:2 together with the education rules and regulations, curriculum frameworks and other statutes define a constitutionally adequate education, we defer to the legislature's judgment. We note, however, that if the current system of delivery in combination with the statutory definition establishes a constitutionally adequate education, there would be no need for any local education taxes as the State would be required to pay for implementing the *entire* statutory scheme. Indeed, if that is the case, we question whether $837 million, the amount currently allotted for public education under House Bill 616, is facially sufficient to fund the school system as required by that statutory scheme. Alternatively, if, as the State asserts, the education rules and regulations, curriculum frameworks and other statutes provide some level of education beyond that of a constitutionally adequate education, the point of demarcation cannot currently be determined.

Any definition of constitutional adequacy crafted by the political branches must be sufficiently clear to permit common understanding and allow for an objective determination of costs. Whatever the State identifies as comprising constitutional adequacy it must pay for. None of that financial obligation can be shifted to local school districts, regardless of their relative wealth or need.

The trial court found House Bill 616 facially unconstitutional in part because it does not contain a definition of constitutional adequacy. House Bill 616 simply modifies the adequacy aid formula. Although the State must define constitutional adequacy in accord with this opinion, House Bill 616 standing alone need not necessarily contain such a definition for the bill itself to pass constitutional muster. Viewed together, however, the current education funding and "definitional" statutory framework falls well short of the constitutional requirements established in this court's *Claremont* decisions.

Because the definition of a constitutionally adequate education is essential to all other issues, including the cost of a constitutionally adequate education and the method by which to raise the necessary funds, we stay that portion of the case containing the trial court's findings that the legislature has failed to determine the cost, failed to satisfy the requirement of accountability and established a non-uniform tax rate. As to the core definitional issues, we will retain jurisdiction with the expectation that the political branches will define with specificity the components of a constitutionally adequate education before the end of fiscal year 2007. Should they fail to do so, we will then be required to take further action to enforce the mandates of Part II, Article 83 of the New Hampshire Constitution. Such appropriate remedies may include: (1) invalidating the funding mechanism established in House Bill 616 as set forth in the concurring opinion of Justice Galway; (2) appointing a special master to aid in the determination of the definition of a constitutionally adequate education, *see Below v. Secretary of State*, 148 N.H. 1, 2–3 (2002) ("the supreme court has been called upon to establish a new district plan for the New Hampshire Senate . . . because the New Hampshire Legislature failed to [do so] following the 2000 census"); or (3) implementing the remedy outlined in the concurring opinion of Justice Duggan and remanding the case to the trial court "for further factual development and a determination of whether the State is providing sufficient funding to pay for a constitutionally adequate education."

Respectful of the roles of the legislative and executive branches, each time this court has been requested to define the substantive content of a constitutionally adequate public education, we have properly demurred. Deference, however, has its limits. We agree with Justice Galway's concern that this court or any court not take over the legislature's role in shaping educational and fiscal policy. For almost thirteen years we have refrained from doing so and continue to refrain today. However, the judiciary has a responsibility to ensure that constitutional rights not be hollowed out and, in the absence of action by other branches, a judicial remedy is not only appropriate but essential. *Petition of Below*, 151 N.H. 135 (2004).

We urge the legislature to act.

Affirmed in part; and stayed in part.

Amended Law in Response to the *Londonderry* Decision

193-E:1 Policy and Purpose.

I. It is the policy of the state of New Hampshire that public elementary and secondary education shall provide all students with the opportunity to acquire the knowledge and skills necessary to prepare them for successful participation in the social, economic, scientific, technological, and political systems of a free government, now and in the years to come; an education that is consistent with the curriculum and student proficiency standards specified in state school approval rules and New Hampshire curriculum frameworks.

II. Respecting New Hampshire's long tradition of community involvement, it is the purpose of this chapter to ensure that appropriate means are established to provide an adequate education through an integrated system of shared responsibility between state and local government. In this system, the state establishes, through school approval and student proficiency standards and curriculum guidelines, the framework for the delivery of educational services at the local level. School districts then have flexibility in implementing diverse educational approaches tailored to meet student needs.

193-E:2 Criteria for an Adequate Education.

An adequate education shall provide all students with the opportunity to acquire:

I. Skill in reading, writing, and speaking English to enable them to communicate effectively and think creatively and critically.

II. Skill in mathematics and familiarity with methods of science to enable them to analyze information, solve problems, and make rational decisions.

III. Knowledge of the biological, physical, and earth sciences to enable them to understand and appreciate the world around them.

IV. Knowledge of civics and government, economics, geography, and history to enable them to participate in the democratic process and to make informed choices as responsible citizens.

V. Grounding in the arts, languages, and literature to enable them to appreciate our cultural heritage and develop lifelong interests and involvement in these areas.

VI. Sound wellness and environmental practices to enable them to enhance their own well-being, as well as that of others.

VII. Skills for lifelong learning, including interpersonal and technological skills, to enable them to learn, work, and participate effectively in a changing society.

193-E:2-a Substantive Educational Content of an Adequate Education.

I. Beginning in the school year 2008–2009, the specific criteria and substantive educational program that deliver the opportunity for an adequate education shall be defined and identified as the school approval standards in the following areas:

(a) English/language arts and reading.

(b) Mathematics.

(c) Science.

(d) Social studies.

(e) Arts education.

(f) World languages.

(g) Health education.

(h) Physical education.

(i) Technology education, and information and communication technologies.

II. The standards shall cover kindergarten through twelfth grade and shall clearly set forth the opportunities to acquire the communication, analytical and research skills and competencies, as well as the substantive knowledge expected to be possessed by students at the various grade levels, including the credit requirement necessary to earn a high school diploma.

III. Public schools and public academies shall adhere to the standards identified in paragraph I.

IV. The school approval standards for the areas identified in paragraph I shall constitute the opportunity for the delivery of an adequate education. The general court shall periodically, but not less frequently than every 10 years, review, revise, and update, as necessary, the standards identified in paragraph I and shall ensure that the high quality of the standards is maintained. Changes made by the board of education to the school approval standards through rulemaking after the effective date of this section shall not be included within the standards that constitute the opportunity for the delivery of an adequate education without prior adoption by the general court. The board of education shall provide written notice to the speaker of the house of representatives, the president of the senate, and the chairs of the house and senate education committees of any changes to the school approval standards adopted pursuant to RSA 541-A.

V. The general court requires the state board of education and the department of education to institute procedures for maintaining, updating, improving, and refining curriculum frameworks for each area of education identified in paragraph I. The curriculum frameworks shall present educational goals, broad pedagogical approaches and strategies for assisting students in the development of the skills, competencies, and knowledge called for by the academic standards for each area of education identified in paragraph I. The curriculum frameworks shall serve as a guide and reference to what New Hampshire students should know and be able to do in each area of education. The frameworks do not establish a statewide curriculum. It is the responsibility of local teachers, administrators, and school boards to identify and implement approaches best suited for the students in their communities to acquire the skills and knowledge included in the frameworks, to determine the scope, organization, and sequence of course offerings, and to choose the methods of instruction, the activities, and the materials to be used.

VI. In this section, "school approval standards" shall mean the applicable criteria that public schools and public academies shall meet in order to be an approved school, as adopted by the state board of education through administrative rules.

Post Problem Discussion

1. Are there any other changes that you feel need to be made to the state's definition in RSA 193-E to meet constitutional requirements given the court's *Londonderry* decision?

2. In *Londonderry*, the court for the first time in New Hampshire's school funding litigation mentions potential remedies that it may impose if the legislature does not act to define a constitutionally adequate education. Which of these remedies do you think is the best approach for the court to take? What are some of the potential political, or public policy consequences of the court instituting the remedies it mentions? See Section 2.08 for more discussion.

3. The court's statements about potential judicial remedies again fueled debate about a constitutional amendment to remove the court from education funding issues. As a legislator, would your opinion about the need for an amendment change given this decision? Why or why not? How about if you were a school board member or administrator?

4. Do you think that the state would be able to develop an objective cost of an adequate education based on the definition of an adequate education in the revised RSA 193-E? Why or why not?

Activity 3: Defining Adequacy in Your State

A number of states have made efforts to define an adequate education. Take the following steps to explore the issue in your state:

> **Step One**—Research your state statutes and regulations to determine if your state has defined an adequate education.
>
> **Step Two**—Compare your state definition to the one developed in New Hampshire. What are the differences and similarities? Does your state definition meet the requirements noted in the *Londonderry* case? If not, what changes would need to be made?
>
> **Step Three**—If your state does not have a definition in place, what do you think should be included in a definition? Alternatively, are there reasons why the state should not define educational adequacy at all?

§ 2.07 The Cost of an Adequate Education

One of the issues that the New Hampshire Supreme Court has not addressed, that some other state courts have, is the how much an adequate education costs, and whether the state funds that amount. Various New Hampshire statutes have purported to determine and fund adequacy, and the New Hampshire legislature has hired a number of experts to calculate adequacy costs, but the New Hampshire Supreme Court has not addressed these issues.

There are a number of methods used by states to determine adequacy costs and funding methods. The following activity gives you a chance to explore these methods and your state's involvement.

Activity 4: Determining the Cost of Adequacy in Your State

> **Step 1**—Review *School Finance Litigation & Adequacy Studies*, 27 U. Ark. Little Rock L. Rev. 69 (2004), online to get an overview of adequacy methods used by states.
>
> **Step 2**—Research your state statutes and regulations on adequacy. Does your state have specific statutes or regulations delineating the cost of an adequate education?

Step 3—If so, research the methods that your state used to determine the cost of an adequate education. Often, states hire outside experts or have legislative committees or staff perform these functions, and there are reports available online describing the methods that were used. The following websites are a clearinghouse of information about adequacy costs in states that may be of some help: www.schoolfunding.info and www.educationjustice .org.

Step 4—Answer the following:

1. What costing method or approach did your state use to determine the cost of an adequate education? Do you think the cost would be different if another approach was used?
2. If your state has not developed a cost or a method, what method do you think it should follow?
3. Have your courts addressed the cost of an adequate education or the methods that should be used to determine the cost?
4. What is the status of school funding litigation in your state? Has the litigation changed the way schools are funded?

§ 2.08 Remedies

In *Claremont II* and in *Londonderry*, the New Hampshire Supreme Court ruled that the State had not met its constitutional obligations. Rather than impose a specific substantive remedy that would cure the constitutional violation, it gave the Legislature and the Governor time to do so. In *Claremont II*, the court stayed the case until the end of the next legislative session to allow for this process to occur. In *Claremont IV*, the court denied the state's request to extend that timeline for two years.

In *Londonderry*, the court mentions potential remedies that it may impose if the Legislature does not act to define a constitutionally adequate education, but again defers to the Legislature and the Governor stating:

> Respectful of the roles of the legislative and executive branches, each time this court has been requested to define the substantive content of a constitutionally adequate public education, we have properly demurred. Deference, however, has its limits. We agree with [the dissent's] concern that this court or any court not take over the legislature's role in shaping educational and fiscal policy. For almost thirteen years we have refrained from doing so and continue to refrain today. However, the judiciary has a responsibility to ensure that constitutional rights not be hollowed out and, in the absence of action by other branches, a judicial remedy is not only appropriate but essential. Petition of Below, 151 N.H. 135 (2004).
>
> We urge the legislature to act.

Londonderry Sch. Dist. SAU No. 12 v. State, 907 A.2d at 996.

After the court issued its decision, the Legislature and the Governor did act and passed the laws in Problem 5 of this book. The plaintiffs tried to challenge the sufficiency of the laws before the court, but the court found the proceeding moot and stated that the plaintiffs would need to start over with the trial court if they wanted to bring such a challenge. *Londonderry Sch. Dist. SAU #12 v. State*, 958 A.2d 930 (N.H. 2008).

Other state courts have taken similar approaches to remedies and ordered other branches of government to act, as opposed to ordering a specific substantive remedy. Some courts have been more direct than others in what they order the other branches of government to do. Some good examples of cases to review online are *Campaign for Fiscal Equity v. State (CFE II)*, 801 N.E.2d 326, 349 (N.Y. 2003) (ordering the defendants to determine the cost of providing a sound basic education in New York City, create a funding scheme which allowed for adequate resources to every district to provide that education, and provide a system of accountability to ensure it is provided); *Campbell County School District v. State*, 907 P.2d 1238, 1279 (Wyo. 1995) (ordering defendants to determine the "proper educational package" each Wyoming student is entitled to have, the cost of that educational package, and to take necessary action to "fund that package"); *Abbeville Cnty. Sch. Dist. v. State*, 767 S.E.2d 157, 178 (S.C. 2014), *reh'g denied*, 2015 S.C. LEXIS 50 (Jan. 23, 2015) (reviewing other court decisions on remedies and ordering the parties to "reappear before this Court within a reasonable time from the issuance of this opinion, and present a plan to address the constitutional violation announced today, with special emphasis on the statutory and administrative pieces necessary to aid the myriad troubles facing these districts at both state and local levels.").

Activity 5: Remedies in School Funding Cases in Your State

Step 1—Review the court decisions mentioned in this section and the discussions in those cases about remedies.

Step 2—Research your state court decisions on school funding or educational adequacy.

Step 3—Answer the following:

1. Have your state courts ordered any remedies? If so, how do the orders compare to the remedies noted in the cases in this section? Why do you think the court took the approach that it did with respect to remedies?
2. If your state courts have not addressed remedies, what remedies, if any, do you think it should order to fix any constitutional deficiencies that exist?
3. What are the pros and cons of courts getting involved in school funding cases and ordering remedies?

Chapter 3

Employment

Synopsis

§ 3.01 Introduction

Schools employ a variety of personnel including teachers, principals, specialists, pathologists, counselors, therapists, psychologists, office staff, janitorial staff, and sometimes school security. Some school personnel may specialize in certain areas, such as assisting students with specific types of disabilities, while others have more general responsibilities. This Chapter focuses on employment issues relating primarily to teachers, though the same concepts apply to many other school employees.

Generally speaking, the teacher employment continuum starts with the teacher obtaining a post-secondary degree. Teachers, and most other types of school employees who are responsible for providing services to students, or supervising students, must also meet state licensing or certification requirements. Every state has a detailed licensure/certification process set forth in state statutes and regulations. Such licensure/certification requirements are generally prerequisites for employment for specific positions at public schools.

Once licensed, a teacher is eligible for employment, which often involves collective bargaining agreements and contractual provisions. While federal law plays a role in employment issues — for example, in prohibiting discrimination in hiring or firing employees, requiring due process, or protecting First Amendment rights — the issues in school employment are primarily governed by state law. As a result, this Chapter provides examples of state laws to illustrate concepts, but each state will have its own specific requirements.

Teacher Employment Continuum

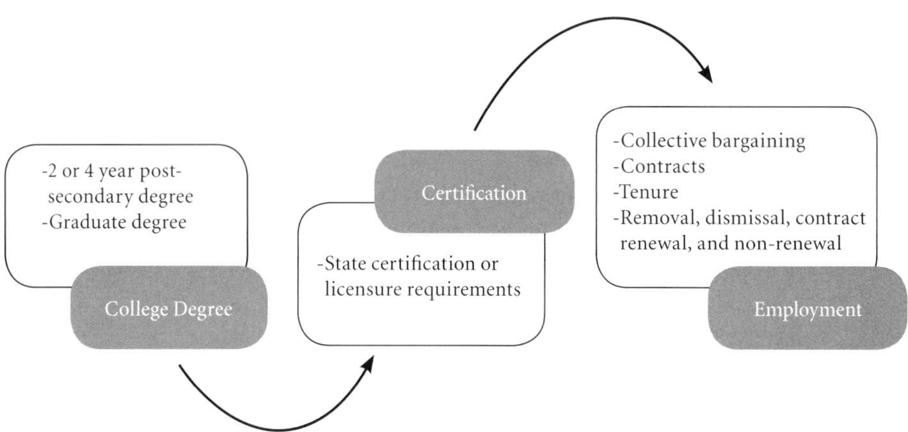

§ 3.02 Licensure/Certification Requirements

Licensure/certification requirements vary from state to state and can apply to many types of employees (e.g., teachers, principals, administrators). Each state defines its requirements through statutes and regulations. Kansas statutes are illustrative. Kansas grants authority to its State Board of Education to issue regulations for teacher licensure subject to a minimum statutory mandate that licensure include an examination:

> (a) The state board of education shall prescribe an examination designed to insure that the licensure of a person as a teacher is a reliable indicator that the person has the basic knowledge and qualifications necessary to engage in the profession of teaching in this state.
>
> (b) In order to comply with the requirements of subsection (a), the state board of education shall select an examination which will measure the basic knowledge and qualifications of applicants for licensure as teachers and shall provide for administration and validation of the examination. The examination shall be administered to applicants at least two times each calendar year at various locations within the state.

Kan. Stat. Ann. § 72-2162(a)–(b) (2019).

Generally speaking, state licensure/certification requirements for teachers include a background check for criminal violations. Substantive requirements generally include a two or four year degree from a post-secondary institution, and demonstrating some level of knowledge or ability to teach.[1] On the latter requirement, Title I of the Elementary and Secondary Education Act ("ESEA"), as amended by

---

1. *See* Diana Pullin, *Key Questions in Implementing Teacher Testing and Licensing*, 30 J.L. & Educ. 383, 384 (2001).

the No Child Left Behind Act ("NCLB") in 2002, required all teachers who taught "core academic subjects" to be "highly qualified" (referred to as "HQT"). HQT had three essential criteria: (1) attaining a bachelor's degree or better in the subject taught; (2) obtaining full state teacher certification; and (3) demonstrating knowledge in the subjects taught.

In 2015, the ESEA was amended by the Every Student Succeeds Act ("ESSA"). The amendments removed or changed many of NCLB's requirements. Under the ESSA, HQT is no longer required. State certification requirements are now left up to the states to determine. The only federal requirement is that states seeking funding under ESSA must provide assurances in the state plans that they submit to the federal government that (1) teachers and paraprofessionals who receive funding from ESSA meet state certification requirements as determined by the state; and (2) "low income and minority children enrolled in schools assisted [with ESSA funds] are not served at disproportionate rates by ineffective, out-of-field, or inexperienced teachers." 20 U.S.C. § 6311(g)(1)(B).

While HQT is no longer required under federal law, some states that previously incorporated HQT requirements into their state certification/licensing standards may still have some of these requirements in place under state law. The following activity allows you to explore your state licensing/certification requirements.

Activity 1: Find Your State's Licensing Requirements

Step One—Go to your state department of education website and search for information about teacher licensure or certification. What are the requirements for regular education teachers? Do they vary based on the subjects taught, or grade level? What are the different kinds of licenses or certifications that are available?

Step Two—NCLB allowed states to develop and use a High Objective Uniform State Standard of Evaluation ("HOUSSE") as a way for experienced teachers to demonstrate that they were highly qualified. Does your state still use HOUSSE? If so, what are its requirements? If not, do state licensing requirements differ for experienced and inexperienced teachers?

Step Three—HQT required teachers to demonstrate knowledge in the subjects that they taught. Does your state have any such requirements now? Some states use Praxis for state certification and licensing requirements. You can access your state's testing requirements online at: www.ets.org/praxis/states

Step Four—Do your state licensing or certification requirements have any provisions related to how a teacher's students perform on statewide accountability tests when assessing the teacher's knowledge or ability to teach? If so, what role does the information play in the licensing or certification process? If not, do you think such information should be considered? Why or why not?

Once a teacher obtains licensure/certification, the state department or board of education that granted the license or certificate generally retains oversight and the power to revoke it under certain conditions. The Kansas statute provides a good illustration:

> Any license issued by the state board of education or institutions under the state board of regents may be canceled by the state board of education in the manner provided by law, on the grounds of immorality, gross neglect of duty, annulling of written contracts with boards of education without the consent of the board which is a party to the contract, or for any cause that would have justified the withholding thereof when the same was granted.

Kan. Stat. Ann. § 72-2155 (2018).

The Kansas approach is typical. Most states have a "morals or fitness for duty" clause that generally goes beyond assessing the teacher's ability to teach. Under such standards, states have denied or revoked teacher licenses or certifications for cheating on the state certification test, providing false information on license or employment applications, and for certain criminal convictions. *See, e.g., Comings v. State Bd. of Educ.*, 100 Cal. Rptr. 73 (Cal. Ct. App. 1972); *Nanko v. Department of Educ.*, 663 A.2d 312 (Pa. Commw. Ct. 1995); *Pettiford v. South Carolina State Bd. of Educ.*, 62 S.E.2d 780 (1950), *cert. denied,* 341 U.S. 920 (1951); *Patterson v. Superintendent of Public Instruction*, 887 P.2d 411 (Wash. Ct. App. 1994), *review denied*, 894 P.2d 564 (1995).

An issue that arises with these clauses is how far states can go in revoking, or in refusing to issue, teacher licenses/certifications because of teacher conduct outside of school that is unrelated to teaching. The following problem explores these issues.

Problem 1: Revoking Teacher Certification for Out of School Conduct

Ms. Sherry is a language arts teacher at Pritikin Elementary School. She received her teacher certification four years ago and has taught at Pritikin Elementary since that time. She graduated from a state university with a Bachelor of Arts degree. Her major was English, and she minored in American Art. She loves to sculpt and paint and does that as often as she can. While she was in college, she was part of a group of students that would paint and sculpt together in their Art professor's studio. The group liked to paint and sculpt the human body. Some students posed as nude models. Others would often paint and sculpt in the nude.

One of the students took videos of the art sessions and recently decided to post the videos on social media, so all the students could remember the good times they had together. The video contains nude images of the students modeling, painting, and sculpting. It also shows some of the artwork that the students created, which includes various body parts and, in some cases, images of people performing sexual acts. The video also includes some of the students explaining their work using some crude language with sexual references.

A parent comes across the video and notifies one of the Pritikin Elementary School Board members about it. The Board member is outraged when she sees Ms. Sherry in the video sculpting male genitalia while in the nude. Ms. Sherry, while nude, also performs a "rap" song describing her work that includes a number of references and gestures that the Board member believes are vulgar and unprofessional. The Board member files a complaint with the State Department of Education and asks the department to revoke Ms. Sherry's teaching certification.

Review the problem materials and determine if the State Department of Education can revoke Ms. Sherry's teaching license under state law. (For purposes of the problem, set aside any potential constitutional issues.)

Problem Materials

- ✓ Hypothetical State Teacher Licensing Statute
- ✓ *Winters v. Arizona Board of Education*, 83 P.3d 1114 (Ariz. Ct. App. 2004)
- ✓ *Thompson v. Wisconsin Department of Public Instruction*, 541 N.W.2d 182 (Wis. Ct. App. 1995)

Hypothetical State Licensing Statute: EDL § 32970

(a) Any person seeking to teach in a public school, including a charter school, or in a school or institution operated by a county or the state shall first obtain a teaching license from the State Department of Education.

(b) The State Department of Education may not grant a license, for 6 years following the date of the conviction, to any person who has been convicted of any Felony under state law, or of an equivalent crime in another state or country.

(c) After written notice and a hearing, the State Department of Education may censure, suspend, suspend with conditions, or revoke a teacher's certificate, upon a finding of immoral or unprofessional conduct, or evidence of the teacher's unfitness for teaching.

Winters v. Arizona Board of Education

83 P.3d 1114 (Ariz. Ct. App. 2004)

The court finds that in order to revoke a teacher certification for out of school conduct, the conduct must relate to the teacher's fitness to teach and have an adverse effect on, or within, the school community.

Hoag, Judge

In this opinion, we hold that the showing of a nexus, or sufficiently rational connection, between the off-campus actions of a teacher and his/her fitness to teach is required before disciplinary action against the teacher may be taken based on such acts.

After receiving his master's degree in education, Claude L. Winters began his first teaching job at Buckeye Union High School in 1997 with a temporary secondary teaching certificate issued by the Arizona Board of Education. In August of 2000, the Board initiated disciplinary proceedings to censure, suspend, suspend with conditions, or revoke the teaching certificate. In its complaint, the Board alleged that disciplinary action was warranted in light of Winters' conduct as illustrated by five separate incidents dating from October 1998 to April 2000.

Incident One: On October 15, 1998, Winters and his twenty-one-year-old neighbor were arrested following a verbal altercation. Both were cited for disorderly conduct. The citations were later dismissed by the Buckeye Magistrate Court.

Incident Two: On May 10, 1999, Winters called the Buckeye Police Department and complained that a rock had been thrown through the front window of his home. Later that same evening, Winters' loaded .357 revolver discharged and damaged a neighbor's air conditioning unit. He was charged with criminal damage and disorderly conduct with a deadly weapon. Under the terms of a plea agreement, he pled no contest to the unlawful discharge of a firearm, a class 2 misdemeanor, and was sentenced to standard probation for one year.

Incident Three: On August 7, 1999, Winters and another neighbor got into a physical altercation in the street outside their homes. Both were charged with disorderly conduct. The charge against Winters was dismissed.

Incident Four: The next day, on August 8, 1999, Winters and a former student became engaged in a verbal confrontation at a local convenience store. Winters was charged with threatening and intimidating the eighteen-year-old. Citing "insufficient evidence-mutual argument," the city prosecutor declined to prosecute.

Incident Five: On April 21, 2000, Winters was arrested and charged with obstructing a criminal investigation, aggravated harassment, interfering with a judicial proceeding, and threatening and intimidating. The arrest stemmed from a dispute between Winters and a neighboring family. Both Winters and his neighbors had previously obtained protective orders against each other. Winters had violated that order of protection by threatening the neighbors' children. He told the children that they "had better sleep with one eye open." He also told the Buckeye Chief of Police "that if nothing was done about the situation, that something might happen." Winters accepted a plea agreement and pled guilty to aggravated harassment, a class 1 misdemeanor. He was sentenced to supervised probation for one year and ordered to participate in anger-management counseling as a condition of probation.

After being served with the Board's complaint, Winters requested and received a hearing before its Professional Practices Advisory Committee ("PPAC"). At the close of the hearing, the PPAC recommended that the Board revoke Winters' teaching certificate. The Board considered the PPAC's recommendation and heard testimony from Winters and arguments from his attorney at two separate Board meetings. On November 26, 2001, a majority of the Board voted to adopt the PPAC's recommendation and revoke Winters' teaching certificate.

After his motion for reconsideration was denied, Winters sought judicial review of the Board's decision in superior court. The trial court affirmed the Board's decision, finding that it was supported by the evidence and not contrary to law, arbitrary, capricious, or an abuse of discretion. Winters timely appeals.

. . . .

Next, Winters argues that his conduct did not constitute "unprofessional conduct" because there was no evidence that it affected the operation of any school or that it adversely affected the teacher-student relationship. We note that, at the time of the Board's action, the term "unprofessional conduct" was neither defined by statute nor by our jurisprudence. In deciding whether Winters' conduct constituted unprofessional conduct, we "may substitute our judgment for agency conclusions regarding the legal effect of its factual findings."

With partial reliance on *Welch v. Board of Education of Chandler Unified School District No. 80 of Maricopa County*, 136 Ariz. 552, 667 P.2d 746 (App. 1983), Winters submits that his off-campus conduct for which he is being disciplined must bear a reasonable relationship to his fitness as a teacher. We agree. *See Welch*, 136 Ariz. at 555, 667 P.2d at 749 (holding that whether actual harm to students or school must be shown or whether inference of unfitness to teach can be inferred from the conduct will be decided on a case-by-case basis).

Although Winters would like us to limit "immoral or unprofessional conduct" to teacher-student interactions, we decline to do so. Instead, we hold that the off-campus acts for which a teacher is being disciplined need not be limited to teacher-student interactions, but must relate to his/her fitness as a teacher and must have an adverse effect on or within the school community. This "nexus" requirement has been adopted by the majority of jurisdictions that have considered this issue. Consistent with our duty to construe a statute, whenever possible, in a reasonable manner, we adopt the nexus requirement for purposes of interpreting "immoral or unprofessional conduct" in A.R.S. § 15-203(A)(20) [the state's license revocation statute].

Our holding is bolstered by the Board's recent amendment to the Arizona Administrative Code ("A.A.C."). Since its decision to revoke Winters' teaching certificate, the Board has detailed the types of conduct constituting "immoral or unprofessional conduct" in A.A.C. R7-2-1308, effective June 28, 2003. Among other activities, the regulation prohibits certificated individuals from "[e]ngag[ing] in conduct which would discredit the teaching profession." A.A.C. R7-2-1308(B)(16). In our opinion, all of the enumerated conduct set forth in A.A.C. R7-2-1308(B) as constituting "immoral or unprofessional conduct" relates to a person's fitness to serve in the capacity of a teacher.

Next, we must consider whether Winters' conduct related to his fitness to hold a teaching certificate. . . . After reviewing the matter, we conclude that Winters' undisputed conduct did relate to his fitness as a teacher. The evidence established his tendency to react with violence and aggression. The frequency of the conduct suggests a pattern of behavior. The fact that these incidents did not occur on school premises does not negate the gravity of Winters' behavior. One conviction involved threatening children and thus directly relates to his fitness as a teacher. Two incidents involved young adults about the age of high school seniors. As a school teacher, Winters would be in regular contact with young people, and his conviction for threats involving harm to children gave the Board reasonable cause for concern and a basis to act "to prevent or control predictable future harm." *Welch*, 136 Ariz. at 555, 667 P.2d at 749.

In *Welch*, the court concluded that a teacher had acted unprofessionally even though "the record [was] devoid of any direct evidence that he was unfit to teach or that the district students were adversely affected by his conduct" and his official school evaluations showed that "he was more than satisfactory in performing his teaching duties." *Id.* at 554–55, 667 P.2d at 748–49. The court determined that the teacher's act of lying to the school board upon its inquiry into his personal relationship with a former student constituted insubordination and unprofessional conduct. *Id.* at 555–56, 667 P.2d at 749–50. We agree with the court's sentiments in *Welch:*

> We are unwilling to hold that a school board must demonstrate with particularity the adverse effects of a teacher's conduct upon his students, his teaching performance or the orderly running of the school as a prerequisite for dismissal in all circumstances. There may be conduct which by itself gives rise to reasonable inferences of unfitness to teach or from which an adverse impact on students can reasonably be assumed. Further, we are concerned that by imposing an absolute requirement that specific harm must be proven prior to dismissal, we would deter school administrators from acting to prevent or control predictable future harm.

Id. at 555, 667 P.2d at 749. . . .

In summary, Winters' conduct demonstrated a marked tendency toward aggression and violence that, as the PPAC noted, could be elicited by a teenage student or a parent. His pattern of hostile conduct is sufficiently related to his fitness to teach. Accordingly, we find that the nexus was implicit in the Board's factual findings and affirm the judgment upholding the decision of the Board to revoke Winters' teaching certificate.

Thompson v. Wisconsin Department of Public Instruction

541 N.W.2d 182 (Wis. Ct. App. 1995)

> *The court rules that a "role model" standard is not appropriate when determining if a nexus exists between a teacher's immoral conduct and the health, welfare, safety, or education of students.*

Myse, Judge

The Wisconsin Department of Public Instruction ("department") appeals a trial court judgment that reversed the decision of the State Superintendent of Public Instruction ("superintendent") to revoke Ray M. Thompson's teaching license. The department contends that the trial court erred because: (1) it refused to use a deferential standard of review to the superintendent's conclusions of law and statutory interpretations; (2) it determined that the superintendent applied the wrong standard to determine whether a nexus existed between Thompson's immoral conduct and the health, welfare, safety or education of any pupil; and (3) it determined that the department did not prove by clear and convincing evidence that Thompson's immoral conduct had a nexus to the health, welfare, safety or education of any pupil.

While we agree with the department that the superintendent's determination is entitled to deference, we conclude that the superintendent applied the wrong standard in determining whether a nexus existed between Thompson's immoral conduct and the health, welfare, safety or education of any pupil. Further, we do not reach the sufficiency of the evidence issue because we conclude that the superintendent should be allowed to review the facts and apply the proper legal standard. Accordingly, we affirm the trial court's judgment in part, reverse it in part and remand the matter to the superintendent for the application of the proper standard.

Thompson has a life teaching license in music for pre-kindergarten through twelfth grade. Thompson was a full-time music teacher for over twenty years in Wisconsin, working primarily for the Oshkosh School District elementary and secondary schools.

However, Thompson was involved in two incidents of unwanted sexual touching that led to license revocation proceedings. The first occurred when Thompson went to Rainbow Park in Oshkosh, a known meeting place for homosexual men. Thompson played "automobile tag" with a man he believed to be homosexual. The man parked his vehicle and walked over to a park bench. Thompson followed and sat down beside him. Thompson then reached over, grabbed the other man around the breast area, fondled his breast and reached down the inner part of his left thigh. When a police car approached, the man ran to the police car and told the officer that he had been assaulted by Thompson. Thompson pled no contest to a disorderly conduct violation.

Approximately two years later, Thompson went to a video bookstore that displayed pornographic movies and materials and served as a meeting place for homosexual men. Thompson entered an unlocked booth occupied by an undercover police officer and immediately began unbuttoning the officer's shirt. The officer protested that he did not want to do anything in the booth, but Thompson persisted and grabbed the officer's genitals. A jury convicted Thompson of fourth-degree sexual assault. In the subsequent license revocation proceeding, the finder of fact found that Thompson's behavior did not reflect a predatory nature and that the assault was not aggravated.

The Oshkosh Board of Education discharged Thompson and the department subsequently issued a Notice of Probable Cause and Intent to Revoke License. Following a five-day hearing and the submission of briefs, hearing examiner Hal Harlowe issued a proposed decision recommending that the revocation action be dismissed. He concluded that there was not clear and convincing evidence that a nexus existed between Thompson's actions and the health, welfare, safety or education of any pupil. *See* Wis. Admin. Code [PI] § 3.04 (1989). However, the superintendent declined to adopt the examiner's recommendation and issued a decision to revoke Thompson's license.

Thompson filed a petition for judicial review, and the trial court held that the superintendent had not complied with Wis. Stat. § 227.46(4) (1989) because he failed to hear the case or review the record prior to issuing his decision. The court stayed the revocation order and remanded the case to the superintendent.

On remand, the superintendent assigned Dr. Thomas Stefonek, a department employee, to read the record and issue a proposed decision. Stefonek agreed with Harlowe that there was not clear and convincing evidence that Thompson's conduct had a nexus to the physical health, welfare or safety of any pupil. However, Stefonek accorded different weight to the expert testimony presented at the hearing and found that the department did prove by clear and convincing evidence that Thompson's immoral conduct had a nexus to the education of pupils and their welfare as it related to the educational process. The basis for Stefonek's conclusion was that Thompson could no longer be an effective role model for the students because the pupils, their parents and the public would lack confidence, respect and regard for Thompson. Accordingly, Stefonek recommended that Thompson's license be revoked. The superintendent adopted Stefonek's recommendation.

On review of this decision, the trial court reversed. The court reviewed the superintendent's conclusions of law de novo. The court held that the superintendent used an improper standard in revoking Thompson's license because he based the decision upon an impossibly high role model standard under which any teacher deemed to be a poor role model could have his or her license revoked. The court further held that the superintendent's decision was not supported by substantial evidence.

The superintendent's decision to revoke Thompson's teaching license was based on the revocation provisions in Wis. Stat. § 118.19 (1989–90) and Wis. Admin. Code [PI] § 3.04 (1989). Section 118.19, Stats., 1989-90, provides in part:

> (1) Any person seeking to teach in a public school or in a school or institution operated by a county or the state shall first procure a certificate or license from the department.
>
> . . . .
>
> (5) After written notice of the charges and of an opportunity for defense, any certificate or license to teach issued by the department may be revoked by the state superintendent for incompetency or immoral conduct on the part of the holder.

The relevant portions of § 3.04 provide:

> (1) DEFINITIONS.

> . . . .
>
> (a) "Immoral conduct" means conduct or behavior which is contrary to commonly accepted moral or ethical standards.
>
> . . . .
>
> (2) STANDARDS FOR REVOCATION.
>
> . . . .
>
> (a) A license may be revoked for immoral conduct if there is clear and convincing evidence that the person engaged in the immoral conduct and there is a nexus between the immoral conduct and the health, welfare, safety or education of any pupil.

. . . .

The proper standard of review regarding the superintendent's determination of whether Thompson's immoral conduct had a nexus to the health, welfare, safety or education of any pupil is disputed. This issue involves a review of the superintendent's interpretation of § 118.19, and PI § 3.04 and application of facts to these laws, which is a question of law.

. . . .

The department agrees that under PI § 3.04 it has the burden to prove by clear and convincing evidence that a nexus exists between Thompson's immoral conduct and the health, welfare, safety or education of any pupil. In this case, Stefonek first determined that Thompson's immoral conduct did not have a nexus to the physical safety of any pupil. However, he concluded that Thompson's immoral conduct had a nexus to the education of pupils because Thompson could no longer be a good role model for students. Stefonek reasoned that the educational experience could not be effective when the pupils, their parents and the public lack confidence, respect and regard for the teacher.

While the superintendent's conclusions of law are subject to various interpretations, the department acknowledged at oral argument that he relied on a standard that has been identified as the "role model standard." Under this standard, a teacher must be a good role model and have the confidence, respect and regard of the pupils, their parents and the community. We conclude that this is an unreasonable interpretation of PI § 3.04 because it would make the requirement of nexus superfluous and permits revocation based solely on public attitudes.

Applying a role model standard reflecting community attitudes effectively eliminates the nexus requirement. All cases of immoral conduct are by definition offensive to community standards. Because a role model rationale assumes all conduct offensive to the community standard hinders the educational process, nexus is subsumed in all cases involving immoral conduct. However, the plain meaning of PI § 3.04 provides that not all immoral conduct should result in license revocation.

The nexus requirement is there for a reason: to make sure there is a direct link between the immoral conduct and the health, welfare, safety or education of any pupil.

Further, a standard based on community attitudes cannot be applied consistently. Community attitudes are difficult to measure, they vary from community to community, and they change over the course of time. This standard is so amorphous as to give no criterion upon which the agency can meaningfully and consistently apply this rationale to license revocation proceedings.

We therefore conclude that the standard used by the superintendent in this case was inappropriate. It is not the superintendent's role to speculate how the general public may perceive specific conduct or determine who is a good role model. Rather, the superintendent, under the terms of PI § 3.04 is obligated to determine whether there is a direct relationship between the immoral conduct and the health, welfare, safety or education of any pupil. If the conduct is of such severity as to adversely affect the atmosphere in which education must exist to be effective, or to endanger the health, welfare or safety of any of the children, revocation is appropriate.

We have no doubt that conduct sufficient to sustain a conviction for fourth-degree sexual assault can be a sufficient basis to warrant revocation of a teacher's license. The superintendent can examine the convictions and their severity to determine whether these offenses would interfere with the educational process. The impact, if any, upon a child's ability to learn based upon the seriousness and nature of these offenses are matters committed to the superintendent under the provision of PI § 3.04. Because these offenses are criminal in nature and involved nonconsensual sexual touching, the superintendent may conclude that the educational process is irretrievably compromised. However, in making this determination, the superintendent must examine the offense and not the community reaction to it.

Thompson suggests that his immoral conduct could not adversely affect the educational process because the public did not know of the conduct in the communities where he was substitute teaching. We disagree. The superintendent need not wait for the public to discover the conduct before initiating revocation proceedings. In an age of rapid mass communications, it is unrealistic to believe the public would forever remain ignorant of his conduct. More importantly, it is immaterial that the public does not know of the conduct because the superintendent is required to examine the conduct and not the public reaction to it.

. . . .

We affirm the trial court's determination that the superintendent applied the wrong standard to decide whether a nexus exists between Thompson's immoral conduct and the health, welfare, safety or education of any pupil. However, we conclude the superintendent is entitled to an opportunity to review the facts of this case and to apply the proper legal standard to Thompson's immoral conduct. *See* Wis. Stat. § 227.57(5). Therefore, we affirm the judgment in part, reverse in part and remand the matter to the superintendent to determine, under the proper standard, whether Thompson's immoral conduct has a direct link to the educational process.

Judgment affirmed in part; reversed in part and cause remanded.

Post Problem Discussion

1. The problem cases mention the need to have a nexus between the immoral or unprofessional conduct and either fitness to teach, or the health, safety, and welfare of students. The problem statute lacks such a requirement. Do you think a court would still view a nexus as necessary, and interpret the problem statute as requiring such a nexus? If so, under what rationale could a court make such an interpretation? If the court reads such a nexus requirement into the problem statute, do you think a nexus exists between Ms. Sherry's acts and her fitness to teach, or the health safety and welfare of students?

2. The majority in the *Thompson* decision concludes that the role model standard is not an appropriate standard because it would make the nexus requirement superfluous and effectively eliminate the requirement. Do you agree with the court's conclusions? Review the dissenting opinion in the case online for a different perspective.

3. Note the definition of "immoral conduct" under Wisconsin law as discussed in the *Thompson* case. In *Epstein v. Benson*, 618 N.W.2d 224 (Wis.Ct.App. 2000), the Wisconsin Court of Appeals applied *Thompson,* and the same Wisconsin morals clause, to the revocation of a teacher's license for shooting her son-in-law in order to protect her daughter and her granddaughters, and for carrying a concealed weapon. What result do you think the court reached on whether or not these actions were "immoral conduct" warranting license revocation? How do you think the results of the criminal proceedings against the teacher for these actions factored into the court's analysis?

4. What are the laws and standards for license revocation for "immoral conduct" in your state? Does your state use a nexus approach, a role model approach, or something different? Would Ms. Sherry's license be revoked under your state's standards?

§ 3.03 Hiring, Collective Bargaining and Contracts

Once licensed, teachers still need to be hired, and that is generally done by contract. Once a contract is offered, it will be governed by common law requirements applicable to all contracts, and often by specific state statutes or regulations addressing teacher contracts as well. Some states use collective bargaining for teacher contracts. While there is no constitutional right to bargain collectively, such a right may be established by state statutes. When this is the case, state law provides the parameters for defining the groups that can bargain collectively (called the bargaining units), the bargaining process, and the scope of what can be bargained.

Under most statutory schema, collective bargaining topics fall into three categories: (1) mandatory, (2) permissive, and (3) prohibited.[2]

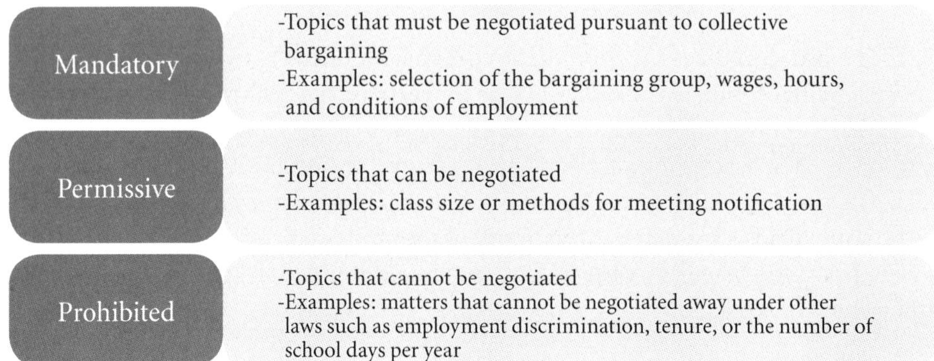

For example, §423.215 of the Michigan statutes, entitled "Collective bargaining; duties of employer and employees' representative; subjects; prohibitions," provides general bargaining authority:

> (1) A public employer shall bargain collectively with the representatives of its employees . . . and may make and enter into collective bargaining agreements with those representatives. Except as otherwise provided in this section, for the purposes of this section, to bargain collectively is the to perform the mutual obligation of the employer and the representative of the employees to meet at reasonable times and confer in good faith with respect to wages, hours, and other terms and conditions of employment, or to negotiate an agreement, or any question arising under the agreement, and to execute a written contract, ordinance, or resolution incorporating any agreement reached if requested by either party, but this obligation does not compel either party to agree to a proposal or make a concession.

Mich. Comp. Laws Serv. §423.215(1) (2019).

This section continues

> (2) A public school employer has the responsibility, authority, and right to manage and direct on behalf of the public the operations and activities of the public schools under its control.

Mich. Comp. Laws Serv. §423.215(2).

2. *See generally* Deborah Tussey, Annotation, *Bargainable or Negotiable Issues in State Public Employment Labor Relations*, 84 A.L.R.3d 242 (2008) (defining and illustrating these terms and including a state jurisdictional table of statutes and cases).

Michigan statutes then prohibit certain areas from being the subject of bargaining in teacher contracts, including, among others, the following: starting day of school; whether to allow inter-district or intra-district open enrollment; whether to contract with third parties for non-instructional support; whether to use volunteers; and whether to institute experimental programs. *Id.* § 423.215(3).

Many state statutes on collective bargaining also include good faith requirements and prohibit unfair labor practices. These provisions are enforced by filing grievances with specified state agencies. State collective bargaining statutes also generally provide dispute resolution provisions to help parties when they reach an impasse in the bargaining process. Some state collective bargaining laws also prohibit employee strikes and/or employer lockouts.[3] The next Activity provides a chance for you to identify the relevant state laws in your jurisdiction.

Activity 2: Find Your State's Collective Bargaining Requirements

Step One—Search your state statutes for collective bargaining provisions that apply to public schools and teachers.

Step Two—If your state statutes address collective bargaining, is it required, permitted, or prohibited for public schools and teachers? You may have to research state court decisions as well to answer this question.

Step Three—If your state statutes permit or require collective bargaining for public schools and teachers, research the statutes and any relevant state court decisions to answer the following:

1. Who has an obligation to bargain?
2. How are bargaining units created and defined?
3. What are the mandatory, prohibited, and permissive topics for bargaining?
4. What is the grievance process for alleged violations?
5. What are the potential penalties or remedies for violations?
6. What must parties in collective bargaining do when they reach an impasse?
7. How are unfair labor practices defined?
8. Are there any provisions regarding strikes or lockouts?

Step Four—If your state statutes prohibit collective bargaining, or do not address collective bargaining at all, how are teacher contracts developed

---

3. *See generally* James Duff, Jr., Annotation, *Labor Law: Right of Public Employees to Strike or Engage in Work Stoppage*, 37 A.L.R.3d 1147 (2008) (including a state jurisdictional table of statutes and cases).

and negotiated? Are there any statutes at all in your state that address the requirements of teacher or administrator contracts? If so, what do they require?

§ 3.04 Termination — Removal, Dismissal and Non-Renewal

Teachers, principals, and many other types of employees in public schools are often employed under contract. The contracts generally last for one school year and are renewed (or not) at a certain point before subsequent school years. States also generally have some type of tenure system that provides certain employees (usually teachers and administrators) with employment related protections once they reach tenured status. Since many public school teachers and administrators are employed pursuant to contracts within tenure systems, public schools must operate within these requirements when ending the employment relationship.

State laws generally provide schools with various methods to address this situation including (1) removal (or suspension) from class or school grounds, (2) dismissal or termination, and (3) contract non-renewal. The legal requirements can vary depending on whether the teacher is tenured or not. The following Table explains these concepts:

Removal	Removal or suspension means removing a teacher from the classroom or from the school building. It is generally used in situations that require immediate action on behalf of the school to prevent the teacher from having any contact or interaction with students (such as when a teacher has been accused of harming a student) while the school investigates and determines what actions to take. Removal can be used if the school decides to initiate dismissal or non-renewal proceedings. The teacher would be removed from the classroom, while the school and teacher go through these proceedings to determine if the teacher will continue to be employed by the school. Removal occurs while the teacher is still under contract. As a result, it can occur only as the terms of the contract or state law allow. States often have statutes or regulations that allow schools to remove or suspend teachers under specific circumstances. *See, e.g.*, Ohio Rev. Code Ann. § 3319.16. When a teacher or employee is removed, he or she is still employed (and generally still paid) by the school.
Dismissal or Termination	Dismissal or termination means ending the employment relationship between the teacher and the school. If the teacher is under contract, then it means terminating the teacher's contract. As with removal, states generally have laws that allow for dismissal/termination of teachers under contract for reasons defined in state law including "just cause." For example, the Ohio statute, Ohio Rev. Code Ann. § 3319.16, provides that teachers in Ohio may be terminated for gross inefficiency or immorality; for willful and persistent violations of reasonable regulations of the board of education; or for other good and just cause. The permissible reasons for dismissal/termination may vary for teachers who are tenured versus those who are not tenured.

Non-Renewal	Non-renewal means the teacher's contract is not renewed for the next school year. The non-renewal process allows the teacher to serve out the term of their current contract (usually to the end of the school year), and then the school does not enter into a new contract with the teacher for the next school year. For tenured teachers, some states require the school to provide notice of contract non-renewal, the reasons for non-renewal, and an opportunity for a hearing on the reasons for non-renewal—particularly if the reasons include the teacher's job performance (as opposed to budget cutbacks, etc.). *See, e.g.*, Ohio Rev. Code Ann. § 3319.16.
Tenure	Tenure generally means that the teacher has been employed for some period of time and receives the benefit of certain employment protections under state law. Tenure protections often include notice and hearing requirements that must be followed before the teacher can be terminated or non-renewed for the next school year. Tenure also often includes "just cause" requirements, which limit the school's ability to end the employment relationship with the teacher.

The following problems explore some of the issues with removal, dismissal, non-renewal, and tenure.

Problem 2: Teacher Removal & Dismissal

Sharon Anderson is a fourth grade teacher at the local elementary school. She has been a teacher at the school district for five years. She has an annual contract with the school district, and she is tenured under state law. On March 1, her principal told her that Superintendent Vasquez was immediately removing her and recommending her immediate dismissal. The principal gave her the memorandum in the problem materials. The reasons given to her verbally by the principal for the removal and dismissal are:

1. She was late to work on three occasions this year without notice in violation of the collective bargaining agreement and her contract. The school principal had to cover for her during class until she arrived.
2. Some (unnamed) parents complained to the Superintendent that she was not teaching her children the basic information and skills that they needed in important subjects like math and reading. The parents reported that the students do a lot of "concept work" and "problem solving projects" instead. The parents do not feel that their children are learning what they need to learn.
3. Parents also complained that she is not strict enough with a few children in the class who cause problems and distract the other children.
4. The test scores for her class on the statewide assessment test have been low or "novice" for the past two years, and these scores contributed to the school status as a "school in need of improvement" under state accountability laws.

The principal told her that there would be a school board meeting on her termination next week, and that, despite the fact that she has a contract, she was being removed from the classroom as of today, and was not allowed to return to school.

Assume that the allegations are true and that Ms. Anderson's teaching contract does not contain any additional information about removal or dismissal beyond what state law requires. Answer the following:

1. Can the school remove Ms. Anderson from the classroom? What rights, if any, does she have in this situation?
2. Can the school dismiss Ms. Anderson if she does not develop a satisfactory improvement plan (as noted in Superintendent Vasquez's memo in the problem materials) even though she is under contract? If so, what rights does she have, and under what circumstances can the school dismiss her?
3. Does Ms. Anderson have any potential legal recourse against the school? If so, what are her potential remedies?

Problem Materials

✓ Memorandum from Superintendent Vasquez

✓ Hypothetical State Statute

✓ *Wilson v. Des Moines Independent Community School District*, 389 N.W.2d 681 (Iowa Ct. App. 1986)

✓ *Sanders v. Board of Education of South Sioux City Community School District*, 263 N.W.2d 461 (Neb. 1978)

Memorandum

To: Sharon Anderson
From: Superintendent Vasquez
Date: March 1, 20xx

Effective today I am exercising my authority to remove you from your teaching duties. You may not return to the classroom or return to your teaching duties until further written notice from me. You have the right to appeal this decision pursuant to ED § 7489:13.

I am also notifying you that I have recommended to the school board that you be dismissed for failing to maintain competency standards and for failing to conform to school regulations. The school board will be holding a hearing on this matter on March 28, 20xx.

It is possible that you may avoid dismissal if you meet with Principal Davis and develop an improvement plan. That plan must then be presented to me for approval. This process must be completed prior to March 28, 20xx.

Hypothetical State Statute

ED 7489:13 Teacher Removal, Dismissal

(a) Dismissal. The school board may dismiss any teacher found by them to be immoral, insubordinate, neglectful of their duties or who has not satisfactorily maintained the competency standards established by the school district; provided, that no tenured teacher shall be so dismissed before the expiration of the period for which said teacher was engaged without having previously been notified of the cause of such dismissal, nor without having previously been granted a full and fair hearing.

(b) Liability of District. The district shall be liable to any teacher dismissed in violation of the provisions of this section to the extent of the full salary for the period for which such teacher was engaged.

(c) Removal of Teacher. Superintendents shall direct and supervise the work of teachers, and for just cause may remove a tenured teacher. Non-tenured teachers may be removed at the discretion of the Superintendent. The person so removed shall continue as an employee of the district unless discharged by the local school board but may not return to the classroom or undertake to perform the duties of such person's position unless reinstated by the superintendent.

(d) Appeal. Any person so removed, unless dismissed by the school board, may appeal to the state board. The board shall prescribe the manner in which appeals shall be made, and when one is made shall investigate the matter in any way it sees fit, and make such orders, as justice requires.

Wilson v. Des Moines Independent Community School District

389 N.W.2d 681 (Iowa Ct. App. 1986)

The court provides a definition of "just cause" and upholds the school district's dismissal of a teacher for just cause.

Schlegel, Judge

Petitioner teacher appeals a district court decision affirming the termination of her employment contract with respondent school district. We are asked on appeal to reverse the lower court on the basis that the termination decision is unsupported by substantial evidence in the record. Petitioner also alleges that the real reason for her dismissal was due to her perceived mental disability, thus rendering the statutory termination notice invalid. We conclude that a preponderance of the evidence establishes "just cause" for termination of petitioner's teaching contract under Iowa Code section 279.15(2) (1985), and therefore affirm the district court.

Petitioner, a nonprobationary teacher in the Des Moines School District, was transferred from North High School to Tech High School in October, 1981. She received her first formal evaluation at Tech in February, 1982, and was given a composite rating of "needs improvement." An assistance team was requested for petitioner for the 1982–83 school year. In September, 1982, petitioner was notified that she required improvement in the areas of planning, meeting individual student's needs, and improving classroom discipline. During the 1982–83 school year, petitioner continued to have problems conforming to the school district's policies. In December, 1982, she went home during school, leaving her students unattended. In

February, 1983, she was warned about her repeated tardiness, her calls to the registrar at inappropriate times contrary to work rules, her problems with fellow faculty members, and her disruptive and inappropriate calls to parents from the school business office. It was also during this month that petitioner was reprimanded for teaching her class from the hall outside the classroom. Despite these warnings and reprimands, petitioner failed to report to work on time on March 30, 1983, and did not notify the registrar until 9:30 a.m. Because of her repeated violation of the work rules regarding tardiness, leaving classes unsupervised, and failure to give proper notification regarding absences, petitioner was suspended for several days.

Due to her work-related behavior, petitioner was evaluated on May 5, 1983, as "not meeting district standards." This rating meant that she had consistently failed to perform tasks and exhibit characteristics as required in the evaluation instrument, and/or had failed to improve sufficiently to meet district standards. In particular, petitioner failed to meet district standards by not demonstrating sensitivity in communicating with staff and in refusing to comply with school regulations and policies. Petitioner was also evaluated as "physically and/or emotionally unable to perform assigned duties," which stemmed from her excessive tardiness and failure to maintain self-control. Finally, at this time, petitioner did not meet district standards by failing "to use appropriate evaluation activities relating to the instructional objectives."

Respondent's superintendent recommended termination of petitioner's contract at this time, but instead, the executive director of personnel sent her a letter notifying her that due to her failure to meet certain standards, as well as her refusal to work on improving her performance, she was suspended for three working days. It was made clear to petitioner at that time that upon her return she would be expected to begin correcting her past behavior.

In September, 1983, petitioner was again assigned an assistance team and was given an improvement plan with specific objectives that essentially included all of the activities discussed above. One of the specific objectives was that petitioner use a clear, reasonable, and fair grading system. However, petitioner continued to have problems with her grading policies.

On November 1, 1983, a conference was held with petitioner concerning an allegation that everyone in her class was getting a grade of A. Petitioner explained that since her evaluation system was in question, she was giving all students that handed in their work, A's. Still, one student, who had never been to class, received a C, and four students who were enrolled received no grade at all. On November 3, 1983, students petitioned the administration objecting to petitioner's grading system.

. . . .

On March 5, 1984, petitioner was given notice of recommendation to terminate her contract. The following were listed in the notice as reasons for considering termination: (1) unsatisfactory performance, (2) unsatisfactory interpersonal relations with students and staff, (3) failure to comply with school regulations, policies and directives, (4) inability to perform assigned duties, and (5) failure to use appropriate evaluation activities. On June 5, 1984, the board of education voted to terminate petitioner's contract effective June 30, 1984, for the reasons stated in the March 5, 1984, notice sent to petitioner. The board also specifically found that, "The evidence in the record does not show that Mrs. Wilson has been treated differently than any other employee in the District or that she is under any physical or emotional disability."

The board's decision was submitted to an adjudicator and he affirmed the termination. The district court, on judicial review, also upheld the termination. Petitioner has now appealed the lower court's decision pursuant to Iowa Code section 279.18.

Judicial review of an adjudicator's decision in teacher termination proceedings is limited to the record made before the board.... Our review is "limited to the specific reasons stated in the superintendent's notice of recommendation of termination." Iowa Code § 279.16; *Smith v. Board of Education*, 293 N.W.2d 221, 225 (Iowa 1980).

Nonprobationary teachers may be discharged for "just cause." A "just cause" for termination is one which:

> [D]irectly or indirectly significantly and adversely affects what must be the ultimate goal of every school system: high quality education for the district's students. It relates to job performance, including leadership and role model effectiveness. It must include the concept that a school district is not married to mediocrity but may dismiss personnel who are neither performing high quality work nor improving in performance. On the other hand, "just cause" cannot include reasons which are arbitrary, unfair or generated out of some petty vendetta.

The burden of proof of "just cause" is, of course, upon the superintendent. If the Board concludes he has carried that burden, and adopts his recommendation, the teacher must then demonstrate, through an appeal to an adjudicator, section 279.17, or upon judicial review, section 279.18, that the board committed error in adopting the recommendation.

We have already set out the facts that the superintendent relied upon in submitting the recommendation for termination and it will serve no purpose to repeat them. The record shows that during the span of well over a year and a half, including two teaching years, petitioner was evaluated and informed of her professional shortcomings. The superintendent constantly made it clear to her that failure to comply with the district's standards may result in sanctions, discipline, or discharge. The record reveals no evidence that demonstrates petitioner's good faith attempt to improve her professional skills or in any way to rise to the standards stressed to her in her evaluations. The superintendent finally listed the specific reasons supporting his recommendation that petitioner's contract be terminated to the board of education, and the board did in fact terminate her contract based upon those reasons. Our examination of the record as a whole establishes by a preponderance of the evidence that petitioner failed to meet the performance standards set by the district for its teaching personnel, and that there was just cause to terminate her contract.

Petitioner alleges on appeal that the reasons listed by the superintendent for her recommended termination, and the subsequent termination, are really a pretext for the real reason she was terminated. She argues that the real reason for her termination was that the administration "perceived" her to be emotionally disabled. She argues therefore that the reasons stated in her notice of termination were inadequate.

We note at the outset that she carries the burden of proof on this issue. However, there is no evidence supporting her allegations and we have already determined that the reasons for termination, as well as the decision to terminate petitioner's contract, are supported by a preponderance of the evidence when the record is viewed as a whole. Therefore, petitioner's argument on this issue is without merit.

Because we conclude the decision to terminate petitioner's teaching contract is supported by a preponderance of the evidence when viewed as a whole, we affirm the district court's judgment.

Sanders v. Board of Education of Sioux City Community School District

263 N.W.2d 461 (Neb. 1978)

The court provides a definition of "just cause" and overturns the school district's dismissal of a teacher for just cause.

McCown, Justice

This is an error proceeding to challenge the action of the defendant, Board of Education of South Sioux City, Nebraska, terminating plaintiff's teaching contract. The District Court found that the action of the defendant board was arbitrary and unreasonable, and that no just cause for termination existed. The District Court set aside the termination and ordered defendant to reinstate the teaching contract of the plaintiff.

The plaintiff, Sharon L. Sanders, after 3 years of teaching physical education in Colorado schools, was employed by the defendant school board commencing with the school year of 1969–70. She taught girls physical education in the junior high school for 3 years. She was transferred to the senior high school for the 1972–73 school year. She taught girls physical education and was director of the girls drill team.

On February 6, 1975, Mrs. Sanders' performance for the 1974–75 year was evaluated by the principal of the senior high school, James Deignan. His overall evaluation was "good" and he recommended that she receive regular salary advancement but no merit increase for the next year. On the instructor evaluation form, Principal Deignan rated Mrs. Sanders "good" or "excellent" on all 12 rating classifications for personal traits. Mrs. Sanders was rated "good" or "excellent" in 15 out of 18 rating categories for instructional methods, and was evaluated as "needs to improve" in 3 areas. These three were "care and appearance of room and equipment"; "definition of goals"; and "all pupil participation." In no area was she rated as nonacceptable.

On February 24, 1975, the school board voted to continue Mrs. Sanders' employment for the 1975–76 school year, but placed her on probationary status. The record does not reflect the significance of that status, but it has no statutory basis. The record reflects that Mrs. Sanders requested, and apparently received, a hearing on the matter, but no record of the hearing was made. There is nothing in the record to reflect the grounds for the "probation" other than the evaluation report of Mr. Deignan. The "comments or suggestions to the instructor" section of that report stated that better organization and discipline were needed. Whatever the reason for the "probation," no suggestions or guidelines for improvement were given to Mrs. Sanders.

On March 22, 1976, Dennis Trump, the high school principal for the year, who had been assistant principal the preceding year, completed his evaluation report on Mrs. Sanders' performance for the 1975–76 school year. Mr. Trump gave Mrs. Sanders an overall rating of "good" and recommended renewal of her contract. His report stated that "improvement has been shown in cooperation and percentage of student participation." Mr. Trump rated Mrs. Sanders "good" or "excellent" in all rating categories except two in which he rated her as "needs to improve." Those two were "classroom control" and "all pupil participation." In the "comments or suggestions to the instructor" section of the report Mr. Trump noted "some time wasted prior to start of class activity. Improvement has been made in number of students participating."

On the same day Mr. Trump's report was made the defendant school board voted to consider terminating the plaintiff's contract at the end of the 1975–76 school year on the ground of "incompetency, neglect of duty, inability to control students, and poor preservation of class equipment." Mrs. Sanders requested a hearing, which was held on May 5, 1976.

The school board presented three witnesses at the hearing. Dr. Ralph Weaver, the Superintendent of Schools, testified that he did not visit individual teacher's classrooms, nor perform any classroom evaluations, and that the responsibility for the evaluation of individual classroom teachers rested with the various principals. He himself dealt with the principals and reports and recommendations from them. He testified, however, that on several occasions Mrs. Sanders was not present when the drill team was practicing, performing, or working out, and that he considered that a neglect of duty.

Mr. Dennis Trump, the principal of the senior high school for the 1975–76 school year, testified that he was primarily responsible for evaluating teachers and visits each classroom at least three times a year. He knew that Mrs. Sanders was on probation, but had not seen her evaluation report from the preceding year. He testified that on several occasions during the 1975–76 school year, students who should have been in Mrs. Sanders' classes, were, instead, outside the gymnasium classroom and in other places in and around the high school building. He also testified that on occasion

Mrs. Sanders had not properly supervised or guarded gymnastics equipment for the safety of students, but acknowledged that he had not called the matter to her attention. Mr. Trump testified that on one occasion during Mrs. Sanders' maternity leave a substitute teacher, in his opinion, had done a better job than Mrs. Sanders. Mr. Trump noted also that on one occasion a drill team class taught by Mrs. Sanders was late in getting started, and that on occasion he had picked up volleyballs in the gymnasium which had not been put away after her classes. Mr. Trump was, nevertheless, of the opinion that Mrs. Sanders' performance had improved, and he recommended that she be retained.

The final witness for the school board was Fred Colvard, the assistant principal of the senior high school. Colvard was in charge of discipline at the high school. He testified that several times he had had to discipline Mrs. Sanders' students for being out of class, and that on occasion Mrs. Sanders had requested his assistance with discipline problems. He testified that on one or two occasions he had seen students working on gymnastics equipment without proper guarding, but had not called it to Mrs. Sanders' attention. Essentially, his testimony as to Mrs. Sanders' conduct agreed with that of Mr. Trump, although Colvard testified that he had not made, or been called upon to make, an evaluation of Mrs. Sanders' teaching performance. He testified that on the basis of his informal observations he was not in a position to say whether she should be retained or terminated.

There were two witnesses for plaintiff. A former student of Mrs. Sanders, who had been in her physical education classes for several years in both junior and senior high school, testified that she had never noticed any discipline problems in class, nor any problems of an insufficient number of students guarding gymnastics equipment, and that Mrs. Sanders was better than the other physical education teachers she had had. She also testified that there were a few students who skipped class on occasion, but that they were people who routinely skipped other classes as well.

Mrs. Sanders herself testified that until the 1974–75 school year she had never had complaints about her teaching. She testified that in the spring of 1975, when she was placed on probation, she was given no specific instructions, suggestions, or guidelines to follow to correct whatever deficiencies there might have been in her teaching. She also testified that her probation was not discussed with her during the 1975–76 school year except in February of 1976, when Mr. Trump indicated to her that he was going to recommend that she be taken off probation. It was her testimony that she did not have an unusual number of discipline problems and that those she had she either handled herself or referred to Mr. Colvard. Mrs. Sanders testified that on one occasion less than four student guards had been in place around the trampoline, and that she immediately corrected the situation when she noticed it. She denied any problem in losing students from her classroom, and explained that if students did not come down to the gymnasium level from the locker room, she had no way of knowing they were present, and she counted them absent. She also testified that all equipment she started the year with was accounted for, although she conceded that on occasion volleyballs would be stuck under the bleachers and she did not find them until later. She also testified that she had never received any complaints from parents about her performance.

At the conclusion of the hearing before the school board on May 5, 1976, the five members of the school board present unanimously voted to terminate Mrs. Sanders' contract.

....

This case is one of first impression in interpreting some of the provisions of section 79–1254, R.R.S.1943, which became effective February 26, 1975. That section deals with the continuation or termination of teachers' contracts and provides in relevant part:

> Except for the first two years of employment * * * any contract of employment between an administrator or a teacher who holds a certificate which is valid for a term of more than one year and a Class I, II, III, or VI district shall be deemed renewed and shall remain in full force and effect until a majority of the members of the board vote on or before May 15 to amend or to terminate the contract for just cause at the close of the contract period. The first two years of the contract shall be a probationary period during which it may be terminated without just cause. * * * The secretary of the board shall, not later than April 15, notify each administrator or teacher in writing of any conditions of unsatisfactory performance * * * which the board considers may be just cause to either terminate or amend the contract for the ensuing school year. Any teacher or administrator so notified shall have the right to file within five days of receipt of such notice a written request with the board of education for a hearing before the board. Upon receipt of such request the board shall order the hearing to be held within ten days, and shall give written notice of the time and place of the hearing to the teacher or administrator. At the hearing evidence shall be presented in support of the reasons given for considering termination or amendment of the contract, and the teacher or administrator shall be permitted to produce evidence relating thereto. The board shall render the decision to amend or terminate a contract based on the evidence produced at the hearing. As used in this section * * * the term just cause shall mean incompetency, neglect of duty, unprofessional conduct, insubordination, immorality, physical or mental incapacity, other conduct which interferes substantially with the continued performance of duties * * *.

The parties have stipulated that only incompetency and neglect of duty are involved here, and none of the other statutory meanings of "just cause" are applicable. It should be noted also that the statute specifically requires that any decision to terminate a teacher's contract must be based only on the evidence produced at the hearing before the school board.

....

The critical issue here is what conduct is sufficient to constitute just cause for the termination of the contract of a tenured teacher under current statutory requirements. There are few, if any, objective criteria for evaluating teacher performance or for determining what constitutes just cause for terminating teaching contracts of tenured teachers. Each case must, therefore, be assessed on its own facts. In this case there is no evidence that Mrs. Sanders violated any directive, regulation, rule, or order given to her by any administrator or the board of education. There is no evidence that the conduct of Mrs. Sanders complained of by the board violated any specific rule or regulation of the school administration. In both of the detailed evaluations of Mrs. Sanders' performance, made by the person charged with that duty by the school administration, there were no areas of performance in which she was not acceptable, and out of almost 20 rating categories, only 2 or 3 were rated as needing improvement. Both of those official evaluations by the administration itself recommended retention. Both were made by professional administrators who presumably had ample knowledge of professional competence and the standards for performance of duty. The evidence at the hearing reflected facts which were thoroughly known by the principal at the time he made his evaluation and report.

. . . .

Evidence that a particular duty was not competently performed on certain occasions, or evidence of an occasional neglect of some duty of performance, in itself, does not ordinarily establish incompetency or neglect of duty sufficient to constitute just cause for termination. Incompetency or neglect of duty are not measured in a vacuum nor against a standard of perfection, but, instead, must be measured against the standard required of others performing the same or similar duties. The conduct of Mrs. Sanders complained of by the board might well be categorized as minimal rather than substantial evidence of incompetence or neglect of duty. However her performance of duty is classified, there is a complete absence of evidence that Mrs. Sanders' performance of her particular duties was below the standard of performance required of other teachers in the high school performing the same or similar duties. Neither is there any expert testimony that Mrs. Sanders' conduct was, or should be, sufficient evidence of incompetency or neglect of duty to constitute just cause for termination of her contract.

The District Court was correct in finding that there was no substantial evidence of incompetency or neglect of duty sufficient to establish just cause for the termination of plaintiff's contract. In the absence of just cause the defendant's action was arbitrary and unreasonable.

The judgment of the District Court was correct and is affirmed.

Post Problem Discussion

1. The *Sanders* and *Wilson* decisions reach different conclusions. What are the differences in the cases that led to different results?

2. Note that the state law in the problem materials provides just cause protections for tenured teachers only. How does your state law compare? Should non-tenured teachers receive similar just cause protections from dismissal or removal? Why or why not?

3. Teacher expertise is central to education. The research repeatedly demonstrates that strong teachers and strong teacher-student relationships are foundational elements of providing students with a quality education.[4] How should the importance of teachers in providing quality education be factored in when deciding how to define just cause, and whether just cause exists in a specific case? Should the just cause standard be more favorable to teachers, or more deferential to school boards/administrators? Should judicial review be deferential toward school board decisions that just cause exists? Why or why not?

4. In 2007, the New York Times ran a series of stories about New York City teachers who had been removed from the classroom and were required to spend their days waiting in a "reassignment center" that they had named the "rubber room" until they had their hearing on the merits of their removal.[5] The room was described as follows:

> The room in question was about 1,100 square feet and on blueprints submitted to the Fire Department was designed to hold 26 people. On this day, it contained upward of 75. It had no windows, no land phone, no Internet access, no wall decorations, not even a clock.

Teachers are not allowed to bring personal items into the room. Some of the teachers were removed for accusations of assault on students, others for incompetence; some had not received specific reasons for their removal. All of them were in limbo waiting for hearings to determine if they could return to the classroom. The article reported that there were 12 reassignment centers and that upwards of 750 teachers (out of 80,000 in the city) were waiting for hearings that could take years to resolve. During this waiting period, the teachers were paid their full salaries and were required to spend the 181 days of the school year from 8:00 am to 3:00 pm in the reassignment center. The full article is available online. What do you think about this approach? What do you think should happen to teachers who are removed and waiting for a hearing on the merits?

Problem 3: Contract Non-Renewal

Assume that Ms. Anderson met with Principal Davis and developed an improvement plan. After that, Superintendent Vasquez decided not to go forward with dismissing Ms. Anderson and cancelled the dismissal hearing. At the same time, Superintendent Vasquez notified Ms. Anderson that the school would be non-renewing her contract.

---

4. *See* Linda Darling-Hammond, *Doing What Matters Most: Investing in Quality Teaching* 8 (1997), http://www.nctaf.org/documents/DoingWhatMattersMost.pdf, stating that "no other intervention can make the difference that a knowledgeable, skillful teacher can make in the learning process."

5. *See* Samuel G. Freedman, *Where Teachers Sit, Awaiting Their Fates*, N.Y. Times, October 10, 2007, www.nytimes.com/2007/10/10/education/10education.html (last visited November 15, 2018).

The school held a hearing on the non-renewal. Read the testimony of Ms. Anderson and Superintendent Vasquez along with the rest of the problem materials, and decide whether the school district complied with the statutory requirements to non-renew Ms. Anderson's contract.

Problem Materials

✓ Memorandum from Superintendent Vasquez

✓ Hypothetical State Statute

✓ Testimony of Ms. Anderson

✓ Ms. Anderson's Improvement Plan

✓ Testimony of Superintendent Vasquez

Memorandum

To: Sharon Anderson
From: Superintendent Vasquez
Date: April 10, 20xx

Pursuant to 7489:14(a), I am notifying you that I will not be re-nominating you for employment at the school district for the 20xx-20xx school year.

Pursuant to our conversation about this matter, I am providing you with a statement of reasons for the non-renewal even though the school district is not required to do so unless requested to do so in writing.

1. You are not being re-nominated due to unsatisfactory performance including the following:
2. Parents have complained about your teaching style and methods.
3. Parents have complained that you are unable to control students in your classroom, which distracts the other children.
4. The test scores for the students in your class on the statewide assessment test for the past two years have been below the proficient level required by state law.
5. You were late to work on three occasions this school year without notice in violation of the collective bargaining agreement, and your contract. The school principal had to cover for you during class, causing disruption in school and in the principal's other daily obligations.

Attached is a copy of the state statute 7489:14(a) explaining your legal rights.

Hypothetical State Statute

ED 7489:14(a) Failure to be Renominated or Reelected.

I. (a) Any teacher who has a professional standards certificate from the state board of education and who has taught for one or more years in the same school district shall be notified in writing on or before April 15 or within 15 days of the adoption of the district budget by the legislative body, whichever is later, if that teacher is not to be re-nominated or reelected, provided that no notification shall occur later than the Friday following the second Tuesday in May.

(b) Any such teacher who has taught for 3 consecutive years or more in the same school district and who has been so notified may request in writing within 10 days of receipt of said notice a hearing before the school board and may in said request ask for reasons for failure to be re-nominated or reelected. For purposes of this section only, a leave of absence shall not interrupt the consecutive nature of a teacher's service, but neither shall such a leave be included in the computation of a teacher's service. Computation of a teacher's service for any other purposes shall not be affected by this section. The notice shall advise the teacher of all of the teacher's rights under this section. The school board, upon receipt of said request, shall provide for a hearing on the request to be held within 15 days. The school board shall issue its decision in writing within 15 days of the close of the hearing.

II. Any teacher who has a professional standards certificate from the state board of education and who has taught for 3 consecutive years or more in any school district in the state shall, after having taught for 2 consecutive years in any other school district in the state, be entitled to all of the rights for notification and hearing in paragraphs I(b), III, and IV of this section.

III. In cases of non-re-nomination because of unsatisfactory performance, the superintendent of the local school district shall demonstrate, at the school board hearing, by a preponderance of the evidence, that the teacher had received written notice that the teacher's unsatisfactory performance may lead to non-re-nomination, that the teacher had a reasonable opportunity to correct such unsatisfactory performance, and that the teacher had failed to correct such unsatisfactory performance. Nothing in this paragraph shall be construed to require the superintendent or the school board to provide a teacher with remedial assistance to correct any deficiencies that form the basis for such teacher's non-re-nomination.

IV. In all proceedings before the school board under this section, the burden of proof for non-renewal of a teacher shall be on the superintendent of the local school district by a preponderance of the evidence.

Teacher Non-Renewal Hearing Testimony—Ms. Anderson

Q. Ms. Anderson, tell us a little bit about your employment at the school.

A. OK. I am a fourth grade teacher at the school district and have been a teacher at the school district for five years now.

Q. When was the first time you had some idea that the school was seeking to terminate your employment relationship?

A. Well, everything seemed to go very well for me with the school until March 1 when the principal told me that I was being immediately removed by the new superintendent and that the superintendent was recommending that I be dismissed. He gave me a memo from the superintendent and told me to work on developing an improvement plan. I must say that it all came as quite a shock. I was really blindsided by it.

Q. Now, is this the memo from the superintendent that you are referring to? [Shows memo from Problem 2]

A. Yes, it is.

Q. Tell us about the improvement plan. Did you complete that task as requested?

A. Yes, I did. I was not sure what to address in the improvement plan, as I was never provided much information about why I was in jeopardy of being dismissed. I was told by the principal that some parents did not like my teaching style, and some were upset by some of the kids in the class who caused discipline problems. I was also told that my class assessment test scores were low. But look, I can't control who is put in my class, and I just so happen to have a number of students with behavioral issues in my class this year. All I can do is follow the school's policies about how to address that. I also can't control how students perform on tests, and, if you ask me, those tests don't really measure much of anything anyway. Just because a student does not test well does not mean they are not doing well academically, or not learning in my class.

Given the information I had, I developed a plan that addressed the subjects the principal told me about. The principal made some suggested changes, which I incorporated, and then the plan was presented to Superintendent Vasquez on March 27.

Q. What happened after that?

A. Superintendent Vasquez called me the next day and told me that the plan was not adequate, but did not explain why. He also told me that the plan did not matter anymore because she had decided not to go forward with the dismissal proceedings, but would be non-renewing my contract instead.

About ten days later, I received the non-renewal notice. I have not been back in the classroom since the March 1 removal, and I miss my students. However, I decided not to challenge the removal given the late date in the school year and the pending non-renewal hearing.

Q. Did you get a chance to work on implementing the improvement plan?

A. No. I have not been teaching for the school, or in the classroom at all, since the March 1 removal, so I have not had any time to work on implementing the items listed in the improvement plan.

Q. Looking at the April 10 non-renewal notice [the notice is the memoranda from Superintendent Vasquez provided in this problem], one of the issues raised is your tardiness. Can you explain that?

A. It could not be helped and was due to last minute illness each time due to my pregnancy. I was only about 30 to 45 minutes late on each occasion.

Q. What about the issues noted here with your teaching methods?

A. I don't know what that is about really. I teach students with the same textbooks as the other fourth grade teachers in the school. I do use different methods than some other teachers I suppose, but I don't see anything wrong with that. I believe that students need to learn how to think for themselves, and they should have more than just basic math and reading instruction by this grade. Some students struggle a bit with the harder material, but they are never going to learn if you keep spoon feeding them answers to test questions all day. I believe that my methods are the current "best practices," and I have not had any parents complain to me about it.

Q. Can you tell us any more about the behavioral issues?

A. I have a handful of students in my class that have behavioral issues. I have worked within the school rules in terms of discipline and have asked for more help with the students from the principal, but I was told that I needed to deal with it on my own. I have sent the students to the principal on a number of occasions only to have them return to class shortly afterwards with nothing happening to the student, so I just stopped doing that. I am frustrated by it, but I can only do so much.

Q. And you mentioned the test scores a minute ago. Anything else to add about that?

A. Not really. Like I said, I understand that my class test scores are low, but I have no control over the students that are placed in my class. About ten of the twenty five students in my class are special education students, and some of them just don't test well.

Q. Anything else to add?

A. No, not really. I just want to be sure that everyone understands that I have not had any problems with the school in the past. My performance has never been questioned in the five years that I have been with the school. I was not aware that there were any problems this year until the principal informed me that I was being removed and subject to dismissal on March 1.

Sharon Anderson Improvement Plan

I, Sharon Anderson, agree to take the following steps to improve:

1. To work with other fourth grade teachers in the school and incorporate some of their teaching methods into my daily instruction.

2. To take at least eight (8) hours of continuing education classes over the summer regarding best practices in teaching basic math and reading skills to fourth grade students and at least eight (8) hours regarding best practices in helping students improve assessment scores.

3. To take steps to discipline students in my class that violate school rules including sending the student to the principal.

____________________*Sharon Anderson*

Teacher Non-Renewal Hearing Testimony—Superintendent Vasquez

Q. How long have you been with the district as a superintendent?

A. I am new to the district this year. My prior experience is as a superintendent in other districts that needed to improve their performance and accountability measures. I am considered something of an expert in that area. I tend to go to districts that need help in that area, help them improve to the point they desire, and then move on to another district.

Q. Is that why you came to this school district?

A. Yes. I was hired as part of the district's effort to improve school performance including teaching performance. I have a special interest in that topic. I expect teachers to be of the highest quality, and this school district wanted to improve in that area.

Q. Relative to Ms. Anderson, how would you assess her performance?

A. One of the things I did when I came into the district was to identify teachers who were not living up to the high standards that we have for teachers. I have some criteria that I have created over the years to assess performance, and it is something of a grid. I looked at the performance of all of the teachers in the district based on the criteria in my grid, and Ms. Anderson did not do well.

Q. What kind of criteria?

A. Oh, a variety of things. Employee evaluations, statewide assessment test scores of the class, parental complaints or commendations, meeting competency requirements, complying with basic employment requirements like showing up for work on time, taking on cafeteria and hall duties when asked, conducting parent conferences as required. There are a number of others that I can't recall right now.

Q. Now, you heard Ms. Anderson's testimony. Can you give us your side of what happened?

A. Sure. As I mentioned, Ms. Anderson was on my list, so to speak, of teachers that I felt the district needed to do something about. I ultimately decided I needed to remove her from the classroom because of repeated complaints from parents that their children were not learning basic reading and math skills, and that the classroom was full of behavioral problems that Ms. Anderson did not address. Her class also consistently scored poorly on the statewide assessment tests.

I just felt that given those circumstances, we could do better with someone else if she was not willing to improve. So I gave her a chance to address her deficiencies in an improvement plan, but the plan was very brief and did not have any specifics about what she would do beyond talking to other teachers and taking some continuing education classes.

I had initially planned on moving to dismiss her, but given that the end of the year was coming, I decided not to proceed with dismissal charges as that would require a showing of incompetence, and I wanted to spare Ms. Anderson from having to go through a hearing demonstrating her incompetency. So, instead of doing that, I decided to non-renew Ms. Anderson's contract for the reasons stated in the memo to her.

Q. Was Ms. Anderson given notice about her unsatisfactory performance?

A. Yes, she was, as part of the removal and dismissal notice I provided when I instructed her to develop an improvement plan. She met with the principal to develop the improvement plan, and he told her about the parental complaints and low-test scores as part of the process of developing the plan. The plan was her chance to correct her performance, and she failed to do so.

Q. Anything else?

A. I would just like to note that Ms. Anderson also failed to address issues regarding her tardiness in her improvement plan. In my opinion, the three times that Ms. Anderson was late without notice and the failure to address it in the improvement plan is itself grounds for non-renewal.

Post Problem Discussion

1. If the school did not meet the statutory requirements in the problem materials, what should the remedy be for Ms. Anderson?

2. Note that the problem statute states that in cases of non-re-nomination because of unsatisfactory performance, the teacher must have had written notice that the teacher's unsatisfactory performance may lead to non-re-nomination, a reasonable opportunity to correct such unsatisfactory performance, and then fail to do so. Why do you think the law includes that requirement? What are the pros and cons of having such a requirement?

3. How should unsatisfactory performance be defined? What would you include and exclude from the definition? For example, should acts such as insubordination or using inappropriate language in front of students be included? Why or why not?

4. In addition to the concepts discussed in Problems 2 and 3, public schools must also abide by constitutional and statutory requirements regarding discrimination. Public schools generally cannot discriminate in hiring or firing on the basis of race, age, sex, disability, religion, citizenship, or political affiliation. *See generally* 67B Am. Jur. 2d, *Schools* § 149 (2018). Do your state laws incorporate these requirements?

Activity 3: Tenure

As noted, some states have tenure systems that provide certain protections to certain employees that meet certain requirements. Some states use different terminology for tenure like probationary and non-probationary, or temporary and permanent. The idea behind tenure for teachers at the elementary and secondary level is to protect teachers from being fired for reasons unrelated to their ability to teach, such as cronyism, or their personal views on social issues, or personality conflicts with a new principal, etc. This protection generally comes in the form of some type of "just cause" requirement that must be met in order to end the teacher's employment, along with a hearing process that must be followed to prove that just cause exists.

In California, certain tenure protections have been subject to litigation. The subject of these cases is whether tenure requirements violate students' right to an education under state constitutional requirements noted in Chapter 2.

Step One—Review *Vergara v. California* 246 Cal. App. 4th 619 (Cal. Ct. App. 2016), *reh'g denied* (May 3, 2016), *review denied* (Aug. 22, 2016) online.

You can also review the website about the case for more information: http://studentsmatter.org/our-case/vergara-v-california-case-summary/.

Step Two—Note the discussion in the *Vergara* case about certain aspects of tenure and the rights of students to receive a quality education from effective teachers. These types of lawsuits have spread to other states including New York and various groups are proposing changes to tenure requirements. Review as an example, the StudentsFirst "Rebalancing Teacher Tenure" position paper at:

http://tntp.org/assets/documents/TNTP_RebalancingTenure_2014.pdf

Step Three—Review your state laws on tenure and compare them to those discussed in *Vergara*, and to the recommendations in the StudentsFirst document.

Step Four—Answer the following:

1. When does tenure apply to teachers in your state, if at all? Does your state have a last in, first out requirement like California?
2. Do you think the additional protections that tenure affords teachers in your state have any impact on the quality of education that is provided to students in your state? Why or why not?
3. Have there been any court challenges or legislative efforts to change tenure in your state? If so, how do they compare to those discussed in the *Vergara* case and the StudentsFirst suggestions?
4. What changes, if any, do you think should be made to tenure requirements in your state? How should they be made? By local school board policies that vary from school to school? By state statutes or regulations? By state court decisions? By federal statute or regulations?

§ 3.05 Constitutional Due Process Protections

In addition to the state law requirements discussed in prior sections, constitutional due process requirements can also arise in employment. In two foundational cases, the United States Supreme Court established the constitutional standards in this area. The following problem explores these issues.

Problem 4: Due Process Requirements For Non-Tenured Teachers

Assume that Ms. Anderson, as described in Problems 2 and 3, is not a tenured teacher. Instead, she has only been with the school district for one school year. During that school year, Superintendent Vasquez informs her that her contract will not be renewed for the following school year. She asks for the reasons for the non-renewal, but Superintendent Vazquez refuses to provide any, citing the state statute in Problem 3 (ED 7489:14(a)). Does Ms. Anderson have any constitutional due process right to receive such information? Does she have any constitutional due process protections?

Problem Materials

✓ State Statutes in Problems 2 and 3

✓ *Board of Regents v. Roth*, 408 U.S. 564 (1972)

✓ *Perry v. Sindermann*, 408 U.S. 593 (1972)

Board of Regents v. Roth

408 U.S. 564 (1972)

The Court finds that a university professor with a one year contract was not deprived of his liberty or property interests when the contract was not renewed.

Mr. Justice Stewart delivered the opinion of the Court.

In 1968 the respondent, David Roth, was hired for his first teaching job as assistant professor of political science at Wisconsin State University-Oshkosh. He was hired for a fixed term of one academic year. The notice of his faculty appointment specified that his employment would begin on September 1, 1968, and would end on June 30, 1969. The respondent completed that term. But he was informed that he would not be rehired for the next academic year.

The respondent had no tenure rights to continued employment. Under Wisconsin statutory law a state university teacher can acquire tenure as a "permanent" employee only after four years of year-to-year employment. Having acquired tenure, a teacher is entitled to continued employment "during efficiency and good behavior." A relatively new teacher without tenure, however, is under Wisconsin law entitled to nothing beyond his one-year appointment. There are no statutory or administrative standards defining eligibility for re-employment. State law thus clearly leaves the decision whether to rehire a no tenured teacher for another year to the unfettered discretion of university officials.

The procedural protection afforded a Wisconsin State University teacher before he is separated from the University corresponds to his job security. As a matter of statutory law, a tenured teacher cannot be "discharged except for cause upon written charges" and pursuant to certain procedures.[6] A nontenured teacher, similarly, is protected to some extent *during* his one-year term. Rules promulgated by the Board of Regents provide that a nontenured teacher "dismissed" before the end of the year may have some opportunity for review of the "dismissal." But the Rules provide no real protection for a nontenured teacher who simply is not re-employed for the next year. He must be informed by February 1 "concerning retention or nonretention for the ensuing year." But "no reason for non-retention need be given. No review or appeal is provided in such case."[7]

In conformance with these Rules, the President of Wisconsin State University-Oshkosh informed the respondent before February 1, 1969, that he would not be rehired for the 1969–1970 academic year. He gave the respondent no reason for the decision and no opportunity to challenge it at any sort of hearing.

The respondent then brought this action in Federal District Court alleging that the decision not to rehire him for the next year infringed his Fourteenth Amendment rights. He attacked the decision both in substance and procedure. First, he alleged that the true reason for the decision was to punish him for certain statements critical of the University administration, and that it therefore violated his right to freedom of speech. Second, he alleged that the failure of University officials

6. [FN 3] Wis. Stat. § 37.31(1) further provided that:

"No teacher who has become permanently employed as herein provided shall be discharged except for cause upon written charges. Within 30 days of receiving the written charges, such teacher may appeal the discharge by a written notice to the president of the board of regents of state colleges. The board shall cause the charges to be investigated, hear the case and provide such teacher with a written statement as to their decision."

7. [FN 4] The Rules, promulgated by the Board of Regents in 1967, provide:

"RULE I—February first is established throughout the State University system as the deadline for written notification of non-tenured faculty concerning retention or non-retention for the ensuing year. The President of each University shall give such notice each year on or before this date."

"RULE II—During the time a faculty member is on probation, no reason for non-retention need be given. No review or appeal is provided in such case.

"RULE III—'Dismissal' as opposed to 'Non-Retention' means termination of responsibilities during an academic year. When a non-tenure faculty member is dismissed he has no right under Wisconsin Statutes to a review of his case or to appeal. The President may, however, in his discretion, grant a request for a review within the institution, either by a faculty committee or by the President, or both. Any such review would be informal in nature and would be advisory only.

"RULE IV—When a non-tenure faculty member is dismissed he may request a review by or hearing before the Board of Regents. Each such request will be considered separately and the Board will, in its discretion, grant or deny same in each individual case."

to give him notice of any reason for nonretention and an opportunity for a hearing violated his right to procedural due process of law.

. . . .

The requirements of procedural due process apply only to the deprivation of interests encompassed by the Fourteenth Amendment's protection of liberty and property. When protected interests are implicated, the right to some kind of prior hearing is paramount. But the range of interests protected by procedural due process is not infinite. . . .

"Liberty" and "property" are broad and majestic terms. They are among the "great [constitutional] concepts . . . purposely left to gather meaning from experience. . . . They relate to the whole domain of social and economic fact, and the statesmen who founded this Nation knew too well that only a stagnant society remains unchanged." For that reason, the Court has fully and finally rejected the wooden distinction between "rights" and "privileges" that once seemed to govern the applicability of procedural due process rights. The Court has also made clear that the property interests protected by procedural due process extend well beyond actual ownership of real estate, chattels, or money. By the same token, the Court has required due process protection for deprivations of liberty beyond the sort of formal constraints imposed by the criminal process.

Yet, while the Court has eschewed rigid or formalistic limitations on the protection of procedural due process, it has at the same time observed certain boundaries. For the words "liberty" and "property" in the Due Process Clause of the Fourteenth Amendment must be given some meaning.

"While this Court has not attempted to define with exactness the liberty . . . guaranteed [by the Fourteenth Amendment], the term has received much consideration and some of the included things have been definitely stated. Without doubt, it denotes not merely freedom from bodily restraint but also the right of the individual to contract, to engage in any of the common occupations of life, to acquire useful knowledge, to marry, establish a home and bring up children, to worship God according to the dictates of his own conscience, and generally to enjoy those privileges long recognized . . . as essential to the orderly pursuit of happiness by free men." In a Constitution for a free people, there can be no doubt that the meaning of "liberty" must be broad indeed.

There might be cases in which a State refused to reemploy a person under such circumstances that interests in liberty would be implicated. But this is not such a case.

The State, in declining to rehire the respondent, did not make any charge against him that might seriously damage his standing and associations in his community. It did not base the nonrenewal of his contract on a charge, for example, that he had been guilty of dishonesty, or immorality. Had it done so, this would be a different case. For "where a person's good name, reputation, honor, or integrity is at stake because of what the government is doing to him, notice and an opportunity to be heard are essential." In such a case, due process would accord an opportunity to refute the charge before University officials. In the present case, however, there is no suggestion whatever that the respondent's "good name, reputation, honor, or integrity" is at stake.

Similarly, there is no suggestion that the State, in declining to re-employ the respondent, imposed on him a stigma or other disability that foreclosed his freedom to take advantage of other employment opportunities. The State, for example, did not invoke any regulations to bar the respondent from all other public employment in state universities. Had it done so, this, again, would be a different case. For "to be deprived not only of present government employment but of future opportunity for it certainly is no small injury. . . ." The Court has held, for example, that a State, in regulating eligibility for a type of professional employment, cannot foreclose a range of opportunities "in a manner . . . that contravene[s] . . . Due Process," and, specifically, in a manner that denies the right to a full prior hearing. In the present case, however, this principle does not come into play.

To be sure, the respondent has alleged that the nonrenewal of his contract was based on his exercise of his right to freedom of speech. But this allegation is not now before us. The District Court stayed proceedings on this issue, and the respondent has yet to prove that the decision not to rehire him was, in fact, based on his free speech activities.

Hence, on the record before us, all that clearly appears is that the respondent was not rehired for one year at one university. It stretches the concept too far to suggest that a person is deprived of "liberty" when he simply is not rehired in one job but remains as free as before to seek another.

The Fourteenth Amendment's procedural protection of property is a safeguard of the security of interests that a person has already acquired in specific benefits. These interests—property interests—may take many forms.

Thus, the Court has held that a person receiving welfare benefits under statutory and administrative standards defining eligibility for them has an interest in continued receipt of those benefits that is safeguarded by procedural due process. *Goldberg v. Kelly*, 397 U.S. 254. Similarly, in the area of public employment, the Court has held that a public college professor dismissed from an office held under tenure provisions, *Slochower v. Board of Education*, 350 U.S. 551, and college professors and staff members dismissed during the terms of their contracts, *Wieman v. Updegraff*, 344 U.S. 183, have interests in continued employment that are safeguarded by due process. Only last year, the Court held that this principle "proscribing summary dismissal from public employment without hearing or inquiry required by due process" also applied to a teacher recently hired without tenure or a formal contract, but nonetheless with a clearly implied promise of continued employment. *Connell v. Higginbotham*, 403 U.S. 207, 208.

Certain attributes of "property" interests protected by procedural due process emerge from these decisions. To have a property interest in a benefit, a person clearly must have more than an abstract need or desire for it. He must have more than a unilateral expectation of it. He must, instead, have a legitimate claim of entitlement to it. It is a purpose of the ancient institution of property to protect those claims upon which people rely in their daily lives, reliance that must not be arbitrarily undermined. It is a purpose of the constitutional right to a hearing to provide an opportunity for a person to vindicate those claims.

Property interests, of course, are not created by the Constitution. Rather, they are created and their dimensions are defined by existing rules or understandings that stem from an independent source such as state law—rules or understandings that secure certain benefits and that support claims of entitlement to those benefits. Thus, the welfare recipients in *Goldberg v. Kelly, supra*, had a claim of entitlement to welfare payments that was grounded in the statute defining eligibility for them. The recipients had not yet shown that they were, in fact, within the statutory terms of eligibility. But we held that they had a right to a hearing at which they might attempt to do so.

Just as the welfare recipients' "property" interest in welfare payments was created and defined by statutory terms, so the respondent's "property" interest in employment at Wisconsin State University-Oshkosh was created and defined by the terms of his appointment. Those terms secured his interest in employment up to June 30, 1969. But the important fact in this case is that they specifically provided that the respondent's employment was to terminate on June 30. They did not provide for contract renewal absent "sufficient cause." Indeed, they made no provision for renewal whatsoever.

Thus, the terms of the respondent's appointment secured absolutely no interest in re-employment for the next year. They supported absolutely no possible claim of entitlement to re-employment. Nor, significantly, was there any state statute or University rule or policy that secured his interest in re-employment or that created any legitimate claim to it. In these circumstances, the respondent surely had an abstract concern in being rehired, but he did not have a *property* interest sufficient to require the University authorities to give him a hearing when they declined to renew his contract of employment.

Our analysis of the respondent's constitutional rights in this case in no way indicates a view that an opportunity for a hearing or a statement of reasons for nonretention would, or would not, be appropriate or wise in public colleges and universities. For it is a written Constitution that we apply. Our role is confined to interpretation of that Constitution.

We must conclude that the summary judgment for the respondent should not have been granted, since the respondent has not shown that he was deprived of liberty or property protected by the Fourteenth Amendment. The judgment of the Court of Appeals, accordingly, is reversed and the case is remanded for further proceedings consistent with this opinion.

It is so ordered.

Perry v. Sindermann

408 U.S. 593 (1972)

The Court finds that the lack of an explicit contract or tenure system does not necessarily defeat a professor's claim for due process and First Amendment protections.

Mr. Justice Stewart delivered the opinion of the Court.

From 1959 to 1969 the respondent, Robert Sindermann, was a teacher in the state college system of the State of Texas. After teaching for two years at the University of Texas and for four years at San Antonio Junior College, he became a professor of Government and Social Science at Odessa Junior College in 1965. He was employed at the college for four successive years, under a series of one-year contracts. He was successful enough to be appointed, for a time, the cochairman of his department.

During the 1968–1969 academic year, however, controversy arose between the respondent and the college administration. The respondent was elected president of the Texas Junior College Teachers Association. In this capacity, he left his teaching duties on several occasions to testify before committees of the Texas Legislature, and he became involved in public disagreements with the policies of the college's Board of Regents. In particular, he aligned himself with a group advocating the elevation of the college to four-year status—a change opposed by the Regents. And, on one occasion, a newspaper advertisement appeared over his name that was highly critical of the Regents.

Finally, in May 1969, the respondent's one-year employment contract terminated and the Board of Regents voted not to offer him a new contract for the next academic year. The Regents issued a press release setting forth allegations of the respondent's insubordination. But they provided him no official statement of the reasons for the nonrenewal of his contract. And they allowed him no opportunity for a hearing to challenge the basis of the nonrenewal.

... The first question presented is whether the respondent's lack of a contractual or tenure right to re-employment, taken alone, defeats his claim that the nonrenewal of his contract violated the First and Fourteenth Amendments. We hold that it does not.

For at least a quarter-century, this Court has made clear that even though a person has no "right" to a valuable governmental benefit and even though the government may deny him the benefit for any number of reasons, there are some reasons upon which the government may not rely. It may not deny a benefit to a person on a basis that infringes his constitutionally protected interests—especially, his interest in freedom of speech. For if the government could deny a benefit to a person because of his constitutionally protected speech or associations, his exercise of those freedoms would in effect be penalized and inhibited. This would allow the government to "produce a result which [it] could not command directly." Such interference with constitutional rights is impermissible.

We have applied this general principle to denials of tax exemptions, and welfare payments. But, most often, we have applied the principle to denials of public employment. We have applied the principle regardless of the public employee's contractual or other claim to a job. Thus, the respondent's lack of a contractual or tenure "right" to re-employment for the 1969–1970 academic year is immaterial to his free speech claim. Indeed, twice before, this Court has specifically held that the nonrenewal of a nontenured public school teacher's one-year contract may not be predicated on his exercise of First and Fourteenth Amendment rights. *Shelton v. Tucker*, 364 U.S. 479; *Keyishian v. Board of Regents*, 385 U.S. 589. We reaffirm those holdings here.

In this case, of course, the respondent has yet to show that the decision not to renew his contract was, in fact, made in retaliation for his exercise of the constitutional right of free speech. The District Court foreclosed any opportunity to make this showing when it granted summary judgment. Hence, we cannot now hold that the Board of Regents' action was invalid.

But we agree with the Court of Appeals that there is a genuine dispute as to "whether the college refused to renew the teaching contract on an impermissible basis—as a reprisal for the exercise of constitutionally protected rights." The respondent has alleged that his nonretention was based on his testimony before legislative committees and his other public statements critical of the Regents' policies. And he has alleged that this public criticism was within the First and Fourteenth Amendments' protection of freedom of speech. Plainly, these allegations present a bona fide constitutional claim. For this Court has held that a teacher's public criticism of his superiors on matters of public concern may be constitutionally protected and may, therefore, be an impermissible basis for termination of his employment. *Pickering v. Board of Education*, 391 U.S. 563.

For this reason we hold that the grant of summary judgment against the respondent, without full exploration of this issue, was improper.

The respondent's lack of formal contractual or tenure security in continued employment at Odessa Junior College, though irrelevant to his free speech claim, is highly relevant to his procedural due process claim. But it may not be entirely dispositive.

We have held today in *Board of Regents v. Roth*, 408 U.S. 564, that the Constitution does not require opportunity for a hearing before the nonrenewal of a nontenured teacher's contract, unless he can show that the decision not to rehire him somehow deprived him of an interest in "liberty" or that he had a "property" interest in continued employment, despite the lack of tenure or a formal contract. In *Roth* the teacher had not made a showing on either point to justify summary judgment in his favor.

Similarly, the respondent here has yet to show that he has been deprived of an interest that could invoke procedural due process protection. As in *Roth*, the mere showing that he was not rehired in one particular job, without more, did not amount to a showing of a loss of liberty. Nor did it amount to a showing of a loss of property.

But the respondent's allegations—which we must construe most favorably to the respondent at this stage of the litigation—do raise a genuine issue as to his interest in continued employment at Odessa Junior College. He alleged that this interest, though not secured by a formal contractual tenure provision, was secured by a no less binding understanding fostered by the college administration. In particular, the respondent alleged that the college had a *de facto* tenure program, and that he had tenure under that program. He claimed that he and others legitimately relied upon an unusual provision that had been in the college's official Faculty Guide for many years:

> "*Teacher Tenure*: Odessa College has no tenure system. The Administration of the College wishes the faculty member to feel that he has permanent tenure as long as his teaching services are satisfactory and as long as he displays a cooperative attitude toward his co-workers and his superiors, and as long as he is happy in his work."

Moreover, the respondent claimed legitimate reliance upon guidelines promulgated by the Coordinating Board of the Texas College and University System that provided that a person, like himself, who had been employed as a teacher in the state college and university system for seven years or more has some form of job tenure. Thus, the respondent offered to prove that a teacher with his long period of service at this particular State College had no less a "property" interest in continued employment than a formally tenured teacher at other colleges, and had no less a procedural due process right to a statement of reasons and a hearing before college officials upon their decision not to retain him.

The respondent alleges that, because he has been employed as a "full-time instructor" or professor within the Texas College and University System for ten years, he should have "tenure" under these provisions.

We have made clear in *Roth, supra,* that "property" interests subject to procedural due process protection are not limited by a few rigid, technical forms. Rather, "property" denotes a broad range of interests that are secured by "existing rules or understandings." A person's interest in a benefit is a "property" interest for due process purposes if there are such rules or mutually explicit understandings that support his claim of entitlement to the benefit and that he may invoke at a hearing. *Ibid.*

A written contract with an explicit tenure provision clearly is evidence of a formal understanding that supports a teacher's claim of entitlement to continued employment unless sufficient "cause" is shown. Yet absence of such an explicit contractual provision may not always foreclose the possibility that a teacher has a "property" interest in re-employment. For example, the law of contracts in most, if not all, jurisdictions long has employed a process by which agreements, though not formalized in writing, may be "implied." Explicit contractual provisions may be supplemented by other agreements implied from "the promisor's words and conduct in the light of the surrounding circumstances." And, "the meaning of [the promisor's] words and acts is found by relating them to the usage of the past."

A teacher, like the respondent, who has held his position for a number of years, might be able to show from the circumstances of this service—and from other relevant facts—that he has a legitimate claim of entitlement to job tenure. Just as this Court has found there to be a "common law of a particular industry or of a particular plant" that may supplement a collective-bargaining agreement, so there may be an unwritten "common law" in a particular university that certain employees shall have the equivalent of tenure. This is particularly likely in a college or university, like Odessa Junior College, that has no explicit tenure system even for senior members of its faculty, but that nonetheless may have created such a system in practice.

In this case, the respondent has alleged the existence of rules and understandings, promulgated and fostered by state officials, that may justify his legitimate claim of entitlement to continued employment absent "sufficient cause." We disagree with the Court of Appeals insofar as it held that a mere subjective "expectancy" is protected by procedural due process, but we agree that the respondent must be given an opportunity to prove the legitimacy of his claim of such entitlement in light of "the policies and practices of the institution." Proof of such a property interest would not, of course, entitle him to reinstatement. But such proof would obligate college officials to grant a hearing at his request, where he could be informed of the grounds for his nonretention and challenge their sufficiency.

Therefore, while we do not wholly agree with the opinion of the Court of Appeals, its judgment remanding this case to the District Court is *Affirmed.*

Post Problem Discussion

1. One of Ms. Anderson's concerns about being non-renewed is likely that it will adversely affect her chances of employment at other schools. In *Roth* and *Sindermann*, the Court touches on the issue of non-retention affecting subsequent employment. In an omitted footnote from *Roth*, the court stated: "Mere proof, for example, that his record of non-retention in one job, taken alone, might make him somewhat less attractive to some other employers would hardly establish the kind of foreclosure of opportunities amounting to a deprivation of 'liberty'." *Roth*, 408 U.S. at 574, n. 13. Given this, what facts do you think Ms. Anderson would need to establish to demonstrate a liberty deprivation in order to be entitled to a statement of reasons for the non-renewal?

2. Assume that at the time Ms. Anderson received her contract, the school principal told Ms. Anderson that if she "does well this school year, the school would be interested in having you stick around long term." Does that change your opinion about whether Ms. Anderson is entitled to any procedural due process protections? Why or why not? If so, what process should be provided?

3. What if Ms. Anderson believed that the real reason for her non-renewal was that she told parents of her special education students that they should be asking the school for an out of district placement at an expensive private school (a topic discussed in detail in Chapter 12), because the school is not providing services that need to be provided. Would that change anything in terms of her procedural due process rights? *See* Section 3.06.

§ 3.06 First Amendment Rights in Employment

As the Court notes in *Perry v. Sindermann*, due process requirements can arise when adverse employment actions are taken against an employee who exercised constitutionally protected rights such as freedom of expression. In a series of cases, the Court has defined the extent and scope of a public employee's right to freedom of expression. For teachers, these rights include the right to academic freedom (discussed in Chapter 4), and the right to speak as citizens about matters of public concern.

As the United States Supreme Court summarized in a case involving an employee's union grievance regarding his termination as chief of police, *Borough of Duryea, Pa. v. Guarnieri*, 131 S. Ct. 2488 (2011):

> When a public employee sues a government employer under the First Amendment's Speech Clause, the employee must show that he or she spoke as a citizen on a matter of public concern. *Connick v. Myers*, 461 U.S. 138, 147 (1983). If an employee does not speak as a citizen, or does not address a matter of public concern, "a federal court is not the appropriate forum in which to review the wisdom of a personnel decision taken by a public agency allegedly in reaction to the employee's behavior." *Ibid.* Even if an employee does speak as a citizen on a matter of public concern, the employee's speech is not automatically privileged. Courts balance the First Amendment interest of the employee against "the interest of the State, as an employer, in promoting the efficiency of the public services it performs through its employees." *Pickering v. Bd. of Ed. of Township High Sch. Dist.*, 391 U.S. 563 (1968).
>
> This framework "reconcile[s] the employee's right to engage in speech and the government employer's right to protect its own legitimate interests in performing its mission." There are some rights and freedoms so fundamental to liberty that they cannot be bargained away in a contract for public employment. "Our responsibility is to ensure that citizens are not deprived of [these] fundamental rights by virtue of working for the government." Nevertheless, a citizen who accepts public employment "must accept certain limitations on his or her freedom." *Garcetti v. Ceballos*, 547 U.S. 410, 418 (2006). The government has a substantial interest in ensuring that all of its operations are efficient and effective. That interest may require broad authority to supervise the conduct of public employees. "When someone who is paid a salary so that she will contribute to an agency's effective operation begins to do or say things that detract from the agency's effective operation, the government employer must have some power to restrain her." *Waters v. Churchill*, 511 U.S. 661, 675 (1994) (plurality opinion). Restraints

are justified by the consensual nature of the employment relationship and by the unique nature of the government's interest.

The following problem explores some of these issues.

Problem 5: "Teaching Chitlins in the Ghetto of Charlotte"

Sylvia Jones is an eighth grade teacher in the Charlotte Middle School. She has been at the school for eight years. She has been recognized as one of the school's superior teachers at various times over the years. Ms. Jones grew up in the Charlotte area, and, after obtaining her master's degree in education, she returned to the area to teach at the middle school. She is a teachers' union building representative, which means she helps protect the collective bargaining rights of teachers who may have disputes with administrators. She is also the chair of the teachers' budget committee, which helps put together the budget for the school to present to the school board for approval.

Ms. Jones maintains a Facebook listing. In the "activities section" of the listing, Ms. Jones listed "teaching chitlins in the ghetto of Charlotte." In the "About Me" section of the listing, she wrote, "I teach in the most ghetto school in Charlotte. Everyone would like to just forget about us including the school board. How do you feel about the way the school board leaves ghetto children behind?" She also included that she was a union building representative and the chair of the teacher budget committee.

Ms. Jones did not block public viewing of her listing or comments, so anyone on the internet could view them. A news reporter saw the Facebook comments and called the school superintendent for a comment. The superintendent promptly removed Ms. Jones from the classroom and initiated a termination hearing. At the hearing, Ms. Jones admitted to making the comments. The board voted to terminate her employment stating that school district employees need to be beyond reproach and Ms. Jones' comments were inappropriate, unprofessional, and demeaning to the school, and to her students.[8]

Does the school board's action violate Ms. Jones' constitutional rights?

Problem Materials

✓ *Pickering v. Board of Education of Township High School*, 391 U.S. 563 (1968)

✓ *Garcetti v. Ceballos*, 547 U.S. 410 (2006)

✓ *Lane v. Franks*,573 U.S. 228 (2014)

---

8. This fact pattern is based on the following news story: Ann Doss Helms, *Teacher's Disciplined for Facebook Postings*, Raleigh News & Observer, November 12, 2008, https://www.heraldonline.com/news/local/article12241319.html (last visited November 15, 2018).

Pickering v. Board of Education of Township High School

391 U.S. 563 (1968)

The Court rules that a teacher cannot constitutionally be compelled to relinquish the First Amendment right that they would otherwise enjoy as a citizen to comment on matters of public interest in connection with the public school where the teacher works.

Mr. Justice Marshall delivered the opinion of the Court.

Appellant Marvin L. Pickering, a teacher in Township High School District 205, Will County, Illinois, was dismissed from his position by the appellee Board of Education for sending a letter to a local newspaper in connection with a recently proposed tax increase that was critical of the way in which the Board and the district superintendent of schools had handled past proposals to raise new revenue for the schools. Appellant's dismissal resulted from a determination by the Board, after a full hearing, that the publication of the letter was "detrimental to the efficient operation and administration of the schools of the district" and hence, under the relevant Illinois statute, Ill. Rev. Stat., c. 122, § 10-22.4 (1963), that "interests of the school require[d] [his dismissal]."

Appellant's claim that his writing of the letter was protected by the First and Fourteenth Amendments was rejected. . . . For the reasons detailed below we agree that appellant's rights to freedom of speech were violated and we reverse.

In February of 1961 the appellee Board of Education asked the voters of the school district to approve a bond issue to raise $4,875,000 to erect two new schools. The proposal was defeated. Then, in December of 1961, the Board submitted another bond proposal to the voters which called for the raising of $5,500,000 to build two new schools. This second proposal passed and the schools were built with the money raised by the bond sales. In May of 1964 a proposed increase in the tax rate to be used for educational purposes was submitted to the voters by the Board and was defeated. Finally, on September 19, 1964, a second proposal to increase the tax rate was submitted by the Board and was likewise defeated. It was in connection with this last proposal of the School Board that appellant wrote the letter to the editor that resulted in his dismissal.

. . . .

The letter constituted, basically, an attack on the School Board's handling of the 1961 bond issue proposals and its subsequent allocation of financial resources between the schools' educational and athletic programs. It also charged the superintendent of schools with attempting to prevent teachers in the district from opposing or criticizing the proposed bond issue.

The Board dismissed Pickering for writing and publishing the letter. Pursuant to Illinois law, the Board was then required to hold a hearing on the dismissal. At the hearing the Board charged that numerous statements in the letter were false and that the publication of the statements unjustifiably impugned the "motives, honesty, integrity, truthfulness, responsibility and competence" of both the Board and the school administration

. . . .

To the extent that the Illinois Supreme Court's opinion may be read to suggest that teachers may constitutionally be compelled to relinquish the First Amendment rights they would otherwise enjoy as citizens to comment on matters of public interest in connection with the operation of the public schools in which they work, it proceeds on a premise that has been unequivocally rejected in numerous prior decisions of this Court. "[T]he theory that public employment which may be denied altogether may be subjected to any conditions, regardless of how unreasonable, has been uniformly rejected." *Keyishian v. Board of Regents*, *supra*, 385 U.S. at 605-606, 87 S.Ct. at 685. At the same time it cannot be gainsaid that the State has interests as an employer in regulating the speech of its employees that differ significantly from those it possesses in connection with regulation of the speech of the citizenry in general. The problem in any case is to arrive at a balance between the interests of the teacher, as a citizen, in commenting upon matters of public concern and the interest of the State, as an employer, in promoting the efficiency of the public services it performs through its employees.

. . . .

An examination of the statements in appellant's letter objected to by the Board reveals that they, like the letter as a whole, consist essentially of criticism of the Board's allocation of school funds between educational and athletic programs, and of both the Board's and the superintendent's methods of informing, or preventing the informing of, the district's taxpayers of the real reasons why additional tax revenues were being sought for the schools. The statements are in no way directed towards any person with whom appellant would normally be in contact in the course of his daily work as a teacher. Thus no question of maintaining either discipline by immediate superiors or harmony among coworkers is presented here. Appellant's employment relationships with the Board and, to a somewhat lesser extent, with the superintendent are not the kind of close working relationships for which it can persuasively be claimed that personal loyalty and confidence are necessary to their proper functioning. Accordingly, to the extent that the Board's position here can be taken to suggest that even comments on matters of public concern that are substantially correct, may furnish grounds for dismissal if they are sufficiently critical in tone, we unequivocally reject it.

We next consider the statements in appellant's letter which we agree to be false. The Board's original charges included allegations that the publication of the letter damaged the professional reputations of the Board and the superintendent and would foment controversy and conflict among the Board, teachers, administrators, and the residents of the district. However, no evidence to support these allegations was introduced at the hearing. So far as the record reveals, Pickering's letter was greeted by everyone but its main target, the Board, with massive apathy and total disbelief. The Board must, therefore, have decided, perhaps by analogy with the law of libel, that the statements were *per se* harmful to the operation of the schools.

However, the only way in which the Board could conclude, absent any evidence of the actual effect of the letter, that the statements contained therein were *per se* detrimental to the interest of the schools was to equate the Board members' own interests with that of the schools. Certainly an accusation that too much money is being spent on athletics by the administrators of the school system . . . cannot reasonably be regarded as *per se* detrimental to the district's schools. Such an accusation reflects rather a difference of opinion between Pickering and the Board as to the preferable manner of operating the school system, a difference of opinion that clearly concerns an issue of general public interest.

In addition, the fact that particular illustrations of the Board's claimed undesirable emphasis on athletic programs are false would not normally have any necessary impact on the actual operation of the schools, beyond its tendency to anger the Board. For example, Pickering's letter was written after the defeat at the polls of the second proposed tax increase. It could, therefore, have had no effect on the ability of the school district to raise necessary revenue, since there was no showing that there was any proposal to increase taxes pending when the letter was written.

More importantly, the question whether a school system requires additional funds is a matter of legitimate public concern on which the judgment of the school administration, including the School Board, cannot, in a society that leaves such questions to popular vote, be taken as conclusive. On such a question free and open debate is vital to informed decision-making by the electorate. Teachers are, as a class, the members of a community most likely to have informed and definite opinions as to how funds allotted to the operation of the schools should be spent. Accordingly, it is essential that they be able to speak out freely on such questions without fear of retaliatory dismissal.

In addition, the amounts expended on athletics which Pickering reported erroneously were matters of public record on which his position as a teacher in the district did not qualify him to speak with any greater authority than any other taxpayer. The Board could easily have rebutted appellant's errors by publishing the accurate figures itself, either via a letter to the same newspaper or otherwise. We are thus not presented with a situation in which a teacher has carelessly made false statements about matters so closely related to the day-to-day operations of the schools that any harmful impact on the public would be difficult to counter because of the teacher's presumed greater access to the real facts. Accordingly, we have no occasion to consider at this time whether under such circumstances a school board could reasonably require that a teacher make substantial efforts to verify the accuracy of his charges before publishing them.

What we do have before us is a case in which a teacher has made erroneous public statements upon issues then currently the subject of public attention, which are critical of his ultimate employer but which are neither shown nor can be presumed to have in any way either impeded teacher's proper performance of his daily duties in the classroom or to have interfered with the regular operation of the schools generally. In these circumstances we conclude that the interest of the school administration in limiting teachers' opportunities to contribute to public debate is not significantly greater than its interest in limiting a similar contribution by any member of the general public.

The public interest in having free and unhindered debate on matters of public importance—the core value of the Free Speech Clause of the First Amendment—is so great that it has been held that a State cannot authorize the recovery of damages by a public official for defamatory statements directed at him except when such statements are shown to have been made either with knowledge of their falsity or with reckless disregard for their truth or falsity. The same test has been applied to suits for invasion of privacy based on false statements where a "matter of public interest" is involved. It is therefore perfectly clear that, were appellant a member of the general public, the State's power to afford the appellee Board of Education or its members any legal right to sue him for writing the letter at issue here would be limited by the requirement that the letter be judged by the standard laid down in *New York Times*.

This Court has also indicated, in more general terms, that statements by public officials on matters of public concern must be accorded First Amendment protection despite the fact that the statements are directed at their nominal superiors. *Garrison v. Louisiana*, 379 U.S. 64 (1964); *Wood v. Georgia*, 370 U.S. 375 (1962). In *Garrison*, the *New York Times* test was specifically applied to a case involving a criminal defamation conviction stemming from statements made by a district attorney about the judges before whom he regularly appeared.

While criminal sanctions and damage awards have a somewhat different impact on the exercise of the right to freedom of speech from dismissal from employment, it is apparent that the threat of dismissal from public employment is nonetheless a potent means of inhibiting speech. We have already noted our disinclination to make an across-the-board equation of dismissal from public employment for remarks critical of superiors with awarding damages in a libel suit by a public official for similar criticism. However, in a case such as the present one, in which the fact of employment is only tangentially and insubstantially involved in the subject matter of the public communication made by a teacher, we conclude that it is necessary to regard the teacher as the member of the general public he seeks to be.

In sum, we hold that, in a case such as this, absent proof of false statements knowingly or recklessly made by him, a teacher's exercise of his right to speak on issues of public importance may not furnish the basis for his dismissal from public employment. Since no such showing has been made in this case regarding appellant's letter, his dismissal for writing it cannot be upheld and the judgment of the Illinois Supreme Court must, accordingly, be reversed and the case remanded for further proceedings not inconsistent with this opinion.

Garcetti v. Ceballos

547 U.S. 410 (2006)

The Court rules that the plaintiff's speech was made pursuant to his official duties as a district attorney, and not as a private citizen, so it was not protected by the First Amendment.

Justice Kennedy delivered the opinion of the Court.

It is well settled that "a State cannot condition public employment on a basis that infringes the employee's constitutionally protected interest in freedom of expression." *Connick v. Myers*, 461 U.S. 138, 142 (1983). The question presented by the instant case is whether the First Amendment protects a government employee from discipline based on speech made pursuant to the employee's official duties.

Respondent Richard Ceballos has been employed since 1989 as a deputy district attorney for the Los Angeles County District Attorney's Office. During the period relevant to this case, Ceballos was a calendar deputy in the office's Pomona branch, and in this capacity he exercised certain supervisory responsibilities over other lawyers. In February 2000, a defense attorney contacted Ceballos about a pending criminal case. The defense attorney said there were inaccuracies in an affidavit used to obtain a critical search warrant. The attorney informed Ceballos that he had filed a motion to traverse, or challenge, the warrant, but he also wanted Ceballos to review the case. According to Ceballos, it was not unusual for defense attorneys to ask calendar deputies to investigate aspects of pending cases.

After examining the affidavit and visiting the location it described, Ceballos determined the affidavit contained serious misrepresentations. . . . Ceballos spoke on the telephone to the warrant affiant, a deputy sheriff from the Los Angeles County Sheriff's Department, but he did not receive a satisfactory explanation for the perceived inaccuracies. He relayed his findings to his supervisors, petitioners Carol Najera and Frank Sundstedt, and followed up by preparing a disposition memorandum. The memo explained Ceballos' concerns and recommended dismissal of the case. On March 2, 2000, Ceballos submitted the memo to Sundstedt for his review. A few days later, Ceballos presented Sundstedt with another memo, this one describing a second telephone conversation between Ceballos and the warrant affiant.

Based on Ceballos' statements, a meeting was held to discuss the affidavit. Attendees included Ceballos, Sundstedt, and Najera, as well as the warrant affiant and other employees from the sheriff's department. The meeting allegedly became heated, with one lieutenant sharply criticizing Ceballos for his handling of the case.

Despite Ceballos' concerns, Sundstedt decided to proceed with the prosecution, pending disposition of the defense motion to traverse. The trial court held a hearing on the motion. Ceballos was called by the defense and recounted his observations about the affidavit, but the trial court rejected the challenge to the warrant.

Ceballos claims that in the aftermath of these events he was subjected to a series of retaliatory employment actions. The actions included reassignment from his calendar deputy position to a trial deputy position, transfer to another courthouse, and denial of a promotion. Ceballos initiated an employment grievance, but the grievance was denied based on a finding that he had not suffered any retaliation. Unsatisfied, Ceballos sued in the United States District Court for the Central District of California, asserting, as relevant here, a claim under Rev. Stat. § 1979, 42 U.S.C. § 1983. He alleged petitioners violated the First and Fourteenth Amendments by retaliating against him based on his memo of March 2.

. . . .

As the Court's decisions have noted, for many years "the unchallenged dogma was that a public employee had no right to object to conditions placed upon the terms of employment—including those which restricted the exercise of constitutional rights." That dogma has been qualified in important respects. The Court has made clear that public employees do not surrender all their First Amendment rights by reason of their employment. Rather, the First Amendment protects a public employee's right, in certain circumstances, to speak as a citizen addressing matters of public concern.

Pickering and the cases decided in its wake identify two inquiries to guide interpretation of the constitutional protections accorded to public employee speech. The first requires determining whether the employee spoke as a citizen on a matter of public concern. If the answer is no, the employee has no First Amendment cause of action based on his or her employer's reaction to the speech. If the answer is yes, then the possibility of a First Amendment claim arises. The question becomes whether the relevant government entity had an adequate justification for treating the employee differently from any other member of the general public. This consideration reflects the importance of the relationship between the speaker's expressions and employment. A government entity has broader discretion to restrict speech when it acts in its role as employer, but the restrictions it imposes must be directed at speech that has some potential to affect the entity's operations.

To be sure, conducting these inquiries sometimes has proved difficult. This is the necessary product of "the enormous variety of fact situations in which critical statements by teachers and other public employees may be thought by their superiors . . . to furnish grounds for dismissal." The Court's overarching objectives, though, are evident.

When a citizen enters government service, the citizen by necessity must accept certain limitations on his or her freedom. *See, e.g., Waters v. Churchill*, 511 U.S. 661, 671 (1994) (plurality opinion) ("[T]he government as employer indeed has far broader powers than does the government as sovereign"). Government employers, like private employers, need a significant degree of control over their employees' words and actions; without it, there would be little chance for the efficient provision of public services. *Cf. Connick v. Meyer*, ("[G]overnment offices could not function if every employment decision became a constitutional matter"). Public employees, moreover, often occupy trusted positions in society. When they speak out, they can express views that contravene governmental policies or impair the proper performance of governmental functions.

At the same time, the Court has recognized that a citizen who works for the government is nonetheless a citizen. The First Amendment limits the ability of a public employer to leverage the employment relationship to restrict, incidentally or intentionally, the liberties employees enjoy in their capacities as private citizens. *See Perry v. Sindermann*, 408 U.S. 593, 597 (1972). So long as employees are speaking as citizens about matters of public concern, they must face only those speech restrictions that are necessary for their employers to operate efficiently and effectively.

. . . .

The Court's decisions, then, have sought both to promote the individual and societal interests that are served when employees speak as citizens on matters of public concern and to respect the needs of government employers attempting to perform their important public functions. Underlying our cases has been the premise that while the First Amendment invests public employees with certain rights, it does not empower them to "constitutionalize the employee grievance."

With these principles in mind we turn to the instant case. Respondent Ceballos believed the affidavit used to obtain a search warrant contained serious misrepresentations. He conveyed his opinion and recommendation in a memo to his supervisor. . . . The memo concerned the subject matter of Ceballos' employment, but this, too, is nondispositive. The First Amendment protects some expressions related to the speaker's job. . . .

The controlling factor in Ceballos' case is that his expressions were made pursuant to his duties as a calendar deputy. That consideration—the fact that Ceballos spoke as a prosecutor fulfilling a responsibility to advise his supervisor about how best to proceed with a pending case—distinguishes Ceballos' case from those in which the First Amendment provides protection against discipline. We hold that when public employees make statements pursuant to their official duties, the employees are not speaking as citizens for First Amendment purposes, and the Constitution does not insulate their communications from employer discipline.

Ceballos wrote his disposition memo because that is part of what he, as a calendar deputy, was employed to do. It is immaterial whether he experienced some personal gratification from writing the memo; his First Amendment rights do not depend on his job satisfaction. The significant point is that the memo was written pursuant to Ceballos' official duties. Restricting speech that owes its existence to a public employee's professional responsibilities does not infringe any liberties the employee might have enjoyed as a private citizen. It simply reflects the exercise of employer control over what the employer itself has commissioned or created. Contrast, for example, the expressions made by the speaker in *Pickering*, whose letter to the newspaper had no official significance and bore similarities to letters submitted by numerous citizens every day.

Ceballos did not act as a citizen when he went about conducting his daily professional activities, such as supervising attorneys, investigating charges, and preparing filings. In the same way he did not speak as a citizen by writing a memo that addressed the proper disposition of a pending criminal case. When he went to work and performed the tasks he was paid to perform, Ceballos acted as a government employee. The fact that his duties sometimes required him to speak or write does not mean his supervisors were prohibited from evaluating his performance.

This result is consistent with our precedents' attention to the potential societal value of employee speech. Refusing to recognize First Amendment claims based on government employees' work product does not prevent them from participating in public debate. The employees retain the prospect of constitutional protection for their contributions to the civic discourse. This prospect of protection, however, does not invest them with a right to perform their jobs however they see fit.

Our holding likewise is supported by the emphasis of our precedents on affording government employers sufficient discretion to manage their operations. Employers have heightened interests in controlling speech made by an employee in his or her professional capacity. Official communications have official consequences, creating a need for substantive consistency and clarity. Supervisors must ensure that their employees' official communications are accurate, demonstrate sound judgment, and promote the employer's mission. Ceballos' memo is illustrative. It demanded the attention of his supervisors and led to a heated meeting with employees from the sheriff's department. If Ceballos' superiors thought his memo was inflammatory or misguided, they had the authority to take proper corrective action.

. . . When an employee speaks as a citizen addressing a matter of public concern, the First Amendment requires a delicate balancing of the competing interests surrounding the speech and its consequences. When, however, the employee is simply performing his or her job duties, there is no warrant for a similar degree of scrutiny. To hold otherwise would be to demand permanent judicial intervention in the conduct of governmental operations to a degree inconsistent with sound principles of federalism and the separation of powers.

. . . .

Proper application of our precedents thus leads to the conclusion that the First Amendment does not prohibit managerial discipline based on an employee's expressions made pursuant to official responsibilities. Because Ceballos' memo falls into this category, his allegation of unconstitutional retaliation must fail.

Two final points warrant mentioning. First, as indicated above, the parties in this case do not dispute that Ceballos wrote his disposition memo pursuant to his employment duties. We thus have no occasion to articulate a comprehensive framework for defining the scope of an employee's duties in cases where there is room for serious debate. We reject, however, the suggestion that employers can restrict employees' rights by creating excessively broad job descriptions. The proper inquiry is a practical one. Formal job descriptions often bear little resemblance to the duties an employee actually is expected to perform, and the listing of a given task in an employee's written job description is neither necessary nor sufficient to demonstrate that conducting the task is within the scope of the employee's professional duties for First Amendment purposes.

Second, JUSTICE SOUTER suggests today's decision may have important ramifications for academic freedom, at least as a constitutional value. There is some argument that expression related to academic scholarship or classroom instruction implicates additional constitutional interests that are not fully accounted for by this Court's customary employee-speech jurisprudence. We need not, and for that reason do not, decide whether the analysis we conduct today would apply in the same manner to a case involving speech related to scholarship or teaching.

Exposing governmental inefficiency and misconduct is a matter of considerable significance. As the Court noted in *Connick*, public employers should, "as a matter of good judgment," be "receptive to constructive criticism offered by their employees." The dictates of sound judgment are reinforced by the powerful network of legislative enactments—such as whistle-blower protection laws and labor codes—available to those who seek to expose wrongdoing. Cases involving government attorneys implicate additional safeguards in the form of, for example, rules of conduct and constitutional obligations apart from the First Amendment. These imperatives, as well as obligations arising from any other applicable constitutional provisions and mandates of the criminal and civil laws, protect employees and provide checks on supervisors who would order unlawful or otherwise inappropriate actions.

We reject, however, the notion that the First Amendment shields from discipline the expressions employees make pursuant to their professional duties. Our precedents do not support the existence of a constitutional cause of action behind every statement a public employee makes in the course of doing his or her job.

The judgment of the Court of Appeals is reversed, and the case is remanded for proceedings consistent with this opinion.

JUSTICE SOUTER, with whom JUSTICE STEVENS and JUSTICE GINSBURG join, dissenting.

The Court holds that "when public employees make statements pursuant to their official duties, the employees are not speaking as citizens for First Amendment purposes, and the Constitution does not insulate their communications from employer discipline." I respectfully dissent. I agree with the majority that a government employer has substantial interests in effectuating its chosen policy and objectives, and in demanding competence, honesty, and judgment from employees who speak for it in doing their work. But I would hold that private and public interests in addressing official wrongdoing and threats to health and safety can outweigh the government's stake in the efficient implementation of policy, and when they do public employees who speak on these matters in the course of their duties should be eligible to claim First Amendment protection ....

This ostensible domain beyond the pale of the First Amendment is spacious enough to include even the teaching of a public university professor, and I have to hope that today's majority does not mean to imperil First Amendment protection of academic freedom in public colleges and universities, whose teachers necessarily speak and write "pursuant to . . . official duties." *See Grutter v. Bollinger*, 539 U.S. 306, 329 (2003) ("We have long recognized that, given the important purpose of public education and the expansive freedoms of speech and thought associated with the university environment, universities occupy a special niche in our constitutional tradition"); *Keyishian v. Board of Regents of Univ. of State of N.Y.*, 385 U.S. 589, 603 (1967) ("Our Nation is deeply committed to safeguarding academic freedom, which is of transcendent value to all of us and not merely to the teachers concerned. That freedom is therefore a special concern of the First Amendment, which does not tolerate laws that cast a pall of orthodoxy over the classroom. 'The vigilant protection of constitutional freedoms is nowhere more vital than in the community of American schools'" (quoting *Shelton v. Tucker*, 364 U.S. 479, 487 (1960))); *Sweezy v. New Hampshire*, 354 U.S. 234, 250 (1957) (a governmental enquiry into the contents of a scholar's lectures at a state university "unquestionably was an invasion of [his] liberties in the areas of academic freedom and political expression—areas in which government should be extremely reticent to tread").

Lane v. Franks

573 U.S. 228 (2014)

The Court rules that the plaintiff's speech is protected, even though the content of the speech involved his employment, because the speech was "outside the scope of his ordinary job duties."

Justice Sotomayor delivered the opinion of the Court.

Almost 50 years ago, this Court declared that citizens do not surrender their First Amendment rights by accepting public employment. Rather, the First Amendment protection of a public employee's speech depends on a careful balance "between the interests of the [employee], as a citizen, in commenting upon matters of public concern and the interest of the State, as an employer, in promoting the efficiency of the public services it performs through its employees." *Pickering v. Board of Ed. of Township High School Dist. 205, Will Cty.*, 391 U.S. 563, 568, (1968). In *Pickering*, the Court struck the balance in favor of the public employee, extending First Amendment protection to a teacher who was fired after writing a letter to the editor of a local newspaper criticizing the school board that employed him. Today, we consider whether the First Amendment similarly protects a public employee who provided truthful sworn testimony, compelled by subpoena, outside the course of his ordinary job responsibilities. We hold that it does.

I

In 2006, Central Alabama Community College (CACC) hired petitioner Edward Lane to be the Director of Community Intensive Training for Youth (CITY), a statewide program for underprivileged youth. CACC hired Lane on a probationary basis. In his capacity as Director, Lane was responsible for overseeing CITY's day-to-day operations, hiring and firing employees, and making decisions with respect to the program's finances. At the time of Lane's appointment, CITY faced significant financial difficulties. That prompted Lane to conduct a comprehensive audit of the program's expenses. The audit revealed that Suzanne Schmitz, an Alabama State Representative on CITY's payroll, had not been reporting to her CITY office. After unfruitful discussions with Schmitz, Lane shared his finding with CACC's president and its attorney. They warned him that firing Schmitz could have negative repercussions for him and CACC.

Lane nonetheless contacted Schmitz again and instructed her to show up to the Huntsville office to serve as a counselor. Schmitz refused; she responded that she wished to "'continue to serve the CITY program in the same manner as [she had] in the past.'" Lane fired her shortly thereafter. Schmitz told another CITY employee, Charles Foley, that she intended to "'get [Lane] back'" for firing her. She also said that if Lane ever requested money from the state legislature for the program, she would tell him, "'[y]ou're fired.'"

Schmitz' termination drew the attention of many, including agents of the Federal Bureau of Investigation, which initiated an investigation into Schmitz' employment with CITY. In November 2006, Lane testified before a federal grand jury about his reasons for firing Schmitz. In January 2008, the grand jury indicted Schmitz on four counts of mail fraud and four counts of theft concerning a program receiving federal funds. The indictment alleged that Schmitz had collected $177,251.82 in federal funds even though she performed "'virtually no services,'" "'generated virtually no work product,'" and "'rarely even appeared for work at the CITY Program offices.'" It further alleged that Schmitz had submitted false statements concerning the hours she worked and the nature of the services she performed.

Schmitz' trial, which garnered extensive press coverage, commenced in August 2008. Lane testified, under subpoena, regarding the events that led to his terminating Schmitz. The jury failed to reach a verdict. Roughly six months later, federal prosecutors retried Schmitz, and Lane testified once again. This time, the jury convicted Schmitz on three counts of mail fraud and four counts of theft concerning a program receiving federal funds. The District Court sentenced her to 30 months in prison and ordered her to pay $177,251.82 in restitution and forfeiture.

Meanwhile, CITY continued to experience considerable budget shortfalls. In November 2008, Lane began reporting to respondent Steve Franks, who had become president of CACC in January 2008. Lane recommended that Franks consider layoffs to address the financial difficulties. In January 2009, Franks decided to terminate 29 probationary CITY employees, including Lane. Shortly thereafter, however, Franks rescinded all but 2 of the 29 terminations—those of Lane and one other employee—because of an "ambiguity in [those other employees'] probationary service." Franks claims that he "did not rescind Lane's termination . . . because he believed that Lane was in a fundamentally different category than the other employees: he was the director of the entire CITY program, and not simply an employee." In September 2009, CACC eliminated the CITY program and terminated the program's remaining employees. Franks later retired, and respondent Susan Burrow, the current Acting President of CACC, replaced him while this case was pending before the Eleventh Circuit.

In January 2011, Lane sued Franks in his individual and official capacities under Rev. Stat. § 1979, 42 U.S.C. § 1983, alleging that Franks had violated the First Amendment by firing him in retaliation for his testimony against Schmitz. Lane sought damages from Franks in his individual capacity and sought equitable relief, including reinstatement, from Franks in his official capacity.

. . . .

II

Speech by citizens on matters of public concern lies at the heart of the First Amendment, which "was fashioned to assure unfettered interchange of ideas for the bringing about of political and social changes desired by the people." This remains true when speech concerns information related to or learned through public employment. After all, public employees do not renounce their citizenship when they accept employment, and this Court has cautioned time and again that public employers may not condition employment on the relinquishment of constitutional rights. There is considerable value, moreover, in encouraging, rather than inhibiting, speech by public employees. For "[g]overnment employees are often in the best position to know what ails the agencies for which they work." "The interest at stake is as much the public's interest in receiving informed opinion as it is the employee's own right to disseminate it."

Our precedents have also acknowledged the government's countervailing interest in controlling the operation of its workplaces. *See, e.g., Pickering,* 391 U.S., at 568. "Government employers, like private employers, need a significant degree of control over their employees' words and actions; without it, there would be little chance for the efficient provision of public services." *Garcetti,* 547 U.S., at 418.

Pickering provides the framework for analyzing whether the employee's interest or the government's interest should prevail in cases where the government seeks to curtail the speech of its employees. It requires "balanc[ing] . . . the interests of the [public employee], as a citizen, in commenting upon matters of public concern and the interest of the State, as an employer, in promoting the efficiency of the public services it performs through its employees." In *Pickering,* the Court held that a teacher's letter to the editor of a local newspaper concerning a school budget constituted speech on a matter of public concern. And in balancing the employee's interest in such speech against the government's efficiency interest, the Court held that the publication of the letter did not "imped[e] the teacher's proper performance of his daily duties in the classroom" or "interfer[e] with the regular operation of the schools generally." The Court therefore held that the teacher's speech could not serve as the basis for his dismissal.

In *Garcetti,* we described a two-step inquiry into whether a public employee's speech is entitled to protection:

> "The first requires determining whether the employee spoke as a citizen on a matter of public concern. If the answer is no, the employee has no First Amendment cause of action based on his or her employer's reaction to the speech. If the answer is yes, then the possibility of a First Amendment claim arises. The question becomes whether the relevant government entity had an adequate justification for treating the employee differently from any other member of the general public."

In describing the first step in this inquiry, *Garcetti* distinguished between employee speech and citizen speech. Whereas speech as a citizen may trigger protection, the Court held that "when public employees make statements pursuant to their official duties, the employees are not speaking as citizens for First Amendment purposes, and the Constitution does not insulate their communications from employer discipline." Applying that rule to the facts before it, the Court found that an internal memorandum prepared by a prosecutor in the course of his ordinary job responsibilities constituted unprotected employee speech.

III

Against this backdrop, we turn to the question presented: whether the First Amendment protects a public employee who provides truthful sworn testimony, compelled by subpoena, outside the scope of his ordinary job responsibilities. We hold that it does.

A

The first inquiry is whether the speech in question—Lane's testimony at Schmitz' trials—is speech as a citizen on a matter of public concern. It clearly is.

1

Truthful testimony under oath by a public employee outside the scope of his ordinary job duties is speech as a citizen for First Amendment purposes. That is so even when the testimony relates to his public employment or concerns information learned during that employment.

In rejecting Lane's argument that his testimony was speech as a citizen, the Eleventh Circuit gave short shrift to the nature of sworn judicial statements and ignored the obligation borne by all witnesses testifying under oath. Sworn testimony in judicial proceedings is a quintessential example of speech as a citizen for a simple reason: Anyone who testifies in court bears an obligation, to the court and society at large, to tell the truth. When the person testifying is a public employee, he may bear separate obligations to his employer—for example, an obligation not to show up to court dressed in an unprofessional manner. But any such obligations as an employee are distinct and independent from the obligation, as a citizen, to speak the truth. That independent obligation renders sworn testimony speech as a citizen and sets it apart from speech made purely in the capacity of an employee.

In holding that Lane did not speak as a citizen when he testified, the Eleventh Circuit read *Garcetti* far too broadly. It reasoned that, because Lane learned of the subject matter of his testimony in the course of his employment with CITY, *Garcetti* requires that his testimony be treated as the speech of an employee rather than that of a citizen. It does not.

The sworn testimony in this case is far removed from the speech at issue in *Garcetti*—an internal memorandum prepared by a deputy district attorney for his supervisors recommending dismissal of a particular prosecution. The *Garcetti* Court held that such speech was made pursuant to the employee's "official responsibilities" because "[w]hen [the employee] went to work and performed the tasks he was paid to perform, [he] acted as a government employee. The fact that his duties sometimes required him to speak or write does not mean that his supervisors were prohibited from evaluating his performance."

But *Garcetti* said nothing about speech that simply relates to public employment or concerns information learned in the course of public employment. The *Garcetti* Court made explicit that its holding did not turn on the fact that the memo at issue "concerned the subject matter of [the prosecutor's] employment," because "[t]he First Amendment protects some expressions related to the speaker's job." In other words, the mere fact that a citizen's speech concerns information acquired by virtue of his public employment does not transform that speech into employee—rather than citizen—speech. The critical question under *Garcetti* is whether the speech at issue is itself ordinarily within the scope of an employee's duties, not whether it merely concerns those duties.

It bears emphasis that our precedents dating back to *Pickering* have recognized that speech by public employees on subject matter related to their employment holds special value precisely because those employees gain knowledge of matters of public concern through their employment. In *Pickering*, for example, the Court observed that "[t]eachers are . . . the members of a community most likely to have informed and definite opinions as to how funds allotted to the operation of the schools should be spent. Accordingly, it is essential that they be able to speak out freely on such questions without fear of retaliatory dismissal." Most recently, in *San Diego v. Roe*, [543 U. S. 77 (2004),] the Court again observed that public employees "are uniquely qualified to comment" on "matters concerning government policies that are of interest to the public at large."

The importance of public employee speech is especially evident in the context of this case: a public corruption scandal. The United States, for example, represents that because "[t]he more than 1000 prosecutions for federal corruption offenses that are brought in a typical year . . . often depend on evidence about activities that government officials undertook while in office," those prosecutions often "require testimony from other government employees." Brief for United States as *Amicus Curiae* 20. It would be antithetical to our jurisprudence to conclude that the very kind of speech necessary to prosecute corruption by public officials—speech by public employees regarding information learned through their employment—may never form the basis for a First Amendment retaliation claim. Such a rule would place public employees who witness corruption in an impossible position, torn between the obligation to testify truthfully and the desire to avoid retaliation and keep their jobs.

Applying these principles, it is clear that Lane's sworn testimony is speech as a citizen.

2

Lane's testimony is also speech on a matter of public concern. Speech involves matters of public concern "when it can 'be fairly considered as relating to any matter of political, social, or other concern to the community,' or when it 'is a subject of legitimate news interest; that is, a subject of general interest and of value and concern to the public.'" The inquiry turns on the "content, form, and context" of the speech.

The content of Lane's testimony—corruption in a public program and misuse of state funds—obviously involves a matter of significant public concern. And the form and context of the speech—sworn testimony in a judicial proceeding—fortify that conclusion. "Unlike speech in other contexts, testimony under oath has the formality and gravity necessary to remind the witness that his or her statements will be the basis for official governmental action, action that often affects the rights and liberties of others."

. . . .

We hold, then, that Lane's truthful sworn testimony at Schmitz' criminal trials is speech as a citizen on a matter of public concern.

B

This does not settle the matter, however. A public employee's sworn testimony is not categorically entitled to First Amendment protection simply because it is speech as a citizen on a matter of public concern. Under *Pickering,* if an employee speaks as a citizen on a matter of public concern, the next question is whether the government had "an adequate justification for treating the employee differently from any other member of the public" based on the government's needs as an employer.

As discussed previously, we have recognized that government employers often have legitimate "interest[s] in the effective and efficient fulfillment of [their] responsibilities to the public," including "'promot[ing] efficiency and integrity in the discharge of official duties,'" and "'maintain[ing] proper discipline in public service.'" We have also cautioned, however, that "a stronger showing [of government interests] may be necessary if the employee's speech more substantially involve[s] matters of public concern."

Here, the employer's side of the *Pickering* scale is entirely empty: Respondents do not assert, and cannot demonstrate, any government interest that tips the balance in their favor. There is no evidence, for example, that Lane's testimony at Schmitz' trials was false or erroneous or that Lane unnecessarily disclosed any sensitive, confidential, or privileged information while testifying. In these circumstances, we conclude that Lane's speech is entitled to protection under the First Amendment. The Eleventh Circuit erred in holding otherwise and dismissing Lane's claim of retaliation on that basis.

....

For the foregoing reasons, the judgment of the United States Court of Appeals for the Eleventh Circuit is affirmed in part and reversed in part, and the case is remanded for further proceedings consistent with this opinion.

It is so ordered.

Post Problem Discussion

1. What do these cases tell us about whether the school board's actions in our problem violate Ms. Jones' constitutional rights? Was she speaking as a citizen? Did her speech concern a matter of public concern? Given the facts, would the school board be justified in disciplining her even if she was speaking as a citizen on a matter of public concern?

2. Review the dissents in *Garcetti* by Justice Souter and Justice Breyer online. What do they add to the discussion about the appropriate legal standards to apply to Ms. Jones' comments? What implications do the *Garcetti* and *Lane* cases have regarding academic freedom? See Section 4.04 for more on academic freedom.

3. How does the substance of the expression affect the First Amendment analysis? Another teacher in the news article upon which the problem is based reportedly wrote in his Facebook listing that his favorite activity was "drinking." Yet another wrote, "I am pissed today because I hate my students." Would your analysis of these teachers' First Amendment claims (and their potential success or failure) be any different from Ms. Jones' claims? Why or why not?

4. Does the impact of Ms. Jones' remarks on the students at the school make any difference in the success or failure of her claims under the First Amendment? For example, what if Ms. Jones' students rallied to support her? Say dozens of her students show up at the termination hearing to testify on her behalf, and ask the board to keep her because she is such a good teacher. How, if at all, does that affect the First Amendment analysis?

Chapter 4

Instruction & Curricular Issues

Synopsis

§ 4.01 Introduction

Curriculum is the core of education. All branches and all levels of government have a role in curriculum issues. State and federal statutes and regulations establish content and proficiency standards that local schools must meet when developing and implementing their curriculum. Courts play an oversight and central role setting the constitutional parameters, typically around the First and Fourteenth Amendments. Early court cases focused on the question of who is in control of schooling and curriculum choices. *See Meyer v. Nebraska*, 262 U.S. 390 (1923); *Pierce v. Society of Sisters*, 268 U.S. 510 (1925). These cases are still used as the basis for parental due process claims regarding their liberty interest in directing the upbringing and education of their children. Most other court cases dealing with curriculum involve First Amendment issues at least in part—what books, who assigns, who decides, who can opt in and out. There is also some crossover with curriculum issues and questions of educational adequacy, discussed in Chapter 2.

As important as the substance of curriculum are considerations of the participants present in the curriculum discussion and debate. As with other education matters, various levels of government—federal, state, local—and various individual participants—teachers, administrators, parents, school board members, and students—all play a role in setting the parameters for curriculum, and the actual curriculum. This Chapter focuses on both the controversial issues embedded in the decisions about the substantive curriculum, and on the significance and hierarchical relationships of the various decision-makers.

§ 4.02 The Curriculum in Statute

A. State Law

States generally have statutory and regulatory requirements regarding the curriculum that schools must provide. Often, the requirements provide frameworks that allow local schools some flexibility in the courses that are developed and offered to students. Each state's curriculum frameworks and requirements will be different as they address required courses, required subject matter, required learning results, and, in some cases, requirements for approaching alternative courses or materials. The excerpts here from New Mexico illustrate an overall approach authorizing curriculum frameworks, and then a specific example grounded in New Mexico's history and population.

Core Curriculum Framework; Purpose; Curriculum,

N.M. Stat. Ann. § 22-13-1.5

A. School districts and charter schools may create core curriculum frameworks to provide high quality curricula in kindergarten through grade six to prepare students for pre-advanced placement and advanced placement coursework in grades seven through twelve.

B. The framework shall include:

(1) a curriculum that is aligned with state academic content and performance standards that is challenging, specific as to content and sequential from grade to grade, similar to a core curriculum sequence;

(2) in-depth professional development for teachers that includes vertical teaming in content areas; and

(3) content, materials and instructional strategies or methodologies that current research demonstrates are likely to lead to improved student achievement in pre-advanced placement and advanced placement coursework in grades seven through twelve.

C. The framework may be selected from previously developed curricula or may be developed by the school district or charter school.

D. A school district or charter school that meets department eligibility requirements may apply to the department for support of its core curriculum framework. Applications shall be in the form prescribed by the department and shall include the following information:

(1) a statement of need;

(2) goals and expected outcomes of the framework;

(3) a detailed description of the curriculum to be implemented;

(4) a detailed work plan and budget for the framework;

(5) documentation of the research upon which the anticipated success of the framework is based;

(6) a description of any partnership proposed to implement the framework, supported by letters of commitment from the partner;

(7) an evaluation plan; and

(8) any other information that the department requires.

E. The department shall award grants within ninety days of the deadline for receipt of grant applications.

F. The department shall adopt and promulgate rules to implement the provisions of this section.

Chapter 22. Public Schools Article 23.

Bilingual Multicultural Education

N.M. Stat. Ann. § 22-23-1.1

22-23-1.1. Legislative findings. The legislature finds that:

A. While state and federal combined funding for New Mexico's bilingual multicultural education programs was forty-one million dollars ($41,000,000) in 2003, the funds do not directly support bilingual multicultural education program instruction;

B. The state's bilingual multicultural education program goals are for all students, including English language learners, to:

(1) become bilingual and biliterate in English and a second language, including Spanish, a Native American language, where a written form exists and there is tribal approval, or another language; and

(2) meet state academic content standards and benchmarks in all subject areas;

C. Districts do not fully understand how to properly assess, place and monitor students in bilingual multicultural education programs so that the students may become academically successful;

D. Because inaccurate reporting on student participation in bilingual multicultural education programs has a direct impact on state and federal funding, accountability measures are necessary to track bilingual multicultural education program funds;

E. The federal No Child Left Behind Act of 2001 [20 USCS § 6301 et seq.] does not preclude using state funds for bilingual multicultural education programs;

F. Article 12, Section 8 of the constitution of New Mexico recognizes the value of bilingualism as an educational tool;

G. Professional development is needed for district employees, including teachers, teacher assistants, principals, bilingual directors or coordinators, associate superintendents, superintendents and financial officers in the areas of:

(1) research-based bilingual multicultural education programs and implications for instruction;

(2) best practices of English as a second language, English language development and bilingual multicultural education programs; and

(3) classroom assessments that support academic and language development;

H. Parents in conjunction with teachers and other district employees shall be empowered to decide what type of bilingual multicultural education program works best for their children and their community. Districts shall also provide parents with appropriate training in English or in the home or heritage language to help their children succeed in school;

I. Because research has shown that it takes five to seven years to acquire academic proficiency in a second language, priority should be given to programs that adequately support a child's linguistic development. The state shall, therefore, fund bilingual multicultural education programs for students in grades kindergarten through three before funding bilingual multicultural education programs at higher grade levels;

J. A standardized curriculum, including instructional materials with scope and sequence, is necessary to ensure that the bilingual multicultural education program is consistent and building on the language skills the students have previously learned. The instructional materials for Native American bilingual multicultural education programs shall be written, when permitted by the Indian nation, tribe or pueblo, and if written materials are not available, an oral standardized curriculum shall be implemented;

K. Equitable and culturally relevant learning environments, educational opportunities and culturally relevant instructional materials for all students participating in the program. For Native American students enrolled in public schools, equitable and culturally relevant learning environments, educational opportunities and culturally relevant instructional materials are required to satisfy a goal of the Indian Education Act [22-23A-1 NMSA 1978]; and

L. The Bilingual Multicultural Education Act [22-23-1 NMSA 1978] will ensure equal education opportunities for students in New Mexico. Cognitive and affective development of the students is encouraged by:

(1) using the cultural and linguistic backgrounds of the students in a bilingual multicultural education program;

(2) providing students with opportunities to expand their conceptual and linguistic abilities and potentials in a successful and positive manner; and

(3) teaching students to appreciate the value and beauty of different languages and cultures.

B. Federal Law

Title I of the Elementary and Secondary Education Act ("ESEA"), as amended by the Every Student Succeeds Act ("ESSA"), plays a role in curriculum decisions by conditioning certain federal funds on states developing content and achievement standards in areas like language arts, mathematics, and science, along with statewide assessment tests that are aligned with those standards. 20 U.S.C. § 6311. These requirements, in turn, influence curriculum standards and frameworks at the state level, which influence the actual curriculum, and what is taught, at the local level.

Activity 1: Find Curriculum Requirements

Take the following steps to explore the curriculum requirements in your state:

Step One—Search your state statutes and regulations. What, if anything, do they say about curriculum requirements in your state?

Step Two—Go to the website for your state department of education and look for information about ESEA (often referred to as "Title I"), ESSA, accountability, assessment, and curriculum.

Step Three—Find your state curriculum frameworks or guidelines for public schools on your state department of education website. These documents often contain content and proficiency/achievement standards that are aligned with your statewide assessment test(s). If your state adopted the Common Core standards, you can find information about them on this website: http://www.corestandards.org/standards-in-your-state/.

Step Three—Review the curriculum guidelines or frameworks. What do they say about the substantive requirements for curriculum subjects like math, language arts, and science? Does your state have frameworks for other topics like social studies, art, technology, or career development? Did your state adopt the Common Core standards? If so, what changes did they make to prior state standards?

Step Four—Find the curriculum for a local public school online for an example of how a local school implements the state standards and consider the relationship between the local curriculum and state and federal requirements.

§ 4.03 The Curriculum in Real Life

A. English as a Second Language

Emma Lazarus' poem on the Statue of Liberty proclaims,

Give me your tired, your poor,
Your huddled masses yearning to breathe free,

The wretched refuse of your teeming shore.
Send these, the homeless, tempest-tost to me,
I lift my lamp beside the golden door!

And indeed, over the years, millions of immigrants have come to America, bringing with them their quest to live in America, and their native cultures and languages. As the children from various societies entered public school, issues around language added to the complexity of education. In 1919, the State of Nebraska passed a law that prohibited teaching students any language other than English until after the student had passed the eighth grade. *Meyer v. Nebraska*, 262 U.S. at 397. A private parochial school teacher was convicted of a misdemeanor for violating the law, and the state supreme court upheld the conviction noting:

> The salutary purpose of the statute is clear. The Legislature had seen the baneful effects of permitting foreigners, who had taken residence in this country, to rear and educate their children in the language of their native land. The result of that condition was found to be inimical to our own safety. To allow the children of foreigners, who had emigrated here, to be taught from early childhood the language of the country of their parents was to rear them with that language as their mother tongue. It was to educate them so that they must always think in that language, and, as a consequence, naturally inculcate in them the ideas and sentiments foreign to the best interests of this country.
>
> The statute, therefore, was intended not only to require that the education of all children be conducted in the English language, but that, until they had grown into that language and until it had become a part of them, they should not in the schools be taught any other language. The obvious purpose of this statute was that the English language should be and become the mother tongue of all children reared in this state. The enactment of such a statute comes reasonably within the police power of the state.

Id. at 398. The United States Supreme Court reversed stating:

> The Supreme Court of the state has held that "the so-called ancient or dead languages" are not "within the spirit or the purpose of the act." Latin, Greek, Hebrew are not proscribed; but German, French, Spanish, Italian, and every other alien speech are within the ban. Evidently the Legislature has attempted materially to interfere with the calling of modern language teachers, with the opportunities of pupils to acquire knowledge, and with the power of parents to control the education of their own.
>
> It is said the purpose of the legislation was to promote civic development by inhibiting training and education of the immature in foreign tongues and ideals before they could learn English and acquire American ideals, and "that the English language should be and become the mother tongue

> of all children reared in this state." It is also affirmed that the foreign born population is very large, that certain communities commonly use foreign words, follow foreign leaders, move in a foreign atmosphere, and that the children are thereby hindered from becoming citizens of the most useful type and the public safety is imperiled.
>
> That the state may do much, go very far, indeed, in order to improve the quality of its citizens, physically, mentally and morally, is clear; but the individual has certain fundamental rights which must be respected. The protection of the Constitution extends to all, to those who speak other languages as well as to those born with English on the tongue. Perhaps it would be highly advantageous if all had ready understanding of our ordinary speech, but this cannot be coerced by methods which conflict with the Constitution—a desirable end cannot be promoted by prohibited means.
>
> ....
>
> No emergency has arisen which renders knowledge by a child of some language other than English so clearly harmful as to justify its inhibition with the consequent infringement of rights long freely enjoyed. We are constrained to conclude that the statute as applied is arbitrary and without reasonable relation to any end within the competency of the state.

Meyer, 262 U.S. at 401–402.

Since that time, the debate has continued about the best way to educate students whose native language is not English. According to the 2018 Condition of Education Report by the National Center of Education Statistics, 9.5 percent of students in public elementary and secondary schools fit into the category of English language learners (or "ELL" students) in the Fall of 2015.[1] This amounts to 4.8 million students, which is up from 3.8 million in the Fall of 2000.

Not surprisingly, courts are involved with language issues in public schools. In 1974, the United States Supreme Court decided a case brought on behalf of young non-English speaking Chinese students in San Francisco. The Court ruled that schools cannot ignore the needs of limited English speaking children and must adopt some program that will offer them "a meaningful opportunity to participate in the educational program" offered by the school district. *Lau v. Nichols*, 414 U.S. 563, 568 (1974).

Lau became part of the vocabulary for planning at the state and district level to respond to these demonstrated needs, and fostered an era of *Lau* plans and programs. The basic principle of *Lau* was codified in a federal law called the Equal Educational Opportunities Act, which prohibits any State from "deny[ing] equal educational

1. *The Condition of Education Report 2018*, National Center of Education Statistics, available at https://nces.ed.gov/pubsearch/pubsinfo.asp?pubid=2018144 (last visited November 18, 2018).

opportunity to an individual on account of his or her race, color, sex, or national origin" by failing "to take appropriate action to overcome language barriers that impede equal participation by its students in its instructional programs." 20 U.S.C. § 1703(f). The plaintiffs in *Lau* did not ask for a specific approach to be imposed, and courts reviewing the issue after *Lau* continue to recognize a lack of expert consensus as to a "best" approach. For example, writing in 1981, the Fifth Circuit observed:

> The state of the art in the area of language remediation may well be such that respected authorities legitimately differ as to the best type of educational program for limited English speaking students and we do not believe that Congress in enacting § 1703(f) intended to make the resolution of these differences the province of federal courts. The court's responsibility, insofar as educational theory is concerned, is only to ascertain that a school system is pursuing a program informed by an educational theory recognized as sound by some experts in the field or, at least, deemed a legitimate experimental strategy.

Castaneda v. Pickard, 648 F.2d 989 (5th Cir. 1981). (*Castaneda* and § 1703 are both subjects of the *Horne v. Flores*, 129 S. Ct. 2579 (2009), opinion, included with Problem 1.)

The ESSA provides funds for states to provide language assistance programs to ELL students to help ensure that they attain English proficiency, and to help them meet the same academic content and achievement standards that all students are expected to meet under state and federal law. 20 U.S.C. §§ 6311-6212, 6825-6826. The following problem gives you a chance to explore ELL requirements in more detail.

Problem 1: El Plan de Estudios en la Vida Real

You have been asked to review your state's requirements for ELL students to ensure that they meet ESSA and 20 U.S.C. § 1703 requirements. Portions of the ESSA requirements are in the problem materials along with a Supreme Court case regarding § 1703. Review this information and then research your state's requirements to determine if any changes need to be made to come into compliance.

You should be able to access your state's ESSA plan on your state's department of education website. This plan should detail the state's ELL efforts with respect to accountability and assessment requirements. You should also search your state statutes and regulations for ELL requirements.

Problem Materials

✓ *Lau v. Nichols*, 414 U.S. 563 (1974)

✓ *Horne v. Flores*, 129 S. Ct. 2579 (2009)

✓ ESSA excerpts,

✓ Additional online research on your state's ELL requirements.

Lau v. Nichols

414 U.S. 563 (1974)

The Supreme Court finds that failure to address the language issues presented by Chinese-speaking minority students violates civil rights protections under the Civil Rights Act of 1964.

Mr. Justice Douglas delivered the opinion of the Court,

The San Francisco, California, school system was integrated in 1971 as a result of a federal court decree. The District Court found that there are 2,856 students of Chinese ancestry in the school system who do not speak English. Of those who have that language deficiency, about 1,000 are given supplemental courses in the English language. About 1,800, however, do not receive that instruction.

This class suit brought by non-English-speaking Chinese students against officials responsible for the operation of the San Francisco Unified School District seeks relief against the unequal educational opportunities, which are alleged to violate, inter alia, the Fourteenth Amendment. No specific remedy is urged upon us. Teaching English to the students of Chinese ancestry who do not speak the language is one choice. Giving instructions to this group in Chinese is another. There may be others. Petitioners ask only that the Board of Education be directed to apply its expertise to the problem and rectify the situation.

The District Court denied relief. The Court of Appeals affirmed, holding that there was no violation of the Equal Protection Clause of the Fourteenth Amendment or of 601 of the Civil Rights Act of 1964, 78 Stat. 252, 42 U.S.C. § 2000d, which excludes from participation in federal financial assistance, recipients of aid which discriminate against racial groups, 483 F.2d 791. One judge dissented. A hearing en banc was denied, two judges dissenting.

We granted the petition for certiorari because of the public importance of the question presented.

... The Court of Appeals reasoned that "[e]very student brings to the starting line of his educational career different advantages and disadvantages caused in part by social, economic and cultural background, created and continued completely apart from any contribution by the school system." Yet in our view the case may not be so easily decided. This is a public school system of California and 71 of the California Education Code states that "English shall be the basic language of instruction in all schools." That section permits a school district to determine "when and under what circumstances instruction may be given bilingually." That section also states as "the policy of the state" to insure "the mastery of English by all pupils in the schools." And bilingual instruction is authorized "to the extent that it does not interfere with the systematic, sequential, and regular instruction of all pupils in the English language."

Moreover, 8573 of the Education Code provides that no pupil shall receive a diploma of graduation from grade 12 who has not met the standards of proficiency in "English," as well as other prescribed subjects. Moreover, by 12101 of the Education Code children between the ages of six and 16 years are (with exceptions not material here) "subject to compulsory full-time education."

Under these state-imposed standards there is no equality of treatment merely by providing students with the same facilities, textbooks, teachers, and curriculum; for students who do not understand English are effectively foreclosed from any meaningful education.

Basic English skills are at the very core of what these public schools teach. Imposition of a requirement that, before a child can effectively participate in the educational program, he must already have acquired those basic skills is to make a mockery of public education. We know that those who do not understand English are certain to find their classroom experiences wholly incomprehensible and in no way meaningful.

We do not reach the Equal Protection Clause argument which has been advanced but rely solely on 601 of the Civil Rights Act of 1964, 42 U.S.C. § 2000d, to reverse the Court of Appeals.

That section bans discrimination based "on the ground of race, color, or national origin," in "any program or activity receiving Federal financial assistance." The school district involved in this litigation receives large amounts of federal financial assistance. The Department of Health, Education, and Welfare (HEW), which has authority to promulgate regulations prohibiting discrimination in federally assisted school systems, 42 U.S.C. § 2000d-1, in 1968 issued one guideline that "[s]chool systems are responsible for assuring that students of a particular race, color, or national origin are not denied the opportunity to obtain the education generally obtained by other students in the system." In 1970 HEW made the guidelines more specific, requiring school districts that were federally funded "to rectify the language deficiency in order to open" the instruction to students who had "linguistic deficiencies."

By 602 of the Act HEW is authorized to issue rules, regulations, and orders to make sure that recipients of federal aid under its jurisdiction conduct any federally financed projects consistently with 601. HEW's regulations, 45 CFR 80.3(b)(1), specify that the recipients may not

> "(ii) Provide any service, financial aid, or other benefit to an individual which is different, or is provided in a different manner, from that provided to others under the program; . . .
>
> "(iv) Restrict an individual in any way in the enjoyment of any advantage or privilege enjoyed by others receiving any service, financial aid, or other benefit under the program."

Discrimination among students on account of race or national origin that is prohibited includes "discrimination . . . in the availability or use of any academic . . . or other facilities of the grantee or other recipient."

Discrimination is barred which has that effect even though no purposeful design is present: a recipient "may not . . . utilize criteria or methods of administration which have the effect of subjecting individuals to discrimination" or have "the effect of defeating or substantially impairing accomplishment of the objectives of the program as respect individuals of a particular race, color, or national origin."

It seems obvious that the Chinese-speaking minority receive fewer benefits than the English-speaking majority from respondents' school system which denies them a meaningful opportunity to participate in the educational program—all earmarks of the discrimination banned by the regulations. In 1970 HEW issued clarifying guidelines, 35 Fed. Reg. 11595, which include the following:

> "Where inability to speak and understand the English language excludes national origin-minority group children from effective participation in the educational program offered by a school district, the district must take affirmative steps to rectify the language deficiency in order to open its instructional program to these students."
>
> "Any ability grouping or tracking system employed by the school system to deal with the special language skill needs of national origin-minority group children must be designed to meet such language skill needs as soon as possible and must not operate as an educational dead end or permanent track."

Respondent school district contractually agreed to "comply with title VI of the Civil Rights Act of 1964 . . . and all requirements imposed by or pursuant to the Regulation" of HEW which are "issued pursuant to that title . . ." and also immediately to "take any measures necessary to effectuate this agreement." The Federal Government has power to fix the terms on which its money allotments to the States shall be disbursed. Whatever may be the limits of that power, they have not been reached here. Senator Humphrey, during the floor debates on the Civil Rights Act of 1964, said:

> "Simple justice requires that public funds, to which all taxpayers of all races contribute, not be spent in any fashion which encourages, entrenches, subsidizes, or results in racial discrimination."

We accordingly reverse the judgment of the Court of Appeals and remand the case for the fashioning of appropriate relief.

Reversed and remanded.

Horne v. Flores

557 U.S. 433 (2009)

The Supreme Court reviews the long history of the Arizona ELL litigation and remands for consideration within its specified parameters of whether enforcement of the prior judgment is equitable.

Justice Alito delivered the opinion of the Court.

These consolidated cases arise from litigation that began in Arizona in 1992 when a group of English Language-Learner (ELL) students in the Nogales Unified School District (Nogales) and their parents filed a class action, alleging that the State was violating the Equal Educational Opportunities Act of 1974 (EEOA), § 204(f), 88 Stat. 515, 20 U.S.C. § 1703(f), which requires a State "to take appropriate action to overcome language barriers that impede equal participation by its students in its instructional programs." In 2000, the District Court entered a declaratory judgment with respect to Nogales, and in 2001, the court extended the order to apply to the entire State. Over the next eight years, petitioners repeatedly sought relief from the District Court's orders, but to no avail. We granted certiorari after the Court of Appeals for the Ninth Circuit affirmed the denial of petitioners' motion for relief under Federal Rule of Civil Procedure 60(b)(5), and we now reverse the judgment of the Court of Appeals and remand for further proceedings.

As we explain, the District Court and the Court of Appeals misunderstood both the obligation that the EEOA imposes on States and the nature of the inquiry that is required when parties such as petitioners seek relief under Rule 60(b)(5) on the ground that enforcement of a judgment is "no longer equitable." Both of the lower courts focused excessively on the narrow question of the adequacy of the State's incremental funding for ELL instruction instead of fairly considering the broader question whether, as a result of important changes during the intervening years, the State was fulfilling its obligation under the EEOA by other means. The question at issue in these cases is not whether Arizona must take "appropriate action" to overcome the language barriers that impede ELL students. Of course it must. But petitioners argue that Arizona is now fulfilling its statutory obligation by new means that reflect new policy insights and other changed circumstances. Rule 60(b)(5) provides the vehicle for petitioners to bring such an argument.

In 1992, a group of students enrolled in the ELL program in Nogales and their parents (plaintiffs) filed suit in the District Court for the District of Arizona on behalf of "all minority 'at risk' and limited English proficient children . . . now or hereafter, enrolled in the Nogales Unified School District . . . as well as their parents and guardians." The plaintiffs sought a declaratory judgment holding that the State of Arizona, its Board of Education, and its Superintendent of Public Instruction (defendants) were violating the EEOA by providing inadequate ELL instruction in Nogales.

> "No State shall deny equal educational opportunity to an individual on account of his or her race, color, sex, or national origin, by—
>
> . . . .
>
> "(f) the failure by an educational agency to take *appropriate action* to overcome language barriers that impede equal participation by its students in its instructional programs." 20 U.S.C. § 1703 (emphasis added).

By simply requiring a State "to take appropriate action to overcome language barriers" without specifying particular actions that a State must take, "Congress intended to leave state and local educational authorities a substantial amount of latitude in choosing the programs and techniques they would use to meet their obligations under the EEOA." *Castaneda v. Pickard*, 648 F.2d 989, 1009 (5th Cir. 1981).

In August 1999, after seven years of pretrial proceedings and after settling various claims regarding the structure of Nogales' ELL curriculum, the evaluation and monitoring of Nogales' students, and the provision of tutoring and other compensatory instruction, the parties proceeded to trial. In January 2000, the District Court concluded that defendants were violating the EEOA because the amount of funding the State allocated for the special needs of ELL students (ELL incremental funding) was arbitrary and not related to the actual funding needed to cover the costs of ELL instruction in Nogales. Defendants did not appeal the District Court's order.

In the years following, the District Court entered a series of additional orders and injunctions. In October 2000, the court ordered the State to "prepare a cost study to establish the proper appropriation to effectively implement" ELL programs. In June 2001, the court applied the declaratory judgment order statewide and granted injunctive relief accordingly. . . .

In January 2005, the court gave the State 90 days to "appropriately and constitutionally fun[d] the state's ELL programs taking into account the [Rule's] previous orders." The State failed to meet this deadline, and in December 2005, the court held the State in contempt. Although the legislature was not then a party to the suit, the court ordered that "the legislature has 15 calendar days after the beginning of the 2006 legislative session to comply with the January 28, 2005 Court order. Everyday thereafter . . . that the State fails to comply with this Order, [fines] will be imposed until the State is in compliance." The schedule of fines that the court imposed escalated from $500,000 to $2 million per day.

The defendants did not appeal any of the District Court's orders, and the record suggests that some state officials supported their continued enforcement. . . .

In March 2006, after accruing over $20 million in fines, the state legislature passed HB 2064, which was designed to implement a permanent funding solution to the problems identified by the District Court in 2000. Among other things, HB 2064 increased ELL incremental funding (with a 2-year per-student limit on such funding) and created two new funds—a structured English immersion fund and a compensatory instruction fund—to cover additional costs of ELL programming. Moneys in both newly created funds were to be offset by available federal moneys. HB 2064 also instituted several programming and structural changes.

The Governor did not approve of HB 2064's funding provisions, but she allowed the bill to become law without her signature. Because HB 2064's incremental ELL funding increase required court approval to become effective, the Governor requested the attorney general to move for accelerated consideration by the District Court. . . . The State Board of Education joined the Governor in opposing HB 2064. Together, the State Board of Education, the State of Arizona, and the plaintiffs are respondents here.

With the principal defendants in the action siding with the plaintiffs, the Speaker of the State House of Representatives and the President of the State Senate (Legislators) filed a motion to intervene as representatives of their respective legislative bodies.... The District Court granted the Legislators' motion for permissive intervention, and the Legislators and superintendent (together, petitioners here) moved to purge the District Court's contempt order in light of HB 2064. Alternatively, they moved for relief under Federal Rule of Civil Procedure 60(b)(5) based on changed circumstances.

In April 2006, the District Court denied petitioners' motion....

In an unpublished decision, the Court of Appeals for the Ninth Circuit vacated the District Court's April 2006 order, the sanctions, and the imposition of fines, and remanded for an evidentiary hearing to determine whether Rule 60(b)(5) relief was warranted.

On remand, the District Court denied petitioners' Rule 60(b)(5) motion. Holding that HB 2064 did not establish "a funding system that rationally relates funding available to the actual costs of all elements of ELL instruction," *id.*, at 1165, the court gave the State until the end of the legislative session to comply with its orders. The State failed to do so, and the District Court again held the State in contempt....

The Court of Appeals affirmed. 516 F.3d 1140. It acknowledged that Nogales had "made significant strides since 2000," *id.*, at 1156, but concluded that the progress did not warrant Rule 60(b)(5) relief....

We granted certiorari, and now reverse.

....

Federal Rule of Civil Procedure 60(b)(5) permits a party to obtain relief from a judgment or order if, among other things, "applying [the judgment or order] prospectively is no longer equitable." Rule 60(b)(5) may not be used to challenge the legal conclusions on which a prior judgment or order rests, but the Rule provides a means by which a party can ask a court to modify or vacate a judgment or order if "a significant change either in factual conditions or in law" renders continued enforcement "detrimental to the public interest."...

Rule 60(b)(5) serves a particularly important function in what we have termed "institutional reform litigation."...

Institutional reform injunctions often raise sensitive federalism concerns. Such litigation commonly involves areas of core state responsibility, such as public education. *See Missouri v. Jenkins*, 515 U.S. 70, 99 (1995) ("[O]ur cases recognize that local autonomy of school districts is a vital national tradition, and that a district court must strive to restore state and local authorities to the control of a school system operating in compliance with the Constitution" (citations omitted)); *United States v. Lopez*, 514 U.S. 549, 580 (1995) (Kennedy, J., concurring).

Federalism concerns are heightened when, as in these cases, a federal court decree has the effect of dictating state or local budget priorities....

It goes without saying that federal courts must vigilantly enforce federal law and must not hesitate in awarding necessary relief. But in recognition of the features of institutional reform decrees, we have held that courts must take a "flexible approach" to Rule 60(b)(5) motions addressing such decrees. . . .

For these reasons, a critical question in this Rule 60(b)(5) inquiry is whether the objective of the District Court's 2000 declaratory judgment order—*i.e.*, satisfaction of the EEOA's "appropriate action" standard—has been achieved. If a durable remedy has been implemented, continued enforcement of the order is not only unnecessary, but improper. We note that the EEOA itself limits court-ordered remedies to those that "are *essential* to correct particular denials of equal educational opportunity or equal protection of the laws." 20 U.S.C. § 1712 (emphasis added).

The Court of Appeals did not engage in the Rule 60(b)(5) analysis just described. Rather than applying a flexible standard that seeks to return control to state and local officials as soon as a violation of federal law has been remedied, the Court of Appeals used a heightened standard that paid insufficient attention to federalism concerns. And rather than inquiring broadly into whether changed conditions in Nogales provided evidence of an ELL program that complied with the EEOA, the Court of Appeals concerned itself only with determining whether increased ELL funding complied with the original declaratory judgment order. The court erred on both counts.

. . . .

Because the lower courts—like the dissent—misperceived both the nature of the obligation imposed by the EEOA and the breadth of the inquiry called for under Rule 60(b)(5), these cases must be remanded for a proper examination of at least four important factual and legal changes that may warrant the granting of relief from the judgment: the State's adoption of a new ELL instructional methodology, Congress' enactment of NCLB, structural and management reforms in Nogales, and increased overall education funding.

. . . .

At the time of the District Court's original declaratory judgment order, ELL instruction in Nogales was based primarily on "bilingual education," which teaches core content areas in a student's native language while providing English instruction in separate language classes. In November 2000, Arizona voters passed Proposition 203, which mandated statewide implementation of a "structured English immersion" (SEI) approach. Proposition 203 defines this methodology as follows:

> "'Sheltered English immersion' or 'structured English immersion' means an English language acquisition process for young children in which nearly all classroom instruction is in English but with the curriculum and presentation designed for children who are learning the language . . . . Although teachers may use a minimal amount of the child's native language when necessary, no subject matter shall be taught in any language other than English, and children in this program learn to read and write solely in English."

Ariz. Rev. Stat. Ann. § 15-751(5) (2009).

In HB 2064, the state legislature attended to the successful and uniform implementation of SEI in a variety of ways. It created an "Arizona English language learners task force" within the State Department of Education to "develop and adopt research based models of structured English immersion programs for use by school districts and charter schools." § 15-756.01(C). It required that all school districts and charter schools select one of the adopted SEI models, § 15-756.02(A), and it created an "Office of English language acquisition services" to aid school districts in implementation of the models. § 15-756.07(1). It also required the State Board of Education to institute a uniform and mandatory training program for all SEI instructors. § 15-756.09.

Research on ELL instruction indicates there is documented, academic support for the view that SEI is significantly more effective than bilingual education. Findings of the Arizona State Department of Education in 2004 strongly support this conclusion. In light of this, a proper analysis of petitioners' Rule 60(b)(5) motion should include further factual findings regarding whether Nogales' implementation of SEI methodology—completed in all of its schools by 2005—constitutes a "significantly changed circumstance" that warrants relief.

Congress' enactment of NCLB represents another potentially significant "changed circumstance." NCLB marked a dramatic shift in federal education policy. It reflects Congress' judgment that the best way to raise the level of education nationwide is by granting state and local officials flexibility to develop and implement educational programs that address local needs, while holding them accountable for the results. NCLB implements this approach by requiring States receiving federal funds to define performance standards and to make regular assessments of progress toward the attainment of those standards. 20 U.S.C. § 6311(b)(2). NCLB conditions the continued receipt of funds on demonstrations of "adequate yearly progress." *Ibid.*

As relevant here, Title III (the English Language Acquisition, Language Enhancement, and Academic Achievement Act) requires States to ensure that ELL students "attain English proficiency, develop high levels of academic attainment in English, and meet the same challenging State academic content and student academic achievement standards as all children are expected to meet." § 6812(1). It requires States to set annual objective achievement goals for the number of students who will annually progress toward proficiency, achieve proficiency, and make "adequate yearly progress" with respect to academic achievement, § 6842(a), and it holds local schools and agencies accountable for meeting these objectives, § 6842(b).

Petitioners argue that through compliance with NCLB, the State has established compliance with the EEOA. They note that when a State adopts a compliance plan under NCLB—as the State of Arizona has—it must provide adequate assurances that ELL students will receive assistance "to achieve at high levels in the core academic subjects so that those children can meet the same . . . standards as all children are expected to meet." § 6812(2). They argue that when the Federal Department of

Education approves a State's plan—as it has with respect to Arizona's—it offers definitive evidence that the State has taken "appropriate action to overcome language barriers" within the meaning of the EEOA. § 1703(f).

The Court of Appeals concluded, and we agree, that because of significant differences in the two statutory schemes, compliance with NCLB will not necessarily constitute "appropriate action" under the EEOA. 516 F.3d at 1172-1176. Approval of a NCLB plan does not entail substantive review of a State's ELL programming or a determination that the programming results in equal educational opportunity for ELL students. See § 6823. Moreover, NCLB contains a saving clause, which provides that "[n]othing in this part shall be construed in a manner inconsistent with any Federal law guaranteeing a civil right." § 6847.

This does not mean, however, that NCLB is not relevant to petitioners' Rule 60(b)(5) motion. To the contrary, we think it is probative in four principal ways. First, it prompted the State to institute significant structural and programming changes in its delivery of ELL education, leading the Court of Appeals to observe that "Arizona has significantly improved its ELL infrastructure." These changes should not be discounted in the Rule 60(b)(5) analysis solely because they do not require or result from increased funding. Second, NCLB significantly increased federal funding for education in general and ELL programming in particular. These funds should not be disregarded just because they are not state funds. Third, through its assessment and reporting requirements, NCLB provides evidence of the progress and achievement of Nogales' ELL students. This evidence could provide persuasive evidence of the current effectiveness of Nogales' ELL programming.

Fourth and finally, NCLB marks a shift in federal education policy. See Brief for Petitioner Speaker of the Arizona House of Representatives et al. 7-16. NCLB grants States "flexibility" to adopt ELL programs they believe are "most effective for teaching English." § 6812(9). Reflecting a growing consensus in education research that increased funding alone does not improve student achievement, NCLB expressly refrains from dictating funding levels. Instead, it focuses on the demonstrated progress of students through accountability reforms. The original declaratory judgment order, in contrast, withdraws the authority of state and local officials to fund and implement ELL programs that best suit Nogales' needs, and measures effective programming solely in terms of adequate incremental funding. This conflict with Congress' determination of federal policy may constitute a significantly changed circumstance, warranting relief. *See Railway Employees v. Wright*, 364 U.S. 642, 651 (1961) (noting that a court decree should be modified when "a change in law brings [the decree] in conflict with statutory objectives").

Structural and management reforms in Nogales constitute another relevant change in circumstances. These reforms were led by Kelt Cooper, the Nogales superintendent from 2000 to 2005, who "adopted policies that ameliorated or eliminated many of the most glaring inadequacies discussed by the district court." Among other things, Cooper "reduce[d] class sizes," "significantly improv[ed] student/teacher ratios," "improved teacher quality," "pioneered a uniform system of textbook and curriculum planning," and "largely eliminated what had been a severe shortage of instructional materials." The Court of Appeals recognized that by "[u]sing careful financial management and applying for 'all funds available,' Cooper was able to achieve his reforms with limited resources." But the Court of Appeals missed the legal import of this observation—that these reforms might have brought Nogales' ELL programming into compliance with the EEOA even without sufficient ELL incremental funding to satisfy the District Court's original order. . . .

Entrenched in the framework of incremental funding, both courts refused to consider that Nogales could be taking "appropriate action" to address language barriers even without having satisfied the original order. This was error. The EEOA seeks to provide "equal educational opportunity" to "all children enrolled in public schools." § 1701(a). Its ultimate focus is on the quality of educational programming and services provided to students, not the amount of money spent on them. Accordingly, there is no statutory basis for precluding petitioners from showing that Nogales has achieved EEOA-compliant programming by means other than increased funding—for example, through Cooper's structural, curricular, and accountability-based reforms. The weight of research suggests that these types of local reforms, much more than court-imposed funding mandates, lead to improved educational opportunities. Cooper even testified that, without the structural changes he imposed, "additional money" would not "have made any difference to th[e] students" in Nogales.

. . . .

A fourth potentially important change is an overall increase in the education funding available in Nogales. . . .

This was clear legal error. As we have noted, the EEOA's "appropriate action" requirement does not necessarily require any particular level of funding, and to the extent that funding is relevant, the EEOA certainly does not require that the money come from any particular source. In addition, the EEOA plainly does not give the federal courts the authority to judge whether a State or a school district is providing "appropriate" instruction in other subjects. . . . Accordingly, the analysis of petitioners' Rule 60(b)(5) motion should evaluate whether the State's budget for general education funding, in addition to any local revenues, is currently supporting EEOA-compliant ELL programming in Nogales.

Because the lower courts engaged in an inadequate Rule 60(b)(5) analysis, and because the District Court failed to make up-to-date factual findings, the analysis of the lower courts was incomplete and inadequate with respect to all of the changed circumstances just noted. These changes are critical to a proper Rule 60(b)(5) analysis, however, as they may establish that Nogales is no longer in violation of the EEOA and, to the contrary, is taking "appropriate action" to remove language barriers in its schools. If this is the case, continued enforcement of the District Court's original order is inequitable within the meaning of Rule 60(b)(5), and relief is warranted.

. . . .

There is no question that the goal of the EEOA—overcoming language barriers—is a vitally important one, and our decision will not in any way undermine efforts to achieve that goal. If petitioners are ultimately granted relief from the judgment, it will be because they have shown that the Nogales School District is doing exactly what this statute requires—taking "appropriate action" to teach English to students who grew up speaking another language.

....

We reverse the judgment of the Court of Appeals and remand the cases for the District Court to determine whether, in accordance with the standards set out in this opinion, petitioners should be granted relief from the judgment.

It is so ordered.

Justice Breyer, with whom Justice Stevens, Justice Souter, and Justice Ginsburg join, dissenting.

....

I disagree with the Court for several reasons. For one thing, the "institutional reform" label does not easily fit this case. For another, the review standards the Court enunciates for "institutional reform" cases are incomplete and, insofar as the Court applies those standards here, they effectively distort Rule 60(b)(5)'s objectives. Finally, my own review of the record convinces me that the Court is wrong regardless. *The lower courts did "fairly consider" every change in circumstances that the parties called to their attention.* The record more than adequately supports this conclusion. In a word, I fear that the Court misapplies an inappropriate procedural framework, reaching a result that neither the record nor the law adequately supports. In doing so, it risks denying schoolchildren the English-learning instruction necessary "to overcome language barriers that impede" their "equal participation." 20 U.S.C. § 1703(f).

....

ESSA (formerly NCLB) Excerpt

20 U.S.C. § 6311

Chapter 70. Strengthening and Improvement of Elementary and Secondary Schools

BASIC PROGRAM REQUIREMENTS

§ 6311. State plans

(a) **Filing for grants**

(1) **In general.** For any State desiring to receive a grant under this part, the State educational agency shall file with the Secretary a plan that is—

...

(b) **Challenging academic standards and academic assessments**

(1) **Challenging State academic standards**

(A) **In general.** Each State, in the plan it files under subsection (a), shall provide an assurance that the State has adopted challenging academic content standards and aligned academic achievement standards (referred to in this chapter as "challenging State academic standards"), which achievement standards shall include not less than 3 levels of achievement, that will be used by the State, its local educational agencies, and its schools to carry out this part. A State shall not be required to submit such challenging State academic standards to the Secretary.

(B) **Same standards.** Except as provided in subparagraph (E), the standards required by subparagraph (A) shall—

(i) apply to all public schools and public school students in the State; and

(ii) with respect to academic achievement standards, include the same knowledge, skills, and levels of achievement expected of all public school students in the State.

(C) **Subjects.** The State shall have such academic standards for mathematics, reading or language arts, and science, and may have such standards for any other subject determined by the State.

(D) **Alignment**

(i) **In general.** Each State shall demonstrate that the challenging State academic standards are aligned with entrance requirements for credit-bearing coursework in the system of public higher education in the State and relevant State career and technical education standards.

(ii) **Rule of construction.** Nothing in this chapter shall be construed to authorize public institutions of higher education to determine the specific challenging State academic standards required under this paragraph.

. . .

(F) **English language proficiency standards.**Each State plan shall demonstrate that the State has adopted English language proficiency standards that—

(i) are derived from the 4 recognized domains of speaking, listening, reading, and writing;

(ii) address the different proficiency levels of English learners; and

(iii) are aligned with the challenging State academic standards.

(G) **Prohibitions**

(i) **Standards review or approval.** A State shall not be required to submit any standards developed under this subsection to the Secretary for review or approval.

(ii) **Federal control.** The Secretary shall not have the authority to mandate, direct, control, coerce, or exercise any direction or supervision over any of the challenging State academic standards adopted or implemented by a State.

(H) **Existing standards.** Nothing in this part shall prohibit a State from revising, consistent with this section, any standards adopted under this part before or after December 10, 2015.

(2) **Academic assessments**

(A) **In general.** Each State plan shall demonstrate that the State educational agency, in consultation with local educational agencies, has implemented a set of high-quality student academic assessments in mathematics, reading or language arts, and science. The State retains the right to implement such assessments in any other subject chosen by the State.

(B) **Requirements.** The assessments under subparagraph (A) shall—

(i) except as provided in subparagraph (D), be—

(I) the same academic assessments used to measure the achievement of all public elementary school and secondary school students in the State; and

(II) administered to all public elementary school and secondary school students in the State;

(ii) be aligned with the challenging State academic standards, and provide coherent and timely information about student attainment of such standards and whether the student is performing at the student's grade level;

(iii) be used for purposes for which such assessments are valid and reliable, consistent with relevant, nationally recognized professional and technical testing standards, objectively measure academic achievement, knowledge, and skills, and be tests that do not evaluate or assess personal or family beliefs and attitudes, or publicly disclose personally identifiable information;

(iv) be of adequate technical quality for each purpose required under this chapter and consistent with the requirements of this section, the evidence of which shall be made public, including on the website of the State educational agency;

(v)(I) in the case of mathematics and reading or language arts, be administered—

(aa) in each of grades 3 through 8; and

(bb) at least once in grades 9 through 12;

(II) in the case of science, be administered not less than one time during—

(aa) grades 3 through 5;

(bb) grades 6 through 9; and

(cc) grades 10 through 12; and

(III) in the case of any other subject chosen by the State, be administered at the discretion of the State;

. . .

(vii) provide for—

(I) the participation in such assessments of all students;

. . .

(III) the inclusion of English learners, who shall be assessed in a valid and reliable manner and provided appropriate accommodations on assessments administered to such students under this paragraph, including, to the extent practicable, assessments in the language and form most likely to yield accurate data on what such students know and can do in academic content areas, until such students have achieved English language proficiency, as determined under subparagraph (G);

. . .

(ix) notwithstanding clause (vii)(III), provide for assessments (using tests in English) of reading or language arts of any student who has attended school in the United States (not including the Commonwealth of Puerto Rico) for 3 or more consecutive school years, except that if the local educational agency determines, on a case-by-case individual basis, that academic assessments in another language or form would likely yield more accurate and reliable information on what such student knows and can do, the local educational agency may make a determination to assess such student in the appropriate language other than English for a period that does not exceed 2 additional consecutive years, provided that such student has not yet reached a level of English language proficiency sufficient to yield valid and reliable information on what such student knows and can do on tests (written in English) of reading or language arts;

(x) produce individual student interpretive, descriptive, and diagnostic reports, consistent with clause (iii), regarding achievement on such assessments that allow parents, teachers, principals, and other school leaders to understand and address the specific academic needs of students, and that are provided to parents, teachers, and school leaders, as soon as is practicable after the assessment is given, in an understandable and uniform format, and to the extent practicable, in a language that parents can understand;

(xi) enable results to be disaggregated within each State, local educational agency, and school by—

(I) each major racial and ethnic group;

(II) economically disadvantaged students as compared to students who are not economically disadvantaged;

(III) children with disabilities as compared to children without disabilities;

(IV) English proficiency status;

(V) gender; and

(VI) migrant status,

. . .

(F) **Language assessments**

(i) **In general.** Each State plan shall identify the languages other than English that are present to a significant extent in the participating student population of the State and indicate the languages for which annual student academic assessments are not available and are needed.

(ii) **Secretarial assistance.** The State shall make every effort to develop such assessments and may request assistance from the Secretary if linguistically accessible academic assessment measures are needed. Upon request, the Secretary shall assist with the identification of appropriate academic assessment measures in the needed languages, but shall not mandate a specific academic assessment or mode of instruction.

(G) **Assessments of English language proficiency**

(i) **In general.** Each State plan shall demonstrate that local educational agencies in the State will provide for an annual assessment of English proficiency of all English learners in the schools served by the State educational agency.

(ii) **Alignment.** The assessments described in clause (i) shall be aligned with the State's English language proficiency standards described in paragraph (1)(F).

. . .

(3) **Exception for recently arrived English learners**

(A) **Assessments.** With respect to recently arrived English learners who have been enrolled in a school in one of the 50 States in the United

States or the District of Columbia for less than 12 months, a State may choose to—

(i) exclude—

(I) such an English learner from one administration of the reading or language arts assessment required under paragraph (2); and

(II) such an English learner's results on any of the assessments required under paragraph (2)(B)(v)(I) or (2)(G) for the first year of the English learner's enrollment in such a school for the purposes of the State-determined accountability system under subsection (c); or

(ii)(I) assess, and report the performance of, such an English learner on the reading or language arts and mathematics assessments required under paragraph (2)(B)(v)(I) in each year of the student's enrollment in such a school; and

(II) for the purposes of the State-determined accountability system—

(aa) for the first year of the student's enrollment in such a school, exclude the results on the assessments described in subclause (I);

(bb) include a measure of student growth on the assessments described in subclause (I) in the second year of the student's enrollment in such a school; and

(cc) include proficiency on the assessments described in subclause (I) in the third year of the student's enrollment in such a school, and each succeeding year of such enrollment.

(B) **English learner subgroup.** With respect to a student previously identified as an English learner and for not more than 4 years after the student ceases to be identified as an English learner, a State may include the results of the student's assessments under paragraph (2)(B)(v)(I) within the English learner subgroup of the subgroups of students (as defined in subsection (c)(2)(D)) for the purposes of the State-determined accountability system.

[Note: §6311 has more provisions related to the details of the ELL subgroup and reporting requirements. You can view these online if you would like more detail.]

20 U.S.C. §6312

The purposes of this part are—

(1) to help ensure that English learners, including immigrant children and youth, attain English proficiency and develop high levels of academic achievement in English;

(2) to assist all English learners, including immigrant children and youth, to achieve at high levels in academic subjects so that all English learners can meet the same challenging State academic standards that all children are expected to meet;

(3) to assist teachers (including preschool teachers), principals and other school leaders, State educational agencies, local educational agencies, and schools in establishing, implementing, and sustaining effective language instruction educational programs designed to assist in teaching English learners, including immigrant children and youth;

(4) to assist teachers (including preschool teachers), principals and other school leaders, State educational agencies, and local educational agencies to develop and enhance their capacity to provide effective instructional programs designed to prepare English learners, including immigrant children and youth, to enter all-English instructional settings; and

(5) to promote parental, family, and community participation in language instruction educational programs for the parents, families, and communities of English learners.

Review 20 U.S.C. § 6325 and 20 U.S.C. § 6326 online.

These provisions allow states to provide sub-grants to local school districts for ELL services, and impose conditions on those funds.

Post Problem Discussion

1. If you determine that changes need to be made to your state's requirements, how should they be made? Are new state statutes or regulations required? Does your state's ESSA plan need to be modified?

2. How much discretion should local school districts have in implementing ELL requirements? Should there be a uniform system or method for educating ELL students that all local school districts must follow, or should local school districts be given flexibility on the methods that they use as long as the methods produce the results required in statewide accountability and assessment requirements?

3. Some states, notably California and Arizona, have used a referendum approach to gain control of English language questions for schools. Arizona statute now provides, in part, as to "English Language Education for Children in Public Schools":

> Subject to the exceptions provided in section 15-753, all children in Arizona public schools shall be taught English by being taught in English and all children shall be placed in English language classrooms. Children who are English learners shall be educated through sheltered English immersion during a temporary transition period not normally intended to exceed one year. Local schools shall be permitted but not required to place in the same classroom English learners of different ages but whose degree of English proficiency is similar. Local schools shall be encouraged to mix together in the same classroom English learners from different native-language groups

> but with the same degree of English fluency. Once English learners have acquired a good working knowledge of English and are able to do regular school work in English, they shall no longer be classified as English learners and shall be transferred to English language mainstream classrooms. As much as possible, current per capita supplemental funding for English learners shall be maintained. Foreign language classes for children who already know English shall be completely unaffected, as shall special educational programs for physically- or mentally-impaired students.

A.R.S. § 15-752. What role, if any, does the possibility of a state referendum play in your consideration of your state's requirements, and potential changes to those requirements?

§ 4.04 Curriculum in Constitutional Context

The *Meyer* and *Pierce v. Society of Sisters* cases set the stage for the constitutional parameters of a discussion about curriculum. In *Meyer*, the Supreme Court laid this foundation: "The power of the state to compel attendance at some school and to make reasonable regulations for all schools, including a requirement that they shall give instructions in English is not questioned. Nor has challenge been made of the state's power to prescribe curriculum for institutions which it supports." 262 U.S. at 402. While the powers noted in *Meyer* are generally not subjected to constitutional challenges, the parameters of those powers remain in play.

Parents disagreeing with the information provided to their children at school is an ongoing issue for public elementary and secondary schools. On one side of the issue, parents may try to assert a due process right to direct the educational upbringing of their children under *Meyer* and *Pierce* as a way of objecting to information being provided to their children at school. These claims are generally unsuccessful in court. As the Sixth Circuit Court of Appeals noted, "[w]hile parents may have a fundamental right to decide *whether* to send their child to a public school, they do not have a fundamental right generally to direct *how* a public school teaches their child. Whether it is the school curriculum, the hours of the school day, school discipline, the timing and content of examinations, the individuals hired to teach at the school, the extracurricular activities offered at the school or, as here, a dress code, these issues of public education are generally 'committed to the control of state and local authorities.'" *Blau v. Fort Thomas Pub. Sch. Dist.*,401 F.3d 381, 395–96 (6th Cir. 2005).

However, sometimes school board members or school officials agree with the parental concerns, or they themselves object to certain information, and they ban the information from being provided or taught at school. These actions raise a related issue of the right of students to receive information under the First Amendment. Another related issue is the academic freedom of teachers to teach the information, or assign the materials. The following problems explore these issues.

Problem 2: Banning Bastard Out of Carolina

Ms. Bragdon, a tenth grade language arts teacher at VeryRural High School has assigned her class the book and film "Bastard Out of Carolina" as required reading and viewing for the semester. All assigned reading and materials must be approved by the principal, and Ms. Bragdon followed all the proper steps in getting her materials approved. One of the parents, Ms. Merrill, noticed her son reading *Bastard* and became very upset because she does not think the material is appropriate for her son or other students at the school. VeryRural is in a small town, with a population that is 80% White, 16% Native American, and 4% Black. Ms. Merrill did not have any trouble enlisting other parents of all racial and ethnic backgrounds to her cause. She and her friends contacted the principal and school board chair demanding that the book and film be removed from the required materials list and be banned from use at the school. The parent group has not mentioned anything about the library.

You are the school board's attorney. The Board is leaning towards removing the book and film from the required reading and banning it from being used at school at all in order to avoid any problems with parents. The Board seeks your advice on whether these actions would be constitutional. Review the problem materials and answer the following:

1. Would removing the book and film from the required materials list, and banning the book and film from use at school, violate the First Amendment? Is the analysis different if the ban includes or excludes having the book in the school's library?
2. Are there any alternatives to removing or banning the book and film that the school board could try to utilize to resolve the problem?

Problem Materials

✓ Excerpt from publisher of *Bastard Out of Carolina*

✓ *Board of Education of Island Trees Union Free School District No. 26 v. Pico*, 457 U.S. 853 (1982)

✓ *Virgil v. School Board of Columbia County*, 862 F.2d 1517 (11th Cir. 1989)

✓ *Monteiro v. Tempe Union High School District*, 158 F.3d 1022 (9th Cir. 1998)

Bastard Out of Carolina *by Dorothy Allison*

Greenville County, South Carolina, a wild, lush place, is home to the Boatwright family—rough-hewn men who drink hard and shoot up each other's trucks, and indomitable women who marry young and age all too quickly. At the heart of this astonishing novel is Ruth Anne Boatwright, known simply as Bone, a South Carolina bastard with an annotated birth certificate to tell the tale. Observing everything with the mercilessly keen eye of a child, Bone finds herself caught in a family triangle that will test the loyalty of her mother, Anney. Her stepfather, Daddy Glen, calls Bone

> "cold as death, mean as a snake, and twice as twisty," yet Anney needs Glen. At first gentle with Bone, Daddy Glen becomes steadily colder and more furious—until their final, harrowing encounter, from which there can be no turning back. (Quoted from Book Description by the Publisher)

Reading the entire book is preferable, but the above description sets the stage.

Board of Education of Island Trees Union Free School District No. 26 v. Pico

457 U.S. 853 (1982)

> *A plurality opinion concludes that under the First Amendment, a local school board may not remove books that it finds "anti-American, anti-Christian, anti-[Semitic], and just plain filthy" from the school library shelves because they "dislike the ideas" in those books.*

BRENNAN, J., announced the judgment of the Court and delivered an opinion, in which MARSHALL and STEVENS, JJ., joined and in all but Part II-A(1) of which BLACKMUN, J., joined. BLACKMUN, J., filed an opinion concurring in part and concurring in the judgment. WHITE, J., filed an opinion concurring in the judgment. BURGER, C.J., filed a dissenting opinion, in which POWELL, REHNQUIST, and O'CONNOR, JJ., joined. POWELL, J., filed a dissenting opinion. REHNQUIST, J., filed a dissenting opinion, in which BURGER, C.J., and POWELL, J., joined. O'CONNOR, J., filed a dissenting opinion.

The principal question presented is whether the First Amendment imposes limitations upon the exercise by a local school board of its discretion to remove library books from high school and junior high school libraries.

. . . .

In September 1975, petitioners Ahrens, Martin, and Hughes attended a conference sponsored by Parents of New York United (PONYU), a politically conservative organization of parents concerned about education legislation in the State of New York. At the conference these petitioners obtained lists of books described by Ahrens as "objectionable," and by Martin as "improper fare for school students." It was later determined that the High School library contained nine of the listed books, and that another listed book was in the Junior High School library.[2] In February 1976, at a meeting with the Superintendent of Schools and the Principals of the High School and Junior High School, the Board gave an "unofficial direction" that

---

2. [FN 3]The nine books in the High School library were: Slaughter House Five, by Kurt Vonnegut, Jr.; The Naked Ape, by Desmond Morris; Down These Mean Streets, by Piri Thomas; Best Short Stories of Negro Writers, edited by Langston Hughes; Go Ask Alice, of anonymous authorship; Laughing Boy, by Oliver LaFarge; Black Boy, by Richard Wright; A Hero Ain't Nothin' But A Sandwich, by Alice Childress; and Soul On Ice, by Eldridge Cleaver. The book in the Junior High School library was A Reader for Writers, edited by Jerome Archer. Still another listed book, The Fixer, by Bernard Malamud, was found to be included in the curriculum of a 12th-grade literature course.

the listed books be removed from the library shelves and delivered to the Board's offices, so that Board members could read them. When this directive was carried out, it became publicized, and the Board issued a press release justifying its action. It characterized the removed books as "anti-American, anti-Christian, anti-[Semitic], and just plain filthy," and concluded that "[it] is our duty, our moral obligation, to protect the children in our schools from this moral danger as surely as from physical and medical dangers."

A short time later, the Board appointed a "Book Review Committee," consisting of four Island Trees parents and four members of the Island Trees schools staff, to read the listed books and to recommend to the Board whether the books should be retained, taking into account the books' "educational suitability," "good taste," "relevance," and "appropriateness to age and grade level." In July, the Committee made its final report to the Board, recommending that five of the listed books be retained and that two others be removed from the school libraries. As for the remaining four books, the Committee could not agree on two, took no position on one, and recommended that the last book be made available to students only with parental approval. The Board substantially rejected the Committee's report later that month, deciding that only one book should be returned to the High School library without restriction, that another should be made available subject to parental approval, but that the remaining nine books should "be removed from elementary and secondary libraries and [from] use in the curriculum." The Board gave no reasons for rejecting the recommendations of the Committee that it had appointed.

Respondents reacted to the Board's decision by bringing the present action under 42 U.S.C. § 1983 in the United States District Court for the Eastern District of New York....

Respondents claimed that the Board's actions denied them their rights under the First Amendment. They asked the court for a declaration that the Board's actions were unconstitutional, and for preliminary and permanent injunctive relief ordering the Board to return the nine books to the school libraries and to refrain from interfering with the use of those books in the schools' curricula.

....

We emphasize at the outset the limited nature of the substantive question presented by the case before us. Our precedents have long recognized certain constitutional limits upon the power of the State to control even the curriculum and classroom. For example, *Meyer v. Nebraska*, 262 U.S. 390 (1923), struck down a state law that forbade the teaching of modern foreign languages in public and private schools, and *Epperson v. Arkansas*, 393 U.S. 97 (1968), declared unconstitutional a state law that prohibited the teaching of the Darwinian theory of evolution in any state-supported school. But the current action does not require us to re-enter this difficult terrain, which *Meyer* and *Epperson* traversed without apparent misgiving. For as this case is presented to us, it does not involve textbooks, or indeed any books that Island Trees students would be required to read. Respondents do not seek in this

Court to impose limitations upon their school Board's discretion to prescribe the curricula of the Island Trees schools. On the contrary, the only books at issue in this case are *library* books, books that by their nature are optional rather than required reading. Our adjudication of the present case thus does not intrude into the classroom, or into the compulsory courses taught there. Furthermore, even as to library books, the action before us does not involve the *acquisition* of books. Respondents have not sought to compel their school Board to add to the school library shelves any books that students desire to read. Rather, the only action challenged in this case is the *removal* from school libraries of books originally placed there by the school authorities, or without objection from them.

....

In sum, the issue before us in this case is a narrow one, both substantively and procedurally. It may best be restated as two distinct questions. First, does the First Amendment impose *any* limitations upon the discretion of petitioners to remove library books from the Island Trees High School and Junior High School? Second, if so, do the affidavits and other evidentiary materials before the District Court, construed most favorably to respondents, raise a genuine issue of fact whether petitioners might have exceeded those limitations? If we answer either of these questions in the negative, then we must reverse the judgment of the Court of Appeals and reinstate the District Court's summary judgment for petitioners. If we answer both questions in the affirmative, then we must affirm the judgment below. We examine these questions in turn.

The Court has long recognized that local school boards have broad discretion in the management of school affairs. *See, e.g., Meyer v. Nebraska*; *Pierce v. Society of Sisters*, 268 U.S. 510, 534 (1925). *Epperson v. Arkansas* reaffirmed that, by and large, "public education in our Nation is committed to the control of state and local authorities," and that federal courts should not ordinarily "intervene in the resolution of conflicts which arise in the daily operation of school systems." *Tinker v. Des Moines School Dist.*, 393 U.S. 503, 507 (1969), noted that we have "repeatedly emphasized . . . the comprehensive authority of the States and of school officials . . . to prescribe and control conduct in the schools." We have also acknowledged that public schools are vitally important "in the preparation of individuals for participation as citizens," and as vehicles for "inculcating fundamental values necessary to the maintenance of a democratic political system." *Ambach v. Norwick*, 441 U.S. 68, 76–77 (1979). We are therefore in full agreement with petitioners that local school boards must be permitted "to establish and apply their curriculum in such a way as to transmit community values," and that "there is a legitimate and substantial community interest in promoting respect for authority and traditional values be they social, moral, or political."

At the same time, however, we have necessarily recognized that the discretion of the States and local school boards in matters of education must be exercised in a manner that comports with the transcendent imperatives of the First Amendment In sum, students do not "shed their constitutional rights to freedom of speech or expression at the schoolhouse gate," *id.*, at 506, and therefore local school boards must discharge their "important, delicate, and highly discretionary functions" within the limits and constraints of the First Amendment.

. . . .

Of course, courts should not "intervene in the resolution of conflicts which arise in the daily operation of school systems" unless "basic constitutional values" are "directly and sharply [implicated]" in those conflicts. *Epperson v. Arkansas*, 393 U.S., at 104. But we think that the First Amendment rights of students may be directly and sharply implicated by the removal of books from the shelves of a school library. Our precedents have focused "not only on the role of the First Amendment in fostering individual self-expression but also on its role in affording the public access to discussion, debate, and the dissemination of information and ideas." And we have recognized that "the State may not, consistently with the spirit of the First Amendment, contract the spectrum of available knowledge." *Griswold v. Connecticut*, 381 U.S. 479, 482 (1965). In keeping with this principle, we have held that in a variety of contexts "the Constitution protects the right to receive information and ideas." This right is an inherent corollary of the rights of free speech and press that are explicitly guaranteed by the Constitution, in two senses. First, the right to receive ideas follows ineluctably from the *sender's* First Amendment right to send them: "The right of freedom of speech and press . . . embraces the right to distribute literature, and necessarily protects the right to receive it." "The dissemination of ideas can accomplish nothing if otherwise willing addressees are not free to receive and consider them. It would be a barren marketplace of ideas that had only sellers and no buyers."

More importantly, the right to receive ideas is a necessary predicate to the *recipient's* meaningful exercise of his own rights of speech, press, and political freedom. Madison admonished us:

> "A popular Government, without popular information, or the means of acquiring it, is but a Prologue to a Farce or a Tragedy; or, perhaps both. Knowledge will forever govern ignorance: And a people who mean to be their own Governors, must arm themselves with the power which knowledge gives." 9 Writings of James Madison 103 (G. Hunt ed. 1910).

As we recognized in *Tinker*, students too are beneficiaries of this principle:

> "In our system, students may not be regarded as closed-circuit recipients of only that which the State chooses to communicate. . . . [School] officials cannot suppress 'expressions of feeling with which they do not wish to contend.'" 393 U.S., at 511 (quoting *Burnside v. Byars*, 363 F.2d 744, 749 (5th Cir. 1966)).

In sum, just as access to ideas makes it possible for citizens generally to exercise their rights of free speech and press in a meaningful manner, such access prepares students for active and effective participation in the pluralistic, often contentious society in which they will soon be adult members. Of course all First Amendment rights accorded to students must be construed "in light of the special characteristics of the school environment." *Tinker v. Des Moines School Dist.*, 393 U.S., at 506. But the special characteristics of the school *library* make that environment especially appropriate for the recognition of the First Amendment rights of students.

. . . .

Petitioners emphasize the inculcative function of secondary education, and argue that they must be allowed *unfettered* discretion to "transmit community values" through the Island Trees schools. But that sweeping claim overlooks the unique role of the school library. It appears from the record that use of the Island Trees school libraries is completely voluntary on the part of students. Their selection of books from these libraries is entirely a matter of free choice; the libraries afford them an opportunity at self-education and individual enrichment that is wholly optional. Petitioners might well defend their claim of absolute discretion in matters of *curriculum* by reliance upon their duty to inculcate community values. But we think that petitioners' reliance upon that duty is misplaced where, as here, they attempt to extend their claim of absolute discretion beyond the compulsory environment of the classroom, into the school library and the regime of voluntary inquiry that there holds sway.

In rejecting petitioners' claim of absolute discretion to remove books from their school libraries, we do not deny that local school boards have a substantial legitimate role to play in the determination of school library content. We thus must turn to the question of the extent to which the First Amendment places limitations upon the discretion of petitioners to remove books from their libraries. In this inquiry we enjoy the guidance of several precedents. *West Virginia Board of Education v. Barnette* stated:

> "If there is any fixed star in our constitutional constellation, it is that no official, high or petty, can prescribe what shall be orthodox in politics, nationalism, religion, or other matters of opinion. . . . If there are any circumstances which permit an exception, they do not now occur to us." 319 U.S. 624, 642.

This doctrine has been reaffirmed in later cases involving education. For example, *Keyishian v. Board of Regents*, noted that "the First Amendment . . . does not tolerate laws that cast a pall of orthodoxy over the classroom"; *see also Epperson v. Arkansas*, 393 U.S., at 104–105. And *Mt. Healthy City Board of Ed. v. Doyle*, 429 U.S. 274 (1977), recognized First Amendment limitations upon the discretion of a local school board to refuse to rehire a nontenured teacher. The school board in *Mt. Healthy* had declined to renew respondent Doyle's employment contract, in part because he had exercised his First Amendment rights. Although Doyle did not have tenure, and thus "could have been discharged for no reason whatever," *Mt. Healthy* held that he could "nonetheless establish a claim to reinstatement if the decision not to rehire him was made by reason of his exercise of constitutionally protected First Amendment freedoms." *Id.*, at 283–284. We held further that once Doyle had shown "that his conduct was constitutionally protected, and that this conduct was a 'substantial factor' . . . in the Board's decision not to rehire him," the school board was obliged to show "by a preponderance of the evidence that it would have reached the same decision as to respondent's reemployment even in the absence of the protected conduct." *Id.*, at 287.

With respect to the present case, the message of these precedents is clear. Petitioners rightly possess significant discretion to determine the content of their school libraries. But that discretion may not be exercised in a narrowly partisan or political manner. If a Democratic school board, motivated by party affiliation, ordered the removal of all books written by or in favor of Republicans, few would doubt that the order violated the constitutional rights of the students denied access to those books. The same conclusion would surely apply if an all-white school board, motivated by racial animus, decided to remove all books authored by blacks or advocating racial equality and integration. Our Constitution does not permit the official suppression of *ideas*. Thus whether petitioners' removal of books from their school libraries denied respondents their First Amendment rights depends upon the motivation behind petitioners' actions. If petitioners *intended* by their removal decision to deny respondents access to ideas with which petitioners disagreed, and if this intent was the decisive factor in petitioners' decision, then petitioners have exercised their discretion in violation of the Constitution. To permit such intentions to control official actions would be to encourage the precise sort of officially prescribed orthodoxy unequivocally condemned in *Barnette*. On the other hand, respondents implicitly concede that an unconstitutional motivation would *not* be demonstrated if it were shown that petitioners had decided to remove the books at issue because those books were pervasively vulgar. And again, respondents concede that if it were demonstrated that the removal decision was based solely upon the "educational suitability" of the books in question, then their removal would be "perfectly permissible." In other words, in respondents' view such motivations, if decisive of petitioners' actions, would not carry the danger of an official suppression of ideas, and thus would not violate respondents' First Amendment rights.

By "decisive factor" we mean a "substantial factor" in the absence of which the opposite decision would have been reached. *See Mt. Healthy City Board of Ed. v. Doyle*, 429 U.S. 274, 287 (1977).

As noted earlier, nothing in our decision today affects in any way the discretion of a local school board to choose books to *add* to the libraries of their schools. Because we are concerned in this case with the suppression of ideas, our holding today affects only the discretion to *remove* books. In brief, we hold that local school boards may not remove books from school library shelves simply because they dislike the ideas contained in those books and seek by their removal to "prescribe what shall be orthodox in politics, nationalism, religion, or other matters of opinion." *West Virginia State Board of Education v. Barnette*, 319 U.S., at 642. Such purposes stand inescapably condemned by our precedents.

. . . .

Construing these claims, affidavit statements, and other evidentiary materials in a manner favorable to respondents, we cannot conclude that petitioners were "entitled to a judgment as a matter of law." The evidence plainly does not foreclose the possibility that petitioners' decision to remove the books rested decisively upon disagreement with constitutionally protected ideas in those books, or upon a desire on petitioners' part to impose upon the students of the Island Trees High School and Junior High School a political orthodoxy to which petitioners and their constituents adhered. Of course, some of the evidence before the District Court might lead a finder of fact to accept petitioners' claim that their removal decision was based upon constitutionally valid concerns. But that evidence at most creates a genuine issue of material fact on the critical question of the credibility of petitioners' justifications for their decision: On that issue, it simply cannot be said that there is no genuine issue as to any material fact.

The mandate shall issue forthwith.

Affirmed.

Virgil v. School Board

862 F.2d 1517 (11th Cir. 1989)

The court finds that a public school did not violate the First Amendment when it removed books from the required reading for an elective high school class when the reason for the removal was alleged vulgarity and sexual explicitness.

Anderson, Circuit Judge:

This case presents the question of whether the first amendment prevents a school board from removing a previously approved textbook from an elective high school class because of objections to the material's vulgarity and sexual explicitness. We conclude that a school board may, without contravening constitutional limits, take such action where, as here, its methods are "reasonably related to legitimate pedagogical concerns." Accordingly, we affirm the judgment of the district court.

The essential facts were stipulated by the parties to this dispute. Since about 1975 the educational curriculum at Columbia High School has included a course entitled "Humanities to 1500" offered as part of a two-semester survey of Western thought, art and literature. In 1985 the school designed the course for eleventh- and twelfth-grade students and prescribed as a textbook Volume I of *The Humanities: Cultural Roots and Continuities*. This book contained both required and optional readings for the course.

Among the selections included in Volume I of *Humanities* which were neither required nor assigned are English translations of *Lysistrata*, written by the Greek dramatist Aristophanes in approximately 411 B.C., and *The Miller's Tale*, written by the English poet Geoffrey Chaucer around 1380–1390 A.D. During the fall semester of the 1985–86 school year, a portion of *Lysistrata* was read aloud in class during a session of the Humanities course.

In the spring of 1986, after the first semester had ended, the Reverend and Mrs. Fritz M. Fountain, the parents of a student who had taken the class in the fall of 1985, filed a formal complaint concerning Volume I of *Humanities* with the School Board of Columbia County. The Fountains also submitted a Request for Examination of School Media. Their objections centered upon *Lysistrata* and *The Miller's Tale*.

In response to this parental complaint, the School Board on April 8, 1986 adopted a Policy on Challenged State Adopted Textbooks to address any complaints regarding books in use in the curriculum. Pursuant to the new policy, the School Board appointed an advisory committee to review Volume I of *Humanities*. Upon examination, the committee recommended that the textbook be retained in the curriculum, but that *Lysistrata* and *The Miller's Tale* not be assigned as required reading.

At its April 22, 1986 meeting the School Board considered the advisory committee's report. Silas Pittman, Superintendent of the Columbia County School System, offered his disagreement with the committee's conclusion, and recommended that the two disputed selections be deleted from Volume I or that use of the book in the curriculum be terminated. Adopting the latter proposal, the School Board voted to discontinue any future use of Volume I in the curriculum.

Pursuant to the Board decision, Volume I of *Humanities* was placed in locked storage and has been kept there ever since. Volume II was used as the course textbook for the rest of the second semester of the 1985–86 academic year, as well as for both semesters of the "Humanities" course during the 1986–87 term. Since the Board's removal decision, both Volumes I and II have been available in the school library for student use, along with other adaptations and translations of *Lysistrata* and *The Miller's Tale*.

On November 24, 1986 parents of students at Columbia High School filed an action against the School Board and the Superintendent seeking an injunction against the textbook removal and a declaration that such action violated their first amendment rights....

The district court found that the two principal factors giving rise to the School Board's decision were "the sexuality in the two selections" and their "excessively vulgar ... language and subject matter." In the court's view, the other reasons stipulated by the Board members "simply amplify why they believed that vulgar and sexually explicit materials could properly be removed from the curriculum." *Id.* The court acknowledged that "the School Board's decision reflects its own restrictive views of the appropriate values to which Columbia High School students should be exposed," *id.*, and expressed the difficulty it had in "apprehend[ing] the harm which could conceivably be caused to a group of eleventh- and twelfth-grade students by exposure to Aristophanes and Chaucer." *Id.* Nonetheless, the court held that the deferential standard recently established in *Hazelwood School District v. Kuhlmeier* had been met, as the removal decision was "reasonably related" to the "legitimate pedagogical concern" of denying students access to "potentially sensitive topics" such as sexuality.

It has long been clear that public school students do not "shed their constitutional rights to freedom of speech or expression at the schoolhouse gate." At the same time, the Supreme Court has held that the rights of students in public schools are not automatically coextensive with the rights of adults, *Hazelwood*, and has recognized the central role of public schools in transmitting values necessary to the development of an informed citizenry. *Bethel School District No. 403 v. Fraser*, 478 U.S. 675 (1986) (affirming that the essence of public education is "prepar[ing] pupils for citizenship in the Republic" through "inculcation of fundamental values"); *Board of Education v. Pico*, 457 U.S. 853, 876 (1982) (Blackmun, J., concurring in part and concurring in judgment) ("It therefore seems entirely appropriate that the State use 'public schools [to] . . . inculcat[e] fundamental values necessary to the maintenance of a democratic political system'").

In matters pertaining to the curriculum, educators have been accorded greater control over expression than they may enjoy in other spheres of activity. *See Hazelwood School District v. Kuhlmeier* (upholding restriction of expression in school-sponsored student newspaper or in other activities which "may fairly be characterized as part of the school curriculum"). *See also Board of Education v. Pico*, 457 U.S. 853, 869 (plurality opinion) (indicating that broad school board discretion in matters of curriculum may be defended by reliance upon school board's duty to inculcate community values); *Pratt v. Independent School District*, 670 F.2d 771, 775 (8th Cir. 1982) (school board's "comprehensive powers and substantial discretion" include "the authority to determine the curriculum that is most suitable for students and the teaching methods that are to be employed, including the educational tools to be used").

Still, courts that have addressed the issue have failed to achieve a consensus on the degree of discretion to be accorded school boards to restrict access to curricular materials.

The most direct guidance from the Supreme Court is found in the recent case of *Hazelwood School District v. Kuhlmeier*. In *Hazelwood* the Court upheld the authority of a high school principal to excise two pages from a school-sponsored student newspaper on the grounds that articles concerning teenage pregnancy and divorce were inappropriate for the level of maturity of the intended readers, the privacy interests of the articles' subjects were insufficiently protected, and the controversial views contained therein might erroneously be attributed to the school. *Hazelwood* established a relatively lenient test for regulation of expression which "may fairly be characterized as part of the school curriculum." Such regulation is permissible so long as it is "reasonably related to legitimate pedagogical concerns."

In applying that test the Supreme Court identified one such legitimate concern which is relevant to this case: "a school must be able to take into account the emotional maturity of the intended audience in determining whether to disseminate student speech on potentially sensitive topics . . . [e.g.] the particulars of teenage sexual activity." *See also Bethel School District v. Fraser* (recognizing interest in protecting minors from exposure to "sexually explicit" speech and "vulgar" or "offensive" spoken language); *Pico* (plurality opinion finding that removal of books from library would be permissible if decision were based on determination that books were "pervasively vulgar" or not "educational[ly] suitab[le]") and (Blackmun, J., concurring in part and concurring in judgment) (removal permissible if motivated by concern that material "contains offensive language . . . or because it is psychologically or intellectually inappropriate for the age group").

In applying the *Hazelwood* standard to the instant case, two considerations are particularly significant. First, we conclude that the Board decisions at issue were curricular decisions. The materials removed were part of the textbook used in a regularly scheduled course of study in the school. Plaintiffs argue that this particular course was an elective course, and not a required course. However, common sense indicates that the overall curriculum offered by a school includes not only the core curriculum (i.e., required courses) but also such additional, elective courses of study that school officials design and offer. Each student is expected to select from the several elective courses which school officials deem appropriate in order to fashion a curriculum tailored to his individual needs.

One factor identified in *Hazelwood* as relevant to the determination of whether an activity could fairly be characterized as part of the curriculum is whether "the public might reasonably perceive [the activity] to bear the imprimatur of the school." It is clear that elective courses designed and offered by the school would be so perceived. Moreover, we can take judicial notice that the journalism class which was considered in *Hazelwood* itself to be part of the curriculum was surely an elective course.

Plaintiffs further point out that the materials removed in this case not only were part of an elective course, but were optional, not required readings. For the reasons just mentioned, we conclude that the optional readings removed in this case were part of the school curriculum. Just as elective courses are designed by school officials to supplement required courses, optional readings in a particular class are carefully selected by the teacher as relevant and appropriate to supplement required readings in order to further the educational goals of the course. This is especially true in the instant circumstances, where the optional readings were included within the text itself, and thus had to accompany the student every time the text was taken home. Such materials would obviously carry the imprimatur of school approval.

The second consideration that is significant in applying the *Hazelwood* standard to this case is the fact that the motivation for the Board's removal of the readings has been stipulated to be related to the explicit sexuality and excessively vulgar language in the selections. It is clear from *Hazelwood* and other cases that this is a legitimate concern. School officials can "take into account the emotional maturity of the intended audience in determining . . . [the appropriateness of] potentially sensitive topics" such as sex and vulgarity. *Hazelwood*.[3]

---

3. [FN 8] Appellants argue that this case is most analogous to the removal of books from a library, and thus that it is governed by *Board of Education v. Pico*, 457 U.S. 853 (1982) (plurality opinion). We disagree. *Pico* involved a school library, and the plurality took special note of the "unique role of the school library" as a repository for "voluntary inquiry." More significantly, the *Pico* plurality held

Since the stipulated motivation of the School Board relates to legitimate concerns, we need only determine whether the Board action was *reasonably* related thereto. It is of course true, as plaintiffs so forcefully point out, that *Lysistrata* and *The Miller's Tale* are widely acclaimed masterpieces of Western literature. However, after careful consideration, we cannot conclude that the school board's actions were not reasonably related to its legitimate concerns regarding the appropriateness (for this high school audience) of the sexuality and vulgarity in these works. Notwithstanding their status as literary classics, *Lysistrata* and *The Miller's Tale* contain passages of exceptional sexual explicitness, as numerous commentators have noted. In assessing the reasonableness of the Board's action, we also take into consideration the fact that most of the high school students involved ranged in age from fifteen to just over eighteen, and a substantial number had not yet reached the age of majority. We also note that the disputed materials have not been banned from the school. The *Humanities* textbook and other adaptations of *Lysistrata* and *The Miller's Tale* are available in the school library. No student or teacher is prohibited from assigning or reading these works or discussing the themes contained therein in class or on school property. Under all the circumstances of this case, we cannot conclude that the Board's action was not reasonably related to the stated legitimate concern.

We decide today only that the Board's removal of these works from the curriculum did not violate the Constitution. Of course, we do not endorse the Board's decision. Like the district court, we seriously question how young persons just below the age of majority can be harmed by these masterpieces of Western literature. However, having concluded that there is no constitutional violation, our role is not to second guess the wisdom of the Board's action.

The judgment of the district court is *Affirmed*.

Monteiro v. Tempe Union High School District

158 F.3d 1022 (9th Cir. 1998)

In a case that involves both equal protection claims and claims of a hostile racial environment as to the assignment of texts using a racially derogatory term, the court affirms the denial of relief as to equal protection but remands as to hostile environment.

Reinhardt, Circuit Judge:

More and more frequently we are faced with cases in which two fundamental constitutional rights appear to be at odds. At such times, the job of federal judges is

---

that a school board may not remove books from a school library where a constitutionally impermissible motive—board members' opposition to the content of ideas expressed in the disputed materials—was the "decisive factor" underlying the decision to remove. By virtue of the parties' stipulated reasons for the Board action in this case, the motive at issue in *Pico* is absent here. We make no suggestion as to the appropriate standard to be applied in a case where one party has demonstrated that removal stemmed from opposition to the ideas contained in the disputed materials.

particularly difficult. Here, we confront a case presenting some elements of such a clash. The setting is a freshman English class in Tempe, Arizona, and the competing interests are the First Amendment rights of high school students to receive information or ideas—even when contained in literary works that may in today's world appear to have racist overtones—and the rights of those same students to receive a public education that neither fosters nor acquiesces in a racially hostile environment.

Jane Doe was a student in a freshman English class at McClintock High School, which is part of the defendant Tempe Unified Union High School District ("School District"). The class' required reading included two classic literary works—the novel *The Adventures of Huckleberry Finn*, by Mark Twain, and the short story *A Rose for Emily*, by William Faulkner. The complaint, brought on Doe's behalf by her mother, Kathy Monteiro, alleged that each of these literary works "contains repeated use of the profane, insulting and racially derogatory term 'nigger.'" It also alleged that neither work is a necessary component of a freshman English class and that none of the assignments in the curriculum refers to Caucasians in a derogatory manner.

According to the complaint, Doe and other similarly situated African-American students suffered psychological injuries and lost educational opportunities due to the required reading of the literary works. The complaint alleged that the School District had notice that Doe suffered these injuries but refused to offer a remedy other than to allow her to study alone in the library while the works were being discussed in class. It further alleged that the assignment of the literary works "created and contributed to a racially hostile educational environment," including increased racial harassment by other students. Finally, it alleged that by its conduct the School District intentionally discriminated against Doe.

In her complaint, Monteiro sought a declaratory judgment, urging that the conduct of the School District violated Doe's rights under the Equal Protection Clause of the Fourteenth Amendment and Title VI of the Civil Rights Act of 1964. She also requested a temporary and permanent injunction "prohibiting [the defendants] from committing similar unlawful acts in the future." Monteiro did not, however, seek the exclusion of the literary works from a voluntary reading list or from inclusion in classroom discussions in which Jane Doe and other African American students [are] *not* held as a captive student audience or consigned to a separate and unequal educational environment.

Finally, she requested compensatory monetary damages, equitable relief in the form of compensatory education, and attorney fees.

In a memorandum order filed January 2, 1997, the district court dismissed the complaint on the ground that Doe failed to state a claim under either the Equal Protection Clause or Title VI because the complaint did not contain specific allegations of fact necessary to sustain a claim of discriminatory intent. The district court also dismissed as moot Monteiro's request for injunctive relief "regarding removal of the literary works from particular English classes" because Doe was no longer a member of the freshman English class. . . .

The amended complaint reiterates the contentions made in the initial complaint and seeks the same relief. It contains additional allegations, however, regarding the hostile racial environment at the school and the notice afforded the District of the complained-of conduct. It alleges with more particularity that Doe and other African-American students were subjected to racial harassment, orally and by the use of graffiti, prior to the time the literary works were introduced into the classroom, and that such harassment increased as a result of the assignment of those works as required reading. In particular, it alleges that African-American students were called "nigger" by their white peers with increased frequency and intensity after the literary works were assigned. Finally, it alleges that the school district, when notified of incidents of racial harassment, refused to accept the complaints or to take any appropriate remedial measures regarding them.

. . . .

Monteiro's amended complaint alleges violations of the Equal Protection clause and Title VI of the Civil Rights Act of 1964.[4]

The amended complaint requests relief on the basis of two distinct acts, or rather failures to act, on the part of the District. The first involves the District's assignment of the two disputed literary works as mandatory reading, and its subsequent refusal to remove them from that part of the curriculum. The second involves the District's refusal to take action in response to complaints by Doe and other African-American students regarding incidents of racial harassment at the school. Each incorporates the facts that underlie the other. We will address the two distinct claims in turn.

A. Assignment of and Failure to Remove the Literary Works

A significant portion of the amended complaint, like the original, is based on the District's assignment of *Huckleberry Finn* and *A Rose for Emily* as required reading and its subsequent refusal to remove them from the mandatory curriculum. In addition to seeking removal, Monteiro's amended complaint seeks monetary damages as a result of the past assignment of the literary works and an injunction preventing the school from "committing similar unlawful acts in the future." We consider here whether the District's conduct, the requirement that students read books that were determined by the appropriate school authorities to have educational value, and the refusal to remove those books from a mandatory curriculum, can form the basis for a complaint alleging discriminatory conduct under the Equal Protection Clause and Title VI.

We approach this question in light of a number of considerations. The first is the threat to First Amendment freedoms posed by efforts to prevent school boards from assigning the reading of literary works on the ground that individuals or groups may

---

4. [FN 3] Title VI provides in relevant part: "No person in the United States shall, on the ground of race, color, or national origin, be excluded from participation in, be denied the benefits of, or be subjected to discrimination under and program or activity receiving Federal financial assistance." 42 U.S.C. § 2000d.

find the contents injurious or offensive. The second is the broad discretion afforded school boards to establish curricula they believe to be appropriate to the educational needs of their students. The third is the awareness that words can hurt, particularly in the case of children, and that words of a racist nature can hurt especially severely. The fourth is the knowledge that the historic prejudice against African-Americans that has existed in this nation since its inception has not yet been eradicated—by any means. The fifth is the requirement that young African-Americans, like all students, be afforded a public education free from racially discriminatory conduct on the part of educational authorities.

The Supreme Court has addressed on a number of occasions the balancing of a school's discretion in determining educational matters with a students' First Amendment rights. *See, e.g., Hazelwood Sch. Dist. v. Kuhlmeier* (holding that school board regulation of curriculum-related speech does not raise First Amendment concerns if regulation is "reasonably related to legitimate pedagogical concerns"); *Bethel Sch. Dist. No. 403 v. Fraser* (holding that punishment of student's "lewd speech" at assembly does not constitute violation); *Board of Educ., Island Trees Union Free Sch. Dist. v. Pico* (holding that students' First Amendment right of access to information is violated when schools remove books from library in content-based manner). In doing so, the Court has recognized that school boards generally retain a broad discretion in managing school affairs, *Kuhlmeier; Pico* (agreeing with proposition that local school boards may establish and apply their curricula such a way as to transmit community values); but it has also consistently noted that the school board's discretion "in matters of education must be exercised in a manner that comports with the transcendent imperatives of the First Amendment."

Unlike the cases cited above, the case before us does not involve an action taken by a school board that arguably abridges the First Amendment rights of its students. Instead, it is a third party, a parent or a class of parents, that seeks to limit the educational materials the school officials may furnish to the students—and require them to read. Here we consider whether the school board's interest in exercising its broad discretion in assigning the literary works in question and the students' First Amendment interest in reading those works are collectively outweighed by the constitutional and statutory interests of students who assert that they are injured by the mandatory assignments. To resolve this controversy, we must consider whether the assignment of material deemed to have educational value by school authorities may in itself serve as the basis for an injunction by a court or an award of damages, when the challenge to the material is founded on its message or the language it employs. In other words, may courts ban books or other literary works from school curricula on the basis of their content? We answer that question in the negative, even when the works are accused of being racist in whole or in part.

To begin with, Monteiro's amended complaint—and other lawsuits threatening to attach civil liability on the basis of the assignment of a book—would severely restrict a student's right to receive material that his school board or other educational authority determines to be of legitimate educational value. The amended complaint requests, under the threat of civil liability, that the school remove the literary works from the classroom. Certainly when a school board identifies information that it believes to be a useful part of a student's education, that student has the right to receive the information. Indeed, the Eighth Circuit has concluded that a school board's removal of material from the classroom curriculum solely on the basis of its message has a powerful symbolic effect on a student or teacher's First Amendment rights—despite the material's availability in the library—and is, therefore, unconstitutional. Because ours is not a case in which a school board has decided on the basis of its own evaluations to remove literary materials, we need not now decide the question resolved by the Eighth Circuit. We have no hesitation in concluding, however, that a student's First Amendment rights are infringed when books that have been determined by the school district to have legitimate educational value are removed from a mandatory reading list because of threats of damages, lawsuits, or other forms of retaliation. In this case, the relief that Monteiro's complaint seeks, injunctive relief as well as monetary damages, would unquestionably restrict the students' First Amendment freedoms and significantly interfere with the District's discretion to determine the composition of its curriculum.

There is an even more serious consequence for McClintock High School, as well as for all schools, that would flow from allowing the judicial system to process complaints that seek to enjoin or attach civil liability to a school district's assignment of a book. As the Supreme Court has recognized, at least since *New York Times Co. v. Sullivan*, were the plaintiff to succeed in this litigation or even to succeed in forcing the defendants to engage in a trial over such well-established literary works, the threat of future litigation would inevitably lead many school districts to "buy their peace" by avoiding the use of books or other materials that express messages—or simply use terms—that could be argued to cause harm to a group of students.

It is not surprising that this conflict arises over *Huckleberry Finn*. According to the American Library Association, Twain's slim volume describing the effects of racism and slavery in antebellum society is the most frequently banned book in the United States, as well as one of the nation's most respected literary works. Black parents all over the country have asserted, as does Monteiro, that the book's use of the word "nigger" some 215 times "has a negative effect on the self-esteem of young black students" and that it therefore "has no place in the classroom." Recent years have seen efforts to remove the work from libraries and reading lists in school districts in a number of states, including Pennsylvania, Ohio, and California, as well as Arizona. Although some districts voted to retain the book, many others have removed it from the curriculum due to concerns about the use of racial stereotypes and epithets.

There is, of course, an extremely wide—if not unlimited—range of literary products that might be considered injurious or offensive, particularly when one considers that high school students frequently take Advanced Placement courses that are equivalent to college-level courses. White plaintiffs could seek to remove books by Toni Morrison, Maya Angelou, and other prominent Black authors on the ground that they portray Caucasians in a derogatory fashion; Jews might try to impose civil liability for the teachings of Shakespeare and of more modern English poets where writings exhibit a similar anti-Semitic strain. Female students could attempt to make a case for damages for the assignment of some of the works of Tennessee Williams, Hemingway, or Freud, and male students for the writings of Andrea Dworkin or Margaret Atwood. The number of potential lawsuits that could arise from the highly varied educational curricula throughout the nation might well be unlimited and unpredictable. Many school districts would undoubtedly prefer to "steer far" from any controversial book and instead substitute "safe" ones in order to reduce the possibility of civil liability and the expensive and time-consuming burdens of a lawsuit—even one having but a slight chance of success. In short, permitting lawsuits against school districts on the basis of the content of literary works to proceed past the complaint stage could have a significant chilling effect on a school district's willingness to assign books with themes, characters, snippets of dialogue, or words that might offend the sensibilities of any number of persons or groups.

Further, any school board attempting to remove books from its curriculum on the ground that the works might offend would likely be vulnerable to First Amendment actions brought by students desiring to study those books, and possibly teachers, as well. Schools could be caught between those seeking to remove *Huckleberry Finn* and those seeking to study it. It would clearly not be in the best interests of our public education system and its students to have such competing lawsuits become a part of our legal landscape.

The number and range of books that might become the subject of litigation must be considered in light of the fact that the literary works at issue here contained only one offensive term, albeit a most injurious one. Moreover, the term is one that was widely used in an earlier era, and that might well appear in any work of fiction attempting to portray life in those times with any accuracy. The amended complaint does not allege that the two literary works are otherwise offensive or that they in any other way convey racist or offensive messages. Nor does it contend that the curriculum itself was racist or that the manner in which the assigned books, or any other books, were taught caused injury to African-American students. To put it in the most elementary terms, it is the literary works, and only the literary works, that Monteiro seeks to put on trial in the principal portion of her complaint—and it is solely because of the recitation in those works of a once commonly used racial epithet that she seeks to do so. Monteiro's complaint indeed raises most serious First Amendment concerns.

Nevertheless, as we said at the outset, there are important countervailing considerations that also must be weighed. We are aware that books can hurt, and that words can hurt—particularly racist epithets. It is now uncontroversial to observe that some of the most lauded works of literature convey, explicitly or in a more subtle manner, messages of racism and sexism, or other ideas that if accepted blindly would serve to maintain or promote the invidious inequalities that exist in our world today. We also recognize that the younger a person is, the more likely it is that those messages will help form that person's thinking, and that the feelings of minority students, especially younger ones, are extremely vulnerable when it comes to books that are racist or have racist overtones. In addition, we acknowledge that we have all too often failed to afford our African-American citizens the equal treatment that the Fourteenth Amendment requires, particularly in the area of public education. Nevertheless, for our courts or even our school boards to prohibit the assignment of literary works that may in some respects be racially offensive is simply not the proper solution.

First, the fact that a student is required to read a book does not mean that he is being asked to agree with what is in it. It cannot be disputed that a necessary component of any education is learning to think critically about offensive ideas—without that ability one can do little to respond to them. Second, it is important for young people to learn about the past—and to discover both the good and the bad in our history. Third, if all books with messages that might be deemed harmful were removed, the number of "acceptable" works might be highly limited. Because sexism and racism, and other forms of inequality, exist in almost every culture—and because our values tend to change and are not immutable—and because the dispute over what ideas are proper or improper will always be a matter of intense controversy—it would be folly to think that there is a certain "safe" set of books written by particular authors that all will find acceptable. Next, we reject the notion that putting books on trial in our courts is the proper way to determine the appropriateness of their use in the classroom. Such judgments are ordinarily best left to school boards and educational officials charged with educating young people and determining which education materials are appropriate for which students, and under what circumstances. Therefore, although we recognize that books—and words—are powerful tools that can convey extremely injurious messages, we conclude that the assignment of a literary work determined to have intrinsic educational value by the duly authorized school authorities cannot constitute the type of discriminatory conduct prohibited by the Fourteenth Amendment and Title VI, regardless of the fact that the work may be deemed to contain racist ideas or language.

We do not, of course, suggest that racist actions on the part of teachers implementing a curriculum could not comprise discriminatory conduct for the purposes of Title VI or the Fourteenth Amendment. Nor do we preclude the prosecution of actions alleging that schools have pursued policies that serve to promote racist attitudes among their students, or have sought to indoctrinate their young charges with racist concepts. We conclude only that allegations that a school required that a book be read, and then refused to remove it from the curriculum, fails to provide the basis for a claim of discrimination under the Equal Protection Clause or Title VI, even when the school district is also accused of a failure to take steps to remedy a hostile racial environment. It is simply not the role of courts to serve as literary censors or to make judgments as to whether reading particular books does students more harm than good.

We close this part of our discussion with two observations. First, we view with considerable skepticism charges that reading books causes evil conduct. It is all too easy to allege cause-and-effect when one event follows another. Here, for example,

Monteiro alleges that racial harassment, including verbal insults, increased "as a result of" the assignment of *Huckleberry Finn* and *A Rose for Emily*. The "as a result" link is wholly unsupported by any factual allegations. If racial harassment indeed increased during the school term, there are many other more likely causes that all of the interested parties might do well to explore. Second, the function of books and other literary materials, as well as of education itself, is to stimulate thought, to explore ideas, to engender intellectual exchanges. Bad ideas should be countered with good ones, not banned by the courts. One of the roles of teachers is to guide students through the difficult process of becoming educated, to help them learn how to discriminate between good concepts and bad, to benefit from the errors society has made in the past, to improve their minds and characters. Those who choose the books and literature that will influence the minds and hearts of our nation's youth and those who teach young people in our schools bear an awesome responsibility. We can only encourage them to exercise their authority wisely and well, and to be sensitive to the needs and concerns of all of their students.

In light of the above, we affirm the district court's rejection of the amended complaint as it relates to the District's assignment of and refusal to remove the two literary works in question.

. . . .

Post Problem Discussion

1. In *Virgil*, the court finds that the *Hazelwood* standard applies. In a footnote, the court distinguishes the *Pico* case due to the fact that *Pico* involved library books that were not part of the curriculum. You will learn more about the *Hazelwood* standard in Chapter 9. Do you agree with the court's analysis? Why or why not?

2. In *Monteiro*, the Ninth Circuit frames the issue as requiring the consideration of "whether the assignment of material deemed to have educational value by school authorities may in itself serve as the basis for an injunction by a court or an award of damages, when the challenge to the material is founded on its message or the language it employs." *Monteiro*, 158 F.3d at 1028. The Court then cites to a line of Supreme Court decisions that includes both *Hazelwood* and *Pico*, but in a footnote not included in the text here observes:

> We find *Pico* to be particularly helpful in identifying the First Amendment interests that are involved in this case. *Pico* held that a school board could not remove books from a school library if it did so "in a narrowly partisan or political manner." 457 U.S. at 870–71. It based its decision on two First Amendment principles that we find are also relevant in the context of a school curriculum. The first is the well-established rule that the right to receive information is an inherent corollary of the rights of free speech and press, because the right to distribute information necessarily protects the right to receive it. 457 U.S. at 866; *see Virginia State Bd. of Pharmacy v. Virginia Citizens Consumer Council, Inc.*, 425 U.S. 748, 756, 96 S.

> Ct. 1817, 48 L. Ed. 2d 346 (1976) ("Freedom of speech presupposes a willing speaker. But where a speaker exists, as is the case here, the protection afforded is to the communication, to its source and to its recipients both.") (right to receive advertising). The second involves the students' rights to receive a broad range of information so that they can freely form their own thoughts: "more importantly, the right to receive ideas is a necessary predicate to the *recipient's* meaningful exercise of his own rights of speech, press, and political freedom." 457 U.S. at 867 (emphasis added). The Supreme Court has long recognized that the freedom to receive ideas, and its relation to the freedom of expression, is particularly relevant in the classroom setting: The classroom is peculiarly "the marketplace of ideas." The Nation's future depends upon leaders trained through wide exposure to that robust exchange of ideas which discovers truth "out of a multitude of tongues, [rather] than through any kind of authoritative selection."

Monteiro, 158 F.3d at 1027 n.5. Which approach (*Monteiro* or *Virgil)* makes more sense to you and why? If you were a judge and could choose between these approaches, which would you follow?

3. What is the difference between the *Pico* and *Hazelwood* standards? Would the result in *Virgil* have been different if the materials at issue were just in the library as opposed to being part of the assigned reading and the court applied the *Pico* standard? Would the result in our problem be different under the *Pico* or *Hazelwood* standards?

4. The court in *Virgil* noted that it did not agree with the school board's decision, but upheld it because there was no constitutional violation, noting that its role is not to "second guess the wisdom of the Board's action." Does *Monteiro* change the level of involvement, or the standard of review, because of the plaintiff's claim of racial discrimination?

Problem 3: Academic Freedom

Assume that the VeryRural High School Board votes to remove the book and film from the required reading and bans them from being used at school. Can Ms. Bragdon, the tenth grade language arts teacher who originally assigned the book, successfully challenge the school board's decision based on her right to academic freedom? Does she have any academic freedom right to use the materials or discuss the book in her class? May the school board terminate her employment if she does so?

Problem Materials

- ✓ *Keyishian v. Board of Regents*, 385 U.S. 589 (1967)
- ✓ *Boring v. Buncombe County Board of Education*, 136 F.3d 364 (4th Cir. 1998), *cert. denied*, 525 U.S. 813 (1998)
- ✓ *Cockrel v. Shelby County School District*, 270 F.3d 1036 (6th Cir. 2001), *cert. denied*, 537 U.S. 813 (2002)

Keyishian v. Board of Regents

385 U.S. 589 (1967)

The Court finds unconstitutional a state law requiring faculty to certify that they are not members of the Communist party.

Mr. Justice Brennan delivered the opinion of the Court.

Appellants were members of the faculty of the privately owned and operated University of Buffalo, and became state employees when the University was merged in 1962 into the State University of New York, an institution of higher education owned and operated by the State of New York. As faculty members of the State University their continued employment was conditioned upon their compliance with a New York plan, formulated partly in statutes and partly in administrative regulations, which the State utilizes to prevent the appointment or retention of "subversive" persons in state employment.

Appellants Hochfield and Maud were Assistant Professors of English, appellant Keyishian an instructor in English, and appellant Garver, a lecturer in Philosophy. Each of them refused to sign, as regulations then in effect required, a certificate that he was not a Communist, and that if he had ever been a Communist, he had communicated that fact to the President of the State University of New York. Each was notified that his failure to sign the certificate would require his dismissal. Keyishian's one-year-term contract was not renewed because of his failure to sign the certificate. Hochfield and Garver, whose contracts still had time to run, continue to teach, but subject to proceedings for their dismissal if the constitutionality of the New York plan is sustained. Maud has voluntarily resigned and therefore no longer has standing in this suit.

Appellant Starbuck was a nonfaculty library employee and part-time lecturer in English. Personnel in that classification were not required to sign a certificate but were required to answer in writing under oath the question, "Have you ever advised or taught or were you ever a member of any society or group of persons which taught or advocated the doctrine that the Government of the United States or of any political subdivisions thereof should be overthrown or overturned by force, violence or any unlawful means?" Starbuck refused to answer the question and as a result was dismissed.

Appellants brought this action for declaratory and injunctive relief, alleging that the state program violated the Federal Constitution in various respects....

....

We do not have the benefit of a judicial gloss by the New York courts enlightening us as to the scope of this complicated plan. In light of the intricate administrative machinery for its enforcement, this is not surprising. The very intricacy of the plan and the uncertainty as to the scope of its proscriptions make it a highly efficient in terrorem mechanism. It would be a bold teacher who would not stay as far as possible from utterances or acts which might jeopardize his living by enmeshing him in this intricate machinery. The uncertainty as to the utterances and acts proscribed increases that caution in "those who believe the written law means what it says." The result must be to stifle "that free play of the spirit which all teachers ought especially to cultivate and practice * * *." That probability is enhanced by the provisions requiring an annual review of every teacher to determine whether any utterance or act of his, inside the classroom or out, came within the sanctions of the laws. For a memorandum warns employees that under the statutes "subversive" activities may take the form of "[t]he writing of articles, the distribution of pamphlets, the endorsement of speeches made or articles written or acts performed by others," and reminds them "that it is a primary duty of the school authorities in each school district to take positive action to eliminate from the school system any teacher in whose case there is evidence that he is guilty of subversive activity. School authorities are under obligation to proceed immediately and conclusively in every such case."

There can be no doubt of the legitimacy of New York's interest in protecting its education system from subversion. But "even though the governmental purpose be legitimate and substantial, that purpose cannot be pursued by means that broadly stifle fundamental personal liberties when the end can be more narrowly achieved." The principle is not inapplicable because the legislation is aimed at keeping subversives out of the teaching ranks. In *De Jonge v. State of Oregon*, 299 U.S. 353, 365, the Court said:

> "The greater the importance of safeguarding the community from incitements to the overthrow of our institutions by force and violence, the more imperative is the need to preserve inviolate the constitutional rights of free speech, free press and free assembly in order to maintain the opportunity for free political discussion, to the end that government may be responsive to the will of the people and that changes, if desired, may be obtained by peaceful means. Therein lies the security of the Republic, the very foundation of constitutional government."

Our Nation is deeply committed to safeguarding academic freedom, which is of transcendent value to all of us and not merely to the teachers concerned. That freedom is therefore a special concern of the First Amendment, which does not tolerate laws that cast a pall of orthodoxy over the classroom. "The vigilant protection of constitutional freedoms is nowhere more vital than in the community of American schools." The classroom is peculiarly the "marketplace of ideas." The Nation's future depends upon leaders trained through wide exposure to that robust exchange of ideas which discovers truth "out of a multitude of tongues, [rather] than through any kind of authoritative selection." In *Sweezy v. State of New Hampshire*, 354 U.S. 234, 250, we said:

> "The essentiality of freedom in the community of American universities is almost self-evident. No one should underestimate the vital role in a democracy that is played by those who guide and train our youth. To impose any strait jacket upon the intellectual leaders in our colleges and universities

> would imperil the future of our Nation. No field of education is so thoroughly comprehended by man that new discoveries cannot yet be made. Particularly is that true in the social sciences, where few, if any, principles are accepted as absolutes. Scholarship cannot flourish in an atmosphere of suspicion and distrust. Teachers and students must always remain free to inquire, to study and to evaluate, to gain new maturity and understanding; otherwise our civilization will stagnate and die."

We emphasize once again that "[p]recision of regulation must be the touchstone in an area so closely touching our most precious freedoms," *N.A.A.C.P. v. Button*, 371 U.S. 415, 438, "[f]or standards of permissible statutory vagueness are strict in the area of free expression. . . . Because First Amendment freedoms need breathing space to survive, government may regulate in the area only with narrow specificity." New York's complicated and intricate scheme plainly violates that standard. When one must guess what conduct or utterance may lose him his position, one necessarily will "steer far wider of the unlawful zone. . . ." For "[t]he threat of sanctions may deter . . . almost as potently as the actual application of sanctions." *N.A.A.C.P. v. Button, supra*, 371 U.S., at 433. The danger of that chilling effect upon the exercise of vital First Amendment rights must be guarded against by sensitive tools which clearly inform teachers what is being proscribed.

The regulatory maze created by New York is wholly lacking in "terms susceptible of objective measurement." It has the quality of 'extraordinary ambiguity' found to be fatal to the oaths considered in *Cramp* and *Baggett v. Bullitt*. "[M]en of common intelligence must necessarily guess at its meaning and differ as to its application. . . ." Vagueness of wording is aggravated by prolixity and profusion of statutes, regulations, and administrative machinery, and by manifold cross-references to interrelated enactments and rules.

We therefore hold that § 3021 of the Education Law and subdivisions 1(a), 1(b) and 3 of § 105 of the Civil Service Law as implemented by the machinery created pursuant to § 3022 of the Education Law are unconstitutional.

Boring v. Buncombe County Board of Education

136 F.3d 364 (4th Cir. 1998), *cert. denied*, 525 U.S. 813 (1998)

The Fourth Circuit finds that a high school teacher's choice of a play in the school curriculum is not protected by the First Amendment.

WIDENER, CIRCUIT JUDGE:

The only issue in this case is whether a public high school teacher has a First Amendment right to participate in the makeup of the school curriculum through the selection and production of a play. We hold that she does not, and affirm the judgment of the district court dismissing the complaint.

Margaret Boring was a teacher in the Charles D. Owen High School in Buncombe County, North Carolina. In the fall of 1991, she chose the play *Independence* for four students in her advanced acting class to perform in an annual statewide competition. She stated in her amended complaint that the play "powerfully depicts the dynamics within a dysfunctional, single-parent family—a divorced mother and three daughters; one a lesbian, another pregnant with an illegitimate child." She alleged that after selecting the play, she notified the school principal, as she did every year, that she had chosen *Independence* as the play for the competition. She does not allege that she gave the principal any information about the play other than the name.

The play was performed in a regional competition and won 17 of 21 awards. Prior to the state finals, a scene from the play was performed for an English class in the school. Plaintiff informed the teacher of that class that the play contained mature subject matter and suggested to the teacher that the students bring in parental permission slips to see the play. Following that performance, a parent of one of the students in the English class complained to the school principal, Fred Ivey, who then asked plaintiff for a copy of the script. After reading the play, Ivey informed plaintiff that she and the students would not be permitted to perform the play in the state competition.

Plaintiff and the parents of the actresses performing the play met with Ivey urging him not to cancel the production. Ivey then agreed to the production of the play in the state competition, but with certain portions deleted. The complaint states that the students performed the play in the state competition and won second place. The complaint does not state, but we assume, that the play was performed in accordance with Ivey's instructions.

. . . .

In June 1992, Ivey requested the transfer of Margaret Boring from Owen High School, citing "personal conflicts resulting from actions she initiated during the course of this school year." Superintendent Yeager approved the transfer stating that she had failed to follow the school system's controversial materials policy in producing the play. Plaintiff states that the purpose of the controversial materials policy is to give the parents some control over the materials to which their children are exposed in school. She alleges that at the time of the production, the controversial materials policy did not cover dramatic presentations, and that the school's policy was amended subsequently to include dramatic presentations.

Plaintiff appealed the transfer to the Board of Education. A hearing was held on September 2, 1992, following which the Board upheld the transfer. . . .

The district court held that the play was a part of the school curriculum and:

> Since plaintiff has not engaged in protected speech, her transfer in retaliation for the play's production did not violate Constitutional standards.

With this holding, the plaintiff takes issue on appeal as follows:

> Whether the district court erred in holding that plaintiff's act of selecting, producing and directing a play did not constitute "speech" within the meaning of the First Amendment.

We begin our discussion with the definition of curriculum:

> all planned school activities including besides courses of study, organized play, athletics, dramatics, clubs, and homeroom program.

Webster's Third New International Dictionary, 1971, p. 557.

Not only does Webster include dramatics within the definition of curriculum, the Supreme Court does the same. In *Hazelwood School District v. Kuhlmeier*, 484 U.S. 260 (1988), a case involving student speech in a school newspaper which was edited by the principal of a high school, the Court distinguished cases which require a school to tolerate student speech from those cases in which the school must affirmatively promote student speech. Although in different context, the reasoning of the Court as to what constitutes the school curriculum is equally applicable here.

> The latter question concerns educators' authority over school-sponsored publications, theatrical productions, and other expressive activities that students, parents, and members of the public might reasonably perceive to bear the imprimatur of the school. These activities may fairly be characterized as part of the school curriculum, whether or not they occur in a traditional classroom setting, so long as they are supervised by faculty members and designed to impart particular knowledge or skills to student participants and audiences [footnote omitted].

Hazelwood, 484 U.S. at 271, 108 S.Ct. at 570.

It is plain that the play was curricular from the fact that it was supervised by a faculty member, Mrs. Boring; it was performed in interscholastic drama competitions; and the theater program at the high school was obviously intended to impart particular skills, such as acting, to student participants. These factors demonstrate beyond doubt that "students, parents, and members of the public might reasonably perceive [the production of the play *Independence*] to bear the imprimatur of the school." *Hazelwood*, 484 U.S. at 271.

So there is no difference between Webster's common definition and that of *Hazelwood*.

With these thoughts in mind, we are of opinion that the judgment of the district court is demonstrably correct.

Plaintiff's selection of the play *Independence*, and the editing of the play by the principal, who was upheld by the superintendent of schools, does not present a matter of public concern and is nothing more than an ordinary employment dispute. That being so, plaintiff has no First Amendment rights derived from her selection of the play *Independence*.

This principle was illustrated in *Connick v. Myers*, 461 U.S. 138 (1983), in which the Court upheld the firing of an assistant district attorney who had circulated a questionnaire questioning the manner in which the district attorney operated that office. The Court held that "if Myers' questionnaire cannot be fairly characterized as constituting speech on a matter of public concern, it is unnecessary for us to scrutinize the reasons for her discharge." *Connick* at 146. Because the questionnaire almost wholly concerned internal office affairs rather than matters of public concern, the court held that, to that extent, it would not upset the decision of the district attorney in discharging Myers. It stated:

> We hold only that when a public employee speaks not as a citizen upon matters of public concern, but instead as an employee upon matters of personal interest, absent the most unusual circumstances, a federal court is not the appropriate forum in which to review the wisdom of a personnel decision taken by a public agency allegedly in reaction to the employee's behavior.

Connick at 147.

We followed *Connick* in *DiMeglio v. Haines*, 45 F.3d 790 (1995), in which we upheld the transfer of a public employee who had insisted on advising some affected citizens as to the merits of a zoning dispute contrary to the instructions of his employer. We stated "a government employer, no less than a private employer, is entitled to insist upon the legitimate, day-to-day decisions of the office without fear of reprisals in the form of lawsuits from disgruntled subordinates who believe that they know better than their superiors how to manage office affairs." *DiMeglio* at 806.

In a case on facts so near to those in the case at hand as to be indistinguishable, the Fifth Circuit came to the conclusion we have just recited in *Kirkland v. Northside Independent School District*, 890 F.2d 794 (5th Cir. 1989), *cert. denied*, 496 U.S. 926 (1990). *Kirkland* was a case in which the employment contract of a high school history teacher was not renewed. He alleged the nonrenewal was a consequence of, and in retaliation for, his use of an unapproved reading list in his world history class. The high school had provided the teacher with a supplemental reading list for his history class along with a copy of the guidelines used to develop and amend that list. He was aware of the guidelines and understood that if he was dissatisfied, a separate body of reading material could be used in his class if he obtained administrative approval. The teacher, however, used his own substitute list and declined to procure the approval of the school authorities for his substitute list. The authorities at his high school then recommended that his contract not be renewed at the end of the next academic year, which was affirmed by the board of trustees, much like Margaret Boring's transfer was affirmed by the school board in this case after a recommendation by the administrative authorities.

The court held that to establish his constitutional claim, Kirkland must have shown that his supplemental reading list was constitutionally protected speech; not different from Mrs. Boring's selection of the play *Independence* in this case. It went on to hold that under *Connick v. Myers*, 461 U.S. 138 (1983), the question of whether a public employee's speech is constitutionally protected depends upon the public or private nature of such speech. It decided that the selection of the reading list by the teacher was not a matter of public concern and stated that:

> Although, the concept of academic freedom has been recognized in our jurisprudence, the doctrine has never conferred upon teachers the control of public school curricula.

890 F.2d at 800. And the *Kirkland* court recognized that *Hazelwood* held that public school officials, consistent with the First Amendment, could place reasonable restrictions upon the subject matter of a student published newspaper and also that schools are typically not public forums.

The court stated that "[w]e hold only that public school teachers are not free, under the first amendment, to arrogate control of curricula," 890 F.2d at 802, and concluded as follows:

> In summary, we conclude that Kirkland's world history reading list does not present a matter of public concern and that this case presents nothing more than an ordinary employment dispute. Accordingly, Kirkland's conduct in disregarding Northside's administrative process does not constitute protected speech. . . .

890 F.2d at 802.

Since plaintiff's dispute with the principal, superintendent of schools and the school board is nothing more than an ordinary employment dispute, it does not constitute protected speech and has no First Amendment protection. Her case is indistinguishable from Kirkland's.

The plaintiff also contends that the district court erred in holding that the defendants had a legitimate pedagogical interest in punishing plaintiff for her speech. Of course, by speech, she means her selection and production of the play *Independence.*

As we have previously set out, the play was a part of the curriculum of Charles D. Owen High School, where plaintiff taught. So this contention of the plaintiff is in reality not different from her first contention, that is, she had a First Amendment right to participate in the makeup of the high school curriculum, which could be regulated by the school administration only if it had a legitimate pedagogical interest in the curriculum. While we are of opinion that plaintiff had no First Amendment right to insist on the makeup of the curriculum, even assuming that she did have, we are of opinion that the school administration did have such a legitimate pedagogical interest and that the holding of the district court was correct.

Pedagogical is defined as "2: of or relating to teaching or pedagogy. EDUCATIONAL." *Webster's Third New International Dictionary*, 1971, p. 1663. There is no doubt at all that the selection of the play *Independence* was a part of the curriculum of Owen High School.

The makeup of the curriculum of Owen High School is by definition a legitimate pedagogical concern. Not only does logic dictate this conclusion, in only slightly different context the Eleventh Circuit has so held as a matter of law: "Since the purpose of a curricular program is by definition 'pedagogical'. . . ." *Searcey v. Harris*, 888 F.2d 1314, 1319 (11th Cir. 1989). *Kirkland*, 890 F.2d at 795, held the same in the same context present here.

If the performance of a play under the auspices of a school and which is a part of the curriculum of the school, is not by definition a legitimate pedagogical concern, we do not know what could be.

In our opinion, the school administrative authorities had a legitimate pedagogical interest in the makeup of the curriculum of the school, including the inclusion of the play *Independence*. The holding of the district court was correct and the plaintiff's claim is without merit.

The question before us is not new. From Plato to Burke, the greatest minds of Western civilization have acknowledged the importance of the very subject at hand and have agreed on how it should be treated. . . .

And Justice Frankfurter, in concurrence, related the four essential freedoms of a university, which should no less obtain in public schools unless quite impracticable or contrary to law:

> It is an atmosphere in which there prevail "the four essential freedoms" of a university—to determine for itself on academic grounds who may teach, what may be taught, how it shall be taught, and who may be admitted to study.

Sweezy v. New Hampshire, 354 U.S. 234, 255, 263–264 (1957).

We agree with Plato and Burke and Justice Frankfurter that the school, not the teacher, has the right to fix the curriculum. Owens being a public school does not give the plaintiff any First Amendment right to fix the curriculum she would not have had if the school were private. *Connick*, 461 U.S. at 147.

Someone must fix the curriculum of any school, public or private. In the case of a public school, in our opinion, it is far better public policy, absent a valid statutory directive on the subject, that the makeup of the curriculum be entrusted to the local school authorities who are in some sense responsible, rather than to the teachers, who would be responsible only to the judges, had they a First Amendment right to participate in the makeup of the curriculum.

The judgment of the district court is accordingly, *Affirmed*.

Cockrel v. Shelby County School District

270 F.3d 1036 (6th Cir. 2001), *cert. denied*, 537 U.S. 813 (2002)

The Sixth Circuit finds that the school district's interest in efficient operation of its schools does not outweigh a fifth grade teacher's First Amendment rights to invite controversial speakers on an issue of public concern.

Moore, Circuit Judge.

Plaintiff Donna Cockrel, a tenured fifth-grade teacher at Simpsonville Elementary School in the Shelby County, Kentucky School District was terminated on July 15, 1997 by the District's superintendent, Dr. Leon Mooneyhan. . . .

While the School District alleged numerous reasons for its decision to terminate Cockrel, she claims that the District fired her due to her decision to invite Woody

Harrelson, the television and film actor most famous for his role as "Woody" on the network television show "Cheers," and others to her classroom to give presentations on the environmental benefits of industrial hemp. . . .

Cockrel claims that on at least three occasions during her seven-year tenure at Simpsonville Elementary she organized outside speakers to come to her class to speak about industrial hemp. Cockrel further claims that both Principal Slate and Superintendent Mooneyhan knew that she organized industrial hemp presentations. While Principal Slate alleges that he never knew industrial hemp was being discussed in Cockrel's class, he does admit that Cockrel's lesson plans, on at least one occasion, specifically mentioned that hemp was to be discussed.

On or about April 9, 1996, following Cockrel's decision to end the 1995–96 school year with a project entitled "Saving the Trees," in which the use of industrial hemp fibers as a possible alternative to wood pulp was to be discussed, Cockrel was contacted by a representative of the Cable News Network ("CNN") and asked if she would permit CNN's cameras to film her class presentation for use in a larger program on tree conservation. Cockrel claims that she then immediately informed Slate of CNN's potential visit to their school, though Slate does not recall this conversation.

In early May 1996, Joe Hickey, president of the Kentucky Hemp Growers Association, informed Cockrel that Woody Harrelson might visit Kentucky with CNN, and that Harrelson might also visit her classroom. Cockrel claims that she was given no specific information as to when Harrelson might visit her classroom, and that it was not until the morning of May 30, 1996, the last day of the school year, that she was notified that Harrelson would be visiting Simpsonville Elementary School that day. Cockrel informed Principal Slate of the impending visit, and he agreed to allow it, though Slate claims that he was only told that the presentation to be given was about agriculture.

Harrelson arrived at the school later that morning with an "entourage, including representatives of the Kentucky Hemp Museum and Kentucky Hemp Growers Cooperative Association, several hemp growers from foreign countries, CNN, and various Kentucky news media representatives." As stated in Cockrel's complaint, Harrelson spoke with the children about his opposition to marijuana use, yet he distinguished marijuana from industrial hemp and advocated the use of industrial hemp as an alternative to increased logging efforts. As part of the presentation, products made from hemp were shown to the children, as were hemp seeds, a banned substance in the state of Kentucky. Harrelson's visit received both local and national media attention. One student who did not have parental permission to be videotaped or photographed by the news media was included by the press in a class photograph with Harrelson.

Following Harrelson's visit and the media attention it garnered, parents and teachers wrote numerous letters to members of the Shelby County School District voicing their concern and dismay regarding the industrial hemp presentation.

Several of the letters noted the mixed message the school was sending on drug use as Harrelson's presentation occurred on the same day that many Simpsonville Elementary School students were graduating from the Drug Abuse Resistance Education ("D.A.R.E.") program offered in the school.

. . . .

In the months following Harrelson's visit, Simpsonville Elementary School adopted a new visitors policy for "controversial" topics that required advance approval by school administration and written consent by students' parents. This policy was put to use when, during the next school year, Cockrel informed Slate that Harrelson would be making a second visit to her classroom to discuss industrial hemp. Cockrel met all of the requirements of the new visitors policy, including providing the requisite advance notice to Principal Slate and obtaining permission from the parents of her students for their children to attend the presentation. Slate did not attempt to discourage Cockrel from having another class presentation on industrial hemp, nor did he tell her that Harrelson should not be invited back to the school. According to Cockrel, however, Superintendent Mooneyhan did tell her earlier in the school year that it would not be in her best interests if Harrelson made any more visits to her class. . . . Harrelson was met by a group of parents outside the school who were protesting his visit. Due to school scheduling problems, Harrelson was only able to speak to the students for a few minutes before the students had to leave for lunch. Harrelson's visit again garnered national media attention from CNN. . . .

. . . .

In the months following Harrelson's initial visit, and shortly after his second visit in January 1997, Slate sat in on Cockrel's class for purposes of conducting evaluations. That school year, Cockrel was the only tenured teacher at Simpsonville Elementary to be reviewed after two years, whereas tenured teachers in the School District are typically reviewed only once every three years. Slate stated in his deposition that the reason for Cockrel's early review was his perception that things had been "going downhill" between the two of them for the previous two years. Slate further explained that Cockrel was neither communicating nor cooperating with him and the rest of the staff and faculty of Simpsonville Elementary, nor was she adequately following the school's curriculum and policies.

Citing examples of this downward trend in Cockrel's attitude and performance, Slate testified that Cockrel did not want Deputy Yeager, the police officer in charge of the D.A.R.E. program at Simpsonville who had spoken out against the Harrelson visits, in her classroom instructing her students. She asked Slate to find someone else to teach the D.A.R.E. program. Slate further stated that two teachers had approached him to let him know that Cockrel was calling him names outside his presence. In addition, a parent notified Slate that her child had heard Cockrel call Slate a name in class. Slate also noted that there were many times when Cockrel simply refused to speak with him or failed to attend meetings.

In the 1996–97 school year, during and after the news that Harrelson would be visiting her class once again, five students, at their parents' request, were transferred out of Cockrel's class. Each time Slate attempted to inform Cockrel of a student's transfer, Cockrel would refuse to talk with him, sometimes walking right past him when he tried to speak with her, or turning her back to him, or refusing to meet with him in his office when he so requested.

. . . .

A little more than a month later, Principal Slate issued a "summative evaluation" of Cockrel's performance, stating that Cockrel did not meet the requisite level of performance in five of the forty-three categories of evaluation. . . . Based on this evaluation, Slate recommended to Superintendent Mooneyhan that Cockrel be terminated. Cockrel was terminated by Mooneyhan on July 15, 1997.

. . . .

On June 4, 1998, Cockrel filed suit in the United States District Court for the Eastern District of Kentucky. Cockrel brought a claim pursuant to 42 U.S.C. § 1983 in which she alleged that she was terminated in retaliation for exercising her First Amendment right of free speech when discussing the potential environmental benefits of industrial hemp. . . .

Donna Cockrel, a teacher in the Shelby County Public School District, is a public employee. For a public employee to establish a claim of First Amendment retaliation, this court has held that she must demonstrate:

> (1) that [she] was engaged in a constitutionally protected activity; (2) that the defendant's adverse action caused [her] to suffer an injury that would likely chill a person of ordinary firmness from continuing to engage in that activity; and (3) that the adverse action was motivated at least in part as a response to the exercise of [her] constitutional rights.

Leary v. Daeschner, 228 F.3d 729, 737 (6th Cir. 2000). To demonstrate that she was engaging in constitutionally protected speech, Cockrel must show that her speech touched on matters of public concern, and that her "interest in commenting upon matters of public concern . . . outweigh[s] the interest of the State, as an employer, in promoting the efficiency of the public services it performs through its employees." If the plaintiff can establish the three elements of her First Amendment retaliation claim, the burden of persuasion then shifts to the defendants, who must show, by a preponderance of the evidence, that they "would have taken the same action even in the absence of the protected conduct."

. . . .

Given our determination that Cockrel's decision to bring industrial hemp advocates into her class is speech, the next question we must ask is whether that speech is constitutionally protected. As stated earlier, speech of a public employee is protected by the First Amendment only if it touches on matters of public concern, and only if "the employee's interest in commenting upon matters of public concern . . .

outweigh[s] the interest of the State, as an employer, in promoting the efficiency of the public services it performs through its employees." If Cockrel's speech cannot meet both of these standards, then her First Amendment retaliation claim cannot go forward.

In determining whether Cockrel's speech touched on a matter of public concern, we turn to *Connick v. Myers*, 461 U.S. 138 (1983), the Supreme Court's most instructive case on this issue. In *Connick*, the Court stated that matters of public concern are those that can "be fairly considered as relating to any matter of political, social, or other concern to the community." There is no question that the issue of industrial hemp is a matter of great political and social concern to many citizens of Kentucky, and we believe that Cockrel's presentations clearly come within the Supreme Court's understanding of speech touching on matters of public concern.

In support of this conclusion, we first turn to the district court's opinion, which unequivocally stated "that the issue of industrial hemp is politically charged and of great concern to certain citizens." Second, in the past year alone, industrial hemp advocacy in Kentucky has made news on several occasions, revealing the significant extent to which industrial hemp has become an important and publicly debated issue in the State. In October, presidential candidate Ralph Nader, in a campaign stop in Kentucky, spoke out in favor of the legalization of industrial hemp and of the benefits it would have for small family farmers. In December, after the Drug Enforcement Agency confiscated industrial hemp being grown on the Pine Ridge, South Dakota Indian Reservation, members of the Kentucky Hemp Growers Association, including former Kentucky governor Louie B. Nunn, traveled to South Dakota and, in a ceremony at the base of Mount Rushmore, delivered legally imported industrial hemp to the tribe as a sign of its solidarity. These examples only scratch the surface of the extent to which industrial hemp has become an issue of contentious political and economic debate in Kentucky.

While discussion of industrial hemp plainly meets the broad concept of "public concern" as defined by the Supreme Court, some courts have focused on other portions of the Supreme Court's *Connick* decision in concluding that a teacher's classroom speech does not touch on matters of public concern. *See Boring v. Buncombe County Bd. of Educ.*, 136 F.3d 364, 368–69 (4th Cir.) (en banc), *cert. denied*, 525 U.S. 813 (1998); *Kirkland v. Northside Indep. Sch. Dist.*, 890 F.2d 794, 797–99 (5th Cir. 1989), *cert. denied*, 496 U.S. 926 (1990). These cases pay particular attention to the following portion of the *Connick* Court's holding:

> [W]hen a public employee speaks not as a citizen upon matters of public concern, but instead as an employee upon matters only of personal interest, absent the most unusual circumstances, a federal court is not the appropriate forum in which to review the wisdom of a personnel decision taken by a public agency allegedly in reaction to the employee's behavior.

Connick, 461 U.S. at 147. Based upon this language, the Fourth and Fifth Circuits have determined that a teacher, in choosing what he will teach his students, is not speaking as a citizen, but rather as an employee on matters of private interest. *Boring*, 136 F.3d at 368–69; *Kirkland*, 890 F.2d at 800.

We believe that the Fourth and Fifth Circuits have extended the holding of *Connick* beyond what the Supreme Court intended. Under the courts' analyses in *Boring* and *Kirkland*, a teacher, regardless of what he decides to include in his curriculum, is speaking as an employee on a private matter. *Boring*, 136 F.3d at 368–69; *Kirkland*, 890 F.2d at 800. This essentially gives a teacher no right to freedom of speech when teaching students in a classroom, for the very act of teaching is what the employee is paid to do. Thus, when teaching, even if about an upcoming presidential election or the importance of our Bill of Rights, the Fourth and Fifth Circuits' reasoning would leave such speech without constitutional protection, for the teacher is speaking as an employee, and not as a citizen.

The facts in *Connick* indicate that the Fourth and Fifth Circuits have read the Supreme Court's language too broadly. In *Connick*, an assistant district attorney, following a disagreement with a supervisor, prepared a questionnaire seeking the opinions of her co-workers on issues such as "office transfer policy, office morale, the need for a grievance committee, the level of confidence in supervisors, and whether employees felt pressured to work in political campaigns." *Connick*, 461 U.S. at 141. Connick was later fired for circulating the questionnaire on the grounds of insubordination. *Id.* The Court held that, while many of the questions simply reflected the plaintiff's efforts to gather information to use against her supervisors in her private employment dispute, Myers's question regarding the pressure to work on political campaigns *did* touch on a matter of public concern. Thus, the Court held that, even though Myers was speaking as an employee out of her private interest in combating her supervisors' decision to transfer her, the fact that one of her questions dealt with the fundamental constitutional right not to be coerced into campaigning for a political candidate was enough to make this particular issue touch on a matter of public concern. *Id.*

If the Fourth and Fifth Circuits' interpretation of *Connick* were correct, then any time a public employee was speaking as an employee, like Myers was when she asked her question about employees being pressured to campaign, the speech at issue would not be protected. As the Supreme Court made clear in its analysis, however, the key question is not whether a person is speaking in his role as an employee or a citizen, but whether the employee's speech in fact touches on matters of public concern. *Id.* 148–49. Thus, even if a public employee were acting out of a private motive with no intent to air her speech publicly, as was the case with Myers, so long as the speech relates to matters of "political, social, or other concern to the community," as opposed to matters "only of personal interest," it shall be considered as touching upon matters of public concern.

In Cockrel's case, although she was speaking in her role as an employee when presenting information on the environmental benefits of industrial hemp, the content of her speech, as discussed *supra*, most certainly involved matters related to the political and social concern of the community, as opposed to mere matters of private interest. Thus, contrary to the analyses in *Boring* and *Kirkland*, we hold that Cockrel's speech does touch on matters of public concern.

Having held that Cockrel's speech touches on matters of public concern, we must now weigh the employee's interest in speaking against the employer's interest in regulating the speech to determine if the speech is constitutionally protected. In *Pickering v. Board of Education*, 391 U.S. 563 (1968), the Supreme Court endeavored to strike a balance between a public employee's speech rights on matters of public interest (in that case a public school teacher's speech outside of school) and the State's interest as an employer in maintaining a productive workplace. In accordance with the balancing test created in *Pickering*, public employee speech, even if touching on matters of public concern, will not be constitutionally protected unless the employee's interest in speaking on these issues "outweigh[s] 'the interest of the State, as an employer, in promoting the efficiency of the public services it performs through its employees.'" In striking the balance between the State's and the employee's respective interests, this court has stated that it will "consider whether an employee's comments meaningfully interfere with the performance of her duties, undermine a legitimate goal or mission of the employer, create disharmony among co-workers, impair discipline by superiors, or destroy the relationship of loyalty and trust required of confidential employees."

Before engaging in a "particularized balancing" of the competing interests at stake in this case, it is important to note that "if an employee's speech substantially involve[s] matters of public concern, an employer may be required to make a particularly strong showing that the employee's speech interfered with workplace functioning before taking action." In this case, it is clear that Cockrel's speech did substantially involve matters of public concern, and thus the defendants will have to make a stronger showing that their interests in regulating plaintiff's speech outweighed Cockrel's interests in speaking.

Weighing in plaintiff's favor in this analysis is the fact that her speech substantially involved matters of significant public concern in Kentucky. Defendants claim, however, that their "interest in maintaining loyalty, efficient operation of the schools, and workplace harmony" outweighs the plaintiff's interest in speaking about industrial hemp. We first note that the defendants do not claim that Cockrel's presentations on industrial hemp meaningfully interfered with the performance of her teaching duties. Defendants would have a difficult time making this argument, however, considering they openly acknowledged in a public statement to CNN that there was "educational value" in teaching students about industrial hemp as an alternative crop. We further note that defendants' purported interest in "maintaining loyalty" is inapposite in this case. While this circuit has stated that it would consider in its balancing whether employee speech operated to "destroy the relationship of loyalty and trust required of confidential employees," a public school teacher, we believe, is hardly the type of confidential employee the court had in mind. Thus, any loyalty concerns that the defendants may have will not be taken into consideration in our weighing of the competing interests at stake.

Turning to the defendants' proffered interests in an efficient operation of the school and a harmonious work environment, there is evidence that plaintiff's speech has led to problems in both of these areas. For example, following Harrelson's first visit to Simpsonville, numerous members of the school's faculty and staff circulated and or signed letters addressed to school officials criticizing Cockrel's actions in advocating the use of industrial hemp to her students. Cockrel thereafter expressed her displeasure with her co-workers' sentiments on several occasions. As discussed earlier, following D.A.R.E. officer Yeager's criticism of the Harrelson visits, Cockrel no longer wanted the officer in her classroom instructing her students. Cockrel asked Slate to find a replacement for Yeager as well. Cockrel's termination letter detailed several instances of disputes Cockrel had with co-workers, including an instance in which Cockrel jerked a phone away from a co-worker who had signed one of the letters speaking out against the Harrelson visit, and an incident in which Cockrel told two co-workers "not to waste their breath after they said 'good morning' to [her.]" At least one of these co-workers had also signed a letter critical of Cockrel's decision to speak about industrial hemp.

Many parents and members of the school community also expressed great concern over Cockrel's decision to invite speakers to her class who advocated the use of industrial hemp. Parents wrote letters to Principal Slate and Superintendent Mooneyhan in opposition to Cockrel's industrial hemp presentations, and a small number came to Simpsonville Elementary to protest on the final two occasions Harrelson was scheduled to visit. In addition, the PTA passed a position statement recommending that Cockrel no longer teach in the Shelby County School District.

Although this evidence of a contentious and periodically disrupted work environment weighs in favor of the defendants, the amount of weight we should give this evidence is an entirely different question. We are troubled by the fact that, whereas school officials gave plaintiff prior approval to host all three of the industrial hemp presentations at issue in this case, defendants now forward concerns of school efficiency and harmony as reasons supporting their decision to discharge Cockrel. Principal Slate approved all of Harrelson's scheduled visits in advance, and Slate openly stated that he had no problem with Cockrel teaching her students about industrial hemp. Cockrel also met the conditions of the new visitors policy implemented after the initial Harrelson visit, including obtaining the permission of each student's parents before a child could participate in the presentation. We do not believe that defendants can use the outcry within the school community protesting Cockrel's speech, speech that was approved by school officials in advance, as a shield for their decision to discharge her. While ordinarily we would give substantial weight to the government employer's concerns of workplace efficiency, harmony, and discipline in conducting our balancing of the employee's and employer's competing interests, we cannot allow these concerns to tilt the *Pickering* scale in favor of the government, absent other evidence, when the disruptive consequences of the employee speech can be traced back to the government's express decision permitting the employee to engage in that speech.

Accordingly, we hold that, on balance, the defendants' interests in an efficient operation of the school and a harmonious workplace do not outweigh the plaintiff's interests in speaking about the benefits of industrial hemp, an issue of substantial political and economic concern in Kentucky. Thus, because Cockrel's speech touches on matters of public concern and because the balancing of interests under *Pickering* weighs in her favor, her speech is constitutionally protected. We now proceed with an examination of the remainder of the elements of plaintiff's First Amendment retaliation claim.

....

[The court goes on to conclude that the remaining elements of Cockrel's claim (that the defendants' adverse action caused her to suffer an injury that would likely chill a person of ordinary firmness from continuing to engage in that activity and that defendants' decision to discharge her was motivated, at least in part, by the exercise of her free speech rights) were met. The court also finds that the defendants did not meet their burden at the summary judgment stage of showing that they would have discharged Cockrel regardless of her decision to engage in constitutionally protected speech. As a result, the court remands the case to the trial court for further proceedings.]

Post Problem Discussion

1. Does the answer to the questions in this problem depend on whether you apply the approach used in *Cockrel* or the approach used in *Boring*? Or, do you come to the same conclusion under either approach? If you come to different results, which approach do you favor and why?

2. *Boring* and *Cockrel* rely on *Connick v. Meyer* and *Pickering v. Board of Education* in their analysis. Review Section 3.06 of Chapter 3, and the *Garcetti v. Ceballos* and *Lane v. Franks* cases in that section. Do *Garcetti* and *Lane* change the analysis in *Boring* or *Cockrel*? Do these cases mean that there is no right to academic freedom, since a teacher's right to teach certain material, or to express certain views while teaching, would be done pursuant to their official duties as a teacher, and not as a citizen? Justice Souter dissented in *Garcetti* and raised concerns about the impact the case would have on academic freedom. *Garcetti,* 547 U.S. at 438. As a result, the Court reserved the question of whether its holding applied to "speech related to scholarship or teaching." *Id.* at 425.

The Ninth Circuit Court of Appeals picked up on this concern and ruled that *Garcetti* did not apply to claims of academic freedom for a university professor. *Demers v. Austin,* 746 U.S. 402, 406 (9th Cir. 2014). Rather, the court said that such speech was governed by *Pickering v. Board of Education*, as long as it was related to scholarship or teaching, and addressed a matter of public concern. If those two requirements are met, then the Ninth Circuit ruled that courts should apply the balancing test noted in *Connick* and *Pickering* to determine if the teacher's interest "in commenting upon matters of public concern" outweighs "the interest of the

State, as an employer, in promoting the efficiency of the public services it performs through its employees." *Id.* at 412. However, courts are not uniform on the issue. *See, e.g., Evans-Marshall v. Bd. of Educ. of Tipp City Exempted Vill. Sch. Dist.*, 624 F.3d 332 (6th Cir. 2010) (applying *Garcetti* to public school teacher's statements in class); *Brammer-Hoelter v. Twin Peaks Charter Acad.*, 492 F.3d 1192, 1205 (10th Cir. 2007) (applying *Garcetti* but finding some of a teacher's comments made outside of school to be eligible for First Amendment protection); *Lee v. York Cnty. Sch. Div.*, 484 F.3d 687 (4th Cir. 2007) (applying *Pickering-Connick* standard as articulated in *Boring* and not *Garcetti* to case involving school's removal of teacher's material from school bulletin board).

Should the approach in *Demers* be followed with public elementary and secondary school teachers as well, or just with university professors? What standard do you think should apply to Ms. Bragdon's claims over her right to assign Bastard out of Carolina to her students?

3. In *Mayer v. Monroe*, 474 F.3d 477 (7th Cir. 2007), *cert. denied*, 128 S.Ct. 160 (2007), the Seventh Circuit ruled that a school district did not violate a teacher's First Amendment rights in terminating her for expressing her opinions about a war where her viewpoint departed from the curriculum adopted by the school, which permitted teaching about controversy related to the war as long as teachers kept their personal opinions to themselves. An important factor in *Mayer*'s analysis was that the students were "captive audiences." The court, noting the *Cockrel* and *Garcetti* decisions, stated:

> Whether teachers in primary and secondary schools have a constitutional right to determine what they say in class is not a novel question in this circuit. We held in *Webster v. New Lenox School District No. 122*, 917 F.2d 1004 (7th Cir. 1990), that public-school teachers must hew to the approach prescribed by principals (and others higher up in the chain of authority). Ray Webster wanted to teach his social-studies class that the world is much younger than the four-billion-year age given in the textbook the class was using; he proposed that the pupils consider the possibility of divine creation as an alternative to the scientific understanding. We held that Webster did not have a constitutional right to introduce his own views on the subject but must stick to the prescribed curriculum—not only the prescribed subject matter, but also the prescribed perspective on that subject matter. . . .
>
> This is so in part because the school system does not "regulate" teachers' speech as much as it *hires* that speech. Expression is a teacher's stock in trade, the commodity she sells to her employer in exchange for a salary. A teacher hired to lead a social-studies class can't use it as a platform for a revisionist perspective that Benedict Arnold wasn't really a traitor, when the approved program calls him one; a high-school teacher hired to explicate *Moby-Dick* in a literature class can't use *Cry, The Beloved Country* instead, even if Paton's book better suits the instructor's style and point of view; a math teacher can't decide that calculus is more important than

> trigonometry and decide to let Hipparchus and Ptolemy slide in favor of Newton and Leibniz.
>
> Beyond the fact that teachers hire out their own speech and must provide the service for which employers are willing to pay—which makes this an easier case for the employer than *Garcetti*, where speech was not what the employee was being paid to create—is the fact that the pupils are a captive audience. Education is compulsory, and children must attend public schools unless their parents are willing to incur the cost of private education or the considerable time commitment of home schooling. Children who attend school because they must ought not be subject to teachers' idiosyncratic perspectives. Majority rule about what subjects and viewpoints will be expressed in the classroom has the potential to turn into indoctrination; elected school boards are tempted to support majority positions about religious or patriotic subjects especially. But if indoctrination is likely, the power should be reposed in someone the people can vote out of office, rather than tenured teachers. At least the board's views can be debated openly, and the people may choose to elect persons committed to neutrality on contentious issues. That is the path Monroe County has chosen; Mayer was told that she could teach the controversy about policy toward Iraq, drawing out arguments from all perspectives, as long as she kept her opinions to herself. The Constitution does not entitle teachers to present personal views to captive audiences against the instructions of elected officials. To the extent that *James v. Board of Education*, 461 F.2d 566 (2d Cir. 1972), and *Cockrel v. Shelby County School District*, 270 F.3d 1036, 1052 (6th Cir. 2001), are to the contrary, they are inconsistent with later authority and unpersuasive.
>
> ....
>
> [T]he first amendment does not entitle primary and secondary teachers, when conducting the education of captive audiences, to cover topics, or advocate viewpoints, that depart from the curriculum adopted by the school system.

Do you find the court's analysis in *Mayer* persuasive? How should the fact that students in elementary and secondary schools are "captive audiences" be factored into the academic freedom analysis? Does it follow that teachers or professors at post-secondary institutions where students are not "compelled" to attend should have greater academic freedom? Why or why not?

Chapter 5

Attendance, Assignment & Placement

Synopsis

§5.01 Introduction

Previous chapters generally surveyed the federal, state, and local roles regarding education. The primary responsibility for education rests with state and local governments, with state constitutions setting the broad educational commitments, and state statutes and regulations providing implementation requirements. These state requirements include compulsory attendance provisions, which obligate parents of children between certain ages to ensure that their child attends school.

For example, the Illinois Constitution provides:

> A fundamental goal of the People of the State is the educational development of all persons to the limits of their capacities. The state shall provide for an efficient system of high quality public educational institutions and services. Education in public schools through the secondary level shall be free. There may be such other free education as the General Assembly provides by law. The State has the primary responsibility for financing the system of public education.

Ill. Const., art. X, §1 (amended 1970). State statutes then provide for compulsory education and exceptions to required attendance:

> Sec. 26-1. Compulsory school age—Exemptions. Whoever has custody or control of any child between the ages of 7 and 17 years (unless the child has already graduated from high school) shall cause such child to attend some public school in the district wherein the child resides the entire time it is in session during the regular school term, except as provided in Section 10-19.1

> [105 ILCS 5/10-19.1], and during a required summer school program established under Section 10-22.33B [105 ILCS 5/10-22.33B]; provided, that the following children shall not be required to attend the public schools:
>
> 1. Any child attending a private or a parochial school where children are taught the branches of education taught to children of corresponding age and grade in the public schools, and where the instruction of the child in the branches of education is in the English language;
>
> 2. Any child who is physically or mentally unable to attend school, such disability being certified [the statute goes on to delineate ways to certify a disability]. . . .
>
> 3. Any child necessarily and lawfully employed according to the provisions of the law regulating child labor may be excused from attendance at school by the county superintendent of schools or the superintendent of the public school which the child should be attending. . . .
>
> 4. Any child over 12 and under 14 years of age while in attendance at confirmation classes;
>
> 5. Any child absent from a public school on a particular day or days or at a particular time of day for the reason that he is unable to attend classes or to participate in any examination, study or work requirements on a particular day or days or at a particular time of day, because the tenets of his religion forbid secular activity on a particular day or days or at a particular time of day . . . ; and
>
> 6. Any child 16 years of age or older who (i) submits to a school district evidence of necessary and lawful employment pursuant to paragraph 3 of this Section and (ii) is enrolled in a graduation incentives program pursuant to Section 26-16 of this Code [105 ILCS 5/26-16] or an alternative learning opportunities program established pursuant to Article 13B of this Code [105 ILCS 5/13B].

105 ILCS 5/26-1.

State statutes vary, and your state may have slightly different requirements and exceptions. Some state statutes provide for the length of school terms, school admission, and school assignment criteria as discussed in further detail in this Chapter. Also, states vary on how they enforce compulsory attendance requirements. The following activity lets you explore these issues in your state.

Activity 1: Find Your State's Compulsory Attendance Law

Step One—Find your state's compulsory attendance law. How does it compare to the Illinois statute?

Step Two—Research your state education regulations (these will be issued by your state department of education or state board of education and are available online). Do any of the regulations address compulsory attendance?

Step Three—Answer the following:

1. What are the ages of required attendance? Is it 7 to 17 like the Illinois statute, or something different? Why do you think the ages are what they are in your state? What would be the effect of changing the ages in your state to 5 to 18? How about 3 to 21?
2. What are the exceptions to attendance in your state? Are there any exceptions that surprised you? Are there any exceptions that you think should be in the law that are not?
3. Most compulsory attendance statutes obligate parents or guardians to ensure that the student attends school (as opposed to just requiring the student to attend). Consider the Illinois statute as an example: "Whoever has custody or control of any child . . . shall cause such child to attend. . . ." What does your state statute say in this regard? Why do you think these statutes obligate parents or guardians instead of, or in addition to, students?
4. What is the penalty for non-compliance with your state's compulsory attendance statute? How is it enforced?

§ 5.02 Compulsory Attendance

Compulsory attendance is the norm, but there are exceptions often set out in state statutes, as noted in the Illinois statute above, or in district policy. However, sometimes the issue rises to a constitutional level, as was the case in *Wisconsin v. Yoder* (included in Problem 1), where the United States Supreme Court found that a state compulsory education law violated Amish parents' substantive due process and free exercise rights. After *Yoder*, some states included an "Amish Exception" in their state compulsory education laws.[1] The following problem explores these issues.

Problem 1: Amish Exceptions to Compulsory Attendance

Charles and Mary Hall have five children ages one through six. The six year old, Charles Jr., just started first grade at Local Elementary School. Charles and Mary are very concerned with the secular education that Charles Jr. is receiving at Local Elementary. Devout Christians, the Halls believe that the public school is corrupting Charles Jr. and that continuing to send him to Local Elementary would violate tenets of their Christian religion. As a result, they remove him from school and refuse to send him back.

The Halls have found several other parents who attend their church and hold the same beliefs as they do. These parents all eventually decide to team up to start

1. James G. Dwyer, *Parents' Religion and Children's Welfare: Debunking the Doctrine of Parents' Rights*, 82 Calif. L. Rev. 1371, 1390 (December 1994).

a school called Mary's School of Christ. Mary Hall and two of the other mothers provide instruction to the students by using their Church's "Christian Curriculum" materials, which they bought from an online source. None of the mothers are certified teachers; Mary has an associate's degree in communications, one mother graduated from high school, and the third dropped out of high school after finishing tenth grade.

The Halls are ultimately contacted by representatives from the local public school and the state department of education regarding Charles Jr.'s absence from school, and the creation of Mary's School of Christ. They are told that Mary's School of Christ does not meet any of the state requirements for private schools, and they will be considered to be in violation of the state compulsory attendance laws unless they fit into one of the exceptions in the law. The Halls apply for the Amish exemption, but they are denied by the state department and state board of education.

The Halls contend that the denial violates their constitutional rights. They seek your advice on whether they can successfully challenge the denial or the constitutionality of the statute itself. What do you advise?

Problem Materials

✓ Hypothetical State Compulsory Attendance Law

✓ *Wisconsin v. Yoder*, 406 U.S. 205 (1972)

✓ *Fellowship Baptist Church v. Benton*, 815 F.2d 485 (8th Cir. 1987)

Hypothetical Compulsory Attendance Law with Amish Exceptions

Ed § 91754

I. A parent or guardian of any child shall cause such child to attend the public school to which the child is assigned in the child's resident district from the time the child is six (6) years of age until they reach eighteen (18) years of age, or graduate high school, unless one or more of the following exceptions apply:

. . . .

4) The parents or guardians are members or representatives of a congregation of a recognized church or religious denomination established for ten years or more which professes principles or tenets that differ substantially from the objectives, goals, and philosophy of education embodied in standards set forth in state law. Said parents or guardians may file with the state department of education proof of the existence of such conflicting tenets or principles, together with the names, ages, and addresses of all persons of compulsory school age desiring to be exempted from the compulsory education law. The state department of education, subject to the approval of the state board of education, may exempt the members of the congregation

or religious denomination from compliance with any or all requirements of the compulsory education law and the educational standards laws of the state. . . .

Wisconsin v. Yoder

406 U.S. 205 (1972)

The Supreme Court recognizes the unique religious history of the Amish and refuses to uphold a state statute that would require Amish children to attend high school.

Mr. Chief Justice Burger delivered the opinion of the Court.

. . . .

Respondents Jonas Yoder and Wallace Miller are members of the Old Order Amish religion. . . . Wisconsin's compulsory school-attendance law required them to cause their children to attend public or private school until reaching age 16 but the respondents declined to send their children, ages 14 and 15, to public school after they completed the eighth grade. The children were not enrolled in any private school, or within any recognized exception to the compulsory-attendance law, and they are conceded to be subject to the Wisconsin statute.

On complaint of the school district administrator for the public schools, respondents were charged, tried, and convicted of violating the compulsory-attendance law in Green County Court and were fined the sum of $5 each. Respondents defended on the ground that the application of the compulsory-attendance law violated their rights under the First and Fourteenth Amendments. The trial testimony showed that respondents believed, in accordance with the tenets of Old Order Amish communities generally, that their children's attendance at high school, public or private, was contrary to the Amish religion and way of life. They believed that by sending their children to high school, they would not only expose themselves to the danger of the censure of the church community, but, as found by the county court, also endanger their own salvation and that of their children. The State stipulated that respondents' religious beliefs were sincere.

. . . .

As a result of their common heritage, Old Order Amish communities today are characterized by a fundamental belief that salvation requires life in a church community separate and apart from the world and worldly influence. This concept of life aloof from the world and its values is central to their faith. . . .

Formal high school education beyond the eighth grade is contrary to Amish beliefs, not only because it places Amish children in an environment hostile to Amish beliefs with increasing emphasis on competition in class work and sports and with pressure to conform to the styles, manners, and ways of the peer group, but also because it takes them away from their community, physically and emotionally, during the crucial and formative adolescent period of life. . . .

The Amish do not object to elementary education through the first eight grades as a general proposition because they agree that their children must have basic skills in the "three R's" in order to read the Bible, to be good farmers and citizens, and to be able to deal with non-Amish people when necessary in the course of daily affairs. They view such a basic education as acceptable because it does not significantly expose their children to worldly values or interfere with their development in the Amish community during the crucial adolescent period. . . .

There is no doubt as to the power of a State, having a high responsibility for education of its citizens, to impose reasonable regulations for the control and duration of basic education. *See, e.g., Pierce v. Society of Sisters*, 268 U.S. 510, 534 (1925). Providing public schools ranks at the very apex of the function of a State. Yet even this paramount responsibility was, in *Pierce*, made to yield to the right of parents to provide an equivalent education in a privately operated system. There the Court held that Oregon's statute compelling attendance in a public school from age eight to age 16 unreasonably interfered with the interest of parents in directing the rearing of their offspring, including their education in church-operated schools. As that case suggests, the values of parental direction of the religious upbringing and education of their children in their early and formative years have a high place in our society. Thus, a State's interest in universal education, however highly we rank it, is not totally free from a balancing process when it impinges on fundamental rights and interests, such as those specifically protected by the Free Exercise Clause of the First Amendment, and the traditional interest of parents with respect to the religious upbringing of their children so long as they, in the words of *Pierce*, "prepare [them] for additional obligations."

It follows that in order for Wisconsin to compel school attendance beyond the eighth grade against a claim that such attendance interferes with the practice of a legitimate religious belief, it must appear either that the State does not deny the free exercise of religious belief by its requirement, or that there is a state interest of sufficient magnitude to override the interest claiming protection under the Free Exercise Clause.

The essence of all that has been said and written on the subject is that only those interests of the highest order and those not otherwise served can overbalance legitimate claims to the free exercise of religion. We can accept it as settled, therefore, that, however strong the State's interest in universal compulsory education, it is by no means absolute to the exclusion or subordination of all other interests.

We come then to the quality of the claims of the respondents concerning the alleged encroachment of Wisconsin's compulsory school-attendance statute on their rights and the rights of their children to the free exercise of the religious beliefs they and their forebears have adhered to for almost three centuries. In evaluating those claims we must be careful to determine whether the Amish religious faith and their mode of life are, as they claim, inseparable and interdependent. A way of life, however virtuous and admirable, may not be interposed as a barrier to reasonable state regulation of education if it is based on purely secular considerations. . . .

Giving no weight to such secular considerations, however, we see that the record in this case abundantly supports the claim that the traditional way of life of the Amish is not merely a matter of personal preference, but one of deep religious conviction, shared by an organized group, and intimately related to daily living. . . .

The record shows that the respondents' religious beliefs and attitude toward life, family, and home have remained constant—perhaps some would say static—in a period of unparalleled progress in human knowledge generally and great changes in education. . . .

The impact of the compulsory-attendance law on respondents' practice of the Amish religion is not only severe, but inescapable, for the Wisconsin law affirmatively compels them, under threat of criminal sanction, to perform acts undeniably at odds with fundamental tenets of their religious beliefs.

In sum, the unchallenged testimony of acknowledged experts in education and religious history, almost 300 years of consistent practice, and strong evidence of a sustained faith pervading and regulating respondents' entire mode of life support the claim that enforcement of the State's requirement of compulsory formal education after the eighth grade would gravely endanger if not destroy the free exercise of respondents' religious beliefs.

. . . .

We turn, then, to the State's broader contention that its interest in its system of compulsory education is so compelling that even the established religious practices of the Amish must give way. Where fundamental claims of religious freedom are at stake, however, we cannot accept such a sweeping claim; despite its admitted validity in the generality of cases, we must searchingly examine the interests that the State seeks to promote by its requirement for compulsory education to age 16, and the impediment to those objectives that would flow from recognizing the claimed Amish exemption.

The State advances two primary arguments in support of its system of compulsory education. It notes, as Thomas Jefferson pointed out early in our history, that some degree of education is necessary to prepare citizens to participate effectively and intelligently in our open political system if we are to preserve freedom and independence. Further, education prepares individuals to be self-reliant and self-sufficient participants in society. We accept these propositions.

However, the evidence adduced by the Amish in this case is persuasively to the effect that an additional one or two years of formal high school for Amish children in place of their long-established program of informal vocational education would do little to serve those interests.

The State attacks respondents' position as one fostering "ignorance" from which the child must be protected by the State. No one can question the State's duty to protect children from ignorance but this argument does not square with the facts disclosed in the record. Whatever their idiosyncrasies as seen by the majority, this record strongly shows that the Amish community has been a highly successful social unit within our society, even if apart from the conventional "mainstream." Its members are productive and very law-abiding members of society; they reject public welfare in any of its usual modern forms. The Congress itself recognized their self-sufficiency by authorizing exemption of such groups as the Amish from the obligation to pay social security taxes.

. . . .

Insofar as the State's claim rests on the view that a brief additional period of formal education is imperative to enable the Amish to participate effectively and intelligently in our democratic process, it must fall. The Amish alternative to formal secondary school education has enabled them to function effectively in their day-to-day life under self-imposed limitations on relations with the world, and to survive and prosper in contemporary society as a separate, sharply identifiable, and highly self-sufficient community for more than 200 years in this country. . . .

In these terms, Wisconsin's interest in compelling the school attendance of Amish children to age 16 emerges as somewhat less substantial than requiring such attendance for children generally. For, while agricultural employment is not totally outside the legitimate concerns of the child labor laws, employment of children under parental guidance and on the family farm from age 14 to age 16 is an ancient tradition that lies at the periphery of the objectives of such laws. There is no intimation that the Amish employment of their children on family farms is in any way deleterious to their health or that Amish parents exploit children at tender years. Any such inference would be contrary to the record before us. Moreover, employment of Amish children on the family farm does not present the undesirable economic aspects of eliminating jobs that might otherwise be held by adults.

. . . .

. . . [T]this case involves the fundamental interest of parents, as contrasted with that of the State, to guide the religious future and education of their children. The history and culture of Western civilization reflect a strong tradition of parental concern for the nurture and upbringing of their children. This primary role of the parents in the upbringing of their children is now established beyond debate as an enduring American tradition. If not the first, perhaps the most significant statements of the Court in this area are found in *Pierce v. Society of Sisters*, in which the Court observed:

> "Under the doctrine of *Meyer v. Nebraska*, 262 U.S. 390, 43 S.Ct. 625, 67 L. Ed. 1042, we think it entirely plain that the Act of 1922 unreasonably interferes with the liberty of parents and guardians to direct the upbringing and education of children under their control. As often heretofore pointed out, rights guaranteed by the Constitution may not be abridged by legislation which has no reasonable relation to some purpose within the competency of the State. The fundamental theory of liberty upon which all governments in this Union repose excludes any general power of the State to standardize

> its children by forcing them to accept instruction from public teachers only. The child is not the mere creature of the State; those who nurture him and direct his destiny have the right, coupled with the high duty, to recognize and prepare him for additional obligations." 268 U.S., at 534–535, 45 S.Ct., at 573.

The duty to prepare the child for "additional obligations," . . . must be read to include the inculcation of moral standards, religious beliefs, and elements of good citizenship. *Pierce*, of course, recognized that, where nothing more than the general interest of the parent in the nurture and education of his children is involved, it is beyond dispute that the State acts "reasonably" and constitutionally in requiring education to age 16 in some public or private school meeting the standards prescribed by the State.

However read, the Court's holding in *Pierce* stands as a charter of the rights of parents to direct the religious upbringing of their children. And, when the interests of parenthood are combined with a free exercise claim of the nature revealed by this record, more than merely a "reasonable relation to some purpose within the competency of the State" is required to sustain the validity of the State's requirement under the First Amendment. To be sure, the power of the parent, even when linked to a free exercise claim, may be subject to limitation . . . if it appears that parental decisions will jeopardize the health or safety of the child, or have a potential for significant social burdens. But, in this case, the Amish have introduced persuasive evidence undermining the arguments the State has advanced to support its claims. . . .

For the reasons stated we hold, with the Supreme Court of Wisconsin, that the First and Fourteenth Amendments prevent the State from compelling respondents to cause their children to attend formal high school to age 16. Our disposition of this case, however, in no way alters our recognition of the obvious fact that courts are not school boards or legislatures, and are ill-equipped to determine the "necessity" of discrete aspects of a State's program of compulsory education. This should suggest that courts must move with great circumspection in performing the sensitive and delicate task of weighing a State's legitimate social concern when faced with religious claims for exemption from generally applicable educational requirements. It cannot be overemphasized that we are not dealing with a way of life and mode of education by a group claiming to have recently discovered some "progressive" or more enlightened process for rearing children for modern life.

Fellowship Baptist Church v. Benton

815 F.2d 485 (8th Cir. 1987)

The Eighth Circuit finds that the state's denial of the Amish Exception to the plaintiffs does not violate their constitutional rights.

In this appeal, the Court is presented with a broad-based attack on Iowa's compulsory school laws. Plaintiffs are two fundamentalist Baptist church schools, the churches' pastors and principals, and several of the schools' teachers, parents and students. . . .

[T]he state has determined that parents of children in the plaintiff schools are not entitled to the "Amish exemption" to the above requirements, *see* Iowa Code § 299.24, and plaintiffs argue this determination is unconstitutional.

. . . .

An understanding of plaintiffs' religious beliefs and practices is essential to the proper evaluation of plaintiffs' claims. The evidence presented by plaintiffs to the district court unquestionably revealed that their religious beliefs stem from the Bible. They view Christ as the Head of their church and all of its ministries, and adhere to the doctrine of separation of church and state. Their schools were created in response to these beliefs. Neither church has a doctrine which requires members to send their children to the church school, however, and parents are not subject to discipline for removing their children from the church schools. Enrollment in the schools is not limited to those who belong to the church, and both schools have enrolled pupils whose parents are not members of the church. Moreover, several members send some of their children to the church school, while others attend the public schools.

. . . .

Plaintiffs believe themselves to be "in the world but not of the world," but they do not segregate themselves from modern communities. They live in ordinary residential neighborhoods and they interact with their neighbors and others not of their faith. They believe they are called by God to perform certain occupations in life, but these include ordinary occupations such as nurse, lawyer, engineer and accountant, and there is no evidence that they object to the licensing of these occupations. They own and use radios, televisions, motor vehicles and other modern conveniences and advancements. Their dress and lifestyle, while conservative, is not distinctive.

Plaintiffs do, however, object to certain state regulation of their churches' ministries, including the reporting, teacher certification and "equivalent instruction" requirements of Iowa's compulsory school laws.

. . . .

[W]hile plaintiffs attempt to analogize their situation to that of the Amish in the *Yoder* case, the burden the certification requirement imposes upon the plaintiffs is not nearly as great as the burden placed upon the plaintiffs in *Yoder*. The *Yoder* Court found that requiring the Amish to attend public school after the eighth grade would "ultimately result in the destruction of the Old Order Amish church community as it exists in the United States today." The Court also found that the Amish believed that by sending their children to high school, they not only would expose themselves to the censure of the church community, but would also endanger their own salvation and that of their children.

Unlike the Old Order Amish in *Yoder*, plaintiffs expect and encourage their children to attend college, and have no objection to college-educated teachers per se. . . .

Under these circumstances, the *Yoder* Court's admonition that courts "move with great circumspection in performing the sensitive and delicate task of weighing a State's legitimate social concern when faced with religious claims for exemption from generally applicable education requirements" is particularly instructive. "Courts are not school boards or legislatures, and are ill-equipped to determine the 'necessity' of discrete aspects of a State's program of compulsory education."

. . . .

Plaintiffs' final constitutional challenge involves the state's denial of plaintiff parents' request to be exempted from the above requirements through the "Amish exemption." As the district court noted, this exemption has been granted only to parents of children attending Amish schools and one conservative Mennonite school, all of which are located in distinct geographical areas of the state and which follow the style of life and religious tenets described by the Supreme Court in *Yoder*. In *Johnson v. Charles City Community Schools Board of Education*, 368 N.W.2d 74 (Iowa 1985), the Iowa Supreme Court specifically ruled that plaintiff parents were not entitled to the exemption because they failed to prove that their church "professes principles or tenets that differ substantially from the 'objectives, goals, and philosophy of education' embodied in the areas of study listed in [the Amish exception law]," which must be taught in grades one through eight.

The Court found that no tenet of plaintiffs' church was in conflict with teaching subjects such as English-language arts, social studies, mathematics and science; plaintiffs sought only to teach those subjects in their own way, and nothing in [the law] prevented plaintiffs from doing so. Holding that plaintiffs had not established any substantial dissimilarity between their educational goals and those embodied in [the law] . . . the *Charles City* Court approved the administrative denial of plaintiffs' request for an exemption.

Plaintiffs argue before this Court, as they did before the district court and before the Iowa Supreme Court, that this denial violates the equal protection clause. They further contend that granting the exemption to the Amish but not to them violates the establishment clause because the effect is to advance the Amish religion and to inhibit the plaintiffs'.

Because religion is a fundamental right, any classification of religious groups is subject to strict scrutiny. That is, the state must show the classification has been precisely tailored to serve a compelling state interest. . . .

The equal protection clause directs that "all persons similarly circumstanced shall be treated alike." "But so too, 'the Constitution does not require things which are different in fact or opinion to be treated in law as though they were the same.'"

In creating an exemption to its compulsory school laws based upon religious beliefs, Iowa treads the fine line between the free exercise clause and the establishment clause noted by the Supreme Court in *Yoder*:

> The Court must not ignore the danger that an exception from a general obligation of citizenship on religious grounds may run afoul of the Establishment Clause, but that danger cannot be allowed to prevent any exception. . . .

The Court found an exception for the Amish warranted based upon what can only be described as their very unique circumstances and their centuries-old insulated, isolated lifestyle. As the Court itself noted, the Amish had made a convincing showing, "one that probably few other religious groups or sects could make," concerning the nature of their religious beliefs, the severe burden placed upon those beliefs by the state's requirements and the adequacy of the continuing informal vocational education which they preferred to serve the state's interest in the education of their children.

Both the district court and the Iowa Supreme Court recognized that resolving plaintiffs' equal protection challenge required the court to determine whether plaintiffs and the Amish were so similarly situated that the denial of the exemption to the plaintiffs violated the constitution. Both courts analyzed the factors upon which the Supreme Court relied in *Yoder* to create an exemption to Wisconsin's compulsory attendance laws for the Amish who opposed sending their children to high school, and compared plaintiffs' position to that of the Amish. Both courts concluded that plaintiffs were properly denied the exemption. . . .

We agree with these observations. The Supreme Court has recently recognized the validity of a clear line where religious practices are concerned. We have previously addressed the factual dissimilarities between the plaintiffs and the Amish, and they will not be repeated here. The record in this case contains additional specific evidence of the beliefs and lifestyles of those who have been granted the exemption in Iowa, and we find more dissimilarities than similarities between these individuals and the plaintiffs. Accordingly, we agree with the district court that the denial of the [Amish] exemption to the plaintiffs does not violate their right to equal protection of the laws.

We also find no establishment clause violation on the facts of this case. As the *Yoder* Court stated, narrow exemptions such as Iowa has adopted successfully traverse the "tightrope" created by the tension between the free exercise clause and the establishment clause. This narrowly drawn accommodation to one religious view does not require the state, under the establishment clause, to accommodate all others. The *Yoder* Court cited the need for "preserving doctrinal flexibility and recognizing the need for a sensible and realistic application of the Religion Clauses," *Wisconsin v. Yoder, supra*, and we believe that such an approach in this case supports to the conclusion that the "Amish exemption" as interpreted by the Iowa Supreme Court is constitutional.

Post Problem Discussion

1. Is *Yoder* likely to be one of a kind? Is there another religious group that can command this kind of attention in a constitutional balance?

2. Since 1972, many states have broadened the exceptions to compulsory attendance. For example, the Illinois statute exempts, among others, a child "attending a private or a parochial school where children are taught the branches of education taught to children of corresponding age and grade in the public schools, and where the instruction of the child in the branches of education is in the English language." 105 ILCS 5/26-1. Could the Halls or Mary's School of Christ fit under this exception?

3. In *Yoder*, the court notes the religious nature of the Amish objection to attend school. "It cannot be overemphasized that we are not dealing with a way of life and mode of education by a group claiming to have recently discovered some 'progressive' or more enlightened process for rearing children for modern life." *Yoder*, 406 U.S. at 235. Along those lines, our problem statute (which is a mixture of actual state statutes) requires "members or representatives of a congregation of a recognized church or religious denomination established for ten years or more." If we remove the religious aspect from the equation, do parents have any remaining right to refuse to comply with compulsory attendance laws?

§ 5.03 Conditions of Admission, Placement, and Exit

States also have conditions for admission to schools at the K-12 level, typically set by state statute or regulation, though in some cases, admission may be limited by policies set by a local school board. *See, e.g.*, Ala. Admin. Code § 290-3-1-.02(7)(b) (providing for local school board to adopt "policies of admission and attendance within the framework of state law and State Board of Education policies"; and requiring policies "be clearly stated, followed implicitly and given publicity in the area to be served in the spring and fall before schools officially open").

Admission requirements generally include residency provisions, which are discussed in Section 5.05. Other requirements are health-related such as those requiring students to be immunized against communicable diseases. For example, Pennsylvania statutes list the immunizations that children must have for attendance and upon entry into the seventh grade; Pennsylvania then provides exceptions:

> (a) *Medical exemption.* Children need not be immunized if a physician or the physician's designee provides a written statement that immunization may be detrimental to the health of the child. When the physician determines that immunization is no longer detrimental to the health of the child, the child shall be immunized according to this subchapter.

> (b) *Religious exemption.* Children need not be immunized if the parent, guardian or emancipated child objects in writing to the immunization on religious grounds or on the basis of a strong moral or ethical conviction similar to a religious belief.

28 Pa. Code §§ 23.83 to 23.84.

Some states also go a step further and have provisions that prohibit students who have not been immunized for health or religious reasons from attending school during the outbreak of a communicable disease for which immunization is required. *See, e.g.*, N.H. Rev. Stat. Ann. § 141-C:20-d. While these types of requirements can be controversial, courts have generally upheld state statutes that require certain immunizations for school admission. *See, e.g.*, *Zucht v. King*, 260 U.S. 174 (1922); *Davis v. State*, 451 A.2d 107 (Md. 1982); *Wright v. DeWitt School District*, 385 S.W.2d 644 (Ark. 1965); *Board of Education v. Maas*, 152 A.2d 394 (N.J. App. Div. 1959); *Seubold v. Ft. Smith Special School Dist.*, 237 S.W.2d 884 (Ark. 1951).

Once admitted to public schools, students must be placed in an appropriate grade or class. This is generally thought to be within the discretion of the school, though disputes do arise, for example, parents who want their children to start Kindergarten before the stated admission date. More serious issues have arisen regarding students placed in special classes or schools based on disability, or race or ethnicity, or language ability, or some combination of these factors. *See, e.g.*, *Larry P. v. Riles*, 793 F.2d 969, 973 (9th Cir. 1984) (rejecting the use of IQ tests to place black children in classes for the "educable mentally retarded"). These topics are discussed further in Section 5.07 and in Chapter 12.

Exit conditions generally include requirements that students take certain courses and achieve a set number of credit hours to graduate. States also have minimum ages before a student can stop attending school without graduating as part of their compulsory attendance requirements.

Some states have high school exit exams that require students to achieve a certain score on a test before they can graduate. Some of these tests have been challenged in litigation, as illustrated by the extended litigation in *Debra P.*, which challenged the constitutionality of the Florida state competency test. *See Debra P. v. Turlington*, 474 F. Supp. 244, (M.D. Fla. 1979) (enjoining the use of the test for four years), *aff'd in part and vacated in part*, 644 F.2d 397, 402 (5th Cir. 1981) (requiring the state to show that the test measured what was "actually studied in the classrooms of the state" and that any disproportionate negative impact on black students was not the result of past discrimination); *Debra P. v. Turlington*, 564 F. Supp. 177, 186 (M.D. Fla. 1983) (lifting the injunction upon finding the test "instructionally valid and therefore constitutional" and results not a vestige of prior discrimination); *Debra P. v. Turlington*, 730 F.2d 1405, 1412, 1416 (11th Cir. 1984) (finding the district court to be not clearly erroneous).

The *Debra P.* requirement that students be tested on material that they "actually studied in the classrooms of the state" remains constitutionally significant and the validity and applicability of high-stakes exit exams are an area of ongoing attention. *See, e.g., Student No. 9 v. Board of Educ.*, 802 N.E.2d 105, 107 (Mass. 2004) (refusing to enjoin the application of the state regulations requiring plaintiff students to "to pass the tenth grade English language arts and mathematics sections of the Massachusetts Comprehensive Assessment System examination (MCAS exam) in order to graduate from high school").

Activity 2: Find the Admission and Exit Conditions in Your State

Step One—Research your state statutes for any admission requirements for public schools; also identify any high school exit exam requirements for graduation.

Step Two—Research your state education regulations for any admission requirements for public schools. If your state has a high school exit exam, identify the implementing state regulations.

Step Three—Answer the following:

1. Do your state's admission requirements include immunization or vaccination requirements? If so, are there exceptions for health or religious reasons? Are there other exceptions?
2. If there are exceptions, do your state statutes or regulations have provisions prohibiting students who were not vaccinated from attending school during outbreaks? What do you think about these provisions?
3. Do your state admission requirements include anything about the placement of students in particular grades or classes, or anything about gender or race? (See Section 5.07 for more on this topic.)
4. Has there been any litigation over your state's admission requirements in state or federal court? If so, what were the legal claims and what was the result? Do you agree or disagree with the analysis and result?
5. Does your state have a high school exit exam? Does it have a certain required score to be able to graduate and obtain a high school diploma? If so, what does it cover? Has there been any litigation over the exit exam? If so, what were the legal claims and what was the result? Do you agree or disagree with the analysis and result?

§ 5.04 Homeschooling

Homeschooling is on the increase nationally. This appears to be in part because of wider acceptance under state law exempting homeschooled children from compulsory attendance. *See, e.g.*, Ohio Rev. Code Ann. § 3321.04 (2012) (exempting from compulsory attendance a child "being instructed at home by a person qualified to teach the branches in which instruction is required, and such additional branches" under specified conditions). Despite the growth in homeschooling, it remains controversial in some respects with some expressing concern about the lack of state or local school supervision, and others contending that parents should have the right to educate their children how they see fit, particularly when that instruction involves religious topics that are not permitted in public schools.[2] States differ in what requirements they place on parents when allowing homeschooling, some having virtually no requirements, and others having very detailed and stringent requirements. Some require the instruction that is provided at home to be equivalent to the instruction the student would receive at a public school.[3]

Homeschooling cases come to court on a variety of issues. Courts have held it reasonable for parents to be required to obtain approval from the state or local public school before homeschooling their children. *See, e.g., State v. Bowman*, 653 P.2d 254 (Or. Ct. App. 1982) (upholding compulsory attendance statutes as applied to parent regarding home school exemption). However, courts have varied on how far states can go in terms of homeschooling requirements and oversight. For example, some courts have found that home visits by the state, or by the local school district, as a condition of approving homeschooling plans are valid, while others have found that such restrictions are overly intrusive. *Compare Brunelle v. Lynn Pub. Schs*, 702 N.E.2d 1182 (Mass. 1998) (holding that state could not require home visits as a condition of approval of home-schooling plans), *with Matter of Kilroy*, 467 N.Y.S.2d 318 (Fam. Ct. 1983) (indicating court would enter order for neglect absent agreement for home visit).

Beyond review requirements, homeschooling cases often display multiple layers of concern around children's welfare. For example, in *Jonathan L. v. Superior Court*, 165 Cal. App. 4th 1074 (2008), the court considered a case that arose out of a dependency proceeding in which California charged the parents with abuse, neglect, and failure to prevent sexual abuse. The children in *Jonathan L.* were being homeschooled by the parent who was alleged to be neglectful. The court held that the state statute permitted homeschooling, but that permission could be overridden to protect the safety of a child in a dependency proceeding. The holding was limited to dependency (or abuse and neglect) proceedings, where the safety of the child was at issue. Homeschooling disputes also arise in other contexts such as custody battles. *See, e.g., Morgan v. Morgan*, 964 So. 2d 24 (Ala. Civ. App. 2007).

Activity 3: Find Your State's Homeschool Requirements

Step One—Research your state statutes for homeschool requirements.

Step Two—Research your state education regulations for homeschool requirements.

---

2. *See* Samantha Lebeda, *Rights of Parents Homeschooling: Depriving Children of Social Development?* 16 J. CONTEMP. LEGAL ISSUES 99 (Spring 2005).

3. *See* Kimberly A. Yuracko, *Education Off the Grid: Constitutional Constraints on Homeschooling*, 96 CAL. L. REV. 123 (2008).

Step Three—Answer the following:

1. Does your state have express requirements for homeschooling? Does it expressly consider homeschooling to be an exception to compulsory education requirements?
2. What does your state require parents to do in order to be able to homeschool? Does it have detailed requirements at the state level, or is it left to local school discretion in how to deal with parents who homeschool?
3. Does your state require that certain topics or information be taught to students who are homeschooled?
4. Does your state require parents to file any reports demonstrating what they are teaching and what the child is learning? If so, are the reports assessed in any way by the state, or by a local school official? What happens if the state or school official determines that the teaching is not appropriate, or that the student is not learning?
5. Are schools obligated to allow homeschool students to take traditional public school classes or participate in extracurricular activities? Can homeschoolers move in and out of school at will?

Step Four—Go back to Problem 1 and reconsider the fact pattern in light of your state's homeschool requirements. Would the Halls be able to homeschool their children in your state and teach them solely from their church's curriculum materials?

§ 5.05 Residency

Most states provide by statute that students attend the public school that is located in the school district where their parent(s) reside. Within the district, students generally attend the school that is the geographically closest school to their residence (sometimes referred to as the "neighborhood school"). There are exceptions to this general framework. Some states, or school districts within some states, have programs like magnet schools or charter schools, where admission is based on factors other than residency in a certain geographic area. The general residency framework is still widely used, and it is a good starting point for learning about residency issues. The following problem explores some issues with general residency requirements.

Problem 2: Residency Requirements

Yusef has just completed his sixth grade year of school. Next year, he is to attend seventh grade at the Hubert Middle School. Hubert has a bad reputation for behavioral issues, violence, and teachers who are not in control of their classrooms. Yusef's parents are divorced, and he lives with his mother; his father lives out of state. Yusef's aunt (his mother's sister, Aunt Maryam) lives in a school district that is only fifteen miles away in Newtown. Yusef's mother's job is also located in Newtown. Unlike Hubert Middle School, Newtown Middle School has a great reputation, and scores on state assessments to support it. Yusef's mother decides that it would be in Yusef's best interest to attend Newtown Middle. Aunt Maryam agrees to allow Yusef to live with her during the weeks that school is in session so that he can do so.

When Aunt Maryam and Yusef visit Newtown Middle to register Yusef, the school secretary tells them that Yusef cannot attend Newtown Middle because state law requires minors to reside in the district with a parent or guardian. Aunt Maryam is neither a parent nor a guardian, and Yusef's mother lives in another district. Aunt Maryam tells the secretary that Yusef's mother will also be living with her during the school year. The secretary then allows them to complete the paperwork necessary for Yusef's enrollment.

The day before school is scheduled to start, the principal at Newtown calls Aunt Maryam to tell her that Yusef cannot attend because he does not meet the residency requirements under state law. The principal adds that the superintendent has also reviewed Yusef's situation and determined that it is not in Yusef's best interest to attend school in the Newtown district.

Assume that Yusef's mother will be living with Aunt Maryam during the week during the school year, but will also keep her home in the Hubert district. She and Yusef will return there on weekends, during school vacations, and summer break.

Review the problem materials and answer the following:

1. Is the superintendent's decision correct?
2. Is the statute constitutional?
3. Would other factual information be helpful to you in answering these questions? If so, what?

Problem Materials

✓ Hypothetical State Residency Statute

✓ *Martinez v. Bynum*, 461 U.S. 321 (1983)

Hypothetical State Residency Statute

Ed. § 915202. Residence

1. Definitions. For the purposes of this chapter, "parent" means the parent or guardian with legal custody.

2. General Rule. A student is eligible to attend schools in the school administrative unit where the students' parent resides, or where the student resides upon reaching the age of 18 years or upon becoming an emancipated minor.

3. Exceptions:

. . . .

(c) Students not living at Home. A student other than a state ward, a state agency client or a homeless child, residing with another person who is not the student's parent, is considered a resident of the school district where the student resides if the superintendent of the district determines that it is in the best interest of the student because of the following:

A. It is undesirable and impractical for that student to reside with the student's parent, or that other extenuating circumstances exist which justify residence in the unit; and

B. That person is residing in the school administrative unit for other than just education purposes.

4. Residency. A "resident" of a school district means a natural person who is domiciled in the school district and who, if temporarily absent, demonstrates an intent to maintain a principal dwelling place in the school district indefinitely and to return there, coupled with an act or acts consistent with that intent. A person may have only one legal residence at a given time.

Martinez v. Bynum

461 U.S. 321 (1983)

The Court finds that bona fide state residency requirements are constitutional and the state residency law at issue is a bona fide residency law.

Justice Powell delivered the opinion of the Court.

This case involves a facial challenge to the constitutionality of the Texas residency requirement governing minors who wish to attend public free schools while living apart from their parents or guardians.

Roberto Morales was born in 1969 in McAllen, Texas, and is thus a United States citizen by birth. His parents are Mexican citizens who reside in Reynosa, Mexico. He left Reynosa in 1977 and returned to McAllen to live with his sister, petitioner Oralia Martinez, for the primary purpose of attending school in the McAllen Independent School District. Although Martinez is now his custodian, she is not—and does not desire to become—his guardian. As a result, Morales is not entitled to tuition-free admission to the McAllen schools. Sections 21.031(b) and (c) of the Texas Education Code would require the local school authorities to admit him if he or "his parent, guardian, or the person having lawful control of him" resided in the school district, but denies tuition-free admission for a minor who lives apart from a "parent, guardian, or other person having lawful control of him under an order of a court" if his presence in the school district is "for the primary purpose of attending the public free schools." Respondent McAllen Independent School District therefore denied Morales' application for admission in the fall of 1977 ....

This Court frequently has considered constitutional challenges to residence requirements. On several occasions the Court has invalidated requirements that condition receipt of a benefit on a minimum period of residence within a jurisdiction, but it always has been careful to distinguish such durational residence requirements from bona fide residence requirements.

....

We specifically have approved bona fide residence requirements in the field of public education. The Connecticut statute before us in *Vlandis v. Kline*, 412 U.S. 441 (1973), for example, was unconstitutional because it created an irrebuttable presumption of nonresidency for state university students whose legal addresses were outside of the State before they applied for admission. The statute violated the Due Process Clause because it in effect classified some bona fide state residents as nonresidents for tuition purposes. But we "fully recognize[d] that a State has a legitimate interest in protecting and preserving the right of its own bona fide residents to attend [its colleges and universities] on a preferential tuition basis." This "legitimate interest" permits a "State [to] establish such reasonable criteria for in-state status as to make virtually certain that students who are not, in fact, bona fide residents of the State, but who have come there solely for educational purposes, cannot take advantage of the in-state rates." Last Term, in *Plyler v. Doe*, 457 U.S. 202 (1982), we reviewed an aspect of Tex. Educ. Code—the statute at issue in this case. Although we invalidated the portion of the statute that excluded undocumented alien children from the public free schools, we recognized the school districts' right "to apply ... established criteria for determining residence."

A bona fide residence requirement, appropriately defined and uniformly applied, furthers the substantial state interest in assuring that services provided for its residents are enjoyed only by residents. Such a requirement with respect to attendance in public free schools does not violate the Equal Protection Clause of the Fourteenth Amendment. It does not burden or penalize the constitutional right of interstate travel, for any person is free to move to a State and to establish residence there. A bona fide residence requirement simply requires that the person does establish residence before demanding the services that are restricted to residents.

There is a further, independent justification for local residence requirements in the public-school context. As we explained in *Milliken v. Bradley*, 418 U.S. 717 (1974):

> "No single tradition in public education is more deeply rooted than local control over the operation of schools; local autonomy has long been thought essential both to the maintenance of community concern and support for public schools and to quality of the educational process.... Local control over the educational process affords citizens an opportunity to participate in decision-making, permits the structuring of school programs to fit local needs, and encourages 'experimentation, innovation, and a healthy competition for educational excellence.'"

The provision of primary and secondary education, of course, is one of the most important functions of local government. Absent residence requirements, there can be little doubt that the proper planning and operation of the schools would suffer significantly. The State thus has a substantial interest in imposing bona fide residence requirements to maintain the quality of local public schools.

The central question we must decide here is whether 21.031(d) is a bona fide residence requirement. Although the meaning may vary according to context, "residence" generally requires both physical presence and an intention to remain. As the Supreme Court of Maine explained over a century ago:

> "When . . . a person voluntarily takes up his abode in a given place, with intention to remain permanently, or for an indefinite period of time; or, to speak more accurately, when a person takes up his abode in a given place, without any present intention to remove therefrom, such place of abode becomes his residence. . . ." *Inhabitants of Warren v. Inhabitants of Thomaston* 43 Me. 406, 418 (1857).

This classic two-part definition of residence has been recognized as a minimum standard in a wide range of contexts time and time again.

Section 21.031 is far more generous than this traditional standard. It compels a school district to permit a child such as Morales to attend school without paying tuition if he has a bona fide intention to remain in the school district indefinitely, for he then would have a reason for being there other than his desire to attend school: his intention to make his home in the district. Thus 21.031 grants the benefits of residency to all who satisfy the traditional requirements. The statute goes further and extends these benefits to many children even if they (or their families) do not intend to remain in the district indefinitely. As long as the child is not living in the district for the sole purpose of attending school, he satisfies the statutory test. For example, if a person comes to Texas to work for a year, his children will be eligible for tuition-free admission to the public schools. Or if a child comes to Texas for six months for health reasons, he would qualify for tuition-free education. In short, 21.031 grants the benefits of residency to everyone who satisfies the traditional residence definition and to some who legitimately could be classified as nonresidents. Since there is no indication that this extension of the traditional definition has any impermissible basis, we certainly cannot say that 21.031(d) violates the Constitution.

The Constitution permits a State to restrict eligibility for tuition-free education to its bona fide residents. We hold that 21.031 is a bona fide residence requirement that satisfies constitutional standards. The judgment of the Court of Appeals accordingly is Affirmed.

Post Problem Discussion

1. *Martinez* answers the question left open in *Plyler* (in Chapter 1), that is, some bona fide residency requirements imposed by states are acceptable. Why do you think states have these kinds of residency statutes?

2. If you find that the superintendent's decision was correct, under what circumstances would it be in Yusef's best interest to attend school in Newtown?

3. Some states have complicated provisions to ascertain residency in situations with children of divorced parents, wards of the state, temporary residents, or homeless residents. *See, e.g.*, N.H. Rev. Stat. Ann. § 193:12 (addressing residency issues for children of divorced or separated parents, children in state institutions, children living with relatives on state recommendation, homeless children, etc.).

Does your state have any provisions addressing these issues? If not, what do schools do when presented with a situation where one parent lives in one school district and the other lives in another district?

4. Does Yusef and his mom staying with Aunt Maryam in Newtown during the week make them residents under the state statute? The analysis should remind you of the domicile analysis for diversity of citizenship jurisdiction in Civil Procedure. If you think that they are not residents based upon the facts, what could Yusef and his mom do to become residents?

5. One option that often arises in class discussions about this problem is if Aunt Maryam could become Yusef's guardian. Take a look at your state laws to see what would be required for guardianship and if those requirements would be met given the facts.

6. The federal government has laid out certain parameters that states and local schools must follow regarding residency requirements for homeless students under The McKinney-Vento Homeless Assistance Act, 42 U.S.C. §§ 11431 et seq. Problem 2 in Chapter 1 dealt with some of the requirements of this law. What do your state residency laws say about homeless students?

Activity 4: Find Your State Charter School Laws

Step One—Go to your state department of education website and review the information provided about charter schools.

Step Two—Review your state statutes and regulations about charter schools.

Step Three—Find a charter school operating in your state and review information about the school on its website, including its admissions policies.

Step Four—Answer the following:

1. What do your state laws say about charter school admissions?
2. What are the admissions requirements for the charter school you selected?
3. What state laws are charter schools exempt from in your state?
4. What additional requirements apply to charter schools that do not apply to public schools in your state?

§ 5.06 Race and Gender in Public School Assignment and Attendance

Issues of race, ethnicity, and segregation follow the historical trail from the rejection of the idea of separate but equal to current caselaw on the role of race in student participation in selected public schools. The intransigent achievement gap between Black, Latino, and Native American students and White and Asian students evinces the continuing significance of this history.

The first inroads into desegregation came in higher education, with the graduate and professional school cases setting the tone for the elementary and secondary cases that followed. Litigation in the late 1940s and into the 1950s challenged the assignment (or rejection) of students based on race and ethnicity and changed the law on segregation. One early landmark decision that is illustrative of the situation of the times is *Mendez v. Westminister Sch. Dist.*, 64 F. Supp. 544 (D. Cal. 1946), *aff'd*, 161 F.2d 774 (9th Cir. 1947), where federal courts in California found that:

> A paramount requisite in the American system of public education is social equality. It must be open to all children by unified school association regardless of lineage. We think that under the record before us the only tenable ground upon which segregation practices in the defendant school districts can be defended lies in the English language deficiencies of some of the children of Mexican ancestry as they enter elementary public school life as beginners. But even such situations do not justify the general and continuous segregation in separate schools of the children of Mexican ancestry from the rest of the elementary school population. . . .

Mendez v. Westminister Sch. Dist., 64 F. Supp. 544, 549 (D. Cal. 1946).

While *Mendez* was decided on the basis of noncompliance with state law and was based on Spanish-speaking not race, *Mendez*, 64 F. Supp. at 546, it was followed by the four cases that made their way to the Supreme Court challenging the law in Kansas, South Carolina, Virginia, and Delaware, which did focus on directly on race. In *Brown*, the United States Supreme Court rejected its prior holding in *Plessy v. Ferguson* supporting "separate but equal," finding that:

> in the field of public education the doctrine of "separate but equal" has no place. Separate educational facilities are inherently unequal. Therefore, we hold that the plaintiffs and others similarly situated for whom the actions have been brought are, by reason of the segregation complained of, deprived of the equal protection of the laws guaranteed by the Fourteenth Amendment. This disposition makes unnecessary any discussion whether such segregation also violates the Due Process Clause of the Fourteenth Amendment.

Brown v. Board of Educ., 347 U.S. 483, 495 (1954). Having ruled that education should not be segregated in *Brown I*, in *Brown II*, the Court held that such desegregation should be accomplished with "all deliberate speed" under the purview and authority of the lower courts. *Brown II*, 349 U.S. 294, 301 (1955).

After *Brown*, states and local districts approached desegregation reluctantly at best. An early response by many schools was the adoption of "freedom-of-choice" or "freedom of transfer" plans, where students chose their public schools. This approach was rejected by the Supreme Court in 1965, with the Court explicitly finding an "affirmative duty" for schools to "convert to a unitary system in which racial discrimination would be eliminated root and branch. . . . The constitutional rights of Negro school children articulated in *Brown I* permit no less than this; and it was to this end that *Brown II* commanded school boards to bend their efforts." *Green v. County Sch. Bd.*, 391 U.S. 430, 437–38 (1968); *Monroe v. Board of Comm'rs*, 391 U.S. 450 (1968) (regarding freedom of transfer). *Green* also set out factors to be considered in evaluating effectiveness in complying with *Brown* including student assignment, staff, faculty, extracurricular activities, and transportation. *Green*, 391 U.S. at 435.

For the next decade or so, the Court continued to hold to its view that schools must achieve "the greatest possible degree of actual desegregation, taking into account the practicalities of the situation." *Davis v. Board of Sch. Comm'rs*, 402 U.S. 33, 37 (1971), an approach labeled "all-out desegregation." *See Keyes v. School Dist.*, 413 U.S. 189 (1973); *see also* James S. Liebman, *Desegregating Politics: "All-Out" School Desegregation Explained*, 90 Colum. L. Rev. 1463 (1990). Cases in this period emphasized that the lower court remedies should focus on effectiveness and supported remedies that included reference to mathematical formulas as a starting point, busing, magnet schools, and the like. Desegregation was found to be a constitutional concern and issue in the north as well as the south. Later decisions of the Supreme Court began to move from "all-out" desegregation, finding, for example, that the remedy for Detroit's segregation did not properly include cross-district busing to suburban districts. *See Milliken v. Bradley*, 418 U.S. 717 (1974). The courts also began to find that some districts had met their obligations for unitary status. *See generally, e.g., Missouri v. Jenkins*, 515 U.S. 70 (1995); *Freeman v. Pitts*, 503 U.S. 467 (1992); *Board of Educ. v. Dowell*, 498 U.S. 237 (1991).

More recently, attention has turned to a different aspect of race, namely affirmative actions taken to assure racial diversity. In two cases decided in 2003, the Court rejected a university admissions plan with race-conscious bonus points, *see Gratz v. Bollinger*, 539 U.S. 244 (2003), but upheld an admissions plan for law school admission where admission was based on individual holistic review narrowly tailored to achieve a compelling interest in a diverse student body. *Grutter v. Bollinger*, 539 U.S. 306 (2003). In 2007, the Court found *Gratz* and *Grutter* do not control decisions regarding public high schools. *Parents Involved in Cmty. Sch. v. Seattle Sch. Dist. No. 1*, 551 U.S. 701 (2007).

The following Table provides a brief overview of selected cases concerning segregation/ desegregation and affirmative action. The Table is only a sketch and cannot possibly reflect what Liebman and others call the "rich and complicated history of school desegregation." 90 Colum. L. Rev. 1463, 1470, n.98 and references therein.

Selected Segregation/Desegregation/Affirmative Action Cases

1849	*Roberts v. City of Boston*, 59 Mass. 198 (1849)	Separate but equal doctrine in early Massachusetts school case.
1896	*Plessy v. Ferguson*, 163 U.S. 537 (1896)	Law requiring separate but equal railway coaches ruled constitutional.
1938	*Missouri ex rel. Gaines v. Canada*, 305 U.S. 337 (1938)	Prohibiting African-American students from University of Missouri law school ruled unconstitutional because there was no other public law school alternative in the state.
1946–47	*Mendez v. Westminister Sch. Dist.*, 64 F. Supp. 544 (D. Cal. 1946), *aff'd*, 161 F.2d 774 (9th Cir. 1947)	Segregation of Mexican-Americans based on native language ruled unconstitutional.
1950	*Sweatt v. Painter*, 339 U.S. 629 (1950)	A separate law school cannot provide a substantially equal opportunity, requiring the University of Texas to admit African-Americans.
1950	*McLaurin v. Board of Regents of Oklahoma*, 339 U.S. 637 (1950)	Students in education graduate schools are to be treated equally in seating, facilities, etc.
1954	*Brown v. Board of Educ.*, 347 U.S. 483 (1954)	Separate but equal is not equal.
1955	*Brown v. Board of Educ.*, 349 U.S. 294 (1955)	Desegregation should be achieved with all deliberate speed.
1958	*Cooper v. Aaron*, 358 U.S. 1 (1958)	Potential violence does not provide grounds to justify delay in desegregation.
1964	*Griffin v. County Sch. Bd.*, 377 U.S. 218 (1964)	Closing of public schools while supporting tuition grants for private schools is unconstitutional, representing "entirely too much deliberation and not enough speed." *Id.* at 229.
1968	*Green v. County Sch. Bd.*, 391 U.S. 430 (1968)	An approach to desegregation that allows freedom of choice may be constitutional if it works, but not if ineffective in moving to unitary system.
1972	*Cisneros v. Corpus Christi Independent Sch. Dist.*, 350 F. Supp. 1241 (S.D. Tex. 1972)	*Brown* applies to Mexican-American students.
1971	*Swann v. Charlotte-Mecklenburg Bd. of Educ.*, 402 U.S. 1 (1971)	In light of lack of desegregation progress, remedial plans to address de jure segregation can include busing, magnet schools, and use of "mathematical ratios" as starting point. *Id.* at 25.
1973	*Keyes v. School Dist.*, 413 U.S. 189 (1973)	Segregation identified in a northern city, Denver; "intentionally segregative policy . . . practiced in a meaningful . . . segment of a school system, can be viewed as creating unconstitutional desegregation." *Id.* at 191, 208–09.

Selected Segregation/Desegregation/Affirmative Action Cases (*continued*)

1974	*Milliken v. Bradley*, 418 U.S. 717 (1974)	Court-ordered remedy for segregation in Detroit (intradistrict) that reaches to suburban districts (interdistrict) not appropriate absent showing that the suburban districts had themselves contributed to unconstitutional violations.
1978	*Regents of the Univ. of Cal. v. Bakke*, 438 U.S. 265 (1978)	White applicant previously denied admission in program with racial set aside of 16/100 seats in medical school, ordered admitted to medical school. Plurality opinion. Powell opinion supports view that "attaining a diverse student body was the only interest asserted by the university that survived scrutiny."
1991	*Board of Educ. v. Dowell*, 498 U.S. 237 (1991)	Court-ordered desegregation plans not "to operate in perpetuity." *Id.* at 248.
1992	*Freeman v. Pitts*, 503 U.S. 467 (1992)	Court "need not retain active control over every aspect of school administration until a school district has demonstrated unitary status in all facets of its system." *Id.* at 471. The question is whether there has been compliance "in good faith with the desegregation decree since it was entered, and whether the vestiges of past discrimination have been eliminated to the extent practicable." *Id.* at 492
1995	*Missouri v. Jenkins*, 515 US 70 (1995)	After eighteen years of desegregation litigation, remedial orders that included focus on "desegregative attractiveness, coupled with suburban comparability" are beyond court's authority. *Id.* at 91.
2003	*Gratz v. Bollinger*, 539 U.S. 244 (2003)	College admissions plan with race-conscious bonus points invalidated.
2003	*Grutter v. Bollinger*, 539 U.S. 306 (2003)	University of Michigan Law School's use of racial factors found constitutional where individual holistic review narrowly tailored to achieve a compelling interest in a diverse student body.
2007	*Parents Involved in Cmty. Sch. v. Seattle Sch. Dist. No. 1*, 551 U.S. 701 (2007) (*PICS*)	*Gratz* and *Grutter* do not control decisions in public high schools, where districts may not constitutionally rely exclusively on a student's race in assigning him/her to a particular district school to achieve racial balance.
2012	*Fisher v. University of Texas at Austin*	University's use of race as a factor in undergraduate admissions process must be subjected to strict scrutiny review by courts and the University receives no deference from courts in proving that the means it chose to attain diversity are narrowly tailored to its goal. University must demonstrate that its admissions process evaluates applicants as an individual and not in a way that makes an applicant's race or ethnicity "the defining feature of his or her application."
2014	*Schuette v. Coalition to Defend Affirmative Action*	State Constitutional Amendment that prohibits state universities from using racial preferences as part of its admissions process does not violate the United States Constitution's Equal Protection Clause.

The following problem explores the issue of how, if at all, public elementary and secondary schools can consider race in assigning students.

Problem 3: The Majestic Equality of the Law Goes to School

You are the attorney for a school district, MidCity, with twenty one high schools and 35,000 students. The district prides itself on a mixed student population that is approximately 20% White, 15% Asian, 25% Black, and 30% Hispanic; in the remaining mixed group, the highest percentage is 5% Russian immigrants. The neighborhoods in the district tend to be predominantly race or ethnicity based, reflecting a geographical as well as historical cultural and racial division. The racial composition of the twenty one high schools reflects the neighborhoods and is thus not diverse. There are demonstrated and wide disparities in resources, teacher quality, and educational opportunities within the schools. Schools with predominantly Black or Latino student populations are uniformly at the lowest levels in all of the categories that the state and school district use to measure quality schools. Conversely, schools with mostly white and Asian student populations are at the highest levels.

MidCity is compact. Most of the schools are neighborhood schools. In many cases, it would be possible to use public transportation to go from one neighborhood or school to another, or even walk, in some instances. MidCity has not been subject to court ordered desegregation in the past.

The school board wants to know if it can change the student populations of its schools by using race as a factor for assigning a student to a school. They particularly want to know if they must let students stay in their neighborhood schools. They believe that more racial diversity in schools will help address the disparities. They also believe that diversity is good for all students in their community. Review the problem materials and advise the board on their options.

Problem Materials

- ✓ Review the *Brown* decisions in Chapter 1.
- ✓ *Mendez v. Westminister School District*, 64 F. Supp. 544 (C.D. Cal. 1946), *aff'd*, 161 F.2d 774 (9th Cir. 1947)
- ✓ *Grutter v. Bollinger*, 539 U.S. 306 (2003)
- ✓ *Parents Involved in Community Schools v. Seattle School District No. 1*, 551 U.S. 701 (2007) *(PICS)*
- ✓ Review Policy Excerpt from National School Boards Association & the College Board, *Not Black and White* available online http://www.collegeboard.com/prod_downloads/prof/not-black-white-collegeboard.pdf.

Mendez v. Westminster

64 F. Supp. 544 (C.D. Cal. 1946), *aff'd*, 161 F.2d 774 (9th Cir. 1947)

The court finds that segregating Mexican or Latin grade school children who cannot speak English violates equal protection.

Opinion by McCormick.

Gonzalo Mendez, William Guzman, Frank Palomino, Thomas Estrada and Lorenzo Ramirez, as citizens of the United States, and on behalf of their minor children, and as they allege in the petition, on behalf of "some 5000" persons similarly affected, all of Mexican or Latin descent, have filed a class suit pursuant to Rule 23 of Federal Rules of Civil Procedure, 28 U.S.C.A. following section 723c, against the Westminister, Garden Grove and El Modeno School Districts, and the Santa Ana City Schools, all of Orange County, California, and the respective trustees and superintendents of said school districts.

The complaint, grounded upon the Fourteenth Amendment to the Constitution of the United States and Subdivision 14 of Section 24 of the Judicial Code, Title 28, Section 41, subdivision 14, 28 U.S.C.A. 41, alleges a concerted policy and design of class discrimination against "persons of Mexican or Latin descent or extraction" of elementary school age by the defendant school agencies in the conduct and operation of public schools of said districts, resulting in the denial of the equal protection of the laws to such class of persons among which are the petitioning school children.

Specifically, plaintiffs allege:

> "That for several years last past respondents have and do now in furtherance and in execution of their common plan, design and purpose within their respective Systems and Districts, have by their regulation, custom and usage and in execution thereof adopted and declared: That all children or persons of Mexican or Latin descent or extraction, though Citizens of the United States of America, shall be, have been and are now excluded from attending, using, enjoying and receiving the benefits of the education, health and recreation facilities of certain schools within their respective Districts and Systems but that said children are now and have been segregated and required to and must attend and use certain schools in said Districts and Systems reserved for and attended solely and exclusively by children and persons of Mexican and Latin descent, while such other schools are maintained attended and used exclusively by and for persons and children purportedly known as White or Anglo-Saxon children.
>
> "That in execution of said rules and regulations, each, every and all the foregoing children are compelled and required to and must attend and use the schools in said respective Districts reserved for and attended solely and exclusively by children of Mexican and Latin descent and are forbidden, barred and excluded from attending any other school in said District or System solely for the reason that said children or child are of Mexican or Latin descent."

. . . .

It is conceded by all parties that there is no question of race discrimination in this action. It is, however, admitted that segregation per se is practiced in the above-mentioned school districts as the Spanish-speaking children enter school life and as they advance through the grades in the respective school districts. It is also admitted by the defendants that the petitioning children are qualified to attend the public schools in the respective districts of their residences.

. . . .

The concrete acts complained of are those of the various school district officials in directing which schools the petitioning children and others of the same class or group must attend. The segregation exists in the elementary schools to and including the sixth grade in two of the defendant districts, and in the two other defendant districts through the eighth grade. The record before us shows without conflict that the technical facilities and physical conveniences offered in the schools housing entirely the segregated pupils, the efficiency of the teachers therein and the curricula are identical and in some respects superior to those in the other schools in the respective districts.

The ultimate question for decision may be thus stated: Does such official action of defendant district school agencies and the usages and practices pursued by the respective school authorities as shown by the evidence operate to deny or deprive the so-called non-English-speaking school children of Mexican ancestry or descent within such school districts of the equal protection of the laws?

The defendants at the outset challenge the jurisdiction of this court under the record as it exists at this time. We have already denied the defendants' motion to dismiss the action upon the "face" of the complaint. No reason has been shown which warrants reconsideration of such decision.

. . . .

Are the actions of public school authorities of a rural or city school in the State of California, as alleged and established in this case, to be considered actions of the State within the meaning of the Fourteenth Amendment so as to confer jurisdiction on this court to hear and decide this case under the authority of Section 24, Subdivision 14 of the Judicial Code, *supra*? We think they are.

In the public school system of the State of California the various local school districts enjoy a considerable degree of autonomy. Fundamentally, however, the people of the State have made the public school system a matter of State supervision. Such system is not committed to the exclusive control of local governments. . . .

. . . .

We therefore turn to consider whether under the record before us the school boards and administrative authorities in the respective defendant districts have by their segregation policies and practices transgressed applicable law and Constitutional safeguards and limitations and thus have invaded the personal right which every public school pupil has to the equal protection provision of the Fourteenth Amendment to obtain the means of education.

We think the pattern of public education promulgated in the Constitution of California and effectuated by provisions of the Education Code of the State prohibits segregation of the pupils of Mexican ancestry in the elementary schools from the rest of the school children.

Section 1 of Article IX of the Constitution of California directs the legislature to "encourage by all suitable means the promotion of intellectual, scientific, moral, and agricultural improvement" of the people. Pursuant to this basic directive by the people of the State many laws stem authorizing special instruction in the public schools for handicapped children. See Division 8 of the Education Code. Such legislation, however, is general in its aspects. It includes all those who fall within the described classification requiring the special consideration provided by the statutes regardless of their ancestry or extraction. The common segregation attitudes and practices of the school authorities in the defendant school districts in Orange County pertain solely to children of Mexican ancestry and parentage. They are singled out as a class for segregation. Not only is such method of public school administration contrary to the general requirements of the school laws of the State, but we think it indicates an official school policy that is antagonistic in principle to Sections 16004 and 16005 of the Education Code of the State.

Obviously, the children referred to in these laws are those of Mexican ancestry. And it is noteworthy that the educational advantages of their commingling with other pupils is regarded as being so important to the school system of the State that it is provided for even regardless of the citizenship of the parents. We perceive in the laws relating to the public educational system in the State of California a clear purpose to avoid and forbid distinctions among pupils based upon race or ancestry except in specific situations not pertinent to this action. Distinctions of that kind have recently been declared by the highest judicial authority of the United States "by their very nature odious to a free people whose institutions are founded upon the doctrine of equality." They are said to be "utterly inconsistent with American traditions and ideals." *Kiyoshi Hirabayashi v. United States*, 320 U.S. 81, 63 S.Ct. 1375, 1385, 87 L.Ed. 1774.

Our conclusions in this action, however, do not rest solely upon what we conceive to be the utter irreconcilability of the segregation practices in the defendant school districts with the public educational system authorized and sanctioned by the laws of the State of California. We think such practices clearly and unmistakably disregard rights secured by the supreme law of the land. *Cumming v. Board of Education of Richmond County*, 175 U.S. 528.

"The equal protection of the laws" pertaining to the public school system in California is not provided by furnishing in separate schools the same technical facilities, text books and courses of instruction to children of Mexican ancestry that are available to the other public school children regardless of their ancestry. A paramount requisite in the American system of public education is social equality. It must be open to all children by unified school association regardless of lineage.

We think that under the record before us the only tenable ground upon which segregation practices in the defendant school districts can be defended lies in the

English language deficiencies of some of the children of Mexican ancestry as they enter elementary public school life as beginners. But even such situations do not justify the general and continuous segregation in separate schools of the children of Mexican ancestry from the rest of the elementary school population as has been shown to be the practice in the defendant school districts—in all of them to the sixth grade, and in two of them through the eighth grade.

The evidence clearly shows that Spanish-speaking children are retarded in learning English by lack of exposure to its use because of segregation, and that commingling of the entire student body instills and develops a common cultural attitude among the school children which is imperative for the perpetuation of American institutions and ideals. It is also established by the record that the methods of segregation prevalent in the defendant school districts foster antagonisms in the children and suggest inferiority among them where none exists. One of the flagrant examples of the discriminatory results of segregation in two of the schools involved in this case is shown by the record. In the district under consideration there are two schools, the Lincoln and the Roosevelt, located approximately 120 yards apart on the same school grounds, hours of opening and closing, as well as recess periods, are not uniform. No credible language test is given to the children of Mexican ancestry upon entering the first grade in Lincoln School. This school has an enrollment of 249 so-called Spanish-speaking pupils, and no so-called English-speaking pupils; while the Roosevelt, (the other) school, has 83 so-called English-speaking pupils and 25 so-called Spanish-speaking pupils. Standardized tests as to mental ability are given to the respective classes in the two schools and the same curricula are pursued in both schools and, of course, in the English language as required by State law. Section 8251, Education Code. In the last school year the students in the seventh grade of the Lincoln were superior scholarly to the same grade in the Roosevelt School and to any group in the seventh grade in either of the schools in the past. It further appears that not only did the class as a group have such mental superiority but that certain pupils in the group were also outstanding in the class itself. Notwithstanding this showing, the pupils of such excellence were kept in the Lincoln School. It is true that there is no evidence in the record before us that shows that any of the members of this exemplary class requested transfer to the other so-called intermingled school, but the record does show without contradiction that another class had protested against the segregation policies and practices in the schools of this El Modeno district without avail. . . .

The long-standing discriminatory custom prevalent in this district is aggravated by the fact shown by the record that although there are approximately 25 children of Mexican descent living in the vicinity of the Lincoln School, none of them attend that school, but all are peremptorily assigned by the school authorities to the Hoover School, although the evidence shows that there are no school zones territorially established in the district.

There is no evidence that any discriminatory or other objectionable motive or purpose actuated the School Board in locating or defining such zones.

. . . .

There are other discriminatory customs, shown by the evidence, existing in the defendant school districts as to pupils of Mexican descent and extraction, but we deem it unnecessary to discuss them in this memorandum.

We conclude by holding that the allegations of the complaint (petition) have been established sufficiently to justify injunctive relief against all defendants, restraining further discriminatory practices against the pupils of Mexican descent in the public schools of defendant school districts. *See Morris v. Williams*, 8 Cir., 149 F.2d 703. . . .

Grutter v. Bollinger

539 U.S. 306 (2003)

The Court rules that a race-conscious admissions policy of a state university law school is constitutional.

Justice O'Connor delivered the opinion of the Court, in which Stevens, Souter, Ginsburg, and Breyer, JJ., joined, and in which Scalia and Thomas, JJ., joined in part insofar as it is consistent with the views expressed in Part VII of the opinion of Thomas, J.

This case requires us to decide whether the use of race as a factor in student admissions by the University of Michigan Law School (Law School) is unlawful.

I

A

The Law School ranks among the Nation's top law schools. It receives more than 3,500 applications each year for a class of around 350 students. Seeking to "admit a group of students who individually and collectively are among the most capable," the Law School looks for individuals with "substantial promise for success in law school" and "a strong likelihood of succeeding in the practice of law and contributing in diverse ways to the well-being of others." More broadly, the Law School seeks "a mix of students with varying backgrounds and experiences who will respect and learn from each other." *Ibid.* In 1992, the dean of the Law School charged a faculty committee with crafting a written admissions policy to implement these goals. In particular, the Law School sought to ensure that its efforts to achieve student body diversity complied with this Court's most recent ruling on the use of race in university admissions. *See Regents of Univ. of Cal. v. Bakke*, 438 U.S. 265, 98 S.Ct. 2733, 57 L.Ed.2d 750 (1978). Upon the unanimous adoption of the committee's report by the Law School faculty, it became the Law School's official admissions policy.

The hallmark of that policy is its focus on academic ability coupled with a flexible assessment of applicants' talents, experiences, and potential "to contribute to the learning of those around them." The policy requires admissions officials to evaluate each applicant based on all the information available in the file, including a personal statement, letters of recommendation and an essay describing the ways in which the applicant will contribute to the life and diversity of the Law School. In reviewing an applicant's file, admissions officials must consider the applicant's undergraduate grade point average (GPA) and Law School Admission Test (LSAT) score because they are important (if imperfect) predictors of academic success in law school. The policy stresses that "no applicant should be admitted unless we expect that applicant to do well enough to graduate with no serious academic problems."

The policy makes clear, however, that even the highest possible score does not guarantee admission to the Law School. Nor does a low score automatically disqualify an applicant. Rather, the policy requires admissions officials to look beyond grades and test scores to other criteria that are important to the Law School's educational objectives. So-called "'soft' variables" such as "the enthusiasm of recommenders, the quality of the undergraduate institution, the quality of the applicant's essay, and the areas and difficulty of undergraduate course selection" are all brought to bear in assessing an "applicant's likely contributions to the intellectual and social life of the institution."

The policy aspires to "achieve that diversity which has the potential to enrich everyone's education and thus make a law school class stronger than the sum of its parts." The policy does not restrict the types of diversity contributions eligible for "substantial weight" in the admissions process, but instead recognizes "many possible bases for diversity admissions." The policy does, however, reaffirm the Law School's longstanding commitment to "one particular type of diversity," that is, "racial and ethnic diversity with special reference to the inclusion of students from groups which have been historically discriminated against, like African-Americans, Hispanics and Native Americans, who without this commitment might not be represented in our student body in meaningful numbers." By enrolling a "'critical mass' of [underrepresented] minority students," the Law School seeks to "ensur[e] their ability to make unique contributions to the character of the Law School."

The policy does not define diversity "solely in terms of racial and ethnic status." Nor is the policy "insensitive to the competition among all students for admission to the [L]aw [S]chool." *Ibid.* Rather, the policy seeks to guide admissions officers in "producing classes both diverse and academically outstanding, classes made up of students who promise to continue the tradition of outstanding contribution by Michigan Graduates to the legal profession." *Ibid.*

B

Petitioner Barbara Grutter is a white Michigan resident who applied to the Law School in 1996 with a 3.8 GPA and 161 LSAT score. The Law School initially placed petitioner on a waiting list, but subsequently rejected her application. In December 1997, petitioner filed suit in the United States District Court for the Eastern District of Michigan against the Law School, the Regents of the University of Michigan, Lee Bollinger (Dean of the Law School from 1987 to 1994, and President of the University of Michigan from 1996 to 2002), Jeffrey Lehman (Dean of the Law School), and Dennis Shields (Director of Admissions at the Law School from 1991 until 1998). Petitioner alleged that respondents discriminated against her on the basis of race in violation of the Fourteenth Amendment; Title VI of the Civil Rights Act of 1964, 78 Stat. 252, 42 U.S.C. § 2000d; and Rev. Stat. § 1977, as amended, 42 U.S.C. § 1981.

Petitioner further alleged that her application was rejected because the Law School uses race as a "predominant" factor, giving applicants who belong to certain minority groups "a significantly greater chance of admission than students with similar credentials from disfavored racial groups." Petitioner also alleged that respondents "had no compelling interest to justify their use of race in the admissions process." Petitioner requested compensatory and punitive damages, an order requiring the Law School to offer her admission, and an injunction prohibiting the Law School from continuing to discriminate on the basis of race. Petitioner clearly has standing to bring this lawsuit.

. . . .

We granted certiorari, to resolve the disagreement among the Courts of Appeals on a question of national importance: Whether diversity is a compelling interest that can justify the narrowly tailored use of race in selecting applicants for admission to public universities. *Compare Hopwood v. Texas*, 78 F.3d 932 (C.A.5 1996) (*Hopwood I*) (holding that diversity is not a compelling state interest), *with Smith v. University of Wash. Law School*, 233 F.3d 1188 (C.A.9 2000) (holding that it is).

II

A

We last addressed the use of race in public higher education over 25 years ago. In the landmark *Bakke* case, we reviewed a racial set-aside program that reserved 16 out of 100 seats in a medical school class for members of certain minority groups. The decision produced six separate opinions, none of which commanded a majority of the Court. Four Justices would have upheld the program against all attack on the ground that the government can use race to "remedy disadvantages cast on minorities by past racial prejudice." (joint opinion of Brennan, White, Marshall, and Blackmun, JJ., concurring in judgment in part and dissenting in part). Four other Justices avoided the constitutional question altogether and struck down the program on statutory grounds. (opinion of Stevens, J., joined by Burger, C. J., and Stewart and Rehnquist, JJ., concurring in judgment in part and dissenting in part). Justice Powell provided a fifth vote not only for invalidating the set-aside program, but also for reversing the state court's injunction against any use of race whatsoever. The only holding for the Court in *Bakke* was that a "State has a substantial interest that legitimately may be served by a properly devised admissions program involving the competitive consideration of race and ethnic origin." Thus, we reversed that part of the lower court's judgment that enjoined the university "from any consideration of the race of any applicant."

Since this Court's splintered decision in *Bakke*, Justice Powell's opinion announcing the judgment of the Court has served as the touchstone for constitutional analysis of race-conscious admissions policies. Public and private universities across the

Nation have modeled their own admissions programs on Justice Powell's views on permissible race-conscious policies. We therefore discuss Justice Powell's opinion in some detail.

Justice Powell began by stating that "[t]he guarantee of equal protection cannot mean one thing when applied to one individual and something else when applied to a person of another color. If both are not accorded the same protection, then it is not equal." In Justice Powell's view, when governmental decisions "touch upon an individual's race or ethnic background, he is entitled to a judicial determination that the burden he is asked to bear on that basis is *precisely tailored to serve a compelling governmental interest.*" Under this exacting standard, only one of the interests asserted by the university survived Justice Powell's scrutiny.

First, Justice Powell rejected an interest in "'reducing the historic deficit of traditionally disfavored minorities in medical schools and in the medical profession'" as an unlawful interest in racial balancing. Second, Justice Powell rejected an interest in remedying societal discrimination because such measures would risk placing unnecessary burdens on innocent third parties "who bear no responsibility for whatever harm the beneficiaries of the special admissions program are thought to have suffered." Third, Justice Powell rejected an interest in "increasing the number of physicians who will practice in communities currently underserved," concluding that even if such an interest could be compelling in some circumstances the program under review was not "geared to promote that goal."

Justice Powell approved the university's use of race to further only one interest: "the attainment of a diverse student body." With the important proviso that "constitutional limitations protecting individual rights may not be disregarded," Justice Powell grounded his analysis in the academic freedom that "long has been viewed as a special concern of the First Amendment." Justice Powell emphasized that nothing less than the "'nation's future depends upon leaders trained through wide exposure' to the ideas and mores of students as diverse as this Nation of many peoples." In seeking the "right to select those students who will contribute the most to the 'robust exchange of ideas,'" a university seeks "to achieve a goal that is of paramount importance in the fulfillment of its mission." Both "tradition and experience lend support to the view that the contribution of diversity is substantial."

Justice Powell was, however, careful to emphasize that in his view race "is only one element in a range of factors a university properly may consider in attaining the goal of a heterogeneous student body." For Justice Powell, "[i]t is not an interest in simple ethnic diversity, in which a specified percentage of the student body is in effect guaranteed to be members of selected ethnic groups," that can justify the use of race. Rather, "[t]he diversity that furthers a compelling state interest encompasses a far broader array of qualifications and characteristics of which racial or ethnic origin is but a single though important element."

In the wake of our fractured decision in *Bakke*, courts have struggled to discern whether Justice Powell's diversity rationale, set forth in part of the opinion joined by no other Justice, is nonetheless binding precedent under *Marks*. In that case, we explained that "[w]hen a fragmented Court decides a case and no single rationale explaining the result enjoys the assent of five Justices, the holding of the Court may be viewed as that position taken by those Members who concurred in the judgments on the narrowest grounds." As the divergent opinions of the lower courts demonstrate, however, "[t]his test is more easily stated than applied to the various opinions supporting the result in [*Bakke*]."

We do not find it necessary to decide whether Justice Powell's opinion is binding under *Marks*. It does not seem "useful to pursue the *Marks* inquiry to the utmost logical possibility when it has so obviously baffled and divided the lower courts that have considered it." More important, for the reasons set out below, today we endorse Justice Powell's view that student body diversity is a compelling state interest that can justify the use of race in university admissions.

B

The Equal Protection Clause provides that no State shall "deny to any person within its jurisdiction the equal protection of the laws." U.S. Const., Amdt. 14, § 2. Because the Fourteenth Amendment "protect[s] *persons*, not *groups*," all "governmental action based on race-a *group* classification long recognized as in most circumstances irrelevant and therefore prohibited-should be subjected to detailed judicial inquiry to ensure that the *personal* right to equal protection of the laws has not been infringed." *Adarand Constructors, Inc. v. Peña*, 515 U.S. 200, 227 (1995) (emphasis in original; internal quotation marks and citation omitted). We are a "free people whose institutions are founded upon the doctrine of equality." *Loving v. Virginia*, 388 U.S. 1, 11 (1967) (internal quotation marks and citation omitted). It follows from that principle that "government may treat people differently because of their race only for the most compelling reasons." *Adarand Constructors, Inc. v. Peña*, 515 U.S., at 227.

We have held that all racial classifications imposed by government "must be analyzed by a reviewing court under strict scrutiny." This means that such classifications are constitutional only if they are narrowly tailored to further compelling governmental interests. "Absent searching judicial inquiry into the justification for such race-based measures," we have no way to determine what "classifications are 'benign' or 'remedial' and what classifications are in fact motivated by illegitimate notions of racial inferiority or simple racial politics." *Richmond v. J.A. Croson Co.*, 488 U.S. 469, 493 (1989) (plurality opinion). We apply strict scrutiny to all racial classifications to "'smoke out' illegitimate uses of race by assuring that [government] is pursuing a goal important enough to warrant use of a highly suspect tool."

Strict scrutiny is not "strict in theory, but fatal in fact." Although all governmental uses of race are subject to strict scrutiny, not all are invalidated by it. As we have explained, "whenever the government treats any person unequally because of his or her race, that person has suffered an injury that falls squarely within the language and spirit of the Constitution's guarantee of equal protection." But that observation "says nothing about the ultimate validity of any particular law; that determination is the job of the court applying strict scrutiny." When race-based action is necessary to further a compelling governmental interest, such action does not violate the constitutional guarantee of equal protection so long as the narrow-tailoring requirement is also satisfied.

Context matters when reviewing race-based governmental action under the Equal Protection Clause. In *Adarand Constructors, Inc. v. Peña*, we made clear that strict scrutiny must take "'relevant differences' into account." 515 U.S., at 228. Indeed, as we explained, that is its "fundamental purpose." *Ibid.* Not every decision influenced by race is equally objectionable, and strict scrutiny is designed to provide a framework for carefully examining the importance and the sincerity of the reasons advanced by the governmental decisionmaker for the use of race in that particular context.

III

A

With these principles in mind, we turn to the question whether the Law School's use of race is justified by a compelling state interest. Before this Court, as they have throughout this litigation, respondents assert only one justification for their use of race in the admissions process: obtaining "the educational benefits that flow from a diverse student body." Brief for Respondent Bollinger et al. i. In other words, the Law School asks us to recognize, in the context of higher education, a compelling state interest in student body diversity.

We first wish to dispel the notion that the Law School's argument has been foreclosed, either expressly or implicitly, by our affirmative-action cases decided since *Bakke*. It is true that some language in those opinions might be read to suggest that remedying past discrimination is the only permissible justification for race-based governmental action. See, *e.g., Richmond v. J.A. Croson Co., supra*, at 493, 109 S.Ct. 706 (plurality opinion) (stating that unless classifications based on race are "strictly reserved for remedial settings, they may in fact promote notions of racial inferiority and lead to a politics of racial hostility"). But we have never held that the only governmental use of race that can survive strict scrutiny is remedying past discrimination. Nor, since *Bakke*, have we directly addressed the use of race in the context of public higher education. Today, we hold that the Law School has a compelling interest in attaining a diverse student body.

... The Law School's educational judgment that such diversity is essential to its educational mission is one to which we defer. The Law School's assessment that diversity will, in fact, yield educational benefits is substantiated by respondents and their *amici*. Our scrutiny of the interest asserted by the Law School is no less strict for taking into account complex educational judgments in an area that lies primarily within the expertise of the university. Our holding today is in keeping with our tradition of giving a degree of deference to a university's academic decisions, within constitutionally prescribed limits.

We have long recognized that, given the important purpose of public education and the expansive freedoms of speech and thought associated with the university environment, universities occupy a special niche in our constitutional tradition. In announcing the principle of student body diversity as a compelling state interest, Justice Powell invoked our cases recognizing a constitutional dimension, grounded in the First Amendment, of educational autonomy: "The freedom of a university to make its own judgments as to education includes the selection of its student body." *Bakke, supra*, at 312. From this premise, Justice Powell reasoned that by claiming "the right to select those students who will contribute the most to the 'robust exchange of ideas,'" a university "seek[s] to achieve a goal that is of paramount importance in the fulfillment of its mission." Our conclusion that the Law School has a compelling interest in a diverse student body is informed by our view that attaining a diverse student body is at the heart of the Law School's proper institutional mission, and that "good faith" on the part of a university is "presumed" absent "a showing to the contrary."

As part of its goal of "assembling a class that is both exceptionally academically qualified and broadly diverse," the Law School seeks to "enroll a 'critical mass' of minority students." The Law School's interest is not simply "to assure within its student body some specified percentage of a particular group merely because of its race or ethnic origin." That would amount to outright racial balancing, which is patently unconstitutional. Rather, the Law School's concept of critical mass is defined by reference to the educational benefits that diversity is designed to produce.

These benefits are substantial. As the District Court emphasized, the Law School's admissions policy promotes "cross-racial understanding," helps to break down racial stereotypes, and "enables [students] to better understand persons of different races." These benefits are "important and laudable," because "classroom discussion is livelier, more spirited, and simply more enlightening and interesting" when the students have "the greatest possible variety of backgrounds."

We have repeatedly acknowledged the overriding importance of preparing students for work and citizenship, describing education as pivotal to "sustaining our political and cultural heritage" with a fundamental role in maintaining the fabric of society. *Plyler v. Doe*, 457 U.S. 202, 221 (1982). This Court has long recognized that "education . . . is the very foundation of good citizenship." *Brown v. Board of Education*, 347 U.S. 483, 493 (1954). For this reason, the diffusion of knowledge and opportunity through public institutions of higher education must be accessible to all individuals regardless of race or ethnicity.

Moreover, universities, and in particular, law schools, represent the training ground for a large number of our Nation's leaders. Individuals with law degrees occupy roughly half the state governorships, more than half the seats in the United States Senate, and more than a third of the seats in the United States House of Representatives. See Brief for Association of American Law Schools as *Amicus Curiae* 5-6. The pattern is even more striking when it comes to highly selective law schools. A handful of these schools accounts for 25 of the 100 United States Senators, 74

United States Courts of Appeals judges, and nearly 200 of the more than 600 United States District Court judges.

In order to cultivate a set of leaders with legitimacy in the eyes of the citizenry, it is necessary that the path to leadership be visibly open to talented and qualified individuals of every race and ethnicity. All members of our heterogeneous society must have confidence in the openness and integrity of the educational institutions that provide this training. As we have recognized, law schools "cannot be effective in isolation from the individuals and institutions with which the law interacts." Access to legal education (and thus the legal profession) must be inclusive of talented and qualified individuals of every race and ethnicity, so that all members of our heterogeneous society may participate in the educational institutions that provide the training and education necessary to succeed in America.

B

Even in the limited circumstance when drawing racial distinctions is permissible to further a compelling state interest, government is still "constrained in how it may pursue that end: [T]he means chosen to accomplish the [government's] asserted purpose must be specifically and narrowly framed to accomplish that purpose." The purpose of the narrow tailoring requirement is to ensure that "the means chosen 'fit' th[e] compelling goal so closely that there is little or no possibility that the motive for the classification was illegitimate racial prejudice or stereotype."

Since *Bakke*, we have had no occasion to define the contours of the narrow-tailoring inquiry with respect to race-conscious university admissions programs. That inquiry must be calibrated to fit the distinct issues raised by the use of race to achieve student body diversity in public higher education. Contrary to Justice KENNEDY's assertions, we do not "abando[n] strict scrutiny," (see dissenting opinion). Rather, as we have already explained,, we adhere to *Adarand's* teaching that the very purpose of strict scrutiny is to take such "relevant differences into account."

To be narrowly tailored, a race-conscious admissions program cannot use a quota system-it cannot "insulat[e] each category of applicants with certain desired qualifications from competition with all other applicants." Instead, a university may consider race or ethnicity only as a "'plus' in a particular applicant's file," without "insulat[ing] the individual from comparison with all other candidates for the available seats." In other words, an admissions program must be "flexible enough to consider all pertinent elements of diversity in light of the particular qualifications of each applicant, and to place them on the same footing for consideration, although not necessarily according them the same weight."

We find that the Law School's admissions program bears the hallmarks of a narrowly tailored plan. As Justice Powell made clear in *Bakke*, truly individualized consideration demands that race be used in a flexible, nonmechanical way. It follows from this mandate that universities cannot establish quotas for members of certain racial groups or put members of those groups on separate admissions tracks. Nor can universities insulate applicants who belong to certain racial or ethnic groups from the competition for admission. *Ibid.* Universities can, however, consider race or ethnicity more flexibly as a "plus" factor in the context of individualized consideration of each and every applicant.

We are satisfied that the Law School's admissions program, like the Harvard plan described by Justice Powell, does not operate as a quota. Properly understood, a "quota" is a program in which a certain fixed number or proportion of opportunities are "reserved exclusively for certain minority groups." Quotas "'impose a fixed number or percentage which must be attained, or which cannot be exceeded,' and "insulate the individual from comparison with all other candidates for the available seats." In contrast, "a permissible goal . . . require[s] only a good-faith effort . . . to come within a range demarcated by the goal itself," and permits consideration of race as a "plus" factor in any given case while still ensuring that each candidate "compete[s] with all other qualified applicants."

Justice Powell's distinction between the medical school's rigid 16-seat quota and Harvard's flexible use of race as a "plus" factor is instructive. Harvard certainly had minimum *goals* for minority enrollment, even if it had no specific number firmly in mind. See *Bakke, supra*, at 323, 98 S.Ct. 2733 (opinion of Powell, J.) ("10 or 20 black students could not begin to bring to their classmates and to each other the variety of points of view, backgrounds and experiences of blacks in the United States"). What is more, Justice Powell flatly rejected the argument that Harvard's program was "the functional equivalent of a quota" merely because it had some "'plus'" for race, or gave greater "weight" to race than to some other factors, in order to achieve student body diversity. 438 U.S., at 317-318, 98 S.Ct. 2733.

The Law School's goal of attaining a critical mass of underrepresented minority students does not transform its program into a quota. As the Harvard plan described by Justice Powell recognized, there is of course "some relationship between numbers and achieving the benefits to be derived from a diverse student body, and between numbers and providing a reasonable environment for those students admitted." "[S]ome attention to numbers," without more, does not transform a flexible admissions system into a rigid quota. Nor, as Justice Kennedy posits, does the Law School's consultation of the "daily reports," which keep track of the racial and ethnic composition of the class (as well as of residency and gender), "sugges[t] there was no further attempt at individual review save for race itself" during the final stages of the admissions process. To the contrary, the Law School's admissions officers testified without contradiction that they never gave race any more or less weight based on the information contained in these reports. Moreover, as Justice Kennedy concedes, between 1993 and 1998, the number of African-American, Latino, and Native-American students in each class at the Law School varied from 13.5 to 20.1 percent, a range inconsistent with a quota.

The Chief Justice believes that the Law School's policy conceals an attempt to achieve racial balancing, and cites admissions data to contend that the Law School discriminates among different groups within the critical mass. But, as The Chief Justice concedes, the number of underrepresented minority students who ultimately enroll in the Law School differs substantially from their representation in the applicant pool and varies considerably for each group from year to year.

That a race-conscious admissions program does not operate as a quota does not, by itself, satisfy the requirement of individualized consideration. When using race as a "plus" factor in university admissions, a university's admissions program must remain flexible enough to ensure that each applicant is evaluated as an individual and not in a way that makes an applicant's race or ethnicity the defining feature of his or her application. The importance of this individualized consideration in the context of a race-conscious admissions program is paramount. See *Bakke*, 438 U.S., at 318, n. 52 (opinion of Powell, J.) (identifying the "denial . . . of th[e] right to individualized consideration" as the "principal evil" of the medical school's admissions program).

Here, the Law School engages in a highly individualized, holistic review of each applicant's file, giving serious consideration to all the ways an applicant might contribute to a diverse educational environment. The Law School affords this individualized consideration to applicants of all races. There is no policy, either *de jure* or *de facto*, of automatic acceptance or rejection based on any single "soft" variable. Unlike the program at issue in *Gratz v. Bollinger, post*, 539 U.S. 244, the Law School awards no mechanical, predetermined diversity "bonuses" based on race or ethnicity. See *post*, 539 U.S., at 271-272 (distinguishing a race-conscious admissions program that automatically awards 20 points based on race from the Harvard plan, which considered race but "did not contemplate that any single characteristic automatically ensured a specific and identifiable contribution to a university's diversity"). Like the Harvard plan, the Law School's admissions policy "is flexible enough to consider all pertinent elements of diversity in light of the particular qualifications of each applicant, and to place them on the same footing for consideration, although not necessarily according them the same weight." *Bakke, supra*, at 317 (opinion of Powell, J.).

We also find that, like the Harvard plan Justice Powell referenced in *Bakke*, the Law School's race-conscious admissions program adequately ensures that all factors that may contribute to student body diversity are meaningfully considered alongside race in admissions decisions. With respect to the use of race itself, all underrepresented minority students admitted by the Law School have been deemed qualified. By virtue of our Nation's struggle with racial inequality, such students are both likely to have experiences of particular importance to the Law School's mission, and less likely to be admitted in meaningful numbers on criteria that ignore those experiences.

The Law School does not, however, limit in any way the broad range of qualities and experiences that may be considered valuable contributions to student body diversity. To the contrary, the 1992 policy makes clear "[t]here are many possible bases for diversity admissions," and provides examples of admittees who have lived or traveled widely abroad, are fluent in several languages, have overcome personal adversity and family hardship, have exceptional records of extensive community service, and have had successful careers in other fields. The Law School seriously considers each "applicant's promise of making a notable contribution to the class by way of a particular strength, attainment, or characteristic-*e.g.*, an unusual intellectual achievement, employment experience, nonacademic performance, or personal background." All applicants have the opportunity to highlight their own potential diversity contributions through the submission of a personal statement, letters of recommendation, and an essay describing the ways in which the applicant will contribute to the life and diversity of the Law School.

What is more, the Law School actually gives substantial weight to diversity factors besides race. The Law School frequently accepts nonminority applicants with grades and test scores lower than underrepresented minority applicants (and other nonminority applicants) who are rejected. This shows that the Law School seriously weighs many other diversity factors besides race that can make a real and dispositive difference for nonminority applicants as well. By this flexible approach, the Law School sufficiently takes into account, in practice as well as in theory, a wide variety of characteristics besides race and ethnicity that contribute to a diverse student body. Justice Kennedy speculates that "race is likely outcome determinative for many members of minority groups" who do not fall within the upper range of LSAT scores and grades. But the same could be said of the Harvard plan discussed approvingly by Justice Powell in *Bakke*, and indeed of any plan that uses race as one of many factors.

Petitioner and the United States argue that the Law School's plan is not narrowly tailored because race-neutral means exist to obtain the educational benefits of student body diversity that the Law School seeks. We disagree. Narrow tailoring does not require exhaustion of every conceivable race-neutral alternative. Nor does it require a university to choose between maintaining a reputation for excellence or fulfilling a commitment to provide educational opportunities to members of all racial groups. Narrow tailoring does, however, require serious, good faith consideration of workable race-neutral alternatives that will achieve the diversity the university seeks.

We agree with the Court of Appeals that the Law School sufficiently considered workable race-neutral alternatives. The District Court took the Law School to task for failing to consider race-neutral alternatives such as "using a lottery system" or "decreasing the emphasis for all applicants on undergraduate GPA and LSAT scores." But these alternatives would require a dramatic sacrifice of diversity, the academic quality of all admitted students, or both.

The Law School's current admissions program considers race as one factor among many, in an effort to assemble a student body that is diverse in ways broader than race. Because a lottery would make that kind of nuanced judgment impossible, it would effectively sacrifice all other educational values, not to mention every other kind of diversity. So too with the suggestion that the Law School simply lower admissions standards for all students, a drastic remedy that would require the Law School to become a much different institution and sacrifice a vital component of its educational mission. The United States advocates "percentage plans," recently adopted by public undergraduate institutions in Texas, Florida, and California, to guarantee admission to all students above a certain class-rank threshold in every high school in the State. The United States does not, however, explain how such plans could work for graduate and professional schools. Moreover, even assuming such plans are race-neutral, they may preclude the university from conducting the individualized assessments necessary to assemble a student body that is not just racially diverse, but diverse along all the qualities valued by the university. We are satisfied that the Law School adequately considered race-neutral alternatives currently capable of producing a critical mass without forcing the Law School to abandon the academic selectivity that is the cornerstone of its educational mission.

We acknowledge that "there are serious problems of justice connected with the idea of preference itself." Narrow tailoring, therefore, requires that a race-conscious admissions program not unduly harm members of any racial group. Even remedial race-based governmental action generally "remains subject to continuing oversight to assure that it will work the least harm possible to other innocent persons competing for the benefit." To be narrowly tailored, a race-conscious admissions program must not "unduly burden individuals who are not members of the favored racial and ethnic groups."

We are satisfied that the Law School's admissions program does not. Because the Law School considers "all pertinent elements of diversity," it can (and does) select nonminority applicants who have greater potential to enhance student body diversity over underrepresented minority applicants. As Justice Powell recognized in *Bakke*, so long as a race-conscious admissions program uses race as a "plus" factor in the context of individualized consideration, a rejected applicant.

> "will not have been foreclosed from all consideration for that seat simply because he was not the right color or had the wrong surname. . . . His qualifications would have been weighed fairly and competitively, and he would have no basis to complain of unequal treatment under the Fourteenth Amendment." 438 U.S., at 318, 98 S.Ct. 2733.

We agree that, in the context of its individualized inquiry into the possible diversity contributions of all applicants, the Law School's race-conscious admissions program does not unduly harm nonminority applicants.

We are mindful, however, that "[a] core purpose of the Fourteenth Amendment was to do away with all governmentally imposed discrimination based on race. Accordingly, race-conscious admissions policies must be limited in time. This requirement reflects that racial classifications, however compelling their goals, are potentially so dangerous that they may be employed no more broadly than the interest demands. Enshrining a permanent justification for racial preferences would offend this fundamental equal protection principle. We see no reason to exempt race-conscious admissions programs from the requirement that all governmental use of race must have a logical end point. The Law School, too, concedes that all "race-conscious programs must have reasonable durational limits."

In the context of higher education, the durational requirement can be met by sunset provisions in race-conscious admissions policies and periodic reviews to determine whether racial preferences are still necessary to achieve student body diversity.

Universities in California, Florida, and Washington State, where racial preferences in admissions are prohibited by state law, are currently engaged in experimenting with a wide variety of alternative approaches. Universities in other States can and should draw on the most promising aspects of these race-neutral alternatives as they develop.

The requirement that all race-conscious admissions programs have a termination point "assure[s] all citizens that the deviation from the norm of equal treatment of all racial and ethnic groups is a temporary matter, a measure taken in the service of the goal of equality itself." We take the Law School at its word that it would "like nothing better than to find a race-neutral admissions formula" and will terminate its race-conscious admissions program as soon as practicable. It has been 25 years since Justice Powell first approved the use of race to further an interest in student body diversity in the context of public higher education. Since that time, the number of minority applicants with high grades and test scores has indeed increased. We expect that 25 years from now, the use of racial preferences will no longer be necessary to further the interest approved today.

IV

In summary, the Equal Protection Clause does not prohibit the Law School's narrowly tailored use of race in admissions decisions to further a compelling interest in obtaining the educational benefits that flow from a diverse student body. Consequently, petitioner's statutory claims based on Title VI and 42 U.S.C. § 1981 also fail. *See Bakke, supra*, at 287, 98 S.Ct. 2733 (opinion of Powell, J.) ("Title VI ... proscribe[s] only those racial classifications that would violate the Equal Protection Clause or the Fifth Amendment"); *General Building Contractors Assn., Inc. v. Pennsylvania*, 458 U.S. 375, 389-391, 102 S.Ct. 3141, 73 L.Ed.2d 835 (1982) (the prohibition against discrimination in § 1981 is co-extensive with the Equal Protection Clause). The judgment of the Court of Appeals for the Sixth Circuit, accordingly, is affirmed.

It is so ordered.

JUSTICE SCALIA, with whom JUSTICE THOMAS joins, concurring in part and dissenting in part.

I join the opinion of THE CHIEF JUSTICE. As he demonstrates, the University of Michigan Law School's mystical "critical mass" justification for its discrimination by race challenges even the most gullible mind. The admissions statistics show it to be a sham to cover a scheme of racially proportionate admissions.

I also join Parts I through VII of JUSTICE THOMAS's opinion. I find particularly unanswerable his central point: that the allegedly "compelling state interest" at issue here is not the incremental "educational benefit" that emanates from the fabled "critical mass" of minority students, but rather Michigan's interest in maintaining a "prestige" law school whose normal admissions standards disproportionately exclude blacks and other minorities. If that is a compelling state interest, everything is.

....

Justice Thomas, with whom Justice Scalia joins as to Parts I-VII, concurring in part and dissenting in part.

Frederick Douglass, speaking to a group of abolitionists almost 140 years ago, delivered a message lost on today's majority:

> "[I]n regard to the colored people, there is always more that is benevolent, I perceive, than just, manifested towards us. What I ask for the negro is not benevolence, not pity, not sympathy, but simply *justice.* The American people have always been anxious to know what they shall do with us.... I have had but one answer from the beginning. Do nothing with us! Your doing with us has already played the mischief with us. Do nothing with us! If the apples will not remain on the tree of their own strength, if they are worm-eaten at the core, if they are early ripe and disposed to fall, let them fall! . . . And if the negro cannot stand on his own legs, let him fall also. All I ask is, give him a chance to stand on his own legs! Let him alone! . . . [Y]our interference is doing him positive injury." What the Black Man Wants: An Address Delivered in Boston, Massachusetts, on 26 January 1865, reprinted in 4 The Frederick Douglass Papers 59, 68 (J. Blassingame & J. McKivigan eds.1991) (emphasis in original).

Like Douglass, I believe blacks can achieve in every avenue of American life without the meddling of university administrators. Because I wish to see all students succeed whatever their color, I share, in some respect, the sympathies of those who sponsor the type of discrimination advanced by the University of Michigan Law School (Law School). The Constitution does not, however, tolerate institutional devotion to the status quo in admissions policies when such devotion ripens into racial discrimination. Nor does the Constitution countenance the unprecedented deference the Court gives to the Law School, an approach inconsistent with the very concept of "strict scrutiny."

No one would argue that a university could set up a lower general admissions standard and then impose heightened requirements only on black applicants. Similarly, a university may not maintain a high admissions standard and grant exemptions to favored races. The Law School, of its own choosing, and for its own purposes, maintains an exclusionary admissions system that it knows produces racially disproportionate results. Racial discrimination is not a permissible solution to the self-inflicted wounds of this elitist admissions policy.

The majority upholds the Law School's racial discrimination not by interpreting the people's Constitution, but by responding to a faddish slogan of the cognoscenti. Nevertheless, I concur in part in the Court's opinion. First, I agree with the Court insofar as its decision, which approves of only one racial classification, confirms that further use of race in admissions remains unlawful. Second, I agree with the Court's holding that racial discrimination in higher education admissions will be illegal in 25 years. I respectfully dissent from the remainder of the Court's opinion and the judgment, however, because I believe that the Law School's current use of race violates the Equal Protection Clause and that the Constitution means the same thing today as it will in 300 months.

. . . .

[Dissenting opinions are omitted for space purposes. You can review them online.]

Parents Involved in Community Schools v. School District No. 1

551 U.S. 701 (2007)

The Court rules that public high schools may not constitutionally rely exclusively on a student's race in assigning him/her to a particular district school to achieve racial balance.

Chief Justice Roberts announced the judgment of the Court, and delivered the opinion of the Court with respect to Parts I, II, III–A, and III–C, and an opinion with respect to Parts III–B and IV, in which Justice Scalia, Justice Thomas, and Justice Alito join.

The school districts in these cases voluntarily adopted student assignment plans that rely upon race to determine which public schools certain children may attend. The Seattle school district classifies children as white or nonwhite; the Jefferson County school district as black or "other." In Seattle, this racial classification is used to allocate slots in oversubscribed high schools. In Jefferson County, it is used to make certain elementary school assignments and to rule on transfer requests. In each case, the school district relies upon an individual student's race in assigning that student to a particular school, so that the racial balance at the school falls within a predetermined range based on the racial composition of the school district as a whole. Parents of students denied assignment to particular schools under these plans solely because of their race brought suit, contending that allocating children to different public schools on the basis of race violated the Fourteenth Amendment guarantee of equal protection. The Courts of Appeals below upheld the plans. We granted certiorari, and now reverse.

I

Both cases present the same underlying legal question—whether a public school that had not operated legally segregated schools or has been found to be unitary may choose to classify students by race and rely upon that classification in making school assignments. Although we examine the plans under the same legal framework, the specifics of the two plans, and the circumstances surrounding their adoption, are in some respects quite different.

A

Seattle School District No. 1 operates 10 regular public high schools. In 1998, it adopted the plan at issue in this case for assigning students to these schools. The plan allows incoming ninth graders to choose from among any of the district's high schools, ranking however many schools they wish in order of preference.

Some schools are more popular than others. If too many students list the same school as their first choice, the district employs a series of "tiebreakers" to determine who will fill the open slots at the oversubscribed school. The first tiebreaker selects for admission students who have a sibling currently enrolled in the chosen school. The next tiebreaker depends upon the racial composition of the particular school and the race of the individual student. In the district's public schools approximately 41 percent of enrolled students are white; the remaining 59 percent, comprising all other racial groups, are classified by Seattle for assignment purposes as nonwhite. If an oversubscribed school is not within 10 percentage points of the district's overall white/nonwhite racial balance, it is what the district calls "integration positive," and the district employs a tiebreaker that selects for assignment students whose race "will serve to bring the school into balance." If it is still necessary to select students for the school after using the racial tiebreaker, the next tiebreaker is the geographic proximity of the school to the student's residence.

Seattle has never operated segregated schools—legally separate schools for students of different races—nor has it ever been subject to court-ordered desegregation. It nonetheless employs the racial tiebreaker in an attempt to address the effects of racially identifiable housing patterns on school assignments. Most white students live in the northern part of Seattle, most students of other racial backgrounds in the southern part. Four of Seattle's high schools are located in the north—Ballard, Nathan Hale, Ingraham, and Roosevelt—and five in the south—Rainier Beach, Cleveland, West Seattle, Chief Sealth, and Franklin. One school—Garfield—is more or less in the center of Seattle.

For the 2000–2001 school year, five of these schools were oversubscribed—Ballard, Nathan Hale, Roosevelt, Garfield, and Franklin—so much so that 82 percent of incoming ninth graders ranked one of these schools as their first choice. Three of the oversubscribed schools were "integration positive" because the school's white enrollment the previous school year was greater than 51 percent—Ballard, Nathan Hale, and Roosevelt. Thus, more nonwhite students (107, 27, and 82, respectively) who selected one of these three schools as a top choice received placement at the school than would have been the case had race not been considered, and proximity been the next tiebreaker. Franklin was "integration positive" because its nonwhite enrollment the previous school year was greater than 69 percent; 89 more white students were assigned to Franklin by operation of the racial tiebreaker in the 2000–2001 school year than otherwise would have been. *Ibid.* Garfield was the only oversubscribed school whose composition during the 1999–2000 school year was within the racial guidelines, although in previous years Garfield's enrollment had been predominantly nonwhite, and the racial tiebreaker had been used to give preference to white students.

Petitioner Parents Involved in Community Schools (Parents Involved) is a nonprofit corporation comprising the parents of children who have been or may be denied assignment to their chosen high school in the district because of their race. . . . Parents Involved commenced this suit in the Western District of Washington, alleging that Seattle's use of race in assignments violated the Equal Protection Clause of the Fourteenth Amendment Title VI of the Civil Rights Act of 1964, and the Washington Civil Rights Act.

. . .

B

Jefferson County Public Schools operates the public school system in metropolitan Louisville, Kentucky. In 1973 a federal court found that Jefferson County had maintained a segregated school system, and in 1975 the District Court entered a desegregation decree. Jefferson County operated under this decree until 2000, when the District Court dissolved the decree after finding that the district had achieved unitary status by eliminating "[t]o the greatest extent practicable" the vestiges of its prior policy of segregation.

In 2001, after the decree had been dissolved, Jefferson County adopted the voluntary student assignment plan at issue in this case. Approximately 34 percent of the district's 97,000 students are black; most of the remaining 66 percent are white. The plan requires all nonmagnet schools to maintain a minimum black enrollment of 15 percent, and a maximum black enrollment of 50 percent.

At the elementary school level, based on his or her address, each student is designated a "resides" school to which students within a specific geographic area are assigned; elementary resides schools are "grouped into clusters in order to facilitate integration." The district assigns students to nonmagnet schools in one of two ways: Parents of kindergartners, first graders, and students new to the district may submit an application indicating a first and second choice among the schools within their cluster; students who do not submit such an application are assigned within the cluster by the district. "Decisions to assign students to schools within each cluster are based on available space within the schools and the racial guidelines in the District's current student assignment plan." If a school has reached the "extremes of the racial guidelines," a student whose race would contribute to the school's racial imbalance will not be assigned there. After assignment, students at all grade levels are permitted to apply to transfer between nonmagnet schools in the district. Transfers may be requested for any number of reasons, and may be denied because of lack of available space or on the basis of the racial guidelines.

When petitioner Crystal Meredith moved into the school district in August 2002, she sought to enroll her son, Joshua McDonald, in kindergarten for the 2002–2003 school year. His resides school was only a mile from his new home, but it had no available space—assignments had been made in May, and the class was full. Jefferson County assigned Joshua to another elementary school in his cluster, Young Elementary. This school was 10 miles from home, and Meredith sought to transfer Joshua to a school in a different cluster, Bloom Elementary, which—like his resides school—was only a mile from home. Space was available at Bloom, and intercluster transfers are allowed, but Joshua's transfer was nonetheless denied because, in the words of Jefferson County, "[t]he transfer would have an adverse effect on desegregation compliance" of Young.

Meredith brought suit in the Western District of Kentucky, alleging violations of the Equal Protection Clause of the Fourteenth Amendment. The District Court found that Jefferson County had asserted a compelling interest in maintaining racially diverse schools, and that the assignment plan was (in all relevant respects) narrowly tailored to serve that compelling interest. The Sixth Circuit affirmed in a *per curiam* opinion relying upon the reasoning of the District Court, concluding that a written opinion "would serve no useful purpose." We granted certiorari.

II

[The Court finds that the plaintiffs have standing to address the issues in the case] . . .

III

A

It is well established that when the government distributes burdens or benefits on the basis of individual racial classifications, that action is reviewed under strict scrutiny. As the Court recently reaffirmed, "'racial classifications are simply too pernicious to permit any but the most exact connection between justification and classification.'" In order to satisfy this searching standard of review, the school districts must demonstrate that the use of individual racial classifications in the assignment plans here under review is "narrowly tailored" to achieve a "compelling" government interest.

Without attempting in these cases to set forth all the interests a school district might assert, it suffices to note that our prior cases, in evaluating the use of racial classifications in the school context, have recognized two interests that qualify as compelling. The first is the compelling interest of remedying the effects of past intentional discrimination. Yet the Seattle public schools have not shown that they were ever segregated by law, and were not subject to court-ordered desegregation decrees. The Jefferson County public schools were previously segregated by law and were subject to a desegregation decree entered in 1975. In 2000, the District Court that entered that decree dissolved it, finding that Jefferson County had "eliminated the vestiges associated with the former policy of segregation and its pernicious effects," and thus had achieved "unitary" status. Jefferson County accordingly does not rely upon an interest in remedying the effects of past intentional discrimination in defending its present use of race in assigning students. *See* Tr. of Oral Arg. in No. 05–915, at 38.

Nor could it. We have emphasized that the harm being remedied by mandatory desegregation plans is the harm that is traceable to segregation, and that "the Constitution is not violated by racial imbalance in the schools, without more." Once Jefferson County achieved unitary status, it had remedied the constitutional wrong that allowed race-based assignments. Any continued use of race must be justified on some other basis.

The second government interest we have recognized as compelling for purposes of strict scrutiny is the interest in diversity in higher education upheld in *Grutter*, 539 U.S., at 328, 123 S.Ct. 2325. The specific interest found compelling in *Grutter* was student body diversity "in the context of higher education." The diversity interest was not focused on race alone but encompassed "all factors that may contribute to student body diversity." We described the various types of diversity that the law school sought:

> "[The law school's] policy makes clear there are many possible bases for diversity admissions, and provides examples of admittees who have lived or traveled widely abroad, are fluent in several languages, have overcome personal adversity and family hardship, have exceptional records of extensive community service, and have had successful careers in other fields."

The Court quoted the articulation of diversity from Justice Powell's opinion in *Regents of Univ. of Cal. v. Bakke*, 438 U.S. 265, 98 S.Ct. 2733, 57 L.Ed.2d 750 (1978), noting that "it is not an interest in simple ethnic diversity, in which a specified percentage of the student body is in effect guaranteed to be members of selected ethnic groups, that can justify the use of race." Instead, what was upheld in *Grutter* was consideration of "a far broader array of qualifications and characteristics of which racial or ethnic origin is but a single though important element."

The entire gist of the analysis in *Grutter* was that the admissions program at issue there focused on each applicant as an individual, and not simply as a member of a particular racial group. The classification of applicants by race upheld in *Grutter* was only as part of a "highly individualized, holistic review," As the Court explained, "[t]he importance of this individualized consideration in the context of a race-conscious admissions program is paramount." The point of the narrow tailoring analysis in which the *Grutter* Court engaged was to ensure that the use of racial classifications was indeed part of a broader assessment of diversity, and not simply an effort to achieve racial balance, which the Court explained would be "patently unconstitutional."

In the present cases, by contrast, race is not considered as part of a broader effort to achieve "exposure to widely diverse people, cultures, ideas, and viewpoints," race, for some students, is determinative standing alone. The districts argue that other factors, such as student preferences, affect assignment decisions under their plans, but under each plan when race comes into play, it is decisive by itself. It is not simply one factor weighed with others in reaching a decision, as in *Grutter*; it is *the* factor. Like the University of Michigan undergraduate plan struck down in *Gratz*, 539 U.S., at 275, 123 S. Ct. 2411, the plans here "do not provide for a meaningful individualized review of applicants" but instead rely on racial classifications in a "nonindividualized, mechanical" way, *id.*, at 276, 280, 123 S.Ct. 2411 (O'Connor, J., concurring).

Even when it comes to race, the plans here employ only a limited notion of diversity, viewing race exclusively in white/nonwhite terms in Seattle and black/"other" terms in Jefferson County. The Seattle "Board Statement Reaffirming Diversity Rationale" speaks of the "inherent educational value" in "[p]roviding students the opportunity to attend schools with diverse student enrollment," But under the Seattle plan, a school with 50 percent Asian—American students and 50 percent white students but no African—American, Native—American, or Latino students would qualify as balanced, while a school with 30 percent Asian-American, 25 percent African-American, 25 percent Latino, and 20 percent white students would not. It is hard to understand how a plan that could allow these results can be viewed as being concerned with achieving enrollment that is "'broadly diverse,'" *Grutter, supra*, at 329, 123 S.Ct. 2325.

Prior to *Grutter*, the courts of appeals rejected as unconstitutional attempts to implement race-based assignment plans—such as the plans at issue here—in primary and secondary schools. After *Grutter*, however, the two Courts of Appeals in these cases, and one other, found that race-based assignments were permissible at the elementary and secondary level, largely in reliance on that case.

In upholding the admissions plan in *Grutter*, though, this Court relied upon considerations unique to institutions of higher education, noting that in light of "the expansive freedoms of speech and thought associated with the university environment, universities occupy a special niche in our constitutional tradition." The Court explained that "[c]ontext matters" in applying strict scrutiny, and repeatedly noted that it was addressing the use of race "in the context of higher education." The Court in *Grutter* expressly articulated key limitations on its holding—defining a specific type of broad-based diversity and noting the unique context of higher education—but these limitations were largely disregarded by the lower courts in extending *Grutter* to uphold race-based assignments in elementary and secondary schools. The present cases are not governed by *Grutter*.

B

Perhaps recognizing that reliance on *Grutter* cannot sustain their plans, both school districts assert additional interests, distinct from the interest upheld in *Grutter*, to justify their race-based assignments. In briefing and argument before this Court, Seattle contends that its use of race helps to reduce racial concentration in schools and to ensure that racially concentrated housing patterns do not prevent nonwhite students from having access to the most desirable schools. Jefferson County has articulated a similar goal, phrasing its interest in terms of educating its students "in a racially integrated environment." Each school district argues that educational and broader socialization benefits flow from a racially diverse learning environment, and each contends that because the diversity they seek is racial diversity—not the broader diversity at issue in *Grutter*—it makes sense to promote that interest directly by relying on race alone.

The parties and their *amici* dispute whether racial diversity in schools in fact has a marked impact on test scores and other objective yardsticks or achieves intangible socialization benefits. The debate is not one we need to resolve, however, because it is clear that the racial classifications employed by the districts are not narrowly tailored to the goal of achieving the educational and social benefits asserted to flow from racial diversity. In design and operation, the plans are directed only to racial balance, pure and simple, an objective this Court has repeatedly condemned as illegitimate.

The plans are tied to each district's specific racial demographics, rather than to any pedagogic concept of the level of diversity needed to obtain the asserted educational benefits. In Seattle, the district seeks white enrollment of between 31 and 51 percent (within 10 percent of "the district white average" of 41 percent), and nonwhite enrollment of between 49 and 69 percent (within 10 percent of "the district minority average" of 59 percent). In Jefferson County, by contrast, the district seeks black enrollment of no less than 15 or more than 50 percent, a range designed to be "equally above and below Black student enrollment systemwide," *McFarland I*, 330 F.Supp.2d, at 842, based on the objective of achieving at "all schools . . . an African—American enrollment equivalent to the average district-wide African—American enrollment" of 34 percent,. In Seattle, then, the benefits of racial diversity require enrollment of at least 31 percent white students; in Jefferson County, at least 50 percent. There must be at least 15 percent nonwhite students under Jefferson County's plan; in Seattle, more than three times that figure. This comparison makes clear that the racial demographics in each district—whatever they happen to be—drive the required "diversity" numbers. The plans here are not tailored to achieving a degree of diversity necessary to realize the asserted educational benefits; instead the plans are tailored, in the words of Seattle's Manager of Enrollment Planning, Technical Support, and Demographics, to "the goal established by the school board of attaining a level of diversity within the schools that approximates the district's overall demographics."

The districts offer no evidence that the level of racial diversity necessary to achieve the asserted educational benefits happens to coincide with the racial demographics of the respective school districts—or rather the white/nonwhite or black/"other" balance of the districts, since that is the only diversity addressed by the plans. Indeed, in its brief Seattle simply assumes that the educational benefits track the racial breakdown of the district. When asked for "a range of percentage that would be diverse," however, Seattle's expert said it was important to have "sufficient numbers so as to avoid students feeling any kind of specter of exceptionality." The district did not attempt to defend the proposition that anything outside its range posed the "specter of exceptionality." Nor did it demonstrate in any way how the educational and social benefits of racial diversity or avoidance of racial isolation are more likely to be achieved at a school that is 50 percent white and 50 percent Asian-American, which would qualify as diverse under Seattle's plan, than at a school that is 30 percent Asian-American, 25 percent African-American, 25 percent Latino, and 20 percent white, which under Seattle's definition would be racially concentrated.

Similarly, Jefferson County's expert referred to the importance of having "at least 20 percent" minority group representation for the group "to be visible enough to make a difference," and noted that "small isolated minority groups in a school are not likely to have a strong effect on the overall school." The Jefferson County plan, however, is based on a goal of replicating at each school "an African—American enrollment equivalent to the average district-wide African-American enrollment." Joshua McDonald's requested transfer was denied because his race was listed as "other" rather than black, and allowing the transfer would have had an adverse effect on the racial guideline compliance of Young Elementary, the school he sought to leave. At the time, however, Young Elementary was 46.8 percent black. The transfer might have had an adverse effect on the effort to approach districtwide racial proportionality at Young, but it had nothing to do with preventing either the black or "other" group from becoming "small" or "isolated" at Young.

In fact, in each case the extreme measure of relying on race in assignments is unnecessary to achieve the stated goals, even as defined by the districts. For example, at Franklin High School in Seattle, the racial tiebreaker was applied because nonwhite enrollment exceeded 69 percent, and resulted in an incoming ninth-grade class in 2000–2001 that was 30.3 percent Asian—American, 21.9 percent African—American, 6.8 percent Latino, 0.5 percent Native—American, and 40.5 percent Caucasian. Without the racial tiebreaker, the class would have been 39.6 percent Asian—American, 30.2 percent African—American, 8.3 percent Latino, 1.1 percent Native—American, and 20.8 percent Caucasian. When the actual racial breakdown is considered, enrolling students without regard to their race yields a substantially diverse student body under any definition of diversity.

In *Grutter*, the number of minority students the school sought to admit was an undefined "meaningful number" necessary to achieve a genuinely diverse student body. Although the matter was the subject of disagreement on the Court, the majority concluded that the law school did not count back from its applicant pool to arrive at the "meaningful number" it regarded as necessary to diversify its student body. Here the racial balance the districts seek is a defined range set solely by reference to the demographics of the respective school districts.

This working backward to achieve a particular type of racial balance, rather than working forward from some demonstration of the level of diversity that provides the purported benefits, is a fatal flaw under our existing precedent. We have many times over reaffirmed that "[r]acial balance is not to be achieved for its own sake. *Grutter* itself reiterated that "outright racial balancing" is "patently unconstitutional."

Accepting racial balancing as a compelling state interest would justify the imposition of racial proportionality throughout American society, contrary to our repeated recognition that "[a]t the heart of the Constitution's guarantee of equal protection lies the simple command that the Government must treat citizens as individuals, not as simply components of a racial, religious, sexual or national class." Allowing racial balancing as a compelling end in itself would "effectively assur[e] that race will always be relevant in American life, and that the 'ultimate goal' of 'eliminating entirely from governmental decisionmaking such irrelevant factors as a human being's race' will never be achieved." An interest "linked to nothing other than proportional representation of various races . . . would support indefinite use of racial classifications, employed first to obtain the appropriate mixture of racial views and then to ensure that the [program] continues to reflect that mixture."

The validity of our concern that racial balancing has "no logical stopping point," is demonstrated here by the degree to which the districts tie their racial guidelines to their demographics. As the districts' demographics shift, so too will their definition of racial diversity.

The Ninth Circuit below stated that it "share[d] in the hope" expressed in *Grutter* that in 25 years racial preferences would no longer be necessary to further the interest identified in that case. But in Seattle the plans are defended as necessary to address the consequences of racially identifiable housing patterns. The sweep of the mandate claimed by the district is contrary to our rulings that remedying past societal discrimination does not justify race-conscious government action.

The principle that racial balancing is not permitted is one of substance, not semantics. Racial balancing is not transformed from "patently unconstitutional" to a compelling state interest simply by relabeling it "racial diversity." While the school districts use various verbal formulations to describe the interest they seek to promote—racial diversity, avoidance of racial isolation, racial integration—they offer no definition of the interest that suggests it differs from racial balance. See, *e.g.*, App. in No. 05–908, at 257a ("Q. What's your understanding of when a school suffers from racial isolation?" "A. I don't have a definition for that"); *id.*, at 228a–229a ("I don't think we've ever sat down and said, 'Define racially concentrated school exactly on point in quantitative terms.' I don't think we've ever had that conversation"); Tr. in *McFarland I*, at 1–90 (Dec. 8, 2003) ("Q." "How does the Jefferson County School Board define diversity . . . ?" "A. Well, we want to have the schools that make up the percentage of students of the population").

Jefferson County phrases its interest as "racial integration," but integration certainly does not require the sort of racial proportionality reflected in its plan. Even in the context of mandatory desegregation, we have stressed that racial proportionality is not required, and here Jefferson County has already been found to have eliminated the vestiges of its prior segregated school system.

The en banc Ninth Circuit declared that "when a racially diverse school system is the goal (or racial concentration or isolation is the problem), there is no more effective means than a consideration of race to achieve the solution." For the foregoing reasons, this conclusory argument cannot sustain the plans. However closely related race-based assignments may be to achieving racial balance, that itself cannot be the goal, whether labeled "racial diversity" or anything else. To the extent the objective is sufficient diversity so that students see fellow students as individuals rather than solely as members of a racial group, using means that treat students solely as members of a racial group is fundamentally at cross-purposes with that end.

C

The districts assert, as they must, that the way in which they have employed individual racial classifications is necessary to achieve their stated ends. The minimal effect these classifications have on student assignments, however, suggests that other means would be effective. Seattle's racial tiebreaker results, in the end, only in shifting a small number of students between schools. Approximately 307 student assignments were affected by the racial tiebreaker in 2000–2001; the district was able to track the enrollment status of 293 of these students. App. in No. 05–908, at 162a. Of these, 209 were assigned to a school that was one of their choices, 87 of whom were assigned to the same school to which they would have been assigned without the racial tiebreaker. Eighty-four students were assigned to schools that they did not list as a choice, but 29 of those students would have been assigned to their respective school without the racial tiebreaker, and 3 were able to attend one of the oversubscribed schools due to waitlist and capacity adjustments. In over one-third of the assignments affected by the racial tiebreaker, then, the use of race in the end made no difference, and the district could identify only 52 students who were ultimately affected adversely by the racial tiebreaker in that it resulted in assignment to a school they had not listed as a preference and to which they would not otherwise have been assigned.

As the panel majority in *Parents Involved VI* concluded:

> "[T]he tiebreaker's annual effect is thus merely to shuffle a few handfuls of different minority students between a few schools—about a dozen additional Latinos into Ballard, a dozen black students into Nathan Hale, perhaps two dozen Asians into Roosevelt, and so on. The District has not met its burden of proving these marginal changes . . . outweigh the cost of subjecting hundreds of students to disparate treatment based solely upon the color of their skin." 377 F.3d, at 984-985.

Similarly, Jefferson County's use of racial classifications has only a minimal effect on the assignment of students. Elementary school students are assigned to their first- or second-choice school 95 percent of the time, and transfers, which account for roughly 5 percent of assignments, are only denied 35 percent of the time—and presumably an even smaller percentage are denied on the basis of the racial guidelines, given that other factors may lead to a denial. Jefferson County estimates that the racial guidelines account for only 3 percent of assignments. As Jefferson County explains, "the racial guidelines have minimal impact in this process, because they 'mostly influence student assignment in subtle and indirect ways.'"

While we do not suggest that *greater* use of race would be preferable, the minimal impact of the districts' racial classifications on school enrollment casts doubt on the necessity of using racial classifications. In *Grutter*, the consideration of race was viewed as indispensable in more than tripling minority representation at the law school—from 4 to 14.5 percent. Here the most Jefferson County itself claims is that "because the guidelines provide a firm definition of the Board's goal of racially integrated schools, they 'provide administrators with the authority to facilitate, negotiate and collaborate with principals and staff to maintain schools within the 15–50% range.'" Classifying and assigning schoolchildren according to a binary conception of race is an extreme approach in light of our precedents and our Nation's history of using race in public schools, and requires more than such an amorphous end to justify it.

The districts have also failed to show that they considered methods other than explicit racial classifications to achieve their stated goals. Narrow tailoring requires "serious, good faith consideration of workable race-neutral alternatives," and yet in Seattle several alternative assignment plans—many of which would not have used express racial classifications—were rejected with little or no consideration. Jefferson County has failed to present any evidence that it considered alternatives, even though the district already claims that its goals are achieved primarily through means other than the racial classifications.

IV

[This portion of Section IV of the opinion addresses Justice Breyer's dissent and has been removed. You can view this portion of the decision and Justice Breyer's dissent online.]

. . . .

If the need for the racial classifications embraced by the school districts is unclear, even on the districts' own terms, the costs are undeniable. "[D]istinctions between citizens solely because of their ancestry are by their very nature odious to a free people whose institutions are founded upon the doctrine of equality." Government action dividing us by race is inherently suspect because such classifications promote "notions of racial inferiority and lead to a politics of racial hostility," "reinforce the belief, held by too many for too much of our history, that individuals should be judged by the color of their skin," and "endorse race-based reasoning and the conception of a Nation divided into racial blocs, thus contributing to an escalation of racial hostility and conflict." As the Court explained in *Rice v. Cayetano*, 528 U.S. 495, 517, 120 S.Ct. 1044, 145 L.Ed.2d 1007 (2000), "[o]ne of the principal reasons race is treated as a forbidden classification is that it demeans the dignity and worth of a person to be judged by ancestry instead of by his or her own merit and essential qualities."

All this is true enough in the contexts in which these statements were made—government contracting, voting districts, allocation of broadcast licenses, and electing state officers—but when it comes to using race to assign children to schools, history will be heard. In *Brown v. Board of Education*, 347 U.S. 483, 74 S.Ct. 686, 98 L. Ed. 873 (1954) (*Brown I*), we held that segregation deprived black children of equal educational opportunities regardless of whether school facilities and other tangible factors were equal, because government classification and separation on grounds of race themselves denoted inferiority. It was not the inequality of the facilities but the fact of legally separating children on the basis of race on which the Court relied to find a constitutional violation in 1954. See *id.*, at 494, 74 S.Ct. 686 ("'The impact [of segregation] is greater when it has the sanction of the law'"). The next Term, we accordingly stated that "full compliance" with *Brown I* required school districts "to achieve a system of determining admission to the public schools *on a nonracial basis.*"

Before *Brown*, schoolchildren were told where they could and could not go to school based on the color of their skin. The school districts in these cases have not carried the heavy burden of demonstrating that we should allow this once again—even for very different reasons. For schools that never segregated on the basis of race, such as Seattle, or that have removed the vestiges of past segregation, such as Jefferson County, the way "to achieve a system of determining admission to the public schools on a nonracial basis," *Brown II, supra*, at 300–301, 75 S.Ct. 753, is to stop assigning students on a racial basis. The way to stop discrimination on the basis of race is to stop discriminating on the basis of race.

The judgments of the Courts of Appeals for the Sixth and Ninth Circuits are reversed, and the cases are remanded for further proceedings.

It is so ordered.

. . . .

Justice Kennedy, concurring in part and concurring in the judgment.

The Nation's schools strive to teach that our strength comes from people of different races, creeds, and cultures uniting in commitment to the freedom of all. In these cases two school districts in different parts of the country seek to teach that principle by having classrooms that reflect the racial makeup of the surrounding community. That the school districts consider these plans to be necessary should remind us our highest aspirations are yet unfulfilled. But the solutions mandated by these school districts must themselves be lawful. To make race matter now so that it might not matter later may entrench the very prejudices we seek to overcome. In my view the state-mandated racial classifications at issue, official labels proclaiming the race of all persons in a broad class of citizens—elementary school students in one case, high school students in another—are unconstitutional as the cases now come to us.

I agree with The Chief Justice that we have jurisdiction to decide the cases before us and join Parts I and II of the Court's opinion. I also join Parts III–A and III–C for reasons provided below. My views do not allow me to join the balance of the opinion by The Chief Justice, which seems to me to be inconsistent in both its approach and its implications with the history, meaning, and reach of the Equal Protection Clause. Justice Breyer's dissenting opinion, on the other hand, rests on what in my respectful submission is a misuse and mistaken interpretation of our precedents. This leads it to advance propositions that, in my view, are both erroneous and in fundamental conflict with basic equal protection principles. As a consequence, this separate opinion is necessary to set forth my conclusions in the two cases before the Court.

I

The opinion of the Court and Justice Breyer's dissenting opinion (hereinafter dissent) describe in detail the history of integration efforts in Louisville and Seattle. These plans classify individuals by race and allocate benefits and burdens on that basis; and as a result, they are to be subjected to strict scrutiny. The dissent finds that the school districts have identified a compelling interest in increasing diversity, including for the purpose of avoiding racial isolation. The plurality, by contrast, does not acknowledge that the school districts have identified a compelling interest here. For this reason, among others, I do not join Parts III–B and IV. Diversity, depending on its meaning and definition, is a compelling educational goal a school district may pursue.

It is well established that when a governmental policy is subjected to strict scrutiny, "the government has the burden of proving that racial classifications 'are narrowly tailored measures that further compelling governmental interests.'" "Absent searching judicial inquiry into the justification for such race-based measures, there is simply no way of determining what classifications are 'benign' or 'remedial' and what classifications are in fact motivated by illegitimate notions of racial inferiority or simple racial politics." And the inquiry into less restrictive alternatives demanded by the narrow tailoring analysis requires in many cases a thorough understanding of how a plan works. The government bears the burden of justifying its use of individual racial classifications. As part of that burden it must establish, in detail, how decisions based on an individual student's race are made in a challenged governmental program. The Jefferson County Board of Education fails to meet this threshold mandate.

Petitioner Crystal Meredith challenges the district's decision to deny her son Joshua McDonald a requested transfer for his kindergarten enrollment. The district concedes it denied his request "under the guidelines," which is to say, on the basis of Joshua's race. Yet the district also maintains that the guidelines do not apply to "kindergartens," and it fails to explain the discrepancy. Resort to the record, including the parties' stipulation of facts, further confuses the matter.

The discrepancy identified is not some simple and straightforward error that touches only upon the peripheries of the district's use of individual racial classifications. To the contrary, Jefferson County in its briefing has explained how and when it employs these classifications only in terms so broad and imprecise that they cannot withstand strict scrutiny. While it acknowledges that racial classifications are used to make certain assignment decisions, it fails to make clear, for example, who makes the decisions; what if any oversight is employed; the precise circumstances in which an assignment decision will or will not be made on the basis of race; or how it is determined which of two similarly situated children will be subjected to a given race-based decision.

When litigation, as here, involves a "complex, comprehensive plan that contains multiple strategies for achieving racially integrated schools," these ambiguities become all the more problematic in light of the contradictions and confusions that result.

One can attempt to identify a construction of Jefferson County's student assignment plan that, at least as a logical matter, complies with these competing propositions; but this does not remedy the underlying problem. Jefferson County fails to make clear to this Court—even in the limited respects implicated by Joshua's initial assignment and transfer denial—whether in fact it relies on racial classifications in a manner narrowly tailored to the interest in question, rather than in the far-reaching, inconsistent, and ad hoc manner that a less forgiving reading of the record would suggest. When a court subjects governmental action to strict scrutiny, it cannot construe ambiguities in favor of the State.

As for the Seattle case, the school district has gone further in describing the methods and criteria used to determine assignment decisions on the basis of individual racial classifications. The district, nevertheless, has failed to make an adequate showing in at least one respect. It has failed to explain why, in a district composed of a diversity of races, with fewer than half of the students classified as "white," it has employed the crude racial categories of "white" and "non-white" as the basis for its assignment decisions.

The district has identified its purposes as follows: "(1) to promote the educational benefits of diverse school enrollments; (2) to reduce the potentially harmful effects of racial isolation by allowing students the opportunity to opt out of racially isolated schools; and (3) to make sure that racially segregated housing patterns did not prevent non-white students from having equitable access to the most popular oversubscribed schools." Yet the school district does not explain how, in the context of its diverse student population, a blunt distinction between "white" and "non-white" furthers these goals. As the Court explains, "a school with 50 percent Asian—American students and 50 percent white students but no African—American, Native—American, or Latino students would qualify as balanced, while a school with 30 percent Asian—American, 25 percent African—American, 25 percent Latino, and 20 percent white students would not." Far from being narrowly tailored to its purposes, this system threatens to defeat its own ends, and the school district has provided no convincing explanation for its design. Other problems are evident in Seattle's system, but there is no need to address them now. As the district fails to account for the classification system it has chosen, despite what appears to be its ill fit, Seattle has not shown its plan to be narrowly tailored to achieve its own ends; and thus it fails to pass strict scrutiny.

II

Our Nation from the inception has sought to preserve and expand the promise of liberty and equality on which it was founded. Today we enjoy a society that is remarkable in its openness and opportunity. Yet our tradition is to go beyond present achievements, however significant, and to recognize and confront the flaws and injustices that remain. This is especially true when we seek assurance that opportunity is not denied on account of race. The enduring hope is that race should not matter; the reality is that too often it does.

This is by way of preface to my respectful submission that parts of the opinion by The Chief Justice imply an all-too-unyielding insistence that race cannot be a factor in instances when, in my view, it may be taken into account. The plurality opinion is too dismissive of the legitimate interest government has in ensuring all people have equal opportunity regardless of their race. The plurality's postulate that "[t]he way to stop discrimination on the basis of race is to stop discriminating on the basis of race," is not sufficient to decide these cases. Fifty years of experience since *Brown v. Board of Education*, 347 U.S. 483, 74 S.Ct. 686, 98 L.Ed. 873 (1954), should teach us that the problem before us defies so easy a solution. School districts can seek to reach *Brown*'s objective of equal educational opportunity. The plurality opinion is at least open to the interpretation that the Constitution requires school districts to ignore the problem of *de facto* resegregation in schooling. I cannot endorse that conclusion. To the extent the plurality opinion suggests the Constitution mandates that state and local school authorities must accept the status quo of racial isolation in schools, it is, in my view, profoundly mistaken.

The statement by Justice Harlan that "[o]ur Constitution is color-blind" was most certainly justified in the context of his dissent in *Plessy v. Ferguson*, 163 U.S. 537, 559, 16 S.Ct. 1138, 41 L.Ed. 256 (1896). The Court's decision in that case was a grievous error it took far too long to overrule. *Plessy*, of course, concerned official classification by race applicable to all persons who sought to use railway carriages. And, as an aspiration, Justice Harlan's axiom must command our assent. In the real world, it is regrettable to say, it cannot be a universal constitutional principle.

In the administration of public schools by the state and local authorities it is permissible to consider the racial makeup of schools and to adopt general policies to encourage a diverse student body, one aspect of which is its racial composition. If school authorities are concerned that the student-body compositions of certain schools interfere with the objective of offering an equal educational opportunity to all of their students, they are free to devise race-conscious measures to address the problem in a general way and without treating each student in different fashion solely on the basis of a systematic, individual typing by race.

School boards may pursue the goal of bringing together students of diverse backgrounds and races through other means, including strategic site selection of new schools; drawing attendance zones with general recognition of the demographics of neighborhoods; allocating resources for special programs; recruiting students and faculty in a targeted fashion; and tracking enrollments, performance, and other statistics by race. These mechanisms are race conscious but do not lead to different treatment based on a classification that tells each student he or she is to be defined by race, so it is unlikely any of them would demand strict scrutiny to be found permissible. Executive and legislative branches, which for generations now have considered these types of policies and procedures, should be permitted to employ them with candor and with confidence that a constitutional violation does not occur whenever a decisionmaker considers the impact a given approach might have on students of different races. Assigning to each student a personal designation according to a crude system of individual racial classifications is quite a different matter; and the legal analysis changes accordingly.

Each respondent has asserted that its assignment of individual students by race is permissible because there is no other way to avoid racial isolation in the school districts. Yet, as explained, each has failed to provide the support necessary for that proposition. "The history of racial classifications in this country suggests that blind judicial deference to legislative or executive pronouncements of necessity has no place in equal protection analysis". And individual racial classifications employed in this manner may be considered legitimate only if they are a last resort to achieve a compelling interest.

In the cases before us it is noteworthy that the number of students whose assignment depends on express racial classifications is limited. I join Part III–C of the Court's opinion because I agree that in the context of these plans, the small number of assignments affected suggests that the schools could have achieved their stated ends through different means. These include the facially race-neutral means set forth above or, if necessary, a more nuanced, individual evaluation of school needs and student characteristics that might include race as a component. The latter approach would be informed by *Grutter*, though of course the criteria relevant to student placement would differ based on the age of the students, the needs of the parents, and the role of the schools.

. . . .

B

To uphold these programs the Court is asked to brush aside two concepts of central importance for determining the validity of laws and decrees designed to alleviate the hurt and adverse consequences resulting from race discrimination. The first is the difference between *de jure* and *de facto* segregation; the second, the presumptive invalidity of a State's use of racial classifications to differentiate its treatment of individuals.

In the immediate aftermath of *Brown* the Court addressed other instances where laws and practices enforced *de jure* segregation. But with reference to schools, the effect of the legal wrong proved most difficult to correct. To remedy the wrong, school districts that had been segregated by law had no choice, whether under court supervision or pursuant to voluntary desegregation efforts, but to resort to extraordinary measures including individual student and teacher assignment to schools based on race. So it was, as the dissent observes, that Louisville classified children by race in its school assignment and busing plan in the 1970's.

Our cases recognized a fundamental difference between those school districts that had engaged in *de jure* segregation and those whose segregation was the result of other factors. School districts that had engaged in *de jure* segregation had an affirmative constitutional duty to desegregate; those that were *de facto* segregated did not. The distinctions between *de jure* and *de facto* segregation extended to the remedies available to governmental units in addition to the courts. For example, in *Wygant v. Jackson Bd. of Ed.*, 476 U.S. 267, 274, 106 S.Ct. 1842, 90 L.Ed.2d 260 (1986), the plurality noted: "This Court never has held that societal discrimination alone is sufficient to justify a racial classification. Rather, the Court has insisted upon some showing of prior discrimination by the governmental unit involved before allowing limited use of racial classifications in order to remedy such discrimination." The Court's decision in *Croson, supra*, reinforced the difference between the remedies available to redress *de facto* and *de jure* discrimination:

> "To accept [a] claim that past societal discrimination alone can serve as the basis for rigid racial preferences would be to open the door to competing claims for 'remedial relief' for every disadvantaged group. The dream of a Nation of equal citizens in a society where race is irrelevant to personal opportunity and achievement would be lost in a mosaic of shifting preferences based on inherently unmeasurable claims of past wrongs."

From the standpoint of the victim, it is true, an injury stemming from racial prejudice can hurt as much when the demeaning treatment based on race identity stems from bias masked deep within the social order as when it is imposed by law. The distinction between government and private action, furthermore, can be amorphous both as a historical matter and as a matter of present-day finding of fact. Laws arise from a culture and vice versa. Neither can assign to the other all responsibility for persisting injustices.

Yet, like so many other legal categories that can overlap in some instances, the constitutional distinction between *de jure* and *de facto* segregation has been thought to be an important one. It must be conceded its primary function in school cases was to delimit the powers of the Judiciary in the fashioning of remedies. The distinction ought not to be altogether disregarded, however, when we come to that most sensitive of all racial issues, an attempt by the government to treat whole classes of persons differently based on the government's systematic classification of each individual by race. There, too, the distinction serves as a limit on the exercise of a power that reaches to the very verge of constitutional authority. Reduction of an individual to an assigned racial identity for differential treatment is among the most pernicious actions our government can undertake. The allocation of governmental burdens and benefits, contentious under any circumstances, is even more divisive when allocations are made on the basis of individual racial classifications.

Notwithstanding these concerns, allocation of benefits and burdens through individual racial classifications was found sometimes permissible in the context of remedies for *de jure* wrong. Where there has been *de jure* segregation, there is a cognizable legal wrong, and the courts and legislatures have broad power to remedy it. The remedy, though, was limited in time and limited to the wrong. The Court has allowed school districts to remedy their prior *de jure* segregation by classifying individual students based on their race. The limitation of this power to instances where there has been *de jure* segregation serves to confine the nature, extent, and duration of governmental reliance on individual racial classifications.

The cases here were argued upon the assumption, and come to us on the premise, that the discrimination in question did not result from *de jure* actions. And when *de facto* discrimination is at issue our tradition has been that the remedial rules are different. The State must seek alternatives to the classification and differential treatment of individuals by race, at least absent some extraordinary showing not present here.

. . . .

This Nation has a moral and ethical obligation to fulfill its historic commitment to creating an integrated society that ensures equal opportunity for all of its children. A compelling interest exists in avoiding racial isolation, an interest that a school district, in its discretion and expertise, may choose to pursue. Likewise, a district may consider it a compelling interest to achieve a diverse student population. Race may be one component of that diversity, but other demographic factors, plus special talents and needs, should also be considered. What the government is not permitted to do, absent a showing of necessity not made here, is to classify every student on the basis of race and to assign each of them to schools based on that classification. Crude measures of this sort threaten to reduce children to racial chits valued and traded according to one school's supply and another's demand.

That statement, to be sure, invites this response: A sense of stigma may already become the fate of those separated out by circumstances beyond their immediate control. But to this the replication must be: Even so, measures other than differential treatment based on racial typing of individuals first must be exhausted.

The decision today should not prevent school districts from continuing the important work of bringing together students of different racial, ethnic, and economic backgrounds. Due to a variety of factors—some influenced by government, some not—neighborhoods in our communities do not reflect the diversity of our Nation as a whole. Those entrusted with directing our public schools can bring to bear the creativity of experts, parents, administrators, and other concerned citizens to find a way to achieve the compelling interests they face without resorting to widespread governmental allocation of benefits and burdens on the basis of racial classifications.

With this explanation I concur in the judgment of the Court.

Post Problem Discussion

1. In 2008, the Los Angeles Times ran a story entitled, *Schools' Racial Makeup Divides San Juan Capistrano.* The subtitle for the story was "Two of the district's elementary campuses are predominantly Latino, while the other two are mostly white. Some parents worry their children are getting shortchanged." The lead paragraph describes the schools with disparate white and Latino enrollment, and the article continues, "Privately, district officials—many of whom came of age during the civil rights struggles of the 1960s—say they are troubled by the schools that are mostly Latino. But they say that any attempt to redraw attendance boundaries would spark a backlash from parents, and that Latino and white parents don't want their kids bused to schools across town to achieve integration." H.G. Reza, *Schools' Racial Makeup Divides San Juan Capistrano*, Los Angeles Times (September 2, 2008).

Given the facts and legal opinions in all that you have read, from *Mendez* to *PICS*, together with the materials on curriculum and achievement in Chapter 4, is there any reason to expect the patterns of education to change?

2. In 2012, the United States Supreme Court decided *Fisher v. Univ. of Texas*, 570 U.S. 297 (2013), which involved a white applicant who was denied admissions and claimed it was due to the University's consideration of race in the admissions process. At issue in the case was the lower court's application of strict scrutiny review. The Supreme Court ruled that the lower courts had not correctly applied the requirements of strict scrutiny in this context and gave inappropriate deference to the University:

> Once the University has established that its goal of diversity is consistent with strict scrutiny, however, there must still be a further judicial determination that the admissions process meets strict scrutiny in its implementation. The University must prove that the means chosen by the University to attain diversity are narrowly tailored to that goal. On this point, the University receives no deference. *Grutter* made clear that it is for the courts, not for university administrators, to ensure that "[t]he means chosen to accomplish the [government's] asserted purpose must be specifically and narrowly framed to accomplish that purpose." True, a court can take account of a university's experience and expertise in adopting or rejecting certain admissions processes. But, as the Court said in *Grutter*, it remains at all times the University's obligation to demonstrate, and the Judiciary's obligation to determine, that admissions processes "ensure that each applicant is evaluated as an individual and not in a way that makes an applicant's race or ethnicity the defining feature of his or her application."
>
> Narrow tailoring also requires that the reviewing court verify that it is "necessary" for a university to use race to achieve the educational benefits of diversity. *Bakke, supra*. This involves a careful judicial inquiry into whether a university could achieve sufficient diversity without using racial classifications. Although "[n]arrow tailoring does not require exhaustion of every *conceivable* race-neutral alternative," strict scrutiny does require a court to examine with care, and not defer to, a university's "serious, good faith consideration of workable race-neutral alternatives." See *Grutter*. Consideration by the university is of course necessary, but it is not sufficient to satisfy strict scrutiny: The reviewing court must ultimately be satisfied that no workable race-neutral alternatives would produce the educational benefits of diversity. If "'a nonracial approach ... could promote the substantial interest about as well and at tolerable administrative expense,'" then the university may not

> consider race. A plaintiff, of course, bears the burden of placing the validity of a university's adoption of an affirmative action plan in issue. But strict scrutiny imposes on the university the ultimate burden of demonstrating, before turning to racial classifications, that available, workable race-neutral alternatives do not suffice.

Id. at 312 (internal citations omitted). What impact do you think this decision will have on the use of race in the college and university admissions process? In the K-12 admissions or student assignment process?

3. In 2014, the United States Supreme Court decided *Schuette v. Coalition to Defend Affirmative Action*, 568 U.S. 1249 (2014). In the aftermath of the Supreme Court's decisions about the University of Michigan's policies in *Gratz v. Bollinger* and *Grutter v. Bollinger*, and the University's changes to its policies as a result of those decisions, the people of the State of Michigan past a constitutional amendment prohibiting the use of racial preferences in public education, employment, and contracting. The amendment states:

"The University of Michigan, Michigan State University, Wayne State University, and any other public college or university, community college, or school district shall not discriminate against, or grant preferential treatment to, any individual or group on the basis of race, sex, color, ethnicity, or national origin in the operation of public employment, public education, or public contracting." *Id.* at 1255. The Sixth Circuit Court of Appeals ruled that the amendment violated Equal Protection requirements of the United States Constitution, but the Supreme Court reversed stating:

> This case is not about how the debate about racial preferences should be resolved. It is about who may resolve it. There is no authority in the Constitution of the United States or in this Court's precedents for the Judiciary to set aside Michigan laws that commit this policy determination to the voters. See *Sailors v. Board of Ed. of County of Kent*, 387 U.S. 105, 109 (1967) ("Save and unless the state, county, or municipal government runs afoul of a federally protected right, it has vast leeway in the management of its internal affairs"). Deliberative debate on sensitive issues such as racial preferences all too often may shade into rancor. But that does not justify removing certain court-determined issues from the voters' reach. Democracy does not presume that some subjects are either too divisive or too profound for public debate.

Id. at 1263. What impact do you think this case will have on the use of racial preferences in admissions policies in colleges, universities, and K-12 public schools?

4. Justice Stevens' dissent in *PICS* begins:

> While I join Justice Breyer's eloquent and unanswerable dissent in its entirety, it is appropriate to add these words.
>
> There is a cruel irony in The Chief Justice's reliance on our decision in *Brown* v. *Board of Education*, 349 U.S. 294, 75 S. Ct. 753, 99 L. Ed. 1083, 71 Ohio Law Abs. 584 (1955). The first sentence in the concluding paragraph

> of his opinion states: "Before *Brown*, schoolchildren were told where they could and could not go to school based on the color of their skin." This sentence reminds me of Anatole France's observation: "[T]he majestic equality of the la[w], forbid[s] rich and poor alike to sleep under bridges, to beg in the streets, and to steal their bread." THE CHIEF JUSTICE fails to note that it was only black schoolchildren who were so ordered; indeed, the history books do not tell stories of white children struggling to attend black schools. In this and other ways, THE CHIEF JUSTICE rewrites the history of one of this Court's most important decisions. . . .

Parents Involved in Cmty. Sch. v. Seattle Sch. Dist. No. 1, 551 U.S. 701, 799 (2007) (internal citations omitted).

Justice Breyer, dissenting for himself, Justices Stevens, Souter, and Ginsburg, begins this way:

> These cases consider the longstanding efforts of two local school boards to integrate their public schools. The school board plans before us resemble many others adopted in the last 50 years by primary and secondary schools throughout the Nation. All of those plans represent local efforts to bring about the kind of racially integrated education that *Brown v. Board of Education*, 347 U.S. 483, 74 S. Ct. 686, 98 L. Ed. 873 (1954), long ago promised—efforts that this Court has repeatedly required, permitted, and encouraged local authorities to undertake. This Court has recognized that the public interests at stake in such cases are "compelling." We have approved of "narrowly tailored" plans that are no less race-conscious than the plans before us. And we have understood that the Constitution *permits* local communities to adopt desegregation plans even where it does not *require* them to do so.
>
> The plurality pays inadequate attention to this law, to past opinions' rationales, their language, and the contexts in which they arise. As a result, it reverses course and reaches the wrong conclusion. In doing so, it distorts precedent, it misapplies the relevant constitutional principles, it announces legal rules that will obstruct efforts by state and local governments to deal effectively with the growing resegregation of public schools, it threatens to substitute for present calm a disruptive round of race-related litigation, and it undermines *Brown*'s promise of integrated primary and secondary education that local communities have sought to make a reality. This cannot be justified in the name of the Equal Protection Clause.

PICS, 551 U.S. at 803. You can read the full text of these dissents online. Do you agree that we have come full circle on these issues?

5. How clear is the Supreme Court opinion in *PICS*? Do you think *PICS* means that K-12 schools cannot constitutionally use race in assigning students? Race exclusively? Race for any reason? What does Justice Kennedy's concurring opinion add to the discussion?

6. Most of the materials in this section address race and ethnicity. There are also legal issues concerning admissions based on gender. The leading case comes from higher education, where a male student sought admission to the state nursing school. The U.S. Supreme Court began its analysis with a review of the precedent:

> Because the challenged policy expressly discriminates among applicants on the basis of gender, it is subject to scrutiny under the Equal Protection Clause of the Fourteenth Amendment. *Reed v. Reed*, 404 U.S. 71, 75 (1971). That this statutory policy discriminates against males rather than against females does not exempt it from scrutiny or reduce the standard of review. *Caban v. Mohammed*, 441 U.S. 380, 394 (1979); *Orr v. Orr*, 440 U.S. 268, 279 (1979). Our decisions also establish that the party seeking to uphold a statute that classifies individuals on the basis of their gender must carry the burden of showing an "exceedingly persuasive justification" for the classification. *Kirchberg v. Feenstra*, 450 U.S. 455, 461 (1981); *Personnel Administrator of Mass. v. Feeney*, 442 U.S. 256, 273 (1979). The burden is met only by showing at least that the classification serves "important governmental objectives and that the discriminatory means employed" are "substantially related to the achievement of those objectives." *Wengler v. Druggists Mutual Ins. Co.*, 446 U.S. 142, 150 (1980).

Mississippi Univ. for Women v. Hogan, 458 U.S. 718, 723–24 (1982). The Court then concluded that in Rob Hogan's case, "considering both the asserted interest and the relationship between the interest and the methods used by the State, we conclude that the State has fallen far short of establishing the 'exceedingly persuasive justification' needed to sustain the gender-based classification. Accordingly, we hold that MUW's policy of denying males the right to enroll for credit in its School of Nursing violates the Equal Protection Clause of the Fourteenth Amendment." *Hogan*, 458 U.S. at 731.

In 1996, the Court decided a gender case where women were claiming discrimination when denied admission to the Virginia Military Institute (VMI). In rejecting the state's defense of the separate programs, the Court said:

> ... generalizations about "the way women are," estimates of what is appropriate for *most women*, no longer justify denying opportunity to women whose talent and capacity place them outside the average description. Notably, Virginia never asserted that VMI's method of education suits *most men*.... In contrast to the generalizations about women on which Virginia rests, we note again these dispositive realities: VMI's "implementing methodology" is not "inherently unsuitable to women," "some women ... do well under [the] adversative model," "some women, at least, would want to attend [VMI] if they had the opportunity," "some women are capable of all of the individual activities required of VMI cadets," and "can meet the physical standards [VMI] now impose[s] on men." It is on behalf of these women that the United States has instituted this suit, and it is for them that a remedy must be crafted, a remedy that will end their exclusion from a

> state-supplied educational opportunity for which they are fit, a decree that will "bar like discrimination in the future."

United States v. Virginia, 518 U.S. 515, 551 (1996) (internal citations omitted). *Hogan* and *VMI* both arose in higher education settings. Should the gender analysis be the same for K-12?

7. In 2006, the U.S. DOE amended its regulations to provide more flexibility for same sex classes and schools in certain situations based on objectives to improve educational opportunities so long as the single-sex approach is even-handed and totally voluntary and so long as "all other students, including students of the excluded sex," are provided with "a substantially equal coeducational class or extracurricular activity in the same subject or activity." *See* 34 C.F.R. 106.34. The adoption of these regulations was controversial, *see, e.g.*, 71 F.R. 62530 (October 25, 2006) (comments on the proposed change); and the issue remains subject to debate and legal challenge, *see, e.g.*, U.S. Dept. of Educ., *Single-Sex Versus Coeducation Schooling: A Systematic Review Final Report* (2005), http://www2.ed.gov/rschstat/eval/other/single-sex/single-sex.pdf; U.S. Dept. of Educ., *Dear Colleague Letter* regarding non-vocational single-sex classes, extracurricular activities, and schools at the elementary and secondary education levels, January 31, 2007, http://www2.ed.gov/about/offices/list/ocr/letters/single-sex-20070131.html; *Doe ex rel. Doe v. Vermilion Parish Sch. Bd.*, 421 Fed. Appx. 366 (5th Cir. 2011) (upholding the denial of an injunction (though remanding on question of mootness and other issues) to a mother and her two daughters in a constitutional challenge of single-sex classes).

Under what circumstances, if any, are single sex classes, or single sex schools constitutional?

Chapter 6

Liability

Synopsis

§6.01 Introduction

Public schools and school employees have numerous sources of legal liabilities. This Chapter focuses primarily on liability as it relates to student tort claims, and student claims under two federal statutes: 42 U.S.C §1983 and 20 U.S.C. §1681 (Title IX). A number of issues arise under these sources of law including:

1. The duty to act with due care;
2. The duty to protect students from harm and to provide a safe educational environment;
3. Liability for harm to students caused by other students;
4. Direct liability of schools (or school districts/boards) for policies and for actions or inactions by the school or school district/board;
5. Indirect liability of schools (or school districts/boards) for the actions of school employees (teachers, principals, etc.); and
6. Defenses and immunities to actions against schools and school employees.

Each of these topics is discussed in this Chapter.

§ 6.02 Torts — Negligence

Torts are common law claims for personal injuries. Torts fall into two basic groups: negligence and intentional torts. Negligence claims for student injuries at school, or school sponsored events, are common. Negligence consists of four elements: (1) duty, (2) breach of duty, (3) actual and proximate cause, and (4) harm.

In the public school context, school employees (teachers, administrators, principals, etc.) owe certain duties to students, and they can be liable for negligence if they breach those duties. Schools, school boards, or school districts (referred to generally in this Chapter as "schools") can be liable directly for their own actions or inactions, and liable indirectly for the negligent acts of their employees under the doctrine of *respondeat superior.*

The duties for schools and school employees include the duty to act with due care so that their actions do not harm students. For example, a teacher who incorrectly mixes chemicals for a science project that explodes and harms students in the class may be liable for negligence, and those actions may also subject the school or school district to liability as well. Likewise, schools have an obligation to use reasonable care in hiring and training employees, in developing policies that affect the actions employees take, or do not take, and in maintaining school grounds.[1]

The duties imposed upon schools and school employees under common law go beyond the general obligation to act with due care. They also include a duty to supervise and to protect students by providing a safe educational environment. These duties come about as a result of the special relationship between students and schools (called *in loco parentis*, which means in the place of a parent), and the fact that compulsory attendance laws require students to attend school. *See, e.g.*, *Rupp v. Bryant*, 417 So. 2d 658 (Fla. 1982); *Miller v. Griesel*, 308 N.E.2d 701 (Ind. 1974).

The duty to supervise and protect generally falls to school employees with some supervisory responsibility for students, such as a superintendent, principal, or teacher. These employees are required to use reasonable care to supervise and protect students from injury. *See, e.g.*, *Ballard v. Polly*, 387 F. Supp. 895 (D.D.C. 1975) (finding school negligent in failing to provide a safe playground for its students); *Dailey v. Los Angeles Unified Sch. Dist.*, 470 P.2d 360 (Cal. 1970) (finding school authorities have duty to supervise conduct of children); *Eastman v. Williams*, 207 A.2d 146 (Vt. 1965) (nature and extent of the duty owed affected by a number of different factors including the student's age).

---

1. *See, e.g.*, Allan E. Korpela, Annotation, *Tort liability of private schools and institutions of higher learning for accidents due to condition of buildings, equipment, or outside premises*, 35 A.L.R.3d 975 (2009); Robin Cheryl Miller, Annotation, *Tort liability of public schools and institutions of higher learning for accidents occurring in physical education classes*, 66 A.L.R.5th 1 (2009); David P. Chapus, Annotation, *Liability of school authorities for hiring or retaining incompetent or otherwise unsuitable teacher*, 60 A.L.R.4th 260 (2008); C.T. Drechsler, Annotation, *Tort liability of public schools and institutions of higher learning*, 86 A.L.R.2d 489 (2008).

The exact nature of the duty often depends on the circumstances. For example, elementary school students may require a greater degree of supervision than would be required for high school students. *See, e.g., Dailey*, 470 P.2d 360; *Miller*, 308 N.E.2d 701; *Besette v. Enderlin Sch. Dist.*, 310 N.W.2d 759 (N.D. 1981). Schools can be liable for failing to adopt sufficient policies regarding school safety or student protection, or for failing to properly train employees on these issues.

Given the nature of schools, courts have recognized that it is virtually impossible to provide constant supervision and prevent every injury. As a result, courts look at two key factors: 1) reasonableness and 2) foreseeability. With reasonableness, the standard is generally what a prudent, or reasonable, person would do under similar circumstances given the age of the children and the circumstances. *Frazer v. St. Tammany Parish Sch. Bd.*, 774 So. 2d 1227, 1232 (La. Ct. App. 2000), *writ denied*, 787 So. 2d 1001 (La. Mar. 23, 2001). Some courts have interpreted the duty to supervise and protect in light of the *in loco parentis* obligations, which means that a teacher's duty is to exercise the same care as a parent of ordinary prudence would observe in comparable circumstances. *See, e.g., Ballard*, 387 F. Supp. 895; *Knicrumah v. Albany City Sch. Dist.*, 241 F. Supp. 2d 199 (N.D.N.Y. 2003).

With foreseeability, the scope of the duty is limited to risks that are reasonably foreseeable or known. As a general rule, schools and school employees have a duty to exercise reasonable care to protect students only from those injuries that can be reasonably anticipated. *Rupp*, 417 So. 2d 658. Foreseeability also plays an important role in the proximate cause aspect of negligence. Even when a duty is found and that duty has been breached, the plaintiffs must still show that the breach caused their injuries. Some courts interpret proximate cause to mean that the injury must have been preventable by the school if the requisite degree of supervision had been exercised. *See, e.g., Bell v. Ayio*, 731 So. 2d 893 (La. Ct. App. 1998). Under this approach, when an injury results from an unforeseen or spontaneous act by a student, the school or school employee is not liable.

A. Student Injuries

One aspect of the duty to supervise students and provide them with a safe educational environment is preventing student injuries that occur as a result of activities at school, such as recess, gym class, field trips, and the like. The following problem addresses some of these issues.

Problem 1: Space Monkey

Louie is a nine-year-old fourth grade student. At recess, he decides to play "space monkey" with his friends, Zach and Charlie. Space monkey is a playground game where students hang upside down, hold their breath, and place their hands around their necks so that they will pass out and feel like they are "floating in space." Other friends stay nearby to catch the student if he/she falls when going unconscious. The three boys go to the monkey bars. Louie begins to hold his breath and choke himself while hanging upside down. Ms. Donovan, a fourth grade substitute teacher who has recess duty that day, sees Louie holding his breath with his hands around his neck. She comes over and asks him what he is doing. Louie explains that he is playing space monkey, and describes the activity to Ms. Donovan. She tells Louie, Zach, and Charlie that space monkey sounds like a very dangerous game and that they should never play it again because they could get hurt. Ms. Donovan tells them to go play on some other playground equipment and then leaves to supervise other children, taking no other action. Ms. Donovan does not tell anyone else at the school about the incident.

The next day, Louie and his friends again go to the monkey bars and play space monkey at recess. This time, Louie reaches unconsciousness before any of the teachers on duty see him. Louie falls down, and his friends are not able to catch him. He hits his head on the ground and is severely injured. Ms. Donovan is not at school on this day, but there are three other teachers on duty for about 100 students at recess.

1. Is Ms. Donovan liable for Louie's injuries? If so, what could she have done to avoid liability?
2. Are any of the teachers on recess duty the day Louie is injured liable for his injuries? If so, what could they have done to avoid liability?
3. Is the school or school district liable? If so, what actions could the school or school district have taken to avoid liability?

Problem Materials

✓ *Partin v. Vernon Parish School Board*, 343 So. 2d 417 (La. Ct. App. 1977)

✓ *Rollins v. Concordia Parish School Board*, 465 So. 2d 213 (La. Ct. App. 1985)

Partin v. Vernon Parish School Board

343 So. 2d 417 (La. Ct. App. 1977)

The court discusses the standards for negligent supervision and finds that the school and teachers are not liable for the student's injury because they met their obligations of due care.

This is a personal injury action instituted by plaintiff wherein she seeks to recover, on her own behalf and on behalf of her minor son, Paul Corcoran Wagner II, hereafter referred to as Paul, damages sustained when Paul allegedly fell on the playground at Simpson Public School in Simpson, Louisiana. . . .

Plaintiff contends that Paul sustained a transverse laceration in the head and body region of the pancreas when he either fell upon, was pushed on or tried balancing on a small tree stump located on the playground at the Simpson Public School. Plaintiff contends that the two teachers were guilty of actionable negligence because they failed in their duty to properly supervise the children and that the school board is liable under the doctrine of respondeat superior. Plaintiff additionally contends that the school board is guilty of independent negligence for having allowed a dangerous condition, i.e., a pine tree stump, to exist on the school playground.

The facts leading up to and surrounding the alleged accident are not in dispute except in two particulars, i.e., how Paul's body came into contact with the tree stump and whether the stump was relatively square and rounded on top or whether it was jagged and knife-like.

The accident happened at about 11:30 a.m. on the morning of September 9, 1974. The previous day, which was a Sunday, Simpson was hit by the fringe winds of a hurricane as a result of which a small dead pine tree located on the very edge of the school playground fell. The trees was described by all witnesses as being about six to ten inches in diameter. Mr. Willard Martin, the school janitor, arrived at the school on the day of the accident at about 7:00 a.m. Upon his arrival be noticed the fallen tree, which was lying partially in the road. He immediately removed the tree and large branches and generally cleaned up the area except for small branches, pine cones, etc. He did not remove the stump which was described by him as about twenty to twenty-four inches in height and almost square and rounded on top. Mr. Martin testified that he did not consider the stump as hazardous and did not report its presence to anyone.

According to the school schedule the first, second and third graders were allowed a noon recess which began about 11:20 a.m. The children, about ninety in number, were taken to the playground under the supervision of Mrs. Gordy, who was the teacher on duty. The playground was described by all witnesses as being about the size of a football field. Upon arrival at the playground Mrs. Gordy immediately saw the stump and the scattered debris, i.e., small branches, twigs, and pine cones, around it and cautioned the children as a group that they should not play there. Mrs. Gordy testified that she was not concerned about the stump, her description thereof being generally in agreement with that of Mr. Martin, however, she was concerned that the children might injure one another if they undertook to throw small twigs, pine cones, etc. Mrs. Gordy stationed herself about 30 or 40 feet away from the stump in the area of the see-saws and remained there during the entire recess. Following Mrs. Gordy's general warning to the group as a whole, she noticed Paul, who was then 7 years old, in the vicinity of the stump and she again warned him that he should play elsewhere. Following this second warning Paul returned to the area and either fell on, was pushed, on, or layed his body over the stump. Mrs. Gordy was sitting near the see-saws, and while taking a rock out of her shoe, looked up and saw Paul on the stump with his hands and feet in the air. Mrs. Gordy assumed that Paul was trying to balance his body on the stump. Upon seeing this Mrs. Gordy immediately went to Paul and again scolded him for disobeying her. At this point we note that only Mrs. Gordy saw Paul on the stump, however, she did not see whether he fell on, was pushed on, or simply laid his body over the stump. The history given to Dr. Edgerton, Paul's treating physician, was to the effect that a little boy pushed Paul and he fell across the stump. Paul testified that he was attempting to climb up on the stump when his foot slipped and he fell. The trial judge did not resolve this controversial fact concluding that regardless of the manner in which Paul's body came into contact with the stump the defendants were not negligent.

. . . .

We likewise find, as did the trial court, that Mrs. Gordy was not guilty of any negligence. There is nothing in the record which would even suggest that Mrs. Gordy was in any way remiss in her duty to supervise the many children under her care at this noon recess. It will be remembered that Mrs. Gordy was supervising the play of some 90 youngsters in an area the size of a football field. She cautioned the children as a group that they should not play in the area of the stump. She again cautioned Paul, himself, that he should play elsewhere. Mrs. Gordy had no reason to know or believe that Paul would not comply with her instructions. Even if Mrs. Gordy had seen Paul when he approached the stump for the second time there is no showing that from her position near the see-saws she could have prevented Paul's contact with the tree stump. As we stated in *Nash v. Rapides Parish School Board*, 188 So. 2d 508 (La. App. 3rd Cir. 1966):

> "As is often the case, accidents such as this, involving school children at play, happen so quickly that unless there was direct supervision of every child (which we recognize as being impossible), the accident can be said to be almost impossible to prevent."

We recognize that a school teacher charged with the duty of supervising the play of children must exercise a high degree of care toward the children, however, the teacher is not the absolute insurer of the safety of the children she supervises. Our law requires that the supervision be reasonable and commensurate with the age of the children and the attendant circumstances. There is no requirement that the supervisor, especially where the play of some ninety children is being monitored, have each child under constant and unremitting scrutiny. Suffice it to say that we find no negligence on the part of Mrs. Gordy.

. . . .

Rollins v. Concordia Parish School Board

465 So. 2d 213 (La. App. 1985)

The court finds a school board liable for a student's playground injuries because the teachers' supervision was inadequate in light of the circumstances involved at the time of the accident.

This appeal involves the issue of whether or not the trial court properly awarded damages and medical expenses to plaintiff for the injuries sustained by her daughter, a fourth grade student, when she fell off a merry-go-round on the school ground during school hours.

On March 2, 1982, Lisa Rollins, a nine-year-old fourth grade student, was riding a merry-go-round on the school grounds, during school hours, with several other girls during a physical education class. The merry-go-round was a used piece of playground equipment that had been disassembled and moved from another school. When it was reassembled on the school ground it was placed lower to the ground because of its intended use by small children. The class consisted of approximately 40 students. The girls in the class were playing on playground equipment and the boys in the class were playing basketball on a basketball court about fifteen feet away. Mrs. Linda Green, a substitute teacher, was supervising the class by walking back and forth between both groups when, at approximately 9:30 A.M., she observed that the merry-go-round was spinning too fast. The merry-go-round was propelled by the girls sitting on it and pushing it with their feet. Recognizing the danger, Mrs. Green told the girls, including Lisa, to slow down and get off. Just as she admonished Lisa and the other girls, she heard two boys begin arguing over a basketball and one of them yelled for Mrs. Green. Mrs. Green turned away from the merry-go-round and walked toward the boys leaving the girls still rapidly spinning on the merry-go-round.

Mrs. Green walked about twenty feet when she heard one of the girls yell that Lisa was hurt, so she returned to help Lisa. When she reached Lisa she asked what happened and Lisa told her that she fell off the merry-go-round and hurt her leg. Mrs. Green carried Lisa to the principal's office, where Dr. Gibson, the school principal, took charge of the situation.

The trial court found the School Board was negligent in not properly supervising the playground activities, that Lisa's injury was aggravated by the lack of immediate medical attention, and that Lisa was guilty of contributory negligence. Applying comparative negligence, . . . the trial court found Lisa to be fifty percent at fault and reduced the damage award for her injuries from $10,000.00 to $5,000.00.

. . . .

The defendants contend that the trial court erred in finding that the School Board was negligent in its failure to provide adequate supervision. On the day of the accident, Mrs. Green, a substitute teacher, was responsible for supervision of two physical education classes containing approximately 40 fourth grade students. The school's standard procedure was to combine two school classes for physical education, which allows one teacher to have a free period. Mrs. Green was not given specific instructions for class activities from the regular teacher, so she gave permission for the boys to play basketball and the girls to play on the playground equipment. The basketball court is approximately fifteen to twenty feet away from the playground equipment so Mrs. Green walked back and forth to supervise both groups. Mrs. Green noticed that Lisa and several other girls were going too fast on the merry-go-round, so she instructed them to slow down and get off. Just after Mrs. Green told the girls to slow down, Mrs. Green heard the boys arguing on the basketball court. Mrs. Green stated that she heard one of the boys yell, "Mrs. Green, he's got my ball." She turned away to walk over to the boys to see what was happening. Mrs. Green testified that she had walked about twenty feet in 30 to 60 seconds, when she heard one of the girls yell that Lisa was hurt. She then returned to the merry-go-round ground where she found Lisa lying next to the merry-go-round. Lisa testified that she fell on the inside of the merry-go-round but that one of the girls helped her up and moved her to the outside of the merry-go-round.

In the case of *Prier v. Horace Mann Ins. Co.*, 351 So. 2d 265 (La. App. 3rd Cir. 1977), *writs den.*, 352 So. 2d 1045 (La.1977), the standard of care imposed upon teachers concerning adequate supervision was explained by our court as follows:

> "Our jurisprudence is settled that a school board is not the insurer of the lives or safety of children. School teachers charged with the duty of superintending children in the school must exercise reasonable supervision over them, commensurate with the age of the children and the attendant circumstances. A greater degree of care must be exercised if the student is required to use or to come in contact with an inherently dangerous object, or to engage in an activity where it is reasonably foreseeable that an accident or injury may occur. The teacher is not liable in damages unless it is shown that he or she, by exercising the degree of supervision required by the circumstances, might have prevented the act which caused the damage, and did not do so. It also is essential to recovery that there be proof of negligence in failing to provide the required supervision and proof of a causal connection between that lack of supervision and the accident . . .". (Citations omitted.)

Defendant argues that the children in this class were adequately supervised as a matter of law as the Louisiana courts have held that a school board provided adequate supervision where only one teacher had the responsibility of supervising anywhere from 50 to 120 children. A review of these and similar cases indicates that the courts actually based their findings of adequate supervision on an examination of whether the supervision was reasonable in light of the age of the children involved and the circumstances surrounding the accident. . . .

Thus, in this case we must determine whether Mrs. Green's supervision of Lisa's physical education class was adequate in light of the particular circumstances involved at the time of the accident. In this analysis, we are guided by the well-established principle that a trial court's finding of negligence is a finding of fact that cannot be overturned unless the court's finding constitutes manifest error.

In the present case, the evidence shows that two regular classes were combined to allow one teacher a free period. Another teacher was available and could have been present to help supervise the class. Mrs. Green saw that the young girls were going too fast on the merry-go-round and obviously feared that someone might get hurt. This is evidenced by her telling the children to slow down and get off the merry-go-round. Instead of making sure the children heeded her warnings, she abandoned what she had already observed to be a perilous situation to deal with another situation that was not urgent or dangerous. Mrs. Green testified that immediately after she first warned the nine-year-old girls to slow down and get off the merry-go-round she heard the boys yelling on the basketball court. She testified that she heard a boy holler, "Mrs. Green, he's got my ball." She then turned away and walked about twenty feet to the basketball court to stop the boys from squabbling over a ball when she heard the girls yell that Lisa was hurt. She estimates that at least thirty seconds elapsed between the time she turned away from the merry-go-round she thought was going too fast and when she heard the girls yell that Lisa was hurt. Mrs. Green testified that she didn't know if the boys were actually fighting or just hollering at each other because she never reached the boys. However, the basketball court was only ten or fifteen feet away from where she was standing. When she heard the noise, she turned and walked about twenty feet toward the boys. Had the boys been actually fighting she would have been able to see them and had they been in danger she probably would not have casually walked over to see what the problem was. The facts of the case show that Mrs. Green abandoned what she had already determined to be a perilous situation to investigate an argument over a basketball.

. . . .

The rapid speed of the merry-go-round and Mrs. Green ordering these nine-year-old children off the merry-go-round, but without herself making sure the children stopped and got off, was an activity where it was reasonably foreseeable that an accident or injury could occur. In these circumstances Mrs. Green failed to exercise a greater degree of care by which she might have prevented the act which caused the injuries.

Under these facts, we cannot say that the trial court was manifestly erroneous in finding that the supervision was inadequate, especially in light of the fact that another teacher was available but not used to help supervise the class.

Contributory Negligence

A determination of contributory negligence is a factual question which can only be altered on appeal by a finding that the conclusions of the trial judge were clearly wrong. The trial judge found that Lisa was contributorily negligent in riding "on the inside of the merry-go-round and apparently trying to get off of the merry-go-round while the machine was in motion." He found her fifty percent at fault and reduced her recovery of damages accordingly. Lisa admitted at trial that she had been facing inward on the merry-go-round and that she broke her leg when she tried to obey the instructions of Mrs. Green and turn facing outward to get off the merry-go-round. Dr. Gibson testified that all the children were warned not to ride the merry-go-round facing inward and he believed that Lisa was aware of these warnings. Since this evidence is supportive of the trial judge's decision, we cannot find that the trial judge was clearly wrong in finding Lisa contributorily negligent and reducing the amount of damages for her injuries by fifty percent.

Post Problem Discussion

1. Both *Partin* and *Rollins* involve situations where a teacher told a student to stop doing something, the student continued the activity, and the student was injured. Why did the court find negligence occurred in *Rollins*, but not *Partin*?

2. As mentioned previously, a school or school employee is ordinarily not liable where the injury results from an unforeseen or unanticipated act by a student. Was Louie's act foreseeable?

3. The day prior to Louie's injury, does the school have any obligation to inform Louie's parents that Ms. Donovan caught him playing space monkey at school? Some

courts have found that schools have an obligation to inform parents when a student expresses a desire to commit suicide. *See, e.g., Eisel v. Board of Educ.*, 597 A.2d 447 (Md. 1991). Is the space monkey game in the suicide category? Would these same arguments apply to Louie, or is the obligation to report suicide distinguishable given the social policies regarding suicide prevention, and school efforts to prevent suicide?

4. As noted in *Rollins*, there are defenses to negligence that may apply to claims against public schools and school employees. These include contributory or comparative negligence and assumption of the risk. Some courts have held that a student may not recover in negligence when their own conduct was a direct cause of the incident. *See, e.g., Danna by Danna v. Sewanhaka Cent. High Sch. Dist.*, 242 A.D.2d 361 (N.Y. App. Div. 1997) (finding injured student who voluntarily entered into fight and struck the first blow precluded from recovering from school district for negligent supervision). Other courts have found that children under the age of fourteen are presumed incapable of negligence for their own behavior given their age, but the presumption can be overcome by evidence that "the child did not use the care which a child of its age, capacity, discretion, knowledge, and experience would ordinarily have exercised under the same or similar circumstances." *Weeks v. Barnard*, 143 S.E.2d 809, 810 (N.C. 1965).

Should Louie be barred from recovery, or have his recovery reduced, since his injuries were self-inflicted? Should he be denied recovery since he was warned by Ms. Donovan and would not have been injured if he had heeded the warning?

B. Injuries by Other Students

Another aspect of the duty to supervise and provide a safe educational environment is protecting students from harm from other students. These obligations can include addressing student fights, students who are harassed or bullied by other students, and even sexual assault or harassment. The legal standards here are the same as discussed in previous sections, but their application differs because the harm occurs from the act/failure to act of another student. As with the discussion in Part A and Problem 1, issues of foreseeability and causation are still often at the forefront of the analysis. Current attention to issues of face-to-face and online bullying are of particular concern and are considered in Problem 2.

Problem 2: Kara and the Bullies

Kara is fifteen and a sophomore at the Alana Falls High School. Three girls at the school have been sending Kara harassing emails and text messages. The emails and text messages call her various derogatory names and slurs, but none of them are racial. They also sent a photo to her cell phone that was doctored to make it look as if she is performing a sexual act on another female student at school. Kara is a lesbian, and the three girls are former friends of Kara's who started harassing her when they found out about her sexual orientation.

The emails, text messages, and photos are all sent after school hours. Kara's mother finds out about these incidents of cyberbullying and contacts the school principal. Soon thereafter, a teacher comes to the principal to report that two of her students were viewing the doctored photo on their cell phones in the school bathroom. The principal speaks to the girls who are harassing Kara and tells them that their actions are not appropriate and not acceptable in the Alana Falls school community. He asks them to stop immediately and warns them that if incidents occur at school, they will be disciplined. The principal did not feel that he had the authority under school policies to discipline the girls for their actions so far since they occurred off school grounds.

Shortly after the principal speaks to the girls, Kara finds a note in her locker that says, "We will get you!" Kara takes it to the principal who again speaks with the same girls, but they all deny writing the note, and the principal does not take any action against the students. The next day, Kara finds a note in her desk in social studies class that says, "Today is the day!" Kara takes that note to the principal who tells Kara that he will call the girls in and speak with them again later in the day. The next class period is physical education, and the three girls are in Kara's class. The principal is not available to speak to the girls before or during the class. After warming up, the class goes outside to play soccer. When the ball comes Kara's way, the three girls converge on Kara, knock her to the ground, fall on top of her, and start hitting her. The gym teacher pulls the three girls off Kara and sends them to the principal's office.

Kara suffers injuries including a broken jaw and broken ribs. Is the school liable for her injuries? Might your analysis be different if Kara, in despair over her treatment, and the school's inability to stop it, committed suicide?

Problem Materials

- ✓ *Busby v. Ticonderoga Central School District*, 258 A.D.2d 762 (N.Y. App. Div. 1999)
- ✓ *Frazer v. St. Tammany Parish School Board*, 774 So. 2d 1227 (La. Ct. App. 2000)

Busby v. Ticonderoga Central School District

258 A.D.2d 762 (N.Y. App. Div. 1999)

The court finds that the school is not liable to a student who is injured when another student punches him because the incident was not foreseeable.

On June 24, 1993, 14-year-old Jeremy Busby was "sucker-punched" in the head by a fellow student, third-party defendant Robert Fleury Jr., while boarding a school bus in front of a high school belonging to defendant Ticonderoga Central School District (hereinafter the District)....

This appeal relates solely to plaintiff's negligent supervision claim against the District. . . . The relevant facts are as follows. On June 24, 1993, the eighth-grade class of the District's middle school attended an orientation program at its high school. Accompanying and supervising these 90-100 students (which included Busby and Fleury) were four teachers and a guidance counselor from the middle school. When the orientation program was concluded, the students and teachers waited outside the high school for the arrival of school buses and dismissal. The students were seated in two sets of temporary bleachers that had been erected for high school graduation. The bleachers were located directly in front of the high school's main entrance, adjacent to the road. The four teachers and guidance counselor were in the immediate area, continuing to supervise the students. According to Busby's deposition testimony, while he was seated in the bleachers, Fleury approached him and said "I'm going to fight you," whereupon a male teacher grabbed Fleury and told him to sit down. Shortly thereafter, the buses arrived, and as Busby was boarding his bus he felt himself grabbed from behind and turned around. He was then punched by Fleury. Not included in his deposition testimony was another incident which Busby subsequently described in his affidavit in opposition to the District's summary judgment motion. While in the bleachers, a friend of Fleury's grabbed Busby's baseball cap and spit into it, and passed it around while others, including Fleury, also spit into it. Busby testified that prior to this incident, he had never had any problems with Fleury and in fact the two were friends. It is also uncontroverted that prior to June 24, 1993, neither boy had any serious disciplinary or behavioral problems at school, and both were considered good students.

We have consistently noted that "[w]here injuries are caused by the intentional acts of fellow students, imposition of liability upon the school under a theory of negligent supervision is justified when a plaintiff can show, usually by virtue of the school's prior knowledge or notice of the dangerous conduct which caused the injury, that the acts of the fellow student could reasonably have been anticipated." The basic premise upon which such liability is imposed is the foreseeability of harm based upon actual or constructive knowledge of a student's dangerous propensity or prior actions. An obvious corollary to this principle is the now familiar rule that, in the absence of any prior knowledge or forewarning, a school will not be held to insure against the consequences of sudden, impulsive, unanticipated acts of other students.

Our difficulty here is precisely with this critical element of foreseeability, as to which we are constrained to find plaintiff's submissions deficient. Assuming, as we must, that Fleury earlier stated to Busby "I'm going to fight you," prompting a teacher to direct Fleury away from Busby, we do not find that this statement, without more, was sufficient to cause the District to anticipate Fleury's eventual act of "sucker punching" Busby or to require it to take any added precautions to protect Busby from Fleury's sudden act, which came as a surprise even to Busby and the other student witnesses. Accordingly, the District's motion for summary judgment should have been granted.

Frazer v. St. Tammany Parish School Board

774 So. 2d 1227 (La. Ct. App. 2000)

The court finds a school board liable for a student's injuries by other students and apportions the damages amongst the defendants.

On September 17, 1993, Andrew Cundiff (Andy), a freshman at Northshore High School, was being transported on a school bus driven by Robert Cerise. During the trip home, Andy and his friend, Eric Fox, were harassed and threatened by other students from his school, specifically Josh Julian, Joe Julian, and Eric Costello. The threats originated from an incident earlier in the week when Andy defended another student, Rachel Main, who also had been harassed by Joe Julian on the bus.

Because Andy and Eric Fox feared the prospect of fighting with the Julian boys, they decided to get off the bus at the home of their friend, Carlos Gierlings. Andy thought getting off at that stop, as opposed to his own regular stop, was the safest solution, because Carlos' house was located close to the bus stop and Carlos' mother was home at that time of day. When the bus stopped near Carlos' house, Andy, Eric Fox, and Carlos got off the bus and were followed by another group of students consisting of Joe Julian, Josh Julian, Curtis Martin, James Embree, and Kevin Knatt. Two other students, Stephen Shockley and Eric Costello, who had left the bus at an earlier stop, followed the bus to the next stop in anticipation of a confrontation between the Julians and Andy Cundiff and Eric Fox.

After Andy got off the bus, he started walking towards Carlos Gierlings' house. After walking a few feet, Andy turned around and saw Josh Julian hit Eric Fox twice in the mouth. Andy noticed Joe Julian was also moving towards Eric Fox. In an attempt to break up what Andy perceived as an unfair fight, Andy ran back towards the group to intercept Joe Julian. As Andy approached the group, he grabbed Joe Julian by the collar to prevent him from getting closer to Eric Fox. However, Andy slipped, and he and Joe both fell to the ground. Once Andy was on the ground, he was kicked and beaten by Joe Julian, Josh Julian, and Eric Costello. By all accounts, Andy was in a defensive position as the three boys beat him.

....

It is well established that a school board, through its agents and teachers, is responsible for reasonable supervision over students. However, this duty to supervise does not make the board the insurer of the safety of the children. Furthermore, constant supervision of all students is not possible nor required for educators to discharge their duty to provide adequate supervision. Before liability can be imposed upon a school board, there must be proof of negligence in providing supervision and also proof of a causal connection between the lack of supervision and the accident. Further, the unreasonable risk of injury must be foreseeable, constructively or actually known, and preventable, if the requisite degree of supervision had been exercised. Said differently, educators are required to exercise only that supervision and discipline expected of a reasonably prudent person under the circumstances at hand. Obviously then, the failure to take every precaution against all foreseeable risk of injury does not necessarily constitute negligence. It is well established that the fact that each student is not personally supervised every moment of each school day does not constitute fault on the part of the school board or its employees.

The record reflects that a few days before the incident, Rachel Main's mother, Linda Hall, telephoned Northshore High School out of concern for her daughter and the events on her bus. Hall spoke to Gwen A. Hopper, one of the assistant principals at Northshore High School. Hall indicated she was concerned that her daughter, who had just moved from California to Slidell, was having problems adjusting to her new surroundings.

According to Hall, Rachel had complained that she was experiencing problems on the school bus with a group of boys who were teasing her every day. Hall testified that she told Hopper that her daughter had been teased, then threatened, and that a boy named "Andy," who had defended her, also had been threatened. Hall did not know the last names of any of the students, but indicated that the father of one of the boys involved owned a liquor store on Frontage Road in Slidell, and that maybe there was an "Eric" or "Andy" involved.

After the phone call, Hopper spoke with Rachel. According to Hopper, Rachel did not appear to be upset about anything said to her by other students nor did she seem to acknowledge any problems on the bus. . . . Stephen Shockley was summoned to the office of Dr. William Morgan, who was the school disciplinarian. Dr. Morgan testified that he spoke with Stephen, who claimed to know nothing about an impending fight between the students on the bus. After this meeting, no further attempt was made to locate the student Hall identified as "Andy" as being the target of a potential fight. Hopper testified that no further action could be taken because the school day had ended and it was time to leave. At that time the School Board did not prepare a list of students who would ride a particular bus, so Hopper had no information on who the student could be.

However, it was the policy of the School Board to take as many steps as possible to prevent a fight when they received information that one was likely to occur. Dr. Morgan testified that if there was going to be a problem on the bus, the procedure was to notify the bus driver. However, in this case Dr. Morgan indicated he was not told by Hopper that the problems between the students were taking place on the bus. As a result, the bus driver, Robert Cerise, was never contacted about the possibility of a fight on his bus.

Cerise testified that had he been informed of the likelihood of a fight, he would have tried to be more aware of what the students were doing on the bus that afternoon. There was testimony from several witnesses that throughout the ride home, Josh Julian, Joe Julian, and Eric Costello made loud threats directed toward Andy Cundiff and Eric Fox, who were seated in the back of the bus. Carlos Gierlings testified that he thought the threats were loud enough for everyone on the bus to hear, since the group making the threats was seated in the middle of the bus and Andy and his friends were in the back of the bus. Andy Cundiff testified that objects were thrown at him and his friends from the group seated half a bus-length away. Despite the testimony of several witnesses who indicated everyone on the bus knew there was going to be a fight, Cerise testified he did not hear any threats or get any indication there was a problem on his bus that afternoon.

The record also indicates that there were several unauthorized students riding on the bus that afternoon. The students did not normally ride this particular bus and did not have written permission in accordance with School Board policy to ride that particular bus on that afternoon. These students boarded the bus to observe the expected confrontation between the Julians and Andy Cundiff. Although Cerise testified he made an attempt to know his riders by eyesight, he failed to notice the presence of the increased number of riders.

According to Carlos Gierlings, everyone on the bus knew there was going to be a fight. He testified that three people regularly got off the bus at his stop, but on that afternoon, as many as eight boys got off the bus. Although Cerise testified that students who got off at a stop other than their regular stop would "raise a flag" in his mind that there was a problem, he failed to notice the increased number of students who left the bus at the stop near Carlos Gierlings' house.

Based on our review of the record, we find the School Board, through its employees, did not follow its own policies of preventing a fight where it had advance notice that there was a problem. Had Cerise been informed by the School Board employees of the potential problem between students on his bus, he could have paid better attention to his riders and prevented unauthorized riders from boarding his bus. At the very least, the absence of students expecting a confrontation could have diminished the possibility of a fight. Further, had Cerise noticed the large group of boys leaving the bus where normally only three left, he could have taken steps to prevent the fight. Significantly, there was substantial testimony that the confrontation broke out not far from the bus and within view of Cerise, who, instead of taking preventative measures, drove away.

The testimony in the record indicates that Joe Julian, Josh Julian, Eric Costello, and Stephen Shockley were all older and physically bigger than Andy. Cerise should have noticed the threats were directed at two smaller students by students who were larger and accompanied by several friends. Such a scenario was more than likely to result in injury to the smaller, outnumbered students, given the threats of physical confrontation that were made during the bus ride. Accordingly, we find the School Board to be 20% at fault in causing the injuries sustained by Andy Cundiff.

....

Based on the foregoing reasons, the judgment of the trial court assessing 100% fault to the School Board is vacated and fault is assessed as follows: 20% to School Board, 25% to Eric Costello, 25% to Joe Julian, 25% to Josh Julian, and 5% to Andy Cundiff.

Post Problem Discussion

1. As mentioned in previous sections, and discussed in detail in Section 6.04, defenses and immunities play a big role in common law claims against schools and school districts. For example, some states provide that schools are immune from such claims altogether, or only allow such claims if there is proof that the school or school personnel were "grossly negligent," or reckless. *See, e.g., B.M.H. v. School Bd.*, 833 F. Supp. 560 (E.D. Va. 1993). Why do you suppose some states take this approach? Would your answer to the school's liability in this problem change if Kara had to establish gross negligence or recklessness as opposed to negligence?

2. In *Frazer*, one of the important facts to the court was that the school did not follow its own policy on fighting. In Kara's case, the principal did not feel that he had the authority under school policies to discipline the girls. Does that make a difference in terms of the school's liability for Kara's injuries?

3. In *Frazer*, the court apportioned the liability between the school and the students who directly caused the injuries. Do you agree with the apportionment? If you were a judge, how would you apportion the liability in Kara's case and why?

§ 6.03 Intentional Torts

Intentional torts also arise in the public school setting. These include the torts of assault, battery, defamation, and intentional infliction of emotional distress. Claims for assault and battery often revolve around school officials coming into contact with students when punishing them (corporal punishment), or when physically restraining them to protect the student or others from harm. As with negligence, there are a number of defenses that may apply to claims of intentional torts. The following problem explores these issues.

Problem 3: "Get Me My Paddle"

Steven is fifteen and in the ninth grade at Mountain Ridge High School. He and two of his friends decide to skip English class so that they can have an extended off-campus lunch period. The school permits students to go off-campus for lunch. Steven and his friends go to an older friend's car in the school parking lot and leave campus. Upon returning to school, Steven and his friends are met by Assistant Principal Jefferson in the parking lot. Steven was smoking a cigarette in the car and forgot to put it out before coming onto campus. Smoking is prohibited on campus. The assistant principal sees Steven smoking and tells Steven to put out the cigarette, and to hand over any other cigarettes he has in his possession.

Steven says that he does not have any other cigarettes. Not believing this, the assistant principal tells Steven to put his hands out on the car so that he can be searched. The search reveals a lighter, but no cigarettes. Steven, unhappy about being searched, starts making rude and derogatory remarks to the assistant principal about the search being unsuccessful. Other students pass by in the parking lot and hear the remarks.

Assistant Principal Jefferson radios another assistant principal and tells him to "get me my paddle." He tells Steven to remain still, with his hands on the car.

About five minutes later, the other assistant principal arrives with the paddle. Assistant Principal Jefferson tells the other students who are watching that "this is what happens when you break school rules and are disrespectful to school authority!" He then paddles Steven four times. In addition, Steven and the other students who skipped school with Steven, receive three days of in-school suspension. Notice of the incident is sent to Steven's parents.

School policies permit corporal punishment in accordance with the policy in the problem materials.

Steven suffers severe bruises and welts from the paddling and brings claims for assault and battery. Will his claims be successful? Why or why not?

Problem Materials

✓ Mountain Ridge Corporal Punishment Policy

✓ *Maddox v. Boutwell*, 336 S.E.2d 599 (Ga. Ct. App. 1985)

✓ *Hinson v. Holt*, 776 So. 2d 804 (Ala. Civ. App. 1998)

Mountain Ridge Corporal Punishment Policy

Subject to the terms of this policy, corporal punishment is authorized as a disciplinary tool at Mountain Ridge High School under the following terms.

1. Corporal punishment is defined as punishment that inflicts pain. Only use of a wooden paddle is authorized to administer corporal punishment. It may not have any holes in it. Swats are to be given on the buttocks area only. No other form of inflicting pain (slap with ruler, holding book overhead) will be allowed.
2. The school principal, or the principal's designee, only may administer corporal punishment. Efforts shall be made in grades 5 and up for corporal punishment to be administered by a member of the same sex as the child receiving the punishment.
3. A child may receive no more than four swats for one offense. A child may not receive more than four swats per day.
4. Any school age child may receive corporal punishment.
5. Corporal punishment will be administered in a private location such as the principal's office.
6. An adult staff member will witness the punishment.
7. Corporal punishment shall not be administered if it requires holding a student or struggling with a student. If a child refuses to take swats, the child will be given an appropriate 1, 2, or 3-day out-of-school suspension.

8. Corporal punishment should be administered to Special Education students only if permitted by the child's I.E.P. and pursuant to the terms of the I.E.P.
9. Notice in writing will be sent home to the parent when corporal punishment has been given. The principal may elect to notify the parents at the time the corporal punishment is to be given.
10. Corporal punishment should be used only after other approaches for correcting behavior have been tried unless the offense is serious enough to justify its use on a first offense.

Maddox v. Boutwell

336 S.E.2d 599 (Ga. Ct. App. 1985)

The court discusses some standards for corporal punishment, along with state law immunities to common law claims, and finds the school is not liable under state law.

. . . .

Corporal punishment in Georgia schools is provided for by OCGA §§ 20-2-730 et seq. In § 20-2-731, it is provided that school boards may authorize the administration of corporal punishment by the adoption of written policies and that such authority is subject to certain limitations, the first of which is "[t]he corporal punishment shall not be excessive or unduly severe." . . . Appellant argued in the trial court and on appeal that Boutwell violated that guideline by administering punishment which was excessive and unduly severe and in bad faith, thereby forfeiting the immunity from civil liability granted by OCGA § 20-2-732. Appellant has also asserted that the violation of that guideline was willful, wanton, and outside the scope of Boutwell's authority, thereby forfeiting the protection of governmental immunity.

The key issue in this case, then, is whether the punishment administered to Stephen was in bad faith and was excessive and unduly severe. If so, the punishment would be outside the established guidelines and, therefore, outside the scope of Boutwell's authority, rendering him liable. If not, both appellees would be protected by both types of immunity.

The essential facts of this case are undisputed. Stephen and another student were sent to Boutwell's office because of disruptive behavior in the classroom. Boutwell gave the students a choice between suspension and a paddling. Both chose paddling and were given four "licks" each with a wooden paddle 24 inches long, 5 inches wide, and 1/4 to 1/2 inch thick.

In an affidavit in opposition to appellees' motion for summary judgment, Stephen swore that the paddling was painful. Both his parents swore that he received "severe bruises" to his buttocks and one thigh.

In support of their motions for summary judgment, appellees introduced the affidavits of both appellees, of the assistant principal who witnessed the punishment, of Stephen's classroom teacher, and of an assistant school superintendent who observed Stephen on the Monday following the punishment. Boutwell's affidavit was discounted by the trial court because his statement that the punishment was not excessive or unduly severe amounted to a self-serving declaration. However, the trial court concluded that the assistant principal's affidavit, in which she averred that the punishment was administered in compliance with applicable guidelines and was not excessive or unduly severe; the assistant superintendent's affidavit, in which he stated that he saw Stephen playing on the next Monday without any outward manifestations of injury or pain; and the classroom teacher's affidavit, in which she swore that both boys returned to the classroom after the punishment without exhibiting any pain, having any problem sitting down, or voicing any complaint about pain, pierced the allegations in appellant's complaint regarding the excessiveness or undue severity of the punishment.

....

We find the trial court to be correct in its conclusion that the affidavits submitted by appellant in opposition to summary judgment did not show the existence of a question of fact. All they showed was that the paddling was painful to Stephen and produced bruises. As the trial court noted, it is to be anticipated that corporal punishment will produce pain and the potential for bruising. Nothing in those affidavits counters the appellees' showing that Stephen experienced no more than the short-term discomfort to be expected from the administration of corporal punishment. We agree, therefore, with the trial court that the evidence in this case demands the conclusion as a matter of law that the punishment administered to Stephen was neither excessive nor unduly severe. Compare *Chrysinger v. Decatur*, 3 Ohio App.3d 286, 445 N.E.2d 260 (1982), where it was held that a mother's testimony that her son's buttocks were badly bruised and blistered, and the student's testimony that he received three licks which turned his skin red, then green, and prevented him from lying on his back for a week, presented a jury question regarding the reasonableness of the punishment.

As to the alleged bad faith on the part of appellee Boutwell in the decision to administer corporal punishment, the trial court noted that Boutwell followed correct procedures in making that decision. The affidavits submitted by appellees set forth the factual setting for the punishment, establishing that the incident for which Stephen was punished was disruption of the classroom caused by his exhibition of a drawing depicting sexual intercourse; that Stephen's mother had recently given prior approval for the use of corporal punishment; and that Stephen and the other boy involved were given the choice of alternative punishment. That evidence pierced the allegations of the complaint regarding bad faith administration of corporal punishment. In opposition, appellant offered only conclusory statements, without a factual predicate, that the punishment was unwarranted. We agree with the trial court's conclusion that Boutwell was entitled to judgment on that issue as well.

....

Hinson v. Holt

776 So. 2d 804 (Ala. Civ. App. 1998)

The court upholds a trial court finding of liability for assault and battery from corporal punishment and rejects claims of immunity because the teacher punished the student with malice.

....

Southside Middle School, where Dustin attended eighth-grade classes in the 1995–96 school term, is a part of the Tallassee city school system. In 1992, the Tallassee City Board of Education adopted the following policy concerning corporal punishment of its students:

> "Reasonable corporal punishment may be administered after consultation with the principal, and only in the presence of another professional staff member. Reasonable corporal punishment shall be administered only as a last resort in the most unusual circumstances and after reasonable corrective measures have been used without success.
>
> "A staff member may, however, use reasonable force against a pupil without advance notice to the principal when it is essential for self-defense, the preservation of order, or for the protection of other persons or the property of the Board."

In addition to this policy, the Tallassee City Board of Education's Code of Conduct, applicable during the 1995–96 school year, placed various student acts into four classes of offenses for disciplinary purposes. Class I offenses included "Use of profane or obscene language not directed toward another person"; Class II offenses included "Threats" and "Use of profane or obscene language or gestures." For Class I offenses, the Code of Conduct listed the following "minimum consequences": for a first offense, a teacher conference with student; for a second offense, a parental contact by the teacher; and for a third offense, office referral, parental contact and student counseling, as well as possible corporal punishment. "Minimum consequences" for Class II offenses included an office referral, a parental conference, a suspension from school, or an in-school suspension of one to three days.

On Friday, September 1, 1995, the fifth day of the 1995–96 school term at Southside Middle School, 13-year-old Dustin reported to his first period eighth-grade physical education class, which was under the direction of a substitute teacher that day. After playing football outdoors during the period, the boys' physical education class returned to the gymnasium, along with the girls' class (which was under Hinson's direction), to change clothes for their next instructional period. As the students walked towards the gym, one student behind Dustin said to another "I will kick your ass." Immediately after that remark was made, Dustin turned around and saw the students behind him laughing. When another student asked Dustin what had been said, Dustin repeated the remark he had overheard; he did not do so in a threatening manner.

Hinson turned around as Dustin uttered the remark, and upon hearing it directed him to "see her at the top of the hill." She then instructed Dustin to dress and to come to a stage inside the gymnasium. Dustin dressed and reported to the stage, and Hinson sent for Coach Bruce Wayne Dean; she informed Coach Dean that she was inflicting corporal punishment on Dustin because he had used profanity. Hinson did not send for, or otherwise consult, the principal of Southside, Ron McDaniel. Moreover, Dustin's disciplinary records show that he had committed no offenses under the Code of Conduct before September 1, 1995.

When Dustin reported to the stage, Hinson directed him to hold onto the top of a chair. Hinson then picked up a wooden paddle that contained holes on that portion of the paddle designed to make contact with a punishee's buttocks, and struck Dustin three times. Three is considered by Tallassee school personnel to be the normal maximum number of blows a student should receive. The force of the third blow was sufficiently strong to cause the chair Dustin was grasping to slide several inches across the stage.

After receiving Hinson's blows, Dustin was in such pain that he was unable to sit through his remaining classes. On the next day, a Saturday, Dustin lay on his stomach, and there is testimony that he could not engage in normal activities. When Dustin's aunt examined his buttocks, she was so shocked by the deep, eggplant-sized black bruises Dustin had received that she and Dustin drove to the home of her employer, a circuit judge from an adjacent county, who examined the bruises with his wife and contacted McDaniel. Dustin was then taken to Tallassee Community Hospital's emergency room for medical treatment, and Dustin's aunt completed a child-abuse incident report. Even on the next school day, which was four days after Hinson's punishment of Dustin, Dustin was still in pain, and his father wrote a note to his teachers asking that they excuse him from being seated in class.

. . . .

At common law, "any touching by one person of the person of another in rudeness or in anger is an assault and battery." However, the Alabama Supreme Court has recognized a qualified privilege for an educator's discipline of a student. In *Suits v. Glover*, 260 Ala. 449, 71 So. 2d 49 (1954), the court affirmed a judgment on a jury verdict in favor of a schoolmaster on his pupil's assault-and-battery claims because evidence in that case justified such a verdict. The *Suits* court noted the following applicable principles of law:

> A schoolmaster is regarded as standing *in loco parentis* and has the authority to administer moderate correction to pupils under his care. To be guilty of an assault and battery, the teacher must not only inflict on the child immoderate chastisement, but he must do so with legal malice or wicked motives or he must inflict some permanent injury. In determining the reasonableness of the punishment or the extent of malice, proper matters for consideration are the instrument used and the nature of the offense

> committed by the child, the age and physical condition of the child, and the other attendant circumstances.

. . . .

Neither are we persuaded that Hinson is immune from liability for assault and battery under the doctrine of discretionary-function immunity applicable to state employees, although that doctrine has been held to apply to employees of city boards of education. Such immunity "protects a State agent from liability for negligence or wantonness while performing discretionary functions." There was considerable dispute concerning Hinson's discretion, under the policy of the Tallassee City Board of Education and the Code of Conduct, to inflict corporal punishment upon Dustin for a single use of the word "ass."

More importantly, however, even if Hinson acted within her discretion in deciding to use a paddle to punish Dustin, the *manner* of her punishment is not necessarily immunized, because "a state officer or employee is not protected under the doctrine of discretionary function immunity if he acts willfully, *maliciously*, fraudulently, or in bad faith." Thus, a showing of legal malice on the part of an educator with respect to the infliction of corporal punishment will not only defeat the privilege enunciated in *Suits*—it will also overcome any substantive immunity arising from the performance of a discretionary function.

Legal malice may be defined as "the intentional doing of a wrongful act without just cause or excuse, either with an intent to injure the other party or under such circumstances that the law will imply an evil intent." Moreover, malice is generally a fact issue; "the existence of malice being a fact which in the nature of things is incapable of positive, direct proof, it must of necessity be rested on inferences and deductions from facts" that can be presented to the trier of fact.

There was sufficient evidence from which the trial court could have concluded that Hinson acted maliciously in corporally punishing Dustin. First, according to the policy of the Tallassee City Board of Education, corporal punishment is not to be administered except "as a *last resort* in the *most unusual circumstances* and after *reasonable corrective measures have been used without success*" (emphasis added). In this case, Dustin was immediately subjected to the maximum corporal punishment for uttering the word "ass" on the fifth day of school. There is no evidence that Dustin had a previous record of such offenses; further, Hinson made no attempt to consult with the principal before inflicting the punishment, and Hinson made no other attempt to correct Dustin before resorting to corporal punishment. Thus, the trial court could have concluded from the evidence that Hinson's infliction of corporal punishment was in direct contravention of the policies of the Tallassee City Board of Education.

Also, in determining the reasonableness of the punishment and the extent of malice, the trier of fact may consider the nature of the offense committed by the student, the age and physical condition of the student, and other attendant circumstances. Here, the evidence reveals that a physical education instructor inflicted three blows to the buttocks of a 13-year-old for using the word "ass," a word that amounts to, at most, a mildly profane reference to the human hindquarters. Taken together, the blows Hinson inflicted on September 1, 1995, were so severe that Dustin developed large, shocking bruises on his buttocks and was unable to sit down in class for the remainder of that school day or the next school day, four days later. In particular, the third of the blows inflicted by Hinson was so severe that the chair Dustin was holding was sent several inches across the stage.

Under the applicable standard of review, we must view this evidence, and the evidence of the Tallassee City Board of Education's policy of reserving the use of corporal punishment as a last resort under unusual circumstances, in a light most favorable to Holt. Applying this principle, we conclude that the evidence in this case was sufficient to support the trial court's finding that Hinson acted with legal malice in punishing Dustin. . . .

. . . .

Based upon the foregoing facts and authorities, the trial court's judgment in favor of Holt is affirmed.

Post Problem Discussion

1. A number of states have statutes that address corporal punishment. Some prohibit it, while others (like the states involved in the problem cases) allow it in certain situations. Do your state laws address corporal punishment? If so, what do you think of how it is addressed?

2. What are the pros and cons of allowing corporal punishment in schools? What measures can schools implementing corporal punishment take to reduce or minimize their liability?

3. In *Hinson*, the court noted that under Alabama law, school officials have some qualified privilege to discipline and focused on whether the conduct at issue was malicious. Why do you think the conduct must rise to that level to be actionable? Why isn't the school official (or the school itself) liable if the student is injured, and the school official caused the injury, even if he or she did not act maliciously?

4. Would the Paul Coverdale Act noted in Section 6.04 below provide a defense for Assistant Principal Jefferson in our problem? Why or why not?

Activity 1: Find Your State Laws on Restraints

Another area where intentional torts can arise is when school staff physically restrain students. Sometimes unplanned restraints occur at school when a student suddenly tries to harm another student, such as a teacher breaking up a fight. Other times, restraints may occur as part of an Individual Education Program/Plan ("IEP"), or a behavior plan for a student who is prone to harm themselves or others.

The latter type of restraints is generally subject to various state laws that require staff training, limit the types of restraints that can be used, and limit the circumstances under which restraints can be used. Local schools may also have policies regarding restraints. The student's behavior plan will also include the specifics about the use of restraints for the particular student.

Step One—Research your state statutes and regulations for requirements regarding the use of physical restraints. Your state department of education may have also issued informal guidance on the use of restraints.

Step Two—Review local school policies about physical restraints online.

Step Three—Answer the following:

1. When are physical restraints allowed, and when are they not allowed, under state law and school policies?
2. Do the state laws, and/or school policies, you reviewed impose any training or certification requirements for staff who restrain students? If so, what are they? If not, what do you think should be required?
3. Have there been any reported problems with student injuries, or staff using restraints inappropriately, in your state?
4. Do you think that your state laws and school policies should be changed in any way? Why or why not?

§ 6.04 Defenses

As noted in prior sections, there are a variety of defenses that can apply to tort claims. These can include contributory negligence, assumption of the risk, justification, self-defense, and immunity. Some form of immunity is often involved with common law tort claims against schools and school employees. In some states, public schools are completely immune from common law claims by students for injuries, because the school is considered an agent of the state under sovereign immunity principles. Claims may still be permitted against school employees in certain circumstances. *B.M.H.*, 833 F. Supp. at 573. Other states have abrogated immunity in full, or in part, by statute or common law. For example, some maintain immunity for official, discretionary, or governmental acts, but not for ministerial or proprietary ones. *See, e.g., Doe v. Petersen*, 903 A.2d 191, 193 (Conn. 2006); Restatement (Second) of Torts § 895C, Comment E (1979). Other states permit claims only for willful and wanton conduct, recklessness, or gross negligence. *See, e.g., Frederick v. Vinton County Bd. of Educ.*, 2004 Ohio 550 (Ohio Ct. App. 2004).

Some states have state statutes that permit claims against municipalities (including schools) only if the terms and conditions of the statute are met. These state laws are similar to the Federal Tort Claims Act at the federal level, and they often limit the kinds of claims that can be brought, and the damages that are available, for injuries.[2]

2. *See* Lawrence Rosenthal, A *Theory of Governmental Damages Liability: Torts, Constitutional Torts, and Takings*, 9 U. Pa. J. Const. L. 797 (2007).

In terms of defenses, many states have "justification" statutes that permit school employees to use reasonable force when necessary to discipline students, or to maintain a safe educational environment.[3] Federal law includes a type of justification defense in the Paul D. Coverdell Teacher Protection Act of 2001, which applies to states that accept funds under the Every Student Succeeds Act ("ESSA"). 20 U.S.C. §§ 7941-7948. The law provides in relevant part:

> (a) Liability protection for teachers
>
> Except as provided in subsection (b), no teacher in a school shall be liable for harm caused by an act or omission of the teacher on behalf of the school if—
>
> (1) the teacher was acting within the scope of the teacher's employment or responsibilities to a school or governmental entity;
>
> (2) the actions of the teacher were carried out in conformity with Federal, State, and local laws (including rules and regulations) in furtherance of efforts to control, discipline, expel, or suspend a student or maintain order or control in the classroom or school;
>
> (3) if appropriate or required, the teacher was properly licensed, certified, or authorized by the appropriate authorities for the activities or practice involved in the State in which the harm occurred, where the activities were or practice was undertaken within the scope of the teacher's responsibilities;
>
> (4) the harm was not caused by willful or criminal misconduct, gross negligence, reckless misconduct, or a conscious, flagrant indifference to the rights or safety of the individual harmed by the teacher.

20 U.S.C. § 7946. The following activity gives you a chance to explore the defenses and immunities available in your state.

Activity 2: Find Your State Defenses and Immunities

Step One—Research your state statutes for ones that provide immunity or defenses to municipalities, public schools, or public school employees, and for those that may authorize claims against municipalities, public schools, or public school employees (e.g., State Tort Claims Acts).

Step Two—Research your state court cases for cases that interpret the statutes you found in Step One, and for cases applying common law immunity or defenses to schools and school employees (meaning immunities or defenses that do not come from the statutes you found in Step One).

Step Three—Answer the following:

1. If your state has statutes that provide immunity, what does the immunity cover? As noted, some states maintain immunity for official,

---

3. *See, e.g.*, Donald H. Henderson, et al., *The Use of Force by Public School Teachers as a Defense Against Threatened Physical Harm*, 54 Ed. Law Rep. 773 (1989).

discretionary, or governmental acts, but not for ministerial or proprietary ones. Some allow claims only for willful and wanton conduct. Some find schools or school districts completely immune, but allow claims against school employees. What do your state statutes say in this regard?

2. Does your state have a justification statute? If so, what types of actions does it permit? How does it compare to the federal provision in the Paul D. Coverdell Teacher Protection Act of 2001?
3. If your state has a tort claims act (or any statute authorizing claims against schools) what does it cover? Does it limit the types of claims that can be brought against schools? Does it limit the amount of damages that can be recovered? Does it include any special requirements? Does it include claims against school officials, or just schools and school districts?
4. Have your state courts interpreted the requirements of the statutes you found? If so, what were the results of the cases, and how do they affect public school and public school employee liability?
5. Have your state courts established or discussed any common law immunities or defenses for public schools or public school employees? If so, what do the immunities or defenses cover? How do the common law immunities or defenses affect the claims that can be brought against public schools or public school employees?

§ 6.05 State Statutory Liability

Another area of liability for public schools with respect to students arises from state statutes. In addition to the State Tort Claims Act statutes discussed in Section 6.04 that permit certain types of claims to be brought against a school, states also create laws that apply to public schools and require schools to take certain actions, or prohibit them from taking certain actions. Violating these laws can lead to some form of liability for the school or for school employees. One such mandatory obligation is the duty imposed by statutes in some states to report knowledge of child abuse or "reasonable cause to suspect that a child has been or is likely to be abused or neglected." 22 M.R.S.A. § 4011-A. Under Maine statute, for example, teachers, guidance counselors, and school officials have such a duty to report. 22 M.R.S.A. § 4011-A(11)-(13). When they act in good faith, they are also granted immunity "from any criminal or civil liability for the act of reporting or participating in the investigation or proceeding." 22 M.R.S.A. § 4012.

Enforcement and remedies under state statutes vary and are sometimes uncertain. Some laws provide for private rights of action that allow students or parents to enforce the law in court. Others are only enforced by the state department of education, or do not have any express enforcement mechanisms.

For example, one area of increasing statutory liability for schools is in the area of bullying. Almost every state has an anti-bullying statute of some kind, over half include cyberbullying, and less than a third specifically include off-campus conduct.[4] In 2011, the U.S. Department of Education released a report analyzing state statutes and model policies for consistency with factors the Department considered valuable and found wide variation in coverage.[5] Of particular note for this chapter is the report's observation that many state statutes do not specifically address victim remedies other than to provide that preexisting remedies are not curtailed.

In some situations, actions that are considered "bullying" may also be considered "harassment" under other state and federal laws, which can lead to other types of claims against the school. The United States Department of Education has also issued a variety of guidance documents and training modules regarding bullying to assist states and schools in addressing the issue.[6] There are also some constitutional limitations on the scope of anti-bullying statutes. For example, in New York, a state statute that prohibited cyberbullying was found unconstitutional under the First Amendment. The law made cyberbullying a crime (as opposed to just prohibiting it and subjecting it to discipline at school). The defendant was a 16-year-old student who posted sexual information about classmates on Facebook. The court applied general First Amendment standards (as opposed to the school specific standards in Chapter 9), and found the statute overbroad and vague. *See People v. Marquan M.*, 24 N.Y.3d 1, 994 N.Y.S.2d 554 (2014).

The following Activity lets you explore these issues in your state.

Activity 3: Find Your State Anti-Bullying Statute

Step One—Research your state statutes and state education regulations. Do they contain any anti-bullying requirements? If so, what are they? Do they address cyberbullying? Do they specifically address off-campus versus on-campus considerations?

Step Two—Pick a local public school from your state that has its policies online. Does it have an anti-bullying policy? Is it consistent with the state law identified in Step One? What does it prohibit and require in terms of bullying, and the school's response to allegations of bullying? Does it address cyberbullying?

Step Three—Research your state court decisions for any that involve bullying or harassment at school, and any that involve the anti-bullying statutes

4. *See* Bully Police, U.S.A., www.bullypolice.org (last visited March 18, 2015).

5. U.S. Dept. of Educ., *Analysis of State Bullying Laws and Policies*, http://www2.ed.gov/rschstat/eval/bullying/state-bullying-laws/state-bullying-laws.pdf (last visited March 15, 2019).

6. See for example, October 21, 2014 Guidance Document on Bullying and Students with Disabilities, http://www2.ed.gov/about/offices/list/ocr/letters/colleague-bullying-201410.pdf (last visited March 20, 2015); September 28, 2012 Guidance Document noting training modules to help classroom teachers combat bullying, http://www.ed.gov/news/press-releases/us-department-education-provides-guidance-help-classroom-teachers-combat-bullying (last accessed March 20, 2015).

and policies you found in Steps One and Two. Are there any decisions like the *Marquan M.* case in your state?

Step Four—Answer the following:

1. How does your state statute and/or local school district policy define bullying? Does it include cyberbullying?
2. What does your state statute and/or local school district policy require schools to do to address bullying? Are there any policy development and/or staff training requirements?
3. What enforcement mechanisms are offered by your state statute and/or local school district policy? Are there any remedies provided to the victim of the bullying? Are schools required to take disciplinary action against students that are found to have bullied other students? Are there any criminal penalties for violating the statute?
4. Do you think that any changes should be made to the state statutes and local school policies you found? Why or why not?

§ 6.06 Federal Statutory Liability

A. Section 1983 Claims

Section 1983 refers to 42 U.S.C. § 1983, a federal statute designed to provide a method for redress of violations of federal law by state actors. *Mitchum v. Foster*, 407 U.S. 225, 238–40 (1972). To establish a § 1983 violation, a plaintiff must show: 1) that an act or omission deprived the plaintiff of a federal right secured by the Constitution or laws of the United States; and 2) that the act or omission was done by a person acting under color of law. *Parratt v. Taylor*, 451 U.S. 527, 535 (1981). Section 1983 does not provide any rights itself. It is merely a vehicle used to bring claims for violations of federal rights established by other federal statutes, or by the United States Constitution. Section 1983 provides monetary and equitable relief for violations of these federal rights, along with attorneys' fees for prevailing plaintiffs.

In a number of foundational cases, the United States Supreme Court established that local governments, including schools and school boards, are persons or state actors under § 1983 along with school officials and school board members. *Monell v. Department of Soc. Services*, 436 U.S. 658 (1978); *Wood v. Strickland*, 420 U.S. 308 (1975). As a result, schools and school officials can be liable for violations of federal law under § 1983 when they are acting under the color of state law. At the same time, the Supreme Court has acknowledged that § 1983 provides certain immunities from liability under the law. For example, school officials can receive qualified immunity from damages under § 1983 claims when their "conduct does not violate clearly established statutory or constitutional rights of which a reasonable person would have known." *Harlow v. Fitzgerald*, 457 U.S. 800, 818 (1982).

Section 1983 claims are often used as vehicles for enforcing federal statutory and constitutional rights against public schools. Claims can arise in a variety of situations including harassment and discrimination, due process, equal protection, and freedom of speech. Section 1983 claims provide some interesting comparisons to the state law tort claims discussed in previous sections. For example, unlike state common law, where courts generally recognize that schools and school officials have a duty to supervise and protect students from harm, most courts have found that such a right does not exist under federal law. Similarly, while state courts have established standards for corporal punishment under state law, some courts have ruled that students do not have the right to bring § 1983 claims alleging violations of substantive due process for corporal punishment (a topic covered in more detail in Chapter 8 Discipline). The following problem explores some of these issues.

Problem 4: Kara's Claims Under Federal Law

Review the fact pattern in Problem 2 in this Chapter. Assume that Kara brings § 1983 claims against the school and school principal alleging that their failure to act violated her substantive due process and equal protection rights under the United States Constitution. The school and principal move to dismiss the claims. You are a judge in a federal circuit that has not yet addressed the subject of liability for peer harassment under § 1983. Review the problem materials and decide which approach you will follow regarding Kara's federal claims and whether or not you will grant the motion to dismiss.

Problem Materials

✓ *Doe v. Covington County Sch. Dist.*, 675 F.3d 849 (5th Cir. 2012)

✓ *Nabozny v. Podlesny*, 92 F.3d 446 (7th Cir. 1996)

Doe v. Covington County School District

675 F.3d 849 (5th Cir. 2012)

The Fifth Circuit Court of Appeals sitting en banc finds that state school compulsory education laws do not create a special relationship between public schools and students under § 1983.

King, Circuit Judge, joined by Edith H. Jones, Chief Judge, E. Grady Jolly, W. Eugene Davis, Jerry E. Smith, Emilio M. Garza, Benavides, Carl E. Stewart, Edith Brown Clement, Prado, Owen, Jennifer Walker Elrod, Leslie H. Southwick, Haynes and Graves, Circuit Judges:

For the third time, the en banc court is called upon to decide whether a public school student has stated a constitutional claim against her school for its failure to protect her from harm inflicted by a private actor. Relying on our prior en banc opinions, the district court found that she had failed to state a claim and dismissed her complaint. A panel of this court reversed in part, concluding that the student had a special relationship with her school under *DeShaney v. Winnebago County Department of Social Services*, 489 U.S. 189 (1989), and that the school was therefore constitutionally obligated to protect her from acts of private violence. The panel nevertheless granted qualified immunity to those defendants sued in their individual capacities. We granted rehearing en banc, thereby vacating the panel opinion. We now hold that the student did not have a *DeShaney* special relationship with her school, and her school therefore had no constitutional duty to protect her from harm inflicted by a private actor. We also hold that the student has failed to state a claim under the state-created danger theory or under a municipal liability theory. We therefore affirm the judgment of the district court.

I. Factual and Procedural Background

During the 2007–2008 school year, Jane Doe ("Jane") attended an elementary school in Covington County, Mississippi. She was nine years old at the time. At some point during the school year, Jane's guardians filled out a "Permission to Check–Out Form," on which they listed the names of the individuals with exclusive permission to "check out" Jane from school during the school day. On six separate occasions between September 2007 and January 2008, school employees allowed a man named Tommy Keyes ("Keyes"), who allegedly bore no relation to Jane and was not listed on her check-out form, to take Jane from school. On these occasions, Keyes took Jane from school without the knowledge or consent of her parents or guardians, sexually molested her, and subsequently returned her to school. On the first five occasions, Keyes signed out Jane as her father. On the final occasion, he signed her out as her mother. The complaint alleges that Keyes was able to gain access to Jane because the policy promulgated by the various school officials permitted school employees to release Jane to Keyes without first verifying Keyes's identification or whether he was among those people listed on her "Permission to Check–Out Form." The complaint contends that this policy created a danger to students and the implementation and execution of the policy constituted deliberate indifference towards the rights and safety of those students, including Jane. This policy is alleged to be the direct and proximate cause of Jane's injury.

The complaint thus assigns a passive role to school employees, alleging that the school violated Jane's constitutional rights by "*allowing* the Defendant, Tommy Keyes, to check the minor child out from school" without verifying his identity or his authorization to take the child. It also alleges that the school policy *permitted* school employees to release students to individuals without checking their identification or authorization, but did not *require* them to do so. The policy thus delegated to school employees the discretion to release a student without verifying an adult's identity or his authorization. Furthermore, the complaint does not claim that any school employee had actual knowledge that Keyes was not authorized to take Jane from school, only that the employees did not check Keyes's identification or verify that he was among the adults listed on Jane's check-out form.

....

The Does asserted due process and equal protection claims under 42 U.S.C. §§ 1983, 1985, and 1986, as well as various state law causes of action.

On the Education Defendants' motion, the district court dismissed the Does' federal claims for failure to state a claim and declined to exercise supplemental jurisdiction over the remaining state law claims. The court concluded that under the Supreme Court's decision in *DeShaney v. Winnebago County Department of Social Services*, 489 U.S. 189, (1989), Jane had no constitutional right to be protected from harm inflicted by a private actor such as Keyes except under one of two narrow exceptions—the "state-created danger" theory and the "special relationship" exception. The district court assumed that the state-created danger theory was available in this circuit, but held that the Does had not sufficiently pleaded a due process violation based on that theory. The court thus determined that the "primary question" was whether the Does could state a claim based on a special relationship between Jane and the Education Defendants, and concluded that the claim was foreclosed by our precedent.

On appeal, a majority of a panel of this court reversed the district court's judgment in part. The majority found that the Does had pleaded a facially plausible claim that the school had violated Jane's substantive due process rights by virtue of its special relationship with her and its deliberate indifference to known threats to her safety. *Doe ex rel. Magee v. Covington Cnty. Sch. Dist. ex rel. Bd. of Educ.*, 649 F.3d 335, 353–54 (5th Cir. 2011). The panel majority, however, affirmed the district court's qualified-immunity dismissal of Jane's constitutional claim against those Education Defendants sued in their individual capacities. We ordered rehearing en banc. For the reasons set forth herein, we now affirm the judgment of the district court.

....

III. Discussion

To state a claim under 42 U.S.C. § 1983, "a plaintiff must (1) allege a violation of a right secured by the Constitution or laws of the United States and (2) demonstrate that the alleged deprivation was committed by a person acting under color of state law." The central issue here is whether the Does have in fact alleged the violation of a constitutional right. Because we find that they have not, we affirm the district court's dismissal of this case.

A. DeShaney Special Relationship

Jane's constitutional claim against the Education Defendants is based not upon Keyes's molestation of Jane, but rather upon the school's allegedly deficient check-out policy, which allowed the molestation to occur. Jane's constitutional claim can proceed, therefore, only if the Education Defendants had a constitutional duty to protect Jane from non-state actors. This duty, in turn, may exist if there is a special relationship, as contemplated by *DeShaney*, between Jane and her school. We begin by reviewing *DeShaney* and its progeny, then consider the application of this law in the context of this case.

1. **DeShaney** *Recognizes a Limited Duty to Protect*

DeShaney v. Winnebago County Department of Social Services, 489 U.S. 189 (1989), arose out of the tragic case of young Joshua DeShaney, who had been placed in state custody after the Winnebago County Department of Social Services suspected his father of child abuse. The agency subsequently returned Joshua to his home after finding insufficient evidence of abuse. Once at home, Joshua continued to endure beatings from his father, and was ultimately left with severe brain damage. Joshua DeShaney and his mother sued the Winnebago County Department of Social Services and various individual defendants, alleging that the Department and its employees had violated Joshua's substantive due process right by failing to protect him from his father's violence even though they knew that he faced a very real danger of harm. The Supreme Court rejected this claim, and held that the plaintiffs could not maintain an action under § 1983 because there had been no constitutional violation. The Court noted that the Fourteenth Amendment was enacted to "protect the people from the State, not to ensure that the State protect[ ] them from each other." The Due Process Clause, the Court explained, "forbids the State itself to deprive individuals of life, liberty, or property without 'due process of law,' but its language cannot fairly be extended to impose an affirmative obligation on the State to ensure that those interests do not come to harm through other means." Thus, the Court concluded that "a State's failure to protect an individual against private violence simply does not constitute a violation of the Due Process Clause."

The Court noted that this categorical rule is subject to at least one very limited exception. Under this exception, a state may create a "special relationship" with a particular citizen, requiring the state to protect him from harm, "when the State takes a person into its custody and holds him there against his will." In such instances, "the Constitution imposes upon it a corresponding duty to assume some responsibility for his safety and general well-being." That special relationship exists when the state incarcerates a prisoner, or involuntarily commits someone to an institution. The *DeShaney* Court reasoned that:

> when the State by the affirmative exercise of its power so restrains an individual's liberty that it renders him unable to care for himself, and at the same time fails to provide for his basic human needs—*e.g.*, food, clothing, shelter, medical care, and reasonable safety—it transgresses the substantive limits on state action set by the Eighth Amendment and the Due Process Clause.

DeShaney, 489 U.S. at 200. The Court stated that "[t]he affirmative duty to protect arises not from the State's knowledge of the individual's predicament or from its expressions of intent to help him, but from the limitation which it has imposed on his freedom to act on his own behalf." *Id.*

In addition to the circumstances of incarceration and involuntary institutionalization recognized by the Court in *DeShaney*, we have extended the special relationship exception to the placement of children in foster care. *Griffith v. Johnston*, 899 F.2d 1427, 1439 (5th Cir. 1990). We reasoned that the state assumes a constitutional duty to care for children under state supervision because "the state's duty to provide services stems from the limitation which the state has placed on the individual's ability to act on his own behalf." *Id.* We have not extended the *DeShaney* special relationship exception beyond these three situations, and have explicitly held that the state does *not* create a special relationship with children attending public schools.

2. Schools and the Special Relationship Exception in the Fifth Circuit

We have twice considered en banc whether the special relationship exception to the *DeShaney* rule applies in the context of public schools. In both cases, we concluded that a public school does not have a special relationship with a student that would require the school to protect the student from harm at the hands of a private actor.

....

Numerous panel decisions have declined to recognize a special relationship between a public school and its students....

We reaffirm, then, decades of binding precedent: a public school does not have a *DeShaney* special relationship with its students requiring the school to ensure the students' safety from private actors. Public schools do not take students into custody and hold them there against their will in the same way that a state takes prisoners, involuntarily committed mental health patients, and foster children into its custody. Without a special relationship, a public school has no *constitutional* duty to ensure that its students are safe from private violence. That is not to say that schools have absolutely no duty to ensure that students are safe during the school day. Schools may have such a duty by virtue of a state's tort or other laws. However, "[s]ection 1983 imposes liability for violations of rights protected by the Constitution, not for violations of duties of care arising out of tort law."

Like our court, each circuit to have addressed the issue has concluded that public schools do not have a special relationship with their students, as public schools do not place the same restraints on students' liberty as do prisons and state mental health institutions....

3. No Special Relationship Exists Here

Against this backdrop, and the many decisions to the contrary, the Does (together with our dissenting colleagues) argue that Jane had a special relationship with her school, and therefore a substantive due process interest. They contend that compulsory school attendance laws, combined with Jane's young age and the affirmative act of placing Jane into Keyes's custody (what the Does describe as the Education Defendants' "active, deliberatively indifferent, conduct"), created a special relationship in this case. None of these factors, however, provides a basis to conclude that the school assumed a constitutional duty to protect Jane. Instead, the Does' argument ignores the contours of the special relationship exception to create a cause of action where none exists.

a. Jane's Young Age

The Does (and the dissenters) rely largely upon Jane's young age to distinguish this case from the many others in which we have held that schools have no special relationship with their students. We do not find Jane's age to be a relevant distinguishing characteristic for purposes of the special relationship analysis.

Although it is true that in our prior cases we have dealt with children older than Jane, we have never relied upon the age of the student at issue to resolve the special relationship analysis. Rather, we have said that schools do not have a special relationship with students because "[p]arents remain the primary source for the basic needs of their children." This is as much true for elementary students as it is for high school students. No matter the age of the child, parents are the primary providers of food, clothing, shelter, medical care, and reasonable safety for their minor children. Thus, school children are returned to their parents' care at the end of each day, and are able to seek assistance from their families on a daily basis, unlike those who are incarcerated or involuntarily committed.

Jane's immaturity is insufficient to distinguish this case from our [prior] decisions . . . The suggestion that we ought to examine an individual's characteristics to determine whether the state has assumed a duty to care for that person is wholly unsupported by precedent. The situations in which the state assumes a duty of care sufficient to create a special relationship are strictly enumerated and the restrictions of each situation are identical. In the circumstances of incarceration, involuntary institutionalization, and foster care, the state has, through an established set of laws and procedures, rendered the person in its care completely unable to provide for his or her basic needs and it assumes a duty to provide for these needs. Neither the Supreme Court nor this court has ever suggested that anything less than such a total restriction is sufficient to create a special relationship with the state, regardless of the age or competence of the individual.

Moreover, the focus upon Jane's young age makes an essentially arbitrary distinction between the thirteen- and fourteen-year-old students in [prior cases] and nine-year-old students like Jane. If we were to accept this argument, schools would be required to evaluate the maturity of each student to determine whether the school has a special relationship with that student. Indeed, some students could "age out" of constitutional protection over the course of one academic year. A constitutional duty to protect a student from harm does not depend on the maturity of the student, a factor not in the control of the state. Through their public school systems, states take on the responsibility of educating students, but, no matter the age of the student, public schools simply do not take on the responsibility of providing "food, clothing, shelter, medical care, and reasonable safety" for the students they educate.

Particularly instructive on this question is the Ninth Circuit's recent decision in *Patel v. Kent School District*, 648 F.3d 965 (9th Cir. 2011). There, a developmentally disabled student had several sexual encounters with a classmate in a restroom adjacent to her classroom. The student's parents had requested that she remain under adult supervision at all times because her disability prevented her from recognizing dangerous situations and caused her to act inappropriately with others. Nevertheless, the student's teacher allowed her to use the restroom alone in order to foster her development. The Ninth Circuit held that compulsory school attendance laws do not create a special relationship between public schools and students that would require schools to protect the students from harm. Of particular import to this case, the Ninth Circuit also rejected the student's contention that the school was required to protect against her "special vulnerabilities." The court reasoned that "[i]n the case of a minor child, custody does not exist until the state has so restrained the child's liberty that the parents cannot care for the child's basic needs," and the student's disability did not prevent her parents from caring for her basic needs. Under the Ninth Circuit's reasoning, the existence of a special relationship does not depend on the characteristics of the individual. Consistent with *Patel*, we conclude that Jane's young age and immaturity do not provide a basis for finding a special relationship with her school.

Our conclusion that no special relationship exists between nine-year-old Jane and her school is consistent with the decisions of our sister circuits, four of which have addressed cases involving children who were approximately the same age or even younger than Jane. While we should have every reason to expect that public schools can and will provide for the safety of public school students, no matter their age, our precedents, and the decisions of every other circuit to have considered this issue, dictate that schools are simply not *constitutionally* required to ensure students' safety from private actors. Despite her young age, Jane was not attending the school through the "affirmative exercise of [state] power," she was attending the school because her parents voluntarily chose to send her there (as one of several ways to fulfill their compulsory education obligations), and they remained responsible for her basic needs.

b. Compulsory School Attendance Laws

The Does also suggest that a special relationship exists because Jane's attendance at school was mandated by compulsory attendance laws. We have specifically held, however, that compulsory school attendance laws do not "alone create a special relationship."

There is no indication that Jane's attendance at the school was somehow more compulsory as a nine-year-old than if she were a teenager. While it may be true that elementary school students are subject to more rules during the school day (a fact not pleaded), their attendance at school is no more or less mandatory than teenagers' attendance. In fact, Jane was subject to exactly the same Mississippi compulsory education laws as was the plaintiff in [a prior case] who voluntarily attended a residential school for the deaf. Mississippi requires parents to enroll their children in school until age seventeen, and parents may fulfill this requirement in several ways, only one of which is to send their child to public school. Miss. Code Ann.

§ 37–13–91(3) (requiring that parent enroll compulsory school-age child in a public school, a "legitimate nonpublic school," or provide a "legitimate home instruction program"). It may well be true that, for the vast majority of parents in Mississippi, the only way for them to fulfill their obligation is to enroll their children in public school. But that practicality does not alter the fact that Jane's parents voluntarily sent her to the school as a means of fulfilling their obligation to educate her. Jane's parents were free at any time to remove Jane from the school if they felt that her safety was being compromised. This reality is a far cry from the situation of incarcerated prisoners, institutionalized mental health patients, or children placed in foster care. Mississippi's compulsory education law is therefore insufficient under our precedent to create a special relationship between the school and Jane, despite Jane's young age.

c. Release of Jane to Keyes

As a final effort to distinguish this case from the many others in this area, the Does contend that the "active, deliberately indifferent, conduct" of school officials in releasing Jane to Keyes formed a special relationship. The dissent similarly argues that a special relationship was created when the school separated Jane from her teachers and classmates and delivered her into Keyes' exclusive custody. This argument, however, has several flaws.

Even assuming that the school had custody over Jane to the exclusion of her legal guardians, which it did not, the school did not *knowingly* transfer that custody to an unauthorized individual. The complaint alleges that the school employee releasing Jane committed an affirmative act, but does not assert that the school employee actually knew that Keyes was unauthorized to take Jane from school. Implicit in the Supreme Court's holding that a state may create a special relationship through an "affirmative exercise of its power," is the requirement that the state actor know that he or she is restricting an individual's liberty. When a state incarcerates a prisoner, institutionalizes a mental health patient, or places a child in foster care, the state knows that it has restricted the individual's liberty and rendered him unable to care for his basic human needs. When a school employee carelessly fails to ensure that an adult is authorized to take an elementary student from the school, no state actor has knowledge that the school has thereby restricted the student's liberty, because the adult taking the student from school may or may not be authorized.

The Does' (and the dissent's) theory also suggests that the same act that creates the special relationship can also violate the duty of care owed to the student. Under the special relationship exception, the state assumes a duty to care for and protect an individual. Once the special relationship is created, it is the failure to fulfill that duty that gives rise to a constitutional violation. An allegation of deliberate indifference may be sufficient to *violate* a constitutional duty, but it is not sufficient to *create* the constitutional duty. Furthermore, this theory suggests that the school's very act of *releasing* Jane into the custody of a private actor somehow created the state custody that is necessary for a *DeShaney* special relationship to exist in the first place. Such a theory is wholly inconsistent with *DeShaney* itself.

The Does point us to no distinguishing characteristics of this case that are sufficient to give rise to a *DeShaney* special relationship between Jane and her school. This case is ultimately no different than [prior cases] and thus requires the same outcome.

4. Conclusion

The question posed to us is whether Jane's school, through its affirmative exercise of state power, assumed a *constitutional* duty to protect Jane from a private actor. We are compelled by our precedent, and by the Supreme Court's guidance in *DeShaney*, to conclude that the school did not assume that duty. The district court correctly held that the Does have failed to state a claim under § 1983 for a constitutional violation under the special relationship exception.

Because we find no special relationship, we do not address whether the school's alleged actions in releasing Jane to Keyes amounted to "deliberate indifference." As this en banc court previously explained in *McClendon v. City of Columbia*, 305 F.3d 314 (5th Cir. 2002), only where a state first creates a special relationship with an individual does the state then have "a constitutional duty to protect that individual from dangers, including, in certain circumstances, private violence." Without a special relationship, the school had no constitutional duty to protect Jane from private actors such as Keyes, and the question of its alleged deliberate indifference is simply immaterial.

Having concluded that the school had no special relationship with Jane that imposed on the school a constitutional duty to protect her from private harm, we now turn to the Does' remaining theories of liability.

B. State—Created Danger

The Does argue that they have stated a viable constitutional claim under the so-called "state-created" danger theory of liability. We find no such viable claim.

. . . .

Under the state-created danger theory, a state actor may be liable under § 1983 if the state actor created or knew of a dangerous situation and affirmatively placed the plaintiff in that situation. *See, e.g., Carlton v. Cleburne Cnty.*, 93 F.3d 505, 508 (8th Cir. 1996) ("In [the state-created danger] cases the courts have uniformly held that state actors may be liable if they affirmatively created the plaintiffs' peril or acted to render them more vulnerable to danger. In other words, the individuals would not have been in harm's way but for the government's affirmative actions.") (citation omitted). In *Wood v. Ostrander*, 879 F.2d 583, 586 (9th Cir. 1989), the Ninth Circuit adopted the state-created danger theory in the context of a § 1983 claim brought against police officers by the passenger of an impounded vehicle, who was raped after officers abandoned her on the side of a road in a high crime area in the early morning hours. Similarly, in *Kneipp v. Tedder*, 95 F.3d 1199 (3d Cir. 1996), the Third Circuit adopted the state-created danger theory in the context of a lawsuit brought against a city and several police officers on behalf of a woman who suffered extensive brain damage when the officers allegedly sent her home "unescorted in a seriously intoxicated state in cold weather."

Unlike many of our sister circuits, we have never explicitly adopted the state-created danger theory. The district court in this case acknowledged our precedent, but held that even if the theory were recognized, the Does had failed to plead facts that would amount to a constitutional violation. The court held that the Does did not contend that the Education Defendants knew that their policy would allow Jane to be checked out of school by an unauthorized adult and sexually assaulted; therefore, the Does had not alleged that the Defendants were deliberately indifferent to a known danger.

. . . .

We decline to use this en banc opportunity to adopt the state-created danger theory in this case because the allegations would not support such a theory. Although we have not recognized the theory, we have stated the elements that such a cause of action would require. The . . . state-created danger theory requires "a plaintiff [to] show [1] the defendants used their authority to create a dangerous environment for the plaintiff and [2] that the defendants acted with deliberate indifference to the plight of the plaintiff." To establish deliberate indifference for purposes of state-created danger, the plaintiff must show that "[t]he environment created by the state actors must be dangerous; they must know it is dangerous; and . . . they must have used their authority to create an opportunity that would not otherwise have existed for the third party's crime to occur." . . .

In support of their state-created danger claim, the Does allege that school officials "received complaints and inquiries and/or had internal discussions and safety meetings concerning checkout policies and procedures and access to students under their care and control by unauthorized individuals," and they therefore "had actual knowledge of the dangers created by their policies, customs and regulations, but they failed to take corrective action to reduce or prevent the danger." According to the Does, the school's failure to adopt a stricter policy amounted to "deliberate indifference." Nevertheless, the Does' allegations cannot make out a state-created danger claim, as they do not demonstrate the existence of "an immediate danger facing a known victim." At most, the Does allege that the school was aware of some general deficiencies in the check-out policy. They do *not* allege that the school knew about an immediate danger to Jane's safety, nor can the court infer such knowledge from the pleadings. Without such allegations, even if we were to embrace the state-created danger theory, the claim would necessarily fail.

We have consistently cautioned against finding liability under the state-created danger theory based upon an ineffective policy or practice in cases where the plaintiff's injury is inflicted by a private actor. . . . We conclude that the Does' allegations do not support a claim under the state-created danger theory, even if that theory were viable in this circuit.

C. Municipal Liability

Finally, the Does maintain that they have stated a viable claim under what they describe as a "pure" municipal liability theory. They argue that municipal liability is available under *Monell v. Department of Social Services of City of New York*, 436 U.S. 658, (1978), because the school promulgated a policy—the ineffective student check-out policy—that was the moving force behind Jane's injury. We disagree.

A claim of municipal liability under Section 1983 "requires proof of three elements: a policymaker; an official policy; and a violation of constitutional rights whose 'moving force' is the policy or custom." We have stated time and again that "[w]ithout an underlying constitutional violation, an essential element of municipal liability is missing." *Becerra v. Asher*, 105 F.3d 1042, 1048 (5th Cir. 1997); *see also Collins v. City of Harker Heights, Tex.*, 503 U.S. 115, 120 (1992) ("[P]roper analysis requires us to separate two different issues when a § 1983 claim is asserted against a municipality: (1) whether plaintiff's harm was caused by a constitutional violation, and (2) if so, whether the city is responsible for that violation."). Thus, even if the ineffective check-out policy was the moving force behind Jane's injury, there can be no § 1983 liability unless Jane suffered a constitutional violation. Jane did not suffer a constitutional violation at the hands of Keyes because Keyes is not a state actor. The only state actions that could give rise to a constitutional violation in this case are the school's failure to prevent Keyes from injuring Jane or the act of releasing Jane to Keyes. As explained above, these state actions are insufficient for purposes of the special relationship and state-created danger theories. The Does now contend that they have alleged a constitutional violation because the school's conduct shocks the conscience.

. . . .

Conduct sufficient to shock the conscience for substantive due process purposes has been described in several different ways. It has been described as conduct that "violates the decencies of civilized conduct"; conduct that is "so brutal and offensive that it [does] not comport with traditional ideas of fair play and decency"; conduct that "interferes with rights implicit in the concept of ordered liberty"; and conduct that "is so egregious, so outrageous, that it may fairly be said to shock the contemporary conscience." Many cases that have applied the standard have involved the use of extreme force by police officers or other state actors. As one court has recently summarized, "[t]he burden to show state conduct that shocks the conscience is extremely high, requiring stunning evidence of arbitrariness and caprice that extends beyond mere violations of state law, even violations resulting from bad faith to something more egregious and more extreme." *J.R. v. Gloria*, 593 F.3d 73, 80 (1st Cir. 2010) (citation and internal quotation marks omitted).

We find that the Does' attempt to employ the shocks the conscience standard is unsuccessful for two reasons. First, the only state action at issue here is the adoption and implementation of an allegedly deficient policy, which allowed school employees to release Jane to Keyes without verifying his identification or his right to take Jane from the school. We conclude that the implementation and execution of such a policy does not, on its own, shock the conscience, particularly when compared to those cases detailed above in which that standard has been successfully applied. The policy simply does not fall within the category of conduct that "is so egregious, so outrageous, that it may fairly be said to shock the contemporary conscience." Far from a policy that shocks the conscience, the check-out policy at issue here appears to be relatively common and to have some logical basis, particularly in small communities such as Covington County, Mississippi. The mere fact that Keyes exploited the check-out system to gain access to Jane does not mean that the school's adoption and implementation of the policy shocks the conscience.

Second, we must be careful not to read the shocks the conscience standard as a separate exception to the *DeShaney* principle. The actual harm inflicted upon Jane in this case was caused by private actor Tommy Keyes, and after *DeShaney*, the state cannot be held constitutionally liable for its "failure to protect an individual against private violence," save for the special relationship theory and, in some circuits, the state-created danger theory. To allow the Does to proceed on a shocks the conscience theory without first demonstrating a constitutional duty to protect would be wholly inconsistent with *DeShaney*. In fact, the *DeShaney* Court itself rejected a similar argument. . . .

As we conclude that the school's adoption and implementation of its check-out policy does not *itself* shock the conscience, a constitutional claim on this basis necessarily fails. Moreover, as we have found that Jane has not alleged an underlying constitutional violation (under either the special relationship theory or the purported state-created danger theory), there is no other potential basis for municipal liability. We therefore reject the Does' municipal liability argument.

D. Qualified Immunity

The district court held in the alternative that, even if the Does had stated a constitutional claim, the Education Defendants sued in their individual capacities were entitled to qualified immunity, because any right to governmental protection based upon a special relationship between Jane and her school was not clearly established at the time that Jane was victimized.

Although no longer mandated as a first step in the qualified immunity analysis, one part of this analysis requires us to "decide whether the facts that a plaintiff has alleged . . . make out a violation of a constitutional right." Because we determine that the Does have failed to state a violation of Jane's constitutional rights, we need not further consider the qualified immunity analysis.

IV. Conclusion

In affirming the dismissal of the Does' complaint, we do not suggest that schools have no obligation to insure that their students remain safe from acts of private violence. State law provides the appropriate legal framework to address Jane's injury. The question we have addressed is simply whether the school's failure to check

Keyes's identity and be certain that he was authorized to take Jane amounted to a *constitutional* violation. Supreme Court precedent, our precedent, and the decisions of every other circuit to address the special relationship exception compel this court to conclude that it does not. In addition, neither the state-created danger theory nor municipal liability provides a viable basis for recovery.

For these reasons, the judgment of the district court is AFFIRMED.

. . . .

WIENER, CIRCUIT JUDGE, joined by DENNIS, CIRCUIT JUDGE, dissenting:

Like the law of nature, the law of man recognizes no more basic or extensive "special relationship" than that between parents and their "very young" children. Central to that relationship is the parents' exclusive right to the custody of their children and the concomitant duty to protect them. It must follow that when a state mandates that parents delegate the custody of their child to a state agency, subdivision, or municipality, such total delegation creates a special relationship between the delegatee and the child in its custody—at least when such child is "very young"—and imposes on such custodial state delegatee a duty to protect that child from violations of her constitutional rights. I am convinced that the parents' custodial delegatee here—the Covington County Elementary School ("the School")—cannot be permitted to evade its duty to protect its very young pupils while they are in its exclusive custody.

As is apparent from the Does' . . . complaint and the majority opinion, this case involves repeated decisions and acts by the School's officials to temporarily subdelegate its exclusive custody of a nine-year-old fourth-grade girl, in the middle of six different school days, over a span of four months, to an unidentified adult, who was not authorized under the School's express policy to check her out, and whose identity it did not even attempt to verify. On each of those six occasions, that adult, Tommy Keyes, proceeded to brutally rape the little girl, Jane Doe, and then return her to the custody of the School—still during the course of the school day. This was no isolated or anecdotal incident, and the School's officials allegedly contributed to its recurrence by failing, each time, to verify Keyes's identity and his lack of authorization.

. . . .

I. Special Relationship

The substantive component of the Due Process Clause of the Fourteenth Amendment protects individuals from state action that "shocks the conscience." Although substantive Due Process does not generally protect individuals from private actors, the Supreme Court stated in *DeShaney* that there is an exception, and that the State does owe an individual a duty of protection when a special relationship exists between the State and the individual:

> [W]hen the State takes a person into its custody and holds him there against his will, the Constitution imposes upon it a corresponding duty to assume some responsibility for his safety and general well-being . . . . The

> rationale for this principle is simple enough: when the State by the affirmative exercise of its power so restrains an individual's liberty that it renders him unable to care for himself, and at the same time fails to provide for his basic human needs—e.g., food, clothing, shelter, medical care, and *reasonable safety*—it transgresses the substantive limits on state action set by the Eighth Amendment and the Due Process Clause.

In this case, Jane attended a public elementary school in Mississippi, where attendance is compulsory and where all the relevant events took place during the school day, not at its end. None disputes that more than compulsory public education is required to establish a special relationship between the State and a student, but this does not justify taking the leap of logic needed to reach the conclusion that a special relationship can *never* exist in the public school setting. When, in *Doe v. Hillsboro Independent School District*, we held that *alone* compulsory attendance does not create a special relationship between a state and a presumably pubescent, thirteen-year-old middle-school student, we quoted the following general explanation from the Supreme Court's decision in *Ingraham v. Wright* as to why public schools are distinguishable from, e.g., prisons and mental institutions:

> Though attendance may not always be voluntary, the public school remains an open institution. *Except perhaps when very young*, the child is not physically restrained from leaving school during school hours; and *at the end of the school day*, the child is invariably free to return home. Even while at school, the child brings with him the support of family and friends and is *rarely apart* from teachers and other pupils who may witness and protest any instances of mistreatment.

Ingraham's latent exception for the "very young" public school attendee is finally before us, in the Does' complaint, for the first time.

The majority attempts to distinguish *Ingraham* based on that case's concern with the application of the Eighth Amendment to corporal punishment in public schools, but our decision in *Hillsboro* expressly recognized the obvious relevance of *Ingraham*'s analysis to the special relationship inquiry. Compounding the majority opinion's error in making this purported distinction, it strangely declares that the Supreme Court's reasoning does "not suggest that a public school is no less an open institution if a student is restrained from freely leaving the school due to her young age or if a student is apart from teachers or other students, whether on campus or off." In fact, though, that is precisely what the Supreme Court's analysis suggests.

Specifically, the *Ingraham* exception can only mean that there may very well be a special relationship between a public school and a student who (1) is "very young,"(2) is "physically restrained" by (and unable to leave freely) the school's custody, and (3) is isolated or kept "apart from teachers and other pupils who may witness and protest any instances of mistreatment"—as is precisely alleged here. Rather than superficially distinguishing what the Supreme Court has said—even in dicta—we should apply it, as I shall now attempt to do.

A. Jane Was of Such a Very Young Age That She Could Not Protect Herself

When Jane was repeatedly checked out of school and brutally raped, she was a very young, pre-pubescent, nine-year-old, fourth-grade girl. The majority refuses to acknowledge the obvious: that the degree of control exercised by a de jure and de facto custodian over very young children is necessarily much greater and more pervasive than over post-puberty teenagers or adults. The majority does not even acknowledge that the Does might be able to establish as much if given the opportunity to adduce evidence, especially expert reports and testimony. But expert testimony is not required to know that very young children like Jane are virtually never capable of protesting or challenging adult authority figures, particularly those whose authority is apparently endorsed by the very persons or institutions that such children trust. Neither are such youngsters generally able to recognize and respond to subtle threats to their safety, which is the prime reason why they, unlike older students, are never permitted to leave school grounds by themselves. The defendants in this case do not assert that the School had a unique policy of allowing very young, fourth-grade students to come and go without restraint; indeed, the School's adoption of a formal check-out policy confirms that just the opposite is true. Add to this truism the two-step factual allegations of the Does' complaint that Jane was *first* taken from her class (and thus separated from the very teacher and classmates who, under *Ingraham*, were her support) and, *second*, turned over to Keyes outside the ken of these putative supporters, and the flaw in the majority's logic becomes all the more apparent. In such isolation, a very young child like Jane could hardly have stood up for herself in light of the actions taken by School officials.

Under the majority's analysis, the age of the schoolchild is categorically irrelevant to the special relationship inquiry: "No matter the age of the child, parents are the primary providers of food, clothing, shelter, medical care, and reasonable safety for their minor children"; and children return home at the end of each school day. But neither the majority nor any decision it cites explains how or why parents' care of children *before and after* the school day can or should preclude the existence of a special relationship *during* school hours. Although Jane's parents were presumably able to provide her with food, clothing, and protection before she left home in the morning and after she returned home at the end of each school day, this in no way enabled them to provide for her safety—reasonable or otherwise—throughout the course of the school day. . . .

This reasoning is all the more powerful when, as here, the schoolchild who suffers injury to her bodily integrity is "very young." To contend that it is primarily up to parents to prevent public schools from handing off their nine-year-old girls to unknown men during the course of the school day would be outrageous. Yet the majority's emphasis on parents' responsibility for their children's needs, including safety from sexual predation, if not wholly irrelevant, can have no other meaning. At the same time, the majority never addresses just what it is that Jane's parents conceivably could have done, or should have done, to safeguard her in this situation. Even if it could somehow be imagined that the parents bear some responsibility, such a conclusion cannot be drawn from the Does' pleadings without the benefit of discovery.

The majority also suggests that the distinction between very young children and older children is "essentially arbitrary." But, far from being arbitrary, distinguishing between pre-pubescent and pubescent or post-pubescent children is not just natural and intuitive-it is grounded in extensive science. This distinction, which is based on biology and is reflected in the differentiation between elementary school and junior high school, has historically been considered important by the medical profession and society at large. In addressing numerous areas, Congress and state legislatures have treated pre-pubescent and post-pubescent children differently and have used age as a proxy for that distinction. The particular *age* selected might appear to be arbitrary (though it could have been informed by expert analysis had this case been allowed to proceed), but not the distinction. A distinction with such deep biological and historical roots, and which remains vital in many legal realms, can hardly be considered "arbitrary."

The majority also contends that it would be impractical to assess every individual's characteristics to determine whether a special relationship exists. Not so: A schoolchild's age is an objective and easily-determined fact. I do not suggest—and we need not decide, in this case—that more subjective factors, such as a specific child's (Jane's) mental acuity or degree of social development, should be a part of the special relationship inquiry. Line-drawing is inevitable in this area, but an approach guided by objective facts does not require line-drawing of unusual difficulty. By contrast, an approach that categorically ignores age—by, for example, ignoring the differences between a nine-year-old grammar school girl and a high school senior twice her age—only heightens the arbitrariness of the line demarcating special relationships. Further, the majority's approach would presumably leave pre-schoolers and even infants in the State's care unprotected—a patently absurd result.

In short, nine-year-old, elementary-school students in general—not just Jane, subjectively—are significantly distinct from teenage, middle- and high-school students in their ability to provide for their own protection from sex offenders when they are mandatorily separated from their legal guardians during the school day. Jane's very young age is thus highly relevant to the existence of a special relationship between herself and the School. This factor need not be sufficient alone, however, because the School also affirmatively exercised its power to restrain Jane's liberty even more strictly, as detailed below.

B. The School Affirmatively Forced Jane into Keyes's Sole Custody at School and Allowed Keyes to Take Her Away from the School Where She Could Not Protect Herself

Under the well-pleaded allegations of the Does' complaint, the State had a special relationship with Jane, not just because of her very young age, but also because of the School's decision, while acting *in loco parentis* to the exclusion of all others, and pursuant to its express policies, (1) first, to separate Jane from her teachers and classmates, and (2) only then to deliver her into the exclusive custody of Keyes for the express purpose of his taking her away from the school grounds and later returning her there, all during the course of the school day. This affirmative exercise of state power is significant under the Supreme Court's analysis in *Ingraham*, quoted by this court in *Doe v. Hillsboro Independent School District.* By actively removing Jane from the classroom and then delivering her in isolation into Keyes's custody, the School rendered Jane (1) *entirely* "apart from teachers and other pupils who may witness and protest any instances of mistreatment," and (2) not "free to return home"—except, exclusively, at Keyes's mercy. This was an affirmative exercise of state power, on six separate occasions, that further disabled Jane and further obliged the State to protect her.

We and other courts have held that a special relationship may exist when a state sub-delegates its delegated custody of an individual to a third party. For example, a state has a special relationship with a minor it places in foster care, a burglary suspect it temporarily places in the custody of a private club owner, and a woman it threatens with arrest and physically places in her intoxicated boyfriend's truck. In none of these or other such cases did a state actor physically hold the victim at the time of the injury (had no de facto "custody"), but the victim "was in the defendant officers' custody at the time she was forced into" the third party's control. The State is therefore considered "a participant in the custody which led to the victim's death [or injury]." The same reasoning has to apply here.

Moreover, these cases demonstrate that the special relationship doctrine is not inflexibly limited to "24/7" incarceration or institutionalization only. Rather than excluding broad areas of state action, such as public schools, from the reach of the special relationship doctrine, we must be sensitive to the factual context in which a case arises. Here, the relevant context includes the School's affirmative decision to (1) isolate the "very young" Jane from her teachers and classmates and (2) deliver Jane into Keyes's exclusive custody, in those sequential steps rendering Jane and her parents utterly helpless.

In light of their decision to separate Jane from her teacher and classmates and then release her to Keyes, the school officials' role was not merely passive or simply negligent, as the majority asserts. The active nature of the School's role is underscored by the check-out policy in question. That policy admittedly—as the majority opinion states—"*permitted* school employees to release students to individuals," but, more importantly, *forced Jane, the student* to be released, giving her, as well as her teacher, her classmates, and her parents, no choice in the matter. Only by examining the relationship between Jane and the State—not the relationship (for these purposes irrelevant) between the State officials who set the School's policies and those who implemented them—does the question of a special relationship in this case come into proper focus.

The majority also reasons that the School's temporary delegation of its exclusive custody of Jane to Keyes does not support the existence of a special relationship because the School did not "*knowingly* transfer that custody to an unauthorized individual." A state-knowledge requirement, the majority continues, is "implicit" in the principle that a special relationship may be created only through an "affirmative exercise" of state power. But such a state-knowledge requirement—for which the majority cites no precedent—would not imply that, for there to be a special relationship, the state must know *all* the circumstances, i.e., each and every discrete fact, surrounding its custody of an individual. As alleged here, the School clearly did affirmatively exercise its powers by separating Jane from her teachers and classmates and delivering her to Keyes, and it did so pursuant to its express policies. School personnel were perfectly aware that they were undertaking these actions—affirmatively, not passively.

It is technically true that the School did not "know" Keyes to be unauthorized, but all it had to do was (1) verify Keyes's identity, and (2) follow its own express policy by viewing Jane's check-out form. Although the School's self-inflicted lack of knowledge could arguably indicate that it was not deliberately indifferent to Jane's safety, that has nothing to do with the special relationship inquiry. For example, a state has a special relationship with and a concomitant duty to protect a prisoner even if the prisoner is injured because of an unknown or unexpected danger to which the official could not have shown deliberate indifference. To conclude, however, that such a prisoner was never in a special relationship to begin with would be illogical. The same is true in this case. My point: the majority has conflated the special relationship and deliberate indifference inquiries.

The majority also asserts that the School's act of releasing Jane into Keyes's custody cannot demonstrate the kind of state custody that is required for a special relationship to exist. This argument ignores the cases discussed above, however, which teach that a special relationship survives a state's delegation of its exclusive custody to a third party.

II. Deliberate Indifference

A state does not violate its substantive due process duty to protect an individual pursuant to a special relationship when it merely acts negligently. Such a violation occurs when the state acts with "deliberate indifference" to that individual's health or safety. Thus, in addition to alleging that a special relationship existed between Jane and the School, the Does needed to allege adequately that the School officials acted, at the very least, with deliberate indifference. "To act with deliberate indifference, a state actor must consciously disregard a known and excessive risk to the victim's health and safety." Even though the majority does not reach this issue, any objective reading of the Does' complaint confirms that they have quite adequately pleaded that the State acted with deliberate indifference to Jane's safety.

The Does allege with specificity that the School adopted and implemented a flawed check-out policy despite its knowledge that the specific policy thus adopted posed excessive risks to students. In particular, the Does allege that the School's check-out policy included a "Permission to Check—Out" form for each student which listed by name the only adults authorized to check out that student during the school day. The Does also allege that (1) the policy did not direct School officials to verify the identity of an adult requesting to check out a student, and (2) the School failed adequately to train and supervise the cognizant officials in the proper administration of the check-out policy. The Does further allege that these "customs and practices guaranteed that verification would not be checked which created an unreasonable danger to the minor child named herein." Thus, when Keyes checked Jane out on multiple occasions as her "father" (and, on at least one occasion, as her "mother"), School officials neither (1) verified Keyes's identity, nor (2) referred to Jane's check-out form, on which Keyes was not listed as an individual authorized to take custody of Jane.

Importantly, the Does' pleadings expressly state that the School's officials were well aware of the risks that their flawed policies engendered, alleging that:

> Upon information and belief, the Education Defendants received complaints and inquiries and/or had internal discussions and safety meetings concerning checkout policies and procedures and access to students under their care and control by unauthorized individuals. The complaints, inquiries, discussions, and/or meetings show that the Education Defendants had actual knowledge of the dangers created by their policies, customs, and regulations, but they failed to take corrective action to reduce or prevent the danger.

These discrete allegations are sufficient to state a claim that School officials acted with deliberate indifference to a known risk to Jane's safety.

True, the Does do not allege that School officials knew that Keyes, in particular, was dangerous. But, "this court has never required state officials to be warned of a specific danger." Indeed, state officials may be deliberately indifferent even if they do not know which particular individual poses the safety risk, or which potential victim will ultimately be injured. An official is deliberately indifferent if he knows of and disregards "a substantial risk of serious harm." And it is such awareness that the Does precisely allege.

The defendants' awareness of this risk to student safety is eminently plausible in light of (1) the alleged complaints, inquiries, discussions, and meetings among the defendants on the subject of unauthorized individuals' access to students; (2) the School's allowing Keyes to check out Jane on at least six occasions, including one occasion when he signed her out as her *mother*, which these officials had to have known was bogus; and (3) the general awareness by schools and school boards—heightened in recent years—of the threat posed in the elementary school setting by deviant adults to young children.

With regard to the last point, we learned in a recent appeal of a nationwide program employing an electronic tracking system to identify whether visitors to primary and secondary schools were registered sex offenders or otherwise presented threats to young students. By 2006, the school year immediately preceding the one at issue here, this program had been endorsed by the U.S. Department of Justice, had received federal grant money, and had already been activated in at least 1,400 schools in some 100 school districts across ten states. In light of the ubiquitous awareness by schools of the threat posed by deviant adults preying on very young schoolchildren, it is certainly "plausible," and indeed highly likely, that the School knew that it was playing with fire. Of course, nothing more than plausibility is required at this stage of the proceedings.

Despite their alleged awareness of the risk, School officials nevertheless checked Jane out to a man whose identity and authority they never bothered to verify. These allegations are sufficient, at least at this initial motion-to-dismiss stage, to state an actionable constitutional claim grounded in deliberate indifference.

III. Conclusion

Any case involving the rape of a child is, of course, a terrible one, so why is this case so shocking? Part of the special horror of this case is the appalling way in which Jane's parents' state-mandated trust in public school officials for the care and safety of their very young child was rewarded. In a case such as this, in which the alleged actions of state officials "shock the conscience," the proper remedy is not merely to compensate the victim in tort, but, additionally, to compensate all of us with a constitutional remedy under 42 U.S.C. § 1983, which is intended "to deter state actors from using the badge of their authority to deprive individuals of their federally guaranteed rights and to provide relief to victims if such deterrence fails."

As one of our Tenth Circuit colleagues has aptly observed, "[w]e do not adequately discharge our duty to interpret the Constitution by merely describing the facts as 'tragic' and invoking state tort law [.]" Neither do we adequately discharge our duty by interpreting the special relationship doctrine so narrowly that a helpless nine-year-old girl, abruptly removed from her classroom by school personnel and wrongly delivered to an unauthorized grown man, falls through the mesh of the Constitution's safety net. The Does have more than adequately alleged discrete facts to show that the State had a constitutional duty to protect Jane and that it failed abysmally in that duty. These are the reasons why I dissent.

Nabozny v. Podlesny

92 F.3d 446 (7th Cir. 1996)

The court rules that schools and school officials may be liable for § 1983 claims for equal protection violations based on student on student harassment, but not for due process claims.

Jamie Nabozny was a student in the Ashland Public School District (hereinafter "the District") in Ashland, Wisconsin throughout his middle school and high school years. During that time, Nabozny was continually harassed and physically abused by fellow students because he is homosexual. Both in middle school and high school Nabozny reported the harassment to school administrators. Nabozny asked the school officials to protect him and to punish his assailants. Despite the fact that the school administrators had a policy of investigating and punishing student-on-student battery and sexual harassment, they allegedly turned a deaf ear to Nabozny's requests. Indeed, there is evidence to suggest that some of the administrators themselves mocked Nabozny's predicament. Nabozny eventually filed suit against several school officials and the District pursuant to 42 U.S.C. § 1983 alleging, among other things, that the defendants: 1) violated his Fourteenth Amendment right to equal protection by discriminating against him based on his gender; 2) violated his Fourteenth Amendment right to equal protection by discriminating against him based on his sexual orientation; 3) violated his Fourteenth Amendment right to due process by exacerbating the risk that he would be harmed by fellow students; and, 4) violated his Fourteenth Amendment right to due process by encouraging an environment in which he would be harmed. The defendants filed a motion for summary judgment, which the district court granted. Nabozny appeals the district court's decision. Because we agree with the district court only in part, we affirm in part, reverse in part, and remand.

. . . .

When Nabozny graduated to the Ashland Middle School in 1988, his life changed. Around the time that Nabozny entered the seventh grade, Nabozny realized that he is gay. Many of Nabozny's fellow classmates soon realized it too. Nabozny decided not to "closet" his sexuality, and considerable harassment from his fellow students ensued. Nabozny's classmates regularly referred to him as "faggot," and subjected him to various forms of physical abuse, including striking and spitting on him. Nabozny spoke to the school's guidance counselor, Ms. Peterson, about the abuse, informing Peterson that he is gay. Peterson took action, ordering the offending students to stop the harassment and placing two of them in detention. However, the students' abusive behavior toward Nabozny stopped only briefly. Meanwhile, Peterson was replaced as guidance counselor by Mr. Nowakowski. Nabozny similarly informed Nowakowski that he is gay, and asked for protection from the student harassment. Nowakowski, in turn, referred the matter to school Principal Mary Podlesny; Podlesny was responsible for school discipline.

Just before the 1988 Winter holiday, Nabozny met with Nowakowski and Podlesny to discuss the harassment. During the meeting, Nabozny explained the nature of the harassment and again revealed his homosexuality. Podlesny promised to protect Nabozny, but took no action. Following the holiday season, student harassment of Nabozny worsened, especially at the hands of students Jason Welty and Roy Grande. Nabozny complained to Nowakowski, and school administrators spoke to the students. The harassment, however, only intensified. A short time later, in a science classroom, Welty grabbed Nabozny and pushed him to the floor. Welty and Grande held Nabozny down and performed a mock rape on Nabozny, exclaiming that Nabozny should enjoy it. The boys carried out the mock rape as twenty other students looked on and laughed. Nabozny escaped and fled to Podlesny's office. Podlesny's alleged response is somewhat astonishing; she said that "boys will be boys" and told Nabozny that if he was "going to be so openly gay," he should "expect" such behavior from his fellow students. In the wake of Podlesny's comments, Nabozny ran home. The next day Nabozny was forced to speak with a counselor, not because he was subjected to a mock rape in a classroom, but because he left the school without obtaining the proper permission. No action was taken against the students involved. Nabozny was forced to return to his regular schedule. Understandably, Nabozny was "petrified" to attend school; he was subjected to abuse throughout the duration of the school year.

The situation hardly improved when Nabozny entered the eighth grade. Shortly after the school year began, several boys attacked Nabozny in a school bathroom, hitting him and pushing his books from his hands. This time Nabozny's parents met with Podlesny and the alleged perpetrators. The offending boys denied that the incident occurred, and no action was taken. Podlesny told both Nabozny and his parents that Nabozny should expect such incidents because he is "openly" gay. Several similar meetings between Nabozny's parents and Podlesny followed subsequent incidents involving Nabozny. Each time perpetrators were identified to Podlesny. Each time Podlesny pledged to take action. And, each time nothing was done. Toward the end of the school year, the harassment against Nabozny intensified to the point that a district attorney purportedly advised Nabozny to take time off from school. Nabozny took one and a half weeks off from school. When he returned, the harassment resumed, driving Nabozny to attempt suicide. After a stint in a hospital, Nabozny finished his eighth grade year in a Catholic school.

The Catholic school attended by Nabozny did not offer classes beyond the eighth grade. Therefore, to attend the ninth grade, Nabozny enrolled in Ashland High School. Almost immediately Nabozny's fellow students sang an all too familiar tune. Early in the year, while Nabozny was using a urinal in the restroom, Nabozny was assaulted. Student Stephen Huntley struck Nabozny in the back of the knee, forcing him to fall into the urinal. Roy Grande then urinated on Nabozny. Nabozny immediately reported the incident to the principal's office. Nabozny recounted the incident to the office secretary, who in turn relayed the story to Principal William Davis. Davis ordered Nabozny to go home and change clothes. Nabozny's parents scheduled a meeting with Davis and Assistant Principal Thomas Blauert. At the meeting, the parties discussed numerous instances of harassment against Nabozny, including the restroom incident.

Rather than taking action against the perpetrators, Davis and Blauert referred Nabozny to Mr. Reeder, a school guidance counselor. Reeder was supposed to change Nabozny's schedule so as to minimize Nabozny's exposure to the offending students. Eventually the school placed Nabozny in a special education class; Stephen Huntley and Roy Grande were special education students. Nabozny's parents continued to insist that the school take action, repeatedly meeting with Davis and Blauert among others. Nabozny's parents' efforts were futile; no action was taken. In the middle of his ninth grade year, Nabozny again attempted suicide. Following another hospital stay and a period living with relatives, Nabozny ran away to Minneapolis. His parents convinced him to return to Ashland by promising that Nabozny would not have to attend Ashland High. Because Nabozny's parents were unable to afford private schooling, however, the Department of Social Services ordered Nabozny to return to Ashland High.

In tenth grade, Nabozny fared no better. Nabozny's parents moved, forcing Nabozny to rely on the school bus to take him to school. Students on the bus regularly used epithets, such as "fag" and "queer," to refer to Nabozny. Some students even pelted Nabozny with dangerous objects such as steel nuts and bolts. When Nabozny's parents complained to the school, school officials changed Nabozny's assigned seat and moved him to the front of the bus. The harassment continued. Ms. Hanson, a school guidance counselor, lobbied the school's administration to take more aggressive action to no avail. The worst was yet to come, however. One morning when Nabozny arrived early to school, he went to the library to study. The library was not yet open, so Nabozny sat down in the hallway. Minutes later he was met by a group of eight boys led by Stephen Huntley. Huntley began kicking Nabozny in the stomach, and continued to do so for five to ten minutes while the other students looked on laughing. Nabozny reported the incident to Hanson, who referred him to the school's "police liaison" Dan Crawford. Nabozny told Crawford that he wanted to press charges, but Crawford dissuaded him. Crawford promised to speak to the offending boys instead. Meanwhile, at Crawford's behest, Nabozny reported the incident to Blauert. Blauert, the school official supposedly in charge of disciplining, laughed and told Nabozny that Nabozny deserved such treatment because he is gay. Weeks later Nabozny collapsed from internal bleeding that resulted from Huntley's beating. Nabozny's parents and counselor Hanson repeatedly urged Davis and Blauert to take action to protect Nabozny. Each time aggressive action was promised. And, each time nothing was done.

Finally, in his eleventh grade year, Nabozny withdrew from Ashland High School. Hanson told Nabozny and his parents that school administrators were unwilling to help him and that he should seek educational opportunities elsewhere. Nabozny left Ashland and moved to Minneapolis where he was diagnosed with Post Traumatic Stress Disorder. In addition to seeking medical help, Nabozny sought legal advice.

....

We will begin our analysis by considering Nabozny's equal protection claims, reserving Nabozny's due process claims for subsequent treatment in the opinion. Wisconsin has elected to protect the students in its schools from discrimination. Wisconsin statute section 118.13(1), regulating general school operations, provides that:

> No person may be denied ... participation in, be denied the benefits of or be discriminated against in any curricular, extracurricular, pupil services, recreational or other program or activity because of the person's sex, race, religion, national origin, ancestry, creed, pregnancy, marital or parental status, sexual orientation or physical, mental, emotional or learning disability.

Since at least 1988, in compliance with the state statute, the Ashland Public School District has had a policy of prohibiting discrimination against students on the basis of gender or sexual orientation. The District's policy and practice includes protecting students from student-on-student sexual harassment and battery. Nabozny maintains that the defendants denied him the equal protection of the law by denying him the protection extended to other students, based on his gender and sexual orientation.

The Equal Protection Clause grants to all Americans "the right to be free from invidious discrimination in statutory classifications and other governmental activity." When a state actor turns a blind eye to the Clause's command, aggrieved parties such as Nabozny can seek relief pursuant to 42 U.S.C. § 1983. In order to establish liability under § 1983, Nabozny must show that the defendants acted with a nefarious discriminatory purpose, and discriminated against him based on his membership in a definable class.... A showing that the defendants were negligent will not suffice. Nabozny must show that the defendants acted either intentionally or with deliberate indifference. To escape liability, the defendants either must prove that they did not discriminate against Nabozny, or at a bare minimum, the defendants' discriminatory conduct must satisfy one of two well-established standards of review: heightened scrutiny in the case of gender discrimination, or rational basis in the case of sexual orientation.

....

A. Gender and Equal Protection

The district court disposed of Nabozny's equal protection claims in two brief paragraphs. Regarding the merits of Nabozny's gender claim, the court concluded that "[t]here is absolutely nothing in the record to indicate that plaintiff was treated differently because of his gender." The district court's conclusion affords two interpretations: 1) there is no evidence that the defendants treated Nabozny differently from other students; or, 2) there is no evidence that the discriminatory treatment was based on Nabozny's gender. We will examine each in turn.

The record viewed in the light most favorable to Nabozny, combined with the defendants' own admissions, suggests that Nabozny was treated differently from other students. The defendants stipulate that they had a commendable record of enforcing their anti-harassment policies. Yet Nabozny has presented evidence that his classmates harassed and battered him for years and that school administrators failed to enforce their anti-harassment policies, despite his repeated pleas for them to do so. If the defendants otherwise enforced their anti-harassment policies, as they contend, then Nabozny's evidence strongly suggests that they made an exception to their normal practice in Nabozny's case.

Therefore, the question becomes whether Nabozny can show that he received different treatment because of his gender. Nabozny's evidence regarding the defendants' punishment of male-on-female battery and harassment is not overwhelming. Nabozny contends that a male student that struck his girlfriend was immediately expelled, that males were reprimanded for striking girls, and that when pregnant girls were called "slut" or "whore," the school took action. Nabozny's evidence does not include specific facts, such as the names and dates of the individuals involved. Nabozny does allege, however, that when he was subjected to a mock rape Podlesny responded by saying "boys will be boys," apparently dismissing the incident because both the perpetrators and the victim were males. We find it impossible to believe that a female lodging a similar complaint would have received the same response.

More important, the defendants do not deny that they aggressively punished male-on-female battery and harassment. The defendants argue that they investigated and punished all complaints of battery and harassment, regardless of the victim's gender. According to the defendants, contrary to the evidence presented by Nabozny, they aggressively pursued each of Nabozny's complaints and punished the alleged perpetrators whenever possible. Like Nabozny, the defendants presented evidence to support their claim. Whether to believe the defendants or Nabozny is, of course, a question of credibility for the fact-finder. In the context of considering the defendants' summary judgment motion, we must assume that Nabozny's version is the credible one. If Nabozny's evidence is considered credible, the record taken in conjunction with the defendants' admissions demonstrates that the defendants treated male and female victims differently.

The defendants also argue that there is no evidence that they either intentionally discriminated against Nabozny, or were deliberately indifferent to his complaints. The defendants concede that they had a policy and practice of punishing perpetrators of battery and harassment. It is well settled law that departures from established practices may evince discriminatory intent. Moreover, Nabozny introduced evidence to suggest that the defendants literally laughed at Nabozny's pleas for help. The defendants' argument, considered against Nabozny's evidence, is simply indefensible.

Our inquiry into Nabozny's gender equal protection claim does not end here, because the district court granted to the defendants qualified immunity. The District itself clearly is not entitled to qualified immunity. *See Owen v. City of Independence, Mo.*, 445 U.S. 622, 650–51 (1980) (denying to municipalities qualified immunity based on good faith constitutional violations). Therefore, we need only consider whether the individual defendants are immune from suit.

In *Harlow v. Fitzgerald*, 457 U.S. 800 (1982), the Supreme Court held that "government officials performing discretionary functions generally are shielded from liability for civil damages insofar as their conduct does not violate clearly established statutory or constitutional rights of which a reasonable person would have known." If the law was not "clearly established," no liability should result because "an official could not reasonably be expected to anticipate subsequent legal developments, nor could be said to 'know' that the law forbade conduct not previously identified as unlawful." *Id.* Thus, the critical questions in this case are whether the law "clearly establishes" the basis for Nabozny's claim, and whether the law was so established in 1988 when Nabozny entered middle school.

The Fourteenth Amendment provides that a State shall not "deny to any person within its jurisdiction the equal protection of the laws." In 1971, the Supreme Court interpreted the Equal Protection Clause to prevent arbitrary gender-based discrimination. *See Reed v. Reed*, 404 U.S. 71, 76 (1971). A few years later, in *Weinberger v. Wiesenfeld*, 420 U.S. 636 (1975), the Court held that discrimination based on "gender-based generalization[s]" in society runs afoul of the Equal Protection Clause.

In Mississippi University for Women v. Hogan, 458 U.S. 718 (1982), building on its earlier precedents, the Court went further in requiring equal treatment regardless of gender. In *Hogan*, the Court struck down a state statute that prevented males from enrolling in a state nursing school as violating the Equal Protection Clause. Rejecting Mississippi's argument that gender-biased enrollment criteria were necessary to compensate for prior discrimination, the Court held that "if the statutory objective is to exclude or 'protect' members of one gender because they are presumed to suffer from an inherent handicap or to be innately inferior, the objective itself is illegitimate." *Hogan* made clear, in 1982, that state-sponsored educational institutions may not discriminate in their protection of men and women based on a stereotype of feminine weakness or inferiority. It is now well settled that to survive constitutional scrutiny, gender based discrimination must be substantially related to an important governmental objective.

Nonetheless, the defendants ask us to affirm the grant of qualified immunity because "there was no clear duty under the equal protection clause for the individual defendants to enforce every student complaint of harassment by other students the same way." The defendants are correct in that the Equal Protection Clause does not require the government to give everyone identical treatment. Nothing we say today suggests anything to the contrary. The Equal Protection Clause does, however, require the state to treat each person with equal regard, as having equal worth, regardless of his or her status. The defendants' argument fails because they frame their inquiry too narrowly. The question is not whether they are required to treat every harassment complaint the same way; as we have noted, they are not. The question is whether they are required to give male and female students equivalent levels of protection; they are, absent an important governmental objective, and the law clearly said so prior to Nabozny's years in middle school.

The defendants bemoan the fact that there is no prior case directly on point with facts identical to this case. Under the doctrine of qualified immunity, liability is not predicated upon the existence of a prior case that is directly on point. The question is whether a reasonable state actor would have known that his actions, viewed in the light of the law at the time, were unlawful. We believe that reasonable persons standing in the defendants' shoes at the time would have reached just such a conclusion.

B. Sexual Orientation and Equal Protection

On the face of the summary judgment order, the fate of Nabozny's sexual orientation equal protection claim is unclear. In the order the district court never specifically discussed Nabozny's sexual orientation claim. There is little doubt, however, that the district court intended for its order to dispose of Nabozny's suit in its entirety. In the interest of judicial economy, rather than remanding the claim back to the district court, we will assume that the court's disposition of Nabozny's sexual orientation claim was synonymous with, and on the same grounds as, the court's disposition of Nabozny's gender claim.

First we must consider whether Nabozny proffered a sufficient evidentiary basis to support his claim. As we noted above, Nabozny's evidence, combined with the defendants' admissions, demonstrates that Nabozny was treated differently. What is more, Nabozny introduced sufficient evidence to show that the discriminatory treatment was motivated by the defendants' disapproval of Nabozny's sexual orientation, including statements by the defendants that Nabozny should expect to be harassed because he is gay.

Next we must consider whether the defendants are entitled to qualified immunity. In other words, we must determine whether reasonable persons in the defendants' positions would have known that discrimination against Nabozny based on his sexual orientation, viewed in the light of the law at the time, was unlawful.

Our discussion of equal protection analysis thus far has revealed a well established principle: the Constitution prohibits intentional invidious discrimination between otherwise similarly situated persons based on one's membership in a definable minority, absent at least a rational basis for the discrimination. There can be little doubt that homosexuals are an identifiable minority subjected to discrimination in our society. Given the legislation across the country both positing and prohibiting homosexual rights, that proposition was as self-evident in 1988 as it is today. In addition, the Wisconsin statute expressly prohibits discrimination on the basis of sexual orientation. Obviously that language was included because the Wisconsin legislature both recognized that homosexuals are discriminated against, and sought to prohibit such discrimination in Wisconsin schools. The defendants stipulate that they knew about the Wisconsin law, and enforced it to protect homosexuals. Therefore, it appears that the defendants concede that they knew that homosexuals are a definable minority and treated them as such.

In this case we need not consider whether homosexuals are a suspect or quasi-suspect class, which would subject the defendants' conduct to either strict or heightened scrutiny. Our court has already ruled that, in the context of the military, discrimination on the basis of sexual orientation is subject to rational basis review. The rational basis standard is sufficient for our purposes herein.

Under rational basis review there is no constitutional violation if "there is any reasonably conceivable state of facts" that would provide a rational basis for the government's conduct. We are unable to garner any rational basis for permitting one student to assault another based on the victim's sexual orientation, and the defendants do not offer us one. Like Nabozny's gender claim, the defendants argue that they did not discriminate against Nabozny.

Absent any rational basis for their alleged discrimination, the defendants are left to argue that the principle that the Constitution prohibits discrimination between similarly situated persons based on membership in a delineable class was somehow unclear back in 1988. We find that suggestion unacceptable. As early as 1886 the Supreme Court held that if the law "is applied and administered by public authority with an evil eye and an unequal hand, so as practically to make unjust and illegal discriminations between persons in similar circumstances, material to their rights, the denial of equal justice is still within the prohibition of the Constitution." *Yick Wo v. Hopkins*, 118 U.S. 356, 373–74 (1886). Further, almost every case that we have cited thus far was decided prior to the events giving rise to this litigation.

. . . .

Therefore, although it presents a closer question than does Nabozny's gender claim, we hold that reasonable persons in the defendants' positions in 1988 would have concluded that discrimination against Nabozny based on his sexual orientation was unconstitutional.

Now we turn to Nabozny's due process arguments. We believe that in order to clarify the nature of Nabozny's due process theories, it is necessary to specify what Nabozny does not argue. However untenable it may be to suggest that under the Fourteenth Amendment a state can force a student to attend a school when school officials know that the student will be placed at risk of bodily harm, our court has concluded that local school administrations have no affirmative substantive due process duty to protect students. *J.O. v. Alton Community Unit School Dist. 11*, 909 F.2d 267, 272–73 (7th Cir. 1990). In *J.O. v. Alton Community Unit School District 11*, we relied on the Supreme Court's opinion in *DeShaney v. Winnebago County Department of Social Services* to conclude that school administrators do not have a "special relationship" with students. Absent a "special relationship," a state actor has no duty to protect a potential victim. *See DeShaney*, 489 U.S. at 200, 109 S. Ct. at 1005–06 ("The affirmative duty to protect arises not from the State's knowledge of the individual's predicament or from its expressions of intent to help him, but from the limitation which it has imposed on his freedom to act on his own behalf."). Nabozny has expressly stated that he does not challenge our holding in *Alton Community*, thereby forfeiting his right to do so. . . . Having clarified Nabozny's forfeiture, we turn to the arguments that were raised by Nabozny.

Nabozny argues that the defendants should be liable because they enhanced his risk of harm, and because their policies encouraged a climate in which he suffered harm. We will consider each theory in turn. First, Nabozny argues that by failing to punish his assailants the defendants exacerbated the risk that he would be harmed, or even encouraged the students to harm him. Nabozny relies on our opinion in *Reed v. Gardner*, 986 F.2d 1122 (7th Cir.), *cert. denied*, 510 U.S. 947, 114 S. Ct. 389, 126 L. Ed. 2d 337 (1993). In *Reed*, we considered a case in which police officers arrested the driver of an automobile, but left an intoxicated passenger on the side of the road with the keys to the car. *Id.* at 1124. After the police left, the intoxicated passenger drove the car onto the road and caused a serious accident. The victims of the accident sued the police officers pursuant to § 1983 for leaving the intoxicated passenger on the side of the road, arguing that the officers' conduct deprived the victims of their Fourteenth Amendment right to due process. We reversed a lower court's dismissal of the complaint, ruling that state actors have a duty to care for citizens if the state actors' conduct "creates, or substantially contributes to the creation of, a danger or renders citizens more vulnerable to a danger than they otherwise would have been." But we noted that the plaintiffs would lose on summary judgment if the defendants could show that the arrested driver was also intoxicated: "[t]he reason is simple: without state intervention, the same danger would exist."

We agree with Nabozny in principle that the defendants could be liable under a due process theory if Nabozny could show that the defendants created a risk of harm, or exacerbated an existing one. After a thorough review of the record, however, we must agree with the district court that Nabozny's claim suffers from a paucity of evidence. Nabozny has presented evidence to show that the defendants failed to act, and that their failure to act was intentional. But, as we noted, *Alton Community* held that the defendants had no affirmative duty to act. The defendants' failure to act left Nabozny in a position of danger, but nothing suggests that their failure to act placed him in the danger, or increased the pre-existing threat of harm. Nabozny has presented "wrenching" facts, but there is insufficient evidence from which a reasonable factfinder could conclude that the defendants' conduct increased the risk of harm to Nabozny beyond that which he would have faced had the defendants taken no action.

Under Nabozny's second theory, he argues that the defendants violated his right to due process by acting with deliberate indifference in maintaining a policy or practice of failing to punish his assailants, thereby encouraging a harmful environment. The district court rejected Nabozny's argument because the harm he suffered was not perpetrated by school employees. On appeal, Nabozny challenges the district court's reasoning, arguing that liability can result regardless whether students or teachers inflicted the harm.

....

Nabozny argues, and presents facts suggesting, that the defendants had a policy or practice of ignoring his pleas for help, and that as a result, he was repeatedly assaulted. Nabozny's theory has one fatal flaw: it rests on a failure to act. Under *Alton Community* the defendants had no duty to act. Therefore, to hold them liable for adopting a practice of failing to act would run directly counter to *Alton Community.*

....

Post Problem Discussion

1. Most courts addressing the issue of substantive due process claims for failing to protect students have followed the approach in *Covington* and *Nabozny.* At least one Federal District Court, *Pagano v. Massapequa Public School*, 714 F. Supp. 641 (E.D.N.Y.1989), took a different view. Which approach did you choose and why?

2. In *Covington*, the court stated that "Despite her young age, Jane was not attending the school through the 'affirmative exercise of [state] power,' she was attending

the school because her parents voluntarily chose to send her there (as one of several ways to fulfill their compulsory education obligations), and they remained responsible for her basic needs. . . . Jane's parents were free at any time to remove Jane from the school if they felt that her safety was being compromised." Are those statements accurate based on what you learned about state compulsory attendance laws in Chapter 5, Section 5.02? What are the "several ways" that the parents could fulfill their compulsory education requirements? Are any of those ways funded by the state, or are the parents responsible for any costs? Do your state compulsory laws allow parents to remove students from school if the parents feel the student's safety is compromised?

3. After the *Covington* decision was issued, a federal district court in Texas reconsidered a prior decision that had denied a school district's motion for summary judgment on a student's due process claim. The student's estate had brought a variety of claims alleging that the school had failed to protect the student from bullying which led to her suicide. The court stated:

> The restraints placed on the Court by *Covington*—and, indeed, by *DeShaney* and its progeny in the Fifth Circuit—are nonetheless troubling. The holding in *Covington* has the undesirable effect here of allowing a school district to affirmatively enact anti-bullying policies which purport to assume responsibility to react to private violence, that is, violence inflicted by other students, yet absolve the same school district of responsibility for enforcement of such policies absent the existence of a special relationship. Sadly, this is not new. *See, e.g., Town of Castle Rock v. Gonzales*, 545 U.S. 748 (2005) (finding that plaintiff had failed to state a due process claim where police failure to enforce restraining order against plaintiff's estranged husband resulted in husband's killing of plaintiff's three daughters).
>
> Further, the effect of *Covington* would seem to undermine state laws requiring schools to adopt—and, presumably, enforce—anti-bullying policies. The Fifth Circuit is content to pass this concern on to the state courts, positing that schools "may have such a duty [to ensure that students are safe during the school day] by virtue of a state's tort or other laws." *Covington*, 675 F.3d at 858. This stance is especially unfortunate here given that the Texas Tort Claims Act forecloses Truong from pursuing a state law remedy in this case. *See* Tex. Civ. Prac. & Rem.Code § 101.001 *et seq.* Following *Covington*, in the absence of a special relationship between the school and the student, public school officials who enact anti-bullying policies do not violate a student's constitutional due process rights by failing to enforce such policies, no matter how pervasive the bullying, no matter how hateful, and no matter how many lives, in addition to Asher's, are lost.

Estate of Brown v. Cypress Fairbanks Indep. Sch. Dist., 863 F. Supp. 2d 632, 638–39 (S.D. Tex. 2012). What recourse does a student have when they are harmed by others at public school if they are unable to bring a § 1983 claim, and state law prohibits claims against school districts?

4. In *Nabozny*, the court allows the equal protection claim to go forward, but not the due process claim, because of the lack of a special relationship and, as a result, a lack of any obligation to protect. Why is the special relationship only required for the due process claim? Why can the equal protection claim go forward when the due process claim cannot? Does Kara have a viable equal protection claim?

5. In addressing the due process claim, the court in *Nabozny* notes that "the defendants could be liable under a due process theory if *Nabozny* could show that the defendants created a risk of harm, or exacerbated an existing one." Why do you think this kind of due process claim could go forward even without the special relationship that the court ruled did not exist? Does Kara have a claim that fits into this category?

6. In *Nabozny* and *Covington*, the courts note that a § 1983 action requires a plaintiff to prove that the defendants acted either intentionally, or with deliberate indifference, as opposed to negligence. "[D]eliberate indifference is a stringent standard of fault, requiring proof that a municipal actor disregarded a known or obvious consequence of his action." *Board of County Comm'rs. v. Brown*, 520 U.S. 397 (1997). Does Kara's situation meet this requirement? See Problem 5 for more about the deliberate indifference standard.

7. *Covington* discusses *Monell v. Department of Social Services*, a decision where the United States Supreme Court ruled that municipalities cannot be vicariously liable for the acts of its employees under § 1983. In the education law context, that means that unlike state common law, where a school board/school district can be vicariously liable for the torts of its employees, it cannot under § 1983. Rather, under § 1983, a plaintiff must be able to trace the action of the employees who actually injured him/her back to a policy or other action of the municipality itself. How would this requirement affect Kara's claims against the school board/district?

B. Title IX Liability

Another form of federal liability for schools comes from Title IX of the Education Amendments Act of 1972, a Spending Clause statute that prohibits gender discrimination by agencies (including schools) that receive federal funds. 20 U.S.C. §§ 1681–88. Title IX provides in relevant part:

> No person in the United States shall, on the basis of sex, be excluded from participation in, be denied the benefits of, or be subjected to discrimination under any educational program or activity receiving Federal financial assistance....

There is an implied private right of action under Title IX, *Cannon v. Univ. of Chicago*, 441 U.S. 677 (1978), and monetary damages are an available remedy. *Franklin v. Gwinnett County Pub. Sch.*, 503 U.S. 60 (1992). In applying Title IX remedies in school situations, courts have incorporated some of the § 1983 standards noted in *Nabozny*. For example, in *Gebser v. Lago Vista Indep. Sch. Dist*, 524 U.S. 274 (1998), the Supreme Court noted that school officials could be liable under Title IX for sexual harassment by a teacher towards a student if the school officials were "deliberately indifferent" to allegations of harassment of which they had actual knowledge.

A year after the Court decided *Gebser*, it extended its analysis to situations where a student alleges sexual harassment by another student at school. In *Davis v. Monroe County Bd. of Educ.*, 526 U.S. 629 (1999), the Court applied *Gebser* and found that a school board could be liable for student on student sexual harassment when it "acts with deliberate indifference to known acts of harassment in its programs or activities," and where the harassment "is so severe, pervasive, and objectively offensive that it effectively bars the victim's access to an educational opportunity or benefit." *Davis*, 526 U.S. at 633 (1999). Since that time, courts have tried to determine the parameters of these requirements.

Problem 5: Kara's Claims Under Federal Law—Part 2

Recall that the original problem regarding Kara included a photo sent to her cell phone, and two students were caught viewing the photo at school. Assume that the doctored picture gets around school and the three girls start to spread rumors at school about Kara's sexual orientation and sexual promiscuity. Male and female students begin teasing Kara at school about receiving sexual favors from her. Assume that Kara's mother informs the principal that students have started teasing Kara at school, but provides no further information about it because Kara will not tell her the details.

1. Does Kara have a viable claim under Title IX based on these facts?
2. What steps should the school take to limit or avoid liability?

Problem Materials

✓ *Gebser v. Lago Vista Ind. Sch. Dist.*, 524 U.S. 274 (1998)

✓ *Davis v. Monroe County Board of Education*, 526 U.S. 629 (1999)

✓ *Vance v. Spencer County Public School District*, 231 F.3d 253 (6th Cir. 2000)

✓ *Rost v. Steamboat Springs Re-2 School District*, 511 F.3d 1114 (10th Cir. 2008)

Gebser v. Lago Vista Independent School District

524 U.S. 274 (1998)

The Court finds that school district liability for monetary damages under Title IX resulting from a teacher's sexual harassment of a student, requires a showing that the school district had actual notice of the teacher's actions, and acted with deliberate indifference.

Justice O'Connor delivered the opinion of the Court, in which Rehnquist, C.J., and Scalia, Kennedy, and Thomas, JJ., joined.

The question in this case is when a school district may be held liable in damages in an implied right of action under Title IX of the Education Amendments of 1972,

86 Stat. 373, as amended, 20 U.S.C. § 1681 *et seq.* (Title IX), for the sexual harassment of a student by one of the district's teachers. We conclude that damages may not be recovered in those circumstances unless an official of the school district who at a minimum has authority to institute corrective measures on the district's behalf has actual notice of, and is deliberately indifferent to, the teacher's misconduct.

I

In the spring of 1991, when petitioner Alida Star Gebser was an eighth-grade student at a middle school in respondent Lago Vista Independent School District (Lago Vista), she joined a high school book discussion group led by Frank Waldrop, a teacher at Lago Vista's high school. Lago Vista received federal funds at all pertinent times. During the book discussion sessions, Waldrop often made sexually suggestive comments to the students. Gebser entered high school in the fall and was assigned to classes taught by Waldrop in both semesters. Waldrop continued to make inappropriate remarks to the students, and he began to direct more of his suggestive comments toward Gebser, including during the substantial amount of time that the two were alone in his classroom. He initiated sexual contact with Gebser in the spring, when, while visiting her home ostensibly to give her a book, he kissed and fondled her. The two had sexual intercourse on a number of occasions during the remainder of the school year. Their relationship continued through the summer and into the following school year, and they often had intercourse during class time, although never on school property.

Gebser did not report the relationship to school officials, testifying that while she realized Waldrop's conduct was improper, she was uncertain how to react and she wanted to continue having him as a teacher. In October 1992, the parents of two other students complained to the high school principal about Waldrop's comments in class. The principal arranged a meeting, at which, according to the principal, Waldrop indicated that he did not believe he had made offensive remarks but apologized to the parents and said it would not happen again. The principal also advised Waldrop to be careful about his classroom comments and told the school guidance counselor about the meeting, but he did not report the parents' complaint to Lago Vista's superintendent, who was the district's Title IX coordinator. A couple of months later, in January 1993, a police officer discovered Waldrop and Gebser engaging in sexual intercourse and arrested Waldrop. Lago Vista terminated his employment, and subsequently, the Texas Education Agency revoked his teaching license. During this time, the district had not promulgated or distributed an official grievance procedure for lodging sexual harassment complaints; nor had it issued a formal anti-harassment policy.

Gebser and her mother filed suit against Lago Vista and Waldrop in state court in November 1993, raising claims against the school district under Title IX, Rev. Stat. § 1979, 42 U.S.C. § 1983, and state negligence law, and claims against Waldrop primarily under state law. They sought compensatory and punitive damages from both defendants. After the case was removed, the United States District Court for the Western District of Texas granted summary judgment in favor of Lago Vista on all claims, and remanded the allegations against Waldrop to state court. In rejecting the Title IX claim against the school district, the court reasoned that the statute "was enacted to counter *policies* of discrimination . . . in federally funded education programs," and that "[o]nly if school administrators have some type of notice of the gender discrimination and fail to respond in good faith can the discrimination be interpreted as a *policy* of the school district." Here, the court determined, the parents' complaint to the principal concerning Waldrop's comments in class was the only one Lago Vista had received about Waldrop, and that evidence was inadequate to raise a genuine issue on whether the school district had actual or constructive notice that Waldrop was involved in a sexual relationship with a student.

Petitioners appealed only on the Title IX claim. . . .

II

Title IX provides in pertinent part: "No person . . . shall, on the basis of sex, be excluded from participation in, be denied the benefits of, or be subjected to discrimination under any education program or activity receiving Federal financial assistance." 20 U.S.C. § 1681(a). The express statutory means of enforcement is administrative: The statute directs federal agencies that distribute education funding to establish requirements to effectuate the nondiscrimination mandate, and permits the agencies to enforce those requirements through "any . . . means authorized by law," including ultimately the termination of federal funding. § 1682. The Court held in *Cannon v. University of Chicago*, 441 U.S. 677 (1979), that Title IX is also enforceable through an implied private right of action, a conclusion we do not revisit here. We subsequently established in *Franklin v. Gwinnett County Public Schools*, 503 U.S. 60 (1992), that monetary damages are available in the implied private action.

In *Franklin*, a high school student alleged that a teacher had sexually abused her on repeated occasions and that teachers and school administrators knew about the harassment but took no action, even to the point of dissuading her from initiating charges. The lower courts dismissed Franklin's complaint against the school district on the ground that the implied right of action under Title IX, as a categorical matter, does not encompass recovery in damages. We reversed the lower courts' blanket rule, concluding that Title IX supports a private action for damages, at least "in a case such as this, in which intentional discrimination is alleged." *Franklin* thereby establishes that a school district can be held liable in damages in cases involving a teacher's sexual harassment of a student; the decision, however, does not purport to define the contours of that liability.

We face that issue squarely in this case. Petitioners, joined by the United States as *amicus curiae*, would invoke standards used by the Courts of Appeals in Title VII cases involving a supervisor's sexual harassment of an employee in the workplace. In support of that approach, they point to a passage in *Franklin* in which we stated: "Unquestionably, Title IX placed on the Gwinnett County Public Schools the duty not to discriminate on the basis of sex, and 'when a supervisor sexually harasses a subordinate because of the subordinate's sex, that supervisor "discriminate[s]" on the basis of sex.' We believe the same rule should apply when a teacher sexually harasses and abuses a student." *Meritor Savings Bank, FSB v. Vinson*, 477 U.S. 57 (1986), directs courts to look to common law agency principles when assessing an employer's liability under Title VII for sexual harassment of an employee by a supervisor. Petitioners and the United States submit that, in light of *Franklin*' s comparison of teacher-student harassment with supervisor-employee harassment, agency principles should likewise apply in Title IX actions.

Whether educational institutions can be said to violate Title IX based solely on principles of *respondeat superior* or constructive notice was not resolved by *Franklin*'s citation of *Meritor.*

In this case, moreover, petitioners seek not just to establish a Title IX violation but to recover *damages* based on theories of *respondeat superior* and constructive notice. It is that aspect of their action, in our view, that is most critical to resolving the case. Unlike Title IX, Title VII contains an express cause of action, § 2000e–5(f), and specifically provides for relief in the form of monetary damages, § 1981a. Congress therefore has directly addressed the subject of damages relief under Title VII and has set out the particular situations in which damages are available as well as the maximum amounts recoverable. § 1981a(b). With respect to Title IX, however, the private right of action is judicially implied, and there is thus no legislative expression of the scope of available remedies, including when it is appropriate to award monetary damages. In addition, although the general presumption that courts can award any appropriate relief in an established cause of action coupled with Congress' abrogation of the States' Eleventh Amendment immunity under Title IX, see 42 U.S.C. § 2000d–7, led us to conclude in *Franklin* that Title IX recognizes a damages remedy, we did so in response to lower court decisions holding that Title IX does not support damages relief at all. We made no effort in *Franklin* to delimit the circumstances in which a damages remedy should lie.

III

Because the private right of action under Title IX is judicially implied, we have a measure of latitude to shape a sensible remedial scheme that best comports with the statute. That endeavor inherently entails a degree of speculation, since it addresses an issue on which Congress has not specifically spoken. To guide the analysis, we generally examine the relevant statute to ensure that we do not fashion the scope of an implied right in a manner at odds with the statutory structure and purpose.

Those considerations, we think, are pertinent not only to the scope of the implied right, but also to the scope of the available remedies. We suggested as much in *Franklin*, where we recognized "the general rule that all appropriate relief is available in an action brought to vindicate a federal right," but indicated that the rule must be reconciled with congressional purpose. The "general rule," that is, "yields where necessary to carry out the intent of Congress or to avoid frustrating the purposes of the statute involved."

Applying those principles here, we conclude that it would "frustrate the purposes" of Title IX to permit a damages recovery against a school district for a teacher's sexual harassment of a student based on principles of *respondeat superior* or constructive notice, *i.e.*, without actual notice to a school district official. Because Congress did not expressly create a private right of action under Title IX, the statutory text does not shed light on Congress' intent with respect to the scope of available remedies. Instead, "we attempt to infer how the [1972] Congress would have addressed the issue had the . . . action been included as an express provision in the" statute.

As a general matter, it does not appear that Congress contemplated unlimited recovery in damages against a funding recipient where the recipient is unaware of discrimination in its programs. . . . Adopting petitioners' position would amount, then, to allowing unlimited recovery of damages under Title IX where Congress has not spoken on the subject of either the right or the remedy, and in the face of evidence that when Congress expressly considered both in Title VII it restricted the amount of damages available.

Congress enacted Title IX in 1972 with two principal objectives in mind: "[T]o avoid the use of federal resources to support discriminatory practices" and "to provide individual citizens effective protection against those practices." The statute was modeled after Title VI of the Civil Rights Act of 1964, which is parallel to Title IX except that it prohibits race discrimination, not sex discrimination, and applies in all programs receiving federal funds, not only in education programs. See 42 U.S.C. § 2000d *et seq.* The two statutes operate in the same manner, conditioning an offer of federal funding on a promise by the recipient not to discriminate, in what amounts essentially to a contract between the Government and the recipient of funds.

That contractual framework distinguishes Title IX from Title VII, which is framed in terms not of a condition but of an outright prohibition. Title VII applies to all employers without regard to federal funding and aims broadly to "eradicat[e] discrimination throughout the economy." Thus, whereas Title VII aims centrally to compensate victims of discrimination, Title IX focuses more on "protecting" individuals from discriminatory practices carried out by recipients of federal funds. That might explain why, when the Court first recognized the implied right under Title IX in *Cannon*, the opinion referred to injunctive or equitable relief in a private action, but not to a damages remedy.

Title IX's contractual nature has implications for our construction of the scope of available remedies. When Congress attaches conditions to the award of federal funds under its spending power, U.S. Const., Art. I, § 8, cl. 1, as it has in Title IX and Title VI, we examine closely the propriety of private actions holding the recipient liable in monetary damages for noncompliance with the condition. Our central concern in that regard is with ensuring that "the receiving entity of federal funds [has] notice that it will be liable for a monetary award." . . . . If a school district's liability for a teacher's sexual harassment rests on principles of constructive notice or *respondeat superior*, it will likewise be the case that the recipient of funds was unaware of the discrimination. It is sensible to assume that Congress did not envision a recipient's liability in damages in that situation.

Most significantly, Title IX contains important clues that Congress did not intend to allow recovery in damages where liability rests solely on principles of vicarious liability or constructive notice. . . .

In the event of a violation, a funding recipient may be required to take "such remedial action as [is] deem[ed] necessary to overcome the effects of [the] discrimination." § 106.3. While agencies have conditioned continued funding on providing equitable relief to the victim, the regulations do not appear to contemplate a condition ordering payment of monetary damages, and there is no indication that payment of damages has been demanded as a condition of finding a recipient to be in compliance with the statute. In *Franklin*, for instance, the Department of Education found a violation of Title IX but determined that the school district came into compliance by virtue of the offending teacher's resignation and the district's institution of a grievance procedure for sexual harassment complaints.

Presumably, a central purpose of requiring notice of the violation "to the appropriate person" and an opportunity for voluntary compliance before administrative enforcement proceedings can commence is to avoid diverting education funding from beneficial uses where a recipient was unaware of discrimination in its programs and is willing to institute prompt corrective measures. The scope of private damages relief proposed by petitioners is at odds with that basic objective. When a teacher's sexual harassment is imputed to a school district or when a school district is deemed to have "constructively" known of the teacher's harassment, by assumption the district had no actual knowledge of the teacher's conduct. Nor, of course, did the district have an opportunity to take action to end the harassment or to limit further harassment.

It would be unsound, we think, for a statute's *express* system of enforcement to require notice to the recipient and an opportunity to come into voluntary compliance while a judicially *implied* system of enforcement permits substantial liability without regard to the recipient's knowledge or its corrective actions upon receiving notice. Moreover, an award of damages in a particular case might well exceed a recipient's level of federal funding. Where a statute's express enforcement scheme hinges its most severe sanction on notice and unsuccessful efforts to obtain compliance, we cannot attribute to Congress the intention to have implied an enforcement scheme that allows imposition of greater liability without comparable conditions.

IV

Because the express remedial scheme under Title IX is predicated upon notice to an "appropriate person" and an opportunity to rectify any violation, 20 U.S.C. § 1682, we conclude, in the absence of further direction from Congress, that the implied damages remedy should be fashioned along the same lines. An "appropriate person" under § 1682 is, at a minimum, an official of the recipient entity with authority to take corrective action to end the discrimination. Consequently, in cases like this one that do not involve official policy of the recipient entity, we hold that a damages remedy will not lie under Title IX unless an official who at a minimum has authority to address the alleged discrimination and to institute corrective measures on the recipient's behalf has actual knowledge of discrimination in the recipient's programs and fails adequately to respond.

We think, moreover, that the response must amount to deliberate indifference to discrimination. The administrative enforcement scheme presupposes that an official who is advised of a Title IX violation refuses to take action to bring the recipient into compliance. The premise, in other words, is an official decision by the recipient not to remedy the violation. That framework finds a rough parallel in the standard of deliberate indifference. Under a lower standard, there would be a risk that the recipient would be liable in damages not for its own official decision but instead for its employees' independent actions. Comparable considerations led to our adoption of a deliberate indifference standard for claims under § 1983 alleging that a municipality's actions in failing to prevent a deprivation of federal rights was the cause of the violation.

Applying the framework to this case is fairly straightforward, as petitioners do not contend they can prevail under an actual notice standard. The only official alleged to have had information about Waldrop's misconduct is the high school principal. That information, however, consisted of a complaint from parents of other students charging only that Waldrop had made inappropriate comments during class, which was plainly insufficient to alert the principal to the possibility that Waldrop was involved in a sexual relationship with a student. Lago Vista, moreover, terminated Waldrop's employment upon learning of his relationship with Gebser. Justice STEVENS points out in his dissenting opinion that Waldrop of course had knowledge of his own actions. Where a school district's liability rests on actual notice principles, however, the knowledge of the wrongdoer himself is not pertinent to the analysis. See Restatement § 280.

Petitioners focus primarily on Lago Vista's asserted failure to promulgate and publicize an effective policy and grievance procedure for sexual harassment claims. They point to Department of Education regulations requiring each funding recipient to "adopt and publish grievance procedures providing for prompt and equitable resolution" of discrimination complaints, 34 C.F.R. § 106.8(b) (1997), and to notify students and others that "it does not discriminate on the basis of sex in the educational programs or activities which it operates," § 106.9(a). Lago Vista's alleged failure to comply with the regulations, however, does not establish the requisite actual notice and deliberate indifference. And in any event, the failure to promulgate a grievance procedure does not itself constitute "discrimination" under Title IX. Of course, the Department of Education could enforce the requirement administratively: Agencies generally have authority to promulgate and enforce requirements that effectuate the statute's nondiscrimination mandate, 20 U.S.C. § 1682, even if those requirements do not purport to represent a definition of discrimination under the statute. We have never held, however, that the implied private right of action under Title IX allows recovery in damages for violation of those sorts of administrative requirements.

V

The number of reported cases involving sexual harassment of students in schools confirms that harassment unfortunately is an all too common aspect of the educational experience. No one questions that a student suffers extraordinary harm when subjected to sexual harassment and abuse by a teacher, and that the teacher's conduct is reprehensible and undermines the basic purposes of the educational system. The issue in this case, however, is whether the independent misconduct of a teacher is attributable to the school district that employs him under a specific federal statute designed primarily to prevent recipients of federal financial assistance from using the funds in a discriminatory manner. Our decision does not affect any right of recovery that an individual may have against a school district as a matter of state law or against the teacher in his individual capacity under state law or under 42 U.S.C. § 1983. Until Congress speaks directly on the subject, however, we will not hold a school district liable in damages under Title IX for a teacher's sexual harassment of a student absent actual notice and deliberate indifference. We therefore affirm the judgment of the Court of Appeals.

It is so ordered.

Davis v. Monroe County Board of Education

526 U.S. 629 (1999)

The Court rules that a school board may be liable for monetary damages under Title IX when it is "deliberately indifferent" to student on student sexual harassment.

Justice O'Connor delivered the opinion of the Court, in which Stevens, Souter, Ginsburg, and Breyer, JJ., joined.

Petitioner brought suit against the Monroe County Board of Education and other defendants, alleging that her fifth-grade daughter had been the victim of sexual harassment by another student in her class. Among petitioner's claims was a claim for monetary and injunctive relief under Title IX of the Education Amendments of 1972 (Title IX).... The District Court dismissed petitioner's Title IX claim on the ground that "student-on-student," or peer, harassment provides no ground for a private cause of action under the statute. The Court of Appeals for the Eleventh Circuit, sitting en banc, affirmed. We consider here whether a private damages action may lie against the school board in cases of student-on-student harassment. We conclude that it may, but only where the funding recipient acts with deliberate indifference to known acts of harassment in its programs or activities. Moreover, we conclude that such an action will lie only for harassment that is so severe, pervasive, and objectively offensive that it effectively bars the victim's access to an educational opportunity or benefit.

....

Petitioner's minor daughter, LaShonda, was allegedly the victim of a prolonged pattern of sexual harassment by one of her fifth-grade classmates at Hubbard Elementary School, a public school in Monroe County, Georgia. According to petitioner's complaint, the harassment began in December 1992, when the classmate, G.F., attempted to touch LaShonda's breasts and genital area and made vulgar statements such as "'I want to get in bed with you'" and "'I want to feel your boobs.'" Similar conduct allegedly occurred on or about January 4 and January 20, 1993. LaShonda reported each of these incidents to her mother and to her classroom teacher, Diane Fort. Petitioner, in turn, also contacted Fort, who allegedly assured petitioner that the school principal, Bill Querry, had been informed of the incidents. Petitioner contends that, notwithstanding these reports, no disciplinary action was taken against G.F.

G.F.'s conduct allegedly continued for many months. In early February, G.F. purportedly placed a door stop in his pants and proceeded to act in a sexually suggestive manner toward LaShonda during physical education class. LaShonda reported G.F.'s behavior to her physical education teacher, Whit Maples. Approximately one week later, G.F. again allegedly engaged in harassing behavior, this time while under the supervision of another classroom teacher, Joyce Pippin. Again, LaShonda allegedly reported the incident to the teacher, and again petitioner contacted the teacher to follow up.

Petitioner alleges that G.F. once more directed sexually harassing conduct toward LaShonda in physical education class in early March, and that LaShonda reported the incident to both Maples and Pippen. In mid-April 1993, G.F. allegedly rubbed his body against LaShonda in the school hallway in what LaShonda considered a sexually suggestive manner, and LaShonda again reported the matter to Fort.

The string of incidents finally ended in mid-May, when G.F. was charged with, and pleaded guilty to, sexual battery for his misconduct. The complaint alleges that LaShonda had suffered during the months of harassment, however; specifically, her previously high grades allegedly dropped as she became unable to concentrate on her studies, and, in April 1993, her father discovered that she had written a suicide note. The complaint further alleges that, at one point, LaShonda told petitioner that she "'didn't know how much longer she could keep [G.F.] off her.'"

Nor was LaShonda G.F.'s only victim; it is alleged that other girls in the class fell prey to G.F.'s conduct. At one point, in fact, a group composed of LaShonda and other female students tried to speak with Principal Querry about G.F.'s behavior. According to the complaint, however, a teacher denied the students' request with the statement, "'If [Querry] wants you, he'll call you.'"

Petitioner alleges that no disciplinary action was taken in response to G.F.'s behavior toward LaShonda. In addition to her conversations with Fort and Pippen, petitioner alleges that she spoke with Principal Querry in mid-May 1993. When petitioner inquired as to what action the school intended to take against G.F., Querry simply stated, "'I guess I'll have to threaten him a little bit harder.'" Yet, petitioner alleges, at no point during the many months of his reported misconduct was G.F. disciplined for harassment. Indeed, Querry allegedly asked petitioner why LaShonda "'was the only one complaining.'"

Nor, according to the complaint, was any effort made to separate G.F. and LaShonda. On the contrary, notwithstanding LaShonda's frequent complaints, only after more than three months of reported harassment was she even permitted to change her classroom seat so that she was no longer seated next to G.F. Moreover, petitioner alleges that, at the time of the events in question, the Monroe County Board of Education (Board) had not instructed its personnel on how to respond to peer sexual harassment and had not established a policy on the issue.

....

We must determine whether a district's failure to respond to student-on-student harassment in its schools can support a private suit for money damages. This Court has indeed recognized an implied private right of action under Title IX. Because we have repeatedly treated Title IX as legislation enacted pursuant to Congress' authority under the Spending Clause, however, private damages actions are available only where recipients of federal funding had adequate notice that they could be liable for the conduct at issue. When Congress acts pursuant to its spending power, it generates legislation "much in the nature of a contract: in return for federal funds, the States agree to comply with federally imposed conditions." *Pennhurst State School and Hospital v. Halderman*, 451 U.S. 1 (1981). In interpreting language in spending legislation, we thus "insis[t] that Congress speak with a clear voice," recognizing that "[t]here can, of course, be no knowing acceptance [of the terms of the putative contract] if a State is unaware of the conditions [imposed by the legislation] or is unable to ascertain what is expected of it."

Invoking *Pennhurst*, respondents urge that Title IX provides no notice that recipients of federal educational funds could be liable in damages for harm arising from student-on-student harassment. Respondents contend, specifically, that the statute only proscribes misconduct by grant recipients, not third parties. Respondents argue, moreover, that it would be contrary to the very purpose of Spending Clause legislation to impose liability on a funding recipient for the misconduct of third parties, over whom recipients exercise little control.

We agree with respondents that a recipient of federal funds may be liable in damages under Title IX only for its own misconduct. . . . We disagree with respondents' assertion, however, that petitioner seeks to hold the Board liable for *G.F.*'s actions instead of its own. Here, petitioner attempts to hold the Board liable for its *own* decision to remain idle in the face of known student-on-student harassment in its schools. In *Gebser*, we concluded that a recipient of federal education funds may be liable in damages under Title IX where it is deliberately indifferent to known acts of sexual harassment by a teacher. . . .

Gebser thus established that a recipient intentionally violates Title IX, and is subject to a private damages action, where the recipient is deliberately indifferent to known acts of teacher-student discrimination. Indeed, whether viewed as "discrimination" or "subject[ing]" students to discrimination, Title IX "[u]nquestionably . . . placed on [the Board] the duty not" to permit teacher-student harassment in its schools, and recipients violate Title IX's plain terms when they remain deliberately indifferent to this form of misconduct.

We consider here whether the misconduct identified in *Gebser*—deliberate indifference to known acts of harassment—amounts to an intentional violation of Title IX, capable of supporting a private damages action, when the harasser is a student rather than a teacher. We conclude that, in certain limited circumstances, it does. As an initial matter, in *Gebser* we expressly rejected the use of agency principles in the Title IX context. . . . Additionally, the regulatory scheme surrounding Title IX has long provided funding recipients with notice that they may be liable for their failure to respond to the discriminatory acts of certain nonagents. The Department of Education requires recipients to monitor third parties for discrimination in specified circumstances and to refrain from particular forms of interaction with outside entities that are known to discriminate. *See, e.g.*, 34 CFR §§ 106.31(b)(6), 106.31(d), 106.37(a)(2), 106.38(a), 106.51(a)(3) (1998).

The common law, too, has put schools on notice that they may be held responsible under state law for their failure to protect students from the tortious acts of third parties. In fact, state courts routinely uphold claims alleging that schools have been negligent in failing to protect their students from the torts of their peers.

This is not to say that the identity of the harasser is irrelevant. On the contrary, both the "deliberate indifference" standard and the language of Title IX narrowly circumscribe the set of parties whose known acts of sexual harassment can trigger some duty to respond on the part of funding recipients. Deliberate indifference makes sense as a theory of direct liability under Title IX only where the funding recipient has some control over the alleged harassment. A recipient cannot be directly liable for its indifference where it lacks the authority to take remedial action.

. . . .

Where, as here, the misconduct occurs during school hours and on school grounds—the bulk of G.F.'s misconduct, in fact, took place in the classroom—the misconduct is taking place "under" an "operation" of the funding recipient. In these circumstances, the recipient retains substantial control over the context in which the harassment occurs. More importantly, however, in this setting the Board exercises significant control over the harasser. . . .

We stress that our conclusion here-that recipients may be liable for their deliberate indifference to known acts of peer sexual harassment-does not mean that recipients can avoid liability only by purging their schools of actionable peer harassment or that administrators must engage in particular disciplinary action. . . .

School administrators will continue to enjoy the flexibility they require so long as funding recipients are deemed "deliberately indifferent" to acts of student-on-student harassment only where the recipient's response to the harassment or lack thereof is clearly unreasonable in light of the known circumstances. The dissent consistently mischaracterizes this standard to require funding recipients to "remedy" peer harassment, and to "ensur[e] that . . . students conform their conduct to" certain rules. Title IX imposes no such requirements. On the contrary, the recipient must merely respond to known peer harassment in a manner that is not clearly unreasonable. This is not a mere "reasonableness" standard, as the dissent assumes. *See post*, at 1688. In an appropriate case, there is no reason why courts, on a motion to dismiss, for summary judgment, or for a directed verdict, could not identify a response as not "clearly unreasonable" as a matter of law.

. . . .

While it remains to be seen whether petitioner can show that the Board's response to reports of G.F.'s misconduct was clearly unreasonable in light of the known circumstances, petitioner may be able to show that the Board "subject[ed]" LaShonda to discrimination by failing to respond in any way over a period of five months to complaints of G.F.'s in-school misconduct from LaShonda and other female students.

. . . .

Applying this standard to the facts at issue here, we conclude that the Eleventh Circuit erred in dismissing petitioner's complaint. Petitioner alleges that her daughter was the victim of repeated acts of sexual harassment by G.F. over a 5-month period, and there are allegations in support of the conclusion that G.F.'s misconduct was severe, pervasive, and objectively offensive. The harassment was not only verbal; it included numerous acts of objectively offensive touching, and, indeed, G.F. ultimately pleaded guilty to criminal sexual misconduct. Moreover, the complaint alleges that there were multiple victims who were sufficiently disturbed by G.F.'s misconduct to seek an audience with the school principal. Further, petitioner contends that the harassment had a concrete, negative effect on her daughter's ability to receive an education. The complaint also suggests that petitioner may be able to show both actual knowledge and deliberate indifference on the part of the Board, which made no effort whatsoever either to investigate or to put an end to the harassment.

On this complaint, we cannot say "beyond doubt that [petitioner] can prove no set of facts in support of [her] claim which would entitle [her] to relief." Accordingly, the judgment of the United States Court of Appeals for the Eleventh Circuit is reversed, and the case is remanded for further proceedings consistent with this opinion.

Vance v. Spencer County Public School District

231 F.3d 253 (6th Cir. 2000)

The court finds that the school did not take sufficient action to address allegations of student on student sexual harassment and is liable under Title IX.

This appeal presents questions concerning the nature and extent of circumstantial evidence needed to permit a reasonable inference of gender discrimination by school officials in the student-on-student sexual harassment context. The Spencer County

School District ("Spencer") appeals from the district court's denial of its post-trial motion for judgment as a matter of law. A jury found that Spencer violated both Title IX of the Education Amendments of 1972, by discriminating against Plaintiff Alma McGowen, a student at one of its schools. For the reasons that follow, this Court AFFIRMS.

In November 1992, Alma McGowen enrolled in Spencer as a sixth grader. On the second day of school, some first graders yelled to her, "Oh, there's that German gay girl, that new girl that just moved here." Alma complained to the Spencer School Counselor, Kathy Whitehead. Whitehead spoke to the children Alma identified and gave presentations on accepting people.

During Alma's sixth grade year, while riding the bus, a high school student asked Alma to describe oral sex. Alma reported the incident to both her mother and Whitehead. Whitehead contacted the high school principal, Murrel Lawson. Lawson expelled the student from the bus for a few days. When the student returned, he continued to curse at Alma and was even more vulgar than before.

During the 1993–1994 school year, Alma attended the Spencer County High School ("Spencer High"). While there, another student, who was the school principal's nephew, confronted Alma in the presence of other students and demanded to know if she was gay. When Alma spoke to David Shelburne, the assistant principal at the high school, he said that the boys considered her cute and they were flirting with her, so she should just "be friendly."

During her seventh grade year, students regularly shoved Alma into walls, grabbed her book bag, and stole and destroyed her homework. Alma reported these incidents to Phyllis Jenkins, the academic counselor, who referred her to Father Ryan, the youth advocate. In response, Father Ryan told her he would see what he could do.

In the fall of the 1993–1994 school year, a male student in her gym class called Alma and other female students "whores" and "motherfuckers," hit them, snapped their bras, and grabbed their butts. He also went into Alma's bag and began to take things from it. When Alma tried to get her pen back from him, the boy stabbed her in the hand with the pen. Alma reported the incident to her gym teacher, who sent her to the principal's office. The office secretary treated Alma's injury. The principal was informed, but did not get involved at that time. A few days later, the student told Alma that he had been talked to, but that he did not get into any trouble because he was a school board member's son.

During the Spring semester of her seventh grade year, Alma's mother wrote two letters concerning her daughter. The first letter concerned an incident in her science class. Some students approached Alma during a bathroom break while the teacher was not in the room. Several of the students called Alma crude names and backed her up against a wall. Two boys held her hands, while other students grabbed her hair and started yanking off her shirt. When a boy stated he was going to have sex with her and began to take his pants off, another boy intervened and assisted

Alma. Alma did not report the incident to her teacher. Alma went home and told her mother about the incident. Alma's mother wrote a letter to the principal, which Alma hand-delivered to the front office the following day.

In response to the letter, the classroom teacher spoke with Alma and five of the boys involved in the incident. With Alma seated between two of the boys, the teacher told Alma to tell the boys what she thought they had done. Alma did not know if anything was done to punish the boys.

During the fall of Alma's eighth grade year, 1994–1995, a female special education student struck Alma. Principal Lawson spoke to the girl. During that same period, Alma spoke with Kirby Smith, the youth advocate who replaced Father Ryan, about other students harassing her. Smith asked Alma for a list of the students in order to address the situation. Smith spoke with the boys who were on the list that Alma gave him.

Later, one of the boys told Alma in front of a class that he told Smith that he had a crush on her and that he could touch Alma in any way he wanted and no one was going to do anything about it. Afterward, the boy did indeed touch Alma on her chest and butt. He also requested sexual favors several times while the teacher was in the room. Alma testified that nothing was done about these incidents.

In December 1994, Alma spoke with Assistant Principal Shelburne and indicated that the boy, who was a part of the problem in her science class, was still harassing her. A few days later, the boy told Alma that although he had been spoken to, he did not "give a damn about it and he would do whatever he wanted to."

Alma testified that the harassment increased to the point that she was propositioned or touched inappropriately in virtually every class. Alma also testified that the more she complained to the principals, even though they spoke to the students, the harassment seemed to increase and she indicated she grew leery of talking to anyone.

In May 1995, pursuant to the Spencer Harassment Policy, Alma filed a complaint alleging violations of Title IX. The complaint listed detailed instances of sexually harassing conduct. Spencer took no action to address the specific harassment allegations before school started in August 1995. Instead, the Title IX Coordinator allowed Alma to complete the remaining few weeks at home. Alma's complaint was not presented to the Spencer's new Superintendent, who began in July 1995. Additionally, Spencer took the position that it did not have enough information to investigate Alma's specific allegations.

At the beginning of the 1995–1996 school year, Spencer discussed its new sexual harassment policy at the high school. From August 16 through August 31, 1995, Alma attended school. She testified that groups of students continued to ask for sexual favors, touch her in ways that made her uncomfortable, and hit her with books. During this same time, Alma attended school sexual harassment presentations. Spencer also provided sexual harassment and discrimination training to all its employees.

Alma was diagnosed with depression. On her last day at the high school, a boy told her he was part of the KKK, as were his family members, and they were going to go to her home and burn it down because all Germans should be burned and sent to hell.

On August 31, 1995, Alma withdrew.

....

On September 1, 1998, a jury trial commenced. At the close of Plaintiff's proof and again at the conclusion of all of the evidence, the Board moved for summary judgment as a matter of law pursuant to Federal Rule of Civil Procedure 50. The trial court denied both motions and submitted the case to the jury. The jury returned its verdict in favor of Alma on all counts and awarded her $220,000.

....

While this action was pending appeal, the Supreme Court decided that recipients of federal funds, like Spencer, may be liable for damages under Title IX for student-on-student sexual harassment. *See Davis v. Monroe County Bd. of Educ.*, 526 U.S. 629, 653 (1999). In the instant action, there is no dispute that Spencer receives federal funding and is therefore liable for Title IX student-on-student sexual harassment. The issue before this Court is whether Plaintiff has satisfied the *prima facie* elements for her claim.

In *Davis*, the Supreme Court established that Title IX may support a claim for student-on-student sexual harassment when the plaintiff can demonstrate the following elements:

> (1) the sexual harassment was so severe, pervasive, and objectively offensive that it could be said to deprive the plaintiff of access to the educational opportunities or benefits provided by the school,
>
> (2) the funding recipient had actual knowledge of the sexual harassment, and
>
> (3) the funding recipient was deliberately indifferent to the harassment.

As explained below, Alma has presented evidence that satisfies each of these three elements.

....

In the instant case, as in *Davis*, Alma has submitted abundant evidence of both verbal and physical sexual harassment. Although one incident can satisfy a claim, Alma has presented several instances that reflect not only severity and pervasiveness, but also circumstances that effectively denied her education. On one occasion, Alma was stabbed in the hand. On another, two male students held Alma while others yanked off her shirt, pulled her hair, and attempted to disrobe. These physical attacks merely layer the testimony regarding verbal propositioning and name calling. In addition, Alma's Title IX complaint, filed with Spencer in May 1995, curiously warranted her completing her studies at home, but not an investigation.

Given the frequency and severity of both the verbal and physical attacks, it is no wonder that Alma was diagnosed with depression. Given this evidence, Alma has satisfied the severity and pervasiveness requirement.

Alma has satisfied the *Davis* notice requirement. In *Davis*, the Supreme Court suggested that both the parent and student had satisfied the actual notice standard where they had made repeated harassment complaints to the teacher and principal. . . . In this case, it is undisputed that Spencer had actual knowledge. Both Alma and her mother made repeated reports to Spencer. Alma informed both her teachers and principals. Alma's mother made repeated reports verbally and in writing, not to mention her Title IX complaint filed with the school. Thus, Alma has satisfied her burden of establishing Spencer's actual knowledge.

The pivotal issue before us is what is required of federal assistance recipients under the "deliberate indifference standard." The recipient is liable for damages only where the recipient itself intentionally acted in clear violation of Title IX by remaining deliberately indifferent to known acts of harassment. "[T]he deliberate indifference must, at a minimum, 'cause [students] to undergo' harassment or 'make them liable or vulnerable' to it."

In describing the proof necessary to satisfy the standard, the Supreme Court stated that a plaintiff may demonstrate defendant's deliberate indifference to discrimination "only where the recipient's response to the harassment or lack thereof is clearly unreasonable in light of the known circumstances." The recipient is not required to "remedy" sexual harassment nor ensure that students conform their conduct to certain rules, but rather, "the recipient must merely respond to known peer harassment in a manner that is not clearly unreasonable." The deliberate indifference standard "does not mean that recipients can avoid liability only by purging their schools of actionable peer harassment or that administrators must engage in particular disciplinary action." The standard does not mean that recipients must expel every student accused of misconduct. Victims do not have a right to particular remedial demands. Furthermore, courts should not second guess the disciplinary decisions that school administrators make.

"The Supreme Court has pointedly reminded us, however, that this is 'not a mere "reasonableness" standard' that transforms every school disciplinary decision into a jury question." In an appropriate case, there is no reason why courts on motion for a directed verdict could not identify a response as not "clearly unreasonable" as a matter of law.

As an initial matter, Spencer alleges that the intent standard governs Title IX student-on-student claims. Essentially, according to Defendant, as long as a school district does something in response to harassment, it has satisfied the standard. Furthermore, according to Defendant, Spencer did something in response to Alma's allegations. After reviewing the record, the briefs of both parties, and the applicable law, and having had the benefit of oral argument, we reject Defendant's understanding of the deliberate indifference standard.

The standard announced by the Supreme Court is a "clearly unreasonable response in light of the known circumstances." If this Court were to accept Spencer's argument, a school district could satisfy its obligation where a student has been raped by merely investigating and absolutely nothing more. Such minimalist response is not within the contemplation of a reasonable response. Although no particular response is required, and although the school district is not required to eradicate all sexual harassment, the school district must respond and must do so reasonably in light of the known circumstances. Thus, where a school district has knowledge that its remedial action is inadequate and ineffective, it is required to take reasonable action in light of those circumstances to eliminate the behavior. Where a school district has actual knowledge that its efforts to remediate are ineffective, and it continues to use those same methods to no avail, such district has failed to act reasonably in light of the known circumstances.

. . . .

In the instant case, Spencer failed to respond in light of the known circumstances. On one occasion, a student's harassing conduct culminated in stabbing Alma in the hand. With the exception of talking to the student, there was no evidence before the jury or this Court that Spencer took any other action whatsoever. On another occasion, two male students held Alma while another took off his pants and others pulled her hair and attempted to rip off her clothes. With respect to that incident, the only evidence before the jury evincing Spencer's response is that a class room teacher spoke to the boys and Alma. There is no evidence before this Court that Spencer ever disciplined the offending students nor informed law enforcement as a result of any of these incidents. On yet another occasion, Alma's mother filed a detailed complaint with Spencer's Title IX coordinator. An investigation, however, never resulted. These three incidents alone reflect a deliberate indifference in light of the known circumstances.

Furthermore, in numerous instances, Spencer continued to use the same ineffective methods to no acknowledged avail. Although "talking to the offenders" produced no results, Spencer continued to employ this ineffective method.

. . . .

In the instant case, Spencer responded to several of Alma's complaints by "talking" to the offenders. However, the harassing conduct not only continued but also increased as a result. In fact, some of Alma's offenders confronted her after they had been "talked" to in order to harass Alma again. [O]nce Spencer had knowledge that its response was inadequate, it was required to take further reasonable action in light of the circumstances to avoid new liability.

. . . .

Although Title IX does not require certain specific responses, it does require a reasonable response, which Spencer failed to provide.

. . . .

Rost v. Steamboat Springs RE-2 School District

511 F.3d 1114 (10th Cir. 2008)

The court addresses the actual notice requirements for allegations of student on student sexual harassment and finds that the school took sufficient action to address known allegations.

K.C. was enrolled in Steamboat Springs Middle School as a seventh-grader in August 2000. She received special education and related services pursuant to the Individuals with Disabilities Education Act, due to an early-childhood brain injury.

Beginning in seventh grade and continuing to eighth grade, K.C. was coerced into performing various sexual acts with a number of boys including Steven Thomas, Nick Mangione, Alex Church, and Thomas Barnes ("the boys") who were all named as individual defendants in the complaint. The boys persistently and continuously pestered her for oral sex, calling her "retard" and stupid, threatened to spread rumors to her peers that she frequently engaged in sexual conduct with others, and threatened to distribute naked photographs of her. A police report indicates that the incidents occurred in a variety of private locations and social settings, and a few of the incidents appeared to be "consensual."

Ms. Rost [K.C.'s parent] did not know of the sexual harassment until K.C. told school officials on January 16, 2003. However, Ms. Rost urged school officials to talk to K.C. during the spring and fall of 2002 because she suspected that something was wrong with K.C. In the spring of 2002, Ms. Rost first became concerned about K.C. because K.C. did not want to attend school anymore. Her mother repeatedly pleaded with school counselor Margie Briggs-Casson to find out what was bothering K.C. She also spoke with Tim Bishop, principal of the middle school, regarding her concerns about K.C. and what she perceived as Ms. Briggs-Casson's lack of responsiveness. She also told Principal Bishop that the boys had tried to break into her home looking for pain medication. At some point, Ms. Briggs-Casson spoke with K.C., and K.C. told her about the harassment saying that "these boys were bothering me," but at that time, K.C. did not know to use the word assault and did not describe the incidents in more specific terms.

In the fall of 2002, K.C. began her freshman year at the Steamboat Springs High School and the harassment continued. Ms. Rost told David Schmidt, principal of the high school, that K.C. said the boys were bothering her and calling her retarded, she hated school and was afraid to go to school, she was afraid to go to a math class in which Steven Thomas was enrolled, and having an aide with her in class caused the boys to tease her. After a series of meetings, Ms. Rost and Principal Schmidt determined that the aide would sit in the back of the math class instead of beside K.C. Neither Ms. Rost nor school officials knew at that time of any sexual harassment of K.C.

On January 16, 2003, K.C. disclosed to Ann Boler, a counselor at the high school, that Steven Thomas was repeatedly calling her to ask for oral sex. She also disclosed that Steven Thomas and Nick Mangione previously coerced her into sexual conduct by threatening to show others naked pictures of her and spread rumors about her. Ms. Boler could not locate the principal or vice-principal, so she immediately contacted Officer Jason Patrick, the school resource officer. Officer Patrick questioned K.C. in Ms. Boler's office for approximately one to two hours. Ms. Boler later informed Principal Schmidt, and together with Officer Patrick, then informed Ms. Rost of K.C.'s disclosures.

Principal Schmidt decided that because none of the incidents occurred on school grounds and the incidents occurred before any of the students were enrolled in high school, Officer Patrick would investigate the sexual assaults. As a result, Principal Schmidt and the school district did not otherwise investigate the assaults. However, Principal Schmidt did maintain daily contact with Officer Patrick regarding the investigation, and the district assisted him in arranging interviews with the students during the investigation.

The investigation was hampered by Ms. Rost's refusal to communicate (or allow K.C. to communicate) further with the school or law enforcement regarding the incident on the advice of counsel. Based on Officer Patrick's report, the district attorney declined to prosecute the case on the rationale that it would be difficult to prove that the activity was not consensual and the trial would expose K.C. to tremendous trauma.

A couple weeks after reporting the abuse to Ms. Boler, K.C. suffered an acute psychotic episode that required hospitalization. Following K.C.'s discharge from the hospital in February 2003, Ms. Rost met with school officials to discuss educational alternatives for K.C. Ms. Rost accepted an offer for a private tutor but declined any option that required K.C. to return to the high school. The following year, as part of a mediation between Ms. Rost and the district regarding educational alternatives for K.C., an independent educational evaluation was conducted which suggested that K.C. attend a different school from Steamboat Springs High School. In the summer of 2004, K.C. suffered two additional acute psychotic episodes, probably as a result of the assaults; one in Chicago during a visit to her sister, and another in Steamboat Springs just before moving to Carbondale, Illinois.

....

Ms. Rost alleges that a genuine issue of fact remains regarding Title IX liability for student-on-student sexual harassment endured by K.C. because the district had actual knowledge of the sexual harassment and was deliberately indifferent to those reports. The district argues that there is no evidence that the district had actual knowledge of the sexual harassment before January 16, 2003. And once the district received the notice, it thoroughly investigated the allegations and worked with Ms. Rost to provide K.C. educational alternatives.

....

Ms. Rost claims that the district received actual notice of the sexual harassment of K.C. on two separate occasions—in the spring of 2002 and in the fall of 2002.

The district court held that K.C.'s complaints that boys were "bothering her" as relayed to the district were insufficient to constitute actual notice of sexual harassment, and that, in the absence of anyone knowing that the sexual harassment was occurring, a negligent failure to investigate Ms. Rost's generalized complaints did not result in Title IX liability. We agree.

K.C. testified in a deposition that she told Margie Briggs-Casson in the spring of 2002 about the assaults, but at that time, she did not know to use the word assault. When asked what she told Ms. Briggs-Casson, K.C. stated, "That these boys were bothering me and no one understood me in town." K.C.'s statement that the boys were bothering her was insufficient to give the district notice that she was being sexually harassed.

. . . .

Ms. Rost testified that she repeatedly pleaded with the counselor, Ms. Briggs-Casson, to find out what was bothering K.C. All Ms. Rost knew was that K.C. hated school and did not want to attend anymore, but K.C. would not tell her why. Ms. Rost also spoke with Principal Bishop regarding her concerns for K.C. and regarding Ms. Briggs-Casson's lack of responsiveness. However, Ms. Rost was unable to provide the school officials with any specifics because she did not know why K.C. was withdrawing as K.C. refused to speak to her mother about the harassment. Ms. Rost's concern for K.C. and complaints about Ms. Briggs-Casson did not give the district actual notice of the sexual harassment.

. . . .

It is undisputed that K.C. disclosed the sexual harassment to Ms. Boler on January 16, 2003, and that this disclosure gave the district actual notice of the harassment. The next question we must answer is whether the school district was "deliberately indifferent to acts of harassment of which it ha[d] actual knowledge."

. . . .

A district is deliberately indifferent to acts of student-on-student harassment "only where the [district's] response to the harassment or lack thereof is clearly unreasonable in light of the known circumstances." Here, once K.C. disclosed the sexual harassment to Ms. Boler, Ms. Boler immediately contacted Officer Patrick, the school resource officer, who questioned K.C. about the harassment. Principal Schmidt determined that because he believed none of the incidents occurred on school grounds and the incidents occurred before any of the students were enrolled at the high school, Officer Patrick should investigate the sexual assaults. Officer Patrick continually interacted with the school to arrange for the interviews of the students. Principal Schmidt had approximately fifty conversations with Officer Patrick regarding the investigation and received a copy of Officer Patrick's report. Though Officer Patrick testified that he might have been initially vague with the school district and not kept it totally involved because he viewed his investigation as separate, he also testified to his interaction with the district. We do not think that the district can be faulted for letting Officer Patrick take the lead in this very serious situation.

Officer Patrick and the school reasonably believed that the harassment occurred away from school, and criminal charges were a possibility. The district's response was not clearly unreasonable as school officials immediately contacted law enforcement officials, cooperated fully in the investigation, and kept informed of the investigation. The district reasonably could believe it did not have responsibility or control over the incidents, and merely because the principal thought that the school could discipline students for conduct occurring outside the school grounds says nothing about whether it was appropriate given what occurred here. *See Davis*, 526 U.S. at 645 (noting harassment creating liability under Title IX "must occur 'under' 'the operations of' a funding recipient, . . . [meaning that] the harassment must take place in a context subject to the school district's control") (quoting 20 U.S.C. § 1681(a); § 1687).[7] This is not a situation where a school district learned of a problem and did nothing. *See Vance v. Spencer County Pub. Sch. Dist.*, 231 F.3d 253, 262 (6th Cir. 2000). Rather, given a complicated situation involving the rights of many parties including the alleged perpetrators, the school district deferred to law enforcement.

. . . .

Finally, it was not clearly unreasonable that the district did not discipline the boys involved. Ms. Rost seems to argue that the district should have expelled the four boys so that K.C. could return to school. However, the Supreme Court has noted that schools need not expel every student accused of sexual harassment to protect themselves from liability, and "victims of peer harassment [do not] have a Title IX right to make particular remedial demands." *Davis*, 526 U.S. at 648. The standard is not that schools must "remedy" peer harassment, but that they "must merely respond to known peer harassment in a manner that is not clearly unreasonable." *Id.* at 648–49.

Many factors in the record counseled caution in determining whether discipline was appropriate in this case, and the district's judgment call not to pursue discipline was not clearly unreasonable and deliberately indifferent. Principal Schmidt determined that discipline was not appropriate in this case since most of the incidents did not occur on school grounds, and the district reasonably could believe it did not have responsibility or control over the incidents. Officer Patrick's investigation and the district attorney's assessment concluded that it would be difficult to prove that the conduct was not consensual. Officer Patrick and Principal Schmidt were unable to further investigate the harassment because Ms. Rost and K.C. refused to

---

7. [FN 1] We do not suggest that harassment occurring off school grounds cannot as a matter of law create liability under Title IX. *Davis* suggests that there must be some nexus between the out-of-school conduct and the school. We do not find a sufficient nexus here, where the only link to the school was an oblique and general reference to harassment or teasing on the school bus or in the halls at school. Moreover, the fact that the boys threatened to post pictures of K.C. at school does not cause the harassment to "take place in a context subject to the school district's control" either. The district's decision to refer the investigation of the harassment to law enforcement officials where the harassment occurred off school grounds and often while the students were not enrolled in school was not clearly unreasonable under the facts of this case.

communicate with them on the advice of counsel. It would be difficult to discipline students where it was unclear which, if any, conduct was consensual and where the victim refuses to clarify details of the incidents. The Supreme Court has noted that administrators need not "engage in particular disciplinary action" under Title IX, but only respond in a manner that is not clearly unreasonable. *Davis*, 526 U.S. at 648–49. In addition, we are discouraged from second-guessing school disciplinary decisions. *Id.* at 648.

Further, Ms. Rost does not contend that further sexual harassment occurred as a result of the district's deliberate indifference after K.C.'s disclosure in January 2003. The Supreme Court has stated that in the case where a district does not engage in the harassment directly, as here, "it may not be liable for damages unless its deliberate indifference subjects its students to harassment. That is, the deliberate indifference must, at a minimum, cause students to undergo harassment or make them liable or vulnerable to it." *Davis*, 526 U.S. at 644–45.

. . . .

Though the facts in this case are tragic, we think the response of the district must be evaluated against a backdrop of the possible. The district's response was not clearly unreasonable so as to be deliberately indifferent to the harassment. Accordingly, we conclude that summary judgment was appropriate on the Title IX claim.

Post Problem Discussion

1. An important part of the deliberate indifference analysis is the school's response to the known allegations of harassment. Why was the school's response insufficient in *Vance*, but sufficient in *Rost*? What additional or different steps should the school have taken in *Vance* to avoid liability? What would the school need to do to have a sufficient response in Kara's case? Is the school under an obligation to "fix" the situation?

2. *Rost* discusses the actual knowledge requirement. What would Kara or Kara's mom need to tell the school in order to meet this requirement? What obligations does the school have to acquire more information? Who needs to have actual knowledge? If Kara tells a teacher what happened, is that enough, or does the principal or superintendent need to be informed? *See Gebser*, 524 U.S. at 290, where the Court stated that notice must be provided to "an official who at a minimum has authority to address the alleged discrimination and to institute corrective measures on the recipient's behalf." Would the school secretary, whom everyone knows knows everything, meet the requirement?

3. How should courts measure when the harassment is severe, pervasive, and offensive enough that it effectively bars educational opportunity or benefit? The requirement was met in *Vance*. How does Kara's situation compare?

4. In *Rost*, the court notes that at least some of the alleged harassment occurred outside of school, and notes that there needs to be a nexus between the out-of-school conduct and the school. Would Kara be able to meet this requirement? Why or why not?

5. How would Kara's Title IX claims differ from her § 1983 claims? If a court finds that the school and school principal were not "deliberately indifferent" under § 1983, does that also foreclose Kara's Title IX claims which also use the "deliberate indifference" standard? Review *Fitzgerald v. Barnstable Sch. Comm.*, 555 U.S. 246 (2009), to help answer this question.

Activity 4: LGBT Students

The facts in the problem set include Kara being harassed because she is a lesbian. During the Obama administration, the Office of Civil Rights for the United States Department of Education issued various guidance documents noting that Title IX included some protections for LGBT students against harassment based on sex or gender stereotypes, and that Title IX extended to "assigned sex, gender identity, and transgender status." Some of the department's guidance changed under the Trump administration in 2017.

State laws may also address some of these issues. This activity gives you a chance to explore these issues in more detail.

Step One—Review the various guidance statements issued by the Office of Civil Rights (OCR) for the United States Department of Education regarding LGBT students and Title IX. These statements cover issues including harassment/discrimination and sex-segregated facilities (bathrooms). You can find these on the OCR website. Some of them are in the form of "Dear Colleague" letters.

Step Two—Review federal court decisions in your judicial circuit regarding LGBT students in public schools that address Title IX, or claims under other federal laws such as Section 1983.

Step Three—Review your state Department of Education website, and your state statutes and regulations for any statutes, regulations, or agency guidance regarding LGBT students.

Step Four—Answer the following:

1. What is OCR's current view regarding the protections afforded to LGBT students under Title IX? Does the department explain the reasons for the changes in its guidance on these issues over the years?
2. Do the court decisions that you reviewed provide any protections or rights to LGBT students under Title IX or Section 1983?
3. What do your state statutes, regulations, or agency guidance statements say about LGBT students? Are your state laws consistent with federal requirements? Are they more protective of LGBT students' rights?
4. What changes, if any, do you think should be made to state or federal laws regarding LGBT students?

§ 6.07 Online Liability

A growing issue for schools is their liability for student actions online. The internet, apps on smartphones, and social media have transformed communication. Students now communicate with their friends through various apps and social media, and they obtain large portions of information from various online sources on a daily basis.

School administrators must maintain discipline and reasonably provide for the safety of the students, faculty, and staff within this electronic rich communication environment with its pervasive reach beyond the schoolhouse gate as well as within it. As noted in Chapter 8, there are a number of issues that arise about whether schools may discipline students from online activities that occur outside of school. A related topic is whether a school is liable for the harm that may occur to the targeted student for these out of school, online activities. Additionally, with more and more schools using technology and online tools to educate students, questions arise about whether the obligation to provide a safe learning environment discussed in Section 6.03 extends to the online environment.

Courts have yet to clearly define the legal standards and school obligations in these areas, but federal statutes and regulations do require schools that accept certain federal monies to develop "Internet safety plans" for students. Among other things, these laws require schools to employ a "technology protection measure" (which means an Internet blocking or filtering device) on all Internet-connected computers to protect minors from visual depictions that are obscene, child pornography, or harmful to minors. Children's Internet Protection Act ("CIPA"), Pub. L. 106-554 (2000), codified in part as 47 U.S.C. § 254(h)(5)–(7) and (l).

The law also requires schools to educate students "about appropriate online behavior, including interacting with other individuals on social networking websites and in chat rooms and cyberbullying awareness and response."47 U.S.C. § 254(h)(5)(B)(iii). The following activity explores these issues.

Activity 5: Protecting Students Online

Step One—Research the Children's Internet Protection Act ("CIPA") and the Neighborhood Children's Internet Protection Act ("N-CIPA"), which is part of CIPA. Draft a short description explaining the technology protection measure requirements and Internet safety plan requirements.

Step Two—Find an acceptable use policy and Internet safety plan for a local public school (most schools make these available online).

Step Three—Answer the following:

1. Do you think that the local school's policy meets the requirements of CIPA and N-CIPA? If you were the school's attorney, what changes, if any, would you recommend to the policy?

2. What does the local school policy say, if anything, about filtering websites? Does it have a process to un-filter websites that have educational value but are inadvertently blocked?
3. Two key undefined terms under CIPA and N-CIPA are "inappropriate matter" and "harmful to minors." Does the local school policy define these terms? If so, what do you think about the definitions? If not, how would you define these terms?
4. Does the policy address how the school will monitor the online activities of minors as required by CIPA and N-CIPA? If so, how?
5. Do you think these approaches are sufficient to address student safety in regard to internet communication?

§ 6.08 Bringing the Pieces Together

In real life, legal claims are not asserted in convenient sections of a casebook. They are generally brought all at once with the attorneys, and the court, dealing with numerous legal theories, standards, and defenses at the same time. The following problem gives an example of how one incident may lead to a number of different claims and explores the issues.

Problem 6: Controlling Classroom Behavior

Mrs. Jones is an eighth grade math teacher at the Sullivan Middle School. Her class has thirty-two students, who can be very difficult and confrontational at times. Most days, she feels that four or five students who tend to cause trouble are in control of the class, making her spend all of her time reprimanding them. Parents of students in the class have complained to her about the noise and disruptions. Mrs. Jones has complained to the assistant principal and to the principal on numerous occasions, but nothing seems to change. She routinely sends students to the principal, and they come back to class the next day, seemingly without punishment.

One day in class, Levi, a student who has been a problem all year for Mrs. Jones, starts poking the student next to him. The neighboring student tells him to stop, but he doesn't. When Mrs. Jones tells him to stop, he says, "Make me!" Mrs. Jones separates the students, puts Levi's desk in the back of the room where it is not near anyone else's, and returns to the front of the class. When she turns around to teach the class again, Levi has gotten out of his seat and is walking towards the other student again. She yells at Levi to return to his seat. Levi does, but five minutes later, when her back is turned, he gets up again. Mrs. Jones yells at him to sit back down. When he does, she takes a roll of duct tape that she had been using to tape up items in class and tapes Levi's ankles to his chair, and the chair to the desk. She says, "That should keep you in your seat," and returns to teaching the class.

A few minutes later, Levi scoots his desk and seat close enough to another student to poke her. When Mrs. Jones walks over to return the desk to the back of the room, Levi grabs her arm and says, "I wouldn't do that if I were you." Mrs. Jones grabs Levi's arm, twists it behind his back, and pulls it up at the same time, causing Levi to be in great pain. She tells him to put his head on the desk, but he yells "no" so she takes her hand and forcefully pushes the side of his face to the desk and keeps it there. She keeps Levi in this position for three or four minutes until he settles down. Then she lets go, goes to the intercom system at the front of the room, and tells the principal that she has been attacked by Levi and to send help. The assistant principal comes in the room a minute or so later with the school resource officer. They remove the tape and escort Levi to the principal's office.

Levi suffered a sprained shoulder and wrist from having his arm twisted behind him, and a black eye and bloody lip from having his face pressed against the desk.

Levi's parents contact you to bring claims against Mrs. Jones and the school.

1. What are the potential state and federal claims? What are the potential defenses?
2. Which, if any, of the claims would be successful?

Research state and federal cases in your judicial circuit to answer these questions. You may also want to review *W.E.T. v. Mitchell*, 2007 U.S. Dist. LEXIS 68376, (M.D.N.C. Sept. 14, 2007), *motion granted in part, dismissed in part by W.E.T. v. Mitchell*, 2008 U.S. Dist. LEXIS 2036 (M.D.N.C. Jan. 10, 2008), where the court discusses a range of state and federal claims based on a teacher taping a student's mouth closed in class, and *Johnson v. Newburgh Enlarged Sch. Dist.*, 239 F.3d 246 (2d Cir. 2001), where the court discusses the qualified immunity defense to § 1983 claims in detail, and finds the defense was properly denied to a teacher who assaulted a student at school.

Problem Materials

✓ *Review cases in this Chapter*

✓ *Review state and federal cases in your state and federal circuit*

Post Problem Discussion

1. What are the advantages and disadvantages of bringing both state and federal claims in Levi's case? Would you consider just bringing state tort claims, or just bringing federal claims? Why or why not?

2. How would you assess the merit of Levi's claims and the potential damages that Levi may recover? How will these factors affect your advice to Levi's parents about bringing claims against the school?

3. How would the state defenses you found in Activity 1 affect potential claims? Would the Coverdale Teacher Protection Act serve as a defense in this case?

Chapter 7

Privacy Rights & Right to Know

Synopsis

§ 7.01 Introduction

This Chapter discusses privacy both in terms of the obligation to protect the privacy of student information, and in terms of assuring that the public business of operating schools is conducted consistent with the public's right to know.

There are constitutional, statutory/regulatory, and common law protections for privacy for individuals and students. The constitutional right of privacy is grounded in the Fourteenth Amendment and in the "penumbra" of various Amendments in the Bill of Rights. *Roe v. Wade*, 410 U.S. 113, 152 (1973); *Griswold v. Connecticut*, 381 U.S. 479 (1965). The jurisprudence around privacy questions and the "zone of privacy" reflect what the Supreme Court describes as "at least two different kinds of interests." One is the "individual interest in avoiding disclosure of personal matters, and another is the interest in independence in making certain kinds of important decisions." *Whalen v. Roe*, 429 U.S. 589, 598–600 (1977). The "important decisions" include "matters relating to marriage, procreation, contraception, family relationships, and child rearing and education." *Paul v. Davis*, 424 U.S. 693, 713 (1976).

In today's society, where it seems everything is accessible online, privacy rights are even more important. The leading general constitutional case on information is *Whalen v. Roe*, which involved a New York statute that required a central system for reporting all prescriptions for controlled substances as a means of controlling the illegitimate use of such drugs. In *Whalen*, the Supreme Court upheld the statute in the face of a challenge that claimed it threatened patient reputation and independence: "neither the immediate nor the threatened impact of the patient-identification requirements in the New York State Controlled Substances Act of 1972 on either the reputation or the independence of patients for whom Schedule II drugs are medically indicated is sufficient to constitute an invasion of any right or liberty protected by the Fourteenth Amendment." 429 U.S. at 603–04.

The Supreme Court has noted the interest in independence exists in the education context as well. For example, *Meyer v. Nebraska*, 262 U.S. 390 (1923), an early education case on independence in education, established the substantive due process right of parents to make important decisions about the education of their children and direct the educational upbringing of their children. This substantive due process right is often involved in constitutional privacy cases, and some courts have found that parents' privacy interests in making decisions about their child's education is subsumed within the substantive due process rights rooted in *Meyer. See, e.g., C.N. v. Ridgewood Bd. of Educ.*, 430 F.3d 159, 182–85 (3d Cir. 2005).

In addition to the constitutional protection of privacy, there are specific protections by state and federal statutes and regulations for educational matters (such as FERPA discussed in Section 7.03). These laws are often very detailed and very significant to the day-to-day operation of schools. State common law tort requirements may also impose duties on schools or school officials to keep certain information confidential.

§ 7.02 Constitutional Privacy Rights

As noted in Section 7.01, the United States Constitution provides parents and students with certain liberty and privacy rights regarding information and decisions about education. These rights are sometimes pitted against efforts in school to collect information about students for various purposes. The following problem explores some of these issues and elaborates on the rights involved.

Problem 1: Student Surveys

Cassie Collins is a tenth grade student at Jamison High School. She works on the school newspaper and has been assigned the task of developing an article for next month's edition. Cassie decides that she wants to do an article about student behaviors and attitudes regarding sex, and how they have changed or not changed as compared to student behaviors in middle school. She creates a survey that asks students fifteen detailed questions about their sexual activities now, as compared to when they were in middle school. The survey also asks students whether they believe that students their age should engage in sexual activities now, as compared to middle school. She hands the survey out to students in the hallways between classes.

Mr. Lee, the tenth grade health teacher, sees Cassie's survey and thinks it is a great idea. Mr. Lee assigns his class the task of completing the survey and returning it to Cassie. The assignment can either be done in class or taken home and returned to Cassie the next day in class. The surveys have a space at the top for the students to include their name if they would like to do so. Cassie included the request for names in case she needed to follow up and interview any of the students for her article.

Yolanda Martin brings the survey home and shows her mom, who becomes furious that the school is asking these kinds of questions and collecting this kind of information about her daughter. She calls the principal and threatens to sue. Does she have a viable constitutional claim?

Problem Materials

✓ *Rhoades v. Penn-Harris-Madison School Corporation*, 574 F. Supp. 2d 888 (N.D. Ind. 2008)

Rhoades v. Penn-Harris-Madison School Corporation

574 F. Supp. 2d 888 (N.D. Ind. 2008)

The court discusses the constitutional right to privacy in the context of a school performing mental health screenings of students, and denies a school's request for summary judgment against claims that such screenings violate constitutional rights.

James T. Moody, District Judge.

This matter is before the court on a motion for summary judgment filed by defendants Penn-Harris-Madison School Corporation ("PHMSC") and five individuals employed by PHMSC at Penn High School: school principal David R. Tydgat; associate principals Dave Risner and Steven Hope; and guidance counselors Marni Cronk and Vickie Marshall. The complaint names these individuals in both their official and individual capacities, and the motion for summary judgment addresses both. For convenience, and because official-capacity claims really are claims against the employing governmental entity, references to PHMSC or "the school defendants" should be understood to include both PHMSC and the individual defendants in the official capacities. When the court addresses claims made against the individual defendants in their individual capacities, it will use either their names or the collective reference "the individual defendants."

The plaintiffs are Chelsea Rhoades, who at the time of the incident involved in this suit was a 15-year-old sophomore at Penn High School, and her parents, Teresa and Michael Allen Rhoades, individually and as Chelsea's parents and next friends. In the complaint they filed initiating this action, plaintiffs claimed that a number of their state and federal constitutional and statutory rights were violated when a "TeenScreen" psychological assessment of Chelsea (and other students) was conducted at school without first obtaining Teresa and Michael Rhoades' written consent....

Factual Overview

A brief summary of the dispute as gleaned from the plaintiffs' amended complaint and the parties' memoranda supporting and opposing summary judgment provides context for the discussion that follows. Although this summary is largely based on facts that are undisputed, it nevertheless should *not* be taken as a statement of undisputed facts. In the analysis and ruling that follows, the court will refer to material facts as necessary that are either undisputed or, if in dispute, taken to exist in the version most favorable to the Rhoades, the non-movants.

In January 2003 a popular student at Penn High School committed suicide. Community reaction to this tragedy included the forming of a "task force," composed of leaders in the community in the business, education and health fields, to research programs and services for the detection and prevention of adolescent suicides. Members of the task force included a former superintendent of PHMSC, and the director of Madison Center, Inc., a mental healthcare provider also named as a defendant in this action. The task force identified the TeenScreen as a "voluntary mental health check-up" that could be used as a screening tool to identify adolescents posing a potential suicide risk. The task force also recommended that a "Yellow Ribbon Suicide Prevention Program" be implemented. Penn High School followed this recommendation and integrated the program into its health education curriculum taught in the tenth grade.

While that integration was taking place, the task force asked Penn High School if it would allow the Madison Center to conduct a "pilot" administration of the TeenScreen to students at the School in the fall of 2003. The School consented, but PHMSC maintains that it provided no funding for administration of the test, "merely a conference room at Penn High School, permission for Madison Center personnel to come on site to administer the test, and coordination with parents and students who would be taking the test." This assertion is contradicted, however, by PHMSC's admission that Penn High School staff mailed a letter and consent form for the TeenScreen to students' parents, which is at least a form of indirect funding.

Only nine parents returned the form consenting to having their children take the TeenScreen. The task force was disappointed with that result, and proposed to Penn High School that when the test was given in the fall of 2004, a "passive consent" form be used. That meant that a form would be mailed to the parents and if the parents did not return the form to indicate that they did *not* want their children to take the TeenScreen, the TeenScreen would be administered. Penn High School agreed to this passive consent procedure, with an additional requirement, however, that each student sign a form at the time of testing indicating that they were taking the test voluntarily . . .

In late October the November issue of the "Kingsman Notes: The Penn High School Newsletter" was mailed to each student's home. The newsletter mentioned that the Madison Center would be administering the TeenScreen to 10th grade students, and attached to the newsletter was a separate letter/opt-out form explaining that the TeenScreen would be administered unless the parents returned the opt-out form by November 8. Although 23 opt-out forms were returned, the court believes that a fact finder could conclude that the "Kingsman Notes" would be treated as "junk mail" in many households and quickly thrown out. The Rhoades deny ever seeing any notice from Penn High School regarding the TeenScreen.

The TeenScreen was administered in November and December, 2004. Associate principal/defendant Hope, and guidance counselors/defendants Cronk and Marshall prepared the testing protocol, that is, arranging the schedule for students to be released from class for testing, and requiring that each student sign an "assent form" before taking the TeenScreen. Chelsea was released from class on December 7, 2004, to take the TeenScreen.

Chelsea's version of that day is that her home room teacher, Mrs. Troyer, announced that all students in the room, with one exception, would be going in groups to Conference Room C to take a test. Students asked Mrs. Troyer what the test was and she told them she didn't know. A memorandum dated November 3, 2004, prepared by guidance counselors/defendants Cronk and Marshall for the home room teachers stated, "[p]lease do not explain what this is to your students. They will receive the letter of explanation in the mail this week."

After Chelsea reported to the conference room, a woman read something about the test while Chelsea was helping a wheelchair-bound friend get situated. Then Chelsea signed the assent form, which was laying on the desk. However, she did not read it, because the woman told her "you need to sign this" and that they all needed to be as quick as possible because many other students needed to take the test. The woman did not tell Chelsea that the test was voluntary and that she could refuse to take it. Chelsea signed the form, thinking it was simply an acknowledgment that she was taking the test. *Id.* Her impression was that she had to sign the form, and that she had to take the test.

After signing the form she was told to sign on to the computer and answer the questions truthfully. Chelsea did so, and after she and the other students completed the test, they were told to wait outside in the hallway. *Id.* After about five minutes a woman came out of the testing room, called Chelsea's name, and walked Chelsea several steps away from the other students. The woman told Chelsea that she had "Obsessive Compulsive Disorder for cleaning and social anxiety disorder," and that she could speak with a counselor, or have her mother call the Madison Center for treatment. Chelsea was very "upset and confused" by this information and dwelled on it all day, becoming more upset the more she thought about it. When she arrived at home she asked her mother to explain to her what Obsessive compulsive disorder and social anxiety disorder were.

Although the complaint, as is typical in notice pleading, is somewhat vague as to the exact nature of each statutory and constitutional violation the Rhoades claim resulted from the factual scenario above, PHMSC's motion identifies and addresses a number of "claims"-that is, legal theories which it believes completely comprise the Rhoades' claim. The plaintiffs have accepted this narrowing by failing to argue, in their response to the motion, that the school defendants left something out. Thus, based on the parties' briefs supporting and opposing summary judgment, the court provides the following outline of the arguments . . .

Analysis

I. Liability of PHMSC

A. Federal Claims Based on Substantive due process

Teresa and Michael Rhoades contend that a violation of their right to substantive due process under the 14th amendment to the United States Constitution occurred when the "TeenScreen" was given to Chelsea without obtaining their prior written consent, depriving them of a liberty interest in directing her upbringing and education, and of a liberty/privacy interest with respect to disclosure of private information.

The substantive due process component of the Fourteenth Amendment "bar[s] certain government actions regardless of the fairness of the procedures used to implement them." *Daniels v. Williams*, 474 U.S. 327, 331 (1986). But providing a concise description of what a plaintiff must prove to establish a violation of substantive due process under the 14th Amendment is not easy: "courts have long struggled to identify the appropriate analysis for substantive-due-process claims." *Khan v. Gallitano*, 180 F.3d 829, 833 (7th Cir. 1999). Even defining whether the right alleged to have been infringed is protected by substantive due process is difficult:

> [T]he development of this Court's substantive-due-process jurisprudence . . . has been a process whereby the outlines of the "liberty" specially protected by the Fourteenth Amendment-never fully clarified, to be sure, and perhaps not capable of being fully clarified-have at least been carefully refined by concrete examples involving fundamental rights found to be deeply rooted in our legal system. This approach tends to rein in the subjective elements that are necessarily present in due-process judicial review.

Washington v. Glucksberg, 521 U.S. 702, 720–22 (1997).

The end result is that an "orderly approach" which attempts to lay out the elements a plaintiff must prove to establish a due process violation is extremely difficult:

> In order to survive summary judgment on a § 1983 claim, Armstrong must present facts to establish that the defendants intentionally or recklessly deprived him of a constitutional right. (Of course, Armstrong must also show that the defendants acted under color of state law and that their actions constituted the legal cause of Armstrong's damages, but the defendants do not appear to contest Armstrong's proof on these elements.) This inquiry involves two separate questions: (1) Did the defendants violate a constitutional right? and (2) Did the defendants act with sufficient culpability?

Unfortunately, this orderly approach deteriorates when the constitutional right exists, if at all, as a matter of substantive due process. Such cases become muddled because any inquiry into substantive due process invokes a "'less rigid and more fluid'" inquiry than "envisaged in other specific and particular provisions of the Bill of Rights." *County of Sacramento*, 118 S.Ct. at 1719 (quoting *Betts v. Brady*, 316 U.S. 455, 462 (1942)). In other words, an investigation into substantive due process involves an appraisal of the totality of the circumstances rather than a formalistic examination of fixed elements: "That which may, in one setting, constitute a denial of fundamental fairness, shocking to the universal sense of justice, may, in other circumstances, and in light of other considerations, fall short of such denial." *Id.* (quoting *Betts*, 316 U.S. at 462).

The court attempts to make something of this muddle, while at the same time trying to limit its analysis to the issues actually raised and presented by the parties' arguments for and against summary judgment, rather than issues which the court might like to have seen raised and argued.

1. Liberty interest in upbringing of children

Teresa and Michael Rhoades claim that PHMSC deprived them of their liberty interest in directing Chelsea's upbringing and education by administering the Teen-Screen exam to her without obtaining their prior written consent. The Supreme Court has recognized for almost 100 years that the due process clause of the Fourteenth Amendment encompasses a liberty interest in the rearing and education of one's children. *Troxel v. Granville*, 530 U.S. 57, 65 (2000); *Carey v. Population Services, Intern.*, 431 U.S. 678 (1977); *Pierce v. Society of Sisters*, 268 U.S. 510, 535 (1925); *Meyer v. Nebraska*, 262 U.S. 390, 399 (1923). In its motion for summary judgment, PHMSC does not claim otherwise. Instead, it argues that the right must be balanced with the state's obligation to educate children, and that two circuits have recently "rejected claims under nearly identical circumstances finding that the balance tips in favor of the school to make curricular decisions including the decision to permit surveys like the Teen Screen."

The cases on which PHMSC relies are *C.N. v. Ridgewood Board of Education*, 430 F.3d 159 (3rd Cir. 2005) and *Fields v. Palmdale School District*, 427 F.3d 1197 (9th Cir. 2005). PHMSC does an excellent job of summarizing the facts, analysis and holding in both cases. Thus, rather than paraphrasing PHMSC's argument, the court quotes it at length:

> In *Fields*, a student working towards a master's degree in psychology who was volunteering at the district as a mental health counselor developed and administered a psychological assessment for first, third, and fifth graders. The parents were given a consent letter stating that the purpose of the survey was to "establish a community baseline measure of children's exposure to early trauma (for example, violence)." *Id.*, 427 F.3d at 1200. The letter stated that the survey was "100% confidential," no information would be used to identify a particular child, and after the study was completed, surveys would be locked in storage and destroyed after five years. The consent letter did not inform parents that some of the survey questions would be about sex. *Id.*, 427 F.3d at 1201.
>
> Following the school's approval of the survey, the volunteer counselor administered the survey during school hours to the children, ages 7–10. *Fields*, 427 F.3d at 1201. When several parents discovered that their children were questioned about sex, they filed suit alleging that "had they known the true nature of the survey, they would not have consented to their children's involvement." *Id.*, 427 F.3d at 1202.
>
> The parents first argued that by administering the survey, the school deprived them of their free-standing fundamental right "to control the upbringing of their children by introducing them to matters of and relating to sex in accordance with their personal and religious values and beliefs."

Id., 427 F.3d at 1203. The 9th Circuit, in affirming the dismissal of the claims against the school responded that while parents have the right to choose the type of "educational forum" that their children attend under *Meyer v. Nebraska*, 262 U.S. 390 (1923) and *Pierce v. Society of Sisters*, 268 U.S. 510 (1925), that "right does not extend beyond the threshold of the school door." *Fields*, 427 F.3d at 1207. The 9th Circuit then went on to find that "[a]ccordingly, *Meyer-Pierce* provides no basis for finding a substantive due process right that could have been violated by the defendants' authorization and administration of the survey." *Id.*, 427 F.3d at 1207. *See also Skoros v. City of New York*, 437 F.3d 1, 41 (2nd Cir. 2006) (Affirming summary judgment for the school in a parental rights claim noting "this precedent affords parents no 'fundamental constitutional right to dictate the curriculum at the public school to which they have chosen to send their children.'").

The second recent case to discuss the issue of parental rights is the 3rd Circuit's decision in *C.N.* In that case the school administered a survey to 7th through 12th grade students about their drug and alcohol use, sexual activity, and other controversial topics. The survey was the result of a multi-year study of local needs by a community task force known as the Community Vision Team which hoped to "understand [students'] needs, attitudes and behavior patterns in order to use the town's programs and resources more effectively." *Id.*, 430 F.3d at 162.

To that end the Vision Team selected a survey designed by a Minneapolis based company which was then purchased and administered by the school. The administration sent parents two letters informing them that the survey would take place and would cover at-risk behaviors such as substance abuse, sexuality, stress, and depression. One of the letters informed parents that the survey was to be voluntary and anonymous. As in Fields, parents claimed that the survey violated their right to privacy and to control the upbringing of their children. *C.N.*, 430 F.3d at 163–167.

Before addressing the constitutional claims, the Third Circuit first addressed whether the survey was voluntary and anonymous. The 3rd Circuit reviewed several factors in determining whether the survey was voluntary: (1) at least one teacher allegedly told students they had to take the survey, a loud speaker announcement at one school said if students did not take the survey, they would receive a cut; (2) instructions read at the high school did not say the survey was voluntary; (3) there was 100% participation in the survey; (4) absent students had to make up the survey; (5) parents received no consent form or instructions about how to exempt their children from participating in the survey; (6) the letters to parents about the survey did not contain the exact date of the survey; and (7) the survey seemed like a test-it was intended to take an entire class period, and no one could leave the classroom while it was being administered. *C.N.*, 430 F.3d at 163–167.

> Based on the foregoing factors the 3rd Circuit noted that "we conclude that the summary judgment record would also support a finding that the survey as intended by the Board and certain School Defendants acting on behalf of the Board was involuntary." *C.N.*, 430 F.3d at 177. However, the Court also found that the "record shows that anonymity and confidentiality-as opposed to voluntariness-were consistently stressed to parents, principals and survey administrators." *Id.*
>
> Therefore for purposes of the *C.N.* case, the survey was involuntary but anonymous. Having made that determination, the court then turned to the "fundamental right of parents to make decisions concerning the care, custody, and control of their children." *C.N.*, 430 F.3d at 182.
>
> Plaintiff Parents complain that the School Defendants, by not requiring parental consent prior to the administration of the survey and failing to provide sufficient information to allow an objecting parent to avoid having their child participate, deprived them of their right to make the important decision whether to allow their child to participate in the survey. Additionally, we understand Plaintiff Parents to complain that the School Defendants' actions intruded upon their parental authority to decide when and how to introduce their children to sensitive topics such as appeared on the survey.

Id., 430 F.3d at 184–185.

In resolving these claims the 3rd Circuit acknowledged that parents do have certain constitutionally guaranteed rights with respect the upbringing of their children, but:

> It does not necessarily follow, however, that the survey violated the Constitution. While the Supreme Court has extended constitutional protection to parental decisions regarding certain matters (see *Troxel*, 530 U.S. 57 (visitation); *Pierce*, 268 U.S. 510 (decision to enroll child in private, religious school rather than public school)), our review of these cases prompts us to conclude that the decision whether to permit a middle or high school student to participate in a survey of this type is not a matter of comparable gravity.
>
> School Defendants in no way indoctrinated the students in any particular outlook on these sensitive topics; at most, they may have introduced a few topics unknown to certain individuals. We thus conclude that the survey's interference with parental decision-making authority did not amount to a constitutional violation.

Id., 430 F.3d at 185.

Thus under *Fields*, the parents lost their challenge to the survey because the rights of parents presented "do[ ] not extend beyond the threshold of the school door." *Id.*, 427 F.3d at 1207. Under *C.N.*, which weighed the facts, even an involuntary survey with no parental consent at all, does not violate parental rights because "the parental decisions alleged to have been usurped by the School Defendants are not of comparable gravity to those protected under existing Supreme Court precedent." *Id.*, 430 F.3d at 185 n. 26.

> Under either of these two approaches, the claims presented in this case fail. Either because the Rhoades have no parental decisional rights "beyond the threshold of the school door" or because "the parental decisions alleged to have been usurped by the School Defendants are not of comparable gravity to those protected under existing Supreme Court precedent." Either way the School Defendants are entitled to judgment as a matter of law with respect to the interference with parental rights claims contained in Count I of the Amended Complaint.

Memorandum pp. 8–12 (footnotes omitted).

As PHMSC forthrightly admits, the Ninth Circuit's "no-rights-beyond-the-threshold-of-the-school- door" approach in *Fields*, was rejected-and rightly so in this court's view-by the Third Circuit in *C.N.*:

> In reaching this conclusion [that there was no constitutional violation], we do not hold, as did the panel in *Fields v. Palmdale School District*, 427 F.3d 1197 (9th Cir. 2005), that the right of parents under the *Meyer- Pierce* rubric "does not extend beyond the threshold of the school door." *Id.* at 1207. Nor do we endorse the categorical approach to this right taken by the *Fields* court, wherein it appears that a claim grounded in *Meyer- Pierce* will now trigger only an inquiry into whether or not the parent chose to send their child to public school and if so, then the claim will fail. Instead, guided by *Gruenke v. Seip*, 225 F.3d 290 (3rd Cir. 2000), wherein this Court stressed that it is primarily the parents' right "to inculcate moral standards, religious beliefs and elements of good citizenship," 225 F.3d at 307, we have determined only that, on the facts presented, the parental decisions alleged to have been usurped by the School Defendants are not of comparable gravity to those protected under existing Supreme Court precedent.

C.N., 430 F.3d at 185 n. 26. This court has found no other cases endorsing the holding in *Fields*, particularly not in this circuit.

This court agrees with *C.N.* that the approach in *Fields* would gut parental rights on the issue of education of any content other than choosing a school. For that reason, and because no other court has endorsed *Fields*, it does not persuade this court that its holding alone dictates a summary judgment in PHMSC's favor.

But even were the court inclined to agree with the holding in *Fields*, there is a substantial factual difference between *Fields* and the present case, also distinguishing this case from *C.N.*, and convincing this court that neither decision indicates that a summary judgment should be granted to PHMSC. The holding in *Fields* was premised on the court's belief that nothing in the relevant Supreme Court precedent indicates that parents have a right to dictate a school's curriculum: "The constitution does not vest parents with the authority to interfere with a public school's decision as to how it will provide information to its students or what information it will provide, in its classrooms or otherwise." *Fields*, 427 F.3d at 1206. *C.N.*'s holding that parental decisions "alleged to have been usurped by the School Defendants are not of comparable gravity to those protected under existing Supreme Court precedent" resulted largely from a finding, similar to that in *Fields*, that all that had occurred was the imparting of information to the students who took the survey:

> We recognize that introducing a child to sensitive topics before a parent might have done so herself can complicate and even undermine parental authority but conclude that the survey in this case did not intrude on parental decision-making authority. . . . School Defendants in no way indoctrinated the students in any particular outlook on these sensitive topics; at most, they may have introduced a few topics unknown to certain individuals.

C.N., 430 F.3d at 185.

The key factual difference between *Fields* and *C.N.* on one hand and the present case on the other, is that the survey in both of those cases was completely anonymous, with no information given to the students thereafter based on their answers to the questions in the survey. *Fields*, 427 F.3d at 1200 n. 1 (consent form sent to parents stated that "survey is 100% confidential and at no time will the information gathered be used to identify your child"); *C.N.*, 430 F.3d at 174–75 ("we find . . . that the survey, as administered and as intended by the Board, was anonymous").

As the court in C.N. noted, "[t]his might be a different case if Plaintiff students actually observed administrators peeking at completed surveys or if the survey setting itself lent support to Plaintiffs' fears of compromised anonymity." *C.N.*, 430 F.3d at 177 n. 20. It is undisputed that the survey in the present case was not anonymous. In fact, it wasn't even a "survey" like those used in *C.N.* and *Fields*, designed to collect data in the aggregate. Instead, the TeenScreen exam which Chelsea took was designed to discover whether she was a suicide risk or had other significant psychological problems. The court in *C.N.* cited one of its prior decisions which explains why this is a different case than an anonymous survey that gathers data in the aggregate:

> School-sponsored counseling and psychological testing that pry into private family activities can overstep the boundaries of school authority and impermissibly usurp the fundamental rights of parents to bring up their children, as they are guaranteed by the Constitution. *See Merriken v. Cressman*, 364 F.Supp. 913, 922 (E.D.Pa. 1973) (questionnaire probing family relationships by school authorities held unconstitutional). Public schools must not forget that "*in loco parentis*" does not mean "displace parents."
>
> It is not educators, but parents who have primary rights in the upbringing of children. School officials have only a secondary responsibility and must respect these rights. State deference to parental control over children is underscored by the Court's admonitions that "[t]he child is not the mere creature of the State," *Pierce*, 268 U.S. at 535, 45 S.Ct. 571, 69 L.Ed. 1070, and

> that it is the parents' responsibility to inculcate "moral standards, religious beliefs, and elements of good citizenship." *Yoder*, 406 U.S. at 233, *Gruenke v. Seip*, 225 F.3d 290, 307 (3rd Cir. 2000).

Because of the fundamental difference between the anonymous surveys at issue in *Fields* and *C.N.* and the non-anonymous psychological screening in the present case, *Fields* and *C.N.* do not indicate that a summary judgment should be granted to PHMSC.

2. Privacy interest in non-disclosure of personal information

Although the nature and scope of the zone of privacy protected by the Constitution are, like most of the Constitutional issues discussed herein, quite amorphous, the Supreme Court appears to have recognized that the liberty protected by the Fourteenth Amendment creates an "individual interest in avoiding disclosure of personal matters." *Whalen v. Roe*, 429 U.S. 589, 599–600, (1977). This is the interest the Rhoades claim was violated in this case, alleging that "Defendants deprived the Plaintiffs of their right to privacy by subjecting [Chelsea] to the 'TeenScreen' examination, without the valid consent of any of the Plaintiffs, by extracting highly personal and private matters from [Chelsea]."

Again analogizing the present case to the Third Circuit's decision in *C.N.*, PHMSC argues that there are two defects in the Rhoades claim entitling PHMSC to summary judgment. In *C.N.*, the court noted that the threshold inquiry for this type of privacy claim is whether the disclosure was involuntary in nature. *C.N.*, 430 F.3d at 180. Second, the court found that where the government's goal was to obtain valuable public health information, the balance against disclosure of private information tipped in the government's favor where the information was disclosed only in the aggregate with personal information highly safeguarded. *Id.* at 180–81. Based on this, PHMSC argues that it is entitled to summary judgment because Chelsea consented to the disclosure by signing an assent form, and because her TeenScreen exam was confidential:

> The present case presents an even more compelling argument. The TeenScreen program was one component of a comprehensive health education curriculum for 10th graders designed in response to the high profile suicide of a student at Penn High School. The test was both voluntary and confidential as noted in the Assent form which C.R. signed. Under these circumstances the School Defendants are entitled to judgment as a matter of law with respect to the invasion of privacy claims contained in Count II of the Amended Complaint.

Memorandum p. 15.

Taking the latter half of this argument first-that the "confidential" nature of the test entitles PHMSC to summary judgment, the court fails to see how PHMSC thinks comparison to *C.N.* is apt. In *C.N.*, the survey was confidential because it was anonymous: data was collected only in the aggregate, and there was no identifying information on the survey booklet, nor information collected, which would allow any particular survey to be linked to a particular student. *Id.* at 167–68, 181. In the present case the TeenScreen was not anonymous: it was used to screen Chelsea for "emotional health concerns," and immediately after taking it she was informed she suffered from obsessive compulsive and social anxiety disorders. Under this circumstance, nothing in *C.N.* suggests that summary judgment should be granted.

That leaves only the issue of whether Chelsea consented to the disclosure, and, if so, whether that consent negates the alleged privacy violation. It is undisputed that before she took the TeenScreen exam, Chelsea signed an "assent" form which, among other provisions, stated: "I have been told that participation in this program is voluntary and that I am not required to do any of these things if I do not want to. I may also refuse to answer any and all questions."

In response, the Rhoades argue that Chelsea's consent was invalid as a factual matter, because she was told to sign the form without being told its nature or purpose, and under circumstances in which she did not have time to review it: they deny that her consent was "knowing, effective, or valid." In addition, the Rhoades argue that regardless of whether her consent was knowing, it was ineffective and void as a matter of law, because of two Indiana statutes which required any such consent to be made by her parents, Ind.Code § 31-32-5-1, and § 20-10.1-4-15(b).

As to the Rhoades' contention that Chelsea's consent was not knowing and voluntary, PHMSC argues that there are facts that suggest otherwise, such as Chelsea's admission during her deposition that she recalls reading part of it and checking the box stating that she understood it. Essentially, however, PHMSC appears to recognize that there is a factual dispute whether Chelsea knowingly executed the form, and argues that it doesn't matter, citing both case law and the Restatement for the proposition that a contract is binding whether or not a party has read it: "Generally, one who assents to a writing is presumed to know its contents and cannot escape being bound by its terms merely by contending that he did not read them." However, Indiana has always recognized that minors can void their contracts at any time. *Mullen v. Tucker*, 510 N.E.2d 711, 714 (Ind.Ct.App. 1987). This is, at bottom, what Chelsea is doing by contending that she did not understand the agreement and knowingly enter into it, making PHMSC's reliance on general contract principles unavailing.

Even if that were not the case, however, there is the Rhoades' contention that regardless whether Chelsea knowingly signed the consent form, Indiana statutes preclude her from being able to give her consent to the TeenScreen exam in the first place. . . .

Although the Rhoades' argument has some merit, the question of statutory interpretation doesn't have to be answered at this juncture, because no matter which interpretation of the statute is correct, there is a question of fact as to whether the survey was required. PHMSC argues that the facts show the test was in fact voluntary, both because of the assent form that was signed, and because of 740 students eligible to take the TeenScreen, only 623 did. The other 117 either had their parents return the opt-out form, were absent from school that day, or refused to sign the assent form.

In the court's view, while this is certainly evidence in PHMSC's favor, it is not enough to negate the existence of a question of fact. There are also facts in the record that do suggest that Chelsea's (and any student's) signing of the "assent" form and taking of the test was under circumstances where the consent was under duress and the test *de facto* required.

....

Because of these circumstances, a question of fact remains as to whether the TeenScreen was effectively required for the students whose parents had not returned the opt-out form. With that question of fact, even if PHMSC is correct that parental consent is not required for a voluntary test, the applicability of the statute has not been ruled out by PHMSC's argument, and so PHMSC has not shown it is entitled to summary judgment on that basis.

....

3. Invasion of Privacy

The tort of invasion of privacy includes four distinct injuries: (1) intrusion upon seclusion, (2) appropriation of likeness, (3) public disclosure of private facts, and (4) false-light publicity. To establish a claim for invasion of privacy by intrusion, "a plaintiff must demonstrate that there was an 'intrusion upon his or her physical solitude or seclusion, as by invading his or her home or other quarters.'" Indiana courts "have narrowly construed the tort of invasion of privacy by intrusion." While the tort "arguably embraces intrusion into emotional solace, [t]here have been no cases in Indiana in which a claim of intrusion was proven without physical contact or invasion of the plaintiff's physical space such as the plaintiff's home," In *Cullison v. Medley*, our Supreme Court held that the tort of invasion of privacy by intrusion "consists of an intrusion upon the plaintiff's *physical* solitude or seclusion as by invading his home or conducting an illegal search." 570 N.E.2d 27, 31 (Ind. 1991) (emphasis added).

As PHMSC observes, the Rhoades' are alleging a claim based upon an intrusion into their familial seclusion. PHMSC argues that it is entitled to summary judgment because the undisputed facts show that the Rhoades suffered no intrusion into their *physical* solitude or seclusion.

The Rhoades' argument in response is that PHMSC is "unduly restrict[ing] the scope of the tort," and that federal courts sitting in Indiana have recognized, relying on *Prosser and Keeton on Torts*, that highly personal questions and demands made by a person in authority can invade a person's psychological solitude and therefore be an invasion of privacy. *See Van Jelgerhuis v. Mercury Finance Co.*, 940 F.Supp. 1344, 1368 (S.D.Ind. 1996) (and cases cited therein).

The problem with the Rhoades' argument is that, in the twelve years since *Van Jelgerhuis*, no Indiana state court appears to have cited it as support for finding a cause of action based on an intrusion into psychological seclusion, and instead the Indiana courts have continued to insist, as recognized only a year ago in *Newman*, that there be some physical intrusion upon a plaintiff's solitude. Thus, the landscape of state law appears different than it did when *Van Jelgerhuis* was decided, or even longer ago when the undersigned decided *Garus v. Rose Acre Farms, Inc.*, 839 F. Supp. 563 (N.D.Ind. 1993). It is not the prerogative of federal courts to expand state tort law beyond the limits that state courts have indicated to be desirable. *See King v. Damiron Corp.*, 113 F.3d 93, 97 (7th Cir. 1997) (and cases cited therein). Because there is no physical invasion of privacy in this case, and because of the Indiana state courts' lengthy practice of requiring that element to exist, this court will not expand the tort of invasion of privacy beyond that limitation. PHMSC will be granted summary judgment on the Rhoades' state-law claim for invasion of privacy.

....

II. Liability of Individual Defendants

A. Federal Constitutional Claims

The individual defendants argue that there is no evidence that they personally participated in the wrongs alleged, a prerequisite to liability, see and that even if they did, they are entitled to qualified immunity.

"Governmental actors performing discretionary functions are 'shielded from liability for civil damages insofar as their conduct does not violate clearly established statutory or constitutional rights of which a reasonable person would have known." Qualified immunity does not exist if the facts, taken in the light most favorable to the plaintiff, show that defendants' conduct violated a constitutional right, and that constitutional right was clearly established at the time of the alleged violation. *Saucier v. Katz*, 533 U.S. 194, 201 (2001). A plaintiff shows that a constitutional right is clearly established by "showing that there is 'a clearly analogous case establishing a right to be free from the specific conduct at issue' or that 'the conduct is so egregious that no reasonable person could have believed that it would not violate clearly established rights.'"

In this opinion, the court has found that, when the facts are viewed most favorably to the Rhoades, the administration of the TeenScreen violated their rights to privacy under the Fourteenth Amendment, the first showing necessary to defeat qualified immunity. As to the second aspect, whether the right violated was clearly established, the Rhoades argue there is no question of whether that is the case, the Supreme Court having recognized in *Troxel* that the fundamental right of parents to make decisions regarding the care, custody, control and upbringing of their children has been established for over 100 years. *Troxel*, 530 U.S. at 65.

If only it were that simple. Although the *existence* of parents' fundamental rights in regard to their children have long been recognized, the substance and contours of those rights are matters of ongoing evolution and are extremely vague and amorphous. As the Rhoades have noted, in determining whether a defendant is entitled to qualified immunity, "the question is whether a reasonable state actor would have known that his actions, viewed in the light of the law at the time, were unlawful." *Nabozny v. Podlesny*, 92 F.3d 446, 456 (7th Cir. 1996). It took this court nearly twenty pages, *supra* pp. 893–903, to analyze and determine whether the facts of this case, viewed in the light most favorable to the Rhoades, establish the violation of a Constitutional right. That itself answers the question whether a reasonable state actor would have understood that his or her actions were unlawful, and that answer is "no." The individual defendants are entitled to qualified immunity, and a summary judgment, on the Rhoades federal claims.

. . . .

Post Problem Discussion

1. As the *Rhoades* court noted, in *C.N. v. Ridgewood Bd. of Education*, the Third Circuit found that an involuntary, anonymous survey did not violate constitutional privacy protections. The court in *Rhoades* denied summary judgment in part because the screening was not anonymous. How do those factors (voluntariness and anonymity) affect your opinion about potential claims against the school in our problem?

2. If you determine that there are no viable claims based on the facts in the problem, are there any circumstances that you could envision that would violate the constitutional privacy protections noted in *Rhoades*, and the cases it discusses? What if Cassie reported the responses from certain students by name in the high school newspaper? Would that cross the constitutional line?

3. If there are viable constitutional claims, what should the remedy be? Remember the discussion in Chapter 6 about § 1983 claims and qualified immunity? The court granted qualified immunity to the individual defendants in *Rhoades*. Would it be granted in claims against Mr. Lee, or other school officials, if claims were brought against them in our problem? See the full *C.N. v. Ridgewood Bd. of Education* case online for a discussion of this issue.

§ 7.03 Privacy Rights Under Federal Statutes & Regulations

At the federal level, the Family Education Rights and Privacy Act ("FERPA") provides privacy protections for student educational records. The statute, and its implementing regulations, have a variety of very specific requirements that schools receiving federal funds must follow. The requirements include providing parents and eligible students (meaning those who are eighteen or older) with the opportunity to inspect and review the student's education records, and to request corrections to the records. 20 U.S.C. § 1232g(a)(1). FERPA also prohibits schools from disclosing personally identifiable information from the student's education records without written consent. 20 U.S.C. § 1232g(b)(1). "Education records" and "personally identifiable information" are specifically defined in the statute and regulations. These definitions become very important when determining if a violation occurred.

There are a number of exceptions to the written consent requirement noted in FERPA,20 U.S.C. § 1232g(b)(1), and in the regulations. There are also certain documents that are explicitly not included as educational records under FERPA. In addition, FERPA permits schools to release "directory information" about students to the public unless the parents or eligible student opt out of such disclosure. See the excerpts with Problem 2 materials in this section for more information.

The United States Supreme Court has interpreted FERPA's requirements in a couple of cases. Problems 2 and 3 explore the parameters of these cases and of FERPA's requirements.

Problem 2: FERPA's Confidentiality Requirements

Jed Chardry is a star football player at Local High. Jed is sixteen. He was stopped for drunk driving three nights before the big game with Local's biggest rival, Next Town High. Jed's parents immediately called the football coach, Will Simms. Coach Simms met with Jed and his parents, and they agreed to sign a "Good Behavior Contract" under which Jed agreed to do twenty hours of community service, to participate in substance abuse counseling, and to attend school, practice, and football games, without participation in any football rallies or parties for the remainder of the term. The Chardrys shared this agreement with Local's police, who agreed to drop the charges. The charges were not a matter of public record, nor were they reported anywhere publicly.

Coach Simms assured the Chardrys that no one would ever know about the contract. The Coach did discuss the Behavior Contract with his Assistant Coach, Karl Mollar, and the contract itself was filed with the coaching records in the Athletic Department offices at Local. When Jed didn't attend any subsequent football rallies and parties, a lot of rumors circulated at Local. Jed himself told his girlfriend, Liz Roth, about the deal. Later, Karen Phelps, the social studies teacher and faculty advisor for the National Honor Society, assigned a "crime and punishment essay" to her class. She told the students their work would not be shared with others, so they could be blunt and honest. Jed wrote his essay on his community service under the Behavior Contract. When Ms. Phelps read Jed's essay, she was very concerned about the "secret deal" that she perceived to be made because Jed was a football star. She discussed both the essay and the deal with the principal. As is so often the way, students *somehow* found out, and the talk is everywhere.

The Chardrys are furious and feel that the Coach and Ms. Phelps betrayed their promises. No one knows how the students learned the details. There is some talk that a student found the Behavior Contract in the Coach's files when the student was looking for something else in the office, but this is not confirmed.

1. What, if any, part of this scenario involves an educational record that should be protected under FERPA?

2. If any part of the record is protected, who exactly owed the obligation to protect the student's privacy?
3. Of what relevance are the students' actions here? The girlfriend?
4. What, if anything, is the remedy against the coach, the teacher, the school?

Problem Materials

✓ Selected provisions of FERPA, 20 U.S.C. § 1232g

✓ Selected provisions of FERPA's Regulations, 34 C.F.R. Part 99

✓ *Owasso Independent School District No. I-011 v. Falvo*, 534 U.S. 426 (2002)

✓ *Gonzaga v. Doe*, 536 U.S. 273 (2002)

20 U.S.C. § 1232g Family Educational and Privacy Rights

This statute protects the privacy of student records in institutions receiving federal funding.

(a). . . .

(3) For the purposes of this section the term "educational agency or institution" means any public or private agency or institution which is the recipient of funds under any applicable program.

(4) (A) For the purposes of this section, the term "education records" means, except as may be provided otherwise in subparagraph (B), those records, files, documents, and other materials which—

(i) contain information directly related to a student; and

(ii) are maintained by an educational agency or institution or by a person acting for such agency or institution.

(B) The term "education records" does not include—

(i) records of instructional, supervisory, and administrative personnel and educational personnel ancillary thereto which are in the sole possession of the maker thereof and which are not accessible or revealed to any other person except a substitute;

(ii) records maintained by a law enforcement unit of the educational agency or institution that were created by that law enforcement unit for the purpose of law enforcement;

(iii) in the case of persons who are employed by an educational agency or institution but who are not in attendance at such agency or institution, records made and maintained in the normal course of business which relate exclusively to such person in that person's capacity as an employee and are not available for use for any other purpose; or

(iv) records on a student who is eighteen years of age or older, or is attending an institution of postsecondary education, which are made or maintained by a physician, psychiatrist, psychologist, or other recognized professional or paraprofessional acting in his professional or paraprofessional capacity, or assisting in that capacity, and which are made, maintained, or used only in connection with the provision of treatment to the student, and are not available to anyone other than persons providing such treatment, except that such records can be personally reviewed by a physician or other appropriate professional of the student's choice.

(5) (A) For the purposes of this section the term "directory information" relating to a student includes the following: the student's name, address, telephone listing, date and place of birth, major field of study, participation in officially recognized activities and sports, weight and height of members of athletic teams, dates of attendance, degrees and awards received, and the most recent previous educational agency or institution attended by the student.

(B) Any educational agency or institution making public directory information shall give public notice of the categories of information which it has designated as such information with respect to each student attending the institution or agency and shall allow a reasonable period of time after such notice has been given for a parent to inform the institution or agency that any or all of the information designated should not be released without the parent's prior consent.

(6) For the purposes of this section, the term "student" includes any person with respect to whom an educational agency or institution maintains education records or personally identifiable information, but does not include a person who has not been in attendance at such agency or institution.

(b) Release of education records; parental consent requirement; exceptions; compliance with judicial orders and subpoenas; audit and evaluation of Federally-supported education programs; recordkeeping.

(1) No funds shall be made available under any applicable program to any educational agency or institution which has a policy or practice of permitting the release of educational records (or personally identifiable information contained therein other than directory information, as defined in paragraph (5) of subsection (a)) of students without the written consent of their parents to any individual, agency, or organization, other than to the following—

(A) other school officials, including teachers within the educational institution or local educational agency, who have been determined by such agency or institution to have legitimate educational interests, including the educational interests of the child for whom consent would otherwise be required;

(B) officials of other schools or school systems in which the student seeks or intends to enroll, upon condition that the student's parents be notified of the transfer, receive a copy of the record if desired, and have an opportunity for a hearing to challenge the content of the record;

....

(E) State and local officials or authorities to whom such information is specifically allowed to be reported or disclosed pursuant to State statute adopted—

....

(2) No funds shall be made available under any applicable program to any educational agency or institution which has a policy or practice of releasing, or providing access to, any personally identifiable information in education records other than directory information, or as is permitted under paragraph (1) of this subsection unless—

(A) there is written consent from the student's parents specifying records to be released, the reasons for such release, and to whom, and with a copy of the records to be released to the student's parents and the student if desired by the parents, or

....

(4) (A) Each educational agency or institution shall maintain a record, kept with the education records of each student, which will indicate all individuals (other than those specified in paragraph (1)(A) of this subsection), agencies, or organizations which have requested or obtained access to a student's education records maintained by such educational agency or institution, and which will indicate specifically the legitimate interest that each such person, agency, or organization has in obtaining this information. Such record of access shall be available only to parents, to the school official and his assistants who are responsible for the custody of such records, and to persons or organizations authorized in, and under the conditions of, clauses (A) and (C) of paragraph (1) as a means of auditing the operation of the system.

(B) With respect to this subsection, personal information shall only be transferred to a third party on the condition that such party will not permit any other party to have access to such information without the written consent of the parents of the student. If a third party outside the educational agency or institution permits access to information in violation of paragraph (2)(A), or fails to destroy information in violation of paragraph (1)(F), the educational agency or institution shall be prohibited from permitting access to information from education records to that third party for a period of not less than five years.

(d) Students' rather than parents' permission or consent. For the purposes of this section, whenever a student has attained eighteen years of age, or is attending an institution of postsecondary education, the permission or consent required of and the rights accorded to the parents of the student shall thereafter only be required of and accorded to the student.

(e) Informing parents or students of rights under this section. No funds shall be made available under any applicable program to any educational agency or institution unless such agency or institution effectively informs the parents of students, or the students, if they are eighteen years of age or older, or are attending an institution of postsecondary education, of the rights accorded them by this section.

(f) Enforcement; termination of assistance. The Secretary shall take appropriate actions to enforce this section and to deal with violations of this section, in accordance with this Act, except that action to terminate assistance may be taken only if the Secretary finds there has been a failure to comply with this section, and he has determined that compliance cannot be secured by voluntary means.

. . . .

(h) Certain disciplinary action information allowable. Nothing in this section shall prohibit an educational agency or institution from—

(1) including appropriate information in the education record of any student concerning disciplinary action taken against such student for conduct that posed a significant risk to the safety or well-being of that student, other students, or other members of the school community; or

(2) disclosing such information to teachers and school officials, including teachers and school officials in other schools, who have legitimate educational interests in the behavior of the student.

(i) Drug and alcohol violation disclosures.

(1) In general. Nothing in this Act or the Higher Education Act of 1965 shall be construed to prohibit an institution of higher education from disclosing, to a parent or legal guardian of a student, information regarding any violation of any Federal, State, or local law, or of any rule or policy of the institution, governing the use or possession of alcohol or a controlled substance, regardless of whether that information is contained in the student's education records, if—

(A) the student is under the age of 21; and

(B) the institution determines that the student has committed a disciplinary violation with respect to such use or possession.

(2) State law regarding disclosure. Nothing in paragraph (1) shall be construed to supersede any provision of State law that prohibits an institution of higher education from making the disclosure described in subsection (a).

34 C.F.R. Part 99 Family Educational Rights and Privacy Act Regulations[1]

§ 99.3 What definitions apply to these regulations?

Disciplinary action or proceeding means the investigation, adjudication, or imposition of sanctions by an educational agency or institution with respect to an infraction or violation of the internal rules of conduct applicable to students of the agency or institution.

Disclosure means to permit access to or the release, transfer, or other communication of personally identifiable information contained in education records by any means, including oral, written, or electronic means, to any party except the party identified as the party that provided or created the record.

Education records

(a) The term means those records that are:

(1) Directly related to a student; and

(2) Maintained by an educational agency or institution or by a party acting for the agency or institution.

(b) The term does not include:

(1) Records that are kept in the sole possession of the maker, are used only as a personal memory aid, and are not accessible or revealed to any other person except a temporary substitute for the maker of the record.

(2) Records of the law enforcement unit of an educational agency or institution, subject to the provisions of § 99.8.

(3) (i) Records relating to an individual who is employed by an educational agency or institution, that:

(A) Are made and maintained in the normal course of business;

(B) Relate exclusively to the individual in that individual's capacity as an employee; and

(C) Are not available for use for any other purpose.

(ii) Records relating to an individual in attendance at the agency or institution who is employed as a result of his or her status as a student

1. Selected terms and sections are included in the excerpt; for full list see the C.F.R (emphasis supplied).

are education records and not excepted under paragraph (b)(3)(i) of this definition.

(4) Records on a student who is 18 years of age or older, or is attending an institution of postsecondary education, that are:

(i) Made or maintained by a physician, psychiatrist, psychologist, or other recognized professional or paraprofessional acting in his or her professional capacity or assisting in a paraprofessional capacity;

(ii) Made, maintained, or used only in connection with treatment of the student; and

(iii) Disclosed only to individuals providing the treatment. For the purpose of this definition, "treatment" does not include remedial educational activities or activities that are part of the program of instruction at the agency or institution; and

(5) Records created or received by an educational agency or institution after an individual is no longer a student in attendance and that are not directly related to the individual's attendance as a student.

(6) Grades on peer-graded papers before they are collected and recorded by a teacher.

Eligible student means a student who has reached 18 years of age or is attending an institution of postsecondary education.

. . . .

Personally Identifiable Information

The term includes, but is not limited to—

(a) The student's name;

(b) The name of the student's parent or other family members;

(c) The address of the student or student's family;

(d) A personal identifier, such as the student's social security number, student number, or biometric record;

(e) Other indirect identifiers, such as the student's date of birth, place of birth, and mother's maiden name;

(f) Other information that, alone or in combination, is linked or linkable to a specific student that would allow a reasonable person in the school community, who does not have personal knowledge of the relevant circumstances, to identify the student with reasonable certainty; or

(g) Information requested by a person who the educational agency or institution reasonably believes knows the identity of the student to whom the education record relates.

Record means any information recorded in any way, including, but not limited to, handwriting, print, computer media, video or audio tape, film, microfilm, and microfiche.

Student, except as otherwise specifically provided in this part, means any individual who is or has been in attendance at an educational agency or institution and regarding whom the agency or institution maintains education records.

§ 99.4 What are the rights of parents?

An educational agency or institution shall give full rights under the Act to either parent, unless the agency or institution has been provided with evidence that there is a court order, State statute, or legally binding document relating to such matters as divorce, separation, or custody that specifically revokes these rights.

§ 99.5 What are the rights of students?

(a) (1) When a student becomes an eligible student, the rights accorded to, and consent required of, parents under this part transfer from the parents to the student.

(2) Nothing in this section prevents an educational agency or institution from disclosing education records, or personally identifiable information from education records, to a parent without the prior written consent of an eligible student if the disclosure meets the conditions in § 99.31(a)(8), § 99.31(a)(10), § 99.31(a)(15), or any other provision in § 99.31(a).

(b) The Act and this part do not prevent educational agencies or institutions from giving students rights in addition to those given to parents.

(c) An individual who is or has been a student at an educational institution and who applies for admission at another component of that institution does not have rights under this part with respect to records maintained by that other component, including records maintained in connection with the student's application for admission, unless the student is accepted and attends that other component of the institution.

§ 99.30 Under what conditions is prior consent required to disclose information?

(a) The parent or eligible student shall provide a signed and dated written consent before an educational agency or institution discloses personally identifiable information from the student's education records, except as provided in § 99.31.

(b) The written consent must:

(1) Specify the records that may be disclosed;

(2) State the purpose of the disclosure; and

(3) Identify the party or class of parties to whom the disclosure may be made.

(c) When a disclosure is made under paragraph (a) of this section:

(1) If a parent or eligible student so requests, the educational agency or institution shall provide him or her with a copy of the records disclosed; and

(2) If the parent of a student who is not an eligible student so requests, the agency or institution shall provide the student with a copy of the records disclosed.

(d) "Signed and dated written consent" under this part may include a record and signature in electronic form that—

(1) Identifies and authenticates a particular person as the source of the electronic consent; and

(2) Indicates such person's approval of the information contained in the electronic consent.

§ 99.31 Under what conditions is prior consent not required to disclose information?

. . . .

(a) An educational agency or institution may disclose personally identifiable information from an education record of a student without the consent required by § 99.30 if the disclosure meets one or more of the following conditions:

(1) (i) (A) The disclosure is to other school officials, including teachers, within the agency or institution whom the agency or institution has determined to have legitimate educational interests.

(B) A contractor, consultant, volunteer, or other party to whom an agency or institution has outsourced institutional services or functions may be considered a school official under this paragraph provided that the outside party—

(1) Performs an institutional service or function for which the agency or institution would otherwise use employees;

(2) Is under the direct control of the agency or institution with respect to the use and maintenance of education records; and

(3) Is subject to the requirements of § 99.33(a) governing the use and redisclosure of personally identifiable information from education records.

(ii) An educational agency or institution must use reasonable methods to ensure that school officials obtain access to only those education records in which they have legitimate educational interests. An educational agency or institution that does not use physical or technological access controls must ensure that its administrative policy for controlling access to education records is effective and that it remains in compliance with the legitimate educational interest requirement in paragraph (a)(1)(i)(A) of this section.

(2) The disclosure is, subject to the requirements of § 99.34, to officials of another school, school system, or institution of postsecondary education where the student seeks or intends to enroll, or where the student is already enrolled so long as the disclosure is for purposes related to the student's enrollment or transfer.

Note: Section 4155(b) of the No Child Left Behind Act of 2001, 20 U.S.C. 7165(b), requires each State to assure the Secretary of Education that it has a procedure in place to facilitate the transfer of disciplinary records with respect to a suspension or expulsion of a student by a local educational agency to any private or public elementary or secondary school in which the student is subsequently enrolled or seeks, intends, or is instructed to enroll.

(3) The disclosure is, subject to the requirements of § 99.35, to authorized representatives of—

(i) The Comptroller General of the United States;

(ii) The Attorney General of the United States;

(iii) The Secretary; or

(iv) State and local educational authorities.

(4) (i) The disclosure is in connection with financial aid for which the student has applied or which the student has received, if the information is necessary for such purposes as to:

(A) Determine eligibility for the aid;

(B) Determine the amount of the aid;

(C) Determine the conditions for the aid; or

(D) Enforce the terms and conditions of the aid.

(ii) As used in paragraph (a)(4)(i) of this section, financial aid means a payment of funds provided to an individual (or a payment in kind of tangible or intangible property to the individual) that is conditioned on the individual's attendance at an educational agency or institution.

(5) (i) The disclosure is to State and local officials or authorities to whom this information is specifically—

(A) Allowed to be reported or disclosed pursuant to State statute adopted before November 19, 1974, if the allowed reporting or disclosure concerns the juvenile justice system and the system's ability to effectively serve the student whose records are released; or

(B) Allowed to be reported or disclosed pursuant to State statute adopted after November 19, 1974, subject to the requirements of § 99.38.

(ii) Paragraph (a)(5)(i) of this section does not prevent a State from further limiting the number or type of State or local officials to whom disclosures may be made under that paragraph.

(6) (i) The disclosure is to organizations conducting studies for, or on behalf of, educational agencies or institutions to:

(A) Develop, validate, or administer predictive tests;

(B) Administer student aid programs; or

(C) Improve instruction.

(ii) Nothing in the Act or this part prevents a State or local educational authority or agency headed by an official listed in paragraph (a)(3) of this section from entering into agreements with organizations conducting studies under paragraph (a)(6)(i) of this section and redisclosing personally identifiable information from education records on behalf of educational agencies and institutions that disclosed the information to the State or local educational authority or agency headed by an official listed in paragraph (a)(3) of this section in accordance with the requirements of § 99.33(b).

(iii) An educational agency or institution may disclose personally identifiable information under paragraph (a)(6)(i) of this section, and a State or local educational authority or agency headed by an official listed in paragraph (a)(3) of this section may redisclose personally identifiable information under paragraph (a)(6)(i) and (a)(6)(ii) of this section, only if—

(A) The study is conducted in a manner that does not permit personal identification of parents and students by individuals other than representatives of the organization that have legitimate interests in the information;

(B) The information is destroyed when no longer needed for the purposes for which the study was conducted; and

(C) The educational agency or institution or the State or local educational authority or agency headed by an official listed in paragraph (a)(3) of this section enters into a written agreement with the organization that—

(1) Specifies the purpose, scope, and duration of the study or studies and the information to be disclosed;

(2) Requires the organization to use personally identifiable information from education records only to meet the purpose or purposes of the study as stated in the written agreement;

(3) Requires the organization to conduct the study in a manner that does not permit personal identification of parents and students, as defined in this part, by anyone other than representatives of the organization with legitimate interests; and

(4) Requires the organization to destroy all personally identifiable information when the information is no longer needed for the purposes for which the study was conducted and specifies the time period in which the information must be destroyed.

(iv) An educational agency or institution or State or local educational authority or Federal agency headed by an official listed in paragraph (a)(3) of this section is not required to initiate a study or agree with or endorse the conclusions or results of the study.

(v) For the purposes of paragraph (a)(6) of this section, the term organization includes, but is not limited to, Federal, State, and local agencies, and independent organizations.

(7) The disclosure is to accrediting organizations to carry out their accrediting functions.

(8) The disclosure is to parents, as defined in § 99.3, of a dependent student, as defined in section 152 of the Internal Revenue Code of 1986.

(9) (i) The disclosure is to comply with a judicial order or lawfully issued subpoena.

(ii) The educational agency or institution may disclose information under paragraph (a)(9)(i) of this section only if the agency or institution makes a reasonable effort to notify the parent or eligible student of the order or subpoena in advance of compliance, so that the parent or eligible student may seek protective action, unless the disclosure is in compliance with—

(A) A Federal grand jury subpoena and the court has ordered that the existence or the contents of the subpoena or the information furnished in response to the subpoena not be disclosed;

(B) Any other subpoena issued for a law enforcement purpose and the court or other issuing agency has ordered that the existence or the contents of the subpoena or the information furnished in response to the subpoena not be disclosed; or

(C) An ex parte court order obtained by the United States Attorney General (or designee not lower than an Assistant Attorney General) concerning investigations or prosecutions of an offense listed in 18 U.S.C. 2332b(g)(5)(B) or an act of domestic or international terrorism as defined in 18 U.S.C. 2331.

(iii) (A) If an educational agency or institution initiates legal action against a parent or student, the educational agency or institution may disclose to the court, without a court order or subpoena, the education records of the student that are relevant for the educational agency or institution to proceed with the legal action as plaintiff.

(B) If a parent or eligible student initiates legal action against an educational agency or institution, the educational agency or institution may disclose to the court, without a court order or subpoena, the student's education records that are relevant for the educational agency or institution to defend itself.

(10) The disclosure is in connection with a health or safety emergency, under the conditions described in § 99.36.

(11) The disclosure is information the educational agency or institution has designated as "directory information", under the conditions described in § 99.37.

(12) The disclosure is to the parent of a student who is not an eligible student or to the student.

(13) The disclosure, subject to the requirements in § 99.39, is to a victim of an alleged perpetrator of a crime of violence or a non-forcible sex offense. The disclosure may only include the final results of the disciplinary proceeding conducted by the institution of postsecondary education with respect to that alleged crime or offense. The institution may disclose the final results of the disciplinary proceeding, regardless of whether the institution concluded a violation was committed.

(14) (i) The disclosure, subject to the requirements in § 99.39, is in connection with a disciplinary proceeding at an institution of postsecondary education. The institution must not disclose the final results of the disciplinary proceeding unless it determines that—

(A) The student is an alleged perpetrator of a crime of violence or non-forcible sex offense; and

(B) With respect to the allegation made against him or her, the student has committed a violation of the institution's rules or policies.

(ii) The institution may not disclose the name of any other student, including a victim or witness, without the prior written consent of the other student.

(iii) This section applies only to disciplinary proceedings in which the final results were reached on or after October 7, 1998.

(15) (i) The disclosure is to a parent of a student at an institution of postsecondary education regarding the student's violation of any Federal, State, or local law, or of any rule or policy of the institution, governing the use or possession of alcohol or a controlled substance if—

(A) The institution determines that the student has committed a disciplinary violation with respect to that use or possession; and

(B) The student is under the age of 21 at the time of the disclosure to the parent.

(ii) Paragraph (a)(15) of this section does not supersede any provision of State law that prohibits an institution of postsecondary education from disclosing information.

(16) The disclosure concerns sex offenders and other individuals required to register under section 170101 of the Violent Crime Control and Law Enforcement Act of 1994, 42 U.S.C. 14071, and the information was provided to the educational agency or institution under 42 U.S.C. 14071 and applicable Federal guidelines.

(b) (1) De-identified records and information. An educational agency or institution, or a party that has received education records or information from education records under this part, may release the records or information without the consent required by § 99.30 after the removal of all personally identifiable information provided that the educational agency or institution or other party has made a reasonable determination that a student's identity is not personally identifiable, whether through single or multiple releases, and taking into account other reasonably available information.

(2) An educational agency or institution, or a party that has received education records or information from education records under this part, may release de-identified student level data from education records for the purpose of education research by attaching a code to each record that may allow the recipient to match information received from the same source, provided that—

(i) An educational agency or institution or other party that releases de-identified data under paragraph (b)(2) of this section does not disclose any information about how it generates and assigns a record code, or that would allow a recipient to identify a student based on a record code;

(ii) The record code is used for no purpose other than identifying a de-identified record for purposes of education research and cannot be used to ascertain personally identifiable information about a student; and

(iii) The record code is not based on a student's social security number or other personal information.

(c) An educational agency or institution must use reasonable methods to identify and authenticate the identity of parents, students, school officials, and any other parties to whom the agency or institution discloses personally identifiable information from education records.

(d) Paragraphs (a) and (b) of this section do not require an educational agency or institution or any other party to disclose education records or information from education records to any party, except for parties under paragraph (a)(12) of this section.

§ 99.37 What conditions apply to disclosing directory information?

(a) An educational agency or institution may disclose directory information if it has given public notice to parents of students in attendance and eligible students in attendance at the agency or institution of:

(1) The types of personally identifiable information that the agency or institution has designated as directory information;

(2) A parent's or eligible student's right to refuse to let the agency or institution designate any or all of those types of information about the student as directory information; and

(3) The period of time within which a parent or eligible student has to notify the agency or institution in writing that he or she does not want any or all of those types of information about the student designated as directory information.

(b) An educational agency or institution may disclose directory information about former students without complying with the notice and opt out conditions in paragraph (a) of this section. However, the agency or institution must continue to honor any valid request to opt out of the disclosure of directory information made while a student was in attendance unless the student rescinds the opt out request.

(c) A parent or eligible student may not use the right under paragraph (a)(2) of this section to opt out of directory information disclosures to—

(1) Prevent an educational agency or institution from disclosing or requiring a student to disclose the student's name, identifier, or institutional email address in a class in which the student is enrolled; or

(2) Prevent an educational agency or institution from requiring a student to wear, to display publicly, or to disclose a student ID card or badge that exhibits information that may be designated as directory information under § 99.3 and that has been properly designated by the educational agency or institution as directory information in the public notice provided under paragraph (a)(1) of this section.

(d) In its public notice to parents and eligible students in attendance at the agency or institution that is described in paragraph (a) of this section, an educational agency or institution may specify that disclosure of directory information will be limited to specific parties, for specific purposes, or both. When an educational agency or institution specifies that disclosure of directory information will be limited to specific parties, for specific purposes, or both, the educational agency or institution must limit its directory information disclosures to those specified in its public notice that is described in paragraph (a) of this section.

(e) An educational agency or institution may not disclose or confirm directory information without meeting the written consent requirements in § 99.30 if a student's social security number or other non-directory information is used alone or combined with other data elements to identify or help identify the student or the student's records.

§ 99.63 Where are complaints filed?

A parent or eligible student may file a written complaint with the Office regarding an alleged violation under the Act and this part. The Office's address is: Family Policy Compliance Office, U.S. Department of Education, 400 Maryland Avenue, S.W., Washington, DC 20202.

§ 99.66 What are the responsibilities of the Office in the enforcement process?

(a) The Office reviews a complaint, if any, information submitted by the educational agency or institution, other recipient of Department funds under any program administered by the Secretary, or third party outside of an educational agency or institution, and any other relevant information. The Office may permit the parties to submit further written or oral arguments or information.

(b) Following its investigation, the Office provides to the complainant, if any, and the educational agency or institution, other recipient, or third party a written notice of its findings and the basis for its findings.

(c) If the Office finds that an educational agency or institution or other recipient has not complied with a provision of the Act or this part, it may also find that the failure to comply was based on a policy or practice of the agency or institution or other recipient. A notice of findings issued under paragraph (b) of this section to an educational agency or institution, or other recipient that has not complied with a provision of the Act or this part—

(1) Includes a statement of the specific steps that the agency or institution or other recipient must take to comply; and

(2) Provides a reasonable period of time, given all of the circumstances of the case, during which the educational agency or institution or other recipient may comply voluntarily.

(d) If the Office finds that a third party outside of an educational agency or institution has not complied with the provisions of § 99.31(a)(6)(iii)(B) or has improperly redisclosed personally identifiable information from education records in violation of § 99.33, the Office's notice of findings issued under paragraph (b) of this section—

(1) Includes a statement of the specific steps that the third party outside of the educational agency or institution must take to comply; and

(2) Provides a reasonable period of time, given all of the circumstances of the case, during which the third party may comply voluntarily.

Owasso Independent School District No. I-011 v. Falvo

534 U.S. 426 (2002)

The Court rules that the peer grading practices used by the school do not violate FERPA, because the student graded papers at issue were not education records under FERPA.

Justice Kennedy delivered the opinion of the Court, in which Rehnquist, C. J., and Stevens, O'Connor, Souter, Thomas, Ginsburg, and Breyer, JJ., joined.

Teachers sometimes ask students to score each other's tests, papers, and assignments as the teacher explains the correct answers to the entire class. Respondent contends this practice, which the parties refer to as peer grading, violates the Family Educational Rights and Privacy Act of 1974 (FERPA or Act), 88 Stat. 571, 20 U.S.C. § 1232g. We took this case to resolve the issue.

Under FERPA, schools and educational agencies receiving federal financial assistance must comply with certain conditions. One condition specified in the Act is that sensitive information about students may not be released without parental consent. The Act states that federal funds are to be withheld from school districts that have "a policy or practice of permitting the release of education records (or personally identifiable information contained therein . . .) of students without the written consent of their parents." The phrase "education records" is defined, under the Act, as "records, files, documents, and other materials" containing information directly related to a student, which "are maintained by an educational agency or institution or by a person acting for such agency or institution." § 1232g(a)(4)(A). The definition of education records contains an exception for "records of instructional, supervisory, and administrative personnel . . . which are in the sole possession of the maker thereof and which are not accessible or revealed to any other person except a substitute." § 1232g(a)(4)(B)(i). The precise question for us is whether peer-graded classroom work and assignments are education records.

Three of respondent Kristja J. Falvo's children are enrolled in Owasso Independent School District No. I-011, in a suburb of Tulsa, Oklahoma. The children's teachers, like many teachers in this country, use peer grading. In a typical case the students exchange papers with each other and score them according to the teacher's instructions, then return the work to the student who prepared it. The teacher may ask the students to report their own scores. In this case it appears the student could either call out the score or walk to the teacher's desk and reveal it in confidence, though by that stage, of course, the score was known at least to the one other student who did the grading. Both the grading and the system of calling out the scores are in contention here.

Respondent claimed the peer grading embarrassed her children. She asked the school district to adopt a uniform policy banning peer grading and requiring teachers either to grade assignments themselves or at least to forbid students from grading papers other than their own. The school district declined to do so, and respondent brought a class action pursuant to 42 U.S.C. § 1983 against the school district, Superintendent Dale Johnson, Assistant Superintendent Lynn Johnson, and Principal Rick Thomas (petitioners). . . .

We granted certiorari to decide whether peer grading violates FERPA. Finding no violation of the Act, we reverse.

At the outset, we note it is an open question whether FERPA provides private parties, like respondent, with a cause of action enforceable under § 1983. We have granted certiorari on this issue in another case. *See Gonzaga Univ. v. Doe*, 534 U.S. 1103, 122 S. Ct. 865. The parties, furthermore, did not contest the § 1983 issue before the Court of Appeals. That court raised the issue *sua sponte*, and petitioners did not seek certiorari on the question. We need not resolve the question here as it is our practice "to decide cases on the grounds raised and considered in the Court of Appeals and included in the question on which we granted certiorari." In these circumstances we assume, but without so deciding or expressing an opinion on the question, that private parties may sue an educational agency under § 1983 to enforce the provisions of FERPA here at issue. . . .

The parties appear to agree that if an assignment becomes an education record the moment a peer grades it, then the grading, or at least the practice of asking students to call out their grades in class, would be an impermissible release of the records under § 1232g(b)(1). Without deciding the point, we assume for the purposes of our analysis that they are correct. The parties disagree, however, whether peer-graded assignments constitute education records at all. The papers do contain information directly related to a student, but they are records under the Act only when and if they "are maintained by an educational agency or institution or by a person acting for such agency or institution." § 1232g(a)(4)(A).

Petitioners, supported by the United States as *amicus curiae*, contend the definition covers only institutional records—namely, those materials retained in a permanent file as a matter of course. They argue that records "maintained by an educational agency or institution" generally would include final course grades, student grade point averages, standardized test scores, attendance records, counseling records, and records of disciplinary actions—but not student homework or classroom work.

Respondent, adopting the reasoning of the Court of Appeals, contends student-graded assignments fall within the definition of education records. That definition contains an exception for "records of instructional, supervisory, and administrative personnel . . . which are in the sole possession of the maker thereof and which are not accessible or revealed to any other person except a substitute." § 1232g(a)(4)(B)(i). The Court of Appeals reasoned that if grade books are not education records, then it would have been unnecessary for Congress to enact the exception. Grade books and the grades within, the court concluded, are "maintained" by a teacher and so are covered by FERPA. The court recognized that teachers do not maintain the grades on individual student assignments until they have recorded the result in the grade books. It reasoned, however, that if Congress forbids teachers to disclose students' grades once written in a grade book, it makes no sense to permit the disclosure immediately beforehand. The court thus held that student graders maintain the grades until they are reported to the teacher.

The Court of Appeals' logic does not withstand scrutiny. Its interpretation, furthermore, would effect a drastic alteration of the existing allocation of responsibilities between States and the National Government in the operation of the Nation's schools. We would hesitate before interpreting the statute to effect such a substantial change in the balance of federalism unless that is the manifest purpose of the legislation. This principle guides our decision.

Two statutory indicators tell us that the Court of Appeals erred in concluding that an assignment satisfies the definition of education records as soon as it is graded by another student. First, the student papers are not, at that stage, "maintained" within the meaning of § 1232g(a)(4)(A). The ordinary meaning of the word "maintain" is "to keep in existence or continuance; preserve; retain." Random House Dictionary of the English Language 1160 (2d ed. 1987). Even assuming the teacher's grade book is an education record—a point the parties contest and one we do not decide here—the score on a student-graded assignment is not "contained therein," § 1232g(b)(1), until the teacher records it. The teacher does not maintain the grade while students correct their peers' assignments or call out their own marks. Nor do the student graders maintain the grades within the meaning of § 1232g(a)(4)(A). The word "maintain" suggests FERPA records will be kept in a filing cabinet in a records room at the school or on a permanent secure database, perhaps even after the student is no longer enrolled. The student graders only handle assignments for a few moments as the teacher calls out the answers. It is fanciful to say they maintain the papers in the same way the registrar maintains a student's folder in a permanent file.

The Court of Appeals was further mistaken in concluding that each student grader is "a person acting for" an educational institution for purposes of § 1232g(a)(4)(A). The phrase "acting for" connotes agents of the school, such as teachers, administrators, and other school employees. Just as it does not accord with our usual understanding to say students are "acting for" an educational institution when they follow their teacher's direction to take a quiz, it is equally awkward to say students are "acting for" an educational institution when they follow their teacher's direction to score it. Correcting a classmate's work can be as much a part of the assignment as taking the test itself. It is a way to teach material again in a new context, and it helps show students how to assist and respect fellow pupils. By explaining the answers to the class as the students correct the papers, the teacher not only reinforces the lesson but also discovers whether the students have understood the material and are ready to move on. We do not think FERPA prohibits these educational techniques. We also must not lose sight of the fact that the phrase "by a person acting for [an educational] institution" modifies "maintain." Even if one were to agree students are acting for the teacher when they correct the assignment, that is different from saying they are acting for the educational institution in maintaining it.

Other sections of the statute support our interpretation. FERPA, for example, requires educational institutions to "maintain a record, kept with the education records of each student." § 1232g(b)(4)(A). This record must list those who have requested access to a student's education records and their reasons for doing so. The record of access "shall be available only to parents, [and] to the school official and his assistants who are responsible for the custody of such records."

Under the Court of Appeals' broad interpretation of education records, every teacher would have an obligation to keep a separate record of access for each student's assignments. Indeed, by that court's logic, even students who grade their own papers would bear the burden of maintaining records of access until they turned in the assignments. We doubt Congress would have imposed such a weighty administrative burden on every teacher, and certainly it would not have extended the mandate to students.

Also, FERPA requires "a record" of access for each pupil. This single record must be kept "with the education records." This suggests Congress contemplated that education records would be kept in one place with a single record of access. By describing a "school official" and "his assistants" as the personnel responsible for the custody of the records, FERPA implies that education records are institutional records kept by a single central custodian, such as a registrar, not individual assignments handled by many student graders in their separate classrooms.

FERPA also requires recipients of federal funds to provide parents with a hearing at which they may contest the accuracy of their child's education records. § 1232g(a)(2). The hearings must be conducted "in accordance with regulations of the Secretary," which in turn require adjudication by a disinterested official and the opportunity for parents to be represented by an attorney. 34 CFR § 99.22 (2001). It is doubtful Congress would have provided parents with this elaborate procedural machinery to challenge the accuracy of the grade on every spelling test and art project the child completes.

Respondent's construction of the term "education records" to cover student homework or classroom work would impose substantial burdens on teachers across the country. It would force all instructors to take time, which otherwise could be spent teaching and in preparation, to correct an assortment of daily student assignments. Respondent's view would make it much more difficult for teachers to give students immediate guidance. The interpretation respondent urges would force teachers to abandon other customary practices, such as group grading of team assignments. Indeed, the logical consequences of respondent's view are all but unbounded. At argument, counsel for respondent seemed to agree that if a teacher in any of the thousands of covered classrooms in the Nation puts a happy face, a gold star, or a disapproving remark on a classroom assignment, federal law does not allow other students to see it.

We doubt Congress meant to intervene in this drastic fashion with traditional state functions. Under the Court of Appeals' interpretation of FERPA, the federal power would exercise minute control over specific teaching methods and instructional dynamics in classrooms throughout the country. The Congress is not likely to have mandated this result, and we do not interpret the statute to require it.

For these reasons, even assuming a teacher's grade book is an education record, the Court of Appeals erred, for in all events the grades on students' papers would not be covered under FERPA at least until the teacher has collected them and recorded them in his or her grade book. We limit our holding to this narrow point, and do not decide the broader question whether the grades on individual student assignments, once they are turned in to teachers, are protected by the Act.

. . . .

Gonzaga University v. Doe

536 U.S. 273 (2002)

The Court rules that there is no private right of action to enforce the protections provided under FERPA in court.

CHIEF JUSTICE REHNQUIST delivered the opinion of the Court, which O'CONNOR, SCALIA, KENNEDY, and THOMAS, JJ., joined.

The question presented is whether a student may sue a private university for damages under Rev. Stat. § 1979, 42 U.S.C. § 1983 to enforce provisions of the Family Educational Rights and Privacy Act of 1974 (FERPA or Act), 20 U.S.C. § 1232g, which prohibit the federal funding of educational institutions that have a policy or practice of releasing education records to unauthorized persons. We hold such an action foreclosed because the relevant provisions of FERPA create no personal rights to enforce under 42 U.S.C. § 1983.

Respondent John Doe is a former undergraduate in the School of Education at Gonzaga University, a private university in Spokane, Washington. He planned to graduate and teach at a Washington public elementary school. Washington at the time required all of its new teachers to obtain an affidavit of good moral character from a dean of their graduating college or university. In October 1993, Roberta League, Gonzaga's "teacher certification specialist," overheard one student tell another that respondent engaged in acts of sexual misconduct against Jane Doe, a female undergraduate. League launched an investigation and contacted the state agency responsible for teacher certification, identifying respondent by name and discussing the allegations against him. Respondent did not learn of the investigation, or that information about him had been disclosed, until March 1994, when he was told by League and others that he would not receive the affidavit required for certification as a Washington schoolteacher.

Respondent then sued Gonzaga and League (petitioners) in state court. He alleged violations of Washington tort and contract law, as well as a pendent violation of § 1983 for the release of personal information to an "unauthorized person" in violation of FERPA. A jury found for respondent on all counts, awarding him $1,155,000, including $150,000 in compensatory damages and $300,000 in punitive damages on the FERPA claim . . . .

The Washington Court of Appeals reversed in relevant part, concluding that FERPA does not create individual rights and thus cannot be enforced under § 1983. The Washington Supreme Court reversed that decision, and ordered the FERPA damages reinstated. The court acknowledged that "FERPA itself does not give rise to a private cause of action," but reasoned that FERPA's nondisclosure provision "gives rise to a federal right enforceable under section 1983."

Like the Washington Supreme Court and the state court of appeals below, other state and federal courts have divided on the question of FERPA's enforceability under § 1983. The fact that all of these courts have relied on the same set of opinions from this Court suggests that our opinions in this area may not be models of clarity. We therefore granted certiorari to resolve the conflict among the lower courts and in the process resolve any ambiguity in our own opinions.

Congress enacted FERPA under its spending power to condition the receipt of federal funds on certain requirements relating to the access and disclosure of student educational records. The Act directs the Secretary of Education to withhold federal funds from any public or private "educational agency or institution" that fails to comply with these conditions. As relevant here, the Act provides: "No funds shall be made available under any applicable program to any educational agency or institution which has a policy or practice of permitting the release of education records (or personally identifiable information contained therein . . .) of students without the written consent of their parents to any individual, agency, or organization." 20 U.S.C. § 1232g(b)(1).

The Act directs the Secretary of Education to enforce this and other of the Act's spending conditions. § 1232g(f). The Secretary is required to establish an office and review board within the Department of Education for "investigating, processing, reviewing, and adjudicating violations of [the Act]." § 1232g(g). Funds may be terminated only if the Secretary determines that a recipient institution "is failing to comply substantially with any requirement of [the Act]" and that such compliance "cannot be secured by voluntary means." §§ 1234c(a), 1232g(f).

Respondent contends that this statutory regime confers upon any student enrolled at a covered school or institution a federal right, enforceable in suits for damages under § 1983, not to have "education records" disclosed to unauthorized persons without the student's express written consent. But we have never before held, and decline to do so here, that spending legislation drafted in terms resembling those of FERPA can confer enforceable rights.

In *Maine v. Thiboutot*, 448 U.S. 1 (1980), six years after Congress enacted FERPA, we recognized for the first time that § 1983 actions may be brought against state actors to enforce rights created by federal statutes as well as by the Constitution. There we held that plaintiffs could recover payments wrongfully withheld by a state agency in violation of the Social Security Act. A year later, in *Pennhurst State School and Hospital* v. *Halderman*, 451 U.S. 1 (1981), we rejected a claim that the Developmentally Disabled Assistance and Bill of Rights Act of 1975 conferred enforceable rights, saying: "In legislation enacted pursuant to the spending power, the typical remedy for state noncompliance with federally imposed conditions is not a private cause of action for noncompliance but rather action by the Federal Government to terminate funds to the State."

We made clear that unless Congress "speaks with a clear voice," and manifests an "unambiguous" intent to confer individual rights, federal funding provisions provide no basis for private enforcement by § 1983.

Since *Pennhurst*, only twice have we found spending legislation to give rise to enforceable rights. In *Wright v. Roanoke Redevelopment and Housing Authority*, 479 U.S. 418 (1987), we allowed a § 1983 suit by tenants to recover past overcharges under a rent-ceiling provision of the Public Housing Act, on the ground that the provision unambiguously conferred "a mandatory [benefit] focusing on the individual family and its income." The key to our inquiry was that Congress spoke in terms that "could not be clearer," and conferred entitlements "sufficiently specific and definite to qualify as enforceable rights under *Pennhurst*." Also significant was that the federal agency charged with administering the Public Housing Act "had never provided a procedure by which tenants could complain to it about the alleged failures [of state welfare agencies] to abide by [the Act's rent-ceiling provision]."

Three years later, in *Wilder v. Virginia Hosp. Ass'n*, 496 U.S. 498 (1990), we allowed a § 1983 suit brought by health care providers to enforce a reimbursement provision of the Medicaid Act, on the ground that the provision, much like the rent-ceiling provision in *Wright*, explicitly conferred specific monetary entitlements upon the plaintiffs. Congress left no doubt of its intent for private enforcement, we said, because the provision required States to pay an "objective" monetary entitlement to individual health care providers, with no sufficient administrative means of enforcing the requirement against States that failed to comply.

Our more recent decisions, however, have rejected attempts to infer enforceable rights from Spending Clause statutes. In *Suter v. Artist M.*, 503 U.S. 347 (1992), the Adoption Assistance and Child Welfare Act of 1980 required States receiving funds for adoption assistance to have a "plan" to make "reasonable efforts" to keep children out of foster homes. A class of parents and children sought to enforce this requirement against state officials under § 1983, claiming that no such efforts had been made. We read the Act "in the light shed by *Pennhurst*," and found no basis for the suit. . . .

Similarly, in *Blessing v. Freestone*, 520 U.S. 329 (1997), Title IV-D of the Social Security Act required States receiving federal child-welfare funds to "substantially comply" with requirements designed to ensure timely payment of child support. Five Arizona mothers invoked § 1983 against state officials on grounds that state child-welfare agencies consistently failed to meet these requirements. We found no basis for the suit, saying,

> "Far from creating an *individual* entitlement to services, the standard is simply a yardstick for the Secretary to measure the *systemwide* performance of a State's Title IV-D program. Thus, the Secretary must look to the aggregate services provided by the State, not to whether the needs of any particular person have been satisfied."

. . . .

We now reject the notion that our cases permit anything short of an unambiguously conferred right to support a cause of action brought under § 1983. Section 1983 provides a remedy only for the deprivation of "rights, privileges, or immunities secured by the Constitution and laws" of the United States. Accordingly, it is *rights*, not the broader or vaguer "benefits" or "interests," that may be enforced under the authority of that section. . . .

We have recognized that whether a statutory violation may be enforced through § 1983 "is a different inquiry than that involved in determining whether a private right of action can be implied from a particular statute." . . . But the inquiries overlap in one meaningful respect — in either case we must first determine whether Congress *intended to create a federal right*. Thus we have held that "the question whether Congress . . . intended to create a private right of action [is] definitively answered in the negative" where "a statute by its terms grants no private rights to any identifiable class." For a statute to create such private rights, its text must be "phrased in terms of the persons benefited." *Cannon v. University of Chicago*, 441 U.S. 677 (1979). We have recognized, for example, that Title VI of the Civil Rights Act of 1964 and Title IX of the Education Amendments of 1972 create individual rights because those statutes are phrased "with an *unmistakable focus* on the benefited class." But even where a statute is phrased in such explicit rights-creating terms, a plaintiff suing under an implied right of action still must show that the statute manifests an intent "to create not just a private *right* but also a private *remedy*."

Plaintiffs suing under § 1983 do not have the burden of showing an intent to create a private remedy because § 1983 generally supplies a remedy for the vindication of rights secured by federal statutes. Once a plaintiff demonstrates that a statute confers an individual right, the right is presumptively enforceable by § 1983. But the initial inquiry—determining whether a statute confers any right at all—is no different from the initial inquiry in an implied right of action case, the express purpose of which is to determine whether or not a statute "confers rights on a particular class of persons." This makes obvious sense, since § 1983 merely provides a mechanism for enforcing individual rights "secured" elsewhere, *i.e.*, rights independently "secured by the Constitution and laws" of the United States. "One cannot go into court and claim a 'violation of § 1983'—for § 1983 by itself does not protect anyone against anything."

....

With this principle in mind, there is no question that FERPA's nondisclosure provisions fail to confer enforceable rights. To begin with, the provisions entirely lack the sort of "rights-creating" language critical to showing the requisite congressional intent to create new rights. Unlike the individually focused terminology of Titles VI and IX ("no person shall be subjected to discrimination"), FERPA's provisions speak only to the Secretary of Education, directing that "no funds shall be made available" to any "educational agency or institution" which has a prohibited "policy or practice." 20 U.S.C. § 1232g(b)(1). This focus is two steps removed from the interests of individual students and parents and clearly does not confer the sort of "*individual* entitlement" that is enforceable under § 1983....

FERPA's nondisclosure provisions further speak only in terms of institutional policy and practice, not individual instances of disclosure. *See* 1232g(b)(1)–(2) (prohibiting the funding of "any educational agency or institution which has a *policy or practice* of permitting the release of education records." Therefore, as in *Blessing*, they have an "aggregate" focus, they are not concerned with "whether the needs of any particular person have been satisfied," and they cannot "give rise to individual rights." Recipient institutions can further avoid termination of funding so long as they "comply substantially" with the Act's requirements. § 1234c(a)....

Our conclusion that FERPA's nondisclosure provisions fail to confer enforceable rights is buttressed by the mechanism that Congress chose to provide for enforcing those provisions. Congress expressly authorized the Secretary of Education to "*deal with violations*" of the Act, § 1232g(f), and required the Secretary to "establish or designate [a] review board" for investigating and adjudicating such violations, § 1232g(g). Pursuant to these provisions, the Secretary created the Family Policy Compliance Office (FPCO) "to act as the Review Board required under the Act and to enforce the Act with respect to all applicable programs." 34 CFR 99.60(a) and (b) (2001). The FPCO permits students and parents who suspect a violation of the Act to file individual written complaints. § 99.63. If a complaint is timely and contains required information, the FPCO will initiate an investigation, §§ 99.64(a)-(b), notify the educational institution of the charge, § 99.65(a), and request a written response, § 99.65. If a violation is found, the FPCO distributes a notice of factual findings and a "statement of the specific steps that the agency or institution must take to comply" with FERPA. §§ 99.66(b) and (c)(1). These administrative [procedures squarely distinguish this case from *Wright* and *Wilder*], where an aggrieved individual lacked any federal review mechanism, and further counsel against our finding a congressional intent to create individually enforceable private rights.

Congress finally provided that "except for the conduct of hearings, none of the functions of the Secretary under this section shall be carried out in any of the regional offices" of the Department of Education. 20 U.S.C. § 1232g(g). This centralized review provision was added just four months after FERPA's enactment due to "concern that regionalizing the enforcement of [FERPA] may lead to multiple interpretations of it, and possibly work a hardship on parents, students, and institutions." 120 Cong. Rec. 39863 (1974) (joint statement).

In sum, if Congress wishes to create new rights enforceable under § 1983, it must do so in clear and unambiguous terms—no less and no more than what is required for Congress to create new rights enforceable under an implied private right of action. FERPA's nondisclosure provisions contain no rights-creating language, they have an aggregate, not individual, focus, and they serve primarily to direct the Secretary of Education's distribution of public funds to educational institutions. They therefore create no rights enforceable under § 1983. Accordingly, the judgment of the Supreme Court of Washington is reversed, and the case is remanded for further proceedings not inconsistent with this opinion.

It is so ordered.

Post Problem Discussion

1. Without a private right of action, how meaningful is FERPA's protection? In *Gonzaga*, the Court's decision took a million dollar verdict away from the plaintiff. What, if any, recourse does the plaintiff have now for the FERPA violations committed by the school in that case?

2. *Gonzaga* is a university level case. FERPA applies to educational institutions receiving federal funds, not just K12 institutions. After the student turns eighteen, the rights, however they may be enforceable, belong to the student. This means that a parent's ability to obtain information from the school about how his/her child is doing at school is limited. What does FERPA say about parental access to information for students who are eighteen and over? Can schools inform parents about serious issues such as potential suicide, drug use, disciplinary infractions, or poor grades without student consent? *See* 34 CFR §§ 99.31(a)(8) & (a)(15).

3. FERPA is not the only protection available to students to protect their privacy. The Protection of Pupil Rights Amendment ("PPRA") 20 U.S.C. § 1232(h), and its implementing regulations, 34 C.F.R. § 98.4, protect the rights of parents and students by requiring that parental consent be secured for U.S. DOE-funded surveys that could reveal information as to:

I. political affiliations or beliefs of the student or the student's parent; mental or psychological problems of the student or the student's family;

II. sex behavior or attitudes;

III. illegal, anti-social, self-incriminating, or demeaning behavior;

IV. critical appraisals of other individuals with whom respondents have close family relationships;

V. legally recognized privileged or analogous relationships, such as those of lawyers, physicians, and ministers;

VI. religious practices, affiliations, or beliefs of the student or student's parent; or

VII. income (other than that required by law to determine eligibility for participation in a program or for receiving financial assistance under such program),

without the prior consent of the student (if the student is an adult or emancipated minor), or in the case of an unemancipated minor, without the prior written consent of the parent. How do these requirements factor into the constitutional privacy issues with surveys discussed in Section 7.02?

4. As the Court noted in *Owasso Indep. Sch. Dist. No. I-011 v. Falvo*, student peer graders did not maintain educational records when they called grades out in class. The Court's decision was based in part on the fact that if the Court were to find otherwise, it would "impose substantial burdens on teachers across the country" and "effect a drastic alteration of the existing allocation of responsibilities between States and the National Government in the operation of the Nation's schools." How are these factors relevant to the Court's interpretation of FERPA?

5. There are sure to be many variations on the *Falvo* facts. How does FERPA treat cases where the whole class (student and teacher participation) is recorded for students who may miss the session? What if the recordings are podcast? Posted on the web?

Problem 3: Directory Information

Lee Chong is a sixth grader at PS 101. PS 101 sent a letter home to Lee's parents. The subject line of the letter said FERPA. The letter gave parents two days to return the attached form to keep their child's information from appearing in the school directory. Lee's parents did not respond. Lee's full name, address, height, weight, sports, and clubs appeared in the directory. Each child got a copy of the directory. It appears that Gerome Lundy, a 28-year-old resident of PS 101 also got a copy. Using the information in the directory, he followed Lee from her home to the school. After school, Lundy lured Lee into his car by telling her that her soccer coach (info from the directory) had asked him to give her a ride to a team supper. The police do find Lundy and bring Lee home, but she has been sexually abused and traumatized. She is now under psychiatric care for the foreseeable future. Review the FERPA statutory provisions in Problem 2 and the problem materials and answer the following:

1. Are there any FERPA violations?
2. Would the situation be different if the Chongs had opted out of the directory after the two-day deadline, but before the directory was distributed?
3. Would the situation be different if the Chongs had opted out within the two-day deadline, and the school had still included Lee in the directory by mistake?

Problem Materials

✓ FERPA (selected provisions included in Problem 2 above)

✓ Selected FERPA regulations (selected provisions included in Problem 2 above)

Post Problem Discussion

1. What are some reasons for allowing schools to disclose directory information about students?

2. What, if any, remedy does Lee have against the school? Could she bring common law tort claims for the disclosure of private information? Would FERPA preempt such claims, or provide the school with a defense to such claims?

3. If you were advising PS 101 about their practices regarding directory information, what, if any, changes would you advise that they make?

4. As noted in this Chapter, the United States Supreme Court determined in *Gonzaga* that plaintiffs cannot enforce FERPA's requirements in court. As a result, FERPA enforcement is left to the Family Policy Compliance Office, an agency within the United States Department of Education. What remedies may this agency pursue for FERPA violations?

§7.04 Online Privacy

In schools today, students routinely use the Internet to access and share information. Schools often have websites providing information to the public about the school, and providing students with access to schoolwork and their teachers. Some schools offer Internet or intranet portals, or virtual classrooms/chatrooms for students to meet and discuss coursework with teachers, or other students. Many parents and students now email their teachers with information about the student or classwork.

For the most part, courts have yet to weigh in and interpret FERPA's requirements to these kinds of electronic communications. The law itself does address some of the issues by including some aspects of electronic communication in the regulatory definitions noted in Section 7.03. Additionally, as noted in Section 6.07 of Chapter 6, the Children's Internet Protection Act ("CIPA") and the Neighborhood Children's Internet Protection Act ("N-CIPA") require schools to develop Internet safety policies. Pub. L. 106-554 (2000), codified in part as 47 U.S.C. § 254(h)(5)–(7) and (l).

Another relevant law is the Children's Online Privacy Protection Act (COPPA), which requires commercial website operators to get parental consent before collecting any personal information from children under thirteen years old. 15 U.S.C. §§ 6501–6506. COPPA allows teachers to act on behalf of a parent during school activities online, but it does not require them to do so.

The following activity gives you a chance to explore some of these issues and legal requirements in more detail.

Activity 1: Online Privacy Issues

Step One—Review the full FERPA statute and regulations online, looking in particular for the definitions and other provisions addressing education records, personally identifiable information, and disclosure.

Step Two—Go back to Activity 5 in Chapter 6 where you reviewed some of the requirements of CIPA and N-CIPA and a local school district policy. Re-review these items.

Step Three—View the FTC's explanation of COPPA's requirements for teachers online at https://www.ftc.gov/tips-advice/business-center/guidance/complying-coppa-frequently-asked-questions#Schools.

Step Four— Answer the following:

1. Is a parent email to a teacher about their child's grades an education record under FERPA? Why or why not?
2. Would a teacher emailing the school district's special education director about behavioral problems she is having with a student violate FERPA? Why or why not? What if the teacher sends the email from her personal computer at home?
3. A sixth grade social studies teacher allows her class to view an interactive audio/video podcast about Ancient Civilizations. There are 20 students in the class and ten computers. The students pair up to view the podcast during class time. The podcast is an interactive session;

students log in and post questions and comments during the podcast, some of which are answered by the podcast speakers, or by other students viewing the podcast in other schools. Any potential FERPA issues? Any potential issues under COPPA, CIPA or N-CIPA?

4. A school district takes pictures of its students at school performing various tasks (working in the science lab, playing soccer, etc.), and posts them on its school website. Does it violate FERPA if they do not receive consent from the parents to use the pictures?
5. How, if at all, does the local Internet school policy you reviewed in Activity 5 in Chapter 6 address FERPA? If you were advising the school, would you recommend any changes to the policy regarding FERPA?
6. How, if at all, does the local Internet school policy you used in Activity 5 in Chapter 6 address the safety and security of minors when using electronic mail, chat rooms, and other forms of direct electronic communications? Hacking? The "unauthorized disclosure, use, and dissemination of personal information regarding minors"? If you were advising the school, would you recommend any changes to the policy regarding these issues?
7. How, if at all, does the policy you used in Activity 5 in Chapter 6 address COPPA and the role of teachers in consenting to the disclosure of student information? If you were advising the school district, would you recommend any changes regarding COPPA's requirements?

§ 7.05 Open Meeting Requirements

While the privacy provisions discussed in prior sections speak to the protection of individual information in the school setting, there are also laws and policies that demand that the public's business be conducted in public. Commonly called "government in the sunshine" or "right to know" provisions, these laws do not contradict individual privacy rights, but rather focus on how certain decisions are made. Within the public process of making decisions, certain information can and must remain private, but other information can and must be public. These laws typically require the school board to provide notice of meetings, to have the meetings in public locations so that members of the public can attend, and to keep minutes of the discussions held at meetings. State statutes often have exceptions that allow the board or agency to go into "non-public" or closed session to deliberate on certain topics and keep certain information protected from public review.

Right to know laws also generally require certain documents to be made available to the public upon request. The documents that are considered public are defined or determined by state law, and often include meeting minutes and documents created, obtained, or reviewed by the school board.

Given today's communication options, issues arise when members communicate outside of scheduled meetings by phone or email. Some state laws expressly address electronic communications.[2] When the issue is not addressed, cases often turn on the definition of "meeting," which generally requires some set number of members to be involved in a discussion about "official acts" or topics relevant to their roles on the school board, or on definitions of "public documents." The following problem addresses some of these topics.

Problem 4: E-Mail and Right to Know Laws

A school district that your law firm represents had a school board meeting last week. At the meeting, all five members of the school board went into "non-public session" and voted to terminate the high school principal's contract, and to find a new principal for the upcoming school year. The reason for termination discussed at the meeting was complaints by parents to the superintendent about inappropriate remarks the principal (a male) made to female students.

The superintendent sent emails to the board members before the meeting about the complaints, and the board members sent emails to the superintendent and to each other about going into nonpublic session at the meeting to discuss terminating the principal. All five school board members participated in some of the email exchanges; other email exchanges were between just the chair and vice-chair of the school board and the superintendent. The school board chair also kept notes of her email discussions that she brought with her to the meeting and reviewed during the non-public session.

The school board provided general notice of the meeting as required by state law, but did not include anything specifically about the principal or his employment status in the notice. It also did not provide the principal with any specific or direct notice about the meeting.

The principal was outraged when he found out about the decision, proclaiming that he was not notified about the meeting, or about the allegations against him. He has asked for copies of the emails and any notes made at the meeting, including the non-public session. He also wants the board to schedule a new meeting where he can attend and address any allegations of impropriety.

Your supervising partner wants you to research the State's Right to Know Law (referred to as § 921-A in the problem materials). Since the courts in your hypothetical state have not interpreted the law's requirements on these issues, your partner wants you to answer some questions based on the language of the statute and the problem cases that offer persuasive authority. While there may be other issues

---

2. *See* John F. O'Conor & Michael J. Baratz, *Some Assembly Required: The Application of State Open Meeting Laws to Email Correspondence*, 12 Geo. Mason L. Rev. 719 (2004); Leanne Holcomb & James Isaac, comment: *Wisconsin's Public-Records Law: Preserving the Presumption of Complete Public Access in the Age of Electronic Records*, 2008 Wis. L. Rev. 515 (2008).

present from the fact pattern, your supervising partner only wants responses to the following:

1. Does the school board have to produce the emails and notes under § 921-A?
2. Was the school supposed to provide notice under § 921-A that the principal's employment would be discussed at the meeting? Was personal notice required?
3. Does the school have to provide the principal with the new meeting that he is asking for under § 921-A?

Problem Materials

✓ Hypothetical State Right to Know Law, § 921

✓ *Lambert v. McPherson*, 90 So. 3d 30 (Ala. Civ. App. Mar. 30, 2012)

Hypothetical State Right to Know Law[3]

§ 921-A:1 Meetings Open to Public

I. For the purpose of this section, a "meeting" shall mean the convening of a quorum of the membership of a public body, to discuss or act upon a matter or matters over which the public body has supervision, control, jurisdiction or advisory power. A quorum means a majority of the public body. "Meeting" shall not include:

(a) Any chance meeting or a social meeting neither planned nor intended for the purpose of discussing matters relating to official business and at which no decisions are made; however, no such chance or social meeting shall be used to circumvent the spirit of this chapter;

(b) Strategy or negotiations with respect to collective bargaining;

(c) Consultation with legal counsel; or

(d) A caucus consisting of elected members of a public body of the same political party who were elected on a partisan basis at a state general election or elected on a partisan basis by a town or city which has adopted a partisan ballot system.

II. All public proceedings shall be open to the public, and all persons shall be permitted to attend any meetings of those bodies or agencies. Except for town meetings, school district meetings and elections, no vote while in open session may be taken by secret ballot. Any person shall be permitted to use recording devices, including, but not limited to, tape recorders, cameras and videotape equipment, at such meetings. Minutes of all such meetings, including names of members, persons appearing before the bodies or agencies, and a brief description of the subject matter discussed and final

3. Based on New Hampshire's Right to Know law, N.H. Rev. Stat. Ann. § 91-A.

decisions, shall be promptly recorded and open to public inspection within 144 hours of the public meeting, and shall be treated as permanent records of any body or agency, or any subordinate body thereof, without exception. Except in an emergency or when there is a meeting of a legislative committee, a notice of the time and place of each such meeting, including a nonpublic session, shall be posted in 2 appropriate places or shall be printed in a newspaper of general circulation in the city or town at least 24 hours, excluding Sundays and legal holidays, prior to such meetings. An emergency shall mean a situation where immediate undelayed action is deemed to be imperative by the chairman or presiding officer of the body or agency who shall employ whatever means are available to inform the public that a meeting is to be held. The minutes of the meeting shall clearly spell out the need for the emergency meeting.

. . . .

§ 921-A:3. Nonpublic Sessions

I. (a) Bodies or agencies shall not meet in nonpublic session, except for one of the purposes set out in paragraph II. No session at which evidence, information or testimony in any form is received shall be closed to the public, except as provided in paragraph II. No body or agency may enter nonpublic session, except pursuant to a motion properly made and seconded.

(b) Any motion to enter nonpublic session shall state on its face the specific exemption under paragraph II which is relied upon as foundation for the nonpublic session. The vote on any such motion shall be by roll call, and shall require the affirmative vote of the majority of members present.

(c) All discussions held and decisions made during nonpublic session shall be confined to the matters set out in the motion.

II. Only the following matters shall be considered or acted upon in nonpublic session:

(a) The dismissal, promotion or compensation of any public employee or the disciplining of such employee, or the investigation of any charges against him, unless the employee affected (1) has a right to a meeting and (2) requests that the meeting be open, in which case the request shall be granted.

(b) The hiring of any person as a public employee.

(c) Matters which, if discussed in public, would likely affect adversely the reputation of any person, other than a member of the body or agency itself, unless such person requests an open meeting. This exemption shall extend to any application for assistance or tax abatement or waiver of a fee, fine, or other levy, if based on inability to pay or poverty of the applicant.

. . . .

III. Minutes of proceedings in nonpublic session shall be kept and the record of all actions shall be promptly made available for public inspection, except as provided in this section. Minutes and decisions reached in nonpublic session shall be publicly disclosed within 72 hours of the meeting, unless, by recorded vote of 2/3 of the members present, it is determined that divulgence of the information likely would affect adversely the reputation of any person other than a member of the body or agency itself, or render the proposed action ineffective, or pertain to terrorism, more specifically, to matters relating to the preparation for and the carrying out of all emergency functions, developed by local or state safety officials that are directly intended to thwart a deliberate act that is intended to result in widespread or severe damage to property or widespread injury or loss of life. This shall include training to carry out such functions. In the event of such circumstances, information may be withheld until, in the opinion of a majority of members, the aforesaid circumstances no longer apply.

§921-A:4 Minutes and Records Available for Public Inspection.

I. Every citizen during the regular or business hours of all such bodies or agencies, and on the regular business premises of such bodies or agencies, has the right to inspect all public records, including minutes of meetings of the bodies or agencies, and to make memoranda, abstracts, and photographic or photostatic copies of the records or minutes so inspected, except as otherwise prohibited by statute.

II. After the completion of a meeting of such bodies or agencies, every citizen, during the regular or business hours of all such bodies or agencies, and on the regular business premises of such bodies or agencies, has the right to inspect all notes, materials, tapes or other sources used for compiling the minutes of such meetings, and to make memoranda, abstracts, photographic or photostatic copies, or tape record such notes, materials, tapes or sources inspected, except as otherwise prohibited by statute.

III. Each body or agency shall keep and maintain all public records in its custody at its regular office or place of business in an accessible place and, if there is no such office or place of business, the public records pertaining to such body or agency shall be kept in an office of the political subdivision in which such body or agency is located or, in the case of a state agency, in an office designated by the secretary of state.

IV. Each public body or agency shall, upon request for any public record reasonably described, make available for inspection and copying any such public record within its files when such records are immediately available for such release. If a public body or agency is unable to make a public record available for immediate inspection and copying, it shall, within 5 business days of request, make such record available, deny the request in writing with reasons, or furnish written acknowledgment of the receipt of the request and a statement of the time reasonably necessary to determine whether the request shall be granted or denied.

V. In the same manner as set forth in §921-A:4, IV, any body or agency which maintains its records in a computer storage system may, in lieu of providing original documents, provide a printout of any record reasonably described and which the agency has the capacity to produce in a manner that does not reveal information which is confidential under this chapter or any other law. Access to work papers, personnel data and other confidential information shall not be provided.

§921-A:5 Exemptions.

The following records are exempted from the provisions of this chapter:

. . . .

IV. Records pertaining to internal personnel practices; confidential, commercial, or financial information; test questions, scoring keys, and other examination data used to administer a licensing examination, examination for employment, or academic examinations; and personnel, medical, welfare, library user, videotape sale or rental, and other files whose disclosure would constitute invasion of privacy. Without otherwise compromising the confidentiality of the files, nothing in this paragraph shall prohibit a body or agency from releasing information relative to health or safety from investigative files on a limited basis to persons whose health or safety may be affected.

. . . .

VIII. Any notes or other materials made for personal use that do not have an official purpose, including notes and materials made prior to, during, or after a public proceeding.

IX. Preliminary drafts, notes, and memoranda and other documents not in their final form and not disclosed, circulated, or available to a quorum or a majority of those entities defined in RSA 91-A:1-a.

§921-A:7 Violation.

Any person aggrieved by a violation of this chapter may petition the superior court for injunctive relief. The courts shall give proceedings under this chapter priority on the court calendar. Such a petitioner may appear with or without counsel. The petition shall be deemed sufficient if it states facts constituting a violation of this chapter, and may be filed by the petitioner or his counsel with the clerk of court or any justice thereof. Thereupon the clerk of court or any justice shall order service by copy of the petition on the person or persons charged. When any justice shall find that time probably is of the essence, he may order notice by any reasonable means, and he shall have authority to issue an order ex parte when he shall reasonably deem such an order necessary to insure compliance with the provisions of this chapter.

§921-A:8 Remedies.

I. If any body or agency or employee or member thereof, in violation of the provisions of this chapter, refuses to provide a public record or refuses access to a public proceeding to a person who reasonably requests the same, such body, agency, or person shall be liable for reasonable attorney's fees and costs incurred in a lawsuit under this chapter provided that the court finds that such lawsuit was necessary in order to make the information available or the proceeding open to the public. Fees shall not be awarded unless the court finds that the body, agency or person knew or should have known that the conduct engaged in was a violation of this chapter or where the parties, by agreement, provide that no such fees shall be paid. In any case where fees are awarded under this chapter, upon a finding that an officer, employee, or other official of a public body or agency has acted in bad faith in refusing to allow access to a public proceeding or to provide a public record, the court may award such fees personally against such officer, employee, or other official.

I-a. The court may award attorneys' fees to a board, agency or employee or member thereof, for having to defend against a person's lawsuit under the provisions of this chapter, when the court makes an affirmative finding that the lawsuit is in bad faith, frivolous, unjust, vexatious, wanton, or oppressive.

II. The court may invalidate an action of a public body or agency taken at a meeting held in violation of the provisions of this chapter, if the circumstances justify such invalidation.

III. In addition to any other relief awarded pursuant to this chapter, the court may issue an order to enjoin future violations of this chapter.

Lambert v. McPherson

90 So. 3d 30 (Ala. Civ. App. 2012)

The court rules that a single email is not a public meeting.

Pittman, Judge.

Charles Gregory Lambert appeals from a judgment of the Limestone Circuit Court dismissing his complaint to enforce the Alabama Open Meetings Act, §36-25A-1 et seq., Ala. Code 1975 ("the Act"). The complaint named as defendants David McPherson, Russell Johnson, Larry Keenum, Beverly Malone, and James Lucas—five of the seven members of the Athens City Board of Education ("the Board"). We affirm.

Facts and Procedural History

After amendment, Lambert's complaint alleged that the defendants had participated in school-board meetings via e-mail, "where decisions were made prior to voting in open meetings"; that such meetings had been held without the required public notice; that the defendants had engaged in improper deliberation about litigation strategy in executive session; and that the defendants had circumvented the Act by conferring with the attorney for the Board via cellular telephone and e-mail. The defendants denied the allegations and asserted various affirmative defenses.

The trial court held a preliminary hearing on the complaint . . . As the only evidence in support of his complaint, Lambert submitted an e-mail message that, the parties stipulated, had been sent on May 21, 2010, by school-board member Larry Keenum to all other board members. The e-mail message is not contained in the record on appeal, but the parties agree that the message expressed Keenum's disagreement with a proposed change to a Board policy concerning renewal of contracts for coaches or other employees of the Board who had supplemental contracts—a matter that had been expected to come before the Board for a decision and that was, in fact, addressed at a meeting of the Board on July 15, 2010.

Section 36-25A-1(a), Ala. Code 1975, provides:

> "It is the policy of this state that the deliberative process of governmental bodies shall be open to the public during meetings as defined in Section 36-25A-2(6). Except for executive sessions permitted in Section 36-25A-7(a) or as otherwise expressly [3] provided by other federal or state statutes, all meetings of a governmental body shall be open to the public and no meetings of a governmental body may be held without providing notice pursuant to the requirements of Section 36-25A-3. No executive sessions are required by this chapter to be held under any circumstances. Electronic communications shall not be utilized to circumvent any of the provisions of this chapter." (Emphasis added.)

Lambert argued that Keenum's e-mail message itself constituted a "meeting" under the Act because, he said, when Keenum "sends out a message to all the board members and he details in it his position on something they're going to vote on, his position about other meetings, and other things that have taken place and how he feels about board policy that's coming up, that constitutes a meeting." In response, the defendants argued that Keenum's e-mail message was not a "meeting," as defined in § 36-25A-2(6)a.3., because it did not involve "deliberation," as defined in § 36-25A-2(1). Section 36-25A-2(6)a.3. defines "meeting," in pertinent part, as

> "[t]he gathering, whether or not it was prearranged, of a quorum of a governmental body or a quorum of a committee or a subcommittee of a governmental body during which the members of the governmental body deliberate specific matters that, at the time of the exchange, the participating members expect to come before the body, committee, or subcommittee at a later date."

Section 36-25A-2(1) defines "deliberation" as

> "[a]n exchange of information or ideas among a quorum of members of a governmental body intended to arrive at or influence a decision as to how the members of the governmental body should vote on a specific matter

> that, at the time of the exchange, the participating members expect to come before the body immediately following the discussion or at a later time."

After hearing arguments, the trial court stated that it was inclined to believe that a single board member cannot "taint the whole board and violate the Open Meetings [Act by] firing away a letter or an email. To me, it is not an exchange of information. It is one-sided That's not a meeting." . . .

Standard of Review

Section 36-25A-9(b), Ala. Code 1975, states the burden of proof that a plaintiff is required to meet at a preliminary hearing conducted pursuant to the Act. The plaintiff must

> "establish by a preponderance of the evidence that a meeting of [a] governmental body occurred and that each defendant attended the meeting." Subsection (b) further requires that "to establish a prima facie case the plaintiff must present substantial evidence of one or more of the following claims:
>
> "(1) That the defendants disregarded the requirements for proper notice of the meeting pursuant to the applicable methods set forth in Section 36-25A-3.
>
> "(2) That the defendants disregarded the provisions of this chapter during a meeting, other than during an executive session.
>
> "(3) That the defendants voted to go into executive session and while in executive session the defendants discussed matters other than those subjects included in the motion to convene an executive session as required by Section 36-25A-7(b).
>
> "(4) That, other than a claim under subdivisions (1) through (3), the defendants intentionally violated other provisions of this chapter."

Section § 36-25A-9(c) provides, in pertinent part, that,

> "[i]f the court finds that the plaintiff has met its initial burden of proof as required in subsection (b) at the preliminary hearing, the court shall establish a schedule for discovery and set the matter for a hearing on the merits."

An appellate court reviews de novo a trial court's determination as to whether a plaintiff presented substantial evidence of one or more claims under the Act at the preliminary hearing.

Discussion

I.

A single e-mail sent by one board member to the other board members, without more, does not constitute a "meeting" as defined in § 36-25A-2(6)a.3. That definition includes three elements: (1) a meeting must involve "a quorum of a governmental body or a quorum of a committee or a subcommittee of a governmental body," (2) "during the which the members of the governmental body deliberate" (3) about "specific matters that, at the time of the exchange, the participating members expect to come before the body, committee, or subcommittee at a later date." Keenum's e-mail message satisfies the first and third elements, but not the second element. The "deliberation" component of a "meeting" is missing because Keenum's e-mail message was a unilateral declaration of his ideas or opinions, not "[a]n exchange of information or ideas among" a quorum of board members concerning a specific matter that the members expected to be presented to the board for a decision. § 36-25A-2(1) and -2(6)a.3.

In *Wood v. Battle Ground School District*, 107 Wash. App. 550, 27 P.3d 1208 (2001), four members of a five-member school board met at the home of one of the members to discuss the new superintendent and his administrative assistant, Jennifer Wood, both of whom were, according to one of the board members, "overpaid, underperforming, and otherwise unqualified." The four board members later exchanged e-mail correspondence as a follow-up to their discussion. The board eventually terminated Wood's employment. Wood sued the board and the four board members, alleging claims of defamation and a violation of Washington's Open Public Meetings Act ("OPMA"). The trial court dismissed the defamation claim and entered a summary judgment in favor of Wood on the OPMA claim.

The Washington Court of Appeals stated that, to enforce the provisions of the OPMA, a plaintiff must show "(1) that a 'member' of a governing body (2) attended a 'meeting' of that body (3) where 'action' was taken in violation of the OPMA, and (4) that the member had 'knowledge' that the meeting violated the OPMA." The OPMA defines "action" as "'the transaction of the official business of a public agency by a governing body including but not limited to receipt of public testimony, deliberations, discussions, considerations, reviews, evaluations, and final actions.'" The court concluded that "the exchange of e-mails can constitute a 'meeting'" but that "the mere use or passive receipt of e-mail does not automatically constitute a 'meeting.'" The court explained that the facts of the case demonstrated more than the board members' passive receipt of information by e-mail:

"Wood has established a prima facie case of 'meeting' by e-mails. The ... e-mail discussions involved a quorum of the five-member Board. For instance, on November 30, [board president] Sharp sent an e-mail to all Board members and another e-mail to three of the members; on December 1, Sharp again e-mailed all the Board members, attaching a response he had received from [board member] Striker about a matter they had discussed; next, on December 3, [board member] Kim e-mailed Sharp and copied three other Board members in response to Sharp's earlier e-mail; and on December 5, Sharp again e-mailed all Board members." With respect to the "deliberation" component of a "meeting," the Washington Court of Appeals held that "the active exchange of information and opinions in these e-mails, as opposed to the mere passive receipt of information, suggests a collective intent to deliberate and/or to discuss Board business." Having determined that Wood had met the threshold requirement of establishing a "meeting" under the OPMA, the court nevertheless reversed the summary judgment in favor of Wood, holding that there were genuine issues of material fact as to whether the board members had exchanged e-mail messages with knowledge that such exchanges violated the OPMA. *See also Roberts v. City of Palmdale*, 5 Cal. 4th 363, 376, 20 Cal. Rptr. 2d 330, 337, 853 P.2d 496, 503 (1993) (construing the "Brown Act," California's open-meetings law, and holding that a meeting implies "collective action . . . not . . . the passive receipt by individuals of their mail"); *Johnston v. Metropolitan Gov't of Nashville*, 320 S.W.3d 299, 312 (Tenn. Ct. App. 2009) (stating that e-mail exchanges between metropolitan council members, in which "members are clearly weighing arguments for and against [a proposed zoning measure] . . . . [and which were] copied to all Council members, mirror the type of debate and reciprocal attempts at persuasion that would be expected to take place at a Council meeting, in the presence of the public and the Council as a whole," and concluding that the e-mails were "'electronic communication . . . used to . . . deliberate public business in circumvention of the spirit or requirements' of the Open Meetings Act. [Tenn. Code Ann.] § 8-44-102(c) (2002)"). See generally John F. O'Connor & Michael J. Baratz, *Some Assembly Required: The Application of State Open Meeting Laws to Email Correspondence*, 12 Geo. Mason L. Rev. 719 (2004).

. . . .

Conclusion

Keenum's e-mail message to the other board members was the only evidence Lambert presented at the preliminary hearing. That communication was a unilateral expression of Keenum's ideas or opinions concerning a specific matter that the members expected to be presented to the Board for a decision—not "[a]n exchange of information or ideas among" a quorum of board members, § 36-25A-2(1), and not, therefore, a "meeting" as contemplated by § 36-25A-2(6)a.3. Accordingly, Lambert failed to meet his initial burden of proof at the preliminary hearing. In addition, the trial court did not act outside the limits of its discretion in disallowing Lambert's untimely amendment to the complaint.

The judgment of the Limestone Circuit Court is affirmed.

Post Problem Discussion

1. Unlike the sample statute in the problem materials, some states have now adopted specific statutory provisions that address e-mail and other electronic communications, and whether they are public documents, or constitute a public meeting under the law. For example, Colorado provides:

> (1)(b) "Meeting" means any kind of gathering, convened to discuss public business, in person, by telephone, electronically, or by other means of communication.
>
> . . . .
>
> (2)(a) All meetings of two or more members of any state public body at which any public business is discussed or at which any formal action may be taken are declared to be public meetings open to the public at all times.

> (b) All meetings of a quorum or three or more members of any local public body, whichever is fewer, at which any public business is discussed or at which any formal action may be taken are declared to be public meetings open to the public at all times.
>
> (d) (III) If elected officials use electronic mail to discuss pending legislation or other public business among themselves, the electronic mail shall be subject to the requirements of this section. Electronic mail communication among elected officials that does not relate to pending legislation or other public business shall not be considered a "meeting" within the meaning of this section.

Colo. Rev. Stat. §§ 24-6-402 (2019).

Others have general definitions of public records that include electronic communications. For example, Virginia provides:

> "Electronic communication" means the use of technology having electrical, digital, magnetic, wireless, optical, electromagnetic, or similar capabilities to transmit or receive information.
>
> ....
>
> "Meeting" or "meetings" means the meetings including work sessions, when sitting physically, or through electronic communication means pursuant to § 2.2-3708.2, as a body or entity, or as an informal assemblage of (i) as many as three members or (ii) a quorum, if less than three, of the constituent membership, wherever held, with or without minutes being taken, whether or not votes are cast, of any public body. Neither the gathering of employees of a public body nor the gathering or attendance of two or more members of a public body (a) at any place or function where no part of the purpose of such gathering or attendance is the discussion or transaction of any public business, and such gathering or attendance was not called or prearranged with any purpose of discussing or transacting any business of the public body, or (b) at a public forum, candidate appearance, or debate, the purpose of which is to inform the electorate and not to transact public business or to hold discussions relating to the transaction of public business, even though the performance of the members individually or collectively in the conduct of public business may be a topic of discussion or debate at such public meeting, shall be deemed a "meeting" subject to the provisions of this chapter.
>
> "Public records" means all writings and recordings that consist of letters, words or numbers, or their equivalent, set down by handwriting, typewriting, printing, photostatting, photography, magnetic impulse, optical or magneto-optical form, mechanical or electronic recording or other form of data compilation, however stored, and regardless of physical form or characteristics, prepared or owned by, or in the possession of a public body or its officers, employees or agents in the transaction of public business.

> Records that are not prepared for or used in the transaction of public business are not public records.

Va. Code Ann. § 2.2-3701 (2019).

What do you think about how these statutes address the issue? Would your answers to the questions in the problem change if these statutes were used instead of the sample statute in the problem?

2. The *Lampert* case cites to *Wood v. Battle Ground School District*, 27 P.3d 1208 (Wash. Ct. App. 2001), for the parameters of a prima facie case of "meeting by e-mails." In *Wood*, the court noted that the e-mail discussions involved a quorum of the Board and "the active exchange of information and opinions in these e-mails, as opposed to the mere passive receipt of information," and said that this exchange "suggests a collective intent to deliberate and/or to discuss Board business." How does this apply to the superintendent and board in the problem school district?

3. Note the potential remedies for violations in § 921-A:8 of the problem statute. Should monetary relief be available as a remedy as well? What are the pros and cons of affording such relief for violations of right to know requirements?

4. What other issues beyond those that the supervising partner asked you to address do you see arising from the fact pattern? How should they be addressed and resolved?

Chapter 8

Student Discipline

Synopsis

§ 8.01 Introduction

School discipline represents an effort to ensure compliance with some rule, standard, or principle of behavior, what some might describe as the social fabric of the school. The source for these standards varies from class agreement, to conduct codes, to rules, ordinances, or statutes. When school discipline is called into question, courts review the source of the standards, caselaw, and constitutional requirements. Constitutional limitations are often of primary importance in these cases, particularly the requirements of due process, both substantive and procedural. Some believe that the courts' increasing involvement in establishing constitutional rights of students *being* disciplined has been detrimental to school climate; others hold the opposite view. In either case, the role of courts in determining the parameters of discipline is well-established. Courts do generally give strong deference to decisions by school officials in discipline cases.

§ 8.02 The Standards for Discipline and the Role of Courts

When addressing school discipline cases, courts must often deal with the convergence of competing interests. On the one hand, schools have a responsibility to provide a safe educational environment for students, and to provide students with appropriate educational services. As noted, courts generally want to defer to school administrators when they punish student activity that interferes with these obligations. On the other hand, students have constitutional, statutory, and regulatory rights in the disciplinary process that courts must honor when reviewing these disciplinary decisions.

In addressing these issues, some courts focus on school officials' inherent authority to discipline students in order to maintain a safe educational environment. Others focus on whether state statutes or school policies prohibit the actions at issue on the theory that students must be provided with notice of the conduct that is subject to discipline. Either way, as the problem materials note, courts generally apply a deferential standard of review and look to see if the discipline was unreasonable, or arbitrary and capricious, given the circumstances.

Problem 1: Defining Conduct Subject to Discipline

James and his friend Terrell are ninth grade students at the New Town High School. They are bored at school and decide to go "Roboating" before their classes to make things more interesting. Roboating is mixing the cold medicine Robitussin with energy drinks that contain high levels of sugar and caffeine, and then drinking large quantities of the mixture at once. James brings the Robitussin to school in his backpack. Terrell brings the energy drinks. They meet in the bathroom before classes start to mix things together and drink. Other students in the bathroom see them and ask to join in. James and Terrell agree to sell five other students multiple "shots" of "Roboat." The students then go their separate ways to class. One of the students gets sick at school from the Roboat. He tells the school nurse what he did, and that James and Terrell supplied the Roboat.

James and Terrell meet with the school principal and admit to what they did. They are suspended from school for ten days under sections 6, 7, and 9 of the school's discipline policy. James and Terrell's parents agree that their sons' conduct is not appropriate, and should be punished, but they feel that a ten day out of school suspension is too severe, and will drastically affect their grades. They contend that the school's policies are unclear and vague about whether this kind of conduct is subject to long term suspension. They believe that the actions are more of a "minor problem" under the discipline policy. They ask you if they have a viable court challenge to the discipline decision, and if they can obtain monetary damages for the harm the suspension has caused James and Terrell and their families.

Problem Materials

✓ New Town High School Discipline Policy

✓ *Hasson v. Boothby*, 318 F. Supp. 1183 (D. Mass. 1970)

✓ *Woodis v. Westark*, 160 F.3d 435 (8th Cir. 1998)

✓ *Wood v. Strickland*, 420 U.S. 308 (1975)

New Town High School Discipline Policy[1]

In order for people to learn, live, and work together in a productive, safe, and student-friendly environment, appropriate behavior is necessary. New Town High School has established realistic and reasonable guidelines for all students to follow, so learning can take place without disruption.

Schools are established for the benefit of all students. The educational purposes of schools are accomplished best in a climate of student behavior that is socially acceptable, and conducive to the learning and teaching process. Student behavior which disrupts this process, or which infringes upon the rights of other individuals, will not be tolerated.

The classroom teacher through discussions with the student handles minor problems. Repeated disruptive incidents will be referred to the principal. When a student is referred to the principal, the course of action will be taken:

1st Visit—discussion with student about problem.

2nd Visit—call to parents.

3rd Visit—in school suspension.

4th Visit—out of school suspension.

Major problems are subject to more severe penalties including out of school suspension or expulsion. The following is a brief summary of reasons for suspension established by the Board of Education:

1. Steals or attempts to steal school or private property.
2. Causes, attempts to cause, or threatens damage or harm to school, school property, or another person.
3. Threatens the use of any real, look alike, or pretend weapon, incendiary device or dangerous object.
4. Possesses, uses, sells or otherwise furnishes or is under the influence of any controlled substance.
5. Possesses or uses tobacco.
6. Commits an obscene act or engages in habitual profanity or vulgarity.
7. Frequent or flagrant willful disobedience, defiance of proper authority or disruptive behavior.
8. Truancy from school.
9. Conduct or activities that given the circumstances deserve swift and severe ramifications.

---

1. This language is fairly common in discipline policies, the version here taken in major part from, e.g., Mount Mahogany Discipline Policy, http://mahogany.alpinedistrict.org/General/discipline.html.

Hasson v. Boothby

318 F. Supp. 1183 (D. Mass. 1970)

The court discusses different approaches to discipline standards, and rules that a school may discipline students for attending a school event with alcohol on their breath, even though the school handbook does not expressly mention alcohol, or prohibit alcohol use.

Introductory note:

The school handbook at issue contained the following relevant language:

> Conduct on the part of any student, either during school hours or at any time outside of school, that brings discredit upon the good name of this school, its faculty and student body, will be considered grounds for disciplinary action as the School Committee may wish to take.
>
> The school placed the students on probation which means the students were forbidden from:
>
> (a) Driving a car to school and parking on the school grounds. (b) Having their car driven to school and parked on the school grounds. (c) Attending dances, plays, musicals, athletic events or any other activities sponsored by the school. (d) Being on the school grounds after school for any reason except authorized makeup work or detention. . . .

Garrity, District Judge.

This action is brought under the Civil Rights Act of 1871, 42 U.S.C. § 1983. The plaintiffs, Patrick M. Hasson, Joseph M. Hickey, Jr. and Robert F. Wheaton, Jr., are junior students at Whitman-Hanson Regional High School (hereinafter the School) in Whitman, Massachusetts.

1. On Friday, April 17, 1970, the first night of a school vacation, the plaintiffs and two other students drank some beer off school premises. The five students then proceeded to the school at around 9:00 P.M., where a dance sponsored by the school was in progress. Upon entering the gymnasium, where the dance was being held, Hasson, Hickey and another student (not a party to this suit) met Ralph Goslin, a teacher and coach of the track team. Apparently Mr. Goslin detected the odor of beer; and both Hasson and Hickey admitted to him that they had consumed some beer. Goslin did not exclude the plaintiffs from the dance. There was no disturbance of any kind involving any of the plaintiffs or their companions at the dance. The plaintiffs were not drunk.

2. On Saturday, April 18, 1970, plaintiff Hasson reported to Goslin, his coach, for track practice. The coach told him he was off the team for the rest of the season. Plaintiff Hickey reported for varsity baseball games during the vacation week. The baseball coach informed him that he would not be allowed to play in two games scheduled for vacation week. Later, plaintiff Wheaton reported to John J. Hrinko, Dr. Boothby's administrative assistant, that he too had drunk some beer with the

others. Wheaton was later informed by the junior varsity baseball coach that he would be excluded from participation for the rest of the season.

3. Upon learning of this incident from the school's athletic director Robert S. Teahan, defendant Boothby directed Hrinko to place all three plaintiffs on probation. During the week of April 27, 1970, Hrinko met individually with each of the plaintiffs (and with the two other students involved) and placed each of them on probation. He sent a letter dated April 29, 1970 to the parents of each plaintiff advising them of this action and the duration of the penalty, one year subject to review. In his letter of April 29, 1970 and in his conversations with the plaintiffs and their parents, Hrinko claimed that a violation of Mass.G.L. c. 272, §40A, which forbids, among other things, the possession of alcoholic beverages on school property, was the basis for the punishment meted out by the administration.

4. Following this action, the parents of the plaintiffs met with the school committee twice, on May 13, 1970 and on August 26, 1970. After these meetings, during which the incident and penalties were discussed, the defendant school committee members refused to terminate probation....

5. In April 1970 the Student Handbook contained certain specific prohibitions and associated penalties. Among the major offenses were "use of profane language towards a teacher", "vandalism" and "smoking". However, involvement with alcohol was not embraced within the specific prohibitions of the handbook, nor was drinking mentioned anywhere else in the handbook.

The plaintiffs do not claim that the conduct for which they were punished, being on school premises with beer on their breaths, is constitutionally protected.... This is not a case where the procedural fairness of the hearing itself is attacked. The plaintiffs admit that the hearings afforded them by the School Committee on May 13 and August 26 were not constitutionally defective. Rather the basic contention of the plaintiffs is that lack of a published rule concerning the use of alcohol rendered punishment as severe as one year's probation violative of the due process clause. The desirability of written rules regulating serious disciplinary offenses and penalties in an academic setting is generally recognized today by both academic and legal commentators....

This growing recognition of the desirability and possible constitutional necessity of prior promulgated rules for the imposition of major penalties by a school administration has been reflected in several recent cases, *e.g.*, *Soglin v. Kauffman*, W.D.Wis., 1968, 295 F. Supp. 978, *aff'd* 7 Cir., 1969, 418 F.2d 163, where the University of Wisconsin relied on a broad misconduct rule to suspend and expel certain students charged with obstructing a Dow Chemical recruitment effort and the court held,

> "Pursuant to appropriate rule or regulation, the University has the power to maintain order by suspension or expulsion of disruptive students. Requiring that such sanctions be administered in accord with preexisting rules does not place an unwarranted burden upon university administrations. We do not require university codes of conduct to satisfy the same rigorous

> standards as criminal statutes. We only hold that expulsion and prolonged suspension may not be imposed on students by a university simply on the basis of allegations of 'misconduct' without reference to any preexisting rule which supplies an adequate guide. The possibility of the sweeping application of the standard of 'misconduct' to protected activities does not comport with the guarantees of the First and Fourteenth Amendments. The desired end must be more narrowly achieved." 418 F.2d at 168.

However, the opposite position, i.e., that students may be severely punished by a school administration under its inherent authority without a prior published rule specifically prohibiting the conduct in question, still retains great vitality. . . . And the Court of Appeals for the First Circuit has indicated in dictum that it is generally inclined to favor this view.

In our opinion neither of the competing doctrines is alone sufficient to solve all the problems raised by the imposition of punishment on a student without a prior promulgated rule. We accept the proposition that a school administration, . . . may punish a student offender without a prior rule specifically forbidding the offending conduct; however, surely such authority cannot be limitless. Moreover, this court believes that the imposition of a severe penalty without a specific promulgated rule might be constitutionally deficient under certain circumstances. What those circumstances are can only be left to the development of the case law in the area. However, at this time the court deems relevant the following factors: (1) prior knowledge of the offending student of the wrongfulness of his conduct and clarity of the public policy involved, (2) potential for a chilling effect on First Amendment rights inherent in the situation, (3) severity of the penalty imposed. Having analyzed the facts of this case in terms of these factors, the court holds that the plaintiffs' rights under the due process clause were not violated by the imposition of a one-year probation, subject to review, for the offense of being on school premises with beer on their breaths, even though no prior published rule forbade such conduct.

First, plaintiffs were aware that involvement with alcohol on or off school premises was wrong and would be punished by school authorities. Each of the plaintiffs was a member of several athletic teams and knew that drinking was forbidden and would be penalized by the athletic department of the school. The notice or warning function of a prior rule was therefore served by the express custom of the athletic department. In addition, plaintiffs are presumed to know the strong public policy against alcohol use by minors as expressed in the pamphlets used in the health course and in the Massachusetts General Laws.

Second, this is not a case where punishment under an overbroad regulation would have the effect of jeopardizing First Amendment rights.

. . . .

There is simply no relationship between the conduct punished here, being present on school premises with beer on one's breath, and First Amendment freedoms deemed so important to the educational process by the Supreme Court in *Tinker v.*

Des Moines Independent Community School Dist., 1969, 393 U.S. 503, 89 S. Ct. 733, 21 L. Ed. 2d 731.

Third, the nature of the penalty imposed is not so severe as to entitle the plaintiffs to full due process protections. The requirements of due process are flexible, and different situations will require different degrees of procedural protection.

. . . .

The court subscribes to the suggestion of one commentator that a distinction between major offenses to which severe penalties may attach and minor offenses, calling only for mild sanctions, is permissible and that major offenses are those with punishments of expulsion or suspension for any significant time. While there was testimony to the effect that extracurricular activities in general, and athletics in particular, can be an important if not integral part of the educational process, nevertheless the court believes that there is a difference between probation as defined above and suspension from school and that this difference has constitutional significance in the circumstances of this case.

Therefore it is ordered that judgment be entered dismissing the complaint.

Woodis v. Westark

160 F.3d 435 (8th Cir. 1998)

The Eighth Circuit upholds the dismissal of a nursing student for violating the school's code of conduct in an episode involving a fraudulent prescription.

Introductory note: The Policy used by the college in this case states:

> Westark College assumes that, by the act of registering, the student agrees to obey all rules and regulations formulated by the College as listed below and to obey all federal, state, and local laws.
>
> Students are expected to conduct themselves in an appropriate manner and conform to standards considered to be in good taste at all times. This implies a consideration for the welfare and reputation of the College and other students enrolled at the College. Students exhibiting behavior problems not compatible with good citizenship can expect to be reprimanded, have certain restrictions imposed, or be denied the privilege to continue as students.

Woodis, 160 F.3d at 438 n.1.

Bright, Circuit Judge

Appellant-plaintiff Rosia Woodis brings this 42 U.S.C. § 1983 action against Westark Community College. Westark expelled Woodis from its nursing college for violating the college's rules, the Standards of Conduct. Woodis asserts two distinct claims: that the Standards are unconstitutionally vague, and that Westark violated her procedural due process rights. The district court granted judgment as a matter of law in favor of Westark dismissing the entire case and Woodis appealed. We affirm.

Ms. Woodis enrolled as a nursing student at Westark to pursue her Licensed Practical Nurse degree ("LPN"). In her third semester in the program, the police arrested Woodis for attempting to obtain a controlled substance with a fraudulent prescription. On October 11, 1996, Dr. Sandi Sanders, then Vice President of Student Affairs, suspended Woodis pending the outcome of the police investigation. Sanders sent a letter to Woodis advising her of this decision and of her due process rights as set forth in the Westark Student Handbook. Woodis appealed the decision to a five-member disciplinary appeals committee, which upheld Woodis' suspension.

On February 24, 1997, Woodis pled nolo contendere to a misdemeanor offense in connection with her criminal conduct. Shortly thereafter, Sanders notified Woodis by letter that her suspension was permanent. With the help of legal counsel, Woodis appealed this decision to a second disciplinary appeals committee and to the President of Westark Joel Stubblefield. Both independently upheld the expulsion of Woodis....

Woodis subsequently filed suit.... Woodis brings her claim pursuant to 42 U.S.C. § 1983....

In examining Woodis' § 1983 claim, certain principles particular to the school setting guide our analysis. Although students do not "shed their constitutional rights ... at the school house gate," the Supreme Court has observed that "maintaining security and order in the schools requires a certain degree of flexibility in school disciplinary procedures." Given the flexibility afforded schools in this area, we must "enter the realm of school discipline with caution," and we must exercise "care and restraint" in reviewing Westark's discretionary decision to expel Woodis from the school's nursing program.

Turning to the specific arguments presented to this court on appeal, Woodis asserts that the Standards of Conduct are void-for-vagueness, as they do not provide adequate notice to Westark students of the proscribed conduct under the school's rules.

....

"The void-for-vagueness doctrine is embodied in the due process clauses of the fifth and fourteenth amendments." A vague regulation violates the Constitution in two significant respects. Such a regulation or enactment fails, (1) to define the offense with sufficient definiteness that ordinary people can understand prohibited conduct; and (2) to establish standards to permit police to enforce the law in a non-arbitrary, non-discriminatory manner. In a facial vagueness challenge, an enactment reaching a substantial amount of constitutionally protected conduct may withstand constitutional scrutiny only if it incorporates a high level of definiteness. An enactment imposing criminal sanctions or implicating constitutionally protected rights demands more definiteness than one which regulates the economic behavior of businesses, or the conduct of students in the school setting.

In examining a facial challenge, this court must first "determine whether the enactment reaches a substantial amount of constitutionally protected conduct."

Where the enactment does not reach constitutionally protected conduct, the overbreadth challenge must fail and the complainant may succeed in a vagueness challenge "only if the enactment is impermissibly vague in all of its applications." Pursuing this line of analysis, the Supreme Court cautioned courts to "examine the complainant's conduct before analyzing other hypothetical applications of the law" because "[a] plaintiff who engages in some conduct that is clearly proscribed cannot complain of the vagueness of the law as applied to . . . others." Therefore, "vagueness challenges that do not involve the First Amendment must be examined in light of the specific facts of the case at hand and not with regard to the statute's facial validity."

Applying these principles to this case, we conclude at the outset that the Standards do not threaten to inhibit the exercise of protected First Amendment rights.

. . . .

The relevant conduct under review here—fraudulent procurement of a controlled substance—constitutes criminal behavior, without First Amendment protection.

Woodis may only succeed in an "as applied" vagueness challenge by "demonstrat[ing] that the [enactment] is impermissibly vague in all of its applications." To withstand a facial challenge, an . . . enactment must define the proscribed behavior with sufficient particularity to provide a person of ordinary intelligence with reasonable notice of prohibited conduct and to encourage non-arbitrary enforcement of the provision. In an "as applied" analysis, we must determine whether the enactment here, the Standards, were sufficiently precise to notify Woodis that her criminal act constituted unacceptable conduct that could lead to expulsion. Woodis cannot maintain a vagueness claim if we determine that she engaged in conduct clearly proscribed by the Standards.

Woodis focuses her vagueness challenge on the phrases "good taste," "appropriate manner," and "good citizenship," the key terms in the Standards defining acceptable conduct under the Westark school rules. Woodis contends that these phrases do not provide the Westark students with notice of proscribed behavior. Nor do they limit the discretion of the Westark administrators in making disciplinary decisions, essentially allowing the school administration to engage in ad hoc, discriminatory enforcement of the school rules.

In response, Westark cites *Felton v. Fayette School Dist.*, 875 F.2d 191 (8th Cir. 1989), for the proposition that the phrase "good citizenship" is at least sufficiently precise to place a student on notice that criminal conduct will subject that student to disciplinary action. In *Felton*, the court rejected a vagueness challenge to a school rule conditioning enrollment in an auto mechanics vocational program on "good citizenship." The *Felton* court concluded the student's conduct, stealing auto parts, was inconsistent with "good citizenship," and that the school had properly excluded him from the activity. *Felton* suggests that a standard based on "good citizenship" apprises the "ordinary" student that criminal conduct may result in disciplinary action, especially where, as here, the criminal conduct related to the student's area of study.

Moreover, in *Esteban v. Central Missouri State College*, 415 F.2d 1077 (8th Cir 1969), we rejected a vagueness challenge to a school regulation which instructed students "to abide by the rules and regulations of the college as well as all local, state and federal laws." Like the regulation in *Esteban*, the Standards specifically state that "by the act of registering, the student agrees to obey all rules and regulations formulated by the College as listed below and to obey all federal, state and local laws." The Standards provide Westark students with clear and precise direction: criminal conduct is inconsistent with the behavior expected of Westark students. Woodis does not dispute that she pled nolo contendere to a misdemeanor charge, and, therefore, that she violated state law. The record also shows that Westark expelled Woodis for engaging in this criminal conduct. In light of the express provision in the Standards prohibiting criminal conduct by students, we conclude that as applied to Woodis, the Standards gave Woodis notice that her conduct would subject her to discipline and, more importantly, placed meaningful bounds on the enforcement decisions of the Westark administrators. Therefore, Woodis' void-for-vagueness claim must fail in the context of this case where the facts do not implicate First Amendment rights. . . .

Wood v. Strickland

420 U.S. 308 (1975)

> *Focusing on possible interpretations of the standards, the Court rules that the School Board appropriately suspended students for spiking the punch at a school function under the standards in place.*

Introductory note:

> The school policy in effect was:
>
> 3. Suspension
>
> . . . Valid causes for suspension from school on first offense: Pupils found to be guilty of any of the following shall be suspended from school on the first offense for the balance of the semester and such suspension will be noted on the permanent record of the student along with reason for suspension. . . .
>
> 4. The use of intoxicating beverage or possession of same at school or at a school sponsored activity.

Wood v. Strickland, 420 U.S. 308, 311 n.3

Mr. Justice White delivered the opinion of the Court.

Respondents Peggy Strickland and Virginia Crain brought this lawsuit against petitioners, . . . claiming that their federal constitutional rights to due process were infringed under color of state law by their expulsion from the Mena Public High School on the grounds of their violation of a school regulation prohibiting the use or possession of intoxicating beverages at school or school activities. . . .

The violation of the school regulation prohibiting the use or possession of intoxicating beverages at school or school activities with which respondents were charged concerned their "spiking" of the punch served at a meeting of an extracurricular school organization attended by parents and students. At the time in question, respondents were 16 years old and were in the 10th grade. The relevant facts begin with their discovery that the punch had not been prepared for the meeting as previously planned. The girls then agreed to "spike" it.

....

Ten days later, the teacher in charge of the extracurricular group and meeting, Mrs. Curtis Powell, having heard something about the "spiking," questioned the girls about it. Although first denying any knowledge, the girls admitted their involvement after the teacher said that she would handle the punishment herself. The next day, however, she told the girls that the incident was becoming increasingly the subject of talk in the school and that the principal, P.T. Waller, would probably hear about it. She told them that her job was in jeopardy but that she would not force them to admit to Waller what they had done. If they did not go to him then, however, she would not be able to help them if the incident became "distorted." The three girls then went to Waller and admitted their role in the affair. He suspended them from school for a maximum two-week period, subject to the decision of the school board. Waller also told them that the board would meet that night, that the girls could tell their parents about the meeting, but that the parents should not contact any members of the board.

Neither the girls nor their parents attended the school board meeting that night. Both Mrs. Powell and Waller, after making their reports concerning the incident, recommended leniency. At this point, a telephone call was received by S.L. Inlow, then the superintendent of schools, from Mrs. Powell's husband, also a teacher at the high school, who reported that he had heard that the third girl involved had been in a fight that evening at a basketball game. Inlow informed the meeting of the news, although he did not mention the name of the girl involved. Mrs. Powell and Waller then withdrew their recommendations of leniency, and the board voted to expel the girls from school for the remainder of the semester, a period of approximately three months.

The board subsequently agreed to hold another meeting on the matter, and one was held approximately two weeks after the first meeting. The girls, their parents, and their counsel attended this session. The board began with a reading of a written statement of facts as it had found them. The girls admitted mixing the malt liquor into the punch with the intent of "spiking" it, but asked the board to forgo its rule punishing such violations by such substantial suspensions. Neither Mrs. Powell nor Waller was present at this meeting. The board voted not to change its policy and, as before, to expel the girls for the remainder of the semester.

....

Petitioners as members of the school board assert here, as they did below, an absolute immunity from liability under § 1983.

....

The nature of the immunity from awards of damages under § 1983 available to school administrators and school board members is not a question which the lower federal courts have answered with a single voice. There is general agreement on the existence of a "good faith" immunity, but the courts have either emphasized different factors as elements of good faith or have not given specific content to the good-faith standard.

As the facts of this case reveal, school board members function at different times in the nature of legislators and adjudicators in the school disciplinary process. Each of these functions necessarily involves the exercise of discretion, the weighing of many factors, and the formulation of long-term policy. "Like legislators and judges, these officers are entitled to rely on traditional sources for the factual information on which they decide and act." As with executive officers faced with instances of civil disorder, school officials, confronted with student behavior causing or threatening disruption, also have an "obvious need for prompt action, and decisions must be made in reliance on factual information supplied by others."

Liability for damages for every action which is found subsequently to have been violative of a student's constitutional rights and to have caused compensable injury would unfairly impose upon the school decisionmaker the burden of mistakes made in good faith in the course of exercising his discretion within the scope of his official duties. School board members, among other duties, must judge whether there have been violations of school regulations and, if so, the appropriate sanctions for the violations. Denying any measure of immunity in these circumstances "would contribute not to principled and fearless decision-making but to intimidation." The imposition of monetary costs for mistakes which were not unreasonable in the light of all the circumstances would undoubtedly deter even the most conscientious school decisionmaker from exercising his judgment independently, forcefully, and in a manner best serving the long-term interest of the school and the students. The most capable candidates for school board positions might be deterred from seeking office if heavy burdens upon their private resources from monetary liability were a likely prospect during their tenure.

. . . .

Therefore, in the specific context of school discipline, we hold that a school board member is not immune from liability for damages under § 1983 if he knew or reasonably should have known that the action he took within his sphere of official responsibility would violate the constitutional rights of the student affected, or if he took the action with the malicious intention to cause a deprivation of constitutional rights or other injury to the student. That is not to say that school board members are "charged with predicting the future course of constitutional law." A compensatory award will be appropriate only if the school board member has acted with such an impermissible motivation or with such disregard of the student's clearly established constitutional rights that his action cannot reasonably be characterized as being in good faith.

The Court of Appeals, based upon its review of the facts but without the benefit of the transcript of the testimony given at the four-day trial to the jury in the District Court, found that the board had made its decision to expel the girls on the basis of *no* evidence that the school regulation had been violated.... The Court of Appeals interpreted the school regulation prohibiting the use or possession of intoxicating beverages as being linked to the definition of "intoxicating liquor" under Arkansas statutes which restrict the term to beverages with an alcoholic content exceeding 5% by weight. Testimony at the trial, however, established convincingly that the term "intoxicating beverage" in the school regulation was not intended at the time of its adoption in 1967 to be linked to the definition in the state statutes or to any other technical definition of "intoxicating." The adoption of the regulation was at a time when the school board was concerned with a previous beer-drinking episode. It was applied prior to respondents' case to another student charged with possession of beer. In its statement of facts issued prior to the onset of this litigation, the school board expressed its construction of the regulation by finding that the girls had brought an "alcoholic beverage" onto school premises. The girls themselves admitted knowing at the time of the incident that they were doing something wrong which might be punished. In light of this evidence, the Court of Appeals was ill advised to supplant the interpretation of the regulation of those officers who adopted it and are entrusted with its enforcement.

When the regulation is construed to prohibit the use and possession of beverages containing alcohol, there was no absence of evidence before the school board to prove the charge against respondents. The girls had admitted that they intended to "spike" the punch and that they had mixed malt liquor into the punch that was served. The third girl estimated at the time of their admissions to Waller that the malt liquor had an alcohol content of 20%. After the expulsion decision had been made and this litigation had begun, it was conclusively determined that the malt liquor in fact had an alcohol content not exceeding 3.2% by weight. Testimony at trial put the alcohol content of the punch served at 0.91%.

Given the fact that there *was* evidence supporting the charge against respondents, the contrary judgment of the Court of Appeals is improvident. It is not the role of the federal courts to set aside decisions of school administrators which the court may view as lacking a basis in wisdom or compassion. Public high school students do have substantive and procedural rights while at school. But § 1983 does not extend the right to relitigate in federal court evidentiary questions arising in school disciplinary proceedings or the proper construction of school regulations. The system of public education that has evolved in this Nation relies necessarily upon the discretion and judgment of school administrators and school board members, and § 1983 was not intended to be a vehicle for federal-court corrections of errors in the exercise of that discretion which do not rise to the level of violations of specific constitutional guarantees.

The judgment of the Court of Appeals is vacated and the case remanded for further proceedings consistent with this opinion.

Post Problem Discussion

1. In *Boothby*, the court discusses the two different approaches for discipline standards: (1) that school administrators have inherent authority to discipline without a prior published rule specifically prohibiting the conduct in question; versus (2) that some preexisting rule must exist to supply an adequate guide for students to know what conduct is subject to discipline under school rules and policies (at least for more severe discipline such as expulsion and prolonged suspension). Which approach do you think is the most appropriate for public schools and why? Would your answer to the questions in this Problem vary under one approach or the other? Issues around notice of conduct subject to discipline are revisited in Problem 5.

2. *Woodis* provides an outline for the kind of analysis that the court may use to consider whether a disciplinary standard is constitutionally sufficient. Would you know what you could and could not do, without likelihood of sanctions, under the Westark policy? Would you know under the New Town High School Policy? At your school?

3. What are the key lessons here for those who work on drafting disciplinary standards?

4. The immunity discussion in *Wood* raises issues of the potential remedy for discipline decisions that do violate the constitution. If James and Terrell's suspensions violate the constitution, what should the remedy be? The parents asked about monetary damages. What is an appropriate monetary award for a ten day out of school suspension?

§ 8.03 Substantive & Procedural Requirements

As noted, student discipline is governed by state and federal constitutional requirements, statutes, regulations, and local school policies. While student expulsion has not typically provided a basis for a substantive due process claim (unlike corporal punishment, which is discussed separately), there is a clear constitutional procedural due process minimum standard for student discipline set forth by the landmark United States Supreme Court opinion *Goss v. Lopez*, 419 U.S. 565 (1975). States have expanded on these constitutional minimum standards through statutes and regulations. Generally speaking, the harsher the potential penalty, the more process and specificity that is required in order to discipline. The following problem highlights some of these issues.

Problem 2: Disciplinary Hearing Process

Kordell Maddox is seventeen and in the eleventh grade at the Harmony High School. On Tuesday, October 11, 20xx, he was arrested at school for damaging school property. Kordell is alleged to have destroyed the high school computer lab by physically breaking computers with some object (like a bat, tire iron, etc.), knocking over furniture, and spray-painting the walls with profanity. Principal Myers discovered the damage on Monday, October 10th and called the police. The police investigated by interviewing teachers, the principal, and Kordell. They also interviewed two other students (Karrie and Steve), who had some information about Kordell's whereabouts at the time the incident occurred, and about potential motives that Kordell may have had to destroy the lab. Based on information obtained in a two day investigation at the school, the police ultimately arrested Kordell.

Principal Myers was present during all of the police interviews about the incident. After the police arrested Kordell, the principal informed Kordell and his parents that based on the information obtained by the police, Kordell would be suspended from school for ten days. When the principal informed Superintendent Harris about the incident, she recommended expulsion and scheduled an expulsion hearing before the school board for October 15. Kordell's parents asked for more time, but Superintendent Harris told them that the school board only met once a month and the matter could not wait until next month.

At the school board hearing, Superintendent Harris presented the evidence for the school. She called Principal Myers to testify for the school. Principal Myers stated that he sat in on the police interviews of Karrie, Kordell, and Steve. Principal Myers also stated that he has his own thoughts about each of the students based on his knowledge of them, and that he and Police Officer Jones shared impressions of each student after each interview. Specifically, Principal Myers testified that Karrie is his niece, so he believes what she says is truthful, and that Steve is Kordell's best friend, so he would likely try to cover for him.

Principal Myers indicated that Kordell has been in all kinds of trouble in the past for various things at school, though nothing of this sort; Kordell is constantly late to class and skips class, often gets into disagreements with teachers and students, and often does not follow school rules about minor things like not wearing hats in class. As a result of this type of behavior, Kordell has been in in-school suspension twice this year already, and five times last year. Kordell was suspended from school once last year for five days for calling a teacher a derogatory name.

The superintendent then presented the police report of Officer Stephan Jones (included in the problem materials) and asked the school board to expel Kordell for the remainder of the school year. The school did not present any other witnesses or evidence.

At the hearing, the school board chair asked Kordell and his parents if they had any evidence to present. Kordell responded "I did not do it. That's all there is to say." Kordell's parents stated that they did not understand why Kordell was being persecuted for something that he did not do and that they felt unqualified to help in this process. They threatened to sue the school for damages if the board expelled Kordell saying that the lawyers they had talked to said that they would take the case if money damages were involved. The school board voted 4 to 1 to expel Kordell for the remainder of the school year.

Did the school comply with the constitutional, statutory, and regulatory standards noted in the problem materials? If you were a judge, or state school board member reviewing the local school board's decision on appeal, would you uphold it? Why or why not?

Problem Materials

- ✓ Hypothetical State Discipline Statute § 76193:13[2]
- ✓ Hypothetical State Discipline Regulations Ed 3127
- ✓ School District Policy
- ✓ Letter to Parents
- ✓ Police Report
- ✓ *Goss v. Lopez*, 419 U.S. 565 (1975)

State Statute

§ 76193:13 Suspension and Expulsion of Pupils

I. (a) The superintendent or a representative designated in writing by the superintendent, is authorized to suspend pupils from school for a period not to exceed 10 school days for gross misconduct or for neglect or refusal to conform to the reasonable rules of the school.

(b) The school board or a representative designated in writing of the school board is authorized, following a hearing, to continue the suspension of a pupil for a period in excess of 10 school days. The school board's designee may be the superintendent or any other individual, but may not be the individual who suspended the pupil for the first 10 days under subparagraph (a).

(c) Any suspension in excess of 10 school days imposed under subparagraph (b) by any person other than the school board is appealable to the school board. The school board shall hold a hearing on the appeal, but shall have discretion to hear evidence or to rely upon the record of a hearing conducted under subparagraph (b). The suspension under subparagraph (b) shall be enforced while that appeal is pending, unless the school board stays the suspension while the appeal is pending.

II. Any pupil may be expelled from school by the local school board for gross misconduct, or for neglect or refusal to conform to the reasonable rules of the school, or for an act of theft, destruction, or violence as defined in state law. . . .

2. The state statute and regulations are modified from various actual laws including New Hampshire's. *See* N.H. Rev. Stat. Ann § 193:13; N.H. Code Admin. R. Ed. 317.

State Education Regulations

Dept. Ed 3127.01 Purpose.

(a) These state regulations rules provide the minimum requirements to assure due process and statewide uniformity in the enforcement of § 76193:13 relative to disciplinary action for gross misconduct, or for neglect or refusal to conform to the reasonable rules of the school.

(b) These rules also provide a standard that local school boards shall use in adopting and implementing a policy relative to pupil conduct and disciplinary procedures.

Dept. Ed 3127.02 Definitions.

(a) "Expulsion" means the permanent denial of a pupil's attendance at school for any of the reasons listed in § 76193:13.

(b) "Gross misconduct" means an act which:

(1) Results in violence to another's person or property;

(2) Poses a direct threat to the safety of others in a safe school zone; or

(3) Is identified in local school district policies.

(c) "Neglect" means the failure of a pupil to pay attention to an announced, posted, or printed school rule.

(d) "Pupil" means a child through age 21 in attendance at a school during the school day.

(e) "Refusal" means the willful defiance of a pupil to comply with an announced, posted, or printed school rule.

(f) "Suspension" means the temporary denial of a student's attendance at school for a specific period of time for gross misconduct or for neglect or refusal to conform to announced, posted, or printed school rules.

Dept. Ed 3127.03 Standard for Expulsion by Local School Board.

(a) A school board which expels a pupil under § 76193:13, shall state in writing its reasons and shall provide a procedure for review as provided by state law.

(b) School boards shall comply with paragraph (a) by specifically naming:

(1) The act leading to expulsion; and

(2) The specific statutory and school policy reference prohibiting that act.

Dept. Ed 3127.04 Disciplinary Procedures.

(a) There shall be the following levels of discipline available to school officials enforcing § 76193:13 relative to the suspension and expulsion of pupils in a safe school zone:

(1) A suspension for gross misconduct or for neglect or refusal to conform to the reasonable rules of the school under § 76193:13, shall be considered a short-term suspension and shall be administered by a superintendent or designee for a period not to exceed 10 school days;

(2) A suspension for an act of theft, destruction, or violence shall be considered a long-term suspension and shall be administered by the school board or designee in order to continue the short term suspension for a period in excess of 10 school days, provided the designee is not the person who suspended the pupil for 10 school days under (1) above, and that designee provides a due process hearing under (d)(2) below;

(3) An expulsion by the local school board for a period determined in writing by the board under § 76193:13; and

(b) Prior to initiating any disciplinary action listed in paragraph (a), each school board shall adopt a policy which prescribes the manner in which the student body shall be informed concerning the content of § 76193:13 through announced, posted, or printed school rules.

(c) If the school and school board have met the requirements of paragraph (b) a pupil appealing a local decision to the state board may not be allowed to claim lack of knowledge of the state law requiring expulsion for bringing or possessing a firearm or other dangerous weapon as defined in these rules.

(d) Due process in disciplinary proceedings shall include, at a minimum, the following:

(1) In a short-term suspension:

a. The superintendent or designee shall inform the pupil of the purpose of the meeting;

b. Oral or written notice of the charges and an explanation of the evidence against the pupil;

c. An opportunity for the pupil to present his/her side of the story;

d. A written statement to the pupil and at least one of the pupil's parents or guardian explaining any disciplinary action taken against the student;

(2) In a long-term suspension of a pupil:

a. Written communication to the pupil and at least one of the pupil's parents or guardian, delivered in person or by mail to the pupil's last known address, of the charges and an explanation of the evidence against the pupil;

b. The superintendent's written or oral recommendation for student action to correct the discipline problem;

c. A hearing in accordance with Ed 3127.04(d)(3). below;

d. A written decision which includes the legal and factual basis for the conclusion that the pupil should be suspended;

e. If the hearing was conducted by the school board's designee, the decision may be appealed to the local school board under § 76193:13; and

f. If the hearing was conducted by the school board, the decision may be appealed to the state board of education;

(3) In an expulsion by the local school board, due process shall include the following minimal requirements:

a. A formal hearing shall be held before any expulsion;

b. Such hearing may be held either before or after the short-term suspension has expired and pending the expulsion hearing;

c. If the hearing is held after the expiration of a short-term suspension, the pupil shall be entitled to return to school after the short-term suspension has expired and pending the expulsion hearing.

d. The school board shall provide written notice to the pupil and at least one of the pupil's parents or guardian, delivered in person or by mail to the pupil's last known address, of the date, time and place for a hearing before the local board;

e. The written notice required by d. above shall include:

1. A written statement of the charges and the nature of the evidence against the pupil; and

2. A superintendent's written recommendation for school board action and a description of the process used by the superintendent to reach his/her recommendation;

f. This notice shall be delivered to the pupil and at least one of the pupil's parents or guardian at least 5 days prior to the hearing.

g. The following hearing procedures shall apply:

1. The pupil, together with a parent or guardian may waive the right to a hearing and admit to the charges made by the superintendent;

2. If the pupil is 18 years of age or older, the concurrence of a parent or guardian shall be unnecessary unless the pupil is subject to a guardianship which would prevent the pupil from waiving the right to a hearing;

3. Formal rules of evidence shall not be applicable, however, school officials shall present evidence in support of the charge(s) and the accused pupil or his/her parent or guardian shall have an opportunity to present any defense or reply;

4. The hearing shall be either public or private and the choice shall be that of the pupil or his parent or guardian; and

5. During the hearing, the pupil, parent, guardian or counsel representing the pupil, shall have the right to examine any and all witnesses;

h. The decision of the school board shall be based on a dispassionate and fair consideration of substantial evidence that the accused pupil committed the act for which expulsion is to imposed and that such acts are, in fact, a proper reason for expulsion;

i. The decision shall state whether the student is expelled and the length of the expulsion. If the decision is to expel the pupil the decision shall include the legal and factual basis for the decision;

j. A statement of the time period for which the student is expelled and any action the student may take to be restored by the board; and

(e) A decision shall include a statement that the pupil has the right to appeal the decision to the state board of education.

Relevant Portion of Harmony High School Discipline Policy[3]

Pursuant to §76193 and Ed 3127, students may be suspended or expelled from school for gross misconduct, or for neglect, or refusal, to conform to the reasonable rules of the school.

"Gross misconduct" means an act which: (1) Results in violence to another's person or property; (2) Poses a direct threat to the safety of others in a safe school zone; or (3) Is of such severity and detriment to the school that it warrants suspension or expulsion.

"Neglect" means the failure of a student to pay attention to an announced, posted, or printed school rule. "Refusal" means the willful defiance of a pupil to comply with an announced, posted, or printed school rule. The school will follow the required procedures in §76193 and Ed 3127 in the discipline process.

Letter to Parents

10/13/20xx
Mr. and Mrs. Maddox
12 Suburban Lane
Pretend, XX 09870

3. Excerpted in part from Derry Cooperative School District No. 1 EPS Code: JFCJ, SAFE SCHOOL ZONE, http://www.derry.k12.nh.us/sb/policies/Jpolicies/JFCJ-P.pdf.

Dear Mr. and Mrs. Maddox:

This is to inform you that your son Kordell has been recommended for expulsion from school for gross misconduct and refusal to conform to school rules in causing damage to the computer lab on or about October 8 or October 9. I made the recommendation to expel after speaking with Principal Myers, and obtaining the information that Principal Myers acquired during the police investigation of this matter. I have enclosed a copy of the police report for you to review.

An expulsion hearing before the school board is scheduled for October 15 in Room 201 of the High School. You have the right to attend this hearing, to be represented by counsel at this hearing, and to present evidence at this hearing. The school board will issue its decision that day. You and Kordell may also waive the right to a hearing if Kordell admits to the charges.

Please contact me if you have any questions or if I can be of any assistance.

Sincerely,
Superintendent Harris

Police Report

On Monday, October 10 and Tuesday, October 11, I performed an investigation at Harmony High School regarding damage to school property. I interviewed a number of teachers and three students, Kordell, Steve, and Karrie. Principal Myers was present for the student interviews as well.

From talking with teachers, I discovered that there was a school event on Friday night and that the teachers were in the building cleaning up until late in the evening. They were near the computer lab at that time and saw no damage. From that, I concluded that the damage must have occurred sometime between early Saturday morning and late Sunday evening.

Principal Myers told me that a student named Karrie told him that she saw a note that a student named Steve opened in class. The note was handed to Steve from a student named Kordell. She was able to see most, but not all, of the note as Steve opened it to read it in class. She sits diagonally behind Steve. She said the note said something about destroying the computer lab and all the people in the lab. She thinks Kordell wrote it because he was mad at the technology teacher for disciplining him in class. Karrie said she decided to come forward with the information about the note after she heard about the lab being destroyed as she thought it was important. I found her to be credible, and believe that she did not have any ulterior motives or reasons to lie.

Next, I interviewed Steve. He said that he and Kordell were very good friends. He said that Kordell did give him a note, but it did not say anything about destroying the computer lab. The note said something about forbidden clues to doing well on a new online game called "Destroy All Humans!" He said that he threw the note away after class. Steve did not know what Kordell did over the weekend. Steve himself was out of town over the weekend playing in a hockey game, which I confirmed. I had suspicions about Steve during the interview. He did not make eye contact, and I felt that he was covering for Kordell.

I then interviewed Kordell. He denied doing any damage to the computer lab. He denied owning spray paint, a baseball bat or any other object like that. He agreed that his father probably had some tools like hammers and tire irons in the garage, but said he had not seen or used any recently. He was vague about what he did over the weekend, only saying he spent most of his time at home, or skateboarding at the local park, or at the mall. He denied writing Steve any kind of note.

I got the sense that Kordell was not being truthful, and I arrested him.

Officer Stephan Jones

Goss v. Lopez

419 U.S. 565 (1975)

The Court rules that a school must provide a student with some form of notice and an opportunity to be heard before instituting disciplinary action.

Mr. Justice White delivered the opinion of the Court.

This appeal by various administrators of the Columbus, Ohio, Public School System (CPSS) challenges the judgment of a three-judge federal court, declaring that appellees—various high school students in the CPSS—were denied due process of law contrary to the command of the Fourteenth Amendment in that they were temporarily suspended from their high schools without a hearing either prior to suspension or within a reasonable time thereafter, and enjoining the administrators to remove all references to such suspensions from the students' records.

Ohio law, Rev. Code Ann. § 3313.64 (1972), provides for free education to all children between the ages of six and 21. Section 3313.66 of the Code empowers the principal of an Ohio public school to suspend a pupil for misconduct for up to 10 days or to expel him. In either case, he must notify the student's parents within 24 hours and state the reasons for his action. A pupil who is expelled, or his parents, may appeal the decision to the Board of Education and in connection therewith shall be permitted to be heard at the board meeting. The Board may reinstate in pupil following the hearing. No similar procedure is provided in § 3313.66 or any other provision of state law for a suspended student. Aside from a regulation tracking the statute, at the time of the imposition of the suspensions in this case the CPSS itself had not issued any written procedure applicable to suspensions. Nor, so far as the record reflects, had any of the individual high schools involved in this case. Each, however, had formally or informally described the conduct for which suspension could be imposed.

The nine named appellees, each of whom alleged that he or she had been suspended from public high school in Columbus for up to 10 days without a hearing pursuant to § 3313.66, filed an action under 42 U.S.C. § 1983 against the Columbus Board of Education and various administrators of the CPSS.

....

At the outset, appellants contend that because there is no constitutional right to an education at public expense, the Due Process Clause does not protect against expulsions from the public school system. This position misconceives the nature of the issue and is refuted by prior decisions. The Fourteenth Amendment forbids the State to deprive any person of life, liberty, or property without due process of law. Protected interests in property are normally "not created by the Constitution. Rather, they are created and their dimensions are defined" by an independent source such as state statutes or rules entitling the citizen to certain benefits. *Board of Regents v. Roth*, 408 U.S. 564, 577 (1972).

....

Here, on the basis of state law, appellees plainly had legitimate claims of entitlement to a public education.

....

All of the schools had their own rules specifying the grounds for expulsion or suspension. Having chosen to extend the right to an education to people of appellees' class generally, Ohio may not withdraw that right on grounds of misconduct absent, fundamentally fair procedures to determine whether the misconduct has occurred.

Although Ohio may not be constitutionally obligated to establish and maintain a public school system, it has nevertheless done so and has required its children to attend.

....

"The Fourteenth Amendment, as now applied to the States, protects the citizen against the State itself and all of its creatures — Boards of Education not excepted." The authority possessed by the State to prescribe and enforce standards of conduct in its schools, although concededly very broad, must be exercised consistently with constitutional safeguards. Among other things, the State is constrained to recognize a student's legitimate entitlement to a public education as a property interest which is protected by the Due Process Clause and which may not be taken away for misconduct without adherence to the minimum procedures required by that Clause.

The Due Process Clause also forbids arbitrary deprivations of liberty. "Where a person's good name, reputation, honor, or integrity is at stake because of what the government is doing to him," the minimal requirements of the Clause must be satisfied. School authorities here suspended appellees from school for periods of up to 10 days based on charges of misconduct. If sustained and recorded, those charges could seriously damage the students' standing with their fellow pupils and their teachers as well as interfere with later opportunities for higher education and employment. It is apparent that the claimed right of the State to determine unilaterally and without process whether that misconduct has occurred immediately collides with the requirements of the Constitution.

....

Appellees were excluded from school only temporarily, it is true, but the length and consequent severity of a deprivation, while another factor to weigh in determining the appropriate form of hearing, "is not decisive of the basic right" to a hearing of some kind. The Court's view has been that as long as a property deprivation is not de minimis, its gravity is irrelevant to the question whether account must be taken of the Due Process Clause.

....

A 10-day suspension from school is not de minimis in our view and may not be imposed in complete disregard of the Due Process Clause.

A short suspension is, of course, a far milder deprivation than expulsion. But, "education is perhaps the most important function of state and local governments," *Brown v. Board of Education*, 347 U.S. 483 (1954), and the total exclusion from the educational process for more than a trivial period, and certainly if the suspension is for 10 days, is a serious event in the life of the suspended child. Neither the property interest in educational benefits temporarily denied nor the liberty interest in reputation, which is also implicated, is so insubstantial that suspensions may constitutionally be imposed by any procedure the school chooses, no matter how arbitrary.

Once it is determined that due process applies, the question remains what process is due. We turn to that question, fully realizing as our cases regularly do that the interpretation and application of the Due Process Clause are intensely practical matters and that "[t]he very nature of due process negates any concept of inflexible procedures universally applicable to every imaginable situation."

....

At the very minimum, therefore, students facing suspension and the consequent interference with a protected property interest must be given some kind of notice and afforded some kind of hearing.

....

It also appears from our cases that the timing and content of the notice and the nature of the hearing will depend on appropriate accommodation of the competing interests involved.... The student's interest is to avoid unfair or mistaken exclusion from the educational process, with all of its unfortunate consequences. The Due Process Clause will not shield him from suspensions properly imposed, but it disserves both his interest and the interest of the State if his suspension is in fact unwarranted. The concern would be mostly academic if the disciplinary process were a totally accurate, unerring process, never mistaken and never unfair. Unfortunately, that is not the case, and no one suggests that it is. Disciplinarians, although proceeding in utmost good faith, frequently act on the reports and advice of others; and the controlling facts and the nature of the conduct under challenge are often disputed. The risk of error is not at all trivial, and it should be guarded against if that may be done without prohibitive cost or interference with the educational process.

The difficulty is that our schools are vast and complex. Some modicum of discipline and order is essential if the educational function is to be performed. Events calling for discipline are frequent occurrences and sometimes require immediate, effective action. Suspension is considered not only to be a necessary tool to maintain order but a valuable educational device. The prospect of imposing elaborate hearing requirements in every suspension case is viewed with great concern, and many school authorities may well prefer the untrammeled power to act unilaterally, unhampered by rules about notice and hearing. But it would be a strange disciplinary system in an educational institution if no communication was sought by the disciplinarian with the student in an effort to inform him of his dereliction and to let him tell his side of the story in order to make sure that an injustice is not done. "[F]airness can rarely be obtained by secret, one-sided determination of facts decisive of rights. . . ." "Secrecy is not congenial to truth-seeking and self-righteousness gives too slender an assurance of rightness. No better instrument has been devised for arriving at truth than to give a person in jeopardy of serious loss notice of the case against him and opportunity to meet it."

We do not believe that school authorities must be totally free from notice and hearing requirements if their schools are to operate with acceptable efficiency. Students facing temporary suspension have interests qualifying for protection of the Due Process Clause, and due process requires, in connection with a suspension of 10 days or less, that the student be given oral or written notice of the charges against him and, if he denies them, an explanation of the evidence the authorities have and an opportunity to present his side of the story. The Clause requires at least these rudimentary precautions against unfair or mistaken findings of misconduct and arbitrary exclusion from school.

There need be no delay between the time "notice" is given and the time of the hearing. In the great majority of cases the disciplinarian may informally discuss the alleged misconduct with the student minutes after it has occurred. We hold only that, in being given an opportunity to explain his version of the facts at this discussion, the student first be told what he is accused of doing and what the basis of the accusation is.

. . . .

Since the hearing may occur almost immediately following the misconduct, it follows that as a general rule notice and hearing should precede removal of the student from school. We agree with the District Court, however, that there are recurring situations in which prior notice and hearing cannot be insisted upon. Students whose presence poses a continuing danger to persons or property or an ongoing threat of disrupting the academic process may be immediately removed from school. In such cases, the necessary notice and rudimentary hearing should follow as soon as practicable, as the District Court indicated.

In holding as we do, we do not believe that we have imposed procedures on school disciplinarians which are inappropriate in a classroom setting.

. . . .

We stop short of construing the Due Process Clause to require, countrywide, that hearings in connection with short suspensions must afford the student the opportunity to secure counsel, to confront and cross-examine witnesses supporting the charge, or to call his own witnesses to verify his version of the incident. Brief disciplinary suspensions are almost countless. To impose in each such case even truncated trial-type procedures might well overwhelm administrative facilities in many places and, by diverting resources, cost more than it would save in educational effectiveness. Moreover, further formalizing the suspension process and escalating its formality and adversary nature may not only make it too costly as a regular disciplinary tool but also destroy its effectiveness as part of the teaching process.

On the other hand, requiring effective notice and informal hearing permitting the student to give his version of the events will provide a meaningful hedge against erroneous action. At least the disciplinarian will be alerted to the existence of disputes about facts and arguments about cause and effect. He may then determine himself to summon the accuser, permit cross-examination, and allow the student to present his own witnesses. In more difficult cases, he may permit counsel. In any event, his discretion will be more informed and we think the risk of error substantially reduced.

Requiring that there be at least an informal give-and-take between student and disciplinarian, preferably prior to the suspension, will add little to the fact-finding function where the disciplinarian himself has witnessed the conduct forming the basis for the charge. But things are not always as they seem to be, and the student will at least have the opportunity to characterize his conduct and put it in what he deems the proper context.

We should also make it clear that we have addressed ourselves solely to the short suspension, not exceeding 10 days. Longer suspensions or expulsions for the remainder of the school term, or permanently, may require more formal procedures. Nor do we put aside the possibility that in unusual situations, although involving only a short suspension, something more than the rudimentary procedures will be required. . . .

Post Problem Discussion

1. *Goss* was preceded by cases in other contexts that offer insight on the issues of discipline and the opportunity for hearing. For example, *Dixon v. Alabama State Bd. of Educ.*, 294 F.2d 150 (5th Cir. 1961), held that students were entitled to some kind of notice before they were expelled from Alabama State College for participating in

a protest at the Montgomery County Courthouse lunch counter. The *Dixon* court concluded, "We are confident that precedent as well as a most fundamental constitutional principle support our holding that due process *requires notice and some opportunity for hearing* before a student at a tax-supported college is expelled for misconduct." The court offered the following "guidance":

> For the guidance of the parties in the event of further proceedings, we state our views on the nature of the notice and hearing required by due process prior to expulsion from a state college or university. They should, we think, comply with the following standards. The notice should contain a statement of the specific charges and grounds which, if proven, would justify expulsion under the regulations of the Board of Education. The nature of the hearing should vary depending upon the circumstances of the particular case. The case before us requires something more than an informal interview with an administrative authority of the college. By its nature, a charge of misconduct, as opposed to a failure to meet the scholastic standards of the college, depends upon a collection of the facts concerning the charged misconduct, easily colored by the point of view of the witnesses. In such circumstances, a hearing which gives the Board or the administrative authorities of the college an opportunity to hear both sides in considerable detail is best suited to protect the rights of all involved. This is not to imply that a full-dress judicial hearing, with the right to cross-examine witnesses, is required. Such a hearing, with the attending publicity and disturbance of college activities, might be detrimental to the college's educational atmosphere and impractical to carry out. Nevertheless, the rudiments of an adversary proceeding may be preserved without encroaching upon the interests of the college. In the instant case, the student should be given the names of the witnesses against him and an oral or written report on the facts to which each witness testifies. He should also be given the opportunity to present to the Board, or at least to an administrative official of the college, his own defense against the charges and to produce either oral testimony or written affidavits of witnesses in his behalf. If the hearing is not before the Board directly, the results and findings of the hearing should be presented in a report open to the student's inspection. If these rudimentary elements of fair play are followed in a case of misconduct of this particular type, we feel that the requirements of due process of law will have been fulfilled.

Dixon, 294 F.2d at 158–59. While *Dixon* dealt with higher education, courts addressing the sufficiency of due process procedures in public secondary and elementary schools have used similar approaches. Most courts use the *Matthews v. Eldridge* balancing test to determine constitutional sufficiency of hearing procedures in student discipline cases and are reluctant to impose additional procedures. *See Mathews v. Eldridge*, 424 U.S. 319 (1976); *see also, e.g., Watson ex rel. Watson v. Beckel*, 242 F.3d 1237, 1240 (10th Cir. 2001); *Palmer ex rel. Palmer v. Merluzzi*, 868 F.2d 90, 95 (3d Cir. 1989); *Newsome v. Batavia Local Sch. Dist.*, 842 F.2d 920, 923–24 (6th Cir. 1988).

Were the *Dixon* guidelines met in Kordell's situation? Did Kordell receive a sufficient hearing? If not, what was lacking?

2. Some courts have ruled that school boards cannot rely solely on police reports as evidence in expulsion hearings when doing so deprives a student of the ability to cross-examine witnesses. *See, e.g.*, *Johnson v. Collins*, 233 F. Supp. 2d 241 (D.N.H. 2002). Others have found that cross-examination is not always required. *See, e.g.*, *Coronado v. Valleyview Pub. Sch. Dist.*, 537 F.3d 791 (7th Cir. 2008); *Brown v. Plainfield Cmty. Consol. Dist. 202*, 522 F. Supp. 2d 1068 (N.D. Ill. 2007) (ruling that student did not have a right to cross-examine unnamed students who provided witness statements).

Do you think the Harmony School District should be allowed to present Officer Jones' report as evidence given the circumstances and facts noted in the problem? Why or why not? What impact would it have on school board expulsion hearings if schools were not allowed to rely on such reports?

3. In the problem materials, Principal Myer's decision to suspend Kordell seems to be colored by his negative view of Kordell based on other disciplinary incidents, and his positive view of his niece because she is his niece. How, if at all, would this influence your decision in reviewing the local school board's decision to expel? Is it inappropriate for a principal to be influenced by these factors? Why or why not?

4. Note that the state regulations in the problem center around 10 day suspensions much like the Court's decision in *Goss*. Why do you think that is so? Do the state regulations in the problem meet the *Goss* standard for suspensions up to 10 days? Do the principal's actions in suspending for 10 days meet the requirements of *Goss*, and the requirements in the state regulations?

5. Note that the materials focus on discipline in public schools. What would happen if the incident occurred in a private school? How would it change the legal standards and requirements that the school must follow in the disciplinary process?[4]

6. What if the incident occurred in a charter school? A California court ruled that a state statute that required a hearing before a student could be expelled did not apply to charter schools. *Scott B. v. Board of Trustees of Orange County High School of the Arts*, 217 Cal. App. 4th 117 (2013), *reh'g denied* (July 8, 2013). The court also seemed to state that constitutional due process protections also would not apply because a student is "dismissed" from a charter school as opposed to being "expelled."

Recall that charter schools are generally a form of public schools, but they are exempt from some state requirements, and they can have different admissions criteria than regular public schools. For example, a charter school may have open

---

4. *See, e.g.*, *Liability of private school or educational institution for breach of contract arising from expulsion or suspension of student*, 47 A.L.R.5th 1 (2008).

enrollment and focus on offering programs for students interested in science.[5] There are even some charter schools that are completely online.[6]

In *Scott B.*, the court noted the due process requirements in *Goss v. Lopez* and then stated:

> Dismissal from a charter school does not implicate these concerns to the same degree as expulsion. Unlike public schools generally, "OCHSA is a school of choice. No student is required to attend." When a student is dismissed from OCHSA, the student is free to immediately enroll in another school without the loss of classroom time. Thus, dismissal from OCHSA need not and should not delay Scott's education. The May 16, 2011 letter informing Scott's mother of his dismissal instructed her to immediately enroll Scott in another school. Scott's transcripts from OCHSA were attached to the letter. The parties have not cited us to any statute requiring a new school be notified of a dismissal from a charter school.

Id. at 124, 158 Cal. Rptr. 3d at 179. What do you think about the court's opinion?

Activity 1: Find Your State and Local Discipline Standards

State and local standards play an important role in the discipline process. This activity gives you a chance to find your state and local standards, and compare them to those used in the problems in this Chapter.

Step One—Find your state discipline statutes and state discipline regulations online.

Step Two—Find a local public school's discipline policy online. It can be from a school you attended, or a public school in your home state, or any public school you would like to use.

Step Three—Answer the following:

1. How do the state discipline statutes and regulations compare to the ones in Problem 2? Do they use similar terminology? Do they have ascending levels of due process requirements for more severe penalties? Do they define certain actions that are subject to discipline? Are there any changes that you think should be made to the state statutes or regulations? Why or why not?
2. How does the local public school district policy compare to the ones in Problem 1 and Problem 2? Does the policy you found comply with the state requirements? Does it go beyond the state's requirements in

---

5. For more information about charter schools see https://nces.ed.gov/fastfacts/display.asp?id=30 (last visited March 23, 2015).

6. See for example the Virtual Learning Academy, http://vlacs.org/ (last visited February 25, 2019).

any way? Are there any changes that you think should be made to the policy? Why or why not?

3. How, if at all, would the discipline process for Kordell in Problem 2 be different if your state laws and local policy were used? Would your answer to Problem 2 regarding Kordell's expulsion change if your state and local standards were used instead of the hypothetical ones in the problem?

4. Do the state discipline statutes and regulations that you found apply to private schools? If not, are there any state laws that address discipline in private schools? How, if at all, are they different from those that apply to public schools?

5. How about charter schools? Are they exempt from discipline requirements in your state? Do they have different discipline requirements than public schools?

§ 8.04 Corporal Punishment

Prior sections have provided some exposure to suspensions and expulsion as a disciplinary punishment. Corporal punishment is physical punishment. Some states specifically authorize corporal punishment; others specifically prohibit it. As noted in Chapter 6, in some situations, schools or school employees may be liable for common law claims under state law for corporal punishment. Another aspect of corporal punishment is whether it violates federal constitutional standards.

In *Ingraham v. Wright*, the United States Supreme Court decided that corporal punishment is not "cruel and unusual punishment" as those terms are used in the Eighth Amendment of the United States Constitution. However, the Supreme Court did not address potential substantive due process claims for corporal punishment. As the problem materials indicate, a number of federal courts have found that corporal punishment can lead to a substantive due process claim. Other courts have found that such claims do not exist when common law claims (like those discussed in Chapter 6) are feasible because the common law claims serve to adequately protect students from excessive punishment. The following problem explores these different perspectives.

Problem 3: Federal Claims for Corporal Punishment

Review Problem 3 in Chapter 6, "Get Me My Paddle," which addressed potential common law claims for injuries Steven incurred from corporal punishment. Assume that you are a judge in a federal circuit that has not yet addressed the issue of whether or not a student may bring a substantive due process claim for corporal punishment. Steven has filed such a claim in your federal court based on the facts in Problem 3 in Chapter 6. The school district has moved to dismiss based on

Ingraham v. Wright and the reasoning in *Fee v. Herndon*. Steven objects and asks the court to follow the approach of the Fourth Circuit Court of Appeals in *Hall v. Tawney*. Review the problem materials and determine how you will rule on the motion to dismiss.

Problem Materials

✓ *Ingraham v. Wright*, 430 U.S. 651 (1977)

✓ *Fee v. Herndon*, 900 F.2d 804 (5th Cir. 1990)

✓ *Hall v. Tawney*, 621 F.2d 607 (4th Cir. 1980)

Ingraham v. Wright

430 U.S. 651 (1977)

The Court rules that the Eighth Amendment does not protect students from severe corporal punishment at school, and that state laws provided sufficient procedural due process protections.

Mr. Justice Powell delivered the opinion of the Court.

This case presents questions concerning the use of corporal punishment in public schools: First, whether the paddling of students as a means of maintaining school discipline constitutes cruel and unusual punishment in violation of the Eighth Amendment; and, second, to the extent that paddling is constitutionally permissible, whether the Due Process Clause of the Fourteenth Amendment requires prior notice and an opportunity to be heard.

. . . .

The use of corporal punishment in this country as a means of disciplining school children dates back to the colonial period. . . .

All of the circumstances are to be taken into account in determining whether the punishment is reasonable in a particular case. Among the most important considerations are the seriousness of the offense, the attitude and past behavior of the child, the nature and severity of the punishment, the age and strength of the child, and the availability of less severe but equally effective means of discipline.

. . . .

Against this background of historical and contemporary approval of reasonable corporal punishment, we turn to the constitutional questions before us.

The Eighth Amendment provides: "Excessive bail shall not be required, nor excessive fines imposed, nor cruel and unusual punishments inflicted." . . . Bail, fines, and punishment traditionally have been associated with the criminal process, and by subjecting the three to parallel limitations the text of the Amendment suggests an intention to limit the power of those entrusted with the criminal-law function of government.

. . . .

Petitioners acknowledge that the original design of the Cruel and Unusual Punishments Clause was to limit criminal punishments, but urge nonetheless that the prohibition should be extended to ban the paddling of schoolchildren. Observing that the Framers of the Eighth Amendment could not have envisioned our present system of public and compulsory education, with its opportunities for noncriminal punishments, petitioners contend that extension of the prohibition against cruel punishments is necessary lest we afford greater protection to criminals than to schoolchildren.

. . . .

The schoolchild has little need for the protection of the Eighth Amendment. Though attendance may not always be voluntary, the public school remains an open institution. Except perhaps when very young, the child is not physically restrained from leaving school during school hours; and at the end of the school day, the child is invariably free to return home. Even while at school, the child brings with him the support of family and friends and is rarely apart from teachers and other pupils who may witness and protest any instances of mistreatment.

The openness of the public school and its supervision by the community afford significant safeguards against the kinds of abuses from which the Eighth Amendment protects the prisoner. In virtually every community where corporal punishment is permitted in the schools, these safeguards are reinforced by the legal constraints of the common law. Public school teachers and administrators are privileged at common law to inflict only such corporal punishment as is reasonably necessary for the proper education and discipline of the child; any punishment going beyond the privilege may result in both civil and criminal liability. As long as the schools are open to public scrutiny, there is no reason to believe that the common-law constraints will not effectively remedy and deter excesses such as those alleged in this case.

We conclude that when public school teachers or administrators impose disciplinary corporal punishment, the Eighth Amendment is inapplicable. The pertinent constitutional question is whether the imposition is consonant with the requirements of due process.

The Fourteenth Amendment prohibits any state deprivation of life, liberty, or property without due process of law. Application of this prohibition requires the familiar two-stage analysis: We must first ask whether the asserted individual interests are encompassed within the Fourteenth Amendment's protection of "life, liberty or property"; if protected interests are implicated, we then must decide what procedures constitute "due process of law." Following that analysis here, we find that corporal punishment in public schools implicates a constitutionally protected liberty interest, but we hold that the traditional common-law remedies are fully adequate to afford due process.

. . . .

It is fundamental that the state cannot hold and physically punish an individual except in accordance with due process of law.

This constitutionally protected liberty interest is at stake in this case. There is, of course a de minimis level of imposition with which the Constitution is not concerned. But at least where school authorities, acting under color of state law, deliberately decide to punish a child for misconduct by restraining the child and inflicting appreciable physical pain, we hold that Fourteenth Amendment liberty interests are implicated.

"[T]he question remains what process is due." Were it not for the common-law privilege permitting teachers, to inflict reasonable corporal punishment on children in their care, and the availability of the traditional remedies for abuse, the case for requiring advance procedural safeguards would be strong indeed. But here we deal with a punishment paddling within that tradition, and the question is whether the common-law remedies are adequate to afford due process.

The concept that reasonable corporal punishment in school is justifiable continues to be recognized in the laws of most States.

. . . .

This is not to say that the child's interest in procedural safeguards is insubstantial. The school disciplinary process is not "a totally accurate, unerring process, never mistaken and never unfair. . . ." *Goss v. Lopez*, 419 U.S. 565 (1975). In any deliberate infliction of corporal punishment on a child who is restrained for that purpose, there is some risk that the intrusion on the child's liberty will be unjustified and therefore unlawful. In these circumstances the child has a strong interest in procedural safeguards that minimize the risk of wrongful punishment and provide for the resolution of disputed questions of justification.

We turn now to a consideration of the safeguards that are available under applicable Florida law.

Florida has continued to recognize, and indeed has strengthened by statute, the common-law right of a child not to be subjected to excessive corporal punishment in school. Under Florida law the teacher and principal of the school decide in the first instance whether corporal punishment is reasonably necessary under the circumstances in order to discipline a child who has misbehaved. But they must exercise prudence and restraint. For Florida has preserved the traditional judicial proceedings for determining whether the punishment was justified. If the punishment inflicted is later found to have been excessive not reasonably believed at the time to be necessary for the child's discipline or training the school authorities inflicting it may be held liable in damages to the child and, if malice is shown, they may be subject to criminal penalties.

Although students have testified in this case to specific instances of abuse, there is every reason to believe that such mistreatment is an aberration. . . . In the ordinary case, a disciplinary paddling neither threatens seriously to violate any substantive rights nor condemns the child "to suffer grievous loss of any kind."

In those cases where severe punishment is contemplated, the available civil and criminal sanctions for abuse considered in light of the openness of the school environment afford significant protection against unjustified corporal punishment. Teachers and school authorities are unlikely to inflict corporal punishment unnecessarily or excessively when a possible consequence of doing so is the institution of civil or criminal proceedings against them.

It still may be argued, of course, that the child's liberty interest would be better protected if the common-law remedies were supplemented by the administrative safeguards of prior notice and a hearing.

. . . .

But even if the need for advance procedural safeguards were clear, the question would remain whether the incremental benefit could justify the cost. Acceptance of petitioners' claims would work a transformation in the law governing corporal punishment in Florida and most other States. Given the impracticability of formulating a rule of procedural due process that varies with the severity of the particular imposition, the prior hearing petitioners seek would have to precede any paddling, however moderate or trivial.

Such a universal constitutional requirement would significantly burden the use of corporal punishment as a disciplinary measure.

. . . .

Elimination or curtailment of corporal punishment would be welcomed by many as a societal advance. But when such a policy choice may result from this Court's determination of an asserted right to due process, rather than from the normal processes of community debate and legislative action, the societal costs cannot be dismissed as insubstantial. We are reviewing here a legislative judgment, rooted in history and reaffirmed in the laws of many States, that corporal punishment serves important educational interests. This judgment must be viewed in light of the disciplinary problems common-place in the schools. As noted in *Goss v. Lopez*, 419 U.S., at 580, 95 S. Ct., at 739: "Events calling for discipline are frequent occurrences and sometimes require immediate, effective action." Assessment of the need for, and the appropriate means of maintaining, school discipline is committed generally to the discretion of school authorities subject to state law. "[T]he Court has repeatedly emphasized the need for affirming the comprehensive authority of the States and of school officials, consistent with fundamental constitutional safeguards, to prescribe and control conduct in the schools." *Tinker v. Des Moines School Dist.*, 393 U.S. 503, 507 (1969).

Petitioners cannot prevail on either of the theories before us in this case. The Eighth Amendment's prohibition against cruel and unusual punishment is inapplicable to school paddlings, and the Fourteenth Amendment's requirement of procedural due process is satisfied by Florida's preservation of common-law constraints and remedies. . . . Affirmed.

Fee v. Herndon

900 F.2d 804 (5th Cir. 1990)

The court rules that a student cannot bring a substantive due process claim for corporal punishment when sufficient state common law claims exist.

Jerry E. Smith, Circuit Judge

A sixth grade special-education student became disruptive during classroom instruction, prompting the use of corporal punishment by the school's principal to restore discipline. The parents, Ronald and Nancy Fee, maintain that the principal beat their emotionally disturbed child so excessively, however, that the student was forced to remain in psychiatric rehabilitation for months. The parents further allege that they incurred large medical costs as a consequence of the hospitalization.

The plaintiffs commenced this action pursuant to 42 U.S.C. § 1983 against the school district and various educators, averring that the fourteenth amendment's substantive due process guarantee operates to ban excessive corporal punishment in public schools. Pendent state-law tort claims were attached to this civil rights suit to raise charges of negligence and excessive force. Indisputably, however, state remedies-both criminal and civil-are available in Texas and proscribe the excessive use of corporal punishment against students, including emotionally handicapped children. That being so, our precedents instruct that the substantive component of the due process clause, though selectively applied in other contexts, is inoperative under the facts herein presented.

We adhere to this circuit's rule that no arbitrary state action exists, by definition, where states affirmatively impose reasonable limitations upon corporal punishment and provide adequate criminal or civil remedies for departures from such laws. Accordingly, we conclude that defendants here, all of whom allegedly acted in contravention of Texas's criminal or civil laws, have not implicated federal substantive due process considerations, irrespective of the argued capriciousness of the corporal punishment imposed. Thus, federal constitutional relief is not among the plaintiffs' available remedies, and consequently we affirm.

Tracy Fee attended special-education classes within the defendant Dickinson Independent School District. The few relevant facts not disputed by the litigants can be reduced succinctly to the following: (1) Tracy attended sixth grade at a public school within the district; (2) he had a documented history of aggressive behavioral problems; (3) he attended special classes for emotionally handicapped children; and (4) he received corporal punishment from the school's principal after his teacher sent him to the principal's office for misbehaving in class. Excluding this narrow area of accord, the facts are dramatically at odds.

. . . .

The Fees allege that Tracy's injuries first became evident to them shortly after his return from school, where he complained of pain and having been beaten by the principal. They called the sheriff's department, and a police officer took pictures of the welts and scrapes on the child's body. The sheriff's department thereafter investigated the incident, but no criminal action was instituted against any defendant.

....

The Fees filed a section 1983 action against Tracy's principal and teacher, the school district, and Dickinson's superintendent and trustees....

....

"Paddling of recalcitrant children has long been an accepted method of promoting good behavior and instilling notions of responsibility and decorum into the mischievous heads of school children." *Ingraham v. Wright*, 525 F.2d 909, 917 (5th Cir. 1976) (en banc), *aff'd*, 430 U.S. 651 (1977). This common law principle, in fact, predates the American Revolution. However, coincidently with the genesis of corporal punishment, reasonable limits traditionally have been imposed upon student discipline so as not to give teachers a license to commit state-sanctioned child abuse. Specifically, post-punishment civil or criminal remedies have targeted public school teachers who departed from the disciplinary norms defined by statute or the common law.

This dispute presents the question of whether the federal Constitution independently shields public school students from excessive discipline, irrespective of state-law safeguards. In *Ingraham*, the Supreme Court declared that twenty swats to a student, which removed him from school for days with bruises and disabled his arm for a week, did not violate *procedural* due process guarantees. That is, while "corporal punishment in public schools implicates a constitutionally protected liberty interest," the state may impose sufficient post-punishment safeguards to satisfy procedural due process concerns, Unfortunately, the *Ingraham* Court declined to address whether teacher discipline can be so capricious as to violate the amorphous substantive due process guarantees inherent in the fourteenth amendment.

We have stated that corporal punishment in public schools "is a deprivation of substantive due process when it is arbitrary, capricious, or wholly unrelated to the legitimate state goal of maintaining an atmosphere conducive to learning." Thus, *reasonable* corporal punishment is not at odds with the fourteenth amendment and does not constitute arbitrary state action. Consistently with this caselaw, Texas has authorized educators to impose a *reasonable* measure of corporal punishment upon students when necessary to maintain school discipline, and the state affords students post-punishment criminal or civil remedies if teachers are unfaithful to this obligation.

Our precedents dictate that injuries sustained incidentally to corporal punishment, irrespective of the severity of these injuries or the sensitivity of the student, do not implicate the due process clause *if* the forum state affords adequate post-punishment civil or criminal remedies for the student to vindicate legal transgressions. The rationale for this rule, quite simply, is that such states have provided all the process constitutionally due. Specifically, states that affirmatively proscribe and remedy mistreatment of students by educators do not, by definition, act "arbitrarily," a necessary predicate for substantive due process relief. That is to say, the Constitution is not a criminal or civil code to be invoked invariably for the crimes or torts of state educators who act in contravention of the very laws designed to thwart abusive disciplinarians.

In *Cunningham v. Beavers*, 858 F.2d 269 (5th Cir. 1988), *cert. denied*, 489 U.S. 1067 (1989), a six-year-old kindergarten student received a total of five paddle swats, causing severe bruising on her buttocks. The child missed six days of school, and her injuries were deemed to be abusive by social welfare workers and her doctor. We held that no deprivation of substantive due process had occurred, because Texas provides adequate state criminal and tort remedies for any excessive punishment that may have been imposed upon the student. *Cunningham*, we conclude, is dispositive here.

In this case, the student's mother authorized the use of corporal punishment against Tracy to cure his disruptive classroom behavior.[7] The litigants agree that the principal and the teacher attempted to discipline the child for his in-class disruptions and that official school policy tolerates only reasonable corporal punishment. Although the injuries are alleged to have been severe, the student's substantive due process guarantees have not been violated under the rationale of *Cunningham*, as Texas does not allow teachers to abuse students with impunity and provides civil and criminal relief against educators who breach statutory and common law standards of conduct. Although the sheriff's department investigated the charges raised, no criminal prosecution commenced here; however, the possibility of state-law civil relief remains.

This circuit has consistently avoided any inquiry into whether five, ten, or twenty swats invokes the fourteenth amendment:

> We think it a misuse of our judicial power to determine, for example, whether a teacher has acted arbitrarily in paddling a particular child for certain behavior or whether in a particular instance of misconduct five licks would have been a more appropriate punishment than ten licks. We note again the possibility of a civil or criminal action in state court against a teacher who has excessively punished a child.

Ingraham, 525 F.2d at 917. Thus, we have avoided having student discipline, a matter of public policy, shaped by the individual predilections of federal jurists rather than by state lawmakers and local officials. We find no constitutional warrant to usurp classroom discipline where states, like Texas, have taken affirmative steps to protect their students from overzealous disciplinarians.

. . . .

7. [FN6] We note, however, that parental consent to corporal punishment is not constitutionally required. *Ingraham*, 430 U.S. at 662 n. 22, 97 S. Ct. at 1408 n. 22 (citing *Baker v. Owen*, 423 U.S. 907, 96 S. Ct. 210, 46 L. Ed. 2d 137 (1975)).

We harbor no opinion as to the severity of the student's injuries in this case. We hold only that since Texas has civil and criminal laws in place to proscribe educators from abusing their charges, and further provides adequate post-punishment relief in favor of students, no substantive due process concerns are implicated because no arbitrary state action exists. Accordingly, we affirm the dismissal of the section 1983 claims asserted against all defendants.

Hall v. Tawney

621 F.2d 607 (4th Cir. 1980)

The court rules that the parents do not have a substantive due process right to refuse to allow schools to paddle their child, but the harm done to the child by the corporal punishment may violate substantive due process regardless of the availability of state common law claims.

James Dickson Phillips, Circuit Judge:

....

The action arose from an incident occurring on December 6, 1974 in which Naomi, then a student at Left Hand Grade School in West Virginia, was paddled by a teacher in that school.... On this appeal, conceding that Ingraham has effectively foreclosed their procedural due process and cruel and unusual punishment claims, plaintiffs press only the substantive due process claims of Naomi and of the parents respectively. We take these in reverse order.

Plaintiffs argue that Naomi's paddling violated the right of her parents to determine the means by which Naomi could be disciplined. They had told school officials, including Tawney, that they did not want Naomi corporally punished.

This issue was decided adversely to plaintiff's claim in *Baker v. Owen*, 395 F. Supp. 294 (M.D.N.C.) (three judge court), *aff'd*, 423 U.S. 907, 96 S. Ct. 210, 46 L. Ed. 2d 137 (1975). There the plaintiff parents had told officials that they did not want their child spanked. Despite this he was given two licks with a drawer divider slightly thicker than a ruler. The court agreed that the parental rights involved came within the protection of the Constitution, but held that they were overborne by the countervailing interest of the state:

> [O]pinion on the merits of the rod is far from unanimous. On such a controversial issue, where we would be acting more from personal preference than from constitutional command, we cannot allow the wishes of a parent to restrict school officials' discretion in deciding the methods to be used in accomplishing the not just legitimate, but essential purpose of maintaining discipline.

Id. at 301.

....

Here plaintiffs allege that the corporal punishment inflicted was not "reasonable," but "severe." *See Baker*, 395 F. Supp. at 301. We do not believe, however, that any constitutional right of parents to choose the means by which their child should be disciplined can be made to turn on the severity of the punishment. The reasons advanced in *Baker* for finding no parental constitutional rights implicated apply alike to all degrees of punishment.

We therefore conclude that the parents' claim was rightly dismissed.

In Ingraham, the Supreme Court denied review to the question, "Is the infliction of severe corporal punishment upon public school students arbitrary, capricious and unrelated to achieving any legitimate educational purpose and therefore violative of the Due Process Clause of the Fourteenth Amendment?" Therefore, the Court said, "[w]e have no occasion in this case . . . to decide whether or under what circumstances corporal punishment of a public school child may give rise to an independent federal cause of action to vindicate substantive rights under the Due Process Clause."

. . . .

That question, unresolved and reserved in *Ingraham* is squarely presented for decision on this appeal. For reasons that follow we conclude that there may be circumstances under which specific corporal punishment administered by state school officials gives rise to an independent federal cause of action to vindicate substantive due process rights under 42 U.S.C. § 1983.

. . . .

We start with the proposition that disciplinary corporal punishment does not per se violate the public school child's substantive due process rights. This is of course implicit in *Ingraham*'s holding that the protectible liberty interest there recognized admits of some corporal punishment, which in turn is based upon a recognition that corporal punishment as such is reasonably related to a legitimate state interest in maintaining order in the schools the critical inquiry in substantive due process analysis. Appellants here concede this much, but contend that the constitutional right is violated at the point where a specific punishment exceeds in severity that reasonably related to the interest.

. . . .

It is of course settled that relief under § 1983 does not depend upon the unavailability of state remedies, but is supplementary to them. Federal and state rights may of course exist in parallel, and federal courts may not avoid the obligation to define and vindicate the federal constitutional right merely because of a coincidence of related rights and remedies in the federal and state systems. Attendant doctrinal difficulties and implications for docket burdens have simply to be accepted.

. . . .

We turn therefore to definition of the constitutionally protected substantive due process right we consider to exist here in addition to the substantive right and remedies provided by state law. First off, the substantive content is quite different than that defining state civil and criminal remedies. Mindful that not every state law tort becomes a federally cognizable "constitutional tort" under § 1983 simply because it is committed by a state official, we do not find the substance of this right in the parallel right defined by state assault and battery law. Instead, we find it grounded in those constitutional rights given protection under the rubric of substantive due process in such cases as *Rochin v. California*, 342 U.S. 165, 72 S. Ct. 205, 96 L. Ed. 183 (1952) (forcible use of stomach pump by police); *Jenkins v. Averett*, 424 F.2d 1228 (4th Cir. 1970) ("reckless" pistol shooting of suspect by police); and *Johnson v. Glick*, 481 F.2d 1028 (2d Cir. 1973) (unprovoked beating of pre-trial detainee by guard):

> the right to be free of state intrusions into realms of personal privacy and bodily security through means so brutal, demeaning, and harmful as literally to shock the conscience of a court. The existence of this right to ultimate bodily security the most fundamental aspect of personal privacy is unmistakably established in our constitutional decisions as an attribute of the ordered liberty that is the concern of substantive due process. Numerous cases in a variety of contexts recognize it as a last line of defense against those literally outrageous abuses of official power whose very variety makes formulation of a more precise standard impossible. Clearly recognized in persons charged with or suspected of crime and in the custody of police officers, we simply do not see how we can fail also to recognize it in public school children under the disciplinary control of public school teachers. Difficult as may be application of the resulting rule of constitutional law in the public school disciplinary context, it would seem no more difficult than in related realms already well established. In any event it is a difficulty that may not be avoided in the face of allegations or proof sufficient to raise the possibility that such an intolerable abuse of official power no matter how aberrant and episodic has occurred through disciplinary corporal punishment.

In the context of disciplinary corporal punishment in the public schools, we emphasize once more that the substantive due process claim is quite different than a claim of assault and battery under state tort law. In resolving a state tort claim, decision may well turn on whether "ten licks rather than five" were excessive, so that line-drawing this refined may be required. But substantive due process is concerned with violations of personal rights of privacy and bodily security of so different an order of magnitude that inquiry in a particular case simply need not start at the level of concern these distinctions imply.

. . . .

As in the cognate police brutality cases, the substantive due process inquiry in school corporal punishment cases must be whether the force applied caused injury so severe, was so disproportionate to the need presented, and was so inspired by malice or sadism rather than a merely careless or unwise excess of zeal that it amounted to a brutal and inhumane abuse of official power literally shocking to the conscience. Not every violation of state tort and criminal assault laws will be a violation of this constitutional right, but some of course may.

. . . .

In ruling on the defendant's motion to dismiss, the district court considered Naomi's substantive due process claim only to the point of concluding, in reliance upon the Fifth Circuit's decision in Ingraham and the Supreme Court's denial of review on the issue, that because corporal punishment per se did not violate substantive due process no cognizable claim was stated under 42 U.S.C. § 1983. It did not analyze the allegations of the complaint to determine whether a cognizable claim based on the specific incident alleged might have been stated, presumably again relying on the Fifth Circuit's view in Ingraham that where state law provides adequate substantive remedies, merely episodic punishments that might violate state law do not give rise to a federal cause of action under § 1983. As our opinion indicates, we disagree with that conclusion and have held instead that a cognizable claim based upon an episodic application of force not authorized by state law or policy may be stated under the substantive due process standard here

When we look to the complaint we cannot say that under that substantive standard it fails to state a claim for relief against Tawney and Claywell, the direct participants in the December 6 paddling incident. Of course, upon full development of a summary judgment or trial record, it may appear that the actual facts of the incident do not support a claim of substantive due process violation. But we cannot say from the bare pleading allegations that "it appears beyond doubt that the plaintiff can prove no set of facts in support of [her] claim which would entitle [her] to relief."

Though admittedly employing conclusory allegations in describing the incident, the complaint in pertinent part stated that Tawney "without apparent provocation" struck the minor plaintiff "with a homemade paddle, made of hard thick rubber and about five inches in width . . . across her left hip and thigh"; that in an ensuing struggle with the plaintiff he "violently shoved the minor plaintiff against a large stationary desk"; that he then "vehemently grasped and twisted the plaintiff's right arm and pushed her into" the presence of the defendant Claywell who then granted permission to Tawney to "again paddle the minor plaintiff"; that "the minor plaintiff was again stricken repeatedly and violently by the defendant Tawney with the rubber paddle, under the supervision and approval of defendant Claywell"; that as a result of this application of force "the minor plaintiff was taken that afternoon to the emergency room of (a nearby hospital) where she was admitted and kept for a period of ten (10) days for the treatment of traumatic injury to the soft tissue of the left hip and thigh, trauma to the skin and soft tissue of the left thigh, and trauma to the soft tissue with ecchyniosis of the left buttock"; that for the injuries inflicted the minor plaintiff was "receiving the treatment of specialists for possible permanent injuries to her lower back and spine and has suffered and will continue to suffer severe pain and discomfort, etc." There were also allegations respecting Tawney's demonstrated attitude toward Naomi and other student members of her family from which malicious motivation might be inferred if the events alleged were proven as fact.

As we have indicated, when exposed to the searching light of full discovery and other pre-trial procedures or eventually, if need be, to the testing of proof on trial, these bare allegations may be exposed as merely that in whole or substantial part, and the actual facts justifying a finding of substantive due process violation simply not present.8 We hold here only that they sufficed to state a claim for relief against Tawney and Claywell under 42 U.S.C. § 1983. Accordingly it was error to dismiss the action against these two defendants as to the minor plaintiff's substantive due process claim.

. . . .

Post Problem Discussion

1. As the Fourth Circuit noted in *Hall, Ingraham* was preceded by *Baker v. Owens*, where the United States Supreme Court affirmed without comment the decision of the District Court of North Carolina, which upheld the spanking of sixth-grader over the objection of the student's mother. The court stated that the "fourteenth amendment liberty embraces the right of parents generally to control means of discipline of their children, but the state has a countervailing interest in the maintenance of order in the schools, in this case sufficient to sustain the right of teachers and school officials to administer reasonable corporal punishment for disciplinary purposes." *Baker v. Owen*, 395 F. Supp. 294, 296 (M.D.N.C. 1975), *aff'd*, 423 U.S. 907 (1975).

Hall relied on *Baker* to reject the parents' substantive due process claim of having a right to refuse to allow the school to paddle their child at all. What do you think about the *Hall* court's decision on that issue? Do parents who do not want their child paddled have any recourse if the school paddles the student anyway?

2. The Fifth Circuit appears to be the only circuit to follow the approach noted in *Fee*. Other circuits have either followed *Hall*, or some modification of the standards noted in *Hall*. For example, in *Wise v. Pea Ridge Sch. Dist.*, 855 F.2d 560 (8th Cir. 1988), the Eighth Circuit set forth some slightly different standards than *Hall* stating:

> We believe that a substantive due process claim in the context of disciplinary corporal punishment is to be considered under the following test: 1) the need for the application of corporal punishment; 2) the relationship between the need and the amount of punishment administered; 3) the extent of injury inflicted; and 4) whether the punishment was administered in a good faith effort to maintain discipline or maliciously and sadistically for the very purpose of causing harm.

Is *Wise* a better approach than *Hall*, or are the differences in the standards of little consequence? Does the fact that most circuits have not followed the Fifth Circuit change your view of which approach to adopt in this problem? Why or why not?

§ 8.05 Academic Discipline

Discipline for behavior can have academic consequences. For example, a student who is suspended may miss key assignments or tests that cannot be made up. Issues also arise where discipline is directly related to academic content or work; for example, situations of cheating or plagiarism. *See, e.g.*, *Napolitano v. Trustees of Princeton University*, 453 A.2d 263 (N.J. Super. Ct. App. Div. 1982) (upholding finding that student had plagiarized and withholding of her degree for a year). So too, students are dismissed from school, particularly in higher education, for failure to meet academic standards. Where academic discipline claims are raised, they typically are grounded in both substantive and procedural due process. Courts tend to be strong in their decisions to defer to the school's judgment and procedures in academic situations. *See, e.g.*, *Megenity v. Stenger*, 27 F.3d 1120 (6th Cir. 1994) (upholding a law school student's dismissal for failure to meet academic standards).

In *Board of Curators of Univ. of Mo. v. Horowitz*, 435 U.S. 78, 90 (1978), a leading case on this topic, which involved dismissal from medical school for failure to meet academic requirements, the United States Supreme Court declined to impose further procedural due process requirements on the University and observed:

> The decision to dismiss respondent, by comparison, rested on the academic judgment of school officials that she did not have the necessary clinical ability to perform adequately as a medical doctor and was making insufficient progress toward that goal. Such a judgment is by its nature more subjective and evaluative than the typical factual questions presented in the average disciplinary decision. Like the decision of an individual professor as to the proper grade for a student in his course, the determination whether to dismiss a student for academic reasons requires an expert evaluation of cumulative information and is not readily adapted to the procedural tools of judicial or administrative decisionmaking.
>
> Under such circumstances, we decline to ignore the historic judgment of educators and thereby formalize the academic dismissal process by requiring a hearing.

Problem 4: The Guitarists

Note: This problem is taken in major part (including quotation without specific attribution) from a real case. Names have been changed, as have some facts.

During the 2006–07 school year, Bennie Rodriguez and Frank Smith were both budding musicians who participated as guitar players in the high school band program at Great High School. A Band class requirement was to perform at various school-wide events, including home basketball games. Great High School's grading policy for Band, provided below, was established by the Band Director and assigned a certain number of points to the different components of the course.

The Band Director specifically forbade guitar solos during the performances. In direct defiance of those rules, and their teacher's explicit orders, Rodriguez and

Smith played two unauthorized guitar pieces (instrumentals, with no words) at a February 10 Band program during a home basketball game. As they were doing so, the Band Director was shouting at them to stop, but they ignored her.

Rodriguez and Smith contend that their actions were a form of protest against the school's rumored decision to remove guitars from Band. They were not awarded any performance points for the February 10 event, and the Band Director referred the matter to the principal, who decided that Rodriguez and Smith had been guilty of disrespect to faculty and staff, which is also a violation of school rules. Under the Great High rules, a student committing a violation could be removed from class for either academic misconduct (e.g., failure to complete homework) or nonacademic misconduct (e.g., possession of tobacco products).

As a penalty, the principal decided to remove the two students from Band class for the remainder of the school year, and to prohibit them from attending any more home basketball games for that year. As a result of these punishments, both received final grades of F for the course. Both students graduated. Rodriguez would have graduated with honors, but for the F in Band.

What is the strongest argument Rodriguez and Smith can make to have their punishment overturned and expunged from their records? Do the Illinois statutes or regulations help them? Do they have viable constitutional claims? Did they get due process?

Problem Materials

✓ *Regents of the University of Michigan v. Ewing*, 474 U.S. 214 (1985)

✓ IL statute, 105 ILCS 5/10-20

✓ IL regulations, 23 Ill. Adm. Code 1.280

✓ Great High Handbook

✓ Great High School Policy

Regents of the University of Michigan v. Ewing

474 U.S. 214 (1985)

> *The Court upholds the university's dismissal of a nursing student where "Considerations of profound importance counsel restrained judicial review of the substance of academic decisions."*

Justice Stevens delivered the opinion of the Court. Justice Powell filed a concurring opinion.

Respondent Scott Ewing was dismissed from the University of Michigan after failing an important written examination. The question presented is whether the University's action deprived Ewing of property without due process of law because its refusal to allow him to retake the examination was an arbitrary departure from the University's past practice. The Court of Appeals held that his constitutional rights were violated. We disagree.

In the fall of 1975 Ewing enrolled in a special 6-year program of study, known as "Inteflex," offered jointly by the undergraduate college and the Medical School. An undergraduate degree and a medical degree are awarded upon successful completion of the program. In order to qualify for the final two years of the Inteflex program, which consist of clinical training at hospitals affiliated with the University, the student must successfully complete four years of study including both premedical courses and courses in the basic medical sciences. The student must also pass the "NBME Part I"—a 2-day written test administered by the National Board of Medical Examiners.

In the spring of 1981, after overcoming certain academic and personal difficulties, Ewing successfully completed the courses prescribed for the first four years of the Inteflex program and thereby qualified to take the NBME Part I. Ewing failed five of the seven subjects on that examination, receiving a total score of 235 when the passing score was 345. (A score of 380 is required for state licensure and the national mean is 500.) Ewing received the lowest score recorded by an Inteflex student in the brief history of that program.

On July 24, 1981, the Promotion and Review Board individually reviewed the status of several students in the Inteflex program. After considering Ewing's record in some detail, the nine members of the Board in attendance voted unanimously to drop him from registration in the program.

In response to a written request from Ewing, the Board reconvened a week later to reconsider its decision. Ewing appeared personally and explained why he believed that his score on the test did not fairly reflect his academic progress or potential. After reconsidering the matter, the nine voting members present unanimously reaffirmed the prior action to drop Ewing from registration in the program.

At this and later meetings Ewing excused his NBME Part I failure because his mother had suffered a heart attack 18 months before the examination; his girlfriend broke up with him about six months before the examination; his work on an essay for a contest had taken too much time; his makeup examination in pharmacology was administered just before the NBME Part I; and his inadequate preparation caused him to panic during the examination.

In August, Ewing appealed the Board's decision to the Executive Committee of the Medical School. After giving Ewing an opportunity to be heard in person, the Executive Committee unanimously approved a motion to deny his appeal for a leave of absence status that would enable him to retake Part I of the NBME examination. In the following year, Ewing reappeared before the Executive Committee on two separate occasions, each time unsuccessfully seeking readmission to the Medical School. On August 19, 1982, he commenced this litigation in the United States District Court for the Eastern District of Michigan.

Ewing's complaint against the Regents of the University of Michigan asserted a right to retake the NBME Part I test.... As a matter of federal law, Ewing alleged that he had a property interest in his continued enrollment in the Inteflex program and that his dismissal was arbitrary and capricious, violating his "substantive due process rights" guaranteed by the Fourteenth Amendment and entitling him to relief under 42 U.S.C. § 1983.

....

The Court of Appeals reversed the dismissal of Ewing's federal constitutional claim. We granted the University's petition for certiorari to consider whether the Court of Appeals had misapplied the doctrine of "substantive due process." We now reverse.

In *Board of Curators, Univ. of Mo. v. Horowitz*, 435 U.S. 78, 91–92 (1978), we assumed, without deciding, that federal courts can review an academic decision of a public educational institution under a substantive due process standard. In this case Ewing contends that such review is appropriate because he had a constitutionally protected property interest in his continued enrollment in the Inteflex program. But remembering Justice Brandeis' admonition not to "'formulate a rule of constitutional law broader than is required by the precise facts to which it is to be applied,'" *Ashwander v. TVA*, 297 U.S. 288, 347 (1936) (concurring opinion), we again conclude, as we did in *Horowitz*, that the precise facts disclosed by the record afford the most appropriate basis for decision. We therefore accept the University's invitation to "assume the existence of a constitutionally protectible property right in [Ewing's] continued enrollment," and hold that even if Ewing's assumed property interest gave rise to a substantive right under the Due Process Clause to continued enrollment free from arbitrary state action, the facts of record disclose no such action.

As a preliminary matter, it must be noted that any substantive constitutional protection against arbitrary dismissal would not necessarily give Ewing a right to retake the NBME Part I. The constitutionally protected interest alleged by Ewing in his complaint and found by the courts below, derives from Ewing's implied contract right to continued enrollment free from arbitrary dismissal. The District Court did not find that Ewing had any separate right to retake the exam....

We recognize, of course, that "mutually explicit understandings" may operate to create property interests. *Perry v. Sindermann*, 408 U.S., at 601. But such understandings or tacit agreements must support "a legitimate claim of entitlement" under "'an independent source such as state law....'" *Id.*, at 602, n. 7 (quoting *Board of Regents v. Roth*, 408 U.S., at 577). The District Court, it bears emphasis, held that the University's liberal retesting custom gave rise to no state-law entitlement to retake the NBME Part I....

It is important to remember that this is not a case in which the procedures used by the University were unfair in any respect; quite the contrary is true. Nor can the Regents be accused of concealing nonacademic or constitutionally impermissible reasons for expelling Ewing; the District Court found that the Regents acted in good faith.

Ewing's claim, therefore, must be that the University misjudged his fitness to remain a student in the Inteflex program. The record unmistakably demonstrates, however, that the faculty's decision was made conscientiously and with careful deliberation, based on an evaluation of the entirety of Ewing's academic career. When judges are asked to review the substance of a genuinely academic decision, such as this one, they should show great respect for the faculty's professional judgment. Plainly, they may not override it unless it is such a substantial departure from accepted academic norms as to demonstrate that the person or committee responsible did not actually exercise professional judgment. *Cf. Youngberg v. Romeo*, 457 U.S. 307, 323 (1982).

Considerations of profound importance counsel restrained judicial review of the substance of academic decisions.

....

Added to our concern for lack of standards is a reluctance to trench on the prerogatives of state and local educational institutions and our responsibility to safeguard their academic freedom, "a special concern of the First Amendment." *Keyishian v. Board of Regents*, 385 U.S. 589, 603 (1967). If a "federal court is not the appropriate forum in which to review the multitude of personnel decisions that are made daily by public agencies," *Bishop v. Wood*, 426 U.S. 341, 349 (1976), far less is it suited to evaluate the substance of the multitude of academic decisions that are made daily by faculty members of public educational institutions—decisions that require "an expert evaluation of cumulative information and [are] not readily adapted to the procedural tools of judicial or administrative decisionmaking." *Board of Curators, Univ. of Mo. v. Horowitz*, 435 U.S., at 89–90.

This narrow avenue for judicial review precludes any conclusion that the decision to dismiss Ewing from the Inteflex program was such a substantial departure from accepted academic norms as to demonstrate that the faculty did not exercise professional judgment.

....

The judgment of the Court of Appeals is reversed, and the case is remanded for proceedings consistent with this opinion.

Illinois State Statutes

§ 105 ILCS 5/10-20. Powers of school board

Sec. 10-20. Powers of school board. The school board has the powers enumerated in the Sections of this Article following this Section. This enumeration of powers is not exclusive, but the board may exercise all other powers not inconsistent with this Act that may be requisite or proper for the maintenance, operation, and development of any school or schools under the jurisdiction of the board. This grant of powers does not release a school board from any duty imposed upon it by this Act or any other law.

§ 105 ILCS 5/10-20.5. Rules

Sec. 10-20.5. Rules. To adopt and enforce all necessary rules for the management and government of the public schools of their district. Rules adopted by the school board shall be filed for public inspection in the administrative office of the district.

§ 105 ILCS 5/10-20.9a. Final Grade; Promotion

Sec. 10-20.9a. Final Grade; Promotion. (a) Teachers shall administer the approved marking system or other approved means of evaluating pupil progress. The teacher shall maintain the responsibility and right to determine grades and other evaluations of students within the grading policies of the district based upon his or her professional judgment of available criteria pertinent to any given subject area or activity for which he or she is responsible. District policy shall provide the procedure and reasons by and for which a grade may be changed; provided that no grade or evaluation shall be changed without notification to the teacher concerning the nature and reasons for such change. If such a change is made, the person making the change shall assume such responsibility for determining the grade or evaluation, and shall initial such change.

(b) School districts shall not promote students to the next higher grade level based upon age or any other social reasons not related to the academic performance of the students. On or before September 1, 1998, school boards shall adopt and enforce a policy on promotion as they deem necessary to ensure that students meet local goals and objectives and can perform at the expected grade level prior to promotion. Decisions to promote or retain students in any classes shall be based on successful completion of the curriculum, attendance, performance based on Illinois Goals and Assessment Program tests, the Iowa Test of Basic Skills, or other testing or any other criteria established by the school board. Students determined by the local district to not qualify for promotion to the next higher grade shall be provided remedial assistance, which may include, but shall not be limited to, a summer bridge program of no less than 90 hours, tutorial sessions, increased or concentrated instructional time, modifications to instructional materials, and retention in grade.

Illinois Administrative Code

23 Ill. Adm. Code 1.280, § 1.280 Discipline

Section 24-24 of the School Code provides for teachers, other certificated educational employees and persons providing a related service for or with respect to a student as determined by the board of education to maintain discipline in the schools.

a) The board of education shall establish and maintain a parent-teacher advisory committee as provided in Section 10-20.14 of the School Code.

b) The board of education shall establish a policy on the administration of discipline in accordance with the requirements of Sections 10-20.14 and 24-24 of the

School Code and disseminate that policy as provided in Section 10-20.14 of the School Code. . . .

School Handbook: Conduct/Discipline

(slightly amended, but taken from Ridge High School)[8]

Student Behavior Expectations

Expectation 1—Students are expected to treat their families, peers, teachers, supervisors, parents, and all other people with respect and dignity at all times.

Expectation 2—Students are expected to come to school and all classes on time, to be prepared with materials and assignments, and to pursue their learning activities at the highest level of accomplishment.

Expectation 3—Students are expected to solve their problems with others in a mature manner, avoiding fighting, threats, and/or any type of intimidating behavior.

Expectation 4—Students are expected to treat the building, grounds, and the entire contents of the school with respect, care, and in a manner that demonstrates they are preserving them for future students.

Expectation 5—Students are expected to demonstrate through their academic achievement and behavior that they attend a school where learning is the top priority.

Expectation 6—Students are expected to conduct themselves in such a manner as not to disturb other students or classes as they move through the building.

Gross Disobedience or Misconduct

In addition to any other rules, regulations, or policies heretofore adopted by the Board of Education pertaining to pupil conduct or discipline, any pupil of this school district may be suspended or expelled for, but not limited to, any of the following actions which are considered to be examples of gross disobedience or misconduct:

1. General misbehavior, blatant refusal to follow instructions of the teachers/administrators; insubordination, racial slurs, insolence to school personnel or other person in authority, use of threats to the safety of persons or property in and about the school premises, assault, theft, extortion, battery, or fighting.
2. Use of obscene, vulgar, or profane language or gestures, verbal abuse, any attempt to intimidate or threaten school personnel or other students.
3. Defacing, damaging, or destroying school property including setting of fires, sounding of false fire alarms, breaking windows, discharge of fireworks or other explosive devices, or threats or attempts to do so.

---

8. Ridgewood High school: Handbook: Conduct/Discipline, www.ridgenet.org/page.php?page=handbook-conduct#student-behavior-expectations (last visited April 7, 2009).

4. The possession, use, or display, of any dangerous or deadly weapon or instrument which resembles a dangerous or deadly weapon.
5. Possession, attempted sale, distribution, or use of tobacco, alcohol, inhalants, narcotics, steroids, look-alike drugs, or other controlled substances or related paraphernalia, on the school grounds, in the school building, or at any school-sponsored activity on or off campus.
6. Conduct in violation of the Criminal Code, or of the laws of the United States, the State of Illinois, or of the Village of Norridge.
7. Repeated incidents of misbehavior, including repeated refusal to comply with school rules, for example, missing Dean's detentions.
8. Disruptive behavior.
9. Truancy, i.e., absence from school or classes (class cuts) without valid cause during a school day or portion thereof even after "available supportive services" have been provided.
10. Acts which directly or indirectly jeopardize the education process or the health, safety, and welfare of school personnel or other students.
11. The possession or transmission of literature or illustrations which are obscene, vulgar or indecent, or which substantially disrupt the educational process.
12. Refusal or failure to proceed to Deans Office when requested.

Guidelines are indicators of a course of action. *Offenses are cumulative* and the administration may skip steps for a specific offense and take actions (including suspension or expulsion) more severe than those listed in the "Statement of Student Conduct Guidelines" if a student has previously violated school rules, regulations or policies.

Great High School Grading Policy

(as filed with the school principal and disseminated to each student in the class)

Every rehearsal, concert, etc. will be assigned a point value. Points will be awarded for presence at the event, appropriate dress, appropriate conduct, etc. Additionally, there will be at least two playing evaluations per quarter for points. The point scale will work as follows:

Daily Rehearsal: 5 points

Performances: 20 points

Playing Evaluations: 25 points

Your conduct at performances is expected to be of the highest standard. We want to look, sound and be professional at all times—anything less is unacceptable. Performance conduct that is not of the highest standard will be dealt with severely. Possible disciplinary actions *range from loss of all points for the performance to lowering of the final grade to dismissal from the band.*

Post Problem Discussion

1. Courts generally defer to school officials' academic decisions on plagiarism. Why do you suppose courts provide such deference to school officials in this area?[9]

2. When academic discipline issues arise in K-12 education, the principles suggested by *Ewing* apply. Do you think these standards are sufficient?

§ 8.06 Discipline for Off-Campus Conduct

School officials generally have the authority to discipline students for actions that occur at school, on the way to or from school, or at school related/sponsored events. *See, e.g., Morse v. Frederick*, 551 U.S. 393 (2007). The law is not as clear on whether school officials can discipline students for activities that occur outside of these parameters. There are a number of older cases that upheld very broad school discipline powers for out of school activities. Examples include students using profane language and fighting with other students when they were at home from school, *Deskins v. Gose*, 85 Mo. 485 (1885), a student using "saucy and disrespectful language" towards school officials when driving his father's cow by the school official's house, *Lander v. Seaver*, 32 Vt. 114 (1859), and a student being drunk and disorderly on the public streets on Christmas day (a school holiday), *Douglas v. Campbell*, 116 S.W. 211, 213 (Ark. 1909).

Over time, courts focused more on whether the out of school conduct impacted the school environment, or general welfare of the school, in some way. That narrowed the school's authority to discipline in some respects, as the analysis was whether there was a connection between the out of school behavior and in school affects, but courts still upheld student discipline for some off school activities. For example, in *R.R. v. Board of Educ. of Shore Reg'l High Sch. Dist.*, 263 A.2d 180 (N.J. Super. Ct. Ch. Div. 1970), a New Jersey court upheld the suspension of a student for fighting another student at the student's home noting:

> There can be no doubt that the establishment of an educational program requires rules and regulations necessary for the maintenance of an orderly instructional program and the creation of an educational environment conducive to learning. Such rules and regulations are equally necessary for the protection of public school students, faculty and property. The power of public school officials to expel or suspend a student is a necessary corollary for the enforcement of such rules and the maintenance of a safe and orderly educational environment conducive to learning. But public school officials cannot exercise this power where the activity which is the subject of the proposed suspension or expulsion does not materially and substantially

9. *See* Roger Billings, *Plagiarism in Academia and Beyond: What Is the Role of the Courts?*, 38 U.S.F. L. Rev. 391 (2004).

> interfere with the requirements of appropriate discipline in the operation of the school.
>
> In New Jersey public school officials have the authority to suspend or expel students for events happening out of school hours. This court is unable to find a New Jersey decision holding that school officials have the right to expel or suspend a pupil for conduct away from school grounds, but the better view is that school authorities have such a right where such is reasonably necessary for the student's physical or emotional safety and well-being, or for reasons relating to the safety and well-being of other students, teachers or public school property.

Similarly, in *Fenton v. Stear*, 423 F. Supp. 767, 772 (W.D. Pa. 1976), a district court in Pennsylvania upheld the discipline of a high school student who called a high school teacher a "prick" when he saw the teacher at a shopping mall. The court noted:

> It is our opinion that when a high school student refers to a high school teacher in a public place on a Sunday by a lewd and obscene name in such a loud voice that the teacher and others hear the insult it may be deemed a matter for discipline in the discretion of the school authorities. To countenance such student conduct even in a public place without imposing sanctions could lead to devastating consequences in the school.

Today, constitutional issues are frequently involved in disciplinary decisions for off-campus activities, and they influence the legal standards. Often, First Amendment standards come into play for off-campus activities, because the off-campus activities involve expression (like calling a principal a derogatory name on some social media platform). The First Amendment issues are discussed in more detail in Chapter 9. The following problem explores issues related to the school's authority to discipline for non-speech related, off-campus activities.

Problem 5: Ben and Clay's Off Campus Activities

Ben is the star quarterback on the Great Brook High School football team. He and his girlfriend Angela have a fight at school in the cafeteria. Clay, an honor student whom Ben frequently picks on at school, sees the argument. The next day, Clay asks Angela to go to a party with him over the weekend, and she agrees. When Ben finds out, he is furious and starts a shouting and shoving match with Clay at school, but they are separated by other students before any fighting occurs. At the party, Clay and Angela decide to make Ben jealous, so they have sex in one of the rooms at the party. Clay uses his cell phone camera to take pictures of them together naked. Clay then sends the pictures to Ben. Unbeknownst to Angela, Clay also sends the pictures to some of his friends, who send them to some of their friends. Before long, most of the students who attend Great Brook High School have seen the pictures.

The next day, Ben goes over to Clay's house and beats him up. The following day at school, Angela is approached by numerous students about the pictures. Some students have their cell phones at school with the pictures on them. Obviously upset, Angela tells the principal about the pictures, saying that she does not think she can continue to come to school if Clay remains at school. She asks the principal to expel Clay from school.

Meanwhile, Clay's parents contact the school about the injuries that Clay suffered when he was attacked by Ben. They express concern about Clay attending school if Ben is present. They ask the school principal to expel Ben.

The problem materials present cases with different approaches to discipline for off-campus activities. Review them and decide if the school can discipline Clay and/or Ben, and if your answer would differ if one court case versus another applied in your jurisdiction.

Assume that the New Town High School Discipline Policy in Problem 1 applies. For purposes of the problem, set aside any potential First Amendment issues, and any child pornography criminal issues.

Problem Materials

✓ New Town High School Discipline Policy in Problem 1

✓ *Smith v. Little Rock School District*, 582 F. Supp. 159 (E.D. Ark. 1984)

✓ *Nicholas B. v. School Commissioner of Worcester*, 587 N.E.2d 211 (Mass. 1992)

✓ *Galveston Independent School District v. Boothe*, 590 S.W.2d 553 (Tex. Civ. App. 1979)

✓ *Howard v. Colonial School District*, 621 A.2d 362 (Del. Super. Ct. 1992)

Smith v. Little Rock School District

582 F. Supp. 159 (E.D. Ark. 1984)

The court rules that the school may suspend a student for a shooting that occurred off-campus under a school policy that prohibits criminal acts committed away from school that may affect school climate.

Roy, District Judge.

This action is brought against the Little Rock School District, the Little Rock School Board, and various officials and administrator of the school system. Plaintiff is a black male, 19 years old, and a former eleventh grade student of Parkview High School, a part of the Little Rock School District.

His complaint requests injunctive and declaratory relief under Title 42, U.S.C., § 1983. Plaintiff alleges that on January 30, 1984, he was suspended from school for the purported violation of Rule No. 5 of the Little Rock School District Student Conduct Code, which reads as follows: "Criminal offenses committed away from school which may affect the school climate."

. . . .

Among other things, the plaintiff contends that Rule 5 gives him no notice as to what acts are detrimental to the school environment; that the school has no authority over his actions when he is outside the bounds of school property. He further contends that he has only been charged with a criminal offense, not found guilty, and that the school board by punishing him is preempting the role of the courts.

At the preliminary hearing the plaintiff admitted, "Yes, I shot Herbert Johnson," and that he used his own 357 Magnum pistol which he had in his pocket. Plaintiff has been charged with murder but it was stipulated that plaintiff had not been convicted of any criminal offense nor admitted that he was guilty of any offense.

The evidence reflected that the Board of Directors of the Little Rock School District ["Board"] made the following findings of fact at a hearing held on February 21, 1984: Plaintiff Gerry Smith fired a gun which caused the death of another person; and an unsafe situation could develop at Parkview High School if plaintiff Smith is allowed to return there. Based on those findings and the evidence presented at the hearing, the Board voted to expel plaintiff Smith from school for the remainder of the semester.

....

When [the superintendent] was questioned as to the bases for his recommendation of expulsion, he testified as follows:

> As I stated earlier, Gerry has a sister at Parkview, the deceased has a brother and sister. I made the judgment for the welfare of the entire student body for any type of trouble that may develop, I am charged with the responsibility of making those decisions there. To maintain peace and tranquility.
>
> I do know my student body very well. I have to be on the alert and look out for anything that happens in the community at any time that may be brought to the school.
>
> It was my feelings and my beliefs and my judgment that it would not be a wholesome environment for Gerry to be there with the brother and sister of the deceased. I did this, I took this step for Gerry's welfare and for the brother and sister of the deceased. And I might mention, Attorney Massie, in talking to Gerry's mother, she agreed with me on the phone that she felt that it was in the best interest that Gerry not return to Parkview.

He also testified that Gerry had been one of the students under his supervision for a number of years and that he had been disciplined for his unruly conduct on several occasions.

All high school students in the Little Rock School District are provided copies of the *Student Rights and Responsibilities Handbook*. The handbook is taught to the students in English classes for the first two weeks of each school year. The handbook contains a Student Conduct Code. The Code describes the types of behavior which will result in school imposed sanctions. The Student Conduct Code applies to criminal offenses committed away from school but which may affect the school climate. That provision is not intended to limit the authority of the Board to act only in situations when a student has been *convicted* of a criminal offense. The Court finds reasonable the argument of school authorities that *if* they were forced to wait for a courtroom adjudication before taking action, the rule would be meaningless. The Student Conduct Code also warns students that "conduct not specifically mentioned might also call for disciplinary action if it is disruptive or harms others."

Other factors considered by the Board are plaintiff's disciplinary record, which was before the Board at the February 21st hearing, and showed that he had been suspended from junior high school or high school six times. These offenses included fighting, using abusive and threatening language to the principal and vice principal, and disruptive behavior in class. The fact that the person who was shot and killed by plaintiff has a brother and a sister who attend Parkview might also tend to cause a very explosive situation at the school, with a potential of harm to the plaintiff himself as well as other students at Parkview.

. . . .

These seem to be the main facts considered by the Board. As to the law, in *O'Rourke v. Walker* (1925), 102 Conn. 130, 128 A. 25, 41 A.L.R. 1308, the court emphasized that the true test of a teacher's right to punish a pupil for conduct off the school campus is not the time or place of the offense, but its effect upon the morale and efficiency of the school, and whether it in fact is detrimental to the good order and to the welfare of the pupils.

In *R.R. v. Board of Education* (1970), 109 N.J.Super. 337, 263 A.2d 180, a high school sophomore was suspended primarily for involvement in a stabbing incident after school hours outside the school grounds. The court held that the school authorities lawfully could suspend him for events happening outside of school hours. In reaching its decision the court stated: "The school officials can suspend or expel a student for conduct outside of school hours when it is reasonably necessary for the punished student's physical or emotional safety or for the safety and well-being of other students, teachers, or public school property."

. . . .

If there is evidence to support the decision of a school board, it is improvident for the court to render a contrary judgment. The burden is on the plaintiff to prove the insufficiency of the evidence in support of the board's decision.

As to whether or not a preliminary injunction should be issued, the Court must consider the four factors enunciated in *Dataphase Systems, Inc., v. CL Systems, Inc.*, 640 F.2d 109, 114 n. 9 (8th Cir. 1981).

As dictated by the mandates of the Eighth Circuit, first, the Court must consider whether the plaintiff will be irreparably harmed absent an injunction. The burden of showing irreparable harm is on the plaintiff. The Court finds that the plaintiff will not be irreparably harmed in this case if an injunction is not issued. The record indicates he has amassed enough high school credits to graduate at the end of the

1984-85 school year, if he is readmitted and attends summer school and the regular term.

Next, the Court must balance the harm plaintiff may suffer as a result of his expulsion against the serious risk to other students which would be presented by plaintiff's presence at the school. The Court finds that the risk of harm to other students and the potential for disruption of educational processes outweigh whatever harm plaintiff Smith may suffer as a result of his expulsion.

As to the probability of success on the merits, the evidence in support of defendants' position appears to outweigh that of the plaintiff's. The school board's action is based not only on the Student Code of Conduct but also upon Arkansas Statutes which establish the responsibilities of the school administrators in carrying out their duties.

. . . .

The last factor to be considered is the public interest in the case. The Court finds that public interest in maintaining safe and productive schools is of paramount importance. The public interest would not be served if the Board were enjoined from removing the plaintiff from the classroom for the balance of this semester, under the circumstances presented in this case.

Accordingly, the Court finds that the motion for relief filed by the plaintiff must be denied. This does not mean that the Court regards lightly the plaintiff's constitutional right to secure an education in our school system—this is a very important right which should be guarded carefully.

. . . .

Nicholas B. v. School Commissioner of Worcester

587 N.E.2d 211 (Mass. 1992)

The court rules that the school may expel the student for fighting with another student off school grounds.

Wilkins, Justice

The plaintiff, whom we have given the pseudonym Nicholas B., appeals from a summary judgment that dismissed his challenge to disciplinary action that the defendant school committee took against him. We transferred his appeal to this court on our own motion.

On October 5, 1989, after hearing evidence in executive session, the school committee found that Nicholas had assaulted a fellow high school student "in violation of the policies, rules and codes of the Worcester Public Schools" and then voted "to expel [Nicholas] for the rest of the school year with a proviso that the case be reevaluated at the end of the school year."

There was evidence before the school committee that, on September 5, 1989, shortly after school was let out, Nicholas committed a battery on a fellow student on a public street near, but not on, school property. The battery was a product of planning by Nicholas and some friends that had occurred earlier that day on school property. The incident was also a continuation of a confrontation that had occurred on school grounds that day between Nicholas's group and a group of which the victim was a member.

Nicholas challenges (1) the school committee's authority to expel him from school for conduct that did not occur on school grounds or at a school event. . . . We reject Nicholas's claim that, because it imposed discipline for conduct not described in its disciplinary rules, the school committee's conduct was arbitrary or capricious. On the facts of this case, the committee was not limited by the provisions of its rules in imposing discipline. School committees have wide discretion in school discipline matters. A court will not reverse a school committee's decision unless the committee acted arbitrarily or capriciously.

Nicholas first argues that his conduct did not fall within any prohibition of the school committee's disciplinary rules. Specifically, he contends that the assault for which the committee disciplined him did not occur on school grounds or at a school event off school grounds and that the prohibitions of the school committee's disciplinary rules apply only to conduct on school grounds or at a school event. We shall not pause to consider whether the disciplinary rules apply by their terms to a battery committed by one student on another student on a street near a school immediately after school has ended for the day, especially where the battery is the continuation of improper conduct that occurred on school grounds. We simply reject the premise of Nicholas's argument that, by artless rulemaking, the school committee has foreclosed itself from disciplining a student for violent conduct against another student in the circumstances of this case.

The misconduct here was unquestionably improper, and Nicholas knew it. He needed no advisory rule to tell him that his conduct was seriously wrong and contrary to school policy. Based on facts that the school committee was warranted in finding, it had ample authority to discipline Nicholas.

. . . .

Galveston Independent School District v. Boothe

590 S.W.2d 553 (Tex. Civ. App. 1979)

The court rules that the school may not discipline a student for possession of marijuana off school grounds because state law and school policies did not provide the student with sufficient notice that such conduct was subject to discipline.

Peden, Justice.

Galveston Independent School District and its Board of Trustees and others appeal from a judgment setting aside the expulsion of David Boothe (based on alleged possession of marijuana near the school) and enjoining the district from either expelling him from school or penalizing him for his absence from school resulting from the expulsion. The trial court found the expulsion void (1) because the school board's rule that he was expelled for violating did not fairly apprise him that he could be expelled for possessing marijuana off the school grounds, and (2) because procedural requirements of the rule were not followed in carrying out the expulsion. We affirm.

Before his first class one morning, David Boothe was sitting in an automobile parked on a street adjacent to the school campus. Mr. Johnson, an employee of the district, approached the car and noticed a bag resting on the console. David admitted owning it. He later told his father it contained marijuana and the parties have stipulated that it did. The amount was one-fourteenth of an ounce....

In their first point of error, the appellants assert that the trial court erred in reaching the conclusion of law that the school board's expulsion of David was void "because it was not authorized by ... the Texas Education Code for the reasons that the pertinent school rules and regulations were not specific enough to apprise him of the nature of the conduct proscribed and that the Board of Trustees did not properly apply said rules and regulations."

....

Justice C.L. Ray, writing for the court in *Texarkana Independent School District v. Lewis*, 470 S.W.2d 727, 733 (Tex.Civ.App.1971, no writ), held:

> While the Board of Trustees has ample authority to suspend or expel students, "it is without authority to suspend a student for any act or conduct, unless, prior thereto, the Board has promulgated a rule, regulation or policy generally covering such act or conduct for which the student is subject to being suspended, or unless the act or conduct constituted incorrigible conduct in violation of this Article. (Article 2904, Vernon's Ann. Revised Civil Statutes, now Sec. 21.301, Tex. Education Code). Such rule, regulation or policy may be informal, preferably written but may be verbal, so long as it fairly apprises the student of the type of prohibited conduct for which he may be suspended from school." Opinion of the Attorney General 1969, No. M-395.

In our case, the Board of Trustees of the Galveston Independent School District has promulgated rules and regulations governing the conduct of students in the Galveston schools and carefully distributed them in a student-parent handbook at the beginning of each school year. This handbook contains rules, policies and regulations relating to expulsion and to the possession of marijuana....

The "Discipline Section" of the district's student-parent handbook states: "Expulsion Administrative action will be taken in cases where students perform asocial acts or are suspected of statutory infractions ...," while the section entitled "Assignment of Demerits/Penalties" lists the penalty for the offense of being "under the influence and/or possession of drugs" as simply "expulsion."

Mr. James Watson, principal of Ball High School, testified that in addition to receiving the handbook the students received verbal instructions and admonitions. Each homeroom teacher went over the handbook with the students in his class. Mr. Dillon, in charge of Human Relations and Security, visited each physical education class and spoke to the students on the dangers of drugs, the importance of adhering to the school's policies, and the problems they would face if they broke the rules. Mr. Watson further admonished the students over the public address system "not to bring marijuana on the campus." Mr. Watson testified that "I said the term marijuana specifically on the P.A. system on two occasions that I can recall, because of the dangers involved and because of the seemingly increased usage and possession of it on the campus."

We agree with the appellees that although the School Board had enacted rules and regulations concerning marijuana possession and expulsion, the district failed to follow them in this case. It appears that the expulsion was not made pursuant to any rule or regulation promulgated by the Board. . . .

Further, David's possession of marijuana was not on the school proper but was in a car parked on an adjacent street. David was verbally warned "not to bring marijuana on the campus," but it has not been shown that possessing marijuana in a car parked on an adjacent street is "on campus." The administrative regulations indicate that the place where possession of marijuana is prohibited is "in our schools." . . .

In their second point of error the appellants maintain that the trial court erred in concluding that David's expulsion was void and unenforceable because it was based on a vague and indefinite rule which contravened his right to due process under the United States Constitution.

They argue that the "vagueness doctrine" is applied only to criminal statutes and to cases involving infringement on basic constitutional rights and is not applicable to student disciplinary matters. We disagree and are in accord with the holding already cited in Texarkana Independent School District v. Lewis, supra, that before a student can be punished by expulsion for violation of a school rule, regulation, or policy, such rule, regulation, or policy must fairly apprise him of the type of prohibited conduct for which he may be expelled.

David was presented with a number of rules and regulations, but they did not fairly notify him that expulsion could result from his possessing marijuana on a street adjacent to the campus. It was made clear that the students were not to bring marijuana "on campus" but not that "on campus" means within 500 feet of the school grounds, regardless of the offense involved.

. . . .

Judgment of the trial court is affirmed.

Howard v. Colonial School District

621 A.2d 362 (Del. Super. Ct. 1992)

The court rules that the school may discipline a student caught dealing drugs to an undercover police officer off school grounds.

Herlihy, Judge.

Bernard Howard [Howard] appeals a decision of the State Board of Education [State Board] which upheld Howard's expulsion by the Colonial Board of Education [Colonial Board]. The Colonial Board expelled Howard for the balance of the 1990–91 school year for selling drugs to an undercover police officer.

Howard raises several issues in his appeal but the primary issue is one of first impression in this State. That issue revolves around the fact that the drug sales were off school property. The question then is the right of the Colonial Board, or any school board for that matter, to discipline for criminal activities conducted off school grounds.

The facts of this case are undisputed. At all times at issue, Howard was 17 years old and a senior in the 1990–91 school year. On three separate occasions in June and July of 1990, Howard sold cocaine to an undercover State Police officer. None of the sales were on school property. . . .

Howard has never denied selling drugs to the undercover officer. The primary issue all along in this matter is the right to expel for non-school-related criminal activities. . . . Howard argues there is no such authority. He points to the District Code of Conduct which does not spell out potential expulsion for such activities.

In contrast, the Colonial Board premises its expulsion of Howard upon (1) the statement in its Code of Conduct that it is not all inclusive and (2) certain broad statutory powers, namely:

> "In each reorganized school district there shall be a school board which shall have the authority to administer and to supervise the free public schools of the reorganized school district and which shall have the authority to determine policy and adopt rules and regulations for the general administration and supervision of the free public schools of the reorganized school district. Such administration, supervision and policy shall be conducted and formulated in accordance with Delaware law and the policies, rules and regulations of the [State Board]." 14 Del.C. § 1043.

The school board of each reorganized school district, subject to this title and in accordance with the policies, rules and regulations of the [State Board], shall, in addition to other duties:

> "(1) Determine the educational policies of the reorganized school district and prescribe rules and regulations for the conduct and management of the schools. . . ." 14 Del.C. § 1049.

The Colonial Board determined that Howard posed, as even an off-campus drug dealer, a threat to the safety and welfare of other District students. The State Board upheld that determination.

It is clear that a school board in this State has authority to expel for drug *possession* in school. This Court in *Rucker v. Colonial School District*, Del.Super., 517 A.2d 703 (1986). upheld the District's "tough" policy on the issue of drugs. *Id.* While the activity condemned in *Rucker* involved in school drug abuse, this Court, in this case, cannot say that a tough policy against students who *deal* drugs off campus is unwarranted or arbitrary.

The local school authorities are in a better position than the courts to determine the impact on their students by the presence of a drug dealer among the student body. Those authorities are responsible for the health, safety and welfare of all of their students. Those authorities also are better able to judge the impact on their students of off-campus criminal activity. Merely because such activity occurred off-campus does not necessarily render the local board powerless to act. That power must be exercised reasonably and without an abuse of discretion.

Selling drugs is a serious offense. If Howard were one year older, he would have been charged with three felonies. The extent of the drug problem in our society is tragically too well known. The legislature has recognized special evils involved in drug sales to minors. 16 Del.C. § 4761. It has also recognized the need to keep drugs away from schools and their surroundings. 16 Del.C. § 4767 (prohibiting possession within 1,000 feet of a school).

While the sales here were not to a minor nor in or within 1,000 feet of a school, this Court cannot say that the Colonial Board acted arbitrarily or capriciously in determining a potential harm to its students by the presence of a 17-year-old drug dealer among its students. The State Board's determination that in this case the Colonial Board's power to expel was correctly used is not erroneous.

It should be noted that this Court is not ruling that all off-campus, non-school activity conduct subjects a student to the threat of expulsion. A clearer Code of Conduct would help to delineate such conduct. However, this Court cannot find that the expulsion here was without authority or justification.

Accordingly, the State Board of Education's affirmance of the Colonial Board of Education's expulsion of Bernard Howard is Affirmed.

Post Problem Discussion

1. In *Nicholas B., Galveston*, and *Howard*, the courts note that the state laws and school policies at issue do not address off-campus activity. Why do the courts in *Nicholas B.* and *Howard* allow expulsion in this circumstance while *Galveston* does not?

2. Recall the discussion in *Hasson v. Boothby* in Problem 1 about the two judicial approaches to reviewing school disciplinary decisions (inherent authority of schools vs. need to provide notice of prohibited activities). Do the different outcomes in the cases in Problem 4 occur because some of the courts follow one approach, and some follow the other? Which approach would more likely allow the school to discipline Ben and Clay?

3. Review the discipline policies in Problems 2 and 4 of this Chapter. Would your opinion about whether the school could discipline Ben and Clay change if that discipline policy were in effect at Harmony High School? Why or why not?

§ 8.07 Drugs, Guns, and Zero Tolerance Policies

In an effort to address substance abuse and violence at school and school-sponsored events, many schools have adopted zero tolerance policies for drugs, weapons, and related issues. Zero tolerance generally means that the school imposes a predetermined disciplinary sanction for certain acts, regardless of the circumstances.

At the federal level, the Gun Free-Schools Act requires states that receive federal funds under the law to expel any student who possess a firearm at school. 20 U.S.C. §§ 7961. In its current form, the law permits the chief school administrator to modify the expulsion on a case-by-case basis and to offer alternative educational services to the student. In response to the Gun Free-Schools Act, all fifty states have some form of zero tolerance policies in place and many of them address issues other than guns in schools.[10] For example, the State of California includes the following in its zero tolerance discipline laws:

- Possessing, selling, or otherwise furnishing a firearm
- Brandishing a knife at another person
- Selling a controlled substance
- Committing or attempting to commit a sexual assault or sexual battery
- Possessing an explosive

Cal. Educ. Code § 48915(c). Many states include some form of weapon beyond guns in their zero tolerance policies. Some use the federal definition of "dangerous weapons" from the United States Criminal Code, which states:

> The term "dangerous weapon" means a weapon, device, instrument, material, or substance, animate or inanimate, that is used for, or is readily capable of, causing death or serious bodily injury, except that such term does not include a pocket knife with a blade of less than 2 1/2 inches in length.

18 U.S.C. § 930(g)(2).

---

10. *See, e.g.*, Paul M. Bogos, Note, *Expelled. No Excuses. No Exceptions—Michigan's Zero-Tolerance Policy in Response to School Violence: M.C.L.A. Section 380.1311*, 74 U. Det. Mercy L. Rev. 357, 358 (1997); Safe and Responsive Schools Project, Indiana University, www.indiana.edu /~safeschl/zero.html (last visited March 9, 2009).

There are ongoing concerns about the effectiveness of zero tolerance policies, and the harsh consequences that can result from not being able to consider the individual circumstances when imposing discipline.[11] The following are some of the more infamous results of zero tolerance policies:[12]

✓ A seventh grade student in Glendale, Arizona was suspended for the remainder of the school term for bringing a homemade rocket made from a potato chip canister to school.

✓ A high school sophomore in Pensacola, Florida was suspended for ten days, and threatened with expulsion, for bringing nail clippers and a nail file to school.

✓ A five year old elementary school student in Deer Lakes, Pennsylvania was suspended for wearing a five-inch plastic ax as part of his firefighter's costume to a Halloween party in his classroom.

✓ A five year old kindergarten student was suspended from school for three days for saying "I'm going to shoot you" to one of his friends, while playing a game of cops and robbers. *S.G. ex rel. A.G. v. Sayreville Bd. of Educ.*, 333 F.3d 417 (3d Cir. 2003), *cert. denied*, 540 U.S. 1104 (2004).

The following activity and problem explores zero tolerance laws, policies, and court decisions in your state.

Activity 2: Zero Tolerance Discipline Policies

Step One—Find your state's school discipline laws and search for provisions on zero tolerance. Look for language that requires the school to take certain actions. For example, "the superintendent shall recommend expulsion for any student who possesses a firearm on school grounds." Also, look for laws that address guns, weapons, or drugs.

Step Two—Find a local public school's discipline policy online. It can be from a school you attended, a public school in your home state, or any public school you would like to use. Search it for zero tolerance provisions. As with Step One, look for language requiring school officials to take certain actions for certain disciplinary infractions.

Step Three—Answer the following:

1. Does your state or school include more than firearms/guns in its zero tolerance laws and policies? If so, what other activities are covered?

---

11. *See, e.g.*, The Civil Rights Project, Opportunities Suspended: The Devastating Consequences of Zero Tolerance School Discipline, Harvard University (2000), www.civilrightsproject.ucla.edu/research/discipline/opport_suspended.php (last visited March 9, 2009); ABA Juvenile Justice Policies, *Zero Tolerance Policy*, available at www.abanet.org/crimjust/juvjus/zerotolreport.html (last visited April 11, 2009).

12. The first three examples are from Russell J. Skiba, *Zero Tolerance, Zero Evidence: An Analysis of School Disciplinary Practice*, Indiana University Education Policy Center (2001), available at www.indiana.edu/~safeschl/ztze.pdf (last visited April 11, 2009).

2. What is the punishment for violating the zero tolerance laws or policies?
3. Have there been any court challenges to the zero tolerance laws/policies? If so, what were the results? If not, do you think the laws/policies meet the constitutional and other legal standards noted in this Chapter?
4. What are the pros and cons of zero tolerance laws/policies in public schools?

Problem 6: Zero Tolerance for Weapons[13]

Wanda is a third grade student at the Penn Elementary School. She is working on a clay sculpture of the White House for a class project. She has trouble cutting and molding the clay in class, and she asks her teacher if she can bring some of her sculpting tools to school the next day. The teacher replies "sure." Wanda brings her sculpting tool kit with her to school the next day. Her parents gave it to her for Christmas to build clay creations at home. The sculpting tools are about five inches long with shaped edges made out of metal. In class, one of the boys, Jay, takes one of the sculpting tools and pretends to stab Wanda saying, "I'm Super Jay and you will be defeated!" The tool accidentally strikes Wanda on the arm and results in a slight scratch with a little bit of blood. The teacher takes the tool away from Jay and sends Jay to the principal's office. She sends Wanda to the school nurse for a band-aid.

Jay tells the principal that he took the tool from Wanda's desk and was "just playing around." The principal goes to Wanda's class and tells her to come to his office with the tools. After Wanda explains what happened, the principal expels her and Jay from school under the school district's zero tolerance policy. Both Wanda's and Jay's parents appeal the decision to the local school board, and to the State Board of Education. Both affirm on the grounds that Wanda and Jay were caught at school in possession of weapons. Do Wanda and Jay have any viable claims in court?

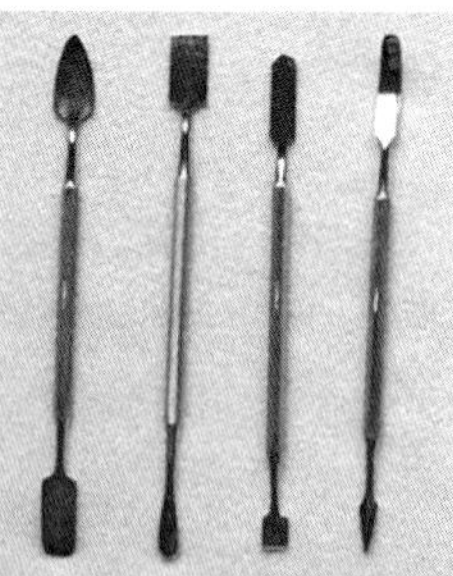

Wanda's Sculpting Tools

13. Picture provided courtesy of Linda Steider, www.steiderstuidos.com.

Problem Materials

✓ Penn School District Zero Tolerance Policy

✓ Hypothetical State Statute

✓ *Vann v. Stewart*, 445 F. Supp. 2d 882 (E.D. Tenn. 2006)

✓ *Colvin v. Lowndes County Mississippi School District*, 114 F. Supp. 2d 504 (N.D. Miss. 1999)

Penn School District Zero Tolerance Policy[14]

Pursuant to state law Ed 8731, all schools in the Penn School District shall have zero tolerance for drugs, weapons, violence, or violent activities. Any student found to possesses any controlled substance, knife, handgun, other firearm, or any other instrument considered to be a dangerous weapon and capable of causing serious bodily harm, or who commits a violent act at any school in the district shall be subject to automatic expulsion for the school year.

Hypothetical State Statute Ed 8731[15]

Any student in any school who possesses any controlled substance, a knife, handgun, other firearm or any other instrument considered to be a dangerous weapon and capable of causing bodily harm or who commits a violent act on educational property shall be subject to automatic expulsion for a school year provided, however, that the superintendent of the school shall be authorized to modify the period of time for such expulsion on a case by case basis. Dangerous weapon means any weapon, device, instrument, material, or substance that is used for, or is readily capable of, causing death or serious bodily injury. School districts shall adopt policies implementing these requirements. School superintendents may modify student expulsions under this provision on a case-by-case basis.

Vann v. Stewart

445 F. Supp. 2d 882 (E.D. Tenn. 2006)

The court upholds the one-year suspension of a high school sophomore for having a small pocket knife on school grounds.

Varlan, District Judge.

Plaintiff Austin Vann alleges that his federal civil rights, along with Tennessee laws, were violated when defendants suspended him from school under Anderson County's zero tolerance policy. Plaintiff was suspended for one calendar year after

---

14. Combined from a selection of actual policies, *see, e.g.*, Pike School http://www.southpike.org/Board%20Policies/JCA%20Student%20Conduct.doc.

15. Modified from actual state laws including Mississippi. Miss. Code Ann. § 37-11-18, *see* www.mscode.com/free/statutes/37/011/0018.htm (last visited April 14, 2009).

he was found with a small pocketknife on school grounds. Defendants generally deny plaintiff's allegations.

. . . .

On April 7, 2004, plaintiff, a sophomore at Anderson County High School, possessed a small pocket knife while on school grounds. Doc. 1-2 at 2. During his first period class, plaintiff discovered the pocket knife in his pocket and showed it to a few classmates, but he did not inform his teacher, nor did he dispose of it. On the other hand, plaintiff did not open the pocket knife or display it in an offensive or threatening manner.

Later that day, the school's assistant principal, Murrel Albright, was informed that plaintiff had threatened a female student with whom plaintiff had carried on a turbulent romantic relationship. Assistant principal Albright called plaintiff into his office and asked him about the allegations. Plaintiff denied making any threats. Assistant principal Albright asked plaintiff whether he possessed "anything he shouldn't have." Plaintiff admitted possessing the pocket knife and gave it to assistant principal Albright.

Upon learning of the pocket knife, assistant principal Albright contacted plaintiff's mother and completed a disciplinary referral form, a zero tolerance report, and a notice of suspension and right to appeal. The disciplinary referral form and zero tolerance report stated that the possession of the pocket knife was a violation of the local zero tolerance policy and that plaintiff was being suspended for one calendar year.

. . . .

The suspension or expulsion of a student from a Tennessee secondary school is regulated by state statute and local school policy. *See* Tenn.Code Ann. §§ 49-6-3401, 49-6-4216. Broadly, certain school officials are permitted to suspend a student from school attendance for "good and sufficient reasons," including "possession of a knife. . . ." § 49-6-3401(a)(8). In addition, Tennessee has authorized the expulsion of a student for committing two types of "zero tolerance" offenses. The procedure for imposing a suspension or expulsion is also mandated by statute. *See* § 49-6-3401(c).

The first type of zero tolerance offense is specified by statute and mandates the expulsion for one year of any student found to be in possession of a firearm, illegal drugs or drug paraphernalia, or any student found to have committed a battery on school personnel. § 49-6-3401(g). The only exception to the one-year expulsion is that the local director of schools may modify the expulsion on "a case-by-case basis." *Id.*

The second type of zero tolerance offense is specified by local school boards pursuant to a statute that directs local school officials to adopt policies to confront certain conduct that threatens "safe and secure learning environments." § 49-6-4216(a)(1). Under the statute, therefore, school officials must file with the state education commissioner "written education policies and procedures" developed by the local school board that protect schools from the influence of "drugs, drug paraphernalia, violence and dangerous weapons" and that impose "severe disciplinary sanctions" for bringing contraband, including dangerous weapons, onto school property. § 49-6-4216(a). Unlike the one-year expulsion for a statutory zero tolerance offense, however, the sanction for a local zero tolerance offense "shall not necessarily result in a presumptive one calendar year expulsion. . . ." § 49-6-4216(b)(1).

In an effort to comply with § 49-6-4216, the Anderson County School Board adopted a zero tolerance policy that prohibited students from possessing any "dangerous weapon." A "dangerous weapon" was broadly defined to include "any dangerous instrument or substance, which is capable of inflicting any injury on any person." *Id.* The stated punishment for violating this local zero tolerance policy is a one calendar year suspension from school attendance. *Id.*

In the instant action, plaintiff was suspended based on the second type of zero tolerance offense-violating the local zero tolerance policy adopted pursuant to § 49-6-4216. Plaintiff admitted possessing a pocket knife while on school property, and there is no dispute that plaintiff's conduct was a violation of the local zero tolerance policy. Thus, the gravamen of plaintiff's claim is that the imposition of the sanction in this case was constitutionally and statutorily flawed.

. . . .

Turning first to plaintiff's due process claims, a state cannot deprive any person of life, liberty, or property, without due process of law. U.S. Const. amend. XIV, § 1. "Protected interests in property are normally 'not created by the Constitution. Rather, they are created and their dimensions defined' by an independent source such as state statutes or rules entitling citizens to certain benefits." *Goss v. Lopez*, 419 U.S. 565, 572–73 (1975) (quoting *Board of Regents v. Roth*, 408 U.S. 564, 577 (1972)).

The Tennessee Constitution guarantees to Tennessee's students "the right to a free public education." In fact, Tennessee requires students to attend school until a certain age. *See* Tenn.Code Ann. § 49-6-3001. Thus, it is undoubted that a Tennessee high school student enjoys a property interest in his high school education. *Seal v. Morgan*, 229 F.3d 567, 574 (6th Cir. 2000). Accordingly, a high school student cannot be deprived of that interest without due process of law. *See Goss*, 419 U.S. at 577, 95 S. Ct. 729.

Due process, however, is comprised of two components, both of which plaintiff claims were violated in his case. Procedural due process requires school officials to provide student with notice and an opportunity to be heard. *See id.* at 581, 95 S. Ct. 729. Plaintiff contends that his right to procedural due process was deprived when school officials failed to consider his argument for a modified punishment in violation of state law and local policy. Substantive due process requires the punishment bear some rational relationship to the offense. *See Seal*, 229 F.3d at 575. Plaintiff contends that his right to substantive due process was deprived when the school officials failed to consider modifying the punishment, yielding a punishment that bore no rational relationship to plaintiff's offense.

Procedural due process requires that a state may not take away a student's public education because of a student's "misconduct without adherence to the minimum procedures required" by the Due Process Clause. *Goss*, 419 U.S. at 574, 95 S. Ct. 729. . . . Plaintiff does not contend that the school discipline procedures required by the Tennessee statute and the Anderson County zero tolerance policy violated plaintiff's right to procedural due process. Instead, plaintiff advances the somewhat novel argument that it was defendants' failure to follow those procedures that resulted in the procedural due process violation. Thus, the issue for the Court's determination is whether the plaintiff's right to procedural due process was violated by defendants' alleged failure to follow the requirements of a valid school policy or state law.

The fact that a valid school policy or state law was not followed is not by itself significant in determining whether procedural due process has been violated. Instead, it is the *degree* of the failure to follow the policy or state law that is significant. Thus, in a school misconduct case, a failure to comply with a valid school discipline policy or state law rises to the level of a procedural due process violation where the failure to comply is so significant or substantial that it could result in "unfair or mistaken findings of misconduct" or an "arbitrary exclusion from school" by denying the student notice and an opportunity to be heard. *See Goss*, 419 U.S. at 581, 95 S. Ct. 729.

Plaintiff argues that members of the DHA and school board considered only whether plaintiff was "guilty or not guilty" and failed to consider whether the one-year suspension was a "reasonable punishment under the circumstances," as Tennessee statute and local policy require. Plaintiff contends that this failure effectively denied him the opportunity to be heard at the hearings because he was only seeking a modification of the length of the suspension and not contesting the underlying finding of misconduct. Defendants, in arguing for summary judgment, contend that plaintiff was given proper notice and hearings were held during which plaintiff, his attorney, and his parents were allowed to address school officials. Furthermore, plaintiff admitted he had possessed the pocket knife, which he acknowledged was a violation of the zero tolerance policy, and that he was aware that a violation of the zero tolerance policy could result in a one-year suspension.

Assuming, *arguendo*, the DHA and school board applied the improper standard when considering plaintiff's case, the Court cannot conclude that such a failure was so significant or substantial that it could result in "unfair or mistaken findings of misconduct" or an "arbitrary exclusion from school," because plaintiff was not denied notice or an opportunity to be heard. *See Goss*, 419 U.S. at 581, 95 S. Ct. 729. Procedural due process ensures that, *at a minimum*, a student will have the opportunity to rebut or otherwise explain the allegations levied against him. Where such an opportunity is provided, procedural due process is satisfied; it does not impose the additional requirement that the student's statements must be accepted. Nor does it guarantee that school officials must apply any specific standard in evaluating the student's conduct.

In this case, the undisputed evidence is that plaintiff received notice of and actively participated in two hearings where he could rebut the finding of misconduct and/or explain his actions. School officials followed a procedure that allowed plaintiff, plaintiff's parents, and plaintiff's attorney to address the allegations of misconduct before the DHA and school board. Before both reviewing authorities, plaintiff was permitted to address the misconduct finding, which he did. Plaintiff challenged the allegation that he had threatened others, but he also admitted possessing the pocket knife in violation of the local zero tolerance policy. Having been allowed to challenge the finding of misconduct, procedural due process was satisfied, even though state law and local policy might require additional procedures. . . .

Turning next to plaintiff's substantive due process claim, in addition to providing protection to a student's property interest in education, as discussed above, the Due Process Clause also provides "heightened protection against government interference with certain fundamental rights and liberty interests." *Washington v. Glucksberg*, 521 U.S. 702, 720 (1997). The right to attend public school, however, is not a fundamental right or liberty interest. *San Antonio Indep. Sch. Dist. v. Rodriguez*, 411 U.S. 1, 33–37 (1973). When a government action does not affect fundamental rights or liberty interests and does not involve suspect classifications, it will be upheld if it is rationally related to a legitimate state interest. *See Vacco v. Quill*, 521 U.S. 793 (1997). In cases involving school discipline, substantive due process is violated only in the rare case that there is no "rational relationship between the punishment and the offense." *Wood v. Strickland*, 420 U.S. 308, 326 (1975). The Court also notes that "[i]t is not the role of the federal courts to set aside decisions of school administrators which the court may view as lacking a basis in wisdom or compassion. . . ." *Id.*

Plaintiff's substantive due process claim flows from his procedural due process claim. That is, he argues that because the DHA and school board failed to consider modifying the one-year suspension according to state law and local policy, the punishment imposed by school officials bears no rational relationship to plaintiff's actual offense. By contrast, defendants, in seeking summary judgment, argue that the one-year suspension does bear a rational relationship to plaintiff's offense when viewed in light of the state's interest in school safety.

The Court cannot conclude that the punishment imposed by school officials in this case bore no rational relationship to plaintiff's offense. State authorities have expressed a legitimate interest in maintaining "safe and secure learning environments." *See* Tenn. Code Ann. §49-6-4216. In an effort to comply with state law adopted pursuant to that interest, local officials adopted a zero tolerance policy that includes a one year suspension for violations. Plaintiff admits that he possessed a pocket knife in violation of the local policy and that he was aware he could receive a one year suspension.

Assuming, *arguendo*, the DHA and school board applied the wrong standard in considering plaintiff's case, the Court cannot conclude that the officials' imposition of a one-year suspension crossed the line of legitimate government action, especially since it imposed a sanction that was specifically recognized in the Tennessee statute and local policy. Even considering plaintiff's contention that the school officials' action might have been harsh or unwise in view of the circumstances, the decision was not so flawed that it bore no rational relationship to plaintiff's offense.

. . . .

Plaintiff alleges federal and state law claims arising from his suspension for violating a local zero tolerance policy. Defendants have moved for summary judgment, and for the reasons discussed herein, that motion will be granted. . . . As a result, this case will be dismissed.

Colvin v. Lowndes County Mississippi School District

114 F. Supp. 2d 504 (N.D. Miss. 1999)

The court rejects the dismissal of a sixth grade student for having a miniature Swiss Army type knife at school.

Davidson, District Judge

The instant case requires this court to address the timely and often controversial topic of school district zero-tolerance policies. In response to numerous instances of school-related crime and violence, several states have implemented laws and countless school districts across the nation have established stringent policies regarding the presence of weapons and drugs on school premises. These "zero-tolerance" policies provide for immediate suspension or expulsion of students that possess weapons or drugs on school grounds. In general, a student found carrying a weapon, such as a gun or a knife, on school property is given no second chance, no appeal, and no guarantee of alternative school programs or education.

The devastation school violence can reap is nowhere more apparent than in the State of Mississippi. While this court is cognizant of the unenviable position of the school boards of this and other states and of their aim to create a school environment conducive to learning, by eliminating the fear of crime and violence, such efforts must be balanced with the constitutional guarantees afforded to the children that enter the school house door.

. . . .

During the 1998–99 school year, Jonathan Colvin was a sixth grade student at New Hope Middle School in New Hope, Mississippi. During this school year, as with many before, Jonathan was struggling to avoid academic failure. . . .

On the morning of February 25, 1999, Jonathan was found to be in possession, on school premises, of a weapon, specifically, a miniature Swiss-army type knife.[16]

16. [FN 3] The "weapon" in question is a miniature Swiss-army knife key chain approximately two inches in length containing a fingernail file, small pair of scissors, and closed-end cuticle knife. The item bears the insignia of a medical or pharmaceutical company and was given to Jonathan by his mother, a registered nurse. . . .

The facts regarding the discovery and presence of the knife are not substantially in dispute. On the day of the incident, Jonathan carried his books and supplies to school in a traditional-style book bag. In preparation for his morning English class, Jonathan reached into his bag to retrieve his textbook. While removing the book, the knife fell to the floor, apparently through a hole in his book bag. Jonathan immediately picked up the knife and placed it in his pocket to avoid losing it. A fellow student observed these events and reported to their teacher that Jonathan had a knife on his person. When confronted, Jonathan admitted having the knife, stated that he was not aware that he had brought it to school, that it apparently fell into his book bag by accident, and handed the knife over to his teacher without incident. Jonathan made no threatening gestures with the knife and fully cooperated with his teacher and the school officials after its discovery.

Following the discovery of the knife, Jonathan's English teacher prepared a discipline referral form which was sent to Assistant Principal Rob Calcote indicating that Jonathan was found in possession of a weapon. Upon questioning by the Assistant Principal, Jonathan admitted having the knife and was subsequently suspended for nine days with a recommendation for expulsion. By letter dated March 9, 1999, the Plaintiffs were notified that a disciplinary hearing had been scheduled for March 15 1999, and informed of their right to attend, to bring witnesses and/or affidavits, or to have counsel of their choosing present.

On March 15, 1999, Jonathan and his father attended the disciplinary hearing, presided over by Hearing Officer Gary S. Goodwin. . . . Officer Goodwin made the following recommendation to the Board of Education:

> It is the opinion of the hearing officer that this student should be expelled from the Lowndes County Schools for a period of one (1) year, with the period of expulsion to be modified, however, by suspending imposition of the expulsion for the school year, except for a period of one (1) day, and that upon return of the student after that day, the student and his parents be made aware that any other violation of the school's rules and regulations will result in imposition of the remainder of the expulsion period.

On April 5, 1999, the Lowndes County School Board overruled the Hearing Officer's recommendation and approved expulsion of Jonathan from the Lowndes County School System for a period of one calendar year.

Prior to the above incident, Jonathan had one disciplinary infraction in his record. Three days before the incident at issue, Jonathan failed to appear for a thirty-minute after school detention and as a consequence, received corporal punishment. Notably, Jonathan received the detention for failing to complete a homework assignment. Numerous school officials and teachers provided testimony regarding Jonathan's attitude and demeanor. Each witness, without fail, testified that Jonathan was a pleasant and respectful student, displaying no aggressive tendencies and posing no disciplinary problems.

. . . .

The Plaintiffs also allege that the School District's action violated Jonathan's constitutional due process rights. For the reasons stated below, this court agrees.

....

In assessing the constitutional parameters of the case *sub judice*, the court finds compelling the reasoning of the Fifth Circuit decision in *Lee v. Macon County Board of Education*, 490 F.2d 458 (5th Cir. 1974). In *Lee*, the court vacated the district court decision affirming the permanent expulsion of two high school students and remanded the case to the district court with instructions to remand to the school board for reconsideration. While the students were afforded a hearing before the school board, the court found that the board, in making its disciplinary decision, merely employed a formalistic acceptance or ratification of the school principal's recommendation, absent any independent assessment of what penalty to impose. The court specifically held that the school board employed "an erroneous legal standard in considering the children's cases," and directed that when a serious penalty is at stake a school board must provide a higher degree of due process than when a student is threatened only with a minor sanction. *Id.* at 459. The opinion is worth quoting:

> Formalistic acceptance or ratification of the principal's request or recommendation as to the scope of punishment, without independent Board consideration of what, under all the circumstances, the penalty should be, is less than full due process. Appropriate punishment is for the Board to determine, in the exercise of its independent judgment.

Id. at 460 (footnote omitted).

While in the instant case, the Board did not defer to the judgment of another official, it did defer to an unwritten blanket policy of expulsion, absent reference to the circumstances of the infraction. It appears clear that the aim of the Fifth Circuit's decision, was to require school boards to fully consider the circumstances surrounding the misdeed as well as the penalty to be prescribed in an effort to provide students with full due process. Employing a blanket policy of expulsion, clearly a serious penalty, precludes the use of independent consideration of relevant facts and circumstances. Certainly, an offense may warrant expulsion, but such punishment should only be handed down upon the Board's independent determination that the facts and circumstances meet the requirements for instituting such judgment. By casting too wide a net, school boards will effectively snare the unwary student.

> The school board may choose not to exercise its power of leniency. In doing so, however, it may not hide behind the notion that the law prohibits leniency for there is no such law. Individualized punishment by reference to all relevant facts and circumstances regarding the offense and the offender is a hallmark of our criminal justice system.

Clinton Municipal Separate School Dist. v. Byrd, 477 So. 2d 237, 241 (Miss. 1985). In a system where criminal offenders are afforded individualized punishment upon review of the facts and circumstances regarding the offense, students in our public school systems, who may also face a daunting punishment, should at least be afforded a thorough review of their case, prior to imposition of penalty.

Initially, the court notes that nothing in the District's written Handbook acknowledges the Board's zero-tolerance policy, although the Board was utilizing the policy by voice vote at its meetings. The Secondary Handbook provides:

> If the Board of Education finds the student guilty of some or all of the charges made against him/her, the school record and previous conduct of the student will be taken into consideration in determining the discipline administered to the student.

Despite the plain language of the Handbook, the President of the Lowndes County School Board testified that the District's zero-tolerance policy requires that the Board impose the same penalty regardless of the circumstances surrounding the offense: a one year expulsion for a weapon or drug infraction.[17] When specifically asked whether the Board considered Jonathan's school record and previous conduct in determining the discipline to be administered, the President of the School Board testified that they did not.

Although the Superintendent of Schools stated that the Board reviews each case on the merits, the President of the School Board testified that he had not seen or reviewed the weapon Jonathan was found in possession of until the trial of this matter. To be sure, the court is not offended by the School Board's decision to overrule the Hearing Officer's recommendation, clearly it had the authority to do so. The court is, however, offended by the manner in which it blindly meted out the student's punishment. Here, Jonathan was expelled for a calendar year, a penalty that this court considers serious and worthy of a higher degree of due process. Nothing in the record reflects independent consideration by the Board of the relevant facts and circumstances surrounding Jonathan's case. According to the minutes of the School Board hearing, the Board acted upon and adopted the recommendation of the Hearing Officer to *expel* Jonathan for one calendar year. Joint Ex. 10. The Officer's recommendation, however was not for expulsion. This provides added concern as to what the Board had knowledge of or thought it was doing when it invoked the expulsion. It appears that the Board simply knew that a weapon was found on school property and instituted a blanket penalty, absent review of relevant facts or circumstances.

---

17. [FN 10] The School District weapons policy is derived from Mississippi Code Annotated section 37-11-18, which provides:

> Any student in any school who possesses any controlled substance . . . , a knife, handgun, other firearm or any other instrument considered to be dangerous and capable of causing bodily harm or who commits a violent act on educational property . . . shall be subject to automatic expulsion for a calendar year . . . ; provided, however, that the superintendent of the school shall be authorized to modify the period of time for such expulsion on a case by case basis.

While this court if fully aware that school disciplinary matters are best resolved in the local community and within the institutional framework of the school system, the court is of the opinion that the Board employed an erroneous standard in considering Jonathan's case. Based on the guiding principles of the Fifth Circuit's decision in *Lee*, the court concludes that the case must be remanded to the Board with directions that it reconsider the question of appropriate penalty, under correct legal standards. Nothing in this court's opinion should be construed to limit the authority of the School Board to enforce its rules and regulations or to enforce its zero-tolerance policy, provided, however, that the correct legal standard is applied and that the student's due process rights are recognized.

Post Problem Discussion

1. The courts in *Vann* and *Colvin* deal with similar situations (students possessing small knives at school), but come to different conclusions. Why?

2. Federal courts have generally been reluctant to overturn zero tolerance policies on constitutional due process theories, regardless of the circumstances. The facts in *Ratner v. Loudon County Public Sch.*, 16 Fed. Appx. 140 (4th Cir. 2001), *cert. denied*, 534 U.S. 1114 (2002), illustrate the troubling results:

> Benjamin Ratner was a thirteen year old eighth grader when one of his middle school classmates told him she had considered killing herself by slitting her wrists. The classmate had "inadvertently" brought a knife to school in her binder. Knowing about previous suicide attempts, Ratner took the binder and left it in his locker. Ratner planned to tell his parents and the girls' parents about the knife after school, but he did not tell any school authority. Nevertheless, the word got around, and at lunchtime the Dean of the School interviewed Ratner about the knife. Ratner admitted he had the knife, explained the circumstances, and gave the binder to the Dean. The Dean "acknowledged that she believed Ratner acted in what he saw as the girl's best interest and that at no time did Ratner pose a threat to harm anyone with the knife." Even with this acknowledgement, Ratner was suspended for the remainder of the school term under the school's zero tolerance policy.

Ratner, 16 Fed. Appx. at 142. Ratner brought due process claims challenging the school's actions. The Fourth Circuit stated:

> However harsh the result in this case, the federal courts are not properly called upon to judge the wisdom of a zero tolerance policy of the sort alleged to be in place at Blue Ridge Middle School or of its application to Ratner. Instead, our inquiry here is limited to whether Ratner's complaint alleges sufficient facts which if proved would show that the implementation of the school's policy in this case failed to comport with the United States Constitution. We conclude that the facts alleged in this case do not so demonstrate.

Concurring specially in the result, Judge Hamilton issued a compelling statement about zero tolerance policies:

> I write separately to express my compassion for Ratner, his family, and common sense. Each is the victim of good intentions run amuck. Ratner's complaint alleges that school suspensions for possession of a weapon on Loudoun County school property are imposed automatically, pursuant to a zero-tolerance policy that precludes consideration of the facts and circumstances of a particular student's conduct in determining a violation of stated policy and the resulting student punishment. There is no doubt that this zero-tolerance/automatic suspension policy, and others like it adopted by school officials throughout our nation, were adopted in large response to the tragic school shootings that have plagued our nation's schools over the past several years. Also, no doubt exists that in adopting these zero-tolerance/automatic suspension policies, school officials had the noble intention of protecting the health and safety of our nation's school children and those adults charged with the profound responsibility of educating them. However, as the oft repeated old English maxim recognizes, "the road to hell is paved with good intentions." The panic over school violence and the intent to stop it has caused school officials to jettison the common sense idea that a person's punishment should fit his crime in favor of a single harsh punishment, namely, mandatory school suspension. Such a policy has stripped away judgment and discretion on the part of those administering it; refuting the well established precept that judgment is the better part of wisdom.
>
> Here, a young man, Ratner, took a binder containing a knife from a suicidal fellow student in an effort to save her life. He put the binder in his locker without even opening it. Indeed, at all times, Ratner never saw the knife. Further, the facts do not offer even the hint of a suggestion that Ratner ever intended to personally possess the knife or harm anyone with it. In fact, the first school official on the scene reported that at no time did Ratner intend to harm anyone with the knife. Yet, based on the school's zero-tolerance/automatic suspension policy, Ratner was suspended from school for nearly four months.
>
> School officials should, without doubt, punish a student for knowingly and intentionally bringing a dangerous weapon on school property. But the question raised by the facts of Ratner's case is one of degree and the law must be flexible enough so that school officials may intrude upon the right to a free appropriate public education *only* in the most justifiable circumstances. Under a facts/circumstances-sensitive examination of this case, Ratner's nearly four-month suspension from middle school is not justifiable. Indeed, it is a calculated overkill when the punishment is considered in light of Ratner's good-faith intentions and his, at best, if at all, technical violation of the school's policy. Suffice it to say that the degree of Ratner's violation of school policy does not correlate with the degree of his

> punishment. Certainly, the oft repeated maxim, "there is no justice without mercy" has been defiled by the results obtained here. But alas, as the opinion for the court explains, this is not a federal constitutional problem.

Ratner, 16 Fed. Appx. at 143-44. Do you agree with the Fourth Circuit's decision, or with Judge Hamilton's impassioned statement? Why isn't the result Judge Hamilton describes a federal constitutional problem?

Chapter 9

Student Expression

Synopsis

§ 9.01 Introduction

Student expression affects public schools in many ways. Students have certain rights to expression under the First Amendment, and sometimes under state constitutions as well. These rights place limits on school officials' ability to restrict student expression. At the same time, the United States Supreme Court has recognized the "special characteristics of the school environment," and, as a result of these characteristics, the Court has afforded school officials some deference in making decisions in this area. As a result, students' rights to expression are not "automatically coextensive with the rights of adults in other settings," and certain speech, which would be protected in other settings, might not be protected in the public school setting. *Bethel School District v. Fraser*, 478 U.S. 675, 682 (1986).

The Supreme Court's student speech decisions began in a milder era, where the expression at issue was wearing black armbands to protest the Vietnam War. Today, the issues are apt to involve threats of school violence or derogatory remarks about students or school officials on social media. The Internet and social media make today's speech instantly available to audiences far beyond those impacted by a speech at a student assembly, or an article in a school print newspaper. This exposure, in turn, raises issues about how far schools can go to discipline students for speech occurring off-campus. The Supreme Court has yet to address all of these issues, and lower courts attempt to do so by applying the Court's existing standards.

§ 9.02 The Classic Cases — A Trilogy Plus One Sets the Standard

For decades, a trilogy of United States Supreme Court cases governed the arena of student speech in public schools — *Tinker v. Des Moines*, which upheld students' right to wear black armbands to protest the Vietnam war; *Bethel v. Fraser*, which upheld the discipline of a student for a "lewd" speech delivered at a school assembly; and *Hazelwood Sch. Dist. v. Kuhlmeier*, which upheld a school's ability to control the content in a student newspaper.

In 2007, the Court added to its student speech decisions with *Morse v. Frederick*, 551 U.S. 393 (2007), commonly referred to as the "Bong Hits 4 Jesus" case. In *Morse*, the Court ruled that a school principal could discipline a student who displayed a banner with that phrase at a school function, because the principal reasonably believed that the banner promoted drug use. The following table summarizes the legal standards established by these four cases:

Case	Holding
Tinker v. Des Moines	School officials may restrict student speech only if there is a reasonable expectation that the speech will cause a substantial disruption of, or a material interference with, school activities, or it will impinge upon the rights of others.
Bethel v. Fraser	School officials may restrict lewd, indecent, vulgar, or plainly offensive student speech, even if there is no expectation of disruption or impingement of others' rights.
Hazelwood v. Kuhlmeier	School officials may restrict school-sponsored speech, as long as the restriction is reasonably related to legitimate pedagogical concerns.
Morse v. Frederick	School officials may restrict student speech that a school official reasonably believed promoted illegal drug use. Deference is given to school officials on whether the speech at issue promotes such activity.

The following problem gives you a chance to apply these Supreme Court standards to various situations.

Problem 1: Applying Free Speech Standards

Review the following fact patterns.[1] For each fact pattern, determine

1. Which Supreme Court precedent/standard applies; and
2. Whether the school's actions are constitutional under the relevant standard.

Fact Pattern #1

A tenth grade High School student records a rap song about two high school coaches that have a reputation amongst students for sexually harassing students. The lyrics are filled with vulgarities, swear words, and derogatory statements about the coaches. They also include statements like "better watch his back," and "you fucking with the wrong one, gonna get a pistol down your mouth." The student uses his personal computer to post the song on his Facebook profile, and on YouTube. None of the student's actions took place on school grounds, or during school hours. School

1. Some of these fact patterns are based on actual court cases or current events.

computers block access to Facebook and YouTube. The school principal finds out about the posts and suspends the student.

Fact Pattern #2

Three girls at the middle school wear **I ♥ Boobies** bracelets to school as part of a breast cancer fundraising raising effort in the community. The principal finds the bracelets to be lewd and offensive and bans them from the school.

Fact Pattern #3

A high school has a "Diversity Day" to promote diversity and respect for others. Part of the day includes a community-wide event held on school grounds after school. The event includes speeches supporting diversity by members of the community and students. A group of students come to the event wearing "Make America Great Again" hats and T-shirts that say "Build the Wall! Keep criminals in Mexico!" One of them asks to give a speech to express her viewpoint that immigrants are draining American resources and taking jobs away from real Americans. School officials tell the students that they cannot wear the shirts at the event, or give a speech.

Fact Pattern #4

A group of white, male, high school students pose for a picture taken by a parent outside of the school's gymnasium as they prepare to attend their high school prom later that Saturday evening. The students all give the Nazi salute for the picture. Several students post the picture on social media. A reporter for the local newspaper comes across the picture, and the paper runs a story about it. The school suspends the students.

Fact Pattern #5

Earl is a high school senior. He volunteers after school for a non-profit group that is working on getting public support to place a referendum on the ballot to legalize marijuana for medicinal purposes. The non-profit has bumper stickers and buttons made to support their efforts that have a picture of a marijuana leaf and say "Vote for *Good* Medicine" underneath the picture. Earl puts the bumper sticker on his car and puts the button on his backpack. The school orders Earl to remove the button and to remove or cover up the bumper sticker while on school grounds.

Fact Pattern #6

A third grade student hands out candy canes with a message about Jesus during her classroom holiday party. The teacher tells the student that she cannot hand them out during class, but could give them to students who wanted them after school, outside of the school building.

Fact Pattern #7

A group of high school students set up a table in the school lobby before school. When students enter the lobby in the morning, they are offered a rubber fetus and a card with anti-abortion information. Students who do not want a fetus are allowed to go on their way. Many students accept the offering and begin throwing them at each other during school. The school prohibits the students from continuing to distribute the dolls on campus.

Fact Pattern #8

John is running for class president at the high school. He has some cards made that say "Vote for John. The safe choice!" He hands out the cards with condoms attached to them as students walk down the halls between classes. The school principal finds out and prohibits John from distributing the cards.

Problem Materials

✓ *Tinker v. Des Moines*, 393 U.S. 503 (1968)

✓ *Bethel School District v. Fraser*, 478 U.S. 675 (1986)

✓ *Hazelwood School District v. Kuhlmeier*, 484 U.S. 260 (1988)

✓ *Morse v. Frederick*, 551 U.S. 393 (2007)

Tinker v. Des Moines

393 U.S. 503 (1968)

The Court finds that the First Amendment protects students' wearing black armbands to protest the Vietnam war, holding that to constitutionally discipline such expression, the school has to show that the speech would reasonably be expected to cause a substantial disruption of, or a material interference with, school activities, or impinge on the rights of others.

Mr. Justice Fortas delivered the opinion of the Court.

Petitioner John F. Tinker, 15 years old, and petitioner Christopher Eckhardt, 16 years old, attended high schools in Des Moines, Iowa. Petitioner Mary Beth Tinker, John's sister, was a 13-year-old student in junior high school.

In December 1965, a group of adults and students in Des Moines held a meeting at the Eckhardt home. The group determined to publicize their objections to the hostilities in Vietnam and their support for a truce by wearing black armbands during the holiday season and by fasting on December 16 and New Year's Eve. Petitioners and their parents had previously engaged in similar activities, and they decided to participate in the program.

The principals of the Des Moines schools became aware of the plan to wear armbands. On December 14, 1965, they met and adopted a policy that any student wearing an armband to school would be asked to remove it, and if he refused he would be suspended until he returned without the armband. Petitioners were aware of the regulation that the school authorities adopted.

On December 16, Mary Beth and Christopher wore black armbands to their schools. John Tinker wore his armband the next day. They were all sent home and suspended from school until they would come back without their armbands. They did not return to school until after the planned period for wearing armbands had expired—that is, until after New Year's Day.

This complaint was filed in the United States District Court by petitioners, through their fathers, under § 1983 of Title 42 of the United States Code. . . .

. . . As we shall discuss, the wearing of armbands in the circumstances of this case was entirely divorced from actually or potentially disruptive conduct by those participating in it. It was closely akin to "pure speech" which, we have repeatedly held, is entitled to comprehensive protection under the First Amendment. . . .

First Amendment rights, applied in light of the special characteristics of the school environment, are available to teachers and students. It can hardly be argued that either students or teachers shed their constitutional rights to freedom of speech or expression at the schoolhouse gate. This has been the unmistakable holding of this Court for almost 50 years. . . .

On the other hand, the Court has repeatedly emphasized the need for affirming the comprehensive authority of the States and of school officials, consistent with fundamental constitutional safeguards, to prescribe and control conduct in the schools. . . .

Our problem lies in the area where students in the exercise of First Amendment rights collide with the rules of the school authorities. . . . Our problem involves direct, primary First Amendment rights akin to "pure speech." The school officials banned and sought to punish petitioners for a silent, passive expression of opinion, unaccompanied by any disorder or disturbance on the part of petitioners. There is here no evidence whatever of petitioners' interference, actual or nascent, with the schools' work or of collision with the rights of other students to be secure and to be let alone. Accordingly, this case does not concern speech or action that intrudes upon the work of the schools or the rights of other students.

Only a few of the 18,000 students in the school system wore the black armbands. Only five students were suspended for wearing them. There is no indication that the work of the schools or any class was disrupted. Outside the classrooms, a few students made hostile remarks to the children wearing armbands, but there were no threats or acts of violence on school premises. . . .

In order for the State in the person of school officials to justify prohibition of a particular expression of opinion, it must be able to show that its action was caused by something more than a mere desire to avoid the discomfort and unpleasantness that always accompany an unpopular viewpoint. Certainly where there is no finding and no showing that engaging in the forbidden conduct would "materially and substantially interfere with the requirements of appropriate discipline in the operation of the school," the prohibition cannot be sustained. . . .

In the present case, the District Court made no such finding, and our independent examination of the record fails to yield evidence that the school authorities had reason to anticipate that the wearing of the armbands would substantially interfere with the work of the school or impinge upon the rights of other students. Even an official memorandum prepared after the suspension that listed the reasons for the ban on wearing the armbands made no reference to the anticipation of such disruption.

On the contrary, the action of the school authorities appears to have been based upon an urgent wish to avoid the controversy which might result from the expression, even by the silent symbol of armbands, of opposition to this Nation's part in the conflagration in Vietnam. It is revealing, in this respect, that the meeting at which the school principals decided to issue the contested regulation was called in response to a student's statement to the journalism teacher in one of the schools that he wanted to write an article on Vietnam and have it published in the school paper. The student was dissuaded.

It is also relevant that the school authorities did not purport to prohibit the wearing of all symbols of political or controversial significance. The record shows that students in some of the schools wore buttons relating to national political campaigns, and some even wore the Iron Cross, traditionally a symbol of Nazism. The order prohibiting the wearing of armbands did not extend to these. Instead, a particular symbol—black armbands worn to exhibit opposition to this Nation's involvement in Vietnam—was singled out for prohibition. Clearly, the prohibition of expression of one particular opinion, at least without evidence that it is necessary to avoid material and substantial interference with schoolwork or discipline, is not constitutionally permissible.

In our system, state-operated schools may not be enclaves of totalitarianism. School officials do not possess absolute authority over their students. Students in school as well as out of school are "persons" under our Constitution. They are possessed of fundamental rights which the State must respect, just as they themselves must respect their obligations to the State. In our system, students may not be regarded as closed-circuit recipients of only that which the State chooses to communicate. They may not be confined to the expression of those sentiments that are officially approved. In the absence of a specific showing of constitutionally valid reasons to regulate their speech, students are entitled to freedom of expression of their views. As Judge Gewin, speaking for the Fifth Circuit, said, school officials cannot suppress "expressions of feelings with which they do not wish to contend." . . .

In *Meyer v. Nebraska*, 262 U.S. 390 (1923), Mr. Justice McReynolds expressed this Nation's repudiation of the principle that a State might so conduct its schools as to "foster a homogeneous people." He said:

> "In order to submerge the individual and develop ideal citizens, Sparta assembled the males at seven into barracks and intrusted their subsequent education and training to official guardians. Although such measures have been deliberately approved by men of great genius, their ideas touching the relation between individual and State were wholly different from those upon which our institutions rest; and it hardly will be affirmed that any

> Legislature could impose such restrictions upon the people of a state without doing violence to both letter and spirit of the Constitution."

This principle has been repeated by this Court of numerous occasions during the intervening years. In *Keyishian v. Board of Regents*, 385 U.S. 589, 603, Mr. Justice Brennan, speaking for the Court, said:

> "'The vigilant protection of constitutional freedoms is nowhere more vital than in the community of American schools.' *Shelton v. Tucker* [364 U.S. 479], at 487. The classroom is peculiarly the 'marketplace of ideas.' The Nation's future depends upon leaders trained through wide exposure to that robust exchange of ideas which discovers truth 'out of a multitude of tongues, [rather] than through any kind of authoritative selection.'"

The principle of these cases is not confined to the supervised and ordained discussion which takes place in the classroom. The principal use to which the schools are dedicated is to accommodate students during prescribed hours for the purpose of certain types of activities. Among those activities is personal intercommunication among the students. This is not only an inevitable part of the process of attending school; it is also an important part of the educational process. A student's rights, therefore, do not embrace merely the classroom hours. When he is in the cafeteria, or on the playing field, or on the campus during the authorized hours, he may express his opinions, even on controversial subjects like the conflict in Vietnam, if he does so without "materially and substantially interfere[ing] with the requirements of appropriate discipline in the operation of the school" and without colliding with the rights of others. But conduct by the student, in class or out of it, which for any reason—whether it stems from time, place, or type of behavior—materially disrupts classwork or involves substantial disorder or invasion of the rights of others is, of course, not immunized by the constitutional guarantee of freedom of speech.

Under our Constitution, free speech is not a right that is given only to be so circumscribed that it exists in principle but not in fact. Freedom of expression would not truly exist if the right could be exercised only in an area that a benevolent government has provided as a safe haven for crackpots. The Constitution says that Congress (and the States) may not abridge the right to free speech. This provision means what it says. We properly read it to permit reasonable regulation of speech-connected activities in carefully restricted circumstances. But we do not confine the permissible exercise of First Amendment rights to a telephone booth or the four corners of a pamphlet, or to supervised and ordained discussion in a school classroom.

If a regulation were adopted by school officials forbidding discussion of the Vietnam conflict, or the expression by any student of opposition to it anywhere on school property except as part of a prescribed classroom exercise, it would be obvious that the regulation would violate the constitutional rights of students, at least if it could not be justified by a showing that the students' activities would materially and substantially disrupt the work and discipline of the school. In the circumstances of the present case, the prohibition of the silent, passive "witness of the armbands," as one of the children called it, is no less offensive to the constitution's guarantees.

As we have discussed, the record does not demonstrate any facts which might reasonably have led school authorities to forecast substantial disruption of or material interference with school activities, and no disturbances or disorders on the school premises in fact occurred. These petitioners merely went about their ordained rounds in school. Their deviation consisted only in wearing on their sleeve a band of black cloth, not more than two inches wide. They wore it to exhibit their disapproval of the Vietnam hostilities and their advocacy of a truce, to make their views known, and, by their example, to influence others to adopt them. They neither interrupted school activities nor sought to intrude in the school affairs or the lives of others. They caused discussion outside of the classrooms, but no interference with work and no disorder. In the circumstances, our Constitution does not permit officials of the State to deny their form of expression.

We express no opinion as to the form of relief which should be granted, this being a matter for the lower courts to determine. We reverse and remand for further proceedings consistent with this opinion.

Reversed and remanded.

Bethel School District v. Fraser

478 U.S. 675 (1986)

The Court holds that the First Amendment does not preclude a school district from exercising its discretion to discipline a student who gives a "lewd" speech at a high school assembly.

Chief Justice Burger delivered the opinion of the Court.

We granted certiorari to decide whether the First Amendment prevents a school district from disciplining a high school student for giving a lewd speech at a school assembly.

On April 26, 1983, respondent Matthew N. Fraser, a student at Bethel High School in Pierce County, Washington, delivered a speech nominating a fellow student for student elective office. Approximately 600 high school students, many of whom were 14-year-olds, attended the assembly. Students were required to attend the assembly or to report to the study hall. The assembly was part of a school-sponsored educational program in self-government. Students who elected not to attend the assembly were required to report to study hall. During the entire speech, Fraser referred to his candidate in terms of an elaborate, graphic, and explicit sexual metaphor.

Two of Fraser's teachers, with whom he discussed the contents of his speech in advance, informed him that the speech was "inappropriate and that he probably should not deliver it," and that his delivery of the speech might have "severe consequences."

During Fraser's delivery of the speech, a school counselor observed the reaction of students to the speech. Some students hooted and yelled; some by gestures graphically simulated the sexual activities pointedly alluded to in respondent's speech. Other students appeared to be bewildered and embarrassed by the speech. One teacher reported that on the day following the speech, she found it necessary to forgo a portion of the scheduled class lesson in order to discuss the speech with the class.

A Bethel High School disciplinary rule prohibiting the use of obscene language in the school provides: "Conduct which materially and substantially interferes with the educational process is prohibited, including the use of obscene, profane language or gestures."

The morning after the assembly, the Assistant Principal called Fraser into her office and notified him that the school considered his speech to have been a violation of this rule. Fraser was presented with copies of five letters submitted by teachers, describing his conduct at the assembly; he was given a chance to explain his conduct, and he admitted to having given the speech described and that he deliberately used sexual innuendo in the speech. Fraser was then informed that he would be suspended for three days, and that his name would be removed from the list of candidates for graduation speaker at the school's commencement exercises.

Fraser sought review of this disciplinary action through the School District's grievance procedures. The hearing officer determined that the speech given by respondent was "indecent, lewd, and offensive to the modesty and decency of many of the students and faculty in attendance at the assembly." The examiner determined that the speech fell within the ordinary meaning of "obscene," as used in the disruptive-conduct rule, and affirmed the discipline in its entirety. Fraser served two days of his suspension, and was allowed to return to school on the third day.

. . . .

It is against this background that we turn to consider the level of First Amendment protection accorded to Fraser's utterances and actions before an official high school assembly attended by 600 students.

The role and purpose of the American public school system were well described by two historians, who stated: "[Public] education must prepare pupils for citizenship in the Republic. . . . It must inculcate the habits and manners of civility as values in themselves conducive to happiness and as indispensable to the practice of self-government in the community and the nation." C. Beard & M. Beard, New Basic History of the United States 228 (1968). In *Ambach v. Norwick*, 441 U.S. 68, 76–77 (1979), we echoed the essence of this statement of the objectives of public education as the "[inculcation of] fundamental values necessary to the maintenance of a democratic political system."

These fundamental values of "habits and manners of civility" essential to a democratic society must, of course, include tolerance of divergent political and religious views, even when the views expressed may be unpopular. But these "fundamental values" must also take into account consideration of the sensibilities of others, and, in the case of a school, the sensibilities of fellow students. The undoubted freedom to advocate unpopular and controversial views in schools and classrooms must be balanced against the society's countervailing interest in teaching students the boundaries of socially appropriate behavior. Even the most heated political discourse in a democratic society requires consideration for the personal sensibilities of the other participants and audiences.

In our Nation's legislative halls, where some of the most vigorous political debates in our society are carried on, there are rules prohibiting the use of expressions offensive to other participants in the debate. . . . Can it be that what is proscribed in the halls of Congress is beyond the reach of school officials to regulate?

The First Amendment guarantees wide freedom in matters of adult public discourse. A sharply divided Court upheld the right to express an antidraft viewpoint in a public place, albeit in terms highly offensive to most citizens. *See Cohen v. California*, 403 U.S. 15 (1971). It does not follow, however, that simply because the use of an offensive form of expression may not be prohibited to adults making what the speaker considers a political point, the same latitude must be permitted to children in a public school. In *New Jersey v. T.L.O.*, 469 U.S. 325 (1985), we reaffirmed that the constitutional rights of students in public school are not automatically coextensive with the rights of adults in other settings. As cogently expressed by Judge Newman, "the First Amendment gives a high school student the classroom right to wear Tinker's armband, but not Cohen's jacket." *Thomas* v. *Board of Educ., Granville Cent. Sch. Dist.*, 607 F.2d 1043, 1057 (2d Cir. 1979).

Surely it is a highly appropriate function of public school education to prohibit the use of vulgar and offensive terms in public discourse. Indeed, the "fundamental values necessary to the maintenance of a democratic political system" disfavor the use of terms of debate highly offensive or highly threatening to others. Nothing in the Constitution prohibits the states from insisting that certain modes of expression are inappropriate and subject to sanctions. The inculcation of these values is truly the "work of the schools." *Tinker.* The determination of what manner of speech in the classroom or in school assembly is inappropriate properly rests with the school board.

The process of educating our youth for citizenship in public schools is not confined to books, the curriculum, and the civics class; schools must teach by example the shared values of a civilized social order. Consciously or otherwise, teachers—and indeed the older students—demonstrate the appropriate form of civil discourse and political expression by their conduct and deportment in and out of class. Inescapably, like parents, they are role models. The schools, as instruments of the state, may determine that the essential lessons of civil, mature conduct cannot be conveyed in a school that tolerates lewd, indecent, or offensive speech and conduct such as that indulged in by this confused boy.

The pervasive sexual innuendo in Fraser's speech was plainly offensive to both teachers and students—indeed to any mature person. By glorifying male sexuality, and in its verbal content, the speech was acutely insulting to teenage girl students. The speech could well be seriously damaging to its less mature audience, many of whom were only 14 years old and on the threshold of awareness of human sexuality. Some students were reported as bewildered by the speech and the reaction of mimicry it provoked.

We hold that petitioner School District acted entirely within its permissible authority in imposing sanctions upon Fraser in response to his offensively lewd and indecent speech. Unlike the sanctions imposed on the students wearing armbands in *Tinker*, the penalties imposed in this case were unrelated to any political viewpoint. The First Amendment does not prevent the school officials from determining that to permit a vulgar and lewd speech such as respondent's would undermine the school's basic educational mission. A high school assembly or classroom is no place for a sexually explicit monologue directed towards an unsuspecting audience of teenage students. Accordingly, it was perfectly appropriate for the school to disassociate itself to make the point to the pupils that vulgar speech and lewd conduct is wholly inconsistent with the "fundamental values" of public school education.

The judgment of the Court of Appeals for the Ninth Circuit is *Reversed*.

Justice Brennan, concurring in the judgment.

Respondent gave the following speech at a high school assembly in support of a candidate for student government office:

> "'I know a man who is firm—he's firm in his pants, he's firm in his shirt, his character is firm—but most . . . of all, his belief in you, the students of Bethel, is firm.
>
> "'Jeff Kuhlman is a man who takes his point and pounds it in. If necessary, he'll take an issue and nail it to the wall. He doesn't attack things in spurts—he drives hard, pushing and pushing until finally—he succeeds.
>
> "'Jeff is a man who will go to the very end—even the climax, for each and every one of you.
>
> "'So vote for Jeff for A.S.B. vice-president—he'll never come between you and the best our high school can be.'"

The Court, referring to these remarks as "obscene," "vulgar," "lewd," and "offensively lewd," concludes that school officials properly punished respondent for uttering the speech. Having read the full text of respondent's remarks, I find it difficult to believe that it is the same speech the Court describes. To my mind, the most that can be said about respondent's speech—and all that need be said—is that in light of the discretion school officials have to teach high school students how to conduct civil and effective public discourse, and to prevent disruption of school educational activities, it was not unconstitutional for school officials to conclude, under the circumstances of this case, that respondent's remarks exceeded permissible limits. . . .

Hazelwood School District v. Kuhlmeier

484 U.S. 260 (1988)

The Court upholds the school's authority to control the content of the student newspaper where the newspaper bore the imprimatur of the school, and the restrictions were reasonably related to legitimate pedagogical concerns.

Justice White delivered the opinion of the Court.

This case concerns the extent to which educators may exercise editorial control over the contents of a high school newspaper produced as part of the school's journalism curriculum.

Petitioners are the Hazelwood School District in St. Louis County, Missouri; various school officials; Robert Eugene Reynolds, the principal of Hazelwood East High School; and Howard Emerson, a teacher in the school district. Respondents are three former Hazelwood East students who were staff members of Spectrum, the school newspaper. They contend that school officials violated their First Amendment rights by deleting two pages of articles from the May 13, 1983, issue of Spectrum.

Spectrum was written and edited by the Journalism II class at Hazelwood East. The newspaper was published every three weeks or so during the 1982–1983 school year. More than 4,500 copies of the newspaper were distributed during that year to students, school personnel, and members of the community.

The Board of Education allocated funds from its annual budget for the printing of Spectrum. . . .

The practice at Hazelwood East during the spring 1983 semester was for the journalism teacher to submit page proofs of each Spectrum issue to Principal Reynolds for his review prior to publication. On May 10, Emerson delivered the proofs of the May 13 edition to Reynolds, who objected to two of the articles scheduled to appear in that edition. One of the stories described three Hazelwood East students' experiences with pregnancy; the other discussed the impact of divorce on students at the school.

Reynolds was concerned that, although the pregnancy story used false names "to keep the identity of these girls a secret," the pregnant students still might be identifiable from the text. He also believed that the article's references to sexual activity and birth control were inappropriate for some of the younger students at the school. In addition, Reynolds was concerned that a student identified by name in the divorce story had complained that her father "wasn't spending enough time with my mom, my sister and I" prior to the divorce, "was always out of town on business or out late playing cards with the guys," and "always argued about everything" with her mother. Reynolds believed that the student's parents should have been given an opportunity to respond to these remarks or to consent to their publication. He was unaware that Emerson had deleted the student's name from the final version of the article.

Reynolds believed that there was no time to make the necessary changes in the stories before the scheduled press run and that the newspaper would not appear before the end of the school year if printing were delayed to any significant extent. He concluded that his only options under the circumstances were to publish a four-page newspaper instead of the planned six-page newspaper, eliminating the two pages on which the offending stories appeared, or to publish no newspaper at all. Accordingly, he directed Emerson to withhold from publication the two pages containing the stories on pregnancy and divorce. He informed his superiors of the decision, and they concurred.

. . . .

Students in the public schools do not "shed their constitutional rights to freedom of speech or expression at the schoolhouse gate." *Tinker.* They cannot be punished merely for expressing their personal views on the school premises—whether "in the cafeteria, or on the playing field, or on the campus during the authorized hours,"—unless school authorities have reason to believe that such expression will "substantially interfere with the work of the school or impinge upon the rights of other students."

We have nonetheless recognized that the First Amendment rights of students in the public schools "are not automatically coextensive with the rights of adults in other settings," and must be "applied in light of the special characteristics of the school environment." A school need not tolerate student speech that is inconsistent with its "basic educational mission," even though the government could not censor similar speech outside the school. Accordingly, we held in *Fraser* that a student could be disciplined for having delivered a speech that was "sexually explicit" but not legally obscene at an official school assembly, because the school was entitled to "disassociate itself" from the speech in a manner that would demonstrate to others that such vulgarity is "wholly inconsistent with the 'fundamental values' of public school education." We thus recognized that "[t]he determination of what manner of speech in the classroom or in school assembly is inappropriate properly rests with the school board," rather than with the federal courts. It is in this context that respondents' First Amendment claims must be considered.

We deal first with the question whether Spectrum may appropriately be characterized as a forum for public expression. The public schools do not possess all of the attributes of streets, parks, and other traditional public forums that "time out of mind, have been used for purposes of assembly, communicating thoughts between citizens, and discussing public questions." Hence, school facilities may be deemed to be public forums only if school authorities have "by policy or by practice" opened those facilities "for indiscriminate use by the general public," or by some segment of the public, such as student organizations. If the facilities have instead been reserved for other intended purposes, "communicative or otherwise," then no public forum has been created, and school officials may impose reasonable restrictions on the speech of students, teachers, and other members of the school community. The government does not create a public forum by inaction or by permitting limited discourse, but only by intentionally opening a nontraditional forum for public discourse.

The policy of school officials toward Spectrum was reflected in Hazelwood School Board Policy 348.51 and the Hazelwood East Curriculum Guide. Board Policy 348.51 provided that "[s]chool sponsored publications are developed within the adopted curriculum and its educational implications in regular classroom activities." The Hazelwood East Curriculum Guide described the Journalism II course as a "laboratory situation in which the students publish the school newspaper applying skills they have learned in Journalism I." The lessons that were to be learned from the Journalism II course, according to the Curriculum Guide, included development of journalistic skills under deadline pressure, "the legal, moral, and ethical restrictions imposed upon journalists within the school community," and "responsibility and acceptance of criticism for articles of opinion." Journalism II was taught by a faculty member during regular class hours. Students received grades and academic credit for their performance in the course.

School officials did not deviate in practice from their policy that production of Spectrum was to be part of the educational curriculum and a "regular classroom activit[y]." The District Court found that Robert Stergos, the journalism teacher during most of the 1982–1983 school year, "both had the authority to exercise and in fact exercised a great deal of control over *Spectrum*." For example, Stergos selected the editors of the newspaper, scheduled publication dates, decided the number of pages for each issue, assigned story ideas to class members, advised students on the development of their stories, reviewed the use of quotations, edited stories, selected and edited the letters to the editor, and dealt with the printing company. Many of these decisions were made without consultation with the Journalism II students. The District Court thus found it "clear that Mr. Stergos was the final authority with respect to almost every aspect of the production and publication of *Spectrum*, including its content." Moreover, after each Spectrum issue had been finally approved by Stergos or his successor, the issue still had to be reviewed by Principal Reynolds prior to publication. Respondents' assertion that they had believed that they could publish "practically anything" in Spectrum was therefore dismissed by the District Court as simply "not credible." These factual findings are amply supported by the record, and were not rejected as clearly erroneous by the Court of Appeals.

. . . .

The question whether the First Amendment requires a school to tolerate particular student speech—the question that we addressed in *Tinker*—is different from the question whether the First Amendment requires a school affirmatively to promote particular student speech. The former question addresses educators' ability to silence a student's personal expression that happens to occur on the school premises. The latter question concerns educators' authority over school-sponsored publications, theatrical productions, and other expressive activities that students, parents, and members of the public might reasonably perceive to bear the imprimatur of the school. These activities may fairly be characterized as part of the school curriculum, whether or not they occur in a traditional classroom setting, so long as they are supervised by faculty members and designed to impart particular knowledge or skills to student participants and audiences.

Educators are entitled to exercise greater control over this second form of student expression to assure that participants learn whatever lessons the activity is designed to teach, that readers or listeners are not exposed to material that may be inappropriate for their level of maturity, and that the views of the individual speaker are not erroneously attributed to the school. Hence, a school may in its capacity as publisher of a school newspaper or producer of a school play "disassociate itself," *Fraser*, not only from speech that would "substantially interfere with [its] work . . . or impinge upon the rights of other students," *Tinker*, but also from speech that is, for example, ungrammatical, poorly written, inadequately researched, biased or prejudiced, vulgar or profane, or unsuitable for immature audiences. A school must be able to set high standards for the student speech that is disseminated under its auspices—standards that may be higher than those demanded by some newspaper publishers or theatrical producers in the "real" world—and may refuse to disseminate student speech that does not meet those standards. In addition, a school must be able to take into account the emotional maturity of the intended audience in determining whether to disseminate student speech on potentially sensitive topics, which might range from the existence of Santa Claus in an elementary school setting to the particulars of teenage sexual activity in a high school setting. A school must also retain the authority to refuse to sponsor student speech that might reasonably be perceived to advocate drug or alcohol use, irresponsible sex, or conduct otherwise inconsistent with "the shared values of a civilized social order," *Fraser*, or to associate the school with any position other than neutrality on matters of political controversy. Otherwise, the schools would be unduly constrained from fulfilling their role as "a principal instrument in awakening the child to cultural values, in preparing him for later professional training, and in helping him to adjust normally to his environment."

Accordingly, we conclude that the standard articulated in *Tinker* for determining when a school may punish student expression need not also be the standard for determining when a school may refuse to lend its name and resources to the dissemination of student expression. Instead, we hold that educators do not offend the First Amendment by exercising editorial control over the style and content of student speech in school-sponsored expressive activities so long as their actions are reasonably related to legitimate pedagogical concerns.

This standard is consistent with our oft-expressed view that the education of the Nation's youth is primarily the responsibility of parents, teachers, and state and local school officials, and not of federal judges. It is only when the decision to censor a school-sponsored publication, theatrical production, or other vehicle of student expression has no valid educational purpose that the First Amendment is so "directly and sharply implicate[d]," as to require judicial intervention to protect students' constitutional rights.

We also conclude that Principal Reynolds acted reasonably in requiring the deletion from the May 13 issue of Spectrum of the pregnancy article, the divorce article, and the remaining articles that were to appear on the same pages of the newspaper. . . .

In sum, we cannot reject as unreasonable Principal Reynolds' conclusion that neither the pregnancy article nor the divorce article was suitable for publication in Spectrum. Reynolds could reasonably have concluded that the students who had written and edited these articles had not sufficiently mastered those portions of the Journalism II curriculum that pertained to the treatment of controversial issues and personal attacks, the need to protect the privacy of individuals whose most intimate concerns are to be revealed in the newspaper, and "the legal, moral, and ethical restrictions imposed upon journalists within [a] school community" that includes adolescent subjects and readers. Finally, we conclude that the principal's decision to delete two pages of Spectrum, rather than to delete only the offending articles or to require that they be modified, was reasonable under the circumstances as he understood them. Accordingly, no violation of First Amendment rights occurred.

Morse v. Frederick

551 U.S. 393 (2007)

Reviewing the trilogy of its prior opinions, the Court rules that a school principal could discipline a student who displayed a "Bong Hits 4 Jesus" banner at a school function where the principal reasonably believed that the banner promoted drug use.

Chief Justice Roberts delivered the opinion of the Court.

At a school-sanctioned and school-supervised event, a high school principal saw some of her students unfurl a large banner conveying a message she reasonably regarded as promoting illegal drug use. Consistent with established school policy prohibiting such messages at school events, the principal directed the students to take down the banner. One student among those who had brought the banner to the event refused to do so. The principal confiscated the banner and later suspended the student. The Ninth Circuit held that the principal's actions violated the First Amendment, and that the student could sue the principal for damages.

Our cases make clear that students do not "shed their constitutional rights to freedom of speech or expression at the schoolhouse gate." At the same time, we have held that "the constitutional rights of students in public school are not automatically coextensive with the rights of adults in other settings," and that the rights of students "must be 'applied in light of the special characteristics of the school environment.'" Consistent with these principles, we hold that schools may take steps to safeguard those entrusted to their care from speech that can reasonably be regarded as encouraging illegal drug use. We conclude that the school officials in this case did not violate the First Amendment by confiscating the pro-drug banner and suspending the student responsible for it.

On January 24, 2002, the Olympic Torch Relay passed through Juneau, Alaska, on its way to the winter games in Salt Lake City, Utah. The torchbearers were to proceed along a street in front of Juneau-Douglas High School (JDHS) while school was in session. Petitioner Deborah Morse, the school principal, decided to permit staff and students to participate in the Torch Relay as an approved social event or class trip. Students were allowed to leave class to observe the relay from either side of the street. Teachers and administrative officials monitored the students' actions.

Respondent Joseph Frederick, a JDHS senior, was late to school that day. When he arrived, he joined his friends (all but one of whom were JDHS students) across the street from the school to watch the event. Not all the students waited patiently. Some became rambunctious, throwing plastic cola bottles and snowballs and scuffling with their classmates. As the torchbearers and camera crews passed by, Frederick and his friends unfurled a 14-foot banner bearing the phrase: "BONG HiTS 4 JESUS." The large banner was easily readable by the students on the other side of the street.

Principal Morse immediately crossed the street and demanded that the banner be taken down. Everyone but Frederick complied. Morse confiscated the banner and told Frederick to report to her office, where she suspended him for 10 days. Morse later explained that she told Frederick to take the banner down because she thought it encouraged illegal drug use, in violation of established school policy. Juneau School Board Policy No. 5520 states: "The Board specifically prohibits any assembly or public expression that . . . advocates the use of substances that are illegal to minors. . . ." In addition, Juneau School Board Policy No. 5850 subjects "[p]upils who participate in approved social events and class trips" to the same student conduct rules that apply during the regular school program.

Frederick administratively appealed his suspension, but the Juneau School District Superintendent upheld it, limiting it to time served (8 days). In a memorandum setting forth his reasons, the superintendent determined that Frederick had displayed his banner "in the midst of his fellow students, during school hours, at a school-sanctioned activity." He further explained that Frederick "was not disciplined because the principal of the school 'disagreed' with his message, but because his speech appeared to advocate the use of illegal drugs."

The superintendent continued:

> "The common-sense understanding of the phrase 'bong hits' is that it is a reference to a means of smoking marijuana. Given [Frederick's] inability or unwillingness to express any other credible meaning for the phrase, I can only agree with the principal and countless others who saw the banner as advocating the use of illegal drugs. [Frederick's] speech was not political. He was not advocating the legalization of marijuana or promoting a religious belief. He was displaying a fairly silly message promoting illegal drug

> usage in the midst of a school activity, for the benefit of television cameras covering the Torch Relay. [Frederick's] speech was potentially disruptive to the event and clearly disruptive of and inconsistent with the school's educational mission to educate students about the dangers of illegal drugs and to discourage their use." *Id.*, at 61a–62a.

Relying on our decision in *Fraser, supra*, the superintendent concluded that the principal's actions were permissible because Frederick's banner was "speech or action that intrudes upon the work of the schools." The Juneau School District Board of Education upheld the suspension.

Frederick then filed suit under 42 U.S.C. § 1983, alleging that the school board and Morse had violated his First Amendment rights. . . .

We granted certiorari on two questions: whether Frederick had a First Amendment right to wield his banner, and, if so, whether that right was so clearly established that the principal may be held liable for damages. We resolve the first question against Frederick, and therefore have no occasion to reach the second.

At the outset, we reject Frederick's argument that this is not a school speech case-as has every other authority to address the question. The event occurred during normal school hours. It was sanctioned by Principal Morse "as an approved social event or class trip," and the school district's rules expressly provide that pupils in "approved social events and class trips are subject to district rules for student conduct." Teachers and administrators were interspersed among the students and charged with supervising them. The high school band and cheerleaders performed. Frederick, standing among other JDHS students across the street from the school, directed his banner toward the school, making it plainly visible to most students. Under these circumstances, we agree with the superintendent that Frederick cannot "stand in the midst of his fellow students, during school hours, at a school-sanctioned activity and claim he is not at school." There is some uncertainty at the outer boundaries as to when courts should apply school-speech precedents, *see Porter v. Ascension Parish School Bd.*, 393 F.3d 608, 615, n. 22 (5th Cir. 2004), but not on these facts.

The message on Frederick's banner is cryptic. It is no doubt offensive to some, perhaps amusing to others. To still others, it probably means nothing at all. Frederick himself claimed "that the words were just nonsense meant to attract television cameras." But Principal Morse thought the banner would be interpreted by those viewing it as promoting illegal drug use, and that interpretation is plainly a reasonable one.

As Morse later explained in a declaration, when she saw the sign, she thought that "the reference to a 'bong hit' would be widely understood by high school students and others as referring to smoking marijuana." She further believed that "display of the banner would be construed by students, District personnel, parents and others witnessing the display of the banner, as advocating or promoting illegal drug use"—in violation of school policy. . . .

We agree with Morse. At least two interpretations of the words on the banner demonstrate that the sign advocated the use of illegal drugs. First, the phrase could be interpreted as an imperative: "[Take] bong hits . . ."—a message equivalent, as Morse explained in her declaration, to "smoke marijuana" or "use an illegal drug." Alternatively, the phrase could be viewed as celebrating drug use—"bong hits [are a good thing]," or "[we take] bong hits"—and we discern no meaningful distinction between celebrating illegal drug use in the midst of fellow students and outright advocacy or promotion.

. . . .

The pro-drug interpretation of the banner gains further plausibility given the paucity of alternative meanings the banner might bear. The best Frederick can come up with is that the banner is "meaningless and funny." . . .

The question thus becomes whether a principal may, consistent with the First Amendment, restrict student speech at a school event, when that speech is reasonably viewed as promoting illegal drug use. We hold that she may.

. . . .

Drawing on the principles applied in our student speech cases, we have held in the Fourth Amendment context that "while children assuredly do not 'shed their constitutional rights . . . at the schoolhouse gate,' . . . the nature of those rights is what is appropriate for children in school." *Vernonia School Dist. 47J v. Acton*, 515 U.S. 646, 655–656 (1995). In particular, "the school setting requires some easing of the restrictions to which searches by public authorities are ordinarily subject." *New Jersey v. T.L.O.*, 469 U.S. 325, 340 (1985). . . . Even more to the point, these cases also recognize that deterring drug use by schoolchildren is an "important—indeed, perhaps compelling" interest. Drug abuse can cause severe and permanent damage to the health and well-being of young people. . . .

Just five years ago, we wrote: "The drug abuse problem among our Nation's youth has hardly abated since *Vernonia* was decided in 1995. In fact, evidence suggests that it has only grown worse." The problem remains serious today. About half of American 12th graders have used an illicit drug, as have more than a third of 10th graders and about one-fifth of 8th graders. Nearly one in four 12th graders has used an illicit drug in the past month. Some 25% of high schoolers say that they have been offered, sold, or given an illegal drug on school property within the past year.

Congress has declared that part of a school's job is educating students about the dangers of illegal drug use. It has provided billions of dollars to support state and local drug-prevention programs and required that schools receiving federal funds under the Safe and Drug-Free Schools and Communities Act of 1994 certify that their drug prevention programs "convey a clear and consistent message that . . . the illegal use of drugs [is] wrong and harmful." 20 U.S.C. § 7114(d)(6) (2000 ed., Supp. IV).

Thousands of school boards throughout the country—including JDHS—have adopted policies aimed at effectuating this message. Those school boards know that peer pressure is perhaps "the single most important factor leading schoolchildren to take drugs," and that students are more likely to use drugs when the norms in school appear to tolerate such behavior. Student speech celebrating illegal drug use at a school event, in the presence of school administrators and teachers, thus poses a particular challenge for school officials working to protect those entrusted to their care from the dangers of drug abuse.

The "special characteristics of the school environment," and the governmental interest in stopping student drug abuse—reflected in the policies of Congress and myriad school boards, including JDHS—allow schools to restrict student expression that they reasonably regard as promoting illegal drug use. *Tinker* warned that schools may not prohibit student speech because of "undifferentiated fear or apprehension of disturbance" or "a mere desire to avoid the discomfort and unpleasantness that always accompany an unpopular viewpoint." The danger here is far more serious and palpable. The particular concern to prevent student drug abuse at issue here, embodied in established school policy, extends well beyond an abstract desire to avoid controversy.

Petitioners urge us to adopt the broader rule that Frederick's speech is proscribable because it is plainly "offensive" as that term is used in *Fraser*. We think this stretches *Fraser* too far; that case should not be read to encompass any speech that could fit under some definition of "offensive." After all, much political and religious speech might be perceived as offensive to some. The concern here is not that Frederick's speech was offensive, but that it was reasonably viewed as promoting illegal drug use.

. . . .

School principals have a difficult job, and a vitally important one. When Frederick suddenly and unexpectedly unfurled his banner, Morse had to decide to act—or not act—on the spot. It was reasonable for her to conclude that the banner promoted illegal drug use—in violation of established school policy—and that failing to act would send a powerful message to the students in her charge, including Frederick, about how serious the school was about the dangers of illegal drug use. The First Amendment does not require schools to tolerate at school events student expression that contributes to those dangers.

The judgment of the United States Court of Appeals for the Ninth Circuit is reversed, and the case is remanded for further proceedings consistent with this opinion.

Justice Alito, with whom Justice Kennedy joins, concurring.

I join the opinion of the Court on the understanding that (1) it goes no further than to hold that a public school may restrict speech that a reasonable observer would interpret as advocating illegal drug use and (2) it provides no support for any restriction of speech that can plausibly be interpreted as commenting on any political or social issue, including speech on issues such as "the wisdom of the war on drugs or of legalizing marijuana for medicinal use."

The opinion of the Court correctly reaffirms the recognition in *Tinker v. Des Moines Independent Community School Dist.*, 393 U.S. 503, 506, (1969), of the fundamental principle that students do not "shed their constitutional rights to freedom of speech or expression at the schoolhouse gate." The Court is also correct in noting that *Tinker*, which permits the regulation of student speech that threatens a concrete and "substantial disruption," does not set out the only ground on which in-school student speech may be regulated by state actors in a way that would not be constitutional in other settings.

But I do not read the opinion to mean that there are necessarily any grounds for such regulation that are not already recognized in the holdings of this Court. In addition to *Tinker*, the decision in the present case allows the restriction of speech advocating illegal drug use; *Bethel School Dist. No. 403 v. Fraser*, 478 U.S. 675 (1986), permits the regulation of speech that is delivered in a lewd or vulgar manner as part of a high school program; and *Hazelwood School Dist. v. Kuhlmeier*, 484 U.S. 260 (1988), allows a school to regulate what is in essence the school's own speech, that is, articles that appear in a publication that is an official school organ. I join the opinion of the Court on the understanding that the opinion does not hold that the special characteristics of the public schools necessarily justify any other speech restrictions.

The opinion of the Court does not endorse the broad argument advanced by petitioners and the United States that the First Amendment permits public school officials to censor any student speech that interferes with a school's "educational mission." This argument can easily be manipulated in dangerous ways, and I would reject it before such abuse occurs. The "educational mission" of the public schools is defined by the elected and appointed public officials with authority over the schools and by the school administrators and faculty. As a result, some public schools have defined their educational missions as including the inculcation of whatever political and social views are held by the members of these groups.

During the *Tinker* era, a public school could have defined its educational mission to include solidarity with our soldiers and their families and thus could have attempted to outlaw the wearing of black armbands on the ground that they undermined this mission. Alternatively, a school could have defined its educational mission to include the promotion of world peace and could have sought to ban the wearing of buttons expressing support for the troops on the ground that the buttons signified approval of war. The "educational mission" argument would give public school authorities a license to suppress speech on political and social issues based on disagreement with the viewpoint expressed. The argument, therefore, strikes at the very heart of the First Amendment.

The public schools are invaluable and beneficent institutions, but they are, after all, organs of the State. When public school authorities regulate student speech, they act as agents of the State; they do not stand in the shoes of the students' parents. It is a dangerous fiction to pretend that parents simply delegate their authority—including their authority to determine what their children may say and hear—to public school authorities. It is even more dangerous to assume that such a delegation of authority somehow strips public school authorities of their status as agents of the State. Most parents, realistically, have no choice but to send their children to a public school and little ability to influence what occurs in the school. It is therefore wrong to treat public school officials, for purposes relevant to the First Amendment, as if they were private, nongovernmental actors standing *in loco parentis.*

For these reasons, any argument for altering the usual free speech rules in the public schools cannot rest on a theory of delegation but must instead be based on some special characteristic of the school setting. The special characteristic that is relevant in this case is the threat to the physical safety of students. School attendance can expose students to threats to their physical safety that they would not otherwise face. Outside of school, parents can attempt to protect their children in many ways and may take steps to monitor and exercise control over the persons with whom their children associate. Similarly, students, when not in school, may be able to avoid threatening individuals and situations. During school hours, however, parents are not present to provide protection and guidance, and students' movements and their ability to choose the persons with whom they spend time are severely restricted. Students may be compelled on a daily basis to spend time at close quarters with other students who may do them harm. Experience shows that schools can be places of special danger.

In most settings, the First Amendment strongly limits the government's ability to suppress speech on the ground that it presents a threat of violence. See *Brandenburg v. Ohio*, 395 U.S. 444 (1969) *(per curiam)*. But due to the special features of the school environment, school officials must have greater authority to intervene before speech leads to violence. And, in most cases, *Tinker's* "substantial disruption" standard permits school officials to step in before actual violence erupts.

Speech advocating illegal drug use poses a threat to student safety that is just as serious, if not always as immediately obvious. As we have recognized in the past and as the opinion of the Court today details, illegal drug use presents a grave and in many ways unique threat to the physical safety of students. I therefore conclude that the public schools may ban speech advocating illegal drug use. But I regard such regulation as standing at the far reaches of what the First Amendment permits. I join the opinion of the Court with the understanding that the opinion does not endorse any further extension.

Post Problem Discussion

1. In *Morse*, the Court gave deference to a school administrator's judgment that a banner could be viewed as promoting illegal drug use. The Court did so because of the "special characteristics of the school environment," the seriousness of drug problems, and the school's interest in stopping student drug abuse. How far should this reasoning go? Some lower courts have extended *Morse* to restrict speech that is reasonably viewed as promoting violence in school in some situations. For example, in *Ponce v. Socorro Indep. Sch. Dist.*, 508 F.3d 765, 771-72 (5th Cir. 2007), the Fifth Circuit Court of Appeals extended *Morse* to "terroristic threats of mass school

violence" because they have the same "unique indicia" that *Morse* found "compelling with respect to drug use," but then in *Bell v. Itawamba County Sch. Bd.*, 799 F.3d 379 (5th Cir. 2015) (en banc), *cert. denied*, 136 S. Ct. 1166 (2016), the court noted that *Tinker* still applied to individual threats of violence. Both cases are in Problem 4, Section 9.05 of this book.

A concurring opinion in *Defoe v. Spiva*, 625 F.3d 324, 338-41 (6th Cir. 2010) (Rogers, J., concurring), advocated extending *Morse* to banning certain racially hostile symbols, like the Confederate flag, in order to reduce racial tension because "racial tension in today's public schools is a concern on the order of the problem of drug abuse." Could the same rationale be extended to prohibit messages that promote sexual activity? Unhealthy decisions like smoking, vaping/Juuling, or eating fatty foods? What are the limits for applying *Morse*?

2. In *Morse*, the Court rejected the student's claim that his situation was not a student speech case because it occurred off school grounds. Relying on the fact that the speech occurred at a school sponsored event, the Court noted: "There is some uncertainty at the outer boundaries as to when courts should apply school-speech precedents, *see Porter v. Ascension Parish Sch. Bd.*, 393 F.3d 608, 615, n. 22 (5th Cir. 2004), but not on these facts." *Morse*, 551 U.S. 393 (2007).

In *Porter*, a student named Adam drew a sketch at home depicting a violent siege on the school, and then put the sketchpad with the sketch in his closet. Two years later, his brother unknowingly took the sketchpad to school. Another student saw Adam's sketch while looking through the sketchpad on the bus, and told the bus driver. The school disciplined Adam. The court ruled that it was not student speech on school premises:

> Given the unique facts of the present case, we decline to find that Adam's drawing constitutes student speech on the school premises. Adam's drawing was completed in his home, stored for two years, and never intended by him to be brought to campus. He took no action that would increase the chances that his drawing would find its way to school; he simply stored it in a closet where it remained until, by chance, it was unwittingly taken to Galvez Middle School by his brother. This is not exactly speech on campus or even speech directed at the campus.

393 F.3d at 615, 620. The court then determined that Adam's speech was protected by the First Amendment, but the school official who disciplined Adam was entitled to qualified immunity because a "reasonable school official facing this question for the first time would find no 'pre-existing' body of law from which he could draw clear guidance and certain conclusions." *Id.* at 620.

Should courts use student speech standards for off-campus speech that does not occur at a school sponsored event, or should the regular First Amendment standards that apply to adults be used instead? What difference do you think it would make if regular adult standards were used? See the post problem discussion for Problem 3 for further discussion of this issue.

3. The substantial disruption/material interference prong of *Tinker* has been described as follows:

> First, the First Amendment does not require school officials to wait until disruption actually occurs before they may act. In fact, they have a duty to prevent the occurrence of disturbances. Second, *Tinker* does not demand a certainty that disruption will occur, but rather the existence of facts which might reasonably lead school officials to forecast substantial disruption. And finally, because of the state's interest in education, the level of disturbance required to justify official intervention is relatively lower in a public school than it might be on a street corner.

Karp v. Becken, 477 F.2d 171, 175 (9th Cir. 1973). Along these lines, lower courts have generally held that if a substantial disruption or material interference has not already occurred, school officials must establish "demonstrable factors" that would give rise to a "reasonable forecast," of such a disruption/interference, or a "well-founded expectation" of such a disruption/interference. *Bell v. Itawamba Cty. Sch. Bd.*, 799 F.3d 379, 390 (5th Cir. 2015) (en banc); *B.H. v. Easton Area Sch. Dist.*, 725 F.3d 293, 321 (3d Cir. 2013) (en banc), *cert. denied*, 134 S. Ct. 1515 (2014). This generally requires a "specific and significant fear of disruption, not just some remote apprehension of disturbance." *Saxe v. State College Area School Dist.*, 240 F.3d 200, 211 (3d Cir. 2001) (Alito, J.).

Based upon these standards, would any of the fact patterns meet *Tinker*'s requirements?

4. Fact pattern #1 is based on *Bell v. Itawamba County Sch. Bd.*, 799 F.3d 379 (5th Cir. 2015) (en banc). Part of the case, and the lyrics of the rap song at issue in the case, are in Problem 4, Section 9.05 of this book. Take a look at the case. Were your answers to the two questions in this problem for fact pattern #1 the same as the court's answers in *Bell*?

5. Lower courts are not uniform on the parameters of what constitutes lewd, vulgar, or offensive speech under *Fraser*. You will learn more about the different approaches that courts use to address this issue in Problem 2, Section 9.03. Fact Pattern #2 is based on a Third Circuit Court of Appeals decision, *B.H. v. Easton Area Sch. Dist.*, 725 F.3d 293 (3d Cir. 2013) (en banc), *cert. denied*, 134 S. Ct. 1515 (2014), which illustrates one such approach. Part of the decision is in Problem 2, Section 9.03. The court, relying in part on the reasoning of Justice Alito's concurring opinion in *Morse*, ruled that a school could prohibit "ambiguous" speech that a "reasonable observer could interpret to be lewd, vulgar, or offensive," as long as it could not also plausibly be interpreted as commenting on a social or political issue. 725 F.3d at 315. If it could be, then *Tinker*'s substantial disruption standard applied.

Under this approach, the court found that a school could not prohibit students from wearing "I ♥ Boobies!" bracelets at school, because wearing them could be interpreted as commenting on the political or social issue of breast cancer awareness, and the school did not have a well-founded expectation of disruption at school regarding the bracelets. Some other courts have come to a different conclusion regarding the same bracelets using different approaches. For example, in *K.J. v. Sauk Prairie Sch. Dist.*, No. 11-CV-622-BBC, 2012 WL 13055058, at *7 (W.D. Wis. Feb. 6, 2012), the court found that a school official's determination that the bracelets were "vulgar" was reasonable given the age of the students and the circumstances, so the court upheld the school's ban on the bracelets. *See also J.A. v. Fort Wayne Cmty. Sch.*, No. 1:12-CV-155 JVB, 2013 WL 4479229, at *7 (N.D. Ind. Aug. 20, 2013) ("when confronted with ambiguously vulgar slogans, federal courts have sided with the school administrators' decision to ban them."). What approach do you think that lower courts should follow?

6. One issue in a number of the fact patterns is whether the speech could be considered school sponsored speech. In *Hazelwood*, the Court said that school sponsored speech is speech that "could reasonably be understood to bear the school's imprimatur." 484 U.S. at 271. In *Morse v. Frederick*, the Court rejected the argument that the "Bong Hits 4 Jesus" banner was school-sponsored speech, stating that "no one would reasonably believe that Frederick's banner bore the school's imprimatur." 551 U.S. at 405.

Lower courts have noted that *Hazelwood* made a "distinction between a school's toleration of student speech that happens to occur on the school premises, and student speech that a school affirmatively promotes." *Fleming v. Jefferson Cty. Sch. Dist. R-1*, 298 F.3d 918, 924 (10th Cir. 2002). As a result, lower courts have used a number of factors to decide whether speech is "school-sponsored" under *Hazelwood*, including: "(1) where and when the speech occurred; (2) to whom the speech was directed and whether recipients were a 'captive audience'; (3) whether the speech occurred during an event or activity organized by the school, conducted pursuant to official guidelines, or supervised and controlled by school officials; and (4) whether the activities where the speech occurred were designed to impart some knowledge or skills to the students." *Morgan v. Swanson*, 659 F.3d 359, 376 (5th Cir. 2011). The age and grade of students are also relevant, because younger students may be less likely to understand the difference between the school tolerating speech and promoting speech. *See, e.g., Walz v. Egg Harbor Twp. Bd. of Educ.*, 342 F.3d 271, 277 (3d Cir. 2003); *Busch v. Marple Newtown Sch. Dist.*, 567 F.3d 89, 96 (3d Cir. 2009).

Is the speech in any of the fact patterns school sponsored speech under these factors?

7. The age and maturity of students can also be a factor with the other student speech standards. Courts have noted that school officials must be able to take the "emotional maturity" of students into account when making decisions about speech regarding controversial or sensitive topics in order to protect students, control behavior, and foster an "environment conducive to learning." *Muller v. Jefferson Lighthouse Sch.*, 98 F.3d 1530, 1537 (7th Cir. 1996). In general, courts agree that "the younger the children, the more latitude the school authorities have in limiting expression." *Zamecnik v. Indian Prairie School District*, 636 F.3d 874, 876 (7th Cir. 2011). "The older and more mature the students are, the more freedom they have to speak." *J.A. v. Fort Wayne Cmty. Sch.*, No. 1:12-CV-155 JVB, 2013 WL 4479229, at *3 (N.D. Ind. Aug. 20, 2013); *Muller*, 98 F.3d at 1538 (while the "marketplace of ideas," is an "important theme in the high school student expression cases, [it] is a less appropriate description of an elementary school, where children are just beginning to acquire the means of expression.").

Does the age and maturity of the students in the fact patterns make any difference in your answers to the questions?

8. Should school officials be allowed to impose viewpoint based restrictions on student speech like the decision to allow speech that promotes diversity, but not allow speech that does not in Fact Pattern #3? If so, what standard should apply to these restrictions? See the notes in Problem 2, Section 9.03 for more on this topic.

§ 9.03 Dress Codes and Student Expression

Courts have generally recognized the discretion of school boards and school officials to adopt and reasonably enforce dress and grooming codes. However, dress codes may contradict constitutional rights of equal protection and First Amendment speech, and this is an area of considerable litigation. Issues often arise when students wear clothing items such as T-shirts, buttons, or hats that convey a message. The following problem addresses these issues.

Problem 2: T-Shirts with a Message

1. During a high school "Diversity Day," James and his friends wear T-shirts with the following symbol on the front:

The back of the shirt says "God Condemns Homosexuals!"

2. Adelina and Raymond, two 17-year-old high school students, wear anti-abortion T-shirts to school as part of a national anti-abortion week initiative.

(The shirts say, "Former Embryo" and "Abortion is Homicide." The back of the homicide T-shirt quotes the American Heritage Dictionary's definition for "homicide.")

You represent the school district. The superintendent calls you and asks if she can take any of the following actions:

a. Tell the students to wear the T-shirts inside out for the day and to not wear the shirts to school again;

b. Send the students home with an unexcused absence, and suspend the students until they agree to return wearing appropriate attire.

In offering your advice, consider whether the age of the students, and the messages of the T-shirts, can or should change the outcome.

Problem Materials

✓ *Boroff v. Van Wert City Board of Education*, 220 F.3d 465 (6th Cir. 2000), *cert. denied*, 532 U.S. 920 (2001)

✓ *Guiles v. Marineau*, 461 F.3d 320 (2d Cir. 2006), *cert. denied*, 551 U.S. 1162 (2007)

✓ *B.H. v. Easton Area School District*, 725 F.3d 293 (3d Cir. 2013) (en banc), *cert. denied*, 134 S. Ct. 1515 (2014)

Boroff v. Van Wert City Board of Education

220 F.3d 465 (6th Cir. 2000), *cert. denied*, 532 U.S. 920 (2001)

The court rules that the school principal did not violate the First Amendment rights of a high school student by prohibiting T-shirts featuring Marilyn Manson pursuant to the school's dress code.

Wellford, Circuit Judge.

This dispute arises out of a high school student's desire to wear "Marilyn Manson" T-shirts to school, and the school's opposing desire to prohibit those T-shirts . . . .

On August 29, 1997, Boroff, then a senior at Van Wert High School, went to school wearing a "Marilyn Manson" T-shirt. The front of the T-shirt depicted a three-faced Jesus, accompanied by the words "See No Truth. Hear No Truth. Speak No Truth." On the back of the shirt, the word "BELIEVE" was spelled out in capital letters, with the letters "LIE" highlighted. Marilyn Manson's name (although not his picture) was displayed prominently on the front of the shirt. At the time, Van Wert High School had in effect a "Dress and Grooming" policy that provided that "clothing with offensive illustrations, drug, alcohol, or tobacco slogans . . . are not acceptable." Chief Principal's Aide David Froelich told Boroff that his shirt was offensive and gave him the choice of turning the shirt inside-out, going home and changing, or leaving and being considered truant. Boroff left school.

On September 4, 1997, which was the next school day, Boroff wore another Marilyn Manson T-shirt to school. Boroff and his mother met that day with Froelich, Principal William Clifton, and Superintendent John Basinger. Basinger told the Boroffs that students would not be permitted to wear Marilyn Manson T-shirts on school grounds. Undaunted, Boroff wore different Marilyn Manson T-shirts on each of the next three school days, September 5, 8, and 9, 1997. The shirts featured pictures of Marilyn Manson, whose appearance can fairly be described as ghoulish and creepy. Each day, Boroff was told that he would not be permitted to attend school while wearing the T-shirts.

Boroff did not attend school for the next four days following September 9, 1997. On the fifth day, September 16, 1997, his mother initiated the present suit in the United States District Court for the Northern District of Ohio, alleging that the administrators' refusal to allow her son to wear Marilyn Manson T-shirts in school violated his First Amendment right to free expression and his Fourteenth Amendment right to due process. . . .

Boroff claims that the administrators' decision that the T-shirts are offensive was manifestly unreasonable and unsupported by the evidence. Boroff relies to a great extent on evidence that similar T-shirts promoting other bands, such as Slayer and Megadeth, were not prohibited, and also on evidence that one other student was not prohibited from carrying a backpack that donned three "Marilyn Manson" patches. Because the T-shirts were not "offensive," Boroff reasons, and because there is no evidence that a substantial disruption would arise from his wearing the T-shirts, then the School violated his First Amendment rights. We disagree.

The standard for reviewing the suppression of vulgar or plainly offensive speech is governed by *Fraser.* The School in this case, according to the affidavit of Principal Clifton, found the Marilyn Manson T-shirts to be offensive because the band promotes destructive conduct and demoralizing values that are contrary to the educational mission of the school. Specifically, Clifton found the "three-headed Jesus" T-shirt to be offensive because of the "See No Truth. Hear No Truth. Speak No Truth." mantra on the front, and because of the obvious implication of the word "BELIEVE" with "LIE" highlighted on the back. The principal specifically stated that the distorted Jesus figure was offensive, because "[m]ocking any religious figure is contrary to our educational mission which is to be respectful of others and others' beliefs." The other T-shirts were treated with equal disapproval. Clifton went on to explain the reasoning behind the School's prohibition of the T-shirts generally:

> Although I do not know if [Boroff] intends to communicate anything when wearing the Marilyn Manson t-shirts, I believe that the Marilyn Manson t-shirts can reasonably be considered a communication agreeing with or approving of the views espoused by Marilyn Manson in its lyrics and those views which have been associated to Marilyn Manson through articles in the press. I find some of the Marilyn Manson lyrics and some of the views associated with Marilyn Manson as reported in articles in the news and entertainment press offensive to our basic educational mission at Van Wert High School. Therefore, I believe that all of the Marilyn Manson t-shirts ... are offensive to and inconsistent with our educational mission at Van Wert High School.

Furthermore, Clifton quotes some of the lyrics from Marilyn Manson songs that the School finds offensive, which include (but certainly are not limited to) lines such as, "you can kill yourself now because you're dead in my mind," "let's jump upon the sharp swords/and cut away our smiles/without the threat of death/there's no reason to live at all," and "Let's just kill everyone and let your god sort them out/ Fuck it/Everybody's someone else's nigger/I know you are so am I/I wasn't born with enough middle fingers." The principal attested that those types of lyrics were contrary to the school mission and goal of establishing "a common core of values that include ... human dignity and worth ... self respect, and responsibility," and also the goal of instilling "into the students, an understanding and appreciation of the ideals of democracy and help them to be diligent and competent in the performance of their obligations as citizens."

Clifton also submitted to the district court magazine articles that portray Marilyn Manson as having a "pro-drug persona" and articles wherein Marilyn Manson himself admits that he is a drug user and promotes drug use. Clifton concludes from his fourteen years of experience that children are genuinely influenced by the rock group and such propaganda.

Affidavits of other School officials support the administration's position that the Marilyn Manson T-shirts, generally speaking, were prohibited because they were "counter-productive and go against the educational mission of the Van Wert City School District community." ... The record is devoid of any evidence that the T-shirts, the "three-headed Jesus" T-shirt particularly, were perceived to express any particular political or religious viewpoint.

Under these circumstances, we find that the district court was correct in finding that the School did not act in a manifestly unreasonable manner in prohibiting the Marilyn Manson T-shirts pursuant to its dress code. The Supreme Court has held that the school board has the authority to determine "what manner of speech in the classroom or in school is inappropriate." *Fraser*, 478 U.S. at 683. The Court has determined that "[a] school need not tolerate student speech that is inconsistent with its 'basic educational mission . . . even though the government could not censor similar speech outside the school.'" *Kuhlmeier*, 484 U.S. at 266. In this case, where Boroff's T-shirts contain symbols and words that promote values that are so patently contrary to the school's educational mission, the School has the authority, under the circumstances of this case, to prohibit those T-shirts.

The dissent would find that the evidence was sufficient for a reasonable jury to infer that the School has engaged in "viewpoint discrimination" by prohibiting the T-shirts, similar to the armband prohibition in *Tinker*. The dissent primarily relies on one sentence in Principal Clifton's affidavit, in which Clifton stated that he found the "three-headed Jesus" T-shirt to be offensive because "it mocks a major religious figure." Under that reasoning, if a jury finds that the School has prohibited the T-shirts because of any viewpoint expressed on the shirts, then the School must show that it reasonably predicted that allowing the T-shirts would have caused a substantial disruption of, or material interference with, school activities. *See Tinker*, 393 U.S. at 509, 89 S. Ct. 733.

In our view, however, the evidence does not support an inference that the School intended to suppress the expression of Boroff's viewpoint, because of its religious implications. Rather, the record demonstrates that the School prohibited Boroff's Marilyn Manson T-shirts generally because this particular rock group promotes disruptive and demoralizing values which are inconsistent with and counterproductive to education. The dissenting judge agrees that "[i]f the only T-shirts at issue in this case were the ones that simply displayed illustrations of Marilyn Manson largely unadorned by text, the judgment of the district court might be sustainable." He reasons, however, that the one T-shirt featuring the distorted Jesus figure may have been prohibited because of the School's disagreement with its religious message. In our view, the School's treatment of the "three-headed Jesus" T-shirt and the others is not distinguishable. The record establishes that all of the T-shirts were banned in the same manner for the same reasons-they were determined to be vulgar, offensive, and contrary to the educational mission of the school.

Guiles v. Marineau

461 F.3d 320 (2nd Cir. 2006), *cert. denied*, 551 U.S. 1162 (2007)

The court rules that a school may not prohibit a middle school student from wearing a T-shirt that is critical of the President of the United States even if it contains messages about drugs and alcohol.

Cardamone, Circuit Judge.

This case requires us to sail into the unsettled waters of free speech rights in public schools, waters rife with rocky shoals and uncertain currents. Plaintiff Zachary Guiles, a 13-year-old student at Williamstown Middle High School (WMHS, Williamstown High School, or school) in Williamstown, Vermont, claims his right under the First Amendment to wear a T-shirt depicting President George W. Bush in an uncharitable light has been violated. The T-shirt, through an amalgam of images and text, criticizes the President as a chicken-hawk president and accuses him of being a former alcohol and cocaine abuser. To make its point, the shirt displays images of drugs and alcohol.

Upon the complaint of another student and her mother, school officials made Guiles put duct tape over the alcohol-and drug-related pictures on the ground that those illustrations violate a school policy prohibiting any display of such images. Plaintiff, through his mother and father, brought the instant action to enjoin the school's application of the policy to his shirt, asserting that the policy violates his freedom to engage in political speech. . . .

We wrestle on this appeal with the question of how far a student's constitutional right freely to express himself on school grounds extends. As the Supreme Court aptly put it, "[o]ur problem lies in the area where students in the exercise of First Amendment rights collide with the rules of the school authorities." *Tinker v. Des Moines*. We begin with several premises. First, we are mindful that the "vigilant protection of constitutional freedoms is nowhere more vital than in the community of [our] schools." Thus neither party disputes that "students have First Amendment rights to political speech in public schools." But while students do not "shed their constitutional rights to freedom of speech or expression at the schoolhouse gate," neither are their rights to free speech "automatically coextensive with the rights of adults." Indeed even for adults it is familiar law that "the right of free speech is not absolute at all times and under all circumstances."

. . . .

We distill the following from *Tinker*, *Fraser*, and *Hazelwood:*

(1) schools have wide discretion to prohibit speech that is less than obscene—to wit, vulgar, lewd, indecent or plainly offensive speech;

(2) if the speech at issue is "school-sponsored," educators may censor student speech so long as the censorship is "reasonably related to legitimate pedagogical concerns;" and

(3) for all other speech, meaning speech that is neither vulgar, lewd, indecent or plainly offensive under *Fraser*, nor school-sponsored under *Hazelwood*, the rule of *Tinker* applies. Schools may not regulate such student speech unless it would materially and substantially disrupt classwork and discipline in the school.

Our articulation of the *Tinker-Fraser-Hazelwood* trilogy is in accord with how other circuits commonly understand these cases. . . .

We turn next to which standard applies to this appeal. That the parties vigorously contest this point is not surprising. Where this case falls on the *Tinker-Fraser-Hazelwood* spectrum primarily determines whether the defendants' censorship of Guiles's T-shirt survives First Amendment scrutiny. For the reasons set out below, we hold that neither *Hazelwood* nor *Fraser* govern, and therefore, the general rule of *Tinker* applies.

We agree with the district court that *Hazelwood* is inapplicable. The deferential standard of *Hazelwood*, which permits schools to regulate student speech so long as the regulation reasonably relates to "legitimate pedagogical concerns," *Hazelwood*, 484 U.S. at 273, 108 S. Ct. 562, comes into play only when the student speech is "school-sponsored" or when a reasonable observer would believe it to be so sponsored. No one disputes that the school did not sponsor Guiles's T-shirt or that the T-shirt could not reasonably be viewed as bearing the school's imprimatur. While we do not doubt that an anti-drug and alcohol policy may be of "legitimate pedagogical concern" to schools, absent school sponsorship, defendants may not look to *Hazelwood* for support.

We disagree with the district judge that *Fraser* governs this case. The district court applied *Fraser*, reasoning that it must ask whether "the images of drugs and alcohol are *offensive* or *inappropriate,*" and concluding that, if so, "then, under *Fraser*, they may be censored." The trial court then accepted the "judgment of the defendants that such images are an inappropriate form of expression for their middle school" and accordingly, upheld the school's censorship of Guiles's T-shirt. *Id.* We believe the district court misjudged the scope of *Fraser* and, consequently, applied it in error.

Fraser's reach is not as great as the trial court presumed. *Fraser* permits schools to censor student speech that is "lewd," "vulgar," "indecent," or "plainly offensive." We thus ask whether the images of a martini glass, a bottle and glass, a man drinking from a bottle, and lines of cocaine constitute lewd, vulgar, indecent, or plainly offensive speech. We think it clear that these depictions on their own are not lewd, vulgar, or indecent. Lewdness, vulgarity, and indecency normally connote sexual innuendo or profanity. *See Merriam-Webster's Third New Int'l Dictionary* 1147, 1301, 2566 (1st ed.1981) (defining (a) "lewd" as "inciting to sensual desire or imagination," (b) "vulgar" as "lewd, obscene, or profane in expression," and (c) "indecent" as "being or tending to be obscene").

We are left then with the question of whether the pictures are plainly offensive. Indeed, the district court held *Fraser* applicable on the basis of its "plainly offensive" language, which it interpreted broadly. What then constitutes plainly offensive speech under *Fraser*? And, can we say that depictions of drugs and alcohol such as those on Guiles's T-shirt are plainly offensive? These are questions of first impression in this Circuit. While what is plainly offensive is not susceptible to precise definition, we hold that the images depicted on Guiles's T-shirt are not plainly offensive as a matter of law.

Dictionaries commonly define the word offensive as that which causes displeasure or resentment or is repugnant to accepted decency. *See Merriam-Webster's Third Int'l Dictionary* 1156; *Black's Law Dictionary* 1110 (7th ed.1999). We doubt the *Fraser* Court's use of the term sweeps as broadly as this dictionary definition, and nothing in *Fraser* suggests that it does. But if it does, then the rule of *Tinker* would have no real effect because it could have been said that the school administrators in *Tinker* found wearing anti-war armbands offensive and repugnant to their sense of patriotism and decency. Yet the Supreme Court held the school could not censor the students' speech in that case.

What is plainly offensive for purposes of *Fraser* must therefore be somewhat narrower than the dictionary definition. Courts that address *Fraser* appear to treat "plainly offensive" synonymously with and as part and parcel of speech that is lewd, vulgar, and indecent—meaning speech that is something less than obscene but related to that concept, that is to say, speech containing sexual innuendo and profanity. In fact, the Supreme Court deemed Fraser's speech could be freely censored because it was imbued with sexual references, bordering on the obscene. *See Fraser*, 478 U.S. at 683, 106 S. Ct. 3159 ("The pervasive *sexual innuendo* in Fraser's speech was *plainly offensive* to both teachers and students." (emphasis added)).

. . . .

Here, the images of a martini glass, alcohol, and lines of cocaine, like the banner in *Frederick*,[2] may cause school administrators displeasure and could be construed as insulting or in poor taste. We cannot say, however, that these images, by themselves, are as plainly offensive as the sexually charged speech considered in *Fraser* nor are they as offensive as profanity used to make a political point. We do not think in light of this discussion that the images on plaintiff's T-shirt are plainly offensive, especially when considering that they are part of an anti-drug political message.

Defendants principally declare that *all* images of illegal drugs and alcohol-even images expressing an *anti-drug* view, such as those on Guiles's T-shirt-are plainly offensive because they undermine the school's anti-drug message. We do not find this argument persuasive.

To begin, sister circuits have rejected similar arguments. In *Newsom v. Albemarle County Sch. Bd.*, 354 F.3d 249, the Fourth Circuit addressed a school dress code that prohibited all images of weapons on clothing. The student in *Newsom* was told not to wear a National Rifle Association T-shirt that depicted "'men shooting guns.'" As in the case before us, the school in *Newsom* relied on the argument that the image conflicted with the school's "message" that "Guns and Schools Don't Mix." In striking the dress code as overly broad, *Newsom* applied *Tinker* instead of *Fraser* and held essentially that while pictures of weapons that promote violence may arguably be regulated, it cannot be said that all such depictions are *per se* offensive. Similarly, in *Castorina ex rel. Rewt v. Madison County School Board*, 246 F.3d 536 (6th Cir. 2001), the Sixth Circuit was confronted with a school's order that reprimanded a student for wearing clothing bearing confederate flags. Confederate flags have been associated with racist ideology, and could undermine the school's mission to promote tolerance. But the Sixth Circuit applied *Tinker* rather than *Fraser* and remanded the case for further fact-finding regarding disruption.

---

2. The court is referring to the Ninth Circuit court of Appeals decision in *Frederick v. Morse*. The Supreme Court had not yet issued its decision in the case. *See* Post Problem Discussion question 5.

The flaw in defendants' position is that it conflates the rule of *Hazelwood* with *Fraser*, and in doing so, eviscerates *Tinker*. Defendants censored the images because they believed such images were contrary to the school's basic educational aim of having an anti-drug school environment. We observe in passing that the witness offered by defendants to opine on their environmental methodology did not point to any specific evidence showing that *anti*-drug and alcohol images are harmful or lead to the use (or increased abuse) of such substances by high school students.

Moreover, the phrase "plainly offensive" as used in *Fraser* cannot be so broad as to be triggered whenever a school decides a student's expression conflicts with its "educational mission" or claims a legitimate pedagogical concern. Were that the rule then *Fraser* would effectively swallow *Hazelwood*'s holding that school officials may censor student speech if (1) the censorship reasonably relates to a legitimate pedagogical concern, *and* (2) *the speech is school-sponsored*. Indeed, if schools were allowed to censor on such a wide-ranging basis, then *Tinker* would no longer have any effect. . . . We therefore decline to adopt defendants' sweeping reading of *Fraser*.

While the exact contours of what is plainly offensive are not so clear to us as the star Arcturus is on a cloudless night, they are evident enough for us to hold that the images of drugs and alcohol on Guiles's T-shirt are not offensive, let alone plainly so, under *Fraser*. We believe this is especially so given that these images are presented as part of an anti-drug T-shirt, and, moreover, a T-shirt with a political message. Indeed the *Fraser* court distinguished its holding from *Tinker* in part on the absence of any political message in Fraser's speech.

Having determined that neither *Hazelwood* nor *Fraser* apply, we turn to *Tinker*. Applying *Tinker* to the facts of this case, we conclude that defendants' censorship of the images on Guiles's T-shirt violated his free speech rights. The parties agree that Guiles's T-shirt did not cause any disruption or confrontation in the school. Nor do defendants contend they had a reasonable belief that it would. Guiles wore the T-shirt on average once a week for two months without any untoward incidents occurring. Only when a fellow student's mother—who had different political views from plaintiff—protested did defendants direct Guiles to cover the drug and alcohol illustrations. Because Guiles's T-shirt did not cause any disruption, defendants' censorship was unwarranted.

We find no merit in defendants' "no harm, no foul contention," namely, that though they directed the images covered, the text and other images remained, and hence, the political message of the T-shirt was left intact. The pictures are an important part of the political message Guiles wished to convey, accentuating the anti-drug (and anti-Bush) message. By covering them defendants diluted Guiles's message, blunting its force and impact. Such censorship may be justified under *Tinker* only when the substantial disruption test is satisfied.

. . . .

Accordingly, for the foregoing reasons, we vacate the district court's order insofar as it denied Guiles's declaratory judgment action seeking to enjoin defendants from enforcing the dress code with regard to his T-shirt. We affirm the district court's holding that the disciplinary action should be expunged from Guiles's record and remand this matter to the district court for further proceedings consistent with this opinion.

B.H. v. Easton Area School District

725 F.3d 293 (3d Cir. 2013) (en banc), *cert. denied*, 134 S. Ct. 1515 (2014)

The Court rules that the school district banning students from wearing "I ♥ Boobies!" bracelets violates the First Amendment as it does not meet the criteria for restricting student speech in either Fraser or Tinker.

Once again, we are asked to find the balance between a student's right to free speech and a school's need to control its educational environment. In this case, two middle-school students purchased bracelets bearing the slogan "I ♥ boobies! (KEEP A BREAST)" as part of a nationally recognized breast-cancer-awareness campaign. The Easton Area School District banned the bracelets, relying on its authority under *Bethel School District No. 403 v. Fraser*, to restrict vulgar, lewd, profane, or plainly offensive speech, and its authority under *Tinker v. Des Moines Independent Community School District*, to restrict speech that is reasonably expected to substantially disrupt the school. The District Court held that the ban violated the students' rights to free speech and issued a preliminary injunction against the ban.

We agree with the District Court that neither *Fraser* nor *Tinker* can sustain the bracelet ban. The scope of a school's authority to restrict lewd, vulgar, profane, or plainly offensive speech under *Fraser* is a novel question left open by the Supreme Court, and one which we must now resolve. We hold that *Fraser*, as modified by the Supreme Court's later reasoning in *Morse v. Frederick*, sets up the following framework: (1) plainly lewd speech, which offends for the same reasons obscenity offends, may be categorically restricted regardless of whether it comments on political or social issues, (2) speech that does not rise to the level of plainly lewd but that a reasonable observer could interpret as lewd may be categorically restricted as long as it cannot plausibly be interpreted as commenting on political or social issues, and (3) speech that does not rise to the level of plainly lewd and that could plausibly be interpreted as commenting on political or social issues may not be categorically restricted. Because the bracelets here are not plainly lewd and because they comment on a social issue, they may not be categorically banned under *Fraser*. The School District has also failed to show that the bracelets threatened to substantially disrupt the school under *Tinker*. We will therefore affirm the District Court.

I.

A. Factual background

As a "leading youth focused global breast cancer organization," the Keep A Breast Foundation tries to educate thirteen- to thirty-year-old women about breast cancer. To that end, it often partners with other merchants to co-brand products that raise awareness. And because it believes that young women's "negative body image[s]" seriously inhibit their awareness of breast cancer, the Foundation's products often "seek[ ] to reduce the stigma by speaking to young people in a voice they can relate to." If young women see such awareness projects and products as cool and trendy, the thinking goes, then they will be more willing to talk about breast cancer openly.

To "start a conversation about that taboo in a light-hearted way" and to break down inhibitions keeping young women from performing self-examinations, the Foundation began its "I ♥ Boobies!" initiative. Part of the campaign included selling silicone bracelets of assorted colors emblazoned with "I ♥ Boobies! (KEEP A BREAST)" and "check y♥ urself! (KEEP A BREAST)." The Foundation's website address (www.keep-a-breast.org) and motto ("art. education. awareness. action.") appear on the inside of the bracelet. *Id.*

As intended, the "I ♥ Boobies" initiative was a hit with young women, quickly becoming one of the Foundation's "most successful and high profile educational campaigns." Two of the young women drawn to the bracelets were middle-school students B.H. and K.M. They purchased the bracelets with their mothers before the 2010–2011 school year—B.H. because she saw "a lot of [her] friends wearing" the bracelets and wanted to learn about them, and K.M. because of the bracelet's popularity and awareness message.

But the bracelets were more than just a new fashion trend. K.M.'s purchase prompted her to become educated about breast cancer in young women. The girls wore their bracelets both to commemorate friends and relatives who had suffered from breast cancer and to promote awareness among their friends. Indeed, their bracelets started conversations about breast cancer and did so far more effectively than the more-traditional pink ribbon. That made sense to B.H., who observed that "no one really notices" the pink ribbon, whereas the "bracelets are new and . . . more appealing to teenagers."

B.H., K.M., and three other students wore the "I ♥ boobies! (KEEP A BREAST)" bracelets at Easton Area Middle School during the 2010–2011 school year. A few teachers, after observing the students wear the bracelets every day for several weeks, considered whether they should take action. The teachers' responses varied: One found the bracelets offensive because they trivialized breast cancer. Others feared that the bracelets might lead to offensive comments or invite inappropriate touching. But school administrators also believed that middle-school boys did not need the bracelets as an excuse to make sexual statements or to engage in inappropriate touching.

In mid- to late September, four or five teachers asked the eighth-grade assistant principal, Amy Braxmeier, whether they should require students to remove the bracelets. The seventh-grade assistant principal, Anthony Viglianti, told the teachers that they should ask students to remove "wristbands that have the word 'boobie' written on them,", even though there were no reports that the bracelets had caused any in-school disruptions or inappropriate comments.

With Breast Cancer Awareness Month approaching in October, school administrators anticipated that the "I ♥ boobies! (KEEP A BREAST)" bracelets might reappear. The school was scheduled to observe Breast Cancer Awareness Month on October 28, so the day before, administrators publicly announced, for the first time, the ban on bracelets containing the word "boobies." Using the word "boobies" in his announcement, Viglianti notified students of the ban over the public-address system, and a student did the same on the school's television station.

Later that day, a school security guard noticed B.H. wearing an "I ♥ boobies! (KEEP A BREAST)" bracelet and ordered her to remove it. B.H. refused. After meeting with Braxmeier, B.H. relented, removed her bracelet, and returned to lunch. No disruption occurred at any time that day.

The following day, B.H. and K.M. each wore their "I ♥ boobies! (KEEP A BREAST)" bracelets to observe the Middle School's Breast Cancer Awareness Day. The day was uneventful—until lunchtime. Once in the cafeteria, both girls were instructed by a school security guard to remove their bracelets. Both girls refused. Hearing this encounter, another girl, R.T., stood up and similarly refused to take off her bracelet. Confronted by this act of solidarity, the security guard permitted the girls to finish eating their lunches before escorting them to Braxmeier's office. Again, the girls' actions caused no disruption in the cafeteria, though R.T. told Braxmeier that one boy had immaturely commented either that he also "love[d] boobies" or that he "love [d] her boobies."

Braxmeier spoke to all three girls, and R.T. agreed to remove her bracelet. B.H. and K.M. stood firm, however, citing their rights to freedom of speech. The Middle School administrators were having none of it. They punished B.H. and K.M. by giving each of them one and a half days of in-school suspension and by forbidding them from attending the Winter Ball. The administrators notified the girls' families, explaining only that B.H. and K.M. were being disciplined for "disrespect," "defiance," and "disruption."

News of the bracelets quickly reached the rest of the Easton Area School District, which instituted a district-wide ban on the "I ♥ boobies! (KEEP A BREAST)" bracelets, effective on November 9, 2010. The only bracelet-related incident reported by school administrators occurred weeks after the district-wide ban: Two girls were talking about their bracelets at lunch when a boy who overheard them interrupted and said something like "I want boobies." He also made an inappropriate gesture with two red spherical candies. The boy admitted his "rude" comment and was suspended for one day.

This was not the first time the Middle School had banned clothing that it found distasteful. Indeed, the School District's dress-code policy prohibits "clothing imprinted with nudity, vulgarity, obscenity, profanity, and double entendre pictures or slogans." Under the policy, seventh-grade students at the Middle School have been asked to remove clothing promoting Hooters and Big Pecker's Bar & Grill, as well as clothing bearing the phrase "Save the ta-tas" (another breast-cancer-awareness slogan). Typically, students are disciplined only if they actually refuse to remove the offending apparel when asked to do so.

....

III.

The School District defends the bracelet ban as an exercise of its authority to restrict lewd, vulgar, profane, or plainly offensive student speech under *Fraser*. As to the novel question of *Fraser*'s scope, jurists seem to agree on one thing: "[t]he mode of analysis employed in *Fraser* is not entirely clear." *Morse*. On this point, we think the Supreme Court's student-speech cases are more consistent than they may first appear. As we explain, *Fraser* involved only *plainly* lewd speech. We hold that, under *Fraser*, a school may also categorically restrict speech that—although not *plainly* lewd, vulgar, or profane—could be interpreted by a reasonable observer as lewd, vulgar, or profane so long as it could not also plausibly be interpreted as commenting on a political or social issue. Because the "I ♥ boobies! (KEEP A BREAST)" bracelets are not plainly lewd and express support for a national breast-cancer-awareness campaign—unquestionably an important social issue—they may not be categorically restricted under *Fraser*.

B. How far does a school's authority under Fraser extend?

The School District asks us to extend *Fraser* in at least two ways: to reach speech that is ambiguously lewd, vulgar, or profane and to reach speech on political or social issues. The first step is justified, but the second is not.

1. Under *Fraser*, schools may restrict ambiguously lewd speech only if it cannot plausibly be interpreted as commenting on a social or political matter.

Although *Fraser* involved plainly lewd, vulgar, profane, or offensive speech that "offends for the same reasons obscenity offends," student speech need not rise to that level to be restricted under *Fraser*. We conclude that schools may also categorically restrict ambiguous speech that a reasonable observer could interpret as lewd, vulgar, profane, or offensive—unless, as explained below, the speech could also plausibly be interpreted as commenting on a political or social issue. After all, *Fraser* made clear that "the determination of what manner of speech in the classroom or in school assembly is inappropriate properly rests with the school board." The Supreme Court's three other student-speech cases suggest that courts should defer to a school's decisions to restrict what a reasonable observer would interpret as lewd, vulgar, profane, or offensive. This makes sense. School officials know the age, maturity, and other characteristics of their students far better than judges do. Our review is restricted to a cold and distant record. And we must take into account that these same officials must often act "suddenly and unexpectedly" based on their experience.

It remains the job of judges, nonetheless, to determine whether a reasonable observer could interpret student speech as lewd, profane, vulgar, or offensive. Whether a reasonable observer could interpret student speech as lewd, profane, vulgar, or offensive depends on the plausibility of the school's interpretation in light of competing meanings; the context, content, and form of the speech; and the age and maturity of the students.

Although this is a highly contextual inquiry, several rules apply. A reasonable observer would not adopt an acontextual interpretation, and the subjective intent of the speaker is irrelevant. And *Fraser* is not a blank check to categorically restrict any speech that touches on sex or any speech that has the potential to offend. After all, a school's mission to mold students into citizens capable of engaging in civil discourse includes teaching students of sufficient age and maturity how to navigate debates touching on sex.

2. *Fraser* does not permit a school to restrict ambiguously lewd speech that can also plausibly be interpreted as commenting on a social or political issue.

A school's leeway to categorically restrict ambiguously lewd speech, however, ends when that speech could also plausibly be interpreted as expressing a view on a political or social issue. Justices Alito and Kennedy's concurrence in *Morse* adopted a similar protection for political speech that could be interpreted as illegal drug advocacy. Their narrower rationale protecting political speech limits and controls the majority opinion in *Morse*, and it applies with even greater force to ambiguously lewd speech.

Justice Alito's concurrence, joined by Justice Kennedy, provided the crucial fourth and fifth votes in the five-to-four majority opinion. But the two justices conditioned their votes on the "understanding that (1) [the majority opinion] goes no further than to hold that a public school may restrict speech that a reasonable observer would interpret as advocating illegal drug use and (2) it provides no support for any restriction of speech that can plausibly be interpreted as commenting on any political or social issue." The purpose of Justice Alito's concurrence was to "ensur[e] that political speech will remain protected within the school setting"

Because the votes of Justices Alito and Kennedy were necessary to the majority opinion and were expressly conditioned on their narrower understanding that speech plausibly interpreted as political or social commentary was protected from categorical regulation, that limitation is a binding part of *Morse*. . . .

Justice Alito would have protected political or social speech reasonably interpreted to advocate illegal drug use, and that protection applies even more strongly to ambiguously lewd speech. . . .

If speech posing such a "grave" and "unique threat to the physical safety of students" can be categorically regulated only when it cannot "plausibly be interpreted as commenting on any political or social issue"—and that regulation nonetheless "stand[s] at the far reaches of what the First Amendment permits"—then there is no reason why ambiguously lewd speech should receive any less protection when it also "can plausibly be interpreted as commenting on any political or social issue." One need not be a philosopher of Mill or Feinberg's stature to recognize that harmful speech posing an "immediately obvious" threat to the "physical safety of students," presents a far graver threat to the educational mission of schools—thereby warranting less protection—than ambiguously lewd speech that might undercut teaching "the appropriate form of civil discourse" to students, . It would make no sense to afford a T-shirt exclaiming "I ♥ pot! (LEGALIZE IT)" protection under *Morse* while declaring that a bracelet saying "I ♥ boobies! (KEEP A BREAST)" is unprotected under *Fraser.*

Those limits are persuasive on their own terms, even if we disregard the controlling limitations of Justice Alito's *Morse* concurrence. *Fraser* reflects the longstanding notions that "not all speech is of equal First Amendment importance" and that "speech on matters of public concern . . . is at the heart of the First Amendment's protection." To be sure, *Fraser* rejected the idea that "simply because an offensive form of expression may not be prohibited to adults making what the speaker considers a political point, the same latitude must be permitted to children in a public school." As we have explained, though, *Fraser* was limited to plainly lewd speech, and that refusal to protect a student's plainly lewd speech where the same speech by an adult would be protected does not extend to political speech that is not plainly lewd. On that score, our conclusion puts us in good company with five justices in *Morse* who were expressly unwilling to permit a categorical exception to *Tinker* that would intrude on political or social speech and two justices who all but said as much.

What's more, this limitation is consistent with our previous intuitions as well as those of the Sixth and Second Circuits. Consequently, we hold that the *Fraser* exception does not permit ambiguously lewd speech to be categorically restricted if it can plausibly be interpreted as political or social speech.

3. Under *Fraser*, schools may restrict plainly lewd speech regardless of whether it could plausibly be interpreted as social or political commentary.

As the Supreme Court made clear in *Fraser*, though, schools may restrict plainly lewd speech regardless of whether it could plausibly be interpreted to comment on a political or social issue. That is true by definition. Plainly lewd speech "offends for the same reasons obscenity offends" because the speech in that category is "no essential part of any exposition of ideas" and thus carries very "slight social value." As with obscenity in general, obscenity to minors, and all other historically unprotected categories of speech, "the evil to be restricted so overwhelmingly outweighs the expressive interests, if any, at stake, that no process of case-by-case adjudication is required" because "the balance of competing interests is clearly struck." In other words, we do not engage in a case-by-case determination of whether obscenity to minors—and by extension, plainly lewd speech under *Fraser*—carries social value. As a result, schools may continue to regulate plainly lewd, vulgar, profane, or offensive speech under *Fraser* even if a particular instance of such speech can "plausibly be interpreted as commenting on any political or social issue." *Morse.*

In response, the School District recites a mantra that has *Fraser* providing schools the ultimate discretion to define what is lewd and vulgar. It relies on the Supreme Court's sentiment that schools may define their "basic educational mission" and prohibit student speech that is inconsistent with that mission. Indeed, before *Morse*, some courts of appeals adopted that broad interpretation of the Supreme Court's student-speech cases. *See, e.g., LaVine v. Blaine Sch. Dist.*, 257 F.3d 981, 988 (9th Cir. 2001) ("[A] school need not tolerate student speech that is inconsistent with its basic educational mission."); *Boroff v. Van Wert City Bd. of Educ.*, 220 F.3d 465, 470 (6th Cir. 2000) ("[W]here Boroff's T-shirts contain symbols and words that promote values that are so patently contrary to the school's educational mission, the School has the authority, under the circumstances of this case, to prohibit those T-shirts [under *Fraser*].").

Whatever the face value of those sentiments, such sweeping and total deference to school officials is incompatible with the Supreme Court's teachings. In *Tinker, Hazelwood*, and *Morse*, the Supreme Court independently evaluated the meaning of the student's speech and the reasonableness of the school's interpretation and actions. There is no reason the school's authority under *Fraser* should receive special treatment. More importantly, such an approach would swallow the other student-speech cases, including *Tinker*, effectively eliminating judicial review of student-speech restrictions. *See Guiles*, 461 F.3d at 327 (making this point). That is precisely why the Supreme Court in *Morse* explicitly rejected total deference to school officials:

> The opinion of the Court does not endorse the broad argument advanced by petitioners and the United States that the First Amendment permits public school officials to censor any student speech that interferes with a school's "educational mission." ... The "educational mission" argument would give public school authorities a license to suppress speech on political and social issues based on disagreement with the viewpoint expressed. The argument, therefore, strikes at the very heart of the First Amendment.

Morse, 551 U.S. at 423 (Alito, J., concurring).

Instead, *Morse* settled on a narrower view of deference, deferring to a school administrator's "reasonable judgment that Frederick's sign qualified as drug advocacy" only if the speech could not plausibly be interpreted as commenting on a political or social issue. Our approach to lewd speech provides the same degree of deference to schools as the Court did in *Morse*. We defer to a school's reasonable judgment that an observer could interpret ambiguous speech as lewd, vulgar, profane, or offensive only if the speech could not plausibly be interpreted as commenting on a political or social issue.

By contrast, there is empirical support for the opposite worry. Some schools, if empowered to do so, might eliminate all student speech touching on sex or merely having the potential to offend. Indeed, the Middle School's administrators seemed inclined to

....

To recap: Under the government's sovereign authority, a school may categorically ban obscenity, fighting words, and the like in schools; the student-speech cases do not supplant the government's sovereign powers to regulate speech. Under *Fraser*, a school may categorically restrict plainly lewd, vulgar, or profane speech that "offends for the same reasons obscenity offends" regardless of whether it can plausibly be interpreted as commenting on social or political issues. As we have explained, plainly lewd speech cannot, by definition, be plausibly interpreted as political or social commentary because the speech offends for the same reason obscenity offends and thus has slight social value. *Fraser* also permits a school to categorically restrict ambiguous speech that a reasonable observer could interpret as having a lewd, vulgar, or profane meaning so long as it could not also plausibly be interpreted as commenting on a social or political issue. But *Fraser* does not permit a school to categorically restrict ambiguous speech that a reasonable observer could interpret as having a lewd, vulgar, or profane meaning and could plausibly interpret as commenting on a social or political issue. And of course, if a reasonable observer could not interpret the speech as lewd, vulgar, or profane, then *Fraser* simply does not apply. As always, a school's other powers over student speech under *Tinker*, *Kuhlmeier*, and *Morse* remain as a backstop.

C. The Middle School's ban on "I ♥ boobies! (KEEP A BREAST)" bracelets

Under this framework, the School District's bracelet ban is an open-and-shut case. The "I ♥ boobies! (KEEP A BREAST)" bracelets are not plainly lewd. The slogan bears no resemblance to Fraser's "pervasive sexual innuendo" that was "plainly offensive to both teachers and students." Teachers had to request guidance about how to deal with the bracelets, and school administrators did not conclude that the bracelets were vulgar until B.H. and K.M. had worn them every day for nearly two months. In addition, the Middle School used the term "boobies" in announcing the bracelet ban over the public address system and the school television station. What's more, the bracelets do not contain language remotely akin to the seven words that are considered obscene to minors on broadcast television. Indeed, the term "boobie" is no more than a sophomoric synonym for "breast." And as the School District also concedes, a reasonable observer would plausibly interpret the bracelets as part of a national breast-cancer-awareness campaign, an undeniably important social issue. Accordingly, the bracelets cannot be categorically banned under *Fraser*.

IV.

Fraser, of course, is only one of four school-specific avenues for regulating student speech. The parties rightly agree that *Kuhlmeier* and *Morse* do not apply: no one could reasonably believe that the Middle School was somehow involved in the morning fashion decisions of a few students, and no one could reasonably interpret the bracelets as advocating illegal drug use.

That leaves only *Tinker* as possible support for the School District's ban. Under *Tinker*'s "general rule," the government may restrict school speech "that threatens a specific and substantial disruption to the school environment" or "inva[des] ... the rights of others." "[I]f a school can point to a well-founded expectation of disruption — especially one based on past incidents arising out of similar speech — the restriction may pass constitutional muster." The School District has the burden of showing that the bracelet ban is constitutional under *Tinker*. That it cannot do.

Tinker meant what it said: "a specific and significant fear of disruption, not just some remote apprehension of disturbance." Tinker's black armbands did not meet this standard, even though the armbands "caused comments, warnings by other students, the poking of fun at them, . . . a warning by an older football player that other, nonprotesting students had better let them alone," and the "wreck[ing]" of a math teacher's lesson period.

Here, the record of disruption is even skimpier. When the School District announced the bracelet ban, it had no more than an "undifferentiated fear or remote apprehension of disturbance." The bracelets had been on campus for at least two weeks without incident. ("[N]one of the three principals had heard any reports of disruption or student misbehavior linked to the bracelets. Nor had any of the principals heard reports of inappropriate comments about 'boobies.'"). That track record "speaks strongly against a finding of likelihood of disruption."

The School District instead relies on two incidents that occurred after the ban. In one, a female student told a teacher that she believed some boys had remarked to girls about their "boobies" in relation to the bracelets—an incident that was never confirmed. In the other, two female students were discussing the bracelets during lunch, and a boy interrupted them to say "I want boobies" while "making inappropriate gestures with two spherical candies." *Id.* The boy was suspended for a day. *Id.*

Even assuming that disruption arising after a school's speech restriction could satisfy *Tinker*—a question we need not decide today—these two isolated incidents hardly bespeak a substantial disruption caused by the bracelets. "[S]tudent expression may not be suppressed simply because it gives rise to some slight, easily overlooked disruption, including but not limited to 'a showing of mild curiosity' by other students, 'discussion and comment' among students, or even some 'hostile remarks' or 'discussion outside of the classrooms' by other students." Given that Tinker's black armband—worn to protest a controversial war and divisive enough to prompt reactions from other students—was not a substantial disruption, neither is the "silent, passive expression" of breast-cancer awareness. If anything, the fact that these incidents did not occur until *after* the School District banned the bracelets suggests that the ban "*exacerbated* rather than contained the disruption in the school."

. . . .

The bracelet ban cannot be upheld on the authority of *Tinker*.

. . . .

School administrators "have a difficult job," and we are well-aware that the job is not getting any easier. Besides the teaching function, school administrators must deal with students distracted by cell phones in class and poverty at home, parental under- and over-involvement, bullying and sexting, preparing students for standardized testing, and ever-diminishing funding. When they are not focused on those issues, school administrators must inculcate students with "the shared values of a civilized social order."

We do not envy those challenges, which require school administrators "to make numerous difficult decisions about when to place restrictions on speech in our public schools." And the School District in this case was not unreasonably concerned that permitting "I ♥ boobies! (KEEP A BREAST)" bracelets in this case might require it to permit other messages that were sexually oriented in nature. But schools cannot avoid teaching our citizens-in-training how to appropriately navigate the "marketplace of ideas." Just because letting in one idea might invite even more difficult judgment calls about other ideas cannot justify suppressing speech of genuine social value.

We will affirm the District Court's order granting a preliminary injunction.

Post Problem Discussion

1. As you see from the cases in the problem materials, courts are not uniform on how to determine what is "lewd, vulgar, indecent or plainly offensive" under *Fraser.* What approach do you think courts should use to make this determination? Under which approach is a school more likely to be able to prohibit students from wearing the T-shirts in the problem?

2. Should schools be able to restrict student speech that other students may view as offensive because it interferes with the rights of others under *Tinker*? In *Tinker,* the Court said that in order to "justify prohibition of a particular expression of opinion," school officials "must be able to show that [their] action was caused by something more than a mere desire to avoid the discomfort and unpleasantness that always accompany an unpopular viewpoint." *Tinker,* 393 U.S. at 509. Notwithstanding this language, some courts have upheld restrictions on offensive speech under *Tinker* because it "impinge[s] upon the rights of other students," which includes the rights to be "secure and to be let alone." *Tinker,* 393 U.S. at 508.

For example, in *West v. Derby Unified Sch. Dist.,* 206 F.3d 1358, 1366 (10th Cir. 2000), the Tenth Circuit Court of Appeals upheld a ban on student displays of the Confederate flag at school because such displays might "interfere with the rights of other students to be secure and let alone." *See also Defoe v. Spiva,* 625 F.3d 324, 332–33 (6th Cir. 2010), *cert. denied,* 132 S. Ct. 399 (2011). Similarly, in *Harper v. Poway Unified School Dist.,* 445 F.3d 1166, 1178 (9th Cir. 2006), *vacated as moot,* 549 U.S. 1262 (2007), the Ninth Circuit Court of Appeals ruled that a student wearing a T-shirt condemning homosexuals "colli[des] with the rights of other students in the most fundamental way." The Ninth Circuit Court of Appeals also ruled that a student could be disciplined for sending an instant message to another student threatening to shoot students at school, because "whatever the scope of the rights of other students to be secure and to be let alone in *Tinker,* without doubt the threat of a school shooting impinges on those rights. They represent the quintessential harm to the rights of other students to be secure." *Wynar v. Douglas Cty. Sch. Dist.,* 728 F.3d 1062, 1072 (9th Cir. 2013).

Other courts have taken a somewhat narrower view. For example, in *Saxe v. State Coll. Area Sch. Dist.,* 240 F.3d 200, 216–17 (3d Cir. 2001), then-Circuit Judge Alito wrote that while the "precise scope of *Tinker*'s 'interference with the rights of others' language is unclear . . . it is certainly not enough that the speech is merely offensive to some listener." Similarly, in *Nuxoll v. Indian Prairie School Dist. #204,* 523 F.3d 668 (7th Cir. 2008), and *Zamecnik v. Indian Prairie School Dist. No. 204,* 636 F.3d 874 (7th Cir. 2011), the Seventh Circuit Court of Appeals ordered a school to allow students who disapprove of homosexuality to wear "Be Happy. Not Gay" T-shirts to school, and awarded nominal damages to the students who had not been allowed to do so. The school banned the shirt under a policy prohibiting derogatory comments "that refer to race, ethnicity, religion, gender, sexual orientation, or disability." The court stated that the shirts were only "tepidly negative," and that calling them derogatory was "too strong a characterization." *Nuxoll,* 523 F.3d at 676. The court went on to say that there is not a "generalized hurt feelings defense to a high school's violation of the First Amendment rights of its students. A particular form of harassment or intimidation can be regulated . . . only if . . . the speech at issue gives rise to a well-founded fear of disruption or interference with the rights of others," and those requirements were not met. *Zamecnik,* 636 F.3d at 877.

Given these different decisions, could a school prohibit James from wearing his anti-gay shirt, or Adelina and Raymond from wearing their anti-abortion shirts, on the grounds that they invade the rights of other students?

3. Some courts have held that offensive speech can provide a well-founded expectation of a substantial disruption under *Tinker* because of the potential reaction to the speech by other students. For example, several courts have upheld bans on displaying the Confederate flag at school because of the potential disruptive impact at school where "racial tension is high and serious racially motivated incidents, such as physical altercations or threats of violence, have occurred." *Barr v. Lafon,* 538 F.3d 554, 568 (6th Cir. 2008); *see also Hardwick v. Heyward,* 711 F.3d 426 (4th Cir. 2013); *Defoe v. Spiva,* 625 F.3d 324 (6th Cir. 2010); *Scott v. Sch. Bd. of Alachua Cty.*, 324 F.3d 1246, 1247 (11th Cir. 2003); *West v. Derby Unified School District* No. 260, 206 F.3d 1358 (10th Cir. 2000).

Similarly, in *Dariano v. Morgan Hill Unified School Dist.*, 767 F.3d 764 (9th Cir. 2014), school officials required some students who wore American flag T-shirts to school during a Cinco de Mayo celebration day to remove the shirts, or to go home for the day with an excused absence, because of concerns for the students' safety. Threats were made against the students because of the shirts, and there were ongoing racial tensions within the school. The Ninth Circuit Court of Appeals ruled that the school's actions were constitutional.

However, other cases have found that there was not a well-founded expectation or a reasonable forecast of disruption for speech that other students might find offensive. *See, e.g., Sypniewski v. Warren Hills Regional Bd. of Educ.*, 307 F.3d 243 (3d Cir. 2002) (student wearing Jeff Foxworthy T-shirt about rednecks); *Castorina v. Madison Cty. Sch. Bd.*, 246 F.3d 536, 541 (6th Cir. 2001) (school did not show a likelihood of violence or disruption over T-shirts with Confederate flags); *Nuxoll v. Indian Prairie School Dist. #204*, 523 F.3d 668, 677 (7th Cir. 2008); *Zamecnik v. Indian Prairie School*

Dist. No. 204, 636 F.3d 874, 876 (7th Cir. 2011) (finding it highly speculative that a student wearing "Be Happy. Not Gay" T-shirt as a way of showing disapproval of homosexuality would provoke incidents of harassment and cause disruption).

In *Saxe*, the Third Circuit Court of Appeals noted that one way to establish a well-founded expectation of disruption was if there had been "past incidents arising out of similar speech." 240 F.3d at 212. Absent past incidents, what evidence would the school need to be able to establish a well-founded expectation of disruption for James wearing his anti-gay T-shirt, or for Adelina and Raymond wearing their anti-abortion shirts?

4. Should it be easier for school officials to prohibit speech than it is for them to punish or discipline students because of their speech? In other words, should a school official be given more discretion or leeway to take the first action in Problem 2 (asking the students to turn their T-shirts inside out and not wear them to school again), then they are for the second action (sending the students home unexcused and suspending them until they agree to return wearing appropriate attire)? *Dariano v. Morgan Hill Unified Sch. Dist.* mentioned in note #3, referenced such a distinction, stating "[s]chool officials have greater constitutional latitude to suppress student speech than to punish it. In [*Karp v. Becken*, 477 F.2d 171 (9th Cir. 1973)], we held that school officials could curtail the exercise of First Amendment rights when they c[ould] reasonably forecast material interference or substantial disruption, but could not discipline the student without show[ing] justification for their action." 767 F.3d at 777.

In *Dariano*, the students were not punished for wearing their American flag shirts to school. They were simply allowed to either turn them inside out for the day, or to go home for the day with an excused absence. The court ruled these actions were constitutional, in part, because they were not punishments. By contrast, in *Karp*, the court overturned a student's suspension for bringing signs to school to protest the school's decision to not renew the contract of an English teacher. The court noted that the student's actions did not violate any school policy and stated, "[a]bsent justification, such as a violation of a statute or school rule, they cannot discipline a student for exercising those rights. The balancing necessary to enable school officials to maintain discipline and order allows curtailment but not necessarily punishment. Consequently, appellant could not be suspended for his activities with the signs." *Karp v. Becken*, 477 F.2d at 176.

Does this mean that school officials could require James, Adelina, or Raymond to turn their T-shirts inside out, and to not wear them again to school, even without some violation of school policy, but could not discipline them absent some type of school policy violation? If so, what advice would you give the school about what a school policy should say about these issues?

5. Note that both *Guiles* and *Boroff* were decided before the Supreme Court decided *Morse v. Frederick*, which originated from the Ninth Circuit as *Frederick v.*

Morse. The *Guiles* court relied in part on the reasoning of the Ninth Circuit Court of Appeals' decision in *Frederick*. The Supreme Court subsequently overturned the Ninth Circuit's decision. Given these events, would the outcome in *Guiles* be different if it were decided today?

Similarly, in *Morse*, the Supreme Court rejected the argument that school officials could ban the "Bong Hits 4 Jesus" banner as offensive under *Fraser*, stating:

> We think this stretches *Fraser* too far; that case should not be read to encompass any speech that could fit under some definition of "offensive." After all, much political and religious speech might be perceived as offensive to some. The concern here is not that Frederick's speech was offensive, but that it was reasonably viewed as promoting illegal drug use.

Morse, 551 U.S. at 409. Justice Alito also stated in his concurring opinion that the Court's decision did not "endorse the broad argument . . . that the First Amendment permits public school officials to censor any student speech that interferes with a school's educational mission." *Id.* at 423. Given these statements, would the outcome in *Boroff* be different if it were decided today?

6. Some public schools require students to wear uniforms as a way of addressing issues that may arise with expressive clothing or clothing colors that are identified with gangs. What are some of the potential constitutional issues with uniform requirements? The following cases provide an overview of some of the issues. *Frudden v. Pilling*, 877 F.3d 821 (9th Cir. 2017); *Frudden v. Pilling*, 742 F.3d 1199 (9th Cir. 2014); *Wilkins v. Penns Grove-Carneys Point Reg'l Sch. Dist.*, 123 Fed. App'x 493 (3d Cir. 2005); *Canady v. Bossier Par. Sch. Bd.*, 240 F.3d 437, 442 (5th Cir. 2001).

7. What standards should apply when schools impose viewpoint based restrictions on student speech? Lower courts are not uniform on the issue. Some have found viewpoint restrictions to be unconstitutional. *See, e.g., Castorina v. Madison Cty. Sch. Bd.*, 246 F.3d 536, 541 (6th Cir. 2001) (student discipline under school dress code for wearing Confederate flag shirts was unconstitutional viewpoint discrimination, because the school allowed students to wear Malcolm X clothing). Some have found that such restrictions are permitted when the speech is school sponsored speech under *Hazelwood*. *Fleming v. Jefferson Cty. Sch. Dist. R-1*, 298 F.3d 918, 926 (10th Cir. 2002) ("we conclude that *Hazelwood* allows educators to make viewpoint-based decisions about school-sponsored speech."). Others have found that a higher standard must be met for viewpoint based restrictions on school sponsored speech. *Peck v. Baldwinsville Cent. Sch. Dist.*, 426 F.3d 617 (2d Cir. 2005) (viewpoint discrimination would be unconstitutional under *Hazelwood* absent an "overriding state interest" even if it related to legitimate pedagogical interests).

What approach do you think courts should take? Should schools be able to restrict speech that is critical of some social or political issue, but permit speech that supports it? Could a school permit only speech that supports the president, and prohibit speech that does not? If so, under what circumstances?

Activity 1: State Constitutional Provisions

As noted in Section 9.01, state constitutions may have provisions that address free speech or free expression. State requirements can be more protective of student rights than the First Amendment, but not less protective. Some states also have statutes or regulations that address student speech or expression in school.

Local schools must take these state requirements and standards into account when they develop policies that affect student expression. The following activity explores some of these issues.

Step One—Choose a state and research whether any state constitutional provisions apply to free speech or expression. Research state court cases to see if these provisions have been applied to students in a public school setting.

Step Two—Research the state's statutes and education regulations to see if they have any provisions that apply to student speech or expression. These could include dress codes, school uniforms, and requirements that schools develop policies regarding harassment, derogatory comments or hate speech.

Step Three—Choose a local school district and identify policies that may affect student expression, such as dress codes, school uniforms, anti-harassment or hate speech policies, and discipline policies that address certain types of speech. (You should be able to find these online.)

Step Four—Answer the following:

1. If the state has constitutional provisions that apply to student speech, have the courts interpreted them to provide more protection to students than the federal requirements, or the same level of protection?
2. Have the state courts used the *Tinker, Bethel*, *Hazelwood,* and *Morse* standards discussed in Section 9.02 when interpreting the state constitutional requirements? If not, how are the standards created by state courts different from those in these United States Supreme Court cases?
3. If your state has statutes or regulations that address student speech or expression, have they been challenged in court? If so, what were the claims and what was the result? If not, do you think any of the statutes or regulations violate students' rights to free speech under your state constitution or the United States Constitution?
4. Do you think that the local school district policies you found are consistent with state laws and state constitutional requirements? Are they consistent with the federal requirements set forth in the United States Supreme Court cases in Section 9.02?

§ 9.04 Online Speech

Today's students spend more and more time online. They communicate using apps and social media. Schools also increasingly use the Internet and electronic devices for educational purposes. The increase of online communications by students, teachers, and school officials raises issues about a school's ability to restrict these communications. Most schools have rules against specified kinds of Internet use in school and use blocking or filtering software for "inappropriate sites." Some schools forbid teachers from contacting students through text, apps, or social media.

The increase of online speech also raises issues about how far schools can go in prohibiting or punishing student speech that occurs off-campus. School officials have had to address issues like students creating fake social media profiles with false and derogatory information about other students or school officials, webpages and instant message icons that show teachers being shot or decapitated, and online threats of school violence. The discipline aspect of this issue is discussed in Chapter 8. As noted in the post problem discussion to Problem 1, courts generally apply *Tinker* to assess off-campus speech that does not occur at a school sponsored event. However, some courts have used the "true threat" standard when the speech involves threats of violence. The true threat standard is addressed in Section 9.05. The following problem gives you a chance to explore some of these issues.

Problem 3: Making Fun of Your Teacher Online

Michael is an eleventh grade student at the high school. He posts the following statement about the eleventh grade band teacher, Mr. Williams, on one of his social media accounts:

> He is an overweight middle-aged man who doesn't like to brush his teeth. He likes to involve himself in everything you do, demands that band be your number one priority, and favors people who brown nose him. He always blames certain students and no one else when things go wrong, even when the students did nothing wrong. I wish he would die.

Michael also sets up a fake social media account in Mr. Williams' name where he places a photo of Hitler in for Mr. Williams' picture. In the profile section, Michael describes Mr. Williams' favorite activities as "playing with little boys and girls" and "harassing big boys and girls." He links the social media profile to his post.

Over one hundred and fifty students from the high school like the post and the fake account, with some posting their own comments saying that they agree with Michael and that the fake account is hilarious. Students talk about the post and fake account at school the next day. A teacher overhears two students talking about it and sends them to the principal's office to tell the principal about it. Mr. Williams' teenage daughter, who also attends the school, sees the post and the fake account while reviewing her social media accounts on her phone at school. She tells her dad, who tells the school principal. The school principal talks to the two students and

Mr. Williams about the post and fake account, views the post, the fake account, and the responding comments, and then talks to Michael about it. After this investigation, the principal suspends Michael for ten days and recommends that the school board expel Michael for the remainder of the school year. Does the school's disciplinary action violate Michael's First Amendment rights?

Problem Materials

- ✓ *J.S. v. Blue Mountain School District*, 650 F.3d 915 (3d Cir. 2011) (en banc), *cert. denied*, 565 U.S. 1156 (2012)
- ✓ *Kowalski v. Berkeley County Sch.*, 652 F.3d 565 (4th Cir. 2011), *cert. denied*, 565 U.S. 1173 (2012)

J.S. v. Blue Mountain School District

650 F.3d 915 (3d Cir. 2011) (en banc), *cert. denied*, 565 U.S. 1156 (2012)

The majority of the Third Circuit sitting en banc applies Tinker to off-campus student speech and finds the school's discipline of that speech violates the First Amendment

Opinion of the Court

This case arose when the School District suspended J.S. for creating, on a weekend and on her home computer, a MySpace profile (the "profile") making fun of her middle school principal, James McGonigle. The profile contained adult language and sexually explicit content. J.S. and her parents sued the School District under 42 U.S.C. § 1983 and state law, alleging that the suspension violated J.S.'s First Amendment free speech rights, that the School District's policies were unconstitutionally overbroad and vague, that the School District violated the Snyders' Fourteenth Amendment substantive due process rights to raise their child, and that the School District acted outside of its authority in punishing J.S. for out-of-school speech.

Because J.S. was suspended from school for speech that indisputably caused no substantial disruption in school and that could not reasonably have led school officials to forecast substantial disruption in school, the School District's actions violated J.S.'s First Amendment free speech rights. We will accordingly reverse and remand that aspect of the District Court's judgment. However, we will affirm the District Court's judgment that the School District's policies were not overbroad or void-for-vagueness, and that the School District did not violate the Snyders' Fourteenth Amendment substantive due process rights.

I.

J.S. was an Honor Roll eighth grade student who had never been disciplined in school until December 2006 and February 2007, when she was twice disciplined for dress code violations by McGonigle. On Sunday, March 18, 2007, J.S. and her friend K.L., another eighth grade student at Blue Mountain Middle School, created a fake profile of McGonigle, which they posted on MySpace, a social networking website. The profile was created at J.S.'s home, on a computer belonging to J.S.'s parents.

The profile did not identify McGonigle by name, school, or location, though it did contain his official photograph from the School District's website. The profile was presented as a self-portrayal of a bisexual Alabama middle school principal named "M—Hoe." The profile contained crude content and vulgar language, ranging from nonsense and juvenile humor to profanity and shameful personal attacks aimed at the principal and his family. For instance, the profile lists M—Hoe's general interests as: "detention, being a tight ass, riding the fraintrain, spending time with my child (who looks like a gorilla), baseball, my golden pen, fucking in my office, hitting on students and their parents." In addition, the profile stated in the "About me" section:

> HELLO CHILDREN[.] yes. it's your oh so wonderful, hairy, expressionless, sex addict, fagass, put on this world with a small dick PRINCIPAL[.] I have come to myspace so i can pervert the minds of other principal's [sic] to be just like me. I know, I know, you're all thrilled[.] Another reason I came to myspace is because—I am keeping an eye on you students (who[m] I care for so much)[.] For those who want to be my friend, and aren't in my school[,] I love children, sex (any kind), dogs, long walks on the beach, tv, being a dick head, and last but not least my darling wife who looks like a man (who satisfies my needs) MY FRAINTRAIN ....

Though disturbing, the record indicates that the profile was so outrageous that no one took its content seriously. J.S. testified that she intended the profile to be a joke between herself and her friends. At her deposition, she testified that she created the profile because she thought it was "comical" insofar as it was so "outrageous."

Initially, the profile could be viewed in full by anyone who knew the URL (or address) or who otherwise found the profile by searching MySpace for a term it contained. The following day, however, J.S. made the profile "private" after several students approached her at school, generally to say that they thought the profile was funny. By making the profile "private," J.S. limited access to the profile to people whom she and K.L. invited to be a MySpace "friend." J.S. and K.L. granted "friend" status to about twenty-two School District students.

The School District's computers block access to MySpace, so no Blue Mountain student was ever able to view the profile from school. McGonigle first learned about the profile on Tuesday, March 20, 2007, from a student who was in his office to discuss an unrelated incident. McGonigle asked this student to attempt to find out who had created the profile. He also attempted—unsuccessfully—to find the profile himself, even contacting MySpace directly.

At the end of the school day on Tuesday, the student who initially told McGonigle about the profile reported to him that it had been created by J.S. McGonigle asked this student to bring him a printout of the profile to school the next day, which she did. It is undisputed that the only printout of the profile that was ever brought to school was one brought at McGonigle's specific request.

On Wednesday, March 21, 2007, McGonigle showed the profile to Superintendent Joyce Romberger and the Director of Technology, Susan Schneider—Morgan. The three met for about fifteen minutes to discuss the profile. McGonigle also showed the profile to two guidance counselors, Michelle Guers and Debra Frain (McGonigle's wife). McGonigle contacted MySpace to attempt to discover what computer had been used to create the profile, but MySpace refused to release that information without a court order. The School District points to no evidence that anyone ever suspected the information in the profile to be true.

McGonigle ultimately decided that the creation of the profile was a Level Four Infraction under the Disciplinary Code of Blue Mountain Middle School, Student—Parent Handbook, as a false accusation about a staff member of the school and a "copyright" violation of the computer use policy, for using McGonigle's photograph. At his deposition, however, McGonigle admitted that he believed the students "weren't accusing me. They were pretending they were me."

J.S. was absent from school on Wednesday, the day McGonigle obtained a copy of the profile. When she returned, on Thursday, March 22, 2007, McGonigle summoned J.S. and K.L. to his office to meet with him and Guidance Counselor Guers. J.S. initially denied creating the profile, but then admitted her role. McGonigle told J.S. and K.L. that he was upset and angry, and threatened the children and their families with legal action. Following this meeting, J.S. and K.L. remained in McGonigle's office while he contacted their parents and waited for them to come to school.

McGonigle met with J.S. and her mother Terry Snyder and showed Mrs. Snyder the profile. He told the children's parents that J.S. and K.L. would receive ten days out-of-school suspension, which also prohibited attendance at school dances. McGonigle also threatened legal action. J.S. and her mother both apologized to McGonigle, and J.S. subsequently wrote a letter of apology to McGonigle and his wife.

McGonigle next contacted MySpace, provided the URL for the profile and requested its removal, which was done. McGonigle also contacted Superintendent Romberger to inform her of his decision regarding J.S. and K.L.'s punishment. Although Romberger could have overruled McGonigle's decision, she agreed with the punishment. On Friday, March 23, 2007, McGonigle sent J.S.'s parents a disciplinary notice, which stated that J.S. had been suspended for ten days. The following week, Romberger declined Mrs. Snyder's request to overrule the suspension.

On the same day McGonigle met with J.S. and her mother, he contacted the local police and asked about the possibility of pressing criminal charges against the students. The local police referred McGonigle to the state police, who informed him that he could press harassment charges, but that the charges would likely be dropped. McGonigle chose not to press charges. An officer did, however, complete a formal report and asked McGonigle whether he wanted the state police to call the students and their parents to the police station to let them know how serious the situation was. McGonigle asked the officer to do this, and on Friday, March 23, J.S. and K.L. and their mothers were summoned to the state police station to discuss the profile.

The School District asserted that the profile disrupted school in the following ways. There were general "rumblings" in the school regarding the profile. More specifically, on Tuesday, March 20, McGonigle was approached by two teachers who informed him that students were discussing the profile in class. Randy Nunemacher, a Middle School math teacher, experienced a disruption in his class when six or seven students were talking and discussing the profile; Nunemacher had to tell the students to stop talking three times, and raised his voice on the third occasion. The exchange lasted about five or six minutes. Nunemacher also testified that he heard two students talking about the profile in his class on another day, but they stopped when he told them to get back to work. Nunemacher admitted that the talking in class was not a unique incident and that he had to tell his students to stop talking about various topics about once a week. Another teacher, Angela Werner, testified that she was approached by a group of eighth grade girls at the end of her Skills for Adolescents course to report the profile. Werner said this did not disrupt her class because the girls spoke with her during the portion of the class when students were permitted to work independently.

The School District also alleged disruption to Counselor Frain's job activities. Frain canceled a small number of student counseling appointments to supervise student testing on the morning that McGonigle met with J.S., K.L., and their parents. Counselor Guers was originally scheduled to supervise the student testing, but was asked by McGonigle to sit in on the meetings, so Frain filled in for Guers. This substitution lasted about twenty-five to thirty minutes. There is no evidence that Frain was unable to reschedule the canceled student appointments, and the students who were to meet with her remained in their regular classes.

On March 28, 2007, J.S. and her parents filed this action against the School District, Superintendent Romberger, and Principal McGonigle. By way of stipulation, on January 7, 2008, all claims against Romberger and McGonigle were dismissed, and only the School District remained as a defendant. After discovery, both parties moved for summary judgment.

After analyzing the above facts, the District Court granted the School District's summary judgment motion on all claims, though specifically acknowledging that *Tinker v. Des Moines Independent Community School District*, 393 U.S. 503 (1969), does not govern this case because no "substantial and material disruption" occurred. Instead, the District Court drew a distinction between political speech at issue in *Tinker*, and "vulgar and offensive" speech at issue in a subsequent school speech case, *Bethel School District v. Fraser*, 478 U.S. 675 (1986). The District Court also noted the Supreme Court's most recent school speech decision, *Morse v. Frederick*, 551 U.S. 393 (2007), where the Court allowed a school district to prohibit a banner promoting illegal drug use at a school-sponsored event.

Applying a variation of the *Fraser* and *Morse* standard, the District Court held that "as vulgar, lewd, and potentially illegal speech that had an effect on campus, we find that the school did not violate the plaintiff's rights in punishing her for it even though it arguably did not cause a substantial disruption of the school." The Court asserted that the facts of this case established a connection between off-campus action and on-campus effect, and thus justified punishment, because: (1) the website was about the school's principal; (2) the intended audience was the student body; (3) a paper copy was brought into the school and the website was discussed in school; (4) the picture on the profile was appropriated from the School District's website; (5) J.S. created the profile out of anger at the principal for disciplining her for dress code violations in the past; (6) J.S. lied in school to the principal about creating the profile; (7) "*although a substantial disruption so as to fall under Tinker did not occur* . . . there was in fact some disruption during school hours"; and (8) the profile was viewed at least by the principal at school.

. . . .

Ultimately, the District Court held that although J.S.'s profile did not cause a "substantial and material" disruption under *Tinker*, the School District's punishment was constitutionally permissible because the profile was "vulgar and offensive" under *Fraser* and J.S.'s off-campus conduct had an "effect" at the school. In a footnote, the District Court also noted that "the protections provided under *Tinker* do not apply to speech that invades the rights of others."

Next, the District Court held that the School District's policies were not vague and overbroad. . . .

The District Court also held that the School District did not violate the Snyders' parental rights under the Fourteenth Amendment. . . .

. . . .

III.

Although the precise issue before this Court is one of first impression, the Supreme Court and this Court have analyzed the extent to which school officials can regulate student speech in several thorough opinions that compel the conclusion that the School District violated J.S.'s First Amendment free speech rights when it suspended her for speech that caused no substantial disruption in school and that could not reasonably have led school officials to forecast substantial disruption in school.

A.

We begin our analysis by recognizing the "comprehensive authority" of teachers and other public school officials. Those officials involved in the educational process perform "important, delicate, and highly discretionary functions. As a result, federal courts generally exercise restraint when considering issues within the purview of public school officials.

The authority of public school officials is not boundless, however. The First Amendment unquestionably protects the free speech rights of students in public school. Indeed, "[t]he vigilant protection of constitutional freedoms is nowhere more vital than in the community of American schools." The exercise of First Amendment rights in school, however, has to be "applied in light of the special characteristics of the school environment," and thus the constitutional rights of students in public schools "are not automatically coextensive with the rights of adults in other settings," Since *Tinker*, courts have struggled to strike a balance between safeguarding students' First Amendment rights and protecting the authority of school administrators to maintain an appropriate learning environment.

The Supreme Court established a basic framework for assessing student free speech claims in *Tinker*, and we will assume, without deciding, that *Tinker* applies to J.S.'s speech in this case. The Court in *Tinker* held that "to justify prohibition of a particular expression of opinion," school officials must demonstrate that "the forbidden conduct would *materially and substantially interfere* with the requirements of appropriate discipline in the operation of the school." *Tinker*, 393 U.S. at 509, 89 S.Ct. 733 (emphasis added) (quotation marks omitted). This burden cannot be met if school officials are driven by "a mere desire to avoid the discomfort and unpleasantness that always accompany an unpopular viewpoint." *Id.* Moreover, "*Tinker* requires a specific and significant fear of disruption, not just some remote apprehension of disturbance." *Saxe v. State Coll. Area Sch. Dist.*, 240 F.3d 200, 211 (3d Cir. 2001). Although *Tinker* dealt with political speech, the opinion has never been confined to such speech. . . .

As this Court has emphasized, with then-Judge Alito writing for the majority, *Tinker* sets the general rule for regulating school speech, and that rule is subject to several *narrow* exceptions. *Saxe*, 240 F.3d at 212 ("Since *Tinker*, the Supreme Court has carved out a number of narrow categories of speech that a school may restrict even without the threat of substantial disruption."). The first exception is set out in *Fraser*, which we interpreted to permit school officials to regulate "'lewd,' 'vulgar,' 'indecent,' and 'plainly offensive' speech *in school*." The second exception to *Tinker* is articulated in *Hazelwood School District v. Kuhlmeier*, which allows school officials to "regulate school-sponsored speech (that is, speech that a reasonable observer would view as the school's own speech) on the basis of any legitimate pedagogical concern." *Saxe*, 240 F.3d at 214.

The Supreme Court recently articulated a third exception to *Tinker*' s general rule in *Morse*. Although, prior to this case, we have not had an opportunity to analyze the scope of the *Morse* exception, the Supreme Court itself emphasized the narrow reach of its decision. In *Morse*, a school punished a student for unfurling, at a school-sponsored event, a large banner containing a message that could reasonably be interpreted as promoting illegal drug use. The Court emphasized that *Morse* was a school speech case, because "[t]he event occurred during normal school hours," was sanctioned by the school "as an approved social event or class trip," was supervised by teachers and administrators from the school, and involved performances by the school band and cheerleaders. The Court then held that "[t]he 'special characteristics of the school environment,' and the governmental interest in stopping student drug abuse . . . allow schools to restrict student expression that they reasonably regard as promoting illegal drug use."

Notably, Justice Alito's concurrence in *Morse* further emphasizes the narrowness of the Court's holding, stressing that *Morse* "stand[s] at the far reaches of what the First Amendment permits." 551 U.S. at 425, (Alito, J., concurring). In fact, Justice Alito only joined the Court's opinion "on the understanding that the opinion does not hold that the special characteristics of the public schools necessarily justify any other speech restrictions" than those recognized by the Court in *Tinker, Fraser, Kuhlmeier*, and *Morse*. Justice Alito also noted that the Morse decision "does not endorse the broad argument . . . that the First Amendment permits public school officials to censor any student speech that interferes with a school's 'educational mission.' This argument can easily be manipulated in dangerous ways, and I would reject it before such abuse occurs." Moreover, Justice Alito engaged in a detailed discussion distinguishing the role of school authorities from the role of parents, and the school context from the "[o]utside of school" context.

B.

There is no dispute that J.S.'s speech did not cause a substantial disruption in the school. The School District's counsel conceded this point at oral argument and the District Court explicitly found that "a substantial disruption so as to fall under *Tinker* did not occur." Nonetheless, the School District now argues that it was justified in punishing J.S. under *Tinker* because of "facts which might reasonably have led school authorities to forecast substantial disruption of or material interference with school activities . . . ." *Tinker*. Although the burden is on school authorities to meet *Tinker*' s requirements to abridge student First Amendment rights, the School District need not prove with absolute certainty that substantial disruption will occur. *Doninger v. Niehoff*, 527 F.3d 41, 51 (2d Cir. 2008) (holding that *Tinker* does not require "actual disruption to justify a restraint on student speech"); *Lowery v. Euverard*, 497 F.3d 584, 591–92 (6th Cir. 2007) ("*Tinker* does not require school officials to wait until the horse has left the barn before closing the door . . . . [It] does not require certainty, only that the forecast of substantial disruption be reasonable."); *LaVine v. Blaine Sch. Dist.*, 257 F.3d 981, 989 (9th Cir. 2001) ("*Tinker* does not require school officials to wait until disruption actually occurs before they may act.").

The facts in this case do not support the conclusion that a forecast of substantial disruption was reasonable. In *Tinker*, the Supreme Court held that "our independent examination of the record fails to yield evidence that the school authorities had reason to anticipate that the wearing of the armbands [to protest the Vietnam War] would substantially interfere with the work of the school or impinge upon the rights of other students." Given this holding, it is important to consider the record before the Supreme Court in *Tinker* and compare it to the facts of this case.

The relevant events in *Tinker* took place in December 1965, the year that over 200,000 U.S. troops were deployed to Vietnam as part of Operation Rolling Thunder. Justice Black dissented in *Tinker*, noting that "members of this Court, like all other citizens, know, without being told, that the disputes over the wisdom of the Vietnam war have disrupted and divided this country as few other issues [e]ver have." In fact, the *Tinker* majority itself noted the school authorities' concern about the effect of the protest on friends of a student who was killed in Vietnam. Justice Black also emphasized the following portions of the record:

> "the [ ] armbands caused comments, warnings by other students, the poking of fun at them, and a warning by an older football player that other, nonprotesting students had better let them alone. There is also evidence that a teacher of mathematics had his lesson period practically 'wrecked' chiefly by disputes with [a protesting student] who wore her armband for her 'demonstration.'"

Based on these facts, Justice Black disagreed with the *Tinker* majority's holding that the armbands did not cause a substantial disruption in school: "I think the record overwhelmingly shows that the armbands did exactly what the elected school officials and principals foresaw they would, that is, took the students' minds off their classwork and diverted them to thoughts about the highly emotional subject of the Vietnam war."

This was the record in *Tinker*, and yet the majority in that case held that "the record does not demonstrate *any facts* which might reasonably have led school authorities to forecast substantial disruption of or material interference with school activities," and thus that the school violated the students' First Amendment rights. Turning to our record, J.S. created the profile as a joke, and she took steps to make it "private" so that access was limited to her and her friends. Although the profile contained McGonigle's picture from the school's website, the profile did not identify him by name, school, or location. Moreover, the profile, though indisputably vulgar, was so juvenile and nonsensical that no reasonable person could take its content seriously, and the record clearly demonstrates that no one did. Also, the School District's computers block access to MySpace, so no Blue Mountain student was ever able to view the profile from school. And, the only printout of the profile that was ever brought to school was one that was brought at McGonigle's express request. Thus, beyond general rumblings, a few minutes of talking in class, and some officials rearranging their schedules to assist McGonigle in dealing with the profile, no disruptions occurred.

In comparing our record to the record in *Tinker*, this Court cannot apply *Tinker*' s holding to justify the School District's actions in this case. As the Supreme Court has admonished, an "undifferentiated fear or apprehension of disturbance is not enough to overcome the right to freedom of expression." If *Tinker*' s black armbands—an ostentatious reminder of the highly emotional and controversial subject of the Vietnam war—could not "reasonably have led school authorities to forecast substantial disruption of or material interference with school activities neither can J.S.'s profile, despite the unfortunate humiliation it caused for McGonigle.

Courts must determine when an "undifferentiated fear or apprehension of disturbance" transforms into a reasonable forecast that a substantial disruption or material interference will occur. The School District cites several cases where courts held that a forecast of substantial and material disruption was reasonable. *See, e.g., Doninger*, 527 F.3d at 50–51 (holding that punishment was justified, under *Tinker*, where a student's derogatory blog about the school was "purposely designed by [the student] to come onto the campus," to "encourage others to contact the administration," and where the blog contained "at best misleading and at worst false information" that the school "need[ed] to correct"; *Lowery*, 497 F.3d at 596 (holding that punishment was justified, under *Tinker*, where students circulated a petition to fellow football players calling for the ouster of their football coach, causing the school to have to call a team meeting to ensure "team unity," and where not doing so "would have been a grave disservice to the other players on the team"); *LaVine*, 257 F.3d at 984, 989–90 (holding that the school district did not violate a student's First Amendment rights when it expelled him on an emergency basis "to prevent [ ] potential violence on campus" after he showed a poem entitled "Last Words" to his English teacher, which was "filled with imagery of violent death and suicide" and could "be interpreted as a portent of future violence, of the shooting of [ ] fellow students").

The School District likens this case to the above cases by contending that the profile was accusatory and aroused suspicions among the school community about McGonigle's character because of the profile's references to his engaging in sexual misconduct. As explained above, however, this contention is simply not supported by the record. The profile was so outrageous that no one could have taken it seriously, and no one did. Thus, it was clearly not reasonably foreseeable that J.S.'s speech would create a substantial disruption or material interference in school, and this case is therefore distinguishable from the student speech at issue in *Doninger*, *Lowery*, and *LaVine*.

Moreover, unlike the students in *Doninger*, *Lowery*, and *LaVine*, J.S. did not even intend for the speech to reach the school—in fact, she took specific steps to make the profile "private" so that only her friends could access it. The fact that her friends happen to be Blue Mountain Middle School students is not surprising, and does not mean that J.S.'s speech targeted the school. Finally, any suggestion that, absent McGonigle's actions, a substantial disruption would have occurred, is directly undermined by the record. If anything, McGonigle's response to the profile *exacerbated* rather than contained the disruption in the school.

The facts simply do not support the conclusion that the School District could have reasonably forecasted a substantial disruption of or material interference with the school as a result of J.S.'s profile. Under *Tinker*, therefore, the School District violated J.S.'s First Amendment free speech rights when it suspended her for creating the profile.

C.

Because *Tinker* does not justify the School District's suspension of J.S., the only way for the punishment to pass constitutional muster is if we accept the School District's argument—and the District Court's holding—that J.S.'s speech can be prohibited under the *Fraser* exception to *Tinker.* The School District argues that although J.S.'s speech occurred off campus, it was justified in disciplining her because it was "lewd, vulgar, and offensive [and] had an effect on the school and the educational mission of the District." The School District's argument fails at the outset because *Fraser* does not apply to off-campus speech. Specifically in *Morse,* Chief Justice Roberts, writing for the majority, emphasized that "[h]ad Fraser delivered the same speech in a public forum outside the school context, it would have been protected." . . . The Court's citation to the *Cohen* decision is noteworthy. The Supreme Court in *Cohen* held, in a non-school setting, that a state may not make a "single four-letter expletive a criminal offense." Accordingly, Chief Justice Roberts's reliance on the *Cohen* decision reaffirms that a student's free speech rights outside the school context are coextensive with the rights of an adult.

Thus, under the Supreme Court's precedent, the *Fraser* exception to *Tinker* does not apply here. In other words, *Fraser*' s "lewdness" standard cannot be extended to justify a school's punishment of J.S. for use of profane language outside the school, during non-school hours.

The School District points out that "a hard copy or printout of the profile *actually* came into the school." However, the fact that McGonigle caused a copy of the profile to be brought to school does not transform J.S.'s off-campus speech into school speech. The flaws of a contrary rule can be illustrated by extrapolating from the facts of *Fraser* itself. As discussed above, the Supreme Court emphasized that Fraser's speech would have been protected had he delivered it outside the school. Presumably, this protection would not be lifted if a school official or Fraser's fellow classmate overheard the off-campus speech, recorded it, and played it to the school principal. Similarly here, the fact that another student printed J.S.'s profile and brought it to school at the express request of McGonigle does not turn J.S.'s off-campus speech into on-campus speech.

Under these circumstances, to apply the *Fraser* standard to justify the School District's punishment of J.S.'s speech would be to adopt a rule that allows school officials to punish any speech by a student that takes place anywhere, at any time, as long as it is *about* the school or a school official, is brought to the attention of a school official, and is deemed "offensive" by the prevailing authority. Under this standard, two students can be punished for using a vulgar remark to speak about their teacher at a private party, if another student overhears the remark, reports it to the school authorities, and the school authorities find the remark "offensive." There is no principled way to distinguish this hypothetical from the facts of the instant case.

Accordingly, we conclude that the *Fraser* decision did not give the School District the authority to punish J.S. for her off-campus speech.

....

Neither the Supreme Court nor this Court has ever allowed schools to punish students for off-campus speech that is not school-sponsored or at a school-sponsored event and that caused no substantial disruption at school. We follow the logic and letter of these cases and reverse the District Court's grant of summary judgment in favor of the School District and denial of J.S.'s motion for summary judgment on her free speech claim. An opposite holding would significantly broaden school districts' authority over student speech and would vest school officials with dangerously overbroad censorship discretion. We will remand to the District Court to determine appropriate relief on this claim.

....

VI.

For the foregoing reasons, the District Court's judgment will be affirmed in part, reversed in part and remanded.

SMITH, CIRCUIT JUDGE, concurring, with whom MCKEE, CHIEF JUDGE, SLOVITER, FUENTES, and HARDIMAN, CIRCUIT JUDGES, join.

Because the school district suspended J.S. for speech that she engaged in at home on a Sunday evening, I fully agree with the majority's conclusion that it violated J.S.'s First Amendment rights. I write separately to address a question that the majority opinion expressly leaves open: whether *Tinker* applies to off-campus speech in the first place. I would hold that it does not, and that the First Amendment protects students engaging in off-campus speech to the same extent it protects speech by citizens in the community at large.

As a general matter, the First Amendment strictly protects speech regardless of whether it is disruptive, offensive, vulgar, or insulting. In *Tinker v. Des Moines Independent Community School District*, 393 U.S. 503 (1969), the Supreme Court considered whether different rules should govern student speech inside public schools. Although it observed that students do not "shed their constitutional rights to freedom of speech or expression at the schoolhouse gate," the Court determined that, "in light of the special characteristics of the school environment" and the need to defer to school officials' authority "to prescribe and control conduct in the schools," the First Amendment's ordinarily strict protection of speech rights should be relaxed in the public-school context. The Court thus concluded that some otherwise-protected speech can be suppressed in the school setting, but only if it "would materially and substantially disrupt the work and discipline of the school."

In later cases, the Court recognized exceptions to *Tinker*, holding that even non-disruptive school speech can be restricted if it is lewd or vulgar, *Bethel Sch. Dist. No. 403 v. Fraser*, if it is school-sponsored and the restriction is "reasonably related to legitimate pedagogical concerns," *Hazelwood Sch. Dist. v. Kuhlmeier*, or if it is reasonably viewed as promoting the use of illegal drugs, *Morse v. Frederick*.

Courts agree that *Fraser, Kuhlmeier*, and *Morse* apply solely to on-campus speech (I use the phrase "on-campus speech" as shorthand for speech communicated at school or, though not on school grounds, at a school-sanctioned event. Indeed, the Supreme Court has expressly recognized that *Fraser* does not extend "outside the school context," and three justices have observed (without objection from the other six) that speech promoting illegal drug use, even if prescribable in a public school, would "unquestionably" be protected if uttered elsewhere. Lower courts, however, are divided on whether *Tinker*' s substantial-disruption test governs students' off-campus expression. In my view, the decisions holding that *Tinker* does not apply to off-campus speech have the better of the argument.

Tinker' s holding is expressly grounded in "the special characteristics of the . . . school environment," and the need to defer to school officials' authority "to prescribe and control conduct in the schools," The Court's later school-speech cases underscored *Tinker*' s narrow reach. *Tinker*, according to the Court's decision in *Fraser*, rests on the understanding that "the constitutional rights of students in public school are not automatically coextensive with the rights of adults in other settings," and that students are a captive audience while at school. *Kuhlmeier*, moreover, described *Tinker* as "address[ing] educators' ability to silence a student's personal expression that happens to occur on the school premises." Finally, in *Morse*, the Court took care to refute the contention that the plaintiff's speech, which took place at a school field trip, did not occur "at school." In concluding that the plaintiff's suit was governed by the *Tinker* line of cases, the Court stressed that the field trip "occurred during normal school hours," that it "was sanctioned by [the principal] as an approved social event or class trip," that "[t]eachers and administrators were interspersed among the students and charged with supervising them," and that the "high school band and cheerleaders performed." If *Tinker* and the Court's other school-speech precedents applied to off-campus speech, this discussion would have been unnecessary. Indeed, in his *Morse* concurrence, Justice Alito essentially recognized that *Tinker*' s substantial-disruption test does not apply to students' off-campus expression . . . .

The Second Circuit addressed a school's punishment of off-campus speech in *Thomas v. Board of Education, Granville Central School District*. There, a public high school suspended students for publishing an "underground" newspaper, which was "saturated with distasteful sexual satire, including an editorial on masturbation and articles alluding to prostitution, sodomy, and castration." . . . The students were suspended after a teacher confiscated a copy of the newspaper that another student had taken to school. In the ensuing § 1983 suit, the Second Circuit concluded that *Tinker* did not control because the newspaper was best viewed as off-campus speech . . . .

The Fifth Circuit followed suit in *Porter v. Ascension Parish School Board*. There, while sitting in the privacy of his own home, a high school student drew a picture of his school being attacked by missiles, helicopters, and armed assailants. The student stored the picture in his closet. The school learned of the drawing when the student's younger brother inadvertently took it there. The school expelled the student. In the civil-rights action that followed, the Fifth Circuit determined that the picture amounted to off-campus speech and thus declined to apply *Tinker*, holding that it governs only "student expression 'that . . . occur[s] on the school premises.' . . ."

I agree with *Thomas* and *Porter*, and I believe that various post- *Tinker* pronouncements of the Supreme Court support their *ratio decidendi*. Applying *Tinker* to off-campus speech would create a precedent with ominous implications. Doing so would empower schools to regulate students' expressive activity no matter where it takes place, when it occurs, or what subject matter it involves—so long as it causes a substantial disruption at school. *Tinker*, for example, authorizes schools to suppress political speech—speech "at the core of what the First Amendment is designed to protect"—if it substantially disrupts school activities. Suppose a high school student, while at home after school hours, were to write a blog entry defending gay marriage. Suppose further that several of the student's classmates got wind of the entry, took issue with it, and caused a significant disturbance at school. While the school could clearly punish the students who acted disruptively, if *Tinker* were held to apply to off-campus speech, the school could also punish the student whose blog entry brought about the disruption. That cannot be, nor is it, the law.

To be sure, *this* case does not involve political speech. J.S. simply published an insulting (and, I would say, mean-spirited) parody of her principal on Myspace. But the lack of political content is irrelevant for First Amendment purposes. There is no First Amendment exception for offensive speech or for speech that lacks a certain quantum of social value. It is worth pointing out, as well, that although speech like J.S.'s may appear to be worthless, it does enable citizens to vent their frustrations in nonviolent ways. We ought not to discount the importance in our society of such a "safety valve."

. . . .

But that is only half the battle. The other half: how can one tell whether speech takes place on or off campus? Answering this question will not always be easy. The answer plainly cannot turn solely on where the speaker was sitting when the speech was originally uttered. Such a standard would fail to accommodate the somewhat "everywhere at once" nature of the internet. So, for example, I would have no difficulty applying *Tinker* to a case where a student sent a disruptive email to school faculty from his home computer. Regardless of its place of origin, speech intentionally directed towards a school is properly considered on-campus speech. On the other hand, speech originating off campus does not mutate into on-campus speech simply because it foreseeably makes its way onto campus. A bare foreseeability standard could be stretched too far, and would risk ensnaring any off-campus expression that happened to discuss school-related matters.

In any event, this case does not require us to precisely define the boundary between on- and off-campus speech, since it is perfectly clear that J.S.'s speech took place off campus . . . .

Having determined that J.S.'s speech took place off campus, I would apply ordinary First Amendment principles to determine whether it was protected. I agree with the majority that this was protected speech. The speech was not defamatory, obscene, or otherwise unprotected. J.S.'s suspension, then, violated the First Amendment.

. . . .

FISHER, CIRCUIT JUDGE, dissenting, with whom SCIRICA, RENDELL, BARRY, JORDAN, and VANASKIE, CIRCUIT JUDGES, join.

Today's holding severely undermines schools' authority to regulate students who "materially and substantially disrupt the work and discipline of the school." *Tinker v. Des Moines Indep. Cmty. Sch. Dist.*. While I agree with the majority's apparent adoption of the rule that off-campus student speech can rise to the level of a substantial disruption, I disagree with the Court's application of that rule to the facts of this case. The majority misconstrues the facts. In doing so, it allows a student to target a school official and his family with malicious and unfounded accusations about their character in vulgar, obscene, and personal language. I fear that our Court leaves schools defenseless to protect teachers and school officials against such attacks and powerless to discipline students for the consequences of their actions . . . .

I respectfully dissent from the majority's ruling that the Blue Mountain School District's ten-day suspension of J.S. for making false accusations against McGonigle violated her First Amendment right to free speech. The majority holds that "[t]he facts in this case do not support the conclusion that a forecast of substantial disruption was reasonable." But the majority makes light of the harmful effects of J.S.'s speech and the serious nature of allegations of sexual misconduct. Broadcasting a personal attack against a school official and his family online to the school community not only causes psychological harm to the targeted individuals but also undermines the authority of the school. It was permissible for the School District to discipline J.S. because substantial disruption was reasonably foreseeable . . . .

I.

I disagree with the majority's assessment that the four opinions of the Supreme Court on student speech "compel the conclusion that the School District violated J.S.'s First Amendment free speech rights." In fact, the Supreme Court has never addressed whether students have the right to make off-campus speech that targets school officials with malicious, obscene, and vulgar accusations. In *Tinker*, the Court examined whether a school had the authority to prevent students from wearing black arm bands on campus in protest of the Vietnam War. In *Bethel School District v. Fraser*, the Court held that a school could suspend a student for giving an obscene and vulgar speech on campus at a school-sponsored event. The Court in *Hazelwood School District v. Kuhlmeier* ruled that a school could exercise editorial control over the contents of a student newspaper so long as it was "reasonably related to legitimate pedagogical concerns." And in *Morse v. Frederick*, the Court determined that a school could sanction a student for unfurling a banner that promoted illegal drug use at a school-approved event. None of these decisions control the facts of this case nor do they compel a conclusion in favor of J.S.

The Supreme Court has only briefly and ambiguously considered whether schools have the authority to regulate student off-campus speech . . . .

I believe that the rule adopted by the Supreme Court in *Tinker* should determine the outcome of this case. Under *Tinker*, we must examine whether J.S.'s speech created a significant threat of substantial disruption at the Middle School. School authorities need not wait until the disruption actually occurs if they are able to "demonstrate any facts which might reasonably have led [them] to forecast substantial disruption of or material interference with school activities." If the Middle School reasonably forecasted substantial disruption, then it had the authority to regulate J.S.'s speech. The majority seems to acknowledge just as much, but finds that "[t]he facts simply do not support the conclusion that the School District could have reasonably forecasted a substantial disruption of or material interference with the school as a result of J.S.'s profile."

The majority reaches this conclusion by contrasting the facts of *Tinker* with those of our case . . . .

Allowing for the expression of beliefs and opinions in a robust but respectful environment encourages engagement, promotes self-improvement, and furthers the search for truth. The Court in *Tinker* embraced the freedom of speech as an essential component of the educational system. "When he is in the cafeteria, or on the playing field, or on the campus during the authorized hours, he may express his opinions, even on controversial subjects like the conflict in Vietnam, if he does so without 'materially and substantially interfer(ing) with the requirements of appropriate discipline in the operation of the school' and without colliding with the rights of others."

B.

J.S., by contrast, targeted her principal and her principal's family with lewd, vulgar, and offensive speech. She created a MySpace page using a photograph of McGonigle that she had taken from the School District website, and she publicly disseminated numerous hurtful accusations. She accused McGonigle of sexual misconduct: "fucking in [his] office," "hitting on students and their parents," and being a "sex addict." She insulted McGonigle by calling him a "dick head," stating that he was "put on this world with a small dick," and calling him a "fagass." And J.S. insulted his family. She stated that his wife "looks like a man" and that his son "looks like a gorilla." She stated that the principal enjoys "riding the fraintrain" and that "it's a slow ride but you'll get there eventually."

The School found this speech to be in violation of school policy because J.S. made "false accusations about the school principal" and violated copyright law in using McGonigle's picture. This constituted a level IV infraction because it involved "making a false accusation about a school staff member," and the School imposed a ten-day suspension.

J.S.'s speech is not the type of speech that the *Tinker* Court so vehemently protected. I agree with the majority that the facts in the record fail to demonstrate substantial disruption at the School. But the profile's *potential* to cause disruption was reasonably foreseeable, and that is sufficient. Two forms of disruption were foreseeable. First, the MySpace page posed a reasonably foreseeable threat of interference with the educational environment. If J.S.'s speech went unpunished, it would undermine McGonigle's authority and disrupt the educational process. Second, J.S.'s speech posed a reasonably foreseeable threat of disrupting the operations of the classroom. It was foreseeable that J.S.'s false accusations and malicious comments would disrupt McGonigle and Frain's ability to perform their jobs . . . .

J.S.'s speech posed a threat of substantial disruption to the educational environment. The majority fails to recognize the effects of accusations of sexual misconduct. J.S. created the profile at the URL ending in: "kidsrockmybed." She accused McGonigle of having sex in his office, "hitting on students and their parents," and being a "sex addict." The profile stated that "I love children [and] sex (any kind)."

Such accusations interfere with the educational process by undermining the authority of school officials to perform their jobs . . . .

Further, accusing school officials of sexual misconduct poses a foreseeable threat of diverting school resources required to correct the misinformation and remedy confusion. It was reasonably foreseeable that the accusations made in the MySpace profile would be shared with parents and teachers. McGonigle's character would come under investigation, and his fitness to occupy a position of trust with adolescent children would be questioned. It is inevitable that as more students and parents learned of the profile, the School would experience disruption. While Superintendent Joyce Romberger may have dismissed the accusations as false because she knew him, students and parents unfamiliar with McGonigle may have had serious questions about McGonigle's character and actions. Parents would become concerned that their children were supervised by a man accused of having sex in his office, being a "sex addict," and "hitting on" their children. It was reasonably foreseeable that school administrators would have to spend a substantial amount of time alleviating these concerns. The Middle School acted reasonably in requesting the removal of the MySpace page, contacting J.S.'s parents, and suspending J.S. for ten days. If such steps were not taken, it is likely that the Middle School would have suffered substantial disruptions because McGonigle's authority would have been severely undermined and school resources would have been diverted to alleviate the inevitable concerns.

The majority also overlooks the substantial disruptions to the classroom environment that follow from personal and harmful attacks on educators and school officials. J.S.'s speech attacked McGonigle and Frain in personal and vulgar terms and broadcasted it to the school community. This kind of harassment has tangible effects on educators. It may cause teachers to leave the school and stop teaching altogether, and those who decide to stay are oftentimes less effective....

In *Wisniewski v. Board of Education of Weedsport Central School District*, the Second Circuit noted that a teacher who was subjected to hostile student speech became distressed and had to stop teaching the student's class. 494 F.3d 34, 35–36 (2d Cir. 2007). Similarly, in *J.S. v. Bethlehem Area School District*, the teacher suffered stress, anxiety, loss of appetite, loss of sleep, loss of weight, and a general sense of loss of well being as a result of viewing the [hostile and offensive student] web site. She suffered from short-term memory loss and an inability to go out of the house and mingle with crowds. [The teacher] suffered headaches and was required to take anti-anxiety/anti-depressant medication.

The teacher was unable to return to school, and the "web site had a demoralizing impact on the school community." In *Schroeder v. Hamilton School District*, a teacher was subjected to anti-homosexual speech from students and parents and suffered a "nervous breakdown that ultimately resulted in his termination." In our case, McGonigle stated that he became distressed after viewing J.S.'s MySpace profile. He stated, "I was very upset and very angry, hurt, and I can't understand why [J.S.] did this to me and my family."

J.S.'s speech had a reasonably foreseeable effect on the classroom environment. In addition to causing a diminution in respect for authority and a diversion of school resources, J.S.'s speech posed reasonably foreseeable psychological harm to McGonigle and Frain that would impact their ability to perform their jobs....

I question the majority's assessment of the facts of this case. Its conclusion that a substantial disruption was not reasonably foreseeable rests on several mischaracterizations: that J.S.'s MySpace profile should be regarded as a "joke"; that her profile should not have been taken seriously; that because J.S. did not identify McGonigle by name, it lessened the impact of her profile; and that J.S. took steps to ensure that her profile remained private and did not reach the school. Each of these findings is flawed....,

Our decision today causes a split with the Second Circuit. In applying *Tinker*, the Second Circuit has held that off-campus hostile and offensive student internet speech that is directed at school officials results in a substantial disruption of the classroom environment. In *Wisniewski*, a middle school student sent messages to fifteen fellow students via an instant messenger program from his home computer during non-school hours. The program used an icon depicting one of his teachers being shot in the head with text below reading "Kill Mr. VanderMolen." The Second Circuit stated that "off-campus conduct can create a foreseeable risk of substantial disruption within a school," and held that it was reasonably foreseeable that the depiction would come to the attention of school authorities and the teacher who was the subject of the drawing. The court reasoned that:

> The potentially threatening content of the icon and the extensive distribution of it, which encompassed 15 recipients, including some of Aaron's classmates, during a three-week circulation period, made this risk at least foreseeable to a reasonable person, if not inevitable. And there can be no doubt that the icon, once made known to the teacher and other school officials, would foreseeably create a risk of substantial disruption within the school environment.

The Second Circuit held that hostile and offensive off-campus student speech posed a reasonably foreseeable threat of substantial disruption within the school.

The Second Circuit confronted a similar scenario in *Doninger v. Niehoff*, 527 F.3d 41 (2d Cir. 2008) (*Doninger* I) and *Doninger v. Niehoff*, 642 F.3d 334, 2011 WL 1532289 (2d Cir. April 25, 2011) (*Doninger* II). A member of the high school student council, upset by scheduling conflicts regarding a student event, posted a message on her blog from her home computer during non-school hours. She stated that the student event was "cancelled due to douchebags in the central office." She urged people to call or write a school official "to piss her off more." The school received numerous calls and emails, some of which were from students who were upset. As a result of the blog post, the school refused to allow the student to run for Junior Class Secretary. The student challenged the school's sanction, but the Second Circuit stated that the student's post, "although created off-campus, was purposely designed by [the student] to come onto the campus." The Court reasoned that her post "foreseeably create[d] a risk of substantial disruption within the school environment." It was reasonably foreseeable that "administrators and teachers would be further diverted from their core educational responsibilities by the need to dissipate misguided anger or confusion over [the student event's] purported cancellation."

The majority claims that these cases are distinguishable. It argues that no one could have taken J.S.'s accusations seriously and that "J.S. did not even intend for the speech to reach the school." The majority misses the mark.

. . . .

The majority's approach does not offer a promising way forward. Internet use among teenagers is nearly universal. *See* Amanda Lenhart, et al., Pew Internet & American Life Project: Teens and Social Media 2 (2007) (stating that 93 percent of teenagers use the internet and 61 percent use it daily). And social networking sites have become one of the main vehicles of social interaction. *See* Amanda Lenhart, et al., Pew Internet and American Life: Teens and Mobile Phones 59 (2010) (stating that 73 percent of teenagers use a social networking site); National School Board Association, Creating & Connecting: Research and Guidelines on Online Social—And Educational—Networking (2007) (stating that teenagers spend an average of 9 hours per week on social networking sites).

The line between "on-campus" and "off-campus" speech is not as clear as it once was. Today, students commonly carry cell phones with internet capabilities onto school grounds. Approximately 66 percent of students receive a cell phone before the age of 14, and slightly less than 75 percent of high school students have cell phones. Amanda Lenhart, et al., Pew Internet and American Life: Teens and Mobile Phones 9 (2010). Twenty-three percent of teenagers between the ages of 12 and 17 who own cell phones use them to access social networking sites like MySpace and Facebook. *Id.* at 56. The majority embraces a notion that student hostile and offensive online speech directed at school officials will not reach the school. But with near-constant student access to social networking sites on and off campus, when offensive and malicious speech is directed at school officials and disseminated online to the student body, it is reasonable to anticipate an impact on the classroom environment. I fear that our Court has adopted a rule that will prove untenable.

....

III.

... I respectfully dissent from the decision that the suspension of J.S. for making false and malicious accusations against her principal in the form of lewd and offensive speech violated her First Amendment rights. In student free speech cases, courts must grapple with the issue of promoting freedom of expression while maintaining a conducive learning environment. I believe the majority has unwisely tipped the balance struck by *Tinker, Fraser, Kuhlmeier,* and *Morse,* thereby jeopardizing schools' ability to maintain an orderly learning environment while protecting teachers and school officials against harmful attacks.

Kowalski v. Berkeley County Sch.

652 F.3d 565 (4th Cir. 2011), *cert. denied*, 565 U.S. 1173 (2012)

The Fourth Circuit applies Tinker and rules that the school did not violate the First Amendment when it disciplined a student who used her home computer to create a website and post comments ridiculing a fellow student.

Niemeyer, Circuit Judge

When Kara Kowalski was a senior at Musselman High School in Berkeley County, West Virginia, school administrators suspended her from school for five days for creating and posting to a MySpace.com webpage called "S.A.S.H.," which Kowalski claims stood for "Students Against Sluts Herpes" and which was largely dedicated to ridiculing a fellow student. Kowalski commenced this action, under 42 U.S.C. § 1983, against the Berkeley County School District and five of its officers, contending that in disciplining her, the defendants violated her free speech and due process rights under the First and Fourteenth Amendments. She alleges, among other things, that the School District was not justified in regulating her speech because it did not occur during a "school-related activity," but rather was "private out-of-school speech."

The district court entered summary judgment in favor of the defendants, concluding that they were authorized to punish Kowalski because her webpage was "created for the purpose of inviting others to indulge in disruptive and hateful conduct," which caused an "in-school disruption."

Reviewing the summary judgment record *de novo*, we conclude that in the circumstances of this case, the School District's imposition of sanctions was permissible. Kowalski used the Internet to orchestrate a targeted attack on a classmate, and did so in a manner that was sufficiently connected to the school environment as to implicate the School District's recognized authority to discipline speech which "materially and substantially interfere[es] with the requirements of appropriate discipline in the operation of the school and collid[es] with the rights of others." *Tinker v. Des Moines Indep. Community Sch. Dist.*, 393 U.S. 503, 513, 89 S. Ct. 733, 21 L. Ed. 2d 731 (1969). Accordingly, we affirm.

I

On December 1, 2005, Kara Kowalski, who was then a 12th grade student at Musselman High School in the Berkeley County School District, returned home from school and, using her home computer, created a discussion group webpage on MySpace.com with the heading "S.A.S.H." Under the webpage's title, she posted the statement, "No No Herpes, We don't want no herpes." Kowalski claimed in her deposition that "S.A.S.H." was an acronym for "Students Against Sluts Herpes," but a classmate, Ray Parsons, stated that it was an acronym for "Students Against Shay's Herpes," referring to another Musselman High School Student, Shay N., who was the main subject of discussion on the webpage.

After creating the group, Kowalski invited approximately 100 people on her MySpace "friends" list to join the group. MySpace discussion groups allow registered users to post and respond to text, comments, and photographs in an interactive fashion. Approximately two dozen Musselman High School students responded and ultimately joined the group. Kowalski later explained that she had hoped that the group would "make other students actively aware of STDs," which were a "hot topic" at her school.

Ray Parsons responded to the MySpace invitation at 3:40 p.m. and was the first to join the group, doing so from a school computer during an after hours class at Musselman High School. Parsons uploaded a photograph of himself and a friend holding their noses while displaying a sign that read, "Shay Has Herpes," referring to Shay N. The record of the webpage shows that Kowalski promptly responded, stating, "Ray you are soo funny!=)" It shows that shortly thereafter, she posted another response to the photograph, stating that it was "the best picture [I]'ve seen on myspace so far! ! ! !" Several other students posted similar replies. Parsons also uploaded to the "S.A.S.H." webpage two additional photographs of Shay N., which he edited. In the first, he had drawn red dots on Shay N.'s face to simulate herpes and added a sign near her pelvic region, that read, "Warning: Enter at your own risk." In the second photograph, he captioned Shay N.'s face with a sign that read, "portrait of a whore."

The commentary posted on the "S.A.S.H." webpage mostly focused on Shay N. The first five comments were posted by other Musselman High School students and ridiculed the pictures of Shay N. One student stated that "shay knows about the sign" and then stated, "wait til she sees the page lol." (The abbreviation "lol" means "laugh out loud" or "laughing out loud.") The next comment replied, "Haha. screw her" and repeatedly stated, "This is great." After expressing her approval of the postings, this student noted the "Shay has herpes sign" and stated, "Kara sent me a few interesting pics . . . Would you be interested in seeing them Ray?" One student posted, "Kara= My Hero," and another said, "your so awesome kara . . . i never thought u would mastermind a group that hates [someone] tho, lol." A few of the posts assumed that Kowalski had posted the photographs of Shay N., but Parsons later clarified that it was he who had posted the photographs.

A few hours after the photographs and comments had been posted to the MySpace .com page, Shay N.'s father called Parsons on the telephone and expressed his anger over the photographs. Parsons then called Kowalski, who unsuccessfully attempted to delete the "S.A.S.H." group and to remove the photographs. Unable to do so, she renamed the group "Students Against Angry People."

The next morning, Shay N.'s parents, together with Shay, went to Musselman High School and filed a harassment complaint with Vice Principal Becky Harden regarding the discussion group, and they provided Harden with a printout of the "S.A.S.H." webpage. Shay thereafter left the school with her parents, as she did not want to attend classes that day, feeling uncomfortable about sitting in class with students who had posted comments about her on the MySpace webpage.

After receiving Shay N.'s complaint, Principal Ronald Stephens contacted the central school board office to determine whether the issue was one that should be addressed with school discipline. A school board official indicated that discipline was appropriate. Principal Stephens then conducted an investigation into the matter, during which he and Vice Principal Harden interviewed the students who had joined the "S.A.S.H." group to determine who posted the photographs and comments. As part of the investigation, Principal Stephens and Vice Principal Harden questioned Parsons, who admitted that he had posted the photographs. Vice Principal Harden met with Kowalski, who admitted that she had created the "S.A.S.H." group but denied that she posted any of the photographs or disparaging remarks.

School administrators concluded that Kowalski had created a "hate website," in violation of the school policy against "harassment, bullying, and intimidation." For punishment, they suspended Kowalski from school for 10 days and issued her a 90-day "social suspension," which prevented her from attending school events in which she was not a direct participant. Kowalski was also prevented from crowning the next "Queen of Charm" in that year's Charm Review, having been elected "Queen" herself the previous year. In addition, she was not allowed to participate on the cheerleading squad for the remainder of the year. After Kowalski's father asked school administrators to reduce or revoke the suspension, Assistant Superintendent Rick Deuell reduced Kowalski's out-of-school suspension to 5 days, but retained the 90-day social suspension.

. . . .

II

Kowalski contends first that the school administrators violated her free speech rights under the First Amendment by punishing her for speech that occurred outside the school . . . she asserts, "The [Supreme] Court has been consistently careful to limit intrusions on students' rights to conduct taking place on school property, at school functions, or while engaged in school-sponsored or school-sanctioned activity." She maintains that "no Supreme Court case addressing student speech has held that a school may punish students for speech away from school—indeed every Supreme Court case addressing student speech has taken pains to emphasize that, were the speech in question to occur away from school, it would be protected."

The Berkeley County School District and its administrators contend that school officials "may regulate off-campus behavior insofar as the off-campus behavior creates a foreseeable risk of reaching school property and causing a substantial disruption to the work and discipline of the school," citing *Doninger v. Niehoff*, 527 F.3d 41 (2d Cir. 2008). Relying on *Doninger*, the defendants note that Kowalski created a webpage that singled out Shay N. for harassment, bullying and intimidation; that it was foreseeable that the off-campus conduct would reach the school; and that it was foreseeable that the off-campus conduct would "create a substantial disruption in the school."

The question thus presented is whether Kowalski's activity fell within the outer boundaries of the high school's legitimate interest in maintaining order in the school and protecting the well-being and educational rights of its students.

. . . It is a "bedrock principle" of the First Amendment that "the government may not prohibit the expression of an idea simply because society finds the idea itself offensive or disagreeable." . . . While students retain significant First Amendment rights in the school context, their rights are not coextensive with those of adults. *See Tinker v. Des Moines Indep. Community Sch. Dist.* Because of the "special characteristics of the school environment," school administrators have some latitude in regulating student speech to further educational objectives. Thus in *Tinker*, the Court held that student speech, consisting of wearing armbands in political protest against the Vietnam War, was protected because it did not "'materially and substantially interfer[e] with the requirements of appropriate discipline in the operation of the school' [or] collid[e] with the rights of others," and thus did not "materially disrupt classwork or involve substantial disorder or invasion of the rights of others." Student speech also may be regulated if it is otherwise "vulgar and lewd. "*See Bethel Sch. Dist. No. 403 v. Fraser.* Finally, the Supreme Court has held that school administrators are free to regulate and punish student speech that encourages the use of illegal drugs. *Morse v. Frederick.*

Although the Supreme Court has not dealt specifically with a factual circumstance where student speech targeted classmates for verbal abuse, in *Tinker* it recognized the need for regulation of speech that interfered with the school's work and discipline, describing that interference as speech that "disrupts classwork," creates "substantial disorder," or "collid[es] with" or "inva[des]" "the rights of others."

In *Tinker*, the Court pointed out at length how wearing black armbands in protest against the Vietnam War was passive and did not create "disorder or disturbance" and therefore did not interfere with the school's work or collide with other students' rights "to be secure and to be let alone." . . . The Court amplified the nature of the disruption it had in mind when it stated:

> [C]conduct by [a] student, in class or out of it, which for any reason—whether it stems from time, place, or type of behavior—materially disrupts classwork or involves substantial disorder or invasion of the rights of others is, of course, not immunized by the constitutional guarantee of freedom of speech . . . .

Thus, the language of *Tinker* supports the conclusion that public schools have a "compelling interest" in regulating speech that interferes with or disrupts the work and discipline of the school, including discipline for student harassment and bullying.

According to a federal government initiative, student-on-student bullying is a "major concern" in schools across the country and can cause victims to become depressed and anxious, to be afraid to go to school, and to have thoughts of suicide. *See* StopBullying.gov, available at www.stopbullying.gov (follow "Recognize the Warning Signs" hyperlink). Just as schools have a responsibility to provide a safe environment for students free from messages advocating illegal drug use, *see Morse*, schools have a duty to protect their students from harassment and bullying in the school environment, *cf. Lowery v. Euverard*, 497 F.3d 584, 596 (6th Cir. 2007) ("School officials have an affirmative duty to not only ameliorate the harmful effects of disruptions, but to prevent them from happening in the first place"). Far from being a situation where school authorities "suppress speech on political and social issues based on disagreement with the viewpoint expressed," school administrators must be able to prevent and punish harassment and bullying in order to provide a safe school environment conducive to learning.

We are confident that Kowalski's speech caused the interference and disruption described in *Tinker* as being immune from First Amendment protection. The "S.A.S.H." webpage functioned as a platform for Kowalski and her friends to direct verbal attacks towards classmate Shay N. The webpage contained comments accusing Shay N. of having herpes and being a "slut," as well as photographs reinforcing those defamatory accusations by depicting a sign across her pelvic area, which stated, "Warning: Enter at your own risk" and labeling her portrait as that of a "whore." One student's posting dismissed any concern for Shay N.'s reaction with a comment that said, "screw her." This is not the conduct and speech that our educational system is required to tolerate, as schools attempt to educate students about "habits and manners of civility" or the "fundamental values necessary to the maintenance of a democratic political system." *Fraser*, 478 U.S. at 681.

While Kowalski does not seriously dispute the harassing character of the speech on the "S.A.S.H." webpage, she argues mainly that her conduct took place at home after school and that the forum she created was therefore subject to the full protection of the First Amendment. This argument, however, raises the metaphysical question of where her speech occurred when she used the Internet as the medium. Kowalski indeed pushed her computer's keys in her home, but she knew that the electronic response would be, as it in fact was, published beyond her home and could reasonably be expected to reach the school or impact the school environment. She also knew that the dialogue would and did take place among Musselman High School students whom she invited to join the "S.A.S.H." group and that the fallout from her conduct and the speech within the group would be felt in the school itself. Indeed, the group's name was "*Students* Against Sluts Herpes" and a vast majority of its members were Musselman students. As one commentator on the webpage observed, "wait til [Shay N.] sees the page lol." Moreover, as Kowalski could anticipate, Shay N. and her parents took the attack as having been made in the school context, as they went to the high school to lodge their complaint.

There is surely a limit to the scope of a high school's interest in the order, safety, and well-being of its students when the speech at issue originates outside the schoolhouse gate. But we need not fully define that limit here, as we are satisfied that the nexus of Kowalski's speech to Musselman High School's pedagogical interests was sufficiently strong to justify the action taken by school officials in carrying out their role as the trustees of the student body's well-being.

Of course, had Kowalski created the "S.A.S.H." group during school hours, using a school-provided computer and Internet connection, this case would be more clear-cut, as the question of where speech that was transmitted by the Internet "occurred" would not come into play. To be sure, a court could determine that speech originating outside of the schoolhouse gate but directed at persons in school and received by and acted on by them was in fact in-school speech. In that case, because it was determined to be in-school speech, its regulation would be permissible not only under *Tinker* but also, as vulgar and lewd in-school speech, under *Fraser*. *See Fraser*, 478 U.S. at 685. *But cf. Layshock v. Hermitage Sch. Dist.*, 650 F.3d 205, 2011 U.S. App. LEXIS 11994, 2011 WL 2305970 (3d Cir. 2011) (en banc) (holding that a school could not punish a student for online speech merely because the speech was vulgar and reached the school). We need not resolve, however, whether this was in-school speech and therefore whether *Fraser* could apply because the School District was authorized by *Tinker* to discipline Kowalski, regardless of where her speech originated, because the speech was materially and substantially disruptive in that it "interfer[ed] . . . with the schools' work [and] colli[ded] with the rights of other students to be secure and to be let alone." *See Tinker*, 393 U.S. at 508, 513.

Given the targeted, defamatory nature of Kowalski's speech, aimed at a fellow classmate, it created "actual or nascent" substantial disorder and disruption in the school. *See Tinker*, 393 U.S. at 508, 513; *Sypniewski v. Warren Hills Reg'l Bd. of Educ.*, 307 F.3d 243, 257 (3d Cir. 2002) (indicating that administrators may regulate student speech any time they have a "particular and concrete basis" for forecasting future substantial disruption) . . . . First, the creation of the "S.A.S.H." group forced Shay N. to miss school in order to avoid further abuse. Moreover, had the school not intervened, the potential for continuing and more serious harassment of Shay N. as well as other students was real. Experience suggests that unpunished misbehavior can have a snowballing effect, in some cases resulting in "copycat" efforts by other students or in retaliation for the initial harassment.

Other courts have similarly concluded that school administrators' authority to regulate student speech extends, in the appropriate circumstances, to speech that does not originate at the school itself, so long as the speech eventually makes its way to the school in a meaningful way. For example, in *Boucher v. School Board of School District of Greenfield*, 134 F.3d 821, 829 (7th Cir. 1998), the Seventh Circuit held that a student was not entitled to a preliminary injunction prohibiting his punishment when the student wrote articles for an independent newspaper that was distributed at school. And again in *Doninger*, the Second Circuit concluded, after a student applied for a preliminary injunction in a factual circumstance not unlike the one at hand, that a school could discipline a student for an out-of-school blog post that included vulgar language and misleading information about school administrators, as long as it was reasonably foreseeable that the post would reach the school and create a substantial disruption there. *See Doninger*, 527 F.3d at 48-49. The court explained, "a student may be disciplined for expressive conduct, even conduct occurring off school grounds, when this CONDUCT 'would foreseeably create a risk of substantial disruption within the school environment,' at least when it was similarly foreseeable that the off-campus expression might also reach campus." *Id.* at 48 (quoting *Wisniewski v. Bd. of Educ.*, 494 F.3d 34, 40 (2d Cir. 2007)). *Cf. J.S. ex rel. Snyder v. Blue Mountain Sch. Dist.*, 650 F.3d 915, 2011 U.S. App. LEXIS 11947 (3d Cir. 2011) (en banc) (divided court assuming without deciding that the *Tinker* substantial disruption test applies to online speech harassing a school administrator).

Thus, even though Kowalski was not physically at the school when she operated her computer to create the webpage and form the "S.A.S.H." MySpace group and to post comments there, other circuits have applied *Tinker* to such circumstances. To be sure, it was foreseeable in this case that Kowalski's conduct would reach the school via computers, smartphones, and other electronic devices, given that most of the "S.A.S.H." group's members and the target of the group's harassment were Musselman High School students. Indeed, the "S.A.S.H." webpage did make its way into the school and was accessed first by Musselman student Ray Parsons at 3:40 p.m., from a school computer during an after hours class. Furthermore, as we have noted, it created a reasonably foreseeable substantial disruption there.

At bottom, we conclude that the school was authorized to discipline Kowalski because her speech interfered with the work and discipline of the school. *See Tinker, Doninger.*

. . . .

V

Kowalski's role in the "S.A.S.H." webpage, which was used to ridicule and demean a fellow student, was particularly mean-spirited and hateful. The webpage called on classmates, in a pack, to target Shay N., knowing that it would be hurtful and damaging to her ability to sit with other students in class at Musselman High School and have a suitable learning experience. While each student in the "S.A.S.H." group might later attempt to minimize his or her role, at bottom, the conduct was indisputably harassing and bullying, in violation of Musselman High School's regulations prohibiting such conduct.

Kowalski asserts that the protections of free speech and due process somehow insulate her activities from school discipline because her activity was not sufficiently school-related to be subject to school discipline. Yet, every aspect of the webpage's design and implementation was school-related. Kowalski designed the website for "students," perhaps even against Shay N.; she sent it to students inviting them to join; and those who joined were mostly students, with Kowalski encouraging the commentary. The victim understood the attack as school-related, filing her complaint with school authorities. Ray Parsons, who provided the vulgar and lewd—indeed, defamatory—photographs understood that the object of the attack was Shay N., and he participated from a school computer during class, to the cheering of Kowalski and her fellow classmates, whom she invited to the affair.

Rather than respond constructively to the school's efforts to bring order and provide a lesson following the incident, Kowalski has rejected those efforts and sued school authorities for damages and other relief. Regretfully, she yet fails to see that such harassment and bullying is inappropriate and hurtful and that it must be taken seriously by school administrators in order to preserve an appropriate pedagogical environment. Indeed, school administrators *are* becoming increasingly alarmed by the phenomenon, and the events in this case are but one example of such bullying and school administrators' efforts to contain it. Suffice it to hold here that, where such speech has a sufficient nexus with the school, the Constitution is not written to hinder school administrators' good faith efforts to address the problem.

The judgment of the district court is

AFFIRMED.

Post Problem Discussion

1. On the same day it decided *J.S. v. Blue Mountain School District*, the Third Circuit Court of Appeals issued another en banc decision in *Layshock v. Hermitage School District*, 650 F.3d 205 (3d Cir. 2011) (en banc), *cert. denied* 132 S. Ct. 1097 (January 17, 2012). The Supreme Court denied *certiorari* on both cases. In *Layshock*, the Third Circuit found that the school violated a student's First Amendment rights by disciplining him for creating a fake internet profile of his school principal on a social networking website. The student created the website at his grandmother's house. The court stated:

> It would be an unseemly and dangerous precedent to allow the state, in the guise of school authorities, to reach into a child's home and control his/her actions there to the same extent that it can control that child when he/she participates in school sponsored activities. Allowing the District to punish Justin for conduct he engaged in while at his grandmother's house using his grandmother's computer would create just such a precedent, and we therefore conclude that the district court correctly ruled that the District's response to Justin's expressive conduct violated the First Amendment guarantee of free expression.

Id. at 216. The case was decided without dissent. The judges who dissented in *Blue Mountain* joined the majority or concurred in *Layshock*. Review the *Layshock* case online. Why did the judges who dissented in *Blue Mountain* join the majority in *Layshock?* Are the decisions consistent with one another?

2. The opinions in *Blue Mountain* represent some of the different views that have developed in this area. The majority in *Blue Mountain* finds that *Tinker* applies, and that *Fraser* does not apply, to off-campus speech even when that speech is vulgar or offensive. A number of other courts have agreed with that approach and applied *Tinker* to off-campus speech that could have otherwise been prohibited under *Fraser* if it had occurred on-campus, or at a school sponsored event. *See, e.g., C.R. v. Eugene Sch. Dist. 4J*, 835 F.3d 1142 (9th Cir. 2016), *cert. denied*, 137 S. Ct. 2117 (2017) (applying *Tinker* and upholding the discipline of a student who sexually harassed another student with vulgar and sexual language off-campus); *Doninger v. Niehoff*, 527 F.3d 41, 49 (2d Cir. 2008) (student calling school officials "douchebags," and encouraging others to contact one official "to piss her off more" contained the sort of language that could be prohibited under *Fraser*, but was instead subject to *Tinker*, since it occurred off-campus in a student blog post).

What are the implications of this analysis in terms of the school's ability to discipline students for off-campus expression? Could Michael (the student in our problem) be disciplined by the school under the *Tinker* standard? Under *Fraser*?

3. The concurring opinion in *Blue Mountain* advocates that *Tinker* should not apply to off-campus speech and that the "First Amendment protects students engaging in off-campus speech to the same extent it protects speech by citizens in the community at large." The concurring opinion notes *Thomas v. Bd. of Educ., Granville Cent. Sch. Dist.*, 607 F.2d 1043 (2d Cir. 1979) as an example of a court following this approach. What are the implications of this analysis in terms of the school's ability to discipline students for off-campus expression? Could the school discipline Michael in our problem under these standards?

4. The dissenting opinion in *Blue Mountain* agreed with the majority that *Tinker* should apply, but disagreed with the majority's application of that standard to the facts of the case. Part of the dissent's analysis noted the impact that the student's expression had on the teacher that was the target of the student's expression. How do you think the impact on the teacher should be factored into the *Tinker* analysis? Could Michael be disciplined under the dissent's application of *Tinker*?

5. On the same day the United States Supreme Court denied certiorari in *Blue Mountain* and *Layshock*, it also denied certiorari in *Kowalski*. In *Kowalski*, the Fourth Circuit applied *Tinker* and ruled that the school did not violate the student's First Amendment rights for disciplining the student. Why does it have a different outcome than *Blue Mountain*? Do you think *Kowalski* or *Blue Mountain* reach the correct result?

6. Note that the *Kowalski* decision imposes an additional threshold test before applying *Tinker*, in that it requires the speech to have a sufficient nexus to the school in order for *Tinker* to apply. This standard is in line with the nexus standard discussed for the discipline of off-campus conduct in Problem 5, Chapter 8. Some other courts have followed a similar approach. *See, e.g., D.J.M. v. Hannibal Public School District # 60*, 647 F.3d 754, 766 (8th Cir. 2011) (must be reasonably foreseeable that speech would reach school property); *S.J.W. v. Lee's Summit R-7 Sch. Dist.*, 696 F.3d 771, 777–78 (8th Cir. 2012) (location of speech less important than whether speech was directed at school, or would impact school environment); *Doninger v. Niehoff*, 527 F.3d 41, 48 (2d Cir. 2008); *Wisniewski v. Bd. of Educ. of the Weedsport Cent. Sch. Dist.*, 494 F.3d 34, 39 (2d Cir. 2007). Should courts require this additional threshold be met before applying *Tinker*? What standard should apply if the threshold is not met?

7. *S.J.W. v. Lee's Summit R-7 Sch. Dist.*, 696 F.3d 771, 774 (8th Cir. 2012), is an example of a court finding off-campus student website blog posts that "discuss, satirize, and vent" about school events, and other students, caused an actual disruption under *Tinker*. In that case, the entire student body found out about the posts on a particular day, numerous school computers were used to access or to attempt to access the blog that day, teachers experienced difficulty managing their classes because students were distracted and upset by the blog, local media arrived on campus that day to cover the event, and parents contacted the school with concerns. How does this compare to the facts of our problem with Michael?

§ 9.05 True Threats

In today's world of school shootings, school officials are generally apt to punish student speech that threatens any type of violent act at school, and courts generally uphold those decisions. *See, e.g., Fleming v. Jefferson County Sch. Dist. R-1*, 298 F.3d 918 (10th Cir. 2002); *Lavine v. Blaine Sch. Dist.*, 257 F.3d 981 (9th Cir. 2001). However, the analysis used by courts is not uniform. Some decisions apply *Tinker*, some apply *Morse*, and others look to see if the speech in question meets the "true threat" standard first established by the Supreme Court in *Watts v. United States*, 394 U.S. 705 (1969). Under the true threat analysis, if the court determines that the speech is a true threat, it is not protected speech. Even within those decisions using the true threat approach, the analysis is not consistent. Some courts focus on whether a reasonable person *in the speaker's* position would foresee that the recipient would view the remarks as a threat, while other courts focus on whether a reasonable person *in the recipient's* position would perceive the remarks as a threat.[3]

The following problem explores these issues.

Problem 4: Convincing the Supreme Court to Resolve True Threat Issues in Schools

Review the cases in the problem materials and answer the following:

1. What are the differences in the cases in terms of the standards they apply and the outcomes?
2. What standard would you propose that the Supreme Court adopt to address student speech with violent content? The *Tinker* standard? *Morse?* A true threat standard? Should it depend on the circumstances, the words used, and their context? Should it depend upon whether the speech occurred on or off campus?
3. If you advocate for the true threat standard, from which perspective should the speech be judged, the speaker or the recipient? Or should the Court adopt a multi-factor test?

Problem Materials

✓ *Ponce v. Socorro Indep. Sch. Dist.*, 508 F.3d 765 (5th Cir. 2007)

✓ *Lavine v. Blaine School District*, 257 F.3d 981 (9th Cir. 2001), *cert. denied*, 536 U.S. 959 (2002)

✓ *Doe v. Pulaski County Special School District*, 306 F.3d 616 (8th Cir. 2002) (en banc)

✓ *Bell v. Itawamba County. Sch. Bd.*, 799 F.3d 379 (5th Cir. 2015) (en banc), *cert. denied*, 136 S. Ct. 1166 (2016)

Ponce v. Socorro Independent School District

508 F.3d 765 (5th Cir. 2007)

The court relies on Morse and rules that student speech that school administrators determine to be a "terroristic threat" is not protected speech.

This appeal presents the question of whether student speech that threatens a Columbine-style attack on a school is protected by the First Amendment. Today we follow the lead of the United States Supreme Court in *Morse v. Frederick*, and hold

3. Sarah E. Redfield, *Threats Made, Threats Posed, School and Judicial Analysis In Need of Redirection*, 2003 B.Y.U. Educ. & L. J. 663 (2003).

that it is not because such speech poses a direct threat to the physical safety of the school population. . . .

While enrolled as a sophomore at Montwood High School, a minor student identified as E.P. kept an extended notebook diary, written in the first-person perspective, in which he detailed the "author's" creation of a pseudo-Nazi group on the Montwood High School Campus, and at other schools in the Socorro Independent School District ("SISD" or "School District"). The notebook describes several incidents involving the pseudo-Nazi group, including one in which the author ordered his group "to brutally injure two homosexuals and seven colored" people and another in which the author describes punishing another student by setting his house on fire and "brutally murder[ing]" his dog. The notebook also details the group's plan to commit a "[C]olumbine shooting" attack on Montwood High School or a coordinated "shooting at all the [district's] schools at the same time." At several points in the journal, the author expresses the feeling that his "anger has the best of [him]" and that "it will get to the point where [he] will no longer have control." The author predicts that this outburst will occur on the day that his close friends at the school graduate.

On August 15, 2005, E.P. told another student (the "informing student") about the notebook and supposedly showed him some of its contents. The informing student told a teacher about the notebook. After waiting a day, the teacher told Assistant Principal Jesus Aguirre ("Aguirre") about the notebook. Aguirre called the informing student into his office and questioned the student about the conversation with E.P. Aguirre then decided to call E.P. into his office for a meeting.

During the meeting, Aguirre told E.P. that students had complained to him that E.P. was writing threats in his diary. E.P. denied these accusations and instead explained that he was writing a work of fiction. Aguirre asked E.P. for permission to search his backpack and E.P. consented. Aguirre discovered the notebook and briefly reviewed its contents. E.P. continued to maintain that the notebook was a work of fiction.

Aguirre called E.P.'s mother to tell her about the notebook. She too maintained that the notebook was fiction, and explained that she also engaged in creative writing. Aguirre informed her that he would read the notebook in detail and "call her the next day with an administrative decision based on the safety and security of the student body." Aguirre then released E.P. back into the general student population to complete the school day. Aguirre took the notebook home and read it several times. He found several lines in the notebook alarming and ultimately determined that E.P.'s writing posed a "terroristic threat" to the safety and security of the students and the campus.

As a "terroristic threat," Aguirre determined that the writing violated the Student Code of Conduct. He therefore suspended E.P. from school three days and recommended that he be placed in the school's alternative education program at KEYS Academy. E.P.'s parents unsuccessfully appealed the decision to the Principal of the Montwood High School, the Assistant Superintendent of Instructional Services, and finally to the School Board's designated committee. To prevent E.P. from being transferred to KEYS Academy, E.P.'s parents placed him in private school, where he completed his sophomore year without incident.

. . . .

We are guided by the Supreme Court's recent decision in *Morse v. Frederick*. But before applying *Morse* to the case before us, some extended analysis of the case and particularly of Justice Alito's concurring, and controlling, opinion is necessary. That concurring opinion appears to have two primary purposes: providing specificity to the rule announced by the majority opinion, and, relatedly, ensuring that political speech will remain protected within the school setting. Taken together, the majority and concurring opinions in *Morse* explain well why the actions of the school administrators here satisfy the requirements of the First Amendment.

In *Morse*, a student at Juneau-Douglas High School unfurled a 14-foot banner bearing the phrase "BONG HiTS 4 JESUS" during a school-sanctioned and supervised event. The principal confiscated the banner and suspended Frederick. Frederick filed suit under 42 U.S.C. § 1983 against the principal and the School Board, claiming that the principal's actions violated his First Amendment rights. Applying the standard first set out in *Tinker v. Des Moines Independent Community School District*, the Ninth Circuit agreed, concluding that the school punished Frederick without demonstrating that his speech gave rise to a risk of substantial disruption.

The Supreme Court reversed, holding that Frederick's suspension violated no constitutional right. In reaching this conclusion, the Court expressly declined to apply the *Tinker* standard of "risk of substantial disturbance" to drug speech. The Court's refusal to apply *Tinker* rested on the relative magnitude of the interest it considered to be at stake, *viz.*, prevention of the "serious and palpable" danger that drug abuse presents to the health and well-being of students. Because the already significant harms of drug use are multiplied in a school environment, the Court found "that deterring drug use by schoolchildren is an 'important-indeed, perhaps compelling' interest," not arising from an "undifferentiated fear or apprehension of disturbance" or "a mere desire to avoid the discomfort and unpleasantness that always accompany an unpopular viewpoint," as was the case in *Tinker*. Accordingly, on the Court's reasoning, school administrators need not evaluate the potential for disruption caused by speech advocating drug use; it is *per se* unprotected because of the scope of the harm it potentially foments.

The Court's evaluation of the harm led to an evidently potent remedy. To the extent that preventing a harmful activity may be classified as an "important-indeed, perhaps compelling interest," speech advocating that activity may be prohibited by school administrators with little further inquiry. But the Court did not provide a detailed account of how the particular harms of a given activity add up to an interest sufficiently compelling to forego *Tinker* analysis. As a result of this ambiguity, speech advocating an activity entailing arguably marginal harms may be included within the circle of the majority's rule. Political speech in the school setting, the important constitutional value *Tinker* sought to protect, could thereby be compromised by overly-anxious administrators.

It is against this background of ambiguity that Justice Alito's concurring opinion opens. It begins by making two interpretive points about the majority opinion:

> (a) [the majority opinion] goes no further than to hold that a public school may restrict speech that a reasonable observer would interpret as advocating illegal drug use and (b) it provides no support for any restriction of speech that can plausibly be interpreted as commenting on any political or social issue, including speech on issues such as the wisdom of the war on drugs or of legalizing marijuana for medicinal use.

Morse, 127 S. Ct. at 2636 (Alito, J., concurring) (internal citation and quotation marks omitted). By making these points, the concurring opinion makes clear from the outset that the majority is focused on the particular harm to students of speech advocating drug use; the concurring opinion is not itself announcing a general rule defining the requirements for applying *Tinker* whenever the safety of the school population is threatened in some other context. On this reading, the majority opinion "does not hold that the special characteristics of the public schools *necessarily* justify any other speech restrictions." But importantly, Justice Alito's concurring opinion goes on to expound with further clarity why some harms are in fact so great in the school setting that requiring a school administrator to evaluate their disruptive potential is unnecessary. In doing so it provides the specificity necessary for determining the harms that are so serious as to merit the *Morse* analysis.

The central paragraph of Justice Alito's concurring opinion states:

> [A]ny argument for altering the usual free speech rules in the public schools cannot rest on a theory of delegation but must instead be based on some special characteristic of the school setting. *The special characteristic that is relevant in this case is the threat to the physical safety of students.* School attendance can expose students to threats to their physical safety that they would not otherwise face. Outside of school, parents can attempt to protect their children in many ways and may take steps to monitor and exercise control over the persons with whom their children associate. Similarly, students, when not in school, may be able to avoid threatening individuals and situations. During school hours, however, parents are not present to provide protection and guidance, and students' movements and their ability to choose the persons with whom they spend time are severely restricted. Students may be compelled on a daily basis to spend time at close quarters with other students who may do them harm. *Experience shows that schools can be places of special danger.*

Id. at 2638 (emphasis added). On Justice Alito's analysis, the heightened vulnerability of students arising from the lack of parental protection and the close proximity of students with one another make schools places of "special danger" to the physical safety of the student. And it is this particular threat that functions as the basis for restricting the First Amendment in schools: "school officials must have greater authority to intervene before speech leads to violence." The limits of that authority are often, but not always, adequately determined by *Tinker*, which "in most cases . . . permits school officials to step in before actual violence erupts." As such, *Tinker* will not always allow school officials to respond to threats of violence appropriately.

The concurring opinion therefore makes explicit that which remains latent in the majority opinion: speech advocating a harm that is demonstrably grave and that derives that gravity from the "special danger" to the physical safety of students arising from the school environment is unprotected. But, because this is a content-based regulation, the concurring opinion is at pains to point out that the reasoning of the court cannot be extended to other kinds of regulations of content, for permitting such content-based regulation is indeed at "the far reaches of what the First Amendment permits." Instead, *Tinker*'s focus on the result of speech rather than its content remains the prevailing norm. The protection of the First Amendment in public schools is thereby preserved.

The constitutional concerns of this case—focusing on content—fall precisely within the student speech area demarcated by Justice Alito in *Morse*. That area consists of speech pertaining to grave harms arising from the particular character of the school setting. The speech in question here is not about violence aimed at specific persons, but of violence bearing the stamp of a well-known pattern of recent historic activity: mass, systematic school-shootings in the style that has become painfully familiar in the United States. *LaVine v. Blaine Sch. Dist.*, 257 F.3d 981, 987 (9th Cir. 2001) ("[W]e live in a time when school violence is an unfortunate reality that educators must confront on an all too frequent basis."). Such shootings exhibit the character that the concurring opinion identifies as particular to schools. As the concurring opinion points out, school attendance results in the creation of an essentially captive group of persons protected only by the limited personnel of the school itself. *See Morse*, 127 S. Ct. at 2638. This environment makes it possible for a single armed student to cause massive harm to his or her fellow students with little restraint and perhaps even less forewarning. Indeed, the difficulty of identifying warning signs in the various instances of school shootings across the country is intrinsic to the harm itself. *Cf. LaVine*, 257 F.3d at 987 ("After Columbine, Thurston, Santee and other school shootings, questions have been asked how teachers or administrators could have missed telltale 'warning signs,' why something was not done earlier and what should be done to prevent such tragedies from happening again."). We therefore "find it untenable in the wake of Columbine and Jonesboro that any reasonable school official who came into possession of [E.P.'s diary] would not have taken some action based on its violent and disturbing content." *Doe v. Pulaski County Special Sch. Dist.*, 306 F.3d 616, 626 n. 4 (8th Cir. 2002). Our recent history demonstrates that threats of an attack on a school and its students *must* be taken seriously.

Lack of forewarning and the frequent setting within schools give mass shootings the unique indicia that the concurring opinion found compelling with respect to drug use. If school administrators are permitted to prohibit student speech that advocates illegal drug use because "illegal drug use presents a grave and in many ways unique threat to the physical safety of students," then it defies logical extrapolation to hold school administrators to a stricter standard with respect to speech that gravely and uniquely threatens violence, including massive deaths, to the school population as a whole.

Of course, we do not remotely suggest that "schools can[] expel students just because they are 'loners,' wear black and play video games." *LaVine*, 257 F.3d at 987. We do hold, however, that when a student threatens violence against a student body, his words are as much beyond the constitutional pale as yelling "fire" in crowded theater, *see Schenck v. United States*, 249 U.S. 47, 52, 39 S. Ct. 247, 63 L. Ed. 470 (1919), and such specific threatening speech to a school or its population is unprotected by the First Amendment. School administrators must be permitted to react quickly and decisively to address a threat of physical violence against their students, without worrying that they will have to face years of litigation second-guessing their judgment as to whether the threat posed a real risk of substantial disturbance.

IV.

Because we conclude that no constitutional violation has occurred, our inquiry ends here. Our role is to enforce constitutional rights, not "to set aside decisions of the school administrators which [we] may view as lacking a basis in wisdom or compassion." Because the journal's threatening language is not protected by the First Amendment, SISD's disciplinary action against E.P. violated no protected right and, accordingly, the Ponces have failed to show that they have a "substantial likelihood" of success on the merits.

Accordingly, the preliminary injunction is VACATED and the case is REMANDED to the district court for further proceedings not inconsistent with this holding.

VACATED AND REMANDED.

Lavine v. Blaine School District

257 F.3d 981 (9th Cir. 2001), *cert. denied*, 536 U.S. 959 (2002)

The court applies the Tinker standard and upholds the school district's decision to expel a student due to the violent content of a poem written at home by the student because of the "potential for substantial disruption."

This case has its genesis in a high school student's poem, which led to his temporary, emergency expulsion from school. It arises against a backdrop of tragic school shootings, occurring both before and after the events at issue here, and requires us to evaluate through a constitutional prism the actions school officials took to address what they perceived was the student's implied threat of violent harm to himself and others. Given the knowledge the shootings at Columbine, Thurston and

Santee high schools, among others, have imparted about the potential for school violence (as rare as these incidents may be when taken in context), we must take care when evaluating a student's First Amendment right of free expression against school officials' need to provide a safe school environment not to overreact in favor of either. Schools must be safe, but they are educational institutions after all, and speech—including creative writing and poetry—is an essential part of the educational fabric. Although this is a close case in retrospect, we conclude that when the school officials expelled James LaVine they acted with sufficient justification and within constitutional limits, not to punish James for the content of his poem, but to avert perceived potential harm.

In the fall of 1998, James LaVine was in eleventh grade and a student in Vivian Bleecker's sixth period English class at Blaine High School. One evening in June or July 1998, James wrote the first draft of a poem he entitled "Last Words." The final version reads:

> As each day passed,
> I watched,
> love sprout, from the most,
> unlikely places,
> wich reminds,
> me that,
> beauty is in the eye's,
> of the beholder.
> As I remember,
> I start to cry,
> for I,
> had leared,
> this to late,
> and now,
> I must spend,
> each day,
> alone,
> alone for supper,
> alone at night,
> alone at death.
> Death I feel,
> crawlling down,
> my neck at,
> every turn,
> and so,
> now I know,
> what I must do.
> I pulled my gun,
> from its case,

and began to load it.
I remember,
thinking at least I won't,
go alone,
as I,
jumpped in,
the car,
all I could think about,
was I would not,
go alone.
As I walked,
hrough the,
now empty halls,
I could feel,
my hart pounding.
As I approached,
the classroom door,
I drew my gun and,
threw open the door,
Bang, Bang, Bang-Bang.
When it all was over,
28 were,
dead,
and all I remember,
was not felling,
any remorce,
for I felt,
I was,
lensing my soul,
I quickly,
turned and ran,
as the bell rang,
all I could here,
were screams,
screams of friends,
screams of co workers,
and just plain,
screams of shear horor,
as the students,
found their,
slayen classmates,
2 years have passed,
and now I lay,
29 roses,

down upon,
these stairs,
as now,
I feel,
I may,
strike again.
No tears,
shall be shead,
in sarrow,
for I am,
alone,
and now,
I hope,
I can feel,
remorce,
for what I did,
without a shed,
of tears,
for no tear,
shall fall, from your face,
but from mine,
as I try,
to rest in peace,
Bang!

Around that time, several school shootings had occurred—including the tragedy at Thurston High School in nearby Springfield, Oregon—and were frequent topics in the news. The morning after James wrote the poem, he showed it to his mother. She warned James not to turn the poem in to his teachers at school, because "with everything that was on the news . . . whoever read it might overreact."

James forgot about the poem until he rediscovered it in his living room on September 30, 1998. He made some editorial changes and brought it to school on Friday, October 2. He showed the poem to several of his friends, some of whom liked it and some of whom did not. At that point, he decided to ask his English teacher, Ms. Bleecker, her opinion of "Last Words."

James had not been in school for the three days prior to October 2. At the end of his sixth period English class, he turned in several assignments and the poem. James asked Bleecker if she would read the poem and tell him what she thought. Bleecker thanked James for the poem and said she looked forward to reading it. The poem was not an assignment or an "extra credit" project, but James had turned in other poems to his previous English teachers at Blaine High School and appreciated their feedback.

That evening, Bleecker read "Last Words" and became concerned. Her impression of James up to that time was that he was a very quiet student. She thought the poem might be "James' way of letting somebody know that . . . maybe something's hurting him, maybe he's upset about something, maybe he's afraid." The next morning (Saturday), Bleecker contacted Karen Mulholland, James' school counselor, to discuss the contents of the poem. Mulholland was similarly concerned and set up a meeting that evening with Bleecker and Tim Haney, the school's vice principal.

During his time at Blaine High School, James had frequently confided in Mulholland, who is also a school psychologist. In 1996, James told her that he thought about suicide. Mulholland made James promise her that he would talk to her before he tried to kill himself. Thereafter, Mulholland kept an eye out for James and tried to make time to help him when he needed it. In fall 1998, James told her about several incidents that had occurred in his home. In particular, on September 12, James and his father had had an argument about James' car. James' father, Bruce, had thrown a rock in the direction of James and his car. James called the police, who filed charges against Bruce. As a result of the charges, a court issued a no-contact order that led to James moving out of his home temporarily to live with his sister. James had also missed school on September 17, 1998 to participate in the resulting legal proceedings. In addition, in the preceding weeks, James had broken up with his girlfriend. The school authorities had become aware of this because the ex-girlfriend's mother had called the school to report that James was stalking her daughter.

Mulholland disclosed these events to Haney and Bleecker. Haney also reviewed James' disciplinary file, which recorded several additional incidents, including a fight in February 1998 and an episode of insubordination with a teacher in March 1997. Moreover, Haney said that a few weeks before October 2, 1998, he had personally disciplined James for wearing to school a T-shirt emblazoned with the words "eat shit and die." Haney's impression of James at that time was that he was a "good kid, but . . . somewhat of a 'loner.'"

Given the content of the poem, and his knowledge of James' suicidal thoughts, family situation and past incidents, Haney decided at the Saturday meeting to call James' home to find out if James would be attending the school's home-coming dance that evening. Haney learned that James would not be attending the dance. Haney, nonetheless, decided to contact the Blaine Police Department for guidance about the situation. At the police department's suggestion, the school officials called Washington State's Child Protective Services, which then suggested they call the Community Mental Health Crisis Line. The Crisis Line in turn put them in touch with Dr. Charles Dewitt, the psychiatrist on duty for that evening. Dr. Dewitt suggested James be picked up by the police for evaluation.

The Whatcom Sheriff's Department, the law enforcement agency having jurisdiction over James' neighborhood, dispatched deputy sheriffs to the LaVines' family farm to conduct a welfare check of James. A deputy sheriff interviewed James to determine whether a medical evaluation was needed. James told the deputy that "he often writes poetry and has his teachers review them. He has never written this type of poem in the past and had no explanation why he wrote this one." James further told the officer he had no access to weapons and had no intention of carrying out any of the acts in the poem. James' mother assured the deputy that James had no access to weapons and was not a danger to himself or others. The deputy found no probable cause to commit James involuntarily, and James was unwilling to undergo a voluntary psychological examination. The deputy telephoned Dr. Dewitt and reported his observations. Based upon Dr. Dewitt's conversation with the deputy and with the school officials, Dr. Dewitt concluded, "[in] my professional opinion on a more probable than not basis based upon the information provided to me by the District and the law enforcement [officers] who had personally observed him, there were insufficient grounds for anyone to make a determination that James LaVine was in imminent danger of causing serious harm to himself and others." Dr. Dewitt accordingly decided not to commit James.

On Sunday, Haney met with Principal Dan Newell regarding James and informed him of James' background. By then, Newell had been informed that the sheriff and mental health professionals had decided not to commit James. That Sunday, based upon the information he had, Newell decided to "emergency expel" James under Washington Administrative Code § 180-40-295. Haney left a message with James' parents that day telling them to attend a meeting the next morning at the school. At 8:00 a.m. on Monday, Newell told James and his father that James was being emergency expelled from school. This expulsion was formally expressed in a letter of the same date.... That letter in relevant part states:

This letter is to inform you of the following violations of the Blaine High School Discipline Policy by your son James:

> On October 2, 1998 at 2:50 p.m., your son James presented a paper to his English teacher, which implied extreme violence to our student body.
>
> This violation of [sic] was of a nature significant enough to be classified as dangerous to your son and/or a threat to other students and/or a threat of serious disruption to the education process. Therefore I impose the sanction of emergency expulsion.

After James' father was informed of the emergency expulsion, he became hostile and began using foul language. James, too, became upset, used profanity and ran out of the office.

....

James and his father filed suit in federal court on July 6, 1999, claiming the Blaine School District, Tim Haney, Dan Newell and Karen Mulholland (collectively "the school" or "defendants") violated James' constitutional rights by expelling him and maintaining documentation in his school file.... As we noted at the outset, we live in a time when school violence is an unfortunate reality that educators must confront on an all too frequent basis. The recent spate of school shootings have put our nation on edge and have focused attention on what school officials, law enforcement and others can do or could have done to prevent these kinds of tragedies. After Columbine, Thurston, Santee and other school shootings, questions have been asked about how teachers or administrators could have missed telltale "warning signs," why something was not done earlier and what should be done to prevent such tragedies from happening again. Although schools are being asked to do more to prevent violence, the Constitution sets limits as to how far they can go. Just as the Constitution does not allow the police to imprison all suspicious characters, schools cannot expel students just because they are "loners," wear black and play video games. Schools must achieve a balance between protecting the safety and well-being of their students and respecting those same students' constitutional rights.

The LaVines, in this lawsuit, argue that the school failed to reach the proper balance when it expelled James....

To determine whether the school violated James' First Amendment rights, we must consider what those rights are. Public school students are protected by the First Amendment and do not "shed their constitutional rights to freedom of speech or expression at the schoolhouse gate." *Tinker.* The First Amendment rights of public school students, however, "'are not automatically coextensive with the rights of adults in other settings'" and must be "'applied in light of the special characteristics of the school environment.'" *Hazelwood.*

In the school context, we have granted educators substantial deference as to what speech is appropriate. "The daily administration of public education is committed to school officials. *Epperson.* That responsibility carries with it the inherent authority to prescribe and control conduct in the schools." States have a compelling interest in their educational system, and a balance must be met between the First Amendment rights of students and preservation of the educational process.... With that said, deference does not mean abdication; there are situations where school officials overstep their bounds and violate the Constitution. In deciding whether school officials have infringed a student's First Amendment rights, we must first determine what type of student speech is at issue. In *Chandler,* we "discerned three distinct areas of student speech," each of which is governed by different Supreme Court precedent:

(1) vulgar, lewd, obscene and plainly offensive speech is governed by *Fraser*;

(2) school-sponsored speech is governed by *Hazelwood*; and

(3) speech that falls into neither of these categories is governed by *Tinker.*

James' poem clearly falls within the third category. "Last Words" is not vulgar, lewd, obscene or plainly offensive. It was not a "speech or speech-related activity that 'students, parents, and members of the public might reasonably perceive to bear the imprimatur of the school.'" It was not an assignment, it was not published in a school publication and James showed it only to several students and his teacher, Ms. Bleecker.

To suppress speech falling within *Chandler*'s "all other speech" category, school officials must justify their decision by showing "facts which might reasonably have led school authorities to forecast substantial disruption of or material interference with school activities." *Tinker. Tinker* does not require school officials to wait until disruption actually occurs before they may act. "In fact, they have a duty to prevent the occurrence of disturbances." Forecasting disruption is unmistakably difficult to do. *Tinker* does not require certainty that disruption will occur, "but rather the existence of facts which might reasonably lead school officials to forecast substantial disruption."

In applying *Tinker*, we look to the totality of the relevant facts. We look not only to James' actions, but to all of the circumstances confronting the school officials that might reasonably portend disruption. When we look to all of the relevant facts here, we conclude that the school did not violate the First Amendment when it emergency expelled James.

The school had a duty to prevent any potential violence on campus to James or to other students. When the school officials made their decision not to allow James to attend class on Monday morning, they were aware of a substantial number of facts that in isolation would probably not have warranted their response, but in combination gave them a reasonable basis for their actions. The school was aware that James previously had suicidal ideations that he had shared with school officials. The officials were aware that James was involved in a domestic dispute where he was forced to move out of his family home. James told Mulholland that his filing charges against his father caused financial pressure on his family because of the legal costs associated with his father's defense, and that in turn his family placed pressure upon him to rescind his allegations. The school was also aware that in the past weeks James had broken up with his girlfriend and he was reportedly stalking her. Moreover, James had had several disciplinary problems in the past, at least one of which involved some violence. Further, in the three days prior to turning in the poem, James had been absent from school, a cause of concern.

Last, and maybe most importantly, there was the poem itself. "Last Words" is filled with imagery of violent death and suicide. At its extreme it can be interpreted as a portent of future violence, of the shooting of James' fellow students. Even in its most mild interpretation, the poem appears to be a "cry for help" from a troubled teenager contemplating suicide. Taken together and given the backdrop of actual school shootings, we hold that these circumstances were sufficient to have led school authorities reasonably to forecast substantial disruption of or material interference with school activities—specifically, that James was intending to inflict injury upon himself or others.

....

Given the potential for substantial disruption, we cannot fault the school's response.... Under § 180-40-295, if school officials have "good and sufficient reason to believe that the student's presence poses an immediate and continuing danger to the student, other students, or school personnel or an immediate and continuing threat of substantial disruption of the educational process," they can emergency expel the student until they deem it safe for the student to return. Here, after emergency expelling James, the school allowed him to return to classes as soon as he was evaluated by a psychiatrist who determined in his professional opinion that James was not a threat to himself or others. Considering all of the relevant facts and the totality of the circumstances, we hold that the school's emergency expulsion was reasonable and did not violate the First Amendment.

....

That said, even though we conclude that emergency expelling James did not violate the First Amendment, the same cannot be said for the school's placement and maintenance in James' file of what the district court characterized as "negative documentation." The school need not permanently blemish James' record and harm his ability to secure future employment. We recognize that the school may have had justification to document contemporaneously the reasons for its emergency expulsion, but the revised October 5, 1998 letter was written and maintained in James' file after the perceived threat had subsided, the school had allowed James to return to classes and had satisfied itself that James was not a threat to himself or others. As such, it created a permanent indictment of James without reference to the later, ameliorating events and thus went beyond the school's legitimate documentation needs. Accordingly, we affirm the district court's injunction prohibiting the placement or maintenance of any such negative documentation in James' file.

Doe v. Pulaski County Special School District

306 F.3d 616 (8th Cir. 2002) (en banc)

The court applies a true threat standard and finds that the school district did not violate the First Amendment by expelling a student for the content of a letter written by the student.

We granted en banc review to determine whether a school board ran afoul of a student's free speech rights when it expelled him for an offensive and vulgar letter that the student had prepared at home. The expelled student described in the letter how he would rape, sodomize, and murder a female classmate who had previously broken up with him. After a bench trial, the district court ordered the expelled student reinstated, concluding that the letter was not a "true threat" and that it therefore was protected speech under the First Amendment. A divided panel of our court affirmed the district court's decision. We vacated the panel decision, ordered en banc rehearing, and now hold that the school board did not violate the student's First Amendment rights when it expelled him.

J.M., a male, and K.G., a female, began "going together" during their seventh-grade year at Northwood Junior High School. As one would expect from typical junior high students, the two primarily saw each other at school and church, and their relationship was marked by multiple breakups during the school year. Sometime during the summer vacation after the end of the seventh-grade year, K.G. "broke up" with J.M. for the final time because she was interested in another boy.

Frustrated by the breakup and upset that K.G. would not go out with him again, J.M. drafted two violent, misogynic, and obscenity-laden rants expressing a desire to molest, rape, and murder K.G. According to J.M., he intended to write a rap song with lyrics similar in theme to the more vulgar and violent rap songs performed by controversial "rappers" such as Eminem, Juvenile, and Kid Rock, but found that his "song" fit no particular beat or rhythm. J.M. ultimately penned the documents as letters, signing them at their conclusion. J.M. prepared both letters at his home, where they remained until J.M.'s best friend, D.M., discovered one of them approximately a month before the youths were to begin their eighth-grade year at Northwood.

D.M. found the letter in J.M.'s bedroom while he was searching for something on top of a dresser. Before D.M. had a chance to read the letter, J.M. snatched it from his hand. D.M. asked to read the letter, and J.M. handed it back to him and gave D.M. permission to read the letter. D.M. asked for a copy of the letter, but J.M. refused to give him one.

K.G. also learned about the existence and contents of the letter, but it was not made clear during the trial when or how she learned about it. K.G. testified that she first learned about *a* letter during a telephone conversation with J.M. She claimed that J.M. told her that another boy had written a letter that stated she would be killed. J.M. claimed instead that K.G. learned about the letter from D.M. Either way, the testimony clearly established that J.M. voluntarily discussed the letter with K.G. during two or three telephone conversations and that J.M. admitted to K.G. in their final telephone conversation that he, not another boy, had written the letter.

Concerned about the letter, K.G. enlisted D.M.'s help in obtaining it from J.M. About a week before the start of school, D.M. spent the night at J.M.'s house and took the letter from J.M.'s room on the following morning. D.M. did so without J.M.'s knowledge or permission. D.M. delivered the letter to K.G. on the second day back from summer vacation, and K.G. read it in gym class in the presence of some other students. One of those students went immediately to the school resource officer, Officer James Kesterson, and reported that threats had been made against K.G. Officer Kesterson accompanied the student back to the gym where he found K.G. frightened and crying. K.G. told Officer Kesterson that J.M. had threatened her and explained how she obtained the letter. Officer Kesterson conducted an investigation and informed school administrators about the situation.

Bob Allison, the principal, conducted his own investigation and learned that D.M. had taken the letter from J.M. and delivered it to K.G. at school. After the investigation, Principal Allison recommended that J.M. be expelled from Northwood for the remainder of his eighth-grade year. Allison based his recommendation on Rule 36 of the district's Handbook for Student Conduct and Discipline, which prohibits students from making terrorizing threats against others. The rule requires that a violator be recommended for expulsion.

J.M. and his parents appealed the principal's recommendation .... The school board voted at the conclusion of the hearing to expel J.M. from both Northwood and the alternative school for the remainder of his eighth-grade year, essentially adopting Principal Allison's initial recommendation.

. . . .

As a general matter, the First Amendment prohibits governmental actors from directing what persons may see, read, speak, or hear. Free speech protections do not extend, however, to certain categories or modes of expression, such as obscenity, defamation, and fighting words. The government is permitted to regulate speech that falls within these categories because the speech is "'of such slight social value as a step to truth that any benefit that may be derived from them is clearly outweighed by the social interest in order and morality.'" Of course the rule remains that the government's proscription of speech within these categories may not, in general, be based on the content of the speech or the speaker's viewpoint.

In *Watts v. United States*, 394 U.S. 705 (1969), the Supreme Court recognized that threats of violence also fall within the realm of speech that the government can proscribe without offending the First Amendment. Although there may be some political or social value associated with threatening words in some circumstances, the government has an overriding interest in "protecting individuals from the fear of violence, from the disruption that fear engenders, and from the possibility that the threatened violence will occur." Our task, therefore, is to determine "[w]hat is a threat . . . from what is constitutionally protected speech." *Watts*, 394 U.S. at 707. The Court in *Watts*, however, set forth no particular definition or description of a true threat that distinguishes an unprotected threat from protected speech. Thus, the lower courts have been left to ascertain for themselves when a statement triggers the government's interest in preventing the disruption and fear of violence associated with a threat.

The federal courts of appeals that have announced a test to parse true threats from protected speech essentially fall into two camps. *See United States v. Fulmer*, 108 F.3d 1486, 1490–91 (1st Cir. 1997) (describing the differing circuit approaches to ascertaining a true threat). All the courts to have reached the issue have consistently adopted an objective test that focuses on whether a reasonable person would interpret the purported threat as a serious expression of an intent to cause a present or future harm. *See id.* The views among the courts diverge, however, in determining from whose viewpoint the statement should be interpreted. Some ask whether a reasonable person standing in the shoes of the speaker would foresee that the recipient would perceive the statement as a threat, whereas others ask how a reasonable person standing in the recipient's shoes would view the alleged threat.

Our court is in the camp that views the nature of the alleged threat from the viewpoint of a reasonable recipient. In *United States v. Dinwiddie*, we emphasized the fact intensive nature of the true threat inquiry and held that a court must view the relevant facts to determine "whether the recipient of the alleged threat could reasonably conclude that it expresses 'a determination or intent to injure presently or in the future.'" We also set forth in *Dinwiddie* a nonexhaustive list of factors relevant to how a reasonable recipient would view the purported threat. Those factors include: 1) the reaction of those who heard the alleged threat; 2) whether the threat was conditional; 3) whether the person who made the alleged threat communicated it directly to the object of the threat; 4) whether the speaker had a history of making threats against the person purportedly threatened; and 5) whether the recipient had a reason to believe that the speaker had a propensity to engage in violence.

In affirming the district court's conclusion that the letter constituted protected speech, our vacated panel opinion discussed *Dinwiddie*'s factors but ultimately relied on the Ninth Circuit's definition of a true threat in *Lovell v. Poway Unified Sch. Dist.*, 90 F.3d 367 (9th Cir. 1996). In *Lovell*, the Ninth Circuit explained that its test is "'whether a reasonable person would foresee that the statement would be interpreted by those to whom the maker communicates the statement as a serious expression of intent to harm or assault.'" Our panel reasoned that the Ninth Circuit, in focusing on whether a reasonable speaker would know of the threatening nature of his or her statement, provided the most concise standard to separate a true threat from protected speech.

The panel's implicit rejection of the *Dinwiddie* true threat inquiry has some support. The First Circuit rejected the reasonable recipient approach, reasoning that it creates the peril that a speaker's constitutional rights could turn on a recipient's unique sensitivity or characteristic that is, or may be, unknown to the speaker. The notion underlying the First Circuit's decision is that the reasonable recipient test is less conducive to the robust and wide-open public debate envisioned by the First Amendment because a speaker may find it necessary to tone down his or her speech in fear of triggering a recipient's unknown sensitivity.

While a panel is normally bound to follow our circuit's prior panel decisions, we, as an en banc court, are free to overrule a prior decision or alter the law of our circuit when we determine such a course is necessary. Given our panel's reliance on the reasonable speaker approach, and the First Circuit's criticism of the reasonable recipient approach, we find it appropriate to address whether we should adhere to the true threat inquiry we previously adopted in *Dinwiddie*. The debate over the approaches appears to us to be largely academic because in the vast majority of cases the outcome will be the same under both tests. The result will differ *only* in the extremely rare case when a recipient suffers from some unique sensitivity *and* that sensitivity is unknown to the speaker. Absent such a situation, a reasonably foreseeable response from the recipient and an actual reasonable response must, theoretically, be one and the same. We have come across no case where such a situation has ever been presented. Moreover, we find no overarching problem with our *Dinwiddie* approach because the recipient's reaction still must be a reasonable one even if he or she suffers some unique sensitivity, thus alleviating much of the First Circuit's concern. Finally, because neither party contends that one test or the other determines the outcome in this case, it is an inappropriate vehicle to use to alter our approach to ascertaining true threats. Accordingly, we adhere to *Dinwiddie*'s inquiry and hold that a true threat is a statement that a reasonable recipient would have interpreted as a serious expression of an intent to harm or cause injury to another.

Before we address whether a reasonable recipient would view the letter as a threat, we are faced with a threshold question of whether J.M. intended to communicate the purported threat. The district court's conclusion that the letter was protected speech turned on its finding that J.M. never intended to deliver the letter to K.G.; in other words, that J.M. never intended to communicate the purported threat to K.G. In determining whether a statement amounts to an unprotected threat, there is no requirement that the speaker intended to carry out the threat, nor is there any requirement that the speaker was capable of carrying out the purported threat of violence. However, the speaker must have intentionally or knowingly communicated the statement in question to someone before he or she may be punished or disciplined for it. *Id.* The requirement is satisfied if the speaker communicates the statement to the object of the purported threat *or* to a third party.

Requiring less than an intent to communicate the purported threat would run afoul of the notion that an individual's most protected right is to be free from governmental interference in the sanctity of his home and in the sanctity of his own personal thoughts. In *Stanley*, the Supreme Court recognized that the First Amendment means, at a minimum, that the government has no business telling an individual what he may read or view in the privacy of his own home. The government similarly has no valid interest in the contents of a writing that a person, such as J.M., might prepare in the confines of his own bedroom. After all, "[o]ur whole constitutional heritage rebels at the thought of giving government the power to control" the moral contents of our minds. *Id.* It is only when a threatening idea or thought is communicated that the government's interest in alleviating the fear of violence and disruption associated with a threat engages.

We conclude here that J.M. intended to communicate the letter and is therefore accountable if a reasonable recipient would have viewed the letter as a threat. Although J.M. snatched the letter out of D.M.'s hands when D.M. first found it, J.M. handed the letter back to D.M. and *permitted* D.M. to read it. J.M.'s decision to let D.M. read the letter is even more problematic for J.M. given his testimony that he knew there was a good possibility that D.M. would tell K.G. about the letter because D.M. and K.G. were friends. J.M. also discussed the letter in more than one phone conversation with K.G., and J.M. admitted to K.G. that he wrote the letter and that it talked of killing her. J.M. made similar admissions to K.G.'s best friend who would be likely to convey the information to K.G. One can hardly say, based on J.M.'s willingness to let D.M. read the letter and his overt discussion of the letter and its contents with K.G. and K.G.'s best friend that J.M. intended to keep the letter, and the message it contained, within his own lockbox of personal privacy.

We turn next to the question of whether a reasonable recipient would have perceived the letter as a threat. There is no question that the contents of the letter itself expressed an intent to harm K.G., and we disagree entirely, but respectfully, with the district court's assessment that the words contained in it were only "arguably" threatening. The letter exhibited J.M.'s pronounced, contemptuous and depraved hate for K.G. J.M. referred to or described K.G. as a "bitch," "slut," "ass," and a "whore" over 80 times in only four pages. He used the f-word no fewer than ninety times and spoke frequently in the letter of his wish to sodomize, rape, and kill K.G. The most disturbing aspect of the letter, however, is J.M.'s warning in two passages, expressed in unconditional terms, that K.G. should not go to sleep because he would be lying under her bed waiting to kill her with a knife. Most, if not all, normal thirteen-year-old girls (and probably most reasonable adults) would be frightened by the message and tone of J.M.'s letter and would fear for their physical well-being if they received the same letter.

The fact that J.M. did not personally deliver the letter to K.G. did not dispel its threatening nature. Although J.M. did not personally hand the letter to K.G., J.M. titled the letter "F____ that bitch [K.G.]," and he wrote the letter as though he was speaking directly to her. As a consequence, the letter was extremely intimate and personal, and the violence described in it was directed unequivocally at K.G.

There is also no indication that J.M. ever attempted to alleviate K.G.'s concerns about the letter during the period between when he told her about the letter and when she received it at school. Prior to K.G. obtaining the letter, J.M. had discussed its contents with her in phone conversations, and he testified at trial that he knew K.G. might have taken the threat as being truthful. It readily appears that J.M. wanted K.G. to be scared as retribution for her treatment of him. In fact, K.G.'s best friend testified at trial that J.M. told her, before D.M. obtained the letter and delivered it, that J.M. wanted to hide under K.G.'s bed and kill her. J.M. told this to K.G.'s best friend knowing the friend would likely pass the message along to K.G. (Trial Tr. at 239–41). J.M. also shared the letter with D.M. suspecting that D.M. would pass the information it contained to K.G. J.M. ultimately apologized to K.G., but his apology came only after he was expelled by the school board and during the pendency of the district court proceeding. The crescendoing events that presaged K.G.'s receipt of the actual letter would not have given a reasonable person in K.G.'s shoes much solace that J.M. did not want or intend to harm her.

Based on the tone of the letter, and the situation surrounding its communication, we are not surprised that those who read it interpreted it as a threat. *Watts*, 394 U.S. at 708, 89 S. Ct. 1399 (recognizing the reaction of the listener is relevant to whether the speech is protected). D.M. was concerned enough by the letter that he purloined it from his friend's home because he "felt that something should be done about it." A girl present when K.G. first read the letter immediately went to Officer Kesterson because she thought someone needed to know about the letter and the threats contained therein. School officials conducted an investigation and ultimately instituted expulsion proceedings because they believed the letter amounted to a "terrorizing threat." As for K.G., she broke down crying and was scared to leave the gym after she read the letter. She also slept with the lights on for the first couple of nights after the incident. The junior high principal who observed K.G. shortly after K.G. received the letter described K.G. as being extremely frightened. He explained that K.G. remained frightened enough of J.M. that she went home early when J.M. returned to school after the district court temporarily reinstated him.

J.M.'s previous portrayal of himself as a tough guy with a propensity for aggression made his threat more credible and contributed to K.G.'s reaction. Before the breakup, J.M. had told K.G., as well as K.G.'s best friend and D.M., that he was a member of the "Bloods" gang. K.G. also testified at trial that J.M. once shot a cat while she was speaking to him on the phone and that J.M.'s penchant for violence towards animals heightened her concern over the letter. . . .

Viewing the entire factual circumstances surrounding the letter, we conclude that a reasonable recipient would have perceived J.M.'s letter as a serious expression of an intent to harm K.G. As such, the letter amounted to a true threat, and the school's administrators and the school board did not violate J.M.'s First Amendment rights by initiating disciplinary action based on the letter's threatening content. The district court's contrary conclusion was erroneous. Had we been sitting as the school board, we might very well have approached the situation differently, for it appears to us that the board's action taken against J.M. was unnecessarily harsh. Other options have occurred to us that could have furthered the district's interest in protecting its students, as well as have punished J.M., but also have aided him in understanding the severity and inappropriateness of his conduct. However, "[i]t is not the role of the federal courts to set aside decisions of school administrators which the court may view as lacking a basis in wisdom or compassion." Those judgments are best left to the voters who elect the school board.

We reverse the judgment of the district court and remand the case to the district court with instructions to dissolve the injunctive relief afforded J.M. and to dismiss J.M.'s First Amendment claim against the school district.

Bell v. Itawamba School Board

799 F.3d 379 (5th Cir. 2015) (en banc), *cert. denied*, 136 S. Ct. 1166 (2016)

The court rules that the school may discipline a student under Tinker for a rap song which was recorded outside of school and posted on the student's personal Facebook page and YouTube.

Rhesa Hawkins Barksdale, Circuit Judge:

Away from school or a school function and without using school resources (off-campus speech), Taylor Bell, a student at Itawamba Agricultural High School in Itawamba County, Mississippi, posted a rap recording containing threatening language against two high school teachers/coaches on the Internet (first on his publicly accessible Facebook profile page and then on YouTube), intending it to reach the school community. In the recording, Bell names the two teachers and describes violent acts to be carried out against them. Interpreting the language as threatening, harassing, and intimidating the teachers, the Itawamba County School Board took disciplinary action against Bell.

Bell claims being disciplined violated his First Amendment right to free speech. On cross-motions for summary judgment, the district court ruled, inter alia: the school board, as well as the school-district superintendent, Teresa McNeece, and the school principal, Trae Wiygul, acting in their official capacities (the school board), acted reasonably as a matter of law.

Primarily at issue is whether, consistent with the requirements of the First Amendment, off-campus speech directed intentionally at the school community and reasonably understood by school officials to be threatening, harassing, and intimidating to a teacher satisfies the almost 50–year–old standard for restricting student speech, based on a reasonable forecast of a substantial disruption. See *Tinker v. Des Moines Indep. Cmty. Sch. Dist.*, 393 U.S. 503, 514 (1969) (infringing otherwise-protected school speech requires "facts which might reasonably have led school authorities to forecast substantial disruption of or material interference with school activities"). Because that standard is satisfied in this instance, the summary judgment is AFFIRMED.

I.

On Wednesday, 5 January 2011, Bell, a high-school senior, posted a rap recording on his public Facebook profile page (and later on YouTube), using what appears to be a representation of a Native American as the rap recording's cover image. (His high-school mascot is a Native American.) The recording, in part, alleges misconduct against female students by Coaches W. and R. Although there are three different versions of the transcribed rap recording in the summary-judgment record, the school board stipulated, at the preliminary-injunction hearing for this action, to the accuracy of the following version provided by Bell, who refers to himself in the recording as "T–Bizzle." (Accordingly, except for deleting part of both coaches' names, the numerous spelling and grammatical errors in the following version are not noted.)

> Let me tell you a little story about these Itawamba coaches / dirty ass niggas like some fucking coacha roaches / started fucking with the white and know they fucking with the blacks / that pussy ass nigga W[.] got me turned up the fucking max /
>
> Fucking with the students and he just had a baby / ever since I met that cracker I knew that he was crazy / always talking shit cause he know I'm from daw-city / the reason he fucking around cause his wife ain't got no tidies /
>
> This niggha telling students that they sexy, betta watch your back / I'm a serve this nigga, like I serve the junkies with some crack / Quit the damn basketball team / the coach a pervert / can't stand the truth so to you these lyrics going to hurt
>
> What the hell was they thinking when they hired Mr. R[.] / dreadlock Bobby Hill the second / He the same see / Talking about you could have went pro to the NFL / Now you just another pervert coach, fat as hell / Talking about you

> gangsta / drive your mama's PT Cruiser / Run up on T–Bizzle / I'm going to hit you with my rueger
>
> Think you got some game / cuz you fucking with some juveniles / you know this shit the truth so don't you try to hide it now / Rubbing on the black girls ears in the gym / white hoes, change your voice when you talk to them / I'm a dope runner, spot a junkie a mile away / came to football practice high / remember that day / I do / to me you a fool / 30 years old fucking with students at the school
>
> Hahahah / You's a lame / and it's a dam shame / instead you was lame / eat shit, the whole school got a ring mutherfucker
>
> Heard you textin number 25 / you want to get it on / white dude, guess you got a thing for them yellow bones / looking down girls shirts / drool running down your mouth / you fucking with the wrong one / going to get a pistol down your mouth / Boww
>
> OMG / Took some girls in the locker room in PE / Cut off the lights / you motherfucking freak / Fucking with the youngins / because your pimpin game weak / How he get the head coach / I don't really fucking know / But I still got a lot of love for my nigga Joe / And my nigga Makaveli / and my nigga codie / W[.] talk shit bitch don't even know me
>
> Middle fingers up if you hate that nigga / Middle fingers up if you can't stand that nigga / middle fingers up if you want to cap that nigga / middle fingers up / he get no mercy nigga

At the very least, this incredibly profane and vulgar rap recording had at least four instances of threatening, harassing, and intimidating language against the two coaches:

1. "betta watch your back / I'm a serve this nigga, like I serve the junkies with some crack";
2. "Run up on T–Bizzle / I'm going to hit you with my rueger";
3. "you fucking with the wrong one / going to get a pistol down your mouth / Boww"; and
4. "middle fingers up if you want to cap that nigga / middle fingers up / he get no mercy nigga".

Bell's use of "rueger" [sic] references a firearm manufactured by Sturm, Ruger & Co.; to "cap" someone is slang for "shoot".

A screenshot of Bell's Facebook profile page, taken approximately 16 hours after he posted the rap recording, shows his profile, including the rap recording, was open to, and viewable by, the public. In other words, anyone could listen to it.

On Thursday, 6 January, the day after the recording was posted, Coach W. received a text message from his wife, informing him about the recording; she had learned about it from a friend. After asking a student about the recording, the coach listened to it at school on the student's smartphone (providing access to the Internet). The coach immediately reported the rap recording to the school's principal, Wiygul, who informed the school-district superintendent, McNeece. The next day, Friday, 7 January, Wiygul, McNeece, and the school-board attorney, Floyd, questioned Bell about the rap recording, including the veracity of the allegations, the extent of the alleged misconduct, and the identity of the students involved. Bell was then sent home for the remainder of the day . . . .

[*Bell was subsequently suspended from school on the grounds that the rap threatened, harassed, and intimidated school employees. Bell filed an action in federal court challenging the decision under the First Amendment, among other claims. The federal district court granted summary judgment for the school.*]

. . . .

In challenging the summary judgment, Bell claims the school board violated his First Amendment free-speech rights by temporarily suspending him and placing him in an alternative school for the six weeks remaining in the grading period. In support, he contends: *Tinker* does not apply to off-campus speech, such as his rap recording; and, even if it does, *Tinker*'s "substantial disruption" test is not satisfied. For the reasons that follow, we hold: *Tinker* applies to the off-campus speech at issue; there is no genuine dispute of material fact precluding ruling, as a matter of law, that a school official reasonably could find Bell's rap recording threatened, harassed, and intimidated the two teachers; and a substantial disruption reasonably could have been forecast, as a matter of law.

1.

As our court explained in *Morgan v. Swanson,* student-speech claims are evaluated "in light of the special characteristics of the school environment, beginning by categorizing the student speech at issue". 659 F.3d at 375 (footnotes and internal quotation marks omitted). We must thus decide whether Bell's speech falls under *Tinker,* or one of the Court's above-described exceptions. *See, e.g., Saxe v. State Coll. Area Sch. Dist.*, 240 F.3d 200, 214 (3d Cir.2001) (employing a similar approach, noting "[s]peech falling outside of . . . categories [such as those in *Fraser* and *Hazelwood*] is subject to *Tinker*'s general rule").

The parties do not assert, and the record does not show, that the school board disciplined Bell based on the lewdness of his speech or its potential perceived sponsorship by the school; therefore, *Fraser* and *Hazelwood* are not directly on point. Bell's speech likewise does not advocate illegal drug use or portend a Columbine-like mass, systematic school-shooting. And, as Justice Alito noted, when the type of violence threatened does not implicate "the special features of the school environment", *Tinker*'s "substantial disruption" standard is the appropriate vehicle for analyzing such claims. *Morse*, 551 U.S. at 425, (citing *Tinker,* 393 U.S. at 508–09, 89 S.Ct. 733) ("[I]n most cases, *Tinker*'s 'substantial disruption' standard permits school officials to step in before actual violence erupts".). Although threats against, and harassment and intimidation of, teachers certainly pose a "grave . . . threat to the physical safety" of members of the school community, *id.*, violence forecast by a student against a teacher does not reach the level of the above-described exceptions necessitating divergence from *Tinker*'s general rule. We therefore analyze Bell's speech under *Tinker. See Ponce*, 508 F.3d at 771–72 & n. 2 ("[B]ecause [threats of violence against individual teachers] are relatively discrete in scope and directed at adults, [they] do not amount to the heightened level of harm that was the focus of both the majority opinion and Justice Alito's concurring opinion in *Morse*".); *see also Wisniewski v. Bd. of Educ. of Weedsport Cent. Sch. Dist.*, 494 F.3d 34, 38 (2d Cir.2007) (analyzing threats of violence to individual teachers under *Tinker*); *Boim v. Fulton Cnty. Sch. Dist.*, 494 F.3d 978, 982–83 (11th Cir.2007) (same).

2.

In claiming *Tinker* does not apply to off-campus speech, Bell asserts: *Tinker* limits its holding to speech inside the "schoolhouse gate"; and each of the Court's subsequent decisions reinforces this understanding.

"Experience shows that schools can be places of special danger." *Morse*, 551 U.S. at 424 (Alito, J., concurring). Over 45 years ago, when *Tinker* was decided, the Internet, cellphones, smartphones, and digital social media did not exist. The advent of these technologies and their sweeping adoption by students present new and evolving challenges for school administrators, confounding previously delineated boundaries of permissible regulations. *See, e.g., Wynar v. Douglas Cnty. Sch. Dist.*, 728 F.3d 1062, 1064 (9th Cir.2013) ("With the advent of the Internet and in the wake of school shootings at Columbine, Santee, Newtown and many others, school administrators face the daunting task of evaluating potential threats of violence and keeping their students safe without impinging on their constitutional rights."). Students now have the ability to disseminate instantaneously and communicate widely from any location via the Internet. These communications, which may reference events occurring, or to occur, at school, or be about members of the school community, can likewise be accessed anywhere, by anyone, at any time. Although, under other circumstances, such communications might be protected speech under the First Amendment, off-campus threats, harassment, and intimidation directed at teachers create a tension between a student's free-speech rights and a school official's duty to maintain discipline and protect the school community. These competing concerns, and differing standards applied to off-campus speech across circuits, as discussed infra, have drawn into question the scope of school officials' authority.

Greatly affecting this landscape is the recent rise in incidents of violence against school communities. See *LaVine v. Blaine Sch. Dist.*, 257 F.3d 981, 987 (9th Cir.2001) ("[W]e live in a time when school violence is an unfortunate reality that educators must confront on an all too frequent basis".). School administrators must be vigilant and take seriously any statements by students resembling threats of violence, *Ponce*, 508 F.3d at 771, as well as harassment and intimidation posted online and made away from campus. This now-tragically common violence increases the importance of clarifying the school's authority to react to potential threats before violence erupts. *See Morse,* 551 U.S. at 408 (pressing that dangerous speech, such as speech advocating drug use, is substantially different from the political speech at issue in *Tinker*, because it presents a "far more serious and palpable" danger than an "undifferentiated fear or apprehension of disturbance" or "a mere desire to avoid the discomfort and unpleasantness that always accompany an unpopular viewpoint" (citation and internal quotation marks omitted)); *see also Ponce,* 508 F.3d at 772 ("School administrators must be permitted to react quickly and decisively to address a threat of physical violence . . . without worrying that they will have to face years of litigation second-guessing their judgment as to whether the threat posed a real risk of substantial disturbance.").

In the light of these competing interests and increasing concerns regarding school violence, it is necessary to establish the extent to which off-campus student speech may be restricted without offending the First Amendment. Our holding concerns the paramount need for school officials to be able to react quickly and efficiently to protect students and faculty from threats, intimidation, and harassment intentionally directed at the school community. *See, e.g., Morse*, 551 U.S. at 425, 127 S.Ct. 2618 (Alito, J., concurring) ("[D]ue to the special features of the school environment, school officials must have greater authority to intervene before speech leads to violence."); *Lowery v. Euverard*, 497 F.3d 584, 596 (6th Cir.2007) ("School officials have an affirmative duty to not only ameliorate the harmful effects of disruptions, but to prevent them from happening in the first place.").

a.

Despite Bell's recognizing the wealth of precedent across numerous circuits contrary to his position, he asserts: *Tinker* does not apply to speech which originated, and was disseminated, off-campus, without the use of school resources. Bell's position is untenable; it fails to account for evolving technological developments, and conflicts not only with our circuit's precedent, but with that of every other circuit to have decided this issue.

Since *Tinker* was decided in 1969, courts have been required to define its scope. As discussed below, of the six circuits to have addressed whether *Tinker* applies to off-campus speech, five, including our own, have held it does. (For the other of the six circuits (the third circuit), there is an intra-circuit split. See *Layshock v. Hermitage Sch. Dist.*, 650 F.3d 205, 219–20 (3d Cir.2011) (en banc) (Jordan, J., concurring) (discussing that *Tinker*'s applicability to off-campus speech remains unresolved in the third circuit); *see also J.S. v. Blue Mountain Sch. Dist.*, 650 F.3d 915, 931 & n. 8 (3d Cir.2011) (en banc) (divided court assuming, without deciding, that the *Tinker* substantial-disruption test applies to online speech harassing a school administrator).) The remainder of the circuits (first, sixth, seventh, tenth, eleventh, D.C.) do not appear to have addressed this issue.

Although the Supreme Court has not expressly ruled on this issue, our court, 43 years ago, applied *Tinker* to analyze whether a school board's actions were constitutional in disciplining students based on their off-campus speech. *E.g., Shanley* [*v. Northeast Independent School Dist.*], 462 F.2d at 970 [(5th Cir. 1972)] ("When the

Burnside/Tinker standards are applied to this case . . .".); *see also Sullivan v. Hous. Indep. Sch. Dist.*, 475 F.2d 1071, 1072 (5th Cir.1973) ("This case arises from the unauthorized distribution of an underground newspaper *near a high school campus*, and presents the now-familiar clash between claims of First Amendment protection on the one hand and the interests of school boards in maintaining an atmosphere in the public schools conducive to learning, on the other." (emphasis added)); *Wisniewski*, 494 F.3d at 39 (interpreting *Sullivan* as applying *Tinker* to off-campus speech); *Porter v. Ascension Parish Sch. Bd.*, 393 F.3d 608, 615 n. 22, 619 n. 40 (5th Cir.2004) (same).

In *Shanley*, students distributed newspapers containing articles they authored "during out-of-school hours, and without using any materials or facilities owned or operated by the school system", "near but outside the school premises on the sidewalk of an adjoining street, separated from the school by a parking lot." 462 F.2d at 964. In concluding the students' speech was protected, our court ruled: "[T]he activity punished here does not even approach the 'material and substantial' disruption . . . either in fact or in reasonable forecast [and] [a]s a factual matter . . . there were no disturbances of any sort, on or off campus, related to the distribution of the [newspaper]". *Id.* at 970.

Further, as noted supra, four other circuits have held that, under certain circumstances, *Tinker* applies to speech which originated, and was disseminated, off-campus. Therefore, based on our court's precedent and guided by that of our sister circuits, *Tinker* applies to off-campus speech in certain situations.

b.

Therefore, the next question is under what circumstances may off-campus speech be restricted. Our court's precedent is less developed in this regard. For the reasons that follow, and in the light of the summary-judgment record, we need not adopt a specific rule: rather, Bell's admittedly intentionally directing at the school community his rap recording containing threats to, and harassment and intimidation of, two teachers permits *Tinker*'s application in this instance.

i.

In 1972 in *Shanley*, our court expressly declined to adopt a rule holding a school's attempt to regulate off-campus speech under *Tinker* was per se unconstitutional. 462 F.2d at 974. Our court explained: "[E]ach situation involving expression and discipline will create its own problems of reasonableness, and for that reason we do not endeavor here to erect any immovable rules, but only to sketch guidelines". *Id.* Likewise, in 1973 in *Sullivan*, our court considered *Tinker*, but did not address any parameters for its application to off-campus speech. 475 F.2d at 1076–77.

Our court's far more recent, 2004 opinion in *Porter*, however, provides valuable insight in this regard. There, the school expelled a student after his brother brought to school a sketchpad containing a two-year-old drawing of the school's being attacked by armed personnel. 393 F.3d at 611. The depiction, albeit violent in nature, "was completed [at] home, stored for two years, and *never intended* by [the creator of the drawing] to be brought to campus". *Id.* at 615 (emphasis added). After concluding

Tinker applied to the school's regulations, our court held the speech was protected because the student *never intended* for the drawing to reach the school, describing its introduction to the school community as "accidental and unintentional". *Id.* at 618, 620 ("Because [the student's] drawing was composed off-campus, displayed only to members of his own household, stored off-campus, and not purposefully taken by him to [school] or publicized in a way certain to result in its appearance at [school], we have found that the drawing is protected by the First Amendment".). Of importance for the issue at hand, and after describing precedent from our and other circuits' applying *Tinker* to off-campus speech, our court stated its holding was "not in conflict with this body of case law" regarding the First Amendment and off-campus student speech because the drawing's being "composed off-campus and remain[ing] off-campus for two years until it was *unintentionally* taken to school by his younger brother takes the present case outside the scope of these precedents". *Id.* at 615 n. 22 (emphasis added).

Porter instructs that a speaker's intent matters when determining whether the off-campus speech being addressed is subject to *Tinker.* A speaker's intention that his speech reach the school community, buttressed by his actions in bringing about that consequence, supports applying *Tinker*'s school-speech standard to that speech.

In addition, those courts to have considered the circumstances under which *Tinker* applies to off-campus speech have advocated varied approaches. *E.g., Wynar,* 728 F.3d at 1069 (holding that, regardless of the location of the speech, "when faced with an identifiable threat of school violence [(threats communicated online via MySpace messages)], schools may take disciplinary action in response to off-campus speech that meets the requirements of *Tinker*"); *Snyder,* 650 F.3d at 940 (Smith, J., concurring) (noting that any standard adopted "cannot turn solely on where the speaker was sitting when the speech was originally uttered [because s]uch a standard would fail to accommodate the somewhat 'everywhere at once' nature of the [I]nternet", and advocating allowing schools to discipline off-campus speech "[r]egardless of its place of origin" so long as that speech was "intentionally directed towards a school"); *Kowalski,* 652 F.3d at 573 (applying *Tinker* when a "sufficiently strong" nexus exists between the student's speech and the school's pedagogical interests "to justify the action taken by school officials in carrying out their role as the trustees of the student body's well-being"); *D.J.M.*, 647 F.3d at 766 (applying *Tinker* because "it was reasonably foreseeable that [the student's] threats about shooting specific students in school would be brought to the attention of school authorities and create a risk of substantial disruption within the school environment"); *Doninger,* 527 F.3d at 48 (holding *Tinker* applies to speech originating off-campus if it "would foreseeably create a risk of substantial disruption within the school environment, at least when it was similarly foreseeable that the off-campus expression might also reach campus" (internal quotation marks omitted)).

The pervasive and omnipresent nature of the Internet has obfuscated the on-campus/off-campus distinction advocated by Bell, "mak[ing] any effort to trace First Amendment boundaries along the physical boundaries of a school campus a recipe for serious problems in our public schools". *Layshock*, 650 F.3d at 220–21 (Jordan, J., concurring). Accordingly, in the light of our court's precedent, we hold *Tinker* governs our analysis, as in this instance, when a student intentionally directs at the school community speech reasonably understood by school officials to threaten, harass, and intimidate a teacher, even when such speech originated, and was disseminated, off-campus without the use of school resources.

This holding is consistent with our circuit's precedent in *Shanley* and *Sullivan*, that of our sister circuits, and our reasoning in *Porter*. Further, in holding *Tinker* applies to the off-campus speech in this instance, because such determinations are heavily influenced by the facts in each matter, we decline: to adopt any rigid standard in this instance; or to adopt or reject approaches advocated by other circuits.

ii.

Turning to the matter before us, there is no genuine dispute of material fact that Bell intended his rap recording to reach the school community. He admitted during the disciplinary-committee hearing that one of the purposes for producing the recording was to "increase awareness of the [alleged misconduct]" and that, by posting the rap recording on Facebook and YouTube, he knew people were "gonna listen to it, somebody's gonna listen to it", remarking that "students all have Facebook". In short, Bell produced and disseminated the rap recording knowing students, and hoping administrators, would listen to it.

Further, regardless of whether Bell's statements in the rap recording qualify as "true threats", as discussed in part II.B., they constitute threats, harassment, and intimidation, as a layperson would understand the terms. The Oxford English Dictionary defines: "threaten" as "to declare (usually conditionally) one's intention of inflicting injury upon" another, 17 Oxford English Dictionary 998 (2d ed.1989); "harass" as "[t]o wear *out*, tire *out*, or exhaust with fatigue, care, [or] trouble", 6 *id.* at 1100 (emphasis in original); and "intimidate" as "[t]o render timid, inspire with fear; [or] to force to or deter from some action by threats or violence", 8 *id.* at 7–8. See also Black's Law Dictionary 1708 (10th ed.2014) (defining "threat" as "[a] communicated intent to inflict harm or loss on another or on another's property"); *id.* at 831 (defining "harassment" as "[w]ords, conduct, or action . . . that, being directed at a specific person, annoys, alarms, or causes substantial emotional distress to that person and serves no legitimate purpose"); *Elonis v. United States*, —U.S.—, 135 S. Ct. 2001, 2011–12, 192 L.Ed.2d 1 (2015) (explaining that a "threat" can have different definitions based on context (for example, the difference between its use in criminal statutes and its being protected speech under the First Amendment)).

A reasonable understanding of Bell's statements satisfies these definitions; they: threatened violence against the two coaches, describing the injury to be inflicted (putting the pistol down their mouths and pulling the trigger, and "capping" them), described the specific weapon (a "rueger" [sic], which, as discussed *supra*, is a type of firearm), and encouraged others to engage in this action; and harassed and intimidated the coaches by forecasting the aforementioned violence, warning them to "watch [their] back[s]" and that they would "get no mercy" when such actions were taken. Accordingly, as further discussed *infra*, there is no genuine dispute of material fact that Bell threatened, harassed, and intimidated the coaches by intentionally directing his rap recording at the school community, thereby subjecting his speech to *Tinker.*

3.

Having held *Tinker* applies in this instance, the next question is whether Bell's recording either caused an actual disruption or reasonably could be forecast to cause one. Taking the school board's decision into account, and the deference we must accord it, this question becomes whether a genuine dispute of material fact exists regarding the reasonableness of finding Bell's rap recording threatening, harassing, and intimidating; and, if no genuine dispute precludes that finding, whether such language, as a matter of law, reasonably could have been forecast to cause a substantial disruption.

a.

As noted by our court in *Shanley*, "in deference to the judgment of the school boards, we refer ad hoc resolution of . . . issues [such as this one] to the neutral corner of 'reasonableness'". 462 F.2d at 971; see also *id.* at 975 ("[T]he balancing of expression and discipline is an exercise in judgment for school administrations and school boards, subject only to the constitutional requirement of reasonableness under the circumstances".). For the reasons discussed *supra*, there is no genuine dispute of material fact that the school board's finding the rap recording threatened, harassed, and intimidated the two coaches was objectively reasonable.

b.

Next, we consider whether the school board's disciplinary action against Bell, based on its finding he threatened, harassed, and intimidated two coaches, satisfies *Tinker.* Arguably, a student's threatening, harassing, and intimidating a teacher inherently portends a substantial disruption, making feasible a per se rule in that regard. We need not decide that question because, in the light of this summary-judgment record, and for the reasons that follow, Bell's conduct reasonably could have been forecast to cause a substantial disruption.

i.

As discussed *supra*, *Tinker* allows a school board to discipline a student for speech that either causes a substantial disruption or reasonably is forecast to cause one. 393 U.S. at 514, 89 S.Ct. 733. The *Tinker* test is satisfied when: an actual disruption occurs; or the record contains facts "which might reasonably have led school authorities to forecast substantial disruption of or material interference with school activities". *Id.* "*Tinker* requires a specific and significant fear of disruption, not just some remote apprehension of disturbance." *Saxe,* 240 F.3d at 211. "School officials must be able to show that their actions were caused by something more than a mere desire to avoid the discomfort and unpleasantness that always accompany an unpopular viewpoint." *A.M. v. Cash*, 585 F.3d 214, 221 (5th Cir.2009) (alterations and internal quotation marks omitted). "Officials must base their decisions on fact, not intuition", *id.* at 221–22 (internal quotation marks omitted); and those decisions are entitled to deference, *Shanley*, 462 F.2d at 967 ("That courts should not interfere with the day-to-day operations of schools is a platitudinous but eminently sound maxim which this court has reaffirmed on many occasions."). *See also Wood* [*v. Strickland*], 420 U.S. at 326 [(1975)] ("It is not the role of the federal courts to set aside decisions of school administrators which the court may view as lacking a basis in wisdom or compassion.").

As our court has held: "While school officials must offer facts to support their proscription of student speech, *this is not a difficult burden, and their decisions will govern if they are within the range where reasonable minds will differ*". *Cash*, 585 F.3d at 222 (emphasis added) (internal citations and quotation marks omitted). Accordingly, school authorities are not required expressly to forecast a "substantial or material disruption"; rather, courts determine the possibility of a reasonable forecast based on the facts in the record. See, e.g., *id.* at 217, 222; see also *Tinker*, 393 U.S. at 514 ("[T]he record does not demonstrate any facts which *might reasonably have led* school authorities to forecast substantial disruption of or material interference with school activities, and no disturbances or disorders on the school premises in fact occurred". (emphasis added)).

Factors considered by other courts in determining, pursuant to *Tinker*, the substantiality vel non of an actual disruption, and the objective reasonableness vel non of a forecasted substantial disruption, include: the nature and content of the speech, the objective and subjective seriousness of the speech, and the severity of the possible consequences should the speaker take action, e.g., *Wynar*, 728 F.3d at 1070–71; the relationship of the speech to the school, the intent of the speaker to disseminate, or keep private, the speech, and the nature, and severity, of the school's response in disciplining the student, *e.g., Doninger*, 527 F.3d at 50–52; whether the speaker expressly identified an educator or student by name or reference, and past incidents arising out of similar speech, *e.g., Kowalski*, 652 F.3d at 574; the manner in which the speech reached the school community, *e.g., Boim*, 494 F.3d at 985; the intent of the school in disciplining the student, *Snyder*, 650 F.3d at 926, 929 (majority opinion), 951 (Fisher, J., dissenting); and the occurrence of other in-school disturbances, including administrative disturbances involving the speaker, such as "[s]chool officials ha[ving] to spend considerable time dealing with these concerns and ensuring that appropriate safety measures were in place", *D.J.M.*, 647 F.3d at 766, brought about "because of the need to manage" concerns over the speech, *Doninger*, 527 F.3d at 51.

ii.

Applying this precedent to the summary-judgment record at hand, and for the reasons that follow, a substantial disruption reasonably could have been forecast as a matter of law. Viewing the evidence in the requisite light most favorable to Bell, including his assertions that he wanted only to raise awareness of alleged misconduct by two teachers (Bell admitted at the disciplinary-committee hearing that his recording was meant to "increase awareness of the situation" and that he was "*foreshadowing something that might happen*" (emphasis added)), the manner in which he voiced his concern—with threatening, intimidating, and harassing language—must be taken seriously by school officials, and reasonably could be forecast by them to cause a substantial disruption. The speech pertained directly to events occurring at school, identified the two teachers by name, and was understood by one to threaten his safety and by neutral, third parties as threatening. (Bell agreed at the disciplinary-committee hearing that "certain statements" were made to his mother "outside the school setting" that "'put a pistol down your mouth'[,] that is a direct threat".) The possible consequences were grave—serious injury to, including the possible death of, two teachers. Along that line, Bell admitted he intended the speech to be public and to reach members of the school community, which is further evidenced by his posting the recording to Facebook and YouTube.

As noted, the school district's Discipline—Administrative Policy lists "[h]arassment, intimidation, or threatening other students and/or teachers" as a severe disruption. Although we may not rely on ipse dixit in evaluating the school board's actions, *Shanley,* 462 F.2d at 970, the school-district's policy demonstrates an awareness of Tinker 's substantial-disruption standard, and the policy's violation can be used as evidence supporting the reasonable forecast of a future substantial disruption. *See, e.g., Morse*, 551 U.S. at 408–10 (relying on, inter alia, the student's violation of established school policy in holding the school board did not violate the student's First Amendment right); *Fraser,* 478 U.S. at 678 (noting that the "[t]he school disciplinary rule proscribing 'obscene' language and the prespeech admonitions of teachers gave adequate warning to [the student] that his lewd speech could subject him to sanctions").

Further, even after finding Bell threatened, intimidated, and harassed two teachers, the school board's response was measured—temporarily suspending Bell and placing him in an alternative-education program for the remainder of the nine-week grading term (about six weeks). The reasonableness of, and amount of care given to, this decision is reinforced by the school board's finding, differently from the disciplinary committee's, that Bell's statements also constituted threats.

And finally, numerous, recent examples of school violence exist in which students have signaled potential violence through speech, writings, or actions, and then carried out violence against school communities, after school administrators and parents failed to properly identify warning signs.

In determining objective reasonableness vel non for forecasting a substantial disruption, the summary-judgment record and numerous related factors must be considered against the backdrop of the mission of schools: to educate. It goes without saying that a teacher, which includes a coach, is the cornerstone of education. Without teaching, there can be little, if any, learning. Without learning, there can be little, if any, education. Without education, there can be little, if any, civilization. It equally goes without saying that threatening, harassing, and intimidating a teacher impedes, if not destroys, the ability to teach; it impedes, if not destroys, the ability to educate. It disrupts, if not destroys, the discipline necessary for an environment in which education can take place. In addition, it encourages and incites other students to engage in similar disruptive conduct. Moreover, it can even cause a teacher to leave that profession. In sum, it disrupts, if not destroys, the very mission for which schools exist—to educate.

If there is to be education, such conduct cannot be permitted. In that regard, the real tragedy in this instance is that a high-school student thought he could, with impunity, direct speech at the school community which threatens, harasses, and intimidates teachers and, as a result, objected to being disciplined.

Put succinctly, "with near-constant student access to social networking sites on and off campus, when offensive and malicious speech is directed at school officials and disseminated online to the student body, it is reasonable to anticipate an impact on the classroom environment". *Snyder*, 650 F.3d at 951–52 (Fisher, J., dissenting). As stated, the school board reasonably could have forecast a substantial disruption at school, based on the threatening, intimidating, and harassing language in Bell's rap recording.

B.

In considering Bell's First Amendment claim, and our having affirmed summary judgment for the school board under *Tinker*, it is unnecessary to decide whether Bell's speech also constitutes a "true threat" under *Watts v. United States*, 394 U.S. 705 (1969) (holding hyperbolic threats on the President's life are not "true threats"). *See Elonis*, 135 S.Ct. at 2012 (declining to address the First Amendment question (whether the speech was a "true threat" not protected by that amendment) after resolving the case on other grounds).

III.

For the foregoing reasons, the judgment is AFFIRMED.

E. Grady Jolly, specially concurring:

In determining the contours of constitutionally permissible school discipline, older cases are relevant for block building, but only block building, as we decide what speech schools may discipline under the First Amendment. In *Tinker*, there was no threat to kill a teacher, no threat of violence, and no lewd or slanderous comments regarding a teacher. *Tinker* also did not address the intersection between on-campus speech and off-campus speech. When *Tinker* refers to a disruption, it is saying that student ideas may be expressed on campus unless they are so controversial that the expression creates a disruption. Those principles are controlling where the facts fit, but *Tinker's* admonitions—or the admonitions in various precedents—are not equally forceful in every case. The same can be said of *Morse*. It is perhaps more applicable here than *Tinker*, because it speaks in terms of physical and moral danger to students. *Morse* makes clear that such danger does not require proof of disruptive effects that the speech may cause, as would be required in the case of mere expression of non-lethal statements.

It is true that in a footnote in *Ponce* we indicated that individual threats of violence are more appropriately analyzed in the light of *Tinker* as opposed to threats of mass violence, which we analyzed under *Morse*. These are evolving principles, however, and we now have before us a different case from *Tinker, Morse, Ponce, or Porter*. *Tinker* may well be a relevant precedent here. But that does not mean that all aspects of a political speech case must be slavishly applied to a case of threats to kill teachers. We should apply reasonable common sense in deciding these continually arising school speech and discipline cases, as we would in any case dealing with the evolving common law, which takes into account the technological and societal environs of the times. When *Tinker* was written in 1969, the use of the Internet as a medium for student speech was not within the Court's mind. It is also true that this issue was not in the forefront of the Court's mind when *Porter* was written in 2004, or even when *Morse* and *Ponce* were written. Ever since *Morse*, the use, the extent and the effect of the online speech seem to have multiplied geometrically.

Judges should also view student speech in the further context of public education today—at a time when many schools suffer from poor performance, when disciplinary problems are at their highest, and when schools are, in many ways, at their most ineffective point. Judges should take into account the effect the courts have had on these problems in school discipline. Increasing judicial oversight of schools has created unforeseen consequences, for teachers and for schools as much as for students. Students feel constraints on conduct and personal speech to be more and more permissive. Teachers will decide not to discipline students, given the likelihood of protracted litigation and its pressures on the time and person of those who work hard to keep up with the increasing demands placed on them as teachers. Schools will not take on the risk of huge litigation costs when they could use these resources on school lunches, textbooks, or other necessary school resources to educate children, all of which are sorely lacking in so many, many instances.

Judges can help to address these concerns by speaking clearly, succinctly and unequivocally. I would decide this case in the simplest way, consonant with our cases and the cases in other circuits, by saying as little as possible and holding:

> Student speech is unprotected by the First Amendment and is subject to school discipline when that speech contains an actual threat to kill or physically harm personnel and/or students of the school; which actual threat is connected to the school environment; and which actual threat is communicated to the school, or its students, or its personnel.

With these comments, I join Judge Barksdale's opinion.

[Note: Other concurring opinions and dissenting opinions were omitted for space purposes. You can review them online.]

Post Problem Discussion

1. As you can imagine, being a judge who has to decide these cases can be difficult, and there are often strongly held views on each side of the issue. Consider the extraordinary dissenting opinion written by Judges Reinhardt and Kleinfeld in *Lavine* when the Ninth Circuit declined to hear the case en banc. It begins by stating:

> After today, members of the black trench coat clique in high schools in the western United States will have to hide their art work. They have lost their free speech rights. If a teacher, administrator, or student finds their art disturbing, they can be punished, even though they say nothing disruptive, defamatory or indecent and do not intend to threaten or harm anyone. School officials may now subordinate students' freedom of expression to a policy of making high schools cozy places, like daycare centers, where no one may be made uncomfortable by the knowledge that others have dark thoughts, and all the art is of hearts and smiley faces. The court has adopted a new doctrine in First Amendment law, that high school students may be punished for non-threatening speech that administrators believe may indicate that the speaker is emotionally disturbed and therefore dangerous.

Lavine v. Blaine Sch. Dist., 279 F.3d 719, 721 (9th Cir. 2002). View the full dissent online. Which view do you agree with, the majority or the dissent and why?

2. The relevant Washington state school discipline regulations at issue in *Lavine* provided:

> Notwithstanding any other provision of this chapter, a student may be expelled immediately by a school district superintendent or a designee of the superintendent in emergency situations: Provided, That the superintendent or designee has good and sufficient reason to believe that the student's presence poses an immediate and continuing danger to the student, other students, or school personnel or an immediate and continuing threat of substantial disruption of the educational process. An emergency expulsion shall continue until rescinded by the superintendent or his or her designee, or until modified or reversed pursuant to the hearing provisions set forth in WAC 180-40-305 or the appeal provisions set forth in WAC 180-40-315.

Wash. Admin. Code 180-40-295 (2009). Did the student's actions in *Lavine* meet these requirements? Does this statute meet the constitutional due process standards required for discipline noted in Chapter 8?

3. The original Fifth Circuit Court of Appeals panel decision in *Bell* ruled that the school could not discipline the student under *Tinker, Morse*, or the true threat standard. It determined that the rap at issue was not a true threat and that the *Tinker* substantial disruption standard was not met. *See Bell v. Itawamba County Sch. Bd.*, 774 F.3d 280 (5th Cir. 2014), *reh'g en banc granted*, 782 F.3d 712 (5th Cir. 2015). The court stated:

> even assuming *arguendo* that the *Tinker* "substantial-disruption" test could be applied to a student's off-campus speech, the summary-judgment evidence establishes that no substantial disruption ever occurred, nor does it "demonstrate any facts which might reasonably have led school authorities

> to forecast substantial disruption of or material interference with school activities." Viewing the evidence in the light most favorable to the School Board, there was no commotion, boisterous conduct, interruption of classes, or any lack of order, discipline and decorum at the school, as a result of Bell's posting of his song on the Internet. Indeed, the School Board's inability to point to any evidence in the record of a disruption directly undermines its argument *and* the district court's conclusion that the summary-judgment evidence supports a finding that a substantial disruption occurred or reasonably could have been forecasted. At the preliminary injunction hearing, Wildmon explained that his students "seem[ed] to act normal" after the posting of the song, and Rainey testified that most of the talk amongst students had not been about Bell's song but rather about his suspension and transfer to alternative school. No evidence was offered that Bell or any other student listened to the song on campus, aside from the single instance when Wildmon had a student play the song for him on his cellphone. The only particularized evidence of a purported disruption that the defendants or the district court identified as stemming from Bell's song was that Rainey and Wildmon have altered their teaching styles in order to ensure they are not perceived as engaging in inappropriate conduct with female students. However, the teachers' alteration of their teaching styles in order to avoid accusations of sexual harassment does not constitute the material and substantial disruption of school work or discipline that would justify the restriction of student speech under *Tinker*.
>
> Furthermore, even if we were to credit the School Board's unsupported assertion that it indeed forecasted a disruption as a result of Bell's song the summary-judgment evidence nevertheless shows that there are no facts that "might reasonably have led" the School Board to make such a forecast. The summary-judgment evidence conclusively shows that Bell's song was composed, recorded, and posted to the Internet entirely off campus. School computers blocked Facebook and school policy prohibited possession of telephones, thus diminishing the likelihood that a student would access the song on campus. Moreover, as discussed at greater length *infra*, the violent lyrics contained in Bell's song were plainly rhetorical in nature, and could not reasonably be viewed as a genuine threat to the coaches, as underscored by the Disciplinary Committee's own determination that whether Bell's song constituted a threat was "vague."

Why does the en banc decision come to a different conclusion about the *Tinker* substantial disruption standard being met?

4. Courts that apply *Tinker* to off-campus speech that involves threats of violence are more likely to defer to a school administrator's forecast of a substantial disruption than they are with speech that is merely rude or derogatory like the speech in *Blue Mountain*. *See, e.g., Wisniewski v. Bd. of Educ. of Weedsport Cent. Sch. Dist.*, 494 F.3d 34, 37–38 (2d Cir. 2007) (instant message icon about killing teacher);

D.J.M. v. Hannibal Pub. Sch. Dist. No. 60, 647 F.3d 754 (8th Cir. 2011) (instant messages about shooting students); *Wynar v. Douglas Cnty. Sch. Dist.*, 728 F.3d 1062, 1064 (9th Cir. 2013) (same). Why do you think courts do so?

5. Given the different standards that courts have applied to off-campus speech, if you were representing a school district, what advice would you provide school officials about what they can and cannot do in this area? Would the advice vary depending on the content of the speech? Would it depend upon which judicial circuit governed the school district?

Chapter 10

Search, Seizure & Interrogation

Synopsis

§ 10.01 Introduction

Student discipline, discussed in Chapter 8, often depends on a lawful and constitutional method of gathering information about the alleged misconduct. Potentially incriminating information uncovered in school investigations may be relevant to school discipline proceedings, and to criminal proceedings, raising questions around the applicability of the protections of the Fourth and Fifth Amendments to students in public schools.

Generally, before intruding into an individual's privacy, the Fourth Amendment requires a showing of probable cause and a search warrant prior to a search. The approach in school settings is less demanding. Like the speech cases, the school search cases begin with a series of classics, starting with *T.L.O. v. New Jersey*, which replaced the probable cause standard with a less rigorous standard of "reasonableness, under all the circumstances, of the search." Such a search must be "justified at its inception," and "reasonably related in scope to the circumstances which justified the interference in the first place." *T.L.O. v. New Jersey*, 469 U.S. 325, 341 (1985).

Courts apply this *T.L.O.* standard to most search situations in public schools. Some searches (such as random, suspicionless searches for drugs or weapons) have different standards as discussed in Section 10.05. Searches involving police officers, or school resource officers, ("SROs") may be subject to the probable cause standard. *See* Section 10.04. School officials must also be mindful of the Fifth Amendment rights of those whom they interrogate, and consider whether *Miranda* warnings should be provided to students before questioning them. This is particularly true when police officers or SROs are involved. *See* Section 10.07.

§ 10.02 Applying *T.L.O.*

In *T.L.O.*, a high school teacher found two girls smoking in a bathroom—a violation of school rules—and took the girls to the principal's office. When the vice-principal met with the girls, one confessed, but T.L.O. denied smoking. The vice-principal then demanded to see her purse, where he found cigarettes. As he pulled the cigarettes from the purse, he also saw rolling papers. Suspecting the rolling papers were used for marijuana, the vice principal looked further. A closer search then revealed other evidence suggesting drug-dealing, including a marijuana pipe, plastic bags, $1 bills, index cards with names of students who owed T.L.O. money, and letters implicating T.L.O. in drug dealing. The vice-principal notified T.L.O.'s mother and turned this evidence over to the police.

At the school, T.L.O. was subject to a three-day suspension for smoking cigarettes, and a seven-day suspension for the marijuana offenses. At the police station, with her mother present, T.L.O. confessed. The confession plus the evidence from the school led to delinquency charges in juvenile court, where T.L.O. sought suppression of the evidence. The case proceeded to the U.S. Supreme Court, which defined the issue as: "what limits, if any, the Fourth Amendment places on the activities of school authorities." *T.L.O.*, 469 U.S. at 332. The Court set forth the two part standard noted in the Introduction in § 10.01. Since *T.L.O.*, state and federal courts have applied this two-part standard to a variety of scenarios from searching students, student lockers, or vehicles on campus, to searching cell phones and electronic devices. The following problem explores some of these issues.

Problem 1: "?420"—"YBYSA!"

Dylan walks by his high school principal on the way to class in the morning. The principal smells marijuana and tells Dylan to come with her to her office. In her office, she asks Dylan if he smoked marijuana that morning, and he says "no." Dylan's cell phone then buzzes in his coat pocket, and the principal tells Dylan to give her the phone. The principal looks at the phone, sees a text message that says "?420," and asks Dylan what that means. He says, "I dunno." She tells Dylan to empty his pockets, which he does, revealing nothing questionable. The principal tells Dylan that she will be keeping his cell phone for the day, and will be watching him. Dylan returns to class.

The principal then asks Aminah, a student in the office who is helping with morning announcements, what the message means. Aminah tells her that it means, "Do you have any marijuana?" She asks Aminah how to reply yes in text lingo, and Aminah tells her to type in "YBYSA!" which means "you bet your sweet ass!" The student replies to the principal's text, and with Aminah's help texting, the principal arranges for the student to meet her behind the dugouts on the school's baseball field in about a half hour with money and rolling papers.

The principal goes to that location and James, a junior at the school, shows up. She searches James' coat pockets and finds rolling papers and some money. She asks

James if he was looking for Dylan, and James says "yes." She then radios to her office to determine the make, model, and license plate of Dylan's car, which is parked on campus. With that information, she locates the car and searches it (the doors were left unlocked) finding several ounces of marijuana under the seat, and in the trunk under the spare tire.

Do any of the principal's actions violate the Fourth Amendment?

Problem Materials

✓ *New Jersey v. T.L.O.*, 469 U.S. 325 (1985)

✓ *Klump v. Nazareth Area School District*, 425 F. Supp. 2d 622 (E.D. Pa. 2006)

✓ *S.V.J. v. State*, 891 So. 2d 1221 (Fla. Dist. Ct. App. 2005)

New Jersey v. T.L.O.

469 U.S. 325 (1985)

The Court rules that school officials are not required to have probable cause, or a warrant, to search students. Rather, the search must simply be reasonable under the circumstances.

JUSTICE WHITE delivered the opinion of the Court, in which BURGER, C.J., and POWELL, REHNQUIST, and O'CONNOR, JJ., joined, and in Part II of which BRENNAN, MARSHALL, and STEVENS, JJ., joined.

. . . .

Although we originally granted certiorari to decide the issue of the appropriate remedy in juvenile court proceedings for unlawful school searches, our doubts regarding the wisdom of deciding that question in isolation from the broader question of what limits, if any, the Fourth Amendment places on the activities of school authorities prompted us to order reargument on that question. Having heard argument on the legality of the search of T.L.O.'s purse, we are satisfied that the search did not violate the *Fourth Amendment.*

In determining whether the search at issue in this case violated the Fourth Amendment, we are faced initially with the question whether that Amendment's prohibition on unreasonable searches and seizures applies to searches conducted by public school officials. We hold that it does.

It is now beyond dispute that "the Federal Constitution, by virtue of the Fourteenth Amendment, prohibits unreasonable searches and seizures by state officers." Equally indisputable is the proposition that the Fourteenth Amendment protects the rights of students against encroachment by public school officials. . . .

To hold that the Fourth Amendment applies to searches conducted by school authorities is only to begin the inquiry into the standards governing such searches. Although the underlying command of the Fourth Amendment is always that searches and seizures be reasonable, what is reasonable depends on the context within which a search takes place. The determination of the standard of reasonableness governing any specific class of searches requires "balancing the need to search against the invasion which the search entails." On one side of the balance are arrayed the individual's legitimate expectations of privacy and personal security; on the other, the government's need for effective methods to deal with breaches of public order.

We have recognized that even a limited search of the person is a substantial invasion of privacy. *Terry v. Ohio*, 392 U.S. 1, 24–25 (1967). We have also recognized that searches of closed items of personal luggage are intrusions on protected privacy interests, for "the Fourth Amendment provides protection to the owner of every container that conceals its contents from plain view." *United States v. Ross*, 456 U.S. 798, 822–823 (1982). A search of a child's person or of a closed purse or other bag carried on her person, no less than a similar search carried out on an adult, is undoubtedly a severe violation of subjective expectations of privacy.

. . . .

Although this Court may take notice of the difficulty of maintaining discipline in the public schools today, the situation is not so dire that students in the schools may claim no legitimate expectations of privacy. We have recently recognized that the need to maintain order in a prison is such that prisoners retain no legitimate expectations of privacy in their cells, but it goes almost without saying that "[the] prisoner and the schoolchild stand in wholly different circumstances, separated by the harsh facts of criminal conviction and incarceration." We are not yet ready to hold that the schools and the prisons need be equated for purposes of the Fourth Amendment.

Nor does the State's suggestion that children have no legitimate need to bring personal property into the schools seem well anchored in reality. . . . Against the child's interest in privacy must be set the substantial interest of teachers and administrators in maintaining discipline in the classroom and on school grounds. . . . Maintaining order in the classroom has never been easy, but in recent years, school disorder has often taken particularly ugly forms: drug use and violent crime in the schools have become major social problems. Even in schools that have been spared the most severe disciplinary problems, the preservation of order and a proper educational environment requires close supervision of schoolchildren, as well as the enforcement of rules against conduct that would be perfectly permissible if undertaken by an adult. "Events calling for discipline are frequent occurrences and sometimes require immediate, effective action." Accordingly, we have recognized that maintaining security and order in the schools requires a certain degree of flexibility in school disciplinary procedures, and we have respected the value of preserving the informality of the student-teacher relationship.

How, then, should we strike the balance between the schoolchild's legitimate expectations of privacy and the school's equally legitimate need to maintain an environment in which learning can take place? It is evident that the school setting requires some easing of the restrictions to which searches by public authorities are ordinarily subject. The warrant requirement, in particular, is unsuited to the school environment: requiring a teacher to obtain a warrant before searching a child suspected of an infraction of school rules (or of the criminal law) would unduly interfere with the maintenance of the swift and informal disciplinary procedures needed in the schools. Just as we have in other cases dispensed with the warrant requirement when "the burden of obtaining a warrant is likely to frustrate the governmental purpose behind the search," we hold today that school officials need not obtain a warrant before searching a student who is under their authority.

The school setting also requires some modification of the level of suspicion of illicit activity needed to justify a search. Ordinarily, a search—even one that may permissibly be carried out without a warrant—must be based upon "probable cause" to believe that a violation of the law has occurred. . . . Where a careful balancing of governmental and private interests suggests that the public interest is best served by a Fourth Amendment standard of reasonableness that stops short of probable cause, we have not hesitated to adopt such a standard.

We join the majority of courts that have examined this issue in concluding that the accommodation of the privacy interests of schoolchildren with the substantial need of teachers and administrators for freedom to maintain order in the schools does not require strict adherence to the requirement that searches be based on probable cause to believe that the subject of the search has violated or is violating the law. Rather, the legality of a search of a student should depend simply on the reasonableness, under all the circumstances, of the search. Determining the reasonableness of any search involves a twofold inquiry: first, one must consider "whether the . . . action was justified at its inception," second, one must determine whether the search as actually conducted "was reasonably related in scope to the circumstances which justified the interference in the first place." Under ordinary circumstances, a search of a student by a teacher or other school official will be "justified at its inception" when there are reasonable grounds for suspecting that the search will turn up evidence that the student has violated or is violating either the law or the rules of the school. Such a search will be permissible in its scope when the measures adopted are reasonably related to the objectives of the search and not excessively intrusive in light of the age and sex of the student and the nature of the infraction.

This standard will, we trust, neither unduly burden the efforts of school authorities to maintain order in their schools nor authorize unrestrained intrusions upon the privacy of schoolchildren. By focusing attention on the question of reasonableness, the standard will spare teachers and school administrators the necessity of schooling themselves in the niceties of probable cause and permit them to regulate their conduct according to the dictates of reason and common sense. At the same time, the reasonableness standard should ensure that the interests of students will be invaded no more than is necessary to achieve the legitimate end of preserving order in the schools.

There remains the question of the legality of the search in this case. We recognize that the "reasonable grounds" standard applied by the New Jersey Supreme Court in its consideration of this question is not substantially different from the standard that we have adopted today. Nonetheless, we believe that the New Jersey court's application of that standard to strike down the search of T.L.O.'s purse reflects a somewhat crabbed notion of reasonableness. Our review of the facts surrounding the search leads us to conclude that the search was in no sense unreasonable for Fourth Amendment purposes.

Because the search resulting in the discovery of the evidence of marihuana dealing by T.L.O. was reasonable, the New Jersey Supreme Court's decision to exclude that evidence from T.L.O.'s juvenile delinquency proceedings on Fourth Amendment grounds was erroneous.

Klump v. Nazareth Area School District

425 F. Supp. 2d 622 (E.D. Pa. 2006)

The court rules that a school principal was justified in taking a student's cell phone, but violated the Fourth Amendment by calling and texting other students with the cell phone to obtain information.

GARDNER, DISTRICT JUDGE.

The events giving rise to plaintiffs' First Amended Complaint occurred on March 17, 2004. At that time, plaintiff Christopher Klump was a student at Nazareth Area High School.

The high school has a policy which permits students to carry, but not use or display cell phones during school hours. On March 17, 2004 Christopher's cell phone fell out of his pocket and came to rest on his leg. Upon seeing Christopher's cell phone, Shawn Kimberly Kocher, a teacher at the high school, enforced the school policy prohibiting use or display of cell phones by confiscating the phone. These events occurred at approximately 10:15 a.m.

Subsequently, Ms. Kocher, along with Assistant Principal Margaret Grube, began making phone calls with Christopher's cell phone. Ms. Kocher and Ms. Grube called nine other Nazareth Area High School students listed in Christopher's phone number directory to determine whether they, too, were violating the school's cell phone policy.

Next, defendants Kocher and Grube accessed Christopher's text messages and voice mail. Finally, defendants Kocher and Grube held an America Online Instant Messaging conversation with Mr. Klump's younger brother without identifying themselves as being anyone other than the primary user of the cell phone, Christopher Klump.

On March 22, 2004, Christopher Klump's parents, plaintiffs Toby Klump and Leigh Klump, met with Ms. Kocher, Ms. Grube, and Assistant Superintendent Diane Dautrich regarding the events of March 17. During that meeting, Ms. Grube told Mr. and Mrs. Klump that while she was in possession of their son's phone, Christopher received a text message from his girlfriend requesting that he get her a "f***in' tampon". The term "tampon", Ms. Grube later averred, is a reference to a large marijuana cigarette and prompted her subsequent use of the phone to investigate possible drug use at the school.

Based upon the foregoing facts, plaintiffs filed a Complaint in the Northampton County Court of Common Pleas. The lawsuit was removed to federal court by defendants on July 29, 2004. Plaintiffs' First Amended Complaint alleges ten causes of action stemming from the violation of various state and federal protections.

. . . .

In Count VI, plaintiffs assert a violation of Christopher Klump's Fourth Amendment rights by defendants Grube and Kocher. Plaintiffs aver that by accessing Christopher's phone number directory, voice mail, and text messages, and subsequently using the phone to call individuals listed in the directory, defendants Grube and Kocher violated Christopher's Fourth Amendment right to be free from unreasonable searches and seizures. In addition, plaintiffs assert that defendants are liable for damages pursuant to 42 U.S.C. § 1983.

. . . .

Although students are protected by the Fourth Amendment, the probable cause requirement does not apply to students at school. *New Jersey v. T.L.O.* The Supreme Court has held that a student search must nevertheless satisfy the reasonableness requirement of the Fourth Amendment. In the context of searches conducted by school officials, this means that the search must be justified at its inception and reasonable in scope. To be justified at its inception, there must be "reasonable grounds for believing that the search will turn up evidence that the student has violated or is violating either the law or the rules of the school."

Here, defendant Kocher was justified in seizing the cell phone, as plaintiff Christopher Klump had violated the school's policy prohibiting use or display of cell phones during school hours. In calling other students, however, defendants Grube and Kocher were conducting a search to find evidence of other students' misconduct, which they may not do under the standard articulated above. They had no reason to suspect at the outset that such a search would reveal that Christopher Klump himself was violating another school policy; rather, they hoped to utilize his phone as a tool to catch other students' violations.

Further, we must accept plaintiffs' allegation that the school officials did not see the allegedly drug-related text message until after they initiated the search of Christopher's cell phone. Accordingly, based upon the averments of the Complaint, which we must accept as true at this stage, there was no justification for the school officials to search Christopher's phone for evidence of drug activity.

Moreover, the law in this area is not as unsettled as defendants suggest. It is clear, based on the case law cited by defendants, that students have a Fourth Amendment right to be free from unreasonable searches and seizures by school officials. Although the meaning of "unreasonable searches and seizures" is different in the school context than elsewhere, it is nonetheless evident that there must be some basis for initiating a search. A reasonable person could not believe otherwise. Accordingly, we deny defendants' motion to dismiss Count VI against defendants Grube and Kocher on the basis of qualified immunity.

S.V.J. v. State

891 So. 2d 1221 (Fla. Dist. Ct. App. 2005)

The court rules that school officials must have more than a gut feeling or hunch that something is wrong to constitute a reasonable suspicion to justify a search.

Silberman, Judge.

S.V.J. appeals the Juvenile Probation Order entered following her no contest plea to possession of marijuana. She argues that the trial court erred in denying her dispositive motion to suppress the marijuana found in her purse. We agree and reverse.

S.V.J. attended Brandon Alternative School, a school for students exhibiting disruptive behavior. In the afternoon of December 8, 2003, S.V.J. and another student engaged in a fight. The school resource officer separated the students and took S.V.J. to an administrator's office. Mr. Arroyo, an administrative assistant at the school, testified that after he spoke briefly with S.V.J., he stepped out of his office for a short time to check on the flow of traffic in the hallway. When he re-entered the office, S.V.J. "looked startled" or "surprised" and put her purse under her arm and her jacket over her shoulder. He stated that "[i]t appeared she was hiding her purse." Although he normally did not search students after a fight, he decided to have a female school official search S.V.J.'s purse. The search revealed marijuana inside the purse.

Mr. Arroyo acknowledged that no complaint had been made regarding S.V.J. and a weapon, any drug use, or sales; he had no idea what might have been in the purse; and the only reason he had someone search the purse was because of S.V.J.'s startled reaction when he re-entered the office. The person who performed the search testified that she did so upon Mr. Arroyo's instruction and that she did not know what might be in the purse. At the conclusion of the testimony, the trial court denied the motion to suppress. The court stated that based on the school environment, the fight, and S.V.J.'s demeanor, the search was reasonable at its inception and in scope.

Although we "defer to the factual findings of the trial court that are supported by competent, substantial evidence," we review the court's application of the law to its factual findings using the de novo standard of review. For school searches, reasonable suspicion is needed to justify the search. For reasonable suspicion to exist, the search "must be justified at its inception, and the search must be reasonably related in scope to the reason for the search."

A court may use various factors to determine whether a search is justified at its inception. Such factors may include

> The child's age, history and record in school; the prevalence and seriousness of the problem in the school to which the search was directed; the exigencies in making a search without delay and further investigation; the probative value and reliability of the information used as a justification for the search; and the particular teacher or school official's experience with the student.

In *A.B. v. State*, 440 So. 2d 500, 501 (Fla. 2d DCA 1983), this court stated that these factors are simply a starting point and "not a complete and exhaustive list of all possible considerations." The court noted that the "experience of the involved school officials with the type of problem to which the search was directed" would be another pertinent factor to consider. *Id.*

Ordinarily, a search of a student by a school official is "'justified at its inception' when there are reasonable grounds for suspecting that the search will turn up evidence that the student has violated or is violating either the law or the rules of the school." The State must "elicit specific and articulable facts which, when taken together with rational inferences from those facts, reasonably warrant the intrusion." A "gut feeling" or hunch that something is wrong does not constitute a reasonable suspicion to justify the search.

Based on the testimony presented at the suppression hearing, S.V.J. argues, and we agree, that the State did not elicit specific and articulable facts that warranted the search. Although the school is for children exhibiting disruptive behavior and students at the school are routinely searched upon arrival for possible weapons, the search of S.V.J. did not occur as part of the arrival procedure. Mr. Arroyo described S.V.J.'s movement and demeanor immediately prior to the search, but he acknowledged that he had no idea what S.V.J. might have had in her possession. He did not give any indication of what he suspected might be in the purse or why the search might reveal evidence of a violation of the law or school rules. None of the witnesses articulated any facts demonstrating a reasonable suspicion that S.V.J. may have been in possession of a weapon, drugs, or other contraband or even that the contents of her purse were somehow connected with the fight.

As acknowledged in *A.B.*, a court may consider various factors in determining whether a search of a student is justified. Here, the evidence simply did not justify the search. Instead, the evidence showed that the search was conducted based on a mere hunch that S.V.J. might have something of interest in her purse. Because the motion to suppress should have been granted, we reverse the Juvenile Probation Order and remand with directions that the trial court discharge S.V.J. Reversed and remanded with directions.

Post Problem Discussion

1. In a footnote in *T.L.O.* omitted from the excerpt in this book, the Court said "We do not address the question, not presented by this case, whether a schoolchild has a legitimate expectation of privacy in lockers, desks, or other school property provided for the storage of school supplies. Nor do we express any opinion on the standards (if any) governing searches of such areas by school officials or by other public authorities acting at the request of school officials." *T.L.O.*, 469 U.S. at 338, n.5. Should the legal standards be any different in these situations than the general *T.L.O.* standard?

2. The *S.V.J.* court discusses some of the criteria that courts have used to assess reasonableness and notes that school officials must have more than a "gut feeling or a hunch." Does the principal in our problem have more than a hunch that she would find something in Dylan's car?

3. *T.L.O.* began its journey to the Supreme Court through an effort to exclude the evidence that school administrators gave to the police. Should the exclusionary rule apply to other kinds of hearings, such as school disciplinary proceedings? For example, in *Scanlon v. Las Cruces Public Schs.*, 172 P.3d 185 (N.M. Ct. App. 2007), Jarrett Scanlon had been suspended from school for one year for possession of marijuana, and of a decorative sword (weapon), in a car in a parking lot on school grounds. Part of the legal challenge was to the warrantless search, and the subsequent use of the evidence in a school disciplinary proceeding. A New Mexico Court of Appeals ruled that the school had not improperly searched the car, but even if it had, "the exclusionary rule does not apply in school disciplinary proceedings because the purpose of the exclusionary rule is not advanced in such proceedings." *Scanlon*, 172 P.3d at 187.

4. What constitutes a search? In most cases, a school official or police officer is searching a person or place for items by looking in car or locker, patting down a student or telling them to empty their pockets, but what other kinds of school activities could constitute searches? Consider *Brannum v. Overton Sch. Bd.*, 516 F.3d 489 (6th Cir. 2008), where the Sixth Circuit Court of Appeals found that a school security surveillance video tape of students changing in the school locker rooms was an unreasonable search. Do you agree with the court's analysis? What implications might the decision have for school surveillance on campus, or on school buses?

§ 10.03 Strip Searches

Courts applying *T.L.O.* have generally noted that the reasonableness of a search depends in part on the context. The more intrusive the search, the more suspicion and information the school official should have to justify the search. Perhaps the most intrusive type of search is a strip search. A number of Circuit Courts of Appeal have addressed strip searches over the years with mixed results.[1] In 2009, the Supreme Court addressed the issue in *Safford Unified Sch. Dist. #1 v. Redding*, 557 U.S. 364 (2009).

---

1. *See, e.g., Phaneuf v. Fraikin*, 448 F.3d 591 (2d Cir. 2006); *Cornfield by Lewis v. Consolidated High School District No. 230*, 991 F.2d 1316 (7th Cir. 1993); *Williams v. Ellington*, 936 F.2d 881, 882-883, 887 (6th Cir. 1991).

Problem 2: Searching for Answers

Lydia is an eighth grade student at the middle school. On the way to school, she overhears two other eighth grade students on the bus talking about the final exam in their science class that day, and how they downloaded all the test answers from a website that is run by a former student at the school. Upon arriving at school, Lydia goes to the principal's office and tells her what she heard. The principal has the two students (both are boys) come into her office and questions them about the answer sheet. Both deny having the answers or knowing anything about it. The principal has the students empty their backpacks and their pockets, but does not find anything. She has the students roll up their sleeves so she can see if they wrote answers on their clothes, hands, or arms. No luck. She then calls in Mr. Peterson, the assistant principal, and tells him what is happening and that the boys need to be "searched further." She leaves the room. Mr. Peterson tells the boys to take off all their clothes except their underwear and to hop up and down. The boys complain, but they are told that they will be suspended from school if they do not comply, so they comply.

Does the search violate the Fourth Amendment? Does your answer depend on the result of the search? For example, does it matter if the answer sheet falls to the ground when the boys start hopping up and down, versus the search not producing any information?

Problem Materials

✓ *Safford Unified Sch. Dist. #1 v. Redding*, 557 U.S. 364 (2009)

Safford Unified Sch. Dist. #1 v. Redding

557 U.S. 364 (2009)

The Supreme Court rules that the strip search of a 13-year-old student for prescription strength Ibuprofen is unconstitutional.

Justice Souter delivered the opinion of the Court, in which Roberts, C.J., and Scalia, Kennedy, Breyer, and Alito, JJ., joined, and in which Stevens and Ginsburg, JJ., joined as to Parts I-III.

The issue here is whether a 13-year-old student's Fourth Amendment right was violated when she was subjected to a search of her bra and underpants by school officials acting on reasonable suspicion that she had brought forbidden prescription and over-the-counter drugs to school. Because there were no reasons to suspect the drugs presented a danger or were concealed in her underwear, we hold that the search did violate the Constitution, but because there is reason to question the clarity with which the right was established, the official who ordered the unconstitutional search is entitled to qualified immunity from liability

The events immediately prior to the search in question began in 13-year-old Savana Redding's math class at Safford Middle School one October day in 2003. The assistant principal of the school, Kerry Wilson, came into the room and asked

Savana to go to his office. There, he showed her a day planner, unzipped and open flat on his desk, in which there were several knives, lighters, a permanent marker, and a cigarette. Wilson asked Savana whether the planner was hers; she said it was, but that a few days before she had lent it to her friend, Marissa Glines. Savana stated that none of the items in the planner belonged to her.

Wilson then showed Savana four white prescription-strength ibuprofen 400-mg pills, and one over-the-counter blue naproxen 200-mg pill, all used for pain and inflammation but banned under school rules without advance permission. He asked Savana if she knew anything about the pills. Savana answered that she did not. Wilson then told Savana that he had received a report that she was giving these pills to fellow students; Savana denied it and agreed to let Wilson search her belongings. Helen Romero, an administrative assistant, came into the office, and together with Wilson they searched Savana's backpack, finding nothing.

At that point, Wilson instructed Romero to take Savana to the school nurse's office to search her clothes for pills. Romero and the nurse, Peggy Schwallier, asked Savana to remove her jacket, socks, and shoes, leaving her in stretch pants and a T-shirt (both without pockets), which she was then asked to remove. Finally, Savana was told to pull her bra out and to the side and shake it, and to pull out the elastic on her underpants, thus exposing her breasts and pelvic area to some degree. No pills were found.

. . . .

The Fourth Amendment "right of the people to be secure in their persons . . . against unreasonable searches and seizures" generally requires a law enforcement officer to have probable cause for conducting a search. "Probable cause exists where 'the facts and circumstances within [an officer's] knowledge and of which [he] had reasonably trustworthy information [are] sufficient in themselves to warrant a man of reasonable caution in the belief that' an offense has been or is being committed," and that evidence bearing on that offense will be found in the place to be searched.

In *T.L.O.*, we recognized that the school setting "requires some modification of the level of suspicion of illicit activity needed to justify a search," and held that for searches by school officials "a careful balancing of governmental and private interests suggests that the public interest is best served by a Fourth Amendment standard of reasonableness that stops short of probable cause." We have thus applied a standard of reasonable suspicion to determine the legality of a school administrator's search of a student, and have held that a school search "will be permissible in its scope when the measures adopted are reasonably related to the objectives of the search and not excessively intrusive in light of the age and sex of the student and the nature of the infraction." . . .

Perhaps the best that can be said generally about the required knowledge component of probable cause for a law enforcement officer's evidence search is that it raise a "fair probability," or a "substantial chance," of discovering evidence of criminal activity. The lesser standard for school searches could as readily be described as a moderate chance of finding evidence of wrongdoing.

In this case, the school's policies strictly prohibit the nonmedical use, possession, or sale of any drug on school grounds, including "'[a]ny prescription or over-the-counter drug, except those for which permission to use in school has been granted pursuant to Board policy.'" A week before Savana was searched, another student, Jordan Romero (no relation of the school's administrative assistant), told the principal and Assistant Principal Wilson that "certain students were bringing drugs and weapons on campus," and that he had been sick after taking some pills that "he got from a classmate." On the morning of October 8, the same boy handed Wilson a white pill that he said Marissa Glines had given him. He told Wilson that students were planning to take the pills at lunch.

Wilson learned from Peggy Schwallier, the school nurse, that the pill was Ibuprofen 400 mg, available only by prescription. Wilson then called Marissa out of class. Outside the classroom, Marissa's teacher handed Wilson the day planner, found within Marissa's reach, containing various contraband items. Wilson escorted Marissa back to his office.

In the presence of Helen Romero, Wilson requested Marissa to turn out her pockets and open her wallet. Marissa produced a blue pill, several white ones, and a razor blade. Wilson asked where the blue pill came from, and Marissa answered, "'I guess it slipped in when she gave me the IBU 400s.'" When Wilson asked whom she meant, Marissa replied, "'Savana Redding.'" *Ibid.* Wilson then enquired about the day planner and its contents; Marissa denied knowing anything about them. Wilson did not ask Marissa any follow-up questions to determine whether there was any likelihood that Savana presently had pills: neither asking when Marissa received the pills from Savana nor where Savana might be hiding them.

Schwallier did not immediately recognize the blue pill, but information provided through a poison control hotline indicated that the pill was a 200-mg dose of an anti-inflammatory drug, generically called naproxen, available over the counter. At Wilson's direction, Marissa was then subjected to a search of her bra and underpants by Romero and Schwallier, as Savana was later on. The search revealed no additional pills.

It was at this juncture that Wilson called Savana into his office and showed her the day planner. Their conversation established that Savana and Marissa were on friendly terms: while she denied knowledge of the contraband, Savana admitted that the day planner was hers and that she had lent it to Marissa. Wilson had other reports of their friendship from staff members, who had identified Savana and Marissa as part of an unusually rowdy group at the school's opening dance in August, during which alcohol and cigarettes were found in the girls' bathroom. Wilson had reason to connect the girls with this contraband, for Wilson knew that Jordan Romero had told the principal that before the dance, he had been at a party at Savana's house where alcohol was served. Marissa's statement that the pills came from Savana was thus sufficiently plausible to warrant suspicion that Savana was involved in pill distribution.

This suspicion of Wilson's was enough to justify a search of Savana's backpack and outer clothing. If a student is reasonably suspected of giving out contraband pills, she is reasonably suspected of carrying them on her person and in the carryall that has become an item of student uniform in most places today. If Wilson's reasonable suspicion of pill distribution were not understood to support searches of outer clothes and backpack, it would not justify any search worth making. And the look into Savana's bag, in her presence and in the relative privacy of Wilson's office, was not excessively intrusive, any more than Romero's subsequent search of her outer clothing.[2]

Here it is that the parties part company, with Savana's claim that extending the search at Wilson's behest to the point of making her pull out her underwear was constitutionally unreasonable. The exact label for this final step in the intrusion is not important, though strip search is a fair way to speak of it. Romero and Schwallier directed Savana to remove her clothes down to her underwear, and then "pull out" her bra and the elastic band on her underpants. Although Romero and Schwallier stated that they did not see anything when Savana followed their instructions, we would not define strip search and its Fourth Amendment consequences in a way that would guarantee litigation about who was looking and how much was seen. The very fact of Savana's pulling her underwear away from her body in the presence of the two officials who were able to see her necessarily exposed her breasts and pelvic area to some degree, and both subjective and reasonable societal expectations of personal privacy support the treatment of such a search as categorically distinct, requiring distinct elements of justification on the part of school authorities for going beyond a search of outer clothing and belongings.

Savana's subjective expectation of privacy against such a search is inherent in her account of it as embarrassing, frightening, and humiliating. The reasonableness of her expectation (required by the Fourth Amendment standard) is indicated by the consistent experiences of other young people similarly searched, whose adolescent vulnerability intensifies the patent intrusiveness of the exposure. The common reaction of these adolescents simply registers the obviously different meaning of a search exposing the body from the experience of nakedness or near undress in other school circumstances. Changing for gym is getting ready for play; exposing for a search is responding to an accusation reserved for suspected wrongdoers and fairly understood as so degrading that a number of communities have decided that strip

2. [FN 3] There is no question here that justification for the school officials' search was required in accordance with the *T.L.O.* standard of reasonable suspicion, for it is common ground that Savana had a reasonable expectation of privacy covering the personal things she chose to carry in her backpack, and that Wilson's decision to look through it was a "search" within the meaning of the Fourth Amendment.

searches in schools are never reasonable and have banned them no matter what the facts may be.

The indignity of the search does not, of course, outlaw it, but it does implicate the rule of reasonableness as stated in *T.L.O.*, that "the search as actually conducted [be] reasonably related in scope to the circumstances which justified the interference in the first place." The scope will be permissible, that is, when it is "not excessively intrusive in light of the age and sex of the student and the nature of the infraction."

Here, the content of the suspicion failed to match the degree of intrusion. Wilson knew beforehand that the pills were prescription-strength ibuprofen and over-the-counter naproxen, common pain relievers equivalent to two Advil, or one Aleve. He must have been aware of the nature and limited threat of the specific drugs he was searching for, and while just about anything can be taken in quantities that will do real harm, Wilson had no reason to suspect that large amounts of the drugs were being passed around, or that individual students were receiving great numbers of pills.

Nor could Wilson have suspected that Savana was hiding common painkillers in her underwear. Petitioners suggest, as a truth universally acknowledged, that "students . . . hid[e] contraband in or under their clothing," Reply Brief for Petitioners 8, and cite a smattering of cases of students with contraband in their underwear, *id.*, at 8-9. But when the categorically extreme intrusiveness of a search down to the body of an adolescent requires some justification in suspected facts, general background possibilities fall short; a reasonable search that extensive calls for suspicion that it will pay off. But nondangerous school contraband does not raise the specter of stashes in intimate places, and there is no evidence in the record of any general practice among Safford Middle School students of hiding that sort of thing in underwear; neither Jordan nor Marissa suggested to Wilson that Savana was doing that, and the preceding search of Marissa that Wilson ordered yielded nothing. Wilson never even determined when Marissa had received the pills from Savana; if it had been a few days before, that would weigh heavily against any reasonable conclusion that Savana presently had the pills on her person, much less in her underwear.

In sum, what was missing from the suspected facts that pointed to Savana was any indication of danger to the students from the power of the drugs or their quantity, and any reason to suppose that Savana was carrying pills in her underwear. We think that the combination of these deficiencies was fatal to finding the search reasonable.

In so holding, we mean to cast no ill reflection on the assistant principal, for the record raises no doubt that his motive throughout was to eliminate drugs from his school and protect students from what Jordan Romero had gone through. Parents are known to overreact to protect their children from danger, and a school official with responsibility for safety may tend to do the same. The difference is that the Fourth Amendment places limits on the official, even with the high degree of deference that courts must pay to the educator's professional judgment.

We do mean, though, to make it clear that the *T.L.O.* concern to limit a school search to reasonable scope requires the support of reasonable suspicion of danger or of resort to underwear for hiding evidence of wrongdoing before a search can reasonably make the quantum leap from outer clothes and backpacks to exposure of intimate parts. The meaning of such a search, and the degradation its subject may reasonably feel, place a search that intrusive in a category of its own demanding its own specific suspicions.

A school official searching a student is "entitled to qualified immunity where clearly established law does not show that the search violated the Fourth Amendment." To be established clearly, however, there is no need that "the very action in question [have] previously been held unlawful." The unconstitutionality of outrageous conduct obviously will be unconstitutional, this being the reason, as Judge Posner has said, that "[t]he easiest cases don't even arise." *K.H. v. Morgan*, 914 F.2d 846, 851 (7th Cir. 1990). But even as to action less than an outrage, "officials can still be on notice that their conduct violates established law . . . in novel factual circumstances." *Hope v. Pelzer*, 536 U.S. 730, 741 (2002).

T.L.O. directed school officials to limit the intrusiveness of a search, "in light of the age and sex of the student and the nature of the infraction," and as we have just said at some length, the intrusiveness of the strip search here cannot be seen as justifiably related to the circumstances. But we realize that the lower courts have reached divergent conclusions regarding how the *T.L.O.* standard applies to such searches.

A number of judges have read *T.L.O.* as the en banc minority of the Ninth Circuit did here. The Sixth Circuit upheld a strip search of a high school student for a drug, without any suspicion that drugs were hidden next to her body. *Williams v. Ellington*, 936 F.2d 881, 882–883, 887 (1991). And other courts considering qualified immunity for strip searches have read *T.L.O.* as "a series of abstractions, on the one hand, and a declaration of seeming deference to the judgments of school officials, on the other," *Jenkins v. Talladega City Bd. of Ed.*, 115 F.3d 821, 828 (11th Cir. 1997) (en banc), which made it impossible "to establish clearly the contours of a Fourth Amendment right . . . [in] the wide variety of possible school settings different from those involved in *T.L.O.*" itself. *Ibid. See also Thomas v. Roberts*, 323 F.3d 950 (11th Cir. 2003) (granting qualified immunity to a teacher and police officer who conducted a group strip search of a fifth grade class when looking for a missing $26).

We think these differences of opinion from our own are substantial enough to require immunity for the school officials in this case. We would not suggest that entitlement to qualified immunity is the guaranteed product of disuniform views of the law in the other federal, or state, courts, and the fact that a single judge, or even a group of judges, disagrees about the contours of a right does not automatically render the law unclear if we have been clear. That said, however, the cases viewing school strip searches differently from the way we see them are numerous enough, with well-reasoned majority and dissenting opinions, to counsel doubt that we were sufficiently clear in the prior statement of law. We conclude that qualified immunity is warranted.

The strip search of Savana Redding was unreasonable and a violation of the Fourth Amendment, but petitioners Wilson, Romero, and Schwallier are nevertheless protected from liability through qualified immunity. Our conclusions here do not resolve, however, the question of the liability of petitioner Safford Unified School District #1 under *Monell v. Department of Soc. Servs.*, 436 U.S. 658, 694 (1978), a claim the Ninth Circuit did not address. The judgment of the Ninth Circuit is therefore affirmed in part and reversed in part, and this case is remanded for consideration of the *Monell* claim.

It is so ordered.

JUSTICE THOMAS, concurring in the judgment in part and dissenting in part.

I agree with the Court that the judgment against the school officials with respect to qualified immunity should be reversed. Unlike the majority, however, I would hold that the search of Savana Redding did not violate the Fourth Amendment. The majority imposes a vague and amorphous standard on school administrators. It also grants judges sweeping authority to second-guess the measures that these officials take to maintain discipline in their schools and ensure the health and safety of the students in their charge. This deep intrusion into the administration of public schools exemplifies why the Court should return to the common-law doctrine of *in loco parentis* under which "the judiciary was reluctant to interfere in the routine business of school administration, allowing schools and teachers to set and enforce rules and to maintain order." *Morse v. Frederic* k, 551 U.S. 393, 414 (2007) (THOMAS, J., concurring). But even under the prevailing Fourth Amendment test established by *New Jersey v. T.L.O.*, 469 U.S. 325 (1985), all petitioners, including the school district, are entitled to judgment as a matter of law in their favor.

Post Problem Discussion

1. In *Redding*, the Court notes that the strip search was not warranted to find the Ibuprofen pills. Would the search have been warranted if the school was looking for LSD? Guns? Are there any circumstances that would justify a strip search under the Supreme Court decision?

2. How does the fact that the principal and assistant principal in our problem were looking for answers to a final exam influence your decision? Would your answer be different if the item were different (say answers to the SAT, or a note threatening to burn down the school)?

3. In *Redding*, the Court discusses the § 1983 claim and qualified immunity. These topics are covered in more detail in Chapter 6, Section 6.06. If you find that the search in our problem violates the Fourth Amendment, would the principal and assistant principal be entitled to qualified immunity? Why or why not?

4. What do you think about Justice Thomas' opinion? What are the pros and cons to his approach for schools and school administrators? For students?

5. Some states have statutes that prohibit strip searching students. Iowa has such a statute. It provides that:

> A school official shall not conduct a search which involves:
>
> a. A strip search.
>
> b. A body cavity search.
>
> c. The use of a drug sniffing animal to search a student's body.
>
> d. The search of a student by a school official not of the same sex as the student.

Iowa Code § 808A.2. How does your state address the issue?

§ 10.04 School-Related Police Searches

Police officers and school administrators often have a good working relationship. School officials call upon police officers to come on to school grounds for various reasons related to school safety. Information is often exchanged about the school in general and individual students in particular. Police officers may well be involved in searching students, either on their own initiative, or at the request of, or in the presence of, school officials.

In general, the rule is that police officers are subject to the probable cause standard when they search a student, rather than the lesser reasonableness standard announced in *T.L.O.* In *T.L.O.*, the Supreme Court specifically declined to rule on "the question of the appropriate standard for assessing the legality of searches conducted by school officials in conjunction with or at the behest of law enforcement agencies." *T.L.O.*, 469 U.S. at 342 n.7. However, some schools have school resource officers ("SROs"), who spend most of their time on campus, and are paid (in part or in full) by the school.

Questions arise about which standard should apply to SROs given their continuous presence on school grounds, and rather unique relationship with the school. The search standard that applies to SROs has been the subject of litigation and the decisions vary. A related topic is the standard that should apply when school officials search students while working with the police in an investigation and provide the fruits of their efforts to the police.

Problem 3: Standards for Police Searches at School

Consider the following fact patterns. For each decide whether the *T.L.O.* or probable cause standard applies and whether the standard is met.

Fact Pattern #1

The Palm City School District employs an SRO at its high school. The SRO is a police officer with the city police department, but he spends ninety percent of his time at the school, and ninety percent of his salary is paid by the school. In investigating a stolen vehicle, the police department uncovered evidence that leads them to believe that a student at the high school may be involved. The department contacts the SRO, who tells the principal. The principal calls the student into her office, and the SRO asks the student questions about the night the vehicle was stolen. The police officer then asks the student to empty his pockets to see if the student has any items from the stolen vehicle. Nothing turns up. The officer then informs the student that blood and broken glass were found at the scene of the crime and asks the student to take off his jacket and roll up his sleeves. The student does so and reveals cuts on his knuckles and a two-inch cut on his right arm that the student says he received "goofing around with his friends." The officer then asks the student to submit a blood sample for DNA testing. The student asks, "Do I have to?" The officer replies, "If you want to clear yourself from this situation, you do." The student agrees and goes with the officer to the school nurse who draws some blood for the DNA test.

Fact Pattern #2

A student anonymously calls the school secretary and says that another student named Zoe has a knife in her purse. The secretary tells the principal and the principal radios the school's SRO, who goes to Zoe's class, removes her from class and searches her purse, uncovering a bag of marijuana, but no knife. Zoe is expelled from school for drug possession.

Fact Pattern #3

Two students tell a principal they saw another student named Armando with folded pieces of tinfoil that they believe contain a drug called Ecstasy. The principal approaches Armando, takes him to her office, searches him, and finds the Ecstasy. Armando tells the principal that he bought the drugs from Dana the previous day in the student parking lot. The principal calls the police and tells them what occurred. The police tell her that they are on the way over and that she should call Dana into her office to question him and to search him for drugs. The principal asks if the police officer would like to do the search, and the officer replies that they likely would not have probable cause to search Dana given that the drug sale occurred yesterday.

The principal calls Dana into her office. She searches him and finds a plastic baggie with dozens of tin foil pieces. When the police arrive, the principal turns over the Ecstasy she found on Armando and the plastic baggie she found on Dana. Both are arrested and taken to the police station.

Fact Pattern #4

Principal Adams finds an eleventh grade student named Drew trying to leave campus in violation of school policy. The principal sees other students, but she is not able to catch them. The principal brings Drew into the office and tells him to wait in the office until he returns. He then tells Drew to hand over his cell phone because he wants to be sure that Drew is not sitting in the office texting his friends to watch out for the principal. Drew complies.

The principal then gives the cell phone to the SRO who goes through all of the text messages that were sent and received from the phone for the past two weeks. The text messages include information about a sexual encounter that Drew had with his girlfriend who is under the age of 16. The SRO goes into the principal's office and arrests Drew for statutory rape.

Problem Materials

✓ *State v. Alaniz*, 815 N.W.2d 234 (N.D. 2012)

✓ *State v. Heirtzler*, 789 A.2d 634 (N.H. 2001)

State v. Alaniz

815 N.W.2d 234 (N.D. 2012)

The court discusses the various standards that apply to searches at school when SROs are involved

VandeWalle, Chief Justice.

Christian Antonio Alaniz, Jr., appealed from an order deferring imposition of sentence entered after he conditionally pled guilty to possession of a controlled substance and possession of drug paraphernalia. Alaniz argues the district court erred in denying his motion to suppress evidence because there was not probable cause to justify the search of his person and the exception to the probable cause requirement for warrantless searches by school officials did not apply. We affirm.

I

Troy Vanyo is a police officer with the Grand Forks Police Department and is assigned to work as a school resource officer at a high school in Grand Forks. Vanyo testified he works full time at the high school during the school year and the school district pays $42,000 per year to the police department to help fund three school resource officers.

On February 17, 2011, Vanyo had received information about possible drug use involving students in an area approximately a block and a half from the high school. Vanyo testified that he and Ryan Rupert, a school security guard, decided to pay extra attention to the area. Rupert patrolled the area on foot and saw two students acting suspiciously. One of the students was later identified as Alaniz. Rupert notified Vanyo about his observations and Vanyo drove in his patrol car to the area where Rupert saw the students. Vanyo saw the two students Rupert had contacted him about and Rupert advised Vanyo the students were attempting to evade Rupert. The students walked to a town square area and Vanyo followed in his patrol car. Vanyo testified the students were seated when they saw him, stood up, and quickly walked toward a stage area in the town square. Vanyo told Rupert of the students' location and Rupert said he would investigate further. Vanyo returned to the high school and Rupert advised Vanyo that he was behind the stage area and he smelled something "funny."

Vanyo waited for the students to return to the high school, and he notified the associate principal when the first student returned. Later, Vanyo observed Alaniz waiting to talk to the attendance secretary and he informed the school principal that Alaniz was the other individual he observed in the town square and suspected was involved in drug activity. The principal took Alaniz into a detention room and Vanyo followed them. Vanyo testified the principal questioned Alaniz, Vanyo testified he told Alaniz something like "if you have anything on you, you need to lay it on the table now," and Alaniz emptied his pockets, which contained a glass pipe and synthetic marijuana. Vanyo arrested Alaniz and transported him to the Grand Forks County Correctional Center. Vanyo testified the questioning and arrest lasted approximately five minutes.

Alaniz was charged with possession of a controlled substance, a class C felony, and possession of drug paraphernalia, a class C felony. Alaniz moved to suppress the evidence, arguing the police failed to advise him of his rights under *Miranda v. Arizona*, 384 U.S. 436, 86, there was not probable cause justifying the search of his person, and the exception to the probable cause requirement for searches by school officials did not apply. The district court denied Vanyo's motion, ruling the reasonableness standard for searches by school officials applied and the search was reasonable. Alaniz entered a conditional guilty plea under N.D.R.Crim.P. 11(a)(2) and reserved his right to appeal the court's denial of his suppression motion.

II

Alaniz argues the district court erred as a matter of law in finding that the school official exception to the probable cause requirement for warrantless searches applies because the investigation occurred off of school property by a police officer in his squad car, Vanyo was acting as a city police officer and not a school official, and the search was conducted at the behest of the police investigation. Alaniz contends there was not probable cause justifying the search and it violated his Fourth Amendment right to be free from unreasonable searches and seizures.

Under the Fourth Amendment of the United States Constitution, an individual has a right to be free from unreasonable searches and seizures. In *New Jersey v. T.L.O.*, 469 U.S. 325, the United States Supreme Court held the Fourth Amendment applies to searches conducted by school authorities but also held probable cause was not necessary to support the search and a lower level of reasonableness was required to justify searches by school officials.

. . . .

Generally, a search by a teacher or other school official is justified at its inception "when there are reasonable grounds for suspecting that the search will turn up evidence that the student has violated or is violating either the law or the rules of the school." In *Safford Unified School Dist. No. 1 v. Redding*, 557 U.S. 364, the Court further elaborated on what it meant by reasonable grounds . . . .

Perhaps the best that can be said generally about the required knowledge component of probable cause for a law enforcement officer's evidence search is that it raise a "fair probability" or a "substantial chance" of discovering evidence of criminal activity. The lesser standard for school searches could as readily be described as a moderate chance of finding evidence of wrongdoing.

However, the holding in *T.L.O.* was limited to searches conducted by school authorities acting alone and on their own authority. The Court stated, "[t]his case does not present the question of the appropriate standard for assessing the legality of searches conducted by school officials in conjunction with or at the behest of law enforcement agencies, and we express no opinion on that question." *T.L.O.*, 469 U.S. at 342 n.7.

Other courts have addressed this issue and have held there are three categories of school searches based on the amount of police involvement: (1) when school officials initiate the search or police involvement is minimal, the reasonableness standard applies; (2) when the search involves school resource officers acting on their own initiative or at the direction of other school officials to further educationally related goals, the reasonableness standard applies; and (3) when "outside" police officers initiate the search, warrant and probable cause requirements apply. . . .

In determining how much police involvement occurred and which standard applies, courts have considered various factors, including whether the officer was in uniform, whether the officer has an office on the school campus, how much time the officer is at the school each day, whether the officer is employed by the school system or an independent law enforcement agency, what the officer's duties are at the school, who initiated the investigation, who conducted the search, whether other school officials were involved, and the officer's purpose in conducting the search. We agree with the rationale used by these courts to determine which standard should apply to school searches.

. . . .

Cases involving school searches are fact specific, and under the circumstances of this case, the relevant facts support application of the reasonableness standard. Vanyo did not initiate the investigation; rather, he was contacted by Rupert after Rupert saw two students acting suspiciously. Vanyo is a school resource officer, the school district pays the police department to fund the resource officer program, and Vanyo is assigned to the school full time during the school year. One of the goals of the resource officer program is to provide a clean, safe, and secure learning environment by providing school security and preventing criminal acts on the school campus. After Vanyo returned to the school, he saw Alaniz standing in line to talk to the attendance secretary, he identified Alaniz as one of the students he observed acting suspiciously, and he informed the principal about what he saw and let the principal decide how to handle the situation. The principal removed Alaniz from the line and questioned him in the detention room. Vanyo was not involved in questioning Alaniz, except for telling Alaniz he should put anything he had on his person on the table.

In other cases with similar facts, courts have held the reasonableness standard applies. In *D.L.D.*, 694 S.E.2d at 398, an officer assigned to the high school was reviewing surveillance video footage with the assistant principal when they saw two students enter a bathroom while another student stood outside the entrance. The officer had made "numerous arrests" for controlled substances in that bathroom. The principal told the officer they should investigate, the students were exiting the bathroom when they approached, but one of the students went back into the bathroom when he saw the officer and principal. The officer followed the student into the bathroom and saw him put something in his pants. The officer notified the principal about what he saw and the principal told the officer they needed to check it out. The officer frisked the student and found marijuana inside a container. The court held the reasonableness standard applied because the facts show the officer was working in conjunction with and at the direction of the principal to maintain a safe and educational environment at the school.

Vanyo, like the officer in *D.L.D.*, was a school resource officer, who was working with other school officials to investigate violations of school rules and the law to maintain a safe and educational environment. Vanyo also advised the principal of the situation and let the principal decide what to do. The facts in this case are similar to those in *D.L.D.*, and support application of the reasonableness standard.

However, Alaniz argues this case is similar to *F.P. v. State*, 528 So.2d 1253, 1255 (Fla. Dist. Ct. App. 1988), where the court held the school exception did not apply because the search was carried out at the behest of police. In *F.P.*, a school resource officer was advised by a police investigator that there was evidence F.P. stole a vehicle and had the keys in his possession. The resource officer saw F.P. in school and took him to her office, where F.P. eventually gave her the keys to the vehicle. The facts in this case are different from the facts in *F.P.* The resource officer in *F.P.* was acting at the request of the outside police officer and other school officials were not involved. Here, Vanyo was acting based on information from school officials, there was no involvement from outside police officers, and the school principal questioned Alaniz and decided how to handle the situation. Under the facts and circumstances of this case, we conclude the reasonableness standard applies.

To determine whether a search was reasonable, we must consider whether the search was justified at its inception and whether the search was reasonably related in scope to the circumstances that justified the interference in the first place. *T.L.O.* A search is justified at its inception when there is a moderate chance the search will turn up evidence the student has violated or is violating the law or school rules. *Safford*. The search is permissible in scope when the "measures adopted are reasonably related to the objectives of the search and not excessively intrusive in light of the age and sex of the student and the nature of the infraction." *T.L.O.*

Here, Rupert observed two students in an area where drug activity had been reported and the two students acted suspiciously, attempted to evade him, and walked to another location. Vanyo also observed the students and the students walked away when they saw him in his patrol vehicle. Rupert went to the location where Vanyo had observed the students and Rupert smelled a "funny" odor. The students returned to the school shortly thereafter. Based on these facts, the search was justified at its inception because there was a moderate chance the search would turn up evidence Alaniz was violating the law or school rules by possessing controlled substances.

The search also was not excessively intrusive in light of Alaniz's age, gender, and nature of the suspicion. Alaniz was eighteen years old. He was not physically searched. Alaniz emptied his pockets after Vanyo told him he should put anything he had on the table. We conclude the search was reasonable and the district court did not err in denying Alaniz's motion to suppress.

State v. Heirtzler

789 A.2d 634 (N.H. 2001)

The court finds that a school principal was acting as an agent of the police, so the probable cause and warrant requirements apply.

Broderick, J.

The defendant, Joseph Heirtzler, was charged with possession and distribution of a controlled drug. The State appeals an order of the Superior Court granting his motion to suppress evidence obtained as a result of an interrogation and search conducted by a school official. We affirm.

The record supports the following facts. Londonderry Police Officer Michael Bennette was assigned as the school resource officer for Londonderry High School (school). One reason for Bennette's assignment was the Londonderry Police Department's (department) perception that the school was investigating criminal matters, which should have been reported to and handled by the department. As the school resource officer, Bennette remained under the direct control and supervision of the department, and his job essentially was to investigate criminal activity on school grounds. The department's policy was to investigate reports of criminal activity at the school in the same manner as other criminal complaints.

Prior to assuming his assignment at the school, Bennette met with school officials to discuss the parameters of his job. He made clear that cases were to be reported and prosecuted, not "whitewashed" by school officials. Bennette told school officials to contact him when cases involved criminal activity or required criminal investigation. They agreed, but asserted that administrative and disciplinary matters involving students fell within the sole authority and control of the school. According to Bennette, the school principal was keenly aware of the difference between administrative duties and law enforcement within the school.

Because of the number of searches conducted at the school under its search policy, Bennette could not handle the investigation of every potential criminal matter. The school, therefore, agreed to investigate the less serious potential criminal matters, including searches.... Bennette's testimony regarding this agreement was as follows:

> Q: Drug investigation. Do you recall me asking you: "Is it fair to say that, in your mind at least, you delegated some of the responsibility of investigating these cases to the school administration?" Your answer is, "Yeah," right?
>
> A: Yes.

This delegation of responsibility, according to Bennette, would occur at his direction after he assessed the information brought to his attention to determine "what level it [rose] to." Bennette stated at his deposition that if the safety level and threat were high, such as in cases involving a report that a student possessed a knife or gun, he would conduct the investigation and any necessary search. If the information involved drugs, however, he would pass it along to school officials for action. Essentially, if Bennette lacked probable cause to pursue a less serious criminal matter and perhaps make an arrest, he would deem it a school issue and turn the information over to school officials. Once he turned the information over, he had no further involvement unless the school requested it. He testified, however, that when officials seized contraband from a student they would contact him.

Bennette conceded that a "silent understanding" existed between him and school officials that passing information to the school when he could not act was a technique used to gather evidence otherwise inaccessible to him due to constitutional restraints. . . .

At the time of his arrest for possession and distribution of a controlled drug, the defendant was a student at the school. During science class, his teacher observed him pass what appeared to be a folded piece of tinfoil to another student. The student removed something from the tinfoil, put it in a piece of cellophane and passed the folded tinfoil back to the defendant. After class ended, the teacher contacted Bennette and told him what she had observed. Bennette testified that although he may have had articulable suspicion to investigate further, he ultimately decided that he did not have enough information to warrant further investigation. Instead, Bennette passed the information to O'Neill for action.

After receiving the information from Bennette, O'Neill told him that the matter was a school administrative issue. O'Neill testified that although the situation could involve drugs or illegal substances, since it did not involve criminal activity of a more serious nature, it was the school's administrative duty to act upon the information. O'Neill and another assistant principal, Robert Shaps, called the defendant to the office, questioned him and asked if they could search him. The defendant complied with the search request and a piece of paper wrapped in tinfoil was found in his cigarette pack. After further questioning, the defendant stated that the piece of paper might be LSD. Once the search produced the potential presence of an illegal drug, O'Neill contacted Bennette and turned the matter over to him.

In his motion to suppress, the defendant argued that O'Neill and Shaps were acting as agents of the police and thus their interrogation and search had to conform with the procedural safeguards afforded criminal suspects when the State acts.

Alternatively, the defendant argued that even if O'Neill and Shaps were not acting as agents of the State, they lacked reasonable grounds to interrogate and search him.

. . . .

A warrantless search or seizure is presumptively illegal and the prosecution has the burden of establishing that it falls within a recognized exception to the warrant requirement. The acquisition of evidence by an individual acting as an agent of the police must be reviewed by the same constitutional standards that govern law enforcement officials. This "agency rule" prevents the police from having a private individual conduct a search or seizure that would be unlawful if performed by the police themselves. Because we uphold the trial court's suppression order under the State Constitution, we need not undertake a separate federal constitutional analysis and look to federal caselaw for guidance only.

An agency relationship requires "proof of some affirmative action by a police officer or other governmental official that preceded the interrogation [of the defendant, which] can reasonably be seen to have induced the third party to conduct the interrogation that took place." In *Bruneau*, we explained that two varieties of governmental action would qualify to prove the existence of an agency relationship. First, an agreement between a private party and the government that the private party should act to obtain evidence from a defendant will suffice as affirmative action and inducement. . . .

Whether formal or informal, the agreement must "evince an understanding that the third party will be acting on the government's behalf or for the government's benefit." Second, prior governmental requests for help may be an affirmative action inducing a third party to act. In both "varieties," the government will have acted in a way that may be understood to have formed an inducement for a third party to engage in obtaining evidence for the government's use or benefit.

The fundamental concern of the agency rule is to curb unconstitutional activity by government; it is meant to prevent the government from circumventing the rights of a defendant by securing private parties to do what it cannot. . . .

A finding of agency relies upon the unique position of the fact-finder, who assesses first-hand all of the verbal and nonverbal aspects of the evidence presented. The determination of whether, based upon the underlying facts, an agency relationship exists requires the application of law, however, and we must therefore consider whether this part of the agency analysis calls for *de novo* review. As the issue of whether an agency relationship exists is essentially fact-driven, a deferential standard of review is appropriate. Therefore, whether or not we would have made a similar finding, we will uphold a trial court's finding of an agency relationship unless it is unsupported by the record or clearly erroneous.

We begin by examining the scope of school officials' administrative duties. School officials are "responsible for administration and discipline within the school and must regularly conduct inquiries concerning both violations of school rules and violations of law." Their administrative duties, however, do not include enforcing the law or investigating criminal matters. School officials are not law enforcement officers and they should not be charged with knowing the intricacies of constitutional criminal procedure.

Because they are not law enforcement officers, when school officials search for contraband in order to foster a safe and healthy educational environment, they are afforded greater flexibility than if a law enforcement officer performed the same search. If school officials agree to take on the mantle of criminal investigation and enforcement, however, they assume an understanding of constitutional criminal law equal to that of a law enforcement officer. In such circumstances, even if school officials *claim* their actions fall within the ambit of their administrative authority, they should be charged with abiding by the constitutional protections required in criminal investigations. In sum, the role of school officials is to foster a safe and healthy educational environment. In order to do so, it is necessary that they be afforded some flexibility to swiftly resolve potential problems affecting this environment. However, enforcing the law or investigating criminal matters is outside the scope of a school official's administrative authority.

The presence of law enforcement personnel within schools requires school officials to establish a working relationship with them. It is here that school officials should be vigilant not to assume responsibilities beyond the scope of their administrative authority....

In this case, the trial court concluded that [Bennette's] decision to report the incident was an affirmative action that can reasonably be seen to have induced O'Neill and Shaps to interrogate and search the defendant. The evidence also supports a finding that there was a prior agreement between [the school] and the [department]. In fact, [Bennette] testified . . . to such prior agreement when he conceded that it was his job to report suspicious criminal activity to the school administrators when he could not take action himself.

The record supports the trial court's conclusion that a prior agreement existed between the department and school officials for purposes of establishing that an agency relationship existed. Bennette testified that he delegated the responsibility of investigating less serious, potential criminal matters—drug cases—to school officials, and O'Neill confirmed that this was a "fair" characterization of the arrangement between the school and the department. Thus, while Bennette was responsible for investigating more serious crimes, such as possession of a dangerous weapon, the school accepted responsibility for investigating less serious ones. Bennette also conceded that a "silent understanding" existed between him and school officials that passing information to the school when he could not act was a technique used to gather evidence otherwise inaccessible to him due to constitutional restraints. The school, by "a mere wink or nod" or something more concrete, agreed to investigate certain potential criminal matters on the State's behalf or for its benefit.

Recognizing that the trier of fact is in the best position to assess the relationship between law enforcement and school officials under an agency analysis, we conclude that the record also supports the trial court's finding that Bennette's actions induced the school officials to conduct the interrogation and search of the defendant. Accordingly, we find no error with the trial court's order granting the defendant's motion to suppress.

Post Problem Discussion

1. As noted, the role of police officers or SROs in school is evolving, and courts are not uniform in what standards apply to searches of students at school. Some courts have found that the *T.L.O.* standard applies in some situations. Other courts have found that if a police officer performs the search, the probable cause standard applies, regardless of the police officer's relationship with the school, and regardless of the circumstances. *See, e.g., State v. KLM*, 628 S.E.2d. 651 (Ga. Ct. App. 2006). Which approach do you think is most appropriate in the public school environment and why?

2. What are the ramifications of allowing an SRO to be subject to the lower *T.L.O.* standard? Are there any unintended consequences that could occur? If so, what?

3. Fact Pattern #4 is similar to the facts in Problem 1. Did you reach the same conclusion? Why or why not? Did the SRO's involvement make a difference in the outcome? Does the different conduct (drugs in Problem 1, sex in Fact Pattern #4) change anything in the analysis?

4. The court in *Heirtzler* finds that the school officials were acting as agents of the police and, as a result, they must follow the higher probable cause standards that apply to police. How do you think this ruling would affect the way schools and police go about investigating, searching, or interrogating students?

§ 10.05 Random, Suspicionless Searches

T.L.O. is grounded in the idea of individualized suspicion. It is the legal standard for searches where school officials believe a particular student (or group of students) have contraband on their person, in their cars, lockers, etc., or may otherwise be violating school rules, or the law. Two cases that followed *T.L.O.* set a path for more generalized searches, particularly for drugs and weapons, such as sniffing dogs, random locker and car searches, suspicionless drug testing, and metal detectors.

The cases, *Vernonia Sch. Dist. v. Acton* and *Board of Educ. of Independent Sch. Dist. No. 92 v. Earls*, establish a three-part balancing test for assessing the constitutionality of random, suspicionless searches for students at public schools: 1) the students' expectation of privacy, 2) the intrusiveness of the search, and 3) the school's special or significant need for the search. Courts are still determining the parameters of these kinds of searches as they balance these three interests in different situations. Sometimes the facts of a situation can lead to the application of both the *T.L.O.* and the *Vernonia/Earls* standards. The following problem explores some of these issues.

Problem 4: Random Searches at School

Review the following fact patterns. For each, determine if the search is constitutional.

Fact Pattern #1

A high school having trouble with drug use and drug sales on campus decides to have a private company bring in drug sniffing dogs. One school day, the dogs come to campus and sniff each car in the school parking lot, each locker in the school, and each student while sitting in class. If the dog alerts by a car or a locker, the car or locker is searched by school officials. If a dog alerts by a student, the student is asked to empty his or her pockets and remove their socks and shoes. The endeavor results in ten cars and six lockers being searched. Drugs are found in each of them. Twenty-four students are asked to empty their pockets and remove their socks and shoes. Fourteen of them are found to have drugs or drug paraphernalia on them.

Fact Pattern #2

The Lakes Region High School has a policy of randomly searching students in selected classrooms to look for drugs, weapons, cigarettes, and other prohibited contraband. One day during the school year, all of the students in Ms. Doe's classroom are ordered to leave the room after removing everything from their pockets and placing all of their belongings, including their backpacks and purses, on the desks in front of them. While the students wait in the hall outside the classroom, school personnel search the items that the students left behind. They find marijuana in a purse and condoms in a backpack.

Fact Pattern #3

Foundation High School has had issues with students smoking and using drugs and alcohol on campus. All of these activities are prohibited on school grounds. A particular problem for the school is students using drugs and alcohol and smoking in their cars as they come to school and as they are parking in the school lot. Students often throw beer cans in the woods beside the parking lot and throw their cigarettes on the ground to put them out. School officials patrol the lot, but it is too big for them to effectively monitor it. All students who park in the school lot must obtain a parking permit. The school implements a policy that requires all students who obtain a permit to consent to weekly urinalysis testing for drugs, alcohol, and nicotine. Positive results on the test are referred to the school and lead to the school revoking the student's parking permit for one week for the first offense, one month for the second, and permanently for the third.

Fact Pattern #4

The Pressley Area High School had an incident earlier in the school year where a student brought a gun to school. After the incident, the school installed metal detectors in all of the entrances and exits. The school board also directed the school resource officer to walk through the halls in school with a hand-held metal detector throughout the school day to randomly scan students as they walk by him in the hall.

Problem Materials

✓ *Vernonia School District v. Acton*, 515 U.S. 646 (1995)

✓ *Board of Education of Independent School District No. 92 v. Earls*, 536 U.S. 822 (2002)

Vernonia School District v. Acton

515 U.S. 646 (1995)

The Supreme Court upholds random drug-testing of student athletes.

Justice Scalia delivered the opinion of the Court, in which Rehnquist, C.J., and Kennedy, Thomas, Ginsburg, and Breyer, JJ., joined.

The Student Athlete Drug Policy adopted by School District 47J in the town of Vernonia, Oregon, authorizes random urinalysis drug testing of students who participate in the District's school athletics programs. We granted certiorari to decide whether this violates the Fourth and Fourteenth Amendments to the United States Constitution.

....

Drugs had not been a major problem in Vernonia schools. In the mid-to-late 1980's, however, teachers and administrators observed a sharp increase in drug use. Students began to speak out about their attraction to the drug culture, and to boast that there was nothing the school could do about it. Along with more drugs came more disciplinary problems. Between 1988 and 1989 the number of disciplinary referrals in Vernonia schools rose to more than twice the number reported in the early 1980's, and several students were suspended. Students became increasingly rude during class; outbursts of profane language became common.

Not only were student athletes included among the drug users but, as the District Court found, athletes were the leaders of the drug culture. This caused the District's administrators particular concern, since drug use increases the risk of sports-related injury. Expert testimony at the trial confirmed the deleterious effects of drugs on motivation, memory, judgment, reaction, coordination, and performance. The high school football and wrestling coach witnessed a severe sternum injury suffered by a wrestler, and various omissions of safety procedures and misexecutions by football players, all attributable in his belief to the effects of drug use.

Initially, the District responded to the drug problem by offering special classes, speakers, and presentations designed to deter drug use. It even brought in a specially trained dog to detect drugs, but the drug problem persisted. According to the District Court:

> "The administration was at its wits end and . . . a large segment of the student body, particularly those involved in interscholastic athletics, was in a state of rebellion. Disciplinary actions had reached 'epidemic proportions.' The coincidence of an almost three-fold increase in classroom disruptions

> and disciplinary reports along with the staff's direct observations of students using drugs or glamorizing drug and alcohol use led the administration to the inescapable conclusion that the rebellion was being fueled by alcohol and drug abuse as well as the student's misperceptions about the drug culture."

At that point, District officials began considering a drug-testing program....

The Policy applies to all students participating in interscholastic athletics. Students wishing to play sports must sign a form consenting to the testing and must obtain the written consent of their parents. Athletes are tested at the beginning of the season for their sport. In addition, once each week of the season the names of the athletes are placed in a "pool" from which a student, with the supervision of two adults, blindly draws the names of 10% of the athletes for random testing. Those selected are notified and tested that same day, if possible....

The samples are sent to an independent laboratory, which routinely tests them for amphetamines, cocaine, and marijuana. Other drugs, such as LSD, may be screened at the request of the District, but the identity of a particular student does not determine which drugs will be tested. The laboratory's procedures are 99.94% accurate. The District follows strict procedures regarding the chain of custody and access to test results....

If a sample tests positive, a second test is administered as soon as possible to confirm the result. If the second test is negative, no further action is taken. If the second test is positive, the athlete's parents are notified, and the school principal convenes a meeting with the student and his parents, at which the student is given the option of (1) participating for six weeks in an assistance program that includes weekly urinalysis, or (2) suffering suspension from athletics for the remainder of the current season and the next athletic season. The student is then retested prior to the start of the next athletic season for which he or she is eligible. The Policy states that a second offense results in automatic imposition of option (2); a third offense in suspension for the remainder of the current season and the next two athletic seasons.

In the fall of 1991, respondent James Acton, then a seventh grader, signed up to play football at one of the District's grade schools. He was denied participation, however, because he and his parents refused to sign the testing consent forms. The Actons filed suit, seeking declaratory and injunctive relief from enforcement of the Policy on the grounds that it violated the Fourth and Fourteenth Amendments to the United States Constitution and Article I, § 9, of the Oregon Constitution....

As the text of the Fourth Amendment indicates, the ultimate measure of the constitutionality of a governmental search is "reasonableness." At least in a case such as this, where there was no clear practice, either approving or disapproving the type of search at issue, at the time the constitutional provision was enacted, whether a particular search meets the reasonableness standard "'is judged by balancing its intrusion on the individual's Fourth Amendment interests against its promotion of legitimate governmental interests.'" Where a search is undertaken by law enforcement officials to discover evidence of criminal wrongdoing, this Court has said that reasonableness generally requires the obtaining of a judicial warrant, Warrants cannot be issued, of course, without the showing of probable cause required by the Warrant Clause. But a warrant is not required to establish the reasonableness of *all* government searches; and when a warrant is not required (and the Warrant Clause therefore not applicable), probable cause is not invariably required either. A search unsupported by probable cause can be constitutional, we have said, "when special needs, beyond the normal need for law enforcement, make the warrant and probable-cause requirement impracticable."

We have found such "special needs" to exist in the public school context. . . . The school search we approved in *T.L.O.*, while not based on probable cause, *was* based on individualized *suspicion* of wrongdoing. As we explicitly acknowledged, however, "'the Fourth Amendment imposes no irreducible requirement of such suspicion.'"

The first factor to be considered is the nature of the privacy interest upon which the search here at issue intrudes. . . . What expectations are legitimate varies, of course, with context, depending, for example, upon whether the individual asserting the privacy interest is at home, at work, in a car, or in a public park. In addition, the legitimacy of certain privacy expectations vis-a-vis the State may depend upon the individual's legal relationship with the State. . . . Central, in our view, to the present case is the fact that the subjects of the Policy are (1) children, who (2) have been committed to the temporary custody of the State as schoolmaster.

Traditionally at common law, and still today, unemancipated minors lack some of the most fundamental rights of self-determination—including even the right of liberty in its narrow sense, *i.e.*, the right to come and go at will. They are subject, even as to their physical freedom, to the control of their parents or guardians. When parents place minor children in private schools for their education, the teachers and administrators of those schools stand *in loco parentis* over the children entrusted to them.

. . . .

Fourth Amendment rights, no less than First and Fourteenth Amendment rights, are different in public schools than elsewhere; the "reasonableness" inquiry cannot disregard the schools' custodial and tutelary responsibility for children. For their own good and that of their classmates, public school children are routinely required to submit to various physical examinations, and to be vaccinated against various diseases. . . .

Legitimate privacy expectations are even less with regard to student athletes. School sports are not for the bashful. They require "suiting up" before each practice or event, and showering and changing afterwards. Public school locker rooms, the usual sites for these activities, are not notable for the privacy they afford. The locker rooms in Vernonia are typical: No individual dressing rooms are provided; shower heads are lined up along a wall, unseparated by any sort of partition or curtain; not even all the toilet stalls have doors. As the United States Court of Appeals for the

Seventh Circuit has noted, there is "an element of 'communal undress' inherent in athletic participation."

There is an additional respect in which school athletes have a reduced expectation of privacy. By choosing to "go out for the team," they voluntarily subject themselves to a degree of regulation even higher than that imposed on students generally. In Vernonia's public schools, they must submit to a preseason physical exam (James testified that his included the giving of a urine sample), they must acquire adequate insurance coverage or sign an insurance waiver, maintain a minimum grade point average, and comply with any "rules of conduct, dress, training hours and related matters as may be established for each sport by the head coach and athletic director with the principal's approval." Somewhat like adults who choose to participate in a "closely regulated industry," students who voluntarily participate in school athletics have reason to expect intrusions upon normal rights and privileges, including privacy.

Having considered the scope of the legitimate expectation of privacy at issue here, we turn next to the character of the intrusion that is complained of. We recognized in *Skinner v. Railway Labor Executives' Assn.*, 489 U.S. 602 (1989), that collecting the samples for urinalysis intrudes upon "an excretory function traditionally shielded by great privacy." . . . We noted, however, that the degree of intrusion depends upon the manner in which production of the urine sample is monitored. Under the District's Policy, male students produce samples at a urinal along a wall. They remain fully clothed and are only observed from behind, if at all. Female students produce samples in an enclosed stall, with a female monitor standing outside listening only for sounds of tampering. These conditions are nearly identical to those typically encountered in public restrooms, which men, women, and especially school children use daily. Under such conditions, the privacy interests compromised by the process of obtaining the urine sample are in our view negligible.

The other privacy-invasive aspect of urinalysis is, of course, the information it discloses concerning the state of the subject's body, and the materials he has ingested. In this regard it is significant that the tests at issue here look only for drugs, and not for whether the student is, for example, epileptic, pregnant, or diabetic. Moreover, the drugs for which the samples are screened are standard, and do not vary according to the identity of the student. And finally, the results of the tests are disclosed only to a limited class of school personnel who have a need to know; and they are not turned over to law enforcement authorities or used for any internal disciplinary function.

. . . .

Finally, we turn to consider the nature and immediacy of the governmental concern at issue here, and the efficacy of this means for meeting it. In both *Skinner* and *Treasury Employees v. Von Raab*, 489 U.S. 656 (1989), we characterized the government interest motivating the search as "compelling." *Skinner* (interest in preventing railway accidents); *Von Raab*, in ensuring fitness of customs officials to interdict drugs and handle firearms). . . . Relying on these cases, the District Court held that because the District's program also called for drug testing in the absence of individualized suspicion, the District "must demonstrate a 'compelling need' for the program." The Court of Appeals appears to have agreed with this view. It is a mistake, however, to think that the phrase "compelling state interest," in the Fourth Amendment context, describes a fixed, minimum quantum of governmental concern, so that one can dispose of a case by answering in isolation the question: Is there a compelling state interest here? Rather, the phrase describes an interest that appears *important enough* to justify the particular search at hand, in light of other factors that show the search to be relatively intrusive upon a genuine expectation of privacy. Whether that relatively high degree of government concern is necessary in this case or not, we think it is met.

That the nature of the concern is important—indeed, perhaps compelling—can hardly be doubted. Deterring drug use by our Nation's schoolchildren is at least as important as enhancing efficient enforcement of the Nation's laws against the importation of drugs, which was the governmental concern in *Von Raab*, or deterring drug use by engineers and trainmen, which was the governmental concern in *Skinner.* School years are the time when the physical, psychological, and addictive effects of drugs are most severe.... And of course the effects of a drug-infested school are visited not just upon the users, but upon the entire student body and faculty, as the educational process is disrupted. In the present case, moreover, the necessity for the State to act is magnified by the fact that this evil is being visited not just upon individuals at large, but upon children for whom it has undertaken a special responsibility of care and direction. Finally, it must not be lost sight of that this program is directed more narrowly to drug use by school athletes, where the risk of immediate physical harm to the drug user or those with whom he is playing his sport is particularly high....

As for the immediacy of the District's concerns: We are not inclined to question—indeed, we could not possibly find clearly erroneous—the District Court's conclusion that "a large segment of the student body, particularly those involved in interscholastic athletics, was in a state of rebellion," that "disciplinary actions had reached 'epidemic proportions,'" and that "the rebellion was being fueled by alcohol and drug abuse as well as by the student's misperceptions about the drug culture." That is an immediate crisis....

As to the efficacy of this means for addressing the problem: It seems to us self-evident that a drug problem largely fueled by the "role model" effect of athletes' drug use, and of particular danger to athletes, is effectively addressed by making sure that athletes do not use drugs. Respondents argue that a "less intrusive means to the same end" was available, namely, "drug testing on suspicion of drug use." We have repeatedly refused to declare that only the "least intrusive" search practicable can be reasonable under the Fourth Amendment.... Taking into account all the factors we have considered above—the decreased expectation of privacy, the relative unobtrusiveness of the search, and the severity of the need met by the search—we conclude Vernonia's Policy is reasonable and hence constitutional.

We caution against the assumption that suspicionless drug testing will readily pass constitutional muster in other contexts. . . .

We may note that the primary guardians of Vernonia's schoolchildren appear to agree. The record shows no objection to this districtwide program by any parents other than the couple before us here—even though, as we have described, a public meeting was held to obtain parents' views. We find insufficient basis to contradict the judgment of Vernonia's parents, its school board, and the District Court, as to what was reasonably in the interest of these children under the circumstances. . . .

Board of Education of Independent School District No. 92 v. Earls

536 U.S. 822 (2002)

The Supreme Court upholds random drug testing of students in extracurricular activities.

Justice Thomas delivered the opinion of the Court, which Rehnquist, C.J., and Scalia, Kennedy, and Breyer, JJ., joined.

The Student Activities Drug Testing Policy implemented by the Board of Education of Independent School District No. 92 of Pottawatomie County requires all students who participate in competitive extracurricular activities to submit to drug testing. Because this Policy reasonably serves the School District's important interest in detecting and preventing drug use among its students, we hold that it is constitutional.

. . . .

In the fall of 1998, the School District adopted the Student Activities Drug Testing Policy (Policy), which requires all middle and high school students to consent to drug testing in order to participate in any extracurricular activity. In practice, the Policy has been applied only to competitive extracurricular activities sanctioned by the Oklahoma Secondary Schools Activities Association, such as the Academic Team, Future Farmers of America, Future Homemakers of America, band, choir, pompom, cheerleading, and athletics. Under the Policy, students are required to take a drug test before participating in an extracurricular activity, must submit to random drug testing while participating in that activity, and must agree to be tested at any time upon reasonable suspicion. The urinalysis tests are designed to detect only the use of illegal drugs, including amphetamines, marijuana, cocaine, opiates, and barbiturates, not medical conditions or the presence of authorized prescription medications.

At the time of their suit, both respondents attended Tecumseh High School. Respondent Lindsay Earls was a member of the show choir, the marching band, the Academic Team, and the National Honor Society. Respondent Daniel James sought to participate in the Academic Team. Together with their parents, Earls and James brought a 42 U.S.C. § 1983 action against the School District, challenging the Policy both on its face and as applied to their participation in extracurricular activities. They alleged that the Policy violates the Fourth Amendment as incorporated by the Fourteenth Amendment and requested injunctive and declarative relief. They also argued that the School District failed to identify a special need for testing students who participate in extracurricular activities, and that the "Drug Testing Policy neither addresses a proven problem nor promises to bring any benefit to students or the school." . . .

. . . .

The Fourth Amendment to the United States Constitution protects "[t]he right of the people to be secure in their persons, houses, papers, and effects, against unreasonable searches and seizures." Searches by public school officials, such as the collection of urine samples, implicate Fourth Amendment interests. We must therefore review the School District's Policy for "reasonableness," which is the touchstone of the constitutionality of a governmental search.

. . . .

Given that the School District's Policy is not in any way related to the conduct of criminal investigations, . . . respondents do not contend that the School District requires probable cause before testing students for drug use. Respondents instead argue that drug testing must be based at least on some level of individualized suspicion. . . . It is true that we generally determine the reasonableness of a search by balancing the nature of the intrusion on the individual's privacy against the promotion of legitimate governmental interests. . . . But we have long held that "the Fourth Amendment imposes no irreducible requirement of [individualized] suspicion." . . . Therefore, in the context of safety and administrative regulations, a search unsupported by probable cause may be reasonable "when 'special needs, beyond the normal need for law enforcement, make the warrant and probable-cause requirement impracticable. . . .

Significantly, this Court has previously held that "special needs" inhere in the public school context. *See Vernonia*, 515 U.S. 646 (1995); *T.L.O.*, 469 U.S. 325, 341 (1985). . . . While schoolchildren do not shed their constitutional rights when they enter the schoolhouse, *see Tinker*, 393 U.S. 503 (1968), Fourth Amendment rights . . . "are different in public schools than elsewhere; the 'reasonableness' inquiry cannot disregard the schools' custodial and tutelary responsibility for children." *Vernonia*. . . . In particular, a finding of individualized suspicion may not be necessary when a school conducts drug testing.

In *Vernonia*, this Court held that the suspicionless drug testing of athletes was constitutional. The Court, however, did not simply authorize all school drug testing, but rather conducted a fact-specific balancing of the intrusion on the children's Fourth Amendment rights against the promotion of legitimate governmental interests. . . . Applying the principles of *Vernonia* to the somewhat different facts of this case, we conclude that Tecumseh's Policy is also constitutional.

We first consider the nature of the privacy interest allegedly compromised by the drug testing. As in *Vernonia*, the context of the public school environment serves as the backdrop for the analysis of the privacy interest at stake and the reasonableness of the drug testing policy in general.... A student's privacy interest is limited in a public school environment where the State is responsible for maintaining discipline, health, and safety. Schoolchildren are routinely required to submit to physical examinations and vaccinations against disease.... Securing order in the school environment sometimes requires that students be subjected to greater controls than those appropriate for adults....

In any event, students who participate in competitive extracurricular activities voluntarily subject themselves to many of the same intrusions on their privacy as do athletes. Some of these clubs and activities require occasional off-campus travel and communal undress. All of them have their own rules and requirements for participating students that do not apply to the student body as a whole. For example, each of the competitive extracurricular activities governed by the Policy must abide by the rules of the Oklahoma Secondary Schools Activities Association, and a faculty sponsor monitors the students for compliance with the various rules dictated by the clubs and activities. This regulation of extracurricular activities further diminishes the expectation of privacy among schoolchildren.... We therefore conclude that the students affected by this Policy have a limited expectation of privacy.

Next, we consider the character of the intrusion imposed by the Policy.... Under the Policy, a faculty monitor waits outside the closed restroom stall for the student to produce a sample and must "listen for the normal sounds of urination in order to guard against tampered specimens and to insure an accurate chain of custody." This procedure is virtually identical to that reviewed in *Vernonia*, except that it additionally protects privacy by allowing male students to produce their samples behind a closed stall. Given that we considered the method of collection in *Vernonia* a "negligible" intrusion, the method here is even less problematic.

In addition, the Policy clearly requires that the test results be kept in confidential files separate from a student's other educational records and released to school personnel only on a "need to know" basis.... Moreover, the test results are not turned over to any law enforcement authority. Nor do the test results here lead to the imposition of discipline or have any academic consequences. Given the minimally intrusive nature of the sample collection and the limited uses to which the test results are put, we conclude that the invasion of students' privacy is not significant.

Finally, this Court must consider the nature and immediacy of the government's concerns and the efficacy of the Policy in meeting them. This Court has already articulated in detail the importance of the governmental concern in preventing drug use by schoolchildren. The drug abuse problem among our Nation's youth has hardly abated since *Vernonia* was decided in 1995. In fact, evidence suggests that it has only grown worse. As in *Vernonia*, "the necessity for the State to act is magnified by the fact that this evil is being visited not just upon individuals at large, but upon children for whom it has undertaken a special responsibility of care and direction." The health and safety risks identified in *Vernonia* apply with equal force to Tecumseh's children. Indeed, the nationwide drug epidemic makes the war against drugs a pressing concern in every school.

Additionally, the School District in this case has presented specific evidence of drug use at Tecumseh schools. . . . Furthermore, this Court has not required a particularized or pervasive drug problem before allowing the government to conduct suspicionless drug testing. . . . Given the nationwide epidemic of drug use, and the evidence of increased drug use in Tecumseh schools, it was entirely reasonable for the School District to enact this particular drug testing policy. We reject the Court of Appeals' novel test that "any district seeking to impose a random suspicionless drug testing policy as a condition to participation in a school activity must demonstrate that there is some identifiable drug abuse problem among a sufficient number of those subject to the testing, such that testing that group of students will actually redress its drug problem." Among other problems, it would be difficult to administer such a test. As we cannot articulate a threshold level of drug use that would suffice to justify a drug testing program for schoolchildren, we refuse to fashion what would in effect be a constitutional quantum of drug use necessary to show a "drug problem."

Finally, we find that testing students who participate in extracurricular activities is a reasonably effective means of addressing the School District's legitimate concerns in preventing, deterring, and detecting drug use. While in *Vernonia* there might have been a closer fit between the testing of athletes and the trial court is finding that the drug problem was "fueled by the 'role model' effect of athletes' drug use," such a finding was not essential to the holding.

Within the limits of the Fourth Amendment, local school boards must assess the desirability of drug testing schoolchildren. In upholding the constitutionality of the Policy, we express no opinion as to its wisdom. Rather, we hold only that Tecumseh's Policy is a reasonable means of furthering the School District's important interest in preventing and deterring drug use among its schoolchildren. Accordingly, we reverse the judgment of the Court of Appeals.

Post Problem Discussion

1. Is a sniff a search? The United States Supreme Court decisions indicate that it depends on the circumstances. In *Illinois v. Caballes*, 543 U.S. 405, 409 (2005), the Court ruled that the use of dogs sniffing cars as part of a lawful traffic stop generally does not implicate legitimate privacy interests and "does not rise to the level of a constitutionally cognizable infringement." Then, in *Florida v. Jardines*, 133 S. Ct. 1409, 1417–18 (2013), the Court ruled that the government's use of trained police dogs to investigate a home by sniffing outside the home and its immediate surroundings was a search within the meaning of the Fourth Amendment.

In the context of public schools and students, some courts have said yes, *see, e.g., B.C. v. Plumas Unified Sch. Dist.*, 192 F.3d 1260 (9th Cir. 1999), some have said no, *see, e.g., Doe v. Renfrow*, 475 F. Supp. 1012 (D. Ind. 1979), *aff'd in part and remanded in part*, 631 F.2d 91 (7th Cir. 1980). Some courts have focused on what is being sniffed and found that dogs sniffing inanimate objects (cars, lockers, etc.) was not a search, but dogs sniffing students was a search particularly when the dog sniff involved the dog touching the person. *See Horton v. Goose Creek Indep. Sch. Dist.*, 690 F.2d 470 (5th Cir. 1982), *cert. denied*, 463 U.S. 1207 (1983).

In *Burlison v. Springfield Pub. Schs.*, 708 F.3d 1034, 1039–40 (8th Cir. 2013), *cert. denied*, 134 S. Ct. 151 (2013), a school district utilized a program with police dogs similar to some of our problem fact patterns. Classrooms were chosen at random. Students in the classroom were notified to leave the room and to leave all of their belongings in the room. Then, trained police dogs sniffed the room and student belongings. The Eighth Circuit Court of Appeals found that this approach did not violate the Fourth Amendment:

> Assuming that C.M.'s belongings were seized in this case when the school police officer directed that they be left in the classroom for approximately five minutes while the drug dog survey occurred, we conclude that the seizure was part of a reasonable procedure to maintain the safety and security of students at the school. Since C.M. is a high school student, he has a "lesser expectation of privacy" than the general public. He was only separated from his belongings for a short period of time while the deputy sheriff safely and efficiently completed the drug dog walkabout. Requiring students to be separated from their property during such a reasonable procedure avoids potential embarrassment to students, ensures that students are not targeted by dogs, and decreases the possibility of dangerous interactions between dogs and children.
>
> C.M.'s freedoms were not unreasonably curtailed by his brief separation from his possessions because he normally would not have been able to access or move his backpack during class time without permission. In [*Doe v. Little Rock Sch. Dist.*, 380 F.3d 349, 352 (8th Cir. 2004)], we concluded that a school's search policy was unconstitutional where it required all students to leave their belongings in a classroom and allowed school personnel to search each student's property. We noted that a drug dog procedure like the one completed in C.M.'s school in April 2010 would not raise the same type of constitutional issues. That is because such a drug dog survey is "minimally intrusive, and provide[s] an effective means for adducing the requisite degree of individualized suspicion to conduct further, more intrusive searches." The drug dog procedure at C.M.'s school was the type of minimally intrusive activity which we referenced in *Little Rock*. C.M. was separated from his backpack only for a short period of time and school personnel were only to search a student's belongings if a drug dog alerted twice on the same property.

> The district and its officials have shown an immediate need for a drug dog procedure because there is substantial evidence showing there was a drug problem in district buildings.

Given these decisions, what advice would you give a school board if they were considering using dogs to help address drug problems at school? Would the approaches taken in Fact Patterns #1 and #2 be constitutional?

2. Does subjecting all students to random, suspicionless drug testing go too far? *Vernonia* and *Earls* deal with extracurricular activities and sports. Does that distinction matter in the outcome of any of our fact patterns?

3. Should schools need some level of individual suspicion before having students turn out their pockets and leave their items behind to be searched as in fact pattern #2? Or is the level of privacy and intrusion analogous to going to a major sporting event, concert, or vacation resort (i.e., Disney, SeaWorld, etc.) post-9/11, where everyone's handbags and backpacks are now generally searched before entering?

§ 10.06 State Constitutions

Some state courts have interpreted their state constitutions to provide more privacy protection to students than the *T.L.O., Vernonia/Earls* standards noted in this Chapter. *See York v. Wahkiakum Sch. Dist. No.* 200, 178 P.3d 995 (Wash. 2008). Others have found that their state constitutions are not more protective than the federal standards noted in this Chapter. *See, e.g., State v. Drake*, 662 A.2d 265 (N.H. 1995), or *Hageman v. Goshen County Sch. Dist.*, 256 P.3d 487 (2011). The following activity allows you to explore the standards in your state.

Activity 1: Find Your State's Search and Seizure Standards

Step One—Research your state court decisions for search and seizure cases in public schools.

Step Two—Research your state constitution and statutes to find the state provision analogous to the Fourth Amendment, and any statutes that apply to searching students in public schools.

Step Three—Answer the following:

1. Do your state court decisions adopt the federal standards discussed in this Chapter (*T.L.O., Vernonia/Earls*)?
2. If not, what standards do your state courts use? Are the standards more protective of student privacy rights? Does your state require probable cause? A warrant? Individualized suspicion for all searches?
3. If so, have your state courts addressed any of the issues in the fact patterns in this Chapter? Were the outcomes similar or different from the conclusions you reached in the problems?

§ 10.07 Student Interrogation

In *Miranda v. Arizona*, the United States Supreme Court held that suspects that are in custody must be warned of their Fifth Amendment right to remain silent before being interrogated by law enforcement officials. *Miranda v. Arizona*, 384 U.S. 436 (1966). The key components to when *Miranda* applies are 1) custodial interrogation, and 2) performed by law enforcement officials.

Are *Miranda* warnings required for student suspects? Courts have generally found that students who are questioned by school officials are not in custody for *Miranda* purposes and/or that school officials are not law enforcement officers. However, things can become murky when school resource officers or police officers are involved, especially when school officials are working in connection with police while investigating and questioning the student.

Problem 5: Finding the PANDA Lab

Principal Morris receives a tip that an eleventh grade honor student named Kelli was in the school bathroom taking "PANDA," a mixture of various prescription drugs. Principal Morris calls Kelli into her office and asks Kelli about it. Kelli, who is 16 years old, denies using PANDA, but when Principal Morris asks Kelli to empty her pockets and dump out her purse, Kelli starts crying and says "my boyfriend Michael gave it to me and told me to try it, so I did!" Upon further questioning, Principal Morris learns that PANDA is becoming very popular with students at the school, and Michael is one of the suppliers of the drug to students. Principal Morris takes the PANDA pills from Kelli and tells her that she is going to have to think about an appropriate disciplinary measure. She sends Kelli to the in-school suspension room to wait while she thinks it over.

Principal Morris then meets with the SRO and tells him what she learned. The SRO and principal then conference call with the drug enforcement officer at the police station and learn that there has been an influx of PANDA in the area, and that there likely is a major outside supplier who has come into the area and set up a "PANDA lab" to mix and make the pills. The officer suspects that the pills are then provided to a few students like Michael to sell to other students at school. The police have been working for a while to figure out who the major supplier is so that they can halt the source of the drug, but so far they have not had any luck. The SRO and drug enforcement officer discuss possible ways of having Michael lead them to the supplier. During the discussion, Principal Morris suggests that she could probably trick Michael, who is 17 years old, into giving her the information. They all agree to give the principal's plan a try. They agree that Michael is more likely to talk if the SRO and police are not involved, so the SRO leaves Principal Morris' office.

Principal Morris calls Michael into her office. She tells Michael the following:

> Michael, come in. I am glad you are here today. I hope that you will be able to help us. Have a seat. I am sorry to have to tell you this, but Kelli is

> seriously ill. She is in the hospital right now. The doctors said that she took some bad drugs that were contaminated with some toxic type substances, but they are not sure exactly what kind of substances. They need to know exactly what was in the drugs so that they can figure out what kind of antidote to give to her. Without the right medication, they are not sure what will happen to Kelli. I know that you are her boyfriend and that you are very close to her. Do you have any idea where those drugs could have come from, or what was in them?

At first, Michael says he does not know anything about it. Principal Morris continues on to say "we are not looking so much for the person that gave her the drugs as we are the person that made the drugs so that we can figure out what is in the drugs." Michael then says that he may have heard about a place that is making drugs, but that he is not sure and does not want to get anyone in trouble. After more questioning by Principal Morris, Michael ultimately breaks down in tears and admits that he gave the drugs to Kelli. He also tells the principal the address where he picks up the drugs. He asks Principal Morris if Kelli will be okay and if he can go see her. Principal Morris has Michael write down the information and she provides it to the SRO, who provides it to the police. Michael is subsequently expelled from school, and the police bring criminal charges against him for selling PANDA to students.

Was Principal Morris obligated to provide Kelli or Michael *Miranda* warnings?

Problem Materials

✓ *J.D.B. v. North Carolina*, 131 S. Ct. 2394 (2011)

✓ *In re Tag*, 663 S.E.2d 392 (Ga. App. 2008)

✓ *J.D. v. Commonwealth of Virginia*, 591 S.E.2d 721 (Va. Ct. App. 2004)

✓ *State v. Tinkham*, 719 A.2d 580 (N.H. 1998)

J.D.B. v. North Carolina

131 S. Ct. 2394 (2011)

The Court rules that a suspect's age is a factor in determining if a student is in custody for Miranda purposes.

Sotomayor, J., delivered the opinion of the Court, in which Kennedy, Ginsburg, Breyer, and Kagan, JJ., joined.

This case presents the question whether the age of a child subjected to police questioning is relevant to the custody analysis of *Miranda v. Arizona*, 384 U.S. 436 (1966). It is beyond dispute that children will often feel bound to submit to police questioning when an adult in the same circumstances would feel free to leave. Seeing no reason for police officers or courts to blind themselves to that commonsense reality, we hold that a child's age properly informs the *Miranda* custody analysis.

I

A

Petitioner J.D.B. was a 13-year-old, seventh-grade student attending class at Smith Middle School in Chapel Hill, North Carolina when he was removed from his classroom by a uniformed police officer, escorted to a closed-door conference room, and questioned by police for at least half an hour.

This was the second time that police questioned J.D.B. in the span of a week. Five days earlier, two home break-ins occurred, and various items were stolen. Police stopped and questioned J.D.B. after he was seen behind a residence in the neighborhood where the crimes occurred. That same day, police also spoke to J.D.B.'s grandmother—his legal guardian—as well as his aunt.

Police later learned that a digital camera matching the description of one of the stolen items had been found at J.D.B.'s middle school and seen in J.D.B.'s possession. Investigator DiCostanzo, the juvenile investigator with the local police force who had been assigned to the case, went to the school to question J.D.B. Upon arrival, DiCostanzo informed the uniformed police officer on detail to the school (a so-called school resource officer), the assistant principal, and an administrative intern that he was there to question J.D.B. about the break-ins. Although DiCostanzo asked the school administrators to verify J.D.B.'s date of birth, address, and parent contact information from school records, neither the police officers nor the school administrators contacted J.D.B.'s grandmother.

The uniformed officer interrupted J.D.B.'s afternoon social studies class, removed J.D.B. from the classroom, and escorted him to a school conference room. There, J.D.B. was met by DiCostanzo, the assistant principal, and the administrative intern. The door to the conference room was closed. With the two police officers and the two administrators present, J.D.B. was questioned for the next 30 to 45 minutes. Prior to the commencement of questioning, J.D.B. was given neither *Miranda* warnings nor the opportunity to speak to his grandmother. Nor was he informed that he was free to leave the room.

Questioning began with small talk—discussion of sports and J.D.B.'s family life. DiCostanzo asked, and J.D.B. agreed, to discuss the events of the prior weekend. Denying any wrongdoing, J.D.B. explained that he had been in the neighborhood where the crimes occurred because he was seeking work mowing lawns. DiCostanzo pressed J.D.B. for additional detail about his efforts to obtain work; asked J.D.B. to explain a prior incident, when one of the victims returned home to find J.D.B. behind her house; and confronted J.D.B. with the stolen camera. The assistant principal urged J.D.B. to "do the right thing," warning J.D.B. that "the truth always comes out in the end."

Eventually, J.D.B. asked whether he would "still be in trouble" if he returned the "stuff." In response, DiCostanzo explained that return of the stolen items would be helpful, but "this thing is going to court" regardless. ("[W]hat's done is done[;] now you need to help yourself by making it right"); DiCostanzo then warned that he may need to seek a secure custody order if he believed that J.D.B. would continue to break into other homes. When J.D.B. asked what a secure custody order was, DiCostanzo explained that "it's where you get sent to juvenile detention before court."

After learning of the prospect of juvenile detention, J.D.B. confessed that he and a friend were responsible for the break-ins. DiCostanzo only then informed J.D.B. that he could refuse to answer the investigator's questions and that he was free to leave. Asked whether he understood, J.D.B. nodded and provided further detail, including information about the location of the stolen items. Eventually J.D.B. wrote a statement, at DiCostanzo's request. When the bell rang indicating the end of the schoolday, J.D.B. was allowed to leave to catch the bus home.

B

Two juvenile petitions were filed against J.D.B., each alleging one count of breaking and entering and one count of larceny. J.D.B.'s public defender moved to suppress his statements and the evidence derived therefrom, arguing that suppression was necessary because J.D.B. had been "interrogated by police in a custodial setting without being afforded *Miranda* warning[s]," and because his statements were involuntary under the totality of the circumstances test.... After a suppression hearing at which DiCostanzo and J.D.B. testified, the trial court denied the motion, deciding that J.D.B. was not in custody at the time of the schoolhouse interrogation and that his statements were voluntary. As a result, J.D.B. entered a transcript of admission to all four counts, renewing his objection to the denial of his motion to suppress, and the court adjudicated J.D.B. delinquent.

A divided panel of the North Carolina Court of Appeals affirmed. The North Carolina Supreme Court held, over two dissents, that J.D.B. was not in custody when he confessed, "declin[ing] to extend the test for custody to include consideration of the age . . . of an individual subjected to questioning by police." We granted certiorari to determine whether the *Miranda* custody analysis includes consideration of a juvenile suspect's age.

II

A

Any police interview of an individual suspected of a crime has "coercive aspects to it." Only those interrogations that occur while a suspect is in police custody, however, "heighte[n] the risk" that statements obtained are not the product of the suspect's free choice.

By its very nature, custodial police interrogation entails "inherently compelling pressures." *Miranda*, 384 U.S., at 467. Even for an adult, the physical and psychological isolation of custodial interrogation can "undermine the individual's will to resist and . . . compel him to speak where he would not otherwise do so freely." Indeed, the pressure of custodial interrogation is so immense that it "can induce a frighteningly high percentage of people to confess to crimes they never committed." That risk is all the more troubling—and recent studies suggest, all the more acute—when the subject of custodial interrogation is a juvenile.

Recognizing that the inherently coercive nature of custodial interrogation "blurs the line between voluntary and involuntary statements," this Court in *Miranda* adopted a set of prophylactic measures designed to safeguard the constitutional guarantee against self-incrimination. Prior to questioning, a suspect "must be warned that he has a right to remain silent, that any statement he does make may be used as evidence against him, and that he has a right to the presence of an attorney, either retained or appointed." And, if a suspect makes a statement during custodial interrogation, the burden is on the Government to show, as a "prerequisit[e]" to the statement's admissibility as evidence in the Government's case in chief, that the defendant "voluntarily, knowingly and intelligently" waived his rights.

Because these measures protect the individual against the coercive nature of custodial interrogation, they are required "'only where there has been such a restriction on a person's freedom as to render him "in custody."'" As we have repeatedly emphasized, whether a suspect is "in custody" is an objective inquiry.

> "Two discrete inquiries are essential to the determination: first, what were the circumstances surrounding the interrogation; and second, given those circumstances, would a reasonable person have felt he or she was at liberty to terminate the interrogation and leave. Once the scene is set and the players' lines and actions are reconstructed, the court must apply an objective test to resolve the ultimate inquiry: was there a formal arrest or restraint on freedom of movement of the degree associated with formal arrest." *Thompson v. Keohane*, 516 U.S. 99, 112 (1995) (internal quotation marks, alteration, and footnote omitted).

Rather than demarcate a limited set of relevant circumstances, we have required police officers and courts to "examine all of the circumstances surrounding the interrogation," including any circumstance that "would have affected how a reasonable person" in the suspect's position "would perceive his or her freedom to leave." On the other hand, the "subjective views harbored by either the interrogating officers or the person being questioned" are irrelevant. The test, in other words, involves no consideration of the "actual mindset" of the particular suspect subjected to police questioning.

The benefit of the objective custody analysis is that it is "designed to give clear guidance to the police." Police must make in-the-moment judgments as to when to administer *Miranda* warnings. By limiting analysis to the objective circumstances of the interrogation, and asking how a reasonable person in the suspect's position would understand his freedom to terminate questioning and leave, the objective test avoids burdening police with the task of anticipating the idiosyncrasies of every individual suspect and divining how those particular traits affect each person's subjective state of mind.

B

The State and its *amici* contend that a child's age has no place in the custody analysis, no matter how young the child subjected to police questioning. We cannot agree. In some circumstances, a child's age "would have affected how a reasonable person" in the suspect's position "would perceive his or her freedom to leave." That is, a reasonable child subjected to police questioning will sometimes feel pressured to submit when a reasonable adult would feel free to go. We think it clear that courts can account for that reality without doing any damage to the objective nature of the custody analysis.

A child's age is far "more than a chronological fact." It is a fact that "generates commonsense conclusions about behavior and perception." Such conclusions apply broadly to children as a class. And, they are self-evident to anyone who was a child once himself, including any police officer or judge.

Time and again, this Court has drawn these commonsense conclusions for itself. We have observed that children "generally are less mature and responsible than adults," that they "often lack the experience, perspective, and judgment to recognize and avoid choices that could be detrimental to them," that they "are more vulnerable or susceptible to . . . outside pressures" than adults, and so on. Addressing the specific context of police interrogation, we have observed that events that "would leave a man cold and unimpressed can overawe and overwhelm a lad in his early teens." Describing no one child in particular, these observations restate what "any parent knows"—indeed, what any person knows—about children generally.

. . . .

Indeed, even where a "reasonable person" standard otherwise applies, the common law has reflected the reality that children are not adults. In negligence suits, for instance, where liability turns on what an objectively reasonable person would do in the circumstances, "[a]ll American jurisdictions accept the idea that a person's childhood is a relevant circumstance" to be considered. . . . As this discussion establishes, "[o]ur history is replete with laws and judicial recognition" that children cannot be viewed simply as miniature adults. We see no justification for taking a different course here. So long as the child's age was known to the officer at the time of the interview, or would have been objectively apparent to any reasonable officer, including age as part of the custody analysis requires officers neither to consider circumstances "unknowable" to them, nor to "anticipat[e] the frailties or idiosyncrasies" of the particular suspect whom they question. The same "wide basis of community experience" that makes it possible, as an objective matter, "to determine what is to be expected" of children in other contexts, likewise makes it possible to know what to expect of children subjected to police questioning.

In other words, a child's age differs from other personal characteristics that, even when known to police, have no objectively discernible relationship to a reasonable person's understanding of his freedom of action. *Alvarado*, holds, for instance, that a suspect's prior interrogation history with law enforcement has no role to play in the custody analysis because such experience could just as easily lead a reasonable person to feel free to walk away as to feel compelled to stay in place. Because the effect in any given case would be "contingent [on the] psycholog[y]" of the individual suspect, the Court explained, such experience cannot be considered without compromising the objective nature of the custody analysis. A child's age, however, is different. Precisely because childhood yields objective conclusions like those we have drawn ourselves—among others, that children are "most susceptible to influence," and "outside pressures,"—considering age in the custody analysis in no way involves a determination of how youth "subjectively affect[s] the mindset" of any particular child.

In fact, in many cases involving juvenile suspects, the custody analysis would be nonsensical absent some consideration of the suspect's age. This case is a prime example. Were the court precluded from taking J.D.B.'s youth into account, it would be forced to evaluate the circumstances present here through the eyes of a reasonable person of average years. In other words, how would a reasonable adult understand his situation, after being removed from a seventh-grade social studies class by a uniformed school resource officer; being encouraged by his assistant principal to "do the right thing"; and being warned by a police investigator of the prospect of juvenile detention and separation from his guardian and primary caretaker? To describe such an inquiry is to demonstrate its absurdity. Neither officers nor courts can reasonably evaluate the effect of objective circumstances that, by their nature, are specific to children without accounting for the age of the child subjected to those circumstances.

Indeed, although the dissent suggests that concerns "regarding the application of the *Miranda* custody rule to minors can be accommodated by considering the unique circumstances present when minors are questioned in school," (opinion of Alito, J.), the effect of the schoolhouse setting cannot be disentangled from the identity of the person questioned. A student—whose presence at school is compulsory and whose disobedience at school is cause for disciplinary action—is in a far different position than, say, a parent volunteer on school grounds to chaperone an event, or an adult from the community on school grounds to attend a basketball game. Without asking whether the person "questioned in school" is a "minor," the coercive effect of the schoolhouse setting is unknowable....

Reviewing the question *de novo* today, we hold that so long as the child's age was known to the officer at the time of police questioning, or would have been objectively apparent to a reasonable officer, its inclusion in the custody analysis is consistent with the objective nature of that test. This is not to say that a child's age will be a determinative, or even a significant, factor in every case. It is, however, a reality that courts cannot simply ignore.

III

....

The question remains whether J.D.B. was in custody when police interrogated him. We remand for the state courts to address that question, this time taking account of all of the relevant circumstances of the interrogation, including J.D.B.'s age at the time. The judgment of the North Carolina Supreme Court is reversed, and the case is remanded for proceedings not inconsistent with this opinion.

It is so ordered.

In re T.A.G.

663 S.E.2d 392 (Ga. App. 2008)

The court rules that a school principal was acting as an agent of the police and was required to provide a student with Miranda warnings.

The State filed a delinquency petition against 13-year-old T.A.G., alleging that he robbed two individuals. Before the adjudicatory hearing, T.A.G. moved to suppress several incriminating statements that he made before he was advised of his *Miranda* rights. The juvenile court denied the motion as to one statement, but granted it as to another. The State appeals the partial grant of T.A.G.'s motion to suppress, and for reasons that follow, we affirm.

On appeal, we construe the evidence in favor of the juvenile court's suppression ruling. The juvenile court—not this Court—makes factual and credibility determinations, and we will uphold those determinations unless they are clearly erroneous.

So viewed, the evidence shows that in November 2006, administrators at Loganville Middle School received a report that two students had been robbed in the boys' bathroom during a school basketball game. T.A.G. was implicated, and an assistant principal, whose job duties included investigating conduct violations, interviewed him. Only the principal and T.A.G. were present during the interview. Although T.A.G. initially denied participating in the crimes, he eventually admitted during the interview that he took money from one of the victims. He insisted, however, that he did not steal from the other victim.

The assistant principal informed another assistant principal involved in the investigation about T.A.G.'s admission, and he took T.A.G. to her office. After further questioning by the second assistant principal, T.A.G. admitted not only taking money from the first victim, but removing money from the other victim's wallet, as well. The administrators then prepared disciplinary paperwork, and T.A.G. went home.

The record shows that the school "resource officer"—a police officer assigned to the school—was present during the second interview with T.A.G. At the time, the officer was wearing a shirt that identified him as a police officer, as well as a gun and police utility belt. Both administrators and the officer all testified that the officer asked no questions during the interview and was present for safety purposes. At one point during the interview, however, the second assistant principal asked the officer whether T.A.G. could be charged with a crime. The officer responded that robbery would be an appropriate charge. The assistant principal explained that she typically confers with the officer about possible charges, and they "kind of work together on that."

The record further shows that the officer learned about the robbery allegations that morning, and one of the administrators told him she would "look into it and keep him posted." According to the officer, he generally does not participate in school investigations because once he "become[s] involved . . . it changes the rules you play by." After school officials completed their interviews, however, they provided the witness statements to the officer, who determined whether criminal charges should be brought.

T.A.G. moved to suppress his statements to both administrators on the ground that he had not been advised of his *Miranda* rights. Concluding that T.A.G. made the statement to the first assistant principal without police involvement, the juvenile court denied the motion as to that statement. With respect to the second interview, however, the juvenile court found that the second assistant principal was acting as an agent of the police at the time, that a law enforcement officer was involved in the interview, and that T.A.G. was in custody. It further found that the police were trying to "usurp [*Miranda*] by having the school officials do all the interrogating while they stand by and don't ask a question, but . . . then . . . take all the statements that were obtained [by the] school officials and make that part of the [police] investigation." It thus excluded the statement.

On appeal, both parties rely heavily on our Supreme Court's decision in *State v. Young*, 234 Ga. 488, 216 S.E.2d 586 (1975), which addressed the application of Fourth Amendment search and seizure law—and the associated exclusionary rule—in the public school setting. Analyzing whether evidence seized by a high school principal should be excluded from a student's criminal trial, the Court noted that three groups of persons exist: private individuals; governmental agents whose conduct constitutes state action covered by the Fourth Amendment; and law enforcement personnel who are governed by both the Fourth Amendment and the exclusionary rule. . . .

Under *Young*, if the school official acts without law enforcement involvement, the exclusionary rule does not apply, even if the official's conduct violates the Fourth Amendment. The violation results not in evidence suppression, but in some other remedy afforded by law, such as a civil damages claim. If police personnel become involved in the school action, however, a Fourth Amendment violation results in exclusion of the evidence. And "[f]or purposes of *Young*, a police officer assigned to work at a school as a school resource officer should be considered a law enforcement officer, not a school official."

Although the *Young* decision focuses on the Fourth Amendment, we have applied its reasoning in a case involving a claimed violation of the Fifth Amendment right against self-incrimination. . . . Thus, the juvenile court first considered whether law enforcement was involved in obtaining T.A.G.'s statement to the second official. Answering this question affirmatively, the juvenile court concluded that the police officer assigned to the school was involved and that the assistant principal was acting as an agent of law enforcement at the time. The State challenges both of these findings.

(a) *Involvement.* The State argues that the officer was merely present during the second interview with T.A.G. and took no part in the questioning. Undoubtedly, administrators made a concerted effort to limit the officer's role during student interviews, and the officer testified that he generally did not participate in school investigations. Police involvement, however, need not be substantial . . . *any* involvement or participation by law enforcement officers brings a case within *Young*'s third category, implicating the exclusionary rule.

Although an officer's mere presence in the room, without more, might not constitute police participation, at least some evidence supports the juvenile court's finding that the officer was more involved here. Specifically, the armed officer was invited into the interview after T.A.G. confessed to one robbery, but was maintaining innocence as to the other. At that point, T.A.G. had been in the school's front office for approximately five hours, he had already been interviewed, and the second administrator was preparing to question him again. During the interview, and in front of T.A.G., the officer advised the assistant principal on what type of criminal charges might be brought against T.A.G. The juvenile then confessed to the second robbery. Under these circumstances, the juvenile court was authorized to find that the officer was more than merely present and, in fact, participated in the interview process.

(b) *Agent of the police.* Moreover, even if the officer avoided direct involvement, some evidence supports the juvenile court's finding that the second administrator acted as an instrument or agent of police during the interview. This agency determination "must be resolved on a case-by-case basis, by viewing the totality of the circumstances."

According to the administrators, they interviewed T.A.G. as part of their school conduct investigation, and they only involved the officer to ensure the safety of themselves and the students. The second administrator, however, also admitted that, in conjunction with such investigations, she often conferred with the officer about possible criminal charges, as well as questions to ask during an interview. As she testified: "[N]ormally I'll ask the questions and if I miss something or if I didn't ask a good question then . . . [the officer will] tell me later or I can ask him later about it, . . . go back and ask them another question to get more information or something that . . . I missed." Furthermore, she and the officer knew that different "rules" would apply if the police became involved, so they decided that the officer should not ask questions. And the fruits of the investigation were ultimately turned over to the police.

Given the totality of these circumstances, we cannot reverse the juvenile court's finding that the second assistant principal acted as an agent or instrument of the police in interviewing T.A.G. . . .

2. "Under *Miranda*, persons must be advised of their rights against self-incrimination after being taken into custody or otherwise deprived of their freedom of action in any significant way." Absent such advice, statements made during a custodial interrogation to law enforcement officers or their agents generally will be excluded from evidence.

As discussed above, the juvenile court found that T.A.G. was questioned by an agent of the police with the involvement and participation of the school resource officer. It then considered whether T.A.G. was in custody, and thus entitled to his *Miranda* warnings, during the second interview. The issue of custody focuses on "the objective circumstances attending the particular interrogation at issue, and not upon the subjective views of either the person being interrogated or the interrogating officer." The relevant inquiry is whether a reasonable person in the suspect's position would have believed that his freedom "was curtailed in a significant way."

On appeal, the State argues that the resource officer's mere presence during the interview did not "elevate an otherwise non-custodial questioning into a custodial interrogation." The juvenile court, however, rejected the "mere presence" argument, finding that the officer was involved in the process and that the administrator acted on his behalf.

Furthermore, once T.A.G. admitted during the first interview that he had robbed one student, he was taken into a room with an armed police officer and questioned again by a second administrator. Particularly given the prior confession, the juvenile court was authorized to conclude that a reasonable person in T.A.G.'s position would have believed he was not free to leave the office, that "the detention would not be temporary," and that he was in custody. It follows that the trial court properly suppressed T.A.G's pre-*Miranda* statement to the second assistant principal.

Judgment affirmed.

J.D. v. Commonwealth of Virginia

591 S.E.2d 721 (Va. Ct. App. 2004)

The court rules that the school principal was not acting as a law enforcement official and that the student was not in custody, so Miranda warnings were not required.

A jury found J.D., a juvenile, guilty of petit larceny. On appeal, J.D. challenges the trial court's denial of his motion to suppress incriminating statements. J.D. contends his statements, which he made in the office of his school's assistant principal, were admitted in violation of the Supreme Court's holding in *Miranda v. Arizona*, 384 U.S. 436 (1966), and that the statements were compelled and involuntary in violation of his Fifth Amendment rights. Finding no error in the trial court's denial of the motion to suppress, we affirm J.D.'s conviction . . . .

In May of 2001, J.D. was a fourteen-year-old student at Albemarle High School, where his father was a teacher. A series of thefts had occurred at the school during that month. School authorities identified J.D. and three other students as suspects in a theft that had occurred during the latter part of the month.

At about 2:30 p.m. on May 25, 2001, Steven Wright, an associate principal at the school, summoned J.D. to his office and questioned him about the most recent theft. In addition, Lawrence Lawill, the principal at Albemarle High School, was present during portions of Wright's questioning of J.D. The record does not indicate that Lawill participated in the interview. Officer Stuart Snead, the school resource police officer, was present while Wright conducted the interview of J.D. The officer was silent during the interview. He did not instruct Wright about questioning J.D. He and Wright had no prior discussions about potential criminal charges against J.D.

During the interview, J.D. was not told he could not leave the office nor was he restrained in any way. Wright told J.D. to tell what, if anything, he knew about the thefts. J.D. made oral and written statements acknowledging his involvement in the theft of a video camera that was school property. He then assisted Wright in the recovery of the camera.

J.D.'s father joined Wright and J.D. in Wright's office at about 4:45 p.m., after the school day had ended. Wright explained that he was investigating the theft of property at the school and showed J.D.'s father the merchandise J.D. had helped to recover. J.D.'s father instructed J.D. to tell him the truth about what had happened. J.D.'s subsequent statements were consistent with those he made before his father came to Wright's office.

On cross-examination Wright testified that a student can be disciplined for refusing to obey an assistant principal at Albemarle High School. The punishment imposed in such a situation would depend upon the circumstances. Wright also indicated that he had no way to require or force a student to talk. J.D. testified he believed he had no option but to report to Wright's office and to cooperate because "if you don't do it you suffer different consequences from detention to suspension." J.D. offered no further testimony regarding the content or circumstances of his conversation with Wright.

J.D. argues that the admission of his statement violated the principles announced in *Miranda v. Arizona*, 384 U.S. 436 (1966). . . . Fundamentally, the *Miranda* rule "does not apply outside the context of the inherently coercive custodial interrogations for which it was designed." . . .

Steven Wright, in questioning J.D., was not acting as a police officer or as a governmental agent with law enforcement authority. Numerous appellate courts from other states have concluded that a school principal or other school official who questions a student about a possible violation of law or school regulation does not, absent other circumstances, act as a law enforcement officer or agent of the state with law enforcement authority.

J.D. cites several out-of-state cases for the proposition that a school official is required to give a student *Miranda* warnings prior to questioning if any resulting statement is to be admissible in a criminal proceeding. In each of these cases, however, it was a police or security officer who interviewed the student, not a principal or other school official....

We agree with the weight of authority and conclude that Wright was not a law enforcement officer, nor was he acting as an agent of a law enforcement governmental agency, when he interviewed J.D. Wright did not act at the direction of the police. In the course of his duties as assistant principal, Wright initiated and conducted the investigation regarding the recent thefts at the school. Although Wright had Snead present at the interview, Snead did not participate. Snead offered Wright no advice about how to conduct the questioning or what to do with the information Wright might obtain.

Additionally, the *Miranda* holding applies only when the suspect is in custody. "Whether a suspect is 'in custody' under *Miranda* is determined by the circumstances of each case, and 'the ultimate inquiry is simply whether there is a "formal arrest or restraint on freedom of movement" of the degree associated with formal arrest.'"

J.D. was not "in custody" for *Miranda* purposes at the time Wright interviewed him. J.D. was not restrained during the meeting, which took place in Wright's office....

Because J.D. was not "in custody" when Wright questioned him and because Wright was not a law enforcement officer or state officer acting in that capacity, *Miranda* has no application here. Accordingly, the trial court did not err in finding that *Miranda* did not require the exclusion of J.D.'s statements....

State v. Tinkham

719 A.2d 580 (N.H. 1998)

The court rules that a school principal was not acting as an agent of the police and Miranda warnings were not required.

The defendant, Frederick L. Tinkham, Jr., appeals his conviction in Superior Court of unlawful sale of a controlled drug. The defendant argues that the Superior Court erred by denying his motion to suppress. We affirm.

On September 15, 1995, two students at Kingswood Regional High School reported to the principal, Deborah Brooks, that they saw a plastic bag containing marijuana in a book bag belonging to a fellow student. Brooks approached the student and discovered marijuana upon searching her bag. The student eventually told Brooks that she had purchased the drugs from the defendant during the previous day in the student parking lot for a concert she was attending with other students later that evening. Brooks brought the bag of marijuana to the Wolfeboro Police Department and told the police that she was planning to question the defendant.

Brooks returned to school and brought the defendant into her office. After the assistant principal joined them, Brooks explained to the defendant that she had reason to believe that he was carrying an illegal substance and asked him to empty his book bag. The defendant complied. While searching the defendant's bag, Brooks discovered a small wooden cylindrical object with a peculiar odor. She seized the item and told the defendant that she would give it to the police. Brooks also asked the defendant to empty his pockets and show her the contents of his socks and shoes, but she did not find any illegal substances.

Following the search, Brooks explained to the defendant that a student confessed to buying marijuana from him on the previous day. The defendant admitted giving a bag of marijuana to someone in exchange for money, but claimed that he received the marijuana from someone else whose name he would not reveal. Brooks then asked him to write a statement on a "student referral form," a form used when disciplinary action is taken against a student, which provides space for the school administrator and the student to write their versions of the events at issue. Although there is some dispute as to the level of the defendant's cooperation in filling out the form, he eventually wrote, "Someone told me to give a bag [of] pot to someone for someone else and exchanged money and then left." Brooks informed the defendant that he would be suspended for five days and that further action would likely be taken. Brooks then contacted the police and told them about the item she seized from the defendant's book bag as well as the details of her conversation with the defendant.

In November 1995, the defendant was charged with selling marijuana to another student on school property. Prior to trial, the defendant moved to suppress the wooden container seized from his book bag and the student referral form containing his statement....

On appeal, the defendant contends ... that his statement should have been suppressed because Brooks failed to provide the defendant with *Miranda* warnings before questioning him....

Miranda warnings advise a defendant of his constitutional rights, and must be administered when an individual is subject to a custodial interrogation by law enforcement agents....

Although school principals are "responsible for administration and discipline within the school," and "must regularly conduct inquiries concerning both violations of school rules and violations of law," they are not law enforcement agents. They are "neither trained nor equipped to conduct police investigations," and, unlike law enforcement agents, enforcing the law is not their primary mission. "Law enforcement officers are responsible for the investigation of criminal matters and maintenance of general public order," while school officials, in comparison, "are charged with fostering a safe and healthy educational environment that facilitates learning and promotes responsible citizenship." Our conclusion that Brooks is not a law enforcement officer is in accordance with the reasoning of the many jurisdictions that have refused to require public school officials to administer *Miranda* warnings.

We next address whether Brooks acted as an agent of the police, because a school official acting as an instrument or agent of the police may be required to administer *Miranda* warnings. "[T]he existence of an agency relationship under Part I, Article

15 of the State Constitution requires proof of some affirmative action by a police officer or other governmental official that preceded the interrogation and can reasonably be seen to have induced the third party to conduct the interrogation." Here, there was no affirmative act by any police officer inducing Brooks to question the defendant. In fact, it was Brooks who approached the Wolfeboro police and told them of her conversation with the student who implicated the defendant, and that she planned on questioning the defendant when she returned to school. The record does not reflect that the Wolfeboro police made any suggestions to Brooks or directed her course of action. *See State v. Bruneau*, 552 A.2d 585, 589 (1988) (noting that third party was not police agent because he initiated contact with police, and police took no affirmative steps to enlist his help). Moreover, "[t]he fact that the school administrators had every intention of turning the marihuana over to the police does not make them agents or instrumentalities of the police in questioning [the defendant]."

We therefore conclude that because Brooks was neither a law enforcement officer nor an agent of the police, *Miranda* warnings were not required. The need to question students about possible misconduct is necessary to maintain a safe school environment and demands that school officials receive some latitude in their questioning. Thus, the trial court properly denied the defendant's motion to suppress.

Post Problem Discussion

1. How do Kelli and Michael's age factor into whether they were in custody for *Miranda* purposes? Would your conclusion about custody be different if they were younger, say 12, 13 or 14 years old?

2. On the issue of whether Principal Morris is acting as an agent of the police, what is the reason for the different outcomes in *T.A.G.* and *State v. Heirtzler* in Problem 3 (which found that the school officials were acting as agents), and *Tinkham* and *J.D.* (which found that the principals were not acting as agents)? Which case is more like our situation in this problem?

3. Would your answer to the question in this problem be any different if the SRO was present during the questioning of Kelli and/or Michael? If the SRO conducted the questioning?

Some courts have found that even SROs do not have to give *Miranda* warnings when they are investigating a violation of school rules, because they are not acting as law enforcement officials. *See, e.g., In re L.A.*, 21 P.3d 952 (Kan. 2001). Other courts have found that SROs do have to provide *Miranda* warnings particularly when they know that the information obtained in questioning will lead to criminal charges. *In re R.H.*, 791 A.2d 331 (Pa. 2002). Which of these approaches should apply to Michael or Kelli?

4. Why was the student in *T.A.G.* found to be in custody, while the student in *J.D.* was not? Would a reasonable person in Michael or Kelli's position feel that they were free to leave under the circumstances?

5. Do you think that Michael would have provided the information to Principal Morris if she had to give Michael *Miranda* warnings before talking to him? Should the answer to that question influence whether or not Principal Morris has to provide *Miranda* warnings to Michael?

6. In the criminal context, police are permitted to trick suspects into confessing in some situations, but it can also raise questions about the voluntariness of a confession. *See, e.g., Illinois v. Perkins*, 496 U.S. 292 (1990); *Minnesota v. Murphy*, 465 U.S. 420, 430 (1984). As a federal district court noted

> Police trickery and deception are interrelated aspects of the voluntariness inquiry, and are relevant to both the waiver and due process analysis. The issue is not, however, whether the police used tricks or deceit, but whether tricks or deceit led a suspect to believe that he could speak without consequences (*Miranda* waiver) or whether they undermined his ability to make a rational choice about confessing (due process).

United States v. McFarland, 424 F. Supp. 2d 427, 436 (N.D.N.Y. 2006). Should the analysis be any different in the school context when a student is questioned by a school official or an SRO? Do you think Principal Morris' trickery influenced the voluntariness of Michael's confession? If so, what should the remedy be?

Chapter 11

Religion

Synopsis

§ 11.01 Introduction and Overview

The First Amendment provides that "Congress shall make no law respecting an establishment of religion, or prohibiting the free exercise thereof." U.S. Const., Amend. I. As state actors, public schools are subject to these requirements, which apply to state and local governments under the Fourteenth Amendment. *See Everson v. Board of Educ.*, 330 U.S. 1 (1947). The Religion Clauses are the subject of significant Supreme Court jurisprudence in cases that involve schools directly, and also in cases that involve other public entities.

The core principles are that the protection of freedom of conscience and belief is "absolute," and that religious conduct is also protected but "remains subject to regulation for the protection of society" where the state's regulatory power "must be so exercised as not, in attaining a permissible end, unduly to infringe the protected freedom." *Cantwell v. Connecticut*, 310 U.S. 296, 303–04 (1940).

In this context, the Establishment Clause and the Free Exercise Clause may sometimes be at odds in the public school setting, placing public schools in something of a paradox. Public schools cannot promote or endorse religion, yet they must also not substantially burden or inhibit the free exercise of religion. The same government action can run afoul of both clauses. For example, mandatory school prayer establishes a religion and could also interfere with a student's free exercise of some other religious opportunity. Tensions with First Amendment speech rights can also arise when school officials prevent students from expressing religious messages.

The short version is that public schools are required to be neutral towards religion, but the case law and relevant statutory provisions provide a more complicated approach. Religion issues with public schools generally fall into three categories:

Category One — Interaction with private religious schools

This category includes:

✓ Public schools providing services, materials, or transportation to students at private religious schools.

✓ State funding of private schools through vouchers or tuition reimbursement to parents.

✓ Students who attend private religious schools or who are home-schooled and claim free exercise violations for being denied benefits available to public school students.

Category Two — Religious activities at public schools or school-sponsored events

This category includes:

✓ School prayer, reciting the Pledge of Allegiance, school holiday celebrations.

✓ Teaching evolution vs. creationism at school.

✓ Displaying religious symbols at school and wearing religious clothing or items.

Category Three — Using public school facilities

This category includes:

✓ Students and outside groups using public school grounds for religious meetings and events after school hours.

Establishment Clause and Free Exercise Clause issues can arise within each of these categories, and when they do, judicial resolution of these issues depends in part on the legal standard employed by the courts.

A. Establishment Clause Legal Standards

The Establishment Clause is often referred to as the separation of church and state. In *Everson v. Board of Educ.*, 330 U.S. 1, 15–16 (1947), the United States Supreme Court described the Establishment Clause as follows:

> The "establishment of religion" clause of the First Amendment means at least this: Neither a state nor the Federal Government can set up a church. Neither can pass laws which aid one religion, aid all religions, or prefer one religion over another. Neither can force nor influence a person to go to or to remain away from church against his will or force him to profess a belief or disbelief in any religion. No person can be punished for entertaining

> or professing religious beliefs or disbeliefs, for church attendance or non-attendance. No tax in any amount, large or small, can be levied to support any religious activities or institutions, whatever they may be called, or whatever form they may adopt to teach or practice religion. Neither a state nor the Federal Government can, openly or secretly, participate in the affairs of any religious organizations or groups and *vice versa*. In the words of Jefferson, the clause against establishment of religion by law was intended to erect "a wall of separation between church and State."

The legal standards used by the Supreme Court in Establishment Clause cases have evolved and changed over the years. The standard used by the Court in a particular case depends in part on the circumstances. The standards currently used by the Court in education cases are outlined in the following table:

Name of Legal Standard	Requirements	When Used by Courts
Lemon Test	*Lemon* looks to the purpose and effect of the law and whether it fosters an excessive entanglement with religion. *Lemon v. Kurtzman*, 403 U.S. 602 (1971). In subsequent cases, the Court modified the *Lemon* test to some extent by recasting some of the criteria and interpretations. *See Agostini v. Felton*, 521 U.S. 203 (1997), in Problem One of this Chapter.	Though it is much maligned by scholars, legal commentators, and some judges, the *Lemon* test (or some version thereof) is still the primary test used by courts in Establishment Clause cases. Example cases: ✓ *Lemon v. Kurtzman* ✓ *Aguilar v. Felton* ✓ *Agostini v. Felton*
Endorsement Test	The endorsement test looks at whether a law or the actions of school officials endorse or disapprove of religion. It is an objective test, with the Court evaluating whether a "reasonable observer" who is aware of the "history and context" underlying a challenged action would conclude that the message communicated is one of either endorsement or disapproval of religion.	The endorsement test has been used to assess the constitutionality of student prayer, displays of religious symbols, school holiday displays and celebrations, and religious topics in the school curriculum. Example cases: ✓ *Wallace v. Jaffree* ✓ *Edwards v. Aguillard* ✓ *School District of Grand Rapids v. Ball* ✓ *Santa Fe Independent Sch. Dist. v. Doe*
Coercion Test	The coercion test is the standard used by the Court in *Lee v. Weisman*, 505 U.S. 577 (1992) (student prayer at high school graduation). Under the coercion test, public schools may not coerce or pressure students into supporting or participating	The coercion test arises in cases involving school prayer and other religious activities. Example cases: ✓ *Lee v. Weisman*

Name of Legal Standard	Requirements	When Used by Courts
	in religious activities, such as prayer. It is best understood as a constitutional floor, because the Court has noted that coercion is not necessary to show an Establishment Clause violation. Laws or actions by school officials that are not coercive can still be unconstitutional if they fail one or more of the other Establishment Clause tests.	
Child Benefit Test	The first test developed by the United States Supreme Court in older Establishment Clause cases such as *Everson v. Board of Educ.*, 330 U.S. 1 (1947). The Court evaluates whether the law or governmental action at issue benefits children rather than the religious school they attended. The Court has used a version of this test in more recent cases like *Zobrest v. Catalina Foothills*, 509 U.S. 1 (1993), and *Mitchell v. Helms*, 530 U.S. 793 (2000), and, in doing so, has focused on the concept of government neutrality.	When public schools or state governments provide transportation, textbooks, or services to students who attend private religious schools. Example cases: ✓ *Everson v. Board of Educ.* ✓ *Board of Educ. v. Allen* ✓ *Zobrest v. Catalina Foothills Sch. Dist.* ✓ *Mitchell v. Helms*

While having various tests or legal standards can be confusing, there is a certain amount of overlap among all of them, and the cases often use very similar language regardless of which "test" is applied. There are a number of themes and principles that arise from the tests to help guide a constitutional analysis of Establishment Clause issues for public schools. They are:

Theme/Principle	Explanation
Neutrality	Public schools must not favor or promote one religion over another, or religion over non-religion.
Endorsement	Public schools must not endorse nor discourage religion.
Coercion	Public schools must not coerce students into supporting or participating in religious activities or events.
Purpose or Effect	The purpose or effect of actions taken by the public school must neither advance nor inhibit religion.
Entanglement	Public school officials cannot become excessively entangled with religious issues.

The cases and problems in this Chapter further elaborate and explain these principles.

B. Free Exercise Legal Standards

The Free Exercise Clause inquiry in education is generally whether public school officials took actions that prohibited the free exercise of religion by students, or imposed substantial burdens on the exercise of religion.

Prior to 1990, the United States Supreme Court utilized a strict scrutiny type test to evaluate free exercise claims. When the state met the compelling interest requirement of that test, the Court would generally balance the state's interest against the individual's interest and the level of governmental coercion involved, to assess the constitutionality of the law or action at issue. *See, e.g., Wisconsin v. Yoder*, 406 U.S. 205 (1972); *Sherbert v. Verner*, 374 U.S. 398 (1963). The Court changed the standard in *Employment Div. v. Smith*, 494 U.S. 872 (1990), when it determined that a law does not have to be justified by a compelling interest if it is 1) neutral, meaning that it does not target religiously motivated conduct; and 2) generally applicable and does not selectively burden religious conduct. *See also Church of Lukumi Babalu Aye, Inc. v. City of Hialeah*, 508 U.S. 520 (1993).

In *Smith*, and in subsequent cases, the Court noted two situations where strict scrutiny would still apply in free exercise claims. One is a "hybrid situation," where there is a combination of rights involved, such as the free exercise rights and substantive due process right of a parent to direct the religious upbringing of their child, as was the issue in *Yoder*. The second situation is when the law is not neutral and targets religion, as was the issue in *Church of Lukumi*, 508 U.S. 520 (1993), where the Court applied strict scrutiny to a city ordinance that prohibited ritualistic animal sacrifice because its objective was to suppress religious practices, and it was targeting conduct motivated by religious beliefs.

The following graphic summarizes the cases and free exercise standards:

Cases	Standard
Employment Div., Dep't of Human Res. of Or. v. Smith, 494 U.S. 872 (1990)	Rational basis standard. Applies when the law or governmental action at issue is neutral, and of general applicability. Under this standard, laws are generally upheld even if they impinge incidentally upon individual religious practices.
Church of Lukumi Babalu Aye, Inc. v. City of Hialeah, 508 U.S. 520 (1993)	Strict scrutiny still applies when the law or action targets religion (or is not neutral towards religion).
Wisconsin v. Yoder, 406 U.S. 205 (1972)	Strict scrutiny applies in "hybrid" situations where rights (such as free exercise and substantive due process) are combined.
Sherbert v. *Verner*, 374 U.S. 398 (1963)	Strict scrutiny applies to laws or government actions that force individuals to choose between following their religious beliefs and receiving governmental benefits. To date, the Supreme Court has only applied *Sherbert* in the context of unemployment benefits.

§ 11.02 Category One: Interaction with Private Religious Schools

A. Providing Materials and Services to Students at Religious Schools

In *Everson*, 330 U.S. 1 (1947), the United States Supreme Court ruled that a state statute that permitted public school districts to reimburse parents for money spent on bus fares to send their children to Catholic schools did not violate the Establishment Clause. Subsequent United States Supreme Court cases have upheld the provision of certain materials (such as textbooks and computers) and services (such as remedial reading and sign language interpreters) to private religious schools in certain situations, but not in others. The legal standards that govern these types of activities have also varied: the child benefit test, the *Lemon* test, and the endorsement test have been used in different cases. The following problem explores the legal parameters of this area of the Establishment Clause.

Problem 1: Religious Organizations Providing Services to Public School Students

Background

Assume for purposes of this problem that under state law, a public school that is found to be "in need of improvement" because of its performance on statewide assessment tests must offer "supplemental educational services" to certain students. Supplemental educational services are to be provided in addition to instruction provided during the school day to help students improve their test results on subsequent tests. The law allows public schools, private schools, and private or non-profit organizations, including those with religious affiliations, to become providers of supplemental services to students. The state Department of Education develops a process to allow providers to apply to be on a state approved list. Parents of eligible children at schools in need of improvement are then able to choose one of the providers from the list, and the public school then enters into an agreement with the provider to deliver supplemental services for a fee.

Fact Pattern

The Geyser Elementary school must offer supplemental educational services to some of its students due to its status as a school in need of improvement under state law. The state list of private supplemental service providers has eleven providers including one that is a religiously affiliated organization named Pinnacle Testing Development. Pinnacle provides its education services in an auxiliary room in a non-denominational church several miles away from Geyser Elementary. The room contains numerous Christian religious symbols and references to Jesus and God. While the instruction itself is not focused on religion, the instructors occasionally incorporate non-denominational religious stories into their lessons.

Pinnacle contends that these stories help students develop a positive attitude about self-improvement, which helps students score higher on the statewide assessments.

The sessions end at the same time the church is closing in the afternoon. The minister of the church ends each day with a prayer that she recites over the church intercom system, which can be heard throughout the church. Students are not required to stay or participate in the prayer and may go outside if they do not want to listen to the prayer. Over the past three years, Pinnacle has the best student improvement rate in the state.

Twenty-three out of the thirty-nine eligible students from Geyser sign up to participate in the Pinnacle sessions; of these, twelve have family members that are part of the Pinnacle parish. The school district enters into an agreement with Pinnacle and provides transportation to the local church for the sessions.

After discovering the religious symbols, religious stories, and prayer, one of the parents asks that her child be reassigned to another provider on the approved state list. The school accommodates her request but is not able to offer transportation to the new provider, because it only has enough funds to transport to one provider. The school offers to provide supplemental services to the student at the public school.

The parent attends the next school board meeting to voice her concerns and threatens to sue the school, noting that she does not want her tax dollars going to support a religious organization.

Answer the following:

1. Does the school violate the Establishment Clause by sending students to the Pinnacle Testing Development program upon request? If so, what facts would need to change so that it does not violate the Establishment Clause? What types of actions could the school take to remove any religious aspects of the program without becoming excessively entangled in religion?
2. Does including the Pinnacle Testing Development program on the state list of supplemental providers violate the Establishment Clause? If so, what facts would need to change so that it does not violate the Establishment Clause? What types of actions could the state take to ensure religious neutrality by supplemental providers without becoming excessively entangled in religion?
3. Does the school violate the Establishment Clause by providing transportation only to the Pinnacle Testing Development program?
4. Would the school violate the Establishment Clause if it refused to send students to the Pinnacle Testing Development program because of its religious affiliation or the religious messages it conveys during student sessions? Similarly, would the state violate the Establishment Clause if it refused to include Pinnacle on the list of supplemental providers?

5. Would your answer to any of these questions differ if you applied the *Lemon* test, the *Lemon* test as modified by *Agostini*, or the child benefit test used in *Zobrest* and *Mitchell*? What about the endorsement test?

Problem Materials

✓ *Lemon v. Kurtzman*, 403 U.S. 602 (1971)

✓ *Zobrest v. Catalina Foothills School District*, 509 U.S. 1 (1993)

✓ *Agostini v. Felton*, 521 U.S. 203 (1997)

✓ *Mitchell v. Helms*, 530 U.S. 793 (2000)

Lemon v. Kurtzman

403 U.S. 602 (1971)

The Court rules that a Pennsylvania statute that provided for state reimbursement to non-public schools for the cost of teachers' salaries, secular textbooks, and instructional materials and a Rhode Island statute that provided for state payment of teacher salary supplements violate the Establishment Clause under the excessive entanglement prong of the Lemon test.

Mr. Chief Justice Burger delivered the opinion of the Court.

Pennsylvania has adopted a statutory program that provides financial support to nonpublic elementary and secondary schools by way of reimbursement for the cost of teachers' salaries, textbooks, and instructional materials in specified secular subjects. Rhode Island has adopted a statute under which the State pays directly to teachers in nonpublic elementary schools a supplement of 15% of their annual salary. Under each statute state aid has been given to church-related educational institutions. We hold that both statutes are unconstitutional.

The Rhode Island Statute

The Rhode Island Salary Supplement Act . . . authorizes state officials to supplement the salaries of teachers of secular subjects in nonpublic elementary schools by paying directly to a teacher an amount not in excess of 15% of his current annual salary. . . .

In order to be eligible for the Rhode Island salary supplement, the recipient must teach in a nonpublic school at which the average per-pupil expenditure on secular education is less than the average in the State's public schools during a specified period. Appellant State Commissioner of Education also requires eligible schools to submit financial data. If this information indicates a per-pupil expenditure in excess of the statutory limitation, the records of the school in question must be examined in order to assess how much of the expenditure is attributable to secular education and how much to religious activity.

The Act also requires that teachers eligible for salary supplements must teach only those subjects that are offered in the State's public schools. They must use "only teaching materials which are used in the public schools." Finally, any teacher applying for a salary supplement must first agree in writing "not to teach a course in religion for so long as or during such time as he or she receives any salary supplements" under the Act.

....

The Pennsylvania Statute

Pennsylvania has adopted a program that has some but not all of the features of the Rhode Island program. . . . The statute authorizes appellee state Superintendent of Public Instruction to "purchase" specified "secular educational services" from nonpublic schools. Under the "contracts" authorized by the statute, the State directly reimburses nonpublic schools solely for their actual expenditures for teachers' salaries, textbooks, and instructional materials. A school seeking reimbursement must maintain prescribed accounting procedures that identify the "separate" cost of the "secular educational service." These accounts are subject to state audit. . . .

There are several significant statutory restrictions on state aid. Reimbursement is limited to courses "presented in the curricula of the public schools." It is further limited "solely" to courses in the following "secular" subjects: mathematics, modern foreign languages, physical science, and physical education. Textbooks and instructional materials included in the program must be approved by the state Superintendent of Public Instruction. Finally, the statute prohibits reimbursement for any course that contains "any subject matter expressing religious teaching, or the morals or forms of worship of any sect."

....

In the absence of precisely stated constitutional prohibitions, we must draw lines with reference to the three main evils against which the Establishment Clause was intended to afford protection: "sponsorship, financial support, and active involvement of the sovereign in religious activity." Every analysis in this area must begin with consideration of the cumulative criteria developed by the Court over many years. Three such tests may be gleaned from our cases. First, the statute must have a secular legislative purpose; second, its principal or primary effect must be one that neither advances nor inhibits religion; finally, the statute must not foster "an excessive government entanglement with religion."

Inquiry into the legislative purposes of the Pennsylvania and Rhode Island statutes affords no basis for a conclusion that the legislative intent was to advance religion. On the contrary, the statutes themselves clearly state that they are intended to enhance the quality of the secular education in all schools covered by the compulsory attendance laws. There is no reason to believe the legislatures meant anything else. . . . [W]e find nothing here that undermines the stated legislative intent; it must therefore be accorded appropriate deference. . . .

The two legislatures, however, have also recognized that church-related elementary and secondary schools have a significant religious mission and that a substantial portion of their activities is religiously oriented. They have therefore sought to create statutory restrictions designed to guarantee the separation between secular and religious educational functions and to ensure that State financial aid supports only the former. All these provisions are precautions taken in candid recognition that these programs approached, even if they did not intrude upon, the forbidden areas under the Religion Clauses. We need not decide whether these legislative precautions restrict the principal or primary effect of the programs to the point where they do not offend the Religion Clauses, for we conclude that the cumulative impact of the entire relationship arising under the statutes in each State involves excessive entanglement between government and religion.

....

Our prior holdings do not call for total separation between church and state; total separation is not possible in an absolute sense. Some relationship between government and religious organizations is inevitable. Fire inspections, building and zoning regulations, and state requirements under compulsory school-attendance laws are examples of necessary and permissible contacts.... Judicial caveats against entanglement must recognize that the line of separation, far from being a "wall," is a blurred, indistinct, and variable barrier depending on all the circumstances of a particular relationship.

....

In order to determine whether the government entanglement with religion is excessive, we must examine the character and purposes of the institutions that are benefited, the nature of the aid that the State provides, and the resulting relationship between the government and the religious authority.... Here we find that both statutes foster an impermissible degree of entanglement.

(a) Rhode Island program

The District Court made extensive findings on the grave potential for excessive entanglement that inheres in the religious character and purpose of the Roman Catholic elementary schools of Rhode Island, to date the sole beneficiaries of the Rhode Island Salary Supplement Act.

The church schools involved in the program are located close to parish churches. This understandably permits convenient access for religious exercises since instruction in faith and morals is part of the total educational process. The school buildings contain identifying religious symbols such as crosses on the exterior and crucifixes, and religious paintings and statues either in the classrooms or hallways. Although only approximately 30 minutes a day are devoted to direct religious instruction, there are religiously oriented extracurricular activities. Approximately two-thirds of the teachers in these schools are nuns of various religious orders. Their dedicated efforts provide an atmosphere in which religious instruction and religious vocations are natural and proper parts of life in such schools. Indeed, as the District Court found, the role of teaching nuns in enhancing the religious atmosphere has led the parochial school authorities to attempt to maintain a one-to-one ratio between nuns and lay teachers in all schools rather than to permit some to be staffed almost entirely by lay teachers. . . .

The substantial religious character of these church-related schools gives rise to entangling church-state relationships of the kind the Religion Clauses sought to avoid. Although the District Court found that concern for religious values did not inevitably or necessarily intrude into the content of secular subjects, the considerable religious activities of these schools led the legislature to provide for careful governmental controls and surveillance by state authorities in order to ensure that state aid supports only secular education.

The dangers and corresponding entanglements are enhanced by the particular form of aid that the Rhode Island Act provides. Our decisions from *Everson v. Board of Educ.*, 330 U.S. 1 (1947), to *Board of Educ. V. Allen*, 392 U.S. 236 (1968), have permitted the States to provide church-related schools with secular, neutral, or non-ideological services, facilities, or materials. Bus transportation, school lunches, public health services, and secular textbooks supplied in common to all students were not thought to offend the Establishment Clause. . . .

In Allen the Court refused to make assumptions, on a meager record, about the religious content of the textbooks that the State would be asked to provide. We cannot, however, refuse here to recognize that teachers have a substantially different ideological character from books. In terms of potential for involving some aspect of faith or morals in secular subjects, a textbook's content is ascertainable, but a teacher's handling of a subject is not. We cannot ignore the danger that a teacher under religious control and discipline poses to the separation of the religious from the purely secular aspects of pre-college education. The conflict of functions inheres in the situation.

. . . .

We need not and do not assume that teachers in parochial schools will be guilty of bad faith or any conscious design to evade the limitations imposed by the statute and the First Amendment. We simply recognize that a dedicated religious person, teaching in a school affiliated with his or her faith and operated to inculcate its tenets, will inevitably experience great difficulty in remaining religiously neutral. Doctrines and faith are not inculcated or advanced by neutrals. With the best of intentions such a teacher would find it hard to make a total separation between secular teaching and religious doctrine. What would appear to some to be essential to good citizenship might well for others border on or constitute instruction in religion. Further difficulties are inherent in the combination of religious discipline and the possibility of disagreement between teacher and religious authorities over the meaning of the statutory restrictions.

We do not assume, however, that parochial school teachers will be unsuccessful in their attempts to segregate their religious beliefs from their secular educational responsibilities. But the potential for impermissible fostering of religion is present. The Rhode Island Legislature has not, and could not, provide state aid on the basis of a mere assumption that secular teachers under religious discipline can avoid conflicts. The State must be certain, given the Religion Clauses, that subsidized teachers do not inculcate religion—indeed the State here has undertaken to do so. To ensure that no trespass occurs, the State has therefore carefully conditioned its aid with pervasive restrictions. An eligible recipient must teach only those courses that are offered in the public schools and use only those texts and materials that are found in the public schools. In addition the teacher must not engage in teaching any course in religion.

A comprehensive, discriminating, and continuing state surveillance will inevitably be required to ensure that these restrictions are obeyed and the First Amendment otherwise respected. Unlike a book, a teacher cannot be inspected once so as to determine the extent and intent of his or her personal beliefs and subjective acceptance of the limitations imposed by the First Amendment. These prophylactic contacts will involve excessive and enduring entanglement between state and church.

. . . .

(b) Pennsylvania program

The Pennsylvania statute also provides state aid to church-related schools for teachers' salaries. The complaint describes an educational system that is very similar to the one existing in Rhode Island. According to the allegations, the church-related elementary and secondary schools are controlled by religious organizations, have the purpose of propagating and promoting a particular religious faith, and conduct their operations to fulfill that purpose. Since this complaint was dismissed for failure to state a claim for relief, we must accept these allegations as true for purposes of our review.

As we noted earlier, the very restrictions and surveillance necessary to ensure that teachers play a strictly non-ideological role give rise to entanglements between church and state. The Pennsylvania statute, like that of Rhode Island, fosters this kind of relationship. Reimbursement is not only limited to courses offered in the public schools and materials approved by state officials, but the statute excludes "any subject matter expressing religious teaching, or the morals or forms of worship of any sect." In addition, schools seeking reimbursement must maintain accounting procedures that require the State to establish the cost of the secular as distinguished from the religious instruction.

The Pennsylvania statute, moreover, has the further defect of providing state financial aid directly to the church-related school. This factor distinguishes both *Everson* and *Allen*, for in both those cases the Court was careful to point out that state aid was provided to the student and his parents—not to the church-related school. *Board of Education v. Allen; Everson v. Board of Education*. . . .

Zobrest v. Catalina Foothills School District

509 U.S. 1 (1993)

The Court rules that a public school providing a sign language interpreter to a student with a disability under the IDEA at a parochial school does not violate the Establishment Clause.

Chief Justice Rehnquist delivered the opinion of the Court.

Petitioner James Zobrest, who has been deaf since birth, asked respondent school district to provide a sign language interpreter to accompany him to classes at a Roman Catholic high school in Tucson, Arizona, pursuant to the Individuals with Disabilities Education Act (IDEA) and its Arizona counterpart. The United States Court of Appeals for the Ninth Circuit decided, however, that provision of such a publicly employed interpreter would violate the Establishment Clause of the First Amendment. We hold that the Establishment Clause does not bar the school district from providing the requested interpreter.

The [district] court . . . granted respondent summary judgment, on the ground that "[t]he interpreter would act as a conduit for the religious inculcation of James—thereby, promoting James' religious development at government expense." "That kind of entanglement of church and state," the District Court concluded, "is not allowed."

The Court of Appeals affirmed by a divided vote, applying the three-part test announced in *Lemon* v. *Kurtzman*, 403 U.S. 602 (1971). . . . Turning to the second prong of the *Lemon* inquiry, though, the Court of Appeals determined that the IDEA, if applied as petitioners proposed, would have the primary effect of advancing religion and thus would run afoul of the Establishment Clause. "By placing its employee in the sectarian school," the Court of Appeals reasoned, "the government would create the appearance that it was a 'joint sponsor' of the school's activities." This, the court held, would create the "symbolic union of government and religion" found impermissible in *School Dist. of Grand Rapids v. Ball*, 473 U.S. 373. . . . We granted certiorari, and now reverse.

. . . .

We have never said that "religious institutions are disabled by the First Amendment from participating in publicly sponsored social welfare programs." For if the Establishment Clause did bar religious groups from receiving general government benefits, then "a church could not be protected by the police and fire departments, or have its public sidewalk kept in repair." Given that a contrary rule would lead to such absurd results, we have consistently held that government programs that neutrally provide benefits to a broad class of citizens defined without reference to religion are not readily subject to an Establishment Clause challenge just because sectarian institutions may also receive an attenuated financial benefit. Nowhere have we stated this principle more clearly than in *Mueller v. Allen*, 463 U.S. 388 (1983), and *Witters v. Washington Dept. of Services for Blind*, 474 U.S. 481 (1986), two cases dealing specifically with government programs offering general educational assistance.

In *Mueller*, we rejected an Establishment Clause challenge to a Minnesota law allowing taxpayers to deduct certain educational expenses in computing their state income tax, even though the vast majority of those deductions (perhaps over 90%) went to parents whose children attended sectarian schools. Two factors, aside from States' traditionally broad taxing authority, informed our decision. We noted that the law "permits *all* parents—whether their children attend public school or private—to deduct their children's educational expenses." . . . We also pointed out that under Minnesota's scheme, public funds become available to sectarian schools "only as a result of numerous private choices of individual parents of school age children," thus distinguishing *Mueller* from our other cases involving "the direct transmission of assistance from the State to the schools themselves."

Witters was premised on virtually identical reasoning. In that case, we upheld against an Establishment Clause challenge the State of Washington's extension of vocational assistance, as part of a general state program, to a blind person studying at a private Christian college to become a pastor, missionary, or youth director. Looking at the statute as a whole, we observed that "[a]ny aid provided under Washington's program that ultimately flows to religious institutions does so only as a result of the genuinely independent and private choices of aid recipients." The program, we said, "creates no financial incentive for students to undertake sectarian education." We also remarked that, much like the law in *Mueller*, "Washington's program is 'made available generally without regard to the sectarian nonsectarian, or public nonpublic nature of the institution benefited.'" In light of these factors, we held that Washington's program—even as applied to a student who sought state assistance so that he could become a pastor—would not advance religion in a manner inconsistent with the Establishment Clause.

That same reasoning applies with equal force here. The service at issue in this case is part of a general government program that distributes benefits neutrally to any child qualifying as "handicapped" under the IDEA, without regard to the "sectarian nonsectarian, or public nonpublic nature" of the school the child attends. By according parents freedom to select a school of their choice, the statute ensures that a government paid interpreter will be present in a sectarian school only as a result of the private decision of individual parents. In other words, because the IDEA creates no financial incentive for parents to choose a sectarian school, an interpreter's presence there cannot be attributed to state decisionmaking. Viewed against the backdrop of *Mueller* and *Witters*, then, the Court of Appeals erred in its decision. When the government offers a neutral service on the premises of a sectarian school as part of a general program that "is in no way skewed towards religion," *Witters, supra*, at 488, it follows under our prior decisions that provision of that service does not offend the Establishment Clause. Indeed, this is an even easier case than *Mueller* and *Witters* in the sense that, under the IDEA, no funds traceable to the government ever find their way into sectarian schools' coffers. The only indirect economic benefit a sectarian school might receive by dint of the IDEA is the handicapped child's tuition—and that is, of course, assuming that the school makes a profit on each student; that, without an IDEA interpreter, the child would have gone to school elsewhere; and that the school, then, would have been unable to fill that child's spot.

....

The extension of aid to petitioners, however, does not amount to "an impermissible 'direct subsidy'".... And, as we noted above, any attenuated financial benefit that parochial schools do ultimately receive from the IDEA is attributable to "the private choices of individual parents." Handicapped children, not sectarian schools, are the primary beneficiaries of the IDEA; to the extent sectarian schools benefit at all from the IDEA, they are only incidental beneficiaries. Thus, the function of the IDEA is hardly "to provide desired financial support for nonpublic, sectarian institutions.'"

Second, the task of a sign language interpreter seems to us quite different from that of a teacher or guidance counselor. Notwithstanding the Court of Appeals' intimations to the contrary, the Establishment Clause lays down no absolute bar to the placing of a public employee in a sectarian school. Such a flat rule, smacking of antiquated notions of "taint," would indeed exalt form over substance. Nothing in this record suggests that a sign language interpreter would do more than accurately interpret whatever material is presented to the class as a whole. In fact, ethical guidelines require interpreters to "transmit everything that is said in exactly the same way it was intended." James' parents have chosen of their own free will to place him in a pervasively sectarian environment. The sign language interpreter they have requested will neither add to nor subtract from that environment, and hence the provision of such assistance is not barred by the Establishment Clause.

The IDEA creates a neutral government program dispensing aid not to schools but to individual handicapped children. If a handicapped child chooses to enroll in a sectarian school, we hold that the Establishment Clause does not prevent the school district from furnishing him with a sign language interpreter there in order to facilitate his education. The judgment of the Court of Appeals is therefore *Reversed.*

Agostini v. Felton

521 U.S. 203 (1997)

The Court modifies the Lemon test by including the excessive entanglement prong in the inquiry regarding the law's effect. It also changes its interpretation of the purpose and effect test resulting in actions that were once unconstitutional now being permissible under the Establishment Clause.

O'Connor, J., delivered the opinion of the Court.

In *Aguilar v. Felton*, 473 U.S. 402 (1985), this Court held that the Establishment Clause of the First Amendment barred the city of New York from sending public school teachers into parochial schools to provide remedial education to disadvantaged children pursuant to a congressionally mandated program. On remand, the District Court for the Eastern District of New York entered a permanent injunction reflecting our ruling. Twelve years later, petitioners—the parties bound by that injunction—seek relief from its operation. Petitioners maintain that *Aguilar* cannot be squared with our intervening Establishment Clause jurisprudence and ask that we explicitly recognize what our more recent cases already dictate: *Aguilar* is no longer good law. We agree with petitioners that *Aguilar* is not consistent with our subsequent Establishment Clause decisions....

In 1965, Congress enacted Title I of the Elementary and Secondary Education Act of 1965.... Title I channels federal funds, through the States, to "local educational agencies" (LEA's). The LEA's spend these funds to provide remedial education, guidance, and job counseling to eligible students. Title I funds must be made available to *all* eligible children, regardless of whether they attend public schools, and the services provided to children attending private schools must be "equitable in comparison to services and other benefits for public school children."

Petitioner Board of Education of the City of New York (Board), an LEA, first applied for Title I funds in 1966 and has grappled ever since with how to provide Title I services to the private school students within its jurisdiction.... [The Board's] plan called for the provision of Title I services on private school premises during school hours. Under the plan, only public employees could serve as Title I instructors and counselors. Assignments to private schools were made on a voluntary basis and without regard to the religious affiliation of the employee or the wishes of the private school. As the Court of Appeals in *Aguilar* observed, a large majority of Title I teachers worked in nonpublic schools with religious affiliations different from their own. The vast majority of Title I teachers also moved among the private schools, spending fewer than five days a week at the same school.

Before any public employee could provide Title I instruction at a private school, she would be given a detailed set of written and oral instructions emphasizing the secular purpose of Title I and setting out the rules to be followed to ensure that this purpose was not compromised. Specifically, employees would be told that (i) they were employees of the Board and accountable only to their public school supervisors; (ii) they had exclusive responsibility for selecting students for the Title I program and could teach only those children who met the eligibility criteria for Title I; (iii) their materials and equipment would be used only in the Title I program; (iv) they could not engage in team teaching or other cooperative instructional activities with private school teachers; and (v) they could not introduce any religious matter into their teaching or become involved in any way with the religious activities of the private schools. All religious symbols were to be removed from classrooms used for Title I services. The rules acknowledged that it might be necessary for Title I teachers to consult with a student's regular classroom teacher to assess the student's particular needs and progress, but admonished instructors to limit those consultations to mutual professional concerns regarding the student's education. To ensure compliance with these rules, a publicly employed field supervisor was to attempt to make at least one unannounced visit to each teacher's classroom every month.

In 1978, six federal taxpayers—respondents here—sued the Board. . . . In a 5-4 decision, this Court [ruled in *Aguilar*] that the Board's Title I program necessitated an "excessive entanglement of church and state in the administration of [Title I] benefits." . . .

. . . .

Our more recent cases have undermined the assumptions upon which . . . *Aguilar* relied. To be sure, the general principles we use to evaluate whether government aid violates the Establishment Clause have not changed since *Aguilar* was decided. For example, we continue to ask whether the government acted with the purpose of advancing or inhibiting religion, and the nature of that inquiry has remained largely unchanged. Likewise, we continue to explore whether the aid has the "effect" of advancing or inhibiting religion. What has changed since we decided. . . . *Aguilar* is our understanding of the criteria used to assess whether aid to religion has an impermissible effect.

As we have repeatedly recognized, government inculcation of religious beliefs has the impermissible effect of advancing religion. Our cases subsequent to *Aguilar* have, however, modified in two significant respects the approach we use to assess indoctrination. First, we have abandoned the presumption erected in *Meek v. Pittenger*, 421 U.S. 349 (1975), and *Ball*, 473 U.S. 373 (1985), that the placement of public employees on parochial school grounds inevitably results in the impermissible effect of state sponsored indoctrination or constitutes a symbolic union between government and religion. [*See Zobrest v. Catalina Foothills*, 509 U.S. 1 (1993)]. . . .

Second, we have departed from the rule relied on in *Ball* that all government aid that directly aids the educational function of religious schools is invalid. In *Witters* v. *Washington Dept. of Servs. For Blind*, 474 U.S. 481 (1986), we held that the Establishment Clause did not bar a State from issuing a vocational tuition grant to a blind person who wished to use the grant to attend a Christian college and become a pastor, missionary, or youth director. Even though the grant recipient clearly would use the money to obtain religious education, we observed that the tuition grants were "'made available generally without regard to the sectarian nonsectarian, or public nonpublic nature of the institution benefited.'" The grants were disbursed directly to students, who then used the money to pay for tuition at the educational institution of their choice. In our view, this transaction was no different from a State's issuing a paycheck to one of its employees, knowing that the employee would donate part or all of the check to a religious institution. In both situations, any money that ultimately went to religious institutions did so "only as a result of the genuinely independent and private choices of" individuals. *Ibid.* The same logic applied in *Zobrest*, where we allowed the State to provide an interpreter, even though she would be a mouthpiece for religious instruction, because the IDEA's neutral eligibility criteria ensured that the interpreter's presence in a sectarian school was a "result of the private decision of individual parents" and "[could] not be attributed to *state* decisionmaking." 509 U. S., at 10 (emphasis added). Because the private school would not have provided an interpreter on its own, we also concluded that the aid in *Zobrest* did not indirectly finance religious education by "reliev[ing] the sectarian schoo[l] of costs [it] otherwise would have borne in educating [its] students." *Id.*, at 12.

Zobrest and *Witters* make clear that, under current law, . . . New York City's Title I program in *Aguilar* will not, as a matter of law, be deemed to have the effect of advancing religion through indoctrination. . . .

Nor under current law can we conclude that a program placing full time public employees on parochial campuses to provide Title I instruction would impermissibly finance religious indoctrination. In all relevant respects, the provision of instructional services under Title I is indistinguishable from the provision of sign language interpreters under the IDEA. Both programs make aid available only to eligible recipients. That aid is provided to students at whatever school they choose to attend. Although Title I instruction is provided to several students at once, whereas an interpreter provides translation to a single student, this distinction is not constitutionally significant. Moreover, as in *Zobrest*, Title I services are by law supplemental to the regular curricula. These services do not, therefore, "reliev[e] sectarian schools of costs they otherwise would have borne in educating their students."

. . . .

[I]t is clear that Title I services are allocated on the basis of criteria that neither favor nor disfavor religion. The services are available to all children who meet the Act's eligibility requirements, no matter what their religious beliefs or where they go to school. The Board's program does not, therefore, give aid recipients any incentive to modify their religious beliefs or practices in order to obtain those services.

We turn now to *Aguilar*'s conclusion that New York City's Title I program resulted in an excessive entanglement between church and state. Whether a government aid program results in such an entanglement has consistently been an aspect of our Establishment Clause analysis. We have considered entanglement both in the course of assessing whether an aid program has an impermissible effect of advancing religion, *Walz v. Tax Comm'n of City of New York*, 397 U.S. 664 (1970), and as a factor separate and apart from "effect," *Lemon v. Kurtzman*, 403 U.S. 602 (1971). Regardless of how we have characterized the issue, however, the factors we use to assess whether an entanglement is "excessive" are similar to the factors we use to examine "effect." That is, to assess entanglement, we have looked to "the character and purposes of the institutions that are benefited, the nature of the aid that the State provides, and the resulting relationship between the government and religious authority." Similarly, we have assessed a law's "effect" by examining the character of the institutions benefited (*e.g.*, whether the religious institutions were "predominantly religious") and the nature of the aid that the State provided (*e.g.*, whether it was neutral and non-ideological). Indeed, in *Lemon* itself, the entanglement that the Court found "independently" to necessitate the program's invalidation also was found to have the effect of inhibiting religion. Thus, it is simplest to recognize why entanglement is significant and treat it—as we did in *Walz*—as an aspect of the inquiry into a statute's effect.

Not all entanglements, of course, have the effect of advancing or inhibiting religion. Interaction between church and state is inevitable and we have always tolerated some level of involvement between the two. Entanglement must be "excessive" before it runs afoul of the Establishment Clause. . . . The pre-*Aguilar* Title I program does not result in an "excessive" entanglement that advances or inhibits religion. As discussed previously, the Court's finding of "excessive" entanglement in *Aguilar* rested on three grounds: (i) the program would require "pervasive monitoring by public authorities" to ensure that Title I employees did not inculcate religion; (ii) the program required "administrative cooperation" between the Board and parochial schools; and (iii) the program might increase the dangers of "political divisiveness." Under our current understanding of the Establishment Clause, the last two considerations are insufficient by themselves to create an "excessive" entanglement. They are present no matter where Title I services are offered, and no court has held that Title I services cannot be offered off campus. Further, the assumption underlying the first consideration has been undermined. In *Aguilar*, the Court presumed that full time public employees on parochial school grounds would be tempted to inculcate religion, despite the ethical standards they were required to uphold. Because of this risk *pervasive* monitoring would be required. But after *Zobrest* we no longer presume that public employees will inculcate religion simply because they happen to be in a sectarian environment. Since we have abandoned the assumption that properly instructed public employees will fail to discharge their duties faithfully, we must also discard the assumption that *pervasive* monitoring of Title I teachers is required. There is no suggestion in the record before us that unannounced monthly visits of public supervisors are insufficient to prevent or to detect inculcation of religion by public employees. Moreover, we have not found excessive entanglement in cases in which States imposed far more onerous burdens on religious institutions than the monitoring system at issue here.

To summarize, New York City's Title I program does not run afoul of any of three primary criteria we currently use to evaluate whether government aid has the effect of advancing religion: it does not result in governmental indoctrination; define its recipients by reference to religion; or create an excessive entanglement. We therefore hold that a federally funded program providing supplemental, remedial instruction to disadvantaged children on a neutral basis is not invalid under the Establishment Clause when such instruction is given on the premises of sectarian schools by government employees pursuant to a program containing safeguards such as those present here. The same considerations that justify this holding require us to conclude that this carefully constrained program also cannot reasonably be viewed as an endorsement of religion. Accordingly, we must acknowledge that *Aguilar*, as well as the portion of *Ball* addressing Grand Rapids' Shared Time program, are no longer good law.

. . . .

Mitchell v. Helms

530 U.S. 793 (2000)

A plurality of the Court upholds a law called the "Chapter 2 program" that allows private religious schools (along with public and non-religious private schools) to be eligible to receive state provided computers. (Part of Justice O'Connor's concurring opinion is also included to demonstrate where the plurality fell short of convincing a majority of the Court.)

Justice Thomas announced the judgment of the Court and delivered an opinion, in which The Chief Justice, Justice Scalia, and Justice Kennedy join.

As we indicated in *Agostini*, and have indicated elsewhere, the question whether governmental aid to religious schools results in governmental indoctrination is ultimately a question whether any religious indoctrination that occurs in those schools could reasonably be attributed to governmental action. . . . We have also indicated that the answer to the question of indoctrination will resolve the question whether a program of educational aid "subsidizes" religion, as our religion cases use that term.

In distinguishing between indoctrination that is attributable to the State and indoctrination that is not, we have consistently turned to the principle of neutrality, upholding aid that is offered to a broad range of groups or persons without regard to their religion. If the religious, irreligious, and areligious are all alike eligible for governmental aid, no one would conclude that any indoctrination that any particular recipient conducts has been done at the behest of the government. For attribution of indoctrination is a relative question. If the government is offering assistance to recipients who provide, so to speak, a broad range of indoctrination, the government itself is not thought responsible for any particular indoctrination. To put the point differently, if the government, seeking to further some legitimate secular purpose, offers aid on the same terms, without regard to religion, to all who adequately further that purpose, then it is fair to say that any aid going to a religious recipient only has the effect of furthering that secular purpose. The government, in crafting such an aid program, has had to conclude that a given level of aid is necessary to further that purpose among secular recipients and has provided no more than that same level to religious recipients.

As a way of assuring neutrality, we have repeatedly considered whether any governmental aid that goes to a religious institution does so "only as a result of the genuinely independent and private choices of individuals." *Agostini*. We have viewed as significant whether the "private choices of individual parents," as opposed to the "unmediated" will of government, determine what schools ultimately benefit from the governmental aid, and how much. For if numerous private choices, rather than the single choice of a government, determine the distribution of aid pursuant to neutral eligibility criteria, then a government cannot, or at least cannot easily, grant special favors that might lead to a religious establishment. Private choice also helps guarantee neutrality by mitigating the preference for pre-existing recipients that is arguably inherent in any governmental aid program, . . . and that could lead to a program inadvertently favoring one religion or favoring religious private schools in general over nonreligious ones.

The principles of neutrality and private choice, and their relationship to each other, were prominent not only in *Agostini*, but also in *Zobrest*, *Witters*, and *Mueller*. The heart of our reasoning in *Zobrest*, upholding governmental provision of a sign-language interpreter to a deaf student at his Catholic high school, was . . . the private choices helped to ensure neutrality, and neutrality and private choices together eliminated any possible attribution to the government even when the interpreter translated classes on Catholic doctrine.

Witters and *Mueller* employed similar reasoning. In *Witters*, we held that the Establishment Clause did not bar a State from including within a neutral program providing tuition payments for vocational rehabilitation a blind person studying at a Christian college to become a pastor, missionary, or youth director. We explained:

> Any aid . . . that ultimately flows to religious institutions does so only as a result of the genuinely independent and private choices of aid recipients. Washington's program is made available generally without regard to the sectarian-nonsectarian, or public-nonpublic nature of the institution benefited and . . . creates no financial incentive for students to undertake sectarian education. . . . [T]he fact that aid goes to individuals means that the decision to support religious education is made by the individual, not by the State.

The tax deduction for educational expenses that we upheld in *Mueller* was, in these respects, the same as the tuition grant in *Witters*. We upheld it chiefly because it "neutrally provides state assistance to a broad spectrum of citizens," and because "numerous, private choices of individual parents of school-age children," determined which schools would benefit from the deductions. We explained that "[w]here, as here, aid to parochial schools is available only as a result of decisions of individual parents no 'imprimatur of state approval' can be deemed to have been conferred on any particular religion, or on religion generally."

Agostini's second primary criterion for determining the effect of governmental aid is closely related to the first. The second criterion requires a court to consider whether an aid program "define[s] its recipients by reference to religion." As we briefly explained in *Agostini*, this second criterion looks to the same set of facts as does our focus, under the first criterion, on neutrality, but the second criterion uses those facts to answer a somewhat different question—whether the criteria for allocating the aid "reate[e] a financial incentive to undertake religious indoctrination." In *Agostini* we set out the following rule for answering this question:

> This incentive is not present, however, where the aid is allocated on the basis of neutral, secular criteria that neither favor nor disfavor religion, and is made available to both religious and secular beneficiaries on a nondiscriminatory basis. Under such circumstances, the aid is less likely to have the effect of advancing religion.

The cases on which *Agostini* relied for this rule, and *Agostini* itself, make clear the close relationship between this rule, incentives, and private choice. For to say that a program does not create an incentive to choose religious schools is to say that the private choice is truly "independent." When such an incentive does exist, there is a greater risk that one could attribute to the government any indoctrination by the religious schools.

We hasten to add, what should be obvious from the rule itself, that simply because an aid program offers private schools, and thus religious schools, a benefit that they did not previously receive does not mean that the program, by reducing the cost of securing a religious education, creates, under *Agostini*'s second criterion, an "incentive" for parents to choose such an education for their children. For *any* aid will have some such effect.

....

If aid to schools, even "direct aid," is neutrally available and, before reaching or benefiting any religious school, first passes through the hands (literally or figuratively) of numerous private citizens who are free to direct the aid elsewhere, the government has not provided any "support of religion." Although the presence of private choice is easier to see when aid literally passes through the hands of individuals—which is why we have mentioned directness in the same breath with private choice, there is no reason why the Establishment Clause requires such a form.

....

Applying the two relevant *Agostini* criteria, we see no basis for concluding that Jefferson Parish's Chapter 2 program "has the effect of advancing religion." Chapter 2 does not result in governmental indoctrination, because it determines eligibility for aid neutrally, allocates that aid based on the private choices of the parents of schoolchildren, and does not provide aid that has an impermissible content. Nor does Chapter 2 define its recipients by reference to religion.

....

Because Chapter 2 aid is provided pursuant to private choices, it is not problematic that one could fairly describe Chapter 2 as providing "direct" aid.... Nor, for reasons we have already explained, is it of constitutional significance that the schools themselves, rather than the students, are the bailees of the Chapter 2 aid. The ultimate beneficiaries of Chapter 2 aid are the students who attend the schools that receive that aid, and this is so regardless of whether individual students lug computers to school each day or, as Jefferson Parish has more sensibly provided, the schools receive the computers. Like the Ninth Circuit, and unlike the dissent, we "see little difference in loaning science kits to students who then bring the kits to school as opposed to loaning science kits to the school directly."

Finally, Chapter 2 satisfies the first *Agostini* criterion because it does not provide to religious schools aid that has an impermissible content. The statute explicitly bars anything of the sort, providing that all Chapter 2 aid for the benefit of children in private schools shall be "secular, neutral, and nonideological," § 7372(a)(1), and the record indicates that the Louisiana SEA and the Jefferson Parish LEA have faithfully enforced this requirement insofar as relevant to this case. . . .

In short, Chapter 2 satisfies both the first and second primary criteria of *Agostini*. It therefore does not have the effect of advancing religion. For the same reason, Chapter 2 also "cannot reasonably be viewed as an endorsement of religion," *Agostini, supra*, at 235. Accordingly, we hold that Chapter 2 is not a law respecting an establishment of religion. Jefferson Parish need not exclude religious schools from its Chapter 2 program. To the extent that *Meek* and *Wolman* conflict with this holding, we overrule them.

. . . .

Justice O'Connor, with whom Justice Breyer joins, concurring in the judgment.

. . . .

I write separately because, in my view, the plurality announces a rule of unprecedented breadth for the evaluation of Establishment Clause challenges to government school-aid programs. Reduced to its essentials, the plurality's rule states that government aid to religious schools does not have the effect of advancing religion so long as the aid is offered on a neutral basis and the aid is secular in content. The plurality also rejects the distinction between direct and indirect aid, and holds that the actual diversion of secular aid by a religious school to the advancement of its religious mission is permissible. Although the expansive scope of the plurality's rule is troubling, two specific aspects of the opinion compel me to write separately. First, the plurality's treatment of neutrality comes close to assigning that factor singular importance in the future adjudication of Establishment Clause challenges to government school-aid programs. Second, the plurality's approval of actual diversion of government aid to religious indoctrination is in tension with our precedents and, in any event, unnecessary to decide the instant case.

. . . .

I do not quarrel with the plurality's recognition that neutrality is an important reason for upholding government-aid programs against Establishment Clause challenges. Our cases have described neutrality in precisely this manner, and we have emphasized a program's neutrality repeatedly in our decisions approving various forms of school aid. Nevertheless, we have never held that a government-aid program passes constitutional muster *solely* because of the neutral criteria it employs as a basis for distributing aid. . . .

[Justice O'Connor goes on to explain that she also disagrees with the plurality's conclusion regarding the actual diversion of government aid to religious indoctrination being consistent with the Establishment Clause. That part of the plurality's opinion is omitted, as is Justice O'Connor's discussion of it. Both are available online.]

Post Problem Discussion

1. What is the difference between the standards noted by the Court in *Lemon* and those noted in *Zobrest, Agostini*, and *Mitchell*? Is it fair to say that the decisions after *Lemon* eased restrictions on state or public schools providing funds or services to religious schools? If so, what impact, if any, do you think this would have on school administrators?

2. If the Supreme Court were to consider the facts in the *Lemon* case again today under the standards in *Zobrest, Agostini*, and *Mitchell*, would they still find that the Rhode Island and Pennsylvania statutes violate the Establishment Clause? Why or why not?

3. Justice O'Connor concurred in *Mitchell* to note her disagreement with using a neutrality test as the sole factor for Establishment Clause cases. As noted, Justice Thomas did not write for a majority of the court in *Mitchell*. Why do you think the Court is unwilling to use neutrality as the sole factor?

4. As a plurality opinion, *Mitchell*'s precedential value is limited to some extent. The Supreme Court has noted that in a plurality opinion, "the holding of the Court may be viewed as that position taken by those Members who concurred in the judgments on the narrowest grounds." *Marks v. United States*, 430 U.S. 188, 193 (1977). Given O'Connor's concurring opinion, what are the narrowest grounds supported by the Court in *Mitchell*? You may want to view the full opinion with concurring opinions and dissenting opinions online answer the question.

B. Vouchers

The neutrality concept that played a role in some of the Court's decisions in Problem One, and became a focal point for the plurality in *Mitchell*, soon took center stage in the debate on vouchers. Voucher programs generally provide financial assistance to parents who send students to private schools. In an older case, *Committee for Public Educ. & Religious Liberty v. Nyquist*, 413 U.S. 756 (1973), the Supreme Court ruled that a state reimbursement program that allowed parents of children at private schools, including religious schools, to receive tuition reimbursement and tax credits for some of the costs of attending the school violated the effect prong of the *Lemon* test. The Court rejected the argument that the plan was constitutional because it provided funds to parents who were free to spend the money they received in any manner they wished, noting:

> if the grants are offered as an incentive to parents to send their children to sectarian schools by making unrestricted cash payments to them, the

> Establishment Clause is violated whether or not the actual dollars given eventually find their way into the sectarian institutions.

Nyquist, 413 U.S. at 786.

Almost thirty years later, the Court came to a different conclusion in *Zelman v. Simmons-Harris*, 536 U.S. 639, 649 (2002). In *Zelman*, the lower courts ruled that an Ohio voucher program was unconstitutional under *Nyquist*, but the Supreme Court overruled the lower courts, noting that the funds were made available on neutral terms (without any reference to religion) to parents who made a "true private choice" on where to spend the funds.

Zelman was a controversial decision that has engendered further litigation at the state and federal levels. Since *Zelman*, a number of state courts have addressed whether or not voucher programs violate state constitutional provisions. Many state constitution religion clauses have stricter requirements when it comes to state or government involvement with religion. A number of states have *Blaine Amendments* in their state constitutions' religion clauses, which directly prohibit or place severe limitations on government involvement in religion. The Supreme Court has noted that Blaine Amendments may have their origins in animus towards sectarian schools and, in particular, Catholic sectarian schools, but it has yet to determine whether or not such provisions would violate federal requirements. *See Mitchell v. Helms*, 530 U.S. 793, 828 (2000).

Additionally, at the federal level, the Supreme Court was faced with the issue of whether certain state funding programs were now required under the Free Exercise Clause to allow funds to be spent on religious programs given the ruling in *Zelman* that it would not violate the Establishment Clause to do so. The Court addressed this issue in *Locke v. Davey*, 540 U.S. 712 (2004).

The following problem explores these issues further and your state requirements.

Problem 2: Vouchers in Your State

You are legal counsel for the Governor's office in your state. The Governor wants to implement a voucher plan for preschool students in the state to help parents with low to moderate incomes afford preschool. While the Governor does not have a specific plan yet, her campaign focused on increasing access to preschool for students, and she wants to develop a specific proposal soon. Her idea is to create a state-funded scholarship where parents can apply for funds up to a certain limit that will be set each year. The parents can then use the funds to pay for the costs of any private preschool. The program would be administered under the authority of the state department of education, which would grant funds to applicants based on certain criteria.

The Governor's idea has been met with skepticism from school boards, superintendents, and teachers' unions in the state. These groups raised a concern about the constitutionality of such a plan under the state and federal constitution, since roughly sixty percent of the state's private preschools are run by religious schools or churches. The Governor is ambivalent about funding religious programs and needs legal guidance to determine her options.

She wants you to provide her with the legal framework so that her staff can develop a plan that will meet her goals and meet the state and federal constitutional requirements in your state.

She has the following specific questions:

1. Are there any criteria that the scholarship administrators should/should not consider when awarding funds? Specifically, can administrators consider whether the preschool will provide religious instruction? Can they develop criteria that would allow funds to be provided to parents who send their children to religious programs only if the program could provide evidence that the majority of instruction provided was secular or non-religious?
2. Can the scholarship funds be limited to parents who will send their students to non-religious private schools? Would it violate the Establishment Clause or Free Exercise Clause of the First Amendment to do so?
3. Could the scholarship funds be provided directly to private religious schools that parents choose, or do the funds need to be provided directly to the parents?
4. Does your state constitution have a Blaine Amendment, or any kind of religion clause? If so, have state courts interpreted the requirements to be the same as federal requirements, or different from the federal requirements? If different, how are they different and will they have any impact on the provisions of the plan?

Problem Materials

✓ *Zelman v. Simmons-Harris*, 536 U.S. 639 (2002)

✓ *Locke v. Davey*, 540 U.S. 712 (2004)

✓ Research your state religion clauses and state court interpretations

Zelman v. Simmons-Harris

536 U.S. 639 (2002)

The Court rules that a state voucher program that provides funds directly to parents to make choices about what school their child attends does not violate the Establishment Clause.

Chief Justice Rehnquist delivered the opinion of the Court.

The State of Ohio has established a pilot program designed to provide educational choices to families with children who reside in the Cleveland City School District. The question presented is whether this program offends the Establishment Clause of the United States Constitution. We hold that it does not.

. . . .

The program provides two basic kinds of assistance to parents of children in a covered district. First, the program provides tuition aid for students in kindergarten through third grade, expanding each year through eighth grade, to attend a participating public or private school of their parent's choosing. Second, the program provides tutorial aid for students who choose to remain enrolled in public school.

The tuition aid portion of the program is designed to provide educational choices to parents who reside in a covered district. Any private school, whether religious or nonreligious, may participate in the program and accept program students so long as the school is located within the boundaries of a covered district and meets statewide educational standards. . . .

The program has been in operation within the Cleveland City School District since the 1996–1997 school year. In the 1999–2000 school year, 56 private schools participated in the program, 46 (or 82%) of which had a religious affiliation. None of the public schools in districts adjacent to Cleveland have elected to participate. More than 3,700 students participated in the scholarship program, most of whom (96%) enrolled in religiously affiliated schools. . . .

The Establishment Clause of the First Amendment, applied to the States through the Fourteenth Amendment, prevents a State from enacting laws that have the "purpose" or "effect" of advancing or inhibiting religion. There is no dispute that the program challenged here was enacted for the valid secular purpose of providing educational assistance to poor children in a demonstrably failing public school system. Thus, the question presented is whether the Ohio program nonetheless has the forbidden "effect" of advancing or inhibiting religion.

To answer that question, our decisions have drawn a consistent distinction between government programs that provide aid directly to religious schools, and programs of true private choice, in which government aid reaches religious schools only as a result of the genuine and independent choices of private individuals, *Mueller v. Allen*, 463 U.S. 388 (1983); *Witters v. Washington Dept. of Servs. for Blind*, 474 U.S. 481 (1986); *Zobrest v. Catalina Foothills School Dist.*, 509 U.S. 1 (1993). While our jurisprudence with respect to the constitutionality of direct aid programs has "changed significantly" over the past two decades, our jurisprudence with respect to true private choice programs has remained consistent and unbroken. Three times we have confronted Establishment Clause challenges to neutral government programs that provide aid directly to a broad class of individuals, who, in turn, direct the aid to religious schools or institutions of their own choosing. Three times we have rejected such challenges.

In *Mueller*, we rejected an Establishment Clause challenge to a Minnesota program authorizing tax deductions for various educational expenses, including private school tuition costs, even though the great majority of the program's beneficiaries (96%) were parents of children in religious schools. . . . Then, viewing the program as a whole, we emphasized the principle of private choice, noting that public funds were made available to religious schools "only as a result of numerous, private choices of individual parents of school-age children." This, we said, ensured that "'no imprimatur of state approval' can be deemed to have been conferred on any particular religion, or on religion generally." We thus found it irrelevant to the constitutional inquiry that the vast majority of beneficiaries were parents of children in religious schools.... That the program was one of true private choice, with no evidence that the State deliberately skewed incentives toward religious schools, was sufficient for the program to survive scrutiny under the Establishment Clause.

In *Witters*, we used identical reasoning to reject an Establishment Clause challenge to a vocational scholarship program that provided tuition aid to a student studying at a religious institution to become a pastor. Looking at the program as a whole, we observed that "[a]ny aid ... that ultimately flows to religious institutions does so only as a result of the genuinely independent and private choices of aid recipients."

Finally, in *Zobrest*, we applied *Mueller* and *Witters* to reject an Establishment Clause challenge to a federal program that permitted sign-language interpreters to assist deaf children enrolled in religious schools.... Looking once again to the challenged program as a whole, we observed that the program "distributes benefits neutrally to any child qualifying as 'disabled.'" Its "primary beneficiaries," we said, were "disabled children, not sectarian schools."

We further observed that "[b]y according parents freedom to select a school of their choice, the statute ensures that a government-paid interpreter will be present in a sectarian school only as a result of the private decision of individual parents." Our focus again was on neutrality and the principle of private choice, not on the number of program beneficiaries attending religious schools....

Mueller, *Witters*, and *Zobrest* thus make clear that where a government aid program is neutral with respect to religion, and provides assistance directly to a broad class of citizens who, in turn, direct government aid to religious schools wholly as a result of their own genuine and independent private choice, the program is not readily subject to challenge under the Establishment Clause. A program that shares these features permits government aid to reach religious institutions only by way of the deliberate choices of numerous individual recipients. The incidental advancement of a religious mission, or the perceived endorsement of a religious message, is reasonably attributable to the individual recipient, not to the government, whose role ends with the disbursement of benefits....

We believe that the program challenged here is a program of true private choice, consistent with *Mueller*, *Witters*, and *Zobrest*, and thus constitutional. As was true in those cases, the Ohio program is neutral in all respects toward religion. It is part of a general and multifaceted undertaking by the State of Ohio to provide educational opportunities to the children of a failed school district. It confers educational assistance directly to a broad class of individuals defined without reference to religion, *i.e.*, any parent of a school-age child who resides in the Cleveland City School District. The program permits the participation of *all* schools within the district, religious or nonreligious. Adjacent public schools also may participate and have a financial incentive to do so. Program benefits are available to participating families on neutral terms, with no reference to religion. The only preference stated anywhere in the program is a preference for low-income families, who receive greater assistance and are given priority for admission at participating schools.

....

Respondents suggest that even without a financial incentive for parents to choose a religious school, the program creates a "public perception that the State is endorsing religious practices and beliefs." But we have repeatedly recognized that no reasonable observer would think a neutral program of private choice, where state aid reaches religious schools solely as a result of the numerous independent decisions of private individuals, carries with it the *imprimatur* of government endorsement.... The argument is particularly misplaced here since "the reasonable observer in the endorsement inquiry must be deemed aware" of the "history and context" underlying a challenged program. Any objective observer familiar with the full history and context of the Ohio program would reasonably view it as one aspect of a broader undertaking to assist poor children in failed schools, not as an endorsement of religious schooling in general.

....

Respondents finally claim that we should look to *Committee for Public Ed. & Religious Liberty v. Nyquist*, 413 U.S. 756 (1973), to decide these cases. We disagree for two reasons. First, the program in *Nyquist* was quite different from the program challenged here. *Nyquist* involved a New York program that gave a package of benefits exclusively to private schools and the parents of private school enrollees. Although the program was enacted for ostensibly secular purposes, we found that its "function" was "*unmistakably* to provide desired financial support for nonpublic, sectarian institutions." Its genesis, we said, was that private religious schools faced "increasingly grave fiscal problems." The program thus provided direct money grants to religious schools. It provided tax benefits "unrelated to the amount of money actually expended by any parent on tuition," ensuring a windfall to parents of children in religious schools. It similarly provided tuition reimbursements designed explicitly to "offe[r] ... an incentive to parents to send their children to sectarian schools." Indeed, the program flatly prohibited the participation of any public school, or parent of any public school enrollee. Ohio's program shares none of these features.

Second, were there any doubt that the program challenged in *Nyquist* is far removed from the program challenged here, we expressly reserved judgment with respect to "a case involving some form of public assistance (*e.g.*, scholarships) made available generally without regard to the sectarian-nonsectarian, or public-nonpublic nature of the institution benefited." That, of course, is the very question now before us, and it has since been answered, first in *Mueller*, then in *Witters*, and again in *Zobrest*. To the extent the scope of *Nyquist* has remained an open question in light of these later decisions, we now hold that *Nyquist* does not govern neutral educational assistance programs that, like the program here, offer aid directly to a broad class of individual recipients defined without regard to religion.

In sum, the Ohio program is entirely neutral with respect to religion. It provides benefits directly to a wide spectrum of individuals, defined only by financial need and residence in a particular school district. It permits such individuals to exercise genuine choice among options public and private, secular and religious. The program is therefore a program of true private choice. In keeping with an unbroken line of decisions rejecting challenges to similar programs, we hold that the program does not offend the Establishment Clause.

The judgment of the Court of Appeals is reversed.

It is so ordered.

Locke v. Davey

540 U.S. 712 (2004)

The Court rules that a state scholarship program that excludes students pursuing a degree in theology does not violate the Free Exercise Clause.

Chief Justice Rehnquist delivered the opinion of the Court.

The State of Washington established the Promise Scholarship Program to assist academically gifted students with postsecondary education expenses. In accordance with the State Constitution, students may not use the scholarship at an institution where they are pursuing a degree in devotional theology. We hold that such an exclusion from an otherwise inclusive aid program does not violate the Free Exercise Clause of the First Amendment.

The Washington State Legislature . . . created the Promise Scholarship Program, which provides a scholarship, renewable for one year, to eligible students for postsecondary education expenses. . . . To be eligible for the scholarship, a student must meet academic, income, and enrollment requirements. . . . Finally, the student must enroll "at least half time in an eligible postsecondary institution in the state of Washington," and may not pursue a degree in theology at that institution while receiving the scholarship. Private institutions, including those religiously affiliated, qualify as "eligible postsecondary institution[s]" if they are accredited by a nationally recognized accrediting body. A "degree in theology" is not defined in the statute, but, as both parties concede, the statute simply codifies the State's constitutional prohibition on providing funds to students to pursue degrees that are "devotional in nature or designed to induce religious faith."

. . . .

Respondent, Joshua Davey, was awarded a Promise Scholarship, and chose to attend Northwest College. Northwest is a private, Christian college affiliated with the Assemblies of God denomination, and is an eligible institution under the Promise Scholarship Program. Davey had "planned for many years to attend a Bible college and to prepare [himself] through that college training for a lifetime of ministry, specifically as a church pastor." To that end, when he enrolled in Northwest College, he decided to pursue a double major in pastoral ministries and business management/administration. There is no dispute that the pastoral ministries degree is devotional and therefore excluded under the Promise Scholarship Program.

. . . .

A divided panel of the United States Court of Appeals for the Ninth Circuit reversed. The court concluded that the State had singled out religion for unfavorable treatment and thus under our decision in *Church of Lukumi Babalu Aye, Inc. v. Hialeah*, the State's exclusion of theology majors must be narrowly tailored to achieve a compelling state interest. Finding that the State's own antiestablishment concerns were not compelling, the court declared Washington's Promise Scholarship Program unconstitutional. We granted certiorari, and now reverse.

The Religion Clauses of the First Amendment provide: "Congress shall make no law respecting an establishment of religion, or prohibiting the free exercise thereof." These two Clauses, the Establishment Clause and the Free Exercise Clause, are frequently in tension. Yet we have long said that "there is room for play in the joints" between them. In other words, there are some state actions permitted by the Establishment Clause but not required by the Free Exercise Clause.

This case involves that "play in the joints" described above. Under our Establishment Clause precedent, the link between government funds and religious training is broken by the independent and private choice of recipients. As such, there is no doubt that the State could, consistent with the Federal Constitution, permit Promise Scholars to pursue a degree in devotional theology, and the State does not contend otherwise. The question before us, however, is whether Washington, pursuant to its own constitution, which has been authoritatively interpreted as prohibiting even indirectly funding religious instruction that will prepare students for the ministry, can deny them such funding without violating the Free Exercise Clause.

Davey urges us to answer that question in the negative. He contends that under the rule we enunciated in *Church of Lukumi Babalu Aye, Inc. v. Hialeah*, the program is presumptively unconstitutional because it is not facially neutral with respect to religion. We reject his claim of presumptive unconstitutionality, however; to do otherwise would extend the *Lukumi* line of cases well beyond not only their facts but their reasoning. In *Lukumi*, the city of Hialeah made it a crime to engage in certain kinds of animal slaughter. We found that the law sought to suppress ritualistic animal sacrifices of the Santeria religion. In the present case, the State's disfavor of religion (if it can be called that) is of a far milder kind. It imposes neither criminal nor civil sanctions on any type of religious service or rite. It does not deny to ministers the right to participate in the political affairs of the community. And it does not require students to choose between their religious beliefs and receiving a government benefit. *See ibid.; Hobbie v. Unemployment Appeals Comm'n of Fla.*, 480 U.S. 136 (1987); *Thomas v. Review Bd. of Indiana Employment Security Div.*, 450 U.S.

707 (1981); *Sherbert v. Verner*, 374 U.S. 398 (1963). The State has merely chosen not to fund a distinct category of instruction.

. . . .

Even though the differently worded Washington Constitution draws a more stringent line than that drawn by the United States Constitution, the interest it seeks to further is scarcely novel. In fact, we can think of few areas in which a State's antiestablishment interests come more into play. Since the founding of our country, there have been popular uprisings against procuring taxpayer funds to support church leaders, which was one of the hallmarks of an "established" religion. Most States that sought to avoid an establishment of religion around the time of the founding placed in their constitutions formal prohibitions against using tax funds to support the ministry. . . . The plain text of these constitutional provisions prohibited *any* tax dollars from supporting the clergy. We have found nothing to indicate, as Justice Scalia contends, that these provisions would not have applied so long as the State equally supported other professions or if the amount at stake was *de minimis*. That early state constitutions saw no problem in explicitly excluding *only* the ministry from receiving state dollars reinforces our conclusion that religious instruction is of a different ilk.

Far from evincing the hostility toward religion which was manifest in *Lukumi*, we believe that the entirety of the Promise Scholarship Program goes a long way toward including religion in its benefits. The program permits students to attend pervasively religious schools, so long as they are accredited. As Northwest advertises, its "concept of education is distinctly Christian in the evangelical sense." It prepares *all* of its students, "through instruction, through modeling, [and] through [its] classes, to use . . . the Bible as their guide, as the truth," no matter their chosen profession. And under the Promise Scholarship Program's current guidelines, students are still eligible to take devotional theology courses. Davey notes all students at Northwest are required to take at least four devotional courses, "Exploring the Bible," "Principles of Spiritual Development," "Evangelism in the Christian Life," and "Christian Doctrine,", and some students may have additional religious requirements as part of their majors.

In short, we find neither in the history or text of Article I, § 11 of the Washington Constitution, nor in the operation of the Promise Scholarship Program, anything that suggests animus towards religion. Given the historic and substantial state interest at issue, we therefore cannot conclude that the denial of funding for vocational religious instruction alone is inherently constitutionally suspect.

Without a presumption of unconstitutionality, Davey's claim must fail. The State's interest in not funding the pursuit of devotional degrees is substantial and the exclusion of such funding places a relatively minor burden on Promise Scholars. If any room exists between the two Religion Clauses, it must be here. We need not venture further into this difficult area in order to uphold the Promise Scholarship Program as currently operated by the State of Washington.

. . . .

Post Problem Discussion

1. In *Zelman*, the Court relied heavily on the concepts of neutrality and private choice and rejected the argument that the voucher program could be perceived by a reasonable observer as endorsing religion. What are the parameters and limits of this approach? Assume that parochial schools in a particular state are less expensive than non-parochial private schools, their average annual tuition being $7,500 compared to $12,500 for non-parochial schools. Could the state develop a voucher program that provided $7,500 per student to all parents who want their children to attend private school, or does the "coincidental" amount suggest some favoritism towards religion? What if a state politician campaigns on getting religion "back in the schools" and then sponsors a voucher plan? How does legislative intent factor into a reasonable observer's perception?

2. In *Davey*, the Court found that the state scholarship at issue did not target religion and distinguished the case from *Church of Lukumi*. Given the Court's decision in *Davey*, what type of state action would be deemed to target religion?

3. Legal and constitutional issues about vouchers, like other religious topics, remain current. The Associated Press, in a story entitled *School Vouchers Spark Growing Court Fights in US*, reported the issues this way:

> For all the arguments in favor of vouchers, there are opponents who say vouchers erode public schools by taking away money, violate the separation of church and state by giving public dollars to religious-based private schools, and aren't a proven way to improve test scores.
>
> Even among supporters, there's dissension over whether vouchers should only be offered to low-income students on a limited basis or made available to anyone. There's also division among black and Hispanic leaders as to whether vouchers help or hurt kids in urban schools.

Is one side clearly correct in legal terms? Is there a middle ground?

C. Public School Benefits and Free Exercise Rights

As noted in Chapter 5, all fifty states have some form of a compulsory education law that requires students between certain ages to attend either public or private school or be homeschooled. Generally speaking, the state and federal requirements for private and home schools are not the same as the state and federal requirements that public schools must meet. For example, private schools do not have to meet the requirements of the Individuals with Disabilities Education Act unless they accept the placement of students with disabilities from public schools; nor do they have to comply with the federal Equal Access Act's requirements of allowing outside groups, including religious groups, to use school facilities under certain circumstances.

Similarly, students who attend private schools, or who are homeschooled, are often not entitled to the same rights or benefits that they would receive if they attended public school. For example, students with disabilities who attend private school on their own (as opposed to the public school placing the student at the private school to receive special education services) are not entitled to the same special education services that they would receive if they attended public school.[1] Students who are homeschooled are not entitled to any special education services at all from the public school unless that is the student's special education placement, or state law otherwise requires some level of services. *See, e.g., Hooks v. Clark County Sch. Dist.*, 228 F.3d 1036 (9th Cir. 2000), *cert. denied*, 532 U.S. 971 (2001).

Parents may decide on a private school, or homeschooling, for a variety of reasons including religious ones. Free Exercise issues can arise when parents decide to send their child to a religious school, or to be homeschooled, for religious reasons and discover that their child will not receive services that they would have received if they attended public school. In a series of cases involving public benefits such as unemployment compensation, the United States Supreme Court stated that individuals cannot be forced to forgo their religious beliefs in order to obtain a public benefit that they would otherwise be entitled to receive. *See Hobbie v. Unemployment Appeals Comm'n*, 480 U.S. 136 (1987); *Thomas v. Review Bd. of Ind. Employment Sec. Div.*, 450 U.S. 707 (1981); *Sherbert v. Verner*, 374 U.S. 398 (1963). However, lower courts have been reluctant to apply this same concept to the educational benefits received at public school. The following problem explores this issue in the context of a free exercise challenge.

Problem 3: Public School Benefits and Free Exercise

Sheila Hatam is a sixth grade student who has been identified as a child with a learning disability under the Individuals with Disabilities Education Act (IDEA). During the last school year, she attended PS#60 for fifth grade and received services pursuant to an IEP. The services included reading instruction for two hours per week, speech instruction for one hour per week, and occupational therapy for one hour per week.

After Sheila attended sixth grade at her neighborhood middle school for about a month, the Hatams determined that the content of the curriculum at the middle school was inappropriate, as it contained readings and information that violate their religious beliefs. The Hatams decided to homeschool Sheila for the rest of the sixth grade and beyond so that they could provide her with religious instruction consistent with their own beliefs. Sheila will be homeschooled with a group of five other students whose families are members of the same church as the Hatam family. The group will receive instructional material and guidance on instruction from their church and use the Sunday school room at their church.

---

1. *See* 34 C.F.R. § 300.137 (2007). A student may be entitled to claim reimbursement for the costs of the private school if they claim that the public school did not provide them with FAPE and the private school is appropriate under the IDEA. *See* 34 C.F.R. § 300.148. *See* Chapter 12, Section 12.4, for more information.

The school district notifies the Hatams that under state and federal law, students who are homeschooled are not entitled to receive any special education services from the public school. They also inform the Hatams that if they decide to reenroll Sheila in public school full time, she would be eligible to receive all of her special education services again. Similarly, the school also informs the Hatams that, as a homeschooled student, Sheila will no longer be eligible to participate in the after school extracurricular activities she enjoyed last year including soccer, art club, and drama. Further, the school informs the parents that while the school does offer a "curriculum advisor" for homeschool parents to assist the parents in choosing curricula that will meet state standards for a high school diploma, that advisor is not able to assist parents who provide religious instruction to their children due to Establishment Clause concerns.

The Hatams sue in a federal district court claiming the school's actions and the state laws that authorize them violate their free exercise rights under the First Amendment. The parents argue that in order to receive the same benefits as other children, the law requires them to send their daughter to public school where she will be exposed to information that violates the family's religious beliefs. The Hatams also contend that not providing them with a curriculum advisor because they are offering religious instruction, when one is provided to those who provide secular instruction, targets them because of their religious beliefs, which violates their free exercise rights.

You are a judge at the district court. Assume you are in a jurisdiction where there are no binding circuit court precedents.

1. How would you rule on the denial of special education services, extracurricular activities, and the curriculum advisor, and why?
2. Which legal standard(s) would you apply to reach your decision? *Smith*? *Lukumi*? *Sherbert*? *Yoder*?

Problem Materials

- ✓ *Employment Division Department of Human Resources of Oregon v. Smith*, 494 U.S. 872 (1990)
- ✓ *Church of Lukumi Babalu Aye, Inc. v. Hialeah*, 508 U.S. 520 (1993)
- ✓ *Wisconsin v. Yoder*, 406 U. S. 205 (1972) (in Chapter 5 Problem 1)
- ✓ *Gary S. v. Manchester School District*, 374 F.3d 15 (1st Cir. 2004)
- ✓ *Davey v. Locke* (in Problem 2 materials)

Employment Division Department of Human Resources of Oregon v. Smith

494 U.S. 872 (1990)

The Court rules that a neutral law of general applicability does not have to meet the strict scrutiny tests developed in prior cases.

Justice Scalia delivered the opinion of the Court.

This case requires us to decide whether the Free Exercise Clause of the First Amendment permits the State of Oregon to include religiously inspired peyote use within the reach of its general criminal prohibition on use of that drug, and thus permits the State to deny unemployment benefits to persons dismissed from their jobs because of such religiously inspired use.

. . . .

Respondents' claim for relief rests on our decisions in *Sherbert v. Verner, supra, Thomas v. Review Bd. of Indiana Employment Security Div., supra*, and *Hobbie v. Unemployment Appeals Comm'n of Florida*, in which we held that a State could not condition the availability of unemployment insurance on an individual's willingness to forgo conduct required by his religion. As we observed in *Smith I*, however, the conduct at issue in those cases was not prohibited by law. We held that distinction to be critical, for "if Oregon does prohibit the religious use of peyote, and if that prohibition is consistent with the Federal Constitution, there is no federal right to engage in that conduct in Oregon," and "the State is free to withhold unemployment compensation from respondents for engaging in work-related misconduct, despite its religious motivation." Now that the Oregon Supreme Court has confirmed that Oregon does prohibit the religious use of peyote, we proceed to consider whether that prohibition is permissible under the Free Exercise Clause.

. . . .

The free exercise of religion means, first and foremost, the right to believe and profess whatever religious doctrine one desires. Thus, the First Amendment obviously excludes all "governmental regulation of religious beliefs as such." The government may not compel affirmation of religious belief, punish the expression of religious doctrines it believes to be false, impose special disabilities on the basis of religious views or religious status, or lend its power to one or the other side in controversies over religious authority or dogma.... But the "exercise of religion" often involves not only belief and profession but the performance of (or abstention from) physical acts: assembling with others for a worship service, participating in sacramental use of bread and wine, proselytizing, abstaining from certain foods or certain modes of transportation. It would be true, we think (though no case of ours has involved the point), that a State would be "prohibiting the free exercise [of religion]" if it sought to ban such acts or abstentions only when they are engaged in for religious reasons, or only because of the religious belief that they display. It would doubtless be unconstitutional, for example, to ban the casting of "statues that are to be used for worship purposes," or to prohibit bowing down before a golden calf.

Respondents in the present case, however, seek to carry the meaning of "prohibiting the free exercise [of religion]" one large step further. They contend that their religious motivation for using peyote places them beyond the reach of a criminal law that is not specifically directed at their religious practice, and that is concededly constitutional as applied to those who use the drug for other reasons. They assert, in other words, that "prohibiting the free exercise [of religion]" includes requiring any individual to observe a generally applicable law that requires (or forbids) the performance of an act that his religious belief forbids (or requires). As a textual matter, we do not think the words must be given that meaning. It is no more necessary to regard the collection of a general tax, for example, as "prohibiting the free exercise [of religion]" by those citizens who believe support of organized government to be sinful, than it is to regard the same tax as "abridging the freedom . . . of the press" of those publishing companies that must pay the tax as a condition of staying in business. It is a permissible reading of the text, in the one case as in the other, to say that if prohibiting the exercise of religion (or burdening the activity of printing) is not the object of the tax but merely the incidental effect of a generally applicable and otherwise valid provision, the First Amendment has not been offended.

Our decisions reveal that the latter reading is the correct one. We have never held that an individual's religious beliefs excuse him from compliance with an otherwise valid law prohibiting conduct that the State is free to regulate. . . .

Subsequent decisions have consistently held that the right of free exercise does not relieve an individual of the obligation to comply with a "valid and neutral law of general applicability on the ground that the law proscribes (or prescribes) conduct that his religion prescribes (or proscribes)." . . . In *Prince v. Massachusetts*, 321 U.S. 158 (1944), we held that a mother could be prosecuted under the child labor laws for using her children to dispense literature in the streets, her religious motivation notwithstanding. We found no constitutional infirmity in "excluding [these children] from doing there what no other children may do." In *Braunfeld v. Brown*, 366 U.S. 599 (1961) (plurality opinion), we upheld Sunday-closing laws against the claim that they burdened the religious practices of persons whose religions compelled them to refrain from work on other days. In *Gillette v. United States*, 401 U.S. 437, 461 (1971), we sustained the military Selective Service System against the claim that it violated free exercise by conscripting persons who opposed a particular war on religious grounds.

Our most recent decision involving a neutral, generally applicable regulatory law that compelled activity forbidden by an individual's religion was *United States v. Lee*, 455 U.S., at 258–261. There, an Amish employer, on behalf of himself and his employees, sought exemption from collection and payment of Social Security taxes on the ground that the Amish faith prohibited participation in governmental support programs. We rejected the claim that an exemption was constitutionally required. There would be no way, we observed, to distinguish the Amish believer's objection to Social Security taxes from the religious objections that others might have to the collection or use of other taxes. "If, for example, a religious adherent believes war is a sin, and if a certain percentage of the federal budget can be identified as devoted to war-related activities, such individuals would have a similarly valid claim to be exempt from paying that percentage of the income tax. The tax system could not function if denominations were allowed to challenge the tax system because tax payments were spent in a manner that violates their religious belief."

The only decisions in which we have held that the First Amendment bars application of a neutral, generally applicable law to religiously motivated action have involved not the Free Exercise Clause alone, but the Free Exercise Clause in conjunction with other constitutional protections, such as freedom of speech and of the press, or the right of parents, acknowledged in *Pierce v. Society of Sisters*, 268 U.S. 510 (1925), to direct the education of their children, *see Wisconsin v. Yoder*, 406 U.S. 205 (1972) (invalidating compulsory school-attendance laws as applied to Amish parents who refused on religious grounds to send their children to school). . . .

The present case does not present such a hybrid situation, but a free exercise claim unconnected with any communicative activity or parental right. Respondents urge us to hold, quite simply, that when otherwise prohibitable conduct is accompanied by religious convictions, not only the convictions but the conduct itself must be free from governmental regulation. We have never held that, and decline to do so now. There being no contention that Oregon's drug law represents an attempt to regulate religious beliefs, the communication of religious beliefs, or the raising of one's children in those beliefs, the rule to which we have adhered ever since *Reynolds* plainly controls. "Our cases do not at their farthest reach support the proposition that a stance of conscientious opposition relieves an objector from any colliding duty fixed by a democratic government."

Respondents argue that even though exemption from generally applicable criminal laws need not automatically be extended to religiously motivated actors, at least the claim for a religious exemption must be evaluated under the balancing test set forth in *Sherbert v. Verner*, 374 U.S. 398 (1963). Under the *Sherbert* test, governmental actions that substantially burden a religious practice must be justified by a compelling governmental interest. Applying that test we have, on three occasions, invalidated state unemployment compensation rules that conditioned the availability of benefits upon an applicant's willingness to work under conditions forbidden by his religion. We have never invalidated any governmental action on the basis of the *Sherbert* test except the denial of unemployment compensation. Although we have sometimes purported to apply the *Sherbert* test in contexts other than that, we have always found the test satisfied. In recent years we have abstained from applying the Sherbert test (outside the unemployment compensation field) at all. . . .

Even if we were inclined to breathe into *Sherbert* some life beyond the unemployment compensation field, we would not apply it to require exemptions from a generally applicable criminal law. The *Sherbert* test, it must be recalled, was developed in a context that lent itself to individualized governmental assessment of the reasons for the relevant conduct. As a plurality of the Court noted in Roy, a distinctive feature of unemployment compensation programs is that their eligibility criteria invite consideration of the particular circumstances behind an applicant's unemployment: "The statutory conditions [in *Sherbert* and *Thomas*] provided that a person was not eligible for unemployment compensation benefits if, 'without good cause,' he had quit work or refused available work. The 'good cause' standard created a mechanism for individualized exemptions." As the plurality pointed out in

Roy, our decisions in the unemployment cases stand for the proposition that where the State has in place a system of individual exemptions, it may not refuse to extend that system to cases of "religious hardship" without compelling reason.

Whether or not the decisions are that limited, they at least have nothing to do with an across-the-board criminal prohibition on a particular form of conduct. Although, as noted earlier, we have sometimes used the *Sherbert* test to analyze free exercise challenges to such laws, we have never applied the test to invalidate one. We conclude today that the sounder approach, and the approach in accord with the vast majority of our precedents, is to hold the test inapplicable to such challenges. The government's ability to enforce generally applicable prohibitions of socially harmful conduct, like its ability to carry out other aspects of public policy, "cannot depend on measuring the effects of a governmental action on a religious objector's spiritual development." To make an individual's obligation to obey such a law contingent upon the law's coincidence with his religious beliefs, except where the State's interest is "compelling"—permitting him, by virtue of his beliefs, "to become a law unto himself"—contradicts both constitutional tradition and common sense.

. . . .

Because respondents' ingestion of peyote was prohibited under Oregon law, and because that prohibition is constitutional, Oregon may, consistent with the Free Exercise Clause, deny respondents unemployment compensation when their dismissal results from use of the drug. The decision of the Oregon Supreme Court is accordingly reversed.

It is so ordered.

Church of Lukumi Babalu Aye, Inc. v. Hialeah

508 U.S. 520 (1993)

The Court rules that city ordinances that prohibited animal sacrifices targeted religion and are subject to strict scrutiny.

Justice Kennedy delivered the opinion of the Court, except as to Part II-A-2 [which is not included in the excerpt of the opinion in this book].

The principle that government may not enact laws that suppress religious belief or practice is so well understood that few violations are recorded in our opinions. Concerned that this fundamental non-persecution principle of the First Amendment was implicated here, however, we granted certiorari. Our review confirms that the laws in question were enacted by officials who did not understand, failed to perceive, or chose to ignore the fact that their official actions violated the Nation's essential commitment to religious freedom. The challenged laws had an impermissible object; and in all events the principle of general applicability was violated because the secular ends asserted in defense of the laws were pursued only with respect to conduct motivated by religious beliefs. We invalidate the challenged enactments and reverse the judgment of the Court of Appeals.

This case involves practices of the Santeria religion, which originated in the 19th century....

The Santeria faith teaches that every individual has a destiny from God, a destiny fulfilled with the aid and energy of the *orishas*. The basis of the Santeria religion is the nurture of a personal relation with the *orishas*, and one of the principal forms of devotion is an animal sacrifice....

Petitioner Church of the Lukumi Babalu Aye, Inc. (Church), ... and its congregants practice the Santeria religion.... The prospect of a Santeria church in their midst was distressing to many members of the Hialeah community, ... the city council adopted three substantive ordinances addressing the issue of religious animal sacrifice....

In addressing the constitutional protection for free exercise of religion, our cases establish the general proposition that a law that is neutral and of general applicability need not be justified by a compelling governmental interest even if the law has the incidental effect of burdening a particular religious practice. *Employment Div., Dept. of Human Resources of Or. v. Smith, supra.* Neutrality and general applicability are interrelated, and, as becomes apparent in this case, failure to satisfy one requirement is a likely indication that the other has not been satisfied. A law failing to satisfy these requirements must be justified by a compelling governmental interest and must be narrowly tailored to advance that interest. These ordinances fail to satisfy the *Smith* requirements. We begin by discussing neutrality.

In our Establishment Clause cases we have often stated the principle that the First Amendment forbids an official purpose to disapprove of a particular religion or of religion in general. These cases, however, for the most part have addressed governmental efforts to benefit religion or particular religions, and so have dealt with a question different, at least in its formulation and emphasis, from the issue here. Petitioners allege an attempt to disfavor their religion because of the religious ceremonies it commands, and the Free Exercise Clause is dispositive in our analysis.

At a minimum, the protections of the Free Exercise Clause pertain if the law at issue discriminates against some or all religious beliefs or regulates or prohibits conduct because it is undertaken for religious reasons.... Although a law targeting religious beliefs as such is never permissible, if the object of a law is to infringe upon or restrict practices because of their religious motivation, the law is not neutral, and it is invalid unless it is justified by a compelling interest and is narrowly tailored to advance that interest.... The record in this case compels the conclusion that suppression of the central element of the Santeria worship service was the object of the ordinances.... [T]he neutrality inquiry leads to one conclusion: The ordinances had as their object the suppression of religion. The pattern we have recited discloses animosity to Santeria adherents and their religious practices; the ordinances by their own terms target this religious exercise; the texts of the ordinances were gerrymandered with care to proscribe religious killings of animals but to exclude almost all secular killings; and the ordinances suppress much more religious conduct than is necessary in order to achieve the legitimate ends asserted in their defense. These ordinances are not neutral, and the court below committed clear error in failing to reach this conclusion.

We turn next to a second requirement of the Free Exercise Clause, the rule that laws burdening religious practice must be of general applicability. All laws are selective to some extent, but categories of selection are of paramount concern when a law has the incidental effect of burdening religious practice. The Free Exercise Clause "protect[s] religious observers against unequal treatment," and inequality results when a legislature decides that the governmental interests it seeks to advance are worthy of being pursued only against conduct with a religious motivation.

The principle that government, in pursuit of legitimate interests, cannot in a selective manner impose burdens only on conduct motivated by religious belief is essential to the protection of the rights guaranteed by the Free Exercise Clause. The principle underlying the general applicability requirement has parallels in our First Amendment jurisprudence. In this case we need not define with precision the standard used to evaluate whether a prohibition is of general application, for these ordinances fall well below the minimum standard necessary to protect First Amendment rights.

. . . .

Gary S. v. Manchester School District

374 F.3d 15 (1st Cir. 2004)

The First Circuit finds that denying a student who attends Catholic school the special education services that he would have received if he attended public school does not violate the Free Exercise Clause.

Levin H. Campbell, Senior Circuit Judge.

Appealing from an adverse judgment of the district court, the parents of Andrew S., a disabled child who is attending a Catholic elementary school, assert that the Individuals with Disabilities Education Act (IDEA), is unconstitutional as applied to their son. While he, like other disabled children who go to private schools, receives some educational services under federal and state law, he is not entitled by law to the panoply of services available to disabled public school students under the rubric of free and appropriate public education (FAPE), nor to the due process hearing provided to public school students alone. Appellants argue that the difference in treatment of their disabled son, who is attending a religious school, from other disabled students, who are attending public schools, violates the Free Exercise Clause of the First Amendment to the federal constitution. . . .

Appellants' lead argument on appeal is that the district court erred in determining that the federal law did not violate Andrew's and his parents' free exercise rights under the First Amendment. They reject the district court's assertion that the Supreme Court's decision in *Employment Div. Dep't of Human Res. of Oregon v.*

Smith, is controlling. *Smith*, according to the district court, exempted most "neutral laws of general applicability" from the compelling interest test. In the district court's view,

> [A] law ordinarily need not be justified by a compelling interest if it is "neutral" in that it is not targeted at religiously motivated conduct and "generally applicable" in that it does not selectively burden religious conduct. *See Church of Lukumi Babalu Aye, Inc. v. City of Hialeah*, 508 U.S. 520, 532–35, 542–43 (1993).

IDEA and its regulations, the district court says, do not target religiously motivated conduct and is "generally applicable" in that it does not selectively burden religious conduct. For these reasons, and because appellants' First Amendment claim is not "hybrid," *i.e.* is not linked to a separate constitutional claim, the district court found no violation of free exercise rights. *Id.* We do not disagree.

Appellants reject the district court's analysis. They ask us to read *Smith* as limited to instances of socially harmful or criminal conduct. They point out that *Smith* did not purport to overrule the Supreme Court's holdings in the cases of *Hobbie v. Unemployment Appeals Comm'n, Thomas v. Review Bd. of the Indian Employment Sec. Div.*, and *Sherbert v. Verner*, 374 U.S. 398, (1963). . . . Appellants have likened the denial of educational disability benefits here to those situations, asking us similarly to apply strict scrutiny. If we do, appellants contend, we will find that Andrew's attendance at a Catholic school is mandated by his parents' sincerely-held religious beliefs. No compelling governmental interest is served, they say, by withholding from him the identical benefits granted to his peers at public schools.

It is not always easy to predict what analytical framework the Supreme Court will apply to the various, factually dissimilar free exercise cases that arise. *Smith* rejected a free exercise claim involving the religiously-based use of peyote, an illegal substance. Writing for five of the Justices, Justice Scalia endorsed the constitutionality of neutral, generally applicable laws even when they impinged incidentally upon individual religious practices. *Smith*, 494 U.S. at 881, 885. The *Smith* majority expressly limited *Hobbie, Thomas* and *Sherbert* to the unemployment compensation field. *Smith*, 494 U.S. at 883–84. While, as appellants point out, Justice Scalia in *Smith* also distinguished *Hobbie, Thomas* and *Sherbert* on the narrower ground that the use of peyote was illegal, the majority's overall message is unmistakably contrary to appellants' present argument that *Hobbie, Thomas* and *Sherbert*—and, in particular, the "compelling interest" test—are broadly applicable here. *Smith*, insofar as can be told from reading the Court's more recent precedent, remains good law, albeit reflective when written of the thinking of a narrow majority of justices, some of whom no longer serve.

We also agree, for the reasons the district court stated, that this case is not a "hybrid" one. Hence, we conclude that the district court analyzed the case under the correct standard. While we could perhaps leave the free exercise analysis there, an even more fundamental reason causes us to reject appellants' First Amendment arguments. We cannot accept appellants' contention that providing to all disabled attendees at private schools, both sectarian and secular, fewer benefits than those granted to public school attendees is truly analogous to denying unemployment benefits to persons fired because of their religiously-inspired insistence upon celebrating the Sabbath or not producing weapons.

The state unemployment benefits denied in *Hobbie, Thomas, Sherbert* were public benefits, available to all. Plaintiffs would have received them had their religiously-motivated refusal to work on a certain day or at a certain job not been erroneously viewed by local authorities as misconduct. While appellants say their son's attendance at a Catholic school is likewise a religiously-motivated act, there is a basic difference. He and they are not being deprived of a *generally available* public benefit. Rather, the benefits to which appellants lay claim under the First Amendment are benefits the federal government has earmarked solely for students enrolled in the nation's public schools—benefits still available for Andrew were he sent to a public school, though not otherwise. Since the early days of public education in this country, public financial aid has commonly been limited to public rather than independent schools. While the parents of private school attendees pay the same taxes as public school parents, the former's tax money normally supports their own children's education only if they transfer them to a public school. To be sure, parents have a protected right to send their children to private schools if they so desire. *Pierce v. Soc'y of Sisters*, 268 U.S. 510, 534–35 (1925). But as the very term "private" denotes, it is not ordinarily expected that such schools will be publicly funded, and there is no precedent requiring such funding.

Given the traditional pattern that has so far prevailed of financing public education via the public schools, it would be unreasonable and inconsistent to premise a free exercise violation upon Congress's mere failure to provide to disabled children attending private religious schools the identical financial and other benefits it confers upon those attending public schools. Unlike unemployment benefits that are equally available to all, private school parents can have no legitimate expectancy that they or their children's schools will receive the same federal or state financial benefits provided to public schools. Thus, the non-receipt of equal funding and programmatic benefits cannot be said to impose any cognizable "burden" upon the religion of those choosing to attend such schools. Persons opting to attend private schools, religious or otherwise, must accept the disadvantages as well as any benefits offered by those schools. They cannot insist, as a matter of constitutional right, that the disadvantages be cured by the provision of public funding. It follows that denying the benefits here, to which appellants have no cognizable entitlement, do not burden their free exercise rights.

Indeed, if we were to find a burden here on appellants' right of free exercise, it would follow logically that we should find free exercise violations whenever a state, city or town refuses to fund programs of other types at religious schools, at least insofar as the absence of funding adversely affects students with parents who believe their faith requires attendance at a religious school. Yet, as noted *supra*, it is clear there is no federal constitutional requirement that private schools be permitted to share with public schools in state largesse on an equal basis.

Accordingly, we see no basis for holding that the federal government violates appellants' free exercise rights under the First Amendment by favoring disabled public school attendees in respect to IDEA's programs and benefits. In so doing, the federal government does no more than state and local governments do everyday by funding public school programs while providing lesser or, more likely, no funding to private schools, religious and otherwise. This methodology leaves all parents with ultimate recourse to the public schools whenever the balance of services associated with attendance at a private school appears to them to be unsatisfactory; but the option thus available can necessitate their having to choose, as here, between alternatives each of which may seem imperfect. In any event, we cannot say that the federal government's structuring of benefits here violates appellants' free exercise rights.

. . . .

We AFFIRM the decision of the district court.

Post Problem Discussion

1. In *Smith* and in *Gary S.*, the courts note that the *Sherbert* line of cases has only been applied in the context of unemployment benefits. Why do you think courts have been reluctant to apply *Sherbert* in other areas?

2. In *Gary S.*, the court distinguishes the special education benefits at issue in the case and the unemployment benefits in *Sherbert*, noting that unemployment benefits are "generally available benefits." Why are unemployment benefits considered generally available, but special education benefits are not?

3. In *Gary S.*, the court rejects the argument that the student fits into a *Yoder* "hybrid" situation. Do you agree? What is the difference between *Yoder* and *Gary S.*? Don't both involve the substantive due process right to direct a child's educational upbringing and free exercise rights?

4. Does the denial of the curriculum advisor target religion? Is it more like the situation in *Lukumi*, or the situation in *Locke v. Davey*?

§ 11.03 Category Two: Religious Activities at Public Schools or School-Sponsored Events

The second category of religious issues in schools involves religious activities in the public school or at events and activities sponsored by the public school. Over the years, the Supreme Court and lower courts have addressed the constitutionality of a number of such religious activities including school prayer, reciting the Pledge of Allegiance, displaying religious symbols, and teaching creationism in schools.

A. School Prayer

When public schools began in the United States, religion was very common in the classroom. Students often began and ended their days with prayers and learned topics from the Bible in school.[2] Over time, the focus on religion in schools dissipated in some places and remained in others, based on state and local decision making and preferences regarding religion.

In *Engel v. Vitale*, 370 U.S. 421 (1962), the United States Supreme Court ruled the New York Board of Regents could not require a school prayer that said, "Almighty God, we acknowledge our dependence upon Thee, and we beg Thy blessings upon us, our parents, our teachers, and our country." *Engel*, 370 U.S. at 422. The Court noted that "the constitutional prohibition against laws respecting an establishment of religion must at least mean that in this country, it is no part of the business of government to compose official prayers for any group of the American people to recite as a part of a religious program carried on by government." *Engel*, 370 U.S. at 425. The Court rejected the school's arguments that its actions were constitutional because the prayer was "non-denominational" and because all pupils were not required to participate, saying that the "Establishment Clause, unlike the Free Exercise Clause, does not depend upon any showing of direct governmental compulsion and is violated by the enactment of laws which establish an official religion whether those laws operate directly to coerce nonobserving individuals or not." *Engel*, 370 U.S. at 439.

The next year, in *Abington v. Schemp*, 374 U.S. 203 (1963), the Court ruled that beginning the school day by reading verses from the Bible and reciting the Lord's Prayer violated the Establishment Clause even though the school permitted students to be excused from such activities by written request of a parent or guardian. *Abington*, 374 U.S. at 205. A central theme in both *Engel* and *Abington* was the fact that the school sponsored the prayer or religious activities at issue which crossed the line in terms of establishing religion. More recent cases have tested the parameters of what constitutes "school sponsored" prayer. The following problem explores these issues.

Problem 4: Student Initiated Prayer at the Senior Prom

The student council at Altec High School approaches the high school principal before the student senior prom saying that they wanted one of the student's parents who is a minister to begin the prom with a prayer. The prom is held at the school gym. The principal refuses, suggesting that the students should have the prayer as a group activity before they come to the prom, because school sponsored prayer at the prom would violate the Constitution. The students contend that it violates their Free Exercise rights to not be able to pray and ask the principal to change her mind. She responds, "I can't have anything to do with it," and walks away.

---

2. *See, e.g.*, Steven K. Green, *All Things Not Being Equal: Reconciling Student Religious Expression in the Public Schools*, 42 U.C. Davis L. Rev. 843 (2009).

At the prom the following week, the principal begins the night by welcoming the students and encouraging them to engage in safe behaviors during the night. She then turns the microphone over to the student president, who traditionally begins the prom by explaining the events of the evening and introducing the band. The student president says the following:

> I am honored to be here tonight representing the school as student president. I am going to tell you about the schedule tonight and introduce the band to you in a minute. First, I'd like to say that I look forward to a fun and safe night. We have with us tonight a very special guest, Sean Jameson's dad. Sean is vice-president of student council. Many of you know our guest as our church minister, but he is here tonight as Sean's dad, and I'd like him to say a few words to help get us started this evening.

The minister then comes to the stage, recites a Bible passage that he believes is relevant to the evening, and he gives a brief prayer asking the Lord to watch over the students and to protect them from harm during prom night. During this time, the principal is in attendance near the stage where Reverend Jameson is leading the prayer. Several students and teachers in attendance complain and ask the principal to stop the prayer. She declines and bows her head to participate in the prayer herself saying "a little prayer never hurt anyone."

1. Do any of the principal's actions violate the Establishment Clause?
2. Could the principal have prevented or stopped the prayer without violating the Free Exercise Clause?
3. Would your answer change if the high school prom were held off-campus instead of on school grounds? Why or why not?
4. Assume that, because of this incident, the school board decides that it should develop a policy regarding student led prayer at school events. What should the policy say?

Problem Materials

✓ *Lee v. Weisman*, 505 U.S. 577 (1992)

✓ *Santa Fe Independent School District v. Doe*, 530 U.S. 290 (2000)

Lee v. Weisman

505 U.S. 577 (1992)

The Court rules that a prayer by clergy at a high school graduation ceremony violates the Establishment Clause.

Kennedy, J., delivered the opinion of the Court, in which Blackmun, Stevens, O'Connor, and Souter, JJ., joined.

School principals in the public school system of the city of Providence, Rhode Island, are permitted to invite members of the clergy to offer invocation and benediction prayers as part of the formal graduation ceremonies for middle schools and for high schools. The question before us is whether including clerical members who offer prayers as part of the official school graduation ceremony is consistent with the Religion Clauses of the First Amendment, provisions the Fourteenth Amendment makes applicable with full force to the States and their school districts.

Deborah Weisman graduated from Nathan Bishop Middle School, a public school in Providence, at a formal ceremony in June, 1989. . . . It has been the custom of Providence school officials to provide invited clergy with a pamphlet entitled "Guidelines for Civic Occasions," prepared by the National Conference of Christians and Jews. The Guidelines recommend that public prayers at nonsectarian civic ceremonies be composed with "inclusiveness and sensitivity," though they acknowledge that "[p]rayer of any kind may be inappropriate on some civic occasions." The principal gave Rabbi Gutterman the pamphlet before the graduation, and advised him the invocation and benediction should be nonsectarian.

. . . .

These dominant facts mark and control the confines of our decision: State officials direct the performance of a formal religious exercise at promotional and graduation ceremonies for secondary schools. Even for those students who object to the religious exercise, their attendance and participation in the state-sponsored religious activity are, in a fair and real sense, obligatory, though the school district does not require attendance as a condition for receipt of the diploma.

This case does not require us to revisit the difficult questions dividing us in recent cases, questions of the definition and full scope of the principles governing the extent of permitted accommodation by the State for the religious beliefs and practices of many of its citizens. For without reference to those principles in other contexts, the controlling precedents as they relate to prayer and religious exercise in primary and secondary public schools compel the holding here that the policy of the city of Providence is an unconstitutional one. We can decide the case without reconsidering the general constitutional framework by which public schools' efforts to accommodate religion are measured. Thus, we do not accept the invitation of petitioners and amicus the United States to reconsider our decision in Lemon v. Kurtzman, supra. The government involvement with religious activity in this case is pervasive, to the point of creating a state-sponsored and state-directed religious exercise in a public school. Conducting this formal religious observance conflicts with settled rules pertaining to prayer exercises for students, and that suffices to determine the question before us.

The principle that government may accommodate the free exercise of religion does not supersede the fundamental limitations imposed by the Establishment Clause. It is beyond dispute that, at a minimum, the Constitution guarantees that government may not coerce anyone to support or participate in religion or its exercise, or otherwise act in a way which "establishes a [state] religion or religious faith, or tends to do so." The State's involvement in the school prayers challenged today violates these central principles.

That involvement is as troubling as it is undenied. A school official, the principal, decided that an invocation and a benediction should be given; this is a choice attributable to the State, and, from a constitutional perspective, it is as if a state statute decreed that the prayers must occur. The principal chose the religious participant, here a rabbi, and that choice is also attributable to the State. The reason for the choice of a rabbi is not disclosed by the record, but the potential for divisiveness over the choice of a particular member of the clergy to conduct the ceremony is apparent.

Divisiveness, of course, can attend any state decision respecting religions, and neither its existence nor its potential necessarily invalidates the State's attempts to accommodate religion in all cases. The potential for divisiveness is of particular relevance here, though, because it centers around an overt religious exercise in a secondary school environment where, as we discuss below, subtle coercive pressures exist, and where the student had no real alternative which would have allowed her to avoid the fact or appearance of participation.

The State's role did not end with the decision to include a prayer and with the choice of clergyman. Principal Lee provided Rabbi Gutterman with a copy of the "Guidelines for Civic Occasions" and advised him that his prayers should be nonsectarian. Through these means, the principal directed and controlled the content of the prayers. . . . It is a cornerstone principle of our Establishment Clause jurisprudence that it is no part of the business of government to compose official prayers for any group of the American people to recite as a part of a religious program carried on by government, and that is what the school officials attempted to do.

. . . .

These concerns have particular application in the case of school officials, whose effort to monitor prayer will be perceived by the students as inducing a participation they might otherwise reject. Though the efforts of the school officials in this case to find common ground appear to have been a good faith attempt to recognize the common aspects of religions, and not the divisive ones, our precedents do not permit school officials to assist in composing prayers as an incident to a formal exercise for their students. And these same precedents caution us to measure the idea of a civic religion against the central meaning of the Religion Clauses of the First Amendment, which is that all creeds must be tolerated, and none favored. The suggestion that government may establish an official or civic religion as a means of avoiding the establishment of a religion with more specific creeds strikes us as a contradiction that cannot be accepted.

The degree of school involvement here made it clear that the graduation prayers bore the imprint of the State, and thus put school-age children who objected in an untenable position. We turn our attention now to consider the position of the students, both those who desired the prayer and she who did not.

To endure the speech of false ideas or offensive content and then to counter it is part of learning how to live in a pluralistic society, a society which insists upon open discourse towards the end of a tolerant citizenry. And tolerance presupposes some mutuality of obligation. It is argued that our constitutional vision of a free society requires confidence in our own ability to accept or reject ideas of which we do not approve, and that prayer at a high school graduation does nothing more than offer a choice. By the time they are seniors, high school students no doubt have been required to attend classes and assemblies and to complete assignments exposing them to ideas they find distasteful or immoral or absurd, or all of these. Against this background, students may consider it an odd measure of justice to be subjected during the course of their educations to ideas deemed offensive and irreligious, but to be denied a brief, formal prayer ceremony that the school offers in return. This argument cannot prevail, however. It overlooks a fundamental dynamic of the Constitution.

The First Amendment protects speech and religion by quite different mechanisms. Speech is protected by ensuring its full expression even when the government participates, for the very object of some of our most important speech is to persuade the government to adopt an idea as its own. The method for protecting freedom of worship and freedom of conscience in religious matters is quite the reverse. In religious debate or expression, the government is not a prime participant, for the Framers deemed religious establishment antithetical to the freedom of all. The Free Exercise Clause embraces a freedom of conscience and worship that has close parallels in the speech provisions of the First Amendment, but the Establishment Clause is a specific prohibition on forms of state intervention in religious affairs, with no precise counterpart in the speech provisions. The explanation lies in the lesson of history that was and is the inspiration for the Establishment Clause, the lesson that, in the hands of government, what might begin as a tolerant expression of religious views may end in a policy to indoctrinate and coerce. A state-created orthodoxy puts at grave risk that freedom of belief and conscience which are the sole assurance that religious faith is real, not imposed.

The lessons of the First Amendment are as urgent in the modern world as in the 18th century, when it was written. One timeless lesson is that, if citizens are subjected to state-sponsored religious exercises, the State disavows its own duty to guard and respect that sphere of inviolable conscience and belief which is the mark of a free people. To compromise that principle today would be to deny our own tradition and forfeit our standing to urge others to secure the protections of that tradition for themselves.

As we have observed before, there are heightened concerns with protecting freedom of conscience from subtle coercive pressure in the elementary and secondary public schools. Our decisions in *Engel v. Vitale*, and *School Dist. of Abington, supra*, recognize, among other things, that prayer exercises in public schools carry a particular risk of indirect coercion. The concern may not be limited to the context of schools, but it is most pronounced there. What to most believers may seem nothing more than a reasonable request that the nonbeliever respect their religious practices, in a school context may appear to the nonbeliever or dissenter to be an attempt to employ the machinery of the State to enforce a religious orthodoxy.

We need not look beyond the circumstances of this case to see the phenomenon at work. The undeniable fact is that the school district's supervision and control of a high school graduation ceremony places public pressure, as well as peer pressure, on attending students to stand as a group or, at least, maintain respectful silence during the invocation and benediction. This pressure, though subtle and indirect, can be as real as any overt compulsion. Of course, in our culture, standing or remaining silent can signify adherence to a view or simple respect for the views of others. And no doubt some persons who have no desire to join a prayer have little objection to standing as a sign of respect for those who do. But for the dissenter of high school age, who has a reasonable perception that she is being forced by the State to pray in a manner her conscience will not allow, the injury is no less real. There can be no doubt that for many, if not most, of the students at the graduation, the act of standing or remaining silent was an expression of participation in the rabbi's prayer. That was the very point of the religious exercise. It is of little comfort to a dissenter, then, to be told that, for her, the act of standing or remaining in silence signifies mere respect, rather than participation. What matters is that, given our social conventions, a reasonable dissenter in this milieu could believe that the group exercise signified her own participation or approval of it.

Finding no violation under these circumstances would place objectors in the dilemma of participating, with all that implies, or protesting. We do not address whether that choice is acceptable if the affected citizens are mature adults, but we think the State may not, consistent with the Establishment Clause, place primary and secondary school children in this position.... To recognize that the choice imposed by the State constitutes an unacceptable constraint only acknowledges that the government may no more use social pressure to enforce orthodoxy than it may use more direct means.

There was a stipulation in the District Court that attendance at graduation and promotional ceremonies is voluntary. Petitioners and the United States, as amicus, made this a center point of the case, arguing that the option of not attending the graduation excuses any inducement or coercion in the ceremony itself. The argument lacks all persuasion. Law reaches past formalism. And to say a teenage student has a real choice not to attend her high school graduation is formalistic in the extreme. True, Deborah could elect not to attend commencement without renouncing her diploma; but we shall not allow the case to turn on this point. Everyone knows that, in our society and in our culture, high school graduation is one of life's most significant occasions. A school rule which excuses attendance is beside the point. Attendance may not be required by official decree, yet it is apparent that a student is not free to absent herself from the graduation exercise in any real sense of the term "voluntary," for absence would require forfeiture of those intangible benefits which have motivated the student through youth and all her high school years.

Graduation is a time for family and those closest to the student to celebrate success and express mutual wishes of gratitude and respect, all to the end of impressing upon the young person the role that it is his or her right and duty to assume in the community and all of its diverse parts.

. . . .

The Government's argument gives insufficient recognition to the real conflict of conscience faced by the young student. The essence of the Government's position is that, with regard to a civic, social occasion of this importance, it is the objector, not the majority, who must take unilateral and private action to avoid compromising religious scruples, hereby electing to miss the graduation exercise. This turns conventional First Amendment analysis on its head. It is a tenet of the First Amendment that the State cannot require one of its citizens to forfeit his or her rights and benefits as the price of resisting conformance to state-sponsored religious practice. To say that a student must remain apart from the ceremony at the opening invocation and closing benediction is to risk compelling conformity in an environment analogous to the classroom setting, where we have said the risk of compulsion is especially high. Just as, in *Engel v. Vitale*, and *School Dist. of Abington v. Schempp*, where we found that provisions within the challenged legislation permitting a student to be voluntarily excused from attendance or participation in the daily prayers did not shield those practices from invalidation, the fact that attendance at the graduation ceremonies is voluntary in a legal sense does not save the religious exercise.

. . . .

The prayer exercises in this case are especially improper because the State has in every practical sense compelled attendance and participation in an explicit religious exercise at an event of singular importance to every student, one the objecting student had no real alternative to avoid.

. . . .

Santa Fe Independent School District v. Doe

530 U.S. 290 (2000)

The Court rules that student-led, student-initiated prayer at a high school football game violates the Establishment Clause.

. . . .

Stevens, J., delivered the opinion of the Court, in which O'Connor, Kennedy, Souter, Ginsburg, and Breyer, JJ., joined.

In *Lee v. Weisman*, we held that a prayer delivered by a rabbi at a middle school graduation ceremony violated that Clause. Although this case involves student prayer at a different type of school function, our analysis is properly guided by the principles that we endorsed in *Lee*.

. . . .

In this case the District first argues that this principle is inapplicable to its October policy because the messages are private student speech, not public speech. It reminds us that "there is a crucial difference between *government* speech endorsing religion, which the Establishment Clause forbids, and *private* speech endorsing religion, which the Free Speech and Free Exercise Clauses protect." We certainly agree with that distinction, but we are not persuaded that the pregame invocations should be regarded as "private speech."

These invocations are authorized by a government policy and take place on government property at government-sponsored school-related events. Of course, not every message delivered under such circumstances is the government's own. We have held, for example, that an individual's contribution to a government-created forum was not government speech. *See Rosenberger v. Rector and Visitors of Univ. of Va.*, 515 U.S. 819 (1995). Although the District relies heavily on *Rosenberger* and similar cases involving such forums, it is clear that the pregame ceremony is not the type of forum discussed in those cases. The Santa Fe school officials simply do not "evince either 'by policy or by practice,' any intent to open the [pregame ceremony] to 'indiscriminate use,' . . . by the student body generally." Rather, the school allows only one student, the same student for the entire season, to give the invocation. The statement or invocation, moreover, is subject to particular regulations that confine the content and topic of the student's message. . . .

Granting only one student access to the stage at a time does not, of course, necessarily preclude a finding that a school has created a limited public forum. Here, however, Santa Fe's student election system ensures that only those messages deemed "appropriate" under the District's policy may be delivered. That is, the majoritarian process implemented by the District guarantees, by definition, that minority candidates will never prevail and that their views will be effectively silenced.

Recently, in *Board of Regents of Univ. of Wis. System v. Southworth*, 529 U.S. 217 (2000), we explained why student elections that determine, by majority vote, which expressive activities shall receive or not receive school benefits are constitutionally problematic:

> To the extent the referendum substitutes majority determinations for viewpoint neutrality it would undermine the constitutional protection the program requires. The whole theory of viewpoint neutrality is that minority views are treated with the same respect as are majority views. Access to a public forum, for instance, does not depend upon majoritarian consent. That principle is controlling here.

Like the student referendum for funding in *Southworth*, this student election does nothing to protect minority views but rather places the students who hold such views at the mercy of the majority. Because "fundamental rights may not be submitted to vote; they depend on the outcome of no elections," the District's elections are insufficient safeguards of diverse student speech.

Moreover, the District has failed to divorce itself from the religious content in the invocations. It has not succeeded in doing so, either by claiming that its policy is "'one of neutrality rather than endorsement'" or by characterizing the individual student as the "circuit-breaker" in the process. Contrary to the District's repeated assertions that it has adopted a "hands-off" approach to the pregame invocation, the realities of the situation plainly reveal that its policy involves both perceived and actual endorsement of religion. In this case, as we found in *Lee*, the "degree of school involvement" makes it clear that the pregame prayers bear "the imprint of the State and thus put school-age children who objected in an untenable position."

The District has attempted to disentangle itself from the religious messages by developing the two-step student election process. The text of the October policy, however, exposes the extent of the school's entanglement. The elections take place at all only because the school "board *has chosen to permit* students to deliver a brief invocation and/or message." The elections thus "shall" be conducted "by the high school student council" and "[u]pon advice and direction of the high school principal." The decision whether to deliver a message is first made by majority vote of the entire student body, followed by a choice of the speaker in a separate, similar majority election. Even though the particular words used by the speaker are not determined by those votes, the policy mandates that the "statement or invocation" be "consistent with the goals and purposes of this policy," which are "to solemnize the event, to promote good sportsmanship and student safety, and to establish the appropriate environment for the competition."

In addition to involving the school in the selection of the speaker, the policy, by its terms, invites and encourages religious messages. The policy itself states that the purpose of the message is "to solemnize the event." A religious message is the most obvious method of solemnizing an event. . . . The results of the elections described in the parties' stipulation make it clear that the students understood that the central question before them was whether prayer should be a part of the pregame ceremony. We recognize the important role that public worship plays in many communities, as well as the sincere desire to include public prayer as a part of various occasions so as to mark those occasions' significance. But such religious activity in public schools, as elsewhere, must comport with the First Amendment.

The actual or perceived endorsement of the message, moreover, is established by factors beyond just the text of the policy. Once the student speaker is selected and the message composed, the invocation is then delivered to a large audience assembled as part of a regularly scheduled, school-sponsored function conducted on school property. The message is broadcast over the school's public address system, which remains subject to the control of school officials. It is fair to assume that the pregame ceremony is clothed in the traditional indicia of school sporting events, which generally include not just the team, but also cheerleaders and band members dressed in uniforms sporting the school name and mascot. The school's name is likely written in large print across the field and on banners and flags. The crowd will certainly include many who display the school colors and insignia on their school T-shirts, jackets, or hats and who may also be waving signs displaying the school name. It is in a setting such as this that "[t]he board has chosen to permit" the elected student to rise and give the "statement or invocation."

In this context the members of the listening audience must perceive the pregame message as a public expression of the views of the majority of the student body delivered with the approval of the school administration. In cases involving state participation in a religious activity, one of the relevant questions is "whether an objective observer, acquainted with the text, legislative history, and implementation of the statute, would perceive it as a state endorsement of prayer in public schools." Regardless of the listener's support for, or objection to, the message, an objective Santa Fe High School student will unquestionably perceive the inevitable pregame prayer as stamped with her school's seal of approval.

The text and history of this policy, moreover, reinforce our objective student's perception that the prayer is, in actuality, encouraged by the school. When a governmental entity professes a secular purpose for an arguably religious policy, the government's characterization is, of course, entitled to some deference. But it is nonetheless the duty of the courts to "distinguis[h] a sham secular purpose from a sincere one."

. . . .

School sponsorship of a religious message is impermissible because it sends the ancillary message to members of the audience who are nonadherants "that they are outsiders, not full members of the political community, and an accompanying message to adherants that they are insiders, favored members of the political community." *Lynch v. Donnelly*, 465 U.S., at 688 (1984) (O'Connor, J., concurring). The delivery of such a message—over the school's public address system, by a speaker representing the student body, under the supervision of school faculty, and pursuant to a school policy that explicitly and implicitly encourages public prayer—is not properly characterized as "private" speech.

The District next argues that its football policy is distinguishable from the graduation prayer in *Lee* because it does not coerce students to participate in religious observances. Its argument has two parts: first, that there is no impermissible government coercion because the pregame messages are the product of student choices; and second, that there is really no coercion at all because attendance at an extracurricular event, unlike a graduation ceremony, is voluntary.

The reasons just discussed explaining why the alleged "circuit-breaker" mechanism of the dual elections and student speaker do not turn public speech into private speech also demonstrate why these mechanisms do not insulate the school from the coercive element of the final message. In fact, this aspect of the District's argument exposes anew the concerns that are created by the majoritarian election system. The parties' stipulation clearly states that the issue resolved in the first election was "whether a student would deliver prayer at varsity football games," and the controversy in this case demonstrates that the views of the students are not unanimous on that issue.

One of the purposes served by the Establishment Clause is to remove debate over this kind of issue from governmental supervision or control. We explained in *Lee* that the "preservation and transmission of religious beliefs and worship is a responsibility and a choice committed to the private sphere." The two student elections authorized by the policy, coupled with the debates that presumably must precede each, impermissibly invade that private sphere. The election mechanism, when considered in light of the history in which the policy in question evolved, reflects a device the District put in place that determines whether religious messages will be delivered at home football games. The mechanism encourages divisiveness along religious lines in a public school setting, a result at odds with the Establishment Clause. Although it is true that the ultimate choice of student speaker is "attributable to the students," the District's decision to hold the constitutionally problematic election is clearly "a choice attributable to the State."

The District further argues that attendance at the commencement ceremonies at issue in *Lee* "differs dramatically" from attendance at high school football games, which it contends "are of no more than passing interest to many students" and are "decidedly extracurricular," thus dissipating any coercion....

There are some students, however, such as cheerleaders, members of the band, and, of course, the team members themselves, for whom seasonal commitments mandate their attendance, sometimes for class credit. The District also minimizes the importance to many students of attending and participating in extracurricular activities as part of a complete educational experience. As we noted in *Lee*, "[l]aw reaches past formalism." To assert that high school students do not feel immense social pressure, or have a truly genuine desire, to be involved in the extracurricular event that is American high school football is "formalistic in the extreme." We stressed in *Lee* the obvious observation that "adolescents are often susceptible to pressure from their peers towards conformity, and that the influence is strongest in matters of social convention." High school home football games are traditional gatherings of a school community; they bring together students and faculty as well as friends and family from years present and past to root for a common cause. Undoubtedly, the games are not important to some students, and they voluntarily choose not to attend. For many others, however, the choice between whether to attend these games or to risk facing a personally offensive religious ritual is in no practical sense an easy one. The Constitution, moreover, demands that the school may not force this difficult choice upon these students for "[i]t is a tenet of the First Amendment that the State cannot require one of its citizens to forfeit his or her rights and benefits as the price of resisting conformance to state-sponsored religious practice."

Even if we regard every high school student's decision to attend a home football game as purely voluntary, we are nevertheless persuaded that the delivery of a pregame prayer has the improper effect of coercing those present to participate in an act of religious worship.

....

Post Problem Discussion

1. In *Santa Fe*, the court mentions the actual or perceived endorsement of the message and says, "an objective Santa Fe High School student will unquestionably perceive the inevitable pregame prayer as stamped with her school's seal of approval." Under this standard, would the prayer in our problem at the high school prom also be unconstitutional? Would there be a different result if we applied the *Lemon* test or the coercion test? Would the result of your analysis be different if the principal had interrupted the Reverend instead of joining in the prayer?

2. Under the endorsement standard noted in *Santa Fe*, under what circumstances, if any, could prayer occur at school-sponsored events? Would the *Lemon* test or coercion test allow prayer at school-sponsored events that would not be allowed under the endorsement test?

3. In *Santa Fe*, the Court notes that the Constitution does not "prohibit any public school student from voluntarily praying at any time before, during, or after the school day. But the religious liberty protected by the Constitution is abridged when the State affirmatively sponsors the particular religious practice of prayer." After *Lee* and *Santa Fe*, what are the parameters of student prayer?

4. How do you think the courts should treat events like Christmas (or Holiday) assemblies or parties at public schools? Is your answer influenced by the age or grade of the students? *See, e.g., Skoros v. City of New York*, 437 F.3d 1 (2d Cir. 2006) *cert. denied*, 549 U.S. 1205 (2007).

B. Pledge of Allegiance and Religious Activities

Notwithstanding *Vitale, Abington, Lee*, and *Santa Fe*, some public school schools still include some aspect of prayer or religion in daily school activities. As mandated prayers were invalidated by the courts, some states and schools adopted required moments of silence at the beginning of the school day. In *Wallace v. Jaffree*, 472 U.S. 38 (1985), the Supreme Court ruled a moment of silence unconstitutional because its purpose was to include religion in public schools. State and federal courts have upheld other moment of silence policies that did not have a religious purpose. *See, e.g., Croft v. Perry*, 624 F.3d 157 (5th Cir. 2009).

Sometimes, the religious activities are included as part of patriotic or historical exercises to try to distinguish them from the activities found unconstitutional in court decisions. Like moments of silence, the Pledge of Allegiance is also a center of dispute in the First Amendment context. In *West Virginia State Bd. of Educ. v. Barnette*, 319 U.S. 624 (1943), the Court addressed a challenge to the Pledge by Jehovah's

Witnesses who asserted their religious beliefs and refused to salute a graven image (the flag) at school. The Court ruled that the school could not compel participation in the Pledge nor punish those who did not participate: "The action of the local authorities . . . invades the sphere of intellect and spirit which it is the purpose of the First Amendment to our Constitution to reserve from all official control." *Barnette*, 319 U.S. 624, 642.

In 2002, the Ninth Circuit ruled that the Pledge of Allegiance violated the Establishment Clause by forcing students to recite the words "under God." *Newdow v. U.S. Congress*, 292 F.3d 597 (9th Cir. 2002). The United States Supreme Court subsequently overruled on standing grounds, without reaching the merits of whether the Pledge violated the Establishment Clause. *Elk Grove Unified Sch. Dist. v. Newdow*, 542 U.S. 1 (2004). Other circuit courts have found that the Pledge does not violate the Establishment Clause as long as students are not forced to participate. *See, e.g., Myers v. Loudoun County Pub Schs.*, 418 F.3d 395 (4th Cir. 2005).

The following Activity lets you explore this issue in your state.

Activity 1: Pledge of Allegiance and Religious Activities in Your State

Step One—Review your state statutes and education regulations for provisions regarding the Pledge of Allegiance, prayer, moments of silence or patriotic activities.

Step Two—Review state and federal court cases in your jurisdiction to see if courts have addressed any of these issues. As part of your research, review the *Newdow v. U.S. Congress*, 292 F.3d 597 (9th Cir. 2002), and *Myers v. Loudoun County Public Schools*, 418 F.3d 395 (4th Cir. 2005), decisions.

Step Three—Answer the following:

1. Does your state have any provisions regarding the Pledge of Allegiance or any other religious or patriotic activities in schools? If so, what do they say?
2. Have your state provisions been challenged in court? If so, what was the outcome? Do you agree with it? If the cases involved the Pledge, which approach did the court follow (*Newdow* or *Myers*)?
3. Why do the Ninth and Fourth Circuits come to different conclusions regarding the Pledge violating the Establishment Clause? Is it because they used different legal standards or tests? Or is it because they interpreted or applied the same tests differently? Which court do you agree with and why?
4. The majority Supreme Court opinion in *Newdow* did not address the merits of the constitutionality of the Pledge. If it were to decide the merits of the question today, how do you think the Court would rule and why? Do you think the potential political and emotional effect of finding the Pledge unconstitutional will play any role in the decision?

C. Teaching Religion in Schools — Evolution vs. Creationism

The United States Supreme Court has been quick to note in numerous cases that religion does not have to be completely excluded from public schools. For example, an often quoted statement from *Abington v. Schempp*, 374 U.S. 203, 225 (1963), notes "it might well be said that one's education is not complete without a study of comparative religion or the history of religion and its relationship to the advancement of civilization. It certainly may be said that the Bible is worthy of study for its literary and historic qualities. Nothing we have said here indicates that such study of the Bible or of religion, when presented objectively as part of a secular program of education, may not be effected consistently with the First Amendment."

Along these lines, courts have generally found that courses that contain religious information can withstand constitutional challenge if the material is part of a secular program of instruction and is presented objectively without efforts to indoctrinate or impose religious views on students. Courts have noted, however, that there are limits to teaching certain religious topics such as creationism (the Biblical account of the creation of mankind). The infamous Scopes Monkey trial brought some of the legal issues with teaching creationism to the limelight in the 1920s. Some years later, in *Epperson v. Arkansas*, 393 U.S. 97 (1968), the United States Supreme Court ruled that a state law that prohibited the teaching of evolution in public schools was unconstitutional. The Court noted, "the First Amendment does not permit the State to require that teaching and learning must be tailored to the principles or prohibitions of any religious sect or dogma. . . ." *Epperson*, 393 U.S. at 106.

Subsequent efforts regarding creationism in public schools have focused more on presenting alternatives to evolution. In *Edwards v. Aguillard*, 482 U.S. 578 (1987), the Supreme Court found a state statute that required equal time for teaching evolution and creationism unconstitutional. More recently, a federal district court in Pennsylvania ruled that a school policy that required students to be provided with a statement regarding "intelligent design" as an alternative to evolution violated the Establishment Clause. *Kitzmiller v. Dover Area Sch. Dist*, 400 F. Supp. 2d 707 (M.D. Pa. 2005). The following problem explores these issues in more detail.

Problem 5: Teaching Alternatives to Evolution

You are the attorney for the East Harmony School District. The school board has provided you with the following draft policy. The board notes that the words that have been stricken are words that the majority of the board thought should be taken out of the policy and the words in brackets are words that the majority of the board wanted to include. A minority of the school board wanted to get your view as legal counsel on whether the words should be taken out or added, so the board agreed to send it as to you as follows:

East Harmony School District Policy on the Origins of Mankind

FINAL DRAFT WITH CHANGES NOTED TO LEGAL COUNSEL

> [The purpose of this policy is to promote academic freedom, critical thinking skills by students, and the diversity of ideas. The board is not intending to promote or endorse religion.]
>
> Evolution is a scientific theory that scientists have developed to explain the origins and development of mankind. It has been tested through the scientific method and accepted by many as an explanation of these very important topics. Others do not agree with this [scientific] approach and believe that the origins and development of mankind can only be explained by the involvement of some ~~divine intervention~~ or [higher authority] that transcends science and methods to prove its existence. We believe that as students, you should be exposed to both views and allowed to make your own decision by using the critical thinking skills you are developing, and will continue to develop, as a student and ~~God-fearing~~ citizen of our State.

The board also tells you that the plan will be implemented by having science teachers teach students evolution, but then have the students' research "other possible explanations for the origin and development of mankind" on their own. The students will then complete a written assignment where they explain what they believe to be the origins of mankind.

The Board wants to know:

1. Is the policy constitutional with the proposed changes?
2. Do the proposed changes need to be made in order for the policy to be constitutional?
3. Is the way the board plans on implementing the policy constitutional?
4. If the policy or implementation is not constitutional, what changes need to be made so that it will be constitutional?

Problem Materials

- ✓ *Epperson v. Arkansas*, 393 U.S. 97 (1968)
- ✓ *Edwards v. Aguillard*, 482 U.S. 578 (1987)
- ✓ *Kitzmiller v. Dover Area School District*, 400 F. Supp. 2d 707 (M.D. Pa. 2005)

Epperson v. Arkansas

393 U.S. 97 (1968)

The Court rules a state statute that prohibits teaching evolution in public schools is unconstitutional.

Mr. Justice Fortas delivered the opinion of the Court.

I.

This appeal challenges the constitutionality of the 'anti-evolution' statute which the State of Arkansas adopted in 1928 to prohibit the teaching in its public schools and universities of the theory that man evolved from other species of life. The statute was a product of the upsurge of 'fundamentalist' religious fervor of the twenties. The Arkansas statute was an adaption of the famous Tennessee 'monkey law' which that State adopted in 1925 The constitutionality of the Tennessee law was upheld by the Tennessee Supreme Court in the celebrated *Scopes* case in 1927.

The Arkansas law makes it unlawful for a teacher in any state-supported school or university 'to teach the theory or doctrine that mankind ascended or descended from a lower order of animals,' or 'to adopt or use in any such institution a textbook that teaches' this theory. Violation is a misdemeanor and subjects the violator to dismissal from his position.

The present case concerns the teaching of biology in a high school in Little Rock. According to the testimony, until the events here in litigation, the official textbook furnished for the high school biology course did not have a section on the Darwinian Theory. Then, for the academic year 1965–1966, the school administration, on recommendation of the teachers of biology in the school system, adopted and prescribed a textbook which contained a chapter setting forth 'the theory about the origin * * * of man from a lower form of animal.'

Susan Epperson, a young woman who graduated from Arkansas' school system and then obtained her master's degree in zoology at the University of Illinois, was employed by the Little Rock school system in the fall of 1964 to teach 10th grade biology at Central High School. At the start of the next academic year, 1965, she was confronted by the new textbook (which one surmises from the record was not unwelcome to her). She faced at least a literal dilemma because she was supposed to use the new textbook for classroom instruction and presumably to teach the statutorily condemned chapter; but to do so would be a criminal offense and subject her to dismissal.

She instituted the present action in the Chancery Court of the State, seeking a declaration that the Arkansas statute is void and enjoining the State and the defendant officials of the Little Rock school system from dismissing her for violation of the statute's provisions. H.H. Blanchard, a parent of children attending the public schools, intervened in support of the action.

The Chancery Court, in an opinion by Chancellor Murray O. Reed, held that the statute violated the Fourteenth Amendment to the United States Constitution. The court noted that this Amendment encompasses the prohibitions upon state interference with freedom of speech and thought which are contained in the First Amendment. Accordingly, it held that the challenged statute is unconstitutional because, in violation of the First Amendment, it 'tends to hinder the quest for knowledge, restrict the freedom to learn, and restrain the freedom to teach.' In this perspective, the Act, it held, was an unconstitutional and void restraint upon the freedom of speech guaranteed by the Constitution.

On appeal, the Supreme Court of Arkansas reversed. Its two-sentence opinion is set forth in the margin. It sustained the statute as an exercise of the State's power to specify the curriculum in public schools. It did not address itself to the competing constitutional considerations.

Appeal was duly prosecuted to this Court under 28 U.S.C. § 1257(2). Only Arkansas and Mississippi have such 'anti-evolution' or 'monkey' laws on their books. There is no record of any prosecutions in Arkansas under its statute. It is possible that the statute is presently more of a curiosity than a vital fact of life in these States. Nevertheless, the present case was brought, the appeal as of right is properly here, and it is our duty to decide the issues presented.

II.

At the outset, it is urged upon us that the challenged statute is vague and uncertain and therefore within the condemnation of the Due Process Clause of the Fourteenth Amendment. The contention that the Act is vague and uncertain is supported by language in the brief opinion of Arkansas' Supreme Court. That court, perhaps reflecting the discomfort which the statute's quixotic prohibition necessarily engenders in the modern mind, stated that it 'expressed no opinion' as to whether the Act prohibits 'explanation' of the theory of evolution or merely forbids 'teaching that the theory is true.' Regardless of this uncertainty, the court held that the statute is constitutional.

On the other hand, counsel for the State, in oral argument in this Court, candidly stated that, despite the State Supreme Court's equivocation, Arkansas would interpret the statute 'to mean that to make a student aware of the theory * * * just to teach that there was such a theory' would be grounds for dismissal and for prosecution under the statute; and he said 'that the Supreme Court of Arkansas' opinion should be interpreted in that manner.' He said: 'If Mrs. Epperson would tell her students that 'Here is Darwin's theory, that man ascended or descended from a lower form of being,' then I think she would be under this statute liable for prosecution.'

In any event, we do not rest our decision upon the asserted vagueness of the statute. On either interpretation of its language, Arkansas' statute cannot stand. It is of no moment whether the law is deemed to prohibit mention of Darwin's theory, or to forbid any or all of the infinite varieties of communication embraced within the term 'teaching.' Under either interpretation, the law must be stricken because of its conflict with the constitutional prohibition of state laws respecting an establishment of religion or prohibiting the free exercise thereof. The overriding fact is that Arkansas' law selects from the body of knowledge a particular segment which it proscribes for the sole reason that it is deemed to conflict with a particular religious doctrine; that is, with a particular interpretation of the Book of Genesis by a particular religious group.

III.

The antecedents of today's decision are many and unmistakable. They are rooted in the foundation soil of our Nation. They are fundamental to freedom.

Government in our democracy, state and national, must be neutral in matters of religious theory, doctrine, and practice. It may not be hostile to any religion or to the advocacy of no religion; and it may not aid, foster, or promote one religion or religious theory against another or even against the militant opposite. The First Amendment mandates governmental neutrality between religion and religion, and between religion and nonreligion.

As early as 1872, this Court said: 'The law knows no heresy, and is committed to the support of no dogma, the establishment of no sect.' *Watson v. Jones*, 20 L.Ed. 666, 13 Wall. 679, 728. This has been the interpretation of the great First Amendment which this Court has applied in the many and subtle problems which the ferment of our national life has presented for decision within the Amendment's broad command.

Judicial interposition in the operation of the public school system of the Nation raises problems requiring care and restraint. Our courts, however, have not failed to apply the First Amendment's mandate in our educational system where essential to safeguard the fundamental values of freedom of speech and inquiry and of belief. By and large, public education in our Nation is committed to the control of state and local authorities. Courts do not and cannot intervene in the resolution of conflicts which arise in the daily operation of school systems and which do not directly and sharply implicate basic constitutional values. On the other hand, '[t]he vigilant protection of constitutional freedoms is nowhere more vital than in the community of American schools,' *Shelton v. Tucker*, 364 U.S. 479, 487, (1960). As this Court said in *Keyishian v. Board of Regents*, the First Amendment 'does not tolerate laws that cast a pall of orthodoxy over the classroom.' 385 U.S. 589, 603, (1967).

The earliest cases in this Court on the subject of the impact of constitutional guarantees upon the classroom were decided before the Court expressly applied the specific prohibitions of the First Amendment to the States. But as early as 1923, the Court did not hesitate to condemn under the Due Process Clause 'arbitrary' restrictions upon the freedom of teachers to teach and of students to learn. In that year, the Court, in an opinion by Justice McReynolds, held unconstitutional an Act of the State of Nebraska making it a crime to teach any subject in any language other than English to pupils who had not passed the eighth grade. The State's purpose in enacting the law was to promote civic cohesiveness by encouraging the learning of English and to combat the 'baneful effect' of permitting foreigners to near and educate their children in the language of the parents' native land. The Court recognized these purposes, and it acknowledged the State's power to prescribe the school curriculum, but it held that these were not adequate to support the restriction upon the liberty of teacher and pupil. The challenged statute it held, unconstitutionally interfered with the right of the individual, guaranteed by the Due Process Clause, to engage in any of the common occupations of life and to acquire useful knowledge. *Meyer v. Nebraska*, 262 U.S. 390, (1923). See also Bartels v. Iowa, 262 U.S. 404, (1923).

For purposes of the present case, we need not re-enter the difficult terrain which the Court, in 1923, traversed without apparent misgivings. We need not take advantage of the broad premise which the Court's decision in *Meyer* furnishes, nor need we explore the implications of that decision in terms of the justiciability of the multitude of controversies that beset our campuses today. Today's problem is capable of resolution in the narrower terms of the First Amendment's prohibition of laws respecting an establishment of religion or prohibiting the free exercise thereof.

There is and can be no doubt that the First Amendment does not permit the State to require that teaching and learning must be tailored to the principles or prohibitions of any religious sect or dogma. In *Everson v. Board of Education*, this Court, in upholding a state law to provide free bus service to school children, including those attending parochial schools, said: 'Neither (a State nor the Federal Government) can pass laws which aid one religion, aid all religions, or prefer one religion over another.' 330 U.S. 1, 15 (1947).

At the following Term of Court, in *People of State of Ill. ex rel. McCollum v. Board of Education*, 333 U.S. 203, (1948), the Court held that Illinois could not release pupils from class to attend classes of instruction in the school buildings in the religion of their choice. This, it said, would involve the State in using tax-supported property for religious purposes, thereby breaching the 'wall of separation' which, according to Jefferson, the First Amendment was intended to erect between church and state. *Id.*, at 211. *See also Engel v. Vitale*, 370 U.S. 421, 428 (1962); *Abington School District v. Schempp*, 374 U.S. 203 (1963). While study of religions and of the Bible from a literary and historic viewpoint, presented objectively as part of a secular program of education, need not collide with the First Amendment's prohibition, the State may not adopt programs or practices in its public schools or colleges which 'aid or oppose' any religion. This prohibition is absolute. It forbids alike the preference of a religious doctrine or the prohibition of theory which is deemed antagonistic to a particular dogma. As Mr. Justice Clark stated in *Joseph Burstyn, Inc. v. Wilson*, 'the state has no legitimate interest in protecting any or all religions from views distasteful to them * * *.' 343 U.S. 495, 505 (1952). The test was stated as follows in *Abington School District v. Schempp, supra*, 374 U.S. at 222: '[W]hat are the purpose and the primary effect of the enactment? If either is the advancement or inhibition of religion then the enactment exceeds the scope of legislative power as circumscribed by the Constitution.'

These precedents inevitably determine the result in the present case. The State's undoubted right to prescribe the curriculum for its public schools does not carry with it the right to prohibit, on pain of criminal penalty, the teaching of a scientific theory or doctrine where that prohibition is based upon reasons that violate the First Amendment. It is much too late to argue that the State may impose upon the teachers in its schools any conditions that it chooses, however restrictive they may be of constitutional guarantees. *Keyishian v. Board of Regents*, 385 U.S. 589, 605-606 (1967).

In the present case, there can be no doubt that Arkansas has sought to prevent its teachers from discussing the theory of evolution because it is contrary to the belief of some that the Book of Genesis must be the exclusive source of doctrine as to the origin of man. No suggestion has been made that Arkansas' law may be justified by considerations of state policy other than the religious views of some of its citizens. It is clear that fundamentalist sectarian conviction was and is the law's reason for existence. Its antecedent, Tennessee's 'monkey law,' candidly stated its purpose: to make it unlawful 'to teach any theory that denies the story of the Divine Creation of man as taught in the Bible, and to teach instead that man has descended from a lower order of animals.' Perhaps the sensational publicity attendant upon the Scopes trial induced Arkansas to adopt less explicit language. It eliminated Tennessee's reference to 'the story of the Divine Creation of man' as taught in the Bible, but there is no doubt that the motivation for the law was the same: to suppress the teaching of a theory which, it was thought, 'denied' the divine creation of man.

Arkansas' law cannot be defended as an act of religious neutrality. Arkansas did not seek to excise from the curricula of its schools and universities all discussion of the origin of man. The law's effort was confined to an attempt to blot out a particular theory because of its supposed conflict with the Biblical account, literally read. Plainly, the law is contrary to the mandate of the First, and in violation of the Fourteenth, Amendment to the Constitution.

The judgment of the Supreme Court of Arkansas is reversed.

Edwards v. Aguillard

482 U.S. 578 (1987)

The Court rules that a state law that prohibits teaching evolution in public schools unless "creation science" is also taught violates the Establishment Clause.

Justice Brennan delivered the opinion of the Court.

The question for decision is whether Louisiana's "Balanced Treatment for Creation-Science and Evolution-Science in Public School Instruction" Act (Creationism Act), is facially invalid as violative of the Establishment Clause of the First Amendment.

The Creationism Act forbids the teaching of the theory of evolution in public schools unless accompanied by instruction in "creation science." No school is required to teach evolution or creation science. If either is taught, however, the other must also be taught. The theories of evolution and creation science are statutorily defined as "the scientific evidences for [creation or evolution] and inferences from those scientific evidences."

....

In this case, the Court must determine whether the Establishment Clause was violated in the special context of the public elementary and secondary school system.

States and local school boards are generally afforded considerable discretion in operating public schools. At the same time . . . we have necessarily recognized that the discretion of the States and local school boards in matters of education must be exercised in a manner that comports with the transcendent imperatives of the First Amendment.

The Court has been particularly vigilant in monitoring compliance with the Establishment Clause in elementary and secondary schools. Families entrust public schools with the education of their children, but condition their trust on the understanding that the classroom will not purposely be used to advance religious views that may conflict with the private beliefs of the student and his or her family. Students in such institutions are impressionable, and their attendance is involuntary. The State exerts great authority and coercive power through mandatory attendance requirements, and because of the students' emulation of teachers as role models and the children's susceptibility to peer pressure.

Consequently, the Court has been required often to invalidate statutes which advance religion in public elementary and secondary schools. Therefore, in employing the three-pronged *Lemon* test, 403 U.S. 602 (1971), we must do so mindful of the particular concerns that arise in the context of public elementary and secondary schools. We now turn to the evaluation of the Act under the *Lemon* test.

Lemon's first prong focuses on the purpose that animated adoption of the Act. "The purpose prong of the *Lemon* test asks whether government's actual purpose is to endorse or disapprove of religion." A governmental intention to promote religion is clear when the State enacts a law to serve a religious purpose. This intention may be evidenced by promotion of religion in general, or by advancement of a particular religious belief. If the law was enacted for the purpose of endorsing religion, "no consideration of the second or third criteria [of *Lemon*] is necessary." In this case, appellants have identified no clear secular purpose for the Louisiana Act.

True, the Act's stated purpose is to protect academic freedom. This phrase might, in common parlance, be understood as referring to enhancing the freedom of teachers to teach what they will. The Court of Appeals, however, correctly concluded that the Act was not designed to further that goal. . . . Even if "academic freedom" is read to mean "teaching all of the evidence" with respect to the origin of human beings, the Act does not further this purpose. The goal of providing a more comprehensive science curriculum is not furthered either by outlawing the teaching of evolution or by requiring the teaching of creation science.

While the Court is normally deferential to a State's articulation of a secular purpose, it is required that the statement of such purpose be sincere, and not a sham. . . . It is clear from the legislative history that the purpose of the legislative sponsor, Senator Bill Keith, was to narrow the science curriculum. . . .

. . . .

Stone v. Graham, 449 U.S. 39 (1980), invalidated the State's requirement that the Ten Commandments be posted in public classrooms noting "The Ten Commandments are undeniably a sacred text in the Jewish and Christian faiths, and no legislative recitation of a supposed secular purpose can blind us to that fact. . . ." As a result, the contention that the law was designed to provide instruction on a "fundamental legal code" was "not sufficient to avoid conflict with the First Amendment." Similarly, *Abington School Dist. v. Schempp*, 374 U.S. 203 (1963), held unconstitutional a statute "requiring the selection and reading at the opening of the school day of verses from the Holy Bible and the recitation of the Lord's Prayer by the students in unison," despite the proffer of such secular purposes as the promotion of moral values, the contradiction to the materialistic trends of our times, the perpetuation of our institutions, and the teaching of literature.

As in *Stone* and *Abington*, we need not be blind in this case to the legislature's preeminent religious purpose in enacting this statute. There is a historic and contemporaneous link between the teachings of certain religious denominations and the teaching of evolution. It was this link that concerned the Court in *Epperson v. Arkansas*, 393 U.S. 97 (1968), which also involved a facial challenge to a statute regulating the teaching of evolution. . . .

These same historic and contemporaneous antagonisms between the teachings of certain religious denominations and the teaching of evolution are present in this case. The preeminent purpose of the Louisiana Legislature was clearly to advance the religious viewpoint that a supernatural being created humankind. . . . Furthermore, it is not happenstance that the legislature required the teaching of a theory that coincided with this religious view. The legislative history documents that the Act's primary purpose was to change the science curriculum of public schools in order to provide persuasive advantage to a particular religious doctrine that rejects the factual basis of evolution in its entirety. . . .

. . . .

We do not imply that a legislature could never require that scientific critiques of prevailing scientific theories be taught. Indeed, the Court acknowledged in *Stone* that its decision forbidding the posting of the Ten Commandments did not mean that no use could ever be made of the Ten Commandments, or that the Ten Commandments played an exclusively religious role in the history of Western Civilization. In a similar way, teaching a variety of scientific theories about the origins of humankind to schoolchildren might be validly done with the clear secular intent of enhancing the effectiveness of science instruction. But because the primary purpose of the Creationism Act is to endorse a particular religious doctrine, the Act furthers religion in violation of the Establishment Clause.

. . . .

Kitzmiller v. Dover Area School District

400 F. Supp. 2d 707 (M.D. Pa. 2005)

The court rules that a school district's actions regarding the teaching of "intelligent design" violate the Establishment Clause.

Jones, District Judge.

On October 18, 2004, the Defendant Dover Area School Board of Directors passed by a 6-3 vote the following resolution:

> Students will be made aware of gaps/problems in Darwin's theory and of other theories of evolution including, but not limited to, intelligent design. Note: Origins of Life is not taught.

On November 19, 2004, the Defendant Dover Area School District announced by press release that, commencing in January 2005, teachers would be required to read the following statement to students in the ninth grade biology class at Dover High School:

> The Pennsylvania Academic Standards require students to learn about Darwin's Theory of Evolution and eventually to take a standardized test of which evolution is a part.
>
> Because Darwin's Theory is a theory, it continues to be tested as new evidence is discovered. The Theory is not a fact. Gaps in the Theory exist for which there is no evidence. A theory is defined as a well-tested explanation that unifies a broad range of observations.
>
> Intelligent Design is an explanation of the origin of life that differs from Darwin's view. The reference book, Of Pandas and People, is available for students who might be interested in gaining an understanding of what Intelligent Design actually involves.
>
> With respect to any theory, students are encouraged to keep an open mind. The school leaves the discussion of the Origins of Life to individual students and their families. As a Standards-driven district, class instruction focuses upon preparing students to achieve proficiency on Standards-based assessments

....

After a searching review of Supreme Court and Third Circuit Court of Appeals precedent, it is apparent to this Court that both the endorsement test and the *Lemon* test should be employed in this case to analyze the constitutionality of the ID Policy under the Establishment Clause....

The endorsement test recognizes that when government transgresses the limits of neutrality and acts in ways that show religious favoritism or sponsorship, it violates the Establishment Clause. As Justice O'Connor first elaborated on this issue, the endorsement test was a gloss on *Lemon* that encompassed both the purpose and effect prongs:

> The central issue in this case is whether [the government] has endorsed [religion] by its [actions]. To answer that question, we must examine both what [the government] intended to communicate ... and what message [its conduct] actually conveyed. The purpose and effect prongs of the

> *Lemon* test represent these two aspects of the meaning of the [government's] action.

Lynch v. Donnelly, 465 U.S. at 690, 104 S. Ct. 1355 (O'Connor, J., concurring).

As the endorsement test developed through application, it is now primarily a lens through which to view "effect," with purpose evidence being relevant to the inquiry derivatively. In *County of Allegheny v. ACLU*, 492 U.S. 573 (1989), the Supreme Court instructed that the word "endorsement is not self-defining" and further elaborated that it derives its meaning from other words that the Court has found useful over the years in interpreting the Establishment Clause. The endorsement test emanates from the "prohibition against government endorsement of religion" and it "preclude[s] government from conveying or attempting to convey a message that religion or a particular religious belief is *favored* or *preferred*." The test consists of the reviewing court determining what message a challenged governmental policy or enactment conveys to a reasonable, objective observer who knows the policy's language, origins, and legislative history, as well as the history of the community and the broader social and historical context in which the policy arose.

In elaborating upon this "reasonable observer," the Third Circuit explained that "the reasonable observer is an informed citizen who is more knowledgeable than the average passerby." Moreover, in addition to knowing the challenged conduct's history, the observer is deemed able to "glean other relevant facts" from the face of the policy in light of its context. Knowing the challenged policy's legislative history, the community's history, and the broader social and historical context in which the policy arose, the objective observer thus considers the publicly available evidence relevant to the purpose inquiry, but notably does not do so to ascertain, strictly speaking, what the governmental purpose actually was.

Instead, the observer looks to that evidence to ascertain whether the policy "in fact conveys a message of endorsement or disapproval" of religion, irrespective of what the government might have intended by it. *Lynch*, 465 U.S. at 690, 104 S. Ct. 1355 (O'Connor, J., concurring) ("The central issue in this case is whether [government] has endorsed Christianity by its [actions]. To answer that question, we must examine both what [the government] intended to communicate . . . and what message [its conduct] actually conveyed. The purpose and effect prongs of the *Lemon* test represent these two aspects of the meaning of the [government's] action.").

We must now ascertain whether the ID Policy "in fact conveys a message of endorsement or disapproval" of religion, with the reasonable, objective observer being the hypothetical construct to consider this issue. As the endorsement test is designed to ascertain the objective meaning of the statement that the District's conduct communicated in the community by focusing on how "the members of the listening audience" perceived the conduct, two inquiries must be made based upon the circumstances of this case. First, we will consider "the message conveyed by the disclaimer to the students who are its intended audience," from the perspective of an objective Dover Area High School student. At a minimum, the pertinent inquiry is whether an "objective observer" in the position of a student of the relevant age would "perceive official school support" for the religious activity in question. We find it incumbent upon the Court to additionally judge Defendants' conduct from the standpoint of a reasonable, objective adult observer. This conclusion is based, in part, upon the revelation at trial that a newsletter explaining the ID Policy in detail was mailed by the Board to every household in the District, as well as the Board members' discussion and defense of the curriculum change in public school board meetings and in the media.

The history of the intelligent design movement (hereinafter "IDM") and the development of the strategy to weaken education of evolution by focusing students on alleged gaps in the theory of evolution is the historical and cultural background against which the Dover School Board acted in adopting the challenged ID Policy. As a reasonable observer, whether adult or child, would be aware of this social context in which the ID Policy arose, and such context will help to reveal the meaning of Defendants' actions, it is necessary to trace the history of the IDM.

....

The concept of intelligent design (hereinafter "ID"), in its current form, came into existence after the *Edwards* case was decided in 1987. For the reasons that follow, we conclude that the religious nature of ID would be readily apparent to an objective observer, adult or child.

We initially note that John Haught, a theologian who testified as an expert witness for Plaintiffs and who has written extensively on the subject of evolution and religion, succinctly explained to the Court that the argument for ID is not a new scientific argument, but is rather an old religious argument for the existence of God. He traced this argument back to at least Thomas Aquinas in the 13th century, who framed the argument as a syllogism: Wherever complex design exists, there must have been a designer; nature is complex; therefore nature must have had an intelligent designer. Dr. Haught testified that Aquinas was explicit that this intelligent designer "everyone understands to be God." The syllogism described by Dr. Haught is essentially the same argument for ID as presented by defense expert witnesses Professors Behe and Minnich who employ the phrase "purposeful arrangement of parts."

....

Although proponents of the IDM occasionally suggest that the designer could be a space alien or a time-traveling cell biologist, no serious alternative to God as the designer has been proposed by members of the IDM, including Defendants' expert witnesses.

[The court goes on to detail more evidence regarding ID and its connection to religious views.]

A "hypothetical reasonable observer," adult or child, who is "aware of the history and context of the community and forum" is also presumed to know that ID is a form of creationism. The evidence at trial demonstrates that ID is nothing less than the progeny of creationism. What is likely the strongest evidence supporting the finding of ID's creationist nature is the history and historical pedigree of the book to which students in Dover's ninth grade biology class are referred, *Pandas*. *Pandas* is published by an organization called FTE, as noted, whose articles of incorporation and filings with the Internal Revenue Service describe it as a religious, Christian organization. *Pandas* was written by Dean Kenyon and Percival Davis, both acknowledged creationists, and Nancy Pearcey, a Young Earth Creationist, contributed to the work.

. . . .

The weight of the evidence clearly demonstrates, as noted, that the systemic change from "creation" to "intelligent design" occurred sometime in 1987, *after* the Supreme Court's important *Edwards* decision. This compelling evidence strongly supports Plaintiffs' assertion that ID is creationism re-labeled. Importantly, the objective observer, whether adult or child, would conclude from the fact that *Pandas* posits a master intellect that the intelligent designer is God.

Further evidence in support of the conclusion that a reasonable observer, adult or child, who is "aware of the history and context of the community and forum" is presumed to know that ID is a form of creationism concerns the fact that ID uses the same, or exceedingly similar arguments as were posited in support of creationism. One significant difference is that the words "God," "creationism," and "Genesis" have been systematically purged from ID explanations, and replaced by an unnamed "designer." . . .

Having thus provided the social and historical context in which the ID Policy arose of which a reasonable observer, either adult or child would be aware, we will now focus on what the objective student alone would know. We will accordingly determine whether an objective student would view the disclaimer read to the ninth grade biology class as an official endorsement of religion.

. . . .

After a careful review of the record and for the reasons that follow, we find that an objective student would view the disclaimer as a strong official endorsement of religion. Application of the objective student standard pursuant to the endorsement test reveals that an objective Dover High School ninth grade student will unquestionably perceive the text of the disclaimer, "enlightened by its context and contemporary legislative history," as conferring a religious concept on "her school's seal of approval."

We arrive at this conclusion by initially considering the plain language of the disclaimer, paragraph by paragraph. . . . [The court goes through each paragraph of the policy and explains why it conveys a message of religious endorsement.]

The classroom presentation of the disclaimer provides further evidence that it conveys a message of religious endorsement. It is important to initially note that as a result of the teachers' refusal to read the disclaimer, school administrators were forced to make special appearances in the science classrooms to deliver it. No evidence was presented by any witness that the Dover students are presented with a disclaimer of any type in any other topic in the curriculum. An objective student observer would accordingly be observant of the fact that the message contained in the disclaimer is special and carries special weight. In addition, the objective student would understand that the administrators are reading the statement because the biology teachers refused to do so on the ground that they are legally and ethically barred from misrepresenting a religious belief as science, as will be discussed below. This would provide the students with an additional reason to conclude that the District is advocating a religious view in biology class.

Second, the administrators made the remarkable and awkward statement, as part of the disclaimer, that "there will be no other discussion of the issue and your teachers will not answer questions on the issue." . . . Unlike anything else in the curriculum, students are under the impression that the topic to which they are introduced in the disclaimer, ID, is so sensitive that the students and their teachers are completely barred from asking questions about it or discussing it.

A third important issue concerning the classroom presentation of the disclaimer is the "opt out" feature. Students who do *not* wish to be exposed to the disclaimer and students whose parents do not care to have them exposed it, must "opt out" to avoid the unwanted religious message. . . .

Accordingly, we find that the classroom presentation of the disclaimer, including school administrators making a special appearance in the science classrooms to deliver the statement, the complete prohibition on discussion or questioning ID, and the "opt out" feature all convey a strong message of religious endorsement.

. . . .

In summary, the disclaimer singles out the theory of evolution for special treatment, misrepresents its status in the scientific community, causes students to doubt its validity without scientific justification, presents students with a religious alternative masquerading as a scientific theory, directs them to consult a creationist text as though it were a science resource, and instructs students to forego scientific inquiry in the public school classroom and instead to seek out religious instruction elsewhere. . . .

Our detailed chronology of what a reasonable, objective student is presumed to know has made abundantly clear to the Court that an objective student would view the disclaimer as a strong official endorsement of religion or a religious viewpoint. We now turn to whether an objective adult observer in the Dover community would perceive Defendants' conduct similarly.

[The court determines that an objective Dover citizen would also perceive the school's conduct to endorse religion and then assesses the policy under the *Lemon* Test.]

Although we have found that Defendants' conduct conveys a strong message of endorsement of the Board members' particular religious view, pursuant to the endorsement test, the better practice in this Circuit is for this Court to also evaluate the challenged conduct separately under the *Lemon* test.

We will therefore consider whether (1) Defendants' primary purpose was to advance religion or (2) the ID Policy has the primary effect of promoting religion. Initially, we note that the central [purpose] inquiry is whether the District has shown favoritism toward religion generally or any set of religious beliefs in particular. . . .

The purpose inquiry involves consideration of the ID Policy's language, "enlightened by its context and contemporaneous legislative history[,]" including, in this case, the broader context of historical and ongoing religiously driven attempts to advance creationism while denigrating evolution. . . . The disclaimer's plain language, the legislative history, and the historical context in which the ID Policy arose, all inevitably lead to the conclusion that Defendants consciously chose to change Dover's biology curriculum to advance religion. We have been presented with a wealth of evidence which reveals that the District's purpose was to advance creationism, an inherently religious view, both by introducing it directly under the label ID and by disparaging the scientific theory of evolution, so that creationism would gain credence by default as the only apparent alternative to evolution, for the reasons that follow.

. . . .

Although Defendants attempt to persuade this Court that each Board member who voted for the biology curriculum change did so for the secular purpose of improving science education and to exercise critical thinking skills, their contentions are simply irreconcilable with the record evidence. Their asserted purposes are a sham, and they are accordingly unavailing. . . .

Accordingly, we find that the secular purposes claimed by the Board amount to a pretext for the Board's real purpose, which was to promote religion in the public school classroom, in violation of the Establishment Clause.

. . . .

To briefly reiterate, we first note that since ID is not science, the conclusion is inescapable that the only real effect of the ID Policy is the advancement of religion. Second, the disclaimer read to students "has the effect of implicitly bolstering alternative religious theories of origin by suggesting that evolution is a problematic theory even in the field of science." Third, reading the disclaimer not only disavows endorsement of educational materials but also "juxtaposes that disavowal with an urging to contemplate alternative religious concepts implies School Board approval of religious principles."

The effect of Defendants' actions in adopting the curriculum change was to impose a religious view of biological origins into the biology course, in violation of the Establishment Clause.

Post Problem Discussion

1. In *Edwards*, the Court notes that students at public schools are impressionable, susceptible to peer pressure, and apt to view teachers as role models. How should these factors be considered by courts under the endorsement test? Under the *Lemon* test?

2. In *Kitzmiller*, the court addresses intelligent design from the perspective of students and adults and comes to the same conclusion. What if the results were different for students and adults? For example, say that the actions would be viewed by a reasonably objective student as endorsing religion, but not to a reasonably objective adult? Or vice-versa? If so, which perspective should a court follow?

3. Is there a constitutional way to teach Intelligent Design in public schools?

§ 11.04 Category Three: Using Public School Facilities

Another issue that public schools encounter with religion is student or community organizations using school facilities to meet for religious purposes. Schools often allow student and community groups or organizations to use school facilities before or after school. The constitutional concerns with allowing religious groups to use school facilities are whether it endorses or promotes religion and whether refusing to do so sends the opposite message. Students or groups that are denied the opportunity to meet because the meeting is for religious purposes may claim a violation of free exercise or free speech rights.

In 1981, the United States Supreme Court ruled that a state university that prohibited the use of their grounds or facilities "for purposes of religious worship or religious teaching" violated "the fundamental principle that a state regulation of speech should be content-neutral." *Widmar v. Vincent*, 454 U.S. 263 (1981). The University argued that the Establishment Clause necessitated its approach, but the Court, using freedom of speech standards, disagreed, noting that an "equal access" policy that allowed religious groups to meet on similar terms as other groups would not violate the Establishment Clause under the *Lemon* Test.

A number of cases with similar claims involving student groups at public high schools then made their way to the Circuit Courts of Appeal. Unlike *Widmar*, most of these courts upheld policies that prohibited using school facilities for religious purposes, noting that a high school setting was different than the college campus in *Widmar*, and that high school students were more likely to view religious groups meeting on school grounds as endorsing religion. *See, e.g.*, *Bender v. Williamsport Area Sch. Dist.*, 741 F.2d 538 (3rd Cir 1984).

In 1984, Congress stepped in with the Equal Access Act, 20 U.S.C. § 4071 (1983), a Spending Clause statute that applies many of the concepts in *Widmar* to public secondary schools that receive federal funds. It requires public secondary schools that allow non-curriculum related groups to meet on school premises to provide that opportunity equally without regard to the religious, political, philosophical, or other content of the speech at such meetings. The following problem explores some of the requirements of the Equal Access Act and the First Amendment.

Problem 6: Religious Student Groups at Public Schools

A group of students meets at the Grearyhill Public High School each day before and after school in a multi-purpose room to read and study verses from the Bible and to discuss how these verses relate to their daily lives and activities at school. The group is closely linked with the Bible study group at a local church, and church leaders often advise the students on various issues and even come to the group's meetings at school from time to time.

The school has about ten other non-curriculum oriented student groups that it allows to meet on school grounds before or after school. It also allows outside community groups to use the school facility on request. The school does not have any kind of access policy regarding student groups, but it tries to follow the requirements of the Equal Access Act.

Three or four of the other non-curriculum oriented student groups have had "membership drives" over the past couple of school years that included: 1) students posting signs outside of the room where their group was meeting noting open membership, 2) students handing out brochures that explain the club, and 3) students making announcements about the club during the school's morning announcements to all students over the school intercom system.

The students in the Bible study group decide that they would like to have a membership drive at school. With the assistance of church leaders, they produce a brochure that explains the student Bible group and includes several passages from the Bible that the group believes are appropriate for membership recruitment. The students in the group ask the high school principal if they can distribute the brochures outside of the multi-purpose room before and after school as students walk by, and if they can make an announcement about their membership drive during the school's morning announcements.

The principal reviews the brochure and tells the students that they cannot distribute it on school grounds because of the religious messages that it contains. She also advises that the group can make an announcement, but the announcement cannot include any prayer or any other religious statements (such as reciting a Bible passage or verse, mentioning God or Jesus Christ, etc.).

The student Bible group sues contending the denial violates the Equal Access Act and their rights under the Free Exercise Clause and Free Speech Clause of the First Amendment. The school responds that its actions were necessary under the Establishment Clause.

1. You are the judge. How would you rule and why?
2. What legal standards/tests did you use to answer question #1 and why did you select those standards/tests?

Problem Materials

✓ Equal Access Act, 20 U.S.C. § 4071–4072

✓ *Board of Education of Westside Community Schools. v. Mergens*, 496 U.S. 226 (1990)

✓ *Good News Club v. Milford Central School*, 533 U.S. 98 (2001)

Equal Access Act

20 U.S.C. § 4071 Denial of Equal Access Prohibited

(a) Restriction of limited open forum on basis of religious, political, philosophical, or other speech content prohibited

It shall be unlawful for any public secondary school which receives Federal financial assistance and which has a limited open forum to deny equal access or a fair opportunity to, or discriminate against, any students who wish to conduct a meeting within that limited open forum on the basis of the religious, political, philosophical, or other content of the speech at such meetings.

(b) "Limited open forum" defined

A public secondary school has a limited open forum whenever such school grants an offering to or opportunity for one or more noncurriculum related student groups to meet on school premises during noninstructional time.

(c) Fair opportunity criteria

Schools shall be deemed to offer a fair opportunity to students who wish to conduct a meeting within its limited open forum if such school uniformly provides that—

(1) the meeting is voluntary and student-initiated;

(2) there is no sponsorship of the meeting by the school, the government, or its agents or employees;

(3) employees or agents of the school or government are present at religious meetings only in a nonparticipatory capacity;

(4) the meeting does not materially and substantially interfere with the orderly conduct of educational activities within the school; and

(5) nonschool persons may not direct, conduct, control, or regularly attend activities of student groups.

(d) Construction of subchapter with respect to certain rights

Nothing in this subchapter shall be construed to authorize the United States or any State or political subdivision thereof—

(1) to influence the form or content of any prayer or other religious activity;

(2) to require any person to participate in prayer or other religious activity;

(3) to expend public funds beyond the incidental cost of providing the space for student-initiated meetings;

(4) to compel any school agent or employee to attend a school meeting if the content of the speech at the meeting is contrary to the beliefs of the agent or employee;

(5) to sanction meetings that are otherwise unlawful;

(6) to limit the rights of groups of students which are not of a specified numerical size; or

(7) to abridge the constitutional rights of any person.

(e) Federal financial assistance to schools unaffected

Notwithstanding the availability of any other remedy under the Constitution or the laws of the United States, nothing in this subchapter shall be construed to authorize the United States to deny or withhold Federal financial assistance to any school.

(f) Authority of schools with respect to order, discipline, well-being, and attendance concerns

Nothing in this subchapter shall be construed to limit the authority of the school, its agents or employees, to maintain order and discipline on school premises, to protect the well-being of students and faculty, and to assure that attendance of students at meetings is voluntary.

20 U.S.C. § 4072 Definitions

As used in this subchapter—

(1) The term "secondary school" means a public school which provides secondary education as determined by State law.

(2) The term "sponsorship" includes the act of promoting, leading, or participating in a meeting. The assignment of a teacher, administrator, or other school employee to a meeting for custodial purposes does not constitute sponsorship of the meeting.

(3) The term "meeting" includes those activities of student groups which are permitted under a school's limited open forum and are not directly related to the school curriculum.

(4) The term "noninstructional time" means time set aside by the school before actual classroom instruction begins or after actual classroom instruction ends.

Board of Education of Westside Community Schools. v. Mergens

496 U.S. 226 (1990)

The Court rules that the Equal Access Act does not violate the Establishment Clause and that the school's actions in denying a student religious group to meet at school violated the Act.

O'Connor, J., announced the judgment of the Court and delivered the opinion of the Court with respect to Parts I, II-A, II-B, and II-C, in which Rehnquist, C.J., and White, Blackmun, Scalia, and Kennedy, JJ., joined, and an opinion with respect to Part III, in which Rehnquist, C.J., and White and Blackmun, JJ., joined.

This case requires us to decide whether the Equal Access Act, prohibits Westside High School from denying a student religious group permission to meet on school premises during noninstructional time, and if so, whether the Act, so construed, violates the Establishment Clause of the First Amendment.

. . . .

Students at Westside High School are permitted to join various student groups and clubs, all of which meet after school hours on school premises. The students may choose from approximately 30 recognized groups on a voluntary basis. . . .

. . . .

In January, 1985, respondent Bridget Mergens met with Westside's principal, Dr. Findley, and requested permission to form a Christian club at the school. The proposed club would have the same privileges and meet on the same terms and conditions as other Westside student groups, except that the proposed club would not have a faculty sponsor. According to the students' testimony at trial, the club's purpose would have been, among other things, to permit the students to read and discuss the Bible, to have fellowship, and to pray together. Membership would have been voluntary and open to all students, regardless of religious affiliation.

Findley denied the request, as did associate superintendent Tangdell. In February, 1985, Findley and Tangdell informed Mergens that they had discussed the matter with superintendent Hanson and that he had agreed that her request should be denied. The school officials explained that school policy required all student clubs to have a faculty sponsor, which the proposed religious club would not or could not have, and that a religious club at the school would violate the Establishment Clause.

[*In the first part of the opinion, the Court discusses whether the school permitted one or more "noncurriculum related student groups" to meet on campus before or after classes. It notes that the Equal Access Act does not define the term "noncurriculum related student groups" but after analyzing the legislative history and the student groups at this particular school, concludes the school had done so which meant the requirements of Equal Access Act applied.*]

The remaining statutory question is whether petitioners' denial of respondents' request to form a religious group constitutes a denial of "equal access" to the school's limited open forum. Although the school apparently permits respondents to meet informally after school, respondents seek equal access in the form of official recognition by the school. Official recognition allows student clubs to be part of the student activities program, and carries with it access to the school newspaper, bulletin boards, the public address system, and the annual Club Fair. Given that the Act explicitly prohibits denial of "equal access . . . to . . . any students who wish to conduct a meeting within [the school's] limited open forum" on the basis of the religious content of the speech at such meetings, § 4071(a), we hold that Westside's denial of respondents' request to form a Christian club denies them "equal access" under the Act.

. . . .

Petitioners contend that, even if Westside has created a limited open forum within the meaning of the Act, its denial of official recognition to the proposed Christian club must nevertheless stand because the Act violates the Establishment Clause of the First Amendment, as applied to the States through the Fourteenth Amendment. Specifically, petitioners maintain that, because the school's recognized student activities are an integral part of its educational mission, official recognition of respondents' proposed club would effectively incorporate religious activities into the school's official program, endorse participation in the religious club, and provide the club with an official platform to proselytize other students.

We disagree. In *Widmar v. Vincent*, 454 U.S. 263 (1981), we applied the three-part *Lemon* test to hold that an "equal access" policy, at the university level, does not violate the Establishment Clause. We concluded that "an open-forum policy, including nondiscrimination against religious speech, would have a secular purpose," and would in fact avoid entanglement with religion. We also found that, although incidental benefits accrued to religious groups who used university facilities, this result did not amount to an establishment of religion. First, we stated that a university's forum does not "confer any imprimatur of state approval on religious sects or practices." Indeed, the message is one of neutrality rather than endorsement; if a State refused to let religious groups use facilities open to others, then it would demonstrate not neutrality but hostility toward religion.

. . . .

Second, we noted that "[t]he [University's] provision of benefits to [a] broad . . . spectrum of groups"—both nonreligious and religious speakers—was "an important index of secular effect."

We think the logic of *Widmar* applies with equal force to the Equal Access Act. As an initial matter, the Act's prohibition of discrimination on the basis of "political, philosophical, or other" speech as well as religious speech is a sufficient basis for meeting the secular purpose prong of the *Lemon* test. Congress' avowed purpose—to prevent discrimination against religious and other types of speech—is undeniably secular. . . .

Petitioners' principal contention is that the Act has the primary effect of advancing religion. Specifically, petitioners urge that, because the student religious meetings are held under school aegis, and because the state's compulsory attendance laws bring the students together (and thereby provide a ready-made audience for student evangelists), an objective observer in the position of a secondary school student will perceive official school support for such religious meetings. . . .

We disagree. First, although we have invalidated the use of public funds to pay for teaching state-required subjects at parochial schools, in part because of the risk of creating a crucial symbolic link between government and religion, thereby enlisting—at least in the eyes of impressionable youngsters—the powers of government to the support of the religious denomination operating the school, there is a crucial difference between government speech endorsing religion, which the Establishment Clause forbids, and private speech endorsing religion, which the Free Speech and Free Exercise Clauses protect. We think that secondary school students are mature enough and are likely to understand that a school does not endorse or support student speech that it merely permits on a nondiscriminatory basis. The proposition that schools do not endorse everything they fail to censor is not complicated.

. . . .

Second, we note that the Act expressly limits participation by school officials at meetings of student religious groups, §§ 4071(c)(2) and (3), and that any such meetings must be held during "noninstructional time," § 4071(b). The Act therefore avoids the problems of "the students' emulation of teachers as role models" and "mandatory attendance requirements." To be sure, the possibility of student peer pressure remains, but there is little if any risk of official state endorsement or coercion where no formal classroom activities are involved and no school officials actively participate. Moreover, petitioners' fear of a mistaken inference of endorsement is largely self-imposed, because the school itself has control over any impressions it gives its students. To the extent a school makes clear that its recognition of respondents' proposed club is not an endorsement of the views of the club's participants, students will reasonably understand that the school's official recognition of the club evinces neutrality toward, rather than endorsement of, religious speech.

Third, the broad spectrum of officially recognized student clubs at Westside, and the fact that Westside students are free to initiate and organize additional student clubs, counteract any possible message of official endorsement of or preference for religion or a particular religious belief. Although a school may not itself lead or direct a religious club, a school that permits a student-initiated and student-led religious club to meet after school, just as it permits any other student group to do, does not convey a message of state approval or endorsement of the particular religion. Under the Act, a school with a limited open forum may not lawfully deny access to a Jewish students' club, a Young Democrats club, or a philosophy club devoted to the study of Nietzsche. To the extent that a religious club is merely one of many different student-initiated voluntary clubs, students should perceive no message of government endorsement of religion. Thus, we conclude that the Act does not, at least on its face and as applied to Westside, have the primary effect of advancing religion.

Petitioners' final argument is that, by complying with the Act's requirement, the school risks excessive entanglement between government and religion. The proposed club, petitioners urge, would be required to have a faculty sponsor who would be charged with actively directing the activities of the group, guiding its leaders, and ensuring balance in the presentation of controversial ideas. Petitioners claim that this influence over the club's religious program would entangle the government in day-to-day surveillance of religion of the type forbidden by the Establishment Clause.

Under the Act, however, faculty monitors may not participate in any religious meetings, and nonschool persons may not direct, control, or regularly attend activities of student groups.... Although the Act permits "[t]he assignment of a teacher, administrator, or other school employee to the meeting for custodial purposes," such custodial oversight of the student-initiated religious group, merely to ensure order and good behavior, does not impermissibly entangle government in the day-to-day surveillance or administration of religious activities.

Accordingly, we hold that the Equal Access Act does not on its face contravene the Establishment Clause. Because we hold that petitioners have violated the Act, we do not decide respondents' claims under the Free Speech and Free Exercise Clauses. For the foregoing reasons, the judgment of the Court of Appeals is affirmed.

Good News Club v. Milford Central School

533 U.S. 98 (2001)

The Court rules that the school violated the free speech rights of a religious group by excluding it from meeting after hours at the school. The Court also finds that the Establishment Clause does not justify the school's actions or excuse the free speech violation.

Justice Thomas delivered the opinion of the Court.

....

The State of New York authorizes local school boards to adopt regulations governing the use of their school facilities.... First, district residents may use the school for "instruction in any branch of education, learning or the arts." Second, the school is available for "social, civic and recreational meetings and entertainment events, and other uses pertaining to the welfare of the community, provided that such uses shall be nonexclusive and shall be opened to the general public."

Stephen and Darleen Fournier reside within Milford's district and therefore are eligible to use the school's facilities as long as their proposed use is approved by the school. Together they are sponsors of the local Good News Club, a private Christian organization for children ages 6 to 12. Pursuant to Milford's policy, in September 1996 the Fourniers submitted a request to Dr. Robert McGruder, interim superintendent of the district, in which they sought permission to hold the Club's weekly afterschool meetings in the school cafeteria. The next month, McGruder formally denied the Fourniers' request on the ground that the proposed use—to have "a fun time of singing songs, hearing a Bible lesson and memorizing scripture,"—was "the equivalent of religious worship." According to McGruder, the community use policy, which prohibits use "by any individual or organization for religious purposes," foreclosed the Club's activities.

In response to a letter submitted by the Club's counsel, Milford's attorney requested information to clarify the nature of the Club's activities. The Club sent a set of materials used or distributed at the meetings and the following description of its meeting:

> The Club opens its session with Ms. Fournier taking attendance. As she calls a child's name, if the child recites a Bible verse the child receives a treat. After attendance, the Club sings songs. Next Club members engage in games that involve, *inter alia*, learning Bible verses. Ms. Fournier then relates a Bible story and explains how it applies to Club members' lives. The Club closes with prayer. Finally, Ms. Fournier distributes treats and the Bible verses for memorization.

McGruder and Milford's attorney reviewed the materials and concluded that "the kinds of activities proposed to be engaged in by the Good News Club were not a discussion of secular subjects such as child rearing, development of character and development of morals from a religious perspective, but were in fact the equivalent of religious instruction itself." In February 1997, the Milford Board of Education adopted a resolution rejecting the Club's request to use Milford's facilities "for the purpose of conducting religious instruction and Bible study."

. . . .

When the State establishes a limited public forum, the State is not required to and does not allow persons to engage in every type of speech. The State may be justified "in reserving [its forum] for certain groups or for the discussion of certain topics." *Rosenberger v. Rector and Visitors of Univ. of Va.*, 515 U.S. 819, 829 (1995). The State's power to restrict speech, however, is not without limits. The restriction must not discriminate against speech on the basis of viewpoint, *Rosenberger, supra*, at 829, and the restriction must be "reasonable in light of the purpose served by the forum," *Cornelius v. NAACP Legal Defense & Ed. Fund, Inc.*, 473 U.S. 788, 806 (1985).

Applying this test, we first address whether the exclusion constituted viewpoint discrimination. We are guided in our analysis by two of our prior opinions, *Lamb's Chapel v. Center Moriches Union Free School Dist.*, 508 U.S. 384, and *Rosenberger.* In *Lamb's Chapel*, we held that a school district violated the Free Speech Clause of the First Amendment when it excluded a private group from presenting films at the school based solely on the films' discussions of family values from a religious perspective. Likewise, in *Rosenberger*, we held that a university's refusal to fund a student publication because the publication addressed issues from a religious perspective violated the Free Speech Clause. Concluding that Milford's exclusion of the Good News Club based on its religious nature is indistinguishable from the exclusions in these cases, we hold that the exclusion constitutes viewpoint discrimination. Because the restriction is viewpoint discriminatory, we need not decide whether it is unreasonable in light of the purposes served by the forum.

. . . .

Milford argues that, even if its restriction constitutes viewpoint discrimination, its interest in not violating the Establishment Clause outweighs the Club's interest in gaining equal access to the school's facilities. In other words, according to Milford, its restriction was required to avoid violating the Establishment Clause. We disagree.

We have said that a state interest in avoiding an Establishment Clause violation "may be characterized as compelling," and therefore may justify content-based discrimination. *Widmar v. Vincent*, 454 U.S. 263, 271 (1981). However, it is not clear whether a State's interest in avoiding an Establishment Clause violation would justify viewpoint discrimination. We need not, however, confront the issue in this case, because we conclude that the school has no valid Establishment Clause interest.

We rejected Establishment Clause defenses similar to Milford's in two previous free speech cases, *Lamb's Chapel* and *Widmar*. In particular, in *Lamb's Chapel*, we explained that . . . "there would have been no realistic danger that the community would think that the District was endorsing religion or any particular creed." Likewise, in *Widmar*, where the university's forum was already available to other groups, this Court concluded that there was no Establishment Clause problem.

The Establishment Clause defense fares no better in this case. As in *Lamb's Chapel*, the Club's meetings were held after school hours, not sponsored by the school, and open to any student who obtained parental consent, not just to Club members. As in *Widmar*, Milford made its forum available to other organizations. The Club's activities are materially indistiguishable from those in *Lamb's Chapel* and *Widmar*. Thus, Milford's reliance on the Establishment Clause is unavailing.

. . . .

[W]e have held that "a significant factor in upholding governmental programs in the face of Establishment Clause attack is their *neutrality* towards religion." . . . Milford's implication that granting access to the Club would do damage to the neutrality principle defies logic. For the "guarantee of neutrality is respected, not offended, when the government, following neutral criteria and evenhanded policies, extends benefits to recipients whose ideologies and viewpoints, including religious ones, are broad and diverse." *Rosenberger, supra*, at 839. The Good News Club seeks nothing more than to be treated neutrally and given access to speak about the same topics as are other groups. Because allowing the Club to speak on school grounds would ensure neutrality, not threaten it, Milford faces an uphill battle in arguing that the Establishment Clause compels it to exclude the Good News Club.

. . . .

When Milford denied the Good News Club access to the school's limited public forum on the ground that the Club was religious in nature, it discriminated against the Club because of its religious viewpoint in violation of the Free Speech Clause of the First Amendment. Because Milford has not raised a valid Establishment Clause claim, we do not address the question whether such a claim could excuse Milford's viewpoint discrimination. . . .

The judgment of the Court of Appeals is reversed, and the case is remanded for further proceedings consistent with this opinion.

It is so ordered.

Post Problem Discussion

1. The long-running litigation in *Bronx Household of Faith v. Board of Educ. of City of New York* offers an interesting gloss on this case. Bronx Household of Faith is a small (85-100) 37-year old community Christian church that used the P.S. 15 school auditorium for Sunday worship. The school board's Standard Operating Procedure section 5.11 provided: "No outside organization or group may be allowed to conduct religious services or religious instruction on school premises after school. However, the use of school premises by outside organizations or groups after school for the purpose of discussing religious material or material which contains a religious viewpoint or for distributing such material is permissible." The Board believed this distinguished between worship and viewpoint.

After *Good News*, the court found a likelihood of success on plaintiffs' part and enjoined the Board from keeping them from using the school. The board then amended its procedures to provide "No permit shall be granted for the purpose of holding religious worship services, or otherwise using a school as a house of worship. Permits may be granted to religious clubs for students that are sponsored by outside organizations and otherwise satisfy the requirements of this [regulation] on the same basis that they are granted to other clubs for students that are sponsored by outside organizations." Is this any more constitutional? The district court thought not, the circuit court split but thought so and vacated the injunction. At that point, the congregation again petitioned to use the hall for the following purpose "Hymn singing, prayer, communion, preaching, teaching, fellowship." What do you think the result was this time? What arguments would you make for each side? *Bronx Household of Faith v. Board of Educ. of City of New York*, 400 F. Supp. 2d 581 (S.D.N.Y. 2005); 650 F.3d 30 (2d Cir. 2011), 750 F.3d 184 (2d Cir. 2012).

2. The Equal Access Act only applies to secondary schools, which is why the Act was not at issue in the *Good News Club* case. Why do you think Congress chose to limit the Act to secondary schools? Does the *Good News Club* case effectively impose Equal Access Act type requirements on elementary schools anyway?

3. Should students be permitted to distribute religious materials on school grounds? Courts are split on the issue. Review *Muller by Muller v. Jefferson Lighthouse Sch.*, 98 F.3d 1530 (7th Cir. 1996), *cert. denied*, 520 U.S. 1156, and *Rusk v. Crestview*

Local Sch. Dist., 379 F.3d 418 (6th Cir. 2004), for different perspectives. Which case do you find more persuasive on the issue and why?

4. There are several Courts of Appeals cases that address issues similar to the fact pattern in the problem. Review *Donovan v. Punxsutawney Area School Bd.*, 336 F.3d 211 (3d Cir. 2003) and *Prince v. Jacoby*, 303 F.3d 1074 (9th Cir. 2002), *cert. denied*, 540 U.S. 813 (2003), online. If you were a judge in one of these circuits, how would these decisions impact your ruling?

Chapter 12

Special Education

Synopsis

§ 12.01 Introduction

A. Background

At one time, public schools classified some students with disabilities as "uneducable and untrainable," making them ineligible for public school attendance. *See Pennsylvania Ass'n for Retarded Children v. Pennsylvania*, 343 F. Supp. 279, 282 (E.D. Pa. 1972) (*P.A.R.C.*). Similarly, some schools excluded "exceptional" students who had been labeled as behavioral problems, mentally retarded, emotionally disturbed, or hyperactive. *Mills v. Board of Educ.*, 348 F. Supp. 866 (D.D.C. 1972). These decisions were made without parental involvement or appropriate due process. Parents were given the option of sending children with disabilities to private special education schools at their own expense; often families were unable to do so.

The *P.A.R.C.* and *Mills* cases addressed the lack of appropriate education for students with disabilities in Washington, D.C., and in Pennsylvania. The cases established some basic rights to due process and to a free and appropriate public education. These early cases led to the passage of the federal Education for All Handicapped Children Act ("EHA") in 1975. The EHA prohibited the exclusion of students with disabilities from public schools and required appropriate educational services be provided at public expense and at no cost to the parents. This requirement became known as FAPE—a free and appropriate public education, and it remains in the law today. *See* 20 U.S.C. §§ 1401(9), 1412(a)(1). The EHA also required schools to involve parents in decisions about their child. These requirements also remain the law today. *See generally* 20 U.S.C. §§ 1400 et seq.

Courts interpreted EHA's requirements to apply even to students with severe disabilities. In *Timothy W. v. Rochester*, 875 F.2d 954 (1st Cir. 1989), a school district argued that it did not have to provide services to a student with severe mental retardation and multiple disabilities because he was "not capable of benefiting from an education." The court disagreed, noting:

> The language of the Act could not be more unequivocal. The statute is permeated with the words "*all* handicapped children" whenever it refers to the target population. It never speaks of any exceptions for severely handicapped children. Indeed, as indicated *supra*, the Act gives priority to the most severely handicapped. Nor is there any language whatsoever which requires as a prerequisite to being covered by the Act, that a handicapped child must demonstrate that he or she will "benefit" from the educational program. Rather, the Act speaks of the *state's* responsibility to design a special education and related services program that will meet the unique "needs" of all handicapped children. The language of the Act in its entirety makes clear that a "zero-reject" policy is at the core of the Act, and that no child, regardless of the severity of his or her handicap, is to ever again be subjected to the deplorable state of affairs which existed at the time of the Act's passage, in which millions of handicapped children received inadequate education or none at all. In summary, the Act mandates an appropriate public education for all handicapped children, regardless of the level of achievement that such children might attain.

Timothy W., 875 F.2d at 960–61.

As subsequently amended, the EHA became the Individuals with Disabilities Education Act ("IDEA"), a Spending Clause statute imposing specific requirements on states that accept funds to deliver services to students with disabilities. The IDEA requires students with disabilities be educated with the same high academic standards that apply to students without disabilities to the maximum extent appropriate. *See* 20 U.S.C. §§ 1412(a)(5); 1400(c)(5)(A); 1414(d). Students with disabilities must be provided with the opportunity, consistent with peer-reviewed research based practices, to "be involved in and make progress in the general education curriculum" which is the same curriculum used for students without disabilities. 20 U.S.C. § 1414(d)(1)(A)(i)(IV); 34 C.F.R. § 300.347. The rationale behind these requirements is that the general curriculum contains educational standards with high expectations for all students because of a variety of state and federal requirements.

Not all students with disabilities are eligible for services under the IDEA. The law has a specific definition of disability that must be met before a student is eligible to receive services. *See* Section 12.2(B). Students who are not eligible under the IDEA may still be eligible for protections under Section 504 of the Rehabilitation Act of 1973, a federal law that prohibits schools from discriminating against students with disabilities. 29 U.S.C. § 794. Section 504 has a broader definition of disability than the IDEA. It applies to all schools that accept federal funds, which means it applies to private schools that accept federal funds. The IDEA has some requirements for private schools as well, but they vary depending on whether the school is considered to be a provider of special education services, and whether the public school is placing the student at the private school for services.

Under Section 504, a student must have a "physical or mental impairment that substantially limits a major life activity" like learning, hearing, or speaking. 29 U.S.C. § 705(9); *accord* 42 U.S.C. § 12102(1). Under Section 504, schools must provide eligible students with services and reasonable accommodations designed to meet the students' individual needs as adequately as the needs of students without disabilities. 34 C.F.R. § 104.33. It is also possible for a student to be eligible under both the IDEA and Section 504.

Today, the IDEA and Section 504's special education requirements influence public schools perhaps more than any other laws. The IDEA requires states to develop their own state statutes and regulations to implement the federal requirements and to fill in some areas that the law leaves to the states to address. As a result, schools must deal with federal statutes, federal regulations, state statutes, and state regulations in complying with special education requirements.

B. Key Concepts in the IDEA

The IDEA has a number of key concepts as illustrated in the following Table.

Key Concept	Explanation
FAPE	Free and Appropriate Public Education ("FAPE") requires public schools to provide "appropriate" special education and related services to meet the "unique needs" of students with disabilities at no charge to the parents. 20 U.S.C. § 1401(9).
Unique Needs	Part of FAPE includes providing specialized instruction and related services that meet the student's individual needs. 20 U.S.C. § 1401(29).
Least Restrictive Environment	Schools must educate students with disabilities with children without disabilities to the maximum extent appropriate. 20 U.S.C. § 1412(a)(5).
IEP	An Individualized Education Program is a document that describes the special education and related services that the student will receive. *See generally* 20 U.S.C. § 1414(d).
High Expectations	The IDEA seeks to improve educational outcomes for students with disabilities by giving them access to high academic standards in the general curriculum, requiring the services provided to students with disabilities be based on peer reviewed research, and requiring special education teachers to be highly qualified. 20 U.S.C. §§ 1400(c)(5)(A); 1402(10)(B); 1412(a)(5); 1414(d).
Team Meetings	Decisions about a student in the special education process are made by a team that includes the parents. 20 U.S.C. § 1414(d)(1)(B).

Key Concept	Explanation
Parental Rights	Parents have the right to notice, participation, and consent in the special education process. 34 C.F.R. §§ 300.322, 300.501.
Procedural Safeguards	Schools must follow certain procedures in the special education process to ensure that parents are involved and have an opportunity to participate and consent (or not) to decisions regarding the student. 20 U.S.C. § 1415.
Dispute Resolution	Parents and schools can request an administrative due process hearing to resolve differences that arise in the special education process. 20 U.S.C. § 1415. A party not satisfied with the result of a due process hearing may appeal to state or federal court. Parents may also file complaints and request their state department of education investigate alleged violations of the law. 34 C.F.R § 300.151. Parents and schools may also utilize alternative dispute resolution methods to resolve disputes.

§ 12.02 The Special Education Process

A. Overview

There are five steps in the special education process: 1) referral/child find, 2) evaluation, 3) eligibility, 4) developing an IEP, and 5) placement. For students who are eligible for services, there are additional obligations to monitor the IEP and the services that the student receives, and to review and revise the IEP and services as appropriate (at least annually) to ensure the student receives FAPE.

The process starts with "child find" obligations that require public school districts to have procedures in place to refer all children who are suspected or known to have a disability for further evaluation. 34 C.F.R. §§ 300.111; 300.121. This obligation includes students who attend private schools in the district. When a referral about a student is made, the school district must convene a "team meeting" to make a decision about whether and how to evaluate the student to see if the student has a disability as defined by the IDEA. The team includes the parents. If the team determines evaluations are required, it must seek the parent's written consent to fully evaluate the student to determine eligibility for special education services, and to determine what services would be required for the student to receive FAPE. 34 C.F.R. §§ 300.300-.301; 300.304(b)(1); 300.305.

B. Eligibility for Services

Only students who meet the law's definition of a "child with a disability" are eligible for services under the IDEA. Whether a student is "child with a disability" is a three-part inquiry:

1. The student's disability must fit within one or more of the thirteen categories of disability noted in the law;
2. Most of the categories of disability require that the disability "adversely affect the child's educational performance"; and

3. The student must require special education and related services as a result of the disability.

34 C.F.R. §§ 300.8; 300.306. Each of the thirteen categories of disability in the IDEA has its own definitional requirements that must be met. The interpretation of "adversely affects educational performance" and the determination of whether the student "requires special education as a result of their disability" can be the determining factor in whether a student is eligible under the IDEA as the following problem illustrates.

Problem 1: Eligibility Under the IDEA

Shane is an eight-year-old with ADHD in the second grade at Sunny Day Elementary, the local public school. Shane is having difficulty completing his assignments in class and is not getting along well with other students. Shane can generally complete his assignments with extra time and help from the classroom aide, but Shane does not seem to like the current classroom aide and is resistant to her efforts to provide help. The aide is also the aide for the whole class and is not always able to help Shane. Shane frequently interrupts class and bothers other students. He has been subject to in-class discipline by the teacher on a number of occasions for these actions. He also has problems reading grade level materials.

At his teacher's request, the school calls a team meeting, and the team agrees that Shane should be evaluated for special education eligibility. The results of the evaluations confirm that Shane has ADHD and show that Shane has above average intelligence with an IQ of 128. He scored in the average to above average range on most of the academic achievement tests administered by the school as part of the evaluation process. His lowest scores were in the reading fluency, word identification, and reading comprehension tests, where he scored "low average." He received passing grades in first grade, though his parents feel that the grades are below what he is capable of doing given his intelligence.

Is Shane eligible for services under the IDEA? If so, under which categories? If not, why not?

Problem Materials

- ✓ Relevant IDEA Eligibility Regulations, 34 C.F.R. §§ 300.8, 300.306; 300.309
- ✓ *Corchado v. Board of Education Rochester City School District*, 86 F. Supp. 2d 168 (W.D.N.Y. 2000)
- ✓ *Hood v. Encinitas Union School District*, 486 F.3d 1099 (9th Cir. 2007)

Relevant IDEA Regulations

§ 300.8 34 C.F.R. § 300.8 Child with a Disability

(a) General.

(1) Child with a disability means a child evaluated in accordance with §§ 300.304 through 300.311 as having mental retardation, a hearing

impairment (including deafness), a speech or language impairment, a visual impairment (including blindness), a serious emotional disturbance (referred to in this part as "emotional disturbance"), an orthopedic impairment, autism, traumatic brain injury, an other health impairment, a specific learning disability, deaf-blindness, or multiple disabilities, and who, by reason thereof, needs special education and related services.

(2) (i) Subject to paragraph (a)(2)(ii) of this section, if it is determined, through an appropriate evaluation under §§ 300.304 through 300.311, that a child has one of the disabilities identified in paragraph (a)(1) of this section, but only needs a related service and not special education, the child is not a child with a disability under this part.

(ii) If, consistent with § 300.39(a)(2), the related service required by the child is considered special education rather than a related service under State standards, the child would be determined to be a child with a disability under paragraph (a)(1) of this section.

. . . .

(c) Definitions of disability terms. The terms used in this definition of a child with a disability are defined as follows:

. . . .

(9) Other health impairment means having limited strength, vitality, or alertness, including a heightened alertness to environmental stimuli, that results in limited alertness with respect to the educational environment, that—

(i) Is due to chronic or acute health problems such as asthma, attention deficit disorder or attention deficit hyperactivity disorder, diabetes, epilepsy, a heart condition, hemophilia, lead poisoning, leukemia, nephritis, rheumatic fever, sickle cell anemia, and Tourette syndrome; and

(ii) Adversely affects a child's educational performance.

(10) Specific learning disability.

(i) General. Specific learning disability means a disorder in one or more of the basic psychological processes involved in understanding or in using language, spoken or written, that may manifest itself in the imperfect ability to listen, think, speak, read, write, spell, or to do mathematical calculations, including conditions such as perceptual disabilities, brain injury, minimal brain dysfunction, dyslexia, and developmental aphasia.

(ii) Disorders not included. Specific learning disability does not include learning problems that are primarily the result of visual, hearing, or motor disabilities, of mental retardation, of emotional disturbance, or of environmental, cultural, or economic disadvantage.

(11) Speech or language impairment means a communication disorder, such as stuttering, impaired articulation, a language impairment, or a voice impairment, that adversely affects a child's educational performance.

. . . .

§ 300.306 Determination of eligibility

(a) General. Upon completion of the administration of assessments and other evaluation measures—

(1) A group of qualified professionals and the parent of the child determines whether the child is a child with a disability, as defined in § 300.8, in accordance with paragraph (b) of this section and the educational needs of the child; and

(2) The public agency provides a copy of the evaluation report and the documentation of determination of eligibility at no cost to the parent.

(b) Special rule for eligibility determination. A child must not be determined to be a child with a disability under this part—

(1) If the determinant factor for that determination is—

(i) Lack of appropriate instruction in reading, including the essential components of reading instruction (as defined in section 1208(3) of the ESEA);

(ii) Lack of appropriate instruction in math; or

(iii) Limited English proficiency; and

(2) If the child does not otherwise meet the eligibility criteria under § 300.8(a).

(c) Procedures for determining eligibility and educational need.

(1) In interpreting evaluation data for the purpose of determining if a child is a child with a disability under § 300.8, and the educational needs of the child, each public agency must—

(i) Draw upon information from a variety of sources, including aptitude and achievement tests, parent input, and teacher recommendations, as well as information about the child's physical condition, social or cultural background, and adaptive behavior; and

(ii) Ensure that information obtained from all of these sources is documented and carefully considered.

(2) If a determination is made that a child has a disability and needs special education and related services, an IEP must be developed for the child in accordance with §§ 300.320 through 300.324.

§ 300.309 Determining the existence of a specific learning disability

(a) The group described in § 300.306 may determine that a child has a specific learning disability, as defined in § 300.8(c)(10), if—

(1) The child does not achieve adequately for the child's age or to meet State-approved grade-level standards in one or more of the following areas, when provided with learning experiences and instruction appropriate for the child's age or State-approved grade-level standards:

(i) Oral expression.

(ii) Listening comprehension.

(iii) Written expression.

(iv) Basic reading skill.

(v) Reading fluency skills.

(vi) Reading comprehension.

(vii) Mathematics calculation.

(viii) Mathematics problem solving.

(2) (i) The child does not make sufficient progress to meet age or State-approved grade-level standards in one or more of the areas identified in paragraph (a)(1) of this section when using a process based on the child's response to scientific, research-based intervention; or

(ii) The child exhibits a pattern of strengths and weaknesses in performance, achievement, or both, relative to age, State-approved grade-level standards, or intellectual development, that is determined by the group to be relevant to the identification of a specific learning disability, using appropriate assessments, consistent with §§ 300.304 and 300.305; and

(3) The group determines that its findings under paragraphs (a)(1) and (2) of this section are not primarily the result of—

(i) A visual, hearing, or motor disability;

(ii) Mental retardation;

(iii) Emotional disturbance;

(iv) Cultural factors;

(v) Environmental or economic disadvantage; or

(vi) Limited English proficiency.

(b) To ensure that underachievement in a child suspected of having a specific learning disability is not due to lack of appropriate instruction in reading or math, the group must consider, as part of the evaluation described in §§ 300.304 through 300.306—

(1) Data that demonstrate that prior to, or as a part of, the referral process, the child was provided appropriate instruction in regular education settings, delivered by qualified personnel; and

(2) Data-based documentation of repeated assessments of achievement at reasonable intervals, reflecting formal assessment of student progress during instruction, which was provided to the child's parents.

(c) The public agency must promptly request parental consent to evaluate the child to determine if the child needs special education and related services, and must adhere to the timeframes described in §§300.301 and 300.303, unless extended by mutual written agreement of the child's parents and a group of qualified professionals, as described in §300.306(a)(1)—

(1) If, prior to a referral, a child has not made adequate progress after an appropriate period of time when provided instruction, as described in paragraphs (b)(1) and (b)(2) of this section; and

(2) Whenever a child is referred for an evaluation.

Corchado v. Board of Education Rochester City School District

86 F. Supp. 2d 168 (W.D.N.Y. 2000)

The court rules that the student is eligible for services under the IDEA under the categories of Other Health Impaired and Specific Learning Disabilities.

Feldman, United States Magistrate Judge.

This is an action brought by plaintiff, Beth Corchado, on behalf of her son, Sadrach Corchado, (Sadrach) pursuant to the Individual with Disabilities Education Act (the "IDEA"), 20 U.S.C. §1400 et seq., seeking review of a denial of educational benefits. The sole issue before this Court is whether Sadrach, a fourth grade student attending public school in the City of Rochester, qualifies for special education benefits under IDEA. The defendant determined that Sadrach did not qualify for benefits under IDEA and, on administrative review, an Impartial Hearing Officer (IHO) and a State Review Officer (SRO) agreed. For the reasons that follow, I find that Sadrach does qualify for IDEA benefits and, therefore, direct the defendant to develop and implement an individualized educational plan (IEP) for Sadrach pursuant to the IDEA.

The facts, as set forth in a detailed administrative record, are for the most part undisputed. Sadrach is a ten year old fourth grader who attends public School #33 in the City of Rochester. Born in Puerto Rico after only eight months of gestation, Sadrach suffers from multiple and complex medical difficulties. The SRO summarized briefly Sadrach's medical history in his decision affirming the denial of IDEA benefits:

> [Sadrach] was born in Puerto Rico and has reportedly had a life long seizure disorder, which may have been the combination of congenital measles and birth anoxia. A pediatric neurologist who examined the boy in November, 1994 reported that the child also has an attention deficit

> hyperactivity disorder (ADHD) with aggressive tendencies, a psychomotor delay, mild asthma and learning disabilities with possible mental retardation. He further reported that the child also had a tremor in his bilateral upper extremities. The pediatric neurologist expressed concern that the medication to control the child's seizure disorder was having a significant detrimental effect on his ADHD, and recommended a different combination of medications. . . .

. . . .

Due to academic and health related difficulties, Sadrach repeated the second grade in the 1997–1998 school year. In March of 1998, while Sadrach was repeating second grade, his mother completed a special education referral request seeking special education services for her son. Her request was referred to, and evaluated by, the school district's "Pupil Personnel Services Team" (PPST) who found that "Sadrach could be classified as a student with a 'Other Health Impairment,'" thus making him eligible for special education benefits. The PPST recommendation was referred to the district's Committee on Special Education ("CSE"). In May, 1998, the CSE rejected the PPST recommendation, finding that Sadrach had "made progress such that achievement is described as average for his grade placement" and that his noted medical problems "are not significantly impacting his overall progress."

Sadrach's mother decided to obtain an independent medical evaluation from the Genesee Developmental Unit ("GDU") at the Genesee Hospital. The GDU evaluation team was supervised by Dr. Miriam Halpern, a developmental pediatrician with the GDU . . . The GDU reports are part of the administrative record and will not be repeated at length herein. Suffice it to say that the team members found Sadrach to suffer from significant learning disorders and/or neurological problems. . . . The GDU "Educational Assessment" likewise found significant deficiencies. Testing found Sadrach to be reading at a beginning second grade level, his reading comprehension at an end of first grade level, math problem solving applications at an end of first grade level and math computation at a mid-second grade level. The [GDU evaluation] team concluded that "Sadrach should be considered as an Other Health Impaired Youngster and receive supportive services for all content areas."

After receiving a copy of the GDU assessment report, Sadrach's mother asked the CSE to reconsider its finding that the child was not eligible for special education services. Notwithstanding the GDU evaluation, findings and report, on November 13, 1998, the CSE again concluded that Sadrach was ineligible for special education services. The CSE discounted the GDU report because "the testing was completed in English, which is not Sadrach's dominant language." Relying instead on district testing completed in the Spanish language in May 1998 which found Sadrach to have a full IQ of 130 (very superior range), the CSE concluded that Sadrach was non-disabled. As to his seizures and ADHD, the CSE concluded: "Although he presents with a seizure disorder and is diagnosed with ADHD, it does not appear to negatively impact on his academic performance in the classroom."

Sadrach's mother appealed the decision of the CSE to the IHO. . . . The IHO found that Sadrach "clearly has a number of difficulties," including ADHD (attention deficit hyperactivity disorder), a seizure disorder, asthma, stuttering, articulation problems, a lateral lisp, and "some degree of hearing difficulty." The IHO described the "crux of the issue" as to whether Sadrach's "educational performance was adversely affected by his difficulties to an extent warranting special education." As to this issue, the IHO found that despite his "difficulties," Sadrach "is achieving at his current grade level in regular education." According to the IHO, "if student (sic) is able to achieve satisfactorily academically, his problems do not rise to a level satisfying the definitional standards" for special education services.

. . . .

On March 25, 1999, Sadrach's mother appealed the IHO's ruling. Almost six months later, the SRO officer affirmed the decision of the IHO. After summarizing the record, the SRO found, *inter alia*, that "the child's educational performance has consistently been in the average range and both the private assessment [GDU] and [the school district's] academic evaluations show that the child was functioning at, near or slightly below grade level." The SRO found that although Sadrach's "IQ scores place him in the superior range of intellectual functioning, and his academic performance is in the average range, it is not clear that the child requires special education services." The SRO concluded that "the child's medical conditions did not adversely impact his academic performance to the extent he required special education or related services."

On October 15, 1999, the instant action was commenced in federal court seeking judicial review of the state administrative proceedings. . . .

Eligibility For Services: The purpose of the IDEA is to "ensure that all children with disabilities have available to them a free appropriate public education that emphasizes special education and related services designed to meet their unique needs." 20 U.S.C. § 1400(d). In enacting the IDEA, Congress declared that "[i]mproving educational results for children with disabilities is an essential element of our national policy of ensuring equality of opportunity, full participation, independent living, and economic self-sufficiency for individuals with disabilities." 20 U.S.C. § 1400(c)(1).

Given the broad scope of the legislation, it is not surprising that the Act as well as its implementing regulations take an inclusionary approach in defining the term "child with a disability" and embrace within its scope children who suffer from a wide variety of deficits including hearing impairments, speech or language impairments, visual impairments, serious emotional disturbance, learning disabilities, orthopedic impairments and "other health impairments." Once a child is determined to meet the definitional standard of a "child with a disability," the school district is required to formulate an individualized education program (IEP) "reasonably calculated to enable the child to receive educational benefits." *Board of Educ. v. Rowley*, 458 U.S. 176, 206–07 (1982).

As stated earlier, the issue here is the threshold one: Does Sadrach's documented disabilities meet the eligibility requirements entitling him to the benefits of special education and related services under the IDEA? Sadrach's mother submits that the administrative record in this case demonstrates that her son meets three distinct disability classifications: (1) "Other Health Impaired"; (2) Speech Impaired; and (3) Learning Disabled. Each classification is discussed below.

"Other Health Impaired": Under applicable regulations, a child is eligible for special education services under the "Other Health Impaired" classification if the child has a condition that limits strength, vitality or alertness resulting in limited alertness to the educational environment and adversely effects educational performance. The administrative record in this case thoroughly documents Sadrach's long term seizure disorder. The recurrent seizures caused him to miss many days of school, both as a result of the seizures themselves and so that he could attend medical appointments. Although adjustments in medication appear to have significantly reduced absences, the administrative record pays tribute to the fact that Sadrach continues to have regular uncontrolled seizures which affect his alertness in class. Dr. Halpern testified that during her neurological examination of Sadrach she observed him experience a seizure of approximately thirty seconds. The seizure occurred during a writing exercise.

....

Dr. Halpern was specifically asked her medical opinion as to what effect such seizures have on academic performance. She answered:

> There is no hard and fast rule about how seizures affect performance, however, seizures definitely do disrupt the learning process not just while they occur but for a post seizure period. They affect memory and memory and learning go hand in hand. This means, now [Sadrach's] mother reported at the time of the evaluation that Sadrach was having approximately one seizure every two weeks. Those are noticed by her. My suspicions, therefore, if she notices them twice a month or so, they are probably occurring more often. Which could mean that for a period of time during his day, he is not a learner, he is not physiologically able to encode new information into his memory.

Dr. Halpern's testimony takes on added significance when considered in conjunction with the documented observations and testimony of Sadrach's teachers. For example, Ms. Poventud, Sadrach's second grade teacher at School 33, testified about witnessing Sadrach experience seizures during class and their impact on his alertness.

> On *many occasions* he had silent episodes where the seizures were so unnoticeable that the kids would not notice that he was having a seizure, but he was, I would describe it like he *was spaced out and just staring for a few minutes* and then he would regain his composure and, and *he wouldn't know what we were talking about in class* so I would repeat, I would repeat what

> we, we were discussing whether it was math or science or social studies for his benefit.

Poventud also testified that she noticed "tremor in his hands that was constant." Given that Ms. Poventud is responsible for twenty or more other students in her class, it is unlikely that she (or any teacher, for that matter) would be able to detect and observe each seizure Sadrach suffers. Indeed, in a report Ms. Poventud prepared for the GDU evaluation team she noted that "Sadrach has difficulties focusing in class for prolonged periods of time."

The expert medical opinions of Dr. Halpern are unrebutted in the administrative record. The district did not present any evidence, either in the form of an expert's report or direct testimony from a medical professional, that Sadrach's seizures would not adversely affect his ability to concentrate, focus and learn. Given the strong correlation between the medical opinion of Dr. Halpern and the classroom observations of Ms. Poventud, the record strongly supports a finding that Sadrach has a condition that results in "limited alertness with respect to the educational environment" and which has adverse effects on Sadrach's educational performance.

Learning Disabled: Federal regulations define a "learning disabled" child as one who has a "severe discrepancy between achievement and intellectual ability" in one or more of several listed areas, including "oral expression, listening comprehension, basic reading skills, and reading comprehension." State regulations provide that the required "discrepancy" must be a "discrepancy of 50 percent or more between expected achievement and actual achievement determined on an individual basis."

The district's own psychological testing results acknowledge a startling discrepancy between Sadrach's intellectual ability and his academic achievement. Assuming they are accurate, district test results from May, 1998, establish that Sadrach has an overall I.Q. of 130, placing him in the "very superior" range of intelligence. Absent some underlying learning disorder, one would not expect a child with superior intelligence to have to repeat the second grade and have such relatively low academic achievements. Indeed, Mrs. Greenfield, the school psychologist who served on Sadrach's CSE committee, testified that Sadrach met the 50% "significant discrepancy" standard as to written language skills. Ms. Johnson, a special education teacher and the Chair of Sadrach's CSE, committee testified that the discrepancy between Sadrach's intellectual abilities and his reading test scores "could be described as severe." The regulations do provide that the classification of learning disabled is not warranted if the discrepancy between ability and achievement is primarily the result of visual or hearing, or motor impairment, mental retardation, emotional disturbance or environmental, cultural or economic disadvantage. There simply is nothing in this record, however, to attribute Sadrach's discrepancy to any of the excluded factors.

Based on the foregoing, Sadrach does meet the eligibility requirements for the classification of having a "learning disability."

Impact of Academic Performance on Eligibility for Special Education Services: Although this Court reviewed the administrative record *de novo*, it did give attention and consideration to the IHO and SRO's reasoning that Sadrach's "average" performance in school was an indication that he did not qualify for special education services. The IHO expressed his view in this regard in no uncertain terms:

> The district *properly contends* that, whatever student's difficulties, if student is able to achieve satisfactory academically, his problems do not rise to a level satisfying the definitional standards in the regulations. While the student has a number of problems, the evidence in the record shows he is achieving satisfactorily in school. He is achieving at an average level at his current grade level in regular education.

While the Court, for the reasons set forth in this decision, does not agree with the IHO's view of what the record shows regarding Sadrach's academic "achievements," the IHO's reasoning also signals what this Court believes is a fundamental error in determining eligibility for special education services. The IHO's reasoning, in effect, precludes a child whose academic achievement can be described as "satisfactory" from being able to demonstrate that documented disabilities adversely affected the student's academic performance. This should not and cannot be the litmus test for eligibility under the IDEA. The fact that a child, despite a disability, receives some educational benefit from regular classroom instruction should not disqualify the child from eligibility for special education benefits if the disabilities are demonstrated to "adversely affect *the child's* educational performance." Likewise, not every child who has a disability needs special education services as a result of that disability. Each child is different, each impairment is different, and the effect of the particular impairment on the particular child's educational achievement is different. While Sadrach's academic performance in relation to his peers is one of many tools that may be considered in determining "adverse affect," denying him special education benefits because he is able to pass from grade to grade despite documented impairments that adversely affect *his* educational performance is wrong.

For the reasons set forth in this decision, I find that Sadrach Corchado is eligible for special education under the Other Health Impaired, Speech Impaired and Learning Disabled classifications. Accordingly, plaintiff's cross motion for summary judgment is granted and defendant's cross motion for summary judgment is denied.

Hood v. Encinitas Union School District

486 F.3d 1099 (9th Cir. 2007)

The court rules that a student is not eligible for services because she is achieving at grade-level/average or above average levels in the public school classroom.

Kennedy, Senior Circuit Judge.

Anna Hood and her parents (hereinafter "appellants" or "the Hoods") brought this claim alleging that the Encinitas Union School District (hereinafter "appellee" or "the school district") violated the Individuals with Disabilities Education Act ("IDEA"), by refusing to provide Anna with special education services.... California special education hearing officer denied the Hoods relief, and the district court affirmed.

On appeal, the Hoods offer two grounds under which Anna should be categorized as a child with a disability per 20 U.S.C. § 1401(3) and is therefore entitled to special education. First, they assert that Anna has a "specific learning disability" because she exhibits a severe discrepancy between her achievement and intellectual ability in one or more of the academic areas enumerated in Cal. Educ.Code § 56337 (2002), as calculated per the formula provided in Cal.Code Regs. tit. 5, § 3030(j)(4)(A) (2002), and the discrepancy cannot be corrected through other regular or categorical services offered within the regular instructional program. Second, they assert that Anna has "other health impairments" under 20 U.S.C. § 1401(3)(A) and Cal.Code Regs. tit. 5, § 3030(f). The Hoods argue that Anna, by reason of either her "specific learning disability" or her "other health impairments," needs special education and related services....

After reviewing the evidence before the hearing officer and additional evidence submitted to the district court, we find that the district court's acceptance of the hearing officer's determination that Anna was not legally entitled to receive publically-funded special education was not in clear error. As a result, we affirm.

At the time the California special education hearing officer issued a decision, Anna Hood was 10 years old and, according to her report cards, was performing at grade-level appropriate/average or above average levels in the public school classroom. While Anna's second, third, fourth, and fifth grade reports chronicle her consistent difficulties completing tasks, turning in homework on time, and keeping her belongings organized, Anna's scores on the Stanford Achievement Test (SAT-9) have placed her above the fiftieth percentile with near uniformity.

Meanwhile, Anna's performance on various intelligence tests indicates high intellectual ability. Anna's scores on the Woodson-Johnson Test of Achievement-III, administered by resource specialist Patricia Hotz, measured Anna's achievement in eleven different areas, and in all but one area, Anna's scores were average or better. One (writing sample) was in the "very superior" range, eight were in the "high average" range, one (reading fluency) was in the "average" range, and one (math fluency) was in the "low average" range. She received a Wechsler Intelligence Scale for Children-III verbal score of 127, performance score of 110, and full scale score of 121, as reported by school psychologist Susan Jordan. Anna's consulting neuropsychologist Nancy Markel administered the Comprehensive Test of Nonverbal Intelligence, which produced a geometric I.Q. score of 136, a pictorial I.Q. score of 121, and a nonverbal I.Q. score of 131. These scores place her ability above average.

Anna has been the subject of a number of medical assessments.... In January 2001, Dr. Joseph Gleeson, a pediatric neurologist, ... interpreted Anna's condition as consistent with a possible seizure disorder and prescribed medication accordingly.... After a subsequent visit with Anna in April 2001, Dr. Gleeson stated unequivocally that Anna "had an EEG that had significant abnormalities consistent with epilepsy" and observed that Anna suffered from "increasing distractibility and difficulty staying on task that appeared to come in spells." He recommended that Anna be evaluated for a possible attention deficit disorder because of her reported difficulties staying on task and her increased distractibility. Anna eventually began taking medication for the attention problem.

Prompted by the receipt of Dr. Gleeson's initial report, the school district instituted an accommodation plan in accordance with Section 504 of the Rehabilitation Act of 1973, 29 U.S.C. § 794, in February 2001. The plan included preferential seating in the classroom, use of a graphic organizer and AlphaSmart keyboard, one-step directions, visual support for instruction and concepts, frequent prompts and checks for understanding, and daily teacher checks for homework assignments.

On May 15, 2001, Anna's advocate, Sara Frampton, wrote to the district to request a special education evaluation. In this letter, Frampton acknowledged that "[Anna] ha[d] recently been offered a 504 plan" but expressed her concern that the plan had "not been based on a thorough assessment in all areas of potential or suspected disability." The district's psycho-educational assessment, performed by resource specialist Patricia Hotz and school psychologist Susan Jordan in August and September 2001, included a battery of tests and classroom observations. Jordan and Hotz ultimately issued a report explicitly stating that "Anna has been diagnosed with [a] Seizure Disorder . . . for which she takes medication" and "[Anna's] Seizure Disorder adversely affects her ability to focus and pay attention in the regular classroom." However, Jordan and Hotz concluded that "[b]ased on State and Federal guidelines, Anna does not qualify for Special Education services at this time, as she is performing at least in the *average range* academically, both in the classroom and in one-on-one testing." . . .

On October 5, 2001, Jordan and Hotz convened with Anna's general education teacher, advocate, and mother for an IEP meeting. The school district determined that Anna did not qualify for special education services, specifically concluding that "Anna does not have a learning disability."

[The court details the hearing officer and district court decision. Both found that the student was not eligible under the IDEA.]

Upon review of the record, hearing officer's opinion, and appellate briefs, we conclude that the district court did not clearly err in determining that Anna was not legally entitled to special education based on a "specific learning disability." . . .

Our decision hinges upon appellants' failure to satisfy the second requirement of the "specific learning disability" qualification for special education eligibility, that being whether any existing severe discrepancy between ability and achievement "[could] not be corrected through other regular or categorical services offered within the regular instructional program." Cal. Educ.Code § 56337.[1] Thus, even

1. Authors' note: The California Code discussed in the *Hood* decision is based on the 1997 version of the IDEA which focused on the "severe discrepancy" model for learning disabilities. The

assuming the existence of a severe discrepancy, the law does not entitle Anna Hood to special education if we find that her discrepancy can be corrected in the regular classroom.

. . . .

Classic IDEA jurisprudence and administrative decisions prove useful when contemplating the standard appropriate to assess "correctability" and factors informative to the determination of whether the standard is satisfied. For example, in *Board of Educ. v. Rowley*, 458 U.S. 176, 206–07 (1982), the paradigm IDEA case, the Supreme Court determined that the state satisfies the requirement to provide a handicapped child with a "free appropriate public education" by providing "personalized instruction with sufficient support services to permit the child *to benefit* educationally from that instruction." While it is true that the *Rowley* case dealt with the level of services that must be provided to a student already deemed eligible for special education, rather than special education eligibility itself, "[the Ninth Circuit] ha[s] applied the *Rowley* framework in numerous cases." *Van Duyn v. Baker Sch. Dist. 5J*, 481 F.3d 770, 776 (9th Cir. 2007). This court has emphasized that "states are obligated to provide 'a basic floor of opportunity' through a program 'individually designed to provide educational benefit to a handicapped child,'" rather than "potential-maximizing" education. The Supreme Court explicitly stated in *Rowley* that IDEA does not contain a requirement "that the services so provided be sufficient to maximize each child's potential commensurate with the opportunity provided other children." Just as courts look to the ability of a disabled child to benefit from the services provided to determine if that child is receiving an adequate special education, it is appropriate for courts to determine if a child classified as non-disabled is receiving adequate accommodations in the general classroom—and thus is not entitled to special education services—using the benefit standard. Accordingly, the district court used the correct standard of review when it considered the benefit Anna received in the regular classroom as part of its eligibility analysis.

The Supreme Court in *Rowley* elaborated that "if the child is being educated in the regular classrooms of the public education system, [an IEP] should be reasonably calculated to enable the child to achieve passing marks and advance from grade to grade." The Court was careful to provide in a footnote that it did not intend to suggest that advancement from grade to grade was always dispositive. However, in the case before it, the Court found "[the child]'s academic progress, when considered with the special services and professional consideration accorded by the . . . school administrators, to be dispositive."

California Special Education Hearing Office opinions also indicate the importance of grades and educators' assessments when determining whether a child with

---

IDEA was amended in 2004 to remove the severe discrepancy requirement at the federal level and include the requirements noted in the IDEA regulations in Problem 1. The amendments still allow states to allow schools to use a severe discrepancy model. See Activity 1 for more information.

a severe discrepancy between his ability and achievement is reaping some educational benefit in the general classroom. . . .

Application of this benefit standard to the facts presented in this case indicates that Anna does not qualify for special education due to a "specific learning disability" because any existing severe discrepancy between ability and achievement appears correctable in the regular classroom. As the hearing officer noted, "[i]t [is] virtually undisputed in this case that Anna has been progressing in the general curriculum along with her peers." She received nearly uniformly average or above average grades. At the hearing, Michelle Dennis, Anna's fourth grade teacher, testified that Anna was a highly proficient student. According to the hearing officer, Dennis "was adamant that she would not have considered referring Anna for special education because she was working at or above grade level." Sidney Sickels, Anna's teacher for approximately a month immediately preceding her withdrawal from the school district, testified that Anna was capable of producing work at grade level and that he did not believe that Anna needed to be referred to special education. Dennis Rota, Anna's fifth grade science teacher, agreed. Dr. Beverly Barrett, director of pupil personnel services for the school district, testified that the IEP team did not feel that Anna's conditions had a significant impact on her performance necessitating special education, as she was not performing below grade level. According to this evidence, it appears that the hearing officer was justified in concluding that Anna is receiving the requisite benefit from her education such that the school district is in compliance with the law.

. . . .

The school district asserts that the Section 504 accommodations plan was the appropriate way to meet Anna's needs. At the time when the Hoods withdrew Anna from the school district, the record indicates that Anna had only been in the general classroom with her Section 504 modification plan for the latter portion of the fourth grade and the beginning portion of the fifth grade. Thus, it is difficult to judge its success at meeting Anna's unique needs. The Section 504 plan was directly tailored to address Anna's weaknesses. In her testimony before the hearing officer, Michelle Dennis, Anna's fourth grade teacher, acknowledged that Anna sometimes required additional guidance or extra time to complete tasks. Similarly Sidney Sickels, Anna's fifth grade teacher, and Dennis Rota, Anna's fifth grade science teacher, noted that Anna had problems with missing assignments, completing work in a timely fashion, and organizing tasks. The hearing officer had sufficient reason to conclude that the accommodations that the school district offered Anna via her Section 504 plan, particularly the provisions for daily teacher checks for homework assignments, one-step directions, and use of a graphic organizer, would assist with Anna's difficulties and allow her to excel in the regular classroom. It was certainly not clear error for the district court to accept the hearing officer's judgment.

In addition, we conclude that the district did not clearly err in determining that Anna was not legally entitled to special education based on an "other health impairment," in the form of a seizure disorder or attention deficit disorder. . . . [A]s with all eligibility categories, the child's "other health impairment" must require instruction, services, or both, which cannot be provided with modification of the regular school program per California Education Code § 56026(b). The hearing officer found the evidence that Anna had a seizure disorder and attention deficit disorder to be inconclusive, and ultimately he concluded that "Anna did not require special education to meet her educational needs[,]" which "could be met with appropriate accommodations in the regular education environment." On appeal of the hearing officer's decision, the district court summarily accepted the hearing officer's findings and stated that, because "the evidence was inconclusive[,] . . . Anna did not meet the eligibility criteria specified in § 3030(f)."

. . . .

Similarly, we need not determine whether Anna has an "other health impairment" in the form of a seizure disorder or attention deficit disorder, as, even assuming this to be true, we conclude that the law would not entitle Anna to benefits because it was reasonable for the hearing officer to conclude that any impairment can be accommodated in the general classroom. The school district determined that a Section 504 plan would be sufficient to serve Anna's special needs. To attempt to accommodate Anna, in spite of her medical conditions, in the general classroom is consistent with the concept of mainstreaming, an objective that the school district is legally bound to pursue. Deference to the hearing officer and the policy determination of the school district itself is appropriate, and the district court did not clearly err in upholding the hearing officer's decision that Anna did not qualify for special education due to an "other health impairment."

For the reasons set forth above, the judgment of the court below is Affirmed.

Post Problem Discussion

1. In *Hood*, the court relied on state law, which focused on whether the student's disability could be "corrected through other regular or categorical services offered within the regular instructional program." If it could, then the student was not eligible for special education services, because the student did not require specialized instruction. Other courts have used similar criteria, such as looking at whether a student would be able to do required class work without the specialized instruction that would be provided under the IDEA. *See, e.g., L.J. v. Pittsburg Unified School District*, 850 F.3d 996 (9th Cir. 2017); *Yankton Sch. Dist. v. Schramm*, 93 F.3d 1369 (8th Cir 1996). How would Shane fare under this approach?

2. The court in *Hood* used the *Rowley* standard as part of the legal standard for eligibility. As noted in Section 12.03, *Rowley* is the standard established by the Supreme Court to determine if a school provided FAPE. Should it be part of the eligibility analysis? What are the pros and cons of doing so? For further discussion of this issue, see Mark C. Weber, *The IDEA Eligibility Mess*, 57 Buff. L. Rev. 83 (2009).

3. Part of the analysis in *Hood* was that the student obtained passing grades without special education services. We will see the issue of passing grades again in the discussion of FAPE in Section 12.03. The IDEA's regulations note that students with disabilities can be eligible for services even if they receive passing grades. 34 C.F.R. § 300.101(c). However, a number of courts have found that students who perform at an average level in the classroom are not eligible for special education services, because this academic achievement shows that their disability does not adversely affect their educational performance. *See, e.g., A.J. v. Board of Educ.*, 679 F. Supp. 2d 299 (E.D.N.Y. 2010) (student with Autism performing at average to above average levels in the classroom and progressing academically is not eligible for special education services); *Ashli C. v. State of Hawaii,* Civ. No. 08–00499, 2007 WL 247761 at 9* (D. Haw. January 23, 2007) (student with ADHD who is able to learn and function at an average level in the regular classroom is not eligible for special education services). Presumably, a student who performs at an average level in the classroom will have passing grades.

Note that the *Corchado* case in the problem materials rejects the notion that average academic performance in school precludes eligibility for services, stating "[t]his should not and cannot be the litmus test for eligibility under the IDEA. The fact that a child, despite a disability, receives some educational benefit from regular classroom instruction should not disqualify the child from eligibility for special education benefits. . . ." 86 F. Supp. 2d at 176.

Some courts have noted that there must be some nexus between the student's academic achievement on generalized academic measures like grades and tests and the student's disability in the "adversely affects educational performance" analysis. For example, in *Doe v. Cape Elizabeth Sch. Dist.*, 832 F.3d 69 (1st Cir. 2016), the court ruled that the school improperly relied on a student's overall academic achievements, which included straight A's in her classes, to determine non-eligibility for IDEA services, without assessing the relevance of such achievements to the student's disability in reading fluency skills. Similarly, in *Ms. H. v. Montgomery Cty. Bd. of Educ.*, Civ. No. 2:10cv247–WHA–SRW, 2011 WL 666033, at *11 (M.D. Ala. Feb. 14, 2011), the court noted that low grades could be used to show that a student's disability adversely affects educational performance only to the extent that the low grades may have been caused by the student's disability.

Given this regulation and these court decisions, how should eligibility teams and courts factor in passing grades when deciding if a student is eligible for services?

4. The IDEA does not define "adversely affects educational performance," which leaves it for states to do so with state laws. Some states have developed specific definitions, while others have simply adopted the federal standard without providing any additional clarity on what the term means. This has led to disparities in different judicial circuits on issues like whether educational performance is limited to academic or classroom performance, or if it includes non-academic or functional performance as well, like social-emotional or behavioral issues.

Some courts have determined that non-academic or functional issues are not sufficient unless they impact academic performance, but courts are not uniform on the issue because of differing state requirements. *Compare Maus v. Wappingers Cent. Sch. Dist.*, 688 F. Supp. 2d 282, 294 (S.D.N.Y. 2010) ("Courts in this Circuit applying New York's IDEA-related regulations have uniformly interpreted this clause to require proof of an adverse impact on *academic* performance, as opposed to social development or integration."), *with Mr. I. v. Me. Sch. Admin. Dist. No. 55,* 480 F.3d 1, 11–12 (1st Cir. 2007) (finding that "educational performance in Maine is more than just academics," because Maine regulation defines "educational performance" to include both academic and non-academic areas).

How does your state define educational performance? Do you think that term should include non-academic/functional performance, or should it be limited to academic performance in the classroom?

5. In *Hood*, the court noted that the school district provided the student with services under Section 504. Students who are not eligible for services under the IDEA may be entitled to protection under Section 504, because the definition of disability is broader under Section 504. As noted previously, a student must have a "physical or mental impairment that substantially limits a major life activity" like learning, hearing, or speaking. 29 U.S.C. § 705. Does Shane qualify under Section 504? Could Shane's difficulties be addressed with a 504 plan? What difference does it make if Shane is entitled to services under § 504 as compared to IDEA? For information explaining Section 504 requirements, go to www2.ed.gov/about/offices/list/ocr/504faq.html and www2.ed.gov/about/offices/list/ocr/docs/edlite-FAPE504.html.

Activity 1: Find Your State Requirements

As noted in Section 12.01, states adopt state statutes and regulations to address certain issues that the IDEA requires or allows states to address. As illustrated in the *Hood* case, sometimes the state provisions further define certain federal requirements. One area that the IDEA requires states to address is eligibility under the specific learning disability category. Prior versions of the IDEA used a "severe discrepancy" model to determine eligibility for specific learning disabilities. It required students to have a severe gap between their ability and their achievement in school before they were eligible for IDEA services to help close the gap. Under this approach, states often adopted formulas that needed to be met in order to show a severe discrepancy.

The severe discrepancy model was criticized by some as a "wait to fail" model, since it required students to first fall behind before they would be eligible for services to help them catch up. As a result, in 2004, Congress amended the IDEA to state that schools can no longer be *required* to use severe discrepancy formulas to determine if students have specific learning disabilities. 20 U.S.C. § 1414(b)(6); 34 C.F.R. § 300.307. Instead, the law now includes "response to intervention" ("RTI") provisions noted in the IDEA regulations in Problem 1. However, the law *allows* schools to continue to use severe discrepancy models; it just prohibits states from *requiring* them to do so.

As a result of the 2004 change, states had to decide what changes, if any, needed to be made to state laws to comply with the new requirements. The following activity explores these issues in your state:

> **Step One**—Research your state education statutes and regulations for requirements regarding special education eligibility and specific learning disabilities. Look to see if your state statutes and regulations were amended after 2004.
>
> **Step Two**—Find a local school district policy in your state on eligibility and specific learning disabilities. These should be available online.
>
> **Step Three**—Answer the following:
>
> 1. What approach does your state use for specific learning disabilities? Did it adopt the Response to Intervention ("RTI") provisions in the IDEA regulations in Problem 1?
> 2. Does your state allow schools to continue to use a severe discrepancy model? If so, does your state have any formulas or requirements for schools in evaluating severe discrepancies?
> 3. What approach does the local school follow? Does it have any requirements that are different than, or in addition to, the state and federal requirements?
> 4. RTI was intended to respond to some of the criticism of prior approaches, but it too has its potential problems, particularly where it delays qualification for special education and concomitant delay in rights and protections that flow from that qualification.[2] Which approach (RTI vs. severe discrepancy) do you think is better suited for students with learning disabilities and why?[3]
> 5. It was also hoped that RTI might play a role in ameliorating problems of disproportionality, where students are disproportionately represented by race or ethnicity in certain categories and placements in special education. Such disproportionality has long been a concern among educators and civil rights activists and is identified in the IDEA purpose and substantive sections as an area of concern. *See* 20 U.S.C. §§ 1412(24), 14218. States are now under obligation to track the data on this issue and to report on it. Does your state have a specific statutory approach or stated policy on addressing disproportionality?[4]

---

2. *See, e.g.*, Mark C. Weber, *The IDEA Eligibility Mess*, 57 Buffalo L. Rev. 83, 127–28 (2009) (discussing RTI methodology and learning disabilities).

3. For more information about the two approaches, see Response to Intervention (RTI) vs. the Discrepancy Model by LDInfo.com, available at www.ldinfo.com/rti.htm#compare (last visited April 1, 2019).

4. *See* Sarah E. Redfield & Theresa Kraft, *What Color is Special Education*, http://ssrn.com/author=723634.

§ 12.03 FAPE

If the Team finds the student eligible for special education services, then the process moves on to developing an individualized education program ("IEP"), which details the special education and related services that the student will receive as part of FAPE. There are two major components to FAPE: 1) the services provided must be appropriate for the child based on the child's individual, unique needs; and 2) the services must be provided at public expense and at no cost to the parents.

In 1982, the United States Supreme Court addressed the requirements of FAPE in *Board of Educ. of the Hendrick Hudson Cent. Sch. Dist. v. Rowley*, 458 U.S. 176 (1982). The Court stated that the IDEA provided a "basic floor of opportunity" for students with disabilities and FAPE required "educational instruction specially designed to meet the unique needs of the handicapped child, supported by such services as are necessary to permit the child 'to benefit' from the instruction." *Rowley*, 458 U.S. at 188–89.

In *Rowley*, the question was whether the school's proposed IEP would provide the student with FAPE. The court developed a two-step approach for courts to follow in answering this question:

> First, has the State complied with the procedures set forth in the Act? And second, is the individualized educational program developed through the Act's procedures reasonably calculated to enable the child to receive educational benefits?

A number of courts interpreted *Rowley* to mean that all that is required on the second part of the test is that the student receives "some educational benefit" from the services provided. *See, e.g., Devine v. Indian River County Sch. Bd.*, 249 F.3d 1289, 1292 (11th Cir. 2001). Some courts further defined some benefit to simply be "merely more than *de minimis*." *See, e.g., Thompson R2-J Sch. Dist. v. Luke P.*, 540 F.3d 1143, 1149 (10th Cir. 2008).

Other courts interpreted FAPE to require "meaningful educational benefit" which is generally measured by assessing the student's progress or lack of progress in light of the student's ability. *See, e.g., Deal v. Hamilton County Bd. of Educ.*, 392 F.3d 840, 862, 864 (6th Cir. 2004); *T.R. ex rel. N.R. v. Kingwood Twp. Bd. of Educ.*, 205 F.3d 572 (3d Cir. 2000).

In 2017, the U.S. Supreme Court revisited the issue of FAPE in *Endrew F. v. Douglas Co. Sch. Dist. RE-1*, 137 S. Ct. 988 (2017). The case did not expressly address the "some versus meaningful benefit" debate, but it did rule that the "merely more than de minimis" standard applied by the lower court in that case was not a sufficient standard for FAPE:

> It cannot be the case that the Act typically aims for grade-level advancement for children with disabilities who can be educated in the regular classroom, but is satisfied with barely more than de minimis progress for those who cannot.

> When all is said and done, a student offered an educational program providing "merely more than de minimis" progress from year to year can hardly be said to have been offered an education at all. For children with disabilities, receiving instruction that aims so low would be tantamount to "sitting idly . . . awaiting the time when they were old enough to 'drop out.'" The IDEA demands more. It requires an educational program reasonably calculated to enable a child to make progress appropriate in light of the child's circumstances.

The following problem explores some of the issues in providing FAPE.

Problem 2: Is This FAPE?

Assume Shane (from Problem 1) is found eligible for special education services and the team develops an IEP to address his unique needs. After two years of receiving special education and related services, Shane's parents believe that their son is not making sufficient progress given his high IQ and ability. The school performs a reevaluation to measure his progress, and these tests produce the following results as compared to his initial testing in second grade:

Subject	Testing beginning of 2nd grade. Reported in grade level scores	Testing beginning of 4th grade. Reported in grade level scores
Math	2.0	4.0
Written Language	1.8	3.5
Reading Comprehension	1.9	2.9
Word Identification	1.5	2.3
Reading Fluency	K4	1.6
Spelling	1.7	3.4
Word Attack	1.6	3
Calculations	2	3.8

In addition, the team reports that Shane's behavioral issues have improved through the use of positive behavioral intervention services ("PBIS") that are provided pursuant to his IEP. Shane's grades for the second and third grade are still passing, but they reflect modifications made by his teachers because of the assistance he receives in completing his work. Shane has also been receiving special education services to address his reading, writing, and math in special education classes that only include other students with disabilities and his grades reflect his work in those classes. His parents contend that Shane is not receiving FAPE. They also contend that the school has not provided them with sufficient notice before IEP meetings and did not schedule them at mutually agreed upon times. As a result, they were not able to attend one of the IEP meetings.

Has Shane received FAPE? Does your answer vary depending on whether you apply a "meaningful benefit" versus a "some benefit" standard as noted in the problem cases?

Problem Materials

- ✓ *Board of Education of Hendrick Hudson Central School District. v. Rowley*, 458 U.S. 176 (1982)
- ✓ *Endrew F. v. Douglas Co. Sch. Dist. RE-1*, 137 S. Ct. 988 (March 22, 2017)
- ✓ *D.S. v. Bayonne Board of Education*, 602 F.3d 553 (3d Cir. 2010)
- ✓ *J.L. v. Mercer Island School District*, 592 F.3d 938 (9th Cir. 2010)
- ✓ IDEA regulation, 34 C.F.R. § 300.322 Parent Participation

Board of Education of Hendrick Hudson Central School District v. Rowley

458 U.S. 176 (1982)

The Court rules that the student received FAPE and rejects the notion that FAPE requires maximizing a student's potential.

This case presents a question of statutory interpretation. Petitioners contend that the Court of Appeals and the District Court misconstrued the requirements imposed by Congress upon States which receive federal funds under the Education of the Handicapped Act. We agree and reverse the judgment of the Court of Appeals.

The Education of the Handicapped Act (Act), provides federal money to assist state and local agencies in educating handicapped children, and conditions such funding upon a State's compliance with extensive goals and procedures. The Act represents an ambitious federal effort to promote the education of handicapped children, and was passed in response to Congress' perception that a majority of handicapped children in the United States "were either totally excluded from schools or [were] sitting idly in regular classrooms awaiting the time when they were old enough to 'drop out.'" ...

In order to qualify for federal financial assistance under the Act, a State must demonstrate that it "has in effect a policy that assures all handicapped children the right to a free appropriate public education." That policy must be reflected in a state plan submitted to and approved by the Secretary of Education, which describes in detail the goals, programs, and timetables under which the State intends to educate handicapped children within its borders. ...

The "free appropriate public education" required by the Act is tailored to the unique needs of the handicapped child by means of an "individualized educational program" (IEP). The IEP, which is prepared at a meeting between a qualified representative of the local educational agency, the child's teacher, the child's parents or guardian, and, where appropriate, the child, consists of a written document containing

> "(A) a statement of the present levels of educational performance of such child, (B) a statement of annual goals, including short-term instructional objectives, (C) a statement of the specific educational services to be provided to such child, and the extent to which such child will be able to participate in regular educational programs, (D) the projected date for initiation and anticipated duration of such services, and (E) appropriate objective criteria and evaluation procedures and schedules for determining, on at least an annual basis, whether instructional objectives are being achieved."

. . .

This case arose in connection with the education of Amy Rowley, a deaf student at the Furnace Woods School in the Hendrick Hudson Central School District, Peekskill, N. Y. Amy has minimal residual hearing and is an excellent lipreader. During the year before she began attending Furnace Woods, a meeting between her parents and school administrators resulted in a decision to place her in a regular kindergarten class in order to determine what supplemental services would be necessary to her education. Several members of the school administration prepared for Amy's arrival by attending a course in sign-language interpretation, and a teletype machine was installed in the principal's office to facilitate communication with her parents who are also deaf. At the end of the trial period it was determined that Amy should remain in the kindergarten class, but that she should be provided with an FM hearing aid which would amplify words spoken into a wireless receiver by the teacher or fellow students during certain classroom activities. Any successfully completed her kindergarten year.

As required by the Act, an IEP was prepared for Amy during the fall of her first-grade year. The IEP provided that Amy should be educated in a regular classroom at Furnace Woods, should continue to use the FM hearing aid, and should receive instruction from a tutor for the deaf for one hour each day and from a speech therapist for three hours each week. The Rowleys agreed with parts of the IEP but insisted that Amy also be provided a qualified sign-language interpreter in all her academic classes in lieu of the assistance proposed in other parts of the IEP. Such an interpreter had been placed in Amy's kindergarten class for a 2-week experimental period, but the interpreter had reported that Amy did not need his services at that time. The school administrators likewise concluded that Amy did not need such an interpreter in her first-grade classroom. . . .

When their request for an interpreter was denied, the Rowleys demanded and received a hearing before an independent examiner. After receiving evidence from both sides, the examiner agreed with the administrators' determination that an interpreter was not necessary because "Amy was achieving educationally, academically, and socially" without such assistance. The examiner's decision was affirmed on appeal by the New York Commissioner of Education on the basis of substantial evidence in the record. Pursuant to the Act's provision for judicial review, the Rowleys then brought an action in the United States District Court for the Southern District of New York, claiming that the administrators' denial of the sign-language interpreter constituted a denial of the "free appropriate public education" guaranteed by the Act.

The District Court found that Amy . . . "is not learning as much, or performing as well academically, as she would without her handicap." This disparity between Amy's achievement and her potential led the court to decide that she was not receiving a "free appropriate public education," which the court defined as "an opportunity to achieve [her] full potential commensurate with the opportunity provided to other children."

. . . .

This is the first case in which this Court has been called upon to interpret any provision of the Act. . . .

We are loath to conclude that Congress failed to offer any assistance in defining the meaning of the principal substantive phrase used in the Act. It is beyond dispute that, contrary to the conclusions of the courts below, the Act does expressly define "free appropriate public education":

> "The term 'free appropriate public education' means *special education* and *related services* which (A) have been provided at public expense, under public supervision and direction, and without charge, (B) meet the standards of the State educational agency, (C) include an appropriate preschool, elementary, or secondary school education in the State involved, and (D) are provided in conformity with the individualized education program required under section 1414(a)(5) of this title." § 1401(18).

"Special education," as referred to in this definition, means "specially designed instruction, at no cost to parents or guardians, to meet the unique needs of a handicapped child, including classroom instruction, instruction in physical education, home instruction, and instruction in hospitals and institutions." § 1401(16). "Related services" are defined as "transportation, and such developmental, corrective, and other supportive services . . . as may be required to assist a handicapped child to benefit from special education." § 1401(17).

Like many statutory definitions, this one tends toward the cryptic rather than the comprehensive, but that is scarcely a reason for abandoning the quest for legislative intent. Whether or not the definition is a "functional" one, as respondents contend it is not, it is the principal tool which Congress has given us for parsing the critical phrase of the Act. We think more must be made of it than either respondents or the United States seems willing to admit.

According to the definitions contained in the Act, a "free appropriate public education" consists of educational instruction specially designed to meet the unique needs of the handicapped child, supported by such services as are necessary to permit the child "to benefit" from the instruction. Almost as a checklist for adequacy under the Act, the definition also requires that such instruction and services be provided at public expense and under public supervision, meet the State's educational standards, approximate the grade levels used in the State's regular education, and comport with the child's IEP. Thus, if personalized instruction is being provided with sufficient supportive services to permit the child to benefit from the instruction, and the other items on the definitional checklist are satisfied, the child is receiving a "free appropriate public education" as defined by the Act.

Other portions of the statute also shed light upon congressional intent. Congress found that of the roughly eight million handicapped children in the United States at the time of enactment, one million were "excluded entirely from the public school system" and more than half were receiving an inappropriate education. In addition, as mentioned in Part I, the Act requires States to extend educational services first to those children who are receiving no education and second to those children who are receiving an "inadequate education." When these express statutory findings and priorities are read together with the Act's extensive procedural requirements and its definition of "free appropriate public education," the face of the statute evinces a congressional intent to bring previously excluded handicapped children into the public education systems of the States and to require the States to adopt *procedures* which would result in individualized consideration of and instruction for each child.

Noticeably absent from the language of the statute is any substantive standard prescribing the level of education to be accorded handicapped children. Certainly the language of the statute contains no requirement like the one imposed by the lower courts.... Although we find the statutory definition of "free appropriate public education" to be helpful in our interpretation of the Act, there remains the question of whether the legislative history indicates a congressional intent that such education meet some additional substantive standard. For an answer, we turn to that history.

As suggested in Part I, federal support for education of the handicapped is a fairly recent development. Before passage of the Act some States had passed laws to improve the educational services afforded handicapped children, but many of these children were excluded completely from any form of public education or were left to fend for themselves in classrooms designed for education of their nonhandicapped peers....

This concern, stressed repeatedly throughout the legislative history, confirms the impression conveyed by the language of the statute: By passing the Act, Congress sought primarily to make public education available to handicapped children. But in seeking to provide such access to public education, Congress did not impose upon the States any greater substantive educational standard than would be necessary to make such access meaningful. Indeed, Congress expressly "[recognized] that in many instances the process of providing special education and related services to handicapped children is not guaranteed to produce any particular outcome." Thus, the intent of the Act was more to open the door of public education to handicapped children on appropriate terms than to guarantee any particular level of education once inside. . . .

That the Act imposes no clear obligation upon recipient States beyond the requirement that handicapped children receive some form of specialized education is perhaps best demonstrated by the fact that Congress, in explaining the need for the Act, equated an "appropriate education" to the receipt of some specialized educational services.

. . . .

Respondents contend that "the goal of the Act is to provide each handicapped child with an equal educational opportunity." We think, however, that the requirement that a State provide specialized educational services to handicapped children generates no additional requirement that the services so provided be sufficient to maximize each child's potential "commensurate with the opportunity provided other children." . . .

. . . .

Implicit in the congressional purpose of providing access to a "free appropriate public education" is the requirement that the education to which access is provided be sufficient to confer some educational benefit upon the handicapped child. It would do little good for Congress to spend millions of dollars in providing access to a public education only to have the handicapped child receive no benefit from that education. The statutory definition of "free appropriate public education," in addition to requiring that States provide each child with "specially designed instruction," expressly requires the provision of "such . . . supportive services . . . as may be required to assist a handicapped child *to benefit* from special education." We therefore conclude that the "basic floor of opportunity" provided by the Act consists of access to specialized instruction and related services which are individually designed to provide educational benefit to the handicapped child.

The determination of when handicapped children are receiving sufficient educational benefits to satisfy the requirements of the Act presents a more difficult problem. . . . It is clear that the benefits obtainable by children at one end of the spectrum will differ dramatically from those obtainable by children at the other end, with infinite variations in between. One child may have little difficulty competing successfully in an academic setting with nonhandicapped children while another child may encounter great difficulty in acquiring even the most basic of self-maintenance skills. We do not attempt today to establish any one test for determining the adequacy of educational benefits conferred upon all children covered by the Act. Because in this case we are presented with a handicapped child who is receiving substantial specialized instruction and related services, and who is performing above average in the regular classrooms of a public school system, we confine our analysis to that situation.

The Act requires participating States to educate handicapped children with nonhandicapped children whenever possible. When that "mainstreaming" preference of the Act has been met and a child is being educated in the regular classrooms of a public school system, the system itself monitors the educational progress of the child. Regular examinations are administered, grades are awarded, and yearly advancement to higher grade levels is permitted for those children who attain an adequate knowledge of the course material. The grading and advancement system thus constitutes an important factor in determining educational benefit. Children who graduate from our public school systems are considered by our society to have been "educated" at least to the grade level they have completed, and access to an "education" for handicapped children is precisely what Congress sought to provide in the Act.

When the language of the Act and its legislative history are considered together, the requirements imposed by Congress become tolerably clear. Insofar as a State is required to provide a handicapped child with a "free appropriate public education," we hold that it satisfies this requirement by providing personalized instruction with sufficient support services to permit the child to benefit educationally from that instruction. Such instruction and services must be provided at public expense, must meet the State's educational standards, must approximate the grade levels used in the State's regular education, and must comport with the child's IEP. In addition, the IEP, and therefore the personalized instruction, should be formulated in accordance with the requirements of the Act and, if the child is being educated in the regular classrooms of the public education system, should be reasonably calculated to enable the child to achieve passing marks and advance from grade to grade.

[The Court goes on to discuss the judicial review provisions in the law.]

Therefore, a court's inquiry in suits brought under [the law] is twofold. First, has the State complied with the procedures set forth in the Act? And second, is the individualized educational program developed through the Act's procedures reasonably calculated to enable the child to receive educational benefits? If these requirements are met, the State has complied with the obligations imposed by Congress and the courts can require no more.

. . . .

Applying these principles to the facts of this case, we conclude that the Court of Appeals erred in affirming the decision of the District Court. Neither the District Court nor the Court of Appeals found that petitioners had failed to comply with the procedures of the Act, and the findings of neither court would support a conclusion that Amy's educational program failed to comply with the substantive requirements of the Act. On the contrary, the District Court found that the "evidence firmly establishes that Amy is receiving an 'adequate' education, since she performs better than the average child in her class and is advancing easily from grade to grade." In light of this finding, and of the fact that Amy was receiving personalized instruction and related services calculated by the Furnace Woods school administrators to meet her educational needs, the lower courts should not have concluded that the

Act requires the provision of a sign-language interpreter. Accordingly, the decision of the Court of Appeals is reversed, and the case is remanded for further proceedings consistent with this opinion.

So ordered.

Endrew F. v. Douglas Co. Sch. Dist. RE-1

137 S. Ct. 988 (March 22, 2017)

The Court rules that a "merely more than de minimis" standard is not sufficient for FAPE. Rather, FAPE requires a student to make progress that is appropriate in light of their circumstances.

Chief Justice Roberts delivered the opinion of the Court.

Thirty-five years ago, this Court held that the Individuals with Disabilities Education Act establishes a substantive right to a "free appropriate public education" for certain children with disabilities. *Board of Ed. of Hendrick Hudson Central School Dist., Westchester Cty. v. Rowley*, 458 U.S. 176 (1982). We declined, however, to endorse any one standard for determining "when handicapped children are receiving sufficient educational benefits to satisfy the requirements of the Act." That "more difficult problem" is before us today.

I

A

The Individuals with Disabilities Education Act (IDEA or Act) offers States federal funds to assist in educating children with disabilities. In exchange for the funds, a State pledges to comply with a number of statutory conditions. Among them, the State must provide a free appropriate public education—a FAPE, for short—to all eligible children. § 1412(a)(1).

A FAPE, as the Act defines it, includes both "special education" and "related services." § 1401(9). "Special education" is "specially designed instruction . . . to meet the unique needs of a child with a disability"; "related services" are the support services "required to assist a child . . . to benefit from" that instruction. §§ 1401(26), (29). A State covered by the IDEA must provide a disabled child with such special education and related services "in conformity with the [child's] individualized education program," or IEP. § 1401(9)(D).

The IEP is "the centerpiece of the statute's education delivery system for disabled children." A comprehensive plan prepared by a child's "IEP Team" (which includes teachers, school officials, and the child's parents), an IEP must be drafted in compliance with a detailed set of procedures. § 1414(d)(1)(B) (internal quotation marks omitted). These procedures emphasize collaboration among parents and educators and require careful consideration of the child's individual circumstances. § 1414. The IEP is the means by which special education and related services are "tailored to the unique needs" of a particular child. *Rowley*, 458 U.S., at 181, 102 S.Ct. 3034.

The IDEA requires that every IEP include "a statement of the child's present levels of academic achievement and functional performance," describe "how the child's disability affects the child's involvement and progress in the general education curriculum," and set out "measurable annual goals, including academic and functional goals," along with a "description of how the child's progress toward meeting" those goals will be gauged. §§ 1414(d)(1)(A)(i)(I)-(III). The IEP must also describe the "special education and related services . . . that will be provided" so that the child may "advance appropriately toward attaining the annual goals" and, when possible, "be involved in and make progress in the general education curriculum." § 1414(d)(1)(A)(i)(IV).

Parents and educators often agree about what a child's IEP should contain. But not always. When disagreement arises, parents may turn to dispute resolution procedures established by the IDEA. The parties may resolve their differences informally, through a "[p]reliminary meeting," or, somewhat more formally, through mediation. §§ 1415(e), (f)(1)(B)(i). If these measures fail to produce accord, the parties may proceed to what the Act calls a "due process hearing" before a state or local educational agency. §§ 1415(f)(1)(A), (g). And at the conclusion of the administrative process, the losing party may seek redress in state or federal court. § 1415(i)(2)(A) . . . .

C

Petitioner Endrew F. was diagnosed with autism at age two. Autism is a neurodevelopmental disorder generally marked by impaired social and communicative skills, "engagement in repetitive activities and stereotyped movements, resistance to environmental change or change in daily routines, and unusual responses to sensory experiences." 34 C.F.R. § 300.8(c)(1)(i) (2016); see Brief for Petitioner 8. A child with autism qualifies as a "[c]hild with a disability" under the IDEA, and Colorado (where Endrew resides) accepts IDEA funding. § 1401(3)(A). Endrew is therefore entitled to the benefits of the Act, including a FAPE provided by the State.

Endrew attended school in respondent Douglas County School District from preschool through fourth grade. Each year, his IEP Team drafted an IEP addressed to his educational and functional needs. By Endrew's fourth grade year, however, his parents had become dissatisfied with his progress. Although Endrew displayed a number of strengths—his teachers described him as a humorous child with a "sweet disposition" who "show[ed] concern[] for friends"—he still "exhibited multiple behaviors that inhibited his ability to access learning in the classroom." Endrew would scream in class, climb over furniture and other students, and occasionally run away from school. He was afflicted by severe fears of commonplace things like flies, spills, and public restrooms. As Endrew's parents saw it, his academic and functional progress had essentially stalled: Endrew's IEPs largely carried over the same basic goals and objectives from one year to the next, indicating that he was failing to make meaningful progress toward his aims. His parents believed that only a thorough overhaul of the school district's approach to Endrew's behavioral problems could reverse the trend. But in April 2010, the school district presented Endrew's parents with a proposed fifth grade IEP that was, in their view, pretty much the same as his past ones. So his parents removed Endrew from public school and enrolled him at Firefly Autism House, a private school that specializes in educating children with autism.

Endrew did much better at Firefly. The school developed a "behavioral intervention plan" that identified Endrew's most problematic behaviors and set out particular strategies for addressing them. Firefly also added heft to Endrew's academic goals. Within months, Endrew's behavior improved significantly, permitting him to make a degree of academic progress that had eluded him in public school.

In November 2010, some six months after Endrew started classes at Firefly, his parents again met with representatives of the Douglas County School District. The district presented a new IEP. Endrew's parents considered the IEP no more adequate than the one proposed in April, and rejected it. They were particularly concerned that the stated plan for addressing Endrew's behavior did not differ meaningfully from the plan in his fourth grade IEP, despite the fact that his experience at Firefly suggested that he would benefit from a different approach.

In February 2012, Endrew's parents filed a complaint with the Colorado Department of Education seeking reimbursement for Endrew's tuition at Firefly. To qualify for such relief, they were required to show that the school district had not provided Endrew a FAPE in a timely manner prior to his enrollment at the private school. See § 1412(a)(10)(C)(ii). Endrew's parents contended that the final IEP proposed by the school district was not "reasonably calculated to enable [Endrew] to receive educational benefits" and that Endrew had therefore been denied a FAPE. An Administrative Law Judge (ALJ) disagreed and denied relief.

Endrew's parents sought review in Federal District Court. Giving "due weight" to the decision of the ALJ, the District Court affirmed. The court acknowledged that Endrew's performance under past IEPs "did not reveal immense educational growth." But it concluded that annual modifications to Endrew's IEP objectives were "sufficient to show a pattern of, at the least, minimal progress." Because Endrew's previous IEPs had enabled him to make this sort of progress, the court reasoned, his latest, similar IEP was reasonably calculated to do the same thing. In the court's view, that was all Rowley demanded.

The Tenth Circuit affirmed. The Court of Appeals recited language from Rowley stating that the instruction and services furnished to children with disabilities must be calculated to confer "some educational benefit." The court noted that it had long interpreted this language to mean that a child's IEP is adequate as long as it is calculated to confer an "educational benefit [that is] merely . . . more than de minimis." Applying this standard, the Tenth Circuit held that Endrew's IEP had been "reasonably calculated to enable [him] to make some progress." Accordingly, he had not been denied a FAPE.

II

A

The Court in *Rowley* declined "to establish any one test for determining the adequacy of educational benefits conferred upon all children covered by the Act." The school district, however, contends that *Rowley* nonetheless established that "an IEP need not promise any particular level of benefit," so long as it is "'reasonably calculated' to provide some benefit, as opposed to none."

The district relies on several passages from *Rowley* to make its case. It points to our observation that "any substantive standard prescribing the level of education to be accorded" children with disabilities was "[n]oticeably absent from the language of the statute." The district also emphasizes the Court's statement that the Act requires States to provide access to instruction "sufficient to confer some educational benefit," reasoning that any benefit, however minimal, satisfies this mandate. Finally, the district urges that the Court conclusively adopted a "some educational benefit" standard when it wrote that "the intent of the Act was more to open the door of public education to handicapped children . . . than to guarantee any particular level of education."

These statements in isolation do support the school district's argument. But the district makes too much of them. Our statement that the face of the IDEA imposed no explicit substantive standard must be evaluated alongside our statement that a substantive standard was "implicit in the Act." Similarly, we find little significance in the Court's language concerning the requirement that States provide instruction calculated to "confer some educational benefit. The Court had no need to say anything more particular, since the case before it involved a child whose progress plainly demonstrated that her IEP was designed to deliver more than adequate educational benefits. The Court's principal concern was to correct what it viewed as the surprising rulings below: that the IDEA effectively empowers judges to elaborate a federal common law of public education, and that a child performing better than most in her class had been denied a FAPE. The Court was not concerned with precisely articulating a governing standard for closer cases. And the statement that the Act did not "guarantee any particular level of education" simply reflects the unobjectionable proposition that the IDEA cannot and does not promise "any particular [educational] outcome." No law could do that—for any child.

More important, the school district's reading of these isolated statements runs headlong into several points on which *Rowley* is crystal clear. For instance—just after saying that the Act requires instruction that is "sufficient to confer some educational benefit"—we noted that "[t]he determination of when handicapped children are receiving sufficient educational benefits . . . presents a . . . difficult problem." And then we expressly declined "to establish any one test for determining the adequacy of educational benefits" under the Act. It would not have been "difficult" for us to say when educational benefits are sufficient if we had just said that any educational benefit was enough. And it would have been strange to refuse to set out a test for the adequacy of educational benefits if we had just done exactly that. We cannot accept the school district's reading of *Rowley.*

B

While *Rowley* declined to articulate an overarching standard to evaluate the adequacy of the education provided under the Act, the decision and the statutory language point to a general approach: To meet its substantive obligation under the IDEA, a school must offer an IEP reasonably calculated to enable a child to make progress appropriate in light of the child's circumstances.

The "reasonably calculated" qualification reflects a recognition that crafting an appropriate program of education requires a prospective judgment by school officials. The Act contemplates that this fact-intensive exercise will be informed not only by the expertise of school officials, but also by the input of the child's parents or guardians. Any review of an IEP must appreciate that the question is whether the IEP is reasonable, not whether the court regards it as ideal.

The IEP must aim to enable the child to make progress. After all, the essential function of an IEP is to set out a plan for pursuing academic and functional advancement. See §§ 1414(d)(1)(A)(i)(I)–(IV). This reflects the broad purpose of the IDEA, an "ambitious" piece of legislation enacted "in response to Congress' perception that a majority of handicapped children in the United States 'were either totally excluded from schools or [were] sitting idly in regular classrooms awaiting the time when they were old enough to 'drop out.'" A substantive standard not focused on student progress would do little to remedy the pervasive and tragic academic stagnation that prompted Congress to act.

That the progress contemplated by the IEP must be appropriate in light of the child's circumstances should come as no surprise. A focus on the particular child is at the core of the IDEA. The instruction offered must be "*specially* designed" to meet a child's "*unique* needs" through an "*[i]ndividualized* education program." §§ 1401(29), (14) (emphasis added). An IEP is not a form document. It is constructed only after careful consideration of the child's present levels of achievement, disability, and potential for growth. §§ 1414(d)(1)(A)(i)(I)-(IV), (d)(3)(A)(i)-(iv). As we observed in *Rowley*, the IDEA "requires participating States to educate a wide spectrum of handicapped children," and "the benefits obtainable by children at one end of the spectrum will differ dramatically from those obtainable by children at the other end, with infinite variations in between."

Rowley sheds light on what appropriate progress will look like in many cases. There, the Court recognized that the IDEA requires that children with disabilities receive education in the regular classroom "whenever possible." *Ibid.* (citing § 1412(a)(5)). When this preference is met, "the system itself monitors the educational progress of the child." "Regular examinations are administered, grades are awarded, and yearly advancement to higher grade levels is permitted for those children who attain an adequate knowledge of the course material." Progress through this system is what our society generally means by an "education." And access to an "education" is what the IDEA promises. *Ibid.* Accordingly, for a child fully integrated in the regular classroom, an IEP typically should, as *Rowley* put it, be "reasonably calculated to enable the child to achieve passing marks and advance from grade to grade."

This guidance is grounded in the statutory definition of a FAPE. One of the components of a FAPE is "special education," defined as "specially designed instruction . . . to meet the unique needs of a child with a disability." §§ 1401(9), (29). In determining what it means to "meet the unique needs" of a child with a disability, the provisions governing the IEP development process are a natural source of guidance: It is through the IEP that "[t]he 'free appropriate public education' required by the Act is tailored to the unique needs of" a particular child.

The IEP provisions reflect *Rowley*'s expectation that, for most children, a FAPE will involve integration in the regular classroom and individualized special education calculated to achieve advancement from grade to grade. Every IEP begins by describing a child's present level of achievement, including explaining "how the child's disability affects the child's involvement and progress in the general education curriculum." § 1414(d)(1)(A)(i)(I)(aa). It then sets out "a statement of measurable annual goals . . . designed to . . . enable the child to be involved in and make progress in the general education curriculum," along with a description of specialized instruction and services that the child will receive. §§ 1414(d)(1)(A)(i)(II), (IV). The instruction and services must likewise be provided with an eye toward "progress in the general education curriculum." § 1414(d)(1)(A)(i)(IV)(bb). Similar IEP requirements have been in place since the time the States began accepting funding under the IDEA.

The school district protests that these provisions impose only procedural requirements—a checklist of items the IEP must address—not a substantive standard enforceable in court. But the procedures are there for a reason, and their focus provides insight into what it means, for purposes of the FAPE definition, to "meet the unique needs" of a child with a disability. §§ 1401(9), (29). When a child is fully integrated in the regular classroom, as the Act prefers, what that typically means is providing a level of instruction reasonably calculated to permit advancement through the general curriculum.

Rowley had no need to provide concrete guidance with respect to a child who is not fully integrated in the regular classroom and not able to achieve on grade level. That case concerned a young girl who was progressing smoothly through the regular curriculum. If that is not a reasonable prospect for a child, his IEP need not aim for grade-level advancement. But his educational program must be appropriately ambitious in light of his circumstances, just as advancement from grade to grade is appropriately ambitious for most children in the regular classroom. The goals may differ, but every child should have the chance to meet challenging objectives.

Of course this describes a general standard, not a formula. But whatever else can be said about it, this standard is markedly more demanding than the "merely more than de minimis " test applied by the Tenth Circuit. It cannot be the case that the

Act typically aims for grade-level advancement for children with disabilities who can be educated in the regular classroom, but is satisfied with barely more than de minimis progress for those who cannot.

When all is said and done, a student offered an educational program providing "merely more than de minimis" progress from year to year can hardly be said to have been offered an education at all. For children with disabilities, receiving instruction that aims so low would be tantamount to "sitting idly . . . awaiting the time when they were old enough to 'drop out.'" The IDEA demands more. It requires an educational program reasonably calculated to enable a child to make progress appropriate in light of the child's circumstances. . . .

D

We will not attempt to elaborate on what "appropriate" progress will look like from case to case. It is in the nature of the Act and the standard we adopt to resist such an effort: The adequacy of a given IEP turns on the unique circumstances of the child for whom it was created. This absence of a bright-line rule, however, should not be mistaken for "an invitation to the courts to substitute their own notions of sound educational policy for those of the school authorities which they review."

At the same time, deference is based on the application of expertise and the exercise of judgment by school authorities. The Act vests these officials with responsibility for decisions of critical importance to the life of a disabled child. The nature of the IEP process, from the initial consultation through state administrative proceedings, ensures that parents and school representatives will fully air their respective opinions on the degree of progress a child's IEP should pursue. See §§ 1414, 1415. By the time any dispute reaches court, school authorities will have had a complete opportunity to bring their expertise and judgment to bear on areas of disagreement. A reviewing court may fairly expect those authorities to be able to offer a cogent and responsive explanation for their decisions that shows the IEP is reasonably calculated to enable the child to make progress appropriate in light of his circumstances.

The judgment of the United States Court of Appeals for the Tenth Circuit is vacated, and the case is remanded for further proceedings consistent with this opinion.

It is so ordered.

D.S. v. Bayonne Board of Education

602 F.3d 553 (3d Cir. 2010)

The court applies the "meaningful educational benefit" standard and upholds an administrative law judge finding that a student did not receive FAPE under that standard.

Greenberg, Circuit Judge.

. . . .

A. Legal Standards

The IDEA requires that states to receive federal education funding make available a free and appropriate public education to all children with disabilities residing within their borders. In particular the IDEA specifies that the education the states provide to these children "specially [be] designed to meet the unique needs of the handicapped child, supported by such services as are necessary to permit the child to benefit from the instruction." Although a state is not required to supply an education to a handicapped child that maximizes the child's potential, it must confer an education providing "significant learning" and "meaningful benefit" to the child. Thus, "the provision of merely more than a trivial educational benefit" is insufficient. In addition to establishing educational standards, the IDEA includes a "mainstreaming" component requiring the placement of a student with disabilities in the least restrictive environment that will provide the child with a meaningful educational benefit.

The IDEA contemplates that school districts will achieve these goals by designing and administering a program of individualized instruction for each special education student set forth in an Individualized Education Plan ("IEP"). The IEP is so significant that the courts have characterized it as the "centerpiece" of the IDEA's system for delivering education to disabled children. "An IEP consists of a specific statement of a student's present abilities, goals for improvement of the student's abilities, services designed to meet those goals, and a timetable for reaching the goals by way of the services." A team consisting of the student's parents and teachers, a curriculum specialist from the local school district, and, if requested, a person with special knowledge or expertise regarding the student must develop an IEP. The IEP team will review the IEP at least annually to determine whether the stated goals for the student are being achieved. When appropriate the team will revise the IEP to address, among other things, lack of progress, necessary changes arising from reevaluation of the child, and parental input.

Though the IEP must provide the student with a "basic floor of opportunity," it need not necessarily provide "the optimal level of services" that parents might desire for their child. Nevertheless, "at a minimum, '[t]he IEP must be reasonably calculated to enable the child to receive meaningful educational benefits in light of the student's intellectual potential.'" When a state is unable to provide a free and appropriate public education to a child but a private school can provide that education, the state must reimburse the child's parents for the private school costs.

B. Factual Background

When D.S. was six years old, he began to suffer from epileptic seizures attributable to brain tumors. The treatment for the seizures included the use of large quantities of anti-epileptic medicine. Unfortunately D.S.'s condition and treatment combined to place severe limits on his cognitive abilities as demonstrated by the circumstance that he had a full scale IQ within the mentally retarded range. D.S. began attending Bayonne public schools in the second grade. After D.S. repeated the second grade, Bayonne classified him as "other health impaired" and provided him with a special education program in the third grade during the 2000–2001 school year. D.S. underwent brain surgery in 2001 and 2003, in which the tumors were removed successfully. D.S.'s seizures abated completely following the 2003 operation allowing him to cease taking preventive medication. As a result, although he still suffered from significant learning difficulties, his condition improved. Thereafter D.S. remained a student in the Bayonne schools into the ninth grade during the 2006–2007 school year. At that level the Bayonne schools placed D.S. in the school's self-contained "cluster" program in which special education teachers educate special education students in a classroom environment distinct from that of the general student population.

1. Report of Neuropsychologist Maria DiDonato

Notwithstanding D.S.'s placement in the cluster program, Appellants obviously were dissatisfied with D.S.'s progress in the Bayonne schools for they retained the services of several professionals to evaluate D.S. for a better understanding of his educational needs and abilities. Thus in April and May of 2006, they retained a neuropsychologist, Dr. Maria DiDonato, to administer a series of aptitude and achievement tests to D.S. while he was in the eighth grade. Based on an evaluation of D.S.'s cognitive reasoning skills using the Wechsler Intelligence Scale for Children IV ("WISC IV"), DiDonato determined that D.S. had a full-scale IQ score of 81, within the low average range of intellectual functioning, signaling that his intellectual capacity had improved following the surgeries. Nevertheless, D.S. evidenced below grade level achievement and in the Wechsler Individual Achievement Test II ("WIAT") scored at the 6.6 grade level for basic reading skills, the 4.2 grade level for reading comprehension, the 7.2 grade level for numerical operations, the 5.4 grade level for math reasoning, the 5.5 grade level for spelling, and the 6.2 grade level for written expression.

. . . .

7. Hackler and Wilkinson Evaluations

Though Appellants had obtained numerous evaluations of D.S., the evaluation process was not one-sided for in May 2007 Bayonne designated learning consultant Lucy Hackley and school psychologist Mary Beth Wilkinson to evaluate D.S. to determine his cognitive level. Hackler administered Woodcock-Johnson III ("Woodcock-Johnson") achievement tests to gauge D.S.'s grade-level proficiency in several academic areas. In these tests D.S. scored at the 3.8 grade-level for reading comprehension, the 6.8 grade-level for math calculation, the 5.3 grade-level for math reasoning, the 5.7 grade-level for basic writing skills, and the 5.8 grade-level for written expression. In each of these subject areas in terms of grade-level equivalence D.S. scored lower than he had scored approximately one year earlier when he took the WIAT achievement test that DiDonato administered. Wilkinson's psychological evaluation consisted of an IQ test and a Multidimensional Self Concept Scale exam, which assessed social-emotional adjustment. D.S's IQ was assessed using the WISC-IV test at 78, within the borderline range of intellectual functioning. When D.S. had taken this test approximately one year earlier, the result was a slightly higher IQ score of 81, within the low average range of intellectual functioning. On the Multidimensional Self Concept Scale exam, D.S. received a total score of 70, indicating that he had a very negative self-image.

8. D.S.'s Final Grades for the 2006–2007 School Year

At the completion of the 2006–2007 school year, D.S. received a cumulative final grade point average of 92 for his major subjects. He received scores of 95 in general sciences, 95 in English, 93 in language arts, 87 in math, and 90 in world history. His overall cumulative grade point average in major subjects for the 2006–2007 school year increased over his previous averages for in each of the previous four years D.S. had received an average in the mid to high 80s.

C. Procedural History

1. State Administrative Proceedings

In early 2007, while D.S. was in ninth grade, Appellants concluded that Bayonne was failing to provide D.S. with a free and appropriate public education, a conclusion leading them on March 19, 2007, as we already have indicated, to file their petition for a due process hearing challenging Bayonne's education treatment of D.S. The Department of Education transmitted the case to the New Jersey Office of Administrative Law which assigned an ALJ to the case who conducted the hearing over a period of months in 2007.

At the hearing, the ALJ reviewed the reports that the parties had compiled and heard testimony from D.S.'s father as well as from a number of educators and health professionals who had worked with or evaluated D.S. There was substantial focus at the hearing on determining the significance of D.S.'s high final grades for the 2006–2007 school year in light of the decrease in grade-level proficiency when his 2007 scores on the Woodcock-Johnson tests were compared to his 2006 scores on the WIAT tests. It is clear that Bayonne's witnesses, in particular D.S.'s teachers and his case manager Peraino, believed that D.S.'s high marks in all of his classes demonstrated that D.S. had made academic progress during the 2006–2007 school year. To Bayonne these high marks seemed particularly significant because its Director of Special Services Carol Trojan and its learning consultant Hackler testified that standardized test scores were not a reliable indicator of academic progress. Yet there was a clear and well-defined dispute between the two camps of expert witnesses with respect to the significance of the results of standardized testing when compared to the grades in school . . .

. . . .

The ALJ ultimately concluded that Bayonne had failed to create an IEP for D.S. sufficient to address his educational needs, and that as a result D.S. had not received a free and appropriate public education conferring a meaningful educational benefit in the least restrictive environment, and thus his education did not satisfy federal law. After considering the testimony from the psychologist at the Banyan School and taking into consideration the evaluations and assessments regarding D.S.'s educational and social needs, the ALJ concluded that the Banyan School would be an appropriate placement and ordered his placement there at Bayonne's expense, a direction carried out in April 2008.

2. District Court Proceedings

[The district court] reversed the decision of the ALJ as the Court concluded that Bayonne had provided D.S. with an education that met federal requirements in its public schools. The Court predicated its conclusion principally on the bases that D.S. had received high grades during the 2006–2007 school year, an achievement that it believed the ALJ failed to consider, and its belief that the ALJ "over-relied on D.S.'s standardized test scores when reaching her decision." Furthermore, the Court also considered that D.S.'s teachers were using a multi-sensory learning approach and were following certain of Appellants' consultants' recommendations.

. . . .

We now come to the heart of this appeal. In her decision, the ALJ found, "based on the scoring results from evaluations and assessments and the weight of testimony from teachers and medical experts," that D.S.'s ninth grade IEP failed to incorporate the recommendations necessary to address D.S.'s needs, which included:

> reading goals, individualized basic phonetics training, placement in a multi-sensory reading program that addresses reading comprehension skills (Lindamood-Bell, Wilson, or the Orton-Gillingham), intensive speech/language therapy, intensive auditory therapy regimens, an academic environment for small group language-based classroom instruction, remediation instruction for reading, writing, comprehension and spelling, usage of visual aids, FM desk-top amplification system and other educational supports.

The absence of these recommendations, or any alternatives reasonably calculated to confer an educational benefit to D.S., led the ALJ to find the IEP inappropriate.

The District Court reversed this finding because D.S.'s ninth grade IEP indicated that his teachers were using a multi-sensory learning approach and rephrasing and restating instructions when necessary as recommended by Appellants' educational consultants, the IEP incorporated a number of the consultants' other proposed recommendations, and, most significantly, D.S. received high marks in his ninth grade classes. The Court acknowledged that the IEP failed to contain reading goals and did not include all of the recommendations of the educational consultants, but stated that "even without these goals, D.S. received meaningful educational benefit during the 2006–2007 school year, as evidenced by the high marks D.S. earned."

We agree with the District Court that the IEP did incorporate certain instructional techniques that were consistent with Appellants' consultants' recommendations . . . Nevertheless, we disagree with the District Court that the presence of these generalized instructions in the IEP contradicts the ALJ's ultimate factual conclusions-which a reviewing court is obliged to consider prima facie correct-that (1) in order for D.S.'s ninth grade IEP to be reasonably calculated to enable D.S. to receive a meaningful educational benefit, it needed to incorporate the specific remedial techniques and provisions for accommodations that the teachers and evaluators who worked with him had proposed, and (2) the IEP failed to incorporate these specific remedial techniques and provisions for accommodations.

As we have indicated, the District Court also found that the IEP was appropriate because the high grades that he received in all of his classes demonstrated that he made meaningful academic progress during his ninth grade year. It certainly was reasonable for the Court to consider D.S.'s academic progress in evaluating the appropriateness of the IEP for "evidence of a student's later educational progress may [ ] be considered in determining whether the original IEP was reasonably calculated to afford some educational benefit." Moreover, the Supreme Court has indicated that a special education student who "is being educated in the regular classrooms of a public school system" and who is performing well enough to advance from grade to grade generally will be considered to be receiving a meaningful educational benefit under the IDEA. Nevertheless, though the Court has stated that the "grading and advancement system" constitutes "an important factor in determining educational benefit," it also has made clear that it was not holding "that every handicapped child who is advancing from grade to grade in a regular public school system is automatically receiving a 'free appropriate public education.'"

D.S., however, was not being educated in Bayonne's regular classrooms. To the contrary, Bayonne was giving him all of his academic instruction in classes composed entirely of special education students in its "cluster" program. The District Court apparently did not view this distinction as significant because "[i]n Bayonne, state core curriculum standards underlie the core curriculum content for all of its students, including special education students." *Rowley*, however, does not support the District Court's position that high scores achieved in special education classrooms are unambiguous evidence of an IEP's sufficiency. In this regard it is important to reiterate that in *Rowley* the Supreme Court made its statements regarding the limited significance of grade-to-grade advancement in the situation before it in which the "mainstreaming" preference of the IDEA had been met and the Court was "presented with a handicapped child ... who is performing above average in the *regular classrooms* of a public school system." Thus, our reading of *Rowley* leads us to believe that when the "mainstreaming" preference has not been met so that high grades are achieved in classes with only special education students set apart from the regular classes of a public school system, the grades are of less significance than grades obtained in regular classrooms.

Moreover, quite aside from *Rowley*, our precedents do not afford the significance the District Court afforded to D.S.'s high scores in special education classrooms in this case for we consistently have declined to adopt bright line rules to determine whether a student is receiving a meaningful educational benefit under the IDEA. *See, e.g., Ridgewood Bd. of Educ.*, 172 F.3d at 247 (what benefit is "appropriate" under the

IDEA is gauged in relation to child's potential); *Polk*, 853 F.2d at 184 ("The educational progress of a handicapped child . . . can be understood as a continuum where the point of regression versus progress is less relevant than the conferral of benefit."); *Carlisle Area Sch.*, 62 F.3d at 534 (". . . the [IDEA] requires that school districts prepare the IEP's based on the student's needs; so long as the IEP responds to the needs, its ultimate success or failure cannot retroactively render it inappropriate.").

Overall, we think that it is clear that a court should not place conclusive significance on special education classroom scores, a conclusion that we believe is reinforced by the circumstance that, as here, there may be a disconnect between a school's assessment of a student in a special education setting and his achievements in that setting and the student's achievements in standardized testing. When there is such a disconnect we think that there should be an especially close examination of the appropriateness of the student's education.

We recognize that the District Court reached its conclusion on the basis of testimony from Carol Trojan, Bayonne's Director of Special Services, who testified in the administrative proceedings that D.S., by receiving high marks in his special education classes, demonstrated mastery of the regular ninth grade curriculum just as if he was in a regular classroom, and whose testimony was recorded in the ALJ's decision. Appellants' witnesses, on the other hand, thoughtfully expressed their beliefs that D.S. had not made grade level progress during the 2006–2007 school year. The ALJ chose to credit Appellants' witnesses, and, under the applicable standard of review the District Court was not at liberty to credit the witnesses who expressed a contrary opinion without a showing that there was good reason to do so, a showing that Bayonne did not make.

The District Court also supported its conclusion by stating that the ALJ over-relied on D.S.'s standardized test scores, i.e., his 2006 scores on the WIAT tests and his 2007 scores on the Woodcock-Johnson tests. The Court stated that Appellants had failed to meet their burden of showing that an apt comparison can be made between scores from the two different types of tests. But the ALJ heard testimony regarding the standardized testing and on the basis of that testimony used the test results to measure D.S.'s progress. Moreover, the District Court did not point to nontestimonial evidence that undermined the ALJ's conclusion on this point. If we give as we should "due weight" to the ALJ's determination that D.S.'s ninth grade IEP was not reasonably calculated to enable D.S. to receive a meaningful educational benefit, we find no basis in the record for overturning that determination. Accordingly, the District Court's contradictory determination was clearly erroneous.

V. Conclusion

For the reasons set forth above, we will reverse the order of the District Court . . . and remand the case for entry of judgment in favor of the Appellants to the end that the ALJ's decision . . . that Bayonne was not supplying D.S. with a free and appropriate public education and that the Banyan School would be an appropriate placement so that D.S. be placed in that school at Bayonne's expense, is reinstated. . . .

J.L. v. Mercer Island School District

592 F.3d 938 (9th Cir. 2010)

The Ninth Circuit overrules a district court decision that utilized the "meaningful educational benefit" standard and finds that the "some educational benefit" standard still applies.

BEEZER, CIRCUIT JUDGE:

This appeal stems from Plaintiffs' allegation that Defendant Mercer Island School District ("District") failed to provide K.L. with a free appropriate public education as required by the Individuals with Disabilities Education Act, 20 U.S.C. §§ 1400-1491. The administrative law judge ("ALJ") analyzed Plaintiffs' claims using the free appropriate public education "educational benefit" standard interpreted by the Supreme Court in *Board of Education of the Hendrick Hudson Central School District v. Rowley*, 458 U.S. 176 (1982), and concluded that the District provided a free appropriate public education. The district court concluded that Congress superseded *Rowley* in the 1997 Individuals with Disabilities Education Act amendment and held that K.L. was denied a free appropriate public education. The District appeals.

... We vacate the district court's orders except to the extent that we reverse the district court's conclusion that the District committed procedural violations of the Individuals with Disabilities Education Act that resulted in the denial of a free appropriate public education. We remand to the district court to review the ALJ's determination that the District provided K.L. with educational benefit as required by *Rowley*.

I

K.L. is a student of average intelligence that the District diagnosed with learning disabilities in first grade. For second and third grades, the District educated K.L. in several general education classes upon determining that she would benefit from an education alongside her typically-developing peers for social and academic purposes. To "level the playing field" in K.L.'s mainstreamed general education classes, the District provided K.L. with accommodations. The District also provided K.L. with specially designed instruction (i.e., "special education") in reading and writing in a "resource room" for special students. For fourth and fifth grades, Parents paid for K.L. to attend a private school serving children with reading and writing difficulties.

K.L. returned to the District for her sixth grade education at Islander Middle School. The District reevaluated K.L. and determined that she was still eligible for special education. K.L.'s intelligence quotient ("IQ") revealed that she was in the average range at the low end. In accordance with K.L.'s individualized educational program, the District educated K.L. with specially designed instruction in reading, writing and mathematics. The District provided K.L. with accommodations in her general education classes including peers to help her read and take notes, use of spelling software, modified instructions, alternate exam methods, reduced assignments and extra time for assignments. K.L. ended her sixth grade year with an "A-" in special education reading, an "A-" in special education language arts, a "B+" in special education mathematics, an "A" in special education structured study, an "A-" in general education science, a "pass" in general education art and a "pass" in general education Spanish.

In seventh grade, K.L. continued with largely the same individualized educational program that she followed in sixth grade after her individualized educational program team concluded that the program was effective. At the end of seventh grade, K.L. received an "A-" in special education language arts (i.e., reading and writing), an "A" in special education mathematics, an "A-" in special education structured study, a "B+" in general education biology and an "A" in general education art.

In eighth grade, the District modified K.L.'s individualized educational program and provided 750 minutes per week of specially designed instruction in reading, writing, mathematics and study skills. K.L.'s accommodations basically stayed the same. Halfway through eighth grade, in January 2003, Mother contacted the District regarding K.L.'s frustrations with her language arts class. K.L. considered her language arts class "boring," "stupid" and "too hard." Specifically, K.L. did not like being singled out to give an answer in front of her classmates. In response, K.L.'s language arts teacher changed her teaching style, thereby galvanizing K.L. to increase her classroom participation and self-confidence.

K.L. took a standardized test of basic skills and scored in the second percentile of eighth graders. Although K.L. made progress on all of her eighth grade individualized educational program objectives, she failed to meet all writing objectives, two reading objectives, one mathematics objective and one study skills objective. At the end of eighth grade, K.L. received a "B" in special education language arts, a "B+" in special education mathematics, an "A" in special education structured study, an "A" in general education science, an "A" in general education social studies and a "pass" as a teacher's assistant.

The District reevaluated K.L. after eighth grade in June 2003. K.L.'s IQ showed improvement in mathematics and regression in numerical operations. One of K.L.'s teachers observed that K.L. performed much better in class than her standardized test results showed.... Based on K.L.'s great progress in eighth grade mathematics, K.L. was placed in a ninth grade algebra class with a difficulty level between special education mathematics and general education algebra.

During first semester of ninth grade at Mercer Island High School, not only did K.L. earn good grades, such as an "A-" in algebra, but she also participated in athletics and enjoyed an active (and sometimes distractive) social life. Unfortunately, in March 2004, K.L. missed three weeks of school due to an illness. One of K.L.'s teachers believed that K.L. "was not the same student" after she returned and that she was less motivated. K.L. turned in only half of her algebra homework and her quiz and test grades decreased as a result. At K.L.'s request, her individualized educational program team returned her to special education mathematics and provided her with another resource room period. . . .

At the end of ninth grade, K.L. received a "B" in special education English foundations, an "A-" in special education mathematics, a "C+" in general education history, a "B" in general education chemistry and an "A" as a teacher's assistant. K.L.'s grade point average was a 3.49, which was higher than both the median and mean grade point average for ninth graders in the District. By the end of ninth grade, K.L. met all of her mathematics and study skills individualized educational program objectives, however, she did not meet two of her reading objectives and any of her writing objectives. Nevertheless, K.L.'s individualized educational program team thought that K.L. "had a very successful year, her grades have been high and though at times she is frustrated or afraid, she has managed to tackle the projects with support." Unbeknownst to anyone at the District, Mother completed much of K.L.'s ninth grade homework, sometimes even in K.L.'s absence.

Shortly after ninth grade concluded, in June 2004, the District held an individualized educational program meeting and presented a proposed tenth grade individualized educational program to Parents. The proposed program provided 972 minutes per week of specially designed instruction in reading, writing, mathematics, study skills and transitions. K.L.'s reading goal was to increase reading decoding and comprehension skills on grade-level materials. K.L.'s written language goal was to increase written expression skills in a more independent manner. The individualized educational program provided most of the same accommodations as K.L.'s ninth grade individualized educational program with the addition of access to books on tape. The individualized educational program's transition statement indicated that K.L.'s programming "is aimed at attending a community or technical college." Parents told the District that they were displeased with K.L.'s ninth grade education and were "looking at other options." This was the first time that Parents had ever expressed dissatisfaction with K.L.'s education.

On the same day, Parents applied to Landmark School, a private residential school in Massachusetts exclusively for learning-disabled students. . . .

Later in June 2004, Parents sent the District a letter requesting an independent educational evaluation at the District's expense to be performed by Dr. Deborah Hill. . . .

Dr. Hill evaluated K.L. in early July 2004. Dr. Hill found that K.L. was generally average and had an IQ of 101. K.L. scored in the borderline or extremely low range in written comprehension and written language. Dr. Hill concluded that K.L.'s special education at the District had been inadequate because K.L. needed an intensive approach to remedy her disability. Ultimately, Dr. Hill determined, no public school in Washington could provide K.L. with an appropriate education. Dr. Hill recommended Landmark School because of its focus on improving phonological awareness skills.

. . . .

On June 6, 2005, Plaintiffs filed a due process hearing request pursuant to 20 U.S.C. § 1415(f), seeking reimbursement for K.L.'s Landmark School tuition and expenses. . . .

K.L. completed tenth, eleventh and twelfth grades at Landmark School. K.L.'s total expenses were $46,479.90 for tenth grade, $50,681.24 for eleventh grade and $54,838.54 for twelfth grade.

II

The ALJ conducted the due process hearing over the course of eleven days in September and October 2005. The ALJ concluded that the District provided a free appropriate public education to K.L. as required by *Rowley* and denied tuition reimbursement . . . . The district court reversed and remanded. After examining congressional findings added in the 1997 Individuals with Disabilities Education Act amendment and the definition of "transition services," the district court concluded that Congress sought to supersede the "educational benefit" standard set forth in *Rowley.* The district court's analysis yielded the following new free appropriate public education standard focused on transition services:

> [W]hether the District's approach to [the student's] educational challenges met the IDEA standard of "equality of opportunity, full participation, independent living, and economic self-sufficiency" for the minor and whether the programs developed for her conferred a "meaningful educational benefit" in light of the IDEA's goals.

The district court instructed the ALJ that under the new standard, K.L. did not receive a free appropriate public education in eighth, ninth and tenth grades. *See* ("Parents are correct that the failure of the IEPs to focus on progressing K.L. toward self-sufficiency (i.e., independent living) and her desired goal of post-secondary education represents a failure to confer the benefit contemplated by the IDEA."). The ALJ's only tasks on remand were to determine whether Landmark School was an appropriate placement and to fashion relief.

On remand, the ALJ concluded that K.L.'s placement at Landmark School was appropriate. The ALJ awarded reimbursement for tuition and related expenses for tenth and eleventh grades based on the district court's holding that K.L. did not receive a free appropriate public education in those grades. However, the ALJ equitably reduced tenth grade reimbursement by the cost of seven months of enrollment at Landmark School after finding that Parents unreasonably delayed the District's reevaluation of K.L. prior to her tenth grade year. The ALJ awarded reimbursement for twelfth grade as "compensatory education" based on the district court's holding that K.L. did not receive a free appropriate public education in eighth and ninth grades. Both parties sought district court review of the ALJ's second decision.

The district court mostly upheld the ALJ's decision. The district court did not impose the ALJ's equitable reduction. The district court ordered the District to pay for three years of Landmark School and $160,687.50 in attorneys' fees. This appeal followed.

III

"The IDEA provides federal funds to assist state and local agencies in educating children with disabilities, but conditions such funding on compliance with certain goals and procedures."

. . . .

In 1982, the Supreme Court rendered its seminal decision construing the Act and the scope of a free appropriate public education in *Board of Education of the Hendrick Hudson Central School District v. Rowley*, 458 U.S. 176 (1982). The Court noted that "Congress was rather sketchy in establishing substantive requirements." The Court concluded that states must provide a "basic floor of opportunity" to disabled students, not a "potential-maximizing education." "Congress did not impose upon the States any greater substantive educational standard than would be necessary to make such access meaningful." Phrased another way, states must "confer some educational benefit upon the handicapped child."

To assist courts in this labyrinth of experts, educational policy and charged emotions, the Court established a two-part test to determine whether a state has provided a free appropriate public education. "First, has the State complied with the procedures set forth in the Act? And second, is the individualized educational program developed through the Act's procedures reasonably calculated to enable the child to receive educational benefits?" "If these requirements are met, the State has complied with the obligations imposed by Congress and the courts can require no more."

Congress amended the Act in 1983. Congress did not alter the definition of a free appropriate public education or indicate its disapproval with *Rowley*. . . .

Congress amended the Act again in 1986. Congress did not change the definition of a free appropriate public education,, or indicate disapproval with *Rowley*. . . .

Congress' next amendment came in 1990 when the Act's name was changed to the "Individuals with Disabilities Education Act." Congress again did not change the definition of a free appropriate public education, or indicate disapproval with the *Rowley* free appropriate public education standard. . . .

Congress amended the Individuals with Disabilities Education Act in 1997, the effect of which is disputed in the present litigation. Even though Congress added numerous new findings, Congress did not indicate disapproval with *Rowley*. Congress enacted the same definition of a free appropriate public education for all intents and purposes. Congress newly required, "beginning at age 14, and updated annually, a statement of the transition service needs of the child . . . that focuses on the child's courses of study (such as participation in advanced-placement courses or a vocational education program)." *Id.*

. . . .

V

The District argues that the district court erred in concluding that Congress sought to supersede *Rowley* or otherwise change the free appropriate public education standard.

. . . .

In addition to the "transition services" definition, the district court also relied on three new congressional findings to support its conclusion that the 1997 amendment dramatically changed the free appropriate public education standard. First, Congress found that "[s]ince the enactment and implementation of the Education for All Handicapped Children Act of 1975, this Act has been successful in ensuring children with disabilities and the families of such children access to a free appropriate public education and in improving educational results for children with disabilities." Second, Congress found that "the implementation of this Act has been impeded by low expectations, and an insufficient focus on applying replicable research on proven methods of teaching and learning for children with disabilities." Third, Congress found that "[i]mproving educational results for children with disabilities is an essential element of our national policy of ensuring equality of opportunity, full participation, independent living, and economic self-sufficiency for individuals with disabilities."

. . . .

We conclude that the district court misinterpreted Congress' intent. Had Congress sought to change the free appropriate public education "educational benefit" standard-a standard that courts have followed vis-à-vis *Rowley* since 1982-it would have expressed a clear intent to do so. Instead, three omissions suggest that Congress intended to keep *Rowley* intact. First, Congress did not change the definition of a free appropriate public education in any material respect. If Congress desired to change the free appropriate public education standard, the most logical way to do so would have been to amend the free appropriate public education definition itself. Second, Congress did not indicate in its definition of "transition services," or elsewhere, that a disabled student could not receive a free appropriate public education absent the attainment of transition goals. Third, Congress did not express disagreement with the "educational benefit" standard or indicate that it sought to supersede *Rowley.* In fact, Congress did not even mention *Rowley.*

In re-enacting the free appropriate public education definition in 1997, as Congress had done in the Act's three prior amendments, Congress presumably was aware of *Rowley* and its renowned "educational benefit" free appropriate public education standard.

We hold that the district court erred in declaring *Rowley* superseded. The proper standard to determine whether a disabled child has received a free appropriate public education is the "educational benefit" standard set forth by the Supreme Court in *Rowley.* Our holding is necessary to avoid the conclusion that Congress abrogated *sub silentio* the Supreme Court's decision in *Rowley.* On remand, the district court must review in the first instance the ALJ's determination that the District provided a free appropriate public education as required by *Rowley.*

VI

Although we remand to the district court the issue of substantive compliance with the Individuals with Disabilities Education Act so that the court can consider the matter in the first instance, we need not remand the procedural compliance issues because the district court's analysis did not turn on any disputed legal standards. The district court held that the District failed to confer a free appropriate public education based on procedural violations involving . . . a lack of specified minutes of instruction. . . .

[T]he District argues that the district court erred in concluding that the District committed a procedural violation by not specifying the minutes of instruction to be devoted to each of K.L.'s services in her individualized educational programs. . . . Under the circumstances of this case, we conclude that the amount of time to be devoted to K.L.'s services was appropriate to the specific services provided.

Even if the District did commit a procedural violation by failing to specify minutes, not every procedural violation results in the denial of a free appropriate public education. A procedural violation denies a free appropriate public education if it results in the loss of an educational opportunity, seriously infringes the parents' opportunity to participate in the IEP formulation process or causes a deprivation of educational benefits. Here, Plaintiffs fail to show how K.L. was prejudiced by the District's failure to specify the amount of services she was to receive. They do not allege that she was denied an educational benefit or missed an educational opportunity. Nor do they show that the parents' ability to participate in the individualized educational program formulation process was harmed. Indeed, the record suggests that even though the individualized educational program did not list the amount of services, everyone involved in the individualized educational team-including K.L.'s parents-knew of the amounts.

We hold that the District did not violate the Individuals with Disabilities Education Act by failing to specifying minutes of instruction in K.L.'s individualized educational program. We further hold that any procedural violation that may have occurred did not deny K.L. a free appropriate public education, and reverse the district court.

VII

For the reasons discussed, we conclude that the district court erred in holding that the definition of a free appropriate public education set forth by the Supreme Court in *Rowley* has been superseded, and accordingly, vacate its orders. In addition, we reverse the district court's conclusions that the District committed procedural violations of the Individuals with Disabilities Education Act that resulted in the denial of a free appropriate public education.

. . . .

34 C.F.R. § 300.322 Parent Participation.

(a) Public agency responsibility—general. Each public agency must take steps to ensure that one or both of the parents of a child with a disability are present at each IEP Team meeting or are afforded the opportunity to participate, including—

(1) Notifying parents of the meeting early enough to ensure that they will have an opportunity to attend; and

(2) Scheduling the meeting at a mutually agreed on time and place.

(b) Information provided to parents.

(1) The notice required under paragraph (a)(1) of this section must—

(i) Indicate the purpose, time, and location of the meeting and who will be in attendance; and

(ii) Inform the parents of the provisions in § 300.321(a)(6) and (c) (relating to the participation of other individuals on the IEP Team who have knowledge or special expertise about the child), and § 300.321(f) (relating to the participation of the Part C service coordinator or other representatives of the Part C system at the initial IEP Team meeting for a child previously served under Part C of the Act).

(2) For a child with a disability beginning not later than the first IEP to be in effect when the child turns 16, or younger if determined appropriate by the IEP Team, the notice also must—

(i) Indicate—

(A) That a purpose of the meeting will be the consideration of the postsecondary goals and transition services for the child, in accordance with § 300.320(b); and

(B) That the agency will invite the student; and

(ii) Identify any other agency that will be invited to send a representative.

(c) Other methods to ensure parent participation. If neither parent can attend an IEP Team meeting, the public agency must use other methods to ensure parent participation, including individual or conference telephone calls, consistent with § 300.328 (related to alternative means of meeting participation).

(d) Conducting an IEP Team meeting without a parent in attendance. A meeting may be conducted without a parent in attendance if the public agency is unable to convince the parents that they should attend. In this case, the public agency must keep a record of its attempts to arrange a mutually agreed on time and place, such as—

(1) Detailed records of telephone calls made or attempted and the results of those calls;

(2) Copies of correspondence sent to the parents and any responses received; and

(3) Detailed records of visits made to the parent's home or place of employment and the results of those visits.

....

Post Problem Discussion

1. In *Rowley*, the Court noted, "We do not attempt today to establish any one test for determining the adequacy of educational benefits conferred upon all children covered by the Act." Despite this statement, have lower courts used *Rowley* as a "one-size fits all" test? What other approaches might courts take to determine if a student was provided with FAPE?

2. Numerous commentators have suggested that the *Rowley* standard is outdated given the changes in the IDEA since the decision.[5] The *J.L. v. Mercer Island Sch. Dist.* district court decision may have been the first federal court opinion to agree with these sentiments. The Ninth Circuit rejected the district court's approach and found that *Rowley* and the "some educational benefit" standard still applied. On remand under the "some educational benefit" standard, the district court upheld the original ALJ findings that it had originally overturned under the "meaningful educational benefit" standard and found that the public school had provided FAPE. These findings resulted in a very different outcome for the student. Review Scott F. Johnson, *Rowley Forever More? A Call for Clarity & Change*, 41 J.L. & Educ. 25 (2012), for an in-depth analysis of the *J.L. v. Mercer Island Sch. Dist.* cases and the impact that using the "some" versus the "meaningful" benefit standard had in the case.

Does *Endrew F.* resolve the "some" versus "meaningful" benefit debate? How does the standard in *Endrew F.* compare to the standard in *Rowley, D.S. v. Bayonne Bd. of Educ.*, and *J.L. v. Mercer Island Sch. Dist.*?

3. In *Endrew F.*, the Court stated: "When a child is fully integrated in the regular classroom, as the Act prefers, what that typically means is providing a level of instruction reasonably calculated to permit advancement through the general

---

5. *See, e.g.*, Andrea Blau, *The IDEIA and the Right to an "Appropriate" Education*, 2007 B.Y.U. Educ. & L.J. 1 (2007); Philip T.K. Daniel, *"Some Benefit" or "Maximum Benefit": Does The No Child Left Behind Act Render Greater Educational Entitlement to Students With Disabilities*, 37 J.L. & Educ. 347 (2008); Dixie Snow Huefner, *Updating the FAPE Standard Under IDEA*, 37 J.L. & Educ. 367 (2008); Scott F. Johnson, *Reexamining Rowley: A New Focus in Special Education Law*, 2003 B.Y.U. Educ. & L.J. 561 (2003).

curriculum." 137 S. Ct. at 1000. It included a footnote that added the following caveat: "This guidance should not be interpreted as an inflexible rule. We declined to hold in *Rowley*, and do not hold today, that 'every handicapped child who is advancing from grade to grade . . . is automatically receiving a [FAPE].'" *Id.* at 1002 n.2.

What role did grades and advancement from grade to grade play in the court decisions in the problem materials? What role should they play in deciding if Shane received FAPE.

4. As noted in *J.L. v. Mercer Island Sch. Dist.*, courts use something of a "no harm no foul" approach to procedural violations (meaning those affecting the parents' rights to notice, participation, or consent in the special education process). As a result, not every procedural violation is seen as a denial of FAPE. Courts generally find that a procedural violation results in a denial of FAPE only when it results in the school failing to provide educational benefit, or restricts the parents' ability to participate fully in their child's education. The IDEA codified this approach in 2004, stating that a procedural violation can result in a failure to provide FAPE only when it 1) impedes the child's right to FAPE, 2) significantly impedes parent participation in decision-making about FAPE, or 3) caused a deprivation of educational benefit. 20 U.S.C. § 1415(f)(3)(E). The IDEA still permits a hearing officer or court to order a school to comply with procedural requirements going forward even if none of these criteria are met. *Id.*

Does this approach adequately protect the parental role in the process? What if the school fails to adhere to any of the procedural requirements, but nonetheless provides the student with the services necessary to receive FAPE? Is an order from a hearing officer or court directing the school to follow procedures going forward likely to be effective? Conversely, what would an appropriate remedy be if not a prospective order to follow procedures?

5. If we assume that Shane was not provided FAPE, what should the remedy be? Failure to provide FAPE may support an award to parents for tuition for a unilateral placement at a private special education school as was the case in *D.S. v. Bayonne Bd. of Educ.* This subject is covered in detail in Section 12.04.

Courts are split on whether monetary damages are available for IDEA violations.[6] Do you think courts should award monetary damages for the denial of FAPE? Why or why not?

6. A common remedy for the denial of FAPE is "compensatory education," which provides the student with additional services for some period of time to make up for

---

6. For further explanations of the different court views on the topic, see Terry Jean Seligmann, *A Diller, A Dollar: Section 1983 Damage Claims in Special Education Lawsuits*, 36 GA. L. REV. 465 (2002); Suzanne Soloman, Note, *The Intersection of 42 U.S.C. § 1983 and The Individuals With Disabilities Education Act* 76 FORDHAM L. REV. 3065 (2008); Mark C. Weber, *Disability Harassment in the Public Schools*, 43 WM. & MARY L. REV. 1079, 1113–1119 (2002).

the lack of progress or FAPE in the past. In *Millay v. Surry Sch. Dep't*, 2011 U.S. Dist. LEXIS 31048 (D. Me. Mar. 23, 2011), the Maine Federal District Court summarized how the remedy is viewed in the First Circuit:

> Compensatory education is a surrogate for the warranted education that a disabled child may have missed during periods when his IEP was so inappropriate that he was effectively denied a FAPE. "[C]ompensatory education is not an automatic entitlement but, rather, a discretionary remedy for nonfeasance or misfeasance in connection with a school system's obligations under the IDEA." As a discretionary equitable remedy, the extent of a compensatory education award is very dependent on the particular facts and circumstances of the case.
>
> The nature and extent of compensatory education services which federal courts have recognized varies according to the facts and circumstances of a given case. Such an award may include extra assistance in the form of tutoring, or summer school while students are still within the age of entitlement for regular services under the Act, or an extended period of assistance beyond the statutory age of entitlement. Compensatory education serves to replace the "educational services the child should have received in the first place" and "should aim to place disabled children in the same position they would have occupied but for the school district's violations of IDEA."

Elements of compensatory education may continue after age 21. *See Ferren C. v. Sch. Dist. of Phila.*, 612 F.3d 712 (3d Cir. 2010). What do you think is a reasonable time for a school district to try to provide educational benefit and make some progress? If you were a judge or a hearing officer, what kind of compensatory education would you order for Shane?

§ 12.04 Placement

After the IEP team develops the student's IEP, it must choose a placement that can implement the IEP. The IDEA includes a "least restrictive environment" requirement, which states that students with disabilities should be educated with students without disabilities to the "maximum extent appropriate." 20 U.S.C. § 1412(a)(5). As a result, the public school that the student would attend if they did not have a disability is often the placement of choice by the team. *See* 34 C.F.R. § 300.116 (noting that student's placement should be as close as possible to the student's home, and unless some other arrangement is required, should be the school he or she would attend if non-disabled).

However, if the public school cannot implement the student's IEP or provide the student FAPE, the public school must fund a placement that can. Sometimes this means sending the student to a private special education school. When the public school places a student at a private special education school, the student retains all of the rights that they would have if they attended public school. 34 C.F.R. § 300.146.

Parents who are dissatisfied with the special education services provided (or not provided) to their child by the public school, can also place their child at a private special education school without the agreement or assistance of the public school and then try to recover the tuition and related costs from the public school. This is called a "unilateral placement" when FAPE is at issue, and it is considered to be something of a "self-help" remedy under the law. The parents pay for the placement and all related expenses up front, and then have the option of trying to receive reimbursement for these expenses from the local school district. 34 C.F.R. § 300.148.

In *School Comm. of Burlington v. Department of Educ.*, 471 U.S. 359, 369–70 (1985), the United States Supreme Court determined that unilateral placements were an appropriate remedy under the IDEA for a public school district's failure to provide FAPE, noting:

> We conclude that the Act authorizes such reimbursement. The statute directs the court to "grant such relief as [it] determines is appropriate." The ordinary meaning of these words confers broad discretion on the court. The type of relief is not further specified, except that it must be "appropriate." . . . As already noted, this is principally to provide handicapped children with "a free appropriate public education which emphasizes special education and related services designed to meet their unique needs." . . . In a case where a court determines that a private placement desired by the parents was proper under the Act and that an IEP calling for placement in a public school was inappropriate, it seems clear beyond cavil that "appropriate" relief would include a prospective injunction directing the school officials to develop and implement at public expense an IEP placing the child in a private school.
>
> If the administrative and judicial review under the Act could be completed in a matter of weeks, rather than years, it would be difficult to imagine a case in which such prospective injunctive relief would not be sufficient. As this case so vividly demonstrates, however, the review process is ponderous. A final judicial decision on the merits of an IEP will in most instances come a year or more after the school term covered by that IEP has passed. In the meantime, the parents who disagree with the proposed IEP are faced with a choice: go along with the IEP to the detriment of their child if it turns out to be inappropriate or pay for what they consider to be the appropriate placement. If they choose the latter course, which conscientious parents who have adequate means and who are reasonably confident of their assessment normally would, it would be an empty victory to have a court tell them several years later that they were right but that these expenditures could not in a proper case be reimbursed by the school officials. If that were the case, the child's right to a *free* appropriate public education, the parents' right to participate fully in developing a proper IEP, and all of the procedural safeguards would be less than complete. Because Congress undoubtedly did not intend this result, we are confident that by empowering the

> court to grant "appropriate" relief Congress meant to include retroactive reimbursement to parents as an available remedy in a proper case.

Under *Burlington*, parents are entitled to reimbursement for the tuition and related expenses only if the local school district did not make FAPE available to the child in a timely manner, and if the placement chosen by the parents is appropriate under the IDEA. A subsequent Supreme Court decision determined that the placement chosen by the parents does not have to meet state standards to be appropriate. *Florence County Sch. Dist. v. Carter*, 510 U.S. 7 (1993).

Amendments to the IDEA after the *Burlington* and *Carter* decisions included specific provisions about unilateral placements that require parents to provide schools with notice of their intent to seek unilateral placements and include some other requirements. *See* 20 U.S.C. § 1412(a)(10)(C); 34 C.F.R. § 300.148. Court decisions interpreting these statutory requirements have reached varied results about their meaning and the parameters of unilateral placements under the IDEA. In 2009, the United States Supreme Court weighed in again on the meaning of the statute in *Forest Grove Sch. Dist. v. T.A.*, 557 U.S. 230 (2009). The following problem explores this issue.

Problem 3: Unilateral Placements

Laurie is a third grade student at a public elementary school. She has struggled at school for the past two years, and her parents are not sure why. Many of her difficulties come with peer relationships. Laurie feels that other students pick on her and harass her. Laurie's parents have complained to the school about these issues, but the school has not resolved them to the parents' satisfaction. Laurie begins resisting going to school, and each day becomes a battle with Laurie and her parents over attending school and completing her homework. Desperate and unsure what else to do, the parents remove Laurie from the public school and place her in a private religious school recommended by their church pastor.

At the private school, Laurie does much better with peer relations but struggles academically, and the private school teacher recommends that the parents contact the public school for a special education evaluation. At the parents' request, the public school evaluates Laurie and concludes that she has ADHD and some personality disorders, but is not eligible for special education services because her needs could be met without special education and related services. The parents decide that Laurie needs to attend a school that can address her disabilities, so they enroll her in a private special education school at their expense for the fourth grade and seek reimbursement from the public school.

The school district argues that the parents should be denied reimbursement because Laurie never received special education services at the public school, is not enrolled in the public school, and because the parents did not provide proper notice as required by the IDEA and its implementing regulations. You are the hearing officer in a state and a federal judicial circuit that does not have any court decisions on the topic. How do you rule and why?

Problem Materials

✓ IDEA, 20 U.S.C. § 1412(a)(10)(C)

✓ IDEA regulations, 34 C.F.R. § 300.148

✓ *Forest Grove Sch. Dist. v. T.A.*, 557 U.S. 230 (2009)

20 U.S.C. § 1412(a)(10)(C)[7]

(i) In general

Subject to subparagraph (A), this subchapter does not require a local educational agency to pay for the cost of education, including special education and related services, of a child with a disability at a private school or facility if that agency made a free appropriate public education available to the child and the parents elected to place the child in such private school or facility.

(ii) Reimbursement for private school placement

If the parents of a child with a disability, who previously received special education and related services under the authority of a public agency, enroll the child in a private elementary or secondary school without the consent of or referral by the public agency, a court or a hearing officer may require the agency to reimburse the parents for the cost of that enrollment if the court or hearing officer finds that the agency had not made a free appropriate public education available to the child in a timely manner prior to that enrollment.

(iii) The cost of reimbursement . . . may be reduced or denied—

(I) if—

(aa) at the most recent IEP meeting that the parents attended prior to removal of the child from the public school, the parents did not inform the IEP Team that they were rejecting the placement proposed by the public agency to provide a free appropriate public education to their child, including stating their concerns and their intent to enroll their child in a private school at public expense; or

(bb) 10 business days (including any holidays that occur on a business day) prior to the removal of the child from the public school, the parents did not give written notice to the public agency of the information described in item (aa);

(II) if, prior to the parents' removal of the child from the public school, the public agency informed the parents, through the notice requirements

7. The cases in the problem materials refer to the 1997 amendments to the IDEA and the language of the statute in those amendments. The IDEA was amended again in 2004, but the amendments did not change the relevant portions of the statute which are provided here in Problem 3.

described in section 1415(b)(3) of this title, of its intent to evaluate the child (including a statement of the purpose of the evaluation that was appropriate and reasonable), but the parents did not make the child available for such evaluation; or

(III) upon a judicial finding of unreasonableness with respect to actions taken by the parents.

(iv) Exception

Notwithstanding the notice requirement in clause (iii)(I), the cost of reimbursement—

(I) shall not be reduced or denied for failure to provide such notice if—

(aa) the school prevented the parent from providing such notice;

(bb) the parents had not received notice, pursuant to section 1415 of this title, of the notice requirement in clause (iii)(I); or

(cc) compliance with clause (iii)(I) would likely result in physical harm to the child;

34 C.F.R. § 300.148 Placement of children by parents when FAPE is at issue.

(a) General. This part does not require an LEA to pay for the cost of education, including special education and related services, of a child with a disability at a private school or facility if that agency made FAPE available to the child and the parents elected to place the child in a private school or facility. However, the public agency must include that child in the population whose needs are addressed consistent with §§ 300.131 through 300.144.

(b) Disagreements about FAPE. Disagreements between the parents and a public agency regarding the availability of a program appropriate for the child, and the question of financial reimbursement, are subject to the due process procedures in §§ 300.504 through 300.520.

(c) Reimbursement for private school placement. If the parents of a child with a disability, who previously received special education and related services under the authority of a public agency, enroll the child in a private preschool, elementary school, or secondary school without the consent of or referral by the public agency, a court or a hearing officer may require the agency to reimburse the parents for the cost of that enrollment if the court or hearing officer finds that the agency had not made FAPE available to the child in a timely manner prior to that enrollment and that the private placement is appropriate. A parental placement may be found to be appropriate by a hearing officer or a court even if it does not meet the State standards that apply to education provided by the SEA and LEAs.

(d) Limitation on reimbursement. The cost of reimbursement described in paragraph (c) of this section may be reduced or denied—

(1) If—

(i) At the most recent IEP Team meeting that the parents attended prior to removal of the child from the public school, the parents did not inform the IEP Team that they were rejecting the placement proposed by the public agency to provide FAPE to their child, including stating their concerns and their intent to enroll their child in a private school at public expense; or

(ii) At least ten (10) business days (including any holidays that occur on a business day) prior to the removal of the child from the public school, the parents did not give written notice to the public agency of the information described in paragraph (d)(1)(i) of this section;

(2) If, prior to the parents' removal of the child from the public school, the public agency informed the parents, through the notice requirements described in § 300.503(a)(1), of its intent to evaluate the child (including a statement of the purpose of the evaluation that was appropriate and reasonable), but the parents did not make the child available for the evaluation; or

(3) Upon a judicial finding of unreasonableness with respect to actions taken by the parents.

(e) Exception. Notwithstanding the notice requirement in paragraph (d)(1) of this section, the cost of reimbursement—

(1) Must not be reduced or denied for failure to provide the notice if—

(i) The school prevented the parents from providing the notice;

(ii) The parents had not received notice, pursuant to § 300.504, of the notice requirement in paragraph (d)(1) of this section; or

(iii) Compliance with paragraph (d)(1) of this section would likely result in physical harm to the child; and

(2) May, in the discretion of the court or a hearing officer, not be reduced or denied for failure to provide this notice if—

(i) The parents are not literate or cannot write in English; or

(ii) Compliance with paragraph (d)(1) of this section would likely result in serious emotional harm to the child.

Forest Grove Sch. Dist. v. T.A.

557 U.S. 230 (2009)

The Supreme Court rules that the IDEA does not categorically bar parents from receiving reimbursement when the child has not previously received special education services from the public school.

Justice Stevens delivered the opinion of the Court.

The Individuals with Disabilities Education Act (IDEA or Act), 84 Stat. 175, as amended, 20 U.S.C. § 1400 *et seq.*, requires States receiving federal funding to make a "free appropriate public education" (FAPE) available to all children with disabilities residing in the State, § 1412(a)(1)(A). We have previously held that when a public school fails to provide a FAPE and a child's parents place the child in an appropriate private school without the school district's consent, a court may require the district to reimburse the parents for the cost of the private education. *See School Comm. of Burlington v. Department of Ed. of Mass.*, 471 U.S. 359, 370 (1985). The question presented in this case is whether the IDEA Amendments of 1997 (Amendments), 111 Stat. 37, categorically prohibit reimbursement for private-education costs if a child has not "previously received special education and related services under the authority of a public agency." § 1412(a)(10)(C)(ii). We hold that the Amendments impose no such categorical bar.

Respondent T.A. attended public schools in the Forest Grove School District (School District or District) from the time he was in kindergarten through the winter of his junior year of high school. From kindergarten through eighth grade, respondent's teachers observed that he had trouble paying attention in class and completing his assignments. When respondent entered high school, his difficulties increased.

In December 2000, during respondent's freshman year, his mother contacted the school counselor to discuss respondent's problems with his schoolwork. At the end of the school year, respondent was evaluated by a school psychologist. After interviewing him, examining his school records, and administering cognitive ability tests, the psychologist concluded that respondent did not need further testing for any learning disabilities or other health impairments, including attention deficit hyperactivity disorder (ADHD). The psychologist and two other school officials discussed the evaluation results with respondent's mother in June 2001, and all agreed that respondent did not qualify for special-education services. Respondent's parents did not seek review of that decision, although the hearing examiner later found that the School District's evaluation was legally inadequate because it failed to address all areas of suspected disability, including ADHD.

With extensive help from his family, respondent completed his sophomore year at Forest Grove High School, but his problems worsened during his junior year. In February 2003, respondent's parents discussed with the School District the possibility of respondent completing high school through a partnership program with the local community college. They also sought private professional advice, and in March 2003 respondent was diagnosed with ADHD and a number of disabilities related to learning and memory. Advised by the private specialist that respondent would do best in a structured, residential learning environment, respondent's parents enrolled him at a private academy that focuses on educating children with special needs.

Four days after enrolling him in private school, respondent's parents hired a lawyer to ascertain their rights and to give the School District written notice of respondent's private placement. A few weeks later, in April 2003, respondent's parents requested an administrative due process hearing regarding respondent's eligibility for special-education services. In June 2003, the District engaged a school psychologist to assist in determining whether respondent had a disability that significantly interfered with his educational performance. Respondent's parents cooperated with the District during the evaluation process. In July 2003, a multidisciplinary team met to discuss whether respondent satisfied IDEA's disability criteria and concluded that he did not because his ADHD did not have a sufficiently significant adverse impact on his educational performance. Because the School District maintained that respondent was not eligible for special-education services and therefore declined to provide an individualized education program (IEP), respondent's parents left him enrolled at the private academy for his senior year.

The administrative review process resumed in September 2003. After considering the parties' evidence, including the testimony of numerous experts, the hearing officer issued a decision in January 2004 finding that respondent's ADHD adversely affected his educational performance and that the School District failed to meet its obligations under IDEA in not identifying respondent as a student eligible for special-education services. Because the District did not offer respondent a FAPE and his private-school placement was appropriate under IDEA, the hearing officer ordered the District to reimburse respondent's parents for the cost of the private-school tuition.

The School District sought judicial review pursuant to § 1415(i)(2), arguing that the hearing officer erred in granting reimbursement. The District Court accepted the hearing officer's findings of fact but set aside the reimbursement award after finding that the 1997 Amendments categorically bar reimbursement of private-school tuition for students who have not "previously received special education and related services under the authority of a public agency." § 612(a)(10)(C)(ii), 111 Stat. 63 20 U.S.C. § 1412(a)(10)(C)(ii). The District Court further held that, "[e]ven assuming that tuition reimbursement may be ordered in an extreme case for a student not receiving special education services, under general principles of equity where the need for special education was obvious to school authorities," the facts of this case do not support equitable relief. App. to Pet. for Cert. 53a.

The Court of Appeals for the Ninth Circuit reversed and remanded for further proceedings. . . .

Because the Courts of Appeals that have considered this question have reached inconsistent results, we granted certiorari to determine whether § 1412(a)(10)(C) establishes a categorical bar to tuition reimbursement for students who have not previously received special-education services under the authority of a public education agency.

Justice Rehnquist's opinion for a unanimous Court in *Burlington* provides the pertinent background for our analysis of the question presented. In that case, respondent challenged the appropriateness of the IEP developed for his child by public-school officials. The child had previously received special-education services through the public school. While administrative review was pending, private specialists advised respondent that the child would do best in a specialized private educational setting, and respondent enrolled the child in private school without the school district's consent. The hearing officer concluded that the IEP was not adequate to meet the child's educational needs and that the school district therefore failed to provide the child a FAPE. Finding also that the private-school placement was appropriate under IDEA, the hearing officer ordered the school district to reimburse respondent for the cost of the private-school tuition.

We granted certiorari in *Burlington* to determine whether IDEA authorizes reimbursement for the cost of private education when a parent or guardian unilaterally enrolls a child in private school because the public school has proposed an inadequate IEP and thus failed to provide a FAPE. The Act at that time made no express reference to the possibility of reimbursement, but it authorized a court to "grant such relief as the court determines is appropriate." § 1415(i)(2)(C)(iii). In determining the scope of the relief authorized, we noted that "the ordinary meaning of these words confers broad discretion on the court" and that, absent any indication to the contrary, what relief is "appropriate" must be determined in light of the Act's broad purpose of providing children with disabilities a FAPE, including through publicly funded private-school placements when necessary. Accordingly, we held that the provision's grant of authority includes "the power to order school authorities to reimburse parents for their expenditures on private special-education services if the court ultimately determines that such placement, rather than a proposed IEP, is proper under the Act."

Our decision rested in part on the fact that administrative and judicial review of a parent's complaint often takes years. We concluded that, having mandated that participating States provide a FAPE for every student, Congress could not have intended to require parents to either accept an inadequate public-school education pending adjudication of their claim or bear the cost of a private education if the court ultimately determined that the private placement was proper under the Act. Eight years later, we unanimously reaffirmed the availability of reimbursement in *Florence County School Dist. Four v. Carter*, 510 U.S. 7, (1993) (holding that reimbursement may be appropriate even when a child is placed in a private school that has not been approved by the State).

The dispute giving rise to the present litigation differs from those in *Burlington* and *Carter* in that it concerns not the adequacy of a proposed IEP but the School District's failure to provide an IEP at all. And, unlike respondent, the children in those cases had previously received public special-education services. These differences are insignificant, however, because our analysis in the earlier cases depended on the language and purpose of the Act and not the particular facts involved. Moreover, when a child requires special-education services, a school district's failure to propose an IEP of any kind is at least as serious a violation of its responsibilities under IDEA as a failure to provide an adequate IEP. It is thus clear that the reasoning of *Burlington* and *Carter* applies equally to this case. The only question is whether the 1997 Amendments require a different result.

Congress enacted IDEA in 1970 to ensure that all children with disabilities are provided "'a free appropriate public education which emphasizes special education and related services designed to meet their unique needs [and] to assure that the rights of [such] children and their parents or guardians are protected.'" After examining the States' progress under IDEA, Congress found in 1997 that substantial gains had been made in the area of special education but that more needed to be done to guarantee children with disabilities adequate access to appropriate services. *See* S. Rep. No. 105-17, p. 5 (1997). The 1997 Amendments were intended "to place greater emphasis on improving student performance and ensuring that children with disabilities receive a quality public education." *Id.*, at 3.

Consistent with that goal, the Amendments preserved the Act's purpose of providing a FAPE to all children with disabilities. And they did not change the text of the provision we considered in Burlington, § 1415(i)(2)(C)(iii), which gives courts broad authority to grant "appropriate" relief, including reimbursement for the cost of private special education when a school district fails to provide a FAPE. "Congress is presumed to be aware of an administrative or judicial interpretation of a statute and to adopt that interpretation when it re-enacts a statute without change." Accordingly, absent a clear expression elsewhere in the Amendments of Congress' intent to repeal some portion of that provision or to abrogate our decisions in *Burlington* and *Carter*, we will continue to read § 1415(i)(2)(C)(iii) to authorize the relief respondent seeks.

. . . .

Looking primarily to clauses (i) and (ii), the School District argues that Congress intended § 1412(a)(10)(C) to provide the exclusive source of authority for courts to order reimbursement when parents unilaterally enroll a child in private school. According to the District, clause (i) provides a safe harbor for school districts that provide a FAPE by foreclosing reimbursement in those circumstances. Clause (ii) then sets forth the circumstance in which reimbursement is appropriate—namely, when a school district fails to provide a FAPE to a child who has previously received special-education services through the public school. The District contends that because § 1412(a)(10)(C) only discusses reimbursement for children who have previously received special-education services through the public school, IDEA only authorizes reimbursement in that circumstance. The dissent agrees.

For several reasons, we find this argument unpersuasive. First, the School District's reading of the Act is not supported by its text and context, as the 1997 Amendments do not expressly prohibit reimbursement under the circumstances of this case, and the District offers no evidence that Congress intended to supersede our decisions in *Burlington* and *Carter*. Clause (i)'s safe harbor explicitly bars reimbursement only when a school district makes a FAPE available by correctly identifying a child as having a disability and proposing an IEP adequate to meet the child's needs. The clause says nothing about the availability of reimbursement when a school district fails to provide a FAPE. Indeed, its statement that reimbursement *is not* authorized when a school district provides a FAPE could be read to indicate that reimbursement *is* authorized when a school district does not fulfill that obligation.

Clause (ii) likewise does not support the District's position. Because that clause is phrased permissively, stating only that courts "may require" reimbursement in those circumstances, it does not foreclose reimbursement awards in other circumstances. Together with clauses (iii) and (iv), clause (ii) is best read as elaborating on the general rule that courts may order reimbursement when a school district fails to provide a FAPE by listing factors that may affect a reimbursement award in the common situation in which a school district has provided a child with some special-education services and the child's parents believe those services are inadequate. Referring as they do to students who have previously received special-education services through a public school, clauses (ii) through (iv) are premised on a history of cooperation and together encourage school districts and parents to continue to cooperate in developing and implementing an appropriate IEP before resorting to a unilateral private placement. The clauses of § 1412(a)(10)(C) are thus best read as elucidative rather than exhaustive. . . .

This reading of § 1412(a)(10)(C) is necessary to avoid the conclusion that Congress abrogated *sub silentio* our decisions in *Burlington* and *Carter*. In those cases, we construed § 1415(i)(2)(C)(iii) to authorize reimbursement when a school district fails to provide a FAPE and a child's private-school placement is appropriate, without regard to the child's prior receipt of services. It would take more than Congress' failure to comment on the category of cases in which a child has not previously received special-education services for us to conclude that the Amendments substantially superseded our decisions and in large part repealed § 1415(i)(2)(C)(iii). *See Branch v. Smith*, 538 U.S. 254, 273 (2003) ("[A]bsent a clearly expressed congressional intention, repeals by implication are not favored" (internal quotation marks and citation omitted)). We accordingly adopt the reading of § 1412(a)(10)(C) that is consistent with those decisions.

The School District's reading of § 1412(a)(10)(C) is also at odds with the general remedial purpose underlying IDEA and the 1997 Amendments. . . .

Indeed, by immunizing a school district's refusal to find a child eligible for special-education services no matter how compelling the child's need, the School District's interpretation of § 1412(a)(10)(C) would produce a rule bordering on the irrational. It would be particularly strange for the Act to provide a remedy, as all agree it does, when a school district offers a child inadequate special-education services but to leave parents without relief in the more egregious situation in which the school district unreasonably denies a child access to such services altogether. That IDEA affords parents substantial procedural safeguards, including the right to challenge a school district's eligibility determination and obtain prospective relief, see post, at 11, is no answer. We roundly rejected that argument in *Burlington*, observing that the "review process is ponderous" and therefore inadequate to ensure that a school's failure to provide a FAPE is remedied with the speed necessary to avoid detriment to the child's education. Like *Burlington, see ibid.*, this case vividly demonstrates the problem of delay, as respondent's parents first sought a due process hearing in April 2003, and the District Court issued its decision in May 2005—almost a year after respondent graduated from high school. The dissent all but ignores these shortcomings of IDEA's procedural safeguards.

The School District advances two additional arguments for reading the Act to foreclose reimbursement in this case. First, the District contends that because IDEA was an exercise of Congress' authority under the Spending Clause, U.S. Const., Art. I, § 8, cl. 1, any conditions attached to a State's acceptance of funds must be stated unambiguously. *See Pennhurst State School and Hospital v. Halderman*, 451 U.S. 1, 17 (1981). Applying that principle, we held in *Arlington Central School Dist. Bd. of Ed. v. Murphy*, 548 U.S. 291, 304 (2006), that IDEA's fee-shifting provision, § 1415(i)(3)(B), does not authorize courts to award expert-services fees to prevailing parents in IDEA actions because the Act does not put States on notice of the possibility of such awards. But *Arlington* is readily distinguishable from this case. In accepting IDEA funding, States expressly agree to provide a FAPE to all children with disabilities. *See* § 1412(a)(1)(A). An order awarding reimbursement of private-education costs when a school district fails to provide a FAPE merely requires the district "to belatedly pay expenses that it should have paid all along." *Burlington*, 471 U.S., at 370-371. And States have in any event been on notice at least since our decision in *Burlington* that IDEA authorizes courts to order reimbursement of the costs of private special-education services in appropriate circumstances. *Pennhurst*'s notice requirement is thus clearly satisfied.

Finally, the District urges that respondent's reading of the Act will impose a substantial financial burden on public school districts and encourage parents to immediately enroll their children in private school without first endeavoring to cooperate with the school district. The dissent echoes this concern. *See post*, at 10. For several reasons, those fears are unfounded. Parents "are entitled to reimbursement *only* if a federal court concludes both that the public placement violated IDEA and the private school placement was proper under the Act." *Carter*, 510 U.S., at 15. And even then courts retain discretion to reduce the amount of a reimbursement award if the equities so warrant—for instance, if the parents failed to give the school district adequate notice of their intent to enroll the child in private school. In considering the equities, courts should generally presume that public-school officials are properly performing their obligations under IDEA. *See Schaffer v. Weast*, 546 U.S. 49, 62-63 (2005) (Stevens, J., concurring). As a result of these criteria and the fact that parents who "'unilaterally change their child's placement during the pendency of review proceedings, without the consent of state or local school officials, do so at their own financial risk,'" *Carter*, 510 U.S., at 15, quoting

Burlington, 471 U.S., at 373-374), the incidence of private-school placement at public expense is quite small.

The IDEA Amendments of 1997 did not modify the text of § 1415(i)(2)(C)(iii), and we do not read § 1412(a)(10)(C) to alter that provision's meaning. Consistent with our decisions in *Burlington* and *Carter*, we conclude that IDEA authorizes reimbursement for the cost of private special-education services when a school district fails to provide a FAPE and the private-school placement is appropriate, regardless of whether the child previously received special education or related services through the public school.

When a court or hearing officer concludes that a school district failed to provide a FAPE and the private placement was suitable, it must consider all relevant factors, including the notice provided by the parents and the school district's opportunities for evaluating the child, in determining whether reimbursement for some or all of the cost of the child's private education is warranted. As the Court of Appeals noted, the District Court did not properly consider the equities in this case and will need to undertake that analysis on remand. Accordingly, the judgment of the Court of Appeals is affirmed.

It is so ordered.

Justice Souter, with whom Justice Scalia and Justice Thomas join, dissenting.

I respectfully dissent.

School Comm. of Burlington v. Department of Ed. of Mass., 471 U.S. 359 (1985), held that the Education of the Handicapped Act, 84 Stat. 175, now known as the Individuals with Disabilities Education Act (IDEA), 20 U.S.C. § 1400 *et seq.*, authorized a district court to order reimbursement of private school tuition and expenses to parents who took their disabled child from public school because the school's special education services did not meet the child's needs. We said that, for want of any specific limitation, this remedy was within the general authorization for courts to award "such relief as [they] determin[e] is appropriate." § 1415(e)(2) (1982 ed.) (now codified at § 1415(i)(2)(C)(iii) (2006 ed.)). In 1997, however, Congress amended the IDEA with a number of provisions explicitly addressing the issue of "[p]ayment for education of children enrolled in private schools without consent of or referral by the public agency." § 1412(a)(10)(C). These amendments generally 35] prohibit reimbursement if the school district made a "free appropriate public education" (FAPE) available, § 1412(a)(10)(C)(i), and if they are to have any effect, there is no exception except by agreement, § 1412(a)(10)(B), or for a student who previously received special education services that were inadequate, § 1412(a)(10)(C)(ii). The majority says otherwise and holds that § 1412(a)(10)(C)(ii) places no limit on reimbursements for private tuition. The Court does not find the provision clear enough to affect the rule in *Burlington*, and it does not believe Congress meant to limit public reimbursement for unilaterally incurred private school tuition. But there is no authority for a heightened standard before Congress can alter a prior judicial interpretation of a statute, and the assessment of congressional policy aims falls short of trumping what seems to me to be the clear limitation imposed by § 1412(a)(10)(C)(ii).

Post Problem Discussion

1. If you are inclined to deny reimbursement as a hearing officer, would you consider a partial award of reimbursement to the parents as permitted by the statute and regulations instead of a full denial? Why or why not?

2. What do you think about Justice Souter's dissent? If you were sitting on the Supreme Court as a Justice, would you side with the majority or Justice Souter?

3. Was proper notice provided by the parents to the school? Do the notice requirements in the IDEA apply in this fact pattern?

§ 12.05 Addressing Student Behavior

The IDEA has a variety of requirements that apply to student behavior in school. Some of the provisions require schools to provide special education and related services to address student behavioral issues as part of the obligation to provide FAPE. *See, e.g.*, 34 C.F.R. § 300.324 (IEP must address student's behavior when it impedes his or her learning or that of others). Other provisions provide protections to students with disabilities in the discipline process to ensure that students with disabilities are not punished for behavior caused by their disabilities. 34 C.F.R. § 300.530 (detailing discipline requirements for students with disabilities).

As noted in Chapter 8, public schools must follow a number of legal requirements when disciplining any student. State and federal special education laws place additional requirements on public schools when disciplining students who receive special education services.[8] Much of the focus of the discipline provisions in special education law is on whether or not a "change in placement" has occurred due to the disciplinary action. If the discipline action includes suspension or removal from school for ten days or less, then it is generally not a change in placement. 34 C.F.R. § 300.536. When there is not a change in placement, a student with a disability may be disciplined in the same manner as students without disabilities.[9] 34 C.F.R. § 300.530(d)(3). Discipline action that includes removal or expulsion from school for more than ten consecutive days is a change in placement. When a change in placement occurs, the school district must conduct a *manifestation determination* to

8. A student who has not yet been identified under the IDEA as a student with a disability may still seek the protections of the IDEA with respect to disciplinary procedures if the school district had knowledge that the student is a student with a disability before the behavior that led to the discipline occurred. 20 U.S.C. § 1415(k)(5); 34 C.F.R. § 300.534.

9. A change of placement can also occur if a suspension or removal from school for 10 days or less is part of a pattern that culminates to more than ten days in the school year; then, it is a change in placement. 34 C.F.R. § 300.530(d)(4); 34 C.F.R. § 300.536.

determine if there is a relationship between the child's disability and the behavior subject to discipline. 20 U.S.C. § 1415(k)(1); 34 C.F.R. § 300.530(e).

The manifestation determination is made by the student's IEP team. If the team determines that the behavior is a manifestation of the child's disability, the school must take a number of steps including conducting a *functional behavioral assessment* and developing a *behavioral intervention plan* for the student. 34 C.F.R. § 300.530(e)-(f). The school must also take immediate steps to remedy any deficiencies in the student's IEP related to the behavior. The school district may not impose further discipline on the student for the incident in question since it was a manifestation of their disability.

Exceptions apply for students who carry or possess weapons, or possess, use or sell illegal drugs or controlled substances, and for students who inflict serious bodily harm upon another person. 20 U.S.C. § 1415(k)(1)(G). Schools may also seek an interim alternative educational placement for not more than 45 days for students if the school believes that maintaining the student in his or her current placement is substantially likely to result in injury to the student or to others. 20 U.S.C. § 1415(k)(3)(B); 34 C.F.R. § 300.532-.533. Additionally, in *Honig v. Doe*, 484 U.S. 305 (1988), the United States Supreme Court recognized that schools could seek injunctions to temporarily enjoin a dangerous student from attending school:

> As the EHA's legislative history makes clear, one of the evils Congress sought to remedy was the unilateral exclusion of disabled children by schools, not courts, and one of the purposes of 1415(e)(3),[10] therefore, was "to prevent school officials from removing a child from the regular public school classroom over the parents' objection pending completion of the review proceedings." The stay-put provision in no way purports to limit or pre-empt the authority conferred on courts by 1415(e)(2) . . .
>
> In short, then, we believe that school officials are entitled to seek injunctive relief under 1415(e)(2) in appropriate cases. In any such action, 1415(e)(3) effectively creates a presumption in favor of the child's current educational placement which school officials can overcome only by showing that maintaining the child in his or her current placement is substantially likely to result in injury either to himself or herself, or to others. In the present case, we are satisfied that the District Court, in enjoining the state and local defendants from indefinitely suspending respondent or otherwise unilaterally altering his then current placement, properly balanced respondent's interest in receiving a free appropriate public education in accordance with the procedures and requirements of the EHA against the interests of the

10. Authors' Note: Section 1415(e)(3) was the citation for the "stay put" provision of the IDEA at the time *Honig* was decided. It requires schools to maintain students in their current educational placements during the pendency of an administrative due process hearing. The requirement remains in the IDEA today codified at 20 U.S.C. § 1415(j).

> state and local school officials in maintaining a safe learning environment for all their students.

Honig, 484 U.S. at 328.

If the team determines that the student's behavior was not a manifestation of the student's disability, then the student may be disciplined in the same manner as students without disabilities, except that the student must still be provided with FAPE. 20 U.S.C. § 1415(k)(1); 34 C.F.R. §§ 300.101(a); 300.530(c). As a result, while the student may be expelled or removed from school, or sent to an alternative educational setting, the school district must continue to provide sufficient services to enable the student to progress in the general curriculum and to meet the goals and objectives in the student's IEP. The following problem explores some of the discipline requirements.

Problem 4: Disciplining Special Education Students

Calvin is a fifteen-year-old student in the tenth grade at Riverside Public High School. He has Asperger's Syndrome, ADHD, and has recently been diagnosed with depression. He was found eligible for special education in the third grade under the other health impaired category. His disabilities influence his relationships with his peers at school, and he often acts out impulsively in class and at school. He has been disciplined three times over the past two school years for violating school rules. One of the violations was for fighting with another student. The other two were for bothering other students in class.

Calvin's IEP has provisions to address some of the behavioral issues that have occurred over the years from his impulsiveness and hyperactivity. These provisions include monitoring Calvin's behavior and interaction with peers. The teachers and school staff have a difficult time implementing these provisions because of the high number of students in their classes and shortages in school staff.

On November 4, Calvin finds a pack of matches on his coffee table at home and brings them to school. During morning break, Calvin tells some of the boys in the boys' bathroom that he brought the matches with him. The boys dare Calvin to light a paper towel on fire in the bathroom. After a few minutes of taunting, Calvin does so. One of the other boys, Kern, immediately steps on the paper towel to put it out and tells Calvin he is in "big trouble." As Kern starts to leave the bathroom, Calvin tackles him and stabs him in the arm with a pencil that Calvin had in his pocket. A second boy, Reed, enters the fight, takes the pencil from Calvin, and stabs Calvin in the leg. The other boys break up the donnybrook and tell the principal what happened.

The principal suspends Calvin and Reed from school for ten days. Three days later, the superintendent suspends Calvin and Reed for an additional ten days and recommends that they both be expelled for the remainder of the school year. On November 19, the school conducts a manifestation determination meeting for Calvin. Calvin's parents present a letter from Calvin's psychologist about how Calvin's actions are related to his disability. The school psychologist and some other team members in attendance state that they do not think that Calvin's behavior is related to his disability. The team members conclude that Calvin's behavior was not a manifestation of his disability. Calvin's parents disagree with the decision and contend that the team members did not fairly consider the information from Calvin's psychologist. Three days later, the school board expels Calvin and Reed for the remainder of the school year. Reed is not a student with a disability.

Calvin's parents appeal the team's decision that the behavior is not a manifestation of his disability and note that the school did not comply with the procedural timelines in the process. They also contend that the school members of the team made up their minds to find that Calvin's behavior was not a manifestation before the manifestation determination meeting occurred, and reassert that the Team did not give due weight to Calvin's psychologist's opinion.

You are the hearing officer. How do you rule and why?

Problem Materials

- ✓ IDEA, 20 U.S.C. § 1415(k)
- ✓ *Shelton v. Maya Angelou Public Charter School*, 578 F. Supp. 2d 83 (D.D.C. 2008)[11]
- ✓ *Fitzgerald v. Fairfax County School Board*, 556 F. Supp. 2d 543 (E.D. Va. 2008)

20 U.S.C. § 1415(k)

(k) Placement in alternative educational setting.

(1) Authority of school personnel.

(A) Case-by-case determination. School personnel may consider any unique circumstances on a case-by-case basis when determining whether to order a change in placement for a child with a disability who violates a code of student conduct.

(B) Authority. School personnel under this subsection may remove a child with a disability who violates a code of student conduct from their current placement to an appropriate interim alternative educational setting, another setting, or suspension, for not more than 10 school days (to the extent such alternatives are applied to children without disabilities).

(C) Additional authority. If school personnel seek to order a change in placement that would exceed 10 school days and the behavior that

11. The § 1983 claim that was part of this suit was subsequently dismissed. *Shelton v. Maya Angelou Pub. Charter Sch.*, 656 F. Supp. 2d 82 (D.D.C. 2009).

gave rise to the violation of the school code is determined not to be a manifestation of the child's disability pursuant to subparagraph (E), the relevant disciplinary procedures applicable to children without disabilities may be applied to the child in the same manner and for the same duration in which the procedures would be applied to children without disabilities, except as provided in section 612(a)(1) although it may be provided in an interim alternative educational setting.

(D) Services. A child with a disability who is removed from the child's current placement under subparagraph (G) (irrespective of whether the behavior is determined to be a manifestation of the child's disability) or subparagraph (C) shall—

(i) continue to receive educational services, as provided in section 612(a)(1) as to enable the child to continue to participate in the general education curriculum, although in another setting, and to progress toward meeting the goals set out in the child's IEP; and

(ii) receive, as appropriate, a functional behavioral assessment, behavioral intervention services and modifications, that are designed to address the behavior violation so that it does not recur.

(E) Manifestation determination.

(i) In general. Except as provided in subparagraph (B), within 10 school days of any decision to change the placement of a child with a disability because of a violation of a code of student conduct, the local educational agency, the parent, and relevant members of the IEP Team (as determined by the parent and the local educational agency) shall review all relevant information in the student's file, including the child's IEP, any teacher observations, and any relevant information provided by the parents to determine—

(I) if the conduct in question was caused by, or had a direct and substantial relationship to, the child's disability; or

(II) if the conduct in question was the direct result of the local educational agency's failure to implement the IEP.

(ii) Manifestation. If the local educational agency, the parent, and relevant members of the IEP Team determine that either subclause (I) or (II) of clause (i) is applicable for the child, the conduct shall be determined to be a manifestation of the child's disability.

(F) Determination that behavior was a manifestation. If the local educational agency, the parent, and relevant members of the IEP Team make the determination that the conduct was a manifestation of the child's disability, the IEP Team shall—

(i) conduct a functional behavioral assessment, and implement a behavioral intervention plan for such child, provided that the local educational agency had not conducted such assessment prior to such determination before the behavior that resulted in a change in placement described in subparagraph (C) or (G);

(ii) in the situation where a behavioral intervention plan has been developed, review the behavioral intervention plan if the child already has such a behavioral intervention plan, and modify it, as necessary, to address the behavior; and

(iii) except as provided in subparagraph (G), return the child to the placement from which the child was removed, unless the parent and the local educational agency agree to a change of placement as part of the modification of the behavioral intervention plan.

(G) Special circumstances. School personnel may remove a student to an interim alternative educational setting for not more than 45 school days without regard to whether the behavior is determined to be a manifestation of the child's disability, in cases where a child—

(i) carries or possesses a weapon to or at school, on school premises, or to or at a school function under the jurisdiction of a State or local educational agency;

(ii) knowingly possesses or uses illegal drugs, or sells or solicits the sale of a controlled substance, while at school, on school premises, or at a school function under the jurisdiction of a State or local educational agency; or

(iii) has inflicted serious bodily injury upon another person while at school, on school premises, or at a school function under the jurisdiction of a State or local educational agency.

(H) Notification. Not later than the date on which the decision to take disciplinary action is made, the local educational agency shall notify the parents of that decision, and of all procedural safeguards accorded under this section.

Shelton v. Maya Angelou Public Charter School

578 F. Supp. 2d 83 (D.D.C. 2008)

The court addresses the discipline requirements under the IDEA and finds that the school denied the student FAPE when it failed to conduct a Functional Behavioral Assessment and implement a Behavioral Intervention Plan following the student's suspension.

Colleen Kollar-Kotelly, District Judge

....

Plaintiff Derrick Shelton attended Maya Angelou Public Charter School during the 2006–2007 school year. Plaintiff's Individualized Education Plan ("IEP") identifies him as learning disabled and calls for a total of four (4) hours and twenty-five (25) minutes of specialized instruction and counseling per week: ninety (90) minutes of counseling, one (1) hour of special education consultation, and one (1) hour and fifty-five (55) minutes of advisory services. . . .

On November 17, 2006, Plaintiff was involved in an incident with another MAPCS student (his girlfriend at the time). While Plaintiff asserts that he acted in self-defense, the parties do not dispute that Plaintiff assaulted the other student, was immediately disciplined by being removed from MAPCS, and was not allowed to return to MAPCS as a student after November 17, 2006. On November 22, 2006, MAPCS sent a letter to Plaintiff's father, informing him that Plaintiff had been suspended with the intent to expel. The letter indicated that MAPCS's special education coordinator would be scheduling a manifestation determination review ("MDR") meeting as soon as possible.

Pursuant to the IDEA, an MDR meeting "shall" be held "within 10 school days of any decision to change the placement of a child with a disability because of a violation of a code of student conduct." 20 U.S.C. § 1415(k)(1)(E). It is undisputed that the MDR in Plaintiff's case was not held until December 19, 2006. Before the Hearing Officer below, Plaintiff argued that MAPCS denied him FAPE when it failed to convene an MDR meeting within 10 school days of his suspension; however, the Hearing Officer concluded that MAPCS's delay in convening the MDR meeting was justified and did not constitute a denial of FAPE. In reaching this conclusion, the Hearing Officer credited testimony that Plaintiff's "father wanted to delay the meeting." The Hearing Officer also noted that "once the student retained counsel the MDR was convened on a date proposed by his counsel," and acknowledged that MAPCS offered to provide Plaintiff with tutoring once he had been out of school for ten days. As neither party has contested the Hearing Officer's findings in this respect, the Court does not revisit herein either the Hearing Officer's ultimate conclusion or its factual underpinnings.

As noted above, MAPCS convened the MDR in this case on December 19, 2006. Plaintiff, his parents, and his educational advocate attended the meeting, along with a counselor, Plaintiff's algebra teacher, a psychologist, and the Special Education Coordinator from MAPCS (collectively the "MDR Team"). The MDR Team determined that Plaintiff's behavior on November 17, 2006 was not a manifestation of his disability, concluding that although Plaintiff had previously been suspended, the November 17, 2006 incident was an aberration. During the MDR meeting, Plaintiff's educational advocate expressed a desire to reconvene the MDR Team at a later date to review Plaintiff's IEP. The MDR Team did not discuss a placement for Plaintiff or consider the services that Plaintiff would be provided during the period that he was not attending MAPCS. The MDR Team also did not discuss whether a Functional Behavioral Assessment ("FBA") or Behavioral Intervention Plan ("BIP") should be conducted. The decision to expel Plaintiff from MAPCS was not made at the MDR meeting.

. . . .

The due process hearing in this case was held on March 12, 2007, and Plaintiff was represented by counsel. . . .

The Hearing Officer issued his Determination on April 5, 2007. *See* A.R. at 2-17 (4/5/07 HOD). As noted above, the Hearing Officer found that MAPCS did not deny Plaintiff FAPE by failing to convene the MDR within 10 days following Plaintiff's November 17, 2006 suspension. In contrast, the Hearing Officer found that Plaintiff's counsel sustained Plaintiff's burden of proof in showing that MAPCS denied Plaintiff FAPE when it (1) failed to conduct an FBA and BIP following the MDR meeting, and (2) failed to provide Plaintiff with an alternative placement and/or to provide Plaintiff with continued services following his suspension/expulsion.

. . . .

The purpose of the IDEA is "to ensure that all children with disabilities have available to them a free appropriate public education that emphasizes special education and related services designed to meet their unique needs . . ." "Implicit" in the IDEA's guarantee "is the requirement that the education to which access is provided be sufficient to confer some educational benefit upon the handicapped child." *Board of Educ. of Hendrick Hudson Cent. Sch. Dist. v. Rowley*, 458 U.S. 176, 200 (1982) . . . .

Of particular relevance to the instant case, the IDEA sets forth particular processes by which a school may remove and/or discipline a child with a disability who violates a code of student conduct. As one option, the Act provides:

> If school personnel seek to order a change in placement that would exceed 10 school days and the behavior that gave rise to a violation of the school code is determined not to be a manifestation of the child's disability . . . the relevant disciplinary procedures applicable to children without disabilities may be applied to the child in the same manner and for the same duration in which the procedures would be applied to children without disabilities . . . although it may be provided in an interim alternative setting.

Id. § 1415(k)(1)(C). As another option, "[s]chool personnel may remove a student to an interim alternative educational setting for not more than 45 school days without regard to whether the behavior is determined to be a manifestation of the child's disability, in cases where a child . . . (iii) has inflicted serious bodily injury upon another person while at school . . ." *Id.* § 1415(k)(1)(G). In either situation, however, a child with a disability who is removed from his or her current placement

> shall—(i) continue to receive educational services . . . so as to enable the child to continue to participate in the general education curriculum, although in another setting, and to progress toward meeting the goals set out in the child's IEP; and (ii) receive, *as appropriate*, a functional behavioral assessment, behavioral intervention services and modifications, that are designed to address the behavior violation so that it does not recur.

Id. § 1415(k)(1)(D).

. . . .

As noted above, the IDEA and its implementing regulations provide two options for schools to remove a child for more than 10 school days for violating a school code of conduct. . . . In seeking to expel Plaintiff, MAPCS obviously sought to remove him from MAPCS for more than 45 days. Accordingly, although MAPCS states that it "was not seeking to change the student's placement, it instead sought to and did dismiss" him for his conduct on November 17, 2006, it appears that MAPCS—regardless of how it describes its intent—ordered a change of placement to exceed 10 school days. This conclusion is bolstered by the fact that the IDEA's implementing regulations clarify that, "for purposes of [disciplinary] removals of a child with a disability from the child's current educational placement" a "change in placement occurs if [*inter alia*] [t]he removal is for more than 10 consecutive school days . . ." 34 C.F.R. § 300.536(a). As such, once Plaintiff was out of school for more than 10 consecutive school days following his November 17, 2006 suspension, a change in placement had occurred.

MAPCS also argues that, because Plaintiff's conduct was determined not to be a manifestation of his disability, MAPCS "could either expel the student, requiring no further services or place the student in an alternative setting-requiring some level of services. The defendant properly elected expulsion, requiring no further services." Defendant's argument is neither clear nor correct. There is no dispute that once the MDR Team determined that Plaintiff's conduct was not a manifestation of his disability MAPCS could discipline Plaintiff in the same manner as it disciplined students without disabilities. *See* 20 U.S.C. § 1415(k)(1)(C). Nevertheless, the IDEA explicitly provides that a child with a disability who is removed from his or her current placement under § 1415(k)(1)(C)

> shall—(i) continue to receive educational services . . . so as to enable the child to continue to participate in the general education curriculum, although in another setting, and to progress toward meeting the goals set out in the child's IEP; and (ii) receive, *as appropriate*, a functional behavioral assessment, behavioral intervention services and modifications, that are designed to address the behavior violation so that it does not recur.

Id. § 1415(k)(1)(D). . . .

Accordingly, despite the fact that MAPCS was entitled to discipline Plaintiff in the same manner that disciplined students without disabilities, pursuant to the IDEA and its regulations, Plaintiff was entitled to receive "as appropriate, a functional behavioral assessment, behavioral intervention services and modifications, that are designed to address the behavior so that it does not recur." 20 U.S.C. § 1415(k)(1)(D). Defendant does not proffer any legal support for its claim that it was not required to provide Plaintiff with an FBA and/or BIP because it validly elected to expel him, and the Court is not aware of any. . . .

. . . .

Under 20 U.S.C. § 1415(k)(1)(D) and 34 C.F.R. §§ 300.530(c) and (d), a child with a disability who is removed from his or her current placement based on a disciplinary violation (regardless of whether the conduct is found to be a manifestation of the child's disability), must "continue to receive educational services . . . so as to enable the child to continue to participate in the general educational curriculum, although in another setting, and to progress toward meeting the goals set out in the child's IEP." . . .

Here, as the Hearing Officer concluded, the December 19, 2006 MDR meeting did not discuss continuing services during Plaintiff's suspension or expulsion, and while tutoring was discussed during the resolution meeting, "there was no agreement among the team as to the services that would be provided." Instead, MAPCS's Special Education Coordinator "unilaterally decided the amount of the tutoring after the resolution meeting." In doing so, MAPCS violated its obligation as a local educational agency to ensure that Plaintiff's IEP Team determined the services he received while on suspension or after being expelled, and in particular, the interim alternative educational setting in which he was to receive those services. *Id.*

. . . .

Fitzgerald v. Fairfax County School Board

556 F. Supp. 2d 543 (E.D. Va. 2008)

The court finds that the school did not violate the IDEA and that the student's conduct was not caused by his disability.

T.S. Ellis, III, District Judge

In this IDEA dispute, plaintiff Kevin Fitzgerald (a minor child) and his parents challenge the procedures and finding of the manifestation determination review ("MDR") held by Fairfax County School Board ("FCSB") that allowed Kevin to be suspended from his school for his involvement in a paintball shooting incident at the school. Specifically, plaintiffs contend that FCSB violated the IDEA's procedural provisions in conducting the MDR hearing; they also claim that Kevin's conduct was caused by, or had a direct relationship to, Kevin's disability and hence his suspension from school was an impermissible punishment under the IDEA. . . .

. . . .

During his eleventh grade year, Kevin engaged in the conduct that is central to this dispute. On December 16, 2006, Kevin and some friends met at a restaurant. At Kevin's suggestion, the boys decided to drive by FCHS and shoot at the school building with paintball guns. Kevin had a paintball gun in his car and offered to drive the four other boys to the school. On the way to the school, Kevin made a detour to another boy's vehicle to retrieve two more paintball guns. The five boys then proceeded to FCHS in Kevin's car where they shot paintballs at the windows of the school building and at various vehicles parked on school property, including school buses. At some point during this first visit to the school, one of the paintball guns malfunctioned, so Kevin drove the boys to retrieve supplies, including CO2 and more paintballs, from a vehicle belonging to one of the boys. Kevin and the boys then made a second trip to the school and this time Kevin, who was driving, shot at the school while one of the boys held the wheel of Kevin's car. After this second trip, two of the boys decided to leave and asked Kevin to drive them to another location. Kevin did so, and then he and the remaining two boys returned to FCHS to shoot paintballs at the school a third time. As a result of the three attacks on the school, thirty school windows, two school buses, and one school delivery truck had been hit with paintballs. On their way home from the school, Kevin, still driving, failed to obey a stop sign and was stopped by a police officer. The officer noticed the paintball guns and questioned the boys, who denied any wrongdoing. The officer then allowed Kevin and the boys to proceed on their way. Later, when the officer heard reports of paintball vandalism at FCHS, he advised the administration and school police officer, Officer George Davis, that he believed Kevin and his friends had been involved. Officer Davis then questioned Kevin, who, after Officer Davis assured him that the school was not planning to pursue criminal charges against the boys, admitted his involvement in the affair.

Virginia law requires the school board to "expel from school attendance for a period of not less than one year any student whom such school board has determined ... to have possessed ... a pneumatic gun as defined in on school property." Because a paintball gun is statutorily defined as a type of pneumatic gun, the school principal suspended Kevin with a recommendation of expulsion. This recommendation triggered the provisions of the IDEA, which prohibits disciplining a disabled student for more than ten days if the "conduct in question was caused by, or had a direct and substantial relationship to, the child's disability." 20 U.S.C. § 1415(k)(1)(E)(i)(II). Accordingly, school officials scheduled an MDR hearing for January 5, 2007, to determine whether Kevin's conduct in the paintball gun affair was a manifestation of his emotional disability....

The MDR hearing was held on January 5, 2007, and was attended by the five FCSB members, Kevin, and his parents....

Although Kevin and his parents contended at the MDR hearing that Kevin's conduct in the paintball gun incident was a manifestation of his disability, they did not argue that Kevin had somehow been induced or inveigled by his classmates to participate in the paintball shooting incident. At the conclusion of the MDR hearing, the FCSB members determined, contrary to plaintiffs' view, that Kevin's behavior was not a manifestation of his disability. This MDR finding that Kevin's behavior was not a manifestation of his emotional disability allowed the school to discipline Kevin as it would any other student....

On July 25, 2007, Kevin's parents invoked their right under the due process procedures of the IDEA to a review of the MDR determination that Kevin's behavior was not a manifestation of his disability. Additionally, they raised a number of procedural violations they alleged occurred during the MDR process....

Analysis of plaintiffs' claims appropriately begins with the recognition that the IDEA requires all public schools to provide every disabled child a FAPE....

Importantly, the IDEA does not rely solely on the IEP requirement to achieve the goal of a FAPE; additionally, the IDEA provides a range of procedural safeguards to ensure parental participation in the process. Indeed, "Congress placed every bit as much emphasis on compliance with procedures giving parents . . . a large measure of participation at every stage of the administrative process . . . as it did upon the measurement of the resulting IEP against a substantive standard." *Rowley*, 458 U.S. at 205–06. This reflects, as courts have recognized, that "[t]he core of the statute . . . is the cooperative process that it establishes between parents and schools."

. . . .

Finally, it is clear that a procedural violation of the IDEA is not alone sufficient to show a school failed to provide a child with a FAPE. Thus, a "presumably correct finding" concerning a child with a disability will not be overturned simply because the IDEA's procedural requirements were not strictly followed; rather, the violation must "*actually interfere* with the provision of a FAPE to that child." Put differently, the inquiry does not end when a court finds a procedural violation of the IDEA; instead, a court must then determine "whether [the procedural violation] resulted in the loss of an educational opportunity for the disabled child, or whether, on the other hand, it was a mere technical contravention of the IDEA."

. . . .

[P]laintiffs contend that FCSB violated the IDEA by failing to give plaintiffs an "equal right" to determine whether Kevin's conduct was a manifestation of his disability. In support of their claim, plaintiffs again rely on the text of § 1415, which states that the LEA, the parents, and the relevant members of the IEP team are to meet "to determine . . . if the conduct in question was caused by, or had a direct and substantial relationship to, the child's disability." § 1415(k)(1)(E)(i)(I). It is unclear whether plaintiffs believe this language gives parents a right to vote at an MDR hearing, or whether they believe it requires a manifestation determination to be unanimous. Regardless, either claim would fail. First, as a factual matter, the record reflects that plaintiffs participated at the hearing and voiced their belief that Kevin's conduct was a manifestation of his disability. Thus, they apparently did, in this sense, have an opportunity to "vote" on the issue.

More importantly, as already noted, the IDEA's emphasis on parental involvement does not give parents the right to veto or otherwise block the LEA's ability . . . to discipline a student. Parents have a right to participate and be heard in the MDR hearing, but these proceedings may become adversarial, as parents may well disagree with the school's decision to discipline their child. If parents were required to consent to the LEA's determination, or if parents were allowed to "stack the deck" against the LEA by inviting several individuals who would vote consistently with the parents' views, the LEA would effectively be hamstrung, a result not contemplated by the IDEA. Accordingly, the IDEA does not require the LEA and the parents to reach a consensus regarding the education or discipline of a disabled child.

Instead, if a consensus cannot be reached, the LEA must make a determination, and the parents' only recourse is to appeal that determination.

In conclusion, consensus may be desirable as a goal, but cannot always be reached and is not statutorily required. All the statute requires is parental involvement in the MDR process. Here, the record reflects that plaintiffs attended and participated in Kevin's MDR hearing. Plaintiffs' procedural claim on this ground must therefore fail.

. . . .

Plaintiffs next contend that FCSB violated the IDEA by failing to require all members of Kevin's MDR committee to review all "relevant information" in his student file before the MDR hearing. *See* 20 U.S.C. § 1415(k)(1)(E)(i). In this respect, plaintiffs point to Ms. Allison's testimony that she did not make copies of Kevin's student file for each of the MDR members, but instead had the file available in her office for their review. . . .

As an initial matter, plaintiffs cite no authority for the proposition that all MDR committee members must review every piece of information in the student's file before an MDR hearing. Rather, the statute requires that the MDR committee "shall review all relevant information in the student's file, including the child's IEP, any teacher observations, and any relevant information provided by the parents" to make its manifestation determination. § 1415(k)(1)(E)(i). This language does not require each member to read before the meeting every piece of information in the student's file. All the statute requires is that, before reaching a manifestation determination, the team must review the information pertinent to that decision, including the child's IEP, his teachers' comments, and any information provided by the parents. And this review clearly may occur before or during the course of an MDR hearing.

The record reflects that Kevin's MDR committee did just that. . . .

Accordingly, the IHO correctly determined that the MDR committee satisfied the IDEA's mandate to review all relevant information in Kevin's file before making a manifestation determination, and this procedural claim fails.

Plaintiffs' final procedural argument is that FCSB violated plaintiffs' right to a fundamentally fair MDR process when the MDR committee members . . . met informally to discuss Kevin's MDR before the formal MDR hearing. In short, plaintiffs believe school personnel may not discuss a child's manifestation determination before the formal MDR hearing unless the child's parents are also present. Plaintiffs cite no statute, regulation, or case law in support of their argument, but rely on *Goss v. Lopez*, 419 U.S. 565, 574 (1975), for the general proposition that schools must employ "fundamentally fair procedures" when disciplining students.

As an initial matter, nothing in *Goss* precludes school personnel from discussing a disabled child's case before a formal meeting, but other case law does make clear that "if the school system has already fully made up its mind before the parents ever get involved, it has denied them the opportunity for any meaningful input." Accordingly, "school officials must come to the IEP table with an open mind" and must not make a final determination regarding a disabled child before fully discussing the issues with the child's parents. This does not, however, require school officials to "come to the IEP table with a blank mind." The district court's opinion in *Doyle* is instructive on this distinction. There, the court found no error in the school's research of particular placement options for the disabled child before the child's IEP meeting. The court noted that "while a school system must not finalize its placement decision before an IEP meeting, it can, and should, have given some thought to that placement." Thus, the court found no unlawful predetermination of the child's placement, finding instead that the parents participated fully in drafting the IEP before any placement options were suggested and that the school was "receptive and responsive" to the parents' suggestions throughout the formulation of the child's IEP.

Given that fairness requires open-mindedness, the key question in this case is whether the FCSB personnel merely discussed Kevin's case before the MDR hearing while remaining open-minded about the final determination, or whether they predetermined that Kevin's conduct was not a manifestation of his disability. Plaintiffs claim FCSB "unlawfully predetermined the result of Kevin's MDR," relying heavily on the draft IEP Ms. Wallace prepared for the IEP meeting scheduled for immediately after Kevin's MDR hearing. Ms. Wallace admitted that she prepared only one draft IEP for that meeting, and that the draft IEP predicted that the MDR committee would find that Kevin's conduct was not a manifestation of his disability. This is evident, as the draft IEP recommended home placement, which was possible only if Kevin's conduct was determined not to be a manifestation of his disability.

After hearing and reviewing evidence on this point, the IHO concluded that FCSB did not unlawfully predetermine the outcome of the MDR. . . . [T]he IHO rejected plaintiffs' contention that the school personnel came to the MDR hearing with the outcome predetermined and found "reasonable" Ms. Wallace's testimony that her preparation of the draft IEP was simply a "time saving exercise to improve the efficiency of the MDR." This finding by the IHO, while not explicitly stated as such, appears to be a determination that the IHO found credible Ms. Wallace's testimony that the draft IEP was not a predetermination of the outcome of Kevin's MDR. Credibility determinations are entitled to deference.

Indeed, the record reflects this credibility determination was sound. Ms. Wallace's draft IEP does not alone demonstrate that FCSB had predetermined the outcome of Kevin's MDR. Although she prepared only one draft IEP, which predicted that the team would find Kevin's conduct not to be a manifestation of his disability, this was only a prediction. Ms. Wallace reasonably could have foreshadowed the outcome of Kevin's manifestation determination, given her experiences with him and her knowledge of his misconduct. That one FCSB employee was leaning toward a particular conclusion does not mean her mind was closed to a different conclusion.... Here, had the MDR committee concluded, after careful consideration, that Kevin's conduct was a manifestation of his disability, Ms. Wallace would simply have drafted a different IEP.

The record makes clear that the MDR committee did not approach the hearing with closed minds, but rather carefully considered all information at the hearing *before* making their determination.... The record also reflects that plaintiffs were afforded an opportunity to participate in the MDR hearing, that team members carefully discussed Kevin's background and his role in the paintball incident, and, only at the conclusion of the meeting, did the committee members conclude that Kevin's conduct was not a manifestation of his disability. This record thus reflects not prejudgment, but open-mindedness. Accordingly, plaintiffs' final procedural claim is therefore without merit.

Given that no procedural violations occurred, it follows that Kevin was not denied a FAPE based on any of the alleged violations, and the only remaining question is whether the IHO's affirmance of the MDR committee's manifestation determination was correct. In this regard, a district court must engage in a modified *de novo* review, giving due weight to the administrative findings but ultimately making an "independent decision based on the preponderance of the evidence." *Doyle v. Arlington County Sch. Bd.*, 953 F.2d 100, 103 (4th Cir. 1991). The application of this standard here compels the conclusion that the determination of the MDR committee, upheld by the IHO, was correct.

First, as the IHO correctly noted, Kevin's anxiety was the "primary basis for his disability classification," rather than the occasional "juvenile outburs[s]" of acting inappropriately in class with friends. The evaluations setting forth Kevin's eligibility under the IDEA described his headaches and school absences, but noted no social problems; indeed, Kevin was described as "academically capable and socially popular." The only evidence of any behavioral problems demonstrated that Kevin sometimes made minor poor choices to impress his friends. For instance, Kevin's 2005 and 2006 IEPs, both of which noted that Kevin had "been drawn into inappropriate behaviors in some of his classes and has been known to be negative and sarcastic toward teachers," suggested that Kevin "refrain from conversation with peers that is not on topic of class lesson" and "distance himself from peers who are behaving inappropriately in class." In addition, at the due process hearing, two of Kevin's teachers testified that Kevin was often persuaded by other students to engage in inappropriate behavior, such as laughing, talking out of turn, or otherwise causing classroom distractions. Such in-class juvenile outbursts to impress friends is not atypical of teenage boys in general.

Even assuming Kevin's disability did cause him to be drawn into inappropriate behaviors at times, the record makes pellucidly clear that far from being drawn into the paintball shooting incident, Kevin played a predominant role in planning and executing it. Specifically, the record reflects that Kevin (i) suggested the idea of shooting the school with paintball guns; (ii) offered to drive the boys there; (iii) used a paintball gun stashed in his own car; and (iv) drove to the school not once, but three times, as he had to drive the boys to get supplies to fix a broken paintball gun and later had to take two boys home who no longer wanted to participate. The entire incident lasted over several hours. Nothing in these facts supports plaintiffs' conclusion that Kevin was impulsively drawn into the paintball incident by his friends as a result of his disability. Indeed, as the IHO pointed out, neither Kevin nor his parents ever suggested at the MDR hearing that Kevin had been drawn into his misconduct by his friends. Kevin simply made a bad decision; he must now live with the consequences.

....

Post Problem Discussion

1. The IDEA defines weapon by using the federal criminal code definition of dangerous weapon:

> a weapon, device, instrument, material, or substance, animate or inanimate, that is used for, or is readily capable of, causing death or serious bodily injury, except that such term does not include a pocket knife with a blade of less than 2 1/2 inches in length.

18 U.S.C. § 930(g)(2). Is the pencil used by Calvin and Reed a weapon under this definition? If the pencil is a weapon, how would that change what the school could do in terms of disciplining Calvin? In terms of disciplining Reed? See further discussion on the issue of zero tolerance in Section 8.07.

2. As a hearing officer, if you find that Calvin's behavior is a manifestation of his disability, what should the school do? Does Calvin get to return to school? Is there any remedy for Calvin for the days he was removed from school?

3. If you find that Calvin's behavior is not a manifestation of his disability, what kind of services would the school need to provide to Calvin during his expulsion from school?

4. This problem focused on school discipline in its usual and broadest sense, but there are other ways in which students' behavior is controlled. The past several years have seen growing attention paid to the use of restraints and seclusion in schools. In 2009 the Congressional Research Service introduced its report to Congress as follows:

> GAO found no federal laws restricting the use of seclusion and restraints in public and private schools and widely divergent laws at the state level. Although GAO could not determine whether allegations were widespread, GAO did find hundreds of cases of alleged abuse and death related to the use of these methods on school children during the past two decades. Examples of these cases include a 7 year old purportedly dying after being held face down for hours by school staff, 5 year olds allegedly being tied to chairs with bungee cords and duct tape by their teacher and suffering broken arms

and bloody noses, and a 13 year old reportedly hanging himself in a seclusion room after prolonged confinement.[12]

In March of 2012 the National Disability Rights Network issued another of its ongoing reports and called on the U.S. Department of Education to issue specific guidance on the topic of restraint and seclusion. *See School Is Not Supposed to Hurt: The U.S. Department of Education Must Do More to Protect School Children from Restraint and Seclusion.*[13] In 2012, the Department of Education responded with *Restraint and Seclusion: Resource Document* as non-regulatory guidance.[14] Fifteen principles are offered, which the Department says are applicable to "the restraint or seclusion of any student regardless of whether the student has a disability."

1. Every effort should be made to prevent the need for the use of restraint and for the use of seclusion.
2. Schools should never use mechanical restraints to restrict a child's freedom of movement, and schools should never use a drug or medication to control behavior or restrict freedom of movement (except as authorized by a licensed physician or other qualified health professional).
3. Physical restraint or seclusion should not be used except in situations where the child's behavior poses imminent danger of serious physical harm to self or others and other interventions are ineffective and should be discontinued as soon as imminent danger of serious physical harm to self or others has dissipated.
4. Policies restricting the use of restraint and seclusion should apply to all children, not just children with disabilities.
5. Any behavioral intervention must be consistent with the child's rights to be treated with dignity and to be free from abuse.
6. Restraint or seclusion should never be used as punishment or discipline (e.g., placing in seclusion for out-of-seat behavior), as a means of coercion or retaliation, or as retaliation, or as a convenience.
7. Restraint or seclusion should never be used in a manner that restricts a child's breathing or harms the child.
8. The use of restraint or seclusion, particularly when there is repeated use for an individual child, multiple uses within the same classroom, or multiple uses by the same individual, should trigger a review and, if appropriate, revision

12. The report can be found at GAO Report on Restraint and Seclusion: *Seclusions and Restraints: Selected Cases of Death and Abuse at Public and Private Schools and Treatment Centers*, www.gao.gov/new.items/d09719t.pdf (last visited March 21, 2019).

13. The report can be found at www.ndrn.org/images/Documents/Resources/Publications/Reports/School_is_Not_Supposed_to_Hurt_3_v7.pdf (last visited March 21, 2019).

14. The guidance can be found at www2.ed.gov/policy/seclusion/restraints-and-seclusion-resources.pdf (last visited March 21, 2019).

of strategies currently in place to address dangerous behavior; if positive behavioral strategies are not in place, staff should consider developing them.

9. Behavioral strategies to address dangerous behavior that results in the use of restraint or seclusion should address the underlying cause or purpose of the dangerous behavior.
10. Teachers and other personnel should be trained regularly on the appropriate use of effective alternatives to physical restraint and seclusion, such as positive behavioral interventions and supports and, only for cases involving imminent danger of serious physical harm, on the safe use of physical restraint and seclusion. Every effort should be made to prevent the need for the use of restraint and for the use of seclusion.
11. Every instance in which restraint or seclusion is used should be carefully and continuously and visually monitored to ensure the appropriateness of its use and safety of the child, other children, teachers, and other personnel.
12. Parents should be informed of the policies on restraint and seclusion at their child's school or other educational setting, as well as applicable Federal, State, or local laws.
13. Parents should be notified as soon as possible following each instance in which restraint or seclusion is used with their child.
14. Policies regarding the use of restraint and seclusion should be reviewed regularly and updated as appropriate.
15. Policies regarding the use of restraint and seclusion should provide that each incident involving the use of restraint or seclusion should be documented in writing and provide for the collection of specific data that would enable teachers, staff, and other personnel to understand and implement the preceding principles.

The U.S. Department of Education followed up with a Dear Colleague letter on the topic on December 28, 2016 that said:

> [D]uring the 2013-14 school year, students with disabilities were subjected to mechanical and physical restraint and seclusion at rates that far exceeded those of other students. Specifically, students with disabilities served by the Individuals with Disabilities Education Act (IDEA) represented 12% of students enrolled in public schools nationally, but 67% of the students who were subjected to restraint or seclusion in school. Based on data reported to OCR, approximately 100,000 students were placed in seclusion or involuntary confinement or were physically restrained at school to immobilize them or reduce their ability to move freely, including more than 69,000 students with disabilities served by the IDEA. Data disparity alone does not prove discrimination. The existence of a disparity, however, does raise a question regarding whether school districts are imposing restraint or seclusion in discriminatory ways.

> A school district discriminates on the basis of disability in its use of restraint or seclusion by (1) unnecessarily treating students with disabilities differently from students without disabilities; (2) implementing policies, practices, procedures, or criteria that have an effect of discriminating against students on the basis of disability or defeating or substantially impairing accomplishment of the objectives of the school district's program or activity with respect to students with disabilities; or (3) denying the right to a free appropriate public education (FAPE). When investigating a school district, OCR would examine any available data as well as the school district's policies, practices, procedures, and criteria to determine whether unlawful discrimination has occurred and, if so, would craft an appropriate remedy with the school district.
>
> . . .
>
> OCR would likely find it to be a justified response to restrain or seclude a student with a disability in situations where the student's behavior poses imminent danger of serious physical harm to self or others. OCR would likely not, however, find the repeated use of restraint and seclusion to be a justified response where alternative methods also could prevent imminent danger to self or others.[15]

What does this regulatory guidance mean? Does your state law have any requirements regarding the use of restraints in schools?

§ 12.06 Attorney's Fees and Costs

One remedy under the IDEA is attorney's fees for plaintiffs who prevail in administrative due process hearings and court proceedings. *See* 20 U.S.C. § 1415(i)(3).[16] In *Buckhannon Bd. & Care Home v. West Va. Dep't of Health & Human Res.*, 532 U.S. 598, 605 (2001), the Supreme Court ruled that in order to be a "prevailing party" entitled to attorney's fees under federal civil rights laws, the party must obtain a "judicially sanctioned change in the legal relationship of the parties." The Court rejected the "catalyst theory" that lower courts had employed to award plaintiffs attorney's fees in cases where the plaintiff achieved their desired result because the "lawsuit brought about a voluntary change in the defendant's conduct," but did not result in a court decision ordering the conduct. *Buckhannon*, 532 U.S at 605. The catalyst theory had

15. United States Department of Education Dear Colleague Letter: Restraint and Seclusion of Students with Disabilities at 2-3, 9 (December 28, 2016), available at https://www2.ed.gov/about/offices/list/ocr/letters/colleague-201612-504-restraint-seclusion-ps.pdf (last accessed March 21, 2019).

16. School districts may also recover attorney's fees from parents if there is a finding that the parents' case is 1) frivolous, unreasonable, or without foundation; 2) if the parent or attorney continued to litigate after the case clearly became frivolous, unreasonable or without foundation; or 3) the parents' case was presented from an improper purpose such as to harass, cause unnecessary delay, or increase litigation costs. 20 U.S.C. § 1415(i)(3).

been frequently used to recover fees in special education (and other) cases when the plaintiffs received some or all of the relief they sought in a settlement reached prior to a decision by an administrative due process hearing officer or court.[17]

Buckhannon did not involve the IDEA, but numerous courts have applied *Buckhannon* to IDEA claims and denied attorney's fees claims based on settlement agreements. *See, e.g.*, *Doe v. Boston Pub. Schs.*, 358 F.3d 20 (1st Cir. 2004); *T.D. v. LaGrange Sch. Dist. No. 102*, 349 F.3d 469 (7th Cir. 2003).

Several years after *Buckhannon*, the Supreme Court addressed a related issued under the IDEA, whether prevailing parties could recover the costs of expert witnesses used in administrative or court proceedings. The Court ruled that such costs were not recoverable under the IDEA. *Arlington Cent. Sch. Dist. Bd. of Educ. v. Murphy*, 548 U.S. 291 (2006).

Some states have made expert fees recoverable under state law. *See, e.g.*, N.H. Rev. Stat. Ann. § 186-C:16-b (V)(a). The following Activity explores these issues.

Activity 2: Recovering Fees

Step One—Review the *Buckhannon Bd. & Care Home v. West Va. Dept. of Health & Human Res.*, 532 U.S. 598, 605 (2001), and *Arlington Cent. Sch. Dist. Bd. of Educ. v. Murphy*, 548 U.S. 291 (2006), cases.

Step Two—Research state and federal cases in your jurisdiction to see if courts in your jurisdiction have applied *Buckhannon* to IDEA cases. If you are unable to find any cases in your jurisdiction, review the cases applying *Buckhannon* to IDEA claims noted above in this section.

Step Three—Review your state statutes and regulations for provisions that address attorney's fees and expert fees.

Step Four—Answer the following:

1. Do you agree with the Court's analysis in *Buckhannon* and *Murphy*? Why or why not?
2. Do you agree with the courts that have applied *Buckhannon* to IDEA cases? Why or why not?
3. Does your state have any provisions addressing attorney's fees or expert fees? Do they permit attorney's fees under state law based on a catalyst theory? Do they permit the recovery of expert fees?
4. What effect, if any, do you think eliminating the catalyst theory has had on special education claims?
5. What effect, if any, do you think eliminating expert fees has had on special education claims?

---

17. *See* Mark C. Weber, *Litigation under the Individuals with Disabilities Education Act after Buckhannon Board & Care Home v. West Virginia Department of Health & Human Resources*, 65 Ohio St. L.J. 357 (2004).

Glossary

Act: An enacted statute; when first introduced to the legislature, called a "Bill."

Administrative agency: An agency created by the legislature to implement legislation, generally as part of the executive branch. The Department of Education is an administrative agency: "There is established an executive department to be known as the Department of Education. The Department shall be administered, in accordance with the provisions of this chapter, under the supervision and direction of a Secretary of Education. The Secretary shall be appointed by the President, by and with the advice and consent of the Senate." 20 U.S.C. § 3411. The officers of the department are also set out by statute under 20 U.S.C. § 3412.

Administrative Law Judge (ALJ): A federal or state hearing officer who hears and makes decisions on administrative matters for a federal or state agency.

Administrative Procedure Act (APA): The statute governing procedures of administrative agencies. The federal APA can be found at 5 U.S.C. § 551 et seq. and governs rulemaking, adjudication, and judicial review of agency actions. States have their own administrative procedure acts.

Affirmed: The decision of a higher court upholding the decision of a lower court on appeal.

Alternative school: A school for placement of students unable to function in regular classroom settings. IDEA refers to an "alternative educational setting," 20 U.S.C. § 1415(k).

Americans with Disabilities Act [ADA]: Federal law prohibiting discrimination against individuals with disabilities, 42 U.S.C. § 12101 et seq.

Amicus curiae: The literal meaning is friend of the court. The term is typically used when a person or institution that is not a party, but that has a strong interest in the issue being decided, petitions the court to file a brief to express a certain view in an appeal. So-called "amicus briefs" are most common in public interest litigation.

Appeal: The procedure (the noun appeal) to request (the verb appeal) a higher court to review the judgment of a lower court.

Appellant: The side appealing the lower court's decision.

Appellee: The side opposing the appeal.

Asperger Syndrome: A developmental disability sometimes referred to as high functioning autism; Asperger Syndrome is characterized by the poor communication and social skills evident in autism, but also by at least normal intelligence and language development.

Attention Deficit Disorder [ADD]: A disorder that involves impulsivity and attentional deficits in initiating or maintaining concentration; these difficulties often result in learning and behavioral issues; sometimes called ADD/WO meaning "without" hyperactivity.

Attention Deficit Hyperactivity Disorder [ADHD]: ADD with hyperactivity, that is with excessive movement and restless behavior. ADD and ADHD are not specifically included in the statutory definitional list for child with a disability but may qualify for special education under other categories where appropriate.

Battery: Tort that involves intentional and wrongful physical touching. Education cases that involve statutory or constitutional violations may also involve torts.

Behavioral Intervention Plan [BIP]: A written document in special education practice that outlines how the IEP team and others will try to intervene with the environment and/or the student to alter problematic behaviors presented by a student and identified in the functional behavioral assessment. This term is used in IDEA at 20 U.S.C. § 1415(k)(1)(B) to address an approach to a child's behavior.

Bias: The attribution of negative traits on the basis of race or other group characteristics. Biases can be explicit and self-reported or implicit and unconscious or unknown. Increasing attention is being paid to emerging research on implicit bias and its impact on education decisions.

Case law: Often used to refer to common law, the term is broader and refers to all court decisions including those interpreting or applying the constitution or enacted or statutory law. Cases, or more often, excerpts from cases, can be found as part of casebooks; but the major source is "reporters," which are series of books that contain the full text of court opinions.

Cause of action: Sometimes called a "right to sue," a claim that is sufficient to bring a case to court. The term is also used to mean the elements of such a claim. In *Cannon v. the University of Chicago*, the United States Supreme Court discussed the concept of cause of action at length. It found that a woman who was denied admission to two medical schools had a private cause of action for sex discrimination against the universities under Title IX's prohibitions of sex discrimination by educational institutions receiving federal financial assistance. The court found such a cause of action even though the statute did not expressly provide for one. *See Cannon v. University of Chicago*, 441 U.S. 677, 716 (1979).

Certiorari (Cert.): Latin meaning to be informed of, an order by the appellate court that is used when the court has discretion as to whether to hear an appeal. A writ or petition for certiorari is the most common way that cases proceed to the U.S. Supreme Court, the court of last resort; granting the petition is discretionary. If the writ is denied, the court refuses to hear the appeal, and in effect, the judgment below stands unchanged. If granted, it is an order to the court below to deliver its records in the matter.

Charter school: A self-governing public school operating under its authorizing charter under state law.

Circuit Courts, U.S. Courts of Appeal: Appellate courts in the federal system; the Court of Appeals for the Federal Circuit plus twelve regional appellate courts. For example, the Eleventh Circuit hears appeals from cases in Louisiana, Texas, and Mississippi.

Civil law: As distinguished from criminal law, law that applies to non-criminal actions. Cases involving contracts, property rights, divorce, negligence, and other torts are all examples.

Code/Codification: A compilation of legislative or quasi-legislative acts (statutes, regulations or ordinances), typically arranged in subject-matter order. The U.S. Code is the compilation of federal laws and each state will have its own code, though not all are officially called codes; for example, the Maine statutes are entitled the "Maine Revised Statutes Annotated."

Code of Federal Regulations (C.F.R.): This set of books is the codification of federal regulations by topic. Many of the regulations of the Department of Education appear in Title 34, for example, Code of Federal Regulations, Title 34—Education, Subtitle A—Office Of The Secretary, Department Of Education.

Common law: The origin of our legal system, law created through court opinions, with the cause of action and rules created by the courts rather than by the legislature. One often sees courts talking about schools' obligations to their students in terms of common law obligations.

For example, in discussing whether a claim of a high school student who had been sexually abused by his teacher was a case of constitutional proportions, the court said: "Although, clearly, a school system has an unmistakable duty to create and maintain a safe environment for its students as a matter of **common law**, its in loco parentis status or a state's compulsory attendance laws do not sufficiently restrain students to raise a school's **common law** obligation to the rank of a constitutional duty." *Doe v. Claiborne County Tennessee*, 103 F.3d 495, 510 (6th Cir. 1996). Another example of the use of the common law in the education arena is the effort to define a tort of "educational malpractice," but the courts have been reluctant to develop such a common law cause of action. *See Sellers by Sellers v. School Board*, 141 F.3d 524 (4th Cir. 1998), *cert. denied*, 525 U.S. 871(1998) where the court was clear that there would not be a cause of action for educational malpractice for failure to identify a student's learning disabilities.

Compensatory ed: Services provided beyond the time that eligibility for special education under IDEA has otherwise expired to address situations where students can show that their programs were inappropriate.

Complaint: The original pleading that sets out a cause of action and claim for relief to begin a lawsuit.

Constitution: The fundamental governing principles of a country or state, typically in a written document. In the United States, in addition to the federal constitution, are state constitutions, which may well differ from the U.S. Constitution and from other states.

Count: An individual claim made in a complaint. Parties may win on some counts and lose on others.

Criminal law: As distinguished from civil law, law defining crimes against the state and imposing punishment for those crimes.

Damages: Money remedy recovered in court to compensate a party for injury. The amount involved may be actual damages for the amount of real loss or punitive damages, which are an extra amount intended to punish the party. Occasionally nominal or symbolic damages are awarded to vindicate a right where no real money damage is found.

Declaratory judgment: A binding decision that determines the rights of the parties in a controversy without requiring that additional relief be granted. Declaratory judgment is a remedy provided for by federal statute: "any court of the United States, upon the filing of an appropriate pleading, may declare the rights and other legal relations of any interested party seeking such declaration, whether or not further relief is or could be sought. Any such declaration shall have the force and effect of a final judgment or decree and shall be reviewable as such." 28 U.S.C. § 2201. Declaratory judgment is often the remedy sought in school cases.

For example, in reviewing the background of a case involving students' free speech claim against the state of New York for prohibiting students from having Tupperware parties in their dormitories, the Court recites: "In October 1982, an AFS representative was conducting a demonstration of the company's products in a student's dormitory room at SUNY's Cortland campus. Campus police asked her to leave because she was violating Resolution 66-156. When she refused, they arrested her and charged her with trespass, soliciting without a permit, and loitering. Respondent Fox, along with several fellow students at SUNY/Cortland, sued for **declaratory judgment** that in prohibiting their hosting and attending AFS demonstrations, and preventing their discussions with other 'commercial invitees' in their rooms, Resolution 66-156 violated the First Amendment." *Board of Trustees of State University of New York v. Fox*, 492 U.S. 469, 471 (1989).

De facto: In fact, often distinguished from de jure, in law. The term is most common in the education arena regarding segregation and desegregation.

Default judgment: Judgment for one party because the other party fails to reply or appear when required.

For example, in a case brought by a student against Brown University and one of her professors, as to the professor the court notes: "Adesogan never responded, and the case proceeded solely against Brown. A **default** judgment in the amount of $275,000 was later entered against Adesogan." *Wills v. Brown University*, 184 F.3d 20 (1st Cir. 1999).

Defendant: In a civil proceeding, the person being sued. In a criminal proceeding, the person being prosecuted.

De Jure: See de facto.

De Minimis: Short for "de minimis non curat lex," the law does not care for very small things; de minimis labels a claim as too insignificant to be litigated. There is also the opposite, "non-de minimis."

De novo: New. When a higher court reviews the decision of a lower court it may review only part of the decision, or it may give some deference to parts of the decision, or it may review part or all of the decision de novo or anew, as if it were deciding the case in the first instance. Typically, an appeals court reviews decisions on constitutional issues, questions of law, or mixed questions of law and fact de novo. Whether a decision is reviewed de novo may well make the difference in the outcome, and the issue is often hotly contested.

Deposition: Testimony taken either orally or with written interrogatories, in preparation for trial, but not in court.

Dictum/Dicta: Latin from the term "obiter dictum", "to say by the way"; that is, comments made by a court that are not directly related to the issue before it or that are not necessary to its holding. In some cases, *dicta* are easily identifiable, in other cases they may not be. Often a subsequent opinion will refer to portions of prior caselaw and describe them as *dicta.*

Disproportionality: Representation of racial or ethnic groups of students in special education categories or placement out of proportion to their representation in the school or special education population as a whole. The issue is addressed in IDEA, which requires school districts to track and report on this concern. *See* 20 U.S.C. §§ 1400(c)(12), (13), § 1418.

Distinguish: To point out an essential difference; to prove a case cited as applicable or inapplicable to the current situation. Because precedent is so important, whether a prior case can be distinguished on the law and/or on the facts is crucial to a decision. In a Title IX case about Illinois State University's eliminating men's soccer and wrestling, the Seventh Circuit considers arguments about one of its prior Title IX decisions: "The plaintiffs-appellants contend that our decision in Kelley is **distinguishable** from the facts of this case, and is therefore not controlling. In attempting to **distinguish** Kelley, the plaintiffs-appellants rely on the financial and budgetary considerations that motivated the University of Illinois's athletic department to eliminate men's swimming.... We are not persuaded by the plaintiffs-appellants' attempt to **distinguish** decisions to eliminate athletic programs motivated by financial concerns from those based on considerations of sex. That **distinction** ignores the fact that a university's decision as to which athletic programs to offer necessarily entails budgetary considerations." *Boulahanis v. Board of Regents*, 198 F.3d 633, 637 (7th Cir. 1999).

Docket (docket number): The number assigned in the court's log to each suit filed. These numbers are useful during litigation, but once a decision has been made the case is referred to by its citation.

Due process: A term from the clauses of this name in the United States Constitution and various state constitutions. In the U.S. Constitution, due process is part of the Fifth Amendment and the Fourteenth Amendment. Lawyers speak of two kinds of due process, procedural due process, which, as its name suggests provides a guarantee for fair procedure, and substantive due process, which is invoked to preclude unfair government interference.

> AMENDMENT XIV. CITIZENSHIP; PRIVILEGES AND IMMUNITIES; DUE PROCESS; EQUAL PROTECTION; APPOINTMENT OF REPRESENTATION; DISQUALIFICATION OF OFFICERS; PUBLIC DEBT; ENFORCEMENT
>
> Section 1. All persons born or naturalized in the United States, and subject to the jurisdiction thereof, are citizens of the United States and of the State wherein they reside. No State shall make or enforce any law which shall abridge the privileges or immunities of citizens of the United States; nor shall any State deprive any person of life, liberty, or property, without **due process** of law; nor deny to any person within its jurisdiction the equal protection of the laws.

Educational malpractice: Professional misconduct, typically used in reference to doctors, lawyers, and accountants, here used regarding the education system. On occasion efforts have been made to assert a claim of educational malpractice against educators or schools. These are typically unsuccessful: "In sum, the claims founded on the above secular allegations can be fairly construed as one for **educational malpractice**. Previously, the Colorado Court of Appeals held that Colorado does not recognize a claim for educational malpractice." Noting that authority from other states has consistently refused to recognize educational malpractice as a cognizable claim, the court reasoned: "Whether to create a claim for relief for **education malpractice** is a question of law which, initially, requires determination by the court whether a duty runs from defendant to plaintiff. Initial resolution of the question of the existence of a duty is dictated by public policy and the conceivable workability of a rule of care in a given factual situation. . . . Since education is a collaborative and subjective process whose success is largely reliant on the student, and since the existence of such outside factors as a student's attitude and abilities render it impossible to establish any quality or curriculum deficiencies as a proximate cause to any injuries, we rule that there is no workable standard of care here and defendant would face an undue burden if forced to litigate its selection of curriculum and teaching methods. Accordingly, as a matter of law, we decline to impose such a duty here and uphold the summary judgment refusing to recognize plaintiff's tort claims premised on **educational malpractice** entered by the trial court." *Houston v. Mile High Adventist Academy*, 846 F. Supp. 1449, 1456 (D. Colo. 1994).

Enabling legislation: The legislation that creates or enables an agency. The term is sometimes used more specifically to describe the authority of an agency to adopt certain rules or make certain decisions, which must be within the scope of the enabling legislation.

For example, in discussing a claim of discrimination based on sex and/or parental or marital status, the court reviews the various regulations under Title IX and Title VII: "To be valid, a regulation, such as subsection 2 of 34 C.F.R. § 106.57(a), must be reasonably related to the purpose of the **enabling legislation.** It goes without question, of course . . . that the regulation cannot impose a standard broader than that imposed by this statute [Title IX]." *Mabry v. State Bd. of Community Colleges and Occupational Education*, 813 F.2d 311, 315 (10th Cir. 1987), *cert. denied, Mabry v. State Board for Community Colleges and Occupational Education*, 484 U.S. 849 (1987).

En banc: "In the bench," a decision made by the full panel of the court. A panel of three judges hears the typical federal appeal. When all judges in the panel hear a case, the case is described as being heard by the court "sitting en banc." The controversial decision about the search of two eight-year-old girls is illustrative. Here is the history: "The United States District Court for the Northern District of Alabama . . . granted summary judgment to all defendants on all claims. Parents appealed. The Court of Appeals . . . affirmed in part and reversed in part. On rehearing **en banc**, the Court of Appeals . . . held that law regarding searches of students at school was not clearly established to extent that teacher and school counselor should have known at time that their conduct in strip searching two eight-year old elementary students twice in attempt to find $7 stolen from classmate was unreasonable under Fourth Amendment, and, thus, teacher and counselor were entitled to qualified immunity for their actions." *Jenkins by Hall v. Talladega City Board of Education*, 115 F.3d 821, (11th Cir. 1997), *cert. denied, Jenkins by Hall v. Herring*, 522 U.S. 966 (1997).

English as a second language; English for speakers of other languages [ESL/ESOL]: A method for teaching English to limited-English-speaking students. Approaches to English Language Learners are matters of both federal and state law. *See generally Castaneda v. Pickard*, 648 F.2d 989 (5th Cir. 1981).

Equal Protection: A constitutional guarantee. See due process for the quotation.

Et seq.: Abbreviation for the Latin "et sequentes" and "et sequentia" meaning "and the following." A common use of the term is in statutory citation.

Executive order: An order issued by the president or the governor.

Ex Parte: On behalf of one party; in the name of a case, for that party. Ex parte denotes a proceeding where only one party is present and heard. In judicial proceedings, it is sometimes the case that a restraining order will be obtained ex parte, where the other side cannot be reached in time. In administrative law, ex parte proceedings are often unlawful since the process is intended to work where all evidence and information is provided in a public forum where each side can review and comment.

For example, in a case involving a search of the university newspaper for film or negatives showing those involved in a demonstration, Justice Stewart comments in his dissent: "The decisions of this Court establish that a prior adversary judicial hearing is generally required to assess in advance any threatened invasion of First Amendment liberty. A search by police officers affords no timely opportunity for such a hearing, since a search warrant is ordinarily issued **ex parte** upon the affidavit of a policeman or prosecutor. There is no opportunity to challenge the necessity for the search until after it has occurred and the constitutional protection of the newspaper has been irretrievably invaded." *Zurcher v. Stanford Daily*, 98 S. Ct. 1970, 1986 (1978).

Ex rel.: An abbreviation for "ex relatione," used where one acts for another, "upon relation or information."

For example, where a lawsuit is instituted by the state but based on an individual case, the case would be captioned *People of State of Illinois ex rel. McCollum v. Board of Education of School District No. 71* 333 U.S. 203, (1948) (prohibiting turning over public school classrooms to religious instructors).

Family Educational Rights and Privacy Act [FERPA]: The federal law protecting the confidentiality of student records and providing certain parental/student rights in regard to those records for schools receiving federal financial assistance, 20 U.S.C. § 1232g; 34 C.F.R. Part 99.

Federal courts: Courts of the United States, as distinguished from state, county, or local courts.

Federal Register: The Federal Register is a daily publication of the Government Printing Office with all proposed and adopted rules of federal agencies, as well as other announcements of those agencies. Eventually the adopted rules are codified and published in the Code of Federal Regulations.

Free appropriate public education [FAPE]: Special education and necessary related services provided without charge in conformity with state standards and a student's IEP. This term is defined by statute and regulation, 20 U.S.C. § 1401(9); 34 C.F.R. §§ 104.33.

Holding: The precise issue or principle decided in a case, as contrasted with *dicta*. It is the holding of a case that will bind future decisions.

Inclusion: Educating all children in the same classroom, including children with various disabilities, by adding appropriate services.

Individualized Education Program [IEP]: A single written document laying out the plan for special education and related services for a student with disabilities. This term is defined by statute and regulation, 20 U.S.C. § 1401(11); 34 C.F.R. §§ 300.340–300.350.

Injunction: A court order restraining a party from an act or requiring a party to perform an act. A preliminary injunction may be granted to prevent parties from taking actions that could have irreparable results while the case is being decided. A permanent injunction is granted after there has been a court hearing on the merits of the case.

In loco parentis: In the place of a parent. This is a term often found in school litigation.

For example, in discussing the drug testing in *Vernonia*, the Supreme Court observed, "Central, in our view, to the present case is the fact that the subjects of the Policy are (1) children, who (2) have been committed to the temporary custody of the State as schoolmaster. Traditionally at common law, and still today, unemancipated minors lack some of the most fundamental rights of self-determination—including even the right of liberty in its narrow sense, i.e., the right to come and go at will. They are subject, even as to their physical freedom, to the control of their parents or guardians. See 59 Am.Jur.2d, Parent and Child § 10 (1987). When parents place minor children in private schools for their education, the teachers and administrators of those schools stand **in loco parentis** over the children entrusted to them. In fact, the tutor or schoolmaster is the very prototype of that status. As Blackstone describes it, a parent 'may . . . delegate part of his parental authority, during his life, to the tutor or schoolmaster of his child; who is then **in loco parentis**, and has such a portion of the power of the parent committed to his charge, viz. that of restraint and correction, as may be necessary to answer the purposes for which he is employed.' 1 W. Blackstone, Commentaries on the Laws of England 441 (1769). In *T.L.O.* we rejected the notion that public schools, like private schools, exercise only parental power over their students, which of course is not subject to constitutional constraints. . . . Such a view of things, we said, 'is not entirely "consonant with compulsory education laws"' . . ." *Vernonia School District 47J v. Acton*, 515 U.S. 646, 654-55 (1992).

In re: Regarding, in the matter of.

Inter alia: Among other things.

Intervenor: A person, not a party, who is involved in a court proceeding, voluntarily and with permission of the court.

Ipso facto: By the fact.

Judgment: The official decision of the court.

Jurisdiction: The legal power of a court to hear and decide cases, typically specified by constitution or statute. Jurisdiction encompasses both subject-matter and personal jurisdiction and both must be present for the court to appropriately proceed. Another meaning of jurisdiction is the geographical area over which a court or legislature has authority.

For example, in a Florida search and seizure case involving the student's ability to bring a § 1983 claim in state court, the U.S. Supreme Court discusses the relationship between state and federal law: "Federal law is enforceable in state courts not because Congress has determined that federal courts would otherwise be burdened or that state courts might provide a more convenient forum—although both might well be true—but because the Constitution and laws passed pursuant to it are as much laws in the States as laws passed by the state legislature. The Supremacy Clause makes those laws 'the supreme Law of the Land,' and charges state courts with a coordinate responsibility to enforce that law according to their regular modes of procedure. 'The laws of the United States are laws in the several States, and just as much binding on the citizens and courts thereof as the State laws are. . . . The two together form one system of **jurisprudence**, which constitutes the law of the land for the State; and the courts of the two jurisdictions are not foreign to each other, nor to be treated by each other as such, but as courts of the same country, having jurisdiction partly different and partly concurrent.'" *Howlett by and through Howlett v. Rose*, 496 U.S. 356, 367 (1990).

Jury: A specifically set and chosen number of citizens sworn (jurati) to find the true facts based on evidence before them. The jury in a typical civil or criminal action is referred to as a common or petit jury. See also grand jury.

Least restrictive environment [LRE]: The placement of children with disabilities that allows for their being included in academic and non-academic settings "to the maximum extent appropriate" with students who are not disabled. IDEA requires that there be a continuum of placements, *see* 20 U.S.C. § 1412(a)(5); 34 C.F.R. §§ 300.114-.120.

Legislative history: The record made during the legislative process. The legislative history is subsequently used to help interpret statutes if they are ambiguous.

Legislative process: This term is used somewhat loosely to refer to all or part of the process by which a statute is enacted. The typical federal process includes: preliminary hearings, the introduction of a bill (proposed legislation) into one or both houses of Congress, referral to the relevant legislative committee, hearings by the committee, committee reports about the bill, debates on the floor, vote on the final draft (engrossed bill), transfer to the other house, eventual vote there, referral to conference committee to resolve any differences between the House and Senate versions of the bill, vote, signature by Speaker and President of the Senate and delivery (enrolled bill) to the President for veto or approval. In the case of a veto, a 2/3 vote of the Congress can override, and the statute becomes law. State legislatures will follow a similar process. Along the way, legislative history is being made, including the bill, its various amendments, committee reports, records of floor debate, presidential statements, and the like. The legislative history will be considered in interpreting and applying the statute.

Liable: Responsible, obliged under the law.

Limited English Proficiency (LEP): Descriptor for students whose English is limited and who will be the focus of second language teaching techniques such as bilingual education. These requirements are a result of federal statutes that are now part of No Child Left Behind.

Litigation: The court resolution of matters, either civil or criminal in nature. Litigation follows a prescribed process under set rules of procedure. Typically, the **litigation** begins with the plaintiff's filing a complaint stating the parties and the cause of action and claim for relief; the complaint is served (delivered) to the defendants who must answer the complaint. In the answer, the defendants set forth any affirmative defenses or counterclaims they may have. There are several preliminary points where the litigation can end in response to a motion of one of the parties. One of the earliest points is a motion to dismiss for various reasons such as lack of jurisdiction or failure to state a claim upon which relief can be granted by the court. If the litigation is not dismissed, there typically follows a period of discovery where each side obtains information orally and in writing or through documents about the other's case. A second opportunity to end the litigation typically arises here via a motion for summary judgment. There may also be other pretrial motions and settlement efforts, but eventually the case will proceed to trial and judgment or decision.

Local education agency [LEA]: Public board of education or authority that administers education in various political subdivisions.

Magnet School: A school with a strong emphasis in a particular subject area, for example, music, science, drama, or math. Typically, students attend a magnet school by application and selection rather than attending a school that would be in their residential area.

Moot or mootness: Situation where the facts that gave rise to that case no longer exist. For example, in a case challenging the constitutionality of a North Dakota statute allowing for user fees for school bus transportation, the defendants claimed that the case was moot in regard to the plaintiffs because the bus contract had been signed and the fee was being paid. The Supreme Court found that because invalidating the contract would obviate the need for further payment and because there were two more children in the family, the case was not moot. *Kadrmas v. Dickinson Public Schools*, 487 U.S. 450 (1988).

Motion: A formal request made to the court. See also, motion to dismiss, motion for summary judgment.

Motion for summary judgment: A request by a party that a decision be reached based on the pleadings alone, without having to go through with the entire trial.

A common request in a court case, summary judgment is allowed only when there is no dispute between the parties as to any of the material or significant facts of the case, and the moving party is entitled to judgment in his/her favor as a matter of law

For example, the Supreme Court opinion in *Texas v. Lesage* a claim of a Caucasian applicant claiming unlawful discrimination in the decision not to admit him to the University's psychology program. In reversing the decision of the Fifth Circuit, and thus supporting the decision of the District Court, the Supreme Court described the lower court decision as follows: "It is undisputed that the school considered the race of its applicants at some stage during the review process. The school rejected Lesage's application and offered admission to at least one minority candidate. Lesage filed suit seeking money damages and injunctive relief. He alleged that, by establishing and maintaining a race-conscious admissions process, the school had violated the Equal Protection Clause of the Fourteenth Amendment and . . . 42 U.S.C. § 1981, . . . § 1983 and . . . 42 U.S.C. § 2000d. Petitioners sought **summary judgment**, offering evidence that, even if the school's admissions process had been completely colorblind, Lesage would not have been admitted. . . . The District Court concluded that 'any consideration of race had no effect on this particular individual's rejection,' and that there was 'uncontested evidence that the students ultimately admitted to the program had credentials that the committee considered superior to Respondent's.' . . . It therefore granted **summary judgment** for petitioners with respect to all of Lesage's claims for relief." *Texas v. Lesage*, 528 U.S. 18 (1999).

Motion to dismiss: A request that the court decide that a party may not further litigate a claim.

Motion to suppress: This is a request to the court to disallow evidence that has been improperly gathered, for example, as a result of an inappropriate search.

Next friend: A person who is acting for the benefit of someone else that the court sees as not able to manage his or her own lawsuit; often a parent will serve as next friend.

For example, the caption in the *DesRoches* case, about a student search reads, "James DesRoches, II, a minor, by his father and **next friend**, James DesRoches, Plaintiff-Appellee, v. Michael Caprio; Roy D. Nichols, Jr.; School Board of the City of Norfolk, Defendants-Appellants." *DesRoches by DesRoches v. Caprio*, 156 F.3d 571 (4th Cir. Va. 1998).

No Child Left Behind [NCLB]: Reauthorization of the Elementary and Secondary Education Act (ESEA), the major federal funding legislation for public schools, P.L. 107-110, codified as 20 U.S.C. § 6301 et seq.

Office for Civil Rights (OCR): Part of the Department of Education, the enforcement agency for several federal civil rights statutes that prohibit discrimination including discrimination on the basis of age, disability, race, color, national origin, and sex, as well as for Title II of the ADA prohibiting discrimination on the basis of disabilities by public entities.

Opinion: Most commonly, a decision of a court. An opinion is typically a document that: states the parties to the litigation; describes the legal or procedural context; describes the parties' contentions; refers to relevant statutes and previously decided cases; and, after analysis, ends up with the decision. The term is also used to describe agency determinations. A unanimous opinion is one where all the justices agree. A majority opinion is the prevailing opinion of a numerical preponderance where not all agree. A concurring opinion is an opinion written by one or more justices agreeing with the result but not the reasoning. A dissenting opinion disagrees with the result. A plurality opinion is when less than a majority of the justices agree.

Oral Argument: The formal spoken argument to a court by the attorneys for the parties in the case. Oral argument follows a strict traditional formula and provides the judges with the opportunity to question the attorneys about any concerns the judges may have on the facts or law of the case.

Ordinance: A municipal statute.

Overrule: Supersede. More specifically, the term describes the situation when the same court or a court of higher jurisdiction in the same system, decides a case on the same question of law in direct contradiction to an earlier decision. At that point, the earlier decision is without value. For a court to overrule a prior decision is unusual, but does happen in education cases. One example is in *Agostini v. Felton* where the U.S. Supreme Court overruled its holding in *Aguilar v. Felton*, 473 U.S. 402. In *Aguilar*, the Supreme Court had held that the First Amendment precluded New York City's sending public school teachers into private schools to provide Title I remedial education. Twelve years later, based on what the court described as "intervening Establishment Clause jurisprudence," the court found *Aguilar* to be "no longer good law" and said "We therefore **overrule** Ball and Aguilar to the extent those decisions are inconsistent with our current understanding of the Establishment Clause." *Agostini v. Felton*, 521 U.S. 203, 236 (1997).

Parens patriae: Literally translated as parent of the country, referring to the government's role as sovereign acting for those without legal status of their own. Often the term refers to the role of the states in protecting children.

Per Curiam: Latin, "by the court." A (usually) short opinion, usually for the whole court without an individual author being identified.

Plain meaning: Ordinary meaning. Typically, this phrase is used in reviewing a statute. The courts follow a plain meaning rule, where the court interprets a statute based on the ordinary meaning of the words if this is possible.

For example, in a case involving a dispute over whether a child who had been receiving a free appropriate public education from the school district in his home was then entitled to services from the school district when the parents unilaterally placed the child in a private residential nursing facility, the court found that the parents' argument was precluded by the 1997 amendments to IDEA. . . . The court disagreed with the parents' reading of the term facility: "We disagree. Section 1412(a)(10)(C)(i) expressly applies to unilateral placement in a 'private school or facility.' The Jasas suggest that 'facility' means only an educational facility, but that is contrary to the word's **plain meaning.** It would also render the word 'facility' coterminous with 'school,' violating the principle of statutory construction that avoids creating mere surplusage. . . . " *Jasa v. Millard Public School District #17*, 206 F.3d 813, 815 (8th Cir. 2000).

Plaintiff: In a civil proceeding, the one who initially brings the lawsuit.

Pleadings: Series of documents at the beginning of a lawsuit, setting out the parties' formal allegations of claims and defenses. Pleadings include a complaint, answer, and reply.

Policy: Commonly, the general principles by which an organization or government agency is governed. As a term of art, policy means a standard that controls the operation of a government agency or suggests to the public how the government agency believes the law should and will be applied, but does not carry the full force and effect of law as would a regulation. Sometimes agencies adopt policies as a less formal effort to set out standards and see how they work; sometimes agencies adopt policies because they do not have the statutory authority as an agency to adopt binding regulations. The amount of attention or deference a court will give to policies varies. For example, in a recent Title IX sexual harassment decision, the Supreme Court delineated a stricter liability standard than that in the OCR policies, which policies would have said a school district is liable for harassment by a teacher where the teacher is "aided in carrying out the sexual harassment of students by his or her position of authority with the institution." The court instead imposed a standard of actual notice and deliberate indifference. See 62 F.R. at 12034, 12039; compare, *Gebser v. Lago Vista Independent School District*, 524 U.S. 274, 282-83 (1998).

In other cases, courts do give deference to policies. *See, e.g., Cohen v. Brown University*, 101 F.3d 155 (1st Cir. 1996), *cert. denied*, 520 U.S. 1186 (1997) (highlights the distinction).

Popular name: Some cases or statutes become known by a certain name, even though that is not the exact name of the statute or the case as it would appear in a table of cases or U.S. Code. Title IX is an example. There is a volume of popular names as part of the U.S. Code and also a Shepard's series listing popular case names and popular legislative acts.

Precedent: A previously decided case with similar facts and law that is recognized as relevant to a case currently being decided. The precedent provides authority for the disposition of future cases. If the former and current case cannot be distinguished from each other, then the precedent is considered binding on the current court, unless the early case can be shown to be wrong and is overruled. For example, in a case concerning students' free speech claims as to the mandatory university student fees being used in part to fund certain organizations, the issue of which precedents were applicable was crucial to the decision. The lower courts had relied on a series of cases that the Supreme Court found not apt: "The *Abood* and *Keller* cases, then, provide the beginning point for our analysis. . . . While those **precedents** identify the interests of the protesting students, the means of implementing First Amendment protections adopted in those decisions are neither applicable nor workable in the context of extracurricular student speech at a university." *Board of Regents of University of Wisconsin System v. Southworth*, 529 U.S. 217, 230 (2000) (internal citations omitted).

Prima facie: Latin meaning at the first sight. The term is applied to something that seems to be true when first reviewed. Often courts use the term to describe a situation where the basic elements of a claim have been established.

For example, in reviewing a claim of religious discrimination, the U.S. Supreme Court observed, "Specifically, we are asked to address whether the Court of Appeals erred in finding that Philbrook established a **prima facie** case of religious discrimination and in opining that an employer must accept the employee's preferred accommodation absent proof of undue hardship. We find little support in the statute for the approach adopted by the Court of Appeals, but we agree that the ultimate issue of reasonable accommodation cannot be resolved without further factual inquiry." *Ansonia Board of Education v. Philbrook*, 479 U.S. 60, 66 (1986).

Private school: Schools that are administered primarily by other than local, state, or federal funds and which thus retain mostly separate control over their functioning. Private schools would include parochial (religiously affiliated) schools as well as various secular schools such as boarding schools, military schools, and others.

Procedural: As distinguished from substantive law, procedural refers to the way the judicial system works. Procedural due process is a core term in many education cases and involves the question of whether the parties were provided with the appropriate procedure in constitutional terms.

Proximate cause: Next in the chain of causation. Proximate cause is an important element in proving a claim of negligence.

For example, on appeal of a case involving a student's suicide, the appellate court observed: "The jury returned a verdict for Wyke, finding that the School Board negligently failed to supervise Shawn, that the failure was the **proximate cause** of his death, that the total damages were $500,000, and that the percentage of fault attributable to the School Board was 33%." *Wyke v. Polk County School Board*, 129 F.3d 560, 566 (11th Cir. 1997).

Quid pro quo: Translated as what for what, suggesting giving something of value for something else of value. The term is often used in sexual harassment claims:

"One theory, popularly known as '**quid pro quo**' harassment or discrimination, occurs most often when some benefit or adverse action, such as change in salary at work or a grade in school, is made to depend on providing sexual favors to someone in authority. . . ." *Wills v. Brown University*, 184 F.3d 20, 25 (1st Cir. 1999).

Redressable: Capable of being addressed or fixed. This term has a special connotation in the concept of standing to sue. To be a proper party a person must show that the claim he or she asserts is one that is likely to be redressed by a court decision in his or her favor.

Regulation: A rule enacted by a federal or state administrative agency. When properly enacted, regulations have the force and effect of statutory law and like statutes, they are usually compiled into codes.

The majority of the federal government's regulations are published first in the daily Federal Register and then compiled into the Code of Federal Regulations. To see an example, look at the regulations implementing Title IX's prohibition against sex discrimination in athletics are found at 34 C.F.R.§§ 106.1–.71; see also, *Cohen v. Brown University*, 101 F.3d 155 (1st Cir. 1996), *cert. denied*, 117 S. Ct. 1469 (1997): "This is a class action lawsuit charging Brown University, its president, and its athletics director . . . with discrimination against women in the operation of its intercollegiate athletics program, in violation of Title IX of the Education Amendments of 1972, 20 U.S.C. §§ 1681–1688 . . . and its implementing **regulations**, 34 C.F.R. §§ 106.1–106.71."

Rehearing: A second hearing with the intended purpose of having the court look at something previously overlooked. The term often appears when the full circuit decides to rehear a case previously decided by three of the circuit court members and a rehearing en banc is granted.

Related services: Related services include a variety of services as may be necessary for a student to benefit from special education. This term is defined by statute and regulation, 20 U.S.C. § 1401(22); 34 C.F.R. § 300.24

Remand: A higher court returning a case to a lower court for further proceedings.

Remedy: The means by which a right is enforced or by which a violation of a right is compensated.

Respondeat superior: Let the superior or master answer. The term suggests a legal doctrine where the master will be responsible for acts of his/her servants.

Respondent: In appellate practice, the party against whom the appeal is taken, or, to put it another way, the party who responds to or answers the petition for appeal.

Reverse: A higher court deciding that a lower court ruling or decision is wrong; often used with remand, that is, a case is "reversed and remanded."

Rulemaking: The process of an administrative agency adopting rules or regulations, distinguished from adjudication. Typically, the provisions of the Administrative Procedure Act, 5 U.S.C. § 553, govern agency rulemaking process.

Section 1703(f): Title 20 U.S.C. § 1703(f), part of the Equal Education Opportunity Act, makes it unlawful for an educational agency to fail to take "appropriate action to overcome language barriers that impede equal participation by its students in its instructional programs."

Section 1983: Title 42 U.S.C. § 1983. This civil rights statute provides for a civil action for the deprivation of rights: "Every person who, under color of any statute, ordinance, regulation, custom, or usage, of any State or Territory or the District of Columbia, subjects, or causes to be subjected, any citizen of the United States or other person within the jurisdiction thereof to the deprivation of any rights, privileges, or immunities secured by the Constitution and laws, shall be liable to the party injured in an action at law, suit in equity, or other proper proceeding for redress, except that. . . ." This section is used so often in litigation that it is commonly known just by its section number.

Section 504: Section 504 of the Rehabilitation Act of 1973, 29 U.S.C. § 794, federal law that prohibits discrimination against disabled students.

Slip opinion: The first format in which an opinion or statute is issued. It typically is a single opinion or statute in a paper pamphlet form. A slip opinion next appears in advance sheets that are bound paper volumes with a series of cases from a jurisdiction or on a subject; these are shelved after the regular bound volumes in the library. Advance sheets are cumulated into bound volumes into the same sequence.

Sovereign immunity: Governmental protection from suit. Derived from the idea that a King could do no wrong, the doctrine of sovereign immunity prevents suing the government.

Standard of review: The level of scrutiny used for review.

For administrative agencies, the standard of review is typically governed by the Administrative Procedure Act, 5 U.S.C. § 701 et seq. For courts, the term typically encompasses the scope of review and the depth of scrutiny. For scope, the higher court may review something de novo, i.e. as if it were hearing the case anew, or it may give some deference to all or parts of the lower court opinion. As to depth, the court will invoke a standard of review of rational basis, intermediate scrutiny, or strict scrutiny.

The standard of review is significant. For example, in the Virginia Military Institute case the court grappled with the question of what standard of review to apply to a sex-based claim. The dissent criticizes the majority on the question as follows: "The States and the Federal Government are entitled to know before they act the standard to which they will be held, rather than be compelled to guess about the outcome of Supreme Court peek-a-boo. The Court's intimations are particularly out of place because it is perfectly clear that, if the question of the applicable **standard of review** for sex-based classifications were to be regarded as an appropriate subject for reconsideration, the stronger argument would be not for elevating the standard to **strict scrutiny**, but for reducing it to **rational-basis review**. The latter certainly has a firmer foundation in our past jurisprudence: Whereas no majority of the Court has ever applied **strict scrutiny** in a case involving sex-based classifications, we routinely applied **rational-basis review** until the 1970's." (citations omitted). *U.S. v. Virginia*, 518 U.S. 515, 574–75 (1996).

Standing: Qualification to sue based on having a personal stake in the dispute that will be affected by the decision. This is a constitutional requirement for federal courts. The doctrine of standing requires a person to show that he or she is actually injured by the actions of the defendant, that the injury is caused by those actions, and that the injury is redressable by the courts.

Stare decisis: Latin, "to stand by things decided," the policy of the courts to follow precedent so that once a court has set forth a principle of law as applicable it will follow that principle in subsequent cases with similar facts.

State courts: Courts of the various states, as distinguished from federal, county, or local courts.

State education agency [SEA]: The State Board of Education or other similar state-level agency responsible for implementing education law and policy.

Statute: Law enacted by the legislative body, as distinguished, for example, from rules or regulations enacted by an agency.

Strict construction: Close reading. Strict construction is a principle of interpretation where the constitution or a statute is read narrowly.

Subpoena: An official order to appear at a stated time and place to give testimony. A subpoena that requires the recipient to bring documents is a subpoena duces tecum.

Substantive: As distinguished from procedural, substantive deals with the actual matter at issue. Substantive law deals with issues and duties owed by one person to another or to the government. The term appears often in conjunction with **due process**, where substantive due process is distinguished from procedural due process; see due process, for examples.

Sui generis: Translated from the Latin as a thing of its own kind. A case will be described as being sui generis if it seems to the court unlike others decided. In reaching its conclusion that education is not a fundamental right under the federal constitution the Supreme Court described the analysis as follows: "We are unable to agree that this case, which in significant aspects is **sui generis**, may be so neatly fitted into the conventional mosaic of constitutional analysis under the Equal Protection Clause." Indeed, for the several reasons that follow, we find neither the suspect-classification nor the fundamental-interest analysis persuasive. *San Antonio v. Rodriguez*, 411 U.S. 1, 18 (1973).

Title I: Refers to Title I of the Elementary and Secondary Education Act (ESEA) of 1965, which targeted federal financial resources to schools with high concentrations of economically disadvantaged students. This part of the federal legislation was also known as Chapter I.

Title VI: Title VI of Civil Rights Act of 1964, 42 U.S.C. § 2000d (prohibiting discrimination on the basis of race, color or national origin).

Title VII: Title VII of the Civil Rights Act of 1964, 42 U.S.C. § 2000e (Equal Employment Opportunities).

Title IX: Title IX of the Education Amendments of 1972, 20 U.S.C. § 1681 (prohibiting sex discrimination).

Tort: A civil wrong or injury such as negligence.

Ultra vires: Beyond authority. The term is used in a variety of circumstances, e.g., to describe an agency's action that is not authorized by statute or to describe a party's action beyond the authority of the court's orders.

United States Supreme Court: The highest court in the United States, sometimes referred to as the court of last resort. Some 5000 requests for review are filed annually with the Supreme Court, and typically less than 200 are heard, 30% or so from the state courts and the rest on appeal from the circuit courts. Cases typically reach the Supreme Court by petition for certiorari or on appeal, the latter being primarily available for cases that involve state/federal issues such as where a federal statute is found invalid by a state court or vice versa. The jurisdiction of the Supreme Court is derived from Article III of the United States Constitution and further defined by statute, 28 U.S.C. § 1251 et seq. The Supreme Court has original jurisdiction in disputes between states, 28 U.S.C. § 1251.

Vacate: To annul a former judgment. A higher court will vacate the judgment of the lower court, making it meaningless. Often the court will vacate an opinion and remand for further proceedings.

Warrant: A written order that a person be arrested; a search warrant is such an order for the search of a designated person or place.

Writ of mandamus: A court order demanding performance by another government agency or official of specified acts.

Index

[References are to sections.]

T